The Annals of Kansas.

Daniel W. Wilder

The BiblioLife Network

GUIDE TO FOLD-OUTS, MAPS and OVERSIZED IMAGES

THE

ANNALS OF KANSAS.

BY

DANIEL W. WILDER.

At first, during the period of America's colonization and her controversy with England, and her affirmation and establishment of her programme of political principles, the great national work of the disunited provinces was a struggle for local self-government against despotic centralization beyond the sea. It was an effort against the vicarious rule of the middle ages, which allowed the people no power in the State, the laity none in the Church, the servant none in the family. It was a great effort—mainly unconscious—in favor of the direct government of each State by itself, of the whole people by the whole people; a national protest against Theocracy—the subordination of man in religious affairs to the accident of his history; Monarchy, the subordination of the mass of men to a single man; Aristocracy, the subordination of the many to the few, of the weak to the strong; yes, in part also against Despotocracy, the subordination of the slave who toils to the master that enjoys—in their rights they were equal. This forced men to look inward at the natural rights of man; outward at the general development thereof in history. It led to the attempt to establish a Democracy, which, so far as Measures are concerned, is the government of all, for all, by all; so far as moral Principle is concerned, it is the enactment of God's Justice into human laws. . . . .

One day the North will rise in her majesty, and put Slavery under our feet, and then we shall extend the area of freedom. The blessing of Almighty God will come down upon the noblest people the world ever saw—who have triumphed over Theocracy, Monarchy, Aristocracy, Despotocracy, and have got a Democracy—a government of all, for all, and by all—a Church without a Bishop, a State without a King, a Community without a Lord, and a Family without a Slave.—THE NEBRASKA QUESTION: DISCOURSE BY THEODORE PARKER, FEBRUARY 12, 1854.

TOPEKA, KANSAS:
GEO. W. MARTIN, KANSAS PUBLISHING HOUSE.
1875.

TO

GEORGE W. MARTIN,

A KANSAN,

OF EIGHTEEN YEARS' RESIDENCE,

WHO,

WITH HIS CUSTOMARY NERVE,

HAS

ASSUMED THE FINANCIAL RISK OF BECOMING THE PUBLISHER
OF THIS BOOK,

IT IS

GRATEFULLY DEDICATED.

THE CHILD OF FATE.

By Eugene F. Ware.

[*From the Fort Scott Monitor, April, 1873.*]

I am the child of fate;
  What need it matter me
Where I shall buried be!
  Death cometh soon or late—
Whether on land or sea,
What may it matter me!

That which hope hangs upon
  We can no insight get.
Blindly Fate leads us on,
  Storming life's parapet;
That which our course impels
Naught of the future tells.

Whether upon the land,
Whether upon the strand,
  What may it matter me
  Where I shall buried be!
Death cometh soon or late;
  All are the sport of Fate.

What should it matter me,
  Falling as others fell,
  Shattered by shot or shell,
Either on land or sea,
  Wrecked on the foaming bar,
  Flung from the misplaced car;

Whether by Arctic cliffs,
Where the ice-current drifts,
  Where the bleak night-wind sobs,
  Where the black ice-tide throbs—
What though my bark may be
Sunk in some sullen sea!

Each has his work and way,
Each has his part and play,
  Each has his task to do,
  Both of the good and true.
Though thou art grave or gay,
  Be thou yet brave and true.

Work for the right and just,
With an intrepid trust;
  Then it need matter thee
  Not that thou buried be
Either on land or strand,
  Either 'neath soil or sea.

THE ANNALS OF KANSAS.

EARLY DISCOVERIES.

1542.

Francisco Vasquez de Coronado, a Spaniard, commanded an expedition which marched from Mexico to the northern boundary of Kansas. Albert Gallatin says, in the Transactions of the American Ethnological Society, vol. II, p. 64: "Coronado appears to have proceeded as far north as the 40° of latitude." Gen. J. H. Simpson, U. S. A., in the Smithsonian Report for 1869, p. 337, says: "Coronado continued his explorations northwardly to the 40° of latitude, where he reached a province which the Indians called Quivira." He was in search of gold and silver. Coronado said: "The province of Quivira is 950 leagues (3,230 miles) from Mexico. The place I have reached is the 40° of latitude. The earth is the best possible for all kinds of productions of Spain; for while it is very strong and black, it is very well watered by brooks, springs, and rivers. I found prunes (wild plums) like those of Spain, some of which were black; also, some excellent grapes and mulberries." He traversed "mighty plains and sandy heaths, smooth and wearisome, and bare of wood." "All that way the plains are as full of crooked-back oxen as the mountain Serena in Spain is of sheep." This is the first authentic account of the buffalo. The route of Coronado was through that part of Kansas now embraced in the counties of Barbour, Kingman, Reno, Harvey, McPherson, Marion, Dickinson, Davis, Riley, Pottawatomie, and Nemaha. Coronado left Quivira, or Kansas, in April, 1542.

The following statement is copied from Brantz Mayer's History of Mexico, vol. I, p. 145: Between the years 1540 and 1542, an expedition was undertaken for the subjugation of an important nation which, it was alleged, existed far to the north of Mexico. A Franciscan missionary, Marcos de Naza, reported that he had discovered, north of Sonora, a rich and powerful people inhabiting a realm known as Quivara, or the Seven Cities, whose capital, Cibola, was quite as civilized as an European city. After the report had reached and been considered in Spain, it was determined to send an armed force to this region in order to explore, and if possible to reduce the

Quivarans to the Spanish yoke. Mendoza had designed to entrust this expedition to Pedro de Alvarado, after having refused Cortez permission to lead the adventurers—a task which he had demanded as his right. But when all the troops were enlisted, Alvarado had not yet reached Mexico from Guatemala, and, accordingly, the Viceroy despatched Vasquez de Coronado at the head of the enterprise. At the same time he fitted out another expedition, with two ships, under the orders of Francisco Alarcon, who was to make a reconnoissance of the coast as far as the thirty-sixth degree, and, after having frequently visited the shores, he was, in that latitude, to meet the forces sent by land. Coronado set forth from Culiacan, with three hundred and fifty Spaniards and eight hundred Indians, and, after reaching the source of the Gila, passed the mountains to the Rio del Norte. He wintered twice in the region now called New Mexico, explored it thoroughly from north to south, and then, striking off to the northeast, crossed the mountains, and wandering eastwardly as far north as the fortieth degree of latitude, he unfortunately found neither Quivara nor gold. A few wretched ruins of Indian villages were all the discoveries made by these hardy pioneers, and thus the enchanted kingdom eluded the grasp of Spain forever. The troop of strangers and Indians soon became disorganized, and disbanded; nor was Alarcon more successful by sea than Coronado by land. His vessels explored the shores of the Pacific carefully, but they found no wealthy cities to plunder, nor could the sailors hear of any from the Indians with whom they held intercourse.

Hildreth says (vol. I, p. 48): While De Soto was engaged in this exploration, a not less adventurous expedition was undertaken to regions still more interior and remote. By the orders of Mendoza, Viceroy of Mexico, Vasquez Coronada, with a force of three hundred and fifty Spaniards and eight hundred Indians, set out from Culiacan, on the southeastern shore of the Gulf of California, then the northwestern limit of Spanish-Mexican conquest, whence he penetrated north along the shores of the Gulf to the river Gila, now the southwestern boundary of the United States. That river he followed to its head, and, crossing the mountains, reached the upper waters of the Rio del Norte, which he followed also to their sources, and then struck off northeasterly into the great interior desert as far as the 40th degree of north latitude.

Gen. Simpson gives a map showing Coronado's line of march. He places the Province of Quivira, (Quivira and Coronado are slightly changed in spelling by different writers,) between the Platte and Kansas rivers, and between the 95th and 98th degrees of longitude. As yet no county in our State bears the crowning name of its discoverer.

De Soto discovered the Mississippi in 1541, and was buried in it in 1542.

Some writers say De Soto entered Missouri, and also went into the Indian Territory, to the place where Fort Gibson now stands. Bancroft says (vol. I, p. 51): "The highlands of White River, more than two hundred miles from the Mississippi, were probably the limit of his ramble in this direction. The mountains offered neither gems nor gold; and the disappointed adventurers marched to the south." The American Cyclopædia places "the highlands of the White River" in the "eastern portion of what is now the Indian Territory." It was in the month of August, 1541, that De Soto reached the most northern point of his journey.

Consult the following:

A Relation of the Rev. Father Friar Marco de Nica, touching his Discovery of the Kingdom of Cevola or Cibola. 1539. (Hakluyt's Collection of Voyages, vol. III. London. 1600.)

The Relation of Francis Vasquez de Coronado, Captain General of the People which were sent in the Name of the Emperor's Majesty to the Country of Cibola. 1540. (Hakluyt, vol. III.)

The Rest of this Voyage to Acuco, Tiguex, Cicuic, and Quivira, etc. By Francis Lopez de Gomara. (Hakluyt, vol. III.)

A Brief Relation of Two Notable Voyages: the first made by Friar Augustin Ruyz, a Franciscan, in the Year 1581; the second by Antonio de Espejo, in the Year 1583, who together with his Company discovered a Land, etc., which they named New Mexico. (Hakluyt, vol. III.)

Relation du Voyage de Cibola entrepris en 1540. Par Pedro de Castaneda de Nagera. (Coll. H. Ternaux-Compans. Vol. IX. Paris. 1838.)

Relation du Voyage fait a la Nouvelle-Terre sous les Ordres du General Francisco Vasquez de Coronado, Commandant de l' Expedition. Redigee par le Capitaine Juan Jaramillo. (Coll. H. Ternaux-Compans. Vol. IX.)

1609.

MAY 23.—The second charter of Virginia (7th James I.) granted "all those lands, countries, and territories, situate, lying, and being in that part of America, called Virginia," from Cape or Point Comfort, to the northward, two hundred miles, and to the southward, two hundred miles, and "up into the land throughout from sea to sea." This grant made Kansas English, Point Comfort being on the 37th degree of latitude.

1670.

In writing to the Superior of Missions, in 1670, Father Marquette spoke of the Missouri river, from the report he had of it from the Indians. "Six or seven days below the Ilois" (Illinois river), he says, "is another great river, on which are prodigious nations, who use wooden canoes; we cannot write more till next year, if God does us the grace to lead us there." Among these "prodigious nations" was the Kanzas. (Hale's Kanzas and Nebraska, p. 9.)

1673.

JUNE 10.—Marquette, accompanied by Joliet, a trader of Quebec, and five other Frenchmen, descending the Wisconsin in canoes, entered the Mississippi. They floated down as far as the Arkansas. In returning they ascended the Illinois river. Father Dablon published his narrative of this expedition in 1678—with a map on which appears the name of the Kansa tribe of Indians. Marquette's manuscript map is still preserved at St. Mary's College, Montreal. John Gilmary Shea has translated and published the narrative, and with it a fac simile of the map.

1 6 7 7.

La Salle obtains from the King of France a commission for perfecting the discovery of the Mississippi, and, at the same time, a monopoly of the trade in buffalo skins.

1 6 8 2.

JANUARY 13.—La Salle, who had been detained by ice and winter at the mouth of the Illinois, begins his descent of the Mississippi.

APRIL 9.—La Salle reaches the Gulf of Mexico.

Hildreth says: "Formal possession of the mouth of the river was ceremoniously taken for the King of France. The country on the banks of the Mississippi received the name of Louisiana, in honor of Louis XIV., then at the height of his power and reputation; but the attempt to fix upon the river itself the name of Colbert did not succeed." Colbert was the French Minister of Finance.

Father Membre wrote a narrative of this expedition, which is published in Shea's History of the Mississippi. He says: "We found the Ozage (Missouri) river coming from the west. It is full as large as the river Colbert, into which it empties, troubling it so that from the mouth of the Ozage the water is hardly drinkable."

In 1684, La Salle left France with four ships, to plant a colony at the mouth of the Mississippi. The vessels missed the entrance of the Mississippi, passed to the westward, and landed their company on the coast of Texas, in February, 1685. In January, 1687, La Salle determined to reach Canada by land; but, after three months' wanderings, he was murdered by two mutinous companions.

1 6 8 3.

Hennepin published in France an account of his exploration of the Mississippi, from the mouth of the Illinois to the Falls of St. Anthony. Hildreth says the French missionaries and fur traders had explored the Mississippi, the Fox, the Wisconsin, and the Illinois from their sources to their mouths, while the upper sources of the Connecticut, the Delaware, the Susquehanna, the Potomac, and the James remained as yet unknown to the English colonists.

1 6 9 9.

FEBRUARY 27.—Iberville, born at Quebec, with two brothers, Sauvolle and Bienville, and two hundred colonists, most of them Canadian soldiers, entered the Mississippi, never before entered from the sea.

MAY.—Iberville plants a colony on the Bay of Biloxi, within the limits of the present State of Mississippi. Sauvolle was the first Governor of the infant colony, but soon fell a victim to the climate. Bienville succeeded him as Governor.

Iberville died of yellow fever, in 1707, at St. Domingo.

1 7 1 2.

SEPTEMBER 14.—The whole province of Louisiana, with a monopoly of trade, granted to Anthony Crozat, a wealthy French merchant. Crozat agreed to send every year two ships from France with goods and emigrants. He was to be entitled, also, to import an annual cargo of slaves from Africa, notwithstanding the monopoly of that trade in the hands of a special company. The French Government agreed to pay annually 50,000 livres ($10,000) toward supporting the civil and military establishments.

In the grant, the river "heretofore called Mississippi" is called St. Louis, the "Missourys" is called St. Philip, and the "Ouabache" is called St. Jerome. Louisiana is made "dependent upon the General Government of New France" (Canada).

The following is copied from the grant:

"3. We permit him to search for, open, and dig, all sorts of mines, veins, and minerals, throughout the whole extent of the said country of Louisiana, and to transport the profits thereof into any part of France, during the said fifteen years; and we grant in perpetuity to him, his heirs, and others claiming under him or them, the property of, in and to the mines, veins and minerals which he shall bring to bear, paying us, in lieu of all claim, the fifth part of the gold and silver which the said Sieur Crozat shall cause to be transported to France, at his own charges, into what port he pleases, (of which fifth part we will run the risk of the sea and of war,) and the tenth part of what effects he shall draw from the other mines, veins, and minerals; which tenth he shall transfer and convey to our magazines in the said country of Louisiana. We likewise permit him to search for precious stones and pearls, paying us the fifth part in the same same manner as is mentioned for the gold and silver. . . . .

"7. Our edicts, ordinances, and customs, and the usages of the Mayoralty and Shrievalty of Paris, shall be observed for laws and customs in the said country of Louisiana.

"Given at Fontainebleau, the 14th day of September, in the year of grace 1712, and of our reign the 70th. "LOUIS.

"By the King: PHELIPEAUX, &c.

"Registered at Paris, in the Parliament, the four-and-twentieth of September, 1712."

After five years Crozat resigned his patent.

1717.

The exclusive commerce of Louisiana for twenty-five years, with extensive powers of government and a monopoly of the Canadian fur trade, was bestowed on the Company of the West, otherwise called the Mississippi Company. The American Cyclopædia says: "On the death of Louis XIV., and the accession of the Duke of Orleans to the regency, John Law re-entered Paris with a fortune of more than $500,000, made by gambling. The financial affairs of the French kingdom being at this time in the utmost embarrassment, he soon gained a hearing, and, having secured the patronage of the regent, in 1716 established a bank under royal authority. This institution was authorized to discount bills of exchange, and to issue notes redeemable in specie of fineness equal to that of the current money of the realm. As it accepted at par Government bills, on which there was a discount of nearly eighty per cent., and as there was a general want of private credit, its stock was soon taken, and a very lucrative business established. Law, however, aimed higher than this. He believed that while there was no standard of prices, or of money, credit was everything, and that a state might with safety treat even possible future profits as the basis of a paper currency. With this view he established the Mississippi or West India Company, based on the scheme of colonizing and drawing profit from the French possessions in North America. This company, enlarging its scope, soon absorbed the French East India Company, under the general title of the 'Company of the Indies.' It extended its capital to 624,000 shares of 550 livres each, and engaged itself to lend the King 1,600,000,000 livres at three per cent. An extraordinary fever of stock gambling had been gradually excited by these financial efforts, and the result was that the shares of the company rose to thirty-five or forty times their original value. Great extravagance resulted. Land near Paris rose to the value of 100 years' purchase, and most objects of commerce in the same proportion. But the constant decrease of specie in France, and the constant issue of Government notes, which by May, 1720, had reached the sum of 1,925,000,000 livres, soon undermined the company. A crash came, the shares sank in value, and Law, from the position of the Comptroller-General of Finances, became a fugitive. It seems, however, to be well established that he was a sincere believer in his own scheme, and that he acted honestly, and with a lively desire to promote the public welfare. He laid by no money, and when he left France took with him only 800 louis d'or. . . . He finally died in great poverty in Venice."

1718.

The city of New Orleans founded by Bienville.

1719.

The following is copied from Hale's History: "M. Dutisne, a French officer, was sent from New Orleans, in 1719, by Bienville, the Governor, into the territory west of the Mississippi He visited the village of the Osage Indians, five miles from the Osage river, at eighty leagues above its mouth. Thence he crossed to the northwest, one hundred and twenty miles, over prairies abounding in buffalo, to the villages of the Panionkees or Pawnees. Here were two villages, of about one hundred and thirty cabins, and two hundred and fifty warriors each, who owned nearly three hundred horses. They were not civilized, he says, but readily accessible on receiving a few presents. Fifteen days more westward marching brought him to the Padoucahs, a very brave and warlike nation. Here he erected a cross, with the arms of the King, September 27th, 1719. In his report of his expedition, he gives the details which we have quoted, and notices the salines and masses of rock salt found to this day in the region he travelled over. He found the Osages at the spot which they still occupy. If his measurements were exact, his first Pawnee or Panionkee village was near the mouth of Republican Fork. Fifteen days' westward travel must have been up the valley of one of the forks of the Kanzas river; but the name of the Padoucah Indians is now lost. From the time he reached the Osage villages, Dutisne was exploring the territory of Kanzas."

Dutisne was the first Frenchman who trod this soil. His line of travel in Kansas, coming in along the Osage, was probably through the counties of Linn, Miami, Franklin, Osage, Lyon, Morris, Davis, and then west some two hundred miles. On this supposition he crossed Coronado's route near Fort Riley, thus making that point the junction of the great trails made by the Spanish and French explorers.

1720.

A Spanish force, from New Mexico, ravages an Indian village in Kansas, and is cut to pieces by the Indians.

1723.

The seat of government removed to New Orleans.

1724.

The Pawnee Indians visited by Bourgmont. They inhabit the country on the river Platte, and their hunting ground extends as far south as the Arkansas.

1732.

The Mississippi Company, for 1,450,000 livres, surrender their charter to the Government. Thus the "Mississippi bubble" burst. The Company had held possession of Louisiana for fourteen years, and left it with a population of 5,000 whites, and 2,500 blacks.

1755.

Ste. Genevieve, Mo., settled by the French.

1760.

The English defeat the French in Canada, and complete the conquest of that country. Louisiana alone remains to France.

1762.

November 3.—France cedes Louisiana to Spain. On the same day, all the region east of the Mississippi, except the island of New Orleans, was yielded, by the treaty of Fontainebleau, to England, by France. The navigation of the Mississippi was to be free to both parties. The sovereignty of the eastern half of North America, from Hudson's Bay to the Gulf of Mexico, is vested in the British crown.—Louisiana contains about ten thousand inhabitants.—M. D'Abbadie, Director-General of Louisiana, grants to a company of merchants, of whom Pierre Laclede Liguest was the leader, the exclusive right of trade with the Indians on the Missouri.

1763.

February 10.—Definitive treaty of peace and friendship, similar to the preliminary articles of November 3, 1762.

France cedes Canada and Nova Scotia, or Acadia, to Great Britain. The boundary between the British and French territories "shall be fixed irrevocably by a line drawn along the middle of the river Mississippi from its source to the river Iberville, and from thence by a line drawn along the middle of this river, and the lakes Maurepas and Pontchartrain, to the sea." The nineteenth article provides for the restoration of Cuba to Spain. In consequence of this stipulated restitution, Florida and all Spanish possessions east of the Mississippi are ceded to England.

October 7.—Proclamation of the King of Great Britain, erecting the countries and islands ceded to him by the treaty of February 10 into four Governments, called Quebec, East Florida, West Florida, and Grenada.

1764.

FEBRUARY 15.—Laclede's company establish themselves on the present site of St. Louis. He founds the city, and gives it its name.

APRIL 21.—A letter from Louis XV., King of France, to M. D'Abbadie, in Louisiana, ordering him to deliver up the country and colony of Louisiana to the Governor or officer appointed for that purpose by the King of Spain.

Colonel Bouquet estimates that the Shawnees have 500 fighting men. This tribe of Indians belongs to the Algonquin group, living on the Wabash and other neighboring affluents of the Ohio.

1766.

Don Antonio d'Ulloa, the Spanish Governor, arrives in New Orleans. He was coldly received, and departed in 1767, without having produced his credentials.

1768.

AUGUST 11.—A company of Spanish troops under Captain Rios take possession of St. Louis, in the name of the King of Spain, under whose sway it remained until its transfer to the United States, in 1804. Rios retired early in the summer of 1769.

1769.

JULY 28.—Don Alexander O'Reilly, Captain-General, lands at New Orleans, and the dominion of Spain begins in Louisiana.—Pontiac, the Ottawa chief, visits St. Louis. He was killed soon afterwards at Cohokia, and his remains buried in St. Louis.

1770.

Lieutenant Governor Piernas arrives in St. Louis and extends the Spanish authority over Upper Louisiana.

1780.

Early in this year, Benjamin Franklin, in Paris, writes to John Jay, at Madrid, respecting the value to the United States of the Mississippi river. He says: "Poor as we are, yet, as I know we shall be rich, I would rather agree with the Spaniards to buy at a great price the whole of their right on the Mississippi than sell a drop of its waters. A neighbor might as well ask me to sell my street door."

1782.

NOVEMBER 30.—Provisional articles of peace negotiated at Paris between Great Britain and the United States. Boundaries of the United States defined. The navigation of the Mississippi shall forever remain free and open to the subjects of Great Britain and the citizens of the United States.

The western and southern boundary line is declared to be the middle of the Mississippi river from as far north as the Lake of the Woods and south to the thirty-first degree of north latitude.

1783.

SEPTEMBER 3.—Definitive treaty of peace negotiated at Paris between the United States of America and His Britannic Majesty. The independence of the United States acknowledged. Boundaries established.

September 3, 1783, by treaty with Great Britain, the territory of the United States was declared to extend from the Atlantic ocean westward to the Mississippi river, and from a line along the great lakes on the north southward to the thirty-first parallel and the southern border of Georgia.—*U. S. Census Report, 1870, Vol. 1, p. 573.*

1787.

SEPTEMBER 17.—The Convention of Delegates, in the State House at Philadelphia, adopt the Constitution of the United States.

1790.

The following is copied from James Parton's Life of Jefferson:

"As Secretary of State, in 1790, when there appeared some danger of Great Britain seizing New Orleans, Jefferson gave it as his official opinion to President Washington, that, rather than see Louisiana and Florida added to the British empire, the United States should brave the risks of joining actively in the general war then supposed to be impending. But, not less averse to the French possessing it, he warned them also, in the same year, to let it alone."

1798.

Population of St. Louis, 925 persons.

1800.

MAY 7.—The Ordinance of 1787, amended in 1789, provided that the legislative power should be vested in the Governor and Judges, who were directed to adopt and publish such laws as they considered necessary. The act of May 7, 1800, creating the Territory of Indiana, conferred the same powers upon its officers as had been exercised by the officers of the Northwestern Territory under the Ordinance of '87.

MAY 9.—John Brown born, at Torrington, Litchfield county, Conn. He was of the sixth generation in regular descent from Peter Brown, one of the Pilgrim Fathers who landed from the Mayflower, at Plymouth, in 1620. His grandfather, John Brown, was a captain in the Revolutionary army and died in the service.

OCTOBER 1.—Treaty concluded at St. Ildefonso, the 9th Vendemiaire, an 9, (1st October, 1800,) between Napoleon, the First Consul of the French Republic, and the King of Spain. By the third article of the treaty, the King of Spain agrees to retrocede to the French Republic "the colony or province of Louisiana, with the same extent that it now has in the hands of Spain, and that it had when France possessed it." This treaty was confirmed and enforced by the treaty of Madrid, March 21, 1801. Spain had held Louisiana thirty-seven years — from 1763 to 1800.

1801.

MARCH 29.—A despatch of this date, from Rufus King, American Minister in London, contains an intimation that Spain has ceded Louisiana and Florida to France.

DECEMBER.—Rufus King sends what he believes to be a true copy of one of the treaties making the cession.

1802.

APRIL 18.—Jefferson writes to Livingston that the intimated cession of Louisiana to France—

"Completely reverses all the political relations of the United States, and will form a new epoch in our political course. We have ever looked to France as our natural friend—one with whom we could never have an occasion of difference; but there is on the globe one single spot, the possessor of which is our natural and habitual enemy. It is New Orleans, through which the produce of three-eighths of our territory must pass to market; and from its fertility it will ere long yield more than half of our whole produce, and contain more than half of our inhabitants. France, placing herself in that door, assumes to us the attitude of defiance. Spain might have retained it quietly for years. Her pacific dispositions, her feeble state, would induce her to increase our facilities there, so that her possession of the place would be hardly felt by us, and it would not, perhaps, be very long before some circumstance might arise which might make the cession of it to us the price of something of more worth to her. Not so can it ever be in the hands of France. . The day that France takes possession of New Orleans fixes the sentence which is to restrain her forever within her low-water mark. It seals the union of two nations, who, in conjunction, can maintain exclusive possession of the ocean. From that moment we must marry ourselves to the British fleet and nation. We must turn all our attentions to a maritime force, for which our resources place us on very high ground; and having formed and connected together a power which may render re-enforcement of her settlements here impossible to France, make the first cannon which shall be fired in Europe the signal for tearing up any settlement she may have made, and for holding the two continents of America in sequestration for the common purposes of the united British and American nations."

The whole letter was an argument that it was for the interest of both countries for France to cede Louisiana to the United States.

OCTOBER 16.—The Spanish Intendant of Louisiana issues a proclamation interdicting the privilege, secured by the treaty of 1795, of depositing American merchandise in New Orleans. Hildreth says:

"This interruption to their commerce produced a great commotion in the Western country, and led to emphatic remonstrances from the Governor and Legislature of Kentucky, threatening to drive the Administration to a speedy use of force."

It was the disaffection in the Southwest that led Burr to engage in his conspiracy.

—James Pursley the first hunter and trapper to cross the plains to New Mexico.

—Greeley says, in the American Conflict:

"In 1802, Napoleon Bonaparte, then First Consul, induced the feeble and decaying Bourbons of Spain, then in close alliance with revolutionary France, to retrocede to her Louisiana, almost without consideration; and the French flag once more waved over delighted New Orleans."

1803.

APRIL 10.—Parton says:

"On Easter Sunday, April 10, in the afternoon, after having taken conspicuous part in the revived ceremonies of the occasion (Mr. Monroe being still many leagues from Paris, but expected hourly), the First Consul opened a conversation with two of his ministers upon Louisiana. One of these Ministers, who reports the scene, was that old friend of Jefferson's, Barbe-Marbois,* for whom, twenty-six years before, he had compiled his Notes on Virginia—a gentleman ten years resident at Philadelphia, where he married the daughter of a Governor of Pennsylvania. The other Minister had served in America under Rochambeau during the Revolutionary war.

"'I know,' said the First Consul, speaking with 'passion and vehemence,'—'I know the full value of Louisiana, and I have been desirous of repairing the fault of the French negotiator who abandoned it in 1763. A few lines of a treaty have restored it to me, and I have scarcely recovered it when I must expect to lose it. But if it escapes from me, it shall one day cost dearer to those who oblige me to strip myself of it than to those to whom I wish to deliver it. The English have successively taken from France Canada, Cape Breton, Newfoundland, Nova Scotia, and the richest portions of Asia. They shall not have the Mississippi, which they covet. I have not a moment to lose in putting it out of their reach: I think of ceding it to the United States. I can scarcely say that I cede it to them, for it is not yet in our possession. If, however, I leave the least time to our enemies, I shall only transmit an empty title to those republicans whose friendship I seek. They only ask of me one town in Louisiana: but I already consider the colony as entirely lost; and it appears to me that in the hands of this growing power it will be more useful to the policy and even to the commerce of France, than if I should attempt to keep it.'"

The next morning Bonaparte resumed the conversation:

"'Irresolution and deliberation,' he said, 'are no longer in reason. I renounce Louisiana. It is not only New Orleans that I will cede; it is the whole colony, without any reservation. I renounce it with the greatest regret. To attempt obstinately to retain it would be folly. I direct you to negotiate this affair with the envoys of the United States. Do not even await the arrival of Mr. Monroe; have an interview this very day with Mr. Livingston. But I require a great deal of money for this war, and I would not like to commence it with new contributions. If I should regulate my terms according to the value of those vast regions to the United States, the indemnity would have no limits. I will be moderate, in consideration of the necessity in which I am of making a sale. But keep this to yourself. I want fifty millions of francs, and for less than that sum I will not treat; I would rather make a desperate attempt to keep those fine countries. To-morrow you shall have your full powers.'"

APRIL 30.—Treaty concluded at Paris between the United States and the French republic. France cedes Louisiana to the United States. Treaty negotiated by Robert R. Livingston, James Monroe, and Barbe-Marbois.

The following is copied from the treaty:

"ARTICLE 1. Whereas, by the article the third of the treaty concluded at St. Ildefonso, the first of October, 1800, between the First Consul of the French Republic and his Catholic Majesty, it was agreed as follows: 'His Catholic Majesty agrees and engages on his part, to retrocede to the French Republic, six months after the full and entire execution of the conditions and stipulations herein relative to his Royal Highness the Duke of Parma, the colony or province of Louisiana, with the same extent that it now has in the hands of Spain, and that it had when France possessed it, and such as it should be after the treaties subsequently entered into between Spain and other states;' and whereas, in pursuance of the treaty, and particularly of the third article, the French Republic has an incontestable title to the domain and to the possession of the said territory: The First Consul of the French Republic, desiring to give to the United States a strong proof of his friendship, doth hereby cede to the said United States, in the name of the French Republic, forever and in full sovereignty, the said territory,

---

*MARBOIS had been Secretary to the French embassy in America, and was now at the head of the French treasury.

with all its rights and appurtenances, as fully and in the same manner as they have been acquired by the French Republic in virtue of the above-mentioned treaty, concluded with his Catholic Majesty.

.　.　.　.　.　.　.　.　.　.　.

"ART. 4. There shall be sent by the Government of France a commissary to Louisiana, to the end that he do every act necessary, as well to receive from the officers of his Catholic Majesty [the King of Spain] the said country and its dependencies, in the name of the French Republic, if it has not been already done, as to transmit it, in the name of the French Republic, to the commissary or agent of the United States."

Two conventions, regulating the payment of the consideration, bear the date of the treaty of cession. The first stipulates that the payment of the sixty million livres shall be made in six per cent. stock of the United States, to the amount of $11,250,000. Under the second convention, the claims of citizens of the United States on France are to be paid at the American treasury, to the amount of $3,750,000.

The following is copied from the "Land Laws," compiled in virtue of a resolution of Congress, of April 27, 1810:

"By the grant of Louis XIV. to Crozat, dated 14th September, 1712, all the country drained by the waters emptying directly or indirectly into the Mississippi, is included within the boundaries of Louisiana."

"East of the Mississippi, the United States claim, by virtue of the treaty of 1803, all the territory south of the thirty-first degree of north latitude, and extending eastwardly to the small river Perdido, which lies between Mobile and Pensacola, and was, when Louisiana formerly belonged to France, the boundary between that colony and the Spanish province of Florida. That territory, together with the residue of Louisiana east of the Mississippi, was, by the treaty of 1763, ceded by France to Great Britain, who, by the same treaty, acquired also Spanish Florida. The preliminary articles of that treaty were signed on the third day of November, 1762; and, on the same day, France, by a separate act, ceded to Spain all the residue of Louisiana west of the Mississippi, and including the city and island (so called) of New Orleans. By the treaties of 1783, Great Britain ceded to the United States all that part of the former colony of Louisiana east of the Mississippi which lay north of the thirty-first degree of north latitude; and to Spain, under the name of West and East Florida, both that part of Louisiana east of the Mississippi which lay south of that parallel of latitude, and the old Spanish province of Florida. The thirty-first degree of latitude was, by the subsequent treaty of 1795, between the United States and Spain, confirmed as the boundary between the possessions of the two nations. The title of the United States to the territory in question, under the treaties of St. Ildefonso, and of 1803, is fully established by those facts."

The province of Louisiana thus purchased comprised 1,160,577 square miles. The whole domain of the original thirteen Colonies was only 820,680 square miles. The amount ultimately paid by the United States, in principal and interest, was more than $23,500,000.

Parton says:

"Bonaparte was so well pleased with the bargain that he gave M. Marbois 192,000 francs of the proceeds. Sixty millions, he said, was a pretty good price for a province of which he had not taken possession, and might not be able to retain twenty-four hours. He also said: 'This accession of territory strengthens forever the power of the United States, and I have just given to England a maritime rival that will sooner or later humble her pride.' Strange to relate, the British Government expressed approval of the cession. . . . .

"One consideration embarrassed the President amid the relief and triumph of this peaceful solution of a problem so alarming. He, a strict constructionist, had done an act unauthorized by the constitution. He owned and justified it thus: 'The constitution has made no provision for our holding foreign territory, still less for incorporating foreign nations into our Union. The Executive, in seizing the fugitive occurrence which so much advances the good of their country, have done an act beyond the constitution. The legislature, in casting behind them metaphysical subtleties, and risking themselves like faithful servants, must ratify and pay for it, and throw themselves on their country for doing for them unauthorized what we know they would have done for themselves, had they been in a situation to do it. It is the case of a guardian, investing the money of his ward in purchasing an important adjacent territory, and saying to him when of age: I did this for your good; I pretend to no right to bind you; you may disavow me, and I must get out of the scrape as I can: I thought it my duty to risk myself for you. But we shall not be disavowed by the nation, and their act of indemnity will confirm and not weaken the constitution, by more strongly marking out its lines.' He proposed that the case should be met by an additional article to the constitution."

Parton fails to quote the following, which Jefferson wrote to his Attorney General:

"The less that is said about any constitutional difficulty, the better. Congress should do what is necessary in silence. I find but one opinion about the necessity of shutting up the constitution for some time."

OCTOBER 20.—A session of Congress, called by the President, met October 17. On the 20th, the Senate ratified the treaty and conventions. Ratifications were exchanged, and the bargain became complete.

OCTOBER 31.—Act of Congress authorizing the President "to take possession of the territories ceded by France to the United States," and "for the temporary government thereof." By this act the government is "vested in such person and persons," and "exercised in such manner as the President of the United States shall direct."

NOVEMBER 10.—Two acts providing for the payment of the fifteen million dollars to France were approved.

NOVEMBER 30.—Laussat takes possession of Louisiana. Casa Calvo and Salcedo, the Spanish commissioners, present to him the keys of the city, over which the tri-color flag floated but for the short space of twenty days.

DECEMBER 20.—Formal delivery of the island and city of Orleans made by citizen Laussat, as commissioner of France, to General Wilkinson and C. C. Claiborne, commissioners on the part of the United States. Claiborne had been commissioned by Congress "to the supreme and sole government of the new province." The star-spangled banner supplants the tri-color of France.

1804.

MARCH 10.—The United States authority in Missouri dates from the 10th day of March, 1804. On that day Major Amos Stoddard assumed the duties of Governor of Upper Louisiana.

MARCH 26.—Act of Congress erecting Louisiana into the Territory of Orleans and the District of Louisiana. The division line was the southern boundary of Mississippi Territory and the thirty-third degree of latitude.

"The executive power now vested in the Governor of the Indiana Territory shall extend to and be exercised in the said District of Louisiana. The Governor and Judges of the Indiana territory shall have power to establish in the said District of Louisiana inferior courts, and prescribe their jurisdiction and duties, and to make all laws which they may deem conducive to the good government of the inhabitants thereof."

The following is copied from vol. I, p. 575, U. S. Census Report, 1870:

"By act of March 26, 1804, to take effect October 1, 1804, (the act dividing the 'Province of Louisiana,' ceded by France, into the Territory of Orleans and the District of

2

Louisiana,) the District of Louisiana, being all of the French cession west of the Mississippi river, except the present State of Louisiana, was committed to the government of the officers of the Territory of Indiana."

MAY 14.—The expedition of Lewis and Clarke leaves St. Louis.

Parton says of Jefferson:

"How eagerly he availed himself of his opportunities for increasing the sum of knowledge, his letters exhibit, and the fact is part of the history of that age. It was his thought that sent Meriwether Lewis and William Clarke up the Missouri to its sources in the Rocky Mountains, across those mountains to the Columbia river, and down the Columbia until huge waves, rolling in from the ocean and tossing high their light canoes, notified them that they had reached the Pacific. Counting from the time when Captain John Smith sailed up the Chickahominy in search of the South Sea, the world had waited two hundred years for this exploration. Never was a piece of work of that kind better done or better chronicled, for it was Jefferson who selected the two heroes that conducted it. Captain Lewis was the son of one of his most valued Albemarle neighbors. Lieutenant Clarke was the brother of that General George Rogers Clarke who held back the Indians from joining in the war of the Revolution; and both of them were such masters of all frontier arts that the perilous expedition of two years, four months and ten days was one joyous holiday excursion to them. Returning to St. Louis laden with spoils and trophies, Captain Lewis, besides his journals and other official results, sends off exultingly to the President 'sixty-seven specimens of earths, salts and minerals, and sixty specimens of plants.' It was Jefferson, too, who set on foot the two exploring expeditions of Lieutenant Zebulon Montgomery Pike, whose name lives in that of the peak which he discovered, and in those of ten counties of the United States. Pike was the first American who explored the upper Mississippi beyond the Falls of St. Anthony, noting the sites of the cities now rising on its banks, and shaking hands on the way with 'Monsieur Dubuque,' who was working the lead mines and lording it over a wide domain. Lieut. Pike was the first American to explore the valley of the Arkansas. He said truly, in one of his letters, that the regions which he had traversed were little more known to the world than the wilds in the interior of Africa. In seventy years we behold them populous, and more familiar to our knowledge than the next county."

—Governor Wm. H. Harrison, of Indiana, arrived in St. Louis. Having learned the wants of the people, he returned, and, with the Judges of the Territory of Indiana, passed such acts as were deemed necessary for the new District.

OCTOBER 1.—The Governor and Judges of Indiana Territory enact the following laws for the District of Louisiana: Providing for punishing crimes; establishing justices' courts; a law respecting slaves [the Ordinance of 1787 was not allowed to come over from Indiana]; a law regulating county taxes; one regulating the militia; one establishing recorders' offices; one relating to attorneys; one on constables; one on boatmen; one on defalcation; one regulating court practice; one establishing a court of probate; one establishing courts of judicature; one regulating the oath of office; and one establishing the office of sheriff. They also, April 24, 1805, enacted a law regulating marriages.

Saint Vincennes, on the Wabash, the seat of government of Indiana Territory.

By a treaty made at St. Louis, the Foxes and Sacs were united into one tribe. They ceded all their land east of the Mississippi to the United States. The Fox Indians, or Ottigamies, are a tribe of the Algonquin nations, belonging to the Western group, with the Sacs, Miamis and others. They formerly lived at the south end of Green bay, Wisconsin. In 1825, they lived in Illinois and Missouri. In 1846, their agency was at the Osage river.

1805.

The Territory of Orleans given by Congress the same government with that of Mississippi — the government of a Territory of the first class, having a Legislature chosen by the inhabitants.

MARCH 3.—Act of Congress changing the District of Louisiana to the Territory of Louisiana. It provides for a Governor, Secretary, and three Judges. The legislative power is vested in the Governor and Judges.

Hildreth says:

"The District of Louisiana, hitherto annexed to Indiana, was now erected into a separate Territory of the second class, the power of legislation being vested in the Governor and Judges. A section of this act, by continuing in force until altered or repealed by the Legislature, all existing laws and regulations, gave a tacit confirmation to the system of slavery, already established in the settlements on the Arkansas and Missouri."

JULY.—Aaron Burr visits St. Louis, and excites in General Wilkinson's mind "definite suspicions" as to his designs.

—Governor James Wilkinson ordered by President Jefferson to leave St. Louis and watch the movements of ex-Vice President Aaron Burr.

AUGUST 9.—Zebulon M. Pike leaves St. Louis, with twenty men, on an exploring expedition. He is gone nine months.

1806.

Pike discovers the peak, in the Rocky Mountains, now known by his name.

Lewis and Clarke return.

1808.

JULY.—The Weekly Missouri Republican founded by Joseph Charles.

1811.

DECEMBER 16.—The whole valley of the Mississippi shaken by an earthquake, and the town of New Madrid, Mo., destroyed.

—The first steamboat on the Western rivers built by Mr. Roosevelt, of New York, at Pittsburgh, and named New Orleans.

1812.

APRIL 8.—The Territory of Orleans becomes the State of Louisiana.

JUNE 4.—Act of Congress making the Territory of Louisiana the Territory of Missouri. It provides for a Governor and a Secretary. The legislative power is vested in the Governor, Council, and House of Representatives. The House is elected by the people. The House sends to the President of the United States the names of eighteen persons, and from these the President, with the advice and consent of the Senate, selects nine persons, who form the Council. The judicial power is vested in a Superior Court, in inferior courts, and in justices of the peace. The Judges are appointed by the President.

1816.

JANUARY 19.—The Legislature of Missouri Territory passes a law making the common law of England the law of the Territory.

Governor Reeder, in his message of July 2, 1855, said:

"It appears that the laws of the United States, not inapplicable to our locality; the laws of the Territory of Indiana, made between the 26th of March, 1804, and the 3d of March, 1805, enacted for the District of Louisiana; the laws for the Territory of Louisiana; the laws of the Territory of Missouri; the common law; and the law of the Province of Louisiana at the time of the cession, except so far as the latter have superseded the former, still remain in force in the Territory of Kansas. As the common law, to a considerable extent, was adopted for the Territory by Congress as late as 1812, and by the Missouri Legislature as late as 1816, ... it has, without doubt, suspended and supplied a great amount of the law previously existing."

—Stephen H. Long begins his explorations. He spends eight years in the West, traversing more than 26,000 miles of wilderness. One of the highest summits of the Rocky Mountains is named from him Long's Peak. An account of an expedition from Pittsburgh to the Rocky Mountains, in 1819–20, from the notes of Major Long and others, by Edwin Adams, was published in 1823.

APRIL 29.—By an act of Congress, the Council of Missouri Territory is elected by the people.

In 1817 and 1819, two treaties were made by the Cherokees, which resulted, twenty years later, in their enforced emigration to the Indian country. The Cherokees are a tribe of the Appalachian group of American Indians, and were formerly the occupants of the most salubrious region east of the Mississippi.

1819.

FEBRUARY 22.—Treaty with Spain. The following is copied from vol. I, pp. 573–4, of the Ninth Census of the United States, 1870:

"April 30, 1803, by treaty with France, the 'Province of Louisiana' was ceded. Its western boundary, as finally adjusted, February 22, 1819, by treaty with Spain, ran up the Sabine river to and along the seventeenth meridian (94th Greenwich), to and along the Red river, to and along the twenty-third meridian (100th Greenwich), to and along the Arkansas river, to and along the Rocky Mountains, to and along the twenty-ninth meridian (106th Greenwich), to and along the forty-second parallel to the Pacific ocean. Its northern boundary has conformed to the boundary established between the British possessions and the United States. On the east it was bounded by the Mississippi river as far south as the thirty-first parallel, where different boundaries were claimed. The United States construed the cession of France to include all the territory between the thirty-first parallel and the Gulf of Mexico, and between the rivers Mississippi and Perdido, the latter of which is now the western boundary of the State of Florida. Under this construction of the cession, the 'Province of Louisiana' is now covered by those portions of the States of Alabama and Mississippi which lie south of the thirty-first parallel; by the States of Louisiana, Arkansas, Missouri, Iowa, Nebraska, Oregon, Minnesota west of the Mississippi river, and Kansas [except the small portion thereof south of the Arkansas river and west of the twenty-third meridian (100th Greenwich)]; by the Territories of Dakota, Montana, Idaho, Washington, and that known as the Indian country; and by the portion of the Territory of Colorado lying east of the Rocky Mountains and north of the Arkansas river, and all of the Territory of Wyoming north of the forty-second parallel, and that portion of the Territory of Wyoming which is south of that parallel and east of the Rocky Mountains. In 1800, however, the 'Province of Louisiana' had been ceded by Spain to France, Spain claiming that she ceded to France no territory east of the Mississippi river except the 'Island of New Orleans,' and also contending that her province of West Florida included all of the territory south of the thirty-first parallel and between the Perdido and Mississippi rivers, except the 'Island of New Orleans.' Under this construction, the 'Province of Louisiana' included on the east of the Mississippi river only the territory bounded on the north and east by the 'Rivers Iberville and Amite and by the Lakes Maurepas and Pontchartrain.'"

MARCH 2.—Arkansas Territory created; cut off from Missouri. Bill to admit Missouri as a State introduced in Congress, and lost.

The Western Engineer, with a corps of topographical engineers under Major S. H. Long, was the first steamboat to ascend the Missouri. It was a stern-wheel boat.

1820.

MARCH 6.—The following is section eight of an act approved March 6, 1820, "to authorize the people of Missouri Territory to form a constitution and State government, and for the admission of such State into the Union on an equal footing with the original States, and to prohibit slavery in certain Territories:"

"SEC. 8. That in all that territory ceded by France to the United States, under the name of Louisiana, which lies north of thirty-six degrees and thirty minutes north latitude, not included within the limits of the State contemplated by this act, slavery and involuntary servitude, otherwise than in the punishment of crimes whereof the parties shall have been duly convicted, shall be, and is hereby, forever prohibited: *Provided always*, that any person escaping into the same, from whom labor or service is lawfully claimed, in any State or Territory of the United States, such fugitive may be lawfully reclaimed and conveyed to the person claiming his or her labor or service as aforesaid."

The Territorial Governors of Missouri were: 1805, James Wilkinson; 1807, Meriwether Lewis; 1810, Benjamin Howard; 1813, William Clarke; 1820, Alexander McNair.

JULY 19.—The people of Missouri, in State convention, assent to the act of March 6.

— Grasshopper visitation in Kansas and Missouri.

1821.

MARCH 2.—Missouri admitted, with conditions, by joint resolution.

AUGUST 10.—Conditions accepted. Proclamation admitting Missouri as a State.

1822.

DECEMBER 9.—The Legislature passes an act incorporating St. Louis as a city. It has 4,800 inhabitants.

In the spring of this year, General William H. Ashley, the head of the Rocky Mountain Fur Company, of St. Louis, equipped two boats to ascend the Missouri to the mouth of the Yellowstone.

1823.

The first Santa Fe train from Missouri. It set out from Franklin, now Booneville.

1825.

APRIL 29.—Public reception of La Fayette in St. Louis.

JUNE.—Major Sibley appointed, under an act of Congress, to survey and establish a wagon road from Missouri to Santa Fe. He established the Santa Fe trail, through Independence, Mo., and through Kansas.

JULY 25.—Treaty of peace with the Cheyennes and Arapahoes.

NOVEMBER 7.—Treaty with the Shawnees. The United States give them a tract of land equal to fifty miles square, situated west of the State of Missouri, and within the purchase made from the Osages on the 2d of June, 1825.

DECEMBER 30.—By treaty with the Osage Indians, the tribe is located upon a tract lying between latitude 37° and 38° north, and longitude 94° and 98° west, and watered by the Arkansas, Verdigris and Neosho rivers. The tract contains 7,564,000 acres. The tribe numbered 5,500 persons. The Osages belong to the Sioux or Dacotah family. The name by which they were known to the Algonquins (Ouasash) means bone-men; and the word Osage, of French origin, is a corruption of that name. From early times they have been prominent in this section of the country.

The following statement in regard to treaties with the Osages and Kaws is copied from F. G. Adams's Homestead Guide:

"Treaties made with the Osages and the Kaws both, in 1825, affect portions of this territory—that of the latter tribe nearly the whole of it; showing that the Kaws then claimed to have, in a great measure, supplanted the Pawnees in their right to the occupancy of the country now embraced within the homestead region. The treaty with the Kansas Indians or Kaws, of June 3, 1825, ceded the following-described territory: 'Beginning at the entrance of the Kansas river into the Missouri river, from thence north to the northwest corner of the State of Missouri, from thence westerly to the Nodaway river, thirty miles from its entrance into the Missouri river, from thence to the entrance of the Nemaha into the Missouri river, and with that river (the Nemaha) to its source, from thence to the source of the Kansas river, leaving the old village of the Pania (Pawnee) Republic to the west, from thence on the ridge dividing the waters of the Kansas river from those of the Arkansas, to the western boundary line of the State of Missouri, and with that line thirty miles to the place of beginning.'

"To understand this boundary, it must be remembered that at that time the western line of Missouri extended due north from the mouth of the Kansas river to the Iowa line, leaving what was afterwards called the Platte Purchase, now a part of Missouri, still, till the date of this treaty of 1825, a part of the territory claimed by the Kaws.

"In the above description, the southwestern terminus of that portion of the boundary line extending 'from the head-waters of the Nemaha to the sources of the Kansas river,' was evidently intended to strike the sources of the Smoky Hill. Thus that line crossed the Republican river far below its source, 'leaving the Pawnee Republic to the west,' thereby conceding that the Pawnees of the Republican had a right to the occupancy of the upper portion of the valley of that stream. But, by the treaty of 1833, the Pawnees relinquished to the United States all their right to territory south of the Platte.

"In the above-mentioned treaty with the Kaws, that tribe reserved for their own occupancy the tract on the Kansas river, thirty miles square, which was afterwards ceded to the Pottawatomies; also some twenty individual half-breed reservations, of a square mile each, extending from the principal reservation, near where Topeka is now situated, along the north bank of the Kansas river, to about the mouth of Grasshopper creek.

"The Osage treaty of June 2, 1825, ceded to the United States the territory west of the States of Missouri and Arkansas, north of Red river, south of the Kansas river, and east of the line from the head sources of the Kansas river to Rock Saline. By Rock Saline is meant the salt plains about the line of Kansas and the Indian Territory."

By the treaty of December 30, 1825, the Osages reserved the tract first above described.

1826.

NOVEMBER 20.—The seat of government of Missouri removed from St. Charles to the City of Jefferson.

1827.

A part of the Third regiment U. S. troops stationed at the place where Fort Leavenworth now stands. It was called a cantonment until 1832, when it became a fort. The name of the fort comes from the Colonel of the regiment, Henry H. Leavenworth. Its latitude is 39° 21′ 14″; longitude, 94° 44′.

1828.

MAY 6.—Treaty with the Cherokees.

SEPTEMBER 24.—The Delawares, called in their own language the Lenapes, are one of the Algonquin tribes of American Indians. At the beginning of the sixteenth century they occupied the valley of the Delaware river. In 1751, they are found on the Susquehanna. In 1781, a part settled on the Muskingum, and were ordered to remove to Sandusky. After 1812, they stopped for a time on the Whitewater river, in Indiana. Thence they crossed the Mississippi. On the 24th of September, 1829, a treaty was made, giving the Delawares "the country in the fork of the Kansas and Missouri rivers, extending up the Kansas river to the Kansas [Indians] line, and up the Missouri river to Camp Leavenworth, and thence by a line drawn westwardly, leaving a space ten miles wide, north of the Kansas boundary line, for an outlet." The Delawares relinquish all claim to the country now occupied by them, on James's fork of White river, in Missouri.

1830.

Rev. Isaac McCoy described the Osage and Neosho valleys in letters to the War Department, from 1830 to 1838. Lewis Cass speaks of Mr. McCoy in the North American Review, vol. XXX. Mr. McCoy came here in 1828, and soon after published a pamphlet describing southern Kansas and the northern part of the present Indian Territory.

1831.

AUGUST 8.—By treaty, the Shawnees of Ohio are given lands in Kansas contiguous to the land of the Shawnees of Missouri, if that cession is not sufficiently large.

AUGUST 30.—The Ottawa Indians residing in Ohio cede their lands to the United States and receive "a tract of land to contain thirty-four thousand acres, to be located adjoining the south or west line of the reservation equal to fifty miles square granted to the Shawnees of Missouri and Ohio, on the Kanzas river and its branches."

The Baptist Shawnee Mission, four miles west of the Missouri line, established by the Baptist General Convention of the United States. Rev. Isaac McCoy was appointed an agent for the Government, for colonizing the Indians, and established this and other missions. In 1839, Rev. Francis Barker took charge of this mission. In 1848, the mission erected a church, one of the first frame buildings in Kansas. Mr. Barker still had charge of the mission in March, 1855.

1832.

Independence, Missouri, becomes the outfitting point for western trains.

APRIL 6.—The Wyandotte Indians sell their lands in Ohio to the Government, and remove to the junction of the Kansas and Missouri rivers, in Kansas. They number 687 persons. The Wyandottes are of the Iroquois family, are called Hurons by the French, but call themselves Wendats or Yendats. When the French settled Canada, they were on the island of Montreal, and numbered 40,000. A part of them went to Quebec, and a part south of the great lakes. In 1829, a small band lived on the river Huron, in Michigan, but the principal portion was collected on the headwaters of the Sandusky river.

In 1855, January 31, by treaty, they acquired the right to become citizens, and the Kansas lands of the tribe were divided among them, giving to each person about forty acres.

OCTOBER 24.—The Kickapoos cede their country, on the Osage river, in Missouri, and receive a tract of land with the following boundaries: "Beginning on the Delaware line six miles westwardly of Fort Leavenworth, thence with the Delaware line westwardly sixty miles, thence north twenty miles, thence in a direct line to the west bank of the Missouri, at a point twenty-six miles north of Fort Leavenworth, thence down the west bank of the Missouri river to a point six miles nearly northwest of Fort Leavenworth, and thence to the beginning."

OCTOBER 27.—"The United States cede to the combined tribes of Kaskaskias and Peorias, and the bands united with them, one hundred and fifty sections of land, forever, or as long as they live upon it as a tribe, to include the present Peoria village, west of the State of Missouri, on the waters of the Osage river, to be bounded as follows, to wit: North by the lands assigned to the Shawanoes, west by the western line of the reservation made for the Piankeshaws, Weas and Peorias, and east by lands assigned the Piankeshaws and Weas." The Peorias relinquish their lands in Missouri and Illinois.

OCTOBER 29.—The United States cede to the Piankeshaw and Wea tribes two hundred and fifty sections of land within the limits of the survey of the lands set apart for the Piankeshaws, Weas and Peorias, bounded east by the western boundary line of the State of Missouri for fifteen miles, north by the southern boundary of the lands assigned to the Shawanoes, west by lands assigned to the Peorias and Kaskaskias, and south by the southern line of the original tract surveyed for the Piankeshaws, Weas and Peorias; said tract being intended to include the present villages of the said Piankeshaws and Weas.

NOVEMBER 26.—By a supplemental article to the Kickapoo treaty, it is agreed that the boundary lines of the lands assigned to the Kickapoos "shall begin on the Delaware line, where said line crosses the left branch of Salt creek, thence down said creek to the Missouri river, thence up the Missouri river thirty miles when measured on a straight line, thence westwardly to a point twenty miles from the Delaware line, so as to include in the lands assigned to the Kickapoos at least twelve hundred square miles."

1833.

FEBRUARY 14.—Seven millions of acres of land ceded to the Cherokees.

MAY 13.—The United States agree to convey to the Quapaw Indians one hundred and fifty sections of land west of the State line of Missouri, and between the lands of the Senecas and Shawnees.

OCTOBER 9.—Treaty made with the Pawnees at Grand Pawnee Village, on the Platte river.

The following is copied from F. G. Adams's Homestead Guide:

"The Pawnees were a powerful and warlike tribe, and for a century they maintained sway over the country embraced by the branches of the Kansas river, and over the whole region watered by the Platte, from near the Rocky Mountains to its mouth. They were divided into several villages or bands, one of which, the 'Pawnee Republic,' gave its name to the Republican river. The Otoes, Omahas and other tribes acknowledged the superiority of the Pawnees, and lived under their protection. In 1832, however, all these tribes were ravaged by the small-pox, and it is said that the Pawnees then lost half their population. The following year, by treaty, they disposed of, to the United States, all their claims to the land lying south of the Platte river, and agreed to locate themselves north of that river, and west of the Missouri. This they did. But large bodies of Sioux came down on their new settlements, and drove them back with great slaughter. Some returned to their old villages; others joined their allies, the Otoes and Omahas. They continued to be unfortunate, and by the ravages of wars and disease rapidly dwindled in numbers."

1834.

The first printing press brought to Kansas by Rev. Joseph Meeker. The Ottawa (Franklin county) Republican of May 20, 1875, says:

"The press in question was brought to Franklin county in 1834, when this country was all in Indian reservations, and was set up at the Baptist Mission farm, five miles northeast of Ottawa, and two miles down the Ottawa creek from the J. T. Jones place. It was sent out by the Baptist Home Mission Society, of New York, at the urgent request of Rev. Mr. Meeker, the first missionary to the Ottawa Indians. Mr. Meeker published a small missionary paper in the English and Cherokee languages. In addition to this paper, he wrote and published several school books in the Indian language, a book of the code of laws of the Ottawas, a hymn book, and several Sunday school books, all in the native language. . . . . The type and other material used at the mission farm by Rev. Mr. Meeker were finally scattered broadcast by the Indian children; and Mr. Richmond tells us that he could pick up whole handfuls of type, as late as 1865, near where that zealous missionary and his wife lie buried."

—The first stock of goods landed near the present site of Kansas City, Missouri.

JUNE 30.—Congress enacts that all that part of the United States west of the Mississippi, and not within the States of Missouri and Louisiana or the Territory of Arkansas, shall be taken for the purpose of the act to be Indian country, and certain regulations are prescribed for its government. So much of the laws of the United States as provide for the punishment of crime committed in any place within the exclusive jurisdiction of the

United States are declared to be in force in it, with the proviso that the same shall not extend to crime committed by one Indian against the person or property of another Indian. For the purpose of carrying this act into effect, all that part of the Indian country west of the Mississippi river that is bounded north by the north line of lands assigned to the Osage tribe of Indians, produced east to the State of Missouri, west by the Mexican possessions, south by Red river, and east by the west line of the Territory of Arkansas, is annexed to the Territory of Arkansas; and the residue of the Indian country west of the Mississippi is annexed to the judicial district of Missouri.

1835.

APRIL 20.—First railroad convention in St. Louis.

MAY 29.—Expedition of Colonel Henry Dodge, U. S. A., to the Rocky Mountains. Colonel Dodge left Fort Leavenworth May 29. He followed the west bank of the Missouri nearly to the mouth of the Platte, traced the Platte to its source, went south to the head-waters of the Arkansas, and returned through that valley. In other words, he marked the line of the railroads from Leavenworth and Atchison to near Omaha, took the Union Pacific west, followed the Colorado railroads to Pueblo, and came home by the Atchison, Topeka & Santa Fe line. Fort Dodge is on the return trail.

DECEMBER 29.—The United States agree to convey to the Cherokee Indians "the following additional tract of land, situated between the west line of the State of Missouri and the Osage reservation: Beginning at the southeast corner of the same, and runs north along the east line of the Osage lands fifty miles to the northeast corner thereof, and thence east to the west line of the State of Missouri, thence with said line south fifty miles, thence west to the place of beginning—estimated to contain eight hundred thousand acres of land; but it is expressly understood that, if any of the lands assigned to the Quapaws shall fall within the aforesaid bounds, the same shall be reserved and excepted out of the lands above granted, and a *pro rata* reduction shall be made in the price to be allowed to the United States for the same by the Cherokees." This treaty was confirmed by Congress in 1838, and General Scott marched into their country, in Georgia, with 2,000 troops, and forced their removal.

1836.

JUNE 7.—The western boundary of Missouri was a line drawn north and south from the mouth of the Kansas river. In 1836, June 7, Congress passed an act by which the "Platte Purchase" was added to Missouri. The eastern boundary of this triangle was formed by a line drawn north from the mouth of the Kaw; the western boundary was the Missouri river. This tract of land became slave territory, in violation of the Missouri compromise.

JULY 21.—The office of the St. Louis Observer, an Anti-Slavery paper, edited by Elijah P. Lovejoy, broken into in the night. The presses were overthrown, and the type scattered into the street. Mr. Lovejoy removed to Alton, Illinois, where he was killed, November 8, 1837. The press moved from St. Louis had been destroyed at Alton, and Lovejoy was murdered while defending another press, lately brought to Alton.

1837.

FEBRUARY 11.—The United States agree to convey "to the Pottawatomies of Indiana a tract of country, on the Osage river, southwest of the Missouri river, sufficient in extent, and adapted to their habits and wants."

MARCH 28.—The act of June 7, 1836, takes effect by the proclamation of March 28, 1837, and the western boundary of Missouri is extended to the Missouri river.

MARCH 29.—Launching of the first steamboat built in St. Louis.

OCTOBER 31.—Plan of defences of the western frontier proposed by Charles Gratiot, and published in the report of J. R. Poinsett, Secretary of War. This is another railroad map. The lines of the Missouri Pacific and North Missouri railroads, the route from Kansas City to Omaha, and directly south to Fort Smith—these and other lines in Missouri and Arkansas anticipate with marvellous accuracy the present railroad system. Posts were recommended at Fort Scott and Kansas City.

NOVEMBER 17.—Burning of the State House at Jefferson City, and destruction of official papers and records.

DECEMBER 20.—The United States agree to reserve a location on the head-waters of the Osage river for the Saginaw tribe of Chippewas.

1838.

JANUARY 15.—The United States agree to set apart to the New York Indians "the following tract of country, situated directly west of the State of Missouri: Beginning on the west line of the State of Missouri, at the northeast corner of the Cherokee tract, and running thence north along the west line of the State of Missouri twenty-seven miles to the southerly line of the Miami lands; thence west so far as shall be necessary, by running a line at right angles, and parallel to the west line aforesaid, to the Osage lands, and thence easterly along the Osage and Cherokee lands to the place of beginning; to include one million eight hundred and twenty-four thousand acres of land, being three hundred and twenty acres for each soul of said Indians, as their numbers are at present computed." This land is also intended as a future home for the Senecas, Onondagas, Cayugas, Tuscaroras, Oneidas, St. Regis, Stockbridges, Munsees, and Brothertowns, residing in the State of New York.

1842.

MAY.—Lieutenant John C. Fremont arrived at St. Louis May 22, 1842. Thence he proceeded to Cyprian Chouteau's trading house, on the Kansas river, about six miles west of the Missouri line; latitude 39° 5′ 57″; longitude 94° 39′ 16″; elevation above the sea, about 700 feet. He started thence June 10, with Kit Carson as his guide. On the 12th he seems to have camped near the site of Lawrence:

"We encamped in a remarkably beautiful situation on the Kanzas bluffs, which commanded a fine view of the river valley, here from three to four miles wide. The central portion was occupied by a broad belt of heavy timber, and nearer the hills the prairies were of the richest verdure."

On the 14th, he crossed to the north side of the river, probably at the point where Topeka now stands. On the 16th, he says:

"We were now fairly in the Indian country, and it began to be time to prepare for the chances of the wilderness."

His journey thence was northwest, to the Blue and the Platte. The expedition went as far west as the Wind River mountains; left there August 18; returned by the Platte, and reached the Missouri at the mouth of the Platte, October 1.

JUNE.—Captain Moore, of the U. S. Dragoons, and Dr. Mott, of the Regular army, select Fort Scott as a military post. It was occupied by United States troops until 1854.

1843.

MAY.—Fremont passes up the Kansas river on a second expedition.

DECEMBER 14.—The Wyandottes purchase of the Delawares 23,040 acres of land at the junction of the Missouri and Kansas rivers. This contract was ratified by the United States, July 25, 1848; on the 1st of April, 1850, they agree to pay the Wyandottes $185,000 for the lands promised them.

1844.

"The Commerce of the Prairies," by Josiah Gregg, published in Philadelphia; two volumes.

—Colonel Dodge, of the Third U. S. Dragoons, makes an expedition from Fort Leavenworth to Pike's Peak.

—The Mormons cross the plains, starting near the site of the present city of Atchison.

—General Kearney marches from Fort Leavenworth to Santa Fe.

1846.

JANUARY 14.—The Kansas Indians cede to the United States "two millions of acres of land on the east part of their country, embracing the entire width, thirty miles, and running west for quantity."

JUNE 5 and 17.—The United States grant to the Pottawatomies a tract of land containing 576,000 acres, being thirty miles square, and being the eastern part of the lands ceded to the United States by the Kansas tribe of Indians, January 14, 1846, adjoining the Shawnees on the south, and the Delawares and Shawnees on the east, on both sides of the Kansas river.

AUGUST 8.—President Polk sends a special message to Congress, asking an appropriation of money to pay for territory to be acquired by treaty from Mexico. A bill was reported appropriating $30,000 expenses of negotiations, and $2,000,000 to be used in making a treaty. The House was Democratic by 120 to 72. A few Northern Democrats—among them Hannibal Hamlin, of Maine, Preston King, of New York, and David Wilmot, of Pennsylvania, held a caucus and decided that, inasmuch as Mexico had abolished slavery some twenty years before, all territory acquired from that country should come in free. In accordance with this understanding, Mr. Wilmot offered the following proviso to the first section of the bill:

"*Provided*, That, as an express and fundamental condition to the acquisition of any territory from the republic of Mexico by the United States, by virtue of any treaty that may be negotiated between them, and to the use by the Executive of the moneys herein appropriated, neither slavery nor involuntary servitude shall ever exist in any part of said territory, except for crime, whereof the party shall first be duly convicted."

The bill passed the House with this proviso, by 85 to 80. It then went to the Senate, in the last hours of the session, and remained there without action upon it when the session ended, August 10.

1847.

The Catholic Osage Mission established in what is now Neosho county. The boys' school opened May 1, and the girls' school, October 10.

DECEMBER 24.—Lewis Cass first promulgates the Squatter Sovereignty dogma, in a letter to A. O. P. Nicholson, of Nashville, Tennessee. He says:

"The Wilmot Proviso has been before the country for some time. It has been repeatedly discussed in Congress, and by the public press. I am strongly impressed with the opinion that a great change has been going on in the public mind upon this subject—in my own as well as others'; and that doubts are resolving themselves into convictions, that the principle it involves should be kept out of the national legislature, and left to the people of the Confederacy in their respective local governments.

"Briefly, then, I am opposed to the exercise of any jurisdiction by Congress over this matter; and I am in favor of leaving the people of any territory which may be hereafter acquired the right to regulate it themselves, under the general principles of the constitution."

The letter is published in Niles's Register. This firebrand did not make Cass President in 1848, nor Douglas in 1860. On the 1st of March, 1847, Mr. Cass said, in the Senate, of the Wilmot Proviso: "Last year I should have voted for the proposition, had it come up."

1848.

FEBRUARY 2, 1848, Mexico ceded the territory now covered by the States of California and Nevada; also her claims to the territory covered by the present State of Texas, by the Territories of Utah, Arizona, and New Mexico, by portions of the Territories of Wyoming and Colorado, and by the unorganized territory west of the Indian country, except that part of the Territory of Arizona and that part of the Territory of New Mexico lying south of the River Gila and west of the old boundary of New Mexico, which lands were ceded by Mexico December 30, 1853, and are known as the Gadsden Purchase.—*U. S. Census Report, 1870. Vol. I, p. 574.*

The United States paid to Mexico $15,000,000.

—Major W. H. Emory makes a military reconnoissance from Fort Leavenworth to San Diego.

1849.

Publication of The California and Oregon Trail, by Francis Parkman.

—Fort Laramie, established by a fur company, is transferred to the United States.

1850.

In 1850 the boundaries of the Indian country were as follows: On the east, the present western boundaries of the States of Missouri and Arkansas; on the south, the Red river; on the west, the twenty-third meridian (100th Greenwich) as far north as the Arkansas river, and along that river to the intersection of the Rocky Mountains and the twenty-ninth meridian (106th Greenwich), and along that meridian northward to the proposed southern boundary of the original Territory of Nebraska, which became the northern limit of this country. Within these limits, however, is included that part of the territory ceded by Texas to the United States which was not included in the Territory of New Mexico, being a parcel of land between the Arkansas river on the north and the present northernmost boundary of the State of Texas, and between the twenty-third and twenty-sixth meridians (100th and 103d Greenwich). Including this latter territory, the area of the Indian country at 1850 was 195,274 square miles. By act of May 30, 1854, the Territory of Kansas was erected, and its southern boundary, from the State of Missouri to the twenty-third meridian (100th Greenwich), became the northern limit of the Indian country. The limits of the Indian country remain as they were left by that act; area, 68,991 square miles. A part of the territory above mentioned as ceded by the State of Texas was included in the Territory of Kansas.—*U. S. Census Report, 1870, Vol. I, p. 577.*

Military road established by the Government from Fort Leavenworth to Fort Kearney.

1851.

SEPTEMBER 17.—Treaty with the Cheyennes and Arapahoes. The boundaries of their country are thus defined: "Commencing at the Red Butte, or the place where the road leaves the North fork of the Platte river, thence up the North fork of the Platte river to its source, thence along the main ridge of the Rocky Mountains to the head-waters of the Arkansas river, thence down the Arkansas river to the crossing of the Santa Fe road, thence in a northwesterly direction to the forks of the Platte river, thence up the Platte river to the place of beginning."

1852.

JULY 31.—T. T. Fauntleroy, Colonel of First Dragoons, while in Washington, writes a letter to Major Gen. T. S. Jessup, Quartermaster General, U. S. A. He says: "Some time since," as commanding officer of the post "at Fort Leavenworth, I. T.," he refused to recommend an expenditure for repairs, etc., there, because he "did not consider that post as best suited for the military operations in that quarter." He urges the establishment of a military post "at or near a point on the Kansas river where the Republican fork unites with it"—now Fort Riley. He urges "the discontinuance of the Leavenworth, Scott, Atkinson, Kearney and Laramie posts," and the concentration of troops at the post proposed.—A military camp, called Camp Centre, was soon made at this place.

DECEMBER 13.—Willard P. Hall, of Missouri, offers in the House a bill organizing the Territory of Platte (embracing Kansas and Nebraska).

1853.

FEBRUARY 2.—William A. Richardson, of Illinois, from the Committee on Territories, reports a bill organizing the Territory of Nebraska.

FEBRUARY 10.—Richardson's bill passes the House by 98 to 43. Neither

Hall's nor Richardson's bills proposed to make the new Territory Slave territory.

FEBRUARY 17.—Stephen A. Douglas, in the Senate, reports Richardson's bill without amendment.

MARCH 3.—The Senate puts the Richardson-Douglas bill on the table by 23 to 17.

MARCH 4.—Franklin Pierce inaugurated.

Fort Riley established. It is in latitude 39° 03′ 38″; longitude 96° 24′ 36″; elevation above the Gulf of Mexico, 926 feet. Major Ogden superintends the building of the fort.

JULY 28.—In 1855, a correspondent of the Chicago Press made the statement that a convention was held at Wyandotte July 28, 1853, a Territorial government organized, and a Delegate to Congress nominated. Abelard Guthrie was put forward by the friends of Thomas H. Benton, and Rev. Thomas Johnson by the friends of D. R. Atchison. Guthrie received the nomination. Late in the fall, Thomas Johnson was brought out as a candidate, and was elected by Indian votes. He went to Washington, but the Territory was not organized, and he was not received as a Delegate. The Washington Union spoke of him as "the Rev. Thomas Johnson, a noble specimen of a Western man."

DECEMBER 4.—Augustus C. Dodge, of Iowa, offers in the Senate a bill to organize the Territory of Nebraska.

TERRITORIAL ORGANIZATION.

1854.

JANUARY 4.—Stephen A. Douglas reports Senator Dodge's bill, with material amendments.

JANUARY 23.—Senator Douglas reports a substitute for his former bill, providing for the organization of two Territories, Nebraska and Kansas. The important provision of the bill is the following, copied from section 32:

"That the constitution, and all laws of the United States which are not locally inapplicable, shall have the same force and effect within the said Territory of Kansas as elsewhere within the United States, except the eighth section of the act preparatory to the admission of Missouri into the Union, approved March sixth, eighteen hundred and twenty, which, being inconsistent with the principle of non-intervention by Congress with slavery in the States and Territories, as recognized by the legislation of eighteen hundred and fifty, commonly called the Compromise Measures, is hereby declared inoperative and void; it being the true intent and meaning of this act not to legislate slavery into any Territory or State, nor to exclude it therefrom, but to leave the people thereof perfectly free to form and regulate their domestic institutions in their own way, subject only to the Constitution of the United States: *Provided*, That nothing herein contained shall be construed to revive or put in force any law or regulation which may have existed prior to the act of the sixth of March, eighteen hundred and twenty, either protecting, establishing, prohibiting, or abolishing slavery."

Mr. Douglas advocates his revolutionary measure as embodying "the great principle of Squatter Sovereignty, or non-intervention."

MARCH 2.—Salmon P. Chase thinks the sovereign squatters ought to be free to have freedom. He offers this addition to the 32d section (following the words, "subject only to the Constitution of the United States"):

"Under which the people of the Territory, through their appropriate representatives, may, if they see fit, prohibit the existence of Slavery therein."

Only ten Senators vote for this provision; thirty-six Senators vote against it.

An amendment offered by Mr. Chase, enabling the people of these Territories to choose their own Governor, is also voted down.

The following is copied from Greeley's American Conflict, vol. I, p. 235:

"Within the three months immediately preceding the passage of the Kansas bill, treaties were quietly made at Washington with the Delawares, Otoes, Kickapoos, Kaskaskias, Shawnees, Sacs, Foxes, and other tribes, whereby the greater part of the soil of Kansas lying within one or two hundred miles of the Missouri border was suddenly opened to White appropriation and settlement. These simultaneous purchases of Indian lands by the Government, though little was known of them elsewhere, were thoroughly understood and appreciated by the Missourians of the Western border, who had for some time been organizing 'Blue Lodges,' 'Social Bands,' 'Sons of the South,' and other societies, with intent to take possession of Kansas in behalf of Slavery. They were well assured, and they fully believed, that the object contemplated and desired, in lifting, by the terms of the Kansas-Nebraska bill, the interdict of slavery from Kansas, was to authorize and facilitate the legal extension of slavery into that region. Within a few days after the passage of the Kansas-Nebraska act, hundreds of leading Missourians crossed into the adjacent Territory, selected each his quarter-section or larger area of land, put some sort of mark on it, and then united with his fellow adventurers in a meeting or meetings intended to establish a sort of Missouri pre-emption upon all this region. Among the resolves passed at one of these meetings were the following:

"'That we will afford protection to no Abolitionist as a settler of this Territory.'

"'That we recognize the institution of Slavery as already existing in this Territory, and advise slaveholders to introduce their property as early as possible.'"

MARCH 3.—The Kansas-Nebraska bill passes the Senate by 37 to 14.

MARCH 15.—The Ottoe and Missouria Indians cede to the United States all their country west of the Missouri river, excepting a strip of land on the waters of the Big Blue river, ten miles in width.

APRIL 26.—The following is copied from the Report, made in 1856, by the Congressional Investigating Committee:

"In April [the 26th], 1854, the General Assembly of Massachusetts passed an act entitled 'An act to incorporate the Massachusetts Emigrant Aid Society.' The object of the Society, as declared in the first section of this act, was 'for the purpose of assisting emigrants to settle in the West.' The nominal capital of the corporation was not to exceed five millions of dollars, but no more than four per cent. could be assessed during the year 1854, and no more than ten per cent. in any one year thereafter. No organization was perfected or proceedings had under this law.

"On the 24th day of July, 1854, certain persons in Boston, Massachusetts, concluded articles of agreement and association for an Emigrant Aid Society. The purpose of this association was declared to be, 'assisting emigrants to settle in the West.' Under these articles of association each stockholder was individually liable. To avoid this difficulty, an application was made to the General Assembly of Massachusetts for an act of incorporation, which was granted. On the 21st day of February, 1855, an act was passed to incorporate the New England Emigrant Aid Company. The purpose of this act was declared to be, 'directing emigration westward, and aiding and providing accommodation after arriving at their place of destination.' The capital stock of the corporation was not to exceed one million of dollars. Under this charter a company was organized."

APRIL 26.—The incorporators under the act of this date creating the Massachusetts Emigrant Aid Company are Benjamin C. Clark, Isaac Livermore, Charles Allen, Isaac Davis, William G. Bates, Stephen C. Phillips, Charles C. Hazewell, Alex. H. Bullock, Henry Wilson, James S. Whitney, Samuel E. Sewall, Samuel G. Howe, James Holland, Moses Kimball, James D. Green, Francis W. Bird, Otis Clapp, Anson Burlingame, Eli Thayer, and Otis Rich. One of the most active men in securing the organization was Eli Thayer.

MAY 6.—The Delaware Indians cede to the United States their lands in Kansas, excepting the country sold to the Wyandottes, and excepting the part "lying east and south of a line beginning at a point on the line between the land of the Delawares and the half-breed Kanzas, forty miles in a direct line west to the boundary between the Delawares and Wyandottes, thence north ten miles, thence in an easterly course to a point on the south bank of Big Island creek," on the Missouri river.

MAY 10.—The Shawnees cede to the United States the tract of land set apart for them November 7, 1825, and conveyed to the tribe by deed May 11, 1844, containing 1,600,000 acres, excepting 200,000 acres for homes for the Shawnee people.

MAY 17.—The Ioway tribe of Indians cede to the United States the small strip of land lying between the Kickapoo land and the Grand Nemahaw river, containing 400 sections, but reserving a portion for a permanent home.

MAY 18.—The Kickapoos cede their land in Kansas to the United States, except the western part, containing 150,000 acres.

MAY 22.—Vote on the passage of the bill to organize the Territories of Nebraska and Kansas.

The House voted May 22. The *ayes* are as follows, from the Free States: *Maine*, McDonald; *New Hampshire*, Hibbard; *Connecticut*, Ingersoll; *New York*, Cumming, Cutting, Rowe, Taylor, Tweed (William M.), Walbridge, Walker, Walsh, Westbrook; *Pennsylvania*, Bridges, Dawson, Florence, Jones, Kurtz, McNair, Packer, Robbins, Straub, Witte, Wright; *New Jersey*, Lilly, Vail; *Ohio*, Disney, Green, Olds, Shannon (Wilson); *Indiana*, Davis, Dunham, Eddy, English, Hendricks (Thos. A.), Lane (James H.), Miller; *Illinois*, Allen (James C.), Allen (Willis), Richardson; *Michigan*, Clark, Stuart; *Iowa*, Henn; *California*, Latham, McDougall—from the Free States, 44.

From the Slave States: *Delaware*, Riddle; *Maryland*, Hamilton, May, Shower, Vansant; *Virginia*, Bayly, Bocock, Caskie, Edmundson, Faulkner, Goode, Kidwell, Letcher, Powell, Smith (William), Snodgrass; *North Carolina*, Ashe, Craige, Clingman, Kerr, Ruffin, Shaw; *South Carolina*, Boyce, Brooks (Preston S.), Orr; *Georgia*, Bailey, Chastain, Colquitt, Hillyer, Reese, Stephens (Alex. H.); *Alabama*, Abercrombie, Cobb, Dowdell, Harris, Houston, Phillips, Smith; *Mississippi*, Barry, Barksdale, Singleton, Wright; *Louisiana*, Dunbar, Jones, Perkins; *Kentucky*, Breckinridge (John C.), Chrisman, Cox, Hill, Elliott, Grey, Preston, Stanton; *Tennessee*, Churchwell, Jones, Ready, Smith, Stanton (Frederick P.), Zollicoffer; *Missouri*, Lamb, Lindley, Miller, Oliver (Mordecai), Phelps (John S.); *Arkansas*, Greenwood, Warren; *Florida*, Maxwell; *Texas*, Bell, Smyth—from the Slave States, 69. Total *ayes*, from Free and Slave States, 113.

The *noes* are as follows, from the Free States: *Maine*, Benson, Farley, Fuller, Mayall, Washburn; *New Hampshire*, Kittredge, Morrison; *Massachusetts*, Banks (N. P.), Crocker, De Witt, Dickinson, Edmands, Eliot, Goodrich, Upham, Walley, Wentworth; *Rhode Island*, Davis, Thurston; *Connecticut*, Belcher, Pratt, Seymour; *Vermont*, Meacham, Sabin, Tracy; *New York*, Bennett, Carpenter, Dean, Lyon, Fenton (Reuben E.), Flagler, Hastings, Haven, Hughes, Jones, Matteson, Morgan (Edwin B.), Murray, Oliver, Peck, Peckham, Perkins, Pringle, Sage, Simmons, Smith (Gerrit), Wheeler; *New Jersey*, Pennington, Skelton, Stratton; *Pennsylvania*, Chandler, Curtis, Dick, Drum, Everhart, Gamble, Grow (Galusha A.), Hiester, Howe, McCulloch, Middleswarth, Ritchie, Russell, Trout; *Ohio*, Ball, Campbell (Lewis D.), Edgerton, Ellison, Giddings (Joshua R.), Harlan, Harrison, Johnson, Lindsley, Nichols, Ritchey, Sapp, Stuart, Taylor, Wade (Edward); *Indiana*, Harlan, Mace, Parker; *Illinois*, Knox, Norton, Washburne (E. B.), Wentworth (John), Yates (Richard); *Michigan*, Noble, Stevens; *Wisconsin*, Eastman, Wells—from the Free States, 91.

From the Slave States: *Virginia*, Millson; *North Carolina*, Puryear,

Rogers; *Tennessee*, Bugg, Cullom, Etheridge (Emerson), Taylor; *Louisiana*, Hunt; *Missouri*, Benton (Thomas H.)—from the Slave States, 9. Total *noes* from Free and Slave States, 100. Absent or not voting, 21.

MAY 24.—The Senate finally passes the bill without a division, the call of the ayes and noes being refused. The vote of the Senate on the third reading of the bill was as follows:

Ayes—Atchison (*Mo.*), Badger (*N. C.*), Benjamin (*La.*), Broadhead (*Pa.*), Brown (*Miss.*), Butler (*S. C.*), Cass (*Mich.*), Clay (*Ala.*), Dawson (*Georgia*), Douglas (*Ill.*), Fitzpatrick (*Ala.*), Gwin (*Cal.*), Hunter (*Va.*), Johnson (*Ark.*), Jones (*Iowa*), Jones (*Tenn.*), Mallory (*Fla.*), Mason (*Va.*), Morton (*Fla.*), Norris (*N. H.*), Pearce (*Md.*), John Pettit (*Ind.*), Pratt (*Md.*), Rusk (*Tex.*), Sebastian (*Ark.*), Shields (*Ill.*), Slidell (*La.*), Stuart (*Mich.*), Thompson (*Ky.*), Thomson (*N. J.*), Toombs (*Ga.*), Toucey (*Conn.*), Weller (*Cal.*), Williams (*N. H.*), Wright (*N. J.*) —35.

Noes—Allen (*R. I.*), Bell (*Tenn.*,), Chase (*Ohio*), Clayton (*Del.*), Fish (*N. Y.*), Foot (*Vt.*), Gillette (*Conn.*), Hamlin (*Me.*), James (*R. I.*), Seward (*N. Y.*), Sumner (*Mass.*), Wade (*Ohio*), Walker (*Wis.*) —13.

MAY 30.—The Kaskaskias, Peorias, Piankeshaws and Weas cede to the United States the land given in October, 1832, excepting 160 acres for each soul in said tribes.

MAY 30.—President Pierce signs the Kansas-Nebraska bill. The following is copied from the act:

"SECTION 19. *And be it further enacted*, That all that part of the territory of the United States included within the following limits, except such portions thereof as are hereinafter expressly exempted from the operations of this act, to wit, beginning at a point on the western boundary of the State of Missouri, where the thirty-seventh parallel of north latitude crosses the same; thence west on said parallel to the eastern boundary of New Mexico; thence north on said boundary to latitude thirty-eight; thence following said boundary westward to the east boundary of the Territory of Utah, on the summit of the Rocky Mountains; thence northward on said summit to the fortieth parallel of latitude; thence east on said parallel to the western boundary of the State of Missouri; thence south with the western boundary of said State, to the place of beginning, be, and the same is hereby created into a temporary government by the name of the Territory of Kansas; and when admitted as a State or States, the said Territory, or any portion of the same, shall be received into the Union with or without slavery, as their constitution may prescribe at the time of their admission: *Provided*, That nothing in this act contained shall be construed to inhibit the Government of the United States from dividing said Territory into two or more Territories, in such manner and at such times as Congress shall deem convenient and proper, or from attaching any portion of said Territory to any other State or Territory of the United States: *Provided further*, That nothing in this act contained shall be construed to impair the rights of person or property now pertaining to the Indians in said Territory, so long as such rights shall remain unextinguished by treaty between the United States and such Indians, or to include any territory which by treaty with any Indian tribe is not, without the consent of said tribe, to be included within the territorial limits or jurisdiction of any State or Territory; but all such territory shall be excepted out of the boundaries, and constitute no part of the Territory of Kansas, until said tribe shall signify their assent to the President of the United States to be included within the said Territory of Kansas, or to affect the authority of the Government of the United States to make any regulation respecting such Indians, their lands, property, or other rights, by treaty, law, or otherwise, which it would have been competent to the Government to make if this act had never passed."

Hale says:

"The Territory of Kansas is bounded on the north by Nebraska, on the east by

Missouri, on the south in part by the line of 37°, which divides it from the Cherokee country, and in part by New Mexico, and on the west by the highest ridge of the Rocky Mountains."

KANSAS.—By act of May 30, 1854, formed as a Territory, extending from the western boundary of Missouri westward to the Rocky Mountains, then the eastern boundary of the Territory of Utah; and from the thirty-seventh northward to the fortieth parallel, excepting that part of the Territory of New Mexico north of the thirty-seventh parallel; area, 126,283 square miles. By act of January 29, 1861, that portion of the Territory east of the twenty-fifth meridian, 81,318 square miles, was admitted as a State. By act of February 28, 1861, the remainder of the Territory, 44,965 square miles, was included in the Territory of Colorado.—*U. S. Census Report, 1870, Vol. I, p. 578.*

The distance from the eastern to the western boundary is as great as the distance from Boston, Mass., to Sandusky, Ohio.

The part of the Territory of Kansas not included in the Louisiana Purchase was derived from Mexico. The Spanish title dates back to Columbus, Coronado, Ponce de Leon, or Cortez. The following is copied from Edward Abbott's "Paragraph History:"

"Hernando Cortez, a native of Spain, but for several years a resident of Hispaniola, landed in Mexico in March, 1519, in command of an expedition for the conquest of that country. After a prolonged campaign, marked by many battles and varying fortunes, he finally captured the city of Mexico, and completed the subjugation of the people. His character and policy were such, however, as to surround him with enemies, and, though he was made Governor of Mexico, his administration was brief, and far from prosperous or peaceful. In 1536, he explored parts of California, and of the gulf since called by the same name, and, returning to Spain, died in 1547, in comparative obscurity."

JUNE 5.—The Miami Indians cede to the United States the land given them in 1840 and 1841, excepting 70,000 acres for homes, and 640 acres for school purposes.

JUNE 13.—The Leavenworth Town Company organized, at Weston, Mo. Mr. Gist, President; Major Macklin, U. S. A., Amos Rees, and L. D. Bird, Trustees; Joseph Evans, Treasurer; H. Miles Moore, Secretary.

JUNE 24.—Commission issued to Saunders W. Johnston, of Ohio, as Associate Justice; to Andrew Jackson Isacks, of Louisiana, as United States District Attorney.

JUNE 29.—Commission issued to Andrew H. Reeder, of Easton, Penn., as Governor; to Israel B. Donalson, of Illinois, as United States Marshal; to Daniel Woodson, of Lynchburg, Va., as Secretary; to Madison Brown, of Maryland, as Chief Justice; to Rush Elmore, of Alabama, as Associate Justice. Mr. Brown did not accept the appointment, and Samuel D. Lecompte, of Maryland, was appointed.

JUNE.—A new Emigrant Aid Company organized in Massachusetts, of which Amos A. Lawrence, Eli Thayer and J. M. F. Williams are the Trustees.

JULY 7.—Governor Reeder takes the oath of office before Peter V. Daniel, one of the Justices of the United States Supreme Court, in Washington.

JULY.—The Massachusetts Emigrant Aid Society obtain a charter from the Connecticut Legislature, and operate under it until the next winter, when they procure a new charter from the Massachusetts Legislature.

JULY 17.—The first pioneer party leaves Boston for Kansas.

July 18.—The New York Legislature charters the Emigrant Aid Society of New York and Connecticut.

July 22.—An act of Congress creates the office of Surveyor General of Kansas and Nebraska.

July 24.—Eli Thayer, Amos A. Lawrence, and J. M. F. Williams, of Massachusetts, Trustees of the Emigrant Aid Stock Company; Dr. Thomas H. Webb, Secretary.

July 27.—The Atchison Town Company formed in Missouri. Peter T. Abell, President; J. H. Stringfellow, Secretary; James N. Burnes, Treasurer.

July 29.—The "Platte County Self-Defensive Association" holds a meeting at Weston, Mo. G. Galloway, President; Benj. F. Stringfellow, Secretary. It was an aggressive Pro-Slavery organization. Similar meetings were held at other places on the border.

July 30.—Charles H. Branscomb, of Massachusetts, arrives on the border with the first company of Eastern immigrants, to found the city of Lawrence. Two weeks later they were followed by a second and larger company, with whom came Dr. Charles Robinson and Samuel C. Pomeroy.

July 30.—James Findlay appointed Clerk of the Supreme Court.

July 31.—William Walker, of the Wyandotte Indians, signs a letter, which is published in the papers, as "Provisional Governor, K. T."

August 1.—The first party, of thirty, led by Charles H. Branscomb, arrive at the Wakarusa.

August 2.—Treaty with the Shawnee Indians.

August 21.—A book published with the following title: "Kanzas and Nebraska: The History, Geographical and Physical Characteristics, and Political Position of those Territories; an Account of the Emigrant Aid Companies, and Directions to Emigrants. By Edward E. Hale. With an Original Map from the Latest Authorities. Boston: Phillips, Sampson and Company." The book contains 256 pages. Mr. Hale's is the ablest of the books on Kansas, and many a year will probably go by before any other book on our State is written by a man so eminent and patriotic as the author of "A Man without a Country." The following is copied from the preface:

"I have followed up, as carefully as I could, the memoirs of the early French travellers who first opened to the civilized world the valley of the Missouri. Of more use, in the view in which that valley is now regarded, are the more recent travels of our own countrymen, a body of official reports which deserve very high praise for the skill and gallantry displayed in exploration, and the care with which their history has been written. I have made such use as I could of the travels of Lewis and Clarke, Captain Pike, Colonel Long, Mr. Breckenridge, Major Bonneville, Colonel Fremont, Colonel Emory, Lieutenant Abert, Mr. Parkman, Major Cross, Captain Stansbury, Captain Gunnison, Governor Stevens, Lieutenant Williamson, and others.

"I have used some recent letters published in newspapers, and have been favored with personal narratives of agents of the Emigrant Aid Company.

"In my sketch of the Indian tribes I have followed the invaluable treatise of Mr. Gallatin, the spirited sketches of Mr. Catlin, and Mr. Parkman's interesting journal of his sojourn with the Ogillalah, besides the notices in the travellers I have named.

"It will not be long, I suppose, before historical societies and antiquarian institutes in Kanzas and Nebraska will be collecting materials far more abundant for their history and geography. I shall watch such collections with great interest, as well as with the pride of being the first collector in the field. Working with the disadvantages of a first collector, I have simply tried to make this book accurate as far as it goes."

Mr. Hale's purpose was to send Northern men here to make Kansas Free. He was one of the Committee, with Richard Hildreth, the historian, who reported the "plan of organization and system of operations" of the Massachusetts Emigrant Aid Company, on the 4th of May, 1854.

AUGUST.—A pamphlet of twenty-four pages printed in Boston, by Alfred Mudge & Son, entitled: "Organization, Objects, and Plan of Operations of the Emigrant Aid Company: Also, a description of Kansas for the Information of Emigrants." The officers of the Company are given as follows: Trustees—Amos A. Lawrence, Boston; J. M. F. Williams, Cambridge; Eli Thayer, Worcester. Treasurer—Amos A. Lawrence, Boston. Secretary—Thomas H. Webb, Boston.

AUGUST 23.—Congress appropriates $25,000 for public buildings in Kansas.

AUGUST 26. —John Calhoun, of Illinois, appointed Surveyor General.

AUGUST 29.—Thos. J. B. Cramer appointed Territorial Treasurer.

AUGUST 30.—John Donaldson appointed Auditor of Public Accounts.

—Father John Schoenmakers, of the Osage Mission, now Neosho county, reports a grasshopper raid. They "came down like a fall of snow." They hatched in the spring of 1855, and destroyed all the crops and "all the grass on the prairies," in that vicinity.

SEPTEMBER 1.—The second New England party arrives at the mouth of the Wakarusa.

SEPTEMBER 15.—Appearance of the first newspaper in Kansas, the Leavenworth Herald. It was printed under an elm tree, on the Levee, near the corner of Cherokee street. It was a Pro-Slavery paper. In 1861, it was discontinued. No file of it is known to be in existence. H. Rives Pollard, of Virginia, was at one time its editor.

SEPTEMBER 20.—Chas. Aug. Williams appointed Executive Clerk.

SEPTEMBER 21.—First sale of city lots in Atchison.

SEPTEMBER 28.—Daniel Woodson takes the oath of office as Secretary, in Washington.

OCTOBER 1.—First sermon preached in Lawrence, by Rev. S. Y. Lum.

OCTOBER 3.—Commission issued to Samuel D. Lecompte, of Maryland, as Chief Justice.

OCTOBER 6.—Lawrence is the name given to the "New Boston," "Yankee," or "Wakarusa" settlement, in honor of Amos A. Lawrence, its benefactor.

OCTOBER 7.—Gov. Reeder arrives in the Territory, and establishes the Executive Office temporarily at Fort Leavenworth.

OCTOBER 9.—First sale of town lots in Leavenworth; amount realized, $12,600.

OCTOBER 15.—This is the date of the Kansas Tribune, of Lawrence, the first number of which is printed in Ohio, by John Speer. The articles were written in Kansas, by Mr. Speer. It is a Free-State paper.

—Rush Elmore takes the oath of office as Associate Justice, before Gov. Reeder, at Fort Leavenworth.

OCTOBER 18.—Gov. Reeder, Judges Johnston and Elmore, and Marshal Donalson, go into the Territory, "to examine the same."

OCTOBER 19.—Robert L. Ream appointed Chief Clerk of Surveyor General. Miss Vinnie Ream is his daughter.

OCTOBER 21.—This is the date of the first number of the Kansas Herald of Freedom, published at Wakarusa, by G. W. Brown & Co. It was printed at Conneautville, Crawford county, Pa., where Mr. Brown had been publishing the Courier. No. 2 was printed in Kansas, and is dated Jan. 6, 1855, Lawrence City. No. 1 is a handsomely-printed and well-edited eight-column paper. During a part of 1855 and 1856 the paper was reduced to seven columns. A wood engraving in the centre of the head of the paper has been closely followed in our State seal. This number records the arrival in Kansas, on the 6th of September, of "the second Kansas party." It left Boston August 29th, was conducted by Chas. H. Branscomb, and contained between one and two hundred persons. They were publicly received at Albany and Rochester, New York. At Rochester, a Bible was presented to the emigrants, inscribed "To establish civil and religious liberty in Kansas," and an address delivered by Hon. Wm. C. Bloss.

Bryant's poem, "The Prairies," is copied in the Herald, and the following poem written by Whittier:

THE KANSAS EMIGRANT'S SONG.
AIR—*Auld Lang Syne.*

We cross the prairies as of old
  The pilgrims crossed the sea,
To make the West, as they the East,
  The homestead of the free.

Cho.—The homestead of the free, my boys,
  The homestead of the free;
To make the West, as they the East,
  The homestead of the free.

We go to rear a wall of men
  On Freedom's Southern line,
And plant beside the cotton tree,
  The rugged Northern pine!

We're flowing from our native hills,
  As our free rivers flow;
The blessing of our mother-land
  Is on us as we go.

We go to plant her common schools
  On distant prairie swells,
And give the Sabbaths of the wild
  The music of her bells.

Upbearing, like the ark of old,
  The Bible in our van,
We go to test the truth of God
  Against the fraud of man.

No pause, nor rest, save where the streams
  That feed the Kansas run,
Save where our pilgrim gonfalon
  Shall flout the setting sun.

We'll sweep the prairies as of old
  Our fathers swept the sea,
And make the West, as they the East,
  The homestead of the free.

A letter written from Kansas by Samuel N. Wood is copied from the National Era. Two files of the Herald of Freedom, neither complete, have been examined in preparing this book. One was bought by Chief Justice Kingman of Judge George W. Smith, of Lawrence, and one by Hon. David Dickinson, State Librarian, of James Christian, of Lawrence. Both files are now in the State House, and accessible to the public.

OCTOBER 26.—Birth of Lawrence Carter, the first child born in Lawrence. In June, 1875, the Atchison Champion published the following:

"A BRAVE LAWRENCE BOY.—Yesterday morning an accident happened down the river, that but for the presence of mind and prompt action of Lawrence Carter, fireman on the yard-engine of the A. & N. road, would have proved fatal. A little son of D. G. Lett, about twelve years of age, was playing in the river and accidentally fell off the log on which he stood. The swift current immediately carried him out in the river, and he sank twice under water, when Lawrence Carter jumped from his engine and plunged into the river to save him."

The Lawrence Standard of July 1st, 1875, copies the above, and adds:

"Rev. D. G. Lett until recently was a citizen of Lawrence, and the young man who saved his son's life was the first child born in Lawrence, and was therefore christened Lawrence Carter. A lot was then deeded to the boy by the Town Company. The lot is now in the centre of the city."

OCTOBER 31.—Sterling G. Cato takes the oath of office as Associate Justice.

— Pawnee was a town made by the officers at Fort Riley, viz., Col. Montgomery, Capt. Nathaniel Lyon, Dr. Hammond, Dr. Simmons, Lieut. Long, Robert Wilson, the Sutler, and others, most of them Free-State men, in the fall of 1854. By order of Jeff. Davis, Secretary of War, the boundaries of Fort Riley were so enlarged as to absorb the Free-State town of Pawnee. This was done in the summer of 1855. The order of Davis was not executed until fall, when Col. Cooke arrived from Texas. The settlers were then driven from Pawnee, and the buildings nearly destroyed.

NOVEMBER 6.—David R. Atchison made a speech in Platte county, Mo., of which the Platte Argus, of Nov. 6, gives the following report:

"Gen. Atchison said his mission here to-day was, if possible, to awaken the people of this county to the danger ahead, and to suggest the means to avoid it.

"The people of Kansas, in their first elections, would decide the question whether or not the slaveholder was to be excluded, and it depended upon a majority of the votes cast at the polls. Now if a set of fanatics and demagogues a thousand miles off could afford to advance their money and exert every nerve to abolitionize the Territory and exclude the slaveholder, when they have not the least personal interest, what is your duty? When you reside in one day's journey of the Territory, and when your peace, your quiet, and your property depend upon your action, you can, without an exertion, send five hundred of your young men who will vote in favor of your institutions. Should each county in the State of Missouri only do its duty, the question will be decided quietly and peaceably at the ballot-box. If we are defeated, then Missouri and the other Southern States will have shown themselves recreant to their interests, and will deserve their fate."

NOVEMBER 7.—The Governor returns from his journey into the Territory.

NOVEMBER 8.—The Territory is divided into sixteen election districts, by Gov. Reeder.

NOVEMBER 10.—Proclamation from the Governor for the election of a Delegate to Congress, on the 29th inst.

—The office of Surveyor General opened for business at Fort Leavenworth.

—Marshal Donalson takes the oath of office before Judge Elmore.

—John A. Halderman, Private Secretary of Governor Reeder from November, 1854, to July 1st, 1855.

NOVEMBER 17.—The Leavenworth Herald of this date notes the appearance of the Kansas Pioneer, published at Kickapoo.

NOVEMBER 24.—Executive office removed to the house of Thos. Johnson, at the Shawnee Mission.

NOVEMBER 25.—Proclamation for the formation of the seventeenth election district.

NOVEMBER 29.—Attorney Isacks takes the oath of office before Governor Reeder.

NOVEMBER 29.—First election of Delegate to Congress. Whitfield is the Pro-Slavery candidate; Wakefield and Flenneken are Free-State men.

ELECTION AND CENSUS OF NOVEMBER 29, 1854.

Districts	Place of Voting.	J. W. Whitfield...	J. A. Wakefield ...	R. P. Flenneken.	Scattering	Total..........	No. of Voters by Census........
1	Lawrence	46	188	51	15	300	369
2	Douglas	235	20	6	......	261	199
3	Stinson's.....................................	40	....	7	......	47	101
4	Dr. Chapman's.............................	140	21	....	......	161	47
5	H. Sherman's...............................	63	4	15	......	82	442
6	Fort Scott....................................	105	....	....	......	105	253
7	"110"..	597	....	7	......	604	53
8	Council Grove...............................	16	....	....	......	16	39
9	Reynolds's....................................	9	....	31	......	40	36
10	Big Blue Crossing..........................	2	6	29	......	37	63
11	Marysville	237	....	3	5	245	24
12	Warton's Store..............................	31	9	....	1	41	78
13	Osawkee.......................................	69	1	1	......	71	96
14	Harding's.....................................	130	....	23	......	153	334
15	Penseneau's..................................	267	....	39	......	306	309
16	Leavenworth	222	....	80	......	312	385
17	Shawnee Agency............................	49	....	13	......	62	50
18	....	....	....	....	......	....	28
	Total..................	2,258	248	305	21	2,833	2,905

DECEMBER 1.—A daily mail is established between Weston and Leavenworth, and the Herald hopes that Leavenworth may yet have a post office.

DECEMBER 3.—J. M. Burrell takes the oath of office as Associate Justice.

DECEMBER 4.—Judges of election make returns of election held November 29.

DECEMBER 5.—Topeka founded by C. K. Holliday, M. C. Dickey, F. W. Giles, and others.

—J. W. Whitfield declared by the Governor duly elected Delegate to Congress, and certificate of election issued. Whitfield took his seat. The Thirty-third Congress ended March 3, 1855. The brevity of the session prevented Republicans from making a contest.

—Samuel D. Lecompte takes the oath of office as Chief Justice, before Governor Reeder.

DECEMBER 23.—The first Free-State meeting, reported in the Herald of Freedom, was held at Lawrence. Rev. S. S. Snyder was Chairman, and Charles Robinson Secretary. Resolutions were reported by John Speer and Samuel N. Wood. John A. Wakefield, C. K. Holliday, S. Y. Lum and James S. Emery took part in the meeting.

DECEMBER 25.—At a meeting held in Lafayette county, Missouri, the following resolution was adopted:

"*Resolved*, That we, the shippers, merchants, planters, and citizens generally, of Lafayette county, deem it an act of injustice that steamboats on the Missouri river should give their aid or countenance to the base attempt to abolitionize the Territory of Kansas by aiding or forwarding any persons who may be sent by Abolition societies thereto, or in giving aid or assistance to any such object; and that in our trading, shipping and travelling we will give preference to such boats as will refuse their aid and comfort to such emigration as may be forwarded by any Abolition society for such purposes."

—A book published, with the following title: "A Journey Through Kansas; with Sketches of Nebraska: Describing the Country, Climate, Soil, Mineral, Manufacturing and other Resources. The Results of a Tour made in the Autumn of 1854. By Rev. Chas. B. Boynton and T. B. Mason, Committee from the 'Kansas League,' of Cincinnati. With a new and authentic Map, from Official Sources. Cincinnati: Moore, Wilstach, Keys & Co., 1855." pp. 216. The map is about eight inches by six in size, and shows the region between the Missouri river and the Rocky Mountains. It is "Redrawn from official sources, with emendations, by H. V. Boynton." It is not a book of events or politics, but a pleasant description of a delightful journey. The writers ardently desired that Kansas might be free. Leavenworth, visited in September, 1854, is thus described:

"A squatter city has little resemblance to any other city; it belongs to a distinct genus of cities. This is a large and important one, the capital, as many hope, of Kansas, and is therefore worthy of description. There was one steam-engine, 'naked as when it was born,' but at work, sawing out its clothes. There were four tents, all on one street, a barrel of water or whiskey under a tree, and a pot, on a pole over a fire. Under a tree, a type-sticker had his case before him, and was at work on the first number of the new paper; and within a frame, without a board on side or roof, was the editor's desk and sanctum. When we returned from the Territory to Weston, we saw the 'Notice,' stating that the editor had removed his office from under the elm tree to the corner of 'Broadway and the Levee.' This Broadway was, at that time, much broader than the streets of old Babylon; for, with the exception of the Fort, there was, probably, not a house on either side for thirty miles."

Fort Riley and Council Grove are visited, and Stinson's, "where the town of Tecumseh has been laid out." Lawrence is spoken of as follows:

"Just before sunset we reached the 'Yankee settlement.' A few tents were pitched on the high ground overlooking the Kansas and Waukereusa valleys, others were scattered over the level bottoms below, but not a dwelling beside was to be seen. It was a city of tents alone. We were cordially received by the intelligent and active agent, Dr. Robinson, from whom we learned, with much satisfaction, the plans and expectations of the Company. . . . . We had a comfortable night's rest in Dr. Robinson's tent, and in the morning were introduced to the only 'boarding house on the hill.' Two very intelligent ladies, from Massachusetts, had united their forces and interests, and had taken 'boarders.' In the open air, on some logs of wood, two rough boards were laid across for a table, and on wash-tubs, and kegs, and blocks, they and their boarders were seated round it. This was the first boarding-house in the new city of Lawrence. All were cheerful, hopeful and full of energy, and the scene reminded me of Plymouth Rock."

—During the years 1854 and 1855, by treaties with the Chippewa tribe, nearly all of the lands owned by them were ceded to the United States. A number of reservations, limited in extent, were set apart for the different bands. One of these was in Kansas.

—The Chippewas, or Ojibways, are a tribe of American Indians, the type of the Algonquin stock, and were occupants from our earliest historical period of the basin of Lake Superior.

1855.

JANUARY.—The Easton (Pa.) Argus says:

"We have just seen the seal of the Territory of Kansas, engraved by Robert Lovett, of Philadelphia, according to the design of Gov. Reeder. It consists of a shield with two supporters, surmounted by a scroll motto, and is emblematic of the life of the pioneer and the agriculturist. The lower compartment of the shield contains the buffalo and the hunter; the upper contains the implements of agriculture. The left-hand supporter is a pioneer with his smock frock, leggins, rifle, and tomahawk; whilst on the right is the goddess Ceres with her sheaf; at their feet, and between them, lie a fallen tree and an axe. The motto is a beautiful allusion to the principle on which the Territory was organized, and consists of '*Populi voce,*' thus translated—*Born of the popular will.*"

JANUARY.—Major Dorn, U. S. Indian Agent, concludes treaties with the Seneca, Shawnee and Quapaw Indians.

JANUARY 19.—A tri-weekly mail between Leavenworth and the Fort is paid for by private subscription. Lewis N. Rees, "without fee or reward," acts as postmaster.

JANUARY 22.—Gov. A. H. Reeder issues a precept to certain persons to take a census.

JANUARY 31.—The Wyandottes cede to the United States the country purchased by them of the Delawares, December 14, 1843, with a few special exceptions.

—Teesdale, Elkins & Co., Akron, Ohio, print a "History of Kansas and Emigrant's Guide," by "J. Butler Chapman, Esq., a Resident since its Settlement." Mr. Eugene M. Cole, of Indianola, Shawnee county, a very intelligent printer, owns a well-worn copy of this peculiar book. Has any other new State called out so many books and newspapers? This book contains 116 pages. The writer was known in Kansas, where he spent a few months, as John B. Chapman. He was a candidate for Delegate to Congress, and the projector of "Whitfield City." Of Lawrence, Mr. Chapman says:

"A printing press was established at this town in October, (1854,) by the enterprise of John and Joseph Speer, of Medina, Ohio; and another has followed since, from Pennsylvania; but we know the Speers are the pioneer editors to Lawrence City."

FEBRUARY 1.—The Kansas Free-State Society formed at Lawrence: R. G. Elliott President, E. D. Ladd and John Speer Secretaries.—C. W. Babcock appointed Postmaster at Lawrence.

FEBRUARY 3.—Robert S. Kelley and John H. Stringfellow start the Squatter Sovereign, at Atchison. In 1857, it became a Free-State paper, and was edited by Robert McBratney and Frank G. Adams. John A. Martin bought the office, and changed the name of the paper to the Champion, February 23, 1858. The Daily Champion came out March 22, 1865. This is the oldest newspaper office in the State.

FEBRUARY 9.—There are three Free-Soil newspapers in Lawrence: The Herald of Freedom, Kansas Tribune, and the Kansas Free State. The Tribune is published by John and Joseph L. Speer; the Free State by Robert G. Elliott and Josiah Miller.

FEBRUARY 23.—The Leavenworth Herald says: "Five months ago there was not a building in the place. The town had just been laid off and the brush cut down. Leavenworth now has a hotel, a saw mill, a tailor's shop, a shoemaker, a barber, two blacksmiths, three carpenter shops, several law and two doctors' offices."

A correspondent of the Liberty (Mo.) Tribune says: "Lawrence is the resort of about 400 Abolitionists."

FEBRUARY 26.— Gov. Reeder issues a proclamation defining the judicial districts of the Territory, and assigning the Judges to them. The First District embraces the thirteenth, fourteenth, fifteenth, sixteenth and eighteenth election districts, and is assigned to Chief Justice S. D. Lecompte; the courts to be held at Leavenworth.

The Second Judicial District includes the first, second, third, fourth, fifth, sixth, and seventeenth election districts, and is assigned to Rush Elmore; courts to be held at Tecumseh.

The rest of the Territory, including the seventh, eighth, ninth, tenth, eleventh, and twelfth election districts, is made the Third District, and is assigned to Saunders W. Johnston; courts to be held at Pawnee.

The terms of the courts are prescribed by the same proclamation.

FEBRUARY 28.—Census completed; 8,501; voters, 2,905. Governor Reeder divides the Territory into eighteen districts, appoints judges of election, and orders an election for a Territorial Legislature to be held March 30th.

FEBRUARY.—John Brown, jr., Jason, Owen, Frederick, and Salmon Brown, sons of John Brown, come to Kansas "early in 1855," and settle near the Pottawatomie river, eight miles from Osawatomie.

CENSUS TAKEN IN JANUARY AND FEBRUARY, 1855.

By whom taken.	Districts	Males	Females	Voters	Minors	Natives of United States	Foreign birth	Negroes	Slaves	Total
C. W. Babcock	1	623	339	369	459	887	75			962
O. H. Browne	2	316	203	199	237	506	19	1		519
T. W. Hayes	3	161	91	101	112	215	12		6	252
O. B. Donaldson	4	106	71	47	97	169	2	1	1	177
William Barbee	5	824	583	442	724	1,385	22	27	26	1,407
William Barbee	6	492	318	253	418	791	12	11	11	810
J. B. McClure	7	82	36	53	50	117	1	1	1	118
J. B. McClure	8	56	27	39	28	76	7	13	10	83
M. F. Conway	9	61	25	36	31	66	12	14	3	86
M. F. Conway	10	97	54	63	61	108	23			151
B. H. Twombly	11	33	3	24	5	30	6			36
B. H. Twombly	12	104	40	78	35	109	37	1	7	144
H. B. Jolly	13	168	116	96	145	273	9	14	14	284
Albert Heed	14	655	512	334		301	46	1	35	1,167
H. B. Jolly	15	492	331	308	448	846	16	15	15	873
Charles Leib	16	708	475	385	514	1,042	104	48	33	1,183
Alex. O. Johnson	17	91	59	50	54	143	5	4	23	150
B. H. Twombly	18	59	40	28	51	97	1			99
Total		5,128	3,383	2,905	3,469	7,161	408	151	192	8,601

MARCH.— Dr. Thos. H. Webb, Secretary of the Emigrant Aid Company, offered a prize of fifty dollars for a Kansas song. Eighty-nine were presented; the following poem obtained the prize:

CALL TO KANSAS.

BY LUCY LARCOM.

AIR—*Nelly Bly.*

Yeomen strong, hither throng!
  Nature's honest men;
We will make the wilderness
  Bud and bloom again.
Bring the sickle, speed the plough,
  Turn the ready soil!
Freedom is the noblest pay
  For the true man's toil.
Ho, brothers! come, brothers!
  Hasten all with me;
We'll sing upon the Kansas plains
  A song of Liberty!

Mother, come! here's a home
  In the waiting West;
Bring the seeds of love and peace,
  You who sow them best.
Faithful hearts, holy prayers,
  Keep from taint the air;
Soil a mother's tears have wet
  Golden crops shall bear.
Come, mother! fond mother,
  List, we call to thee;
We'll sing, etc.

Father, haste! o'er the waste
  Lies a pleasant land.
There your fireside's altar-stones,
  Fixed in truth, shall stand.
There your sons, brave and good,
  Shall to freemen grow,
Clad in triple mail of right,
  Wrong to overthrow.
Ho, brothers! come, brothers!
  Hasten all with me;
We'll sing, etc.

Brother brave, stem the wave!
  Firm the prairies tread!
Up the dark Missouri flood
  Be your canvas spread.
Sister true, join us too,
  Where the Kansas flows;
Let the Northern lily bloom
  With the Southern rose.
Brave brother! true sister!
  List, we call to thee;
We'll sing, etc.

One and all, hear our call
  Echo through the land!
Aid us with a willing heart,
  And the strong right hand!
Feed the spark the Pilgrims struck
  On old Plymouth rock!
To the watch-fires of the free
  Millions glad shall flock.
Ho, brothers! come, brothers!
  Hasten all with me;
We'll sing, etc.

MARCH 8.—Governor Reeder issues a proclamation for an election, March 30, of thirteen members of the Council and twenty-six members of the House.

MARCH 13.—Dr. Charles Robinson leaves Boston for Kansas with about two hundred persons.

MARCH.—A few days before the 30th, John Ellis, owner of the Weston and Kickapoo Ferry, had the following bill printed and tacked upon his boat:

SOME illy-disposed persons have tried to injure my Ferry by stating that I refused to cross persons, last fall, to go to the election. This is false; it will be difficult to find one more sound on the "goose" than I am.
Signed,   JOHN ELLIS.

MARCH 30.—About one thousand Missourians, under Samuel Young and Claiborne F. Jackson, arrive in Lawrence to vote, and vote. Mrs. Robinson says: "They were armed with guns, pistols, rifles and bowie-knives. They brought two cannon loaded with musket balls."

RETURNS OF ELECTION OF MARCH 30, 1855, BY DISTRICTS.

District	Place of Voting.	Pro-Slavery vote.	Free-State vote.	Scattering	COUNCIL. No. of District.	COUNCIL. No. of Members.	HOUSE. No. of District.	HOUSE. No. of Members.
1	Lawrence	781	253	......	1	2	2	3
2	Bloomington	318	12	11	2	1	3	2
3	Stinson's, or Tecumseh	366	4	2	3	1	4	1
4	Dr.Chapman's	78	2	......	1	....	1	1
	Bull Creek	377	9	......				
5	Pottawatomie	199	65	......				
	Big Sugar Creek	74	17	7	4	2	7	4
	Little Sugar Creek	34	70	......				
6	Fort Scott	315	35	......	5	1	6	2
7	Isaac B. Titus's	211	23	......	3	....	5	1
8	Council Grove	17	17	......	3		5	
9	Pawnee	23	52	......	6	1	8	1
10	Big Blue	27	42	......	10		8	
	Rock Creek	2	21	......	8		8	
11	Marysville	328	....	......	9		9	1
12	St. Mary's	4	7	......	10		9	
	Silver Lake	12	19	2	1		9	
13	Hickory Point	233	6	......	10		10	1
	Doniphan	313	30	3	7	....	11	
14	Wolf Creek	57	15	6	7	1	11	2
	Burr Oak	256	2	48	8	....	12	2
15	Hayes's	412	....	5	9	1	13	2
16	Leavenworth	899	60	5	10	2	14	3
17	Gum Springs	43	16	......	1	....	....	......
18	Moorestown	48	14	......	7	1	....	......
	Total	5,427	791	89		13		26

ELECTION OF MARCH 30, 1855, BY COUNCIL DISTRICTS.

Total votes cast in Council district	Total votes cast in election district	Total votes in Council dist. for them	No. of votes for them in election district	Free-State Candidates	Total votes in Council dist. for them	No. of votes for them in election district	Pro-Slavery Candidates	No. of Councilmen	Precincts	No. of election district	No. of Council district
1,183	1,034		254	Joel K. Goodin		780	Thomas Johnson	2	Lawrence	1	1
		273	255	Sam. N. Wood		783	Ed. Chapman				
	80		2	Joel K. Goodin		78	Thomas Johnson		Chapman's	4	
			2	Sam. N. Wood		78	Ed. Chapman				
	59		16	Joel K. Goodin	900	42	Thomas Johnson			17	
			16	Sam. N. Wood		43	Ed Chapman				
330	330	12	12	J. A. Wakefield	318	318	A. McDonald	1		2	2
	374		4	A. McDonald		370	H. J. Strickler	1		3	3
	234		23	Wm. F. Johnson		211	H. J. Strickler		Titus's	7	
642	37	44	17	Rice	508	17	H. J. Strickler			8	
	303		9	M. G. Morris		377	A. M. Coffey	2	Bull Creek	5	4
			9	James P. Fox		376	David Lykins				
	266		65	M. G. Morris		199	A. M. Coffey		Pottawatomie		
			63	James P. Fox		199	David Lykins				
	91		17	M. G. Morris		74	A. M. Coffey		Big Sugar Creek		
			16	M. G. Morris		74	David Lykins				
855	855	158	62	James P. Fox	680	31	A. M. Coffey		Little Sugar Creek		
			70	James P. Fox		34	David Lykins				
343	343				343	343	Wm. Barbee				
	69		50	M. F. Conway		23	John Donaldson	1	Big Blue	6	5
	22		42	M. F. Conway		27	John Donaldson	1	Rock Creek	9	6
	331		21	M. F. Conway		2	John Donaldson		Marysville	10	
	31		3	M. F. Conway		328	John Donaldson		Silver Lake	11	
538	11	140	19	M. F. Conway	396	12	John Donaldson		St. Mary's	12	
			7	M. F. Conway		4	John Donaldson		Wolf River	14	
						74	John W. Forman	1	Doniphan		7
478		68	68	John W. Whitehead	478	343	John W. Forman			18	
						61	John W. Forman			14	
302	302				234	234	W. P. Richardson	1	Burr Oak	15	8
412	412				411	411	D. A. M. Grover	1		13	9
	242		6	B. H. Twombly		233	R. R. Rees	2		16	10
			6	A. J. Whitney		233	L. J Eastin				
	964		60	R. H. Twombly		896	R. R. Rees				
1,216		66	59	A. J. Whitney	1,129	893	L. J. Eastin				

ELECTION OF MARCH 30, 1855, BY REPRESENTATIVE DISTRICTS.

No. Representative Dist.	No. of Election District.	Precincts and Place of voting.	No. of Representatives...	Pro-Slavery Candidates.	Their vote in Electn. Dist.	Their vote in Rep. Dist.	Free-State Candidates.	Their vote in Electn. Dist.	Their vote in Rep. Dist.
1	4	Dr. Chapman's............	1	A. S. Johnson............	77		A. F. Powell............	3	
	17	Shawnee Mission.......	...	A. S. Johnson............	43	120	A. F. Powell............	16	19
2	1	Lawrence.................	3	James Whitlock	780		John Hutchinson...	252	
				J. M. Banks............	781		E. D. Ladd............	253	
				A. B. Wade.............	781	781	P. P. Fowler............	254	253
3	2	Bloomington.............	2	G. W. Ward............	318		Isaac Davis............	12	
				O. H. Browne............	318	318	E. G. Macy.............	12	12
4	3	Tecumseh.................	1	D. L Croysdale.........	366	366	C. K. Holliday........	4	4
5	7	I. B. Titus's.............	1	M. W. McGee............	210		H. Rice	23	
	8	Council Grove		M. W. McGee............	12	222	A. I. Baker............	25	49
6	6	Fort Scott..............	2	Joseph C. Anderson..	315		Jno. Hamilton.......	35	35
				S. A. Williams	313	315	William Margraves	16	....
7	5	Bull Creek..............	4	W. A. Heiskell	377		John Serpell	9	
				Allen Wilkinson......	375		Adam Pore	9	
				Henry Younger........	375		S. H. Houser	9	
				Samuel Scott............	377		William Jennings...	9	
		Pottawatomie Creek....	...	Wm. A. Heiskell........	198		John Serpell	61	
				Allen Wilkinson......	198		Adam Pore	54	
				Henry Younger........	198		S. H. Houser	64	
				Samuel Scott............	198		Wm. Jennings.......	62	
		Big Sugar Creek........		Wm. A. Heiskell........	74		John Serpell	17	
				Allen Wilkinson......	74		Adam Pore	16	
				Henry Younger........	74		S. H. Houser	17	
				Samuel Scott............	74		Wm. Jennings.......	17	
		Little Sugar Creek		Wm. A. Heiskell........	33		John Serpell	62	
				Allen Wilkinson......	32		Adam Pore	62	
				Henry Younger........	35		S. H. Houser	64	
				Samuel Scott............	35	684	Wm. Jennings........	66	152
8	9	Pawnee	1	Russell Garrett	18		S. D. Houston	56	
	10	Big Blue................		Russell Garrett	21		S. D. Houston	43	
		Rock Creek		Russell Garrett	2	41	S. D. Houston	21	120
9	11		1	Fr. J. Marshall.........	328				
	12	Silver Lake.............		Fr. J. Marshall.........	12		H. McCartney.........	19	
		St. Mary's...............		Fr. J. Marshall.........	4	344	H. McCartney.........	7	26
10	13	Hickory Point	1	Wm. H. Tebbs ...'....	237	237	C. Hard.............	3	
11	14	Wolf River..............		John H. Stringfellow	57		G. A. Cutler.........	15	
				R. L. Kirk.............	52		John Landis	8	
		Doniphan		J. H. Stringfellow	313		J. Ryan.............	8	
				R. L. Kirk.............	292		G. A. Cutler.........	30	
							John Landis............	25	
	18	Nemaha	...	J. H. Stringfellow.....	48		Joel Ryan.............	18	
				R. L. Kirk	50	420	G. A. Cutler.........	14	
12	14	Burr Oak	2	Joel P. Blair............	256		John Landis............	13	54
				Thos. W. Waterson...	258	258	John Fee.............	2	
13	15	....	2	H. B. C. Harris.........	412				
				J. Weddell................	412	412			
14	16	Leavenworth	3	Wm. G. Mathias........	899		Felix G. Braden......	59	
				H. McMeekin............	899		Samuel France........	59	
				Archy Payne	895	897	F. Browning	59	59

APRIL 5.—Election returns opened by Gov. Reeder, Secretary Woodson, and Clerk Halderman.

APRIL 6.—The Leavenworth Herald announces the result of the first Legislative election in these words:

"All hail! Pro-Slavery Party Victorious. We have met the enemy and they are ours. *Veni, Vidi, Vici.* Free White State Party Used Up."

"The triumph of the Pro-Slavery party is complete and overwhelming. Come on, Southern men; bring your slaves and fill up the Territory. Kansas is saved. Abolitionism is rebuked, her fortress stormed, her flag is draggling in the dust! The tricolored Platform has fallen with a crash; the rotten timbers of its structure were not sufficient to sustain the small fragments of the party."

"Kansas has proved herself to be S. G. Q."

Those letters meant: Sound on the Goose Question.

APRIL 14.—The Parkville (Mo.) Luminary destroyed by a Pro-Slavery mob from Platte City.

APRIL 16.—Gov. Reeder calls an election, May 22, to fill vacancies in the House and Council, in the 1st, 2d, 3d, 7th, 8th and 16th districts, on account of irregularities in the previous election. The Legislature is ordered to meet at the town of Pawnee, in the 9th election district, on the first Monday in July, "in the building which will be provided for that purpose."

APRIL 17.—The Governor leaves for Pennsylvania.

APRIL 30.—Pro-Slavery Vigilance Committee appointed at Leavenworth. Nine resolutions were adopted, the following among them:

"*Resolved,* That we recognize the right of every man to entertain his own sentiments in all questions, and to act them out so long as they interfere with neither public or private rights; but that when the acts of men strike at the peace of our social relations, and tend to subvert the known and recognized rights of others, such acts are in violation of morals, of natural law, and systems of jurisprudence to which we are accustomed to submit.

"*Resolved,* That a Vigilance Committee, consisting of thirty members, shall now be appointed, who shall observe and report all such persons as shall openly act in violation of law and order, and by the expression of Abolition sentiments produce disturbance to the quiet of the citizens or danger to their domestic relations; and all such persons so offending shall be notified and made to leave the Territory."

The report of the meeting in the Leavenworth Herald says: "The meeting was ably and eloquently addressed by Judge Lecompte, Col. J. N. Burnes, of Weston, and D. J. Johnson."

APRIL 30.—Cole McCrea kills Malcolm Clark, at Leavenworth. The Congressional Committee (1856) reported:

"Your committee in their examinations have found that in no case of crime or homicide mentioned in this report, or in the testimony, has any indictment been found against the guilty party, except in the homicide of Clark by McCrea; McCrea being a Free-State man."

McCrea was arrested and imprisoned at Fort Leavenworth, and in jail. The Grand Jury in September failed to find a bill against McCrea. Mrs. Robinson says:

"At the adjourned term of the court, in November, Judge Lecompte had added seven new members to the Grand Jury, and a bill of indictment for murder in the first degree was found against him. Four of the counsel within the bar, and officers acting at this tribunal, including the clerk of the court, were connected with the lynching of Phillips, on the 17th of May."

McCrea escaped from jail, and made his appearance in Lawrence Dec. 1st.

4

—The District Court for the Second District organized at Tecumseh; Rush Elmore, Judge; John A. Halderman appointed U. S. Attorney *pro tem.*, and Ben. I. Newsom Clerk.

—The Herald of Freedom says a drought prevailed from June '54 to May '55, "with scarcely any rain or snow to cool the atmosphere or moisten the earth."

RETURNS OF THE ELECTION OF MAY 22, 1855, TO FILL VACANCIES —CALLED BY GOV. REEDER.

No. of Dist.	Place of Voting.	Pro-Slavery Votes	Free-State Votes	Scattering.	Total.
1	Lawrence		288	18	306
2	Douglas		127	....	127
3	Stinson's		148	1	149
7	"110"		66	13	79
8	Council Grove		33	....	33
16	Leavenworth	560	140	15	715
	Total number of votes cast				1,409

MAY.—The steamers Emma Harmon, Financier No. 2, and the Hartford, arrived at Lawrence. A Government boat, the Excel, was the only one to ascend the river before the Harmon. The Harmon was six days in reaching Topeka, from Lawrence. On the return trip, she went from Lawrence to Kansas City in six hours.

MAY 11.—The Leavenworth Herald publishes, with editorial approval, a communication which says: "Suffer not an avowed Abolitionist to remain within your borders. You [the Pro-Slavery party] have got the start; keep it."

MAY 17.—Lynching of William Phillips. The following account is copied from Gladstone's History:

"A Vigilance Committee was appointed in the spring of 1855, having for its object 'to observe and report all such persons as shall, . . . by the expression of Abolition sentiments, produce disturbance to the quiet of the citizens or danger to their domestic relations; and all such persons so offending shall be notified and made to leave the Territory.' On this committee were several members of the Legislature. The first person 'observed and reported' by the committee as acting so as to endanger 'their domestic relations' (by which delicate expression is meant the institution of slavery) was Mr. William Phillips, a lawyer residing in Leavenworth, whose offence was that he had sworn to a protest against the validity of the election in his district, in consequence of which protest Governor Reeder had ordered a new election. Mr. Phillips was 'notified' to leave the Territory. He refused to do so, whereupon he was seized by a party of Missouri men to the number of fourteen, taken across the river, and carried several miles into Missouri. [To Weston.] They then proceeded to shave one side of his head, next stripped off his clothes, and put him through the horrible ordeal of tarring and feathering. This being completed, they rode him on a rail for a mile and a half, and finally put him up at auction, a negro acting as auctioneer, and went through the mockery of selling him, not at the price of a slave, but for the sum of one dollar. Eight days after this outrage a public meeting was held, at which the following resolution was unanimously adopted:

"'That we heartily endorse the action of the committee of citizens that shaved, tarred and feathered, rode on a rail, and had sold by a negro, Wm. Phillips, the moral perjurer.'

"The meeting was presided over by Mr. Rees, a member of Council in the Kansas Legislature, and the resolution was offered by Mr. Payne, a Judge, and also member of the House of Representatives. The outrage committed against Mr. Phillips was not, therefore, the hasty act of a few murderous ruffians, but one advisedly carried out and afterwards deliberately endorsed by a number of citizens and by members of both houses of the Legislature. Mr. Phillips returned to Leavenworth, but has since, according to accounts received in the autumn of 1856, been shot."

MAY 20.—The Leavenworth Herald devotes a column to the description of the tarring, feathering and riding on a rail of Wm. Phillips. The crime of Phillips was, that he protested against a fraudulent election. The Herald says:

"Our action in the whole affair is emphatically endorsed by the Pro-Slavery party in this district. The joy, exultation and glorification produced by it in our community are unparalleled."

—A public meeting was held to approve of this dastardly outrage. The Herald says:

"On motion of Jarret Todd, R. R. Rees was called to the chair, and C. C. Harrison chosen Secretary. On motion of Judge Payne, five resolutions were unanimously adopted, one of which reads as follows:

"'*Resolved*, That we heartily endorse the action of the citizens that shaved, tarred and feathered, rode on a rail, and had sold by a negro, Wm. Phillips, the moral perjurer.'"

—About this time M. W. Delahay begins the publication of the Territorial Register. His paper does not meet the approbation of the violently Pro-Slavery Herald; hence Delahay is denounced as a "traitor."

JUNE 8.—Free-State Convention at Lawrence. *Committee on Organization:* Wm. Partridge, S. F. Shore, Wm. Jessee. *Committee on Resolutions:* S. N. Wood, John Brown, jr., Jas. P. Fox, Aug. Wattles, A. F. Powell. *Officers:* John A. Wakefield, President; John Brown, jr., J. E. Curtis, and Joseph L. Speer, Vice Presidents; R. G. Elliott and Chas. A. Foster, Secretaries.

Resolutions were adopted in favor of making Kansas a Free State, and against the illegal voting by citizens of Missouri. Also, the following:

"*Resolved*, That in reply to the threats of war so frequently made in our neighboring State, our answer is, We Are Ready."

Speeches were made by Wood, Robinson, Elliott, Foster, Speer, Stockton, and others.

JUNE 11.—W. L. Marcy, Secretary of State, writes a letter to Gov. Reeder, charging him with irregularities in the purchase of Indian lands.

JUNE 25.—Gov. Reeder, having returned to Kansas, denies Mr. Marcy's charges.

JUNE 25.—The Governor declares duly elected John Hutchinson, Erastus D. Ladd and Philip P. Fowler, Representatives from the Second District; John A. Wakefield, to be duly elected, from the Second District, and Augustus Wattles and Wm. Jessee, also Representatives from the same district; Jesse D. Wood, a member of the Council from the Third District; Wm. G. Mathias, A. Payne and H. D. McMeekin, members of the House from the Fourteenth District, and C. K. Holliday, a member of the House from the Fourth District.

JUNE 27.—Executive office removed from Shawnee Manual Labor School.

—Convention of the "National Democracy" at Lawrence; James H. Lane, Chairman; J. N. O. P. Wood, Secretary. They resolved that "the best interests of Kansas require an early organization of the Democratic party upon truly national ground;" fully endorse the Democratic platform of 1852; kindly request citizens of adjoining States to let them alone, and that they cannot permit "the purity of the ballot-box to be polluted by outsiders, or illegal voting from any quarter." E. Chapman, C. W. Babcock, James

Garvin, James S. Emery and Hugh Cameron, were the committee on resolutions.

JULY 2.—The Legislature meets at Pawnee, near Fort Riley, as ordered by the Governor. The executive office established at Pawnee.

—Congress appropriates $25,000 for public buildings in Kansas.

—The Third Judicial District organized at Pawnee, Saunders W. Johnston presiding. A. J. Isacks, U. S. Attorney, present. R. H. Higgins appointed Clerk.

July 3.—M. F. Conway resigns his seat in the Council.—Gov. Reeder's Message is read.—John A. Wakefield and Jesse D. Wood, elected from the Second and Third Council Districts on the 22d of May to fill vacancies, enter their solemn protest against being denied seats.

JULY 4.—Donaldson, McDonald and Strickler admitted to seats in the Council.

S. D. Houston, in the House, protests against the action of the House in refusing seats to John Hutchinson, Erastus D. Ladd, Philip P. Fowler, Augustus Wattles and William Jessee, who have received certificates of election from the Governor. The seats are given to the Pro-Slavery candidates voted for on the 30th of March. The ousted members also protest.

—The Kansas Freeman appears, published by Edward C. K. Garvey & Co., at Topeka. The first paper in Topeka.

—A daily paper published in Lawrence one week, by John Speer. The first daily attempted in the Territory.

JULY 6.—John T. Brady elected Public Printer.—An act to remove the seat of Government to the Shawnee Manual Labor School passes both branches over the Governor's veto. Adjourned to meet at Shawnee July 16th.

JULY 10.—Surveyor General's office removed to Leavenworth City.

JULY 16.—Legislature reassembles at Shawnee.

The following are copies of tables printed at the time:

MEMBERS AND OFFICERS OF THE COUNCIL.

Names.	Age.	Occupation.	Nativity.	How long in Terri'y	Quotations from their Speeches.
T. Johnson, Prest., Supt. of Shawnee Mission	53	Farmer	Va ...	18 years..	Justice to all.
R. R. Rees, Prest. pro tem	43	Lawyer	Ohio.	10 mos ...	Just laws and rigid execution.
John W. Forman	36	Merchant	Ky...	12 years..	The organic act—our charter of liberty.
A. M. Coffey	51	Farmer	Ky...	4 years...	The Union; it must be preserved.
D. Lykins	34	Physician	Ia...	12 years..	Cuba must be annexed.
W. P. Richardson, Maj. Gen. Com'g K. M.	53	Farmer	Ky...	9 years...	Hemp for negro-stealers.
H. J. Strickler, Brig. Gen. K. M.	24	Surv.& civ.eng.	Va...	6 mos	The South and her Institutions.
L. J. Eastin, do., Ed. Leavenworth City Herald	40	Printer	Ky...	9 mos	Negro Slavery for Kansas. "Good."
D. A. N. Grover	26	Lawyer	Ky...	10 years..	Homestead for the squatters.
Wm. Barbee	29	Lawyer	Ky...	1 year.....	Majority shall rule.
John Donaldson	25	Merchant	Ky...	6 mos	The cause I advocate must succeed. It is right; it is just.

MEMBERS AND OFFICERS OF THE COUNCIL—*Concluded.*

Names.	Age	Occupation.	Nativity.	How long in Territ'y	Quotations from their Speeches.
A. McDonald............	37	Lawyer............	Va....	10 mos ...	United we stand.
E. Chapman............	27	Lawyer............	La....	10 mos ...	As an American, I reverence the Constitution, now and forever.
Jno. A. Halderman, Chief Clerk.........	24	Lawyer............	Mo....	14 mos ...	
Charles H. Grover, Assistant Clerk....	24	Lawyer............	Ky...	11 years..	A new treaty with the Delawares.
T. C. Hughes, Eng. Clerk.................	37	Farmer............	Md...	5 mos ...	Down with the National Democracy in Kansas.
S. J. Waful, Eng. Clerk.................	23	Farmer............	N.Y..	14 mos ...	Kansas—May her virgin soil be unpolluted by the foul stain of freesoilism.
C. B. Whitehead, Sergeant-at-Arms.	41	Farmer............	Va....	2 years...	

MEMBERS AND OFFICERS OF THE HOUSE OF REPRESENTATIVES.

Names.	Age	Occupation.	Nativity.	How long in the Territory.	Quotations from their Speeches.
J. M. Banks.................	36	Farmer....	Penn	1 year.....	Justice and truth.
J. P. Blair....................	47	Farmer....	Tenn	6 mos.....	
O. H. Browne..............	34	Farmer....	Md...	1 year.....	Be just, and fear not.
D. L. Croysdale..........	26	Physician	Mo...	1 year.....	
H. B. C. Harris.............	30	Physician	Va....	9 mos...	Act justly, but fearlessly.
W. A. Heiskell.............	47	Merchant	Va....	6 years...	The South—her rights and interests.
S. D. Houston..............	36	Farmer....	Ohio.		
Alex. S. Johnson...........	23	Farmer....	K. T.	23 years..	Peaceably if we can—forcibly if we must.
R. L. Kirk....................	37	Farmer....	Ky...	9 mos......	My country, my whole country.
F. J. Marshall.............	38	Merchant	Va....	4 years...	Be sure you're right, then go ahead.
W. G. Mathias..............	29	Lawyer ...	Md...	10 mos....	No disorganization, no fanaticism.
M. W. McGee..............	36	Merchant	Ky...	1 year.....	Kansas, with Southern institutions.
H. D. McMeekin	33	Merchant	Ky...	5 years...	We fight to conquer.
A. Payne	36	Farmer....	Ky...	1 year.....	Union first—South all the time.
Samuel Scott................	52	Farmer....	Ky...	7 mos......	Onward march to victory.
W. H. Tebbs	32	Physician	Va....	1 year......	Non-intercourse, and Southern rights.
A. B. Wade...................	26	Farmer....	Mo...	1 year.....	
G. W. Ward...................	55	Farmer....	Ky...	1 year.....	Justice and the South.
T. W. Waterson.............	44	Farmer....	Penn	18 mos....	Kansas for the South, now and forever.
Jonah Weddle..............	28	Teacher...	Va....	1 year......	Kansas, the South, and the Union.
Jas. Whitlock...............	37	Farmer....	Mo...	10 mos....	My country's flag.
Samuel A. Williams.......	35	Farmer....	Ky...	6 mos.....	Kansas and the Union.
Allen Wilkinson............	35	Farmer....	Tenn	8 mos......	
H. W. Younger	43	Farmer....	Mo...	8 mos......	Order and liberty.
J.H.Stringfellow, Sp'k'r, Ed.Squatter Sovereign	35	Physician	Va....	1 year......	Squatter rights.
J. C. Anderson, Speaker pro tem.........	25	Lawyer ...	Ky...	10 mos....	Vox populi, vox Dei.
Jas. M. Lyle, Chief Clerk....	22	Lawyer ...	S. C...	6 mos.......	Civil and religious liberty.
John Martin, Assistant Clerk.........	21	Lawyer ...	Tenn	6 mos......	Strict construction of the Constitution.
J. C. Thompson, Engrossing Clerk.......	25	Lawyer ...	Ohio.	1 year......	To the victors belong the spoils.
B. F. Simmons, Enrolling Clerk.........	29	Lawyer ...	N. C..	6 mos......	Union only when it protects our interests.
T. J. B. Cramer, Sergeant-at-Arms...	38	Farmer....	Va....	1 year......	
B. F. Campbell, Doorkeeper	28	Farmer....	N. Y.	10 mos....	Kansas to be the brightest star of all.
John T. Peery, Chaplain...............	88	Minister...	Va.....	12 years..	Religion the corner-stone of civilization.
John T. Brady, Public Printer.......	24	Lawyer ...	Md...	16 mos....	The Constitution.
S. A. Lowe, Eng. Clerk	35	Lawyer ...	Md...	2 years...	Money makes the mare go.

JULY 16.— Gov. Reeder receives notice from Mr. Marcy of the intention to remove him.

JULY 21.— Message from Gov. Reeder, in which he says:

"It seems, then, to be plain that the Legislature are now in session, so far as the place is concerned, in contravention of the act of Congress, and where they have no right to sit, and can make no valid legislation. Entertaining these views, I can give no sanction to any bill that may be passed; and if my views are not satisfactory to the Legislative Assembly, it follows that we must act independently of each other."

A resolution was passed by the Council asking the President to remove Gov. Reeder. On the 23d the House concurred in the resolution.

JULY 23.— S. D. Houston resigns his seat in the House. This left both branches unanimously Pro-Slavery.

JULY 24.— The Chairman of the Judiciary Committee in the Council makes a written report sanctioning the penalty of death as the punishment of persons who decoy slaves from their masters.

JULY 23.— There are four Free-State papers in the Territory — the Herald of Freedom, Free State, and Tribune, at Lawrence, and the Freeman, at Topeka. The Leavenworth Herald, the Kickapoo Pioneer and the Atchison Squatter Sovereign are the Pro-Slavery papers.

JULY 30.— First session of the Supreme Court, at the Shawnee Manual Labor School, Johnson county. Lecompte, Johnston and Elmore present, and A. J. Isacks, U. S. District Attorney. Marcus J. Parrott is appointed Reporter of the decisions of the Court.

JULY 31.— Removal of Gov. Reeder officially announced.

—The appointment of Governor was tendered to John L. Dawson, of Pennsylvania, who declined it.

JULY 31.— Mr. Donaldson, in the Council, offered the following resolution:

"Whereas, Reliable information has been received of the removal of 'Squire A. H. Reeder; and, whereas, this body wish to make suitable arrangements to celebrate the day : therefore,

"Resolved, This body do adjourn."

AUGUST.— S. D. Lecompte and Rush Elmore, Judges, and A. J. Isacks, Attorney, give the Legislature a written opinion declaring that the removal of the seat of government to Shawnee is valid, and the legislation at Shawnee legal.

AUGUST 8.— The Legislature, in joint session, votes to establish the permanent seat of government at Lecompton.

AUGUST 10.— Wilson Shannon, of Ohio, commissioned as Governor.

AUGUST 14–15.— First Convention in Lawrence of Free-State men, made up from the various political parties. Philip C. Schuyler presided ; Chas. Robinson reported the resolutions; and Colonel James H. Lane took an active part. The Convention adopted the following resolution:

"Whereas, The people of Kansas have been, since its settlement, and now are, without any law-making power: therefore, be it

"Resolved, That we, the people of Kansas Territory, in mass meeting assembled, irrespective of party distinctions, influenced by common necessity, and greatly desirous of promoting the common good, do hereby call upon and request all bona fide citizens of Kansas Territory, of whatever political views and predilections, to consult together in their respective election districts, and, in mass conventions or otherwise, elect three delegates for each Representative to which said election district is entitled in the House of Representatives of the Legislative Assembly, by proclamation of Governor Reeder, of date 19th of March, 1855; said delegates to assemble in convention, at the town of Topeka, on the 19th day of September, 1855, then and there to consider and determine upon all subjects of public interest, and particularly upon that having reference to the speedy formation of a State Constitution, with an intention of an immediate application to be admitted as a State into the Union of the United States of America."

A Free-State Convention was also called to meet at Big Springs, Douglas county, September 5.

The following Free-State Executive Committee was appointed: Charles Robinson, Chairman; J. K. Goodin, Secretary; George W. Smith, J. A. Wakefield, L. Macy, F. W. Giles, William Phillips (afterwards murdered), Charles A. Foster, J. P. Fox, J. D. Stockton, W. K. Vail, John Brown, jr., W. A. Ely, G. F. Warren, John Hamilton, Hamilton Smith, Lotan Smith, M. F. Conway, S. D. Houston, L. R. Adams, L. R. Palmer, J. E. Gould, Abelard Guthrie.

—The Emigrant Aid Company have four steam saw mills at Kansas City—one for Manhattan, one for Osawatomie, and one for Hampden, on the Neosho.

AUGUST 16.—Gov. Reeder informs the Legislature that he has received official notice of his removal.

—Acting Governor Woodson continues G. P. Lowry in the office of Executive Clerk.

AUGUST 16.—Rev. Pardee Butler sent from Atchison by the Pro-Slavery men. The Squatter Sovereign gives this account of the affair:

"On Thursday last, one Pardee Butler arrived in town with a view of starting for the East, probably for the purpose of getting a fresh supply of Free-Soilers from the penitentiaries and pest-holes of the Northern States. Finding it inconvenient to depart before morning, he took lodgings at the hotel, and proceeded to visit numerous portions of our town, everywhere avowing himself a Free-Soiler, and preaching the foulest of Abolition heresies. He declared the recent action of our citizens in regard to J. W. B. Kelley, the infamous and unlawful proceedings of a mob; at the same time stating that many persons in Atchison, who were Free-Soilers at heart, had been intimidated thereby, and feared to avow their true sentiments; but that he (Butler) would express his views in defiance of the whole community. On the ensuing morning our townsmen assembled en masse, and, deeming the presence of such persons highly detrimental to the safety of our slave property, appointed a committee of two to wait on Mr. Butler and request his signature to the resolutions passed at the late Pro-Slavery meeting in Atchison. After perusing the said resolutions, Mr. B. positively declined signing them, and was instantly arrested by the committee. After the various plans for his disposal had been considered, it was finally decided to place him on a raft composed of two logs firmly lashed together; that his baggage and a loaf of bread be given him; and, having attached a flag to his primitive bark, emblazoned with mottoes indicative of our contempt for such characters, Mr. Butler was set adrift on the great Missouri, with the letter R legibly painted on his forehead.

"He was escorted some distance down the river by several of our citizens, who, seeing him pass several rock-heaps in quite a skilful manner, bade him adieu, and returned to Atchison. Such treatment may be expected by all scoundrels visiting our town for the purpose of interfering with our time-honored institutions, and the same punishment we will be happy to award all Free-Soilers, Abolitionists, and their emissaries."

The mottoes on the flag were these: "Eastern Emigrant Aid Express. The Rev. Mr. Butler, Agent for the Underground Railroad;" "The way they are served in Kansas;" "For Boston;" "Cargo insured—unavoidable danger of the Missourians and the Missouri River excepted." "Let future

emissaries from the North beware.   Our hemp crop is sufficient to reward
all such scoundrels."

AUGUST 25.—The Legislature, in joint session, elects Probate Judges,
Commissioners, and Sheriffs for all the counties, and District Attorneys for
the three Judicial Districts.   The appointment of Justices of the Peace and
Constables is given to Commissioners chosen by the Legislature.

AUGUST 30.—The following appears in the proceedings of the Legislature:

"Mr. Speaker J. H. Stringfellow, Mr. Anderson in the chair, offered the following concurrent resolution:

"*Whereas,* The signs of the times indicate that a measure is now on foot fraught with
more danger to the interests of the Pro-Slavery party, and to the Union, than any
which has yet been agitated, to wit, the proposition to organize a National Democratic
Party; and

"*Whereas,* Some of our friends have already been misled by it; and

"*Whereas,* The result will be to divide Pro-Slavery Whigs from Democrats, thus weak-
ening our party one-half; and

"*Whereas,* We believe that on the success of our party depends the perpetuity of the
Union: therefore

"*Be it resolved by the House of Representatives, the Council concurring therein,* That it
is the duty of the Pro-Slavery party, the Union-loving men of Kansas Territory, to
know but one issue, Slavery; and that any party making or attempting to make any
other, is, and should be held, as an ally of Abolitionism and Disunionism."

The resolution was adopted.

AUGUST 30.—The Council confirms Acting Gov. Woodson's appointments
of Major Generals, Brigadier Generals, and Colonels; and the appointment
of Thos. J. B. Cramer as Auditor of Public Accounts, and John Donaldson
as Treasurer.   Legislature adjourns.

The private laws fill 212 pages of the statute book.   The cities incorpo-
rated are Leavenworth, Lawrence, Kickapoo, Pawnee and Lecompton.
Among the town companies incorporated are Marysville, Iola, Atchison,
Fort Scott and Paola.

AUGUST 31.—Commissions issued by Gov. Woodson to A. M. Coffey,
Major General; Wm. A. Heiskell, Brigadier General; Wm. Barbee, Brig-
adier General; Wm. C. Yager, Colonel; Geo. W. Johnson, Colonel; S. A.
Williams, Colonel; Skilman Fleming, Colonel; Wm. P. Richardson, Major
General; F. J. Marshall, Brigadier General; Lucien J. Eastin, Brigadier
General; Robt. Clark, Colonel; Jas. E. Thompson, Colonel; David M.
Johnson, Colonel; Archibald Payne, Colonel; Hiram J. Strickler, Adjutant
General; and Thomas J. B. Cramer, Inspector General.   Commissions
were also issued to the county officers appointed by the Legislature, for the
following counties: Doniphan, Atchison, Jefferson, Calhoun, Leavenworth,
Douglas, Johnson, Lykins, Bourbon, Allen, Anderson, Franklin, Shawnee,
Nemaha, Marshall, Riley, and Madison.   Commissions were issued to Chas.
H. Grover, H. A. Hutchinson and John T. Brady, as District Attorneys for
the First, Second and Third Judicial Districts.

SEPTEMBER 1.—Nearly all the acts of the first Legislature, commonly
called the "Bogus Laws," took effect as soon as they were passed.   The
volume of laws, 1058 pages, was published in October.   General Stringfellow, in a letter to the Montgomery (Alabama) Advertiser, uses this
language as to the character of the laws of the Territory in reference to
slavery:

"They have now laws more efficient to protect slave property than any State in the

Union. These laws have just taken effect, and have already silenced Abolitionists ; for, in spite of their heretofore boasting, they know they will be enforced to the very letter, and with the utmost rigor. Not only is it profitable for slaveholders to go to Kansas, but politically it is all-important."

The following is a copy of the "Act to punish offences against slave property :"

"Be it enacted by the Governor and Legislative Assembly of the Territory of Kansas, as follows :

"SECTION 1. That every person, bond or free, who shall be convicted of actually raising a rebellion or insurrection of slaves, free negroes, or mulattoes, in this Territory, shall suffer death.

"SEC. 2. Every free person who shall aid or assist in any rebellion or insurrection of slaves, free negroes, or mulattoes, or shall furnish arms, or do any overt act in furtherance of such rebellion or insurrection, shall suffer death.

"SEC. 3. If any free person shall, by speaking, writing, or printing, advise, persuade, or induce any slaves to rebel, conspire against or murder any citizen of this Territory, or shall bring into, print, write publish or circulate, or cause to be brought into, printed, written, published, or circulated, or shall knowingly aid or assist in the bringing into, printing, writing, publishing or circulating, in this Territory, any book, paper, magazine, pamphlet, or circular, for the purpose of exciting insurrection, rebellion, revolt, or conspiracy on the part of the slaves, free negroes, or mulattoes, against the citizens of the Territory, or any part of them, such person shall be guilty of felony, and suffer death.

"SEC. 4. If any person shall entice, decoy, or carry away out of this Territory any slave belonging to another, with intent to deprive the owner thereof of the services of such slave, or with intent to effect or procure the freedom of such slave, he shall be adjudged guilty of grand larceny, and on conviction thereof, shall suffer death, or be imprisoned at hard labor for not less than ten years.

"SEC. 5. If any person shall aid or assist in enticing, decoying, or persuading, or carrying away, or sending out of this Territory, any slave belonging to another, with intent to procure or effect the freedom of such slave, or with intent to deprive the owner thereof of the services of such slave, he shall be adjudged guilty of grand larceny, and, on conviction thereof, shall suffer death, or be imprisoned at hard labor for not less than ten years.

"SEC. 6. If any person shall entice, decoy, or carry away out of any State or other Territory of the United States any slave belonging to another, with intent to procure or effect the freedom of such slave, or to deprive the owners thereof of the services of such slave, and shall bring such slave into this Territory, he shall be adjudged guilty of grand larceny, in the same manner as if such slave had been enticed, decoyed, or carried away out of this Territory; and in such case the larceny may be charged to have been committed in any county of this Territory into or through which such slave shall have been brought by such person; and on conviction thereof, the person offending shall suffer death, or be imprisoned at hard labor for not less than ten years.

"SEC. 7. If any person shall entice, persuade or induce any slave to escape from the service of his master or owner in this Territory, or shall aid or assist any slave in escaping from the service of his master or owner, or shall aid, assist, harbor or conceal any slave who may have escaped from the service of his master or owner, shall be deemed guilty of felony, and punished by imprisonment at hard labor for a term of not less than five years.

"SEC. 8. If any person in this Territory shall aid or assist, harbor or conceal any slave who has escaped from the service of his master or owner in another State or Territory, such person shall be punished in like manner as if such slave had escaped from the service of his master or owner in this Territory.

"SEC. 9. If any person shall resist any officer while attempting to arrest any slave that may have escaped from the service of his master or owner, or shall rescue such slave when in custody of any officer or other person, or shall entice, persuade, aid or assist such slave to escape from the custody of any officer or other person who may have such slave in custody, whether such slave have escaped from the service of his master or owner in this Territory or in any other State or Territory, the person so offending shall be guilty of felony, and punished by imprisonment at hard labor for a term of not less than two years.

"SEC. 10. If any marshal, sheriff, or constable, or the deputy of any such officer, shall, when required by any person, refuse to aid or assist in the arrest and capture of any slave that may have escaped from the service of his master or owner, whether such slave shall have escaped from his master or owner in this Territory or any State or other Territory, such officer shall be fined in a sum of not less than one hundred nor more than five hundred dollars.

"SEC. 11. If any person print, write, introduce into, publish or circulate, or cause to be brought into, printed, written, published or circulated, or shall knowingly aid or assist in bringing into, printing, publishing or circulating within this Territory, any book, paper, pamphlet, magazine, handbill or circular, containing any statements, arguments, opinions, sentiment, doctrine, advice or innuendo, calculated to produce a disorderly, dangerous or rebellious disaffection among the slaves in this Territory, or to induce such slaves to escape from the service of their masters, or resist their authority, he shall be guilty of felony, and be punished by imprisonment and hard labor for a term not less than five years.

"SEC. 12. If any free person, by speaking or by writing, assert or maintain that persons have not the right to hold slaves in this Territory, or shall introduce into this Territory, print, publish, write, circulate, or cause to be introduced into this Territory, written, printed, published or circulated in this Territory, any book, paper, magazine, pamphlet or circular containing any denial of the right of persons to hold slaves in this Territory, such person shall be deemed guilty of felony, and punished by imprisonment at hard labor for a term of not less than two years.

"SEC. 13. No person who is conscientiously opposed to holding slaves, or who does not admit the right to hold slaves in this Territory, shall sit as a juror on the trial of any prosecution for any violation of any of the sections of this act.

"This act to take effect and be in force from and after the fifteenth day of September, A. D. 1855."

By these laws only a Pro-Slavery man could hold office. Every officer, whether elected or appointed, was compelled to take an oath to support the Organic Act and the Fugitive Slave Law. (Page 516.)

The following is section 13, chapter 92, page 445:

"No person who is conscientiously opposed to the holding of slaves, or who does not admit the right to hold slaves in this Territory, shall be a juror in any cause in which the right to hold any person in slavery is involved, nor in any cause in which any injury done to or committed by any slave is in issue, nor in any criminal proceeding for the violation of any law enacted for the protection of slave property, and for the punishment of crimes committed against the right to such property."

Chapter 22, page 165, defines the terms "hard labor" and "convicts." A person found with a copy of the New York Tribune in his pocket, or who uttered a word against slavery, would probably remember his punishment. Section 2 of this law provides that the keeper "having charge of such convict, shall cause such convict, while engaged at such labor, to be securely confined by a chain six feet in length, of not less than four-sixteenths nor more than three-eighths of an inch links, with a round ball of iron, of not less than four nor more than six inches in diameter, attached, which chain shall be securely fastened to the ankle of such convict with a strong lock and key; and such keeper or other person having charge of such convict, may, if necessary, confine such convict, while so engaged at hard labor, by other chains or other means in his discretion, so as to keep such convict secure and prevent his escape; and when there shall be two or more convicts under the charge of such keeper, or other person, such convicts shall be fastened together by strong chains, with strong locks and keys, during the time such convicts shall be engaged in hard labor without the walls of any jail or prison." The next section of this law provides that the convict may be "employed upon private hiring at labor," for fifty cents a day. This would place the Anti-Slavery man, with his ball and chain, at work in the field by the side of the slave.

Of this code and this Legislature, Mr. Gladstone says:

"Being in haste to give a code of laws to Kansas, they transferred into a volume of more than a thousand pages, the greater part of the laws of their own State, substituting the words 'Territory of Kansas' for 'State of Missouri.' In protection of slavery, they enacted far more rigorous laws than obtain in Missouri, or than were ever before conceived of, making it a felony to utter a word against the institution, or even to have in possession a book or paper which denies the right to hold slaves in Kansas. Some of these laws have already been quoted in this volume. It will have been seen that for every copy of a Free-State newspaper which a person might innocently purchase, the law would justify that person's condemnation to penal servitude for two or five years, dragging a heavy ball and chain at his ankle, and hired out for labor on the public roads, or for the service of private individuals, at the fixed price of fifty cents per diem. So comprehensive did these legislators make their slave code, that by the authority they thus gave themselves, they could, in a very short time, have made every Free-State man in the Territory a chained convict, standing side by side, if they so pleased, with their slaves, and giving years of forced labor for the behoof of their Pro-Slavery fellow-citizens.

"The Legislature proceeded also to appoint officers for the Territory. Even the executive and judiciary were made to hold office from itself; and a Board of Commissioners chosen by the Legislature, instead of the inhabitants themselves, was empowered to appoint the sheriffs, justices of the peace, constables, and all other officers in the various counties into which the Territory was divided.

"Every member of succeeding Legislatures, every judge of election, every voter, must swear to his faithfulness on the test-questions of slavery. Every officer in the Territory, judicial, executive, or legislative, every attorney admitted to practise in the courts, every juryman weighing evidence on the rights of slaveholders, must attest his soundness in the interest of slavery, and his readiness to endorse its most repugnant measures.

"For further security, the members of the Assembly submitted their enactments to the Chief Justice for confirmation. This judicial confirmation was gratefully given; all they had done was declared legal. And the sheriffs and other local officers appointed by the Legislature were equally ready with their aid in the execution of these unjust laws."

The following is copied from the Report of the Special Committee appointed in 1856, to Investigate the Troubles in Kansas:

"The material differences in the Missouri and Kansas statutes are upon the following subjects:

"The qualifications of voters and of members of the Legislative Assembly; the official oath of all officers, attorneys, and voters; the mode of selecting officers, and their qualifications; the slave code, and the qualifications of jurors.

"Upon these subjects the provisions of the Missouri code are such as are usual in many of the States. But, by the 'Kansas Statutes' every officer in the Territory, executive and judicial, was to be appointed by the Legislature, or by some officer appointed by it. These appointments were not merely to meet a temporary exigency, but were to hold over two regular elections, and until after the general election in October, 1857. Thus, by the terms of these 'laws' the people have no control whatever over either the legislative, the executive, or the judicial departments of the Territorial government, until a time, before which, by the natural progress of population, the Territorial government will be superseded by a State government.

"No session of the Legislature is to be held during 1856, but the members of the House are to be elected in October of that year. A candidate, to be eligible at this election, must swear to support the Fugitive Slave Law, and each judge of election, and each voter, if challenged, must take the same oath. The same oath is required of every officer elected or appointed in the Territory, and of every attorney admitted to practise in the courts."

SEPTEMBER 1.—Andrew B. Moore, of Alabama, declines the appointment of Associate Justice, vice Elmore, removed.

SEPTEMBER 1.—Gov. Shannon arrives at Westport, Mo.

SEPTEMBER 5.—Big Springs Convention. Organization of the Free-State party. President, Geo. W. Smith; Vice Presidents, John Fee, J. A. Wakefield, James Salsbury, and Amory Hunting; Secretaries, R. G. Elliott, D. Dodge, and A. G. Adams.

The following resolutions, reported by James H. Lane, were afterwards known as the "Big Springs Platform." It was the first platform of the Free-State party of the Territory:

"*Whereas,* The Free-State party of the Territory of Kansas is about to originate an organization for concert of political action in electing our own officers and moulding our institutions; and,

"*Whereas,* It is expedient and necessary that a platform of principles be adopted and proclaimed to make known the character of our organization, and to test the qualifications of candidates and the fidelity of our members; and,

"*Whereas,* We find ourselves in an unparalleled and critical condition—deprived by superior force of the rights guaranteed by the Declaration of Independence, the Constitution of the United States, and the Kansas Bill; and,

"*Whereas,* The great and overshadowing question, whether Kansas shall become a Free or Slave State, must inevitably absorb all other issues, except those inseparably connected with it; and,

"*Whereas,* The crisis demands the concert and harmonious action of all those who from principle or interest prefer free to slave labor, as well as of those who value the preservation of the Union and the guarantees of Republican institutions by the Constitution: therefore,

"*Resolved,* That, setting aside all the minor issues of partisan politics, it is incumbent upon us to proffer an organization calculated to recover our dearest rights, and into which Democrats and Whigs, native and naturalized citizens, may freely enter without any sacrifice of their respective political creeds, but without forcing them as a test upon others. And that when we shall have achieved our political freedom, vindicated our right of self-government, and become an independent State of the Union, when these issues may become vital as they are now dormant, it will be time enough to divide our organization by these tests, the importance of which we fully recognize in their appropriate sphere.

"*Resolved,* That we will oppose and resist all non-resident voters at our polls, whether from Missouri or elsewhere, as a gross violation of our rights, and a virtual disfranchisement of our citizens.

"*Resolved,* That our true interests, socially, morally and pecuniarily, require that Kansas should be a free State; that free labor will best promote the happiness, the rapid population, the prosperity and the wealth of our people; that slave labor is a curse to the master and the community, if not to the slave; that our country is unsuited to it, and that we will devote our energies as a party to exclude the institution, and to secure for Kansas the constitution of a free State.

"*Resolved,* That the best interests of Kansas require a population of free white men, and that in the organization we are in favor of stringent laws excluding all negroes, bond or free, from the Territory; that nevertheless such measures shall not be regarded as a test of party orthodoxy.

"*Resolved,* That the stale and ridiculous charge of Abolitionism, so industriously imputed to the Free-State party, and so persistently adhered to in spite of all the evidence to the contrary, is without a shadow of a truth to support it, and that it is not more appropriate to ourselves than it is to our opponents, who use it as a term of reproach, to bring odium upon us, pretending to believe in its truth, and hoping to frighten from our ranks the weak and the timid, who are more willing to desert their principles than they are to stand up under persecution and abuse, with a consciousness of right.

"*Resolved,* That we will discountenance and denounce any attempt to encroach upon the constitutional rights of the people of any State, or to interfere with their slaves;

conceding to their citizens the right to regulate their own institutions, and to hold and recover their slaves, without any molestation or obstruction from the people of Kansas."

The following resolutions, offered by James S. Emery, and written by ex-Gov. Reeder, were also adopted:

"*Resolved*, That the body of men who, for the past two months, have been making laws for the people of our Territory, moved, counselled and dictated to by the demagogues of Missouri, are to us a foreign body, representing only the lawless invaders who elected them, and not the people of the Territory; that we repudiate their action as the monstrous consummation of an act of violence, usurpation and fraud, unparalleled in the history of the Union, and worthy only of men unfitted for the duties and regardless of the responsibilities of republicans.

"*Resolved*, That having, by reason of numerical inferiority and want of preparation, been compelled to succumb to the outrageous oppression of armed and organized bands of the citizens of a neighboring State — having been robbed by force of the right of suffrage and self-government, and subjected to a foreign despotism, the more odious and infamous that it involves a violation of compacts with sister States, more sacred and solemn than treaties — we disown and disavow with scorn and indignation the contemptible and hypocritical mockery of a republican government into which this infamous despotism has been converted.

"*Resolved*, That this miscalled Legislature, by their reckless disregard of the Organic Territorial Act, and other Congressional legislation, in expelling members whose title to seats was beyond their power to annul, in admitting members who were not elected, and in legislating at an unauthorized place — by their refusal to allow the people to select any of their own officers, by leaving us no elections save those prescribed by Congress, and therefore beyond their power to abrogate, and even at these selling the right of suffrage at our ballot-boxes to any non-resident who chooses to buy and pay for it — by compelling us to take an oath to support a law of the United States, invidiously pointed out — by stifling the freedom of speech and of the press, thus usurping the power forbidden to Congress, has libelled the Declaration of Independence — violated the Constitutional Bill of Rights, and brought contempt and disgrace upon our republican institutions at home and abroad.

"*Resolved*, That we owe no allegiance or obedience to the tyrannical enactments of this spurious Legislature — that their laws have no validity or binding force upon the people of Kansas, and that every free man among us is at full liberty, consistent with all his obligations as a citizen and a man, to resist them if he chooses so to do.

"*Resolved*, That we will resist them primarily by every peaceable and legal means in our power, until we can elect our own Representatives and sweep them from the statute book; and that as the majority of our Supreme Court have so far forgotten their official duty — have so far cast off the honor of a lawyer and the dignity of a judge as to enter, clothed with the judicial ermine, into a partisan contest, and by extra-judicial decisions giving opinions in violation of all propriety, having prejudged our case before we could be heard, and have pledged themselves to the outlaws in advance, to decide in their favor, we will therefore take measures to carry the question of the validity of these laws to a higher tribunal, where judges are unpledged and dispassionate — where the law will be administered in its purity, and where we can at least have a hearing before the decision.

"*Resolved*, That we will endure and submit to these laws no longer than the best interests of the Territory require, as the least of two evils, and will resist them to a bloody issue as soon as we ascertain that peaceable remedies shall fail, and forcible resistance shall furnish any reasonable prospect of success; and that in the meantime we recommend to our friends throughout the Territory the organization and discipline of volunteer companies and the procurement and preparation of arms.

"*Resolved*, That we cannot and will not quietly submit to surrender our great American birthright — the elective franchise — which, first by violence, and then by chicanery, artifice, weak and wicked legislation, they have so effectually attempted to deprive us of, and that we with scorn repudiate the election law, so called, and will not meet with them on the day they have appointed for the election, but will ourselves fix upon a day for the purpose of electing a Delegate to Congress."

The Convention adopted a resolution offered by John Hutchinson, fully endorsing "the People's Convention of the 14th ult., for a delegate convention of the people of Kansas Territory, to be held at Topeka on the 19th inst., to consider the propriety of forming a State Constitution."

On motion of M. F. Conway, A. H. Reeder was nominated for Congress, by acclamation. It was decided to vote for a Delegate to the Thirty-fourth Congress on the second Tuesday in October.

SEPTEMBER 6.—John Donaldson commissioned as Auditor of Public Accounts.

SEPTEMBER 7.—Surveyor General's office removed to Wyandotte.

—Governor Shannon, the second Governor appointed for the term of four years, takes the oath of office before Secretary Woodson. Commissions issued to the officers of Arapahoe county.

SEPTEMBER 13.—Sterling G. Cato, of Alabama, appointed Judge in place of Elmore, and J. M. Burrill, of Pennsylvania, in place of Johnston.

SEPTEMBER 19-20.—Convention at Topeka to take measures to form a Free-State Constitution. Called to order by Geo. W. Smith, of Lawrence. *Officers:* President, W. Y. Roberts; Vice Presidents, J. A. Wakefield, P. C. Schuyler, L. P. Lincoln, J. K. Goodin, S. N. Latta, R. H. Phelan; Secretaries, E. D. Ladd, J. H. Nesbitt, M. W. Delahay. Among the delegates were Geo. W. Deitzler, Geo. W. Brown, John Speer, Jas. H. Lane, C. K. Holliday, and M. J. Parrott. *Committee on an Address to the People:* J. H. Lane, W. Y. Roberts, Hamilton Smith, P. C. Schuyler, H. Miles Moore, Jas. S. Emery, A. M. Jordan, M. W. Delahay, E. D. Ladd, G. W. Deitzler, J. A. Wakefield, Samuel C. Smith, Thos. J. Addis, J. H. Nesbitt, L. P. Lincoln, John Speer, G. W. Brown, S. N. Latta, James Pierce. An election was called for delegates to a Constitutional Convention at Topeka. *Territorial Executive Committee:* J. H. Lane, Chairman; C. K. Holliday, M. J. Parrott, P. C. Schuyler, G. W. Smith, G. W. Brown, and J. K. Goodin, Secretary.

SEPTEMBER 21.—A book issued with this title: "History of the Shawnee Indians, from the Year 1681 to 1854, inclusive. By Henry Harvey, a Member of the Religious Society of Friends. Cincinnati: Ephraim Morgan & Sons. 1855." pp. 316.

Mr. Harvey quotes from a report made to a Yearly Meeting of Friends, in London, the statement that the basin of the Cumberland was the early home of the Shawnees. He says the Shawnees were a party to the treaty made by William Penn, in 1682. The address to Congress, made at the Huron village, near the mouth of the Detroit river, December 18, 1786, was signed: The Five Nations, Hurons, Ottawas, Twitchtwees, Shawnees, Chippewas, Cherokees, Delawares, and Pottawatomies. The first treaty with the Shawnees was made at the mouth of the Great Miami, January 31, 1786.

In 1830, Mr. Harvey took charge of the Friends' School among the Shawnees in Ohio. In 1833, the Ohio Shawnees came to Kansas. Schools were established by the Friends, the Baptists, and the Methodists. Mr. Harvey took charge of the Friends' School in 1840. He left them in 1842. "In the year 1844," he says, "they were visited by a great flood, which swept off their houses, and a large amount of grain; many of their farms were laid waste." This flood extended through the whole Kansas river valley. In the year 1854, the Shawnees numbered 900 souls, and owned 1,600,000 acres of land.

Mr. Harvey's History contains much valuable information.

ELECTION OF DELEGATE TO CONGRESS, OCTOBER 1, 1855.

Counties.	Townships.	No. of votes cast for J. W. Whit-field.	Scattering.
Atchison	Grasshopper	7	
	Shannon	131	4
Bourbon		242	
Brown		4	
Calhoun		29	
Davis		8	4
Doniphan	Burr Oak	42	
	Iowa	31	
	Wayne	66	
	Washington	59	
	Wolf River	53	
Douglas	Franklin	86	
	Lawrence	42	
	Lecompton	101	
	Willow Springs	103	
Franklin		15	
Jefferson		42	3
Johnson		190	
Leavenworth	Alexandria	42	
	Delaware	239	
	Kickapoo	150	1
	Leavenworth	212	
	Wyandotte	246	5
Lykins		220	
Linn		67	
Madison	(See Wise county.)		
Marshall		171	
Nemaha		6	
Riley		28	
Shawnee	One Hundred and Ten	23	
	Tecumseh	52	
Wise	Council Grove	14	
Total		2,721	17

The Free-State men took no part in this election.

OCTOBER 3.—Meeting of Pro-Slavery men at Leavenworth. A. J. Isacks, J. A. Halderman, D. J. Johnson, W. G. Mathias, R. R. Rees, L. F. Hollingsworth and D. A. N. Grover issued an address, asking the "lovers of law and order" to obey the bogus laws, and declaring it treason to oppose them. It also called for a convention at Leavenworth, Nov. 14.

OCTOBER 9.—Election of delegates to the Topeka Constitutional Convention.

ELECTION OF DELEGATES TO THE TOPEKA CONSTITUTIONAL CONVENTION, OCTOBER 9, 1855.

FIRST DISTRICT.

Candidates.	Blanton.	Palmyra.	Lawrence.
Chas. Robinson	67	16	
Jas. H. Lane	70	16	
G. W. Smith	70	16	[Poll-books mislaid. Total vote, 558.]
J. K. Goodin	61	16	
Edward Jones	30	16	
Morris Hunt	72	16	
Abraham Still	40		
Total	74	16	558

SECOND DISTRICT.

Candidates.	Benicia......	Bloomington
A. Curtiss	27	116
H. Burson..............	27	116
J. A. Wakefield.........	24	116
J. M. Turner	27	116
Total	27	116

THIRD DISTRICT.

Candidates.	Tecumseh..	Camp Creek.....	Topeka	Washington	Brownsville......
W. Y. Roberts	31	7	94	33	19
C. K. Holliday	31	7	104	33	19
J. Cowles	....	....	14	....	....
H. H. Wentworth	....	....	12	....	....
Edward Segraves	....	....	2	....	....
Scattering	....	....	3	....	....
P. C. Schuyler	....	....	....	....	5
Total..........	31	7	119	33	24

FOURTH DISTRICT.

Candidates.	Willow Springs.
S. Mewhinney	55
Wm. Graham............	55
Total.........	55

FIFTH DISTRICT.

Candidates.	Big Sugar.	Pottawatomie.....	Neosho......	Little Osage ...	Osawatomie......	Little Sugar ...	Stanton.....	Alderman's.....	Hampden.
Wm. Turner	24	49	8	16	67	32	35	8	33
Jas. M. Arthur..........	24	49	8	16	67	32	35	9	33
M. T. Morris	23	49	8	16	66	32	35	9	33
Orville C. Brown........	24	49	....	16	66	32	35	....	33
Richard Knight.........	24	49	....	16	67	32	35	....	33
Hamilton Smith.........	23	48	....	16	66	32	35	....	
Hiram Hoover..........	17	....	13	....	....	....	....	13	
David C. Forbes.........	....	....	....	16	....	....	....	....	
N. S. Nichols	....	....	....	....	3	....	....	....	
Wm. S. Nichols.........	....	....	....	....	64	....	7	....	
Isaac Woollard.........	....	....	....	....	....	....	29	....	
Frederick Brown........	24	47	....	16	64	32	35	....	33
Total.............	24	49	13	16	67	32	35	13	33

SIXTH DISTRICT.

Candidates.	House of R. J. Fargird.	Scott Town....	Columbia......
W. R. Griffith..	12	......	......
John Hamilton...	12	27	......
A. W. J. Brown...	12	......	......
Wm. Saunders...	12	......	......
W. J. Griffith..	......	27	......
T. H. Burgess...	......	24	......
A. H. Brown	......	26	......
Jas. H. Phenis..	......	......	20
Total...	12	27	20

SEVENTH DISTRICT.

Candidate.	L. B. Titus's, Council City.
Ph. C. Schuyler.........	60
Total................	62

EIGHTH DISTRICT.

Candidates.	Wabaunsee......
J. H. Pillsbury.............	27
P. C. Schuyler.............	27
Total.................	27

NINTH DISTRICT.

Candidates.	Pawnee........
Robert Klotz.................	53
A. Hunting.................	54
Total.......................	76

TENTH DISTRICT.

Candidates.	Rock Creek....	Big Blue.....
Dr. A. Hunting..	30	64
Robert Klotz..	30	73
Total..	30	80

ELEVENTH DISTRICT.

No returns except Black Vermilion precinct; total, 14.

TWELFTH DISTRICT.

Candidates.	St. Mary's.	Silver Lake.....
M. F. Conway...	19	12
Joseph F. Coles...	....	18
J. S. Thompson...	....	21
Total..	19	21

THIRTEENTH DISTRICT.

Candidates.	Ralls......	Pleasant Hill......
George S. Hillyer......	43	......
William Grigsbee......	41	......
William Hicks......	......	43
J. Whitney......	......	43
Total......	43	43

FOURTEENTH DISTRICT.

Candidates.	Palermo......	Burr Oak.	Doniphan.	Wolf River......
G. A. Cutler......	40	33	18	18
John Landis......	40	33	18	18
D. M. Field......	40	33	18	18
C. M. Stewart......	39	33	18	18
Total......	40	33	18	18

FIFTEENTH DISTRICT.

Candidates.	Crosby's Store......	Precinct......
Caleb May......	29	......
R. H. Crosby......	29	......
Stanford McDaniel......	......	30
James S. Sayle......	......	30
H. B. Gale......	......	28
Charles S. Foster......	......	2
Total......	29	30

SIXTEENTH DISTRICT.

Candidates.	Leavenworth.	W'yandotte...	Ridge	Easton......	Delaware......
M. J. Parrott......	492	38	47	61	22
M. W. Delahay......	495	38	47	61	22
Matt. France......	493	38	47	61	22
S. N. Latta......	493	38	47	61	22
Robt. Riddle......	493	38	47	61	22
D. Dodge......	493	38	47	61	22
Total......	514	38	47	63	22

SEVENTEENTH DISTRICT.

Candidates.	Mission.....	Wakarusa
William Graham...	13	5
Samuel Mewhinney...	13	5
Total...	13	5

RECAPITULATION OF VOTES CAST.

District.	Vote.	District.	Vote.
First district..............................	648	Eleventh district...........................	14
Second district...........................	143	Twelfth district.............................	40
Third district..............................	214	Thirteenth district........................	86
Fourth district............................	55	Fourteenth district........................	133
Fifth district...............................	282	Fifteenth district..........................	59
Sixth district..............................	59	Sixteenth district..........................	684
Seventh district..........................	62	Seventeenth district.....................	18
Eighth district............................	27		
Ninth district	76	Total......................................	2,710
Tenth district.............................	110		

OCTOBER 9.—ELECTION OF A. H. REEDER, DELEGATE TO CONGRESS.

No. Dist....	Place of Voting.	No. Votes....	No. Dist....	Place of Voting.	No. Votes....
1	Lawrence	557	10	Rock Creek	30
	Blanton	77	11	Black Vermilion ....:.......	14
	Palmyra	16	12	St. Mary's....................................	19
2	Bloomington	116		Silver Lake...................................	28
	Benicia...	27		Pleasant Hill................................	43
	Brownsville....................................	24	13	Falls Precinct................................	45
3	Topeka...	131		Hickory Point...............................	11
	Tecumseh......................................	31	14	Burr Oak......................................	33
	Big Springs...................................	35		Doniphan.....................................	43
	Camp Creek..................................	7		Palermo.......................................	32
4	Willow Springs..............................	54		Wolf River...................................	17
	Hampden......................................	33	15	Oceana..	32
	Neosho..	16		Crosby's Store...............................	39
	Stanton	44		Jackson Crane's.............................	30
5	Osawatomie...................................	74	16	Leavenworth.................................	503
	Pottawatomie	56		Wyandotte...................................	38
	Big Sugar Creek.............................	28		Delaware	22
	Little Sugar Creek...........................	41		Easton...	63
6	Scott Town....................................	27		Ridge Point..................................	48
	Columbia......................................	20	17	Wakarusa.....................................	7
	Fuqua's..	12		Mission..	13
7	Council City	62	18	Iowa Point....................................	40
8	Wabaunsee....................................	26		Moorstown	16
	A. I. Baker's.................................	16			
9	Pawnee..	76		Total.....................................	2,849
10	Big Blue.......................................	77			

OCTOBER 16.—Proclamation by the Free-State Committee, giving the
names of the following delegates to the Topeka Constitutional Convention:
First District, Samuel Mewhinney, William Graham; Second, G. W. Smith,
J. H. Lane, J. K. Goodin, C. Robinson, J. S. Emery, Morris Hunt; Third,
J. A. Wakefield, A. Curtiss, J. M. Tuton, H. Burson; Fourth, C. K. Holli-
day, W. Y. Roberts; Fifth, P. C. Schuyler, J. H. Pillsbury; Sixth, James

Phenis, Dr. Burgess, N. Vandever; Seventh, W. T. Turner, Jas. McArthur,
W. T. Morris, O. C. Brown, Richard Knight, F. Brown, H. Smith, W. G.
Nichols; Eighth, Robert Klotz, A. Hunting; Ninth, M. F. Conway, J. G.
Thompson; Tenth, Geo. S. Hillyer, J. Whitney; Fourteenth, Robert Rid-
dle, M. J. Parrott, Matt. France, S. N. Latta, D. Dodge, M. W. Delahay;
Eleventh, G. A. Cutler, John Landis, C. W. Stewart, D. W. Field; Thir-
teenth, R. H. Crosby, Caleb May, Sanford McDaniel, James S. Sayle.

OCTOBER 20.—Thomas J. B. Cramer commissioned as Territorial Treasurer.

OCTOBER 23.—Constitutional Convention meets at Topeka.

The following is an incomplete list of the members of the Topeka Constitutional Convention:

Name.	Age.	Occupation.	Native State.	Residence.	Politics.	From what State.
Arthur, James M...	38	Farmer	Indiana	Sugar Creek..	Dem......	Indiana.
Brown, Orville C....	44	Farmer	New York..	Osawatomie..	Freesoil..	New York.
Burson, H..............	36	Farmer	Virginia ...	Bloomington	Whig ...	Illinois.
Crosby, R. H.........	21	Merchant..	Maine........	Oceana.........	Rep	Minn. Terr.
Curtiss, A.............	32	Lawyer......	New York..	Bloomington	None......	Kentucky.
Cutler, G. A..........	23	Physician ..	Tennessee..	Doniphan	Freesoil..	Missouri.
Delahay, M. W......	27	Lawyer......	Maryland ..	Leavenworth	Dem.......	Alabama.
Dodge, D..............	25	Lawyer......	New York..	Doniphan	Dem.......	New York.
Emery, J. S..........	26	Lawyer......	Maine........	Lawrence......	Dem.......	New York.
Goodin, J. K.........	31	Lawyer......	Ohio.........	Clear Lake...	Dem.......	Ohio.
Holliday, C. K.......	28	Lawyer......	Pennsylv'a	Topeka	Dem.......	Pennsylv.
Hillyer, G. S.........	35	Farmer	Ohio.........	Grassh. Falls.	Whig	Ohio.
Hunt, Morris........	27	Lawyer......	Ohio.........	Lawrence......	Whig	Ohio.
Hunting, Amory...	61	Physician ..	Mass.........	Manhattan...	Rep	RhodeIsl'd.
Hicks, W. H.........	53	Farmer	Pennsylv'a	Dayton	Dem	Indiana.
Klotz, Robert.......	35	Merchant..	Pennsylv'a	Pawnee.........	Dem.......	Pennsylv.
Knight, Richard....	43	Clergyman	England	Lawrence......	FreeSt'te	Mass.
Lane, James H......	33	Lawyer......	Kentucky..	Lawrence......	Dem.......	Indiana.
Latta, S. N...........	30	Lawyer......	Ohio.........	Leavenworth	Whig	Iowa.
Landis, John........	28	Farmer	Kentucky..	Doniphan	Dem.......	Missouri.
McDaniel, Sanford.	30	Farmer	Indiana.....	Round Pr'rie	Dem.......	Missouri.
Mewhinney, Sam'l.	45	Farmer	Ohio.........	Prairie City..	Dem.......	Illinois.
Parrott, M. J........	26	Lawyer......	S. Carolina..	Leavenworth	Dem.......	Ohio.
Roberts, W. Y.......	41	Farmer	Pennsylv'a	Washington..	Dem.......	Pennsylv.
Robinson, C.........	37	Physician ..	Mass.........	Lawrence......	Indep.....	Mass.
Sayle, James L......	37	Farmer	Illinois......	Kickapoo	Rep	Iowa.
Schuyler, P. C......	50	Farmer	New York..	Council City.	Rep	New York.
Smith, G. W.........	50	Lawyer......	Pennsylv'a	Franklin......	Whig	Pennsylv.
Thompson, J. G....	55	Saddler......	Pennsylv'a	Topeka	Dem.......	Pennsylv.
Tuton, J. M..........	33	Clergyman	Tennessee..	Bloomington	Dem.......	Missouri.
Wakefield, J. A......	59	Lawyer......	S. Carolina..	Bloomington	Whig	Iowa.

OFFICERS.

Name.	Age.	Office.	Occupation.	Native State.	Residence.	Politics.	From what State.
Sam'l C. Smith.	27	Secretary	Farmer ...	Mass.	Lawrence ..	Republican.	Mass.
Chas. A. Foster	28	Ass't Sec.	Lawyer....	Mass.	Osawato'ie.	Republican.	Mass.
Sam. F. Tappan	24	Clerk	Mechanic.	Mass.	Lawrence ..	Abolitionist	Mass.
John Dailey....	24	Clerk	Farmer ...	Ind. ..	Topeka......	Democrat ...	Indiana.
James Redpath	22	Reporter ..	Journalist	Engl.	St. Louis....	D. & Emanc.	Louisiana.

ABSENT MEMBERS.

Messrs. Brown, Burgess, Field, France, Graham, Morris, Nichols, Phenis, Riddle,
Hamden, Smith, Stewart, Turner, Vandever.

The Convention was called to order by J. A. Wakefield; prayer by Rev.
Richard Knight; calling of the roll by Joel K. Goodin; twenty-one members, less than a quorum, present.

OCTOBER 23.—The Kansas Daily Freeman issued at Topeka.   E. C. K.

Garvey, publisher; J. F. Cummings, printer. The Weekly Freeman was started in July. The Daily edition was printed during the sessions of the Constitutional Convention. Mr. Cummings still possesses copies of ten numbers of this paper. The size of the paper is eight by twelve inches, with three columns to a page. It was an evening paper.

— Sale of lots at Lecompton.

OCTOBER 24.— James H. Lane elected President of the Convention, receiving fifteen votes, to five for W. Y. Roberts, and four for J. A. Wakefield. Samuel C. Smith was elected Secretary, and Rev. H. B. Burgess, Chaplain. Samuel F. Tappan appeared as reporter for the Herald of Freedom, and John Speer for the Kansas Tribune. Lane's speech, on taking the chair, marked out very briefly the policy the Convention ought to pursue. Why he made the following assertion, it would be difficult now to tell:

"When the Kansas-Nebraska bill was before Congress, no one of its supporters claimed that Kansas could ever become a Slave State; all, from the highest to the lowest, discarded the idea that slavery could ever be extended within her borders. Our Southern friends were among the most prominent in pressing this position before the country."

James Redpath was given a seat as a reporter for the Missouri Democrat, Wm. A. Phillips for the New York Tribune, and Joseph L. Speer for the Chicago Tribune. Mr. Redpath was elected Reporter for the Convention.

OCTOBER 25.— Samuel Collins killed by Patrick Laughlin, near Doniphan. Laughlin claimed originally to be a Free-State man, and became a member of the "Kansas Legion." He afterwards exposed this Free-State organization, and became a violent Pro-Slavery man. Gladstone thus describes the murder:

"Mr. Collins, who owned a saw-mill at Doniphan, was shot on political grounds by a violent Pro-Slavery man, named Patrick Laughlin. Laughlin came, it is said, originally from Ireland, and had rendered himself famous by an exposure, as it was termed, of the Kansas Legion. Laughlin was aided in this attack by three or four armed associates, and Mr. Collins's sons were present, and sought to defend their father. There was considerable interchange of bowie-knife cuts and pistol-firing on this occasion, and the murderer himself was wounded. But the victim being a Free-State man, the law took no cognizance of the murder, and Laughlin found protection, and was rewarded by a situation in a shop in Atchison."

OCTOBER 26.— The printing for the Convention was divided, E. C. K. Garvey, John Speer and M. W. Delahay each receiving a portion.

The vote on striking the word "white" out of the Constitution stood as follows: *Yeas* — Brown, Crosby, Hillyer, Hunting, Knight, Robinson, Schuyler — 7. *Nays* — Arthur, Burson, Curtiss, Cutler, Delahay, Dodge, Hunt, Klotz, Lane, Latta, Landis, McDaniels, Mewhinney, Parrott, Roberts, Sayle, Smith, Thompson, Tuton, Wakefield, Hicks, Emery, Goodin, Holliday, Graham — 25.

OCTOBER 30.— John W. Whitfield receives his certificate as duly elected Delegate to the Thirty-fourth Congress.

NOVEMBER.— John Speer moves the Kansas Tribune from Lawrence to Topeka, and Wm. W. Ross becomes his partner in its publication.

NOVEMBER 5.— Josiah H. Pillsbury having resigned, J. H. Nesbitt was elected and admitted to the Convention as a delegate from the Eighth District.

NOVEMBER 6.—W. R. Griffith admitted as a delegate from the Sixth District, to the Convention. M. F. Conway, elected a delegate, thus far prevented by sickness from taking a seat in the Convention.

NOVEMBER 11.—The Convention completes its labor, and submits a Constitution to the people. The fourth of March is appointed as the time for organizing the State government.

NOVEMBER 14.—A Convention at Leavenworth organizes the "Law-and-Order" party. Gov. Shannon presides. John Calhoun, Surveyor General, makes a bitter Pro-Slavery speech. J. H. Stringfellow, Daniel Woodson and Judge Lecompte are present. Marcus J. Parrott is hissed down.

NOVEMBER.—The scrip issued by the Free-State Executive Committee amounted to $15,265.90. The first Topeka Legislature, as required by the Constitution, made provision for its redemption, but the laws of that body were only on paper, and the scrip was not paid. The following is a copy of a piece of Free-State scrip:

No. 62.   TOPEKA, NOV. 26, 1855. $20.

WOOD CUT: WOMAN HOLDING SCALES.

This is to Certify, That Cyrus K. Holliday, or bearer, is entitled on presentation to receive from the Treasurer of the

STATE OF KANSAS.

Twenty Dollars, with interest at ten per cent. per annum, for account as per bill on file, for the payment of which the faith of the State is pledged.

Attest—J. K. GOODIN, *Sec'y.*

J. H. LANE, *Ch'n Ex. Com., Kansas.*

[The Kansas Freeman Print, Topeka, Kansas.]

Proclaim liberty throughout the land, and to all the inhabitants thereof.

NOVEMBER 21.—Charles W. Dow killed by Franklin N. Coleman, Pro-Slavery, near Hickory Point, Douglas county. The Free-State men held a meeting on the 22d, at the scene of the murder. That night Sheriff Jones arrested Jacob Branson, with whom Dow had lived, for taking part in the Free-State meeting. Jones, with his prisoner and a posse of fourteen men, proceeded towards Lecompton, via Blanton. Near J. B. Abbott's house, at Blanton, Jones's party was confronted by fifteen Free-State men, among them Samuel N. Wood, J. B. Abbott, and Samuel F. Tappan. They requested Branson to leave the Sheriff's party; he did so. Jones sent to Shawnee Mission for aid. A meeting was held in Lawrence, and was addressed by Branson. A mob from Missouri was feared, and the citizens were placed under arms. On the 2d of December, Free-State companies from Bloomington, Wakarusa and Palmyra had arrived in Lawrence. Jones, with a body-guard, rode through Lawrence. Gen. Richardson and staff dined with J. H. Lane. A company of 100 armed Free-State men arrived from Topeka at nine in the evening. On Monday, the 3d, a proclamation was received from Gov. Shannon calling upon all good citizens to aid the Sheriff in the recapture of Branson. It was dated November 29. A public meeting, through Chas. Robinson, Chairman, reported that there was no association of lawless men in Lawrence. The roar of the cannon at Franklin, where the invaders are massed, is occasionally heard in the Free-

State town. On Tuesday, the 4th, it is reported that Judge Cato's court has found bills of indictment against the leading Free-State men. Loaded wagons destined for Lawrence are stopped and robbed of provisions and ammunition. Messengers are sent to Gov. Shannon asking him to remove the mob which is menacing Lawrence. Dr. C. Robinson is elected Commander-in-Chief, and the citizen soldiery is fully organized. On Friday, the 7th, news is received of the murder of Thomas W. Barber, the previous afternoon, while returning to his home, near Bloomington, from Lawrence. He was accompanied by his brother Robert Barber, and his brother-in-law Thos. Pierson. Four miles southwest of Lawrence they met twelve horsemen, who were going to Franklin. The Free-State men refusing to surrender, were fired upon. One ball passed through the body of Thomas W. Barber; he rode a short distance, fell and expired. His body was brought to Lawrence, which he had so lately been engaged in defending. Gov. Shannon arrives, and consults with Robinson and Lane. Shannon, at night, goes to Franklin. John Brown and four sons, all armed, are in Lawrence. On Saturday, the 8th, Governor Shannon again appears, with Col. Boone, of Westport, Mo., and one or two others. News is received that S. C. Pomeroy, who had left Lawrence to go to the Eastern States, is a prisoner at Franklin. The body of Barber is temporarily buried. Robinson and Lane go back to the Pro-Slavery camp with Shannon. Sunday morning, December 9th, was extremely cold. Negotiations with Gov. Shannon were finally completed, and were made known by Lane and Robinson. A supper for Gov. Shannon was arranged for Monday night; he was not present. It was a joyful occasion for the citizens. On Tuesday, the 11th, the volunteer companies from other towns took their departure. Of Gov. Shannon, the Herald of Freedom says: "He came, learned the facts, and, like an honorable man, has done what he could to retrace his steps."

On Saturday, the 15th, a public funeral was given to the remains of Thos. W. Barber. The sermon was preached at the Free-State Hotel by Rev. L. B. Dennis; addresses were delivered by Lane and Robinson. Lane said Dow and Barber were the first martyrs of freedom in Kansas, and monuments should be erected to their memory.

—There was a Hickory Point ten miles south of Lawrence, on the Santa Fe road, and another Hickory Point in Jefferson county. It was at the former place that Dow was killed. The Free-State resistance to an officer, Samuel J. Jones, who was the Sheriff of Douglas county, and Postmaster of Westport, Mo., led to the "Wakarusa War," as it was called, the Pro-Slavery militia being called into the field as a Sheriff's posse to aid him in making arrests and executing the law.

NOVEMBER 27.—Sheriff Jones writes to Gov. Shannon that "open rebellion" exists, and calls for "three thousand men to carry out the laws."

NOVEMBER 27.—Gov. Shannon orders Maj. Gen. Wm. P. Richardson, of the Territorial Militia, "to collect as large a force as you can in your division, and repair without delay to Lecompton, and report yourself to S. J. Jones, Sheriff of Douglas county." A similar order is sent to Hiram J. Strickler, Adjutant General.

NOVEMBER 28.—Gov. Shannon informs President Pierce of a fearful state of affairs. He says: "It is vain to conceal the fact; we are standing on a volcano."

NOVEMBER 28.—Lucian J. Eastin, Brigadier General, orders his brigade to arms, there being "a state of open rebellion" in Douglas county.

NOVEMBER 29.—Proclamation by the Governor, calling upon the citizens to support the laws.

NOVEMBER 29.—At a meeting in Lawrence it is resolved to form a military organization. A Committee of Safety is appointed. Dr. Chas. Robinson is made Commander-in-Chief of the military forces, and Col. James H. Lane is placed second in command.

The Pro-Slavery forces begin to collect at Franklin, near the mouth of the Wakarusa, four miles east of Lawrence. The militia of Richardson and Strickler is at Lecompton, and David R. Atchison, with the Platte County (Missouri) Riflemen, is on the Kaw, north of Lawrence.

The Free-State men at Lawrence send despatches to the President, to Congress, and to Col. Sumner, at Fort Leavenworth. About 800 men are enrolled, among them John Brown and his sons.

Col. Sumner writes to Gov. Shannon that he cannot act until he receives orders from the Government. C. W. Babcock and G. P. Lowry visit Gov. Shannon at Shawnee Mission, on behalf of the people of Lawrence. Gov. Shannon visits the Wakarusa camp, and endeavors to avert bloodshed.

DECEMBER 2.—Despatch from Governor Shannon to Sheriff Jones. It closes thus:

"Let me know the number of warrants you have, and the names of defendants. I will probably accompany Colonel Sumner's command."

DECEMBER 3.—Lawrence beleaguered.

—The Supreme Court meets at Lecompton.

DECEMBER 4.—Jeremiah Burrill and Sterling G. Cato take their seats as Associate Justices. Judge Burrill was in Kansas only a short time. He returned to Greensburg, Pennsylvania, and died in October, 1856. Thomas Cunningham, of Beaver county, Pennsylvania, was appointed his successor. He visited Kansas, and resigned without entering upon the duties of his office.

DECEMBER.—Reeder and Whitfield both claim a seat in Congress; both receive mileage. Neither was allowed a seat.

DECEMBER 6.—Thomas W. Barber, Free-State, shot and killed by Geo. W. Clarke, Pottawatomie Indian Agent, about four miles southwest of Lawrence.

—About 1,500 Missourians are encamped on the Wakarusa. Lawrence nearly surrounded.

DECEMBER 6.—Governor Shannon writes to Colonel Sumner to go to Lawrence, saying: "It is peace, not war, that we want, and you have the power to secure peace." Colonel Sumner replies that he cannot act without orders.

DECEMBER 7.—Governor Shannon in Lawrence.

DECEMBER 8.—Governor Shannon makes a treaty with the Free-State Generals. The paper is signed by Shannon, Robinson and Lane. Robinson and Lane go to Franklin and return without a guard.

DECEMBER 9.—Governor Shannon orders Generals Richardson and Strickler and Sheriff Jones to disband their forces.

—John Brown opposed the Treaty of Peace. He was for fighting and dying, now, if need be.

DECEMBER 15.—At the election on the adoption or rejection of the Topeka Constitution, at Leavenworth, the Pro-Slavery men carried off the ballot-box. They also destroyed the office of the Territorial Register, a Free-State paper, at Leavenworth, edited by Mark W. Delahay.

VOTE ON THE ADOPTION OF THE TOPEKA CONSTITUTION, DECEMBER 15, 1855.

Districts	Precincts.	Constitution.	No Constitution	General Bank'g Law.		Exclusion of Negroes and Mulattoes.		No. of votes cast.
				Yes.	No.	Yes.	No.	
1	Lawrence	348	1	225	83	133	223	356
	Blanton	72	2	59	14	48	20	76
	Palmyra	11	....	9	3	12	....	12
	Franklin	48	....	31	15	48	2	53
2	Bloomington	137	....	122	11	113	15	137
	East Douglas	18	....	13	4	14	4	18
	Topeka	135	....	125	9	69	64	136
3	Washington	42	....	41	1	42	....	42
	Brownsville	24	....	22	2	22	2	24
	Tecumseh	35	....	23	11	35	....	35
4	Prairie City	72	....	39	33	69	3	72
	Little Osage	21	7	16	12	23	7	31
	Big Sugar	18	2	5	16	20	....	21
	Neosho	12	....	6	6	12	....	12
5	Pottawatomie	39	3	21	19	25	18	43
	Little Sugar	42	18	33	13	42	2	60
	Stanton	32	....	4	33	33	5	37
	Osawatomie	56	1	33	20	38	17	59
7	Titus	39	5	32	7	25	15	44
	Juniata	30	....	23	6	10	19	31
	Ohio City	21	....	16	5	20	1	21
8	Mill Creek	20	....	....	20	20	....	20
	St. Mary's	14	....	....	14	14	....	14
	Wabaunsee	19	....	17	1	7	11	19
9	Pawnee	45	....	15	29	40	5	45
	Grasshopper Falls	54	....	19	34	50	3	54
	Doniphan	22	2	5	14	21	....	22
10	Burr Oak	23	....	7	16	22	1	23
	Jesse Padou's	12	....	1	11	12	....	12
11	Oceana	28	....	8	20	28	....	28
	Kickapoo	20	....	7	13	16	4	20
	Pleasant Hill	47	....	37	6	45	1	47
13	Indianola	19	....	....	18	19	....	19
	Whitfield	7	....	3	4	6	....	7
14	Wolf River	24	....	11	12	18	6	....
	St. Joseph Bottom	15	....	4	9	14	1	15
15	Mount Pleasant	32	....	32	1	30	2	33
16	Easton	71	7	53	19	71	....	73
17	Mission	7	....	3	....	1	2	7
	Total	1,731	46	1,120	564	1,287	453	1,778

NOTE.—The poll-book at Leavenworth was destroyed. The vote cast there October 9, 1855, was 514.

DECEMBER 16.—Funeral of Barber.

DECEMBER 22.—A Convention at Lawrence nominates State officers under the Topeka Constitution. The conservative Free-State men bolt, and nominate a "Free-State Anti-Abolition" ticket.

DECEMBER 26.—The Kickapoo Pioneer of this date says:

"But the Abolitionists, or Free-State men, if you please, have become dissatisfied, and are willing to violate the Constitution of their country, which explicitly recognizes Slavery, and disfranchise themselves as loyal citizens, for the purpose of stealing ne- groes, and committing other unconstitutional and unlawful depredations. Should such men receive any compassion from an orderly, Union-loving people? No! It is this class of men that have congregated at Lawrence, and it is this class of men that Kansas must get rid of. And we know of no better method than for every man who loves his country, and the laws by which he is governed, to meet in Kansas and kill off this God- forsaken class of humanity as soon as they place their feet upon our soil."

THE TOPEKA CONSTITUTION.

PREAMBLE.

We, the people of the Territory of Kansas, by our delegates in Convention assembled at Topeka, on the 23d day of October, A. D. 1855, and of the Independence of the United States the eightieth year, having the right of admission into the Union as one of the United States of America, consistent with the Federal Constitution and by virtue of the treaty of cession by France to the United States of the Province of Louisiana, in order to secure to ourselves and our posterity the enjoyment of all the rights of life, liberty and property, and the free pursuit of happiness, do mutually agree with each other to form ourselves into a free and independent State, by the name and style of the STATE OF KANSAS, bounded as follows, to wit: Beginning at a point on the western boundary of the State of Missouri where the thirty-seventh parallel of north latitude crosses the same; thence west on said parallel to the eastern boundary of New Mexico; thence north on said boundary to latitude thirty-eight; thence following said boundary westward to the eastern boundary of the Territory of Utah, on the summit of the Rocky Mountains; thence northward on said summit to the fortieth parallel of said latitude; thence east on said parallel to the western boundary of the State of Missouri; thence south with the western boundary of said State to the place of beginning; and do ordain and establish the following Constitution and Bill of Rights for the govern- ment thereof:

ARTICLE I.—BILL OF RIGHTS.

SECTION 1. All men are by nature free and independent, and have certain inaliena- ble rights, among which are those of enjoying and defending life and liberty, acquiring, possessing, and protecting property, and seeking and obtaining happiness and safety.

SEC. 2. All political power is inherent in the people. Government is instituted for their equal protection and benefit; and they have the right to alter, reform or abolish the same whenever they may deem it necessary; and no special privileges or immuni- ties shall ever be granted that may not be altered, revoked, or repealed by the General Assembly.

SEC. 3. The people have the right to assemble together, in a peaceable manner, to consult, for their common good, to instruct their representatives, and to petition the General Assembly for the redress of grievances.

SEC. 4. The people have the right to bear arms for their defence and security, but standing armies in time of peace are dangerous to liberty, and shall not be kept up; and the military shall be kept in strict subordination to the civil power.

SEC. 5. The right of trial by jury shall be inviolate.

SEC. 6. There shall be no Slavery in this State, nor involuntary servitude, unless for the punishment of crime.

SEC. 7. All men have a natural and indefeasible right to worship Almighty God ac- cording to the dictates of their own conscience. No person shall be compelled to attend, erect or support any place of worship, or maintain any form of worship against his consent; and no preference shall be given by law to any religious society; nor shall any interference with the rights of conscience be permitted. No religious test shall be required as a qualification for office, nor shall any person be incompetent to be a witness on account of his religious belief; but nothing herein shall be construed to dis- pense with oaths and affirmations. Religion, morality, and knowledge, however, being essential to good government, it shall be the duty of the General Assembly to pass suit- able laws to protect every religious denomination in the peaceable enjoyment of its own mode of public worship, and to encourage schools and the means of instruction.

SEC. 8. The privilege of the writ of habeas corpus shall not be suspended, unless in case of rebellion or invasion the public safety requires it.

SEC. 9. All persons shall be bailable by sufficient sureties, unless for capital offences where the proof is evident, or the presumption great. Excessive bail shall not be required, nor excessive fines imposed, nor cruel and unusual punishment inflicted.

SEC. 10. Except in cases of impeachment, and cases arising in the army and navy, or in the militia, when in actual service, in time of war or public danger, and in cases of petit larceny and other inferior offences, no person shall be held to answer for a capital or otherwise infamous crime unless on presentment or indictment of a grand jury. In any trial, in any court, the party accused shall be allowed to appear and defend in person, and with counsel; to demand the nature and cause of the accusation against him, and to have a copy thereof; to meet the witnesses face to face, and to have compulsory process to procure the attendance of witnesses in his behalf, and a speedy public trial by an impartial jury of the county or district in which the offence is alleged to have been committed; nor shall any person be compelled in any criminal case to be a witness against himself, or be twice put in jeopardy for the same offence.

SEC. 11. Every citizen may freely speak, write and publish his sentiments on all subjects, being responsible for the abuse of the right; and no law shall be passed to restrain or abridge the liberty of speech or of the press. In all criminal prosecutions or indictments for libel, the truth may be given in evidence to the jury, and if it shall appear to the jury that the matter charged as libellous is true, and was published with good motives, and for justifiable ends, the party shall be acquitted.

SEC. 12. No person shall be transported out of the State for any offence committed within the same, and no conviction shall work corruption of blood or forfeiture of estate.

SEC. 13. No soldier shall, in time of peace, be quartered in any house without the consent of the owner; nor in time of war, except in a manner prescribed by law.

SEC. 14. The right of the people to be secure in their persons, houses, papers and possessions, against unreasonable searches and seizures, shall not be violated; and no warrant shall issue but upon probable cause, supported by oath or affirmation, particularly describing the place to be searched, and the persons and things to be seized.

SEC. 15. No person shall be imprisoned for debt in any civil action, or mesne or final process, unless in case of fraud.

SEC. 16. All courts shall be open; and every person for an injury done him in his land, goods, person or reputation, shall have remedy by due course of law, and justice administered without denial or delay.

SEC. 17. No hereditary emoluments, honors or privileges shall ever be granted or conferred by this State.

SEC. 18. No power of suspending laws shall ever be exercised, except by the General Assembly.

SEC. 19. The payment of a tax shall not be a qualification for exercising the right of suffrage.

SEC. 20. Private property shall ever be held inviolate, but subservient to the public welfare. When taken in time of war, or other public exigency imperatively requiring its immediate seizure, or for the purpose of making or repairing roads which shall be open to the public use without toll or other charge therefor, a compensation shall be made to the owner in money; and in all other cases where private property shall be taken for public use, a compensation therefor shall first be made in money, first secured by a deposit of money; and such compensation shall be assessed by a jury, without deduction for benefits to any property of the owner.

SEC. 21. No indenture of any negro or mulatto, made and executed out of the bounds of the State, shall be valid within the State.

SEC. 22. This enumeration of rights shall not be construed to impair or deny others retained by the people; and all powers not herein delegated shall remain with the people.

ARTICLE II.—ELECTIVE FRANCHISE.

SECTION 1. In all elections by the people, the vote shall be by ballot; and in all elections in the General Assembly, the vote shall be viva voce.

SEC. 2. Every white male person, and every civilized male Indian who has adopted the habits of the white man, of the age of twenty-one years and upward, who shall be at the time of offering to vote a citizen of the United States; who shall have resided, and had his habitation, domicile, home, and place of permanent abode in the State of Kansas for six months next preceding the election at which he offers his vote; who, at such time, and for thirty days immediately preceding such time, shall have had his actual habitation, domicile, home, and place of abode in the county in which he offers to vote; and who shall have resided in the precinct or election district for at least ten days immediately preceding the election, shall be deemed a qualified elector at all elections under this Constitution, except at elections by general ticket in the State or district prescribed by law, in which case the elector must have the aforesaid qualifications, but a residence in said district for ten days will entitle him to vote: *Provided,* That no soldier, seaman, or marine of the regular army of the United States shall be considered a resident of the State in consequence of being stationed within the same.

SEC. 3. The General Assembly shall, at its first session, provide for the registration of all qualified electors in each county, and thereafter, from time to time, of all who may become qualified electors.

SEC. 4. The Legislature shall have power to exclude from every office of honor, trust or profit, within the State, and from the right of suffrage, all persons convicted of any infamous crime.

SEC. 5. No person shall be deemed capable of holding or being elected to any post of honor, profit, trust or emolument, civil or military, or exercise the right of suffrage under the government of this State, who shall hereafter fight a duel, send or accept a challenge to fight a duel, or who shall be a second to either party, or who shall in any manner aid or assist in such a duel, or who shall be knowingly the bearer of such challenge or acceptance, whether the same occur or be committed in or out of the State.

SEC. 6. No person who may hereafter be collector or holder of public moneys shall be eligible to any office of trust or profit in the State until he shall have accounted for and paid into the proper public treasury all sums for which he may be accountable.

SEC. 7. No State officer or member of the General Assembly of this State shall receive a fee, be engaged as counsel, agent or attorney, in any case or claim against the State.

SEC. 8. No Senator or Representative shall, during the term of office for which he shall have been elected, be appointed to any civil office of profit in this State which shall have been created, or the emoluments of which shall have been increased, during such term, except such offices as may be filled by election by the people.

SEC. 9. All officers, civil and military, in this State, before they enter upon the duties of their respective offices, shall take the following oath or affirmation: "I, —— ——, do swear [or affirm] that I will support the Constitution of the United States, and of the State of Kansas; that I am duly qualified according to the Constitution to exercise the office to which I have been elected [or appointed], and will, to the best of my abilities, discharge the duties thereof faithfully and impartially, according to law."

SEC. 10. Every person shall be disqualified from holding any office of honor or profit in this State, who shall have been convicted of having given or offered any bribe to procure his election, or who shall have made use of any undue influence from power, tumult, or other improper practices.

SEC. 11. All civil officers of the State shall reside within the State, and all district and county officers within their respective districts and counties, and shall have their offices at such places as may be required by law.

SEC. 12. Returns of elections for members of Congress, the General Assembly, and all other officers not otherwise provided for, shall be made to the Secretary of State, in such manner as may be prescribed by law.

SEC. 13. Electors shall in all cases be privileged from arrest during their attendance on elections, and in going to and returning therefrom, except in case of felony, treason, and breach of the peace.

ARTICLE III.—DISTRIBUTION OF POWERS.

SECTION 1. The powers of the Government shall be divided into three separate departments—the Legislative, the Executive (including the Administrative), and the Judicial; and no person charged with official duties under one of these departments shall exercise any of the functions of another, except as in this Constitution expressly provided.

Article IV.—Legislative.

Section 1. The Legislative power of this State shall be vested in the General Assembly, which shall consist of a Senate and House of Representatives.

Sec. 2. The Senators and Representatives shall be chosen annually by the qualified electors of the respective counties or districts for which they are chosen on the first Monday of August, for one year, and their term of office shall commence on the first day of January next thereafter.

Sec. 3. There shall be elected at the first election twenty Senators and sixty Representatives, and the number afterward shall be regulated by law.

Sec. 4. No person shall be eligible to the office of Senator or Representative, who shall not possess the qualifications of an elector.

Sec. 5. No person holding office under the authority of the United States, or any lucrative office under the authority of this State, shall be eligible to, or hold a seat in the General Assembly; but this provision shall not extend to township officers, justices of the peace, notaries public, postmasters, or officers of the militia.

Sec. 6. Each house, except as otherwise provided in this Constitution, shall choose its own officers, determine its own rule of proceeding, punish its members for disorderly conduct, and, with the concurrence of two-thirds, expel a member, but not the second time for the same cause; and shall judge of the qualification, election and return of its own members, and shall have all other powers necessary for its safety, and the undisturbed transaction of business.

Sec. 7. Each house shall keep a journal of its proceedings, and publish the same. The yeas and nays on any question shall, at the request of two members, be entered on the journal.

Sec. 8. Any member of either house shall have the right to protest against any act or resolution thereof; and such protest and reason therefor shall, without alteration, commitment or delay, be entered on the journal.

Sec. 9. All vacancies which may occur in either house shall, for the unexpired term, be filled by election as shall be prescribed by law.

Sec. 10. Senators and Representatives shall, in all cases except treason, felony or breach of the peace, be privileged from arrest during the session of the General Assembly, and in going to and returning from the same; and for words spoken in debate they shall not be questioned in any other place.

Sec. 11. A majority of all the members elected to each house shall be necessary to pass every bill or joint resolution, and all bills and joint resolutions so passed shall be signed by the presiding officers of the respective houses, and presented to the Governor for his approval.

Sec. 12. The doors of each house, and of Committees of the Whole, shall be kept open. Neither house shall, without the consent of the other, adjourn for more than two days, nor to any other place than that in which the two houses shall be sitting, except for personal safety.

Sec. 13. Every bill shall be read by sections on three several days in each house, unless in case of emergency. Two-thirds of the house where such bill is pending may, if deemed expedient, suspend the rules on a call of the yeas and nays; but the reading of a bill by sections on its final passage shall in no case be dispensed with; and the vote on the passage of every bill or joint resolution shall be taken by yeas and nays.

Sec. 14. Every act shall contain but one subject, which shall be clearly expressed in its title. Bills may originate in either house, but may be altered, amended or rejected by the other.

Sec. 15. In all cases where a general law can be made applicable, special laws shall not be enacted.

Sec. 16. No act shall ever be revived or amended by mere reference to its title; but the act revived or the section amended shall be set forth and published at full length.

Sec. 17. No act shall take effect until the same shall have been published and circulated in the counties of the State by authority, except in case of emergency, which emergency shall be declared in the preamble, or the body of the law.

Sec. 18. The election and appointment of all officers, and the filling of all vacancies not otherwise provided for by this Constitution, or the Constitution of the United States, shall be made in such manner as shall be prescribed by law; but no appointing power shall be exercised by the General Assembly, except as provided in this Constitution and in the election of the United States Senator, and in these cases the vote shall be taken viva voce.

SEC. 19. The General Assembly shall not have power to enact laws annulling the contract of marriage in any case where, by law, the courts of this State may have power to decree a divorce.

SEC. 20. The General Assembly shall not have power to pass retroactive laws, or laws impairing the obligation of contracts, but may, by general laws, authorize courts to carry into effect, upon such terms as shall be just and equitable, the manifest intention of parties and officers, by curing omissions, defects and errors in instruments, and proceedings arising out of a want of conformity with the laws of this State.

SEC. 21. The style of the laws of this State shall be: *"Be it enacted by the General Assembly of the State of Kansas."*

SEC. 22. The House of Representatives shall have the sole power of impeachment. All impeachments shall be tried by the Senate, and, when sitting for the purpose, the Senators shall be upon oath or affirmation to do justice according to law and evidence. No person shall be convicted without the concurrence of two-thirds of all the Senators present.

SEC. 23. The Governor, and all other civil officers under the laws of this State, shall be liable to impeachment for any misdemeanor in office, but judgment in such cases shall not extend further than to removal from office, and disqualification to hold any office of honor, profit or trust under this State. The party, whether convicted or acquitted, shall nevertheless be liable to indictment, trial, judgment and punishment, according to law.

SEC. 24. Within one year after the ratification of this Constitution, and within every subsequent two years thereafter, for the term of ten years, an enumeration of all the white inhabitants of this State shall be made, in such manner as shall be directed by law.

SEC. 25. All regular sessions of the General Assembly shall be held at the capital of the State, and shall commence on the first Tuesday of January, annually.

SEC. 26. All bills for raising revenue shall originate in the House of Representatives, subject, however, to amendment or rejection as in other cases.

SEC. 27. The members of the General Assembly shall receive for their services the sum of four dollars per day for each and every day they are actually in attendance at any regular or special session, and four dollars for every twenty miles they shall travel in going to and returning from the place of meeting by the most usually travelled route; and no session of the General Assembly, except the first, under this Constitution, shall extend beyond the term of sixty days, nor any special session more than forty days.

ARTICLE V. — EXECUTIVE.

SECTION 1. The Executive Department shall consist of a Governor, a Lieutenant-Governor, Secretary of State, Treasurer, Auditor, and Attorney General, who shall be chosen by the electors of the State at the same time and place of voting for the members of the General Assembly.

SEC. 2. The Governor, Lieutenant-Governor, Secretary of State, Treasurer, Auditor, Attorney General, and State Printer, shall hold their office for two years. Their terms of office shall commence on the first Tuesday of January next after their election, and continue until their successors are elected and qualified — neither of which officers shall be eligible for re-election more than two out of three consecutive terms; nor shall any person be eligible for the office of Governor who shall not have attained the age of thirty years.

SEC. 3. The returns of every election for the officers named in the foregoing section, shall be sealed up and transmitted to the seat of Government by the returning officers, directed to the Secretary of State, who shall lay the same before the General Assembly at their first meeting thereafter, when they shall open, publish and declare the result thereof, in the presence of a majority of the members of both houses. The person having the highest number of votes shall be declared duly elected, and a certificate thereof given to such person, signed by the presiding officers of both bodies; but if any two or more shall be highest and equal in votes for the same office, one of them shall be chosen by the joint vote of both houses.

SEC. 4. The supreme executive power shall be vested in a Governor.

SEC. 5. He may require information in writing from the officers in the Executive Department upon any subject relating to the duties of their respective offices, and shall see that the laws are faithfully executed.

SEC. 6. He shall communicate at every session by message, to the General Assembly, the condition of the affairs of the State, and recommend such measures as he shall deem expedient for their action.

SEC. 7. He may, on extraordinary occasions, convene the General Assembly by proclamation, and shall state to both houses when assembled the purposes for which they were convened.

SEC. 8. In case of disagreement between the two houses, in respect to the time of adjournment, he shall have power to adjourn the General Assembly to such time as he may think proper, but not beyond the regular meeting thereof.

SEC. 9. He shall be Commander-in-Chief of the military in the State, except when they shall be called into the service of the United States.

SEC. 10. The pardoning power shall be vested in the Governor, under such regulations and restrictions as may be prescribed by law.

SEC. 11. There shall be a seal of the State, the device of which shall be fixed upon by the Governor and other State officers, be kept by the Governor and used by him officially, and shall be called "The Great Seal of the State of Kansas."

SEC. 12. All grants and commissions shall be used in the name and by the authority of the State of Kansas, sealed with the great seal, signed by the Governor, and countersigned by the Secretary of State.

SEC. 13. No member of either house of Congress, or other persons holding office under the authority of this State, or of the United States, shall execute the office of Governor except as herein provided.

SEC. 14. In the case of death, impeachment, resignation, removal or other disability of the Governor, the Lieutenant Governor shall exercise the duties of the office of Governor until another Governor shall be duly qualified; but in such case another Governor shall be chosen at the next annual election for members of the General Assembly, unless such death, resignation, impeachment, removal, or other disability shall occur within three calendar months immediately preceding such next annual election, in which case a Governor shall be chosen at the second succeeding annual election for members of the General Assembly; and in case of the death, impeachment, resignation, removal, or other disability of the Lieutenant Governor, the President of the Senate *pro tem.* shall exercise the office of Governor until a Governor shall be duly qualified as aforesaid.

SEC. 15. The Lieutenant Governor shall be President of the Senate, but shall vote only when the Senate is equally divided, and shall be entitled to the same pay as the Speaker of the House of Representatives; and in case of his death, impeachment, resignation, removal from office, or when he shall exercise the office of Governor, the Senate shall choose a President *pro tem.*

SEC. 16. Should the office of Secretary of State, Treasurer, Auditor or Attorney-General become vacant, for any of the causes specified in the fourteenth and fifteenth sections, the Governor shall fill the vacancy or vacancies until the disability is removed or a successor is elected and qualified. Every such vacancy shall be filled by election, at the first general election that occurs more than thirty days after such vacancy shall have occurred, and the person chosen shall hold the office for the full term fixed in the second section of this article.

SEC. 17. The officers mentioned in this article shall, at stated times, receive for their services compensation to be fixed by law, which shall neither be increased nor diminished during the period for which they shall have been elected.

SEC. 18. The officers of the Executive Department and of the public State institutions shall, at least ten days preceding each regular session of the General Assembly, severally report to the Governor, who shall transmit the same to the General Assembly.

SEC. 19. Every bill which shall have passed both houses shall be presented to the Governor. If he approve, he shall sign the same; but if he shall not approve, he shall return it with his objections to the house in which it shall have originated, who shall enter the objections at large upon the journal, and proceed to reconsider the same. If after such reconsideration two-thirds of that house shall agree to pass the bill, it shall be sent, with the objections, to the other house, by which, likewise, it shall be reconsidered; and if approved by two-thirds of that house, it shall be a law. But in such case the votes of both houses shall be determined by yeas and nays, and the names of the persons voting for or against the bill shall be entered upon the journals of the houses respectively. If any bill shall not be returned by the Governor within five days (Sunday excepted) after it shall have been presented to him, it shall be a law in like manner as if he had signed it, unless the General Assembly, by their adjournment, prevented its return, in which case it shall also be a law, unless sent back within two days after the next meeting.

SEC. 20. Contested elections for Governor, Lieutenant Governor, Judges of the Supreme Court, and all other State officers, shall be determined by the General Assembly in such manner as may be prescribed by law.

SEC. 21. The General Assembly shall have power to provide by law for the election of a Surveyor General, State Geologist, and Superintendent of Common Schools, whose duties shall be prescribed by law.

ARTICLE VI.— JUDICIAL.

SECTION 1. The judicial power of the State shall be vested in a Supreme Court, Courts of Common Pleas, Justices of the Peace, and in such other courts inferior to the Supreme Court as the General Assembly may establish.

SEC. 2. The Supreme Court shall consist of three judges, a majority of whom shall form a quorum. It shall have such original and appellate jurisdiction as may be provided by law. It shall hold at least one term each year at the seat of government, and such other terms as may be provided by law. The Judges of the Supreme Court shall be elected by the electors of the State at large.

SEC. 3. The State shall be divided by the first General Assembly under this Constitution into three Common Pleas districts of compact territory, bounded by county lines, and as nearly equal in population as practicable; and a Judge for each district shall be chosen by the electors thereof, and their term of office shall be for three years.

SEC. 4. The Courts of Common Pleas shall consist of one Judge each, who shall reside within the district for which he is chosen during his continuance in office.

SEC. 5. The jurisdiction of the Court of Common Pleas, and of the Judges thereof, shall be fixed by law.

SEC. 6. A competent number of justices of the peace shall be elected by the electors in each township of the several counties. The term of office shall be for three years, and their powers and duties shall be fixed by law.

SEC. 7. All Judges, other than those provided for in the Constitution, shall be elected by the electors of the judicial district for which they may be created, but not for a longer term of office than three years.

SEC. 8. The Judges of the Supreme Court shall, immediately after the first election under this Constitution, be classified by lot, so that one shall hold for the term of one year, one for the term of three years; and all subsequent elections the term of each of said Judges shall be for three years.

SEC. 9. In case the office of any judge shall become vacant before the expiration of the term for which he was elected, the vacancy shall be filled by appointment by the Governor until a successor shall be elected and qualified; and such successor shall be elected for the residue of the unexpired term at the first annual election that occurs more than thirty days after such vacancy shall have happened.

SEC. 10. The Judges of the Supreme Court and of the Courts of Common Pleas shall, at stated times, receive such compensation as may be provided by law, which shall not be increased nor diminished during their term of office; but they shall receive no fees or perquisites, nor hold any other office of profit and trust under the State, other than a judicial office.

SEC. 11. The General Assembly may increase or diminish the number of the Judges of the Supreme Court, the number of the districts of the Courts of Common Pleas, the number of Judges in any district, or establish other courts, whenever two-thirds of the members elected to each house shall concur therein; but no such change, addition or diminution shall vacate the office of any Judge.

SEC. 12. There shall be elected in each county, by the electors thereof, one Clerk of the Court of Common Pleas, who shall hold his office for the term of three years, and until his successor shall be elected and qualified.

Sec. 13. The General Assembly shall provide by law for the speedy publication of the decisions of the Supreme Court made under this Constitution.

Sec. 14. The Supreme Court shall, upon the decision of every case, give an opinion in writing of each question arising in the record in such case, and the decision of the court thereon.

Sec. 15. There shall be elected by the voters of the State, a Clerk and a Reporter for the Supreme Court, who shall hold their offices for three years, and whose duties shall be prescribed by law.

Sec. 16. Judges may be removed from office by concurrent resolution of both houses of the General Assembly, if two-thirds of the members elected to each house concur therein ; but no such removal shall be made except upon complaint, the substance of which shall be entered upon the journal, nor until the party thereof charged shall have had notice thereof, and an opportunity to be heard.

Sec. 17. The several Judges of the Supreme Court, of the Court of Common Pleas, and of such other courts as may be created by law, shall respectively have and exercise such power and jurisdiction, at chambers or otherwise, as may be provided by law.

Sec. 18. The style of all process shall be, "The State of Kansas." All prosecutions shall be carried on in the name and by the authority of the State of Kansas, and all indictments shall conclude, "against the peace and dignity of the State of Kansas."

Article VII.—Education.

Section 1. The principal of all funds arising from the sale or other disposition of lands or other property granted or entrusted to this State, for educational and religious purposes, shall forever be preserved inviolate and undiminished, and the income arising therefrom shall be faithfully applied to the specific objects of the original grants or appropriations.

Sec. 2. The General Assembly shall make such provision, by taxation or otherwise, as, with the income arising from the school-trust fund, will secure a thorough and efficient system of common schools throughout the State; but no religious or other sect or sects shall ever have any exclusive right to, or control of, any part of the school funds of this State.

Sec. 3. The General Assembly may take measures for the establishment of a University, with such branches as the public convenience may hereafter demand, for the promotion of literature, the arts, sciences, medical and agricultural instruction.

Sec. 4. Provision may be made by law for the support of normal schools, with suitable libraries, and scientific apparatus.

Article VIII.—Public Institutions.

Section 1. It shall be the duty of the General Assembly, at as early a date as possible, to provide State asylums for the benefit, treatment, and instruction of the blind, deaf and dumb, and insane.

Sec. 2. The General Assembly shall make provision for the establishment of an asylum for idiots, to be regulated by law.

Sec. 3. The respective counties of the State shall provide in some suitable manner for those inhabitants who by reason of age, infirmity, or other misfortune, may have claims upon the sympathy and aid of society : under provisions to be made by the laws of the General Assembly.

Sec. 4. The General Assembly shall make provision for the establishment of houses of refuge for the correction, reform and instruction of juvenile offenders.

Sec. 5. It shall be the duty of the General Assembly to make provision as soon as possible for a State General Hospital.

Article IX.—Public Debt and Public Works.

Section 1. No money shall be paid out of the Treasury except in pursuance of an appropriation by law.

Sec. 2. The credit of the State shall never be given or loaned in aid of any individual association or corporation.

Sec. 3. For the purpose of defraying extraordinary expenditures, the State may contract public debts, but such debts shall never in the aggregate exceed one hundred thou. sand dollars, unless authorized by a direct vote of the people at a general election. Every such debt shall be authorized by law, and every such law shall provide for the payment of the annual interest of such debt, and the principal within ten years from the passage of such law ; and such appropriation shall not be repealed until the principal and interest shall have been wholly paid.

SEC. 4. The Legislature may also borrow money to repel invasion, suppress insurrection, or defend the State in time of war; but the money thus raised shall be applied exclusively to the object for which the loan was authorized, or repayment of the debts thereby created.

SEC. 5. No scrip, certificate, or other evidence of State debt whatever, shall be issued, except for such debts as are authorized by the third and fourth sections of this article.

ARTICLE X. — MILITIA.

SECTION 1. The militia shall consist of all able-bodied white male persons between the ages of eighteen and forty years, except such as may be exempt by the laws of the United States, or of this State, and shall be organized, officered, armed, equipped, and trained in such manner as may be provided by law.

SEC. 2. The Governor shall appoint the Adjutant, Quartermaster and Commissary Generals.

SEC. 3. All militia officers shall be commissioned by the Governor, and shall hold their offices not longer than three years.

SEC. 4. The General Assembly shall determine the method of dividing the militia into divisions, brigades, regiments, battalions, and companies, and fix the rank of all officers.

SEC. 5. The militia may be divided into classes, in such manner as shall be prescribed by law.

SEC. 6. No person conscientiously opposed to bearing arms shall be compelled to do military duty; but such person shall pay an equivalent for such exemption, the amount to be prescribed by law.

SEC. 7. The first General Assembly shall offer inducements for the formation, uniforming, and drilling of independent volunteer companies in the different cities and counties in this State.

ARTICLE XI. — FINANCE AND TAXATION.

SECTION 1. The General Assembly shall provide by law for a uniform and equal rate of assessment and taxation; and taxes shall be levied upon all such property, real and personal, as the General Assembly may from time to time prescribe; but all property appropriated and used exclusively for municipal, literary, educational, scientific, or charitable purposes, and personal property to an amount not exceeding one hundred dollars for each head of a family, and all property appropriated and used exclusively for religious purposes to an amount not exceeding $200,000, may by general laws be exempted from taxation.

SEC. 2. The General Assembly shall provide by law for an annual tax sufficient to defray the estimated ordinary expenses of the State for each year.

SEC. 3. Every law imposing a tax shall state distinctly the object of the same, to which it shall be applied.

SEC. 4. On the passage, in either house of the General Assembly, of any law which imposes, continues or renews a tax, or makes, continues or renews an appropriation of public or trust money, or releases, discharges or commutes a claim or demand of the State, the question shall be taken by yeas and nays, which shall be duly entered on the journal; and three-fifths of all the members elected to such house shall, in all such cases, be required to constitute a quorum.

ARTICLE XII. — COUNTY AND TOWNSHIP OFFICERS.

SECTION 1. The General Assembly shall provide by law for the election of county, city, town and township officers.

SEC. 2. All officers whose election or appointment is not provided for by this Constitution, shall be elected by the people, or appointed, as the General Assembly may by law direct.

SEC. 3. Provision shall be made by law for the removal, for misconduct or malversation in office, of all officers whose powers and duties are not local or legislative, and who shall be elected at general elections, and also for supplying vacancies created by such removal.

SEC. 4. The Legislature may declare the cases in which any office shall be deemed vacant, where no provision is made for that purpose in this Constitution.

ARTICLE XIII.—CORPORATIONS.

SECTION 1. The General Assembly shall not create corporations by special act, except for municipal purposes.

SEC. 2. Corporations may be formed under general laws, but such laws may at any time be altered or repealed.

ARTICLE XIV.—JURISPRUDENCE.

SECTION 1. The General Assembly, at its first session, shall constitute three commissioners, whose duty it shall be to revise, reform, simplify and abridge the rules of practice, pleadings, forms and proceedings of the courts of record of this State, and to provide, so far as practicable and expedient, that justice shall be administered by intelligent and uniform proceedings, without any distinction between law and equity.

SEC. 2. The proceedings of the commissioners shall be reported to the General Assembly, and be subject to the action of that body.

ARTICLE XV.—MISCELLANEOUS.

SECTION 1. The first General Assembly shall locate the permanent seat of government.

SEC. 2. Lotteries and the sale of lottery tickets for any purpose whatever shall forever be prohibited in the State.

SEC. 3. No person shall be elected or appointed to any office in this State unless they possess the qualifications of an elector.

SEC. 4. There may be established in the Secretary of State's office a Bureau of Statistics and Agriculture, under such regulations as may be prescribed by law, and provision shall be made by the General Assembly for the organization and encouragement of State and county agricultural associations.

SEC. 5. The first General Assembly shall provide by law for securing to the wife the separate property acquired by her before or after coverture, and the equal right with the husband to the custody of their children during their minority; and in case of death, insanity, intemperance, or gross impropriety of the husband, their exclusive custody.

ARTICLE XVI.—AMENDMENTS TO THE CONSTITUTION.

SECTION 1. All propositions for amendments to the Constitution shall be made by the General Assembly.

SEC. 2. A concurrence of two-thirds of the members elected to each house shall be necessary, after which such proposed amendments shall be entered upon the journals, with the yeas and nays; and the Secretary of State shall cause the same to be published in at least one newspaper in each county in the State where a newspaper is published, for at least six months preceding the next election for Senators and Representatives, when such proposed amendments shall be again referred to the Legislature elected next succeeding said publication. If passed by the second Legislature, by a majority of two-thirds of the members elected to each house, such amendments shall be republished as aforesaid for at least six months prior to the next general election, at which election such proposed amendments shall be submitted to the people for their approval or rejection, and if the majority of the electors voting at such election shall adopt such amendments, the same shall become a part of the Constitution.

SEC. 3. When more than one amendment is submitted at the same time, they shall be so submitted as to enable the electors to vote upon each amendment separately.

SEC. 4. No convention for the formation of a new Constitution shall be called, and no amendment to the Constitution shall be by the General Assembly made, before the year 1865, nor more than once in five years thereafter.

ARTICLE XVII.—BANKS AND CURRENCY.

SECTION 1. No banks shall be established otherwise than under a general banking law.

SEC. 2. If the General Assembly shall enact a general banking law, such law shall provide for the registry and countersigning by the Auditor of State of all paper credit designed to be circulated as money, with ample collateral security, readily convertible into specie, for the redemption of the same in gold or silver, shall be required; which collateral security shall be under the control of the proper officer or officers of State. Such law shall restrict the aggregate amount of all paper credit to be circulated as money, and the aggregate amount to be put in circulation in any one year; and no note issued under the provision of this section shall be of a less denomination than ten dollars.

SEC. 3. The stockholders in every bank or banking company shall be individually liable to an amount over and above their stock equal to their respective shares of stock, for all debts and liabilities of said bank or banking company.

SEC. 4. All bills or notes issued as money shall be at all times redeemable in gold or silver; and no law shall be passed sanctioning, directly or indirectly, the suspension, by any bank or banking company, of specie payments.

SEC. 5. Holders of bank notes shall be entitled, in case of insolvency, to preference of specie payment over all other creditors.

SEC. 6. No bank shall receive, directly or indirectly, a greater rate of interest than shall be allowed by law to individuals loaning money.

SEC. 7. Every bank or banking company shall be required to cease all banking operations within twenty years from the time of its organization, and promptly thereafter to close its business.

SEC. 8. The State shall not be a stockholder in any bank or banking institution.

SEC. 9. All banks shall be required to keep officers and proper offices for the issue and redemption of their paper at some accessible and convenient point within the State.

SEC. 10. The said banking law shall contain a provision reserving the power to alter, amend or repeal said law.

SEC. 11. At the time of submitting this Constitution to the electors for their approval or disapproval, the articles numbered, in relation to a general banking law, shall be submitted as a distinct proposition in the following form: General Banking Law — yes or no; and if a majority of the votes cast shall be in favor of said article, then the same shall form a part of this Constitution; otherwise it shall be void, and form no part thereof.

SCHEDULE.

In order that no inconvenience may arise from the organization and establishment of a State Government, and that the wishes of the people may be fully accomplished, it is declared—

FIRST: That no existing rights, suits, prosecutions, claims and contracts shall be affected by a change in the form of government.

SECOND: That this Constitution shall be submitted to the people of Kansas for ratification on the fifteenth day of December next.

THIRD: That each qualified elector shall express his assent or dissent to the Constitution by voting a written or printed ticket, labelled "Constitution," or, "No Constitution," which election shall be held by the same judges and conducted under the same regulations and restrictions as are hereinafter provided for the election of members of the General Assembly; and the judges therein named shall, within ten days after said election, seal up and transmit to the Chairman of the Executive Committee of Kansas Territory the result of said election, who shall forthwith make proclamation of the same. And in case the Constitution be ratified by the people, the Chairman of the Executive Committee shall cause publication to be made by proclamation that an election will be held on the third Tuesday of January, A. D. 1856, for Governor, Lieutenant Governor, Secretary of State, Treasurer, Auditor, Judges of Supreme Court, State Printer, Attorney General, Reporter of the Supreme Court, Clerk of the Supreme Court, and Members of the General Assembly, which said election shall be held by the same judges, under the same restrictions and conducted in the same manner, as is hereinafter provided for the election of members of the General Assembly; and the judges herein named are hereby required within ten days after said election to seal up and transmit duplicate copies of the returns of said election to the Chairman of the Executive Committee, one of which shall be laid before the General Assembly at its first meeting.

FOURTH: At the same time and place, the qualified voters shall, under the same regulations and restrictions, elect a Member of Congress, to represent the State of Kansas in the Thirty-fourth Congress of the United States; the returns of said election to be made to the Chairman of the Executive Committee, who shall deposit the same in the office of the Secretary of State as soon as he shall enter upon the discharge of the duties of his office.

FIFTH: The General Assembly shall meet on the fourth day of March, A. D. 1856, at the city of Topeka, at 12 M., at which time and place the Governor, Lieutenant Governor, Secretary of State, Judge of the Supreme Court, Treasurer, Auditor, State Printer, Reporter and Clerk of the Supreme Court, and Attorney General, shall appear, take the oath of office, and enter upon the discharge of the duties of their respective offices under this Constitution, and shall continue in office in the same manner and during the same period that they would have done had they been elected on the first Monday of August, A. D. 1856.

SIXTH: Until otherwise provided by law, the State shall be divided into election districts; and the Senators and Representatives shall be apportioned among the several districts as follows:

First District.— Commencing in the Kansas river, at the mouth of Cedar creek; thence up said river to the first tributary above the town of Lawrence; thence up said tributary to its source; thence by a direct line to the west side of Johnson's house; thence by a due south line to the Santa Fe road, and along the middle of said road to a point due south of the source of Cedar creek; thence due north to the source of said Cedar creek, and down the same to the place of beginning.

Second District.—Commencing at the mouth of Big Spring branch, on the south bank of the Kansas river; thence up said branch to its furthest source; thence by a southerly line crossing the Wakarusa river, on the east side of the house of Charles Matney, to the middle of the Santa Fe road; thence along the middle of said road to the line of the First District; thence by the same along the west side of the house of ——Johnson, to the head of the first tributary of the Kansas above the town of Lawrence; and thence by the same tributary to the Kansas river, and up the south bank of said river to the mouth of Big Spring branch, the place of beginning.

Third District.— Commencing at the mouth of Big Spring branch, on the south side of the Kansas river; thence up the same to its furthest source; thence by a southerly line to the north bank of the Wakarusa river, on the east side of the house of Charles Matney; thence up said river and its main branch to the line of the Pottawatomie Reservation; and thence by the southern and western line of said Reservation to the Kansas river, and down the said river to the place of beginning.

Fourth District.—Commencing at the Missouri State line, in the middle of the Santa Fe road; thence along the middle of said road to Rock creek, near the 65th mile of said road; thence south to the line of the Shawnee Reservation ceded by the treaty of 1854; thence due east along the south line of said Reservation and the north lines of the existing Reservations of the Sacs and Foxes, the existing Reservations of the Chippewas and Ottawas, and the Reservations of the Piankeshaws, Weas, Peorias and Kaskaskias, to the Missouri State line; thence up the Missouri State line to the place of beginning.

Fifth District.— Commencing at the Missouri State line, at the southern boundary of the Fourth District; thence west along the same to the northwest corner of the Sac and Fox Reservation; thence due south along the western line thereof, and due south to the south branch of the Neosho river, about seventy miles above the Catholic Osage Mission; thence down said river to the north line of the Reserve for the New York Indians; and east along said line to the head-waters of Little Osage River, or the nearest point thereto; and thence down said river to the Missouri State line, and up said line to the place of beginning.

Sixth District.— Commencing on the Missouri State line, in Little Osage river; thence up the same to the line of the Reserve for the New York Indians, or the nearest point thereto; thence to and by the north line of said Reserve to the Neosho river, and up said river and the south branch thereof to the head; and thence by a due south line to the southern line of the territory; thence by the southern and eastern lines of said Territory to the place of beginning.

Seventh District.—Commencing at the east side of the house of Charles Matney, on the Wakarusa river; thence due south to the middle of the Santa Fe road; thence westwardly along the middle of said road to Rock creek, near the 65th mile of said road; thence due south to the north line of the Sac and Fox Reservation; thence along the north and west lines thereof, and due south to the Neosho river; thence up said river to a point due south of the mouth of Elm creek; thence due north to the mouth of Elm creek, and up said creek to the Santa Fe road, and thence by a direct line in a northerly direction to the southwest corner of the Pottawatomie Reservation; thence along the southern line of said Reservation to the head-waters of the Wakarusa river, or the point nearest thereto; thence to and down the said river to the place of beginning.

Eighth District.—Commencing at the mouth of Elm creek, one of the branches of Osage river; thence up the same to the Santa Fe road; thence by a direct northerly line to the southwest corner of the Pottawatomie Reservation; thence up the western line thereof to Kansas river; thence up said river and the Smoky Hill Fork, beyond the most westerly settlements; thence due south to the line of the Territory; thence by the same to the line of the Sixth District; thence due north to the head of the south branch of the Neosho river; thence down said river to the line of the Seventh District; thence due north to the place of beginning.

Ninth District.—Commencing at Smoky Hill Fork, beyond the most westerly settlements; thence down the same and the Kansas river, to the mouth of Wild Cat creek; thence up said creek to the head-waters thereof; thence due north to the Independence emigrant road; thence up said road to the north line of the Territory; thence west along the same, beyond the most westerly settlements; and thence due north to the place of beginning.

Tenth District.—Commencing at the mouth of Vermilion river; thence up the same beyond the house of Josiah D. Adams; thence due north to the Independence emigrant road; thence up the middle of said road to the line of the Ninth District; thence by the same to the head of Wild Cat creek, and down said creek to the Kansas river; thence down said river to the place of beginning.

Eleventh District.—Commencing in the Vermilion river, opposite the north side of the house of Josiah D. Adams; thence up said river to the head of the main branch; thence due north to the military road from Fort Leavenworth to Fort Kearney; thence along the middle of said road to the crossing of the Vermilion branch of the Blue; thence due north to the northern line of the Territory; thence west along said line to the Independence emigrant road; thence down said road to a point due west of the north end of the house of Josiah D. Adams, and due east to the place of beginning.

Twelfth District.—Commencing at the mouth of Soldier creek, in the Kansas river; thence up said creek to the head of the main branch; thence due north to the military road from Fort Leavenworth to Fort Kearney; thence along the middle of said road to the line of the Eleventh District; thence due south to the head of Vermilion river, down Vermilion river to the mouth, and down Kansas river to the place of beginning.

Thirteenth District.—Commencing in the Kansas river, at a point three miles above the mouth of Stranger creek; thence in a northwardly direction by a line corresponding to, and three miles west of, the several courses of said creek to the line of the late Kickapoo Reservation; thence by the southern and western line of said Reservation to the military road from Fort Leavenworth to Fort Kearney; thence along the middle of said road to the line of the Twelfth District; thence due south to the head of Soldier creek; down Soldier creek to the mouth, and down Kansas river to the place of beginning.

Fourteenth District.—Commencing at the mouth of Independence creek; thence up said creek to the head of the main branch, and thence due west to the line of the late Kickapoo Reservation; thence north along said line, and the line of the late Sac and Fox Reservation, to the north line of the Territory; thence along said line eastwardly to the Missouri river, and down said river to the place of beginning.

Fifteenth District.—Commencing at the mouth of Salt creek, on the Missouri river; thence up said creek to the military road, and along the middle of said road to the lower crossing of Stranger creek; thence up said creek to the line of the late Kickapoo Reservation, and thence along the southern and western line thereof to the line of the Fourteenth District; thence by the same, and down Independence creek, to the mouth thereof, and thence down the Missouri river to the place of beginning.

Sixteenth District.—Commencing at the mouth of Salt creek; thence up said creek to the military road; thence along the middle of said road to the lower crossing of Stranger creek; thence up said creek to the line of the late Kickapoo Reservation, and thence along the same to the line of the Thirteenth District, and thence by the same, along a line corresponding to the course of Stranger creek, and keeping three miles west thereof to the Kansas river; thence down the Kansas river to the Missouri, and up the Missouri river to the place of beginning.

Seventeenth District.—Commencing at the mouth of the Kansas river; thence up the south bank thereof to the mouth of Cedar creek; thence up Cedar creek to its source; and thence due south to the Santa Fe road; along the middle of said road to the Missouri State line; and along said line to the place of beginning.

Eighteenth District.—Commencing in the military road at the crossing of the Vermilion branch of Blue river; thence due north to the line of the Territory; thence east along said line to the Fourteenth District; thence due south along said line to the aforesaid military road, and along the middle of said road to the place of beginning.

SENATORIAL AND REPRESENTATIVE DISTRICTS.

First.—The First Election District shall be entitled to three Senators and eight Representatives.

Second.—The Second Election District shall be entitled to one Senator and three Representatives.

Third.—The Third Election District shall be entitled to one Senator and three Representatives.

Fourth.—The Fourth and Seventeenth Election Districts shall constitute the Fourth Senatorial and Representative District, and be entitled to one Senator and two Representatives.

Fifth.—The Fifth Election District shall be entitled to three Senators and nine Representatives.

Sixth.—The Sixth, Seventh and Eighth Election Districts shall constitute the Sixth Senatorial and Representative District, and be entitled to two Senators and five Representatives.

Seventh.—The Ninth and Tenth Election Districts shall constitute the Seventh Senatorial and Representative District, and be entitled to one Senator and four Representatives.

Eighth.—The Eleventh and Twelfth Election Districts shall constitute the Eighth Senatorial and Representative District, and be entitled to one Senator and three Representatives.

Ninth.—The Thirteenth Election District shall constitute the Ninth Senatorial and Representative District, and be entitled to one Senator and two Representatives.

Tenth.—The Fourteenth and Eighteenth Election Districts shall constitute the Tenth Senatorial and Representative District, and be entitled to two Senators and seven Representatives.

Eleventh.—The Fifteenth Election District shall constitute the Eleventh Senatorial and Representative District, and be entitled to one Senator and five Representatives.

Twelfth.—The Sixteenth Election District shall constitute the Twelfth Senatorial and Representative District, and be entitled to three Senators and nine Representatives.

SEC. 3. Until otherwise provided by law, the election in the several districts shall be held at the following places, and the following-named persons are hereby appointed as judges of the elections.

[Next follow the places for holding the elections, and the names of the judges.]

INSTRUCTIONS TO JUDGES

SEC. 7. The three judges will provide for each poll, ballot-boxes for depositing the ballots cast by electors; shall appoint two clerks, all of whom shall be sworn or affirmed to discharge the duties of their respective offices impartially and with fidelity; and the judges and clerks shall have power to administer the oath or affirmation to each other; and the said judges shall open said election at 9 o'clock A. M., at the place designated in each precinct, and close the same at 6 o'clock P. M. In case any of the officers appointed fail to attend, the officer or officers in attendance shall supply their places, and in the event of all of them failing to attend, the qualified voters shall supply their places; and the said judges shall make out duplicate returns of said election, seal up and transmit the same within ten days to the Chairman of the Executive Committee, one copy of which is to be laid before the General Assembly. If at the time of holding said election it shall be inconvenient, from any cause whatever, that would disturb or prevent the voters of any election precinct in the Territory from the free and peaceable exercise of the elective franchise, the officers are hereby authorized to adjourn said election into any other precinct in the Territory, and to any other day they may see proper, of the necessity of which they shall be the exclusive judges, at which time and place the qualified voters may cast their votes.

SEC. 8. Until otherwise provided by law, the Chairman of the Executive Committee of Kansas Territory shall announce by proclamation the result of the elections, and the names of persons elected to office.

SEC. 9. No person shall be entitled to a seat in the first General Assembly at its organization, except the members whose names are contained in the proclamation of the Chairman of the Executive Committee; but after the General Assembly is organized, seats may be contested in the usual way.

SEC. 10. Certificates of indebtedness may be issued by the Territorial Executive Committee for all necessary expenses accruing in the formation of the State Government, not exceeding twenty-five thousand dollars; provided no certificate shall be issued except for legitimate expenses. All claims shall be made in writing, and shall be numbered and kept on file in the Secretary's office; and all certificates of indebtedness shall be signed· by the President and Secretary, and countersigned by the Treasurer, and numbered to correspond with the numbers of the claim or bill for which it was issued. The certificates shall bear ten per cent. interest per annum.

SEC. 11. The first General Assembly shall provide by law for the redemption of the certificates of indebtedness issued under the provisions of the foregoing section.

SEC. 12. Until the great seal of the State of Kansas is agreed upon and procured, as provided for in the 11th section of the 5th article of this Constitution, the Governor shall use his own private seal as the seal of State.

SEC. 13. At the election for the ratification of this Constitution, and the first election for State officers, a representation in the Congress of the United States and members of the General Assembly of this State, an actual residence in the Territory of thirty days immediately preceding said election shall be sufficient as a qualification for an elector, and an actual residence of ninety days for the candidates; provided said elector and candidates possess all the other qualifications required by the provisions of this Constitution.

SEC. 14. The first Legislature shall provide by law for the enforcement of the provisions of the 6th section of the Bill of Rights on or before the 4th day of July, 1857, as to all persons in the Territory before the adoption of this Constitution; and as to all others, the provisions of said section shall operate from and after the ratification of this Constitution by the people.

ROBERT KLOTZ.	CALEB MAY.	W. Y. ROBERTS.
M. J. PARROTT.	S. MEWHINNEY.	G. W. SMITH.
M. W. DELAHAY.	A. CURTISS.	J. G. THOMPSON.
W. R. GRIFFITH.	A. HUNTING.	G. A. CUTLER.
G. S. HILLYER.	R. KNIGHT.	J. K. GOODIN.
WM. HICKS.	O. C. BROWN.	J. M. TUTON.
S. N. LATTA.	W. GRAHAM.	THOMAS BELL.
JOHN LANDIS.	MORRIS HUNT.	R. H. CROSBY.
H. BURSON.	J. H. NESBITT.	P. C. SCHUYLER.
C. W. STEWART.	C. K. HOLLIDAY.	C. ROBINSON.
J. M. ARTHUR.	DAVID DODGE.	M. F. CONWAY.
J. L. SAYLE.	J. A. WAKEFIELD.	J. S. EMERY.

J. H. LANE, *President.*

SAM. C. SMITH, *Secretary.*
CHAS. A. FOSTER, *Asst. Secretary.*

1856.

JANUARY 12.—Lawrence has a weekly mail to Leavenworth.

—During the winter, the Legislatures of some of the Southern States appropriated money to send men to Kansas. Armed bodies of men came from several Southern States. The Free-State men of Kansas sent men to the Northern States "to plead the cause of the people of Kansas."

JANUARY 15.—Election of State officers under the Topeka Constitution.

ELECTION OF OFFICERS UNDER THE TOPEKA FREE-STATE CONSTITUTION, JANUARY 15, 1856.

Precincts.	Governor C. Robinson	Governor W. Y. Roberts	Lt. Gov. W. Y. Roberts	Lt. Gov. M. J. Parrott	Sec. of State P. C. Schuyler	Sec. of State C. K. Holliday	Auditor G. A. Cutler	Auditor W. R. Griffith	Treasurer J. A. Wakefield	Treasurer E. C. K. Garvey	Att'y Gen. H. Miles Moore	Supreme Judges M. Hunt	Supreme Judges S. N. Latta	Supreme Judges M. F. Conway	Supreme Judges G. W. Smith	Supreme Judges S. W. Johnston	Supreme Judges J. A. Wakefield	Rep. Sup. Court S. B. McKenzie	Rep. Sup. Court E. M. Thurston	Clerk Su. C. S. B. Floyd	Printer John Speer	Printer R. G. Elliott	Rep. to Cong. M. W. Delahay
Washington	1	29		29	1	29	1	29	1	29	30	1	3	1	29	29	27	29	1	30	1	29	30
Doniphan	32		32		32		31		32		32	32	31	31					32	32	32		32
Osawatonie	82		42		82		81		82		81	81	81	82					79	82	82		78
Osage	19	6	19	7	19	7	19	7	19	8	19	19	19	19	7	7		7	19	19	19	7	19
Easton	66	1	66		66		66		64		75	66	73	65					66	76	70		73
Burr Oak	24		24		24		24		24		24	24	24	24					24	24	24		24
St. Joseph Bottom	49		49		50		49		50	3	50	50	50	50	4	4		3	50	50	50	3	50
Padon's House	27		27		27		27		27		27	27	27	27					27	27	27		27
Wolf River	36		36		36		36		36		36	36	36	36					36	36	36		36
East Douglas	28	3	28	3	28	3	28	3	28		31	29	27	28	4	4		4	28	31	28	3	31
Stanton	31		31		31		31		31	4	31	31	31	31					31	31	31		28
Pottawatomie	39		39		39		39		38	17	39	39	39	39	23	23	23	20	39	39	39	4	38
Titus	28		28		28		28		28	33	82	28	32	28	45	45	45	45	28	32	28	24	32
Blanton	52	4	42	4	55	4	54	4	55	2	78	55	55	55	2	2	2	2	55	77	54	45	77
Prairie City	24	25	25	33	27	23	27	24	27		72	27	27	27					27	70	25	2	71
Pleasant Hill	42	50	43	45	43	37	43	45	43	58	45	43	43	43	57	57	48	58	43	45	43	58	44
Mission	10	2		2	10	2	10	2	10		10	10	10	10					10		10		10
Palmyra	25		25	9	25		25		25		25	25	25	25					25	25	25		25
Franklin	8	58	5	59	8	58	8	58	8		66	8	8	8	8		48	58	8	66	8	58	66
Little Sugar Creek	33		35		32		34		34	48	34	34	34	34	61	61	51	61	34	36	33	48	34
Little Osage Creek	19		19		19		19		19	24	19	19	19	19	34	34	51	34	19	19	19	51	19
Topeka	83	61	61	64	77	68	83	62	89		145	84	141	84			33		84	145	96		135
Tecumseh	1	34	3	34	1	34	1	34	8	48	35	1	25		51	51	10	51		35	1	2	35
Kickapoo	3	23	6	23		23	3	23	29	24		14		14	7	7		7	14	65	18	51	26
Brownsville	14	51	94	59	14	51	14	51	14		65	94	14	94	62	48		46	94	65	14	8	65
Leavenworth	94	7	13	7	94	7	94	7	94	51	101	383	101	371	14	14		14	380	101	94	7	65
Lawrence	365	41	14	245	383	43	380		385	7	426	13	379							427	373	53	100
Neosho		14	34			14	13	14	13	36	13	14	13							10	13		395
Slough Creek		1										14	4					14	14	14		14	13
Wyandotte	1	1			35		35				35	35	35						35	35	35		14
Total	1,296	410																					1,628

JANUARY 17.—Printers' Festival in Lawrence. G. W. Brown, Chairman; R. G. Elliott, of the Free State, and James Redpath, of the St. Louis Democrat, Secretaries. Speeches by G. W. Brown, J. Short, Jos. Boyer, M. F. Conway, J. L. Speer, Mr. Greene, James Redpath, John Speer, Miss Annis W. Gleason, W. B. Atwood, Miss Hiscox, Frank B. Swift, B. C. Golliday, C. V. Eskridge, R. G. Elliott, J. H. Greene, Chas. F. Lenhart, Mrs. S. N. Wood, and Mrs. G. W. Brown.

JANUARY 17.—The election under the Topeka Constitution for State officers was held at the house of T. A. Minard, in Easton, Leavenworth county, on the 17th. On Friday morning, January 18th, Stephen Sparks, a Free-State man, while on his way home from the election, with his son and nephew, was surrounded by Ruffians. Capt. R. P. Brown went to their assistance, and rescued them. While Brown and seven others were on their way to Leavenworth they were arrested and taken to Easton, where a Pro-Slavery mob had assembled. Through that day they were guarded. At night all the Free-State men were released except Brown. He was taken out and assaulted with hatchets and knives, then dragged to a wagon and carried to Dunn's liquor shop, in Salt Creek valley. Finding that Brown must die, he was taken to his home, where he soon expired. Capt. Brown had been in Lawrence during the recent Wakarusa war, aiding the Free-State men. He was a member elect of the Free-State Legislature.

JANUARY 20.—Burial of the remains of R. P. Brown, by a few friendly hands, on Pilot Knob, Leavenworth. A writer in the Herald of Freedom says: "Brown was brought to his home about midnight, with three gashes cut in the side of his face — no doubt with a hatchet — exhausted, bleeding, and benumbed with cold. He lingered an hour or two, perfectly sensible, though very weak."

JANUARY 24.—President Pierce, in a Special Message to Congress, endorses the Bogus Legislature, and calls the formation of the Topeka Government revolutionary, and an act of rebellion. He asks for the passage of a bill authorizing the people of Kansas to frame a Constitution.

JANUARY 29.—The Montgomery (Alabama) Advertiser and Gazette says Maj. Jeff. Buford, of Eufala, Alabama, will leave there February 15, with two or three hundred Southern men, bound for Kansas Territory.

FEBRUARY.—The following is the title of a book published this month: "Three Years on the Kansas Border. By a Clergyman of the Episcopal Church. New York and Auburn: 1856." pp. 240.

The writer, a New York man, was a Missionary in the Platte Purchase, in 1851–2. In 1853 he went to Chicago. In October, 1854, he returned, as a Missionary of the Church for Kansas Territory, and was on duty one year. He lived some months at Weston, Mo., preaching at Kickapoo, and occasionally at Leavenworth. In the summer of 1855 he lived on a claim near Mount Pleasant, in Atchison county. The book treats more of home life than of politics. The writer was a Free-State man, but took no part in public affairs. His story of the death of two children, of the severe illness of his wife and himself, and of the sufferings and destitution they passed through in the vain attempt to make a home on the prairie, is a very sad one.

FEBRUARY 1.—Commissions issued by the Governor to the "Kickapoo Rangers."

FEBRUARY 1.—Samuel J. Jones, Sheriff of Douglas county, Kansas, by appointment of the Bogus Legislature, is still Postmaster of Westport, Mo.

—The Leavenworth Herald justifies the brutal murder of R. P. Brown. In an article on the subject, it says: "These higher-law men will not be permitted longer to carry out their illegal and high-handed proceedings. The good sense of the people is frowning it down. And if it cannot be put down in one way, it will in another."

FEBRUARY 2.—Nathaniel P. Banks, Republican, elected Speaker of the House of Representatives, on the 134th ballot. He receives 103 votes, to 100 for Wm. Aiken, of South Carolina.

FEBRUARY 6.—Lane, Chairman of the Committee, announces the election of the following State officers: Governor, Charles Robinson; Lieut. Governor, Wm. Y. Roberts; Secretary of State, Philip C. Schuyler; Auditor, George A. Cutler; Treasurer, John A. Wakefield; Attorney General, H. Miles Moore; Judges of the Supreme Court, S. N. Latta, Morris Hunt, and M. F. Conway; Reporter of the Supreme Court, E. M. Thurston; Clerk Supreme Court, B. Floyd; Printer, John Speer.

FEBRUARY 8.—The Committee announce the election of Mark W. Delahay for Representative to the Thirty-fourth Congress.

FEBRUARY 11.—President Pierce issues a proclamation commanding "all persons engaged in unlawful combinations against the constituted authority of the Territory of Kansas, or of the United States, to disperse and retire peaceably to their respective abodes."

FEBRUARY 16.—Secretary Marcy writes to Governor Shannon to call upon the officers at Fort Leavenworth and Fort Riley to aid him in "the suppression of insurrectionary combinations, or armed resistance to the execution of the laws."

FEBRUARY 18.—Drawing of town lots at Grasshopper Falls.

—There are fifty-eight post offices in Kansas.

FEBRUARY 20.—The Squatter Sovereign says: "In our opinion the only effectual way to correct the evils that now exist is to hang up to the nearest tree the very last traitor who was instrumental in getting up, or participated in, the celebrated Topeka Convention."

FEBRUARY 22.—The National Republican Party organized at Pittsburgh. S. N. Wood appears as a delegate from Kansas, and on his motion, Charles Robinson is placed on the National Committee. Francis P. Blair, sen., presides. Address to the people written by Henry J. Raymond, of the New York Times.

FEBRUARY.—Millard Fillmore nominated by the Americans for President.

FEBRUARY 29.—J. H. Stringfellow commissioned as the captain of a military company in Atchison county. Many military commissions issued in the winter and spring, by the Governor.

MARCH.—The National Era publishes the following poem, written by John G. Whittier:

THE BURIAL OF BARBER.

Bear him, comrades, to his grave;
Never over one more brave ,
    Shall the prairie grasses weep,
In all ages yet to come,
When the millions in our room,
    What we sow in tears, shall reap.

Bear him up the icy hill,
With the Kansas frozen still
    As his noble heart, below,
And the land he came to till
With a freeman's thews and will,
    And his poor hut roofed with snow!

One more look of that dead face,
Of his murder's ghastly trace!
    One more kiss, oh, widowed one!
Lay your left hands on his brow,
Lift your right hands up, and vow
    That his work shall yet be done!

Patience, friends! The eye of God
Every path by Murder trod
    Watches, lidless, day and night;
And the dead man in his shroud,
And his widow weeping loud,
    And our hearts are in His sight.

Every deadly threat that swells
With the roar of gambling hells,
    Every brutal jest and jeer,
Every wicked thought and plan
Of the cruel heart of man,
·   Tho' but whispered, He can hear.

You in suffering, they in crime,
Wait the just award of time,
    Wait the vengeance that is due;
Not in vain a heart shall break,
Not a tear for freedom's sake
    Fall unheeded: God is true.

While the flag, with stars bedeck'd,
Threatens where it should protect,
    And the Law shakes hands with Crime,
What is left ye but to wait,
Match your patience to your fate,
    And abide the better time?

Patience, friends! The human heart
Everywhere shall take your part,
    · Everywhere for you shall pray;
On your side are nature's laws,
And God's life is in the cause
    That you suffer for to-day.

Well to suffer is divine; ·
Pass the watchword down the line,
    Pass the countersign: "ENDURE."
Not to him who rashly dares,
But to him who nobly bears,
    Is the victor's garland sure.

Frozen earth to frozen breast,
Lay your slain one down to rest;
    Lay him down in hope and faith;
And above the broken sod,
Once again, to Freedom's God,
    Pledge yourselves for life or death —

That the State whose walls ye lay,
In your blood and tears to-day,
    Shall be free from bonds of shame,
And your goodly land untrod
By the feet of slavery, shod
    With cursing as with flame!

Plant the Buckeye on his grave,
For the hunter of the slave
    In its shadow cannot rest;
And let martyr mound and tree
Be your pledge and guarantee
    Of the freedom of the West!

MARCH.—Derby & Jackson, New York, publish a book of 400 pages, entitled: "The War in Kansas. A Rough Trip to the Border, among New Homes and a Strange People. By G. Douglas Brewerton." The writer was a correspondent of the New York Herald, and the book is made up from his letters. He was in Kansas in December, 1855, and in January, 1856. He was not a partisan, and his book is now valuable because he wrote down the Northern and Southern versions of our affairs in the very words of the leading actors. Mr. Brewerton was an interviewer, but trusted his pen instead of his imagination. When he meets Gov. Shannon, he obtains a full history from that officer of the Wakarusa War. This sketch fills fifty pages of the book, and perhaps no other narrative of those events is more clear, cool, and straightforward. The book also contains the narrative of Franklin M. Coleman, who killed Dow; James Christian's history of the disturbances; Gov. Robinson's history of the war; the statement of Josiah Miller, editor of the Free State, and the facts relating to the shooting of Thomas W. Barber, from the lips of his brother, Robert F. Barber, and his brother-in-law, Thomas M. Pierson. The following sketch is copied from Brewerton's book:

"Charles Robinson was born in Worcester county, Massachusetts, on the 21st of July, 1818; was educated at Amherst College, but did not, we believe, graduate at that institution; studied medicine at the Medical College in Pittsfield, Massachusetts, where he received his diploma as an M. D., in 1843; practised his profession at Belchertown and Fitchburg, in the same State, until his removal to California, in 1849, by way of the Rocky Mountains. Upon arriving in the El Dorado of the West, Dr. Robinson settled at Sacramento, where he played a prominent part in the 'squatter riots' of 1850, in which, as the reader may perhaps remember, the Mayor of Sacramento, and some eight or ten others, lost their lives. Upon this occasion, Dr. Robinson fought upon the side of 'squatter sovereignty,' and was seriously wounded — it was asserted, mortally, at the time. For his alleged conduct upon this occasion, and while still suffering from a desperate hurt, Dr. Robinson was indicted for murder, assault with intent to kill, and for conspiracy: tried before the District Court of Sacramento, and acquitted. While still in confinement, on board the prison-ship, he was nominated and elected to the Legislature of California, from Sacramento district. This was in 1851. In July of the same year, he sailed from California in the steamship Union, which was wrecked on her passage to the Isthmus; in the difficulties which followed this disaster, Robinson is said to have borne an active and conservative part. After many delays, he finally managed to reach New York city, in September of 1851; was at Havana at the time of the Lopez execution, and a witness to that cold-blooded murder. Upon his return to the East, Dr. Robinson recommenced the practice of medicine, in Fitchburg, where he remained until June of 1854, when he emigrated with his family to Kansas. Here, he settled himself at Lawrence, where he still resides upon his 'claim,' some half a mile distant from the main body of the town. Unlike his compatriot, General Lane, Dr. Robinson — or, as we should now begin to call him, General Robinson — does not call himself a man of property; he says he is simply 'a poor man whose business prospects have been sadly damaged by the war.'

"In Kansas politics, Gen. Robinson was a member of the State Constitutional Convention, is Chairman of the Free-State Executive Committee, and, in addition to this, holds the military rank of Major General and Commander-in-Chief of the Kansas Volunteers — as the Free-State army of Kansas style themselves. He may be regarded as the real head — the thinking one, we mean — and mainspring of the Free-State party; or, to speak more correctly, of all that party who are worth anything. We believe him to be a keen, shrewd, far-seeing man, who would permit nothing to stand in the way of the end which he desired to gain. He is, moreover, cool and determined, and appears to be endowed with immense firmness; we should call him a conservative man, *now;* but conservative rather from policy than from principle. He seems to have strong common sense, and a good ordinary brain, but no brilliancy of talent. In fact, to sum Gen. Robinson up in a single sentence, we consider him the most dangerous enemy which the Pro-Slavery party have to encounter in Kansas.

"In person he is tall, well made, and more than ordinarily handsome; gentlemanly, but by no means winning in his manners, with one of those cold, keen blue eyes that seem to look you through."

Mr. Brewerton gives a sketch of the life of Gen. Lane, with the remark, "these facts may be relied upon, as we have obtained them from General Lane himself." The facts are given elsewhere in this book. The following is Brewerton's opening paragraph:

"James H. Lane was born in Boone county, Kentucky, on the twenty-second of June, 1822. He is a son of Amos Lane, a Western lawyer of considerable celebrity, who figured in the politics of his day as Speaker of the first Legislature of Indiana, and

Member of Congress during the Presidency of General Jackson, where he proved himself one of the warmest supporters of 'Old Hickory's' administration."

The above is copied as a statement of Gen. Lane's in regard to the place and time of his birth. He was generally believed to have been older, and he sometimes created the impression that he was born in Indiana; in fact, it was the prevailing opinion of his friends here that he was born in Indiana. Lane's affidavit is published on page 143 of Proceedings in Impeachment Cases; he swears, April 29, 1862, that he is in his forty-third year. This agrees with his statement to Brewerton, and makes him twenty-four years old when, in 1846, he became Colonel of the Third Indiana Volunteers.

MARCH 4.—Meeting of the Topeka Legislature. *Senate.*—Officers: President, W. Y. Roberts; Chief Clerk, Asaph Allen; Assistant, W. L. Brigdon; Sergeant-at-Arms, J. M. Fuller; Assistant, Harris Stratton; Transcribing Clerks, J. F. Cummings, J. C. Dunn; Chaplain, Paul Shepherd. President *pro tem.,* J. Curtis. *House.*—Called to order by J. H. Lane, Chairman of Executive Committee. Speaker, T. Minard; Clerk, J. K. Goodin; Assistant Clerk, Sam'l F. Tappan; Transcribing Clerks, J. Snodgrass, G. T. Gordon; Sergeant-at-Arms, J. Mitchell; Assistant, J. Swain; Chaplain, C. H. Lovejoy. The State officers are sworn in. Message by Governor Robinson, giving a history of the Free-State movement.

Speer and Ross publish the Daily Tribune, at Topeka.

The Message of Governor Robinson is an able paper, and very valuable now, historically. It is published in full in Mrs. Robinson's "Kansas."

The following is a list of the members of the Legislature:

Senators.—— —— Adams, J. M. Cole, J. Curtis, J. Dailey, —— Dunn, L. Fish, P. Fuller, J. C. Green, Benj. Harding, Geo. S. Hillyer, H. M. Hook, J. M. Irvin, D. E. Jones, S. B. McKenzie, B. W. Miller, J. H. Pillsbury, J. R. Rhaum, T. G. Thornton, W. W. Updegraff—19.

Representatives.—S. N. Hartwell, J. B. Abbott, John Hutchinson, H. F. Saunders, James Blood, C. Hornsby, E. B. Purdam, J. McGhee, M. C. Dickey, W. R. Frost, W. A. Sumnerwell, S. Mewhinney, S. T. Shore, S. R. Baldwin, David Rees, D. W. Cannon, Isaac Landers, J. M. Arthur, H. H. Williams, H. W. Labor, A. B. Marshall, J. D. Adams, T. W. Platt, Rees Furby, B. H. Brock, John Landis, E. R. Zimmerman, W. T. Burnett, L. P. Patty, F. A. Minard, Isaac Cody, Thos. Bowman, John Brown, jr., Henry Todd, J. Hornby, Abraham Barre, Richard Murphy, Wm. Hicks, B. R. Martin, Wm. Bayless, J. W. Stevens, J. K. Edsaul, S. J. Campbell, S. Goslin, H. B. Standiford, Isaac B. Higgins, T. J. Addis, D. Toothman, Wm. McClure, J. B. Wetson, Wm. B. Wade, Alex. Jamieson, A. D. Jones, Wm. Crosby, Stephen Sparks, R. P. Brown (deceased), Adam Fisher—57.

Three commissioners are appointed to prepare a code of laws. James H. Lane and Andrew H. Reeder are elected United States Senators, each receiving 38 votes, with none opposing.

A memorial to Congress is prepared, asking admission into the Union.

MARCH 8.—Adjourned to July 4th.

MARCH 12.—Senator Douglas submits a report extenuating the outrages committed in Kansas, and severely denouncing the action of the New

England Emigrant Aid Society. Senator Collamer presents a minority report.

MARCH 19.—The House of Representatives, at Washington, votes to send a Special Committee to Kansas to inquire into the validity of the pretended Legislature, (the "Bogus," of 1855,) and of the election of Whitfield. The Committee consists of Wm. A. Howard, of Michigan, John Sherman, of Ohio, and Mordecai Oliver, of Missouri.

MARCH 24.—Topeka Constitution presented in the United States Senate, by Lewis Cass.

MARCH 29.—Nearly every boat coming up the Missouri river is overhauled, and searched to see whether there are articles on board which have been pronounced contraband by the Pro-Slavery pirates. All such goods, owned by Northern men, are stolen.

APRIL 5.—In the office of the Milwaukee Sentinel, E. G. Ross, foreman in the job office, receives the present of a rifle from his fellow-printers. It is inscribed to him as an earnest of their good wishes for him, and for freedom in Kansas.

APRIL 7.—Senator Cass presents the Memorial of the Topeka Legislature asking for the admission of Kansas into the Union.

—Topeka Constitution presented in the House by Daniel Mace, of Indiana.

APRIL.—Major Buford arrives with a large body of men from Georgia, Alabama, and South Carolina.

APRIL 12.—The Free-State Hotel, Lawrence, begun in April, 1855, is finished. It is to be kept by Col. Shaler W. Eldridge.

—The Squatter Sovereign says: "We understand that the grand jurors of Doniphan and Atchison counties have found true bills of indictment against all the persons acting in the late disorganizing election in their respective counties. We hope the other counties will follow suit, and teach the Abolition traitors that the laws are now in force, and that all attempts to ruin this country will be strictly dealt with by law."

APRIL 16.—E. B. Whitman and A. D. Searl, of Lawrence, issue a map of Kansas.

APRIL 18.—The Congressional Investigating Committee reach Lawrence.

APRIL 19.—Sheriff Jones attempts to arrest S. N. Wood, in Lawrence, charging him with aiding in the rescue of Branson, in November. Mr. Wood refused to give himself up; he did not recognize the authority. An attempt to take Wood by force failed. On the 20th, Sheriff Jones returned, and called upon a number of the citizens to aid him in making the arrest. They did not answer the summons. On the 23d, Jones returned, bringing with him United States troops. The Lieutenant in command read a letter from Col. Sumner to the Mayor of Lawrence, saying the troops are sent to aid the Sheriff in executing writs. Jones then arrested John Hutchinson, E. D. Lyman, G. F. Warren, J. G. Fuller, F. Hunt, A. F. Smith, and others whom he had summoned on the 20th to assist him. No resistance was made to the Sheriff. About ten o'clock that night Jones was shot and wounded. A public meeting was held on the 24th, and the shooting of Jones severely denounced.

APRIL.—A book published, called "Six Months in Kansas. By a Lady. Boston: John P. Jewett & Co. 1856." The writer was Mrs. Hannah Anderson Ropes, who came to Kansas from Massachusetts in September, 1855. The book contains 231 pages. "Fourth thousand" is on the title page of a copy owned by Leslie J. Perry. It is made up of letters from Mrs. Ropes to her mother, and is admirably written. No little of Mrs. Ropes's time is spent with the sick; and the sufferings of pioneers who live in cabins, deprived of nearly all the comforts of life, even in the "city" of Lawrence, where she lived, are only too truly told. The following account of the funeral of Barber is copied from the book:

"I believe I have forgotten to tell you that the funeral of Mr. Barber was deferred, on account of the important business this week to be attended to. Another week has closed, and the Sabbath calls all people out to pay the last tribute of respect to poor Barber's memory. A December day, but clear, cloudless, dreadfully bright, and windy. . . . . The whole neighborhood seems astir with people, picking their way to one centre, the Hotel, where not as last Monday evening, for rejoicing, they come together, but to mourn with the sufferers of a great sorrow: a widow, made so by violence wholly unprovoked; brothers, bereaved in a manner never to be forgotten — never to be thought of in years to come but with the smartest twinges of pain. The room we enter is a long dining-hall. The walls are of limestone, rough and unplastered. Seats of plank stretch in rows, closely packed, through the whole length, with the exception of a narrow space for the clergyman. The seats are all filled. The atmosphere of the assembly is of the truest sympathy. Each soul seems personally aggrieved and afflicted. Silence is the only, and most emphatic, expression given to this grief. The first break upon that silence is the tread of many feet and a smothered, broken sob, that will not be wholly choked down. Working his way through the crowd, appears a tall man, with white hair, large blue eyes, and a very benevolent countenance. You see at once that he is a Methodist. He has clinging to his arm a small, veiled figure,—everybody knows it is the widow; 'a widow indeed.'

"There comes another smothered sob as she is borne along to the far end of the hall. The man of white hair stoops over her, and tenderly whispers words of peace to her. I do not hear them; she does not. Now she sinks into a seat. A hymn is read, and the crowd sing the tune of 'Martin Luther,' so familiar to everybody, and stretching back over the whole length of the oldest life present. What a relief it is! how it gathers up and rolls away the pent-up emotions of the multitude! Now the white head sinks down over bended knees, to the floor, and his voice utters its prayers and supplications, while the tears course down the cheeks of the speaker and his audience. The sobs of that broken heart grow fainter. Does she find a relief through the channel of other hearts? I believe so. Then follow short speeches from Colonel Lane and General Robinson, and a sad sermon from the white head. All the exercises are remarkably good of the kind. Even Colonel Lane did well.

"The services are over, and the people form a procession. Men with arms reversed take the lead; then the body and its friends; then the whole crowd, mounted in carts drawn by oxen, wagons led by mules, and carriages of every pattern, form into a solemn line, stretching far along the open country. Up over Mount Pleasant curves the road to the ground appropriated for a burial place, two miles away. What a sight it is! One like it could hardly be got up anywhere else, or under any other circumstances. This grand old country, with its lofty trees, its smoothly-terraced hills, its serene repose! The tread of the white man is fresh and new; but to-day the grand old prairie witnesses the burial of its second martyr! Now the soldiers make a wall on either side, with lifted hats, for the mourners to pass through. Gently the coffin is lowered to its last rest, while the words, 'Dust to dust,' 'I am the Resurrection and the Life,' are broken by the wailing wind, and lost to the ears of the audience by the fast-coming sobs of that forlorn, childless, earth-stricken widow! The soldiers now approach; the audience and friends fall back, giving place to them; while, standing about the grave, at the signal of their commander, one division after another bury the contents of their rifles in the last resting-place of their much-loved and honored comrade."

APRIL 25.—Governor Shannon asks Col. Sumner for "a military posse, or guard of thirty men," to be stationed at Lecompton. At later dates troops are asked to be stationed at various places.

APRIL 30.—Rev. Pardee Butler returns to Atchison. He is stripped, tarred, and covered with cotton.

MAY 3.—The Union started in Lecompton, by A. W. Jones and C. A. Faris.

—P. O. Conver edits the Kansas State Journal, at Topeka.

MAY 5.—The Grand Jury of Douglas county recommend that the Herald of Freedom and the Kansas Free State newspapers, and the Free-State Hotel, be abated as nuisances. Robinson, Reeder and others, who had participated in organizing the Free-State Government, are indicted for high treason.

MAY 7.—While Governor Reeder was with the Investigating Committee, at Tecumseh, he was summoned to appear before the Grand Jury, at Lecompton. He did not obey. The next day, at Lawrence, with the Committee, a writ of attachment was served on Governor Reeder for contempt of court. He said he was privileged from arrest. If any man laid hands on him to arrest him he did so at his peril. He was not arrested.

MAY 9.—After the attempt of Deputy United States Marshal W. P. Fain to arrest Reeder failed, Governor Reeder hastened to Kansas City. Col. S. W. Eldridge, of the American Hotel, secreted Reeder till night. The Governor was then shaved and his clothes changed to those of a laborer. Thomas B. and Edward Eldridge then rowed him in a skiff to Liberty, Missouri. Governor Reeder took a deck passage, with the laborers, on the first boat that came down, in due time landed safely at St. Charles, and then made his way across the country to Illinois.

MAY 10.—Governor Robinson, on his way East, with his wife, is arrested at Lexington, Mo. He is taken to Westport, to the Pro-Slavery camp near Lawrence, back to Kansas City, to Leavenworth, on a boat, and then to Lecompton. He is arrested for treason.

—The Herald of Freedom says:

"Kansas is again invaded by armed ruffians. They are gathering in by tens, and fifties, and hundreds. Shannon has regularly enrolled them as Territorial Militia, commissioned their officers, etc. At any moment they may commence the work of devastation."

MAY 11.—Israel B. Donalson, United States Marshal, issues a proclamation. It says the citizens of Lawrence resist arrest, under judicial writs, and law-abiding citizens are commanded to immediately appear at Lecompton "in sufficient numbers for the execution of the law." Citizens of Lawrence ask the Governor for protection.

MAY 12.—Governor Shannon writes to the Lawrence Committee:

"There is no force around or approaching Lawrence, except the legally constituted posse of the United States Marshal, and Sheriff of Douglas county, each of whom, I am informed, has a number of writs for execution against persons now in Lawrence."

MAY 13.—A meeting in Lawrence declares the statements in Donalson's proclamation to be false; that they are law-abiding citizens, but will resist an invading mob. A new Committee of Safety is appointed.

Free-State men are arrested on steamboats and on the prairie, and anar-

7

chy prevails through the Territory. The force of invaders around Lawrence constantly increases. It is the Free-State headquarters, and its citizens are constantly accused of warlike and treasonable intentions.

MAY 14.—The citizens of Lawrence make another protest to the Governor and Marshal.

—During the second week in May, the First District Court held its sessions at Lecompton, Judge Lecompte presiding. Mrs. Robinson makes the following quotations from Judge Lecompte's "extraordinary charge to the Grand Jury:"

"This Territory was organized by an act of Congress, and so far its authority is from the United States. It has a Legislature elected in pursuance of that organic act. This Legislature, being an instrument of Congress by which it governs the Territory, has passed laws. These laws, therefore, are of United States authority and making; and all that resist these laws resist the power and authority of the United States, and are, therefore, guilty of high treason. Now, gentlemen, if you find that any person has resisted these laws, then you must, under your oaths, find bills against them for high treason. · If you find that no such resistance has been made, but that combinations have been formed for the purpose of resisting them, and individuals of influence and notoriety have been aiding and abetting in such combinations, then must you find bills for constructive treason."

Mrs. Robinson says: "To make the matter so plain that even the dullest of his hearers may not fail to comprehend his meaning, he states that some who are 'dubbed Governor, Lieutenant Governor, etc., are such individuals of influence and notoriety.'"

MAY 14.—Gaius Jenkins and George W. Brown arrested. On the 22d, they were taken before Judge Lecompte, at Lecompton, to answer to the charge of treason. Bail was denied, and the cases were continued till September. Gov. Robinson, Judge G. W. Smith, and G. W. Deitzler, were similarly held. John Brown, jr., and H. H. Williams, were arrested soon after, being taken in the field, for bearing arms against the "Government." All were confined in the same camp, at Lecompton.

MAY 15.—Josiah Miller, of the Lawrence Free State newspaper, arrested for treason by South Carolina soldiers, is tried in a military tent near Lecompton, defended by James Christian, and acquitted. The following is a copy of the pass given him, on leaving Lecompton, to prevent his arrest by Ruffians:

LECOMPTON, May 16, 1856.

The bearer of this, Mr. Josiah Miller, is desirous to pass out of this Territory, and in doing so, desires to stop in the town of Lawrence to transact some private business for a short time. He designs going to Kansas City, and thence by boat or horse and buggy at that place. He is now in this Territory not to participate in the rebellion, but to settle up some private business.

Now, therefore, all persons are requested to let the bearer, Mr. Miller, pass without molestation or delay.   WILSON SHANNON,
                                                             Governor of Kansas Territory.
I. B. DONALSON, U. S. Marshal, Territory of Kansas.

—Constant arrests of Free-State men. Armed Missourians pouring into the Territory.

MAY 17.—C. W. Babcock, Lyman Allen and J. A. Perry, a committee appointed by the people of Lawrence, ask the Marshal to put a stop to the depredations committed by a large force of armed men in the vicinity of Lawrence.

MAY 19.—

"Take down your map, sir, and you will find that the Territory of Kansas, more than any other region, occupies the middle spot of North America, equally distant from the Atlantic on the east, and the Pacific on the west; from the frozen waters of Hudson's Bay on the north, and the tepid gulf stream on the south, constituting the precise territorial centre of the whole vast continent. To such advantage of situation, on the very highway between two oceans, are added a soil of unsurpassed richness, and a fascinating, undulating beauty of surface, with a health-giving climate, calculated to nurture a powerful and generous people, worthy to be a central pivot of American institutions.

"A few short months only have passed since this spacious mediterranean country was open only to the savage, who ran wild in its woods and prairies; and now it has already drawn to its bosom a population of freemen larger than Athens crowded within her historic gates, when her sons, under Miltiades, won liberty for mankind on the field of Marathon; more than Sparta contained when she ruled Greece, and sent forth her devoted children, quickened by a mother's benediction, to return with their shields or on them; more than Rome gathered on her seven hills, when, under her kings, she commenced that sovereign sway, which afterwards embraced the whole earth; more than London held, when, on the fields of Crecy and Agincourt, the English banner was carried victoriously over the chivalrous hosts of France."—*The Crime Against Kansas.— Speech of Charles Sumner in the U. S. Senate.*

MAY 21.—John Brown with six sons and a son-in-law in Lawrence.

MAY 21.—In the morning, Deputy Marshal Fain entered Lawrence and arrested George W. Smith and George W. Deitzler, without resistance. He then dismissed his monster posse, telling them he had no further use for them. In the afternoon, Sheriff Jones appeared in Lawrence with a body of armed men. Colonel Eldridge's Free-State Hotel, and the offices of the Herald of Freedom and the Kansas Free State, were destroyed. Stores were broken open and pillaged, and the dwelling-house of Charles Robinson was burned. The wanton destruction of property in Lawrence led to retaliation by bands of Free-State men in different parts of the Territory. The most conspicuous leader of these forces was Captain John Brown.

—The following is copied from Mrs. Robinson's book, pages 243–4:

"Sheriff Jones told Colonel Eldridge the hotel must be destroyed; he was acting under orders; he had writs issued by the First District Court of the United States to destroy the Free-State Hotel, and the offices of the Herald of Freedom, and Free State. The Grand Jury at Lecompton had indicted them as nuisances, and the Court had ordered them to be destroyed. The following is a copy of such indictment:

"'The Grand Jury sitting for the adjourned term of the First District Court, in and for the county of Douglas, in the Territory of Kansas, beg leave to report to the Honorable Court that, from evidence laid before them showing that the newspaper known as the Herald of Freedom, published at the town of Lawrence, has from time to time issued publications of the most inflammatory and seditious character—denying the legality of the Territorial authorities; addressing and commanding forcible resistance to the same; demoralizing the popular mind, and rendering life and property unsafe, even to the extent of advising assassination as a last resort.

"'Also, that the paper known as the Kansas Free State has been similarly engaged, and has recently reported the resolutions of a public meeting in Johnson county, in this Territory, in which resistance to the Territorial laws even unto blood has been agreed upon. And that we respectfully recommend their abatement as a nuisance.

"'Also, that we are satisfied that the building known as the Free-State Hotel, in Lawrence, has been constructed with the view to military occupation and defence, regularly parapeted and port-holed for the use of cannon and small-arms, and could only have been designed as a stronghold of resistance to law, thereby endangering the public safety and encouraging rebellion and sedition in this country; and respectfully recommend that steps be taken whereby this nuisance may be removed.

"'OWEN C. STEWART, *Foreman.*'"

MAY 21.—The following history of the 20th and 21st is copied from the Lecompton Union:

"LAWRENCE TAKEN!—GLORIOUS TRIUMPH OF THE LAW-AND-ORDER PARTY OVER FANATICISM IN KANSAS!—FULL PARTICULARS.—On Tuesday, the 20th, a large force of Law-and-Order men having gathered in and around Lecompton, the Marshal ordered the different camps to concentrate about two miles this side of Lawrence, so as to be ready for the execution of his immediate demands upon the people of Lawrence. At this order we left our sanctum and proceeded to the encampment, equipped for the occasion."

The writer says the cavalry is—

"commanded by Col. H. T. Titus, of this county, originally of Florida. . . . The prison tent has eight occupants. . . . . At half-past four o'clock the cannon were planted without any resistance upon the heights beyond Robinson's house, and within four hundred yards of the big stone hotel. . . . . At eleven, Major Buford's company from Franklin arrived; and by twelve our forces amounted to eight hundred strong, cavalry and infantry, and four six-pound pieces of brass cannon. . . At one o'clock the United States Deputy Marshal selected a small posse and entered town to make arrests. . . . . Only three arrests were made, viz.: Smith, Jenkins, and Deitzler." [Sheriff Jones then summons a posse.] "Jones had a great many writs in his hands, but could find no one against whom he held them. He also had an order from the Court to demand a surrender of their arms, field and side, and a demolition of the two presses and the Free-State Hotel as nuisances. . . . . When they agreed to surrender, our men were marched down in front of the town, and one cannon planted upon their own battlements. . . . About this time a banner was seen fluttering in the breeze over the office of the Herald of Freedom. Its color was a blood-red, with a lone star in the centre, and South Carolina above. . . . . Thus floated victoriously the first banner of Southern rights over the Abolition town of Lawrence, unfurled by the noble sons of Carolina. . . . . Mr. Jones ordered two companies into each printing office to destroy the press. Both presses were broken up and thrown into the streets, the type thrown in the river, and all the material belonging to each office destroyed. After this was accomplished, and the private property removed from the hotel by the different companies, the cannon were brought in front of the house, and directed their destructive blows upon the walls. The building caught on fire, and soon its walls came with a crash to the ground. Thus fell the Abolition fortress; and we hope this will teach the Aid Society a good lesson for the future. . . . We think the conservative men of the North and East have had furnished them, long since, sufficient data to form correct opinions of the motives governing these men. If every man of them had been killed, every house burned, and total and entire extermination had been the motto of the 'Law-and-Order Party,' who would be to blame? 'Impartial decision answers, 'These men have brought the calamity upon their own heads.'"

MAY 22.—Preston S. Brooks, a Member of the House from South Carolina, commits a violent assault upon Charles Sumner, in the U. S. Senate Chamber. The House afterwards voted by 121 to 95 to expel Brooks—less than two-thirds. Brooks resigned, was re-elected, and died January 27, 1857.

MAY 24.—Mr. Doyle and his two sons, Mr. Sherman and Mr. Wilkinson, all Pro-Slavery, were taken from their houses at night, and murdered.

Pate captures two of Brown's sons, John jr., who was a member of the Topeka Legislature, and Jason, and treats them inhumanly. He proceeds towards Lecompton, and encamps on a stream called Black Jack, near Hickory Point, in the southeast corner of Douglas county. Monday morning Capt. Brown with nine men and Capt. Shore with nineteen men left Prairie City, and marched to Black Jack, five miles distant. Pate had fifty men. The fight was opened by Shore and lasted about three hours, and ended in Pate's surrender.

Brown entrenched himself on Middle Ottawa Creek, near Prairie City, and about two miles from the present Baldwin City.

MAY 31.—A Pro-Slavery meeting in Leavenworth appoints a Committee of Safety.

JUNE 1.—Governor Robinson arrives at Lecompton. He had been under arrest since May 10. There were two indictments against him—one for usurping office, and one for high treason.

JUNE 2.—Democratic National Convention at Cincinnati. It resolved that, repudiating all sectionalism, the Democratic party adopts the principles of the Kansas-Nebraska bill—that is, the non-interference of the General Government with Slavery, which was the basis of the Compromise measures. That it recognizes the right of new States to regulate their domestic institutions, with or without Slavery, as they see fit. The administration of Pierce was endorsed, and Buchanan and Breckinridge nominated.

In the Free States, at the election in November, Fremont received 115,868 more votes than Buchanan. In the Slave States, Fremont received only 1,194 votes, while Buchanan received 609,587.

JUNE 2.—Battle of Black Jack, near Palmyra. Free-State men led by Captain John Brown.

JUNE 4.—A party from Lawrence march to Franklin. There is a night skirmish, with small results.

—Whitfield, Reed, Milt. McGee and Coleman are assembled on Bull creek, about twelve miles east of Baldwin City, in the southeast corner of Johnson county.

JUNE 4.—Gov. Shannon issues a proclamation "commanding all persons belonging to military companies unauthorized by law to disperse; otherwise they will be dispersed by United States troops." He writes to Col. Sumner "to defend Franklin and Lehay's house."

JUNE 5.—Col. Sumner proceeds to the camp of Brown, on Ottawa creek, to enforce Shannon's orders. Capt. Brown and Capt. Shore consent to disband, and Whitfield promises to return with his men to Missouri. The other Free-State leaders, encamped at Hickory Point, were Walker, Cracklin, Abbott, Lenhart, Cook, and Hopkins.

JUNE 6.—Col. Sumner returns to Fort Leavenworth. Whitfield leaves for Missouri. Reed, Pate, Bell, and Jenigen, reach Osawatomie, and sack the town. The dwelling-houses are pillaged.

JUNE 7.—Civil war rages throughout the settled portions of the Territory. The Missouri river closed to Free-State immigrants. Steamboats are stopped, and "Yankees" robbed and sent back.

JUNE.—The following is copied from an article on David Starr Hoyt, written by William B. Parsons, and published in the Kansas Magazine of July, 1872—vol. II, p. 45:

"After a few weeks, Hoyt returned to Lawrence, and entered heart and soul into the stirring events which followed. In June he went with a white flag into a Border-Ruffian fort in the south part of Douglas county, known as Fort Saunders, and while returning, still under the protection of the flag, was basely murdered by the men with whom he had been treating. Such was the boasted 'chivalry.'

"Hoyt was among the earliest and bravest of the Kansas martyrs. He left his home with the impression fastened in his mind, that he should be called upon to give up his life somewhere upon the Kansas prairies, and the thought never quickened his pulse, or produced the quiver of a muscle."

The "Relief" business began in 1856. The settlers had raised issues, not crops. Money and clothing came from the North and East in the bountiful way since grown so familiar. Milwaukee raised $3,000, Chicago $20,000. The Grand Kansas Aid Society, organized in Buffalo, J. D. Webster, Chairman, raised $120,000. The Boston Committee, George L. Stearns, Chairman, raised $20,000. The Kansas Aid Committee of Massachusetts raised $78,000. Horace White, of the Chicago Tribune, was the Secretary of that Society.

JUNE 17.—The National Republican Convention held at Philadelphia. The platform is mainly "Free Kansas." It declares that it is "both the right and the duty of Congress to prohibit in the Territories those twin relics of barbarism — polygamy and slavery."

It was also —

"*Resolved*, That Kansas should be immediately admitted as a State of the Union, with her present free Constitution, as at once the most effectual way of securing to her citizens the enjoyment of the rights and privileges to which they are entitled, and of ending the civil strife now raging in that Territory."

It was a ringing and grand platform, and was said to have been written by E. Rockwood Hoar. Fremont and Dayton were nominated. Abram Lincoln received 110 votes for Vice President.

JUNE 19.—Jas. F. Legate arrested in Lawrence, for treason, and taken to Lecompton. The prisoners are confined in tents, about two miles from the town, and guarded by soldiers.

JUNE 21.—An address from the Law-and-Order party, signed by Atchison, Stringfellow, Buford and others, is sent through the South. It asks aid in money and men.

JUNE 23.—Capt. John Brown, jr., and H. H. Williams, both of Osawatomie, are added to the prison camp. Capt. Brown had been in irons, and the cruel treatment he had received had made him insane.

JUNE 23.—Two letters from the Governor to Col. Sumner. In the second he says: "I do hope it will be in your power to attend in person this Topeka Legislature." The Governor leaves Lecompton for St. Louis, on official business.

JUNE 25.—G. A. Grow, of Pennsylvania, presents a bill in the House of Representatives, for the admission of Kansas.

JUNE 27.—Gov. Shannon writes from St. Louis to President Pierce on the military and political situation.

JUNE 29.—Secretary Woodson writes to Col. P. St. George Cooke, commanding at Fort Riley, "to take the field," and "scour the country between Fort Riley and the crossing opposite Topeka, for the purpose of repelling said armed invasion of the Territory."

JULY.—A book is published with this title: "The Kanzas Region, by Max. Greene. New York: Fowler & Wells. 1856." pp. 192. Two maps.

The writer had been a traveller on the Santa Fe trail. The book is pleasantly written, but romantic rather than valuable. It contains very little trustworthy information. There is a town-site flavor about it, the favorite town of Mr. Greene being "Council City, on Switzler's Creek, eighty-eight miles west from Missouri, on the Santa Fe trail." This was the town of the "American Settlement Company." The directors of the company were Theodore Dwight, J. E. Snodgrass, A. H. Jocelyn, Geo. Walter, J. M. Winchell, G. Manning Tracy, I. R. Barbour, Lotan Smith and D. C. Van Norman. "Council City" is now known as Burlingame.

JULY 1.—The prisoners are placed in a log cabin, near Lecompton. The camp was soon moved again.

JULY 1.—Report No. 200, House of Representatives, Thirty-fourth Congress, first session, submitted. It is a book of 1206 pages, and has this title: "Report of the Special Committee appointed to Investigate the Troubles in Kansas; with the Views of the Minority of said Committee. Washington: Cornelius Wendell, Printer. 1856." Twenty thousand copies were printed, but the book has already become rare. Sherman and Howard make the majority, and Oliver the minority report. It is an amazingly full collection of political facts in the history of Kansas, containing the name of nearly every voter in the Territory, and the affidavits of prominent men of both political parties in regard to leading events.

JULY 3.—The House passes Grow's bill for the admission of Kansas, under the Topeka Constitution, by a vote of 99 to 97.

—In the Senate, Mr. Douglas reports a bill to take a census and provide for a Constitutional Convention, to be held in December; adopted, and sent to the House. No action taken in the House.

—Colonel E. V. Sumner, of the First Cavalry, in camp at Topeka, asks the members of the Legislature not to assemble.

JULY 4.—Acting Governor Woodson issues a proclamation forbidding the meeting of the Topeka Legislature. Colonel Sumner says he will sustain the Governor's proclamation.

—The Free-State Legislature reassembles at Topeka. Colonel Edwin V. Sumner, U. S. A., appears in the House, and then in the Senate, and orders each body to disperse. He was ordered to do so by Acting Governor Woodson and President Pierce. The Legislature obeys the order.

JULY 7.—Secretary Woodson asks Major Sedgwick, U. S. A., for a posse to enable Deputy Marshal William P. Fain to execute writs. Military commissions continue to be issued by the Acting Governor.

JULY 8.—Senator Douglas reports a substitute for the bill of the House admitting Kansas. It authorizes the people to form a new Constitution. The Senate passes the substitute, the same day, by 30 to 13.

—The House refuses to recede from its previous action.

The House then passed a bill reorganizing the Territory of Kansas. It was lost in the Senate.

The House refused to vote the army appropriation bill except with a proviso that the army should not be used in putting down Free-State men in Kansas.

—The House and Senate having come to a dead-lock, Congress adjourned on the 18th. It was reassembled by the President, August 21. On the 30th, the army bill passed without the proviso. The House was also defeated in its attempt to have writs of nolle prosequi entered in the cases of the Free-State prisoners in Kansas.

JULY.— Colonel Sumner removed, and General Persifer F. Smith placed in command at Fort Leavenworth. General Smith's health was failing, and he took no active part in the Territory.

—Late in the month, John W. Geary, of Pennsylvania, was appointed Governor.

AUGUST 1.—The House votes that John W. Whitfield is not entitled to a seat as the Delegate from Kansas, by 110 to 92. The vote to give A. H. Reeder a seat was 88 yeas to 113 nays. Whitfield had held the seat up to this time.

"THE CONQUEST OF KANSAS, BY MISSOURI AND HER ALLIES. A History of the Troubles in Kansas, from the Passage of the Organic Act until the close of July, 1856. By William Phillips, Special Correspondent of the New York Tribune, for Kansas. 'Come on, then, gentlemen of the Slave States; since there is no escaping your challenge, I accept it in behalf of Freedom. We will engage in competition for the virgin soil of Kansas, and God give the victory to the side that is stronger in numbers, as it is in right!'—*Speech of Wm. H. Seward, in the United States Senate, 1854.* Boston: Phillips, Sampson & Co. 1856." pp. 414.

The above is a copy of the title-page of Col. Phillips's book, the author's name appearing as William, not William A., Phillips. The book is the most minute and elaborate history we have of the years 1854, '5 and '6, and has always been taken as the standard Free-State record of that period. Col. Phillips was energetic, tireless, and thoroughly in earnest. His book is a flaming and fiery manifesto in behalf of Freedom in Kansas. Kansas was said to be "conquered" to fire the Northern heart, and to prevent the possibility of such an event. The book, and the author's letters in the Tribune, did an immense work in saving Kansas and the whole country from Slavery.

AUGUST 4.—Rules of the First District Court, Samuel D. Lecompte, justice, adopted. They were printed by Millan & Posegate, St. Joseph, Mo., in a pamphlet of 17 pages.

AUGUST 5.—Free-State men take the fort near Osawatomie, driving out the Georgia camp.

AUGUST 7.— James H. Lane, with a party of four hundred immigrants, arrives in Kansas by the overland route, through Iowa and Nebraska. Free-State immigration up the Missouri river had been forcibly stopped. Several colonies came to Kansas through Iowa.

AUGUST 11.—Col. Treadwell has a camp on Washington creek, called Fort Saunders, about twelve miles southwest of Lawrence.

—Free-State men attack Franklin. A wagon-load of burning hay is pushed up to the blockhouse in which the Pro-Slavery men are gathered, and causes them to surrender. This was the second fight at Franklin.

AUGUST 15.—The Georgia camp, at Washington creek, taken by Free-State men.

AUGUST 16.— Capt. Samuel Walker attacks the fortified house of Col. Titus, near Lecompton, captures twenty prisoners, and burns the house.

AUGUST 17.—Sunday. Gov. Shannon and Dr. Rodrique, and Maj.

Sedgwick of the U. S. dragoons, visit Lawrence. Gov. Shannon makes a second treaty of peace. The Free-State prisoners are exchanged.

AUGUST 19. – Murder of Hopps by Fugit. Fugit was arrested in 1857, after Henry J. Adams became Mayor of Leavenworth. A letter in the St. Louis Democrat, dated May 27th, 1857, says:

"Fugit is the same person who made a bet in this city (Leavenworth), last August, that before night he would have a Yankee scalp. He got a horse and rode out into the country a few miles, and met a German, a brother-in-law of Rev. E. Nute, named Hopps. He asked if he was from Lawrence. Hopps replied that he was. Fugit immediately levelled his revolver and fired, the shot taking effect in the temples, and Hopps fell a corpse. The assassin dismounted from his horse, cut the scalp from the back of his head, tied it to a pole, and returned to town, exhibiting it to the people, and boasting of his exploit. The body of the victim was found shortly after, and buried on Pilot Knob, about two miles distant from this city. This same Fugit is one of the party who, when the widow came from Lawrence to look for her husband's corpse, forced her on board of a steamer, and sent her down the river."

AUGUST 21.—Gov. Shannon receives notice of his removal. Acting Governor Woodson calls out the militia. This was the darkest hour for Free-State men, and hundreds of them left Kansas.

The Northern Division of the Pro-Slavery militia is under Gen. Richardson, and the Southern Division under Gen. Coffey.

AUGUST 25.—David Atchison chosen commander of the Pro-Slavery "Army of Law and Order in Kansas Territory." Gov. Woodson issues a proclamation, declaring the Territory in a State of open insurrection and rebellion.

Atchison and Stringfellow concentrate an army at Little Santa Fe, on the Missouri border.

AUGUST 29.—The Missourians under John W. Reed and Rev. Martin White attack Osawatomie, and take it. Their number was about four hundred, and John Brown's forty-one. Capt. Brown's son Frederick was killed. Robbery and fire left nothing of Osawatomie.

AUGUST 30.—Woodson orders Col. Cooke to attack Topeka.

SEPTEMBER 1.—City election at Leavenworth. Wm. Phillips, a Free-State lawyer, who had been tarred and feathered the year before, was now killed in his house. The Free-State candidates did not receive a single vote. Fred. Emory led the Ruffians. Free-State men ordered to leave the city. Wm. E. Murphy, Pro-Slavery, elected Mayor.

SEPTEMBER 3.—Jefferson Davis, Secretary of War, writes to Major-General Persifer F. Smith, Commanding Department of the West, to call upon the Governor (Geary) "for such militia force as you may require to enable you promptly and successfully to execute your orders and suppress insurrection against the Government of the Territory of Kansas. . . . . The position of the insurgents . . . is that of open rebellion against the laws and constitutional authorities. . . . Patriotism and humanity alike require that rebellion should be promptly crushed," etc., etc.

SEPTEMBER 7.—At Glasgow, Mo., Gov. Geary has an interview with ex-Gov. Shannon. Geary is coming up on the steamboat Keystone, and Shannon going down on another boat.

SEPTEMBER.—Organization of the Methodist Episcopal Church by a

Conference of Ministers, held at Lawrence. The Conference embraced
Nebraska until 1860, when a division was made.

ANNUAL STATISTICS FROM 1856 TO 1863.

Year.	Number of Ministers.	Number of Members.	Churches.	Value.	No. Sabbath Schools.	No. Sunday School Scholars.
1856	22	996	5	....	20	407
1857	31	1,033	4	$11,900	14	357
1858	47	1,980	4	15,000	73	1,823
1859	62	2,628	17	29,200	80	2,017
1860	85	3,881	17	34,900	94	3,044
1861	74	3,932	43	49,725	87	2,825
1862	72	3,964	30	39,690	90	2,624
1863	68	4,184	33	40,775	100	3,674

At the first meeting of the Conference, a plan was projected for meeting the educational wants of the rapidly-developing State. The "Kansas Educational Association" was formed, with the object of securing a favorable location for a University. They received a large and valuable tract of land from the "Palmyra Association" of Douglas county, secured a liberal and comprehensive charter, and in 1857 founded "Baker University."—*Annual Register, p. 84.*

SEPTEMBER.—The following statement in regard to the Protestant Episcopal Church in Kansas is copied from a paper by N. O. Preston, in the Annual Register, in 1864:

"The Rev. Hiram Stone came as a missionary of the Episcopal Church to Leavenworth in the autumn of 1856. He entered upon his field of labors with commendable zeal, and worked faithfully for the space of three years. He built a neat church edifice—gathered a respectable and intelligent congregation, embracing forty communicants. In the autumn of 1859, he accepted the chaplaincy of Fort Leavenworth. In April, 1863, the Rev. Mr. Egar was called to the rectorship of the parish, left vacant for three years, and is now engaged in building a Gothic church in that city. The Rev. C. M. Calloway, by a Missionary Society in Philadelphia, was sent to Kansas in the winter of 1856-57, on what may be called a church exploring expedition. After visiting various points in the Territory, and surmounting many difficulties, he returned, and made a full report of his discoveries and impressions. His report was of such a nature—representing the field as "already white for the harvest"—as to induce the Missionary Committee to employ several missionaries to labor in Kansas. The Rev. Mr. Calloway soon returned, located with his family in Topeka, and labored in that city till the autumn of 1860. He succeeded, with funds gathered from churchmen in the East and South, in erecting, of brick, a large and substantial building, one part of which is a rectory, and the other part a female seminary. He organized Grace Church, Topeka, and, as he left, reported twelve communicants.

"The Rev. Charles Reynolds came with his family to Lawrence in 1857, organized Trinity Church in that city, and with funds obtained mainly from the East, built a church edifice of stone, and a substantial parsonage. He also organized Christ Church, Prairie City. He has been a successful laborer in Kansas. In his last printed report, there are twenty-seven communicants in Lawrence, and ten in Prairie City. He is now a chaplain in one of the Kansas regiments, and is engaged, in connexion with other duties, in building a church edifice at Fort Scott.

"The Rev. R. S. Nash came as a missionary to Kansas in the year 1857. He located in Wyandotte, and labored faithfully there till near the close of 1862. He succeeded—with funds gathered mainly from the East—in erecting a beautiful church edifice and a commodious parsonage. He reports twelve communicants. He is now laboring with acceptance at Prairie City, in the capacity of Rector of Christ Church, and Principal of a diocesan male school.

"The Rev. N. O. Preston came to Kansas in May, 1858, located in Manhattan, found three communicants of the Episcopal Church. He labored there two years and eight months, and succeeded with funds mainly collected in New Orleans and Philadelphia, in building a Gothic church. He organized St. Paul's Church, Manhattan, and in his last report to the convention, appear sixteen communicants. By the urgent solicitation of friends in the Diocese, and of others, he removed with his family to Topeka, January 1, 1861, where he is still laboring in the position of Rector of Grace Church, and Principal of the Episcopal Female Seminary. He has succeeded, by the aid of funds contributed through Bishop Lee of Iowa, and from contributions by his parishioners, in erecting a beautiful stone church. He has also succeeded in establishing a flourishing female seminary. The communicants in Grace Church have increased from twelve to thirty.

"The Rev. J. Ryan came to Kansas as a missionary in the spring of 1858, and located at Elwood. He built a church there, and reported, in 1861, ten communicants. He also preached at several other places, and is now dividing his time between Troy and Atchison."

SEPTEMBER 9.—John W. Geary, the third Governor, arrives at Fort Leavenworth, and is received by Gen. P. F. Smith.

—Despatch of Gov. Geary to the President:

"I find that I have not simply to contend against bands of armed ruffians and brigands, whose sole aim and end is assassination and robbery; infatuated adherents and advocates of conflicting political sentiments and local institutions, and evil-disposed persons actuated by a desire to obtain elevated positions, but, worst of all, against the influence of men who have been placed in authority, and have employed all the destructive agents around them to promote their own personal interests at the sacrifice of every just, honorable, and lawful consideration.

"I have barely time to give you a brief statement of facts as I find them. The town of Leavenworth is now in the hands of armed bodies of men, who, having been enrolled as militia, perpetrate outrages of the most atrocious character under the shadow of authority from the Territorial Government.

"Within a few days these men have robbed and driven from their homes unoffending citizens, have fired upon and killed others in their own dwellings, and stolen horses and property, under the pretence of employing them in the public service. They have seized persons who had committed no offence, and, after stripping them of all their valuables, placed them on steamers and sent them out of the Territory.

"In isolated or country places no man's life is safe. The roads are filled with armed robbers, and murders for mere plunder are of daily occurrence. Almost every farmhouse is deserted, and no traveller has the temerity to venture upon the highways without an escort."

—See Executive Documents, 3d sess. Thirty-fourth Congress, Vol. I, part 1, pages 88 and 89.

—In describing the condition of the Territory at the time of his arrival, in his farewell to the people of Kansas, (Senate Doc., 1st sess. Thirty-fifth Congress, No. 17, p. 200,) Gov. Geary says:

"Desolation and ruin reigned on every hand; homes and firesides were deserted; the smoke of burning dwellings darkened the atmosphere; women and children, driven from their habitations, wandered over the prairies and among the woodlands, or sought refuge and protection even among the Indian tribes."

—At the trial of the treason prisoners before the Supreme Court at Lecompton, the Government asks a postponement till April. C. H. Branscomb and M. J. Parrott appeared for the prisoners, and demanded an immediate trial. The cases were continued, and the prisoners released on bail.

SEPTEMBER 10.—Gov. Robinson released on bail of $5,000—just four months from the day he was taken prisoner.

—Gov. Geary arrives at Lecompton.

SEPTEMBER 11.—Gov. Geary issues his inaugural address. It promises justice and fair play. He issues a proclamation disbanding the Territorial militia, and ordering all other armed men to quit the Territory; and also a proclamation ordering all persons qualified to bear arms to enroll themselves and be in readiness for service.

An address is issued, signed by Atchison, Stringfellow, Tebbs, Anderson, Reid, Doniphan, and others, calling upon the people of the Slave States to come to Kansas and drive out the "army of the North."

SEPTEMBER 12.—Gov. Geary orders H. J. Strickler to disarm and disband the militia. He orders Thos. J. B. Cramer, Inspector General, to take charge of the arms. The orders were disregarded. Gov. Geary informs Hon. W. L. Marcy, Secretary of State, of his official acts and purposes. Wm. A. Heiskell, General of the First Brigade, Southern Division, with L. A. Maclean, Adjutant, has 1,000 men at Mission Creek.

By order of Gov. Geary, Capt. Samuel Walker's Free-State infantry company, at Lawrence, and the Pro-Slavery cavalry company of Capt. John Wallis, and the infantry of Capt. John Donaldson, Lecompton, were mustered into the United States' service. The two Pro-Slavery companies were mustered out at Fort Leavenworth, and Walker's at Lawrence, December 1st.

SEPTEMBER 13.—Capt. Harvey, with a Lawrence force, has a fight at Hickory Point, about five miles east of Osawkee, in Jefferson county. The Pro-Slavery men, under Lowe and Robertson, surrender, after a six-hours' fight. The Lawrence men have a gun, lately taken at Franklin. It was a six-pounder, and was originally captured at Sacramento by Col. Doniphan. Lane had been at Hickory Point the day before, and had declined to fight without artillery. Lane was on his way East, by way of Nebraska. He had called the Lawrence men there, and also a Topeka company, under "Capt. Whipple." Whipple, whose real name was Aaron D. Stephens, was afterwards executed at Harper's Ferry, being one of John Brown's men.

Harvey's men, 101 in number, were captured by Col. Cooke, and kept in confinement in the camp of the U. S. troops, on the outskirts of Lecompton.

After a hearing before Judge Cato, he committed the whole party for trial on the charge of murder in the first degree. They were taken to a dilapidated house in Lecompton, and guarded by Col. Titus's militia.

In October, about twenty of Harvey's soldiers were convicted, and sentenced to the Penitentiary for a term of five years. Among them were Frank B. Swift, a native of Maine (afterwards the Captain of the Lawrence Stubbs, and a Captain in the First Kansas), Alfred Paine of Ohio, Sam'l Stewart of Michigan, L. Soley of Massachusetts, —— Crawford, Jer'h Jordan of Pennsylvania, and John Lawrie of Indiana.

SEPTEMBER 14.—John Brown in command of the Free-State men at Lawrence. After a night skirmish, the Missourians retreat.

— Gov. Geary orders Woodson and Strickler to proceed to the Pro-Slavery army on the Wakarusa, and disband it. Gov. Geary, with United States troops, arrives in Lawrence. The people are in arms.

SEPTEMBER 15.—The United States troops left in Lawrence by Gov. Geary, who goes to Franklin. The Pro-Slavery camp is at the junction of the Wakarusa and Kaw rivers. The commander is Gen. John W. Reid, a member of the Missouri Legislature, assisted by David Atchison, B. F. Stringfellow, L. A. Maclean (Chief Clerk of Surveyor General John Calhoun), J. W. Whitfield, Geo. W. Clarke, Wm. A. Heiskell, Wm. P. Richardson, Frank J. Marshall, H. T. Titus, Fred. Emory, Sheriff Jones, and others, with 2,700 men. Judge Cato was in this camp. Gov. Geary assembled the officers and addressed them at length, and ordered the army to be disbanded and dispersed. He told Atchison that he had last seen him as the presiding officer of the United States Senate, and Acting Vice President of the United States.

—Murder of David C. Buffum, a Free-State man, near Lecompton. Gov. Geary visited the wounded man, and had Judge Cato take down his dying declarations. The Governor tried in vain to have the assassins arrested. Arrests of Free-State men were constantly made.

—Carmi W. Babcock, Postmaster at Lawrence, and a Free-State man, is arrested at Topeka, and discharged by the Governor.

SEPTEMBER 18.—Governor Geary, Colonel Cooke and United States soldiers arrest twelve persons and capture property at Topeka, on a warrant from Lecompte.

SEPTEMBER 23.—The Governor addresses a letter to each of the Judges, asking them what they have done. The replies show that very little had been done. In the midst of war, laws are silent. Chief Justice Lecompte replied that he had a "party bias" for the Democratic party, and was proud of it. He said, "To the charge of a Pro-Slavery bias, I am proud, too, of this. I am the steady friend of Southern rights under the Constitution of the United States. I have been reared where Slavery was recognized by the Constitution of my State. I love the institution as entwining itself around all my early and late associations."

OCTOBER.—Publication of Mrs. Robinson's book—"Kansas; Its Interior and Exterior Life. Including a Full View of its Settlement, Political History, Social Life, Climate, Soil, Productions, Scenery, etc. By Sara T. L. Robinson. Boston: Crosby, Nichols and Company. 1856." pp. 366.

Allibone's Dictionary of Authors says this book went through six editions. It was favorably noticed by the London Athenæum, as well as by the Republican press of this country. Mrs. Robinson is an accomplished lady, the wife of Governor Robinson. She possessed the knowledge of events and the literary skill necessary to produce an interesting and trustworthy book, and one which will continue to have a permanent value. The women of Kansas suffered more than the men, and were not less heroic. Their names are not known; they were not elected to office; they had none of the exciting delights of an active, out-door life on these attractive prairies; they endured in silence; they took care of the home, of the sick; if "home they brought her warrior dead, she nor swooned, nor uttered sigh." It is fortunate that a few of these truest heroes have left a printed record of pioneer life in Kansas.

OCTOBER 6.—Pro-Slavery election for Delegate to Congress, members of the Legislature, and on the question of calling a Convention to form a State Constitution. The Free-State men do not vote. Of the 4,276 votes cast for Whitfield, as Delegate, 1,458 were cast at Leavenworth. The vote for a Convention was 2,592; against, 454.

TERRITORIAL ELECTION, OCTOBER 6, 1856.

Name of County.	For Congress.		Convention.		For Council—F.J. Marshall......
	J. W. Whitfield.	A. H. Reeder...	For.	Against	
Atchison........	520	....	545	....	....
Arapahoe........	7	....	....	....	7
Bourbon	188	....	....	....	....
Brown	16	....	15	....	....
Doniphan........	323	....	367	7	....
Douglas........	461	....	4	380	....
Davis........	123	....	....	....	93
Calhoun	52	....	19	....	15
Franklin........	13	....	....	....	....
Jefferson........	222	....	21	7	....
Johnson	132	....	131	....	....
Leavenworth	1,480	....	1,243	47	....
Linn........	142	....	....	....	....
Lykius........	133	....	99	2	....
Madison	13	40	....	....	....
Marshall........	183	....	180	....	185
Nemaha	5	....	....	....	....
Riley	11	....	....	....	25

FOR REPRESENTATIVES.

Name of County.	Name of Candidate.	Vote.	Name of County.	Name of Candidate.	Vote.
Atchison........	Joseph P. Carr.....	428	Calhoun	Jas. Kukendall....	30
	Wm. Young	506		Geo. Young........	22
	Richard L. Kirk..	451	Franklin	A. Laws............	15
	Caleb May...........	100		J. A. Merritt.......	13
	W. P. Lamb........	91		H Howard......	14
	A. Elliott............	107	Jefferson	Wm. H. Tebbs.....	193
	Luther Knox......	84	Johnson....	J. T. Barton	117
Arapahoe	Benj. F. Simmons	10	Leavenworth ...	John W. Martin...	1,301
Bourbon	B. Brantly	176		Wm. G. Mathias..	980
	W. W. Spratt.....	127		M. Walker........	898
	R. G. Roberts.....	60		D. J. Johnson......	669
Brown	X. K. Stout	17		L.F.Hollingsw'th.	516
	B. O'Driscoll......	17		A. R. Kellum.......	510
	T. W. Waterson...	17	Linn........	J. Davis............	143
Doniphan........	X. K. Stout........	316		J. P. Fox	123
	B. O'Driscoll......	296	Lykins........	Martin White.....	127
	T. W. Waterson...	268		J. P. Fox	105
	Jos. C. Anderson..	456	Madison........	Geo. H. Reese......	45
Douglas........	J. C. Thompson...	418		Sol. G. Brown......	40
	Jas. Garvin........	457		R. F. Stiggers......	12
	O. H. Browne	404		A. L. Baker........	12
	H. Butcher..........	447	Marshall........	W. H. Jenkins.....	186
Davis	R. Garrett...........	59		A. G. Burrett	1
	O. J. Chapman....	84	Nemaha	C. Dolman............	12
Riley........	R. Garrett...........	66			

OCTOBER 7.—The Vermont Legislature appropriate $20,000 for the relief of Kansas. Governor Geary writes to the Governor of that State that the money is not needed.

OCTOBER 10.—Colonel Cooke aided William S. Preston, Deputy Marshal, in arresting a large party of Free-State immigrants, "near the Nebraska river," on the northern line of the Territory. Shaler W. Eldridge was the conductor of the party, and among the number were S. C. Pomeroy, Robert Morrow and Richard Realf. Major H. H. Sibley conducted them to North Topeka.

OCTOBER 14.—Governor Geary met the immigrants and released them from arrest.

OCTOBER 17.—Governor Geary leaves Lecompton on a tour of observation.

OCTOBER 20.—Surveyor General's office removed to Lecompton.

OCTOBER.— One of the "Anti-Slavery Tracts" is called "A Ride Through Kanzas. By Thomas Wentworth Higginson." It contains 24 pages, and is made up of letters written by Colonel Higginson from Nebraska and Kansas in September and October, 1856. The letters were originally published with the signature of "Worcester," in the New York Tribune. The pictures of Topeka, Lecompton, Lawrence and Leavenworth are entertaining and valuable. The day is not distant when such brief histories will be republished for permanent preservation by our State Historical Society.

NOVEMBER 1.—Reissue of the Herald of Freedom, at Lawrence. The Free-State paper at Topeka is revived.

NOVEMBER 6.—The Governor arrives at Lecompton, and issues a proclamation setting apart November 20th as a day of Thanksgiving. He had visited many towns, going east as far as Osawatomie, and west to Fort Riley.

NOVEMBER 7.—Owen C. Stewart is discharged as Superintendent of the Capitol. The $50,000 appropriated by Congress had been expended, but the walls of the building had been advanced only a few feet above the foundation.

NOVEMBER 10.—Charles Hays, arrested for the murder of Buffum, and indicted by a Pro-Slavery grand jury at Lecompton for murder in the first degree, was discharged on bail by Lecompte. Gov. Geary regarded this act as a judicial outrage, treated it as a nullity, and ordered Marshal Donalson to rearrest Hays. He declined to obey the order. Col. H. T. Titus then arrested Hays and brought him to Lecompton.

NOVEMBER 13.—The Governor asked the Postmaster General for better mail facilities: "It requires eleven days for a letter to reach this place from Washington City, when a person travelling with expedition can accomplish the same distance in six days."

NOVEMBER 15.—The Free-State prisoners, forty in number, are removed to Tecumseh.

NOVEMBER 17.—While Gov. Geary was attending the Delaware Land sales, at Leavenworth, Lecompte released Hays on a writ of habeas corpus. These facts were made known to President Pierce. He nominated C. O. Harrison, of Kentucky, to supersede Lecompte, but Harrison was not confirmed by the Senate.

DECEMBER 15.— Gov. Geary writes from Leavenworth to President Pierce that $440,000 have been realized from the land sales. The city of Leavenworth, not yet sold, contained 320 acres, and had been appraised by lots, at thirty dollars an acre. Its population was placed at 2,000.

DECEMBER.—Mr. James W. Fox, of the State Printing Office, Topeka, has a bound file of the Kansas Tribune. The first copy in the volume is dated, Lawrence, September 15, 1855, and is No. 29 of Vol. I. John Speer and Samuel N. Wood are the publishers and editors. It is a six-column paper, the columns of a measure wider than usual. This number contains a full report of the proceedings of the Big Springs Convention. Number 31 is dated December 10th, at Topeka. W. W. Ross had taken the place of S. N. Wood.

The next copy is No. 33, dated January 7, 1856. On the fifth of March, 1856, the Tribune began to issue a Daily Edition. The State Legislature was in session at Topeka. The proceedings are published in the Weekly of March 10th. A sale of lots took place at Topeka, April 23d. The highest price paid was $810 for a lot 75 by 150 feet, on the corner of Kansas Avenue and Sixth street. The Tribune of July 9th contains the report of the dispersing of the Legislature by Col. Sumner. In his brief statement to the members of the House, Col. Sumner twice said: "This is the most painful duty of my whole life."

The next paper on this file is No. 1 of Vol. II, dated Topeka, September 5, 1856. A statement is copied from the St. Louis News, that Major Buford has passed through that city on his return to Alabama. Several quotations are made from Southern papers. The True Carolinian, of South Carolina, says W. D. Wilkes believes he will carry with him to Kansas $50,000. The Charleston News says: "South Carolina is still unflagging in her efforts in behalf of Kansas, and her people continue to forward emigrants and means. The Executive Committee of the Charleston Association will despatch another and the fourth corps to-morrow. · They will go under the charge of Capt. Palmer, who conducted the second corps." A Georgia paper says Alpheus Baker, jr., of Alabama, Dr. Jones, and L. F. Johnson, have "recently been engaged in canvassing Central Alabama for the purpose of raising men and money for Kansas. Success has crowned their efforts."

The next number of the Tribune was not issued till October 22d. It records the arrival of P. B. Plumb, of the Xenia (Ohio) News, with a company of twenty-eight young men. Number 3 contains a letter from the Prison at Lecompton, dated October 24th, written by J. H. Kagi. The Prison contains ninety-nine Free-State men. Eighty-eight of Capt. Harvey's men have been indicted for murder in the first degree, and also for manslaughter — the crimes being committed at Hickory Point, Jefferson county, September 13th. Another letter, dated November 17th, gives an account of the trial and sentence — for five years in the Penitentiary — of some thirty of these prisoners. Number 4 announces a visit to Lawrence by Thaddeus Hyatt. On the 29th of December, John Speer retires, and is succeeded by E. G. Ross. J. H. Kagi writes on the 23d, that there are now sixteen Free-State prisoners at Lecompton, and seven at Tecumseh. John Ritchie and some others have escaped.

The file of the Tribune is nearly complete for 1857, and for the first half of 1858.

1857.

JANUARY 6.—The Free-State Legislature, under the Topeka Constitution, met at Topeka. Governor Robinson and Lieutenant Governor Roberts are absent, and there is no quorum.

JANUARY 7.—State Legislature reassembles; quorum present. Organize and appoint a committee to memorialize Congress to admit Kansas under the Topeka Constitution. After adjournment, a Deputy United States Marshal arrests about a dozen of the members, under a writ granted by Judge Cato, and takes them to Tecumseh.

JANUARY 8.—When the State Legislature met, both bodies were without presiding officers and without a quorum. The President of the Senate and the Speaker of the House are prisoners at Tecumseh. A recess was taken till the second Tuesday in June.

—The prisoners are taken before Judge Cato, at Tecumseh (the county seat of Shawnee county), and bound over to appear at the June term.

JANUARY 12.—Second session of the Territorial Legislature, and the first held at Lecompton. Governor Geary's Message has the merit of reading well to-day. Although a Democrat, appointed by President Pierce, it is a fair Message. He promises "'equal and exact justice to all men,' of whatever political or religious persuasion." He prays for peace, promises free speech, and asks for the repeal of many of the Bogus Laws. "Let the people, then, rule in everything. I have every confidence in the virtue, intelligence, and sober thought of the toiling millions." His review of his brief administration has a historic value now. He advocated the building of a railroad to the Gulf of Mexico. "The entire length of such a road would not exceed 600 miles, much less than half the distance to the Atlantic, and at an ordinary speed of railroad travel could be traversed in less than twenty-four hours."

The Free-State men had taken no part in the election of members of this House, and the whole Legislature remained Pro-Slavery.

Governor Geary said there was not a single officer in the Territory amenable to him or to the people, the whole having been either appointed by the Legislature, or holding office for terms extending a long way into the future.

All bills vetoed by Governor Geary were passed over his head by a two-thirds vote, in accordance with a secret agreement at the beginning of the session.

Blake Little, in the Council, succeeds William Barbee, deceased; Frank J. Marshall succeeds J. Donaldson, resigned.

Officers of the Council: Thomas Johnson, President; Richard R. Rees, President *pro tem.;* Thos. C. Hughes, Chief Clerk; C. H. Grover, Assistant Clerk; S. J. Cramer, Sergeant-at-Arms; Wm. Alley, Doorkeeper; D. Scott Boyle, Engrossing Clerk.

Officers of the House: Wm. G. Mathias, Speaker; W. H. Tebbs, Speaker *pro tem.;* Robert C. Bishop, Chief Clerk; D. G. Flemming, Assistant Clerk; John Robertson, Sergeant-at-Arms; J. H. Jackson, Doorkeeper.

JANUARY 12.—Convention of the "National Democratic Party of Kan-

8

sas Territory," at Lecompton. The following-named persons were appointed a committee to prepare an address to the people of the United States: John Calhoun, George W. Clarke, John W. Forman, J. Kuykendall, John H. Stringfellow, A. B. Hazzard, John R. Boyd, E. Ransom, L. A. Maclean, H. B. Harris, A. Coffey, John Donaldson, B. I. Newsom, J. T. Hereford, J. C. Anderson, David R. Atchison, Jeff. Buford, W. H. Tebbs, Samuel J. Jones, Hugh M. Moore, G. W. Purkins, A. J. Isacks. The address was published in pamphlet form.

JANUARY 14.—R. H. Bennett is elected Public Printer.

JANUARY 21.—James Guthrie, Secretary of the Treasury, reports to G. A. Grow, of the House, that the appropriations for public buildings in Kansas have been drawn from the Treasury. Gov. Shannon drew $20,000, Jan. 31, 1856, and $20,000, July 7, 1856. Gov. Geary drew $10,000, Dec. 21, 1856. These facts are reported to the House, by Mr. Grow, Feb. 7, 1857.

JANUARY 22.—An act creating the office of Superintendent of Public Printing.

JANUARY 29.—James Christian succeeds E. Chapman as a member of the Council.

FEBRUARY 3.—A. B. Hazzard elected Superintendent of Printing.

FEBRUARY 7.—The Committee on Territories of the House of Representatives, Washington, report a bill for the payment of property destroyed at Lawrence, May 21, 1856, as asked in the memorial of R. G. Elliott and others.

FEBRUARY 11.—A bill passed dividing the Territory into three judicial districts.

FEBRUARY 12.—The House Committee on Elections (Washington) report that John W. Whitfield is not entitled to a seat as Delegate from Kansas.

The first election for Delegate was held in October, 1854; the second in October, 1855; under this second election John W. Whitfield took his seat in the House; his right to a seat was contested by A. H. Reeder; Whitfield was ousted from his seat by order of the House; the Governor called an election to fill the vacancy, on the first Monday in October, 1856; Whitfield received 4,300 votes, and the Governor gave him a certificate of election to the Thirty-fourth Congress; Reeder also claimed a seat, under the election held in 1855, but the House Committee did not grant his request.

FEBRUARY 14.—Death of General William P. Richardson, member of the Council, announced.

—The cities of Topeka, Atchison and Manhattan incorporated.

FEBRUARY 17.—Hiawatha Town Company incorporated.

—The House of Representatives, at Washington, pass a bill, 98 to 79, declaring void all acts of the Territorial Legislature, on the ground that they are "cruel and oppressive," and that "the said Legislature was not elected by the legal voters of Kansas, but was forced upon them by non-residents, in violation of the organic act of the Territory," and enabling the people to establish a government for themselves. In the Senate, it is laid on the table, by 30 to 20. Bell, Brodhead, Houston, James, Pugh and Stuart vote in the negative, with the Republicans.

In the Senate, the partisans of Lecompte are strong enough to prevent the confirmation of Chief Justice Harrison, nominated by President Pierce to succeed Lecompte, and the latter still holds his office.

Gov. Geary soon becomes very obnoxious to the Legislature. That body sides with Judge Lecompte in his difficulty with the Governor. Thus Geary finds himself abandoned at Washington, and without power in the Territory.

FEBRUARY 19.—First step in the Lecompton Constitution movement. The Legislature passes an act to provide for electing a convention to frame a State Constitution. It provides for a census of voters, to be taken by sheriffs, April 1st, the return to be made in each county, to the probate judge, before the 10th of April. The judge can correct and add to the list from April 10th to May 1st, when it is to be sent to the Governor. Upon the basis of this census, the Governor is to apportion among the precincts the sixty delegates to the convention. The election is to be held the third Monday in June. The delegates are to meet at Lecompton the first Monday in September. The registry of voters is placed entirely in the hands of Pro-Slavery officers.

Gov. Geary vetoes the bill. He says the Legislature "has failed to make any provision to submit the constitution, when framed, to the consideration of the people for their ratification or rejection." The Council passed the bill over the veto by 11 votes for to none against. The House likewise passes it by a two-thirds vote.

—A bill is passed providing for the election of a new Legislature in October.

—Joint session of the Legislature to elect county officers, to fill vacancies.

FEBRUARY 18.—Capt. John Brown reads the following statement "in a clear, ringing tone," to the Massachusetts Legislature:

"I saw, while in Missouri, in the fall of 1855, large numbers of men going to Kansas *to vote*, and also returning after they had so done ; as they said.

"Later in the year, I, with four of my sons, was called out, and travelled, mostly on foot and during the night, to help defend Lawrence, a distance of thirty-five miles ; where we were detained, with some five hundred others, or thereabouts, from five to ten days—say an average of ten days—at a cost of not less than a dollar and a half per day, as wages ; to say nothing of the actual loss and suffering occasioned to many of them, by leaving their families sick, their crops not secured, their houses unprepared for winter, and many without houses at all. This was the case with myself and sons, who could not get houses built after returning. Wages alone would amount to seven thousand five hundred dollars ; loss and suffering cannot be estimated.

"I saw, at that time, the body of the murdered Barber, and was present to witness his wife and other friends brought in to see him with his clothes on, just as he was when killed.

"I, with six sons and a son-in-law, was called out, and travelled, most of the way on foot, to try and save Lawrence, May 20 and 21, and much of the way in the night. From that date, neither I nor my sons, nor my son-in-law, could do any work about our homes, but lost our whole time until we left, in October ; except one of my sons, who had a few weeks to devote to the care of his own and his brother's family, who were then without a home.

"From about the 20th of May, hundreds of men, like ourselves, lost their whole time, and entirely failed of securing any kind of crop whatever. I believe it safe to say, that five hundred Free-State men lost each one hundred and twenty days, which, at one dollar and a half per day, would be—to say nothing of attendant losses—ninety thousand dollars.

"On or about the 30th of May, two of my sons, with several others, were imprisoned without other crime than opposition to bogus legislation, and most barbarously treated for a time, one being held about one month, and the other about four months. Both had their families on the ground. After this, both of them had their houses burned, and all their goods consumed by the Missourians. In this burning all the eight suffered. One had his oxen stolen, in addition."

Redpath says:

"The Captain, laying aside his paper, here said that he had now at his hotel, and would exhibit to the Committee, if they so desired, the chains which one of his sons had worn, when he was driven, beneath a burning sun, by Federal troops, to a distant prison, on a charge of treason. The cruelties he there endured, added to the anxieties and sufferings incident to his position, had rendered him, the old man said, as his eye flashed and his voice grew sterner, 'a maniac — yes, a MANIAC.'

"He paused a few seconds, wiped a tear from his eye, and continued his narration:

"'At Black Jack, the invading Missourians wounded three Free-State men, one of them my son-in-law; and, a few days afterwards, one of my sons was so wounded that he will be a cripple for life.

"'In June, I was present and saw the mangled and disfigured body of the murdered Hoyt, of Deerfield, Massachusetts, brought into our camp. I knew him well.

"'I saw the ruins of many Free-State men's houses in different parts of the Territory, together with grain in the stack, burning, and wasted in other ways, to the amount, at least, of fifty thousand dollars.

"'I saw several other Free-State men, besides those I have named, during the summer, who were badly wounded by the invaders of the Territory.

"'I know that for much of the time during the summer, the travel over portions of the Territory was entirely cut off, and that none but bodies of armed men dared to move at all.

"'I know that for a considerable time the mails on different routes were entirely stopped; and notwithstanding there were abundant troops in the Territory to escort the mails, I know that such escorts were not furnished, as they ought to have been.

"'I saw while it was standing, and afterwards saw the ruins of, a most valuable house, the property of a highly civilized, intelligent, and exemplary Christian Indian, which was burned to the ground by the Ruffians, because its owner was suspected of favoring the Free-State men. He is known as Ottawa Jones, or John T. Jones.

"'In September last, I visited a beautiful little Free-State town called Stanton, on the north side of the Osage (or Marais des Cygnes, as it is sometimes called), from which every inhabitant had fled for fear of their lives, even after having built a strong log house, or wooden fort, at a heavy expense, for their protection. Many of them had left their effects liable to be destroyed or carried off, not being able to remove them. This was to me a most gloomy scene, and like a visit to a sepulchre.

"'Deserted houses and cornfields were to be found in almost every direction south of the Kansas river.

"'I have not yet told all I saw in Kansas.

"'I once saw three mangled bodies, two of which were dead, and one alive, but with twenty bullet and buckshot holes in him, after the two murdered men had lain on the ground, to be worked at by flies, for some eighteen hours. One of these young men was *my own son.*'

"The stern old man faltered. He struggled long to suppress all exhibition of his feelings; and soon, but with a subdued, and in a faltering, tone continued:

"'I saw Mr. Parker, whom I well know, all bruised about the head, and with his throat partly cut, after he had been dragged, sick, from the house of Ottawa Jones, and thrown over the bank of the Ottawa creek for dead.

"'About the first of September, I, and five sick and wounded sons, and a son-in-law, were obliged to lie on the ground, without shelter, for a considerable time, and at times almost in a state of starvation, and dependent on the charity of the Christian Indian I have before named, and his wife.

"'I saw Dr. Graham, of Prairie City, who was a prisoner with the Ruffians on the 2d of June, and was present when they wounded him, in an attempt to kill him, as he was trying to save himself from being murdered by them during the fight at Black Jack.

"'I know that numerous other persons, whose names I cannot now remember, suffered like hardships and exposures to those I have mentioned.

"'I know well that on or about the 14th of September, 1856, a large force of Missourians and other Ruffians, said by Governor Geary to be twenty-seven hundred in number, invaded the Territory, burned Franklin, and, while the smoke of that place was going up behind them, they, on the same day, made their appearance in full view of, and within about a mile, of Lawrence; and I know of no reason why they did not attack that place, except that about one hundred Free-State men volunteered to go out and did go out, on the open plain before the town, and give them the offer of a fight; which, after getting scattering shots from our men, they declined, and retreated back towards Franklin. I saw that whole thing. The Government troops, at this time, were at Lecompton, a distance of twelve miles only from Lawrence, with Governor Geary; and yet, notwithstanding runners had been despatched to advise him, in good time, of the approach and setting out of the enemy, (who had to march some forty miles to reach Lawrence,) he did not, on that memorable occasion, get a single soldier on the ground until after the enemy had retreated to Franklin, and been gone for more than five hours. This is the way he saved Lawrence. And it is just the kind of protection the Free-State men have received from the Administration from the first.'"

FEBRUARY 20.—L. A. Maclean, J. W. Martin, O. C. Stewart, W. H. Tebbs and T. W. Waterson elected Bank Commissioners, on joint ballot. Hiram J. Strickler confirmed as Comptroller of the Treasury.

—Passage of a bill making a new apportionment for the Legislature.

—The Emporia and the Olathe Town Companies incorporated.

FEBRUARY 21.—The Legislature adjourns, at midnight.

MARCH 4.— Gov. Geary sends his resignation to President Buchanan, to take effect March 20th. This act is not publicly known in Kansas.

MARCH 4.—James Buchanan becomes President. The following is copied from his Inaugural Address:

"Congress is neither to legislate Slavery into any Territory or State, nor to exclude it therefrom, but to leave the people thereof perfectly free to form and regulate their domestic institutions in their own way, subject only to the Constitution of the United States. As a natural consequence, Congress has also prescribed, that when the Territory of Kansas shall be admitted as a State, it shall be received into the Union with or without Slavery, as their Constitution may prescribe at the time of their admission. A difference of opinion has arisen in regard to the time when the people of a Territory shall decide this question for themselves. This is happily a matter of but little practical importance, and besides it is a judicial question, which legitimately belongs to the Supreme Court of the United States, before whom it is now pending, and will, it is understood, be speedily and finally settled. To their decision, in common with all good citizens, I shall cheerfully submit, whatever this may be, though it has been my individual opinion that under the Nebraska-Kansas act, the appropriate period will be when the number of actual residents in the Territory shall justify the formation of a Constitution, with a view to its admission as a State into the Union."

This allusion to a judicial decision is only understood by the members of the Supreme Court and the leaders of the Democratic party.

MARCH 6.—The Supreme Court renders the Dred Scott decision. The following summary of the decision is copied from George E. Baker's Life of William H. Seward (New York, 1861):

"An action was commenced in the Circuit Court of the United States, for the District of Missouri, in 1854, by Dred Scott, to establish his freedom, and that of his wife and their two daughters, who were claimed and held as slaves by one Sanford, the defendant. Sanford placed his defence on two grounds: *First*, that Dred Scott was not a citizen of Missouri because he was a negro of African descent; and, *Second*, that Dred and his family were the defendant's slaves. Scott relied on facts mutually admitted—that he was formerly a slave in Missouri; was taken, in 1834, by his then master, to Illinois, and held there in servitude two years, and was thence taken to the territory west of the Mississippi, and north of the Missouri Compromise line, where he was also held in

servitude until the year 1838, when he was brought back to the State of Missouri and
sold as a slave to the defendant before this suit was commenced.

"The Circuit Court decided in Scott's favor as to the jurisdiction of the court, but
against him on the question of his freedom. He then appealed to the Supreme Court.
His case was twice elaborately argued before that tribunal. The court decided substantially that Dred Scott was not a citizen, and for that reason the courts of the
United States had no jurisdiction in the case; and expressed the opinion that free colored persons whose ancestors were imported into this country and sold as slaves, 'had
no rights which the white man was bound to respect,' and were not citizens of the
United States; that there is no difference between property in a slave and other property; that Congress has no power to prohibit Slavery in the Territories; that the Missouri Compromise act was unconstitutional and void; and that the taking of a slave,
by his master, into a free State or a Territory, does not entitle the slave to his freedom.
Two judges, Messrs. McLean and Curtis, dissented from the majority of the court in
their decision and opinions."

MARCH 7.—The New York Times says:

"The most important decision ever made by the Supreme Court of the United States
was pronounced yesterday,—and a summary of its leading points will be found among
our telegraphic despatches. That supreme tribunal of the land decides that the Ordinance of 1787, so far as it prohibited Slavery from the Northwest Territory, was unconstitutional;—that the Missouri Compromise, so far as it excluded Slavery from the
Louisiana Territory north of 36° 30′, was unconstitutional;—that Congress had no power
to prohibit Slavery from *any* portion of the Federal territory, nor to authorize the inhabitants thereof to do so;—that negroes are not citizens of the United States;—and
that the residence of a slave in a Free State does not affect his legal condition upon his
return to a State where Slavery is allowed by law."

MARCH 10.— Gov. Geary writes to Secretary Woodson: "For several
weeks my health has been gradually sinking, and I have had several
hemorrhages of the lungs. I am convinced my life will not be long, if not
promptly cared for. I will be absent a few days from Lecompton."

Gov. Geary feared assassination, and left the Territory secretly, as Gov.
Reeder had done. His best friends of late, at Lecompton, had been the
Free-State prisoners. He had told them of his fears, and they were ready
to protect him. He left in haste, and forgot to pardon and release these
men, as he had agreed to do. His farewell address bears this date. He
reached Washington March 21st. Gladstone copies (page 312) a portion
of an address signed by ninety-eight of these prisoners.

MARCH 10.—Robert J. Walker, of Mississippi, is appointed Governor,
and Fred. P. Stanton, of Tennessee, Secretary of the Territory, by President Buchanan.

—The Free-State Convention, at Topeka, appoints the following Com-
mittee to prepare an address to the American People: James Davis, Lyman
Allen, Rev. C. E. Blood, A. Polley, W. W. Ross, Rev. H. Jones, H. Miles
Moore, M. J. Parrott, C. F. Currier, S. N. Latta, O. B. Holman, C. Robin-
son, E. Fish, L. J. Worden, M. Fennimore, James Blood, Rev. James Gil-
patrick, Rev. J. B. McAfee, I. T. Goodnow, J. A. Wakefield, A. Larzelere,
William Mitchell, J. H. Kagi, J. P. Mitchell, Rev. W. R. Griffith, J. W.
Morris, B. F. Harding, Prof. Walter Oakley, Albert Griffin, J. E. Stewart,
S. B. Prentiss. The Address is a spirited review of the political events in
Kansas.

The Convention adopted the following platform:

"*Whereas*, A body of men, recently assembled at Lecompton, and claiming to be the
Legislative Assembly of Kansas, have adopted a regulation purporting to be a law, for

taking the census and electing delegates to a Constitutional Convention, proposed to be held in that place in September next; and

"*Whereas*, The said Assembly was the creature of fraud, and its members the representatives of a people foreign to the Territory; and

"*Whereas*, The Organic Act does not authorize the Territorial Legislature power, even when legitimately convened, to pass any enabling act to change the government of the same; and

"*Whereas*, The act of this Assembly is partisan in its character, clearly contemplates fraud, for the recurrence of which it offers inadequate security, while it deprives the Executive of the Territory of the power to prevent or remedy such fraud, leaves the control of the census and election in the hands of pretended officers, not chosen by the people of Kansas, who are of violent characters and hostile to the best interests of the Territory; and

"*Whereas*, Said act purports to disfranchise certain bona fide settlers of Kansas, who have filed their declaration of intention to become citizens, and are recognized as voters by the Organic Act; and

"*Whereas*, There is no provision in the said regulation for submitting the Constitution so framed to the vote of the people of the Territory: therefore,

"*Resolved*, That the people of Kansas Territory cannot participate in any election under such regulation without compromising their rights as American citizens, sacrificing the best interests of Kansas, and jeopardizing the public peace.

"*Resolved*, That having suffered under this misrule of persons pretending to be the local officials of this Territory, we have lost all confidence in the integrity of the administration of the laws, however just these laws may appear to some on their face.

"*Resolved*, That with the people of any Territory alone rests the right to change the form of their government, subject to the approval of Congress, given before or after steps for the formation of a State Government have been taken; and further, that a Territorial Government is extra-constitutional, and, at best, under ordinances of Congress, purely temporary.

"*Resolved*, That the Constitution framed at Topeka, by the representatives of the people of Kansas, and ratified by popular vote, is still the choice of a majority of our citizens, as the form of a State Government, and that we maintain and urge on Congress our immediate admission as a State under it.

"*Resolved*, That the policy of the Free-State party has always been averse to any movement of an aggressive character, and that violence has never been resorted to save in self-defence.

"*Resolved*, That we make no tests for membership in the Free-State party, save that of the exclusion of domestic slavery from Kansas by subsequent legislation.

"*Resolved*, That we regard the presence of peaceful relations between our citizens as conducive to their best personal welfare as well as indispensable to the perfect development and expansion of the various economical interests of the Territory. To the end, therefore, that such relations may be obtained and permanently established amongst us, we earnestly appeal to all men of whatever party, to submit all differences of opinion growing out of the question of our future internal domestic institutions, to the test of sound reason and enlightened though friendly discussion, and to the final arbitrament of the ballot-box: *Provided*, That any attempt to abridge or impair the freedom of speech, oral or written, or of the ballot-box, or other constitutional rights, will be held as just cause of departure from this policy.

"*Resolved*, That Congress having presented the principles of Squatter Sovereignty enunciated in the Kansas bill as the basis of the political action of the people of Kansas, we are inflexibly determined to abide by its faithful execution, as we ever have resolutely opposed its violation, and ever will while it remains on the statute book."

The Convention also adopted ten miscellaneous resolutions.

MARCH 25.—Secretary Woodson calls on General P. F. Smith for troops: "The counties of Franklin and Anderson are infested by a predatory band or bands of assassins and robbers."

MARCH 26.—Woodson protests to General Smith against the withdrawal of troops from Lecompton: "A number of writs for the arrest of notorious outlaws are now in the hands of the United States Deputy Marshals," etc.

MARCH 27.—Colonel Sumner writes to Woodson: "I would respectfully suggest whether it would not be safer to pause a little in military matters, until we know the policy of the new Administration."

MARCH 31.—Secretary Woodson writes to Lewis Cass, Secretary of State, in regard to "the depredations of an organized banditti."

APRIL —A book issued with this title: "The Kansas and Nebraska Hand-Book, for 1857–8. With a New and Accurate Map. By Nathan H. Parker. Boston: John P. Jewet & Co." pp. 189. It is a well-printed guide-book, but has little historical value. It copies in full an "Address to the People of the United States and Kansas Territory," issued by the Committee appointed by the Topeka Free-State Convention of March 10th. This address is issued in reply to an address put forth by the Pro-Slavery Convention which met at Lecompton, January 12th. Both addresses were published in pamphlet form.

—In the spring, the Cone Brothers issued the Sumner (Atchison county) Gazette as a Daily, for a short time.

—Secretary Woodson is appointed Receiver of the Delaware Land District — a reward for valuable services.

APRIL 2.—Mr. Stanton takes the oath of office in Washington, before James M. Wayne, of the United States Supreme Court.

APRIL 15.—Secretary Stanton reaches Lecompton.

APRIL 17.—Secretary Stanton issues an Address to the People. He trusts that the Constitutional Convention will submit the Slavery question "to a fair vote of all the actual bona fide residents of the Territory, with every possible security against fraud and violence." He also urges "a general amnesty in reference to all those acts, on both sides, which grew out of the political contest, and which were not corruptly and feloniously committed for personal gain, and to gratify individual malignity." He writes to Hon. Lewis Cass, suggesting that the President issue a proclamation of amnesty.

APRIL.—Louis Weil wrote an article for the Annual Register, from which the following is copied:

"To Leavenworth City, the future Giant City of the West, after the Territory of Kansas was organized, flocked a large German immigration. The dark and troublesome Border-Ruffian days of 1855 and '56 drove them from their homes, but they returned with increased numbers during the year of 1856, and endured all the difficulties throughout that year. In the spring of 1857, a few young Germans met and organized 'The Leavenworth Turnverein.' As yet it was dangerous in those days to express even Free-State sentiments. But the nucleus was formed, around which the freedom-loving Germans of Leavenworth could gather. The Americans were not long in feeling the work of this association. They are a unit, and always ready to defend the right and their cause. We cannot here enumerate the acts of the Leavenworth Turnverein: suffice it to say that no action, political or otherwise, was had in Leavenworth county without their power being felt. The time had passed when Free-State men could be driven from the polls; there was always one company ready to protect the ballot-box. Kansas now ranks the most loyal of all the States, and with pride can the Turners of Leavenworth point to their acts in that struggle which made Kansas what it is to-day. The memorable 'Kickapoo,' the cannon which was used to destroy the Eldridge House in Lawrence, is a trophy of the Leavenworth Turners, and is yet in their possession."

APRIL.— Secretary Stanton issues a proclamation giving the census:

No.	Counties.	Legal voters.	Inhabitants.	No.	Counties.	Legal voters.	Inhabitants.
1	Doniphan	1,086	4,120	9	Riley	353	No return
2	Brown	205	No return	10	Pottawatomie	205	No return
3	Nemaha	140	612	11	Johnson	469	840
4	Atchison	804	2,807	12	Douglas	1,318	3,727
5	Jefferson	555	No return	13	Shawnee	283	No return
6	Leavenworth	1,837	5,529	14	Lykins	413	1,352
7	Calhoun	291	885	15	Linn	413	1,821
8	Marshall	206	415	16	Bourbon	645	2,622

The following diagram, numbering the counties as above, will give a view of the portion of the Territory now taking part in political affairs:

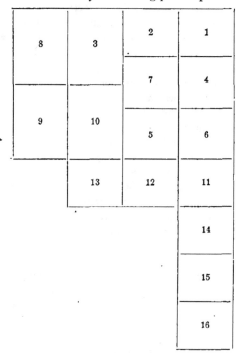

By the Kansas-Nebraska Act, the few people living here determine whether Slavery shall be extended from the Missouri river to the Rocky Mountains.

APRIL 18.—The American edition issued, of a book with the following title: "The Englishman in Kansas; or Squatter Life and Border Warfare. By T. H. Gladstone, Esq., Author of the Letters from Kansas in the 'London Times.' With an Introduction by Fred. Law Olmsted, Author of 'A Journey through the Seaboard Slave States,' 'A Journey through Texas,' etc. New York: Miller & Company. 1857."

Mr. Olmsted says: "Mr. Gladstone is a kinsman of the distinguished ex-Chancellor of the Exchequer of England." He spent the summer of 1856 in Kansas. The book contains 328 pages; is critical and descriptive as well as historical, and is one of the clearest statements ever published of the Free-State side of the question. It contains certain elements that the American narratives lack, and is free from passion. The writer acknowledges his indebtedness to the books of Mr. Phillips and Mrs. Robinson.

Mr. Gladstone had visited New York, Washington, and most of the Southern States, before coming to Kansas, and came here from Mississippi. He says:

"When in South Carolina and other Southern States, I witnessed extraordinary meetings, presided over by men of influence, at which addresses of almost incredible violence were delivered on the necessity of 'forcing slavery into Kansas,' 'of spreading the beneficent influence of Southern institutions over the new Territories,' and of 'driving back at the point of the bayonet the nigger-stealing scum poured down by Northern fanaticism.'"

He was in Washington when the Investigating Committee was appointed, and says: "No member from any one of the Southern States voted in favor of the investigation, but happily a majority was given by the Northern States, and the Committee on Enquiry was appointed." He reached St. Louis in May, and found that the St. Louis papers "contained advertisements, by the half-column, of rifles, revolvers, gunpowder, and lead." The following is copied from the Daily Missouri Republican:

KANSAS.

JUST RECEIVED, by Adams & Co.'s Express, a large and fine assortment of DOUBLE AND SINGLE SHOT-GUNS, which will be sold cheap for cash.

We have also on hand an assortment of our own manufacture of RIFLES, so well known for the past thirty years throughout the Western country. Emigrants to Kansas should not fail to call at ———, and examine our stock before purchasing elsewhere.

Mr. Gladstone arrived on the border the day after the destruction of Lawrence, May 22, 1856. He says:

"It was on that night that I first came in contact with the Missourian patriots. I had just arrived in Kansas City, and shall never forget the appearance of the lawless mob that poured into the place, inflamed with drink, glutted with the indulgence of the vilest passions, displaying with loud boasts the 'plunder' they had taken from the inhabitants, and thirsting for the opportunity of repeating the sack of Lawrence in some other offending place. Men, for the most part, of large frame, with red flannel shirts, and immense boots worn outside their trousers, their faces unwashed and unshaven, still reeking with the dust and smoke of Lawrence, wearing the most savage looks, and giving utterance to the most horrible imprecations and blasphemies; armed, moreover, to the teeth with rifles and revolvers, cutlasses and bowie-knives — such were the men I saw around me. Some displayed a grotesque intermixture in their dress, having crossed their native red rough shirt with the satin vest or narrow dress-coat pillaged from the wardrobe of some Lawrence Yankee, or having girded themselves with the cords and tassels which the day before had ornamented the curtains of the Free-State Hotel. Looking around at these groups of drunken, bellowing, blood-thirsty demons, who crowded around the bar of the hotel, shouting for drink, or vented their furious noise on the levee without, I felt that all my former experiences of border men and Missourians bore faint comparison with the spectacle presented by this wretched crew, who appeared only the more terrifying from the darkness of the surrounding night. The hotel in Kansas City, where we were, was the next, they said, that should fall; the attack was being planned that night, and such, they declared, should be the end of every place which was built by Free-State men, or that harbored 'those rascally Abolitionists.' Happily, this threat was not fulfilled."

The next day Mr. Gladstone went to Leavenworth. Governor Robinson, under arrest for "treason," was a passenger on the same boat. Colonel

Sumner was in command at Fort Leavenworth. The descriptions of the City and Fort are the best we have of those places at that period. The author says:

"Among all the scenes of violence I witnessed, it is remarkable that the offending parties were invariably on the Pro-Slavery side. The Free-State men appeared to me to be intimidated and overawed, in consequence, not merely of the determination and defiant boldness of their opponents, but still more through the sanction given to these acts by the Government."

Retaliation began at a later day, as the writer states.

The fact is stated that the early elections in Kansas were controlled by Missourians, and the writer compares it to an invasion of England by an "army of Frenchmen, larger in number than the aggregate of all our voters, who should, at the point of the sword, choose for us our representatives, and elect without exception as our rulers men from among themselves or pledged to their own political sentiments." Citizens of Kansas who resisted the laws made by the invaders were indicted as traitors, and suffered, many of them, a long and painful imprisonment.

The Pro-Slavery badge is described as a "bunch of hemp, symbolic of a rope, stuck into the button-hole."

The following relates to the election of March 30, 1855:

"A Presbyterian clergyman, the Rev. Frederick Starr, who was an eye-witness of the fraud and intimidation practised at Leavenworth City, and has published a statement of this and preceding events, describes a scene by no means rare on the occasion of this election. 'Some four days later,' he writes, 'I was on my horse, returning from Platte City to Weston, when four wagons came along, and on the bottom sat six men. A pole, about five feet high, stuck upright at the front of the wagon; on its top stuck an inverted empty whiskey bottle; across the stick at right angles was tied a bowie-knife; a black cambric flag, with a death's-head-and-bones daubed on in white paint, and a long streamer of beautiful, glossy Missouri hemp floated from the pole; there was a revolver lashed across the pole, and a powder-horn hanging loosely by it. They bore the piratical symbols of Missouri Ruffians returning from Kansas.'"

The party had been to Fort Riley, to vote.

MAY 3.—Trial before Judge Cato, at Lecompton, for treason, of the Free-State men, Chas. Robinson, G. W. Deitzler, Geo. W. Smith, John Brown, jr., Gaius Jenkins, H. H. Williams and Geo. W. Brown; and of Samuel C. Smith and Samuel F. Tappan for rescuing Jacob Branson from Sheriff Jones, November 26, 1855.

MAY 9.—Robert J. Walker, Governor, takes the oath of office in Washington, before Roger B. Taney, Chief Justice of the Supreme Court of the United States.

MAY 11.—The indictments for treason against Chas. Robinson and others are disposed of, the prosecuting officer entering a *nolle prosequi.*

MAY 13.—J. M. Walden and Edmund Babb start the Quindaro Chindowan, a Free-State paper. Mr. Walden left the paper June 12, 1858. Mrs. C. I. H. Nichols was associate editor.

MAY 19.—General Harney is in command at Fort Leavenworth.

MAY 20.— Secretary Stanton issues the following proclamation:

"*Whereas,* The following returns of the census taken under the act of the Legislative

Assembly, entitled 'An Act to provide for the taking of a Census, and election of Delegates to Convention,' passed the 19th February, 1857, have been made to me, to wit:

Dist.	Counties.	No. of legal voters.	Whole population.
1	Doniphan	1,086	4,120
2	{ Brown	206	No return.
	{ Nemaha	140	512
3	Atchison	804	2,807
4	Leavenworth	1,837	5,529
5	Jefferson	555	No return.
6	Calhoun	291	885
7	Marshall	206	415
8	{ Riley	353	No return.
	{ Pottawatomie	205	641
9	Johnson	496	890
10	Douglas	1,318	3,727
11	{ Shawnee	283	
	{ Richardson		
	{ Davis		
12	Lykins	413	1,352
13		No return.	
14		No return.	
15		No return.	
16	Linn	413	1,821
17		No return.	
18	Bourbon, McGee, Dorn and Allen	645	2,622
19		No return.	
	Total	9,251	

"Now, therefore, I, Frederick P. Stanton, Secretary, and Acting Governor, do hereby proclaim, that according to the provisions of said Act, and the census returns made in pursuance thereof, and upon a proper apportionment among the legal voters of the several districts aforesaid, they are respectively entitled to elect to the Convention provided for in said law, the number of delegates severally herein assigned to them, that is to say, to the—

1st district............Doniphan county.................................. 7 delegates
2d district............Brown and Nemaha.............................. 2 delegates
3d district............Atchison... 5 delegates
4th district............Leavenworth.....................................12 delegates
5th district............Jefferson... 4 delegates
6th district............Calhoun.. 2 delegates
7th district............Marshall... 1 delegate
8th district............Riley and Pottawatomie .... 4 delegates
9th district............Johnson.. 3 delegates
10th district............Douglas .... 8 delegates
11th district............Shawnee, Richardson and Davis......... 2 delegates
12th district............Lykins .... 3 delegates
16th district............Linn .... 3 delegates
18th district............Bourbon, McGee, Dorn and Allen........ 4 delegates

"The proper officers will hold the election for delegates to said Convention on the third Monday of June next, as directed by the law aforesaid, and in accordance with the apportionment herein made and declared."

MAY 24.—Gov. Walker, from the steamboat New Lucy, makes his first speech to Kansans, at Quindaro. Hon. Henry Wilson, of Massachusetts, arrives at Quindaro on the same boat.

MAY 25.—Henry Wilson visits Lawrence, Topeka, and other towns. He urges the Free-State men to vote at the October election, and, after going home, he raised $2,500 to be used in the canvass in Kansas. Thomas J. Marsh, of Massachusetts, came here and disbursed the money.

—The following facts in regard to the Congregationalists in Kansas are copied from an article by Richard Cordley, in the Kansas Annual Register:

"Among the first colonies there was a large proportion of members of Congregational Churches, and still more who had been educated in that faith. As soon as the emigrants began to move from the East, the American Home Missionary Society—never behind the demands of the hour—commissioned Rev. S. Y. Lum, formerly of Middletown, N. Y., as 'a Missionary to Kansas.' He came out in September, 1854, and on the first of October, preached in Lawrence the first sermon probably ever preached to white settlers in the Territory. On the 15th of the same month, a Congregational Church was organized in Lawrence—the first church organized in Kansas, except among the Indians. Seven names were signed to the original Articles of Faith and Covenant. In December, Mr. Lum began to preach at Topeka, where another settlement was commenced. A short time before this, a settlement was formed at the junction of the Kansas and Big Blue rivers, and Rev. C. E. Blood, from Illinois, began preaching to the colony. This colony laid out the town of Manhattan. The next summer, what was called the 'Connecticut Colony' came out, and settled at Wabaunsee, twelve miles below Manhattan. It is doubtful whether any Western colony ever contained so large a proportion of thoroughly educated Christian men, as this colony at Wabaunsee. Rev. Harvey Jones became pastor of the colony.

"Several other Congregational colonies were formed in different parts of the Territory, which we have not time to mention. No other churches were organized, however, till 1856. Seven were organized during this year: Manhattan, in January; Topeka, Osawatomie, and Zeandale, in July; Burlingame, in September; and Bloomington, and Kanwaka, in October.

"April 25th, 1857, a meeting of ministers and delegates was held at Topeka, to form a State organization. They organized the 'General Association of Congregational Ministers and Churches in Kansas.' It is composed of the ministers and delegates from the churches. Each church can send one delegate; or if the church have more than twenty-five members, one delegate for every twenty-five members. Eleven ministers became members of the body. They reported eight churches in the Territory, with a membership of eighty-five. The church at Lawrence had erected a house of worship. In their address to other Congregational bodies, the brethren say: 'It shall be our aim to transplant the principles and institutions of the Puritans to these fertile plains.' The Association adjourned to meet in October."

MAY 25.—Gov. Robert J. Walker reaches Leavenworth, and is received by a large concourse of citizens.

MAY 27.—Senator Wilson, Dr. Samuel G. Howe and Rev. John Pierpont speak in the Unitarian Church, at Lawrence. Gov. Walker and E. O. Perrin, his private secretary, are present, and speak briefly. It was in this speech that the poet Pierpont applied to Kansas the saying of Dr. Boteler of strawberries: "Doubtless God could have made a better berry, but doubtless God never did."

MAY 27.—Gov. Walker reaches Lecompton, via Lawrence, and issues his Inaugural Address. It was a long and adroit speech, and had been read to President Buchanan. In the course of it he said:

"There is a law more powerful than the legislation of man, more potent than passion or prejudice, that must ultimately determine the location of Slavery in this country: it is the isothermal line; it is the law of the thermometer, of latitude or altitude, regulating climate, labor, and productions, and, as a consequence, profit and loss. . . . If, from the operation of these causes, Slavery should not exist here, I trust it by no means follows that Kansas should become a State controlled by the treason and fanaticism of Abolition. She has, in any event, certain constitutional duties to perform to her sister States, and especially to her immediate neighbor—the slaveholding State of Missouri. . . . That Kansas should become hostile to Missouri, an asylum for her fugitive slaves, or a propagandist of Abolition treason, would be alike inexpedient and unjust, and fatal to the continuance of the American Union "

The census for the Lecompton Constitution, prescribing who should vote, was taken only in fifteen counties. Nineteen interior counties, strongly Free-State, had no vote, and could have no delegates in the Convention. These were called the "disfranchised" counties.

June 1.—Albert D. Richardson, correspondent of Cincinnati and Boston papers, arrives in Kansas, stopping at Quindaro.

June.—About the first of the month, the Lawrence Republican is started, with Norman Allen as publisher and T. Dwight Thacher and Mr. Allen as editors.

— Joseph Williams appointed Associate Justice in place of Cunningham.

"In June, 1857, Fort Scott was visited by Norman Eddy, of South Bend, Ind.; George A. Crawford, of Lock Haven, Pa.; D. H. Weir, of Laporte, Ind., and D. W. Holbrook, of Michigan, who negotiated for the purchase of the 'claims' on which the town was located. These were bought of H. T. Wilson, G. W. Jones, N. E. Herson, A. Hornbeck and S. A. Williams. This purchase was made in behalf of the 'Fort Scott Town Company,' consisting originally of George A. Crawford, Norman Eddy, D. H. Weir, D. W. Holbrook, G. W. Jones, Wm. R. Judson, E. S. Lowman, and H. T. Wilson. Blake Little was subsequently made a conditional member of the Company. Joseph Williams soon after purchased the Jones interest. George A. Crawford was chosen first President, and has acted in that capacity ever since. H. T. Wilson was first Treasurer, and has been continued in office to the present time. G. W. Jones was first Secretary. He has been succeeded by Joseph Williams, William R. Judson, and George A. Reynolds. After long delay with the Indian title, the Company acquired title through the Mayor on the 17th of September, 1860, to 320 acres of land. They have since purchased 200 acres, so that their lands now embrace all of section 30, township 25, range 25, except the west half and the northeast fourth of the northwest quarter. The Company had been incorporated by the Legislature in February, 1860. They made donations to the old settlers of the lots on which the houses purchased of the Government were built. They have also given lots to all the religious denominations represented among the citizens; also to the Government a cemetery for the burial of soldiers, and to the county a square for courthouse and jail.

"The Legislature of 1855 incorporated the town. In February, 1860, the Legislature enlarged the corporate limits of the town."—*Annual Register, pp.* 134-5.

June 9.—Meeting of the Free-State Legislature at Topeka. On the 11th, there being no quorum in the House, a quorum was made by declaring vacant the seats of thirteen absent members. This reduced the number in the House to twenty-five. The Message of Governor Robinson was read. The following is quoted from the Message:

"A large and necessary portion of the labors of your codifying committee was destroyed, with much other property, at Lawrence, in May, 1856, when that place was pillaged and partially burned, by a mob brought there by the United States Marshal. When your bodies met, pursuant to adjournment, in July last, your assembly was interfered with and broken up by a large force of United States troops, in battle array, who drove you hence, in gross violation of those constitutional rights which it was your duty to have protected. When you again convened, in January last, at your regular session, your proceedings were again interfered with by a Deputy Marshal, and many of your members arrested. . . . . There is not much of 'popular sovereignty' and 'self-government' here. This usurpation [by the Territorial Legislature] is repudiated by the people, but it is recognized by Congress and the President."

Considerable space is given in the Message to a pointed review of Governor Walker's inaugural.

Both houses adjourn sine die, June 13th.

The following laws were enacted: For taking the census and apportioning the State; for a State election, in August, to fill vacancies; locating the capital at Topeka; establishing a State University at Lawrence; and a joint resolution asking Congress to admit Kansas under the Topeka Constitution. Governor Walker was in Topeka during the session, but did not interfere with the Legislature.

—Free-State Convention at Topeka. J. H. Lane, President; W. F. M. Arny and T. D. Thacher, Secretaries. It endorsed the Topeka movement, and urged Free-State men not to participate in the Lecompton movement, and declared the Territorial laws of no force. The resolutions were reported by George W. Smith, G. W. Deitzler, J. P. Root, A. A. Jamieson, Walter Oakley, C. K. Holliday, C. Robinson, Morris Hunt, and Mark W. Delahay.

ELECTION OF DELEGATES TO THE LECOMPTON CONSTITUTIONAL CONVENTION, JUNE 15.

LEAVENWORTH COUNTY, FOURTH DISTRICT—TWELVE DELEGATES.

Hugh M. Moore	438	M. P. Rively	428
James Doniphan	436	Wm. Christian	445
Jarrett M. Todd	434	Jesse Connell	448
Lucien J. Eastin	431	Greene B. Redman	414
John D. Henderson	428	S. J. Kookagee	413
John W. Martin	424	Wm. Walker	461

DONIPHAN COUNTY, FIRST DISTRICT—SEVEN DELEGATES.

James J. Reynolds	232	Wm. Mathews	233
Daniel Vanderslice	221	Milt. E. Bryant	241
H. W. Forman	234	Thos. J. Keys	233
J. P. Blair	224		

BROWN COUNTY, SECOND DISTRICT—TWO DELEGATES.

Henry Smith	36	'Squire Griffiths	9
Cyrus Dolman	44		

ATCHISON COUNTY, THIRD DISTRICT—FIVE DELEGATES.

James Adkins	185	P. H. Larrey	183
P. R. King	10	I. S. Hascal	173
G. W. Swinney	186	A. McPherson	33
J. T. Hereford	190		

JEFFERSON COUNTY, FIFTH DISTRICT—FOUR DELEGATES.

Alex. Bayne	119	Jno. W. Murphy	3
J. A. Manning	55	Gal. Sprague	11
W. H. Swift	118	T. H. Stewart	81
Thos. Childs	121		

CALHOUN COUNTY, SIXTH DISTRICT—TWO DELEGATES.

H. D. Oden	23	James Kuykendall	20

MARSHALL COUNTY, SEVENTH DISTRICT—ONE DELEGATE.

William H. Jenkins	57	W. S. Blackburn	40

RILEY AND POTTAWATOMIE, EIGHTH DISTRICT—FOUR DELEGATES.

C. R. Mobley	36	John Pipher	2
J. S. Randolph	46	S. Dyer	8
P. Z. Taylor	59	W. H. Davis	31
Robert Wilson	27	George Montague	7

JOHNSON COUNTY, NINTH DISTRICT—THREE DELEGATES.

G. W. McKown	113	J. H. Danforth	75
Batt. Jones	104	J. T. Barton	62

DOUGLAS COUNTY, TENTH DISTRICT—EIGHT DELEGATES.

John Calhoun	180	W. T. Spicely	225
L. S. Boling	182	W. S. Wells	225
A. W. Jones	166	H. Butcher	170
John M. Wallace	173	John Spicer	67
L. A. Prather	88	O. C. Stewart	114

SHAWNEE, RICHARDSON AND DAVIS, ELEVENTH DISTRICT — TWO DELEGATES.

David Lykins...................................... 58 | Henry L. Lyons............................... 17
Wm. A. Heiskell .... 58 | J. T. Bradford................................. 58

LINN COUNTY, SIXTEENTH DISTRICT — THREE DELEGATES.

J. H. Barlow .... 124 | George Overstreet............................ 118
S. H. Hayze...................................... 118 |

BOURBON, ALLEN, M'GEE AND DORN, EIGHTEENTH DISTRICT — FOUR DELEGATES.

James S. Barbee................................ 86 | — Little.. 187
H. T. Wilson.................................... 204 | — Greenwood................................ 123
B. F. Hill... 75 | G. P. Hamilton............................... 166

BRECKINRIDGE COUNTY, FOURTEENTH DISTRICT.

J. H. Pritchard .... 13 | C. H. Withington........................... 13

FRANKLIN COUNTY.

William R. Judson........................... 21 | Alfred Johnson.............................. 1

ANDERSON COUNTY.

R. Gilpatrick.................................... 31 | J. Y. Campbell.............................. 31

LYKINS COUNTY.

David Lykins.................................... 58 | Henry T. Lyons............................ 58
William A. Heiskell.......................... 58 | J. T. Bradford............................... 17

NEMAHA COUNTY.

C. Dolman....................................... 35 | Joseph Brown............................... 11
Henry Smith.................................... 16 | J. H. Steer.................................... 12

Only 2,200 votes were polled. This proved that the Free-State men could have controlled the election, had they voted.

JUNE 18.—Governor Walker issues a grant of land to the Atchison Town Company.

—Governor Walker writes to Wm. G. Mathias, Speaker of the House, and Thomas Johnson, President of the Council, to make a new apportionment of Representatives and Councilmen.

JUNE 24.—Land sales at Paola. Walker and Stanton present.

JUNE 29.—The Pro-Slavery city officers of Leavenworth, elected by violence last fall, are induced to resign. An election on the 29th is carried by Free-State men, for the first time, electing Henry J. Adams Mayor and filling vacancies in the Council. In an affray at the polls, William Haller, Free State, kills James T. Lyle, the Pro-Slavery City Recorder.

JULY 2-3.—National Democratic Convention at Lecompton. Ten counties represented. Epaphroditus Ransom, ex-Governor of Michigan, is nominated for Delegate to Congress.

JULY.—The people of Lawrence refuse to organize the city under the charter granted by the Bogus Legislature, and set up an independent municipal organization.

JULY 10.—Joseph Williams takes the oath of office before Secretary Stanton, as Associate Justice of the Supreme Court. His residence is in Fort Scott.

JULY 12.—President Buchanan writes to Robert J. Walker: "Gen. Harney has been selected to command the expedition to Utah, but we must contrive to leave him with you, at least until you are out of the woods. Kansas is vastly more important at the present moment than Utah."

It was more important to defeat free institutions in Kansas than Mormonism in Utah. Buchanan's letter is given in full in the Report of the Covode Investigating Committee.

JULY 13.—Lawrence holds its independent city election.

JULY 15.—Gov. Walker issues a proclamation, declaring the action of Lawrence rebellious. If they persist, he says they will be guilty of treason, and "involve the Territory in all the horrors of civil war." He sends a body of United States troops there. They encamp near Lawrence, and remain until they are driven away by ridicule—and Walker's "Lawrence War" ends. The Free-State men have become strong and cool enough to laugh when fighting is not necessary.

—Opening of the Delaware Trust Land sales at Osawkee.

—Gov. Walker writes to the Secretary of State that—

"The movement in Lawrence was the beginning of a plan, originating in that city to organize an insurrection throughout the Territory, and especially in all the towns, cities and counties where the Republican party have a majority. Lawrence is the hotbed of all Abolition movements in this Territory. It is the idea established by the Abolition societies at the East, and whilst there are a respectable number of people there, it is filled by a considerable number of mercenaries, who are paid by the Abolition societies to perpetuate and diffuse agitation throughout Kansas, and prevent the peaceful settlement of this question. Having failed in inducing their own so-called Topeka State Legislature to organize this insurrection, Lawrence has commenced it herself, and if not arrested, rebellion will extend throughout the Territory.

. . . .

"In order to send this communication immediately by mail, I must close; assuring you that the spirit of rebellion pervades the great mass of the Republican party in this Territory, instigated—as I entertain no doubt they are—by Eastern societies having in view results most disastrous to the Government and the Union, and that the continued presence of Gen. Harney is indispensable, and was originally stipulated by me, with a large body of dragoons and several batteries."

This letter, like Buchanan's to Walker, was not made public until these Pro-Slavery chieftains had fallen out. Buchanan quotes it in his Special Message of February 2, 1858.

JULY 15–16.—Free-State Convention at Topeka. President, J. H. Lane; Vice Presidents, J. A. Wakefield, H. Miles Moore, T. J. Addis, Albert Griffin, Harris Stratton; Secretaries, Richard J. Hinton, A. D. Richardson. There were 187 delegates present. J. H. Lane declined the nomination for Congress. The resolutions, reported by J. M. Walden, declare in favor of sustaining the Topeka movement, as the first and only choice of the Free-State party of Kansas; deny the validity of the Territorial Legislature; declare that the Pro-Slavery faction is a minority, and that the admission of Kansas under its proposed Constitution would be an act of injustice and despotism, justifying the extremest measures in opposition; asking a resubmission of the Topeka Constitution, in August; calling a convention at Grasshopper Falls, in August. P. C. Schuyler was nominated for Secretary of State, over Walter Oakley, J. P. Root, and A. Wattles; Dr. G. A. Cutler, for Auditor; M. F. Conway, and S. N. Latta, for Judges of the Supreme Court; E. M. Thurston, for Reporter, and A. G. Patrick, for Clerk, of the Supreme Court. M. J. Parrott was nominated for Representative in Congress, receiving 83 votes, to 80 for Henry J. Adams. State Central Com-

9

mittee: J. Blood, A. Curtiss, S. E. Martin, R. Mayfield, W. F. M. Arny, W. R. Griffith, Henry Harvey, J. P. Root, G. S. Hillyer, Albert Griffin, F. G. Adams, H. Miles Moore, A. Larzelere, E. S. Nash.

JULY.—The Kansas Zeitung started in Atchison by Dr. Chas. F. Kob.

JULY 18.—Governor Walker receives the following apportionment of the Legislature, made by the President of the Council and the Speaker of the House:

APPORTIONMENT FOR THE SECOND TERRITORIAL LEGISLATURE FOR THE TERRITORY OF KANSAS.

FOR THE COUNCIL.

No. Dist.	Counties.	No. of members
1	Leavenworth	3
2	Atchison	1
3	Doniphan	
4	Brown, Nemaha, Marshall, Pottawatomie, Riley, and all that part of the Territory of Kansas west of Marshall, Riley and Davis counties	2
5	Jefferson and Calhoun	1
6	Douglas and Johnson	3
7	Shawnee, Richardson, Davis, Wise and Breckinridge	
8	Bourbon, Godfrey, Wilson, Dorn and McGee	2
9	Butler, Hunter, Greenwood, Madison, Weller, Coffey, Woodson and Allen	
10	Anderson, Lykins, Linn and Franklin, and all that part of the Territory of Kansas west of Wise, Butler and Hunter counties	1
	Total	13

THOS. JOHNSON,   WM. G. MATHIAS,
President of the Council.   *Speaker House of Representatives, at Session of 1857.*

FOR THE HOUSE OF REPRESENTATIVES.

No. Dist.	Counties.	No. of members
1	Leavenworth	8
2	Atchison	3
3	Doniphan	5
4	Brown	1
5	Nemaha	
6	Marshall	1
7	Jefferson	2
8	Calhoun	2
9	Pottawatomie and Riley	1
10	Douglas and Johnson, and all that part of the Territory of Kansas west of the counties of Wise, Butler and Hunter	8
11	Shawnee	1
12	Richardson, Davis, Wise and Breckinridge	
13	Weller, Madison, Butler, Hunter and Greenwood	
14	Bourbon, Godfrey, Wilson, Dorn and McGee	3
15	Woodson, Coffey and Allen	
16	Anderson and Franklin	
17	Linn	2
18	Lykins	2
	Total	39

THOS. JOHNSON,   WM. G. MATHIAS,
President of the Council.   *Speaker House of Representatives, at Session of 1857.*

The following diagram, showing the Bogus Apportionment for members of the House, is copied from the Topeka Tribune:

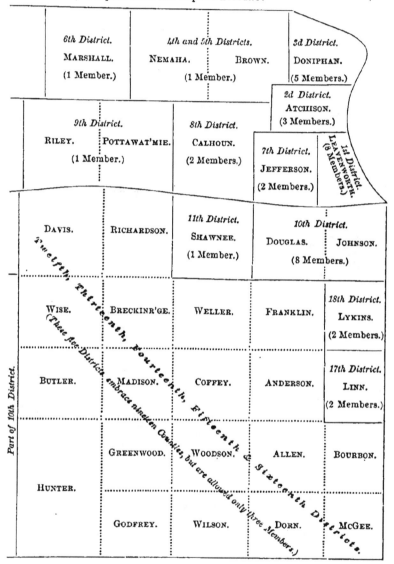

JULY 28.—Geo. W. Sweeney, of Atchison county, elected to the Constitutional Convention, resigns. An election to fill the vacancy was called, to be held August 25th.

JULY 31.—James Stevens was murdered at Leavenworth by John C. Quarles and W. M. Bays. The murderers were hanged by the people the next day, on an elm tree, near Young's saw-mill. Wm. Knighten and Bill Woods, arrested as accomplices in the murder of Stevens, were taken to the Delaware City jail, on the Morning Star.

JULY.—A book issued with this title: "Gov. Geary's Administration in Kansas: With a Complete History of the Territory until July, 1857. By John II. Gihon, M. D., Private Secretary of Gov. Geary. Philadelphia: Chas. C. Rhodes, 1857." pp. 348. This book is a good summary of preceding histories, and a warm defence of all the acts of Gov. Geary. Dr. Gihon came to Kansas Pro-Slavery, and, like thousands of others, hated Slavery as soon as he had seen it. The book has the new-convert ardor, but contains a large amount of valuable matter. The following is copied from page 102:

"On the first of September, 1856, Capt. Frederick Emory, a United States mail contractor, rendered himself conspicuous in Leavenworth, at the head of a band of Ruffians, mostly from western Missouri. They entered houses, stores, and dwellings of Free-State people, and, in the name of 'law and order,' abused and robbed the occupants, and drove them out into the roads, irrespective of age, sex or condition. Under pretence of searching for arms, they approached the house of William Phillips, the lawyer who had previously been tarred and feathered and carried to Missouri. Phillips, supposing he was to be subjected to a similar outrage, resolved not to submit to the indignity, and stood upon his defence. In repelling the assaults of the mob, he killed two of them, when the others burst into the house, and poured a volley of balls into his body, killing him instantly in the presence of his wife and another lady. His brother, who was also present, had an arm badly broken with bullets, and was compelled to submit to an amputation. Fifty of the Free-State prisoners were then driven on board the Polar Star, bound for St. Louis. On the next day a hundred more were embarked by Emory and his men, on the steamboat Emma. During these proceedings, an election was held for Mayor, and Wm. E. Murphy, since appointed Indian Agent by the President, was elected, 'without opposition.'"

Dr. Gihon's book contains Gov. Geary's Message to the Legislature, his Farewell Address, and Gov. Walker's Inaugural Address.

AUGUST 9.—The following is the official vote for the officers under the Topeka Constitution:

FOR JUDGES OF THE SUPREME COURT:
Samuel N. Latta 7,200
Martin F. Conway 7,178

CLERK OF THE SUPREME COURT:
A. G. Patrick 7,200

SECRETARY OF STATE:
Philip C. Schuyler........................... 7,167

REPRESENTATIVE IN CONGRESS:
Marcus J. Parrott............................. 7,267

AUDITOR:
Geo. A. Cutler 7,177

VOTE ON CONSTITUTION:
For Constitution.............................. 7,257

REPORTER OF THE SUPREME COURT:
E. M. Thurston 7,187

Against Constitution........................ 34

MEMBERS OF THE SENATE:

Dist.	Name of Candidate.	Vote.	Dist.	Name of Candidate.	Vote
1	Henry J. Adams........................	1,266	10	Wm. A. Phillips........................	935
1	J. P. Root..............................	1,265	10	Jas. B. Abbott.........................	733
2	Caleb May	403	11	John A. Beam	220
2	David Dodge...........................	403	12	Walter Oakley.........................	692
3	Benj. Harding	220	13	C. F. W. Leonhardt....................	100
3	Alfred Larzelere......................	219	15	J. M. Hendry..........................	313
4	J. B. Smith...........................	165	16	Hamilton Smith........................	271
6	Geo. S. Hillyer.......................	460	17	W. F. M. Arny.........................	189
8	S. D. Houston.........................	149	18	Jas. Montgomery.......................	235
9	Samuel L. Adair.......................	269			

MEMBERS OF THE HOUSE OF REPRESENTATIVES.

Dist.	Name of Candidate.	Vote.	Dist.	Name of Candidate.	Vote.
1	J. C. Green	1,265	8	Dr. Adams	185
1	J. P. Hatterscheidt	1,260	9	Chas. Mayo	271
1	Geo. H. Keller	1,268	9	Edwin S. Nash	271
1	John C. Douglass	1,268	9	Leander Martin	252
1	Stephen Sparks	1,266	10	Robt. Morrow	1,000
1	Wm. Pennock	1,266	10	Geo. W. Deitzler	1,003
1	Patrick Orr	1,265	10	Wm. Hutchinson	927
1	R. G. Elliott	1,265	10	Geo. H. Crocker	994
1	J. M. Funk	1,265	10	E. P. Vaughn	725
1	J. M. Walden	1,268	10	Thaddeus Prentice	647
2	A. Elliott	381	10	Geo. F. Warren	944
2	S. J. H. Snyder	383	11	P. H. Townsend	231
2	H. Martin	383	11	Philip T. Hupp	226
2	W. A. Woodworth	383	12	Henry Harvey	701
2	J. H. Gilbert	382	12	Jeremiah Sabin	648
3	Harris Stratton	217	12	John D. Deleman	703
3	J. B. Wheeler	218	13	D. E. Adams	104
3	Alex. A. Jamieson	219	14	Chris. Columbia	191
3	Benj. H. Brock	219	15	J. W. Stewart	427
3	Thos. Stevenson	219	15	E. W. Robinson	417
3	Mathew Iles	219	15	David B. Jackman	379
4	Ira H. Smith	150	16	R. Austin	273
4	W. W. Guthrie	149	16	Geo. Kellogg	235
5	C. Beary	52	17	Samuel Stewart	221
6	Stephen C. Cooper	520	17	S. F. Stone	170
6	Edward Lynde	518	18	B. B. Newton	233
7	Geo. W. Brassbridge	98	18	Jas. M. Arthur	233
7	Albert Fuller	98	18	E. L. Taylor	231

AUGUST 14.—Mass Convention at Centropolis. Resolutions were adopted urging Free-State men to take part in the October election. G. W. Brown, Richard J. Hinton, M. J. Parrott, W. A. Phillips and M. F. Conway were in the Convention.

AUGUST 20.—Governor Robinson acquitted by the jury; trial before Judge Cato, at Lecompton; charge, "usurpation of office." Colonel Samuel Walker is also acquitted. Judge Cato charged strongly against both.

AUGUST 23.—William Haller escapes from Fort Leavenworth.

AUGUST 26.—Free-State Conventions at Grasshopper Falls. George W. Smith was Chairman of the Mass Convention, and R. G. Elliott, Dr. C. F. Kob, Mr. Miller and E. G. Ross, Secretaries. W. Y. Roberts was Chairman of the Delegate Convention, and A. D. Richardson and E. G. Ross Secretaries. The main question was, whether Free-State men should take part in the Territorial election of October 5th. Robinson, Lane, Holliday and Smith favored it, while Conway, Phillips and Redpath opposed it. The following platform was adopted:

"*Whereas*, It is of the most vital importance to the people of Kansas that the Territorial Government should be controlled by the bona fide citizens thereof; and

"*Whereas*, Governor Walker has repeatedly pledged himself that the people of Kansas should have a full and fair vote, before impartial judges, at the election to be held the first Monday in October, for Delegate to Congress, members of the Legislature, and other officers: therefore,

"*Resolved*, That we, the people of Kansas, in mass convention assembled, agree to participate in said election.

"*Resolved*, That in thus voting we rely upon the faithful fulfilment of the pledge of Governor Walker; and that we, as heretofore, protest against the enactments forced upon us by the voters of Missouri.

"*Resolved*, That this mass meeting recommend the appointment of a committee, to wait upon the Territorial authorities, and urgently insist upon a review and correction of the wicked apportionment endeavored to be forced upon the people of Kansas, for the selection of members of the Territorial Legislature.

"*Resolved*, That General J. H. Lane be authorized and empowered to tender to Governor Walker the force organized by him under the resolution passed by the Convention held at Topeka, on the 15th of July last, to be used for the protection of the ballot-box."

The Delegate Convention unanimously nominated M. J. Parrott for Delegate to Congress, and appointed the following Executive Committee: J. H. Lane, C. K. Holliday, Dr. James Davis, O. E. Learnard, And. Johnson, Geo. W. Hutchinson, W. F. M. Arny, H. Miles Moore, J. P. Root, A. E. Jamieson, Geo. W. Brown, Robt. Riddle, W. R. Frost, Geo. W. Smith, J. K. Goodin, Dr. J. H. Gilpatrick, P. C. Schuyler, Dr. Robertson, Edward Lynde, and C. W. Babcock.

SEPTEMBER 1.—Land office opened at Lecompton.

SEPTEMBER 7.—Meeting of the Lecompton Constitutional Convention, at Lecompton. B. Little was elected President *pro tem.*, and Thos. C. Hughes Secretary *pro tem.*

On the 8th, the following officers were elected: President, John Calhoun; Secretary, Thos. C. Hughes; Assistant Secretary, Jas. H. Nounnan; Reporter, P. H. Carey; Sergeant-at-Arms, Samuel Cramer; Chaplain, Mr. Magee.

On the 10th, D. R. Gilpatrick and J. Y. Campbell were declared entitled to seats from Anderson county. John D. Henderson was elected Public Printer.

On the 11th, adjourned to October 19th. Met on the 19th of October, and finally adjourned on the 3d of November. The Proceedings of the Convention are given in Vol. III, of Reports of Committees of the House of Representatives, 1st sess. Thirty-fifth Congress, 1858. The Constitution adopted is as follows:

THE LECOMPTON CONSTITUTION.

PREAMBLE.

We, the people of the Territory of Kansas, by our representatives in convention assembled, at Lecompton, in said Territory, on Monday, the fourth day of September, one thousand eight hundred and fifty-seven, and of the independence of the United States of America the eighty-second year, having the right of admission into the Union as one of the United States of America, consistent with the Federal Constitution, and by virtue of the treaty of cession by France to the United States of the province of Louisiana, made and entered into on the thirtieth day of April, one thousand eight hundred and three, and by virtue of, and in accordance with, the act of Congress passed May the thirtieth, one thousand eight hundred and fifty-four, entitled "An act to organize the Territories of Nebraska and Kansas," in order to secure to ourselves and our posterity the enjoyment of all the rights of life, liberty and property, and the free pursuit of happiness, do mutually agree with each other to form ourselves into a free, independent and sovereign State by the name and style of the STATE OF KANSAS, and do ordain and establish the following Constitution for the government thereof:

ARTICLE I.—BOUNDARIES.

We do declare and establish, ratify and confirm the following as the permanent boundaries of the said State of Kansas, that is to say: Beginning at a point on the western boundary of the State of Missouri where the thirty-seventh parallel of north latitude crosses the same; thence west on said parallel to the eastern boundary of New Mexico; thence north on said boundary to latitude thirty-eight; thence following said boundary westward to the east boundary of the Territory of Utah, on the summit of the Rocky Mountains; thence northward on said summit to the fortieth parallel of latitude; thence east on said parallel to the western boundary of the State of Missouri; thence south with the western boundary of said State to the place of beginning.

ARTICLE II.—COUNTY BOUNDARIES.

No county now established which borders upon the Missouri river, or upon either bank of the Kansas river, shall ever be reduced by the formation of new counties to less than twenty miles square; nor shall any other county now organized, or hereafter to be organized, be reduced to less than five hundred square miles.

ARTICLE III.—DISTRIBUTION OF POWERS.

The power of the Government of the State of Kansas shall be divided into three separate departments—the Executive, the Legislative, and the Judicial; and no person charged with the exercise of powers properly belonging to one of these departments shall exercise any functions appertaining to either of the others, except in the cases hereinafter expressly directed or permitted.

ARTICLE IV.—EXECUTIVE DEPARTMENT.

SECTION 1. The chief executive power of this State shall be vested in a Governor, who shall hold his office for two years from the time of his installation.

SEC. 2. The Governor shall be elected by the qualified electors of the State. The returns of every election for Governor shall be sealed up and transmitted to the seat of Government, directed to the Secretary of State, who shall deliver them to the Speaker of the House of Representatives at the next ensuing session of the Legislature, during the first week of which session the Speaker shall open and publish them in the presence of both houses of the Legislature. The person having the highest number of votes shall be Governor; but if two or more shall be equal, and having received the highest number of votes, then one of them shall be chosen Governor by the joint ballot of both houses of the Legislature; contested elections for Governor shall be determined by both houses of the Legislature in such manner as may be prescribed by law.

SEC. 3. The Governor shall be at least thirty years of age, shall have been a citizen of the United States for twenty years, shall have resided in this State at least five years next preceding the day of his election, or from the time of the formation of this Constitution, and shall not be capable of holding the office more than four years in any term of six years.

SEC. 4. He shall, at stated terms, receive for his services a compensation which shall be fixed by law, and shall not be increased or diminished during the term for which he shall be elected.

SEC. 5. He shall be commander-in-chief of the army and navy of this State, and of the militia, except when they shall be called into the service of the United States.

SEC. 6. He may require information in writing from officers in the Executive Department on any subject relating to the duties of their respective offices.

SEC. 7. He may, in cases of emergency, convene the Legislature at the seat of Government, or at a different place, if that shall have become, since their last adjournment, dangerous from an enemy or disease; and in case of disagreement between the two houses with respect to the time of adjournment, adjourn them to such time as he may think proper, not beyond the next stated meeting of the Legislature.

SEC. 8. He shall, from time to time, give the Legislature information of the state of the Government, and recommend to their consideration such measures as he may deem necessary and expedient.

SEC. 9. He shall take care that the laws be faithfully executed.

SEC. 10. In all criminal and penal cases, except in those of treason and impeachment, he shall have power to grant reprieves and pardons, and remit fines; and in cases of forfeitures, to stay the collection until the end of the next session of the Legislature, and to remit forfeitures by and with the advice and consent of the Senate. In cases of treason he shall have power to grant reprieves by and with the advice and consent of the Senate, but may respite the sentence until the end of the next session of the Legislature.

SEC. 11. All commissions shall be in the name and by the authority of the State of Kansas, be sealed with the great seal, and signed by the Governor, and attested by the Secretary of State.

SEC. 12. There shall be a seal of this State, which shall be kept by the Governor and used by him officially, and the present seal of this Territory shall be the seal of the State until otherwise directed by the Legislature.

SEC. 13. All vacancies not provided for in this Constitution shall be filled in such manner as the Legislature may prescribe.

SEC. 14. The Secretary of State shall be elected by the qualified electors of the State, and shall continue in office during the term of two years, and until his successor is qualified. He shall keep a fair register of all the official acts and proceedings of the Governor, and shall, when required, lay the same, and all papers, minutes, and vouchers relative thereto, before the Legislature, and shall perform such other duties as may be required by law.

SEC. 15. Every bill which shall have passed both houses of the Legislature shall be presented to the Governor. If he approve, he shall sign it; but if not, he shall return it, with his objections, to the house in which it shall have originated, which shall enter the objections at length upon their journals, and proceed to reconsider it. If, after such reconsideration, two-thirds of the house shall agree to pass the bill, it shall be sent, with the objections, to the other house, by which it shall likewise be reconsidered; if approved by two-thirds of that house, it shall become a law; but in such case, the votes of each house shall be determined by yeas and nays, and the names of the members voting for and against the bill shall be entered upon the journals of each house, respectively. If any bill shall not be returned by the Governor within six days (Sundays excepted) after it shall have been presented to him, the same shall become a law in like manner as if he had signed it, unless the Legislature, by their adjournment, prevent its return, in which case it shall not become a law.

SEC. 16. Every order, resolution, or vote, to which the concurrence of both houses may be necessary, except resolutions for the purpose of obtaining the joint action of both houses, and on questions of adjournment, shall be presented to the Governor, and, before it shall take effect, be approved by him; or, being disapproved, shall be repassed by both houses, according to the rules and limitations prescribed in case of a bill.

SEC. 17. A Lieutenant Governor shall be elected at the same time and for the same term as the Governor, and his qualifications and the manner of his election shall be the same in all respects.

SEC. 18. In case of the removal of the Governor from office, or of his death, failure to qualify, resignation, removal from the State, or inability to discharge the powers and duties of the office, the said office, with its compensation, shall devolve upon the Lieutenant Governor; and the Legislature shall provide by law for the discharge of the Executive functions in other necessary cases.

SEC. 19. The Lieutenant Governor shall be President of the Senate, but shall have no vote except in the case of a tie, when he may give the casting vote; and while acting as such, shall receive a compensation equal to that allowed to the Speaker of the House of Representatives.

SEC. 20. A Sheriff, and one or more Coroners, a Treasurer, and Surveyor, shall be elected in each county by the qualified electors thereof, who shall hold their offices for two years, unless sooner removed, except that the Coroner shall hold his office until his successor be duly qualified.

SEC. 21. A State Treasurer and Auditor of Public Accounts shall be elected by the qualified electors of the State, who shall hold their offices for the term of two years, unless sooner removed.

ARTICLE V.—LEGISLATIVE DEPARTMENT.

SECTION 1. The legislative authority of this State shall be vested in a Legislature, which shall consist of a Senate and House of Representatives.

SEC. 2. No person holding office under the authority of the United States, except Postmasters, or any lucrative office under the authority of this State, shall be eligible to or have a seat in the Legislature; but this provision shall not extend to township officers, Justices of the Peace, Notaries Public, or military officers.

SEC. 3. No person who has been, or may hereafter be, convicted of a penitentiary offence, or of an embezzlement of the public funds, shall hold any office in this State; nor shall any person holding public money, for disbursement or otherwise, have a seat in the Legislature until he shall have accounted for and paid such money into the treasury.

SEC. 4. The members of the House of Representatives shall be elected by the qualified electors, and shall serve for the term of two years from the close of the general election, and no longer.

SEC. 5. The Senators shall be chosen for the term of four years, at the same time, in the same manner, and at the same places as are herein provided for members of the House of Representatives.

SEC. 6. At the first session of the Legislature, the Senate shall, by lot, divide their Senators into two classes; and the seats of the Senators of the first class shall be vacated at the expiration of the second year, and of the second class at the expiration of the fourth year, so that one-half, as near as may be, may be chosen thereafter every two years for the term of four years.

SEC. 7. The number of Senators shall not be less than thirteen nor more than thirty-three; and at any time when the number of Senators is increased, they shall be annexed by lot to one of the two classes, so as to keep them as nearly equal in number as possible.

SEC. 8. The number of members of the House of Representatives shall not be less than thirty-nine nor more than one hundred.

SEC. 9. The style of the laws of this State shall be, "*Be it enacted by the Legislature of the State of Kansas.*"

SEC. 10. Each house may determine the rules of its own proceedings, punish its members for disorderly behavior, and, with the consent of two-thirds, may expel a member; but not a second time for the same offence. The names of the members voting on the question shall be spread upon the journal.

SEC. 11. Each house during the session may, in its discretion, punish by fine or imprisonment, or both, any person not a member, for disrespectful or disorderly behavior in its presence, or for obstructing any of its proceedings: *Provided*, Such fine shall not exceed two hundred dollars, or such imprisonment shall not extend beyond the end of the session.

SEC. 12. Each house of the Legislature shall keep a journal of its proceedings, and cause the same to be published as soon after the adjournment as may be provided by law.

SEC. 13. Neither house during the session of the Legislature shall, without the consent of the other, adjourn for more than three days (Sundays excepted), nor to any other place than that in which they may be sitting.

SEC. 14. The Senate when assembled shall choose its officers, and the House of Representatives shall choose a Speaker and its other officers; and each branch of the Legislature shall be the judge of the qualifications, elections and returns of its members.

SEC. 15. A majority of each house of the Legislature shall constitute a quorum to do business, but a smaller number may adjourn from day to day, and compel the attendance of absent members in such manner as each house may prescribe.

SEC. 16. Each member of the Legislature shall receive from the public treasury such compensation for his services as may be fixed by law; but no increase of compensation shall take effect during the term for which the members are elected when such law passed.

SEC. 17. Bills may originate in either house, but may be altered, amended, or rejected by the other, and all bills shall be read by sections on three several days, except on an extraordinary occasion; two-thirds of the members may dispense with such reading, but in no case shall a bill be passed without having once been read; and every bill having passed both houses shall be signed by the Speaker and President in the presence of their respective houses.

SEC. 18. The Legislature shall provide by law for filling all vacancies that may occur in either house by the death, resignation, or otherwise, of any of its members.

SEC. 19. The doors of each house shall be open, except on such occasions as, in the opinion of the house, the public safety may require secrecy.

SEC. 20. Every law enacted by the Legislature shall embrace but one subject, and that shall be expressed in its title, and any extraneous matter introduced in a bill which shall pass shall be void; and no law shall be amended by its title, but in such case the act or section amended shall be enacted and published at length.

Sec. 21. Every act and joint resolution shall be plainly worded, avoiding, as far as practicable, the use of technical terms.

Sec. 22. The Legislature shall meet every two years, at the seat of Government.

Sec. 23. The Legislature shall provide for an enumeration of inhabitants by law. An apportionment of Representatives in the Legislature shall be provided by law according to population, as nearly equal as may be.

Sec. 24. The Legislature shall have no power to grant divorces, to change the names of individuals, or direct the sales of estates belonging to infants or other persons laboring under legal disabilities, by special legislation, but by general laws shall confer such powers on the courts of justice.

Sec. 25. It shall be the duty of all civil officers of this State to use due diligence in the securing and rendition of persons held to service or labor in this State, either of the States or Territories of the United States; and the Legislature shall enact such laws as may be necessary for the honest and faithful carrying out of this provision of the Constitution.

ELECTION DISTRICTS.

At the first election holden under this Constitution for members of the State Legislature, the Representative and Senatorial Districts shall be as follows: The First Representative District shall consist of Doniphan county, and be entitled to four Representatives; the Second, Atchison, four Representatives; the Third, Leavenworth, eight Representatives; the Fourth, Brown and Nemaha, one Representative; the Fifth, Calhoun and Pottawatomie, one Representative; the Sixth, Jefferson, two Representatives; the Seventh, Marshall and Washington, one Representative; the Eighth, Riley, one Representative; the Ninth, Johnson, four Representatives; the Tenth, Lykins, one Representative; the Eleventh, Linn, two Representatives; the Twelfth, Bourbon, two Representatives; the Thirteenth, McGee, Dorn and Allen, one Representative; the Fourteenth, Douglas, five Representatives; the Fifteenth, Anderson and Franklin, one Representative; the Sixteenth, Shawnee, two Representatives; the Seventeenth, Weller and Coffey, one Representative; the Eighteenth, Woodson, Wilson, Godfrey, Greenwood and Madison, one Representative; the Nineteenth, Breckinridge and Richardson, one Representative; the Twentieth, Davis, Wise, Butler, Hunter, and that portion of country west, one Representative—in all, forty-four Representatives. The First Senatorial District shall be Doniphan county, and be entitled to one Senator; the Second, Atchison, one Senator; the Third, Doniphan and Atchison, one Senator: the Fourth, Leavenworth, three Senators; the Fifth, Brown, Nemaha and Pottawatomie, one Senator; the Sixth, Riley, Marshall, Dickinson and Washington, one Senator; the Seventh, Jefferson and Calhoun, one Senator; the Eighth, Johnson, two Senators; the Ninth, Lykins, Anderson and Franklin, one Senator; the Tenth, Linn, one Senator; the Eleventh, Bourbon and McGee, one Senator; the Twelfth, Douglas, two Senators; the Thirteenth, Shawnee, one Senator; the Fourteenth, Dorn, Allen, Wilson, Woodson, Godfrey, Greenwood, Madison and Coffey, one Senator; the Fifteenth, Richardson, Davis, Wise, Breckinridge, Butler, Hunter, and all west of Davis, Wise, Butler and Hunter, one Senator. The entire number of Senators, nineteen.

ARTICLE VI.—JUDICIARY.

Section 1. The judicial powers of this State shall be vested in one Supreme Court, Circuit Courts, Chancery Courts, Courts of Probate, and Justices of the Peace, and such other inferior courts as the Legislature may from time to time ordain and establish.

Sec. 2. The Supreme Court, except in cases otherwise directed in this Constitution, shall have appellate jurisdiction only, which shall be coextensive with the State, under such restrictions and regulations, not repugnant to this Constitution, as may from time to time be prescribed by law: *Provided*, That the Supreme Court shall have power to issue writs of injunction, mandamus, quo warranto, habeas corpus, and such other remedial and original writs as may be necessary to give a general superintendence and control of inferior jurisdictions.

Sec. 3. There shall be held annually, at the seat of Government, two sessions of the Supreme Court, at such times as the Legislature may direct.

Sec. 4. The Supreme Court shall consist of one Chief Justice and two Associate Justices.

SEC. 5. The Supreme Court may elect a Clerk and Reporter, who shall, respectively, receive such compensation as the Legislature may prescribe.

SEC. 6. The State shall be divided into convenient circuits, and for each circuit there shall be elected a Judge, who shall, at the time of his election, and as long as he continues in office, reside in the circuit for which he has been elected.

SEC. 7. The Circuit Courts shall have original jurisdiction of all matters, civil and criminal, within this State not otherwise excepted in this Constitution; but in civil cases only where the matter in controversy shall exceed the sum of one hundred dollars.

SEC. 8. A Circuit Court shall be held in each county in this State twice in every year, at such times and places as may be prescribed by law; and the Judges of the several Circuit Courts may hold courts for each other when they may deem it advisable, and shall do so when directed by law.

SEC. 9. The Legislature may establish a Court or Courts of Chancery, with original and appellate equity jurisdiction; and until the establishment of such court or courts the said jurisdiction shall be vested in the Judges of the Circuit Courts, respectively; but the Judges of the several Circuit Courts shall have power to issue writs of injunction, returnable to the Court of Chancery.

SEC. 10. The Legislature shall establish within each county in the State a Court of Probate, for the granting of letters testamentary of the administration, and orphans' business, and the general superintendence of the estates of deceased persons, and such other duties as may be prescribed by law; but in no case shall they have jurisdiction in matters of civil or criminal law.

SEC. 11. A competent number of justices of the peace in and for each county shall be elected in such mode and for such term of office as the Legislature may direct. Their jurisdiction in civil matters shall be limited to cases in which the amount does not exceed one hundred dollars; and in all cases tried by justices of the peace the right of appeal shall be secured under such rules and regulations as may be prescribed by law.

SEC. 12. The Chief Justice and Associate Justices of the Supreme Court, and Judges of the Circuit Court, and Courts of Chancery, shall, at stated times, receive for their services a compensation which shall be fixed by law, and shall not be diminished during their continuance in office; but they shall receive no fees, no perquisites of office, nor hold any other office of profit or trust under this State, the United States, or either of the other States, or any other power, during their continuance in office.

SEC. 13. The Chief Justice and Associate Justices of the Supreme Court shall be elected by the qualified voters of the whole State, the Judges of the Circuit Courts by the qualified voters of their respective circuits, and the Judges of the Chancery Courts shall be elected by the qualified voters of their respective chancery divisions, at such times and places as may be prescribed by law; but said election shall not be on the same day that the election of members of the Legislature is held.

SEC. 14. All vacancies in the office of Chief Justice and Associate Justices of the Supreme Court, and Judges of the Circuit Court, Court of Chancery, and Probate Court, shall be filled by appointment made by the Governor for the time being; but the Governor shall, immediately upon the receipt of information of a vacancy aforesaid, order an election to fill such vacancy, first giving sixty days' notice of such election.

SEC. 15. The Chief Justice and Associate Justices of the Supreme Court shall hold their offices for and during the period of six years from the date of their election, and until their successors shall be qualified, and provision shall be made by law for classifying those elected, so that the Chief Justice or one of the said Associate Justices of the Supreme Court shall be elected every two years. The Judges of the Circuit, Chancery and Probate Courts shall hold their offices for and during the term of four years from the date of their election, and until their successors shall be qualified.

SEC. 16. Clerks of the Circuit Courts and Courts of Probate shall be elected by the qualified electors in each county, and all vacancies in such office shall be filled in such manner as the law may direct.

SEC. 17. The Chief Justice and Associate Justices of the Supreme Court, by virtue of their offices, shall be conservators of the peace throughout the State, the Judges of the Circuit Court throughout their respective circuits, and the Judges of the inferior courts throughout their respective counties.

SEC. 18. The style of all process shall be, "The State of Kansas;" and all prosecutions shall be carried on in the name and by the authority of the State of Kansas, and shall conclude, "against the peace and dignity of the same."

SEC. 19. There shall be an Attorney General of the State, who shall be elected by the qualified voters thereof, and as many District Attorneys as the Legislature may deem necessary, to be elected by the qualified voters of their respective circuits, who shall hold their offices for the term of four years from the date of their election, and shall receive for their services such compensation as may be established by law, which shall not be diminished during their continuance in office.

SEC. 20. Vacancies occurring in the office of Attorney General, District Attorneys, Clerk of the Circuit Court, Clerk of the Court of Probate, justices of the peace, and constables, shall be filled in such manner as shall be provided by law.

SEC. 21. The House of Representatives shall have the sole power of impeachment.

SEC. 22. All impeachments shall be tried by the Senate; when sitting for that purpose the Senators shall be on oath or affirmation; and no person shall be convicted without the concurrence of two-thirds of the members present.

SEC. 23. The Governor and all civil officers shall be liable to impeachment for any misdemeanor in office; but judgment in such cases shall not extend further than to removal from office, and of disqualification from office of honor, trust, or profit under the State; but the party convicted shall, nevertheless, be liable and subject to indictment, trial, and punishment according to law.

ARTICLE VII.— SLAVERY.

SECTION 1. The right of property is before and higher than any constitutional sanction, and the right of the owner of a slave to such slave and its increase is the same and as inviolable as the right of the owner of any property whatever.

SEC. 2. The Legislature shall have no power to pass laws for the emancipation of slaves without the consent of the owners, or without paying the owners previous to their emancipation a full equivalent in money for the slaves so emancipated. They shall have no power to prevent immigrants to the State from bringing with them such persons as are deemed slaves by the laws of any one of the United States or Territories, so long as any person of the same age or description shall be continued in slavery by the laws of this State: *Provided*, That such person or slave be the bona fide property of such immigrants: *And provided, also*, That laws may be passed to prohibit the introduction into this State of slaves who have committed high crimes in other States or Territories. They shall have power to pass laws to permit the owners of slaves to emancipate them, saving the rights of creditors, and preventing them from becoming a public charge. They shall have power to oblige the owners of slaves to treat them with humanity, to provide for them necessary food and clothing, to abstain from all injuries to them extending to life or limb, and, in case of their neglect or refusal to comply with the direction of such laws, to have such slave or slaves sold for the benefit of the owner or owners.

SEC. 3. In the prosecution of slaves for crimes of higher grade than petit larceny, the Legislature shall have no power to deprive them of an impartial trial by a petit jury.

SEC. 4. Any person who shall maliciously dismember, or deprive a slave of life shall suffer such punishment as would be inflicted in case the like offence had been committed on a free white person, and on the like proof, except in case of insurrection of such slave.

ARTICLE VIII.— ELECTIONS AND RIGHTS OF SUFFRAGE.

SECTION 1. Every male citizen of the United States, above the age of twenty-one years, having resided in this State one year, and in the county, city, or town in which he may offer to vote, three months next preceding any election, shall have the qualifications of an elector, and be entitled to vote at all elections. And every male citizen of the United States, above the age aforesaid, who may be a resident of the State at the time that this Constitution shall be adopted, shall have the right of voting as aforesaid; but no such citizen or inhabitant shall be entitled to vote except in the county in which he shall actually reside at the time of the election.

SEC. 2. All voting by the people shall be by ballot.

SEC. 3. Electors, during their attendance at elections, going to and returning therefrom, shall be privileged from arrest in all cases except treason, felony, and breach of the peace.

SEC. 4. No elector shall be obliged to do militia duty on the days of election, except in time of war or public danger.

SEC. 5. No elector shall be deemed to have lost his residence in this State by reason of his absence on business of his own, or of the United States, or of this State.

SEC. 6. No person employed in the military, naval or marine service of the United States stationed in this State, shall, by reason of his services therein, be deemed a resident of this State.

SEC. 7. No person shall be elected or appointed to any office in this State, civil or military, who shall not be possessed of the qualifications hereinbefore prescribed for an elector.

SEC. 8. The Legislature shall have power to exclude from the privilege of voting, or being eligible to office, any person convicted of bribery, perjury, or other infamous crimes.

SEC. 9. The first general election in this State shall be held on the day and year provided by this Constitution, and all general elections thereafter on the day and year provided by subsequent legislative enactment.

ARTICLE IX.—FINANCE.

SECTION 1. The rule of taxation shall be uniform, and taxes shall be levied upon such property as the Legislature shall from time to time prescribe.

SEC. 2. The Legislature shall provide for an annual tax sufficient to defray the estimated expenses of the Government for each year; and whenever the expenses of any one year shall exceed the income, the Legislature shall provide for levying a tax for the ensuing year sufficient, with other sources of income, to pay the deficiency as well as the estimated expenses for such ensuing year.

SEC. 3. For the purpose of defraying extraordinary expenditures, the State may contract public debts; but such debts, in the aggregate, shall never exceed five hundred thousand dollars. Every such debt shall be authorized by law for some purpose or purposes, to be distinctly specified therein, and a vote of a majority of all the members elected to both houses shall be necessary to the passage of such law, and such law shall provide for an annual tax to be levied sufficient to pay the interest of such debt created; and such appropriation shall not be repealed, nor the taxes postponed, until the principal and interest of such debt shall have been wholly paid.

SEC. 4. The Legislature may also borrow money for the purpose of repelling invasion, suppressing insurrection, and defending the State in time of war; but the money thus raised shall be applied exclusively to the purposes for which it was raised.

SEC. 5. No scrip, certificate, or other evidence of State debt shall be issued, except for such debts as are authorized by the third or fourth sections of this article.

SEC. 6. The property of the State and counties, both real and personal, and such other property as the Legislature may deem necessary for school, religious or charitable purposes, may be exempted from taxation.

SEC. 7. No money shall at any time be paid out of the treasury except in pursuance of an appropriation by law.

SEC. 8. An accurate statement of the receipts and expenditures of the public money shall be published with the laws of each regular session of the Legislature.

ARTICLE X.—REVENUE.

SECTION 1. All bills for raising revenue shall originate in the House of Representatives.

SEC. 2. Taxation shall be equal and uniform, and all property on which taxes shall be levied shall be taxed in proportion to its value, to be ascertained as directed by legislative enactment, and no one species of property shall be taxed higher than another species of property of equal value on which taxes shall be levied.

SEC. 3. The Legislature shall have power to levy an income tax, and to tax all persons pursuing any occupation, trade, or profession.

SEC. 4. The Legislature shall provide for the classification of the lands of this State into three distinct classes, to be styled, respectively, Class One, Two, Three; and each of these classes shall have a fixed value in so much money, upon which there shall be assessed an ad valorem tax.

SEC. 5. The Legislature shall provide for a capitation or poll-tax, to be paid by every able-bodied male citizen over twenty-one years and under sixty years of age, but nothing herein contained shall prevent the exemption of taxable polls in cases of bodily infirmity.

SEC. 6. The Legislature shall levy a tax on all railroad incomes proceeding from gifts of public lands, at the rate of ten cents on the one hundred dollars.

SEC. 7. No lotteries shall be authorized by law as a source of revenue.

SEC. 8. Whatever donations of lands or money that may be received from the General Government by this State shall be regarded as a source of revenue, subject to a compact made with the United States by special ordinance.

ARTICLE XI.—PUBLIC DOMAIN AND INTERNAL IMPROVEMENT.

SECTION 1. It shall be the duty of the Legislature to provide for the prevention of waste and damage of the public land now possessed or that may hereafter be ceded to the Territory or State of Kansas, and it may pass laws for the sale of any part or portion thereof, and, in such case, provide for the safety, security, and appropriation of the proceeds.

SEC. 2. A liberal system of internal improvements being essential to the development of the resources of the country, shall be encouraged by the Government of this State; and it shall be the duty of the Legislature, as soon as practicable, to ascertain by law proper objects of improvement, in relation to roads, canals and navigable streams, and to provide for a suitable application of such funds as may be appropriated for such improvements.

ARTICLE XII.—CORPORATIONS.

SECTION 1. Corporations may be formed under a general law, but the Legislature may by special act create bodies politic for municipal purposes, where the objects of the corporations cannot be attained under it. All general laws or special acts enacted under the provisions of this section may be altered, amended, or repealed by the Legislature at any time.

SEC. 2. No corporation shall take private property for public use without first having the consent of the owner, or where the necessity thereof being first established by a verdict of a jury, and the value thereof assessed and paid.

SEC. 3. It shall be the duty of the Legislature to provide for the organization of cities and incorporated villages, and to restrict their power of taxation, borrowing money, contracting debts, and loaning their credit, so as to prevent abuses.

SEC. 4. The Legislature may incorporate banks of deposit and exchange, but such banks shall not issue any bills, notes, checks, or other paper as money.

SEC. 5. The Legislature may incorporate one bank of discount and issue, with not more than two branches, provided that the act incorporating said bank and branches thereof shall not take effect until it shall be submitted to the people at the general election next succeeding the passage of the same, and shall have been approved by a majority of the electors voting at such election.

SEC. 6. The said bank and branches shall be mutually liable for each other's debts or liabilities for all paper credits or bills issued representing money; and the stockholders in said bank or branches shall be individually responsible to an amount equal to the stock held by them for all debts or liabilities of said bank or branches; and no law shall be passed sanctioning directly or indirectly the suspension by said bank or its branches of specie payment.

SEC. 7. The State shall not be a stockholder in any bank, nor shall the credit of the State be given or loaned in aid of any person, association, or incorporation, nor shall the State become a stockholder in any corporation or association.

ARTICLE XIII.—MILITIA.

SECTION 1. The militia of this State shall consist of all the able-bodied male citizens of the State between the ages of eighteen and forty-five years, except such citizens as are now, or hereafter may be, exempted by the laws of the United States or of this State.

SEC. 2. Any citizen whose religious tenets conflict with bearing arms shall not be compelled to do militia duty in time of peace, but shall pay such an equivalent for personal services as may be prescribed by law.

SEC. 3. All militia officers shall be elected by the persons subject to military duty within the bounds of their several companies, battalions, regiments, brigades and divisions, under such rules and regulations as the Legislature may from time to time direct and establish.

ARTICLE XIV.—EDUCATION.

SECTION 1. A general diffusion of knowledge being essential to the preservation of the rights and liberties of the people, schools and the means of education shall be forever encouraged in this State.

SEC. 2. The Legislature shall take measures to preserve from waste and damage such lands as have been, or hereafter may be, granted by the United States, or lands or funds which may be received from other sources, for the use of schools within this State, and shall apply the funds which may arise from such lands, or from any other source, in strict conformity with the object of the grant.

SEC. 3. The Legislature shall, as soon as practicable, establish one common school (or more) in each township in the State, where the children of the township shall be taught gratis.

SEC. 4. The Legislature shall have power to make appropriations from the State treasury for the support and maintenance of common schools, whenever the funds accruing from the lands donated by the United States, or the funds received from other sources, are insufficient for that purpose.

SEC. 5. The Legislature shall have power to pass laws for the government of all common schools within this State.

ARTICLE XV.—MISCELLANEOUS.

SECTION 1. Lecompton shall be the seat of government until otherwise directed by law, two-thirds of each house of the Legislature concurring in the passage of such law.

SEC. 2. Every person chosen or appointed to any office under this State, before entering upon the discharge of its duties, shall take an oath or affirmation to support the Constitution of the United States, the Constitution of this State, and all laws made in pursuance thereof, and faithfully to demean himself in the discharge of the duties of his office.

SEC. 3. The laws, public records, and the written, judicial, and legislative proceedings of the State, shall be conducted, promulgated, and preserved in the English language.

SEC. 4. Aliens who are, or may hereafter become, bona fide residents of this State shall enjoy the same rights, in respect to the possession, inheritance, and enjoyment of property, as native-born citizens.

SEC. 5. No county seat shall be removed until the point to which it is proposed to be removed shall be fixed by law, and a majority of the voters of the county voting on the question shall have voted in favor of its removal to such point.

SEC. 6. All property, both real and personal, of the wife, owned or claimed by marriage, and that acquired afterwards by gift, devise, or descent, shall be her separate property; and laws shall be passed more clearly defining the rights of the wife, in relation as well to her separate property as to that held in common with her husband. Laws shall also be passed providing for the registration of the wife's separate property.

SEC. 7. The privilege of free suffrage shall be supported by laws regulating elections, and prohibiting, under adequate penalties, all undue influence thereon from power, bribery, tumult, or other improper practice.

SEC. 8. Treason against the State shall consist only in levying war against it, or adhering to its enemies, giving them aid and comfort. No person shall be convicted of treason unless on the testimony of two witnesses to the same overt act, or his own confession in open court.

BILL OF RIGHTS.

That the great and essential principles of liberty and free government may be recognized and established, we declare:

1. That all freemen, when they form a social compact, are equal in rights, and that no man or set of men are entitled to exclusive separate public emoluments or privileges, but in consideration of public services.

2. All political power is inherent in the people, and all free governments are founded on their authority, and instituted for their benefit; and therefore they have at all times an inalienable and indefeasible right to alter, reform, or abolish their form of government in such manner as they may think proper.

3. That all persons have a natural and indefeasible right to worship Almighty God according to the dictates of their own conscience, and no person can of right be compelled to attend, erect, or support any place of worship, or maintain any ministry, against his consent. That no human authority can in any case whatever interfere with the rights of conscience, and that no preference shall ever be given to any religious establishment or mode of worship.

4. That the civil rights, privileges, or capacities of a citizen shall in nowise be diminished or enlarged on account of his religion.

5. That all elections shall be free and equal.

6. That the right of trial by jury shall remain inviolate.

7. Every citizen may freely speak, write, and publish his sentiments on all subjects, being responsible for the abuse of that right.

8. The people shall be secure in their persons, houses, papers, and possessions, from unreasonable seizures and searches; and no warrant to search any place, or to seize any person or thing, shall issue without probable cause, supported by oath or affirmation. In all criminal prosecutions the accused has a right to be heard by himself or counsel; to demand the nature and cause of the accusation, and have a copy thereof; to be confronted by the witness or witnesses against him; to have compulsory process for obtaining witnesses in his favor, and in all prosecutions by indictments or informations, a speedy public trial by an impartial jury of the county or district in which the offence shall have been committed. He shall not be compelled to give evidence against himself, nor shall he be deprived of his life, liberty, or property, but by due course of law.

9. That no freeman shall be taken or imprisoned, or disseized of his freehold, liberties or privileges, or outlawed or exiled, or in any manner destroyed or deprived of his life, liberty, or property, but by the judgment of his peers, or the law of the land.

10. No person, for the same offence, shall twice be put in jeopardy of life, limb, or liberty; nor shall any person's property be taken or applied to the public use, unless compensation be made therefor.

11. That all penalties shall be reasonable, and proportionate to the nature of the offence.

12. No person shall be held to answer a capital or otherwise infamous crime, unless on the presentment or indictment of a grand jury, or by impeachment, except in cases of rebellion, insurrection, or invasion.

13. That no conviction shall work corruption of blood or forfeiture of estate.

14. That all prisoners shall be bailable by sufficient securities, unless in capital offences, where the proof is evident or the presumption great; and the privileges of habeas corpus shall not be suspended unless, when in the cases of rebellion [insurrection] or invasion, the public safety may require it.

15. That excessive bail shall in no case be required, nor excessive fines imposed.

16. That no "ex post facto" law, nor any law impairing the obligations of contracts, shall ever be made.

17. That forfeitures and monopolies are contrary to the genius of a republic, and shall not be allowed; nor shall any hereditary emolument, privileges or honors ever be granted or conferred in this State.

18. That the citizens have a right, in a peaceable manner, to assemble together for their common good; to instruct their representatives, and to apply to those entrusted with the power of government for redress of grievances, or other purposes, by address or remonstrance.

19. That the citizens of this State shall have a right to keep and bear arms for their common defence.

20. That no soldier shall in time of peace be quartered in any house without the consent of the owner, nor in time of war but in a manner prescribed by law.

21. The military shall be kept in strict subordination to the civil power.

22. Emigration to or from this State shall not be prohibited.

23. Free negroes shall not be permitted to live in this State under any circumstances.

24. This enumeration of rights shall not be construed to deny or disparage others retained by the people; and to guard against any encroachments on the rights herein retained, or any transgression of any of the higher power herein delegated, we declare that everything in this article is excepted out of the general powers of government, and

shall forever remain inviolate, and that all laws contrary thereto, or to the other provisions herein contained, shall be void.

SCHEDULE.

SECTION 1. That no inconvenience may arise by reason of a change from a Territorial to a permanent State Government, it is declared that all rights, actions, prosecutions, judgments, claims, and contracts, as well of individuals as of bodies corporate, except the bill incorporating banks by the last Territorial Legislature, shall continue as if no such change had taken place; and all processes which may have issued under the authority of the Territory of Kansas shall be as valid as if issued in the name of the State of Kansas.

SEC. 2. All laws now in force in the Territory of Kansas, which are not repugnant to this Constitution, shall continue and be of force until altered, amended, or repealed, by a Legislature assembled under the provisions of this Constitution.

SEC. 3. All fines, penalties, and forfeitures to the Territory of Kansas shall inure to the use of the State of Kansas.

SEC. 4. All recognizances heretofore taken shall pass to, and be prosecuted in the name of the State of Kansas, and all bonds executed to the Governor of the Territory, or to any other officer of the Court in his or their official capacity, shall pass to the Governor and corresponding officers of the State authority and their successors in office, and for the use therein expressed, and may be sued for and recovered accordingly; and all the estates or property, real, personal, or mixed, and all judgments, bonds, specialties, choses in action, and claims or debts of whatever description, of the Territory of Kansas, shall inure to, and rest in, the State of Kansas, and be sued for and recovered in the same manner and to the same extent as the same could have been by the Territory of Kansas.

SEC. 5. All criminal prosecutions and penal actions, which may have arisen before the change from a Territorial to a State Government, and which shall then be pending, shall be prosecuted to judgment in the name of the State of Kansas. All actions at law and suits in equity, which may be pending in the courts of the Territory of Kansas, at the time of a change from a Territorial to a State Government, may be continued and transferred to any court of the State, which shall have jurisdiction of the subject-matter thereof.

SEC. 6. All officers, civil and military, holding their offices under authority of the Territory of Kansas, shall continue to hold and exercise their respective offices until they shall be superseded by the authority of the State.

SEC. 7. This Constitution shall be submitted to the Congress of the United States at its next ensuing session, and as soon as official information has been received that it is approved by the same, by the admission of the State of Kansas as one of the sovereign States of the United States, the President of this Convention shall issue his proclamation to convene the State Legislature at the seat of Government, within thirty-one days after publication. Should any vacancy occur, by death, resignation or otherwise, in the Legislature, or other office, he shall order an election to fill such vacancy: *Provided, however,* In case of removal, absence or disability of the President of this Convention to discharge the duties herein imposed on him, the President *pro tempore* of this Convention shall perform said duties, and in case of absence, refusal or disability of the President *pro tempore*, a committee consisting of seven, or a majority of them, shall discharge the duties required of the President of this Convention.

Before this Constitution shall be sent to Congress, asking for admission into the Union as a State, it shall be submitted to all the white male inhabitants of this Territory, for approval or disapproval, as follows: The President of this Convention shall, by proclamation, declare that on the twenty-first day of December, one thousand eight hundred and fifty-seven, at the different election precincts now established by law, or which may be established as herein provided, in the Territory of Kansas, an election shall be held, over which shall preside three judges, or a majority of them, to be appointed as follows: The President of this Convention shall appoint three commissioners in each county in the Territory, whose duty it shall be to appoint three judges of election in the several precincts of their respective counties, and to establish precincts for voting, and to cause polls to be opened, at such places as they may deem proper in their respective counties, at which election the Constitution framed by this Convention shall

10

be submitted to all the white male inhabitants of the Territory of Kansas in the said Territory upon that day, and over the age of twenty-one years, for ratification or rejection, in the following manner and form: The voting shall be by ballot. The judges of said election shall cause to be kept two poll-books by two clerks, by them appointed. The ballots cast at said election shall be endorsed, "Constitution with Slavery," and "Constitution with no Slavery." One of said poll-books shall be returned within eight days to the President of this Convention, and the other shall be retained by the judges of election and kept open for inspection. The President, with two or more members of this Convention, shall examine said poll-books, and if it shall appear upon said examination that a majority of the legal votes cast at said election be in favor of the "Constitution with Slavery," he shall immediately have the same transmitted to Congress of the United States, as hereinbefore provided; but if, upon such examination of said poll-books, it shall appear that a majority of the legal votes cast at said election be in favor of the "Constitution with no Slavery," then the article providing for Slavery shall be stricken from this Constitution by the President of this Convention, and Slavery shall no longer exist in the State of Kansas, except that the right of property in slaves now in this Territory shall in no manner be interfered with, and shall have transmitted the Constitution, so ratified, [to Congress the Constitution, so ratified,] to the Congress of the United States, as hereinbefore provided. In case of the failure of the President of this Convention to perform the duties imposed upon him in the foregoing section, by reason of death, resignation or otherwise, the same duties shall devolve upon the President *pro tem.*

SEC. 8. There shall be a general election upon the first Monday in January, eighteen hundred and fifty-eight, to be conducted as the election provided for in the seventh section of this article, at which election there shall be chosen a Governor, Lieutenant Governor, Secretary of State, State Treasurer, and members of the Legislature, and also a member of Congress.

SEC. 9. Any person offering to vote at the aforesaid election upon said Constitution shall be challenged to take an oath to support the Constitution of the United States, and to support this Constitution, under the penalties of perjury under the Territorial laws.

SEC. 10. All officers appointed to carry into execution the provisions of the foregoing sections shall, before entering upon their duties, be sworn to faithfully perform the duties of their offices, and in failure thereof be subject to the same charges and penalties as are provided in like cases under the Territorial laws.

SEC. 11. The officers provided for in the preceding sections shall receive for their services the same compensation as given to officers performing similar duties under the Territorial laws.

SEC. 12. The Governor and all other officers shall enter upon the discharge of their respective duties as soon after the admission of the State of Kansas, as one of the independent and sovereign States of the Union, as may be convenient.

SEC. 13. Oaths of office may be administered by any judge, justice of the peace, or clerk of any court of record of the Territory or the State of Kansas, until the Legislature may otherwise direct.

SEC. 14. After the year one thousand eight hundred and sixty-four, whenever the Legislature shall think it necessary to amend, alter, or change this Constitution, they shall recommend to the electors at the next general election, two-thirds of the members of each house concurring, to vote for or against calling a convention; and if it shall appear that a majority of all citizens of the State have voted for a convention, the Legislature shall at its next regular session call a convention, to consist of as many members as there may be in the House of Representatives at the time, to be chosen in the same manner, at the same places, and by the same electors that choose the Representatives. Said delegates so elected shall meet within three months after said election, for the purpose of revising, amending, or changing the Constitution; but no alteration shall be made to affect the rights of property in the ownership of slaves.

SEC. 15. Until the Legislature elected in accordance with the provisions of this Constitution shall otherwise direct, the salary of the Governor shall be three thousand dollars, and the salary of Lieutenant Governor shall be double the pay of a State Senator, and the pay of members of the Legislature shall be five dollars per diem, until otherwise provided by the first Legislature, which shall fix the salaries of all officers other than those elected by the people at first election.

SEC. 16. This Constitution shall take effect and be in force from and after its ratification by the people as hereinbefore provided.

Done in convention at Lecompton, in the Territory of Kansas, on the seventh day of November, in the year of our Lord one thousand eight hundred and fifty-seven, and of the independence of the United States of America the eighty-second. In testimony whereof, we have hereunto subscribed our names.

JESSE CONNELL,
JOHN DALE HENDERSON,
HUGH M. MOORE, .
JARRETT TODD,
WILBURN CHRISTISON,
SAMUEL J. KOOKAGEE,
LUCIEN J. EASTIN,
WM. WALKER,
JOHN W. MARTIN,
GREENE B. REDMAN,
    Leavenworth County.

CYRUS DOLMAN,
HENRY SMITH,
    Brown and Nemaha Cos.

W. S. WELLS,
ALFRED W. JONES,
OWEN C. STEWART,
L. S. BOLING,
W. T. SPICELY,
H. BUTCHER,
    Douglas County.

THOS. J. KEY,
SAMUEL P. BLAIR,
JAMES J. REYNOLDS,
WILLIAM MATHEWS,
D. VANDERSLICE,
HARVEY W. FORMAN,
    Doniphan County.

MILTON E. BRYANT,
    Linn County.

JUN. T. HEREFORD,
ISAAC S. HASCAL,
JAMES ADKINS,
    Atchison County.

JACOB T. BRADFORD,
WM. A. HASKELL,
    Lykins County.

THOS. D. CHILDS,
ALEXANDER BAYNE,
W. H. SWIFT,
    Jefferson County.

G. W. McKOWN,
BATT. JONES,
J. H. DANFORTH,
    Johnson County.

WM. H. JENKINS,
    Marshall County.

JOHN S. RANDOLPH,
C. K. MOBLEY,
    Riley County.

HENRY D. ODEN,
    Calhoun County.

SAMUEL G. REED,
RUSH ELMORE,
    Shawnee County.

H. T. WILSON,
B. LITTLE,
    Bourbon County.

J. CALHOUN,
President of the Convention, and Delegate from the County of Douglas.

CHARLES J. McILVAINE, *Secretary of the Convention.*

ORDINANCE.

WHEREAS, The Government of the United States is the proprietor, or will become so, of all or most of the lands lying within the limits of Kansas, as determined under the Constitution; and whereas, the State of Kansas will possess the undoubted right to tax such lands for the support of her State Government, or for other proper and legitimate purposes connected with her existence as a State: Now, therefore, be it ordained by this Convention, on behalf of and by the authority of the people of Kansas, that the right aforesaid to tax such lands shall be and is hereby forever relinquished, if the conditions following shall be accepted and agreed to by the Congress of the United States:

SECTION 1. That sections numbered 8, 16, 24, and 36, in every township in the State, or in case either of said numbered sections are or shall be otherwise disposed of, that other lands, equal thereto in value, and as contiguous as may be, shall be granted to the State, to be applied exclusively to the support of common schools.

SEC. 2. That all salt springs, and gold, silver, copper, lead, or other valuable mines, together with the lands necessary for their full occupation and use, shall be granted to said State for the use and benefit of said State; and the same shall be used or disposed of under such terms and conditions and regulations as the Legislature of said State shall direct.

SEC. 3. That five per centum of the proceeds of the sales of all public lands sold or held in trust or otherwise lying within the said State, whether sold before or after the admission of the State into the Union, after deducting all expenses incidental to the same, shall be paid to the said State of Kansas for the purposes following, to wit: two-fifths to be disbursed under the direction of the Legislature of the State for the purpose of aiding the construction of railroads within said State, and the residue for the support of common schools.

SEC. 4. That seventy-two sections, or two entire townships, shall be designated by the President of the United States, which shall be reserved for the use of a seminary of learning, and appropriated by the Legislature of said State solely to the use of said seminary.

SEC. 5. That each alternate section of land now owned, or which may hereafter be acquired by the United States, for twelve miles on each side of a line of railroad to be established or located from some point on the northern boundary of the State, leading southerly through said State in the direction of the Gulf of Mexico, and on each side of a line of railroad to be located and established from some point on the Missouri river westwardly through said State in the direction of the Pacific ocean, shall be reserved and conveyed to said State of Kansas for the purpose of aiding in the construction of said railroad; and it shall be the duty of the Congress of the United States, in conjunction with the proper authorities of this State, to adopt immediate measures for carrying the several provisions herein contained into full effect.

SEPTEMBER 15.—The committee appointed at Grasshopper Falls issue an address to the people. The following is quoted from it:

"The system of districting and apportionment for members of the Legislature shows an unquestionable determination to introduce voters from abroad. Sixteen counties, strongly Free-State, containing nearly one-half of the entire population of the Territory, are not allowed a single representative in either branch. Of the thirteen members of the Council, all but three, and of the thirty-nine members of the House of Representatives, all but ten, are to be elected in districts bordering on the Missouri line. Topeka is connected with Fort Scott, and Lawrence is attached to the Shawnee Mission, adjoining Westport."

SEPTEMBER 16.—Gov. Walker issues an address to the people of Kansas. He assures the people that the October election shall be fair and free. The two parties of Kansas will then, for the first time, measure their strength, "at the same times and places," at the ballot-box.

OCTOBER 5.—Election of the Territorial Legislature.

	Free-State.	Democratic.	House.	Council.
Leavenworth	1,083	1,370	8 (d.)	3 (d.)
Atchison	315	366	3 (d.)	1 (d.)
Doniphan	574	497	5 (f.)	
Brown	138	72	1 (f.)	
Nemaha	145	30		2 (f.)
Marshall	1	160	1 (d.)	
Pottawatomie	151	16	2 (f.)	
Riley	251	106		
Jefferson	344	189	2 (f.)	
Calhoun	200	39	1 (f.)	1 (f.)
Douglas	1,683	187	8 (f.)	3 (f.)
Johnson	33	1,604		
Shawnee	749	61	1 (f.)	
Richardson	127	....		
Davis	126	30		
Wise and Breckinridge	266	7		
Madison and Butler	69	7		
Bourbon	96	175		
Dorn	....	18		
Coffey	265	48		2 (f.)
McGee	24	1,202	3 (d.)	
Woodson	....	....		
Weller	....	....		
Godfrey	....	....		
Wilson	....	....		
Greenwood	14	13		
Allen	65	20		
Anderson	261	2		
Franklin	345	10		1 (f.)
Lykins	348	59	2 (f.)	
Linn	214	178	2 (f.)	

(f.) Free State   (d.) Democratic.

The one Free-State vote in Marshall county was cast by James White. The illegal votes in Johnson and McGee counties were thrown out. These returns result as follows:

	Free State.	*Democratic.*	*Whole No.*
Council	9	4	13
House	24	15	39

The candidates for the Legislature are given below:

COUNCIL.

County.	*Free-State.*	*Democratic.*
Leavenworth	Robert Crozier............	John A. Halderman.
	Jos. P. Root.................	J. W. Martin.
	J. Wright.................	Alson C. Davis.
Atchison............................	Caleb May.................	Jos. P. Carr.
Doniphan, Brown, Nemaha, Marshall,	Benj. Harding	Frank J. Marshall.
[Riley, and Pottawatomie	Andrew J. Mead..........	Henry S. Creal.
Jefferson and Calhoun.................	A. G. Patrick	C. Buck.
Douglas and Johnson...................	Carmi W. Babcock.......	H. M. Bledsoe.
	Lyman Allen	Wm. H. Hull.
	Edwin S. Nash.............	S. J. Jones.
Anderson, Franklin, Lykins and Linn	H. B. Standiford..........	L. B. Williams.
The seventeen remaining counties......	Oscar E Learnard	Geo. A. Crawford.
	Cyrus K. Holliday	Benj. I. Newsom.

HOUSE.

County.	*Free-State.*	*Democratic.*
Leavenworth	H. Miles Moore	Hugh M. Moore.
	Geo. H. Keller...............	H. B. Denman.
	W. M. McClure	A. B. Hazzard.
	J. P. Hatterscheidt..........	B. Johnson.
	Owen A. Bassett.............	T. B. Whitesides.
	Wm. Pennock...............	A. B. Bartlett.
	R. G. Elliott	S. Armstrong.
	P. R. Orr......................	W. H. Sharp.
Atchison...........................	John P. Wheeler.............	J. H. Miller.
	Caleb Woodworth...........	John Bennett.
	S. J. H. Snyder..............	Jas. Adkins.
Doniphan...........................	Benj. H. Brock...............	And'n Miller.
	Alex. A. Jamieson...........	Sidney Tennent.
	Harris Stratton..............	John Starwalt.
	C. Graham...................	John R. Boyd.
	John B. Wheeler.............	Wm. Word.
Brown and Nemaha...................	E. N. Morrill.................	E. M. Hubbard.
Marshall	W. S. Blackburn	J. P. Miller.
Riley and Pottawatomie..............	Abram Barry.................	Geo. Montague.
	Chas. Jenkins...............	S. G. Menzies.
Jefferson...........................	S. S. Cooper	C. L. Freeman.
	Henry Owen.................	W. W. Gregg.
Calhoun	A. Reynard.................	A. Davidson.
Douglas and Johnson	John Speer	J. H. Danforth.
	G. W. Deitzler	T. B. Sykes.
	Oliver Barber.................	J. P. Thompson.
	H. Appleman...............	U. B. Windsor.
	A. T. Still.................	A. P. Walker.
	G. W. Zinn	W. S. Wells.
	G. Seymour	John Ector.
	John Lockhart...............	L. S. Boling.
Shawnee	Jas. A. Delong	Wm. S. Romigh.
Lykins	A. J. Shannon.............	J. J. Parks.
	John Hanna.................	J. H. King.
Linn	A. Danford.................	J. H. Barlow.
	R. B. Mitchell.............	J. E. Mooney.
The eighteen remaining counties.......	Samuel Stewart	J. Head.
	C. Columbia.................	N. S. Goss.
	John Curtis.................	L. E. Rhodes.

OCTOBER 5.—Election of Delegate in Congress.

LEAVENWORTH COUNTY. Precincts.	E. Ransom...	M.J.Parrott.
Delaware	92	56
Leavenworth.................	275	511
Kickapoo.....................	728	171
Wyandotte	134	200
Stranger	63	168
	1,297	1,046

ATCHISON COUNTY.	E. Ransom...	M.J.Parrott.
Grasshopper	31	55
Walnut	88	22
Mount Pleasant..............	42	80
Shannon......................	205	158
	366	315

DONIPHAN COUNTY.	E. Ransom...	M.J.Parrott.
Centre Township.............	69	57
Iowa..........................	110	113
Wolf River	51	53
Palermo......................	23	50
Washington..................	54	79
Wayne	163	147
Burr Oak	27	75
	497	574

BROWN COUNTY.	E. Ransom...	M.J.Parrott.
Walnut Creek.................	3	46
Locknane.....................	11	10
Irving........................	23	43
Claytonville..................	35	37
	72	136

MARSHALL COUNTY.	E. Ransom...	M.J.Parrott.
Marysville....................	160	1

NEMAHA COUNTY.	E. Ransom...	M.J.Parrott.
Red Vermilion...............	1	44
Richmond....................	8	66
Capioma......................	5	10
Grenada......................	13	7
Wheatland	2	18
	30	145

RILEY COUNTY.	E. Ransom...	M.J.Parrott.
Manhattan....................	5	123
Montague.....................	15	31
Ogden........................	80	79
Randolph.....................	6	18
	106	251

POTTAWATOMIE COUNTY.	E. Ransom...	M.J.Parrott.
Louisville....................	10	30
St George....................	1	22
Pottawatomie................	1	34
Vienna.......................	—	11
Blue	4	51
	16	148

JEFFERSON COUNTY.	E. Ransom...	M.J.Parrott.
Slough Creek.................	46	56
Hickory Point................	35	43
Osawkee......................	44	63
Kaw City	6	—
Kentucky	42	12
Grasshopper Falls............	16	170
	189	344

CALHOUN COUNTY. Precincts.	E. Ransom...	M.J.Parrott.
Half-Day	4	55
Atchison	12	29
Franklin......................	10	94
Douglas......................	13	27
	39	205

JOHNSON COUNTY.	E. Ransom...	M.J.Parrott.
*Oxford......................	—	—
McCamish....................	10	32
Lexington....................	39	19
Monticello...................	48	6
Shawnee	68	13
Spring Hill...................	6	7
Olathe	41	19
	212	96

* For Justice of the Peace 124 votes were polled; all Democratic.

DOUGLAS COUNTY.	E. Ransom...	M.J.Parrott.
Lecompton	138	294
Washington	34	268
Calhoun......................	4	215
Wakarusa	11	905
	187	1,682

SHAWNEE COUNTY.	E. Ransom...	M.J.Parrott.
Tecumseh.....................	52	126
Topeka........................	4	334
Burlingame...................	—	112
Wakarusa	5	91
Brownsville..................	—	86
	61	749

RICHARDSON COUNTY.	E. Ransom...	M.J.Parrott.
Wabaunsee...................	—	74
Alma	—	37
Mission	—	16
	—	127

DAVIS COUNTY.	E. Ransom...	M.J.Parrott.
Ashland	11	33
Chelolah	2	8
Clark Creek..................	—	19
Zeandale.....................	—	46
Riley City....................	17	20
	30	126

BRECKINRIDGE COUNTY.	E. Ransom...	M.J.Parrott.
Emporia	—	137
Americus.....................	—	36
Geo. Newberry's	2	25
J. Nathan Cory's.............	—	41
Agnes City...................	5	27
	7	266

BOURBON COUNTY.	E. Ransom...	M.J.Parrott.
Drywood......................	9	3
Russell.......................	12	2
Fort Scott....................	99	24
Sprattsville	33	47
Osage	22	20
	175	96

DORN COUNTY.	E. Ransom...	M.J.Parrott.
Dorn.........................	18	—

•

ALLEN COUNTY. Precincts.	E. Ransom	M. J. Parrott
Deer Creek	1	33
Cofachique	16	20
Cole Creek	3	12
	20	65
GREENWOOD COUNTY.		
Greenville	8	6
Pleasant Grove	5	8
	13	14
COFFEY COUNTY.		
Neosho City	2	51
Burlington	—	133
LeRoy	26	31
Ottumwa	20	50
	48	265
MADISON COUNTY.		
Columbia	7	69
LYKINS COUNTY.		
Miami	4	23
Stanton	4	60
Paola	51	26
Osawatomie	—	239
	59	348

FRANKLIN COUNTY. Precincts.	E. Ransom	M. J. Parrott
St. Bernard	2	153
Musquito Branch	—	90
Peoria	1	66
Ohio City	7	36
	10	345
ANDERSON COUNTY.		
Cresco	1	35
Addington	—	32
Shannon	1	66
Greeley	—	68
Hyatt	—	60
	2	261
LINN COUNTY.		
Paris Township	65	79
Tate	39	25
Centreville	14	23
Scott	33	—
Mound City	2	63
Potosi	10	4
Jackson	4	12
Breckinridge	11	8
	178	214

Total vote for E. Ransom 3,799
Total vote for M. J. Parrott 7,888

Free-State majority 4,089

Oxford, in Johnson county, near Missouri, polled 1,628 Pro-Slavery votes, nearly all illegal. McGee county polled 1,200 Pro-Slavery votes, nearly all illegal. Kickapoo did the same. Governor Walker set the election returns aside for informality, not for fraud.

OCTOBER.—Baker University established at Palmyra, twelve miles south of Lawrence, now Baldwin City.

—Gerrit Smith, who had been giving $1,000 a month for the relief of Kansas, discontinues the princely donation.

OCTOBER 19.—Governor Walker and Secretary Stanton issue a proclamation rejecting the whole return from Oxford precinct, Johnson county, which represented that 1,628 votes had been cast there on the 5th and 6th instant. This return was a manuscript roll fifty feet long, containing the names of 1,628 persons as having voted at Oxford precinct—a place containing eleven houses. If admitted, by transferring from the Free-State to the Pro-Slavery side three Councilmen and eight Representatives for the district of which this precinct formed a part, it would have changed the party character of the Legislature.

A Free-State meeting was held at Lecompton October 19. Philip C. Schuyler was President, and Richard Realf and O. E. Learnard Secretaries. Resolutions were passed exposing the fraudulent vote cast at Oxford, Kickapoo, and in McGee county.

OCTOBER 20.—A Democratic meeting held in Lecompton passes seventeen resolutions condemning Walker and Stanton. Dr. B. Little, of Bourbon county, is Chairman, and Major G. D. Hand, of Johnson county, Secretary.

OCTOBER 20.—Judge Cato, of the Second District, issues a peremptory mandamus to Governor Walker and Secretary Stanton to compel them to issue certificates of election to the Pro-Slavery candidates for the Legislature in Douglas and Johnson counties, who claimed an election through the fraudulent vote cast at Oxford. A written refusal was sent to Judge Cato.

OCTOBER 22.—Governor Walker and Secretary Stanton issue a proclamation rejecting the returns from McGee county, where three precincts had cast more than 1,200 votes. This county covered the Cherokee Indian land, in the southeastern part of the State.

The Free-State or Republican Party has carried every election in Kansas since this date—usually by two to one.

OCTOBER 27.—Certificate of election issued to Marcus J. Parrott, elected Delegate to the Thirty-fifth Congress.

OCTOBER 31.—The first court ever held in Lawrence now in session; Samuel N. Wood, Justice of the Peace.

NOVEMBER 1.—Robert Crozier sells his interest in the Leavenworth Times to Champion Vaughan.

NOVEMBER 11.—Free-State Convention at Lawrence. The object of the Convention was to organize the Republican party. It was not largely attended.

NOVEMBER 16.—Gov. Walker leaves the Territory, to be "absent on business three or four weeks."

NOVEMBER 19.—Shawnee Indian lands thrown open for purchase and pre-emption.

NOVEMBER 23.—A convention at Topeka declares in favor of setting the Free-State Government in motion. C. K. Holliday is President, and S. N. Frazier and Guilford Dudley Secretaries.

NOVEMBER 24.—Convention at Leavenworth to organize a Free-State Democratic party. It does not meet with success.

NOVEMBER 28.—G. W. Deitzler, John Speer, Lyman Allen, and a majority of the members elected to the Legislature, ask Acting Gov. Stanton to call an extra session of the Legislature, and pledge themselves not to engage in general legislation. The request is concurred in by G. W. Brown, G. W. Smith, C. Robinson and J. H. Lane.

NOVEMBER 28.—Stephen A. Douglas opposes the Lecompton Constitution.

DECEMBER.—Pottawatomies go to Washington to arrange a sale of their lands south of the Kansas river. Land offices at Doniphan and Ogden are open.

DECEMBER 1.—Secretary Stanton calls an Extra Session of the Legislature, to meet December 7th.

—The following is a list of the papers published in the Territory at this date:

Herald, Leavenworth, Pro-Slavery.
Herald of Freedom, Lawrence, Free-State.
Tribune, Topeka, Free-State.
Pioneer, Kickapoo, Pro-Slavery.
Squatter Sovereign, Atchison, now Free-Times, Leavenworth, Free-State.   [State.
Republican, Lawrence, Free-State.
Leader, Centropolis, Free-State.
Chindowan, Quindaro, Free-State.
News, Emporia, Free-State.

Constitutionalist, Doniphan, Pro-Slavery.
Kansas Chief, White Cloud, Free-State.
Zeitung, Atchison, Free-State.
Era, Geary City, Free-State.
Advertiser, Elwood, Neutral.
Young America, Leavenworth, Whig.
National Democrat, Lecompton, Democratic
Gazette, Sumner, Neutral.
Citizen, Wyandotte, Democratic.
Journal, Leavenworth, Pro-Slavery.

—The following papers have suspended:

Freeman, Topeka, Free-State.
Journal, Topeka, Free-State.
Journal, Ottumwa, Free-State.
Free-State, Delaware, Free-State.

Freemen's Champion, Prairie City, Free-Register, Wyandotte, Free-State.   [State.
Union, Lecompton, Pro-Slavery.
Note-Book, Tecumseh, Pro-Slavery.

DECEMBER 2.—Free-State Convention at Lawrence. Charles Robinson presided; Secretaries, William A. Phillips, A. Wattles, and E. G. Macy. Committee on Resolutions: James H. Lane, Champion Vaughan, Wm. V. Barr, J. Rymal, Charles F. Kob, H. Evans, S. Westover, Charles A. Foster, T. Dwight Thacher, G. W. Gilmore, C. K. Holliday, J. K. Goodin, P. B. Plumb, L. F. Carver, G. A. Cutler. The resolutions repudiate the Lecompton Constitution; denounce the proposed elections of December 21 and January 4; ask the Extra Session of the Legislature to submit the Topeka and the Lecompton Constitutions to a vote of the people, and to provide that "the Constitution which shall receive a majority of all the legal votes shall become the fundamental law of the State of Kansas." Secretary Stanton is thanked for calling an Extra Session of the Legislature.

DECEMBER 7.—Meeting of the Legislature at Lecompton; Message from Secretary Stanton, asking for the submission of the whole Constitution to a vote. It is a fair and able statement of the laws and the elections relating to the Lecompton Constitution.

A joint resolution is passed, asking Congress to admit Kansas under the Topeka Constitution.

—At the opening of the Thirty-fifth Congress, M. J. Parrott takes his seat as a Delegate.

—President Buchanan, in his Message, endorses the Lecompton Constitutional Convention, and urges Congress to admit Kansas under that Constitution. He says:

"The Kansas-Nebraska act did not require the submission of any portion of the Constitution to an election, except that which relates to the domestic institution of Slavery."

DECEMBER 8.—*Officers of the Council:* President, C. W. Babcock; Secretary, Joel K. Goodin; Assistant Secretary, G. A. Colton; Sergeant-at-Arms, A. Cutler; Engrossing Clerk, D. H. Weir; Enrolling Clerk, B. T. Hutchins; Chaplain, S. Y. Lum; President *pro tem.*, C. K. Holliday.

Officers of the House: G. W. Deitzler, Speaker; C. F. Currier, Chief Clerk; W. B. Parsons, Assistant Clerk; G. F. Warren, Sergeant-at-Arms; T. A. Blake, Doorkeeper; Henry C. Sargent, Enrolling Clerk; Guilford Dudley,

Engrossing Clerk; Robert Speer, Messenger; Rev. Charles H. Lovejoy, Chaplain.

DECEMBER 9.—Pro-Slavery convention at Lecompton; nomination of the following candidates for State officers under the Lecompton Constitution:

Governor, Frank J. Marshall, of Marshall county; Lieutenant Governor, William G. Mathias, of Leavenworth; Secretary of State, W. T. Spicely, of Douglas county; Auditor, Blake Little, of Bourbon county; Treasurer, T. J. B. Cramer, of Douglas county; for Congress, Joseph P. Carr, of Atchison.

The resolutions declare it to be the duty of every true Democrat to support the Lecompton Constitution; they accuse Secretary Stanton of a "corrupt contract with the Black Republicans in calling an Extra Session of the Legislature," and declare the fullest confidence in the administration of James Buchanan.

"*Resolved*, That though a Reeder, a Geary and a Walker have sought to reduce and prostitute the Democracy to the unholy ends of the Abolitionists, yet we rejoice that their careers have closed in Kansas in contempt and infamy to themselves and without injury to the Democratic party.

"*Resolved*, That in the approaching election we shall hail all who stand by us as National men and sound Democrats, and can only regard all who join in opposition to our Constitution as Black Republicans and enemies to the Union."

DECEMBER 10.—The House admits to seats from Leavenworth county H. Miles Moore, George H. Keller, William M. McClure, J. P. Hatterscheidt, O. A. Bassett, William Pennock, R. G. Elliott, and Patrick R. Orr.

DECEMBER 11.—The Legislature, in joint session, elects W. W. Ross Public Printer and R. G. Elliott Superintendent of Printing. A joint resolution is adopted reaffirming the People's Constitution, framed at Topeka, October 23, 1855. R. Crozier, J. Wright and J. P. Root are admitted to the Council in place of. J. A. Halderman, A. C. Davis and J. W. Martin.

—Lewis Cass, Secretary of State, writes to James W. Denver that Stanton has been removed because he called a special session of the Legislature, and that Denver is appointed in Stanton's place.

DECEMBER 14.—Passage of a joint resolution in relation to the Lecompton Constitution.

DECEMBER 16.—The Legislature, in joint session, elects the following Militia officers: Major General, James H. Lane; Brigadier Generals, I. G. Losee. S. V. Jamieson, Asa Hall, George S. Hillyer, Samuel Walker, L. G. Cleveland, C. W. McDaniel, John H. Whistler; Adjutant, Charles Chadwick; Commissary, Hiram Houser; Inspector, J. Finn Hill; Quartermaster, S. W. Eldridge, Surgeon, S. B. Prentiss.

DECEMBER 16.—Secretary Stanton requests General Harney to send troops to Fort Scott to act as a "posse comitatus to aid in the execution of legal process."

DECEMBER 17.—Passage of an act submitting the Lecompton Constitution to a vote of the people on the 4th of January.

DECEMBER 17.—The Legislature adjourns. Before the adjournment, Stanton receives notice of his removal.

DECEMBER 17.—Governor Walker's letter resigning his office. It is a long statement, addressed to Secretary Cass.

DECEMBER 17.—Troubles at Fort Scott and on the Little Osage. Secretary Stanton sends troops to Fort Scott. The troubles originated in 1856, when the Free-State men were driven from their claims. In the spring of '57, these men came back and attempted to take possession of their claims. Warrants were issued in Fort Scott for their arrest. The Free-State men then organized a Squatter Court, and tried and fined those who had taken their property. Deputy Marshal Little attempted to arrest the "Court," with a posse of forty men. The Free-State men were in a fortified log house. Considerable firing was done on both sides; no one was killed, and no arrests were made. Little retired.

DECEMBER 18.—Secretary Cass briefly replies to Governor Walker.

DECEMBER 18.—Wm. S. Harney, Colonel of Second Dragoons, writes to Secretary Stanton that he will send troops wherever wanted "to insure a full and free vote to the people" at the approaching election. Troops were sent to Doniphan, Atchison, Palermo, and Fort Scott, and requested by Stanton for Shawnee and Oxford.

DECEMBER 19.—Secretary Stanton issues a proclamation appointing commissioners for the election to be held January 4th.

DECEMBER 19.—John Calhoun asks Secretary Denver to be present when the returns are opened of the election to be held on the 21st.

DECEMBER 21.—J. W. Denver takes the oath of office before Judge Sterling G. Cato.

—Secretary Denver issues an address. He quotes from Secretary Cass's letter, and says the elections shall be fairly conducted.

—Secretary Denver asks Howell Cobb, Secretary of the Treasury, to send him eleven thousand dollars, for Legislative expenses. "There is not a dollar now on hand here."

—Election on the Lecompton Constitution. The Free-State men abstain from voting. Calhoun announces the vote as for the "Constitution with slavery," 6,226; "Constitution with no slavery," 569. The Commissioners appointed by the following Legislature to investigate this election reported the illegal vote at Kickapoo, 700; at Delaware City, 145; at Oxford, 1,200; at Shawnee, 675; total, 2,720.

ELECTION OF STATE OFFICERS UNDER THE LECOMPTON CONSTITUTION, DECEMBER 21, 1857.

COUNTIES.	Governor		Lieut. Governor		Secretary of State.		Auditor.		Treasr.		Congress.		Constitution.		
	F. J. Marshall.	Geo. W. Smith.	Wm. G. Mathias.	W. Y. Roberts.	W. T. Spicely.	P. C. Schuyler.	Blake Little.	Joel K. Goodin.	Thos. J.B. Cramer.	A. J. Mead.	Jos. P. Carr.	M. J. Parrott.	With Slavery.	Without Slavery.	To Hell with the Lecmptn. Const.
Doniphan......	674	193	673	193	671	193	673	193	674	193	673	318	537	72	......
Atchison........	......	......	......	......	......	......	......	......	......	......	......	......	368	35	......
Leavenworth.	......	......	......	......	......	......	......	......	......	......	......	......	1735	142	9
Brown and Nemaha.... }	80	223	80	223	80	223	80	223	80	223	80	223	60	24	......
Calhoun	35	205	36	205	36	205	36	205	36	205	35	204	12	51	......
Jefferson........	177	283	177	285	176	269	126	230	176	285	176	287	69	22	......
Marshall	72	47	62	57	62	57	62	57	62	57	62	57	232	41	......
Riley.............	10	181	12	181	11	181	11	182	11	184	11	182	6	14	......
Johnson.........	1755	186	1755	181	1756	180	1756	181	1755	182	1756	227	2075	25	......
Lykins..........	149	368	149	350	149	365	150	353	149	356	148	365	81	12	......
Linn.............	380	360	381	360	383	358	381	360	381	360	382	360	183	46	......
Bourbon	523	281	522	281	523	281	521	281	474	281	522	276	366	78	......
McGee..........	276	......	274	......	276	......	278	......	274	......	278	......	31	1	......
Dorn.............	120	......	120	......	120	......	120	......	120	......	120	......	......	......	......
Allen	21	172	20	167	21	172	21	172	21	172	21	172	20	1	......
Douglas.........	......	......	......	......	......	......	......	......	......	......	......	......	137	35	......
Anderson & Franklin... }	3	577	3	577	4	576	2	567	3	577	3	576	1	1	......
Shawnee	57	333	56	330	49	331	53	333	58	333	57	532	51	7	......
Weller and Coffey....... }	6	348	3	349	3	351	3	349	......	351	6	351	......	......	......
Woodson	......	48	......	48	......	48	......	48	......	48	......	48	......	......	......
Br'kinridge and Rich- ardson...... }	......	84	......	84	......	84	......	84	......	84	......	84	......	......	......
Davis.............	37	77	37	77	35	77	37	77	37	77	38	76	5	1	......

This is a complete record of all the returns in the office of the Secretary of State. There are no returns from Pottawatomie, Washington, Dickinson, Wilson, Greenwood, Godfrey, Madison, Wise, Hunter, and Butler counties.

DECEMBER 21.—C. W. Babcock and G. W. Deitzler, invited by John Calhoun, were present when the returns of the election of December 21st were opened (Jan. 13, 1858), and reported to the Legislature that the vote for the Constitution with Slavery was 6,143; with no Slavery, 569. They report the fraudulent vote at Oxford, Johnson county, as 1,266; at Shawnee, Johnson county, as 729; at Kickapoo, Leavenworth county, 1,017.

On the State ticket they report:

FREE-STATE.

Smith, Gov'r.	Roberts, Lt. Gov.	Schuyler, Sec'y.	Mead, Treas.	Goodin, Aud'r.	Parrott, Cong.
6,875	6,947	6,867	6,885	6,813	7,260

PRO-SLAVERY.

Marshall.	Mathias.	Spicely.	Cramer.	Little.	Carr.
6,545	6,446	6,566	6,514	6,509	6,574

FREE-STATE MAJORITIES.

330	501	301	371	304	696

They report the fraudulent votes on this ticket, at Oxford, Shawnee, Kickapoo, and in other places not named, as amounting to 3,000. But these are included in the foregoing returns. For the Legislature, under the Lecompton Constitution, they report that the Free-State men have elected 29 members of the House, and 13 of the Senate; the Pro-Slavery, 15 in the House, and 6 in the Senate.

The State Legislature under the Lecompton Constitution was elected December 21, 1857. The result was not officially made known until March 19, 1858, when John Calhoun, then in Washington, D. C., published a letter in the Washington Star in which he said he should issue certificates of election to the following persons:

SENATE.

1st district......Doniphan county.........................Sidney Tennent.
2d district......Atchison county ....J. T. Hereford.
3d district......Doniphan and Atchison counties..R. S. Kelley.
4th district......Leavenworth county...................C. Vaughan, G. Sparks, C. Chadwick.
5th district......Brown, Nemaha and Pottawato-
                 mie counties.........................A. Johnson.
6th district......Riley, Marshall, Dickinson and
                 Washington counties................Amory Hunting.
7th district......Jefferson and Calhoun..................A. G. Patrick.
8th district......Johnson ....A. Paine, E. S. Wilkinson.
9th district......Lykins, Anderson and Franklin...H. H. Williams.
10th district......Linn......................................C. A. Hamilton.
11th district......Bourbon and McGee ....Blake Little.
12th district......Douglas...................................Robert Morrow, W. S. Bonnifield.
13th district......Shawnee ....Wm. Oakley.
14th district......Dorn, Allen, etc..........................J. P. Cox.
15th district......Richardson, Davis, Wise, etc.........H. P. Leonard.

HOUSE OF REPRESENTATIVES.

1st district......Doniphan.............................C. B. Whitehead, J. R. Boyd, Albert
                                                      Head, G. R. Wilson.
2d district......Atchison.............................B. Bay, A. Elliott, J. P. Wheeler, J. B.
                                                      Church.
3d district......Leavenworth.........................Wm. Kempf, J. W. Morris, G. J. Park,
                                                      J. H. Noteware, Barz. Gray, George
                                                      W. Gardiner,W. Pennock, P. R. Orr.
4th district......Brown and Nemaha...................E. N. Morrill.
5th district......Calhoun and Pottawatomie...........J. N. Parrott.
6th district......Jefferson.............................H. Owens, S. S. Cooper.
7th district......Marshall and Washington...........J. E. Clardy.
8th district......Riley.................................N. Berry.
9th district......Johnson ....W. J. Sherraff, A. A. Cox, H. W. Jones,
                                                      J. B. Wiley.
10th district......Lykins ....Chas. A. Foster.
11th district ....Linn.................................J. E. Mooney, T. H. Barlow.
12th district......Bourbon .:...........................W. D. Campbell, J. C. Simms.
13th district......McGee, Dorn and Allen..............E. D. Hart.
14th district......Douglas..............................E. S. Lowman, J. E. Stewart, S. T.
                                                      Shore, J. Gardiner, J. A. Wakefield.
15th district......Anderson and Franklin..............Perry Fuller.
16th district......Shawnee.............................J. L. Dolman, R. M. Fish.
17th district......Weller and Coffey...................A. Crocker.
18th district......Woodson, Wilson, etc...............H. Crittenden.
19th district......Breckinridge and Richardson......John R. Swallow.
20th district......Davis, Wise, Butler and Hunter...E. R. McCurdy.

DECEMBER 23 AND 24.—Free-State Convention at Lawrence. Thomas Ewing, jr., M. F. Conway, George W. Smith and Charles Robinson favored the policy of voting for State officers and Members of the Legislature on the 4th of January. In the Convention on the 24th, resolutions to that effect were adopted, and the following State ticket nominated: Governor, Geo. W. Smith; Lieutenant Governor, W. Y. Roberts; Secretary of State, P. C. Schuyler; Treasurer, A. J. Mead; Auditor, Joel K. Goodin; for Congress, M. J. Parrott. These men all opposed the Lecompton movement, but thought it best to take part in the election of State officers.

DECEMBER 24.—A Democratic Convention at Leavenworth utterly repudiates the Lecompton movement, and endorses Walker and Stanton. Among those who take part in the Convention are Saunders W. Johnston

James Christian, John A. Halderman, John P. Slough, H. B. Denman, A. G. Ege, Robert L. Ream, S. W. Driggs, and J. C. Hemingray.

The Convention unanimously adopt a Memorial asking Congress to give the Lecompton Constitution "no countenance nor encouragement whatever, but to reject it in consideration of the regard you have for the people of the Territory." Congress is asked to pass an act similar to the one given the people of Minnesota Territory, by which the people of Kansas may frame a Constitution, submit it to the people, and be admitted under it, after a ratification by the people.

DECEMBER 26.—Secretary Denver issues a proclamation declaring that United States troops shall be so distributed over the Territory "as to preserve order and ensure to every one entitled a fair opportunity of voting."

1858.

The Territory contains, according to the American Cyclopædia, the following Indian reservations: New York Indians, 1,658,000 acres; Pottawatomies, 756,000; Kansas, 256,000; Delawares, 256,000; Otoes and Missouris, 160,000; Kickapoos, 128,000; Sacs and Foxes, 32,000; Wyandottes, 24,960.

JANUARY 2.—Secretary Denver writes to Marshal Dennis that the judges of election, and not his deputies, must decide on the "legality or illegality of the votes offered at the polls."

JANUARY 4.—Third Session of the Territorial Legislature at Lecompton. The following are the members of the Council:

Allen, Babcock, Crozier, Harding, Learnard, Mead, Nash, Patrick, Root, Wright, Carr, Holliday, and Standiford.

Officers of the Council: Carmi W. Babcock, President; Cyrus K. Holliday, President *pro tem.*; Joel K. Goodin, Secretary; Gustavus A. Colton, Assistant Secretary; Abram Cutler, Sergeant-at-Arms; Jacob Branson, Doorkeeper; D. H. Weir, Engrossing Clerk; Benj. T. Hutchins, Enrolling Clerk; S. Y. Lum, Chaplain.

Members of the House:

First Representative District, composed of Leavenworth county: George H. Keller, H. Miles Moore, R. G. Elliott, O. A. Bassett, William M. McClure, William Pennock, Patrick R. Orr, J. P. Hatterscheidt.

Second Representative District, composed of Atchison county: Archibald Elliott, John Bennett.

Third Representative District, composed of Doniphan county: B. H. Brock, C. Graham, H. Stratton, J. B. Wheeler, A. A. Jamieson.

Fourth and Fifth Representative Districts, composed of Brown and Nemaha counties: E. N. Morrill.

Sixth Representative District, composed of Marshall county: J. P. Miller.

Seventh Representative District, composed of Jefferson county: Henry Owens, J. P. Cooper.

Eighth Representative District, composed of Calhoun county: Asa Reynard.

Ninth Representative District, composed of Riley and Pottawatomie counties: Charles Jenkins, Abram Barry.

Tenth Representative District, composed of Douglas and Johnson counties: John Speer, George W. Deitzler, Oliver Barber, Hiram Appleman, Andrew T. Still, George W. Zinn, Gideon Seymour, John Lockhart.

Eleventh Representative District, composed of Shawnee county: James A. Delong.

Twelfth Representative District, composed of Davis, Wise, Richardson and Breckinridge; Thirteenth, composed of Weller, Madison, Butler, Hunter and Greenwood; Fourteenth, composed of Bourbon, Godfrey, Wilson, Dorn and McGee; Fifteenth, composed of Allen, Coffey and Woodson; Sixteenth, composed of Anderson and Franklin: John Curtis, Christopher Columbia, Samuel Stewart.

Seventeenth Representative District, composed of Linn county: A. Danford, R. B. Mitchell.

Eighteenth Representative District, composed of Lykins county: John Hanna, A. J. Shannon—there being a vacancy in the Second District of one member.

Officers of the House: George W. Deitzler, Speaker; Cyrus F. Currier, Chief Clerk; William B. Parsons, Assistant Clerk; Geo. F. Warren, Sergeant-at-Arms; T. A. Blake, Doorkeeper; Robert Speer, Messenger; C. H. Lovejoy, Chaplain.

JANUARY 5.—The Free-State Legislature meets at Topeka. Harris Stratton elected Speaker of the House, and J. P. Root President of the Senate. Gov. Robinson, in his Message, urges the keeping up of the State organization. It is published in the Quindaro Chindowan.

JANUARY 5.—Message received from J. W. Denver, Secretary and Acting Governor. The following, on the Lecompton Constitution, is copied from the Message to show what "sovereigns" and how "perfectly free" the squatters were in "regulating their affairs in their own way":

"Before engaging in the business of legislation, however, I will direct your attention to a Constitution, recently framed by a Convention sitting in this place. The second section of the schedule reads as follows:

"'SEC. 2. All laws now of force in the Territory of Kansas, which are repugnant to this Constitution, shall continue and be of force until altered, amended or repealed by a Legislature assembled under the provisions of this Constitution.'

"This was signed on the 7th day of November, 1857, and, under its provisions, submitted to the people on the 21st day of December last. It was again submitted to a vote of the people by an act of the Legislature, approved December 17, 1857, only one of the political parties voting at a time on these propositions, and the others absenting themselves from the polls. In this condition it will probably be sent to Congress, and it may be as well for you to delay any important legislation until you can ascertain what action Congress will take in the premises; for, should Kansas be admitted as one of the States of the Union, under this Constitution, it would have the effect to nullify all your acts, and revive such as you may have repealed."

Adjourned to Lawrence.

JANUARY 7.—The Free-State Legislature adjourns to Lawrence, and asks the Territorial Legislature to substitute the State for the Territorial organization. Benj. Harding and C. K. Holliday, of the Territorial Council, report adversely. A similar report is made in the House by S. S. Cooper, John Speer, W. P. Badger, E. N. Morrill and H. Miles Moore. Soon after, the State Legislature adjourned.

JANUARY 7.—J. H. Stringfellow writes to the Washington Union against the admission of Kansas under the Lecompton Constitution. To do so, he says, will break down the Democratic party at the North, and seriously endanger the peace and interests of Missouri and Kansas, if not of the whole Union. The Slavery question in Kansas, he says, is settled against the South by immigration.

JANUARY 8.—Legislature meets at Lawrence.

JANUARY 9.—Death announced of Hiram B. Standiford, member of the Council from the Tenth District, Franklin county. He died January 3d. A journal is printed each day. The books containing the journals of the two houses were not printed till 1861.

JANUARY 14.—A proclamation is issued by J. W. Denver, Acting Governor, C. W. Babcock, President of the Council, and George W. Deitzler, Speaker of the House, announcing the following as the result of the election held January 4th on the Lecompton Constitution:

Counties.	Against Constitution.	For Constit'n with Slavery.	For Con. without Slavery.
Leavenworth	1,997	10	3
Atchison	536	4	......
Doniphan	561	1	2
Brown	187	2	......
Nemaha	238	1	......
Marshall	66	......	......
Riley	287	7	......
Pottawatomie	207	2	......
Calhoun	249	......	......
Jefferson	377	1	......
Johnson	292	2	......
Lykins	358	1	1
Linn	510	1	3
Bourbon	268	55	......
Douglas	1,647	21	2
Franklin	304	......	......
Anderson	177	......	......
Allen	191	1	4
Shawnee	832	28	3
Coffey	463	......	4
Woodson	50	......	......
Richardson	177	......	1
Breckinridge	191	......	......
Madison	40	......	......
Davis	21	......	......
Total	10,226	138	23

JANUARY 15.—Champion Vaughan elected Public Printer. He resigns, and William W. Ross is elected.

—General Lane makes a report to the Legislature on the troubles in Bourbon county. (See House Journal, pp. 84–5.)

JANUARY.—The Daily Ledger issued in Leavenworth, by George W. McLane.

JANUARY 20.—Smith, Roberts, Schuyler, Mead, and Goodin, the State officers elected under the Lecompton Constitution, memorialize Congress to defeat that instrument, and not to admit Kansas under it.

JANUARY 21.—The Legislature appoints Henry J. Adams, E. L. Taylor,

Thomas Ewing, J. B. Abbott, Ely Moore, and Dillon Pickering, to investigate the frauds of the last two elections.

Act passed for election of delegates to a Constitutional Convention in March.

Act passed over the Governor's veto, locating the seat of government at Minneola.

JANUARY 21.—John D. Henderson having been arrested in Lawrence, Judge Lecompte grants a habeas corpus for his release. A Deputy Marshal applies to General Harney for troops to execute Lecompte's writ. General Harney refers the matter to Secretary Denver, and Denver replies that he cannot sanction the application of the Marshal.

JANUARY 23.—Joseph P. Carr, of Atchison, resigns his seat in the Council. He had not claimed it.

JANUARY 23.—A newspaper gives the "lifetime of Kansas Governors:"

No. 1: A. H. Reeder, reached here October 6, 1854; removed July 31, 1855. Term of service, ten months.

No. 2: W. Shannon, reached here September 1, 1855; removed August 21, 1856. Term of service, twelve months.

No. 3: J. W. Geary, reached here September 9, 1856; resigned March, 1857. Term of service, six months.

No. 4: R. J. Walker, reached here May 24th, 1857; resigned December 7, 1857. Term of service, seven months.

JANUARY 26.—David Sibbitt elected to the Council in the place of H. B. Standiford, deceased, from the Tenth Council District.

JANUARY 27.—Mr. Holliday presents a resolution asking for the annexation of that part of the Territory of Nebraska lying south of the Platte river.

JANUARY 29.—Fred. P. Stanton publishes a letter in the National Intelligencer, defending his official career in Kansas.

—A census of Oxford, taken by act of the Legislature, shows that it contains only forty-two voters. In October, Oxford polled, according to the returns, 1,628 votes; December 21, 1,266 votes; January 4, 738 votes.

FEBRUARY 2.—President Buchanan sends the Lecompton Constitution to the Senate, with a Message, asking its acceptance. Green, of Missouri, presents the majority report in favor of admission under the Constitution; Douglas, of Illinois, presents a minority report; another minority report was made by Collamer and Wade.

In the House the subject of the Lecompton Constitution was referred to a Select Committee, by a vote of 114 to 111.

In the House, Alex. H. Stephens presents the majority report, signed by eight members of the Committee. Harris, of Illinois, presents the minority report, against admission under the Lecompton Constitution, signed by the other seven members of the Special Committee.

—The Committee investigating the election frauds find the Delaware Crossing returns in a candle-box which had been buried under a wood-pile, at Lecompton. Thomas Ewing, jr., obtained a search-warrant from Judge Josiah Miller, of Lawrence, and Samuel Walker, Sheriff, executed it, and found the candle-box. The returns were buried by Gen. L. A. Maclean,

11

Chief Clerk of Surveyor General John Calhoun. On the night of January 28th, Maclean fled from the Territory, as Calhoun had already done.

FEBRUARY 6.—The following Message is received from Secretary Denver:

To the Council of the Legislative Assembly:

GENTLEMEN: A bill entitled "An act repealing 'An act to punish offences against slave property,'" has been presented to me for my approval.

The act referred to is a very stringent one, perhaps much more so than necessary, but, so long as the Territorial existence continues here, the owners of slaves have a right to claim protection for their property at the hands of the law-making power.

The peculiar character of this property requires the enactment of laws, for its management and control, different, in many respects, from that which is required for any other. I cannot, therefore, give my consent to the repeal of all laws on this subject, until there shall be some other enactment to take their place, so long as Slavery is recognized and allowed to exist in this Territory.

With these objections, the bill is herewith returned to the house in which it originated.   J. W. DENVER, *Acting Governor.*

FEBRUARY 6, 1858.

All acts of Territorial Legislatures abolishing Slavery were vetoed by the Governors.

FEBRUARY 8.—Secretary Denver vetoes the bill removing the Capital to Minneola. The House passes the bill by 28 to 9.

FEBRUARY 10.—Luther C. Challis succeeds Mr. Carr as a member of the Council.

—Passage of a bill for a Constitutional Convention.

FEBRUARY 11.—The Legislature, in joint session, elect Caleb S. Pratt, Ward L. Lewis, and Ashael Hunt, Penitentiary Commissioners.

FEBRUARY 12.—Acts passed establishing codes of civil and criminal procedure.

—The Council confirm J. H. Noteware as Superintendent of Common Schools. The militia officers elected at the Extra Session are re-elected.

FEBRUARY 12.—Henry J. Adams, Thomas Ewing, jr., E. L. Taylor, Dillon Pickering, J. B. Abbott, and H. T. Green, Commissioners to investigate election frauds, report to Governor Denver. They expose in detail the fraudulent vote cast at Kickapoo, Delaware City, Delaware Agency, Shawnee, and Oxford. They decide that the following illegal votes were cast at the election on the acceptance of the Lecompton Constitution, December 21st, 1857: At Kickapoo, 700; Delaware City, 145; Oxford, 1,200; Shawnee, 675: total, 2,720. And the following illegal votes at the election of January 4th, 1858, for officers under the Lecompton Constitution: At Kickapoo, 600; Delaware City, 5; Delaware Agency, 336; Oxford, 696; Shawnee, 821: total, 2,458. Of the returns from Delaware Agency (commonly called "Delaware Crossing"), of the election held January 4th, the Committee say they "were honestly made out by the officers of the election, and subsequently 336 names were forged upon them, by or with the knowledge of John D. Henderson; and that John Calhoun was *particeps criminis,* after the fact."

FEBRUARY 13.—Legislature adjourns.

The volume of general laws of this session contains 469 pages; the special laws fill 398 pages. The city incorporation acts relate to Atchison, Elwood, Geary, Lawrence, Lecompton, Leavenworth, Olathe, Palermo,

Quindaro, Tecumseh, Topeka, and White Cloud. Of town companies, there are 175 incorporated, among them Burlington, Burlingame, Cottonwood Falls, Holton, Humboldt, Marmaton, Mapleton, Minneola, Mound City, Sabetha, Seneca, Spring Hill, and Wyandotte. Much time was given to the passage of private bills for banks, railroads, etc. The most obnoxious of the Pro-Slavery laws were repealed. The bill for a convention to frame a new Constitution was passed so late in the session that Governor Denver insisted that it had failed to become a law.

FEBRUARY 13.—J. E. Johnston, Lieutenant Colonel First Cavalry, having explored the southern boundary of Kansas with the view of ascertaining the practicability of constructing a railroad by this route to the Rio Grande, reports to Secretary Floyd.

FEBRUARY 15.—Two mounted companies ordered to Fort Scott, to report to Judge Williams or to John H. Little, Deputy Marshal.

—The Leavenworth Daily Times issued, by Champion Vaughan and J. Kemp Bartlett.

—Freemen's Champion, published by S. S. Prouty, at Prairie City, is revived, after a temporary suspension.

MARCH 4.—Last meeting of the Topeka Legislature; no quorum present.

—In the spring, James Redpath started the Crusader of Freedom, at Doniphan. It was short-lived.

MARCH 9.—Election of the following delegates to the Constitutional Convention. About 9,000 votes were cast:

Jefferson County.—Edward Lynde, James Monroe, J. C. Todd, A. W. McCauslin.

Shawnee.—A. L. Winans, Lucian Fish, R. M. Fish, H. W. Curtis, Wm. W. Ross, John Ritchie.

Atchison.—Frank G. Adams, Caleb May, G. M. Fuller, C. A. Woodworth, H. S. Baker.

Breckinridge.—P. B. Plumb, Wm. McCulloch, John R. Swallow.

Butler and Hunter.—Samuel Stewart.

Madison.—G. D. Humphrey.

Linn.—A. Danford, Thomas H. Butler, Robt. B. Mitchell, Robt. Ewing.

Brown.—A. B. Anderson, Orville Root, A. W. Williams.

Richardson.—James Fletcher, Henry Harvey.

Anderson.—W. F. M. Arny, Wm. Spriggs, W. L. Webster.

Coffey.—R. A. Kinzie, D. A. Hawkins, J. M. Elliott.

Calhoun.—W. E. Bowker, Adam Fuller.

Lykins.—G. A. Colton, Thomas Roberts, Chas. A. Foster, A. Knapp.

Franklin.—Joel K. Goodin, J. G. Rees.

Wells.—A. H. Shurtleff.

Allen and Bourbon.—W. R. Griffith, M. H. Hudson, G. A. Nuller, A. G. Carpenter, G. W. Campbell.

Douglas and Johnson.—M. F. Conway, E. S. Scudder, Charles H. Branscomb, A. Soule, W. R. Monteith, J. M. Shepherd, John L. Brown, D. Pickering, Charles Mayo, James D. Allen, T. Dwight Thacher, James S. Emery, Samuel N. Wood.

Doniphan, etc.—James H. Lane, Wm. V. Barr, A. Larzelere, W. Fleming, Hugh Robertson, Charles E. Perham, W. D. Beeler, J. F. Hampson.

Riley.—Isaac T. Goodnow, F. N. Blake, Geo. W. Higinbotham.

Pottawatomie.—U. Cook, J. D. Adams.

Davis.—J. H. Pillsbury.

Nemaha.—S. S. Wright, R. U. Torrey.

Woodson.— R. Austin.

Greenwood.— M. L. Ashmore.

Wise.—H. J. Espy.

Leavenworth.—Henry J. Adams, Thomas Ewing, jr., John P. Hatterscheidt, John C. Douglass, James Davis, W. Y. Roberts, J. M. Walden, Wm. H. Coffin, Thomas Trower, H. P. Johnson.

Richardson.—James M. Winchell.

Not Assigned.— B. B. Newton, James Telfer, G. W. K. Twombly.

MARCH 12.—The steamer Minnie Belle arrives at Lawrence. On the 24th of April she had made three trips to Lawrence.

MARCH 13.—The editor of the Herald of Freedom returns after two weeks' absence, and expresses his thanks "to his worthy foreman, T. A. Osborn, Esq., for the very satisfactory manner he has conducted its columns."

MARCH 23.—The Constitutional Convention met at Minneola. Called to order by W. Y. Roberts. The vote for temporary Chairman stood: M. F. Conway, 37; A. Danford, 19. Informal ballot for President: J. H. Lane, 43; H. J. Adams, 9; T. D. Thacher, 7; Thomas Ewing, jr., 5; W. Y. Roberts, 4; D. Pickering, 1. James H. Lane was then elected President by acclamation. Samuel F. Tappan was elected Clerk, B. T. Hutchins Assistant Clerk, George F. Warren Sergeant-at-Arms, John Kimball Assistant, and Richard J. Hinton Reporter. There were seventy-two delegates present. The Convention once decided to adjourn to Topeka, but, on the 24th, it adjourned to Leavenworth, to reassemble on the evening of the 25th.

—The bill of Senator James S. Green, of Missouri, introduced February 19, passed the Senate March 23, by 33 to 25. It proposed to admit Kansas under the Pro-Slavery Constitution framed at Lecompton. The boundaries named in the bill, for the State, were the same as those of the Territory under the Organic Act. For this bill, the House adopted, by 120 to 112, the Crittenden-Montgomery substitute. It proposed to resubmit the Lecompton Constitution to the people of Kansas. If they adopted it, the State was to be admitted; if they rejected it, provision was made for holding a new Constitutional Convention.

MARCH 25.—The Constitutional Convention met at Melodeon Hall, Leavenworth.

MARCH 26.—After appointing the Committees, General Lane resigned the position of President of the Convention. Martin F. Conway was elected President; the opposing candidate was Thomas Ewing, jr.

MARCH 27.—Two Free-State men, Denton and Hedrick, killed by Ruffians at night, near Fort Scott. Hardwick and Brockett were reported as members of the murdering gang.

MARCH 31.—Joseph Medill, of the Chicago Tribune, speaks in an Anti-Lecompton meeting at Leavenworth.

April 1.—The House refuses to reject the Senate bill, 95 voting to reject, and 137 against it. The amendment offered by Crittenden in the Senate, and lost, was adopted by the House by 120 to 112.

The Senate, on motion of Green, rejected the bill thus amended, by 34 to 22.

April 3.—The Leavenworth Constitutional Convention adjourns.

April 7.—On motion of Wm. Montgomery, of Pennsylvania, the House adhered to its amendment, by 119 to 111.

April 13.—The Senate voted, 30 to 24, for a committee of conference.

April 14.—The House voted, 109 to 108, on motion of Wm. H. English, of Indiana, to agree to a conference committee. The committee consisted of James S. Green of Missouri, R. M. T. Hunter of Virginia, and Wm. H. Seward of New York, of the Senate; and William H. English of Indiana, Alex. H. Stephens of Georgia, and William A. Howard of Michigan, on the part of the House.

April.—Wm. A. Phillips founds the town of Salina.

—Morris appointed Receiver, and Moorah Register, at Ogden; Alson C. Davis, United States District Attorney; B. I. Newsom, Agent for Shawnees, and W. P. Badger, for Kickapoos. Isaac Winston appointed United States Marshal. Dennis was removed for opposition to the Lecompton Constitution.

April.—At Fort Scott, troops attempting to arrest Free-State men are fired upon.

April 23.—English reports the following compromise bill. Seward and Howard dissent:

"*Whereas,* The People of Kansas did, by a Convention of Delegates assembled at Lecompton, on the 7th day of November, 1857, for that purpose, form for themselves a Constitution and State Government, which Constitution is republican; and

"*Whereas,* At the same time and place, said Convention did adopt an ordinance which asserts that Kansas, when admitted as a State, will have an undoubted right to tax the lands within her limits belonging to the United States, and proposed to relinquish said asserted right if certain conditions set forth in said ordinance be accepted and agreed to by the Congress of the United States; and

"*Whereas,* Said Constitution and ordinance have been presented to Congress by order of said Convention, and the admission of said Territory into the Union thereon as a State requested; and

"*Whereas,* Said ordinance is not acceptable to Congress, and it is desirable to ascertain whether the people of Kansas concur in the changes in said ordinance hereafter stated, and desire admission into the Union as a State as herein proposed: therefore,

"*Be it enacted, etc.,* That the State of Kansas be and is hereby admitted into the Union on an equal footing with the original States in all respects whatever, but upon this fundamental condition precedent, namely: That the question of admission with the following proposition, in lieu of the ordinance framed at Lecompton, shall be submitted to the vote of the people of Kansas, and assented to by them, or the majority of the voters voting at an election to be held for that purpose, namely: That the following propositions be and the same are hereby offered to said people of Kansas for their free acceptation, etc.

"*And be it further enacted,* That the following propositions be, and the same are hereby offered to the said people of Kansas for their free acceptance or rejection, which, if accepted, shall be obligatory upon the United States and upon the said State of Kansas, to wit:

"*First:* That sections numbered sixteen and thirty-six in every township of public lands in said State, and where either of said sections or any part thereof has been sold or otherwise disposed of, other lands equivalent thereto, and as contiguous as may be, shall be granted to the said State for the use of schools.

"*Second:* That seventy-two sections of land shall be set apart and reserved for the use and support of a State University, to be selected by the Governor of said State, subject to the approval of the Commissioner of the General Land Office, and to be appropriated and applied in such manner as the Legislature of the said State may prescribe for the purpose aforesaid, but for no other purpose.

"*Third:* That ten entire sections of lands, to be selected by the Governor of said State, in legal subdivisions, shall be granted to said State for the purpose of completing the public buildings, or for the erection of others at the seat of Government, under the direction of the Legislature thereof.

"*Fourth:* That all the salt springs within the said State, not exceeding twelve in number, with six sections of land adjoining, or as contiguous as may be to each, shall be granted to said State for its use, the same to be selected by the Governor thereof, within one year after the admission of said State, and when so selected, to be used or disposed of on such terms, conditions and regulations as the Legislature shall direct: *Provided*, That no salt spring, or land, the right whereof is now vested in any individual or individuals, or which may be hereafter confirmed or adjudged to any individual or individuals, shall by this article be granted to said State.

"*Fifth:* That five per centum of the proceeds of the sales of all public lands lying within the said State, which shall be sold by Congress after the admission of said State into the Union, after deducting all the expenses incident to the same, shall be paid to said State, for the purpose of making public roads and internal improvements, as the Legislature shall direct: *Provided*, That the foregoing propositions herein offered to the State of Kansas shall never interfere with the primary disposal of the land of the United States, or with any regulations Congress may find necessary for securing title in said soil to bona fide purchasers thereof, and that no tax shall be imposed on land belonging to the United States, and that in no case shall non-resident proprietors be taxed higher than resident.

"*Sixth:* And that said State shall never tax the lands or property of the United States.

"SECTION 1. That the State of Kansas be and is hereby admitted into the Union, on an equal footing with the original States, with the Constitution framed at Lecompton; and this admission of her into the Union as a State is here declared to be upon this fundamental condition precedent, namely: That the said constitutional instrument shall be first submitted to a vote of the people of Kansas, and assented to by them, or a majority of the voters, at an election to be held for the purpose. At the said election, the voting shall be by ballot, and by endorsing on his ballot, as each voter may please, "For proposition of Congress and admission," or, "Against proposition of Congress and admission." The President of the United States, as soon as the fact is duly made known to him, shall announce the same by proclamation; and thereafter, and without any further proceedings on the part of Congress, the admission of the State of Kansas into the Union on an equal footing with the original States, in all respects whatever, shall be complete and absolute; and said State shall be entitled to one Member in the House of Representatives in the Congress of the United States until the next census be taken by the Federal Government. But, should the majority of the votes be cast for "Proposition rejected," it shall be deemed and held that the people of Kansas do not desire admission into the Union with said Constitution, under the conditions set forth in said proposition; and in that event the people of said Territory are hereby authorized and empowered to form for themselves a Constitution and State Government, by the name of the State of Kansas, according to the Federal Constitution, and may elect Delegates for that purpose whenever, and not before, it is ascertained, by a census duly and legally taken, that the population of said Territory equals the ratio of representation required for a Member of the House of Representatives of the United States; and whenever thereafter such Delegates shall assemble in convention. they shall first determine by a vote whether it is the wish of the people of the proposed State to be admitted into the Union at that time, and, if so, shall proceed to form a Constitution, and take all necessary steps for the establishment of a State Government, in conformity with the Federal Constitution, subject to such limitations and restrictions as to the mode and manner of its approval or ratification by the people of the proposed State as they may have prescribed by law, and shall be entitled to admission into the Union as a State under such Constitution, thus fairly and legally made, with or without Slavery, as said Constitution may prescribe.

"SEC. 2. *And be it further enacted,* That for the purpose of ensuring, as far as possible, that the elections authorized by this act may be fair and free, the Governor, United States District Attorney and Secretary of the Territory of Kansas, and the presiding officers of the two branches of its Legislature, namely, the President of the Council and Speaker of the House of Representatives, are hereby constituted a Board of Commissioners to carry into effect the provisions of this act, and to use all the means necessary and proper to that end. Any three of them shall constitute a Board; and the Board shall have power and authority to designate and establish precincts for voting, or to adopt those already established; to cause polls to be opened at such places as it may deem proper in the respective counties and election precincts of said Territory; to appoint, as judges of election at each of the several places of voting, three discreet and respectable persons, any two of whom shall be competent to act; to require the sheriffs of the several counties, by themselves or deputies, to attend the judges at each of the places of voting, for the purpose of preserving peace and good order, or the said Board may, instead of said sheriffs and their deputies, appoint, at their discretion and in such instances as they may choose, other fit persons for the same purpose. The election hereby authorized shall continue one day only, and shall not be continued later than sundown on that day. The Board shall appoint the day for holding said election, and said Governor shall announce the same by proclamation, and the day shall be as early a one as is consistent with due notice thereof to the people of said Territory, subject to the provisions of this act. The said Board shall have full power to prescribe the time, manner and place of said election, and to direct the time and manner of the returns thereof, which returns shall be made to said Board, whose duty it shall be to announce the result by proclamation; and said Governor shall certify the same to the President of the United States without delay.

"SEC. 3. *And be it further enacted,* That in the election hereby authorized all white male inhabitants of said Territory, over the age of twenty-one years, who possess the qualifications which were required by the laws of said Territory for a legal voter at the last general election for a member of the Territorial Legislature, and none others, shall be allowed to vote; and this shall be the only qualification required to entitle the citizens to the right of suffrage in said elections; and if any person not so qualified shall vote, or offer to vote, or if any person shall vote more than once at said election, or shall make, or cause to be made, any false, fictitious or fraudulent returns, or shall alter or change any returns of said election, such person shall, upon conviction thereof before any court of competent jurisdiction, be kept at hard labor not less than six months, and not more than three years.

"SEC. 4. *And be it further enacted,* That the members of the aforesaid Board of Commissioners, and all persons appointed by them to carry into effect the provisions of this act, shall, before entering upon their duties, take an oath to perform faithfully the duties of their respective offices; and on failure thereof, they shall be liable and subject to the same charges and penalties as are provided in like cases under the Territorial laws.

"SEC. 5. *And be it further enacted,* That the officers mentioned in the preceding section shall receive for their services the same compensation as is given for like services under the Territorial laws."

APRIL 28 AND 29.—Free-State Convention at Topeka, to nominate officers under the Leavenworth Constitution. President, C. B. Lines, Wabaunsee; Vice Presidents, Thos. Ewing, John W. Robinson, R. B. Mitchell, A. Polley; Secretaries, S. F. Tappan, T. D. Thacher, P. B. Plumb, E. Russell. That part of the call asking for the nomination of U. S. Senators was postponed. The following ticket was nominated:

Governor, Henry J. Adams, Leavenworth; Lieutenant Governor, Cyrus K. Holliday, Topeka; Secretary of State, E. P. Bancroft, Emporia; Treasurer, J. B. Wheeler, Doniphan; Auditor, Geo. S. Hillyer, Grasshopper Falls;

Attorney General, Chas. A. Foster, Osawatomie; Superintendent of Public Instruction, J. M. Walden, Quindaro; Commissioner of School Land, J. W. Robinson, Manhattan; Representative in Congress, M. F. Conway, Lawrence; Supreme Judges, Wm. A. Phillips, Lawrence, 2 years; Lorenzo Dow, Topeka, 4 years; Wm. McKay, Wyandotte, 6 years; Reporter of Supreme Court, Albert D. Richardson, Sumner; Clerk of Supreme Court, W. F. M. Arny, Hyatt.

The following platform was adopted:

"*Resolved*, That we, the representatives of the Free-State party, do heartily accept the Leavenworth Constitution, and do pledge ourselves to favor its adoption and ratification by the people.

"*Resolved*, That should Congress accept the application accompanying the Lecompton Constitution, and admit Kansas as a sovereign State into the Union, without the condition precedent that said Constitution, at a fair election, shall receive the ratification of the people of Kansas, then we will put the Leavenworth Constitution, ratified by the people, and the government under it, into immediate and active operation as the organic law and living Government of the State of Kansas; and that we will support and defend the same against any opposition, come from whatever quarter it may.

"*Resolved*, That, at the election upon the Constitution, the voters of Kansas be requested to vote for or against negro suffrage, and for or against separate schools for white and negro children; and if a majority of the votes cast be against negro suffrage, it shall operate as instructions to the first Legislature to submit to the people at once an amendment of the Constitution prohibiting negro suffrage; and if a majority of the votes cast be in favor of separate schools, it shall operate in like manner as instructions to the first Legislature to submit an amendment providing for separate schools for white and negro children, except in districts where the people by general consent shall allow the school to be in common."

The following Central Committee was appointed: J. M. Winchell, John McKee, G. E. Budington, A. D. Richardson, Jos. Thompson, A. Larzelere, W. Crosby, James Richardson, B. B. Newton, J. D. Adams, E. P. Bancroft, W. W. Ross, O. E. Learnard, S. D. Humphrey, W. A. Ela, James Blood, P. H. Townsend, Chas. Mayo, Cyrus Tator, P. P. Elder, W. F. M. Arny, Jesse Brown, W. R. Griffith, B. Jordan.

APRIL 30.—The compromise bill, otherwise known as the "English Swindle" and "Lecompton, junior," passes the House by 112 to 103, and the Senate by 30 to 22. Broderick, Crittenden, Douglas and Stuart vote with the Republicans. The President signed the bill May 4th.

THE LEAVENWORTH CONSTITUTION.

Framed by the Constitutional Convention in session at Leavenworth, signed by the Members thereof, April 3d, 1858, and adopted by the People May 18th, 1858.

ORDINANCE.

By the authority of the people of Kansas, be it ordained by this Convention, irrevocably, that the State of Kansas will never, without the consent of Congress, interfere with the title of the United States to the public domain, or unsold lands within the limits of said State, or the primary right of the United States to dispose of the same, or with any regulation which Congress may prescribe for securing the title thereof to purchasers in good faith; and also, that no tax or other assessment shall be imposed upon the lands belonging to the United States: *Provided*, That the conditions following shall be accepted and agreed to by the Congress of the United States:

First. The sections numbered sixteen and thirty-six in every township, including Indian Reserve of Trust Lands, in said State, (and where either of such sections, or any part thereof, has been sold or otherwise aliened or appropriated, other lands equivalent thereto, as nearly contiguous as possible,) shall be granted to the said State exclusively for the use of the common schools.

Second. That seventy-two sections of land shall be set apart and reserved for the use and support of a State university, and sixty sections for the use and support of four district colleges, to be located in the four equal divisions of the State—said lands to be selected by the Governor of the State, subject to the approval of the Commissioner of the General Land Office.

Third. That thirty-six sections of land, to be selected by the Governor of said State, shall be granted to said State for the purpose of the erection of public buildings at the seat of Government, and the erection of buildings for the various public benevolent institutions created by the State Constitution.

Fourth. That the salt springs, and gold, silver, copper, lead or other valuable mines, not exceeding twelve in number, with six sections of land adjacent, shall be granted to the said State, to be selected, used or alienated as may hereafter be prescribed by law.

Fifth. That five per centum of the net proceeds of the sales of public lands within said State, sold by Congress after the admission of said State into the Union, shall be paid to the said State for the purpose of creating a common school fund, the principal to be held sacred, and the interest to be applied to the education of the children of Kansas.

Sixth. That each alternate section of land now owned, or which may hereafter be acquired, by the United States, lying, for six miles in width, on each side of the following lines of railroads, shall be granted by Congress to the State of Kansas: First—Commencing on the Missouri State line, at some point south of the fourth standard parallel line, and traversing Southern Kansas westwardly. Second—Commencing at some point on the Missouri river, or Missouri State line, and traversing Central Kansas westwardly. Third—Commencing at some point on the Missouri river, and traversing Northern Kansas westwardly. Fourth—Commencing at some point on the Missouri river, and running southerly in the direction of the Gulf of Mexico. *Provided,* That, should the alternate sections along the lines of said railroads be disposed of, an equal number of sections shall be selected from any other public lands contiguous to said railroads; said lands to be reserved and conveyed to the State for the purpose of aiding in the construction of said railroads, under such rules and restrictions as may hereafter be prescribed by law.

The Congress of the United States, in conjunction with the proper authorities of this State, may adopt the necessary measures for carrying the general provisions herein contained into effect.

PREAMBLE.

We, the People of the Territory of Kansas, grateful to Almighty God for our Freedom, by our Delegates in Convention assembled, having the right of admission into the Union as one of the United States of America, consistent with the Federal Constitution, and by virtue of the treaty of cession by France to the United States, of the Province of Louisiana, believing that the time has arrived when our present political condition should cease, and the right of self-government be asserted, in order to secure to ourselves and our posterity all the rights of life, liberty, and property, and the free pursuit of happiness, ordain the following Constitution as the Organic Law of a free and independent State, by the name and style of the STATE OF KANSAS, bounded as follows, to wit: Beginning at a point on the western boundary of the State of Missouri, where the thirty-seventh parallel of north latitude crosses the same; thence west on said parallel to the eastern boundary of New Mexico; thence north on said boundary to latitude thirty-eight; thence following said boundary westward to the eastern boundary of the Territory of Utah, on the summit of the Rocky Mountains; thence northward on said summit to the fortieth parallel of latitude; thence east on said parallel to the western boundary of the State of Missouri; thence south with the western boundary of said State to the place of beginning.

ARTICLE I.—BILL OF RIGHTS.

SECTION 1. All men are by nature equally free and independent, and have certain inalienable rights, among which are those of enjoying and defending life and liberty, acquiring, possessing and protecting property, and seeking and obtaining happiness and safety; and the right of all men to the control of their persons exists prior to law, and is inalienable.

SEC. 2. All political power is inherent in the people, and all free governments are founded on their authority and are instituted for their equal protection and benefit; and they alone have the right, at all times, to alter, reform or abolish their form of government in such manner as they may think proper. No special privileges or immunities shall ever be granted by the General Assembly which may not be altered, revoked or repealed by the same authority.

SEC. 3. The people have a right to assemble, in a peaceable manner, to consult for their common good, to instruct their Representatives, and to petition the General Assembly for the redress of grievances.

SEC. 4. The people have the right to bear arms for their defence and security, but standing armies in time of peace are dangerous to liberty, and shall not be kept up, and the military shall be in strict subordination to the civil power.

SEC. 5. The right of trial by jury shall be inviolate, and extend to persons of every condition.

SEC. 6. There shall be no Slavery in this State, and no involuntary servitude, unless for the punishment of crime, whereof the parties shall have been duly convicted.

SEC. 7. All men have a natural and indefeasible right to worship Almighty God according to the dictates of their own conscience. No person shall be compelled to attend, erect, or support any place of worship, or maintain any form of worship against his consent; and no preference shall be given by law to any religious society; nor shall any interference with the right of conscience be permitted. No religious test shall be required as a qualification for office, nor shall any person be incompetent to be a witness on account of religious belief; but nothing herein contained shall be so construed as to dispense with oaths or affirmations. Religion, morality, and knowledge, however, being essential to good government, it shall be the duty of the Legislature to make suitable provisions for the protection of all religious denominations in the peaceable enjoyment of their modes of worship, and for the encouragement of schools and the means of instruction.

SEC. 8. The privilege of the writ of habeas corpus shall not be suspended unless in case of rebellion or invasion the public safety may require it.

SEC. 9. All persons shall be bailable by sufficient sureties, except for capital offences where the proof is evident or the presumption great. Excessive bail shall not be required, nor excessive fines imposed; no cruel or unusual punishment inflicted.

SEC. 10. Except in cases of impeachment, and cases arising in the army or navy, or in the militia, when in actual service, in time of war or public danger, and cases of petit larceny and other inferior offences, no person shall be held to answer for a capital or otherwise infamous crime, unless upon presentment or indictment of a grand jury. In any trial, in any court, the accused shall be allowed to appear and defend in person, or by counsel; to demand the nature and cause of the accusation against him; to meet the witnesses face to face, and to have compulsory process to procure the attendance of witnesses in his behalf, and a speedy public trial by an impartial jury of the county or district in which the offence is alleged to have been committed; nor shall any person be compelled in a criminal case to be a witness against himself, or be twice put in jeopardy for the same offence.

SEC. 11. Every citizen may freely speak, write and publish his sentiments on all subjects, being responsible for the abuse of such right; and no law shall be passed to restrain or abridge the liberty of speech or of the press. In all prosecutions for libel, the truth of the charge may be given in evidence to the jury, and if it shall appear to the jury that the matter charged as libellous is true, and was published with good motives, and for justifiable ends, the accused shall be acquitted.

SEC. 12. No person shall be transported out of the State for any offence committed within the same, and no conviction in this State shall work a corruption of blood or forfeiture of estate.

SEC. 13. No soldier shall, in time of peace, be quartered in any house without the consent of the owner; nor in time of war, except in a manner prescribed by law.

SEC. 14. The right of the people to be secure in their persons, houses, papers and possessions, against unreasonable searches and seizures, shall be inviolate; and no warrant shall issue but upon probable cause, supported by oath or affirmation, particularly describing the place to be searched and the persons and things to be seized.

SEC. 15. No person shall be imprisoned for debt in any civil action, or mesne or final process, except in cases of fraud.

SEC. 16. All courts shall be open; and every person for an injury done him or his land, goods, person or reputation, shall have remedy by due course of law, and justice administered without denial or delay.

SEC. 17. No hereditary emoluments, honors or privileges shall ever be granted or conferred by this State.

SEC. 18. No power of suspending laws shall be exercised, except by the General Assembly.

SEC. 19. Private property shall ever be held inviolate, but subservient to the public welfare. When taken in time of war, or other public exigencies imperatively requiring its immediate seizure, or for the purpose of making or repairing roads, which shall be open to the public without charge, a just compensation shall be made to the owners in money; and in all other cases where private property shall be taken for public uses, a compensation therefor shall first be made in money, or first secured by depositing money, and such compensation shall be estimated by a jury, without deduction for benefits to any property of the owner.

SEC. 20. The payment of a tax shall not be a qualification for exercising the right of suffrage.

SEC. 21. This enumeration of rights shall not be construed to impair or deny others retained by the people; and all powers not herein delegated, remain with the people.

SEC. 22. No indenture of any persons made and executed out of the bounds of the State, shall be valid within the State.

ARTICLE II.—ELECTIVE FRANCHISE.

SECTION 1. In all elections not otherwise provided for by this Constitution, every male citizen of the United States, of the age of twenty-one years or upwards, who shall have resided in the State six months next preceding such election, and ten days in the precinct in which he may offer to vote, and every male person of foreign birth of the age of twenty-one years or upwards, who shall have resided in the United States one year, in this State six months, and in the precinct in which he may offer to vote, ten days next preceding such election, and who shall have declared his intention to become a citizen of the United States, conformably to the laws of the United States, ten days preceding such election, shall be deemed a qualified elector.

SEC. 2. No soldier, seaman, or mariner, in the army or navy of the United States, or of their allies, shall be deemed to have acquired a residence in this State in consequence of being stationed within the same; nor shall any such soldier, seaman or marine have the right to vote.

SEC. 3. No person shall be deemed to have lost his residence in this State by reason of his absence, either on business of this State or of the United States.

SEC. 4. Every person shall be disqualified from holding office during the term for which he may have been elected, who shall have given or offered a bribe or reward to procure his election.

SEC. 5. Every person who shall give or accept a challenge to fight a duel, or who shall knowingly carry to another person such challenge, or who shall agree to go out of this State to fight a duel, shall be ineligible to any office of trust or profit in this State.

SEC. 6. The General Assembly shall have power to deprive of the right of suffrage and to render ineligible to office, any person convicted of an infamous crime.

SEC. 7. No person holding a lucrative office or appointment under the Constitution or laws of the United States, or of this State, shall be eligible to a seat in the General Assembly, nor shall any person hold more than one lucrative office at the same time, except as in this Constitution expressly permitted: *Provided*, That offices in the militia to which there is attached no annual salary, where the compensation does not exceed ninety dollars per annum, shall not be deemed lucrative.

SEC. 8. No person who may hereafter be collector or holder of public moneys shall be eligible to any office of trust or profit in the State until he shall have accounted for and paid into the proper treasury all sums for which he may be accountable.

SEC. 9. Any person who shall commit a fraud tending to affect the result of any election in this State, shall, on conviction thereof, be forever ineligible as an elector.

ARTICLE III.—DISTRIBUTION OF POWERS.

SECTION 1. The powers of the Government shall be divided into three separate departments—the Legislative, the Executive (including the Administrative), and the Judicial; and no person charged with official duties under one of these departments shall exercise any of the functions of another, except as in this Constitution expressly provided.

ARTICLE IV.—LEGISLATIVE.

SECTION 1. The Legislative power of the State shall be vested in a General Assembly, which shall consist of a Senate and House of Representatives.

SEC. 2. The Senators and Representatives shall be chosen annually by the qualified electors of the respective counties or districts for which they are chosen, on the Tuesday next after the first Monday in November. Their terms of office shall be one year, and shall commence on the first day of January next after their election.

SEC. 3. There shall be elected at the first election twenty-five Senators and seventy-five Representatives, and the number afterward shall be regulated by law; and the General Assembly shall, in all apportionments for members of the Legislature, establish single Representative and single Senatorial Districts.

SEC. 4. No person shall be eligible to the office of Senator or Representative who shall not at the time of his election possess the qualifications of an elector.

SEC. 5. Each house, except as otherwise provided in this Constitution, shall choose its own officers, determine its own rules of proceeding, punish its members for disorderly conduct, and, with the concurrence of two-thirds of all the members elected to the house, expel a member, but not a second time for the same cause; and shall judge of the qualification, election and return of its own members, and have all other powers necessary to secure its safety, and the undisturbed transaction of its business.

SEC. 6. Each house shall keep a journal of its proceedings, which shall be published. The yeas and nays on any question shall, at the request of two members, be taken, and entered on the journal.

SEC. 7. Any member of either house shall have the right to protest against any act or resolution thereof; and such protest and reason therefor shall, without alteration, commitment, or delay, be entered on the journal.

SEC. 8. All vacancies which may occur in either house shall, for the unexpired term, be filled by election as shall be prescribed by law.

SEC. 9. Senators and Representatives shall, in all cases except treason, felony, or breach of the peace, be privileged from arrest during the session of the General Assembly, and in going to and returning from the same; and for words spoken in debate they shall not be questioned in any other place.

SEC. 10. A majority of all the members elected to each house, voting in the affirmative, shall be necessary to pass a bill or joint resolution, and all bills and joint resolutions so passed shall be signed by the presiding officers of the respective houses, and presented to the Governor for his approval.

SEC. 11. The doors of each house, and of committees of the whole, shall be kept open. Neither house shall, without the consent of the other, adjourn for more than two days, nor to any other place than that in which the two houses shall be sitting, except for personal safety.

SEC. 12. Every bill shall be read by sections in each house on three several days, except in case of emergency. Two-thirds of the house where such bill is pending may, if deemed expedient, suspend the rules on a call of the yeas and nays; but the reading of a bill by sections on its final passage shall in no case be dispensed with; and the vote on the final passage of every bill and joint resolution shall be taken by yeas and nays, and entered on the journal.

SEC. 13. Every act shall contain but one subject, which shall be clearly expressed in its title. Bills may originate in either house, but may be altered, amended or rejected by the other.

SEC. 14. In all cases where a general law can be made applicable, special laws shall not be enacted.

SEC. 15. No act shall ever be revived or amended by mere reference to its title, but the act revived or the section amended shall be set forth as amended or revived at full length.

SEC. 16. No general act shall take effect until the same shall have been published and circulated in the counties of the State by authority, except in case of emergency, which emergency shall be declared in the preamble or the body of the law.

SEC. 17. The election and appointment of all officers, and the filling of all vacancies
- not otherwise provided for by this Constitution, or the Constitution of the United States,
shall be made in such manner as shall be prescribed by law; but no appointing power
shall be exercised by the General Assembly, except as provided in this Constitution and
in the election of the United States Senators, and in these cases the vote shall be taken
viva voce.

SEC. 18. The General Assembly shall not have power to enact special laws annulling
the contract of marriage.

SEC. 19. The General Assembly shall not have power to pass retroactive laws, or laws
impairing the obligation of contracts, but may by general laws authorize the courts to
carry into effect, upon such terms as shall be just and equitable, the manifest intention
of parties and officers, by curing omissions, defects and errors in instruments and proceedings arising out of a want of conformity with the laws of this State.

SEC. 20. The style of the laws of this State shall be, "*Be it enacted by the General Assembly of the State of Kansas.*"

SEC 21. The House of Representatives shall have the sole power of impeachment.
All impeachments shall be tried by the Senate, and, when sitting for this purpose, the
Senators shall be upon oath or affirmation to do justice according to law and evidence.
No person shall be convicted without the concurrence of two-thirds of all the Senators
present.

SEC. 22. The Governor, and all other civil officers under the laws of this State, shall
be liable to impeachment for any misdemeanor in office; but judgment in such cases
shall not extend further than to removal from office, and disqualification to hold any
office of honor, trust, or profit under the laws and Constitution of this State. The party,
whether convicted or acquitted, shall nevertheless be liable to indictment, trial, judgment and punishment according to law.

SEC. 23. Within one year after the ratification of this Constitution, and within every
two years subsequently, for the term of ten years, an enumeration of all the inhabitants of this State shall be made in such manner as shall be directed by law.

SEC. 24. All regular sessions of the General Assembly shall be held at the Capital of
the State, and shall commence on the first Monday of January, annually.

SEC. 25. All bills for raising revenue shall originate in the House of Representatives.

SEC. 26. The members of the General Assembly shall receive for their services the
sum of four dollars per day for each and every day they are actually in attendance at
any regular or special session, and four dollars for every twenty miles they shall travel
in going to and returning from the place of meeting, by the usually travelled route; and
no regular session of the General Assembly, except the first under this Constitution,
shall extend beyond the term of sixty days, nor any special session more than forty
days.

SEC. 27. Every bill or resolution shall, before its final passage, be printed for the use
of the General Assembly.

ARTICLE V.—EXECUTIVE.

SECTION 1. The Executive Department shall consist of a Governor, a Lieutenant Governor, Secretary of State, Treasurer of State, Auditor of State, and Attorney General,
who shall be chosen by the electors of the State at the same time and place of voting as
for members of the General Assembly.

SEC. 2. The term of office of the Governor, Lieutenant Governor, Treasurer, Auditor,
Secretary of State and Attorney General, shall commence on the first day of January
next after their election, and shall continue for two years and until their successors are
elected and qualified. No person shall be eligible for the above offices more than two
out of three consecutive terms.

SEC. 3. The returns of every election for the officers named in the preceding section
shall be sealed up and transmitted to the seat of government by the returning officers,
directed to the Secretary of State, who shall lay the same before the General Assembly
at their first meeting thereafter, when they shall open and canvass them and publish
and declare the result thereof in the presence of a majority of the members of both
houses. The persons having the highest number of votes shall be declared duly elected
and the certificate thereof given to such persons, signed by the presiding officers of both
houses; but if any two or more shall have the highest and equal number of votes for the

same office, one of them shall be chosen by a vote of the two houses of the General Assembly in joint session.

SEC. 4. The executive power shall be vested in a Governor.

SEC. 5. He may require information in writing from the officers in the Executive Department upon any subject relating to the duties of their respective offices, and shall see that the laws are faithfully executed.

SEC. 6. He shall communicate at every session by message to the General Assembly the condition of the affairs of the State, and recommend such measures as he shall deem expedient for their action.

SEC. 7. He may on extraordinary occasions convene the General Assembly by proclamation, and shall state in such proclamation the purpose for which they are convened; and the General Assembly shall enter upon no legislative business except that for which they were especially called together.

SEC. 8. In case of disagreement between the two houses in respect to the time of adjournment, he shall have power to adjourn the General Assembly to such time as he may think proper, but not beyond the regular meetings thereof.

SEC. 9. He shall be Commander-in-Chief of the Military in the State, except when they shall be called into the service of the United States.

SEC. 10. The pardoning power shall be vested in the Governor, under such regulations and restrictions as may be prescribed by law.

SEC. 11. There shall be a seal of the State, the device for which shall be agreed upon by the General Assembly, and which shall be kept by the Governor, and used by him officially, and shall be called "The Seal of the State of Kansas."

SEC. 12. All grants and commissions shall be issued in the name and by the authority of the State of Kansas, sealed with the seal thereof, signed by the Governor, and countersigned by the Secretary of State.

SEC. 13. No member of either house of Congress, or other persons holding office under the authority of this State, or of the United States, shall execute the duties of Governor except as herein provided.

SEC. 14. In the case of death, impeachment, resignation, removal, or other disability of the Governor, the Lieutenant Governor shall exercise the duties of the office of Governor, until another Governor shall be duly qualified, or the disability be removed; but in such case another Governor shall be chosen at the next annual election for members of the General Assembly, unless such death, resignation, impeachment, removal or other disability shall occur within three calendar months immediately preceding such next annual election, in which case a Governor shall be chosen at the second succeeding annual election for members of the General Assembly; and in case of the death, impeachment, resignation, removal or other disability of the Lieutenant Governor, the President of the Senate *pro tempore* shall exercise the office of Governor until another Governor shall be duly qualified as aforesaid.

SEC. 15. The Lieutenant Governor shall be President of the Senate, but shall vote only when the Senate is equally divided, and shall be entitled to the same pay as the Speaker of the House of Representatives; and in case of his death, resignation, impeachment, removal from office, or when he shall exercise the office of Governor, the Senate shall choose a President *pro tempore*.

SEC. 16. Should the office of Secretary of State, Auditor of State, Treasurer of State, or Attorney General, become vacant, for any of the causes specified in the fourteenth and fifteenth sections, the Governor shall fill the vacancy or vacancies until the disability is removed or a successor is elected and qualified. Every such vacancy shall be filled by election, at the first general election that occurs more than thirty days after such vacancy shall have occurred, and the person chosen shall hold the office for the full term fixed in the second section of this article.

SEC. 17. The officers mentioned in this article shall, at stated times, receive for their services compensation to be fixed by law, which shall neither be increased or diminished during the period for which they shall have been elected.

SEC. 18. The officers of the Executive Department, and of the public State institutions, shall, at least ten days preceding each regular session of the General Assembly, severally report to the Governor, who shall transmit the same to the General Assembly.

SEC. 19. Every bill which shall have passed both houses shall be presented to the Governor. If he approve, he shall sign the same; but if he shall not approve, he shall return it with his objections to the house in which it shall have originated, which shall enter the objections at large upon the journal, and proceed to reconsider the bill. If after such reconsideration a majority of that house shall agree to pass the bill, it shall be sent, with the objections, to the other house, by which, likewise, it shall be reconsidered, and if approved by a majority of that house, it shall be a law; but in such case the votes of both houses shall be determined by yeas and nays, and the names of the persons voting for or against the bill shall be entered upon the journals of each house respectively. If any bill shall not be returned by the Governor within three days (Sundays excepted) after it shall have been presented to him, it shall be a law in like manner as if he had signed it, unless the General Assembly by adjournment prevent its return, in which case it shall not be a law.

ARTICLE VI.—JUDICIAL.

SECTION 1. The judicial power of the State shall be vested in a Supreme Court, Circuit Courts, County Courts, Justices of the Peace, and in such other courts inferior to the Supreme Court as may be established in the manner hereinafter provided.

SEC. 2. The Supreme Court shall consist of three Judges, a majority of whom shall form a quorum. It shall hold at least one term each year, at the seat of Government, and such other terms, there or elsewhere, as may be required by law.

SEC. 3. The Judges of the Supreme Court shall be elected by the electors of the State at large, at the first election under this Constitution. The term of one of said Judges shall be two years, of another four years, of another six years, and at all subsequent elections the term of each of said Judges shall be six years.

SEC. 4. The Judge having the shortest term to serve, not holding by appointment, shall be Chief Justice.

SEC. 5. The General Assembly shall provide by law for the speedy publication of the decisions of the Supreme Court.

SEC. 6. There shall be elected by the voters of the State, a Clerk, and a Reporter, for the Supreme Court, who shall hold their offices for three years.

SEC. 7. The Circuit Courts shall each consist of one Judge. The State shall be divided into judicial circuits, and a Judge for each circuit shall be elected by the voters thereof. He shall, while in office, reside in the circuit for which he is chosen, and his term of office shall be three years.

SEC. 8. Until otherwise provided by law, there shall be five judicial circuits, as follows: The First, comprising the counties of Leavenworth, Jefferson, Atchison, Doniphan, and Brown; the Second, the counties of Calhoun, Nemaha, Pottawatomie, Marshall, Riley, Washington, and Clay; the Third, the counties of Shawnee, Douglas, Johnson, Lykins, Franklin, and Weller; the Fourth, the counties of Linn, Bourbon, Coffey, Anderson, Allen, Woodson, Wilson, Dorn, and McGee; the Fifth, the counties of Richardson, Breckinridge, Madison, Greenwood, Godfrey, Hunter, Butler, Wise, Davis, and Dickinson.

SEC. 9. The General Assembly may provide by law that that the Judge of one circuit may hold the courts of another circuit in case of necessity or convenience.

SEC. 10. The County Courts shall each consist of one Judge, who shall be elected by the voters of each county. He shall reside in the county; and his term of office shall be two years.

SEC. 11. A sufficient number of Justices of the Peace shall be elected by the voters in each township of the several counties. Their term of office shall be two years.

SEC. 12. All Judges other than those hereinbefore provided for shall be elected by the electors of the judicial district over which their jurisdiction may extend, but not for a term of office longer than six years.

SEC. 13. The jurisdiction of the Supreme Court, the Circuit Courts, the County Courts, the Justices of the Peace, and such other courts as may be created, shall be fixed by law; and the Judges of the courts shall respectively have and exercise such power and jurisdiction at chambers as may be provided by law.

SEC. 14. Judges may be removed from office by concurrent resolution of both houses of the General Assembly, if two-thirds of the members elected to each house concur therein; but no such removal shall be made except upon complaint, the substance of which shall be entered upon the journal, nor until the party charged shall have notice thereof, and an opportunity to be heard.

SEC. 15. In case the office of any Judge shall become vacant before the expiration of the term for which he was elected, the vacancy shall be filled by appointment by the Governor until a successor shall be elected and qualified; and such successor shall be elected for the residue of the unexpired term, at the first annual election that occurs more than thirty days after such vacancy shall have happened.

SEC. 16. The compensation of the Judges of the Supreme Court and of the Circuit Courts shall not be increased or diminished during their term of office, and they shall receive no fees or perquisites, nor hold any office of profit and trust under the State, other than a judicial office.

SEC. 17. The General Assembly may at any time increase the number of the Judges of the Supreme Court, may increase or diminish the number of judicial circuits, or change the circuits, or may establish other courts by a law passed by two-thirds of the members elected to each house; but no such change, addition or diminution shall vacate the office of any Judge.

SEC. 18. There shall be elected in each county, by the electors thereof, one Clerk of the Courts, who shall hold his office for the term of two years, and until his successor shall be elected and qualified. He shall be Clerk of the County Court and Circuit Court in the county in which he is chosen.

SEC. 19. There shall be elected in each county by the voters thereof one County Attorney, who shall hold his office for the term of two years, and until his successor shall be elected and qualified.

SEC. 20. The duties, compensation, fees and perquisites of the officers provided for in this article shall be fixed by law.

SEC. 21. The style of all process shall be, "The State of Kansas." All prosecutions shall be carried on in the name and by the authority of the State of Kansas; and all indictments shall conclude, "against the peace and dignity of the State of Kansas."

ARTICLE VII.—EDUCATION.

SECTION 1. The stability and perpetuity of free republican institutions depend upon the intelligence and virtue of the people; therefore it is declared to be the duty of the State to establish by law, at the earliest possible period, a uniform system of free schools, in which every child in the State shall be entitled to receive a good common school education at the public expense.

SEC. 2. The principal of all school funds, from whatever source, shall be the common property of the State, and may be increased, but shall forever be preserved inviolate and undiminished.

SEC. 3. The income of the school fund shall be devoted exclusively to the support of schools, and, together with any funds raised in any other manner for school purposes, shall be distributed, through the county or township treasurers, to the several school districts, in some equitable proportion to the number of children and youth resident therein, between the ages of five and twenty-one years.

SEC. 4. The school lands shall never be sold until such sale is authorized by a free and fair vote of the people of Kansas, but, subject to a valuation every three years, may be leased at a per centum established by law.

SEC. 5. No religious sect or sects shall ever have any right to, or control of, any part of the school funds of this State.

SEC. 6. The General Assembly shall make such provision, by taxation or otherwise, as, with the income arising from the school fund, will secure, throughout the State, the maintenance of a thorough and uniform system of common schools, which shall be kept up and supported in each district at least four months in each year, and shall be open and free to every child in the State between the ages of five and twenty-one years.

SEC. 7. As the means of the State will admit, educational institutions of a higher grade shall be established by law so as to form a complete system of public instruction, embracing the primary, normal, preparatory, collegiate and university departments.

SEC. 8. At the first election of State officers, and biennially thereafter, the people shall elect a Superintendent of Public Instruction, whose duties and compensation shall be prescribed by law.

SEC. 9. At the first election of State officers, and biennially thereafter, there shall be elected by the people a Commissioner of School Funds, who shall have the charge of the school lands and the principal of the school fund, whose duties and compensation shall be prescribed by law.

ARTICLE VIII.— PUBLIC INSTITUTIONS.

SECTION 1. It shall be the duty of the General Assembly, at as early a date as possible, to provide State Asylums for the benefit, treatment and instruction of the blind, deaf and dumb, and insane.

SEC. 2. The General Assembly shall make provision for the establishment of an asylum for idiots, to be regulated by law.

SEC. 3. The General Assembly shall make provision for the establishment of houses of refuge for the correction, reform and instruction of juvenile offenders.

SEC. 4. It shall be the duty of the General Assembly to make provision as soon as possible for a State Hospital and State Penitentiary: *Provided,* That not more than one of the aforesaid institutions shall be located in any county of this State, the location to be determined by a vote of the electors at large at any general election, and that the directors and superintendents of the same shall be elected by the people.

SEC. 5. The respective counties of the State shall provide in some suitable manner for those inhabitants who, by reason of age, infirmity or other misfortune, may have claims upon the sympathy and aid of society, under provision to be made by the laws of the General Assembly.

ARTICLE IX.— MILITIA.

SECTION 1. The Governor shall be Commander-in-Chief of the military forces of the State, excepting when these forces shall be actually in the service of the United States, and shall have power to call out any part, or the whole, of said military forces to aid in the execution of the laws, to suppress insurrection, and to repel invasion.

SEC. 2. All male citizens of this State, between the ages of eighteen and forty-five years, excepting those who are conscientiously opposed to bearing arms, and such others as may be by law exempted shall be enrolled in the militia, and held to perform such military duty as by law may be required.

SEC. 3. The General Assembly shall provide by law for organizing and disciplining the militia in such manner as it shall deem expedient.

ARTICLE X.— PUBLIC DEBT.

SECTION 1. No money shall be paid out of the Treasury except in pursuance of an appropriation by law.

SEC. 2. The credit of the State shall never be given or loaned in aid of any individual, association or corporation.

SEC. 3. For the purpose of defraying extraordinary expenditures, the State may contract public debts, but such debt shall never in the aggregate exceed one hundred thousand dollars, unless authorized by a direct vote of the people at a general election. Every such debt shall be authorized by law, and every such law shall provide for the payment of the annual interest of such debt, and the principal within ten years from the passage of such law; and such appropriation shall not be repealed until the principal and interest shall have been wholly paid.

SEC. 4. The Legislature may also borrow money to repel invasion, suppress insurrection, or defend the State in time of war; but the money thus raised shall be applied exclusively to the object for which the loan was authorized, or repayment of the debts thereby created.

SEC. 5. No scrip, certificate, or other evidence of State debt whatever, shall be issued, except for such debts as are authorized by the third and fourth sections of this article.

ARTICLE XI.— FINANCE AND TAXATION.

SECTION 1. The levying of taxes by the poll is grievous and oppressive; therefore, the General Assembly shall never levy a poll tax for county or State purposes.

SEC. 2. Laws shall be passed taxing, by a uniform rule, all real and personal property, according to its true value in money; but burying grounds, school houses, and other property used exclusively for educational purposes, houses used exclusively for public worship, not exceeding fifty thousand dollars in value, institutions of public charity, public and municipal property used exclusively for public and municipal purposes, and personal property to an amount not exceeding in value two hundred dollars for each

12

head of a family, may by general laws be exempted from taxation, but all such laws shall be subject to alteration or repeal; and the value of all such property, so exempted, shall from time to time be ascertained and published, as may be directed by law.

SEC. 3. The General Assembly shall provide for raising revenue sufficient to defray the expenses of the State for each year; and also a sufficient sum to pay the interest and such part of the principal of a State debt, if any such debt shall accrue, as may be directed by law.

SEC. 4. No tax shall be levied except in pursuance of law; and every law imposing a tax shall state distinctly the object of the same, to which only it shall be applied.

SEC. 5. The State shall never contract any debt for purposes of internal improvements.

SEC. 6. In the passage in either house of the General Assembly of any law which imposes, continues, or renews a tax, or makes, continues, or renews an appropriation of public or trust moneys, or to release, discharge, or commute a claim or demand of the State, the vote shall be taken by yeas and nays, which shall be duly entered on the journal; and three-fifths of all the members elected to such house shall, in all such cases, be requisite to constitute a quorum.

ARTICLE XII. — COUNTIES, AND COUNTY AND TOWNSHIP OFFICERS.

SECTION 1. The General Assembly shall provide by law for submitting to the people of each county, at an annual election, the question of the location of the county seats; and the General Assembly may change the lines of counties, but shall by law submit such proposed alterations to the electors of the county or counties affected thereby, at a general election; said alterations to be made to township lines, as far as practicable.

SEC. 2. The General Assembly shall provide by law for the creation and election of county, city, town and township officers.

SEC. 3. All officers whose election or appointment is not provided for by this Constitution, shall be elected by the people or appointed, as the General Assembly may by law direct.

SEC. 4. Provision shall be made by law for the removal, for misconduct or malversation in office, of all officers whose powers and duties are not local or legislative, and who shall be elected at general elections, and also for supplying vacancies created by such removal.

SEC. 5. The Legislature may declare the cases in which any office shall be deemed vacant, where no provision is made for that purpose in this Constitution.

ARTICLE XIII. — ELECTIONS.

SECTION 1. All elections shall be free and equal.

SEC. 2. Electors shall, in all cases except treason, felony, and breach of the peace, be privileged from arrest during their attendance on elections, and in going to and returning from them.

SEC. 3. All elections by the people shall be by ballot, and all elections by the General Assembly, or by either branch thereof, shall be viva voce.

SEC. 4. All general elections shall be held on the Tuesday next succeeding the first Monday in November of each year.

SEC. 5. Returns of elections for Members of Congress, the General Assembly, and all other officers not otherwise provided for, shall be made to the Secretary of State, in such manner as may be prescribed by law.

ARTICLE XIV. — CORPORATIONS.

SECTION 1. Corporations may be created under general law, but shall not be created by special acts, except for municipal purposes. All general laws and special acts authorizing or creating corporations may be altered from time to time, or repealed.

SEC. 2. Dues from corporations shall be secured by such individual liability of the stockholders and other means as shall be prescribed by law, and each stockholder of a corporation or joint-stock association, except corporations for charitable purposes and railroad corporations, shall be individually liable over and above the stock by him or her owned, and any amount unpaid thereon to a further sum at least equal in amount to such stock.

SEC. 3. The property of corporations, except for charitable and religious purposes, now existing, and to be hereafter created, shall be subject to taxation the same as the property of individuals.

SEC. 4. All real estate or other property of religious corporations shall vest in trustees, whose election shall be by the members of such corporation.

SEC. 5. The General Assembly shall provide for the organization of cities and villages by general laws, and restrict their power of taxation, assessment, borrowing money, contracting debts, and loaning their credit, so as to prevent the abuse of such power.

SEC. 6. The term corporations as used in this article shall be construed to include all associations and joint-stock companies having any of the powers or privileges of corporations not possessed by individuals or partnerships; and all such corporations shall have the right to sue, and shall be subject to be sued, in all courts, the same as natural persons.

ARTICLE XV.— JURISPRUDENCE.

SECTION 1. The General Assembly at its first session under this Constitution shall constitute a commission, to consist of three persons not members of the Senate or House of Representatives, whose duty it shall be to revise, reform, simplify, and abridge the rules of practice, pleading, and proceeding in the courts of record of this State, abolishing the forms of action known to the common law, and distinctions as to form between proceedings at law and in equity.

SEC. 2. The proceedings of the Commissioners shall be reported to and be subject to the action of the General Assembly.

SEC. 3. All the proceedings of the courts of this State shall be instituted and conducted in the English language, avoiding, as far as practicable, the use of technical terms.

ARTICLE XVI.— MISCELLANEOUS.

SECTION 1. No person shall be taken, imprisoned, or disseized of his freehold, outlawed, exiled, or in any manner deprived of his life, liberty or property, but by the judgment of his peers and the law of the land.

SEC. 2. The printing of the laws and journals, bills, legislative documents and papers for each branch of the General Assembly, and all printing for the Executive and other departments of State, shall be let to the lowest responsible bidder, by such officers and in such manner as shall be prescribed by law.

SEC. 3. The General Assembly shall provide by law for the protection of the rights of women, married and single, in the acquiring and possessing of property, real, personal, and mixed, separate and apart from the husband or other person, and shall also provide for the equal rights of women in the protection, with the husband, of their children, during their minority; also shall provide for the securing of a homestead, which, without the consent of the wife, she cannot be divested of.

SEC. 4. No person shall be elected or appointed to any office in this State unless he possesses the qualification of an elector at the time of his election or appointment.

SEC. 5. There shall be established in the Secretary of State's office a Bureau of Statistics and Agriculture, under such regulations as may be prescribed by law; and provision shall be made by the General Assembly for the organization and encouragement of State and County Agricultural Associations.

SEC. 6. Lotteries, gift enterprises, and the sale of lottery and gift-enterprise tickets, for any purpose whatever, shall be forever prohibited in the State.

SEC. 7. A homestead of one hundred and sixty acres of land, or, in lieu thereof, a house and lot, or other property not exceeding in value two thousand dollars, belonging to any one family, shall by law be exempted from forced sale under any process of law, and shall not be alienated without the joint consent of husband and wife, in cases where that relation exists; but no property shall be exempt from sale for taxes or for the payment of obligations contracted for its purchase.

SEC. 8. This State shall have jurisdiction concurrent with the State of Missouri, on the Missouri river, so far as the said river may be the common boundary of the two States.

SEC. 9. For the purpose of preserving the public health, the General Assembly shall have power to pass general sanitary laws.

SEC. 10. No lease or grant of agricultural land for a longer period than twelve years, hereafter to be made, in which shall be reserved any rent or service of any kind, shall be valid; and all fines, quarter-sales, or other like restraints upon transfer, reserved in any lease of land, hereafter to be made, shall be void, provided that this article shall in no wise interfere with the disposition of the school lands of the State.

SEC. 11. In all cases where it shall be necessary to sell any of the lands granted by Congress, said sales shall not be made without one year's notice through publication in the county or counties where the lands lie, and an advertisement in two or more central newspapers of the State; and there shall be a valuation of said lands by disinterested persons, and no lands shall be sold at a less price than the valuation.

ARTICLE XVII.—BANKS AND CURRENCY.

SECTION 1. No bank shall be established otherwise than under a general banking law.

SEC. 2. If the General Assembly shall enact a general banking law, such law shall provide for the registry and countersigning by the Auditor of State of all bank notes or paper credit designed to be circulated as money.

SEC. 3. It shall be further provided that such bank notes or paper credits shall be amply secured by the deposit with the proper officer of State of bonds of interest-paying States, or the United States.

SEC. 4. All bills or notes issued as money shall be at all times redeemable in gold or silver.

SEC. 5. Holders of bank notes shall be entitled, in case of insolvency, to preference of specie payment, over all other creditors.

SEC. 6. The State shall not be a stockholder in any bank or banking institution.

SEC. 7. All banks shall be required to keep officers and proper offices for the issue and redemption of their paper, at some convenient point within the State.

SEC. 8. Any general banking law passed by the General Assembly of this State may at any time be altered, amended, or repealed.

SEC. 9. No general banking law shall have any force or effect until the same shall have been submitted to a vote of the electors of the State, at some general election, and having been approved by a majority of all the votes given on that subject at such election.

ARTICLE XVIII.—AMENDMENTS.

SECTION 1. Propositions for the amendment of this Constitution may be made by either branch of the General Assembly; and if three-fifths of all the members elected to each house concur therein, such proposed amendments shall be entered on the journals, with the yeas and nays; and the Secretary of State shall cause the same to be published in at least one newspaper in each county of the State where a newspaper is published, for three months preceding the next election for Senators and Representatives, at which time the same shall be submitted to the electors for their approval or rejection; and if a majority of the electors voting on said amendments, at said election, shall adopt such amendments, the same shall become a part of the Constitution. When more than one amendment shall be submitted at the same time, they shall be so submitted as to enable the electors to vote on each amendment separately.

SEC. 2. Whenever three-fifths of the members elected to each branch of the General Assembly shall think it necessary to call a Convention to revise, amend or change this Constitution, they shall recommend to the electors to vote at the next election of members of the General Assembly for or against a Convention; and if a majority of all the electors voting at said election shall have voted for a Convention, the General Assembly shall, at its next regular session, provide by law for calling the same. The Convention shall consist of as many members as the House of Representatives, and shall be chosen in the same manner, and shall meet within three months after their election, at the Capital of the State, for the purpose aforesaid.

SEC. 3. At the general election to be held in the year one thousand eight hundred and sixty-three, and in each tenth year thereafter, the question, "Shall there be a Convention to revise, alter or amend the Constitution?" shall be submitted to the electors of the State; and in case a majority of the electors voting at such election shall decide in favor of a Convention, the General Assembly, at its next regular session, shall provide by law for the election of delegates, and the assembling of such Convention, as provided in the preceding section; but no amendment or revision of this Constitution agreed upon by any Convention in pursuance of this article, shall take effect until the same shall have been submitted to the electors of the State, and adopted by a majority of those voting thereon.

SCHEDULE.

SECTION 1. In order that no inconvenience may arise from the change from a Territorial to a State Government, it is declared that no existing rights, suits, prosecutions (except for political offences), claims or contracts, shall be affected by a change in the form of government, except as otherwise declared in this Constitution. But no debt of the Territory shall be assumed by the State, except by a law passed by a vote of two-thirds of each branch of the General Assembly.

SEC. 2. This Constitution shall be submitted to a vote of the people for approval or rejection, on the third Tuesday of May, one thousand eight hundred and fifty-eight. The vote shall be by ballot, and those in favor of the Constitution shall write or print upon their ballots the words, "For the Constitution," and those opposed to the Constitution shall write or print upon their ballots the words, "Against the Constitution." Said election shall be conducted according to the provisions of section thirteen of an Act of the Legislative Assembly of the Territory of Kansas, passed February —, one thousand eight hundred and fifty-eight, entitled "An act to provide for the election of Delegates to a Convention to frame a State Constitution."

SEC. 3. At the same time and place, and under the provisions of the section aforesaid, of the Act aforesaid, an election shall be held for members of the General Assembly, for State officers, for Judges, and for Member of Congress to represent the State of Kansas in the Thirty-fifth Congress of the United States.

SEC. 4. If this Constitution, upon being submitted to the people, shall be approved by a majority of the legal votes cast thereon, a copy of the same, certified by the President and Secretary of the Convention, together with a Memorial framed by the Convention, asking admission into the Union, and a certified statement of the vote on the ratification thereof, shall be transmitted, as soon as practicable, by the Governor, President of the Council, and Speaker of the House of Representatives of the Territory of Kansas, or any two of them, to the President and Congress of the United States.

SEC. 5. Provided this Constitution shall be ratified by the people, then, upon the admission of Kansas into the Union as a State, this Constitution shall be in full force, the State officers shall immediately enter upon the performance of their duties, and the Governor shall immediately, by proclamation, convene the General Assembly.

SEC. 6. The members of the first General Assembly shall hold their offices until and including December thirty-first, one thousand eight hundred and fifty-nine.

SEC. 7. The State officers and Supreme and District Judges elected under this constitution shall hold their respective offices for the same length of time as though their term of office commenced on January first, one thousand eight hundred and fifty-nine.

SEC. 8. The Governor is authorized to adopt a seal, to be the seal of the State of Kansas, until otherwise provided for by law.

SEC. 9. Until otherwise provided by law, the State shall be divided into Senatorial districts, and Senators apportioned to them as follows: The First District shall consist of Leavenworth county, and shall be entitled to three Senators; the Second District shall consist of Atchison county, and shall be entitled to one Senator; the Third District shall consist of Doniphan county, and shall be entitled to two Senators; the Fourth District shall consist of Jefferson county, and be entitled to one Senator; the Fifth District shall consist of the counties of Brown and Calhoun, and shall be entitled to one Senator; the Sixth District shall consist of the counties of Nemaha, Marshall and Washington, and shall be entitled to one Senator; the Seventh District shall consist of the counties of Pottawatomie and Richardson, and shall be entitled to one Senator; the Eighth District shall consist of the counties of Riley, Clay, Dickinson, Arapahoe, and all the western part of Kansas, not otherwise attached, and shall be entitled to one Senator; the Ninth District shall consist of the counties of Breckinridge, Wise and Davis, and shall be entitled to one Senator; the Tenth District shall consist of the counties of Shawnee and Weller, and shall be entitled to two Senators; the Eleventh District shall consist of the counties of Butler, Hunter, Woodson, Greenwood, Madison, Godfrey and Wilson, and shall be entitled to one Senator; the Twelfth District shall consist of the county of Coffey and shall be entitled to one Senator; the Thirteenth District shall consist of the county of Douglas, and shall be entitled to two Senators; the Fourteenth District shall consist of the county of Johnson, and be entitled to one Senator; the Fifteenth District shall consist of the county of Lykins, and be entitled to one Senator; the Sixteenth District shall consist of the county of Franklin, and be entitled to one Senator; the Seventeenth

District shall consist of the county of Anderson, and be entitled to one Senator; the Eighteenth District shall consist of the county of Linn, and shall be entitled to one Senator; the Nineteenth District shall consist of the county of Bourbon, and shall be entitled to one Senator; the Twentieth District shall consist of the counties of Allen, Dorn and McGee, and shall be entitled to one Senator.

SEC. 10. The State shall be divided into Representative districts, and members apportioned thereto as follows: First District, Leavenworth county, ten members; Second, Atchison, three; Third, Doniphan, five; Fourth, Jefferson, three; Fifth, Brown, two; Sixth, Nemaha, two; Seventh, Pottawatomie, two; Eighth, Calhoun, one; Ninth, Marshall and Washington, one; Tenth, Riley, three; Eleventh, Clay and Dickinson, one; Twelfth, Davis, one; Thirteenth, Wise, one; Fourteenth, Butler and Hunter, one; Fifteenth, Richardson, one; Sixteenth, Breckinridge, two; Seventeenth, Madison, one; Eighteenth, Greenwood, one; Nineteenth, Woodson, one; Twentieth, Coffey, two; Twenty-first, Weller, one; Twenty-second, Shawnee, four; Twenty-third, Douglas, seven; Twenty-fourth, Johnson, three; Twenty-fifth, Lykins, three; Twenty-sixth, Linn, three; Twenty-seventh, Franklin, two; Twenty-eighth, Anderson, two; Twenty-ninth, Allen, one; Thirtieth, Bourbon, three; Thirty-first, McGee, Dorn, Wilson and Godfrey, one; District Number Thirty-two to consist of all the western part of Kansas, not otherwise attached, including the county of Arapahoe, one member.

SEC. 11. The General Assembly at its first session shall provide for receiving proposals for the location of the seat of Government, and shall publish such proposals and also a plan for the purchase of a site by the State, and then submit them to a full and fair vote of the people, at the first general election after such session; and if no proposal or plan submitted shall receive a majority of all the votes cast, then they shall be submitted at each subsequent and general election until such choice shall be made; and when a proposal or plan shall be adopted, the Legislature shall provide for the location at the place or in the manner designated, and for the application of the profits which may accrue to the State therefrom, to the benevolent institutions of the State; and when the seat of Government shall have been thus located, it shall not be changed but by a law ratified by a direct vote of the people; and until the selection provided for in this section shall be made, Topeka shall be the seat of Government.

SEC. 12. The first General Assembly shall provide by law for the submission of the question of universal suffrage to a vote of the people at the first general election of members of the General Assembly, provided that the qualifications of voters at that election shall be the same as at the vote on the submission of the Constitution.

M. F. CONWAY, *President.*

F. G. ADAMS.
H. S. BAKER.
G. M. FULLER.
CALEB MAY.
CALEB A. WOODWORTH.
W. F. M. ARNY.
WILLIAM SPRIGGS.
WM. L. WEBSTER.
WM. R. GRIFFITH.
B. B. NEWTON.
WM. McCULLOCH.
P. B. PLUMB.
J. R. SWALLOW.
A. B. ANDERSON.
ORVILLE ROOT.
A. W. WILLIAMS.
SAMUEL STEWART.
WM. E. BOWKER.
R. A. KINZIE.
J. M. ELLIOTT.
JAMES D. ALLEN.
C. H. BRANSCOMB.
JOHN L. BROWN.
JAMES S. EMERY.
CHARLES MAYO.
WM. R. MONTIETH.
D. PICKERING.
E. S. SCUDDER.

AMASA SOULE.
J. M. SHEPHERD.
T. DWIGHT THACHER.
SAM'L N. WOOD.
WM. V. BARR.
W. D. BEELER.
JOS. F. HAMPSON.
THOS. H. BUTLER.
A. DANFORD.
ROBERT EWING.
ROBT. B. MITCHELL.
CHAS. A. FOSTER.
GUSTAVUS A. COLTON.
ALBURTUS KNAPP.
J. K. GOODIN.
J. G. REES.
URIAH COOK.
EDWARD LYNDE.
JAMES MONROE.
A. W. McCAUSLIN.
JONATHAN C. TODD.
R. U. TORRY.
JAMES FLETCHER.
HENRY HARVEY.
F. N. BLAKE.
ISAAC T. GOODNOW.
G. W. HIGINBOTHAM.
R. M. FISH.

LUCIAN FISH.
W. W. ROSS.
JOHN RITCHIE.
ALFRED L. WINANS.
G. D. HUMPHREY.
A. H. SHURTLEFF.
R. AUSTIN.
H. J. ESPY.
HENRY J. ADAMS.
WM. H. COFFIN.
JOHN C. DOUGLASS.
JAMES DAVIS.
THOS. EWING, JR.
J. P. HATTERSCHEIDT.
H. P. JOHNSON.
J. H. LANE.
ALFRED LARZELERE.
CHAS. S. PERHAM.
HUGH ROBERTSON.
JOSIAH H. PILLSBURY.
M. L. ASHMORE.
W. Y. ROBERTS.
THOMAS TROWER.
JAMES TELFER.
G. W. K. TWOMBLY.
JAMES M. WINCHELL.
J. M. WALDEN.

SAMUEL F. TAPPAN, *Secretary.*

I hereby certify that the above is a correct copy of the Constitution adopted by the Convention at Leavenworth, April 3d, 1858, from the original draft now in my possession.   M. F. CONWAY, *President of the Convention.*
LEAVENWORTH, APRIL 5, 1858.

MAY 12.—James W. Denver takes the oath of office as Governor, and Hugh S. Walsh as Secretary.

Governor Denver orders Samuel Walker, Sheriff of Douglas county, to arrest the band of lawless armed men acting under James Montgomery.

MAY 18.—Vote on the Leavenworth Constitution, State officers and Legislature.

Rev. Richard Cordley starts the Congregational Record, at Lawrence.

MAY 19.—The Marais des Cygnes massacre. Tomlinson says Hamilton's party consisted of twenty-five persons. He gives the following names: Charles A. Hamilton, Dr. John Hamilton, Alvin Hamilton, Luke Yealock, William Yealock, Thomas Jackson, Brockett, Harlin, Beach, and Mattock. They lived near or in West Point, Missouri. They reached the Trading Post, in Linn county, early in the afternoon, and arrested John F. Campbell and G. W. Andrews, who were in the store. William Stillwell was next arrested. They then made other arrests of Free-State men in the vicinity, placed the prisoners in Stillwell's wagon, and started towards Missouri. Soon after, Rev. Charles Reed was arrested, and Andrews was released. The prisoners numbered nine. About three miles from the Trading Post they halted. Brockett then came up, with Snyder, the blacksmith, as a prisoner. The prisoners were ordered to form in line a few yards from the Ruffians. The order to fire was given, and every Free-State man fell. Five were killed instantly, and all the others, except one, badly wounded. The one slightly wounded was, soon after, shot through the head and killed. The others feigned death. The Ruffians robbed the bodies and rode off. The murdered men were William Stillwell, Patrick Ross, Mr. Colpetzer, Michael Robinson, John F. Campbell; the wounded were William Hairgrove, Asa Hairgrove, Charles Reed, Amos Hall, and Charles Snyder.

Robert B. Mitchell with a party of men, among them Montgomery, proceeded to West Point in pursuit of the murderers, but came back without having done anything.

The following poem was written by John G. Whittier, and was published in the Atlantic Monthly, in September, 1858:

LE MARAIS DU CYGNE.*

A blush as of roses
  Where rose never grew!
Great drops on the bunch-grass,
  But not of the dew!
A taint in the sweet air
  For wild bees to shun!
A stain that shall never
  Bleach out in the sun!

Back, steed of the prairies!
  Sweet song-bird, fly back!
Wheel hither, bald vulture!
  Gray wolf, call thy pack!
The foul human vultures
  Have feasted and fled;
The wolves of the Border
  Have crept from the dead.

In the homes of their rearing,
  Yet warm with their lives,
Ye wait the dead only,
  Poor children and wives!
Put out the red forge-fire,
  The smith shall not come;
Unyoke the brown oxen,
  The ploughman lies dumb.

Wind slow from the Swan's Marsh,
  O dreary death-train,
With pressed lips as bloodless
  As lips of the slain!
Kiss down the young eyelids,
  Smooth down the gray hairs;
Let tears quench the curses
  That burn through your prayers.

---

*The massacre of unarmed and unoffending men in Southern Kansas took place near the Marais du Cygne of the French voyageurs.

From the hearths of their cabins,
   The fields of their corn,
Unwarned and unweaponed,
   The victims were torn,—
By the whirlwind of murder
   Swooped up and swept on
To the low, reedy fen-lands,
   The Marsh of the Swan.

With a vain plea for mercy
   No stout knee was crooked;
In the mouths of the rifles
   Right manly they looked.
How paled the May sunshine,
   Green Marais du Cygne,
When the death-smoke blew over
   Thy lonely ravine!

Strong man of the prairies,
   Mourn bitter and wild!
Wail, desolate woman!
   Weep, fatherless child!
But the grain of God springs up
   From ashes beneath,
And the crown of His harvest
   Is life out of death.

Not in vain on the dial
   The shade moves along
To point the great contrasts
   Of right and of wrong;
Free homes and free altars
   And fields of ripe food;
The reeds of the Swan's Marsh,
   Whose bloom is of blood.

On the lintels of Kansas
   That blood shall not dry;
Henceforth the Bad Angel
   Shall harmless go by;
Henceforth to the sunset,
   Unchecked on her way,
Shall liberty follow
   The march of the day.

MAY 21.—Twenty men leave Lawrence for "the gold region in the vicinity of the Rocky Mountains in Kansas." This was the first, or one of the earliest, expeditions to Pike's Peak, or Colorado.

The journey is pleasantly described by William B. Parsons in the Kansas Magazine of June, 1872, vol. I, p. 552.

MAY 29.—Samuel Walker marches to Fort Scott; Montgomery and a large party of mounted men go with him from Raysville, leaving there on the 29th. Arriving in Fort Scott, Walker divided the men into three divisions. Tomlinson says: "One company surrounded Sheriff Hill's house, another the Pro-Slavery Hotel (McKay's), and the third the house of the notorious Clarke"—the murderer of Barber. Clarke defied arrest, but Walker arrested him. After leaving town, Walker arrested Montgomery, for whom also he had a writ. Walker was the Sheriff of Douglas county and a Deputy U. S. Marshal. On the 30th, at Raysville, news was brought to him that Clarke and the other Pro-Slavery men he had arrested in Fort Scott had been released, without a trial, and were again at large. Walker then released Montgomery from arrest.

JUNE.—D. H. Huyett visits Kansas to take sketches for a book.

JUNE 3.—Gaius Jenkins killed by James H. Lane, at Lawrence. The cause of the difficulty was a contested land claim.

JUNE 3.—Gov. Denver announces August 2d as the day of the election under the English bill, or act of Congress of May 4th.

JUNE 5.—Alson C. Davis takes the oath of office as United States Attorney.

JUNE 6.—Capt. James Montgomery enters Fort Scott, at midnight.

JUNE 8.—Conference meeting at West Point, Bates county, Mo. Six delegates went from border counties in Kansas. Bates, Vernon and Jasper counties, Missouri, were represented by about two hundred men. An agreement was signed by the delegates from the two States. It was a pledge against invasion, from either side of the line, and a promise by the Missourians to assist in bringing to justice Capt. Hamilton and all the men engaged in the Marais des Cygnes massacre.

JUNE 15.—Gov. Denver, at Fort Scott, makes an agreement with the citizens of Fort Scott and Bourbon county; he agrees to withdraw the troops, and they to keep the peace.

JUNE 17.—Abram Lincoln addresses a Republican Convention in Springfield, Ill., and says:

"A house divided against itself cannot stand. I believe this Government cannot endure permanently half slave and half free. I do not expect the Union to dissolve; but I do expect it will cease to be divided. It will become all one thing or all the other. Either the opponents of Slavery will arrest the further spread of it, and place it where the public mind will rest in the belief that it is in the course of ultimate extinction, or its advocates will push it forward until it shall become alike lawful in all the States, old as well as new, North as well as South. . . . We are now far into the fifth year since a policy was inaugurated with the avowed object and confident promise of putting an end to Slavery agitation. Under the operation of this policy, that agitation has not only not ceased, but has constantly augmented."

The debate between Lincoln and Douglas, candidates for the United States Senate, takes place this summer, and attracts national attention. It proves to be a canvass for the Presidency.

JUNE 17.—Governor Denver addresses a meeting at Chouteau's Trading Post, Linn county, and agrees to station Major Weaver on the border with a force of sixty men, to protect the eastern line of the county. Governor Robinson and Captain James Montgomery are present, and concur with Governor Denver in his peace policy.

JUNE 18.—United States Marshal Winston removed, and W. P. Fain appointed.

JUNE 22.—J. Calhoun, "President of the Constitutional Convention," issues certificates of election to the members of the Legislature under the Lecompton Constitution, elected December 21, 1857. In a letter from Nebraska City, dated July 2, 1858, General Calhoun writes to Governor Denver:

"For State officers I shall issue no certificates, as I do not deem it my right to do so. If the Constitution go into operation it will be my duty to convene the Legislature, and at its meeting I will lay before that body a statement of the returns, or the returns themselves, and let it determine who are elected State officers."

JUNE 25.—Captain Nathaniel Lyon, commanding United States troops at Fort Scott, writes to Governor Denver that "the agreement made by the people here on the occasion of your late visit has been entered upon in good faith, and to this time fully observed."

JUNE 26.—Commissions issued to A. J. Weaver, Captain, and the other officers of the Linn county company of volunteers, under an act of the Legislature, "to suppress the disturbances in Bourbon county."

JUNE 30.—Hiram J. Strickler commissioned as Librarian of the Territory.

JULY.—Joseph Williams and Rush Elmore Associate Justices until the admission of the State. Elmore was reappointed in place of Cato, who leaves the Territory.

JULY 3.—Governor Denver leaves Leavenworth for Washington.

—Organization of a Board of Education for the city of Leavenworth. George Wetherell taught the first public school, beginning July 5.

—Ward B. Burnett, of New York, appointed Surveyor General, vice John Calhoun.

JULY 8.—The Fort Scott Democrat says Sheriff Roberts has recovered nearly all the horses stolen by Rev. John E. Stewart. This Stewart sometimes took the name of Captain "Plum," and sometimes of Captain Montgomery, and looked upon all horses as Pro-Slavery.

JULY 13.—A. J. Isacks sends to Secretary Walsh the certificates of the members of the Legislature elected under the Lecompton Constitution, received by him from John Calhoun, at Nebraska City, with Calhoun's letter.

JULY 14.—Destructive fire in Leavenworth. The Market Hall, Christian Church and many other buildings burned.

JULY 15.—Major T. W. Sherman writes that the troops will be kept in Fort Scott, as Governor Denver had last requested.

AUGUST 2.—Vote on the Lecompton Constitution, as submitted by the English Bill.

DOUGLAS COUNTY.	Prop. rejected.	Prop. accepted.
Lawrence	718	4
Lecompton	122	27
Franklin	75	3
Bloomington	186	2
Eudora	103	—
Prairie City	123	—
Palmyra	109	—
Willow Springs	157	3
Big Springs	66	—
Coal Creek	57	—
Twin Mound	18	1
Blanton	64	—
	1,785	40
SHAWNEE COUNTY.		
Tecumseh	187	29
Brownville	127	1
Topeka	246	10
Burlingame	115	—
Versailles	14	—
Wakarusa	59	1
	743	41
LEAVENWORTH COUNTY.		
Leavenworth	1,610	138
Delaware	79	75
Wyandotte	203	84
Quindaro	130	16
Easton	60	41
Alexandria	68	14
Kickapoo	53	90
	2,203	456
ATCHISON COUNTY.		
Atchison	151	140
Sumner	221	13
Monrovia	63	8
Pardee	55	8
Allen's	47	14
Independence	17	2
Mt. Pleasant	65	35
Fort William	42	14
	616	260

DONIPHAN COUNTY.	Prop. rejected.	Prop. accepted.
White Cloud	61	9
Iowa Point	106	100
Highland	36	1
Troy	85	93
Elwood	129	38
Palermo	69	7
Wathena	40	37
Doniphan	160	44
Columbus	113	27
Wolf Creek	53	59
Geary City	75	1
	927	421
BROWN COUNTY.		
Hamlin	41	3
Iliawatha	83	1
Plymouth	22	—
Mt. Roy	21	6
Claytonville	68	25
Locknane	28	3
	243	35
NEMAHA COUNTY.		
Seneca	33	5
Central City	89	—
Wheatland	40	—
Granada	35	2
Capioma	30	5
	227	12
LYKINS COUNTY.		
Paola	26	27
Miamiville	70	20
Stanton	31	—
Middle Creek	19	—
Wea	7	6
Richland	11	18
Marysville	20	23
Osawatomie	226	3
	440	99
M'GEE COUNTY.		
Shoal Creek	14	6

BOURBON COUNTY.	Prop. rejected.	Prop. accepted.
Raysville	53	—
Mapleton	84	1
Marmaton	41	—
Barnesville	46	4
Osage	30	—
Mill Creek	26	—
Drywood	50	13
Fort Scott	81	19
Sprattsville	18	—
	429	37

ALLEN COUNTY.		
Cottage Grove	23	—
Deer Creek	23	—
Cofachique	78	18
Humboldt	85	6
Martin's Creek	65	—
Osage	17	—
Wray's	65	—
	268	23

DORN COUNTY.		
Osage Mission	—	9

ANDERSON COUNTY.		
Hyatt	55	—
Shannon	109	3
Cresco	40	1
Addington	32	—
Walker	70	—
	313	4

LINN COUNTY.		
Potosi	44	4
Centreville	79	—
Mound City	150	2
Scott	58	8
Liberty	13	—
Tate	57	2
Breckinridge	21	27
	422	43

FRANKLIN COUNTY.		
Centropolis	155	—
Ohio City	52	3
Ottawa	45	1
Peoria	59	2
Pottawatomie	65	—
	376	6

JOHNSON COUNTY.		
Lexington	29	33
Monticello	14	9
Shawnee	80	41
Oxford	13	16
McCamish	77	5
Spring Hill	37	5
Gardner	100	3
Aubrey	5	6
Olathe	69	31
	424	154

BRECKINRIDGE COUNTY.		
Emporia	104	—
Kansas Centre	33	2
Americus	20	—
Agnes City	20	2
Cottonwood	17	—
	194	4

MADISON COUNTY.	Prop. rejected.	Prop. accepted.
Columbia	75	—
Eagle City	62	—
Hesperia	21	—
	158	—

WISE COUNTY.		
Cottonwood Falls	30	—
Council Grove	26	6
Diamond Springs	9	—
	65	6

HUNTER COUNTY.		
Eldorado	23	—

RILEY COUNTY.		
Randolph	30	—
Ogden	42	17
Manhattan	132	1
Kent	23	2
Republican	31	2
	258	22

JEFFERSON COUNTY.		
Grasshopper Falls	166	6
Oskaloosa	93	15
Osawkee	75	25
Hardtville	77	63
Rising Sun	30	42
	441	151

CALHOUN COUNTY.		
Jefferson Township	61	8
Holton	99	13
Douglas	90	11
	250	32

RICHARDSON COUNTY.		
Mission Creek	19	—
Wabaunsee	71	—
Wilmington	38	—
Alma	16	—
	144	—

WOODSON COUNTY.		
Reeder } Belmont } Neosho Falls }	121	2

DAVIS COUNTY.		
Ashland	27	5
Riley	42	16
Zeandale	54	6
	123	27

COFFEY COUNTY.		
Burlington	120	—
Neosho City	64	1
LeRoy	180	15
Ottumwa	—	2
	364	18

POTTAWATOMIE COUNTY.		
Juniata	39	4
St George	58	3
Louisville	37	1
Shannon	16	—
Vienna	46	—
Pottawatomie	40	—
	236	8

The official result was declared to be 1,788 for the proposition, and 11,300 against it; majority against it, 9,512. The proclamation was signed by J. W. Denver, Hugh S. Walsh, A. C. Davis, and G. W. Deitzler—C. W. Babcock being absent. Some returns were not counted that are given in the foregoing table.

AUGUST.—Jacob Stotler unites with P. B. Plumb in publishing the Emporia News. The News, White Cloud Chief, and Leavenworth Times were established in 1857.

— E. R. Smith appointed United States Mail Agent.

AUGUST 5.—Governor Denver writes to Fort Leavenworth that troops are no longer needed at Fort Scott.

AUGUST 13.—Rush Elmore takes the oath of office as Associate Justice of the Supreme Court.

SEPTEMBER 1.—The Massasoit House opened at Atchison, by Thomas Murphy.

SEPTEMBER.—A Masonic Lodge organized at Emporia. Lawrence D. Bailey, W. M.; C. V. Eskridge, Secretary.

—Frank F. Barclay starts a French paper, L' Estafette du Kansas, at Leavenworth.

—Asa Hairgrove and William Hairgrove, of Linn county, bring suits against Charles A. Hamilton, Algernon Hamilton, James Tate, Lewis Henderson, W. B. Brockett and others, for shooting and dangerously wounding them on the 19th of May.

—Hockaday, Burr & Co. begin outfitting trains at Atchison for Salt Lake.

—Charles Hays, who murdered Buffum in 1856, is arrested at Atchison.

—The Minnie Belle makes a trip to Manhattan.

—"Pike's Peak" becomes the leading topic of the Kansas press.

—Samuel J. Jones, the notorious ex-Sheriff of Douglas county, who led the expedition against Lawrence, May 21, 1856, is appointed Collector of the district Paso del Norte. G. W. Clarke, the murderer of Barber, is made a Purser in the Navy.

—Colonel Titus leaves for Sonora.

—W. W. & E. G. Ross retire from the Topeka Tribune. The paper was revived by Farnsworth & Cummings.

SEPTEMBER 5.—Governor Denver resigns, to take effect October 10th.

SEPTEMBER 18.—Governor Denver writes to Secretary Cass that Captain Weaver's company has been the means of preserving the peace in the southern part of the Territory, but that he intends to discharge it November 6th.

OCTOBER 4.—Election of members of the House (Territorial Legislature), and Territorial Superintendent of Common Schools.

FIRST DISTRICT— LEAVENWORTH COUNTY—*Eight Members.*

Adam Fisher	933	A. M. Clark	1130
Fred. Brown	891	James L. McDowell	1142
W. P. Gambell	934	Lyman Scott	1109
O. B. Holman	839	Charles F. Kob	1011
Pascal S. Parks	916	W. Y. Roberts	1313
I. A. S. Hanford	924	John W. Wright	1002
Philip T. Colby	903	James Medill	1101
George P. Nelson	923	O. M. Marsh	1100

Superintendent of Schools.

Perry Fuller (Dem.)	405	S. W. Greer (F. S.)	436

SECOND DISTRICT—ATCHISON—*Three Members.*

John B. Irvin	492	S. J. H. Snyder	422
H. Weider	534	D. McIntyre	460
L. Dickerson	562	A. D. Richardson	369

Superintendent of Schools.

S. W. Greer 429

THIRD DISTRICT—DONIPHAN—*Five Members.*

Ward L. Lewis	243	John F. Sparks	271
Robert Graham	236	Benjamin Wrigley	272
A. Larzelere	259	Joseph Penny	278
A. J. Allison	237	J. W. Shepherd	275
Thomas Stevenson	242	Wm. C. Croft	255

Iowa, Washington, and Wolf River townships not counted in the official abstract.

Superintendent of Schools.

John Bayless .... 211 | —— Hill .... 194 | S. W. Greer 37

FOURTH AND FIFTH DISTRICTS—BROWN AND NEMAHA.

George Graham	129	H. Sutherland	28
H. H. Patterson	73	Lloyd D. Ashby	2

SIXTH DISTRICT—MARSHALL.

Thrown out; "voted by ballot, contrary to law."

SEVENTH DISTRICT—JEFFERSON—*Two Members.*

Henry Owens	212	Edward Lynde	231
Franklin Finch	279	Daniel W. Guernsey	229
H. G. Turner	97		

Superintendent of Schools.

S. W. Greer .... 17 | Perry Fuller 8

EIGHTH DISTRICT—CALHOUN—*One Member.*

Golden Silvers	163	Martin Anderson	104

Superintendent of Schools.

S. W. Greer 107

NINTH DISTRICT—RILEY AND POTTAWATOMIE—*Two Members.*

Abraham Barry .... 133 | Thomas R. Points .... 231 | Daniel L. Chandler 98

Superintendent of Schools.

J. H. Noteware .... 120 | Isaac T. Goodnow 92

TENTH DISTRICT—DOUGLAS AND JOHNSON—*Eight Members.*

Robert Morrow	1342	P. H. Townsend	986
C. H. Branscomb	1311	A. Curtiss	915
Levi Woodard	1357	H. J. Canniff	976
F. F. Bruner	421	John Lockhart	1015
P. H. Berkaw	437	J. E. Corliss	227
Samuel Shore	417		
J. B. Hovey	1296		
David Martin	443		

Superintendent of Schools.

S. W. Greer .... 1103 | Perry Fuller .... 130 | W. F. M. Arny 6

ELEVENTH DISTRICT—SHAWNEE—*One Member.*

George B. Holmes	311	A. L. Winans	258

Superintendent of Schools.

S. W. Greer .... 347 | W. F. M. Arny .... 89 | Perry Fuller 4

TWELFTH TO SIXTEENTH DISTRICTS — RICHARDSON, DAVIS, WISE, BRECKINRIDGE, WEL-
LER, MADISON, BUTLER, HUNTER, GREENWOOD, BOURBON, GODFREY, WILSON, DORN,
McGEE, WOODSON, COFFEY, ALLEN, ANDERSON, AND FRANKLIN.

L. D. Bailey	898	A. G. Osborn	64
T. R Roberts	975	J. B. Scott	45
William Spriggs	1090	William B. Marshall	35
A. L. Dunn	233		

Superintendent of Schools.

W. F. M. Arny .... 283 | S. W. Greer 49
J. H. Noteware .... 61 | Perry Fuller 1

OCTOBER.—Arapahoe county, covering the Pike's Peak region, is organized by Gov. Denver, and officers appointed.

OCTOBER 10.—On the resignation of Gov. Denver, Secretary Hugh S. Walsh becomes Acting Governor.

OCTOBER 25.—Wm. H. Seward makes a speech at Rochester, New York, in which he says:

"Shall I tell you what this collision means? They who think it is accidental, unnecessary, the work of interested or fanatical agitators, and therefore ephemeral, mistake the case altogether. It is an irrepressible conflict between opposing and enduring forces, and it means that the United States must and will, sooner or later, become either entirely a slaveholding nation, or entirely a free-labor nation. . . . . It is the failure to comprehend this great truth that induces so many unsuccessful attempts at final compromise between the Slave and Free States, and it is the existence of this great fact that renders all such pretended compromises, when made, vain and ephemeral. Startling as this saying may appear to you, fellow-citizens, it is by no means an original or even a modern one."

NOVEMBER 9.—Gov. Denver issues a parting address to the people.

NOVEMBER 10.—A letter from Osage, in the Leavenworth Journal, says: "George W. Clarke, a pet in the Land Office at Fort Scott, was the real cause of all the troubles in that region, and a company of dragoons had to be stationed there to protect him from the merited vengeance of an outraged people." He says Clarke "in the summer of 1856, plundered, robbed and burned out of house and home nearly every Free-State settler in Linn county, while his hands were steeped in innocent blood, and the light of burning buildings marked his course."

NOVEMBER 12.—Capt. James Montgomery learns that he has been indicted for destroying the ballot-box at Sugar Mound, on the 4th of January.

—On the three following days and nights several persons in Linn county are jayhawked, and the crimes are charged to Montgomery's band.

NOVEMBER 16.—The houses of Poyner and Lemon, near Fort Scott, are robbed. Ben. Rice, indicted for the murder of Travis, is arrested and lodged in the Fort Scott jail.

NOVEMBER 19.—Samuel Medary appointed Governor.

NOVEMBER 20.—Jeremiah S. Black, U. S. Attorney General, decides that the Legislature had no right to take the seat of Government away from Lecompton.

NOVEMBER 23.—Hugh S. Walsh, Acting Governor, says: "The notorious James Montgomery, encouraged by the support of a leading Republican press in the Territory, has recommenced his system of marauding and plundering in the county of Linn."

NOVEMBER 25.—Democratic Territorial Convention at Leavenworth. Called to order by Col. Dickey, of Topeka. President, Joel K. Goodin. Vice Presidents, M. C. Dickey, A. J. Isacks, E. S. Dennis, H. P. Petriken, W. H. Gill, Daniel Killen, W. P. Badger, W. P. Campbell, James Garvin, Jeremiah Murphy, Isaac E. Eaton, John H. McDowell, H. Miles Moore, James Christian. Secretaries, Cyrus L. Gorton, R. D. Campbell, S. W. Driggs, Lucien J. Eastin, Frank F. Barclay, C. H. McLaughlin.

Cyrus F. Currier and Alson C. Davis conducted the President to the chair. John A. Halderman, R. N. Sherwood, Saunders W. Johnston, A. C. Davis, S. K. Huson, Dr. James Davis, H. B. Denman, and F. F. Bruner, reported the following resolutions:

"*Whereas,* The causes which have hitherto divided and estranged the people of Kansas no longer exist; and

"*Whereas,* The members of this Convention, animated by a sincere devotion to the Constitution and the Union, the rights of the States and the sovereign and the reserved rights of the people; and being profoundly impressed with the importance and necessity of a political organization which shall embody and render effective these sentiments, we do hereby agree to unite and be known as the Democratic party of Kansas: and as such,

"*Resolved,* That we affirm our abiding faith and confidence in the principles of the Democratic party, as enunciated in the Cincinnati Platform.

"2. That the people of this Territory are indebted to the Democratic party for the passage of the Kansas-Nebraska Act, which opened this magnificent domain to settlement, and recognized their sovereign right and their capacity to form and regulate their institutions in their own way.

"3. That we repudiate the dogma of the Republican party 'that Congress has sovereign power over the Territories of the United States for their government,' as a denial of the right and capacity of the people to govern themselves, and declare our devotion to the principles of popular sovereignty, and our hostility to Congressional despotism.

"4. That great danger is to be apprehended from the negro equality tendencies of the Republican party, as manifested in their conventions; and inasmuch as the slavery question is settled beyond the possibility of further controversy, we hereby declare in favor of the entire exclusion of free negroes from the future State of Kansas.

"5. That in view of the many hardships to which settlers upon public lands are subjected, and the enhanced value which they confer upon the lands held by Government, we would most respectfully but urgently press upon Congress the justice and propriety of selling a quarter-section of land to every actual settler who shall remain upon and improve the land for three consecutive years, at the actual cost of survey, and issuing a patent, and that all public lands in this Territory be withdrawn from the market for three years, and left open to pre-emptors.

"6. That we most respectfully but earnestly urge upon the General Government the necessity of immediately extinguishing the Indian title to the Reservations within this Territory, and opening the same for settlement under the pre-emption law.

"7. That we confidently appeal to the justice and liberality of the General Government in behalf of public improvements in this Territory, and urge that a generous grant of the public lands, and liberal appropriations, be made in aid of railroads, wagon-roads, bridges, and all necessary Territorial and county buildings.

"8. That our rich mineral resources deserve the fostering care of the Government, and that we urge a wise and liberal legislation in aid of the development especially of the iron, copper, lead and gold fields of the Territory.

"9. That in addition to the lands already set apart for school purposes, we claim from the Government such additional grants as will make good the loss from Indian Reservations and pre-emptions before surveys were made; and also ample endowments for a male and female university; and that we respectfully urge the propriety of perfecting the title to the Territory, that the people therein may immediately enjoy the benefits arising from such grant.

"10. That the Democracy of Kansas are in favor of the establishment and liberal endowment of free schools for the education of the children of the Territory.

"11. That indemnity for all losses sustained in the past political troubles in Kansas, should be fully and promptly made by the General Government, and that a commission should be immediately appointed to ascertain and adjust them.

"12. That we demand of the Legislative Assembly of this Territory the immediate revision of the present Representative apportionment, so that the people may be fully and fairly represented in that body."

Among those who took part in the Convention were Samuel A. Stinson, O. B. Holman, P. T. Colby and Judge George W. Purkins.

NOVEMBER 27.—There are now twenty newspapers in the Territory. Lawrence has 2; Lecompton, 1; Topeka, 1; Emporia, 1; Junction City, 1; Wyandotte, 2; Leavenworth, 5; Atchison, 2; Palermo, 1; Troy, 1; White Cloud, 1; Elwood, 1; Fort Scott, 1.

DECEMBER 1.—Samuel Medary takes the oath of office as Governor, before Chief Justice Taney, at Washington. The oath recorded at Lecompton December 18th.

—A meeting of citizens of Bourbon county held at Ray's Mill. W. R. Griffith, President; J. E. Jones, Secretary. They repudiate violence and lawlessness, and pledge themselves to bring the guilty to punishment. A motion to go to Fort Scott and release Ben. Rice was withdrawn.

DECEMBER 11.—Poles for the telegraph are up as far as Leavenworth, via Jefferson and Kansas Cities.

DECEMBER 16.—Captain Montgomery, with sixty-eight men, enters Fort Scott and releases Benjamin Rice, a Free-State prisoner and Jayhawker. J. H. Little, who had fired on Montgomery's men, was killed, and his store jayhawked.

DECEMBER 17.—Gov. Medary arrives at Lecompton.

DECEMBER 20.—John Brown and his men go into Missouri and liberate fourteen slaves. The Governor of Missouri offers a reward of $3,000, and President Buchanan $250, for the arrest of Brown. Brown goes north through Kansas with his negroes. At Holton an attempt by men from Atchison to capture him ends in a failure. The retreat of the Pro-Slavery men is called "The Battle of the Spurs." The next Legislature passed an amnesty act for "criminal offences growing out of any political difference of opinion."

DECEMBER 28.—Gov. Medary informs President Buchanan and the commanding officers at Forts Leavenworth and Riley of the disturbances created by Montgomery in Bourbon, Linn and Lykins counties, and asks for military assistance.

—Sentinel started at Junction City; Benj. H. Keyser, editor; Geo. W. Kingsbury, printer. Soon after, the Statesman appeared, published by Kingsbury and W. S. Blakely. This was succeeded by the Kansas Statesman, by Samuel A. Medary.

DECEMBER 31.—Gov. Robert M. Stewart, of Missouri, telegraphs that he will aid the Governor of Kansas.

DECEMBER 31.—A book published with the following title: "Kansas in Eighteen Fifty-Eight: Being chiefly a history of the Recent Troubles in the Territory. By William P. Tomlinson. 'Kansas, sir, is the Cinderella

of the American family. She is buffeted; she is insulted; she is smitten
and disgraced; she is turned out of the dwelling, and the door locked
against her. There is always, however, a fairy that takes care of the
younger daughter, if she be the most honest, the most virtuous, the meekest
and the most enduring of the domestic household.'—Speech of Wm. H.
Seward in the U. S. Senate, 1858. New York: H. Dayton, Publisher.
1859." The book is dedicated to Rev. Henry Ward Beecher, "the unwavering friend of Kansas." It contains 304 pages. Mr. Tomlinson spent
the summer of 1858 in Linn and Bourbon counties, riding with Montgomery and associating with the Free-State men. His book is a defence of the
course pursued by the Free-State men in the southeast, and a grateful tribute
to James Montgomery. It reads like a romance, and will grow more attractive as the years go by. There are no bad Free-State men in it, and no
good Pro-Slavery men. The writer lived on an Indian pony, and was fasci-
nated with the scenery, the climate, the men and the life he found on the
border—as hundreds of other young men were in those days. The following sketch of Montgomery is compiled from its pages. He was born in
Ohio, in 1813: while a child, his parents removed to Kentucky. He joined
the Campbellite church and became a preacher. In 1854, Montgomery
moved to Missouri, and came into Kansas soon after it was opened for settlement. He settled in Linn county, at the head of Little Sugar creek, a
branch of the Marais des Cygnes. He was a leading Free-State man from
the beginning. In 1856, the Pro-Slavery General Clarke sent a squad of
Ruffians to Montgomery's house to arrest him; Montgomery was absent;
his house was burned. Many attempts were made to arrest Montgomery,
but they failed. Linn was a Pro-Slavery county. The Pro-Slavery leaders
inaugurated the bushwhacking policy; they plundered and drove from
their homes Free-State men. Montgomery made no attempt to retaliate
until 1857, when he formed the "Self-Protective Company," and took the
field. He warned the leading Pro-Slavery men of the county to leave the
Territory. They obeyed, peace followed, and Montgomery returned to his
home.

In December, 1857, the Free-State settlers on the Little Osage river, in
Bourbon county, sent for Montgomery. In the summer of 1856, General
Clarke drove off the Free-State settlers on that river. In 1857, many of
these men came back and attempted to recover their homes. The Pro-
Slavery county officers issued writs for the arrest of these robbed and plundered Free-State men, many of whom had been indicted. They retaliated
by organizing a Free-State "Squatter Court," in opposition to the U. S.
Court of Judge Joe. Williams, at Fort Scott. Pro-Slavery men were
brought before this Court, and compelled to restore the claims and stock
stolen from Free-State settlers. On the 16th of December, 1857, Deputy
U. S. Marshal Little, of Fort Scott, with a formidable posse, attempted to
capture the Squatter Court. A fight ensued; one of Little's men was killed,
two badly wounded, and several horses shot; and Little retired, with his
writs in his pocket, and no prisoners. Montgomery then warned and drove
off the Pro-Slavery men who occupied Free-State claims, on the Little
Osage and the Marmaton, and retired to Raysville, in Bourbon county.

13

Six Free-State men arrested by Little were imprisoned in Fort Scott; after some weeks of imprisonment, all but one, Beason, escaped.

On the 4th of January, 1858, Montgomery destroyed a ballot-box, at Sugar Mound, Linn county. He was opposed to voting for State officers under the Lecompton Constitution, and the box he destroyed was the one containing those ballots.

The troubles on the Little Osage led Governor Denver to order a company of dragoons to Fort Scott. This encouraged the Ruffians to revive their old policy. On the night of the 27th of March, 1858, they made a raid on the Little Osage. Mr. Denton, a Free-State man, was assassinated. He lived two hours, and charged the crime to Brockett and Hardwick. The house of Mr. Davis was then visited, fired into, and Davis slightly wounded. The next victim was Mr. Hedrick, who was instantly killed while standing in the doorway of his own house.

Soon after this, Montgomery with eight men crossed the Marmaton, near Fort Scott, in pursuit of horse-thieves. His presence soon became known, and Captain Anderson, of the regular army, took some thirty of his dragoons, and went out to arrest the irregulars. There was a chase over the prairie. Montgomery halted at a deep ravine on Yellow Paint creek. It could only be approached in front. His men threw themselves from their horses, and formed in line. Three times Anderson was ordered to halt. He continued to advance, and was fired upon. The regulars fired once, wheeled and fled. One dragoon was killed, one mortally wounded; Anderson was wounded, and his horse shot under him. One Free-State man was slightly wounded. This was the first and only time that the Free-State men resisted and fired upon U. S. troops.

The murderers arrested by Samuel Walker, at Fort Scott, having been released, Montgomery decided on striking a blow on that Pro-Slavery stronghold, "to convince the citizens that unless there was a change their town must fall." On the night of June 6th he left his headquarters on the Marmaton, and took up the march for Fort Scott. Attempts were made to fire the Fort and the Pro-Slavery Hotel, but they failed. Citizens came out to extinguish the fires, "but scarcely had they collected before a fire was opened upon them by the men of Montgomery." One dwelling-house "received several bullets," and another "was completely riddled with balls." Had the town been burned, history would have classed this raid with Quantrell's at Lawrence, in 1863. Montgomery retreated with his men to the Big Bend of the Marmaton, five miles off, awaiting an attack at daylight. None was made.

Governor Denver left Lawrence June 9th, with Governor Charles Robinson, Judge John Wright, A. D. Richardson, Lewis N. Tappan, Edmund Babb and others, for Fort Scott. Montgomery joined the party at Moneka, Linn county. At Raysville, Bourbon county, Governor Denver made a speech. His terms of peace are thus reported by Tomlinson:

1. The withdrawal of United States troops from Fort Scott.

2. The election of new county officers in Bourbon county.

3. The stationing of troops along the Missouri frontier, to protect the settlers of the Territory from invasion.

4. The suspension of the execution of all old writs until their legitimacy is authenticated before the proper tribunal.

5. The abandonment of the field by Montgomery and his men, and all other parties of armed men, whether Free-State or Pro-Slavery.

Montgomery immediately accepted these terms.

At Fort Scott Gov. Denver made a speech, and presented the same terms. The Pro-Slavery men were dissatisfied. Judge Wright, a Free-State man, followed Gov. Denver; his statements were disputed by ex-Gov. Ransom, and a bloody collision was nearly provoked. Gov. Denver left Fort Scott June 16th. Montgomery disbanded his men, the troops left Fort Scott, and Capt. Weaver was stationed at the Trading Post with a company of soldiers to protect the border.

Mr. Tomlinson thus describes Montgomery's residence:

"A rude log building, not exceeding ten by twelve in dimensions, situated on a gentle elevation; the height of the structure not over eight feet; the whole covered with a rough shed roof of split strips of oak."

The following portrait of Montgomery is copied from a letter published in the New York Evening Post, in 1858:

"In conversation he talks mildly, in a calm, even voice, using the language of a cultivated, educated gentleman. His antecedents are unexceptionable; he was always a Free-State man, although coming from a Slave State, where he was noted as a good citizen, and for his mild, even temperament. In his daily conduct he maintains the same character now; but when in action, and under fire, he displays a daring fearlessness, untiring perseverance, and an indomitable energy that has given him the leadership in this border warfare. His discretion, courage, and acknowledged ability, have gained him what he will continue to receive—the confidence and support of the southern tier of counties. Montgomery's enrolled company numbers from four to five hundred men, all of whom are old residents of the Territory, and are, consequently, familiar with the peculiar mode of fighting pursued by the Border Ruffians. Some of them are desperate men, and could their histories be told, you would not wonder that they followed their Border-Ruffian persecutors to the bitter end. There are two boys in that company whose dying father charged them to avenge his cowardly murder. Five bullets pierced his body as he stepped from the door-sill to extend the hospitalities of his cabin to his murderers. Others have been robbed at home, or on the highways, and not one of them but what has suffered some outrage or indignity from those villains headed by Brockett, Hamilton, Clarke and Titus. Notwithstanding every incentive to retaliate actuates these men to demand blood for blood, yet Montgomery is able to control and direct them. He truly tempers justice with mercy, and he has always protected women and children from harm, and has never shed blood except in conflict, or in self-defence. Such is the portrait of the Kansas Hero—James Montgomery."

1859.

JANUARY 3.—Meeting of the Territorial Legislature, at Lecompton.

Members of the Council: Lyman Allen, Robert Crozier, Luther D. Challis, Edwin S. Nash, David Sibbet, Cyrus K. Holliday, Benjamin Harding, Andrew J. Mead, A. G. Patrick, Joseph P. Root, Carmi W. Babcock, John Wright, and O. E. Learnard.

Officers of the Council: President, C. W. Babcock; Vice President, C. K. Holliday; Secretary, A. Smith Devenney; Sergeant-at-Arms, P. Wiley; Doorkeeper, Asaph Allen; Assistant Secretary, G. A. Colton; Docket Clerk, E. P. Heberton. Message from Governor Medary. It is a calm and unobjectionable paper.

Members of the House: First District, Wm. Y. Roberts, John W. Wright, Lyman Scott, A. M. Clark, J. L. McDowell, James Medill and O. M. Marsh, of Leavenworth county; Second, Luther Dickerson, Harrison Weider and J. B. Irvin, of Atchison county; Third, A. Larzelere, Ward L. Lewis, A. J. Allison and Thomas Stevenson, of Doniphan county; Fourth and Fifth, George Graham, of Nemaha county; Sixth, T. S. Vaile, of Marshall county; Seventh, Franklin Finch and Edward Lynde, of Jefferson county; Eighth, Golden Silvers, of Calhoun county; Ninth, Abraham Barry, of Riley county; Tenth, Robert Morrow, Charles H. Branscomb, P. H. Townsend, Levi Woodard, H. J. Canniff and A. Curtiss, of Douglas county, and John Lockhart, of Johnson county; Eleventh, George B. Holmes, of Shawnee county; Twelfth and Thirteenth, William Spriggs, of Anderson county; Twelfth, Thirteenth, Fourteenth and Fifteenth, L. D. Bailey, of Breckinridge county; Fourteenth, Fifteenth and Sixteenth, T. R. Roberts, of Bourbon county; Seventeenth, R. B. Mitchell and A. Danford, of Linn county; Eighteenth, M. F. Holaday and William Walters, of Lykins county. John B. Irvin was elected Speaker *pro tem.*, and Chas. H. Branscomb Clerk *pro tem.*

Officers of the House: Speaker, A. Larzelere; Chief Clerk, Byron P. Ayres; Assistant Clerk, P. P. Elder; Sergeant-at-Arms, Geo. F. Warren; Doorkeeper, Geo. W. Smith, jr.; Journal Clerk, A. D. Richardson; Chaplain, Rev. E. Nute; Engrossing Clerk, A. C. Soley; Docket Clerk, John M. Funk; Enrolling Clerk, S. C. Smith.

Governor Medary transmits the report of H. J. Strickler, Commissioner to audit claims for losses during the troubles. The claims presented to the Commissioner amounted to $301,225.11; amount awarded, $254,279.28. They have been sent to Congress, and referred to the Committee on Claims. The Comptroller estimates the taxable property of the Territory at $25,000,000. In the Delaware Land District (Kickapoo Land Office), 1,196,129.19 acres of land have been sold; at the Lecompton Land Office, 1,095,313.09. The town-site property sold in trust for the Delaware Indians amounted to $28,612.25. The Legislature is asked to give its attention to the serious disturbances in Bourbon and Linn counties.

JANUARY 4.—Legislature adjourns to Lawrence.

JANUARY 6.—The Leavenworth Constitution is submitted to the U. S. Senate, with a petition asking the admission of Kansas under it. No action is taken.

JANUARY 7.—Legislature meets at Lawrence. Rev. Charles Reynolds elected Chaplain of the Council. J. J. Ingalls elected Engrossing Clerk.

—Sheriff Samuel Walker reports the disturbances in Linn and Bourbon counties, caused by John Brown and James Montgomery. He says Montgomery will cease fighting if the Pro-Slavery men he had run out will stay out, and his men are not punished for their recent acts.

—Gov. Stewart sends a Special Message to the Missouri Legislature on the invasion of southwest Missouri by Kansans.

JANUARY 8.—Capt. W. S. Walker, U. S. A., is ordered to Fort Scott. Capt. A. I. Weaver is ordered by Gov. Medary to enroll a company of men.

JANUARY 9.—T. Dwight Thacher is elected Public Printer, receiving 24 votes, to 11 for P. B. Plumb. The Secretary of the Territory continued to control the printing; he authorized it to be done by Joel K. Goodin, who employed Geo. W. Brown to do the work.

JANUARY 10.— P. T. Colby, of Quindaro, appointed United States Marshal.

JANUARY 11.—Message from Gov. Medary to the House, in regard to the difficulties in Linn and Bourbon counties. It gives an account of Montgomery's raid on Fort Scott, Dec. 16th, the killing of J. H. Little, release of Benj. Rice, the pillaging of the Fort Scott Hotel and Little's store, and the stealing of fifteen negroes by Capt. Brown. One statement made to him is this: "Good citizens, that formerly sustained those men, begged to have something done to stop the 'Jay-Hawking,' as they termed it, or their counties would be depopulated."

"Montgomery was asked 'if no means could be devised by which he could be induced to desist driving men out of the Territory for opinion's sake?' His reply was, 'that if the Governor would give it to him, in black and white, that none of his men should be arrested for anything that had been done; and that the Pro-Slavery men that he had run out should stay out; and that Sheriff Bull should be removed, and Mr. Moore appointed in his stead—then they would stop, and that he would assist the officers to enforce the laws: if not, he would fight it out.'

"Capt. Brown was fortifying himself on Sugar creek, some twelve miles from the State line. He says he will resist any officers sent to take him."

The Secretary of the Interior authorizes Gov. Medary "to offer a reward of $250 each, for the apprehension of Capts. Montgomery and Brown." The message is referred to a special committee. That committee reported that it would sustain the Governor in all legal measures to restore peace.

JANUARY 12.—The Legislature elects Wm. McKay, Ed. S. Lowman and James McCahon Codifying Commissioners.

JANUARY 12.—Capt. Walker, U. S. A., on orders from Washington, is commanded to return.

JANUARY 15.—The report of H. J. Strickler, Commissioner for Auditing Claims, is published in the House Journal, pp. 83 to 96. He was appointed under an act of 1857, to audit claims for property lost since the organization of the Territory.

JANUARY 16.— Ep. Ransom and 116 citizens of Fort Scott petition the Governor to establish martial law in Linn, Bourbon, Allen and Anderson counties.

JANUARY 16.—Colonel Sumner returns to the command of Fort Leavenworth.

JANUARY 19.—Captain James Montgomery makes a speech in the Congregational Church, Lawrence, defending his course in Linn and Bourbon counties.

JANUARY 21.—Governor Medary writes to Secretary Cass that he has received his commission, dated December 22, 1858.

JANUARY 24.—Charley Fisher, a fugitive slave, is rescued by Free-State men, at Leavenworth. Lewis Ledyard Weld, D. R. Anthony, Champion Vaughan, George W. Gardiner, David H. Bailey, Robert W. Hamer and other Republicans were engaged in giving Fisher his freedom. In Leavenworth, Fisher was a barber. In Mississippi, after the war, he became a

State Senator. One of the cases arising out of this rescue is reported in McCahon's Reports.

JANUARY 25.—Dr. John Doy and Charles Doy, his son, with thirteen Missouri slaves, arrested in Kansas, are taken to Weston, Mo., and placed in the Platte county jail. Charles afterwards escaped.

JANUARY 25.—The telegraph is completed to Leavenworth, via Wyandotte.

JANUARY 31.—Governor Medary writes the following letter to Colonel E. V. Sumner:

"You will furnish Deputy Marshal Colby, the bearer of this, with such military forces as he may think necessary to secure Captain Brown, who is now in Calhoun county, K. T., on his way to Nebraska and Iowa."

FEBRUARY 11.—Governor Medary appoints H. J. Strickler, Auditor, and Robt. B. Mitchell, Treasurer. Legislature adjourns.

FEBRUARY 11.—An act was passed, to authorize the Governor to employ counsel to defend Dr. John Doy; (Wilson Shannon and A. C. Davis defended him, for freeing slaves); an act apportioning the Legislature; providing for Territorial Auditor and a Treasurer; for the adjustment of claims; acts establishing codes of civil and criminal procedure; an act granting amnesty for political offences; for the formation of a Constitution and State Government; defining judicial districts; organizing the counties of Wyandotte and Butler, and repealing the Bogus Laws. A joint resolution was passed, requesting Congress to attach to Kansas that portion of Nebraska south of the Platte river. A bill abolishing and prohibiting Slavery was not signed by Governor Medary. At midnight, when the session closed, a bonfire was made, and copies of the Bogus Statutes, the laws of 1855, burned.

The Executive Committee, under the University law, consists of C. E. Miner, T. Dwight Thacher, Wm. Bishop, Chas. Reynolds, G. W. Hutchinson, Chas. H. Branscomb, James Blood, and Robert Morrow.

Six counties were authorized to issue bonds. The general laws fill 720 pages. There are 233 pages of special laws. The Atchison and Pike's Peak R. R. Co. is incorporated; a University at Lawrence, the cities of Baldwin City, Elwood, Eudora, Wyandotte, Quindaro, White Cloud, and others; and the towns of Grasshopper Falls, Highland, Council Grove, Garnett, Junction City, Salina, Wabaunsee, and others.

FEBRUARY 23.—Celebration at St. Joseph, Mo., of the opening of the Hannibal and St. Joseph Railroad.

MARCH 7.—Governor Medary issues a proclamation, calling an election for or against holding a Constitutional Convention.

MARCH.—Samuel Stover, of Wyandotte, appointed Agent of the Delaware Indians, vice B. F. Robinson.

—John Pettit, of Indiana, confirmed as Chief Justice of Kansas.

MARCH 24.—Trial of John Doy at St. Joseph. The jury does not agree.

MARCH 28.—Election for or against a Constitutional Convention.

APRIL 2.—John Pettit takes the oath as Chief Justice of the Supreme Court, at Leavenworth, before Samuel D. Lecompte.

APRIL 8.—Governor R. M. Stewart, of Missouri, writes to Governor

Medary that he has sent Adjutant General G. A. Parsons to Cass, Bates, and Vernon counties, Mo., to protect the Missouri border from marauding incursions.

APRIL 14.—Governor Medary writes to Governor Stewart that he does not think there is any trouble on this side of the line.

APRIL 16.—Governor Medary in a proclamation declares the following to be the result of the election held March 28—the first of the elections under the Wyandotte Constitution movement:

Counties.	For a Constitution......	Against a Constitution	Total.........
Anderson	176	7	183
Atchison	308	32	340
Bourbon	333	47	380
Breckinridge	313	16	329
Butler	15	2	17
Coffey	184	134	318
Doniphan	343	192	535
Douglas	405	164	569
Franklin	92	1	93
Jackson	107	47	154
Jefferson	219	202	421
Johnson	301	65	366
Leavenworth	989	272	1,261
Linn	341	6	347
Morris	63	14	78
Nemaha	120	39	159
Pottawatomie	66	29	95
Riley	119	54	173
Shawnee	359	67	426
Wabaunsee	121	....	121
Wyandotte	254	31	285
Woodson	77	4	81
Total	5,306	1,425	6,731

Majority for a Constitution and State Government, 3,881. There were no returns from the following counties: Allen, Brown, Broderick, Chase, Clay, Davis, Dickinson, Dorn, El Paso, Fremont, Godfrey, Greenwood, Hunter, Lykins, Madison, Marshall, McGee, Montana, Oro, Osage, Washington, and Wilson. The following returns were sent to the Governor instead of the County Boards, and were not counted:

Townships.	Counties.	For......	Against ...	Total ......
Clinton	Douglas	148	6	154
St. Marysville	Lykins	19	32	51
Humboldt	Allen	70	....	70
Cofachique	Allen	46	16	62
Walnut	Brown	23	3	26
Plymouth	Brown	48	....	48
Irving	Brown	55	....	55
Centropolis	Franklin	24	12	36
Total		433	69	502

APRIL 19.—Governor Medary calls an election for delegates, and their meeting in Convention at Wyandotte.

MAY.—Four steamboats arrive at Lawrence. The Gus Linn went thirty miles up the Smoky Hill river. Col. R. H. Nelson, who was a passenger on the Linn, believed she could have gone with ease 100 miles farther.

MAY 11.—A Democratic Convention at Tecumseh adopts the following platform:

"*Whereas,* The members of this Convention have met in pursuance of a call of the Central Committee of the Democratic party of Kansas, and being animated by a sincere devotion to the Constitution of the Union, the rights of the States and the sovereign and reserved rights of the people; and

"*Whereas,* The Slavery question is practically settled in favor of a Free State, beyond the possibility of further controversy; and

"*Whereas,* We recognize no difference between Pro-Slavery and Free-State men as such: therefore, be it

"*Resolved,* That we affirm our abiding faith and confidence in the principles of the Democratic party, as enunciated by Jefferson, Madison, Jackson and the founders of our Government, and re-enunciated in the Cincinnati platform.

"2. That we affirm the absolute sovereignty of the States of this Union in regard to their domestic institutions, and the perfect compatibility of the confederation of Free and Slave States to exist harmoniously together under the provisions of our Federal Constitution.

"3. That the people of the Territory, according to the true meaning of the Act of Congress known as the 'Kansas-Nebraska Act,' have the sole and exclusive right, in the organization of a State Government, to form and regulate their domestic institutions in their own way, by the will of the majority, fairly and fully expressed at the ballot-box, subject only to the Constitution of the United States.

"4. That non-intervention by Congress with the domestic institutions of the States or Territories is the vital and distinct feature of the Democratic party, and any deviation from that principle, either for or against those institutions, is impolitic, illiberal and unjust.

"5. That we assert the original and essential inferiority of the negro race, and hereby call upon the Constitutional Convention to prohibit negro and mulatto suffrage, and exclude all free negroes from the future State of Kansas.

"6. That said Convention should submit said Constitution to a direct vote of the people, for ratification or rejection.

"7. That the Democratic party condemns all efforts to array the people of this Union against one another, either on account of locality, birth-place or religion, but, on the contrary, practise what in theory it professes, that patriotic spirit which united the people of every clime in the great struggle for American independence.

"8. That the registry law passed by a majority of the late Legislature is anti-Democratic, infamous, and contrary to justice.

"9. That the unequal and oppressive tax law passed by a majority of the late Legislature meets with the unqualified disapprobation of the Democratic party.

"10. That the objects of the pre-emption law would be better effected by giving a homestead to every bona fide settler and cultivator of the public land, without limit as to time; and that we respectfully urge upon the President of the United States the propriety of postponing the public sales of the Government lands in Kansas for at least twelve months."

MAY 12.—A Convention held at Big Springs, to reorganize the Free-State party. George W. Smith called the Convention to order. Robert Riddle, of Jefferson county, presided; George W. Brown was one of the secretaries. Fred. P. Stanton reported the resolutions. They endorse the Big Springs platform of 1855, and favor the continuance of the Free-State party until the Territory becomes a State. E. S. Lowman, P. C. Schuyler, C. V. Eskridge, W. Y. Roberts, H. W. Martin, Ed. S. Nash, Capt. Samuel Shore and other Free-State men favored the movement. The Convention was not large, and was not sustained by the people.

MAY.—Horace Greeley arrives in Leavenworth. He is visited by the Typographical Union and by prominent citizens. He delivers a lecture.

MAY 18.—Convention at Osawatomie. Organization of the Republican party in Kansas. The Convention was called to order by T. Dwight Thacher, of Lawrence. Henry Fox, of Shawnee county, was made the Temporary Chairman, and T. D. Thacher Secretary. *Committee on Credentials:* E. Heath, A. Danford, P. Shepherd, James L. McDowell, John A. Martin, William Spriggs, and A. J. Shannon. *Committee on Permanent Organization:* Branscomb, Fearl, Lawrence, Fletcher, Delahay, McKay, Larzelere, Rapp, Burnett, Pomeroy, Gilpatrick, and Shannon. The Committee reported as follows:

President: Oscar E. Learnard, of Coffey county.

Vice Presidents: Nathan Price, of Doniphan county; Samuel C. Pomeroy, of Atchison; Thomas Ewing, jr., of Leavenworth county; Joseph Speck, of Wyandotte county; Erastus Heath, of Douglas county; Henry Fox, of Shawnee county; D. W. Houston, of Anderson county; and E. G. Jewell, of Bourbon county.

Secretaries: Daniel W. Wilder, of Doniphan county; T. Dwight Thacher, of Douglas county; J. F. Cummings, of Shawnee county; and John A. Martin, of Atchison county.

The Convention was then addressed by Horace Greeley. In the course of his speech Mr. Greeley said:

"The able and gallant Lincoln, of Illinois, whom we had hoped to meet and hear to-day, has happily illustrated the Squatter Sovereignty principle thus: 'If A. wants to make B. a slave, C. must not interfere to prevent him.'"

The following is the conclusion of Mr. Greeley's speech:

"Freemen of Kansas! I would inspire you with no unwarranted, no overweening confidence of success in the great struggle directly before us. I have passed the age of illusions, and no longer presume a party or cause destined to triumph merely because I know it should. On the contrary, when I consider how vast are the interests and influences combined to defeat us—the Three Thousand Millions of property in human flesh and blood—the subserviency of Commerce to this great source of custom and profit—the prevalence of ignorance and of selfishness affecting the many Millions prodigally lavished by the wielders of Federal authority—the lust of Office and the prevalence of Corruption—I often regard the struggle of 1860 with less of hope than of apprehension. Yet, when I think of the steady diffusion of intelligence—the manifest antagonism between the Slavery Extensionists and the interests of Free Labor—when I consider how vital and imminent is the necessity for the passage of the Free Land bill—when I feel how the very air of the Nineteenth Century vibrates to the pulsations of the great heart of Humanity, beating higher and higher with aspirations for Universal Freedom, until even barbarous Russia is intent on striking off the shackles of her fettered Millions—I cannot repress the hope that we are on the eve of a grand, beneficent victory. But, whether destined to be waved in triumph over our next great battle-field, or trodden into its mire through our defeat, I entreat you to keep the Republican flag flying in Kansas, so long as one man can anywhere be rallied to defend it. Defile not the glorious dust of the martyred dead whose freshly-grassed graves lie thickly around us, by trailing that flag in dishonor or folding it in cowardly despair on this soil so lately reddened by their patriotic blood. If it be destined, in the mysterious Providence of God, to go down, let the sunlight which falls lovingly upon their graves catch the last defiant wave of its folds in the free breeze which sweeps over these prairies; let it be burned, not surrendered, when no one remains to uphold it; and let its ashes rest forever with theirs by the banks of the Marais des Cygnes!"

Committee on Platform: A. Larzelere, John A. Martin, Thos. Ewing, jr.,

James McCahon, Chas. F. deVivaldi, W. H. Smythe, C. K. Holliday, T. D. Thacher, D. W. Houston, W. Y. Roberts, A. J. Shannon, T. R. Roberts, Silas Fearl, and Wm. A. Phillips.

Mr. Ewing, Chairman of the Committee, reported the following platform:

"*Whereas*, Since the organization of the Territory of Kansas, the Democratic party has been in the control of the Legislative and Executive Departments of the Government; and

"*Whereas*, It has used those powers, which should have been exerted to foster and sustain, only to oppress our people; violated every principle it claimed to advocate; protected and supported invasions by foreign mobs, which burned our towns, plundered our houses, wasted our sustenance, destroyed our presses, and murdered our people; evinced a total disregard of popular rights and a settled determination to force the institution of negro slavery upon us; attempted to put in execution laws which, for injustice, cruelty and fraud, have scarcely been paralleled in the history of the most barbarous ages; supported that creature of infamous usurpation, the Lecompton Constitution, by Federal bayonets in Kansas, and by official patronage and Executive corruption at the national capital; made an invidious and disgraceful distinction between Slave and Free Constitutions, by offering us a bribe to enter the Union under the former without a Representative population, and refusing us admission under the latter until we had a population of 93,000; appointed corrupt and obnoxious judicial and executive officers over us, whose partisan sympathies and partial decisions have prevented the administration of justice; and by a long train of abuses, crimes and usurpations proved itself the bitter foe of the people of Kansas and the enemy of popular rights everywhere; and

"*Whereas*, The Republican party has on all occasions evinced a devotion to popular rights and an attachment to the best interests of the nation that deserve our approval; and has, by its adherence to the principles of the fathers of the Revolution, and its earnest support of the cause of Freedom in Kansas, won our approbation and gratitude; and

"*Whereas*, We believe the time has come for the people of Kansas to take a position and affiliate with a party national in its organization and objects: therefore,

"*Resolved*, That we, the people of Kansas, in Delegate Convention assembled, do proceed to organize the Republican party, and declare our principles as follows:

"*Resolved*, That we affirm that the only true basis of Free Governments, and of popular rights, for all countries and times, is to be found in the great self-evident truths enunciated by Thomas Jefferson and the Fathers of the Republic, in the Declaration of Independence.

"*Resolved*, That while we declare our submission to the Constitution and Laws of the United States, and disclaim all control over Slavery in the States in which it exists, we hold that the Constitution does not carry Slavery into the Territories, but that it is the creature of special enactment, and has existence only where supported by it; and we reprobate and condemn the perversion of the power of the Supreme Court of the United States to sectional demands and party purposes.

"*Resolved*, That, with the founders of the Republic, we believe that Governments derive their just powers from the consent of the governed, and that it is proper that the people of an organized Territory should be permitted to elect their own officers, and enact their own laws, free from Congressional and Executive control.

"*Resolved*, That Freedom is national, and Slavery sectional, and that we are inflexibly opposed to the extension of Slavery to soil now free.

"*Resolved*, That we condemn the Administration for its feebleness and impotency in the enforcement of the law prohibiting the importation of African slaves into the United States, and demand such further legislation by Congress as will forever suppress the inhuman traffic.

"*Resolved*, That the Wyandotte Constitutional Convention be requested to incorporate in the Bill of Rights in the Constitution a provision that neither Slavery nor involuntary servitude shall ever exist in Kansas, except in punishment of crime.

"*Resolved*, That the passage of a liberal Homestead Bill, giving 160 acres of land to every citizen who will settle upon and improve it, would be a measure just in principle, sound in policy, and productive of the greatest good to the people of the nation; and that we regard the defeat of Mr. Grow's bill in the Senate, by the Democratic party, as a direct blow at the laboring classes of the country, and as unworthy of the liberality of a great Government.

"*Resolved*, That the President, in ordering the public lands in this and other Territories to be sold during a season of universal depression, thus impoverishing thousands of our fellow-citizens, has been guilty of an act of injustice without parallel in the history of a free Government, and that the Republicans, for their generous though unsuccessful effort to secure the postponement of the sales, deserve the thanks of the people of Kansas and the West.

"*Resolved*, That we protest against any action which would put the adopted citizen under greater political disabilities than those imposed by the naturalization laws of the United States.

"*Resolved*, That the people of the West, the Commerce of whose lakes and rivers—in spite of the neglect of Democratic Administrations and Congresses—has grown to be three-fold greater than the whole foreign commerce of the country, will hold, henceforth, the Empire of the Government, and should unite in inaugurating a national policy which will open and improve the rivers and harbors of the country, and highways over the interior of the Continent for the great and growing commerce of the Plains, and that a railroad to the Pacific by the most central and practicable route is imperatively demanded by the interests of the whole country, and the Federal Government ought to render immediate and efficient aid in its construction."

The several delegations selected the following Central Territorial Committee: Jas. Blood, W. W. Lawrence, Douglas county; A. C. Wilder, Wm. Tholen, Leavenworth county; A. Larzelere, Doniphan county; B. Gray, Wyandotte county; H. H. Williams, Lykins county; John Ritchie, Shawnee county; Geo. Graham, Nemaha county; S. D. Houston, Riley county; J. C. Burnett, Bourbon county; S. C. Pomeroy, Atchison county; Wm. A. Phillips, Arapahoe county; John Chip, Johnson county; A. D. Richardson, Mining District. The Committee met and appointed the following Executive Committee: S. C. Pomeroy, Chairman; A. C. Wilder, Secretary; Jas. Blood, Wm. Tholen, John Ritchie.

MAY 18.—The Leavenworth Herald issues a daily.

MAY.— Horace Greeley writes from Leavenworth to the New York Tribune that "the twin curses of Kansas, now that the Border-Ruffians have stopped ravaging her, are Land Speculators and One-Horse Politicians." The latter, he says, "gravitate irresistibly toward the Sham Democracy, in whose embrace the whole tribe will bring up sooner or later." And where did H. G. go? He thinks Leavenworth has 1,000 houses and 10,000 inhabitants, and Lawrence half as many. In another letter Mr. Greeley says:

"I like Kansas—that is natural Kansas—better than I expected to. The soil is richer and deeper; the timber is more generally diffused; the country more rolling, than I had supposed them. . . . I consider Kansas well watered—no Prairie State better. . . . Springs, streams, creeks, rivers, are quite universal."

In a later letter Mr. Greeley says:

"I did not speak long in Lawrence, for I trust words are not there needed. Her people have had practical illustrations of the great issues which divide the country, and are not likely soon to forget them.

"Of course, her pioneers will die or become dispersed; new men will come in or rise up to fill their places, and 'another king arose who knew not Joseph,' will find its parallel in her future."

In an Overland letter, written on the Plains, Mr. Greeley said:

"I believe I have now descended the ladder of artificial life nearly to its lowest round. If the Cheyennes—thirty of whom stopped the last Express down on the route we must traverse, and tried to beg or steal from it—should see fit to capture and strip us, we should of course have further experience in the same line; but for the present the progress I have made during the last fortnight towards the primitive simplicity of human existence may be roughly noted thus:

"May 12th—Chicago.—Chocolate and morning newspapers last seen on the breakfast table.

"23d—Leavenworth.—Room-bells and baths make their last appearance.

"24th—Topeka.—Beefsteak and washbowls (other than tin) last visible. Barber ditto.

"26th—Manhattan.—Potatoes and eggs last recognized among the blessings that 'brighten as they take their flight.'

"27th—Junction City.—Last visitation of a boot-black, with dissolving views of a broad bedroom. Chairs bid us good-bye.

"28th—Pipe Creek.—Benches for seats at meals have disappeared, giving place to bags and boxes. We (two passengers of a scribbling turn) write our letters in the Express wagon that has borne us by day, and must supply us lodgings for the night."

MAY 30.—Samuel N. Wood starts the Press, at Cottonwood Falls. In October, it was removed to Council Grove, and there published about three years.

JUNE 4.—G. O. Chase starts the Atchison Union. It was sold to Adams & Stebbins in the winter of 1861. During the city election, in 1861, the Union and Champion issued Dailies, the latter paper's daily edition taking the name of Union Banner.

JUNE.—Delegates elected to the Wyandotte Convention; 14,000 votes cast; the Republicans elect 35, the Democrats 17 delegates.

JUNE.—The second trial of Dr. Doy resulted in his conviction, for negro-stealing. He was sentenced to the Penitentiary for five years.

—Five counties in southern Nebraska elected delegates to the Wyandotte Convention; one of the delegates, R. W. Furnas, has recently been Governor of Nebraska.

JUNE 25.—The Free Press issued at Elwood, by A. L. Lee and D. W. Wilder. It raises the name of Wm. H. Seward for President, and Abraham Lincoln for Vice President.

JULY 5.—Governor Medary issues a proclamation declaring the vote on the election of delegates to the Wyandotte Convention, as follows:

FIRST DISTRICT — LEAVENWORTH COUNTY — TEN DELEGATES.

Samuel A. Stinson	1778	Samuel Hipple	1770
Marcus J. Parrott	1358	Thomas Ewing, jr.	1328
William Perry	1708	Robert Cole Foster	1761
Roger F. Kelly	1286	George W. Gardiner	1304
John P. Slough	1773	Adam D. McCune	1755
William Engleman	1267	Josiah Kellogg	1325
Frederic Brown	1738	John Wright	1731
John E. Gould	1288	George Dickinson	1288
William C. McDowell	1783	Pascal S. Parks	1735
Charles G. Foster	1298	B. W. Williams	1288

SECOND DISTRICT — ATCHISON COUNTY — THREE DELEGATES.

Robert Graham	433	J. W. Smith	332
R. H. Weightman	342	John J. Ingalls	411
Caleb May	411	F. Lombard	325

THIRD DISTRICT — DONIPHAN COUNTY — FIVE DELEGATES.

Robert J. Porter	651	V. D. Markham	531
Albert L. Lee	526	Benjamin Wrigley	648
John W. Forman	694	E. Fleming	514
Franklin Grube	540	E. M. Hubbard	669
John Stiarwalt	684	William Lewis	558

FOURTH DISTRICT — BROWN COUNTY — ONE DELEGATE.

Samuel A. Kingman	93	Samuel C. Shields	19

FIFTH DISTRICT — NEMAHA COUNTY — ONE DELEGATE.

Thomas S. Wright	74	C. Bre	11

SIXTH DISTRICT — MARSHALL AND WASHINGTON COUNTIES — ONE DELEGATE.

J. A. Middleton	83	J. D. Brumbaugh	63

SEVENTH DISTRICT — JEFFERSON COUNTY — ONE DELEGATE.

C. B. McClelland	278	Henry Buckmaster	249

EIGHTH DISTRICT — JACKSON COUNTY — ONE DELEGATE.

Ephraim Moore	186	Aaron Foster	145

NINTH DISTRICT — RILEY COUNTY — ONE DELEGATE.

S. D. Houston	104	Amory Hunting	34

TENTH DISTRICT — POTTAWATOMIE COUNTY — ONE DELEGATE.

Luther R. Palmer	73	Uriah Cook	69

ELEVENTH DISTRICT — JOHNSON COUNTY — TWO DELEGATES.

J. T. Barton	375	John T. Burris	348
David Martin	346	C. F. Stratton	331

TWELFTH DISTRICT — DOUGLAS COUNTY — SEVEN DELEGATES.

James Blood	762	W. T. Spicely	313
Charles Willemsen	335	N. C. Blood	766
Solon O. Thacher	763	Thomas Majors	328
George A. Reynolds	374	P. H. Townsend	761
L. R. Williams	769	J. L Brown	323
J. Church	324	E. Stokes	760
William Hutchinson	701	R. C. Dix	321

THIRTEENTH DISTRICT — SHAWNEE COUNTY — THREE DELEGATES.

John P. Greer	543	Henry Fox	170
John Ritchie	335	Hiram D. Preston	60
H. D. Preston	325	Edward Hoagland	171
Jeremiah Murphy	50	J. Murphey	153

FOURTEENTH DISTRICT — WABAUNSEE, DAVIS, DICKINSON, AND CLAY COUNTIES — ONE DELEGATE.

Edmund G. Ross	152	J. R. McClure	105

FIFTEENTH DISTRICT — LYKINS COUNTY — TWO DELEGATES.

Benjamin F. Simpson	443	W. P. Dutton	431
Harry Torrey	311	G. W. Cavert	325

SIXTEENTH DISTRICT — FRANKLIN COUNTY — ONE DELEGATE.

James Hanway	217	Joab Toney	115

SEVENTEENTH DISTRICT — OSAGE, BRECKINRIDGE, MORRIS, AND CHASE COUNTIES — TWO
DELEGATES.

James M. Winchell.............................. 316 | Samuel N. Wood................................. 289
William McCulloch............................. 321 | H. J. Espy 280

EIGHTEENTH DISTRICT — LINN COUNTY — TWO DELEGATES.

J. M. Arthur...................................... 455 | Josiah Lamb..................................... 446
H. M. Dobyns .... 315 | J. Farris.. 314

NINETEENTH DISTRICT — ANDERSON COUNTY — ONE DELEGATE.

James G. Blunt.................................. 98 | W. F. M. Arny................................... 93

TWENTIETH DISTRICT — COFFEY AND WOODSON COUNTIES — TWO DELEGATES.

Allen Crocker .... 222 | Hiram Hoover.................................. 127
Samuel E. Hoffman............................ 187 | J. D. Carney.................................... 107

TWENTY-FIRST DISTRICT — MADISON, HUNTER, BUTLER, GREENWOOD, GODFREY, AND
WILSON COUNTIES — ONE DELEGATE.

Returns from Madison county only.
George H. Lillie 49

TWENTY-SECOND DISTRICT — BOURBON, M'GEE, AND DORN COUNTIES — TWO DELEGATES.

Returns from Bourbon county only.
J. C. Burnett..................................... 281 | W. R. Griffith.................................. 294
Ezra Gilbert...................................... 229 | Hugh Glenn..................................... 220

TWENTY-THIRD DISTRICT — ALLEN COUNTY — ONE DELEGATE.

J. H. Signor...................................... 175 | C. S. Clark...................................... 169

WYANDOTTE COUNTY — VOLUNTARY VOTE.

J. E. Bennett .... 295 | J. B. Welborn.................................. 293
W. Y. Roberts.................................... 237 | Fielding Johnson.............................. 240

— Gov. Medary proclaims the election of the following delegates:

Leavenworth County.—Samuel A. Stinson, William Perry, John P. Slough, Frederic Brown, William C. McDowell, Samuel Hipple, Robert C. Foster, Adam D. McCune, John Wright, Pascal S. Parks.

Atchison County.—Robert Graham, Caleb May, John J. Ingalls.

Doniphan County.—Robert J. Porter, John W. Forman, John Stiarwalt, Benj. Wrigley, E. M. Hubbard.

Brown County.—Samuel A. Kingman.

Nemaha County.—Thomas S. Wright.

Marshall and Washington Counties.—J. A. Middleton.

Jefferson County.—C. B. McClelland.

Jackson County.—Ephraim Moore.

Riley County.—S. D. Houston.

Pottawatomie County.—Luther R. Palmer.

Johnson County.—J. T. Barton, John T. Burris.

Douglas County.—James Blood, Solon O. Thacher, L. R. Williams, Wm. Hutchinson, N. C. Blood, P. H. Townsend, Edwin Stokes.

Shawnee County.—John P. Greer, John Ritchie, H. D. Preston.

Wabaunsee, Davis, Dickinson, and Clay Counties.—Edmund G. Ross.

Lykins County.—Benj. F. Simpson, W. P. Dutton.

Franklin County.—James Hanway.

Osage, Breckinridge, Morris, and Chase Counties.—James M. Winchell, Wm. McCulloch.

Linn County.—James M. Arthur, Josiah Lamb.

Anderson County.—James G. Blunt.

Coffey and Woodson Counties.—Samuel E. Hoffman, Allen Crocker.

Madison, Butler, Hunter, Greenwood, Godfrey, and Wilson Counties.—George H. Lillie.
Bourbon, McGee, and Dorn Counties.—William R. Griffith.
Allen County.—James H. Signor.

The Democrats elected seventeen delegates: ten from Leavenworth, four from Doniphan, and one each from Jefferson, Jackson and Johnson. The remaining thirty-five delegates were Free-State men or Republicans.

JULY 5.—Meeting of the Constitutional Convention at Wyandotte. List of Members:

Names.	County.	P. O. Address.	Where born.	Age.	Avocation.
J. M. Arthur	Linn	Centreville	Indiana	42	Farmer.
Josiah Lamb	Linn	Mound City	Indiana	42	Mechanic.
Caleb May	Atchison	Pardee	Kentucky	44	Farmer.
S. A. Kingman	Brown	Hiawatha	Mass	38	Lawyer.
J. J. Ingalls	Atchison	Sumner	Mass	34	Lawyer.
John P. Greer	Shawnee	Topeka	Ohio	38	Lawyer.
R. L. Williams	Douglas	Franklin	Kentucky	42	Merchant.
J. A. Middleton	Marshall	Nottingham	Pennsylv	25	Lawyer.
B. F. Simpson	Lykins	Paola	Ohio	23	Lawyer.
P. H. Townsend	Douglas	Big Springs	New Hamp.	33	Lawyer.
H. D. Preston	Shawnee	Burlingame	New Hamp.	28	Farmer.
J. C. Burnett	Bourbon	Mapleton	Vermont	34	Farmer.
W. R. Griffith	Bourbon	Marmaton	Indiana	39	Farmer.
N. C. Blood	Douglas	Baldwin City	Vermont	42	Merchant.
T. S. Wright	Nemaha	Granada	Pennsylv	50	Lawyer.
G. H. Lillie	Madison	Emporia	Ohio	35	Lawyer.
S. E. Hoffman	Woodson	Neosho	Pennsylv	25	Lawyer.
A. Crocker	Coffey	Burlington	Indiana	34	Farmer.
L. R. Palmer	Pottawatomie	Louisville	New York	40	Physician.
Jas. G. Blunt	Anderson	Walker	Maine	33	Physician.
Jas. Hanway	Franklin	Shermanville	England	49	Farmer.
W. Hutchinson	Douglas	Lawrence	Vermont	35	Farmer.
Jas. Blood	Douglas	Lawrence	Vermont	39	Merchant.
S. O. Thacher	Douglas	Lawrence	New York	28	Lawyer.
Ed. Stokes	Douglas	Clinton	Pennsylv	35	Manufacturer.
S. D. Houston	Riley	Manhattan	Ohio	40	Farmer.
J. P. Slough	Leavenworth	Leavenworth	Ohio	30	Lawyer.
W. McCulloch	Morris	Council Grove	Scotland	44	Farmer.
C. B. McClelland	Jefferson	Oskaloosa	Ohio	30	Merchant.
J. W. Forman	Doniphan	Doniphan	Kentucky	40	Merchant.
J. Stiarwalt	Doniphan	Palermo	Ohio	45	Farmer.
E. M. Hubbard	Doniphan	Highland	Kentucky	30	Merchant.
P. S. Parks	Leavenworth	Kickapoo	Indiana	26	Lawyer.
Fred. Brown	Leavenworth	Leavenworth	Germany	33	Manufacturer.
Sam'l Hipple	Leavenworth	Leavenworth	Pennsylv	28	Land Agent.
S. A. Stinson	Leavenworth	Leavenworth	Maine	26	Lawyer.
Wm. C. McDowell	Leavenworth	Leavenworth	Ohio	31	Lawyer.
A. D. McCune	Leavenworth	Leavenworth	Ohio	31	Farmer.
John Wright	Leavenworth	Leavenworth	Indiana	33	Farmer.
Wm. Perry	Leavenworth	Leavenworth	New York	28	Lawyer.
R. C. Foster	Leavenworth	Delaware	Kentucky	24	Lawyer.
Robt. Graham	Atchison	Atchison	Ireland	55	Merchant.
J. T. Barton	Johnson	Olathe	Virginia	28	Physician.
E. Moore	Jackson	Holton	Ohio	38	Manufacturer.
B. Wrigley	Doniphan	Troy	Ohio	29	Lawyer.
W. P. Dutton	Lykins	Stanton	New Hamp.	42	Farmer.
J. Ritchie	Shawnee	Topeka	Ohio	41	Farmer.
E. G. Ross	Wabaunsee	Glenross	Ohio	32	Printer.
J. H. Signor	Allen	Humboldt	New York	25	Surveyor.
R. J. Porter	Doniphan	Troy	Pennsylv	28	Merchant.
J. M. Winchell	Osage	Superior	New York	35	Farmer.
J. T. Burris	Johnson	Olathe	Ohio	28	Lawyer.

OFFICERS.

Names.	Office.	County.	P.O. Address.	Where born.	Age.	Avocat'n.
J. M. Winchell	President	Osage	Superior	New York	35	Farmer.
John A. Martin	Secretary	Atchison	Atchison	Pennsylv	21	Editor.
G. F. Warren	Sergeant-at-Arms	Douglas	B'ldwin City	Maine		Farmer.

S. A. Kingman was chosen temporary President, and John A. Martin Secretary. James M. Winchell was chosen President, receiving 32 votes, to 13 for J. T. Barton, the Democratic candidate. This is the first Constitutional Convention in the Territory which contains members of both political parties. For Secretary, John A. Martin is elected by 32 votes, to 15 for William Spencer. Assistant Secretary, J. L. Blanchard, of Anderson county; Sergeant-at-Arms, George F. Warren; Doorkeeper, J. M. Funk; Chaplain, Werter R. Davis.

The proceedings were published in the Daily Commercial Gazette, printed at Wyandotte by S. D. Macdonald. Seats are refused to Samuel N. Wood and H. J. Espy, Winchell and McCulloch having been elected from that district. The Constitution of Ohio is adopted as a "model or basis of action," receiving 25 votes, to 23 for Indiana and one for Kentucky. Seats are refused to Bennett and Welborn, of Wyandotte county, that new county being represented as a part of Leavenworth. Ariel E. Drapier is elected Reporter. Seventeen members protest against the exclusion of the Wyandotte delegates. S. O. Thacher is elected President *pro tem.*

Chairmen of Committees: Preamble, Hutchinson; Executive, Greer; Legislative, Thacher; Militia, Blunt; Judiciary, Kingman; Electors, Townsend; Schedule, Burris; Apportionment, Preston; Corporations, Graham; Education, Griffith; Counties, Ritchie; Ordinance, Jas. Blood; Finance, Simpson; Amendments, Houston; Federal Relations, T. S. Wright; Phraseology, Ingalls.

On the 11th, Richard J. Hinton and Robert St. Clair Graham were elected Enrolling Clerks, and Edwin S. Nash Journal Clerk. Credentials are presented of delegates elected from that part of Nebraska south of the Platte. A petition is received asking that the elective franchise be given to women. Mr. Ritchie presents a resolution asking that power be conferred on the Legislature to enact a prohibitory liquor law. Mr. McCune asks for the exclusion of free negroes from a residence in the State. On the 12th, Messrs. Nichols, Reeves, Furnas, Hewett, Keeting, Chambers, Taylor, Niles, Croxton, Cheever, Bennett, Dawson, and Doan, the Nebraska delegates, are given seats as honorary delegates, with the privilege of discussing the northern boundary question. The New England Emigrant Aid Society ask for the allowance of their claim, by the Kingman Claim Commission, of $20,000, the value of the Free-State Hotel destroyed at Lawrence in May, 1856. The claim had been rejected because the owners were not citizens of the Territory. A resolution of Mr. McDowell to exclude free negroes is laid on the table by 26 to 21. On the 15th, the Nebraska delegates were heard. On the 16th it was voted by 25 to 13 that the northern boundary remain unchanged, and the western boundary be the twenty-third meridian. On the 19th, Blunt, Slough, Ingalls, Arthur, and Stinson, protest against the homestead exemption, because "its provisions are unjust, invidious, and open to fraudulent construction." McClelland, Moore, Forman, Wrigley, Barton, Hipple, Hubbard, Brown, and Stiarwalt, protest against the same section "because its passage is calculated to utterly destroy the credit of the citizens of Kansas, and the law is not uniform in its operation." On the 22d, the Report of the Kingman

Commission on Claims is presented, and referred to the Committee on Ordinance and Public Debt. It is published in the proceedings. On the 23d, Topeka is made the temporary capital, the vote standing: Topeka 26, Lawrence 14, Atchison 6. On the 25th, Mr. Hubbard says of Mr. Hutchinson: "He offered me a good lot if I would vote for Lawrence. And then he said the title should be good; and he would make the same offer to any other Democratic member of the Convention. I say, sir, he has sworn to a lie." Mr. Hutchinson had denied offering the bribe. He made no statement now in reply to Mr. Hubbard, and the subject was laid on the table. On the 27th, Stinson, Stiarwalt, McClelland, Slough, McDowell, Forman, Foster, McCune, Moore, Hubbard, Barton, and Wrigley, file a protest against "the apportionment of the State for Representative purposes." On the 28th, it is voted by 35 to 8 to submit the homestead clause to the people. The western boundary line is made the 25th meridian. On the 29th, the Constitution is completed and signed by thirty-four Republican members of the Convention. The proceedings of the Convention were published by S. D. Macdonald, in a volume of 485 pages.

CONSTITUTION OF THE STATE OF KANSAS.

ADOPTED AT WYANDOTTE, JULY 29, 1859.

ORDINANCE.

Whereas, The Government of the United States is the proprietor of a large portion of lands included in the limits of the State of Kansas, as defined by the Constitution; and

Whereas, The State of Kansas will possess the right to tax such lands for the purpose of government, and for other purposes: now, therefore,

Be it ordained by the people of Kansas, That the right of the State of Kansas to tax such lands is relinquished forever, and the State of Kansas will not interfere with the title of the United States to such lands, nor with any regulation of Congress in relation thereto, nor tax non-residents higher than residents: *Provided always,* That the following conditions be agreed to by Congress:

SECTION 1. Sections numbered sixteen and thirty-six, in each township in the State, including Indian Reservations and Trust Lands, shall be granted to the State for the exclusive use of common schools; and when either of said sections, or any part thereof, has been disposed of, other lands of equal value, as nearly contiguous thereto as possible, shall be substituted therefor.

SEC. 2. That seventy-two sections of land shall be granted to the State for the erection and maintenance of a State University.

SEC. 3. That thirty-six sections shall be granted to the State for the erection of public buildings.

SEC. 4. That seventy-two sections shall be granted to the State for the erection and maintenance of charitable and benevolent institutions.

SEC. 5. That all salt springs, not exceeding twelve in number, with six sections of land adjacent to each, together with all mines, with the lands necessary for their full use, shall be granted to the State for works of public improvement.

SEC. 6. That five per centum of the proceeds of the public lands in Kansas, disposed of after the admission of Kansas into the Union, shall be paid to the State for a fund, the income of which shall be used for the support of the common schools.

SEC. 7. That the five hundred thousand acres of land to which the State is entitled under the act of Congress entitled "An act to appropriate the proceeds of the sales of public lands and grant pre-emption rights," approved September 4, 1841, shall be granted to the State for the support of common schools.

SEC. 8. That the lands hereinbefore mentioned shall be selected in such manner as may be prescribed by law; such selections to be subject to the approval of the Commissioner of the General Land Office of the United States.

14

PREAMBLE.

We, the people of Kansas, grateful to Almighty God for our civil and religious privileges, in order to ensure the full enjoyment of our rights as American citizens, do ordain and establish this Constitution of the State of Kansas, with the following boundaries, to wit: Beginning at a point on the western boundary of the State of Missouri, where the thirty-seventh parallel of north latitude crosses the same; thence running west on said parallel to the twenty-fifth meridian of longitude west from Washington; thence north on said meridian to the fortieth parallel of north latitude; thence east on said parallel to the western boundary of the State of Missouri; thence south with the western boundary of said State to the place of beginning.

BILL OF RIGHTS.

SECTION 1. All men are possessed of equal and inalienable natural rights, among which are life, liberty, and the pursuit of happiness.

SEC. 2. All political power is inherent in the people, and all free governments are founded on their authority, and are instituted for their equal protection and benefit. No special privileges or immunities shall ever be granted by the Legislature which may not be altered, revoked or repealed by the same body; and this power shall be exercised by no other tribunal or agency.

SEC. 3. The people have the right to assemble, in a peaceable manner, to consult for their common good, to instruct their Representatives, and to petition the Government, or any department thereof, for the redress of grievances.

SEC. 4. The people have the right to bear arms for their defence and security; but standing armies, in time of peace, are dangerous to liberty, and shall not be tolerated, and the military shall be in strict subordination to the civil power.

SEC. 5. The right of trial by jury shall be inviolate.

SEC. 6. There shall be no slavery in this State; and no involuntary servitude, except for the punishment of crime, whereof the party shall have been duly convicted.

SEC. 7. The right to worship God according to the dictates of conscience shall never be infringed; nor shall any person be compelled to attend or support any form of worship; nor shall any control of or interference with the rights of conscience be permitted, nor any preference be given by law to any religious establishment or mode of worship. No religious test or property qualification shall be required for any office of public trust, nor for any vote at any election, nor shall any person be incompetent to testify on account of religious belief.

SEC. 8. The right to the writ of habeas corpus shall not be suspended, unless the public safety requires it in case of invasion or rebellion.

SEC. 9. All persons shall be bailable by sufficient sureties, except for capital offences, where proof is evident or the presumption great. Excessive bail shall not be required, nor excessive fines imposed, nor cruel or unusual punishment inflicted.

SEC. 10. In all prosecutions, the accused shall be allowed to appear and defend in person or by counsel; to demand the nature and cause of the accusation against him; to meet the witness face to face, and to have compulsory process to compel the attendance of witnesses in his behalf, and a speedy public trial by an impartial jury of the county or district in which the offence is alleged to have been committed. No person shall be a witness against himself, or be twice put in jeopardy for the same offence.

SEC. 11. The liberty of the press shall be inviolate; and all persons may freely speak, write or publish their sentiments on all subjects, being responsible for the abuse of such right; and in all civil or criminal actions for libel, the truth may be given in evidence to the jury, and if it shall appear that the alleged libellous matter was published for justifiable ends, the accused party shall be acquitted.

SEC. 12. No person shall be transported from the State for any offence committed within the same; and no conviction in the State shall work a corruption of blood or forfeiture of estate.

SEC. 13. Treason shall consist only in levying war against the State, adhering to its enemies, or giving them aid and comfort. No person shall be convicted of treason unless on the evidence of two witnesses to the overt act, or confession in open court.

SEC. 14. No soldier shall, in time of peace, be quartered in any house without the consent of the occupant, nor in time of war, except as prescribed by law.

SEC. 15. The right of the people to be secure in their persons and property against unreasonable searches and seizures shall be inviolate, and no warrant shall issue but on probable cause, supported by oath or affirmation, particularly describing the place to be searched and the person or property to be seized.

SEC. 16. No person shall be imprisoned for debt except in case of fraud.

SEC. 17. No distinction shall ever be made between citizens and aliens in reference to the purchase, enjoyment or descent of property.

SEC. 18. All persons, for injuries suffered in person, reputation or property, shall have remedy by due course of law, and justice administered without delay.

SEC. 19. No hereditary emoluments, honors or privileges shall ever be granted or conferred by the State.

SEC. 20. This enumeration of rights shall not be construed to impair or deny others retained by the people, and all powers not herein delegated remain with the people.

ARTICLE I.—EXECUTIVE.

SECTION 1. The Executive Department shall consist of a Governor, Lieutenant Governor, Secretary of State, Auditor, Treasurer, Attorney General, and Superintendent of Public Instruction, who shall be chosen by the electors of the State at the time and place of voting for members of the Legislature, and shall hold their offices for the term of two years from the second Monday in January, next after their election, and until their successors are elected and qualified.

SEC. 2. Until otherwise provided by law, an abstract of the returns of every election, for the offices named in the foregoing section, shall be sealed up and transmitted, by the Clerk of the Board of Canvassers of the several counties, to the Secretary of State, who, with the Lieutenant Governor and Attorney General, shall constitute a Board of State Canvassers, whose duty it shall be to meet at the State capital on the second Tuesday of December succeeding each election for State officers, and canvass the vote for such officers and proclaim the result; but in case any two or more have an equal and the highest number of votes, the Legislature shall, by joint ballot, choose one of said persons so having an equal and the highest number of votes for said office.

SEC. 3. The supreme executive power of the State shall be vested in a Governor, who shall see that the laws are faithfully executed.

SEC. 4. He may require information in writing from the officers of the Executive Department upon any subject relating to their respective duties.

SEC. 5. He may, on extraordinary occasions, convene the Legislature by proclamation, and shall, at the commencement of every session, communicate in writing such information as he may possess in reference to the condition of the State, and recommend such measures as he may deem expedient.

SEC. 6. In case of disagreement between the two houses in respect to the time of adjournment, he may adjourn the Legislature to such time as he may think proper, not beyond its regular meeting.

SEC. 7. The pardoning power shall be vested in the Governor, under regulations and restrictions prescribed by law.

SEC. 8. There shall be a seal of the State, which shall be kept by the Governor, and used by him officially, and which shall be the great seal of Kansas.

SEC. 9. All commissions shall be issued in the name of the State of Kansas; signed by the Governor, countersigned by the Secretary of State, and sealed with the great seal.

SEC. 10. No member of Congress or officer of the State, or of the United States, shall hold the office of Governor except as herein provided.

SEC. 11. In case of death, impeachment, resignation, removal or other disability of the Governor, the power and duties of the office for the residue of the term, or until the disability shall be removed, shall devolve upon the President of the Senate.

SEC. 12. The Lieutenant Governor shall be President of the Senate, and shall vote only when the Senate is equally divided. The Senate shall choose a President *pro tempore* to preside in case of his absence or impeachment, or when he shall hold the office of Governor.

SEC. 13. If the Lieutenant Governor, while holding the office of Governor, shall be impeached or displaced, or shall resign or die, or otherwise become incapable of performing the duties of the office, the President of the Senate shall act as Governor until the vacancy is filled or the disability removed; and if the President of the Senate, for any of the above causes, shall be rendered incapable of performing the duties pertaining to the office of Governor, the same shall devolve upon the Speaker of the House of Representatives.

SEC. 14. Should either the Secretary of State, Auditor, Treasurer, Attorney General or Superintendent of Public Instruction become incapable of performing the duties of his office, for any of the causes specified in the thirteenth section of this article, the Governor shall fill the vacancy until the disability is removed, or a successor is elected and qualified. Every such vacancy shall be filled by election, at the first general election that occurs more than thirty days after it shall have happened, and the person chosen shall hold the office for the unexpired term.

SEC. 15. The officers mentioned in this article shall, at stated times, receive for their services a compensation to be established by law, which shall neither be increased nor diminished during the period for which they shall have been elected.

SEC. 16. The officers of the Executive Department, and of all public State institutions, shall, at least ten days preceding each regular session of the Legislature, severally report to the Governor, who shall transmit such reports to the Legislature.

ARTICLE II.—LEGISLATIVE.

SECTION 1. The Legislative power of the State shall be vested in a House of Representatives and Senate.

SEC. 2. The first House of Representatives under this Constitution shall consist of seventy-five members, who shall be chosen for one year. The first Senate shall consist of twenty-five members, who shall be chosen for two years. After the first election, the number of Senators and Members of the House of Representatives shall be regulated by law; but shall never exceed one hundred Representatives and thirty-three Senators.

SEC. 3. The members of the Legislature shall receive as compensation for their services the sum of three dollars for each day's actual service at any regular or special session, and fifteen cents for each mile travelled by the usual route in going to and returning from the place of meeting; but such compensation shall not in the aggregate exceed the sum of two hundred and forty dollars for each member, as per diem allowance for the first session held under this Constitution, nor more than one hundred and fifty dollars for each session thereafter, nor more than ninety dollars for any special session.

SEC. 4. No person shall be a member of the Legislature who is not at the time of his election a qualified voter of, and resident in, the county or district for which he is elected.

SEC. 5. No member of Congress or officer of the United States shall be eligible to a seat in the Legislature. If any person, after his election to the Legislature, be elected to Congress, or elected or appointed to any office under the United States, his acceptance thereof shall vacate his seat.

SEC. 6. No person convicted of embezzlement or misuse of the public funds shall have a seat in the Legislature.

SEC. 7. All State officers, before entering upon their respective duties, shall take and subscribe an oath or affirmation to support the Constitution of the United States and the Constitution of this State, and faithfully to discharge the duties of their respective offices.

SEC. 8. A majority of each house shall constitute a quorum. Each house shall establish its own rules, and shall be judge of the elections, returns and qualifications of its own members.

SEC. 9. All vacancies occurring in either house shall be filled for the unexpired term by election.

SEC. 10. Each house shall keep and publish a journal of its proceedings. The yeas and nays shall be taken, and entered immediately on the journal, upon the final passage of every bill or joint resolution. Neither house, without the consent of the other, shall adjourn for more than two days, Sundays excepted.

SEC. 11. Any member of either house shall have the right to protest against any bill or resolution; and such protest shall, without delay or alteration, be entered on the journal.

SEC. 12. All bills shall originate in the House of Representatives, and be subject to amendment or rejection by the Senate.

SEC. 13. A majority of all the members elected to each house, voting in the affirmative, shall be necessary to pass any bill or joint resolution.

SEC. 14. Every bill and joint resolution passed by the House of Representatives and Senate, shall, within two days thereafter, be signed by the presiding officers, and presented to the Governor; if he approve it, he shall sign it; but if not, he shall return it to the House of Representatives, which shall enter the objections at large upon its journal, and proceed to reconsider the same. If, after such reconsideration, two-thirds of the members elected shall agree to pass the bill or resolution, it shall be sent, with the objections, to the Senate, by which it shall likewise be reconsidered, and if approved by two-thirds of all the members elected, it shall become a law. But in all such cases the vote shall be taken by yeas and nays, and entered upon the journals of each house. If any bill shall not be returned within three days (Sundays excepted) after it shall have been presented to the Governor, it shall become a law in like manner as if he had signed it, unless the Legislature, by its adjournment, prevent its return, in which case it shall not become a law.

SEC. 15. Every bill shall be read on three separate days in each house, unless in case of emergency. Two-thirds of the house where such bill is pending may, if deemed expedient, suspend the rules; but the reading of the bill by section, on its final passage, shall in no case be dispensed with.

SEC. 16. No bill shall contain more than one subject, which shall be clearly expressed in its title, and no law shall be revived or amended, unless the new act contain the entire act revived, or the section or sections amended, and the section or sections so amended shall be repealed.

SEC. 17. All laws of a general nature shall have a uniform operation throughout the State; and in all cases where a general law can be made applicable, no special law shall be enacted.

SEC. 18. All power to grant divorces is vested in the district courts, subject to regulation by law.

SEC. 19. The Legislature shall prescribe the time when its acts shall be in force, and shall provide for the speedy publication of the same; and no law of a general nature shall be in force until the same be published. It shall have the power to provide for the election or appointment of all officers, and the filling of all vacancies not otherwise provided for in this Constitution.

SEC. 20. The enacting clause of all laws shall be, *"Be it enacted by the Legislature of the State of Kansas;"* and no law shall be enacted except by bill.

SEC. 21. The Legislature may confer upon tribunals transacting the county business of the several counties such powers of local legislation and administration as it shall deem expedient.

SEC. 22. For any speech or debate in either house, the members shall not be questioned elsewhere. No member of the Legislature shall be subject to arrest — except for felony or breach of the peace — in going to or returning from the place of meeting, or during the continuance of the session; neither shall he be subject to the service of any civil process during the session, nor for fifteen days previous to its commencement.

SEC. 23. The Legislature, in providing for the formation and regulation of schools, shall make no distinction between the rights of males and females.

SEC. 24. No money shall be drawn from the treasury except in pursuance of a specific appropriation made by law, and no appropriation shall be for a longer term than one year.

SEC. 25. All sessions of the Legislature shall be held at the State capital, and all regular sessions shall commence annually, on the second Tuesday of January.

SEC. 26. The Legislature shall provide for taking an enumeration of the inhabitants of the State, at least once in ten years. The first enumeration shall be taken in A. D. 1865.

SEC. 27. The House of Representatives shall have the sole power to impeach. All impeachments shall be tried by the Senate, and when sitting for that purpose, the Senators shall take an oath to do justice according to the law and the evidence. No person shall be convicted without the concurrence of two-thirds of the Senators elected.

SEC. 28. The Governor, and all other officers under this Constitution, shall be subject to impeachment for any misdemeanor in office; but judgment in all such cases shall not be extended further than to removal from office, or disqualification to hold any office of profit, honor or trust under this Constitution; but the party, whether convicted or acquitted, shall be liable to indictment, trial, judgment and punishment, according to law.

ARTICLE III.—JUDICIAL.

SECTION 1. The judicial power of the State shall be vested in a Supreme Court, District Courts, Probate Courts, justices of the peace, and such other courts, inferior to the Supreme Court, as may be provided by law; and all courts of record shall have a seal, to be used in the authentication of all process.

SEC. 2. The Supreme Court shall consist of one Chief Justice and two Associate Justices (a majority of whom shall constitute a quorum), who shall be elected by the electors of the State at large, and whose term of office, after the first, shall be six years. At the first election, a Chief Justice shall be chosen for six years, one Associate Justice for four years, and one for two years.

SEC. 3. The Supreme Court shall have original jurisdiction in proceedings in quo warranto, mandamus and habeas corpus, and such appellate jurisdiction as may be provided by law. It shall hold one term each year at the seat of Government, and such other terms at such places as may be provided by law; and its jurisdiction shall be coextensive with the State.

SEC. 4. There shall be appointed by the Justices of the Supreme Court a Reporter and Clerk of said court, who shall hold their offices two years, and whose duties shall be prescribed by law.

SEC. 5. The State shall be divided into five judicial districts, in each of which there shall be elected, by the electors thereof, a District Judge, who shall hold his office for the term of four years. District Courts shall be held at such times and places as may be provided by law.

SEC. 6. The District Courts shall have such jurisdiction in their respective districts as may be provided by law.

SEC. 7. There shall be elected, in each organized county, a Clerk of the District Court, who shall hold his office two years, and whose duties shall be prescribed by law.

SEC. 8. There shall be a Probate Court in each county, which shall be a court of record, and have such probate jurisdiction and care of estates of deceased persons, minors, and persons of unsound minds, as may be prescribed by law, and shall have jurisdiction in cases of habeas corpus. This court shall consist of one Judge, who shall be elected by the qualified voters of the county, and hold his office two years. He shall be his own clerk, and shall hold court at such times and receive for compensation such fees may be prescribed by law.

SEC. 9. Two justices of the peace shall be elected in each township, whose term of office shall be two years, and whose powers and duties shall be prescribed by law. The justices of the peace may be increased in any township by law.

SEC. 10. All appeals from Probate Courts and justices of the peace shall be to the district court.

SEC. 11. All the judicial officers provided for by this article shall be elected at the first election under this constitution, and shall reside in their respective townships, counties or districts during their respective terms of office. In case of vacancy in any judicial office, it shall be filled by appointment of the Governor, until the next regular election that shall occur more than thirty days after such vacancy shall have happened.

SEC. 12. All judicial officers shall hold their offices until their successors shall have been qualified.

SEC. 13. The Justices of the Supreme Court and Judges of the District Court shall, at stated times, receive for their services such compensation as may be provided by law, which shall not be increased during their respective terms of office: *Provided,* Such compensation shall not be less than fifteen hundred dollars to each justice or judge each year; and such justices or judges shall receive no fees or perquisites, nor hold any other office of profit or trust under the authority of the State or the United States during the term of office for which said justices and judges shall be elected, nor practice law in any of the courts of the State during their continuance in office.

SEC. 14. Provisions may be made by law for the increase of the number of judicial districts whenever two-thirds of the members of each house shall concur. Such districts shall be formed of compact territory and bounded by county lines, and such increase shall not vacate the office of any judge.

SEC. 15. Justices of the Supreme Court and Judges of the District Courts may be removed from office by resolution of both houses, if two-thirds of the members of each house concur; but no such removal shall be made except upon complaint, the substance of which shall be entered upon the journal, nor until the party charged shall have had notice and opportunity to be heard.

SEC. 16. The several justices and judges of the courts of record in this State shall have such jurisdiction at chambers as may be provided by law.

SEC. 17. The style of all process shall be, "The State of Kansas;" and all prosecutions shall be carried on in the name of the State.

SEC. 18. Until otherwise provided by law, the First District shall consist of the counties of Wyandotte, Leavenworth, Jefferson, and Jackson; the Second District shall consist of the counties of Atchison, Doniphan, Brown, Nemaha, Marshall, and Washington; the Third District shall consist of the counties of Pottawatomie, Riley, Clay, Dickinson, Davis, Wabaunsee, and Shawnee; the Fourth District shall consist of the counties of Douglas, Johnson, Lykins, Franklin, Anderson, Linn, Bourbon, and Allen; the Fifth District shall consist of the counties of Osage, Coffey, Woodson, Greenwood, Madison, Breckinridge, Morris, Chase, Butler, and Hunter.

SEC. 19. New or unorganized counties shall, by law, be attached for judicial purposes to the most convenient judicial districts.

SEC. 20. Provisions shall be made by law for the selection, by the bar, of a *pvo tem.* Judge of the District Court, when the Judge is absent or otherwise unable or disqualified to sit in any case.

ARTICLE IV.—ELECTIONS.

SECTION 1. All elections by the people shall be by ballot; and all elections by the Legislature shall be viva voce.

SEC. 2. General elections shall be held annually on the Tuesday succeeding the first Monday in November. Township elections shall be held on the first Tuesday of April, until otherwise provided by law.

ARTICLE V.—SUFFRAGE.

SECTION 1. Every white male person, of twenty-one years and upward, belonging to either of the following classes, who shall have resided in Kansas six months next preceding any election, and in the township or ward in which he offers to vote at least thirty days next preceding such election, shall be deemed a qualified elector: *First,* Citizens of the United States. *Second,* Persons of foreign birth who shall have declared their intention to become citizens conformably to the laws of the United States on the subject of naturalization.

SEC. 2. No person under guardianship, non compos mentis, or insane, shall be qualified to vote; nor any person convicted of treason or felony, unless restored to civil rights.

SEC. 3. No soldier, seaman, or marine, in the army or navy of the United States, or of their allies, shall be deemed to have acquired a residence in the State in consequence of being stationed within the same; nor shall any soldier, seaman or marine have the right to vote.

SEC. 4. The Legislature shall pass such laws as may be necessary for ascertaining, by proper proofs, the citizens who shall be entitled to the right of suffrage hereby established.

SEC. 5. Every person who shall give or accept a challenge to fight a duel, or who shall knowingly carry to another person such challenge, or shall go out of the State to fight a duel, shall be ineligible to any office of trust or profit.

SEC. 6. Every person who shall have given or offered a bribe to procure his election, shall be disqualified from holding office during the term for which he may have been elected.

SEC. 7. Electors, during their attendance at elections, and in going to and returning therefrom, shall be privileged from arrest in all cases except treason, felony, or breach of the peace.

ARTICLE VI.—EDUCATION.

SECTION 1. The State Superintendent of Public Instruction shall have the general supervision of the common school funds and educational interests of the State, and perform such other duties as may be prescribed by law. A Superintendent of Public Instruction shall be elected in each county, whose term of office shall be two years, and whose duty and compensation shall be prescribed by law.

SEC. 2. The Legislature shall encourage the promotion of intellectual, moral, scientific and agricultural improvement, by establishing a uniform system of common schools, and schools of higher grade, embracing normal, preparatory, collegiate, and university departments.

SEC. 3. The proceeds of all lands that have been, or may be, granted by the United States to the State, for the support of schools, and the five hundred thousand acres of land granted to the new State, under an act of Congress distributing the proceeds of public lands among the several States of the Union, approved September 4, A. D. 1841, and all estates of persons dying without heir or will, and such per cent. as may be granted by Congress on the sale of lands in this State, shall be the common property of the State, and shall be a perpetual school fund, which shall not be diminished, but the interest of which, together with all the rents of the lands, and such other means as the Legislature may provide, by tax or otherwise, shall be inviolably appropriated to the support of common schools.

SEC. 4. The income of the State school funds shall be disbursed annually, by order of the State Superintendent, to the several County Treasurers, and thence to the Treasurers of the several school districts, in equitable proportion to the number of children and youth resident therein, between the ages of five and twenty-one years: *Provided*, That no school district in which a common school has not been maintained at least three months in each year shall be entitled to receive any portion of such funds.

SEC. 5. The school lands shall not be sold unless such sale shall be authorized by a vote of the people at a general election; but, subject to revaluation every five years, they may be leased for any number of years not exceeding twenty-five, at a rate established by law.

SEC. 6. All money which shall be paid by persons as an equivalent for exemption from military duty; the clear proceeds of estrays, ownership of which shall vest in the taker-up; and the proceeds of fines for any breach of the penal laws, shall be exclusively applied in the several counties in which the money is paid or fines collected, to the support of common schools.

SEC. 7. Provisions shall be made by law for the establishment, at some eligible and central point, of a State University, for the promotion of literature and the arts and sciences, including a normal and agricultural department. All funds arising from the sale or rents of lands granted by the United States to the State for the support of a State University, and all other grants, donations or bequests, either by the State or by individuals, for such purpose, shall remain a perpetual fund, to be called the "University fund;" the interest of which shall be appropriated to the support of the State University.

SEC. 8. No religious sect or sects shall ever control any part of the common school or University funds of the State.

SEC. 9. The State Superintendent of Public Instruction, Secretary of State and Attorney General shall constitute a Board of Commissioners for the management and investment of the school funds. Any two of said Commissioners shall be a quorum.

ARTICLE VII.—PUBLIC INSTITUTIONS.

SECTION 1. Institutions for the benefit of the insane, blind, and deaf and dumb, and such other benevolent institutions as the public good may require, shall be fostered and supported by the State, subject to such regulations as may be prescribed by law. Trustees of such benevolent institutions as may be hereafter created shall be appointed by the Governor, by and with the advice and consent of the Senate; and upon all nominations made by the Governor, the question shall be taken in yeas and nays, and entered upon the journal.

SEC. 2. A Penitentiary shall be established, the directors of which shall be appointed or elected, as prescribed by law.

Sec. 3. The Governor shall fill any vacancy that may occur in the offices aforesaid, until the next session of the Legislature, and until a successor to his appointee shall be confirmed and qualified.

Sec. 4. The respective counties of the State shall provide, as may be prescribed by law, for those inhabitants who, by reason of age, infirmity or other misfortune, may have claims upon sympathy and aid of society.

ARTICLE VIII.—MILITIA.

Section 1. The militia shall be composed of all able-bodied white male citizens between the ages of twenty-one and forty-five years, except such as are exempted by the laws of the United States or of this State; but all citizens, of any religious denomination whatever, who, from scruples of conscience, may be averse to bearing arms, shall be exempted therefrom, upon such conditions as may be prescribed by law.

Sec. 2. The Legislature shall provide for organizing, equipping and disciplining the militia in such manner as it shall deem expedient, not incompatible with the laws of the United States.

Sec. 3. Officers of the militia shall be elected or appointed, and commissioned in such manner as may be provided by law.

Sec. 4. The Governor shall be Commander-in-Chief, and shall have power to call out the militia to execute the laws, to suppress insurrection, and to repel invasion.

ARTICLE IX.— COUNTY AND TOWNSHIP ORGANIZATION.

Section 1. The Legislature shall provide for organizing new counties, locating county seats, and changing county lines; and no county seat shall be changed without the consent of a majority of the electors of the county, nor any county organized, or the lines of any county changed so as to include an area of less than four hundred and thirty-two square miles.

Sec. 2. The Legislature shall provide for such county and township officers as may be necessary.

Sec. 3. All county officers shall hold their offices for the term of two years, and until their successors shall be qualified; but no person shall hold the office of sheriff or county treasurer for more than two consecutive terms.

Sec. 4. Township officers, except justices of the peace, shall hold their offices one year from the Monday next succeeding their election, and until their successors are qualified.

Sec. 5. All county and township officers may be removed from office in such manner and for such cause as shall be prescribed by law.

ARTICLE X.—APPORTIONMENT.

Section 1. In the future apportionment of the State, each organized county shall have at least one Representative; and each county shall be divided into as many districts as it has Representatives.

Sec. 2. It shall be the duty of the first Legislature to make an apportionment, based upon the census ordered by the last Legislative Assembly of the Territory; and a new apportionment shall be made in the year 1866, and every five years thereafter, based upon the census of the preceding year.

Sec. 3. Until there shall be a new apportionment, the State shall be divided into election districts; and the Representatives and Senators shall be apportioned among the several districts as follows, viz.:

First District.—Doniphan county, four Representatives, two Senators.

Second District.—Atchison and Brown counties, six Representatives, two Senators.

Third District.—Nemaha, Marshall, and Washington counties, two Representatives, one Senator.

Fourth District.—Clay, Riley, and Pottawatomie counties, four Representatives, one Senator.

Fifth District.— Dickinson, Davis, and Wabaunsee counties, three Representatives, one Senator.

Sixth District.—Shawnee, Jackson, and Jefferson counties, eight Representatives, two Senators.

Seventh District.—Leavenworth county, nine Representatives, three Senators.

Eighth District.—Douglas, Johnson, and Wyandotte counties, thirteen Representatives, four Senators.

Ninth District.—Lykins, Linn, and Bourbon counties, nine Representatives, three Senators.

Tenth District.—Allen, Anderson, and Franklin counties, six Representatives, two Senators.

Eleventh District.—Woodson and Madison counties, two Representatives, one Senator.

Twelfth District.—Coffey, Osage, and Breckinridge counties, six Representatives, two Senators.

Thirteenth District.—Morris, Chase, and Butler counties, two Representatives, one Senator.

Fourteenth District.—Arapahoe, Godfrey, Greenwood, Hunter, Wilson, Dorn, and McGee counties, one Representative.

ARTICLE XI.—FINANCE AND TAXATION.

SECTION 1. The Legislature shall provide for a uniform and equal rate of assessment and taxation; but all property used exclusively for State, county, municipal, literary, educational, scientific, religious, benevolent, and charitable purposes, and personal property to the amount of at least two hundred dollars for each family, shall be exempted from taxation.

SEC. 2. The Legislature shall provide for taxing the notes and bills discounted or purchased, moneys loaned, and other property, effects, or dues of every description (without deduction), of all banks now existing, or hereafter to be created, and of all bankers, so that all property employed in banking shall always bear a burden of taxation equal to that imposed upon the property of individuals.

SEC. 3. The Legislature shall provide, each year, for raising revenue sufficient to defray the current expenses of the State.

SEC. 4. No tax shall be levied except in pursuance of a law, which shall distinctly state the object of the same, to which object only such tax shall be applied.

SEC. 5. For the purpose of defraying extraordinary expenses, and making public improvements, the State may contract public debts; but such debts shall never, in the aggregate, exceed one million dollars, except as hereinafter provided. Every such debt shall be authorized by law for some purpose specified therein, and the vote of a majority of all the members elected to each house, to be taken by the yeas and nays, shall be necessary to the passage of such law; and every such law shall provide for levying an annual tax sufficient to pay the annual interest of such debt, and the principal thereof, when it shall become due; and shall specifically appropriate the proceeds of such taxes to the payment of such principal and interest; and such appropriation shall not be repealed, nor the taxes postponed or diminished, until the interest and principal of such debt shall have been wholly paid.

SEC. 6. No debt shall be contracted by the State, except as herein provided, unless the proposed law for creating such debt shall first be submitted to a direct vote of the electors of the State, at some general election; and if such proposed law shall be ratified by a majority of all the votes cast at such general election, then it shall be the duty of the Legislature next after such election to enact such law and create such debt, subject to all the provisions and restrictions provided in the preceding section of this article.

SEC. 7. The State may borrow money to repel invasion, suppress insurrection, or defend the State in time of war; but the money thus raised shall be applied exclusively to the object for which the loan was authorized, or to the repayment of the debt thereby created.

SEC. 8. The State shall never be a party in carrying on any works of internal improvement.

ARTICLE XII.—CORPORATIONS.

SECTION 1. The Legislature shall pass no special act conferring corporate powers. Corporations may be created under general laws; but all such laws may be amended or repealed.

SEC. 2. Dues from corporations shall be secured by individual liability of the stockholders to an additional amount equal to the stock owned by each stockholder, and such other means as shall be provided by law; but such individual liabilities shall not apply to railroad corporations, nor corporations for religious or charitable purposes.

SEC. 3. The title to all property of religious corporations shall vest in trustees, whose election shall be by the members of such corporations.

SEC. 4. No right of way shall be appropriated to the use of any corporation until full compensation therefor be first made in money, or secured by a deposit of money, to the owner, irrespective of any benefit from any improvement proposed by such corporation.

SEC. 5. Provision shall be made by general law for the organization of cities, towns and villages; and their power of taxation, assessment, borrowing money, contracting debts, and loaning their credit, shall be so restricted as to prevent the abuse of such power.

SEC. 6. The term corporation, as used in this article, shall include all associations and joint-stock companies having powers and privileges not possessed by individuals and partnerships; and all corporations may sue and be sued in their corporate name.

ARTICLE XIII.—BANKS AND CURRENCY.

SECTION 1. No bank shall be established otherwise than under a general banking law.

SEC. 2. All banking laws shall require, as collateral security for the redemption of the circulating notes of any bank organized under their provision, a deposit with the Auditor of State of the interest-paying bonds of the several States or of the United States, at the cash rates of the New York stock exchange, to an amount equal to the amount of circulating notes which such bank shall be authorized to issue, and a cash deposit in its vaults of ten per cent. of such amount of circulating notes; and the Auditor shall register and countersign no more circulating bills of any bank than the cash value of such bonds when deposited.

SEC. 3. Whenever the bonds pledged as collateral security for the circulation of any bank shall depreciate in value, the Auditor of State shall require additional security, or curtail the circulation of such bank to such extent as will continue the security unimpaired.

SEC. 4. All circulating notes shall be redeemable in the money of the United States. Holders of such notes shall be entitled, in case of the insolvency of such banks, to preference of payment over all other creditors.

SEC. 5. The State shall not be a stockholder in any banking institution.

SEC. 6. All banks shall be required to keep offices and officers for the issue and redemption of their circulation, at a convenient place within the State, to be named on the circulating notes issued by such bank.

SEC. 7. No banking institution shall issue circulating notes of a less denomination than five dollars.

SEC. 8. No banking law shall be in force until the same shall have been submitted to a vote of the electors of the State at some general election, and approved by a majority of all the votes cast at such election.

SEC. 9. Any banking law may be amended or repealed.

ARTICLE XIV.—AMENDMENTS.

SECTION 1. Propositions for the amendment of this Constitution may be made by either branch of the Legislature; and if two-thirds of all the members elected to each house shall concur therein, such proposed amendments, together with the yeas and nays, shall be entered on the journal, and the Secretary of State shall cause the same to be published in at least one newspaper in each county of the State where a newspaper is published, for three months preceding the next election for Representatives, at which time the same shall be submitted to the electors for their approval or rejection; and if a majority of the electors voting on said amendments at said election shall adopt the amendments, the same shall become a part of the Constitution. When more than one amendment shall be submitted at the same time, they shall be so submitted as to enable the electors to vote on each amendment separately; and not more than three propositions to amend shall be submitted at the same election.

SEC. 2. Whenever two-thirds of the members elected to each branch of the Legislature shall think it necessary to call a Convention to revise, amend or change this Constitution, they shall recommend to the electors to vote at the next election of members to the Legislature for or against a Convention; and if a majority of all the electors voting at such election shall have voted for a Convention, the Legislature shall, at the next session, provide for calling the same.

ARTICLE XV.— MISCELLANEOUS.

SECTION 1. All officers whose election or appointment is not otherwise provided for, shall be chosen or appointed as may be prescribed by law.

SEC. 2. The tenure of any office not herein provided for may be declared by law; when not so declared, such office shall be held during the pleasure of the authority making the appointment; but the Legislature shall not create any office the tenure of which shall be longer than four years.

SEC. 3. Lotteries and the sale of lottery tickets are forever prohibited.

SEC. 4. All public printing shall be let, on contract, to the lowest responsible bidder, by such executive officer and in such manner as shall be prescribed by law.

SEC. 5. An accurate and detailed statement of the receipts and expenditures of the public moneys, and the several amounts paid, to whom, and on what account, shall be published, as prescribed by law.

SEC. 6. The Legislature shall provide for the protection of the rights of women, in acquiring and possessing property, real, personal and mixed, separate and apart from the husband; and shall also provide for their equal rights in the possession of their children.

SEC. 7. The Legislature may reduce the salaries of officers who shall neglect the performance of any legal duty.

SEC. 8. The temporary seat of government is hereby located at the city of Topeka, county of Shawnee. The first Legislature under this Constitution shall provide by law for submitting the question of the permanent location of the capital to a popular vote, and a majority of all the votes cast at some general election shall be necessary for such location.

SEC. 9. A homestead, to the extent of one hundred and sixty acres of farming land, or of one acre within the limits of an incorporated town or city, occupied as a residence by the family of the owner, together with all improvements on the same, shall be exempted from forced sale under any process of law, and shall not be alienated without the joint consent of husband and wife, when that relation exists; but no property shall be exempt from sale for taxes, or for the payment of obligations contracted for the purchase of said premises, or for the erection of improvements thereon: *Provided*, The provisions of this section shall not apply to any process of law obtained by virtue of a lien given by the consent of both husband and wife.

SCHEDULE.

SECTION 1. That no inconvenience may arise from the change from a Territorial Government to a permanent State Government, it is declared by this Constitution that all suits, rights, actions, prosecutions, recognizances, contracts, judgments, and claims, both as respects individuals and bodies corporate, shall continue as if no change had taken place.

SEC. 2. All fines, penalties and forfeitures, owing to the Territory of Kansas, or any county, shall inure to the use of the State or county. All bonds executed to the Territory, or any officer thereof, in his official capacity, shall pass over to the Governor, or other officers of the State or county, and their successors in office, or the use of the State or county, or by him or them to be respectively assigned over to the use of those concerned, as the case may be.

SEC. 3. The Governor, Secretary and Judges, and all other officers, both civil and military, under the Territorial Government, shall continue in the exercise of the duties of their respective departments until the said officers are superseded under the authority of this constitution.

SEC. 4. All laws and parts of laws in force in the Territory, at the time of the acceptance of this Constitution by Congress, not inconsistent with this Constitution, shall continue and remain in full force until they expire or shall be repealed.

SEC. 5. The Governor shall use his private seal until a State seal is provided.

SEC. 6. The Governor, Secretary of State, Auditor of State, Treasurer of State, Attorney General, and Superintendent of Public Instruction, shall keep their respective offices at the seat of Government.

SEC. 7. All records, documents, books, papers, moneys, and vouchers, belonging and pertaining to the several Territorial courts and offices, and to the several districts and county offices, at the date of the admission of this State into the Union, shall be disposed of in such manner as may be prescribed by law.

SEC. 8. All suits, pleas, plaints, and other proceedings pending in any court of record, or justice's court, may be prosecuted to final judgment and execution; and all appeals, writs of error, certiorari, injunctions, or other proceedings whatever, may progress and be carried on as if this Constitution had not been adopted; and the Legislature shall direct the mode in which such suits, pleas, plaints, prosecutions, and other proceedings, and all papers, records, books and documents connected therewith, may be removed to the courts established by this Constitution.

SEC. 9. For the purpose of taking the vote of the electors of this Territory for the ratification or rejection of this Constitution, an election shall be held in the several voting precincts in this Territory, on the first Tuesday in October, A. D. 1859.

SEC. 10. Each elector shall express his assent or dissent by voting a written or printed ballot, labelled, "For the Constitution," or, "Against the Constitution." .

SEC. 11. If a majority of all the votes cast at such election shall be in favor of the Constitution, then there shall be an election held in the several voting precincts on the first Tuesday in December, A. D. 1859, for the election of members of the first Legislature, of all State, district and county officers provided for in this Constitution, and for a Representative in Congress.

SEC. 12. All persons having the qualifications of electors, according to the provisions of this Constitution, at the date of each of said elections, and who shall have been duly registered according to the provisions of the registry law of this Territory, and none others, shall be entitled to vote at each of said elections.

SEC. 13. The persons who may be judges of the several voting precincts of this Territory, at the date of the respective elections in this schedule provided for, shall be the judges of the respective elections herein provided for.

SEC. 14. The said judges of election, before entering upon the duties of their office, shall take and subscribe an oath faithfully to discharge their duties as such. They shall appoint two clerks of election, who shall be sworn by one of said judges faithfully to discharge their duties as such. In the event of a vacancy in the board of judges, the same shall be filled by the electors present.

SEC. 15. At each of the elections provided for in this schedule, the polls shall be opened between the hours of nine and ten o'clock, A. M., and closed at sunset.

SEC. 16. The tribunals transacting county business of the several counties shall cause to be furnished to the boards of judges, in their respective counties, two poll books for each election hereinbefore provided for, upon which the clerks shall inscribe the name of every person who may vote at the said elections.

SEC. 17. After closing the polls at each of the elections provided for in this schedule, the judges shall proceed to count the votes cast, and designate the persons or objects for which they were cast, and shall make two correct tally lists of the same.

SEC. 18. Each of the boards of judges shall safely keep one poll book and tally list, and the ballots cast at each election, and shall, within ten days after such election, cause the other poll book and tally list to be transmitted, by the hands of a sworn officer, to the clerk of the board transacting county business in their respective counties, or to which the county may be attached for municipal purposes.

SEC. 19. The tribunals transacting county business shall assemble at the county seats of their respective counties, on the second Tuesday after each of the elections provided for in this schedule, and shall canvass the votes cast at the elections held in the several precincts in their respective counties, and of the counties attached for municipal purposes. They shall hold in safe keeping the poll books and tally lists of said elections. and shall, within ten days thereafter, transmit, by the hands of a sworn officer, to the President of this Convention, at the city of Topeka, a certified transcript of the same, showing the number of votes cast for each person or object voted for at each of the several precincts in their respective counties, and in the counties attached for municipal purposes, separately.

SEC. 20. The Governor of the Territory, and the President and Secretary of this Convention, shall constitute a Board of State Canvassers, any two of whom shall be a quorum; and who shall, on the fourth Monday after each of the elections provided for in this schedule, assemble at said city of Topeka, and proceed to open and canvass the votes cast at the several precincts in the different counties of the Territory, and declare the result; and shall immediately issue certificates of election to all persons (if any) thus elected.

SEC. 21. Said Board of State Canvassers shall issue their proclamation, not less than twenty days next preceding each of the elections provided for in this schedule. Said proclamation shall contain an announcement of the several elections; the qualifications of electors; the manner of conducting said elections and of making the returns thereof, as in this Constitution provided; and shall publish said proclamation in one newspaper in each of the counties of the Territory in which a newspaper may be then published.

SEC. 22. The Board of State Canvassers shall provide for the transmission of authenticated copies of the Constitution to the President of the United States, the President of the Senate, and Speaker of the House of Representatives.

SEC. 23. Upon official information having been by him received of the admission of Kansas into the Union as a State, it shall be the duty of the Governor elect under the Constitution to proclaim the same, and to convene the Legislature, and do all things else necessary to the complete and active organization of the State Government.

SEC. 24. The first Legislature shall have no power to make any changes in county lines.

SEC. 25. At the election to be held for the ratification or rejection of this Constitution, each elector shall be permitted vote on the homestead provision contained in the article on "Miscellaneous," by depositing a ballot inscribed, "For the homestead," or, "Against the homestead;" and if a majority of all the votes cast at said election shall be against said provision, then it shall be stricken from the Constitution.

RESOLUTIONS.

Resolved, That the Congress of the United States is hereby requested, upon the application of Kansas for admission into the Union, to pass an act granting to the State forty-five hundred thousand acres of land to aid in the construction of railroads and other internal improvements.

Resolved, That Congress be further requested to pass an act appropriating fifty thousand acres of land for the improvement of the Kansas river from its mouth to Fort Riley.

Resolved, That Congress be further requested to pass an act granting all swamp lands within the State for the benefit of common schools.

Resolved, That Congress be further requested to pass an act appropriating five hundred thousand dollars, or, in lieu thereof, five hundred thousand acres of land, for the payment of the claims awarded to citizens of Kansas by the claim commissioners appointed by the Governor and Legislature of Kansas, under an act of the Territorial Legislature, passed February 7, 1859.

Resolved, That the Legislature shall make provision for the sale or disposal of the lands granted to the State in aid of internal improvements and for other purposes, subject to the same rights of pre-emption to the settlers thereon as are now allowed by law to settlers on the public lands.

Resolved, That it is the desire of the people of Kansas to be admitted into the Union with this Constitution.

Resolved, That Congress be further requested to assume the debt of this Territory.

Done in Convention at Wyandotte, this 29th day of July, A.D. 1859.

JAMES M. WINCHELL,
President of the Kansas Constitutional Convention, and Delegate from Osage County.

JOHN A. MARTIN, *Secretary.*

ROBERT GRAHAM.	JAMES M. ARTHUR.	P. H. TOWNSEND.
JOHN JAMES INGALLS.	JOSIAH LAMB.	WM. HUTCHINSON.
CALEB MAY.	WM. McCULLOCH.	N. C. BLOOD.
J. A. MIDDLETON.	JAS. G. BLUNT.	EDMUND G. ROSS.
S. D. HOUSTON.	J. C. BURNETT.	JAS. HANWAY.
LUTHER R. PALMER.	WM. R. GRIFFITH.	ALLEN CROCKER.
JOHN TAYLOR BURRIS.	SAM'L A. KINGMAN.	SAM'L E. HOFFMAN.
JOHN P. GREER.	ROBT. J. PORTER.	JAMES A. SIGNOR.
JOHN RITCHIE.	JAMES BLOOD.	GEO. H. LILLIE.
H. D. PRESTON.	S. O. THACHER.	R. L. WILLIAMS.
BENJAMIN F. SIMPSON.	EDWIN STOKES.	W. P. DUTTON.

AMENDMENTS TO THE CONSTITUTION.
ARTICLE II.

Section 2 was amended, November 4, 1873, as follows:

"SECTION 2. The number of Representatives and Senators shall be regulated by law, but shall never exceed one hundred and twenty-five Representatives and forty Senators. From and after the adoption of the amendment, the House of Representatives shall admit one member from each county in which at least two hundred and fifty legal votes were cast at the next preceding general election; and each organized county in which less than two hundred legal votes were cast at the next preceding general election shall be attached to, and constitute a part of, the Representative District of the county lying next adjacent to it on the east."

Section 12 was amended, November 8, 1864, as follows:

"SECTION 12. Bills may originate in either house, but may be amended or rejected by either."

ARTICLE V.

Section 2 was amended, November 5, 1867, as follows:

"SECTION 2. No person under guardianship, non compos mentis, or insane; no person convicted of felony, unless restored to civil rights; no person who has been dishonorably discharged from the service of the United States, unless reinstated; no person guilty of defrauding the Government of the United States, or any of the States thereof; no person guilty of giving or receiving a bribe, or offering to give or receive a bribe; and no person who has ever voluntarily borne arms against the Government of the United States, or in any manner voluntarily aided or abetted in the attempted overthrow of said Government, except all persons who have been honorably discharged from the military service of the United States since the first day of April, A. D. 1861, provided that they have served one year or more therein, shall be qualified to vote or hold office in this State, until such disability shall be removed by a law passed by a vote of two-thirds of all the members of both branches of the Legislature."

Section 3 was amended, November 8, 1864, as follows:

"SECTION 3. For the purpose of voting, no person shall be deemed to have gained or lost a residence by reason of his presence or absence while employed in the service of the United States, nor while engaged in the navigation of the waters of this State or of the United States, or of the high seas; nor while a student of any seminary of learning; nor while kept at any almshouse, or other asylum, at public expense; nor while confined in any public prison: and the Legislature may make provision for taking the votes of electors who may be absent from their townships or wards, in the volunteer military service of the United States, or the militia service of this State; but nothing herein contained shall be deemed to allow any soldier, seaman or marine in the regular army or navy of the United States the right to vote."

ARTICLE XIII.

Section 7 was amended, November, 1861, as follows:

"No banking institution shall issue circulating notes of a less denomination than one dollar."

ARTICLE XV.

Section 4 was amended, November 3, 1868, as follows:

"All public printing shall be done by a State Printer, who shall be elected by the Legislature in joint session, and shall hold his office for two years, and until his successor shall be elected and qualified. The joint session of the Legislature for the election of a State Printer shall be on the third Tuesday of January, A. D. 1869, and every two years thereafter. All public printing shall be done at the capital, and the prices for the same shall be regulated by law."

The following amendment will be voted upon by the people in November, 1875:

SENATE JOINT RESOLUTION NO. 1.

PROPOSED AMENDMENT to section three of the Constitution of the State, regulating the time of electing and compensation of members of the Legislature.

Be it resolved by the Legislature of the State of Kansas, two-thirds of the members elected to each [house] concurring therein:

[SECTION 1.] The following proposition to amend the Constitution of the State of Kansas shall be submitted to the electors of the State at the general election of eighteen hundred and seventy-five:

PROPOSITION ONE: Section twenty-five of article two shall be amended so as to read as follows: Section 25. All sessions of the Legislature shall be held at the State capital, and beginning with the session of eighteen hundred and seventy-seven, all regular sessions shall be held once in two years, commencing on the second Tuesday of January of each alternate year thereafter.

PROPOSITION TWO: Section three of article eleven shall be amended so as to read as follows: Section 3. The Legislature shall provide, at each regular session, for raising sufficient revenue to defray the current expenses of the State for two years.

PROPOSITION THREE: The following shall constitute section twenty-nine of article two: Section 29. At the general election held in eighteen hundred and seventy-six, and thereafter, members of the House of Representatives shall be elected for two years, and members of the Senate shall be elected for four years.

SEC. 2. The following shall be the method of submitting said proposition of amendment: The ballots shall be either written or printed, or partly printed and partly written. In regard to proposition one, the form of the ballots shall be, "For proposition one to amend the Constitution," "Against proposition one to amend the Constitution;" in regard to proposition two, the form of the ballots shall be, "For proposition two to amend the Constitution," "Against proposition two to amend the Constitution;" in regard to proposition three, the form of the ballots shall be, "For proposition three to amend the Constitution," "Against proposition three to amend the Constitution."

SEC. 3. This joint resolution shall take effect and be in force from and after its publication in the statute book.

JULY.—The report made to the Constitutional Convention by Edward Hoogland, Henry J. Adams and Samuel A. Kingman, Commissioners under the act of February 7, 1859, "to provide for the adjustment and payment of claims," was printed by order of the United States House of Representatives in 1861, and is one of the documents of the second session of the Thirty-sixth Congress. It is published in two octavo volumes, and contains 1767 pages.

The first act for the auditing of claims was passed February 23, 1857. Hiram J. Strickler was the Commissioner under this act.

Mr. Hoogland was appointed by the Governor, Mr. Adams elected by the Council, and Judge Kingman chosen by the House. The Legislature, on joint ballot, elected William McKay the Attorney of the Board. The claims allowed by this Commission amount to $412,978.03. The Commissioners believe that more than two hundred lives were lost, and not less than two millions in money, during the Territorial troubles. The Report is made up of affidavits of claimants, who tell the story of their losses in their own way, and it is altogether unique and invaluable as a historical record. Testimony was taken in 463 cases.

Congress made no appropriation.

On certificates of the Commission, the Territorial Auditor issued warrants on the Treasurer to the amount of $349,933.63. The Treasurer issued bonds on the warrants to the amount of $95,700. The Legislature refused to make the Territory responsible for this debt. The first State Legislature, in 1861, took similar action.

JULY 16.—Treaty with "the Swan Creek and Black River band of Chippewas of Kansas Territory." The reservation of 8,320 acres, in Franklin county, Kansas, set apart for the entire band, shall inure to the benefit of that portion of said band now residing thereon. The Munsees, or Christian Indians, are united with said band.

JULY 23.—Dr. John Doy is rescued from the jail in St. Joseph. Dr. Doy afterwards published a book, giving a history of his experience in Kansas and Missouri. His son Charles died suddenly in southern Kansas, and the father in Michigan—neither from disease.

AUGUST 3.—Republican Convention at Lawrence, to nominate a Delegate to Congress. Called to order by S. C. Pomeroy. J. P. Root, of Wyandotte, was elected temporary Chairman, and Albert L. Lee, of Elwood, Secretary. The permanent officers were as follows:

President: Jas. M. Winchell, of Osage county.

Vice Presidents: Chas. Chadwick, of Wyandotte county; Warren W. Guthrie, of Brown county; Chas. B. Lines, of Wabaunsee county; B. F. Simpson, of Lykins county; and Silas Fearl, of Coffey county.

Secretaries: Albert L. Lee, of Doniphan county, and Jacob Stotler, of Breckinridge county.

The vote on candidate for Congress stood thus: M. J. Parrott, 57; M. F. Conway, 26; A. Danford, 11; Chas. A. Foster, 3; S. C. Pomeroy, 3; Benj. Harding, 1, and two blanks. Necessary to a choice, 52. On motion of C. B. Lines, the nomination of Mr. Parrott was made unanimous. On motion of Wm. A. Phillips, of Arapahoe, Mr. Parrott was pledged the support of every Republican voter in the Territory.

AUGUST 17.—Democratic Convention at Topeka. Saunders W. Johnston nominated for Delegate in Congress.

SEPTEMBER 12.—James M. Winchell, President, and John A. Martin, Secretary, issue a proclamation calling an election on the Wyandotte Constitution, to ratify or reject it.

SEPTEMBER.—Anson Burlingamé visits Kansas. The Republicans of Leavenworth gave him a supper. D. R. Anthony presided, and James McCahon acted as toastmaster.

OCTOBER 1.—Treaty with the Sacs and Foxes.

—The State Record started at Topeka by E. G. and W. W. Ross.

OCTOBER 4.—The Wyandotte Constitution adopted. Vote for the Constitution, 10,421; against, 5,530; for the homestead clause, 8,788; against, 4,772.

OCTOBER 5.—Treaty with the Kansas Indians. A portion of their reservation set apart and assigned in severalty to members of the tribe.

OCTOBER 12.—Republican State Convention at Lawrence. William A. Phillips was elected temporary Chairman of the Convention, receiving 31 votes to 29 for James M. Winchell. Leavenworth county appeared in the Convention with two sets of delegates, one favorable to the nomination of H. P. Johnson for Governor, and the other to Henry J. Adams. The mat-

15

ter was compromised, and both candidates killed, by selecting four from each delegation to represent the county in the Convention. *President:* William A. Phillips. *Secretaries:* P. B. Plumb and J. A. Martin. A motion to nominate the Congressman first was defeated, by a vote of 38 to 36. Mr. Vaughan then nominated H. P. Johnson, and Mr. Thacher, Charles Robinson, for Governor. The whole number of votes cast was 77, Robinson receiving 43, and Johnson 34. *Lieutenant Governor:* J. P. Root received 39 votes, Mr. Fish 15, A. Larzelere 14, and 9 scattering. *Secretary of State:* J. W. Robinson 43, James Fletcher 24, and 9 scattering. *Auditor:* On the second ballot George S. Hillyer received 45, and Asa Hairgrove 24. *Treasurer:* On the second ballot Wm. Tholen received 49, and T. P. Herrick 25. *Attorney General:* On the first ballot B. F. Simpson received 37, John C. Douglass 17, D. W. Houston 14, and Ed. S. Lowman 8. *Superintendent of Public Instruction:* W. R. Griffith was nominated on the first ballot, having received 49 votes to 16 for Davis and 8 scattering. *Congressman:* On the first ballot M. F. Conway received 48, and O. E. Learnard 29. *Judges:* Thomas Ewing, jr., Chief Justice, and Samuel A. Kingman and Lawrence D. Bailey, Associates, were nominated by acclamation.

OCTOBER 16.—Captain John Brown, with twenty-one men, takes possession of the town of Harper's Ferry, Virginia.

OCTOBER 18.—Anson Burlingame speaks at Topeka. He also visits Burlingame, Osage county.

OCTOBER 25.—Democratic Convention at Lawrence. Called to order by J. P. Slough. *Temporary Officers:* G. H. Fairchild, Atchison, Chairman; B. P. Ayers, of Linn county, Secretary.

Officers: President, G. H. Fairchild; Vice Presidents, J. Stiarwalt, John Wright, E. Jones, C. E. Haskins, D. Goodin, Jesse Clover, T. J. Fortaine, J. G. Sparrey, J. F. Cooper, C. K. Miner, Seth Killam, Hiram Moran; Secretaries, B. P. Ayers, A. G. Otis, S. A. Medary, A. S. Devenney, A. Jones.

Ballot for Governor: Samuel Medary 43, H. B. Denman 27, C. K. Holliday 10. For Lieutenant Governor, John P. Slough was nominated by acclamation. For Chief Justice, Judge Joseph Williams received 54 votes, Judge Purkins 29. For Member of Congress: John A. Halderman 41, Robert B. Mitchell 35, Robert S. Stevens 5. For Attorney General: Orlin Thurston, of Allen, 39; W. D. Wood, of Doniphan, 21; G. W. Willey, of Lykins, 18. On the second ballot Thurston was declared the nominee. For Auditor: J. K. Goodin 51; C. R. Deming, of Marshall, 25. For Treasurer: R. J. Pease, of Atchison, 44; J. E. Jones, of Bourbon, 31. For Secretary of State: A. P. Walker, of Douglas, 43; J. M. Giffen, of Johnson, 34. For Associate Justices: R. B. Mitchell was nominated by acclamation, and Samuel A. Stinson over H. Miles Moore.

OCTOBER 31.—The Governor sets apart Thursday, November 24th, as a day of Thanksgiving.

NOVEMBER 1.—Governor Medary proclaims the following as the result of the vote on the Wyandotte Constitution, at the election held on the 4th of October:

Names of Counties.	For the Constitution....	Against the Constitution.	For a Homestead........	Against a Homestead.
Allen..	244	159	201	152
Anderson......................................	266	80	206	109
Arapahoe (no returns)................	....	....	....	....
Atchison......................................	694	581	412	587
Bourbon.......................................	464	256	530	102
Breckinridge..............................	545	26	425	19
Brown...	269	103	173	163
Butler..	27	1	28	....
Chase (no returns).....................	....	....	....	....
Clay (no returns).......................	....	....	....	....
Coffey..	434	121	360	115
Davis (no returns).....................	....	....	....	....
Dickinson (no returns)..............	....	....	....	....
Doniphan....................................	743	630	592	690
Douglas......................................	1,412	383	1,325	314
Dorn (no returns).......................	....	....	....	....
Franklin.....................................	301	111	252	111
Greenwood.................................	24	16	33	3
Hunter (no returns)...................	....	....	....	....
Jackson.....................................	224	170	138	185
Jefferson...................................	392	354	345	131
Johnson.....................................	373	377	316	113
Leavenworth..............................	1,143	1,088	1,019	1,045
Linn..	549	157	455	169
Lykins.......................................	492	295	455	225
Madison.....................................	82	4	60	23
Marshall (no returns)................	....	....	....	.
McGee (no returns)....................	....	....	....	....
Morris..	25	50	22	13
Nemaha......................................	200	44	104	63
Osage...	44	....	42	2
Pottawatomie............................	93	68	76	49
Riley..	296	128	202	52
Shawnee.....................................	671	109	666	60
Wabaunsee.................................	110	14	65	17
Wilson (no returns)...................	....	....	....	....
Wyandotte.................................	274	205	166	260
Woodson (no returns)................	....	....	....	....
Total.....................................	10,421	5,530	8,788	4,772

The "Constitution" and "Homestead," therefore, having received a majority of the votes cast, are adopted by the people of Kansas.

NOVEMBER 8.—Territorial election for Delegate in Congress. Saunders W. Johnston was the Democratic and Marcus J. Parrott the Republican candidate.

Name of County.	*Johnston*	*Parrott.*	*Total.*
Arapahoe..	38	22	60
Atchison...	654	531	1,185
Anderson..	105	238	343
Allen..	207	203	410
Brown..	25	272	297
Breckinridge...	145	371	516
Butler..	1	47	48
Bourbon...	251	368	619
Coffey..	170	285	455
Chase...	....	126	126
Clay (attached to Riley).			
Doniphan...	762	768	1,530
Dickinson..	....	....	....
Davis..	127	94	221
Douglas..	353	993	1,346
Dorn (attached to Bourbon).			
Franklin..	172	265	437

VOTE FOR TERRITORIAL DELEGATE IN CONGRESS—*Concluded.*

Name of County.	Johnston	Parrott.	Total.
Greenwood..	....	....	....
Godfrey (attached to Coffey).			
Hunter (attached to Breckinridge).			
Jackson...	179	222	401
Jefferson.................................	355	367	722
Johnson..	482	408	890
Leavenworth	1,391	1,109	2,592
Lykins	355	453	808
Linn..	373	563	936
Madison	6	81	87
Morris	114	41	155
Marshall and Washington.................................	179	146	325
McGee (attached to Bourbon).			
Nemaha..	41	228	270
Osage	1	31	32
Pottawatomie...	33	121	154
Riley	97	298	395
Shawnee	167	535	702
Wabaunsee...	8	121	129
Wyandotte	321	289	610
Woodson	77	87	164
Wilson (attached to Allen).			
Total..	7,232	9,708	16,949

Parrott's majority, 2,746.

NOVEMBER 8.—Election of Territorial Legislature:

COUNCIL.—(*Each District One Member.*)

FIRST DISTRICT — DONIPHAN.
George M. Beebe.............................. 762 | William D. Beeler................................ 748

SECOND DISTRICT — ATCHISON AND JACKSON.
M. R. Benton...................................... 741 | W. J. Marion 815

THIRD DISTRICT — LEAVENWORTH.
William G. Mathias...........................1267 | James L. McDowell 1221

FOURTH DISTRICT — LEAVENWORTH AND JEFFERSON.
J. M. Christison................................1692 | Adam Fisher.......................................1101

FIFTH DISTRICT — BROWN, NEMAHA, POTTAWATOMIE, MARSHALL, AND WASHINGTON.
Luther R. Palmer................................. 476 | Warren W. Guthrie............................. 201
George Graham................................... 187 | Charles R. Deming............................. 182

SIXTH DISTRICT — RILEY, CLAY, DAVIS, DICKINSON, WABAUNSEE, AND MORRIS.
J. B. Woodward................................... 573 | H. N. Williams.................................... 320

SEVENTH DISTRICT — SHAWNEE, OSAGE, AND BRECKINRIDGE.
Chester Thomas................................... 909 | Philip C. Schuyler 238

EIGHTH DISTRICT — DOUGLAS.
James M. Hendry .... 893 | George A. Reynolds............................. 435

NINTH DISTRICT — DOUGLAS, FRANKLIN, AND ANDERSON.
P. P. Elder......................................1492 | Isaiah Pile.. 607

TENTH DISTRICT — WYANDOTTE AND JOHNSON.

Charles G. Keeler.............................. 765 | Alfred Gray.. 702

ELEVENTH DISTRICT — LINN AND LYKINS.

W. W. Updegraff................................. 994 | Joseph H. Barlow............................... 781

TWELFTH DISTRICT — BOURBON, ALLEN, M'GEE, DORN, WOODSON, AND WILSON.

Watson Stewart.................................. 642 | N. S. Goss... 550

THIRTEENTH DISTRICT — COFFEY, MADISON, HUNTER, BUTLER, CHASE, GODFREY, AND
GREENWOOD.

John C. Lambdin .... 341 | Hiram Hoover...................................... 210

HOUSE OF REPRESENTATIVES.

FIRST DISTRICT — DONIPHAN — THREE MEMBERS.

Thomas Vanderslice .... 747 | Carey B. Whitehead............................. 759
Hugh Robertson................................. 752 | Thomas A. Osborn.............................. 731
Philip Burke....................................... 731 | B. O'Driscoll...................................... 728

SECOND DISTRICT — ATCHISON — TWO MEMBERS.

William Noel .... 659 | F. Lombard... 658
R. A. Van Winkle .... 506 | James Auld... 495

THIRD DISTRICT — LEAVENWORTH — FOUR MEMBERS.

Fred. Brown.....................................1314 | Jeremiah Clark..................................1123
Pascal S. Parks ....1372 | Benjamin H. Twombly 1133
John Wright ....1293 | C. H. W. Ettinger..... 1114
J. C. Murphy ....1275 | A. M. Clark 1163

FOURTH DISTRICT — JEFFERSON — TWO MEMBERS.

Edward Lynde................................... 372 | Henry Buckmaster 329
T. A. Blake .... 370 | James H. Jones................................... 328

FIFTH DISTRICT — POTTAWATOMIE AND WABAUNSEE — ONE MEMBER.

Amasa Bartlett.................................. 234 | Charles Jenkins................................... 82

SIXTH DISTRICT — JACKSON — ONE MEMBER.

Byron Steward.................................. 217 | William Cline...................................... 183

SEVENTH DISTRICT — WYANDOTTE — ONE MEMBER.

Wm. L. McMath........... 295 | Thos. J. Williams......... 295 | A. B. Bartlett.............. 39

EIGHTH DISTRICT — BROWN — ONE MEMBER.

H. R. Dutton..................................... 232 | A. B. Anderson................................... 60

NINTH DISTRICT — NEMAHA — ONE MEMBER.

Morton Cave (vote not given in official abstract.)

TENTH DISTRICT — MARSHALL AND WASHINGTON — ONE MEMBER.

J. S. Magill .... 162 | George G. Pierce................................ 160

ELEVENTH DISTRICT — RILEY AND CLAY — ONE MEMBER.

Daniel L. Chandler................................ 268 | George Montague.. 174

TWELFTH DISTRICT — DICKINSON AND DAVIS — ONE MEMBER.

Robert Reynolds.................................... 136 | J. W. Blaine.. 83

THIRTEENTH DISTRICT — BRECKINRIDGE — ONE MEMBER.

Stephen G. Elliott .... 387 | E. C. Stevens...................................... 101

FOURTEENTH DISTRICT — SHAWNEE — TWO MEMBERS.

William H. Fitzpatrick .... 524 | Cyrus K. Holliday.............................. 152
S. R. Caniff.. 524 | N. O. Case 155

FIFTEENTH DISTRICT — DOUGLAS — THREE MEMBERS.

Paul R. Brooks................................... 992 | Edwin Mervin 335
William A. Rankin .... 965 | George W. Zinn................................... 334
Erastus Heath...................................... 991 | L. A. Prather 338

SIXTEENTH DISTRICT — JOHNSON — TWO MEMBERS.

Charles Sims.. 511 | Josiah E. Hayes 385
L. S. Cornwall..................................... 477 | D. W. Scott.. 389

SEVENTEENTH DISTRICT — LYKINS — ONE MEMBER.

Gustavus A. Colton.............................. 471 | George W. Dall................................... 368

EIGHTEENTH DISTRICT — LINN — ONE MEMBER.

J. H. Jones... 490 | John T. Alexander 394

NINETEENTH DISTRICT — LYKINS AND LINN — ONE MEMBER.

William R. Wagstaff........................... 847 | James Montgomery 838

TWENTIETH DISTRICT — ANDERSON — ONE MEMBER.

Thomas Lindsay.................................. 296 | Samuel Anderson 5

TWENTY-FIRST DISTRICT — FRANKLIN — ONE MEMBER.

Henry Shively...................................... 221 | John F. Javens.................................... 216 .

TWENTY-SECOND DISTRICT — COFFEY AND OSAGE — TWO MEMBERS.

O. H. Sheldon...................................... 309 | A. A. Burr.. 177
George W. Nelson................................. 335 | Doc. Howell.. 136

TWENTY-THIRD DISTRICT — MADISON, CHASE, AND MORRIS — ONE MEMBER.

T. S. Huffaker .... 121 | S. N. Wood.................... 86 | S. G. Britton................ 34

TWENTY-FOURTH DISTRICT — BUTLER, GREENWOOD, HUNTER, GODFREY, AND WOODSON
— ONE MEMBER.

P. G. D. Morton................................... 149 | E. I. Brown 124

TWENTY-FIFTH DISTRICT — ALLEN, WILSON, DORN, AND M'GEE — ONE MEMBER.

John W. Scott .... 213 | Nimrod Hawkins.................................. 195

DECEMBER 1.—Abram Lincoln arrives in Elwood, and makes a speech that evening. He was met at St. Joseph by M. W. Delahay and D. W. Wilder. His speech was substantially the same he made soon afterwards at the Cooper Institute, New York, and one of the ablest and clearest ever delivered by an American statesman.

DECEMBER 2.—John Brown executed.

DECEMBER 3.—The Leavenworth Times says: "The Hon. Abe Lincoln is on Kansas soil. He has spoken at Elwood, Troy and Doniphan. Last night he spoke at Atchison. To-day at noon he arrives in Leavenworth. To-night he speaks at Stockton's." He received a public reception, and made two speeches, one on the 3d and one on the 5th.

DECEMBER 5.— Meeting of the 36th Congress. John Sherman, of Ohio, the Republican candidate for Speaker, had approved of an Anti-Slavery book written by Hinton R. Helper, of North Carolina. John B. Clark, of Missouri, offered a resolution declaring any member unfit to be Speaker who had signed a recommendation of Helper's "Compendium of the Impending Crisis." The resolution was long debated, but did not come to a vote.

DECEMBER 5.—In the Senate, Mr. Mason, of Virginia, moved the appointment of a committee to enquire into the facts connected with the seizure of the United States Armory at Harper's Ferry, by John Brown and his confederates; adopted. Mr. Trumbull, of Illinois, moved to include in the investigation the seizure of the Arsenal at Franklin, Mo., by the invaders of Kansas, in 1855; rejected. The committee consisted of Mason, Fitch, Jefferson Davis, Doolittle and Collamer. The majority report, signed by Mason, Fitch and Davis, absolved all persons except Brown and his men from any connexion with the invasion. The committee examined several witnesses from Kansas.

DECEMBER 6.—ELECTION OF STATE OFFICERS AND A REPRESENTATIVE IN CONGRESS, UNDER THE WYANDOTTE CONSTITUTION.

COUNTIES.	John A. Halderman (Repr've in Congress)	Martin F. Conway (Repr've in Congress)	Orlin Thurston (Att'y Gen'l)	Benjamin F. Simpson (Att'y Gen'l)	Robert B. Mitchell (Asso'te J'stice, Two years)	Lawrence D. Bailey (Asso'te J'stice, Two years)	Samuel A. Stinson (Asso'te J'stice, Four years)	Samuel A. Kingman (Asso'te J'stice, Four years)	Joseph Williams (Chief Justice)	Thomas Ewing, jr. (Chief Justice)	J. S. McGill (Supt. of Pub. Instruction)	William R. Griffith (Supt. of Pub. Instruction)	Joel K. Goodin (Auditor)	George S. Hillyer (Auditor)	R. L. Pease (Treasurer)	William Tholen (Treasurer)	A. P. Walker (Sec'y of State)	John W. Robinson (Sec'y of State)	John P. Slough (Lieut. Gov.)	Joseph P. Root (Lieut. Gov.)	Samuel Medary (Governor)	Chas. Robinson (Governor)
Atchison	583	638	581	647	577	649	579	649	579	649	581	646	583	645	586	632	581	645	581	644	585	644
Allen	135	175	141	165	135	174	135	174	134	112	135	175	135	175	135	176	135	175	134	175	136	174
Anderson	87	160	89	162	80	162	92	162	89	150	88	162	88	162	89	162	89	162	89	162	89	160
Brown	95	258	81	273	80	274	71	280	80	271			81	273	81	273	81	272	80	271	81	273
Breckinridge	126	397	110	413	142	356	109	413	111	411	111	413	111	411	110	413	111	413	109	405	122	398
Bourbon	149	214	148	274	148	275	147	275	151	272	149	172	150	273	135	275	147	275	145	273	149	275
Chase	10	105	10	109	35	84	10	109	10	109	10	109	10	92	10	92	10	109	10	109	10	109
Coffey	100	223	99	227	98	228	98	229	97	227	97	229	99	227	98	228	98	228	98	228	101	223
Douglas	341	1,057	325	1,037	333	1,093	328	1,100	341	1,086	330	1,094	330	1,097	324	1,100	333	1,093	324	1,093	334	1,018
Doniphan	382	470	378	473	376	472	373	472	376	472	377	472	380	466	375	472	377	473	327	472	371	476
Di'k'n & Davis	115	30	116	49	116	48	115	49	116	49	116	48	115	49	115	48	115	50	117	50	116	50
Franklin	124	242	122	250	122	250	121	250	129	241	122	249	116	245	122	250	121	249	120	250	121	249
Greenwood	6	23	5	24	6	23	6	23	6	23	6	23	6	23	6	23	6	23	6	23	6	23
Hunter	3	21	3	21	3	21	3	21	3	21	3	21	3	21	3	21	3	21	3	21	3	21
Jackson	169	170	169	170	169	169	169	169	169	170	169	170	169	169	169	170	169	170	169	170	170	169
Jefferson	294	332	292	329	293	331	296	328	294	329	292	331	281	330	293	332	292	332	295	333	293	332
Johnson	426	303	424	307	421	308	423	308	422	309	425	308	425	308	423	310	425	310	424	310	425	306
Leavenworth	1,515	878	1,405	961	1,404	961	1,415	952	1,312	1,098	1,402	961	1,403	965	1,372	1,022	1,406	965	1,433	975	1,404	997
Linn	127	219	131	225	159	199	130	226	118	238	131	224	135	224	131	224	131	225	131	226	132	222
Lykins	195	314	186	301	192	190	313	315	203	306	190	314	190	300	204	314	190	315	189	313	200	312
Madison	7	47	7	47	34	47	5	47	5	48	7	47	7	47	7	47	7	47	7	47	7	47
Marshall	69	39	69	40	69	40	69	40	40	69	68	40	69	40	69	40	69	40	69	40	69	40
Morris	60	52	59	54	66	47	59	54	59	54	59	54	59	54	59	54	59	54	59	54	59	54
Nemaha	62	123	61	128	60	127	60	128	60	127	59	127	66	127	60	128	60	128	60	129	60	128
Osage	2	24	2	12	2	12	2	12	2	14	2	12	2	12	2	12	2	12	2	12	2	24
Pottawatomie	41	128	34	135	34	135	34	135	34	136	34	135	35	134	39	135	34	135	37	131	35	133
Riley	101	228	96	233	97	235	97	234	97	235	94	234	96	235	96	235	113	196	97	232	95	234
Shawnee	187	555	175	567	177	546	177	554	174	567	175	568	175	567	175	566	175	570	173	567	171	569
Wabaunsee	16	121	15	128	16	128	16	128	16	129	16	102	16	127	15	126	16	119	16	119	17	128
Woodson	39	58	39	58	41	56	39	58	40	47	39	58	39	58	39	58	39	58	38	59	37	60
Total	**5,567**	**7,674**	**5,372**	**7,880**	**5,492**	**7,721**	**5,396**	**7,895**	**5,301**	**8,010**	**5,287**	**7,598**	**5,365**	**7,856**	**5,348**	**7,937**	**5,396**	**7,864**	**5,392**	**7,893**	**5,395**	**7,908**

DÉCEMBER 6.—Vote on State Senators. Republicans are marked with a star.

FIRST DISTRICT.

Names.	Doniphan.	Majority...
H. N. Seaver *	424	1
T. A. Osborn *	483	130
C. H. Hatcher	423	....
X. K. Stout	353	....

SECOND DISTRICT.

Names.	Atchison...	Brown......	Total.......	Majority...
John A. Martin *	644	266	910	290
H. R. Dutton *	628	297	925	249
Samuel W. Wade	574	46	620	....
G. O. Chase	596	80	676	....

THIRD DISTRICT.

Names.	Marshall...	Nemaha.....	Total.	Majority :.
R. W. Terry *	40	109	149	21
J. E. Clardy	63	65	128	....

FOURTH DISTRICT.

Names.	Pottawato-mie.....	Riley......	Total.......	Majority :.
S. D. Houston *	136	233	369	242
W. H. Herbert	33	94	127	....

FIFTH DISTRICT.

Names.	Davis.......	Wabaun-see.......	Total.......	Majority...
J. M. Hubbard *	35	109	144	5
Robert Reynolds	122	17	139	....

SIXTH DISTRICT.

Names.	Shawnee...	Jefferson :.	Jackson.....	Total.......	Majority...
H. W. Farnsworth *	492	325	167	984	257
Edward Lynde *	515	318	168	1001	409
C. K. Holliday	253	306	168	727	....
G. A. Buck	144	280	168	592	....

SEVENTH DISTRICT.

Names.	Leavenworth.	Major'ty
John H. McDowell	1445	483
H. B. Denman	1424	435
Jesse Connell	1328	290
David H. Bailey *	962	....
Matt. France *	989	....
Jas. L. McDowell *	1038	....

EIGHTH DISTRICT.

Names.	Douglas	Johnson.	Total	Major'ty
John Lockhart *	1081	297	1378	630
Josiah Miller *	1020	303	1323	594
Robert Morrow *	1068	308	1376	609
O. B. Gunn *	1072	306	1378	635
A. S. Devenney	327	421	748	....
S. O. Hemmenway	305	424	729	....
S. K. Huson	343	424	767	....
G. W. Veale	319	424	743	....

NINTH DISTRICT.

Names.	Bourbon	Linn......	Lykins ..	Total....	Major'ty
J. C. Burnett *	270	218	314	802	341
J. F. Broadhead *	275	201	311	787	321
J. A. Phillips *	275	217	287	779	304
Geo. A. Crawford	141	140	180	461	....
Harry Torrey	140	132	194	466	....
Jos. H. Barlow	140	147	188	475	....

TENTH DISTRICT.

Names.	Allen......	Anderson.	Franklin...	Total.......	Majority ..
P. P. Elder *	169	161	239	569	289
Wm. Spriggs *	169	172	246	587	233
Wm. Pennock	76	81	123	280	....
John R. Goodin	139	84	131	354	....

ELEVENTH DISTRICT.

Names.	Madison...	Woodson...	Total.........	Plurality ..
S. E. Hoffman *	17	45	62	8
Russell Austin	....	30	30	....
John L. Dunn	38	16	54	....

TWELFTH DISTRICT.

Names.	Breckin-ridge.....	Coffey	Osage	Total	Majority
J. W. Kerr *†	409	221	9	639	408
E. P. Bancroft *	383	229	12	624	410
R. M. Ruggles	131	98	2	231	....
John J. Sanders	114	98	2	214	....

† Kerr died before the session, and H. S. Sleeper was chosen to the vacancy.

THIRTEENTH DISTRICT.

Names.	Chase.....	Morris.....	Total	Majority
S. N. Wood *	106	55	161	101
H. J. Espy	8	52	60	....

The vote for Representatives is not announced in the official paper, the Atchison Champion, but a note states that it did not vary materially from that for Senators. The returns are not on file in the Secretary of State's office.

First District.—T. P. Herrick, F. W. Emery, A. Lowe, Republicans; W. C. Kimber, Democrat.

Second District.—William H. Grimes, E. P. Lewis, Thomas Butcher, C. B. Keith, A. Elliott, Ira Smith, Republicans.

Third District.—David C. Auld, D. E. Ballard, Republicans.

Fourth District.—Ambrose W. Mussey, Thomas Price, William H. Smith, F. N. Blake, Republicans.

Fifth District.—Earnest Hoheneck, Abner Allen, Republicans; E. J. Lines, Democrat.

Sixth District.—Henry Buckmaster, Jerome Kunkel, John E. Moore, S. R. Caniff, H. Heberling, H. W. Curtis, A. Ray, William E. Bowker, Republicans.

Seventh District.— R. P. C. Wilson, W. P. Gambell, John Benz, Isaac E. Eaton, N. Humber, L. T. Smith, John D. Crafton, Charles Starns, James M. Calvert, Democrats.

Eighth District.—Amasa Soule, James B. Abbott, E. D. Thompson, W. D. Blackford, D. M. Alexander, Oliver Barber, L. Woodard, J. C. Bartlett, James F. Legate, J. E. Corliss, J. E. Hayes, James McGrew, Alfred Gray, Republicans.

Ninth District.—J. F. Neal, Horatio Knowles, S. B. Mayhern, J. A. Jones, Andrew Stark, J. W. Stewart, Abram Ellis, Cyrus Tator, Gustavus A. Colton, Republicans.

Tenth District.—W. W. H. Lawrence, Jacob Marcell, W. F. M. Arny, S. J. Crawford, B. L. G. Stone, N. B. Blanton, Republicans.

Eleventh District.—George H. Lillie, Alanson K. Hawkes, Republicans.

Twelfth District.— O. H. Sheldon, B. Wheat, W. R. Sanders, G. A. Cutler, R. W. Cloud, G. H. Rees, Republicans.

Thirteenth District.—A. J. Chipman, P. G. D. Morton, Republicans.

Fourteenth District.—John S. Rackliff, Republican.

	RECAPITULATION.	*Republicans.*	*Democrats.*
Senate	....	22	3
House	....	64	11
Total	....	86	14

DECEMBER 6.—Election of District Judges under the Wyandotte Constitution:

FIRST DISTRICT.

Counties.	*William C. McDowell.*	*George W. Gardiner.*
Jackson	182	169
Jefferson	295	316
Leavenworth	1428	964
Total	1905	1449

SECOND DISTRICT.

Counties.	A. L. Lee..	George W. Glick......	S. Tennent.
Atchison	631	599	......
Brown	274	80	......
Marshall	40	4	63
Nemaha	129	46	......
Doniphan	466	359	......
Total	1560	1088	63

THIRD DISTRICT.

Counties.	Jacob Safford......	J. R. Mc-Clure	R. L. Wil-son......
Davis and Dickinson	29	119	15
Pottawatomie	......	31	120
Riley	10	140	177
Wabaunsee	93	16	14
Shawnee	458	79	136
Total	590	385	462

FOURTH DISTRICT.

Counties.	Solon O. Thacher..	James Christian.
Allen	172	136
Anderson	142	97
Bourbon	273	140
Douglas	941	454
Franklin	232	138
Johnson	304	423
Linn	193	152
Lykins	311	192
Total	2568	1732

FIFTH DISTRICT.

Counties.	O.E.Lear-nard......	J. H. Wat-son......
Breckinridge	170	323
Chase	96	31
Greenwood	22	7
Hunter	3	18
Madison	17	37
Coffey	167	143
Morris	50	32
Osage	13	1
Woodson	78	15
Total	616	607

DECEMBER 25.—A book published with this title: "The Public Life of Capt. John Brown, by James Redpath, with an Autobiography of his Child-hood and Youth. Boston: Thayer & Eldridge." pp. 407. The author re-turns thanks to Dr. Thomas H. Webb, of Boston, and Richard J. Hinton, of Kansas, for assistance in preparing the book. It is an earnest and sincere book, and an enthusiastic defence of John Brown's character and acts. It contains much Kansas history, of which Mr. Redpath was an eye-witness. This is the most radical Kansas book published up to this time. Redpath believed that Slavery was a crime, and that it was as much an evil by all means to be put down as murder was, or any other villany. The book had a great sale, and must have convinced as well as startled thousands of men. Like Brown's heroic martyrdom, it hastened the day of emancipation. His statement of Brown's connexion with the Pottawatomie murders is the same as Sanborn's, and is as follows:

"On the 2d of November, 1859, Judge Russell, of Boston, and his wife, arrived in Charlestown, and had an interview with John Brown. The Judge spoke of the charge preferred by an Administration journalist in Kansas against the Captain, which accused him of having killed the Ruffians of Pottawatomie. The old man declared that he did not, in any way, participate in their execution; but thought here, in jail, as he had be-lieved in Kansas, that the act was just and necessary."

John Brown's understanding of Christianity is well shown by the follow-ing incident:

"Brown was visited yesterday by Rev. James II. March, of the M. E. Church. The reverend gentleman having advanced an argument in favor of the institution of Slavery as it now exists, Brown replied to him, saying, 'My dear sir, you know nothing about Christianity; you will have to learn the A B C's in the lesson of Christianity, as I find you entirely ignorant of the meaning of the word. I of course respect you as a gentle-man, but it is as a *heathen* gentleman.'"

On the first of November, 1859, Captain Brown was brought into Court to receive the sentence of death. Here is his last speech:

"I have, may it please the Court, a few words to say.

"In the first place, I deny everything but what I have all along admitted—the design on my part to free the slaves. I intended certainly to have made a clear thing of that matter, as I did last winter, when I went into Missouri, and there took slaves without the snapping of a gun on either side, moved them through the country, and finally left them in Canada. I designed to have done the same thing again, on a larger scale. That was all I intended. I never did intend murder, or treason, or the destruction of prop-erty, or to excite or incite slaves to rebellion, or to make insurrection.

"I have another objection: and that is, it is unjust that I should suffer such a penalty. Had I interfered in the manner which I admit, and which I admit has been fairly proved —(for I admire the truthfulness and candor of the greater portion of the witnesses who have testified in this case)—had I so interfered in behalf of the rich, the powerful, the intelligent, the so-called great, or in behalf of any of their friends, either father, mother, brother, sister, wife, or children, or any of that class, and suffered and sacrificed what I have in this interference, it would have been all right, and every man in this Court would have deemed it an act worthy of reward rather than punishment.

"This Court acknowledges, as I suppose, the validity of the Law of God. I see a book kissed here which I suppose to be the Bible, or, at least, the New Testament. That teaches me that all things 'whatsoever I would that men should do unto me I should do even so to them.' It teaches me further, to 'remember them that are in bonds as bound with them.' I endeavored to act up to that instruction. I say, I am yet too young to understand that God is any respecter of persons. I believe that to have inter-fered as I have done, as I have always freely admitted I have done, in behalf of His despised poor, was not wrong, but right. Now, if it is deemed necessary that I should forfeit my life for the furtherance of the ends of justice, and mingle my blood further with the blood of my children, and with the blood of millions in this slave country whose rights are disregarded by wicked, cruel, and unjust enactments—I submit: so let it be done.

"Let me say one word further.

"I feel entirely satisfied with the treatment I have received on my trial. Considering all the circumstances, it has been more generous than I expected. But I feel no consciousness of guilt. I have stated from the first what was my intention and what was not. I never had any design against the life of any person, nor any disposition to commit treason, or excite slaves to rebel, or make any general insurrection. I never encouraged any man to do so, but always discouraged any idea of that kind.

"Let me say, also, a word in regard to the statements made by some of those connected with me. I hear it has been stated by some of them that I have induced them to join me. But the contrary is true. I do not say this to injure them, but as regretting their weakness. There is not one of them but joined me of his own accord, and the greater part at their own expense. A number of them I never saw, and never had a word of conversation with, till the day they came to me, and that was for the purpose I have stated.

"Now I have done."

1860.

JANUARY 2.—Legislature meets at Lecompton. Message from Governor Medary. It reviews the legislation of the last session, points out defects, and urges needed amendments. "The utmost peace and quiet has pervaded the whole Territory."

The following is a list of the members (Democrats in *Italic*, and Republicans in Roman):

COUNCIL.

1st District .... *Geo. M. Beebe.*	8th District .... Jas. M. Hendry.
2d District .... *W. J. Marion.*	9th District .... P. P. Elder.
3d District .... *V. G. Mathias.*	10th District .... *C. G. Keeler.*
4th District .... *J. M. Christison.*	11th District .... W. W. Updegraff.
5th District .... L. R. Palmer.	12th District .... Watson Stewart.
6th District .... J. B. Woodward.	13th District .... John C. Lambdin.
7th District .... Chester Thomas.	

REPRESENTATIVES.

1st District	{ C. B. Whitehead. / *Thos. Vanderslice.* / Hugh Robertson. }	14th District	{ W. H. Fitzpatrick. / S. R. Caniff. }
2d District	{ *F. Lombard.* / *Wm. Noel.* }	15th District	{ Paul R. Brooks. / Wm. A. Rankin. / Erastus Heath. }
3d District	{ Pascal S. Parks. / Fred. Brown. / *John Wright.* / *John C. Murphy.* }	16th District	{ *Chas. Sims.* / *L. S. Cornwall.* }
		17th District ....G. A. Colton.	
4th District	{ T. A. Blake. / Edward Lynde. }	18th District ....J. H. Jones.	
5th District ....A. Bartlett.		19th District .... *Wm. R. Wagstaff.*	
6th District ....Byron Steward.		20th District ....Thomas Lindsay.	
7th District .... *Wm. L. McMath.*		21st District ....Henry Shively.	
8th District ....H. R. Dutton.		22d District	{ O. H. Sheldon. / G. W. Nelson. }
9th District ....Morton Cave.		23d District ....Sam'l N. Wood.	
10th District .... *J. S. Magill.*		24th District .... *P. G. D. Morton.*	
11th District ....Dan. L. Chandler.		25th District ....John W. Scott.	
12th District .... *Robert Reynolds.*		26th District ....Horatio Knowles.	
13th District ....Steph. G. Elliott.		27th Dist. (Pike's Peak).. *R. Sopris.*	

The Council consisted of 9 Republicans and 4 Democrats, and the House of 23 Republicans and 16 Democrats.

Officers of the Council: W. W. Updegraff, President; John J. Ingalls, Clerk; A. Cutler, Assistant Clerk; H. M. Selden, Sergeant-at-Arms; J. K. Rankin, Doorkeeper.

Officers of the House: Speaker, G. A. Colton; Chief Clerk, M. W. Delahay;

Assistant Clerk, N. J. Chipman; Sergeant-at-Arms, G. F. Warren; Door-keeper, William House; Docket Clerk, John W. Day; Engrossing Clerk, J. L. Wilson; Enrolling Clerk, Andrew Stark; Journal Clerk, H. C. Chase; Second Assistant Clerk, Samuel F. Tappan.

JANUARY 4.—Report received from S. W. Greer, Superintendent of Schools. It is a long and interesting paper. The following table is copied from it:

ABSTRACT OF ANNUAL SCHOOL REPORTS OF COUNTY SUPERINTENDENTS.

Counties.	Number of Districts organized......	No. youths between the age of 5 and 21.	No. of children enrolled in the schools.	No. of months taught in the year......	No. districts in which schools were taught....	Amount of money raised to build school houses......	Amount of public money for schools......	Amount of money raised by private subscription......
Anderson...........	13	558	227	25	12	$371 60	$300 00	$497 09
Bourbon............	7	74	....	12	6	....	....	....
Douglas............	36	1,805	....	92	33	860 33	950 00	7 44
Franklin...........	10	226	....	....	7	....	....	....
Jackson............	11	396	....	....	....	....	....	....
Jefferson..........	18	447	185	33	12	456 34	787 50	15 50
Johnson............	25	543	274	36	16	1,308 00	....	8 44
Leavenworth.......	32	1,436	730	60	24	3,368 75	4,816 17	8 18
Lykins	11	144	52	21	9	....	....	60 00
Nemaha............	6	180	180	20	8	....	....	....
Osage..............	2	50	....	....	2	....	....	....
Pottawatomie	6	182	....	....	5	9 00	....	30 00
Shawnee...........	14	....	....	....	....	....	....	....
Brown	4	204	95	15	2	980 00	3 80	....
Atchison...........	24	591	396	33	....	700 00	....	3,675 00
Doniphan..........	3	165	44	3	7	....	....	....
Total	222	7,029	2,087	351	136	$7,045 23	$6,233 67	$6,883 50

The Legislature votes to adjourn to Lawrence.

JANUARY 5.—Milton R. Benton is given the seat in the Council occupied by W. J. Marion, as a member from the Second District.

JANUARY 5.—Message from the Governor vetoing the joint resolution adjourning the Legislature to Lawrence. The House passes the resolution over the veto by 22 to 7. The Council, on the 6th, passed the resolution by 9 to 4.

JANUARY 7.—The Legislature meets at Lawrence.

JANUARY 18.—The House votes, by 33 to 1, to adjourn; the Council concurs, by 6 to 3.

—Geo. G. Pierce is awarded the seat of Mr. Magill, in the House, as the member from the Tenth District.

—The Council Journal of this Session contains 95 pages; the House Journal 162 pages. The journals of the session immediately following are published separately, as of a new Legislature, and are voluminous.

JANUARY 18.—W. F. M. Arny before the Harper's Ferry Committee, in Washington.

JANUARY 18.—Gov. Medary issues a proclamation summoning the Legislature to meet at Lecompton on the 19th.

JANUARY 19.—Meeting of the Legislature at Lecompton. Both houses re-elect their recent officers. They vote to adjourn to Lawrence.

JANUARY 20.—Message from the Governor. Report received from Auditor Strickler. The Governor vetoes the bill adjourning to Lawrence. It is passed over the veto.

JANUARY 21.—The Legislature meets at Lawrence. The Census Report is published in the Council Journal, pp. 136–40, and the Report of Treasurer Mitchell on pages 140–42. He reports $90,600 issued in Claim bonds to redeem Claim warrants.

FEBRUARY 1.—Wm. Pennington, of New Jersey, is elected Speaker of the House, by the Republicans, on the 44th ballot, receiving 117 votes, to 116 for all others. Sherman withdrew as a candidate.

—A Kansas Historical Society is organized at Lawrence. Samuel A. Kingman delivers the address.

FEBRUARY 6.—Telegraph completed to St. Joseph, via Leavenworth and Atchison, by C. M. Stebbins & Co.

FEBRUARY 7.—Ground broken on the "Kansas Central" Railroad, at Wyandotte.

—A Legislative Committee reports 97,570 as the population of Kansas. The census as made to and reported by the Governor gave a population of 71,770.

FEBRUARY 11.—Mr. Beebe, Democrat, makes a report against the bill abolishing slavery, as follows:

"A minority of your Committee, to whom was referred House Bill No. 6, 'An Act to prohibit Slavery and Involuntary Servitude in the Territory of Kansas,' having had the same under consideration, and having found that there is now invested in this Territory between one-fourth and one-half a million of dollars' worth of property in slaves; and believing that the *immediate* prohibition of an existing right of property in any given article is beyond either the legislative power of the States or Territories, as contravening the letter and spirit of articles four and five of the 'Amendments' to the Federal Constitution, recommend to your honorable body the indefinite postponement of the said bill.   G. M. BEEBE, *a Minority of your Committee.*"

The Council pass the bill by 9 to 4, the noes being Beebe, Christison, Keeler, and Mathias.

FEBRUARY 14.—The President of the U. S. Senate presents the Constitution of Kansas, framed at Wyandotte.

FEBRUARY 17.—The Governor appoints, and the Senate confirms, H. J. Strickler as Auditor.

FEBRUARY 20.—A very long message from Gov. Medary vetoing the bill abolishing Slavery. He quotes the act organizing the Territory, and says: "You claim, under this declaration in the Organic Act, the right to prohibit Slavery in the Territory of Kansas. By so doing, you mistake both the words and the meaning, and misconceive the true spirit of the text."

It is passed over the veto by the following vote:

IN THE HOUSE—*Yeas:* Messrs. Brown, Bartlett, Brooks, Chandler, Caniff, Cornwall, Cave, Dutton, Elliott, Fitzpatrick, Heath, Jones, Knowles, Lindsay, Morton, Nelson, Parks, Pierce, Robertson, Rankin, Steward, Sims, Shively, Sheldon, Scott, Sopris, Wagstaff, Wood, and Mr. Speaker Colton. *Nays:* Messrs. Lombard, Murphy, McMath, Noel, Reynolds, Vanderslice, and Whitehead.

IN THE COUNCIL—*Yeas:* Messrs. Updegraff (President), Benton, Lambdin, Thomas, Hendry, Woodward, Palmer, Stewart, and Elder. *Nays:* Messrs. Christison, Beebe, Keeler, and Mathias.

FEBRUARY 20.—Report of the Special Committee on the Claims Commission; published in House Journal, page 481. A full statement is given of the Territorial bonds issued for claim warrants, and all the facts relating to the transaction. On page 531, a copy is given of the bonds issued. Wm. H. Fitzpatrick issued a minority report, which led to the defeat of the bond scheme.

— Gov. Robinson before the Harper's Ferry Committee.

FEBRUARY 22.—Railroad completed from St. Joseph to Atchison.

FEBRUARY 27.—Lincoln's Cooper Institute speech. The N. Y. Tribune said: "No man ever made such an impression on his first appeal to a New York audience."

FEBRUARY 27.—The Legislature adjourns. The volume of general laws contains 264 pages. Among the Acts passed were the following: Authorizing Doniphan, Douglas, Johnson, and Leavenworth counties, and Leavenworth City, to issue bonds; the name of McGee county is changed to Cherokee; the eastern boundary of Neosho county is defined; the lines are changed of Davis, Chase and Butler counties; Dickinson, Clay, Greenwood, Irving, Marion, Otoe, Peketon, Republic, Shirley, Ottawa, Saline and Washington counties are organized; defining judicial districts; to prohibit the recording of deeds in Land District Recorders' offices, and to secure their record in the office of the Register of Deeds; abolishing slavery. The volume of private laws contains 455 pages. Among the cities incorporated are Denver and Auraria (now in Colorado), Burlingame, Paola, and Troy; among the towns are Alma, Bellemont, Carlyle, Fort Scott, Iola, Irving, Louisville, Marion, Neosho Falls, Osawatomie, Ottumwa, and Stanton. Forty-three bills are passed granting divorces.

FEBRUARY 29.—Senator Seward delivers an elaborate speech in favor of the immediate admission of Kansas.

—This was a very dry year. Large amounts of money and goods were sent from the North and East for the relief of Kansas, and were chiefly distributed by S. C. Pomeroy, at Atchison. The Legislature of New York appropriated $50,000; an appropriation was also made by the Wisconsin Legislature, and every Free State contributed generously.

• MARCH 15.—The Topeka Record publishes a long letter from Governor Robinson in regard to his testimony before the Harper's Ferry Committee. He says: "Not one word of my testimony can be construed against the Free-State party; on the contrary, I fully endorsed that party, with all its actions, and it will so appear in the testimony, if ever printed."

MARCH 16.—Aaron D. Stevens and Albert Hazlett, John Brown's men, executed at Charlestown, Virginia. James Montgomery and a few of his men went from Kansas to rescue these men from prison, but were prevented by the deep snow. Thomas W. Higginson organized a New England and New York party, and they met Montgomery at Harrisburg.

MARCH 20.—Reports of a raid by Missourians in Bourbon county.

MARCH 20.—Iron arrives in Kansas, and track-laying begins on the Elwood and Marysville Railroad. This is the first railroad iron laid down on Kansas soil.

MARCH 25.—James E. Jones, of Fort Scott, takes the office of Register, at the Lecompton Land Office, in place of Ely Moore, deceased.

MARCH 26.—Wm. A. Phillips writes from Lawrence to the Topeka Record, denying that he was engaged in John Brown's revolutionary plans; accusing Governor Robinson of giving his peculiar testimony in order to secure land grants; giving M. F. Conway the credit for repudiating the bogus Missouri Legislature of 1855; and regretting that the Topeka movement was abandoned by the Grasshopper Falls Convention, and the Territorial Government taken possession of.

MARCH 27.—Democratic Convention at Atchison. Dr. W. R. Crane, of Doniphan, President; James A. Burton, of Leavenworth, Secretary. The following Delegates were elected to the Charleston National Convention: John A. Halderman, Isaac E. Eaton, John P. Slough, and H. Miles Moore, Leavenworth; George M. Beebe, Doniphan; Charles W. Blair, Bourbon; William Weer, Wyandotte; James Christian, Douglas; Charles Sims, Johnson; Robert B. Mitchell, Linn; Cyrus K. Holliday, Shawnee; Robert Wilson, Riley. The Convention passed the following resolutions:

"*Resolved*, That the law prohibiting Slavery in this Territory, recently passed by the Republican party in the Territorial Legislature, is in disregard of the decision of the Supreme Court of the United States, in contravention of the Constitutional rights of fifteen of the States of this Union, and calculated to weaken the bonds of the Union.

"*Resolved*, That Samuel Medary, Governor of this Territory, in vetoing this unconstitutional law, and Messrs. Noel, Lombard, Beebe, Mathias, Christison, Keeler, Murphy, Reynolds, Whitehead, Vanderslice, and McMath, members of the Territorial Assembly of Kansas, in sustaining by their votes the Governor's veto, have deserved well of the Democracy of Kansas and of their whole country."

MARCH 29.—Mr. Grow, from the Committee on Territories, recommends the admission of Kansas into the Union, under the Wyandotte Constitution. The following is copied from the report:

"As to population, if there was any doubt on that point, your committee regard it as waived by the action of Congress. A majority of both houses, on the 13th day of April, A. D. 1858, declared by vote that there was sufficient population within the limits now proposed for Kansas to enable it to be admitted as a Slave State; and certainly that *same* population increased by two years' immigration should be, in the judgment of your committee, sufficient for a Free State, unless Congress proposes to establish one rule as to population for the admission of Slave States, and another and a different one for Free States.

" Your committee, therefore, deem it unnecessary to enquire into the precise number of the present population of Kansas, for if under ordinary circumstances there could be any objections on that point, they have, so far as Kansas is concerned, been twice waived by the action of Congress. In addition to the instance just cited, the House of Representatives four years ago passed an act for the admission of the State; and the Senate passed an act for the immediate formation of a State Government, in order to such admission, without regard to population. Since the first action of Congress the population has more than doubled, and has increased very largely since the last."

J. B. Clark, Democrat, of Missouri, in the House, presents a minority report.

APRIL 2.—Leavenworth appropriates money to survey the Smoky Hill route to Pike's Peak.

—Frank M. Tracy, of the Elwood Press, becomes editor of the St. Joseph Free Democrat.

APRIL 3.—The first Pony Express leaves St. Joseph for San Francisco. It is a weekly express.

APRIL 4.—Frank B. Sanborn, of Concord, Mass., an officer of the Kansas Emigrant Aid Society, and a confidential friend of John Brown, arrested to appear before the Harper's Ferry Committee, is released by the Supreme Court of Massachusetts.

APRIL 11.—The House votes to admit Kansas under the Wyandotte Constitution:

Yeas: Charles F. Adams, Adrain, Aldrich, Allen, Alley, Ashley, Babbitt, Barr, Barrett, Beale, Bingham, Blair, Blake, Brayton, Briggs, Buffinton, Burch, Burlingame, Burnham, Butterfield, Campbell, Carey, Carter, Case, Horace F. Clark, Clark B. Cochrane, John Cochrane, Colfax, Conkling, Cooper, Corwin, Covode, Cox, Curtis, Dawes, Delano, Duell, Dunn, Edgerton, Edwards, Eliot, Ely, Etheridge, Farnsworth, Fenton, Ferry, Florence, Foster, Fouke, Frank, French, Gooch, Grow, Gurley, Hale, Hall, Haskin, Helmick, Hickman, Hoard, Holman, Howard, Humphrey, Hutchins, Irvine, Junkin, Francis W. Kellogg, William Kellogg, Kenyon, Kilgore, Killinger, Larrabee, DeWitt C. Leach, Lee, Logan, Longenecker, Loomis, Lovejoy, Marston, Charles D. Martin, McClernand, McKean, McKnight, McPherson, Montgomery, Moorhead, Morrill, Edward Joy Morris, Isaac N. Morris, Morse, Niblack, Nixon, Olin, Palmer, Pendleton, Perry, Pettit, Porter, Potter, Pottle, Rice, Riggs, Christopher Robinson, James C. Robinson, Royce, Schwartz, Scranton, Sedgwick, Spaulding, Spinner, Stanton, Stevens, William Stewart, Stout, Stratton, Tappan, Thayer, Theaker, Thompkins, Train, Trimble, Vallandigham, Vandever, Verre, Waldron, Walton, Cadwallader C. Washburn, Elihu B. Washburne, Israel Washburne, Webster, Wells, Wilson, Windom, Wood, and Woodruff—134.

Nays: Green Adams, Thomas L. Anderson, William C. Anderson, Ashmore, Avery, Barksdale, Bocock, Bonham, Boteler, Boyce, Brabson, Branch, Bristow, Burnett, John B. Clark, Clopton, Cobb, James Craig, Burton Craige, Crawford, Curry, Davidson, H. Winter Davis, Edmundson, English, Garnett, Gartrell, Gilmer, Hamilton, Hardeman, John T. Harris, Hatton, Hawkins, Hill, Hindman, Houston, Hughes, Jackson, Jenkins, Jones, Keitt, Lamar, James M. Leach, Leake, Love, Mallory, Maynard, McQueen, McRae, Miles, Millson, Laban T. Moore, Sydenham Moore, Nelson, Noell, Pugh, Quarles, Reagan, Ruffin, Scott, Sickles, Simms, Singleton, William Smith, William N. H. Smith, Stallworth, Stevenson, Stokes, Thomas, Vance, Whiteley, Winslow, and Woodson—73.

APRIL 11.—Republican Convention at Lawrence to elect Delegates to the Chicago National Convention, and to select Presidential Electors. Called to order by A. C. Wilder. *Temporary Officers:* Edward Lynde, of Jefferson, Chairman; John J. Ingalls, of Atchison, Secretary. *Committee on Credentials:* John A. Martin, Geo. W. Gardiner, James Fletcher, J. C. Burnett, J. C. Lambdin, S. N. Wood, L. R. Palmer. The following is a list of delegates:

Doniphan County.—J. B. Maynard, H. Housel, T. P. Herrick, G. H. Robb, and J. B. Wheeler.

Atchison.—John A. Martin, E. B. Grimes, H. L. Davis, E. P. Lewis, and J. J. Ingalls.

Brown.—Dr. H. Seaborn.

Marshall and Pottawatomie.—L. R. Palmer.

Clay, Dickinson and Davis.—J. B. Woodward.

Riley.—J. W. Robinson and D. L. Chandler.

Wabaunsee.—C. B. Lines.

Shawnee.—R. M. Fish, Dr. James Fletcher, L. Dow, and Chester Thomas.

Jefferson.—E. Lynde and George M. Dix.

Leavenworth.—A. C. Wilder, G. W. Gardiner, G. W. Still, E. McCrillus, Wm. Tholen, A. W. McCauslin, O. E. Brecklin, A. Soule, and George Dickinson.

Douglas.—Wm. A. Phillips, Michael Oswald, J. H. Shimmons, J. C. Steele, J. H. Johnson, and D. M. Alexander.

Johnson.—J. E. Hayes, J. T. Burris, and J. F. Legate.

Wyandotte.—G. E. Budington and S. A. Cobb.

Lykins.—W. W. Updegraff, A. J. Shannon, and W. J. McCowan.

Linn.—Captain James Montgomery.

Bourbon.—J. C. Burnett and P. Hutchins.

Anderson.—J. R. Eaton and Dr. R. Gilpatrick.

Franklin.—W. W. H. Lawrence and P. P. Elder.

Madison.—L. L. Jones, of Lawrence.

Coffey.—Orville L. Ford.

Osage.—H. D. Preston.

Breckinridge.—M. Bailey and J. Stotler.

Morris.—S. N. Wood.

Chase, Greenwood, and Hunter.—P. G. D. Morton.

Butler.—J. C. Lambdin.

Arapahoe.—John Mack.

Nemaha, Jackson, Allen, and Woodson.—Not represented.

Committee on Permanent Organization: Messrs. T. P. Herrick, E. B. Grimes, G. W. Gardiner, G. W. Still, H. Seaborn, L. B. Woodward, M. Bailey, J. H. Johnson, P. P. Elder, J. F. Legate, A. J. Shannon, P. Hutchins, and P. G. D. Morton.

Central Committee: A. Larzelere, E. P. Lewis, A. C. Wilder, E. Lynde, A. Bartlett, S. N. Wood, E. P. Bancroft, Wm. A. Phillips, W. J. McCowan, J. E. Jones, O. E. Learnard.

The Committee on Permanent Organization reported the following as permanent officers of the Convention: President, E. Lynde; Vice Presidents, J. B. Maynard, E. McCrillus, and C. B. Lines; Secretaries, J. Stotler and J. E. Hayes.

On motion of Mr. Martin, the Convention proceeded to ballot for five Delegates.

On motion, Messrs. Martin and Budington were appointed tellers.

Several gentlemen were put in nomination, when the balloting was commenced, the first of which resulted as follows: A. C. Wilder received 58 votes; John A. Martin, 48; W. W. Ross, 41; Wm. A. Phillips, 48; A. G. Proctor, 39; F. N. Blake, 33; J. C. Burnett, 29; J. B. Wheeler, 23; C. Chadwick, 24; L. R. Palmer, 16; scattering, 7.

On motion of Dr. J. W. Robinson, the five gentlemen having the highest number of votes were declared elected by acclamation.

On motion of Mr. Phillips, John P. Hatterscheidt was elected as an additional Delegate to the Chicago Convention.

Mr. Phillips was then called upon the stand and made a few remarks, taking strong ground for Mr. Seward for the next President. He closed by offering a resolution, which was adopted with but one or two dissenting voices:

"*Resolved,* That Wm. H. Seward is the first representative man of the Republican party, and the first choice of the Republicans of Kansas for the Presidency in 1860."

Mr. Fish moved that the Convention now proceed to elect three Presidential Electors for the State of Kansas. Carried.

The Chair appointed Messrs. Updegraff and Elder as tellers.

The first ballot resulted as follows: T. Dwight Thacher, 48; R. Gilpatrick, 41; C. B. Lines, 48; Gardiner, 24; McKay, 24; Seaver, 22; scattering, 6. The three gentlemen receiving the highest number of votes were declared elected.

Mr. Phillips offered a series of resolutions denouncing certain "Territorial bonds and warrants, issued for claims allowed under the commission created and authorized by the Legislature of 1859;" and charging the Territorial officers with "palpable perversions of duty in giving these evidences of Territorial indebtedness for such claims," and calling for "a committee of five to ascertain the precise amount of bonds issued on such claims, and to publish a notification in the Territorial and New York city papers, warning innocent purchasers from investing their means in these spurious bonds, which the people of Kansas have never authorized and do not wish to be responsible for."

These resolutions called forth an excited discussion, which lasted several hours, and was participated in by several members of the Convention. The result was the adoption of the following as a substitute, offered by Mr. C. B. Lines:

"*Whereas*, The Executive officers of this Territory have issued a large amount of bonds and warrants, purporting to be based upon certain claims for losses during the war and troubles in Kansas, and in satisfaction of said claims: therefore,

"*Resolved*, That we believe said bonds and warrants were issued without authority of law, and that the issue thereof involves a gross act of infidelity on the part of public officers to the people of the Territory, and a fraud upon the public.

"*Resolved*, That while we recognize the validity of the claims aforesaid, as against the General Government, so far as they have been or may be established by authority of law, we denounce as unjust and absurd, any attempt that has been, or may be made to collect the first dime of the amount from the people of this Territory."

Organization of the State Central Committee, and address of its members: A. C. Wilder, Chairman, Leavenworth City; E. P. Bancroft, Secretary, Emporia, Breckinridge county; A. Larzelere, Wathena, Doniphan county; Wm. A. Phillips, Lawrence, Douglas county; E. P. Lewis, Sumner, Atchison county; E. Lynde, Grasshopper Falls, Jefferson county; A. Bartlett, St. George, Pottawatomie county; S. N. Wood, Council Grove, Morris county; W. H. H. Lawrence, Minneola, Franklin county; Geo. E. Budington, Quindaro, Wyandotte county; W. J. McCowan, Stanton, Lykins county; J. H. Jones, Twin Springs, Linn county; O. E. Learnard, Burlington, Coffey county.

APRIL 20.—

"On Friday, April 20th, Deputy U. S. Marshal L. Arms was shot by John Ritchie, at Topeka, and immediately expired. The cause of this fatal encounter was the attempt by Arms to arrest Ritchie for an alleged offence committed during the political troubles of 1856. The arrest was in direct violation of the Amnesty Act passed by the Legislature of 1859, and Ritchie had often declared that he would not submit to any such illegal seizure of his person. A preliminary examination was had before Justice Miller on the 21st inst. Ritchie was defended by Lorenzo Dow, J. H. Lane and A. Winants, Esqs., and was discharged. We hope that this is the last of these old and infamous accusations. The citizens at Topeka have held a meeting and passed resolutions approving of Ritchie's defence of his life and liberty."—*Elwood Free Press, April 28th.*

APRIL 28.—The Elwood Free Press of this date says:

"On Monday last, April 23d, the Directors of the Elwood and Marysville R. R. placed on their track the locomotive 'Albany,' an engine which has been used from Boston to the Missouri, as railroads have successively stretched their length toward the setting sun.

"On Tuesday, several cars were brought across the river, and a large concourse of people gathered to celebrate the actual opening of the first section of the Great Pacific Road. Col. M. Jeff. Thompson, President of the Elwood and Marysville road; Willard P. Hall, President of the St. Joseph and Topeka road; Gov. Robert M. Stewart, of Missouri, and others, addressed the crowd on the great topic of the day."

APRIL 28.—Sixth day of the National Democratic Convention, at Charleston. Delegates from the Southern States secede.

MAY 1.—George M. Beebe appointed Secretary in place of Hugh S. Walsh.

MAY 7.—Mr. Wade's motion, in the Senate, to take up the bill for the admission of Kansas, defeated by the following vote:

Yeas: Anthony, Bigler, Bingham, Cameron, Chandler, Clark, Collamer, Dixon, Doolittle, Durkee, Fessenden, Foot, Foster, Grimes, Hale, Hamlin, Harlan, King, Seward, Simmons, Sumner, Ten Eyck, Trumbull, Wade, Wilkinson, and Wilson—26.

Nays: Bayard, Benjamin, Bragg, Bright, Brown, Chestnut, Clingman, Davis, Fitch, Fitzpatrick, Green, Gwin, Hammond, Hemphill, Hunter, Iverson, Andrew Johnson, Lane, Latham, Mallory, Mason, Nicholson, Pierce, Polk, Powell, Rice, Sebastian, Slidell, Thompson, Toombs, Wigfall, and Yulee—32.

MAY 16–18.—The Republican National Convention, at Chicago, nominates Abraham Lincoln for President, and Hannibal Hamlin for Vice President. The following were planks in the platform adopted:

"10. That in the recent vetoes, by their Federal Governors, of the acts of the Legislatures of Kansas and Nebraska, prohibiting Slavery in those Territories, we find a practical illustration of the boasted Democratic principle of Non-Intervention and Popular Sovereignty, embodied in the Kansas-Nebraska bill, and a demonstration of the deception and fraud involved therein.

"11. That Kansas should, of right, be immediately admitted as a State under the Constitution recently formed and adopted by her people, and accepted by the House of Representatives."

MAY 19.—Solon O. Thacher retires from the Lawrence Republican.

—The Emporia News is enlarged. It is published by P. B. Plumb, Jacob Stotler, and Dudley Randall.

MAY 30.—John B. Floyd, Secretary of War, writes to Jeff. Davis, chairman of the Military Committee of the Senate, recommending a wagon-road from Fort Leavenworth, along the Smoky Hill fork, to Denver City.

—Treaty with the Delawares. Eighty acres are assigned to each member of the tribe, to be held in severalty. The Leavenworth, Pawnee and Western Railroad Company to have the preference of purchasing the remainder of the Delaware land, at not less than $1.25 an acre.

JUNE 1.—

POPULATION OF KANSAS, JUNE 1, 1860, AS TAKEN BY THE MARSHAL OF THE TERRITORY.

Counties.	Population.	Cattle.	Swine.	Horses.	Mules.	Sheep.
Leavenworth	12,900	4,970	10,138	1,208	117	1,600
Douglas	9,207	7,977	10,674	1,836	115	614
Doniphan	8,148	5,105	12,700	1,175	73	1,953
Atchison	7,747	6,042	7,300	972	74	1,539
Linn	6,347	5,470	7,500	1,407	85	1,705
Bourbon	6,102	6,480	8,040	1,740	100	2,055
Lykins	5,095	4,550	7,760	1,177	70	600
Johnson	4,513	3,020	3,932	875	87	88
Jefferson	4,446	4,020	9,660	950	77	839
Shawnee	3,405	3,300	4,650	670	25	94
Breckinridge	3,164	3,708	4,033	733	37	508
Allen	3,120	5,043	3,060	951	50	710
Franklin	3,040	3,955	5,560	816	49	780
Coffey	2,845	3,109	3,967	590	25	199
Brown						
Wyandotte	2,609	1,000	1,095	400	15	....
Nemaha	2,551					
Anderson	2,403	2,151	2,894	448	26	864
Marshall	2,275	756	795	150	12	144
Jackson	2,207	1,890	2,000	324	....	672
Godfrey *	1,893	....				
Pottawatomie	1,856					
McGee	1,501	2,073	3,314	507	35	579
Riley	1,268	836	2,320	189	8	6
Davis	1,194	889	1,296	136	19	33
Osage	1,187	1,529	1,822	217	9	65
Wabaunsee	993	....				
Chase	912	680	840	46	8	89
Morris	800	932	1,090	174	27	110
Madison	680	762	940	116	5	8
Butler	640	413	234	59	5	47
Dickinson	403	105	284	23	3	7
Washington	387	....				
Greenwood *	360	564	360	90	2	20
Hunter	194	156	55	19	....	40
Clay	170	112	356	18	1	....
Woodson *	77	1,458	1,667	193	9	194
Dorn	50	40	18	20	2	....
Wilson *	27					
Pike's Peak	34,242	....	....	....	....	....
Total	143,643	83,155	120,352	18,289	1,170	16,252

*The census of these four counties was taken by one assistant, and I presume the farms were all taken in and included in the returns of Greenwood and Woodson.

I cannot give the amount of stock in the counties of Washington, Wabaunsee, Pottawatomie, Nemaha and Brown.

No stock is included in the above returns except such as was owned by farmers and reported with the farms.—*Remarks by the Marshal.*

JUNE 4.—Charles Sumner, after a silence of four years, makes a speech in the Senate for the admission of Kansas. His last speech in the Senate was for Free Kansas, and led to the murderous assault by Preston S. Brooks, of South Carolina. After debate, Mr. Hunter moved to postpone the Kansas Bill. Mr. Fessenden demanded the yeas and nays, and the question was decided in the affirmative by the following vote:

Yeas: Messrs. Bayard, Benjamin, Bigler, Bragg, Bright, Brown, Chestnut, Clingman, Davis, Fitch, Fitzpatrick, Green, Gwin, Hammond, Hemphill, Hunter, Iverson, Johnson of Arkansas, Johnson of Tennessee, Kennedy, Lane, Mallory, Mason, Pearce, Polk, Powell, Rice, Saulsbury, Sebastian, Slidell, Toombs, Wigfall, and Yulee—33.

Nays: Messrs. Anthony, Bingham, Cameron, Chandler, Clark, Collamer,

Dixon, Doolittle, Durkee, Fessenden, Foot, Foster, Grimes, Hale, Hamlin, Harlan, King, Latham, Pugh, Seward, Simmons, Sumner, Ten Eyck, Trumbull, Wade, Wilkinson, and Wilson—27.

This was the usual vote in the Senate on the bill for the admission of Kansas, until the Rebel Senators withdrew, in January, 1861.

JUNE 13.—Ground broken at Atchison for the Atchison and Pike's Peak Railroad.

JUNE 18.—The Democratic Convention reassembles at Baltimore. After another secession, Stephen A. Douglas is nominated for President, and Benjamin Fitzpatrick, of Alabama, for Vice President. Herschel V. Johnson, of Georgia, was afterwards substituted for Mr. Fitzpatrick. The seceders nominate John C. Breckinridge, of Kentucky, for President, and Joseph Lane, of Oregon, for Vice President.

JUNE 20.—The Auburn (Shawnee county) Docket issued, by David B. Emmert.

JULY.—The Independent started at Oskaloosa, by J. W. Roberts and J. W. Day.

JULY 1.—George M. Beebe takes possession of the Secretary's office.

JULY 19.—Celebration at Elwood of the completion of the railroad to Wathena—the first railroad in the Territory.

JULY 25.—Ground broken at Kansas City, Mo., for the Missouri Pacific Railroad.

—William H. Gill retires from the Leavenworth Herald; it is now published by Wm. P. Fain & Co., and edited by Ward Burlingame.

—A Lincoln and Hamlin newspaper at Lexington, Mo., is destroyed by a mob.

AUGUST.—Judge Pettit grants a perpetual injunction on the Provisional Government of Jefferson Territory, or "Pike's Peak."

—S. A. Cobb is the editor of the Wyandotte department of the Quindaro Tribune.

SEPTEMBER.—

"This section of country is now suffering severely from an inundation of grasshoppers, which are destroying what the drought has left. Late corn, buckwheat, potatoes and turnips are fast being destroyed. Many of our farmers are cutting their corn now for the purpose of saving the fodder. Misfortunes never come singly, and Kansas has had enough of them this year to last for several years to come. If it is true that this is a world of compensations, we shall look for rousing crops and unchecked prosperity in Kansas for the next five years, at least, as compensation for the disasters of the last twelve months."—*Emporia News.*

SEPTEMBER 17.—Gordon, the murderer, who was arrested near Denver, by Sheriff Middaugh, and brought to Leavenworth, before Judge Pettit, was discharged for want of jurisdiction. From three to eight o'clock p. m. there was a terrible struggle to take the prisoner from the officers and hang him. James L. McDowell, the Mayor, who had organized a large posse to preserve the peace, at last triumphed.

SEPTEMBER 22.—William H. Seward arrives in St. Joseph, and makes a brief speech. He was met by John A. Martin of Atchison, Martin F. Conway of Lawrence, and A. C. Wilder, David H. Bailey, and John C. Vaughan of Leavenworth.

SEPTEMBER 22.—Drought Convention in Topeka.

SEPTEMBER 24.—Reception of William H. Seward in Leavenworth. He is introduced by A. C. Wilder.

SEPTEMBER 26.—Senator Seward welcomed to Lawrence by George W. Deitzler and Charles Robinson. He makes an elaborate speech. Mr. Seward made a hasty visit to Topeka.

SEPTEMBER 28.—Senator Seward has a public reception at Atchison. He is introduced by John A. Martin.

OCTOBER.—The carrying of the October elections was very satisfactory to the people of Kansas. They read these lines by Whittier with enthusiasm:

> Not vainly we waited and counted the hours—
> The buds of our hope have burst forth into flowers.
> No room for misgivings—no loop-hole of doubt—
> We've heard from the Keystone! The Quakers are out.
>
> The plot has exploded—we've found out the trick:
> The bribe goes a begging; the fusion won't stick.
> When the Wide-Awake lanterns are shining about,
> The rogues stay at home, and the true men come out!
>
> The good State has broken the cords for her spun;
> Her oil-springs and water won't fuse into one;
> The Dutchman has seasoned with Freedom his kraut;
> And slow, late, but certain, the Quakers are out!
>
> Give the flags to the winds!—set the hills all aflame:
> Make way for the man with the patriarch's name!
> Away with misgivings—away with all doubt,
> For LINCOLN goes in when the Quakers come out!

OCTOBER 17.—Railroad Convention held at Topeka.

Officers: President, W. Y. Roberts; Vice Presidents, W. F. M. Arny, Charles Robinson, Judge Medberry, Thomas Ewing, jr., P. T. Abell, A. J. Mead, W. A. Ela. Secretaries, John A. Martin, J. F. Cummings, C. F. de Vivaldi.

The following Schedule was adopted:

"*Resolved*, That a memorial be presented to Congress asking an appropriation of public lands to aid in the construction of the following railroads in Kansas:

"1. A railroad from the western boundary of the State of Missouri, where the Osage Valley & Southern Kansas Railroad terminates, westwardly by way of Emporia, Fremont and Council Grove, to the Fort Riley Military Reservation.

"2. A railroad from the city of Wyandotte (connecting with the P. & G. R. R. and the Pacific R. R.) up the Kansas Valley by way of Lawrence, Lecompton, Tecumseh, Topeka, Manhattan, and the Fort Riley Military Reservation, to the western boundary of the Territory.

"3. A railroad running from Lawrence to the southern boundary of Kansas, in the direction of Fort Gibson and Galveston Bay.

"4. A railroad from Atchison, by way of Topeka, through the Territory, in the direction of Santa Fe.

"5. A railroad from Atchison to the western boundary of Kansas."

About 125 delegates were present, representing the counties of Atchison, Breckinridge, Allen, Doniphan, Davis, Jackson, Lykins, Leavenworth, Morris, Anderson, Coffey, Clay, Douglas, Riley, Pottawatomie, Osage, Jefferson, Wabaunsee, Wyandotte, and Shawnee.

NOVEMBER 6.—Election of Territorial Legislature:

HOUSE OF REPRESENTATIVES.

FIRST DISTRICT — DONIPHAN — THREE MEMBERS.

E. J. Jenkins	924	V. D. Markham	927
W. H. Wilson	931	S. D. Benight	872
R. M. Williams	964	Uriah Griffith	917

SECOND DISTRICT — ATCHISON — TWO MEMBERS.

George H. Fairchild	682	Robert McBratney	460
John Kean	650	A. S. Speck	473

THIRD DISTRICT — LEAVENWORTH — FOUR MEMBERS.

William Perry	1115	David H. Bailey	1116
Wm. P. Fain	1063	Samuel F. Atwood	1082
Charles Starns	1109	Boaz W. Williams	1082
N. Humber	1111	William Kelsey	1104

FOURTH DISTRICT — JEFFERSON — TWO MEMBERS.

Henry Buckmaster	364	Edward Lynde	280
David L. Lakin	400	T. D. Kuykendall	272

FIFTH DISTRICT — POTTAWATOMIE AND WABAUNSEE — ONE MEMBER.

Charles B. Lines	142	John L. Wilson	1

SIXTH DISTRICT — JACKSON — ONE MEMBER.

Martin Anderson	211

SEVENTH DISTRICT — WYANDOTTE — ONE MEMBER.

Wm. Y. Roberts	282	William Weer	163

EIGHTH DISTRICT — BROWN — ONE MEMBER.

Warren W. Guthrie	261	Ira J. Lacock	161

NINTH DISTRICT — NEMAHA — ONE MEMBER.

Chas. C. Coffinberry	161

TENTH DISTRICT — MARSHALL AND WASHINGTON — ONE MEMBER.

J. D. Brumbaugh	157	J. E. Clardy	81	George G. Pierce	151

ELEVENTH DISTRICT — RILEY AND CLAY — ONE MEMBER.

Walter C. Dunton	142	James Boyle	4

TWELFTH DISTRICT — DICKINSON AND DAVIS — ONE MEMBER.

Robert Reynolds	217

THIRTEENTH DISTRICT — BRECKINRIDGE — ONE MEMBER.

George H. Lillie	366	Perry B. Maxson	211

FOURTEENTH DISTRICT — SHAWNEE — TWO MEMBERS.

W. H. Fitzpatrick	284	I. N. Roberts	70
C. K. Holliday	136	J. P. Greer	269
Wm. E. Bowker	284	J. W. Brown	253

FIFTEENTH DISTRICT — DOUGLAS — THREE MEMBERS.

George W. Deitzler	538	Paul H. Berkau	377
John P. Cowles	423	J. G. Scott	243
Alois Thoman	534	G. W. Bell	263

SIXTEENTH DISTRICT — JOHNSON — TWO MEMBERS.

John T. Burris.................................. 343 | J. T. Campbell............................. 333
F. E. Henderson............................. 328 | John Evans................................. 409

SEVENTEENTH DISTRICT — LYKINS — ONE MEMBER.

Benjamin F. Simpson .... 492 | John M. Roberts......................... 331

EIGHTEENTH DISTRICT — LINN — ONE MEMBER.

John T. Snoddy.............. 405 | J. H. Barlow.............. 208 | J. W. Garrett............... 182

NINETEENTH DISTRICT — LYKINS AND LINN — ONE MEMBER.

George W. Miller .... 870 | Robert Ewing............................. 756

TWENTIETH DISTRICT — ANDERSON — ONE MEMBER.

Rufus Gilpatrick............................. 178 | W. F. M. Arny............................. 118
George W. Iler................................. 122 | Isaac Hiner............................... 12

TWENTY-FIRST DISTRICT — FRANKLIN — ONE MEMBER.

James Hanway................................ 244 | D. C. Cutler............................... 11
Harlan P. Welsh............................. 178 | Green Perkins............................. 1

TWENTY-SECOND DISTRICT — COFFEY AND OSAGE — TWO MEMBERS.

D. A. Hawkins................................ 377 | Levi Empie................................. 339
James M. Winchell.......................... 364 | H. D. Preston............................. 1
W. A. Jenkins................................ 348 | John Smith............................... 1

TWENTY-THIRD DISTRICT — MADISON, CHASE, PEKETON, AND MORRIS — ONE MEMBER.

T. S. Huffaker.............. 99 | N. B. Moulton.............. 102 | Samuel N. Wood............ 177

TWENTY-FOURTH DISTRICT — BUTLER, GREENWOOD, HUNTER, GODFREY, AND WOODSON — ONE MEMBER.

Pusey Graves................................ 109 | N. S. Goss................................. 79

TWENTY-FIFTH DISTRICT — ALLEN, WILSON, DORN, AND CHEROKEE — ONE MEMBER.

John W. Scott .... 124 | N. B. Blanton............................. 8
J. W. Tibbet .... 108 | John Wesel............................... 1

TWENTY-SIXTH DISTRICT — BOURBON — ONE MEMBER.

J. C. Burnett................................ 487 | Chas. W. Blair........................... 37
J. T. Neal.................................. 322 | W. R. Griffith...........................

TWENTY-SEVENTH DISTRICT — ARAPAHOE — ONE MEMBER.

E. M. McCook.............1855 | H. H. C. Harrison............557 | C. B. Clemens............1083

NOVEMBER 9.—Russell Hinds, of Linn county, a kidnapper, tried and hung by a vigilance committee.

NOVEMBER 12.— Gov. Dennison, of Ohio, asks the people, on Thanksgiving Day, to contribute for the relief of the people of Kansas.

NOVEMBER 14.—Territorial Relief Convention at Lawrence. Robert S. Mitchell, President; R. G. Elliott and John A. Martin, Secretaries. The following Territorial Committee appointed: S. C. Pomeroy, James L. McDowell, William Y. Roberts, Samuel A. Kingman, F. P. Baker, C. B. Lines, C. S. Lambdin, F. N. Blake, Rev. Wm. Bishop, Dr. Ayres, Lewis Bodwell, Rev. Chas. Reynolds, A. Spaulding, J. C. Burnett. S. C. Pomeroy elected President; Rev. C. Reynolds, Vice President; James L. McDowell, Secretary; George H. Fairchild, Treasurer.

NOVEMBER 19.—George M. Beebe, Secretary and Acting Governor, asks H. J. Strickler, Adjutant General, what force can be put in the field one week from date, to meet the pending difficulties in Linn county. He asks 200 men of General Harney.

NOVEMBER 28.—Governor Medary and General Harney leave Leavenworth for Fort Scott; United States troops ordered to go there.

DECEMBER 8.—The military expedition sent by Governor Stewart, of Missouri, to Fort Scott, in command of General D. M. Frost, is encamped near the State line, in Missouri.

—A Convention at Mound City justifies the hanging of Russell Hinds and Samuel Scott, and the shooting of L. D. Moore.

DECEMBER 20.—Frank M. Tracy, Daniel W. Wilder, and Bernard P. Chenoweth indicted for publishing the Free Democrat, a Free-State paper, at St. Joseph, Mo. Robert Tracy, Joseph Thompson, and Prince Langdon, printers, and C. C. Woolworth, bookseller, also indicted.

DECEMBER 31.—Judge Pettit declares unconstitutional the law abolishing slavery in Kansas. The suit was brought by Samuel Haley against F. R. Foard, to recover a slave woman named Fanny. This was the last blow struck at the people-perfectly-free dogma.

1861.

JANUARY 1.—The report of General Harney to the War Department, on the Fort Scott difficulties, is published. He says: "I am satisfied that the greater part, if not all, the donations which are sent to the sufferers in Kansas goes into the hands of this band," (Montgomery and Jennison,) "and the greater portion of it is perverted from the use intended, by purchasing arms and munitions of war for carrying out their plans."

JANUARY 2.—John C. Douglass commissioned as Territorial Superintendent of Common Schools.

JANUARY 4.—Despatch received at Fort Leavenworth from General Winfield Scott, ordering every man and horse to be ready to start for Baltimore at any moment.

JANUARY 5.—S. C. Pomeroy, President of the Relief Committee, reports total amount of goods received, 867,619 pounds.

JANUARY 7.—The Legislature meets, at Lecompton.

Officers of the Council: W. W. Updegraff, President; John J. Ingalls, Secretary; Jacob Stotler, Assistant Secretary; J. Y. Hewitt, Sergeant-at-Arms; C. L. Caldwell, Doorkeeper.

Officers of the House: Speaker, John W. Scott; Chief Clerk, Alfred Gray; Assistant Clerk, George W. Still; Sergeant-at-Arms, F. D. Sawin; Doorkeeper, H. Gibbs; Docket Clerk, Edwin S. Nash; Journal Clerk, Arthur Gunther; Enrolling Clerk, John L. Wilson. The Clerks were sworn in by Judge Elmore.

JANUARY 8.—The Legislature votes to adjourn to Lawrence.

JANUARY 9.—Meeting of the Legislature at Lawrence.

JANUARY 9.—Meeting of the Relief Committee in Lawrence. S. A.

Kingman declines to serve on the Committee, and W. W. Guthrie is appointed. W. F. M. Arny is made the general shipping agent of the Committee.

JANUARY 10.—Message from George M. Beebe, Acting Governor, Gov. Medary having resigned. The Governor says:

"If God in his wrath shall tolerate the worst portent of this tempest of passion, now so fiercely raging, Kansas ought, and I trust will, declining identification with either branch of a contending family, tendering to each alike the olive offering of good-neighborship, establish, under a Constitution of her own creation, a Government to be separate and independent among the Nations."

Beebe was a Democrat, appointed by Buchanan.

JANUARY 11.—Rev. Chas. Reynolds elected Chaplain of the Council.

JANUARY 16.—J. H. Lane writes to the Lawrence Republican that Missouri and Kansas ought to live at peace. He suggests the appointment of "a mixed commission" to confer with the Legislature of Missouri in regard to the maintenance of friendly relations.

JANUARY 18.—The Relief Committee acknowledge the receipt of goods to the amount of 1,062,552 pounds, besides garments, boots and shoes, and cloth.

JANUARY 19.—James Green, of Missouri, in the Senate, proposes to change the boundary of Kansas. He is opposed by Seward, Douglas, Pugh, Latham and Bigler, and his amendment is lost by 31 to 23.

JANUARY 21.—The bill for the admission of Kansas passes the Senate. *Ayes:* Anthony, Baker, Bigler, Bingham, Bright, Cameron, Chandler, Clark, Collamer, Crittenden, Dixon, Doolittle, Douglas, Durkee, Fessenden, Fitch, Foot, Foster, Grimes, Hale, Harlan, Johnson of Tennessee, King, Latham, Morrill, Pugh, Rice, Seward, Simmons, Sumner, Ten Eyck, Thompson, Trumbull, Wade, Wilkinson, and Wilson—36. *Noes:* Benjamin, Bragg, Clingman, Green, Hemphill, Hunter, Iverson, Johnson of Arkansas, Kennedy, Mason, Nicholson, Polk, Powell, Sebastian, Slidell, and Wigfall—16.

JANUARY 21.—Three military companies organized in Leavenworth.

JANUARY 28.—The House passes the Kansas admission bill, by 117 to 42.

JANUARY 28.—The Leavenworth Daily Conservative started. D. R. Anthony, Publisher; D. W. Wilder, Editor. Mathew Weightman, George F. Prescott, Henry Buckingham and George C. Hume were members of the publishing company.

STATE ORGANIZATION.

1861.

JANUARY 29.—President Buchanan signs the bill, and Kansas becomes a State.

AN ACT FOR THE ADMISSION OF KANSAS INTO THE UNION.

Whereas, The people of the Territory of Kansas, by their representatives in Convention assembled, at Wyandotte, in said Territory, on the twenty-ninth day of July, one thousand eight hundred and fifty-nine, did form for themselves a Constitution and State Government, republican in form, which was ratified and adopted by the people at an election held for that purpose, on Tuesday, the fourth day of October, one thousand eight hundred and fifty-nine, and the said Convention has, in their name and behalf, asked the Congress of the United States to admit the said Territory into the Union as a State, on an equal footing with the other States: therefore,

Be it enacted by the Senate and House of Representatives of the United States of America in Congress assembled:

SECTION 1. That the State of Kansas shall be, and is hereby declared to be, one of the United States of America, and admitted into the Union on an equal footing with the original States in all respects whatever. And the said State shall consist of all the territory included within the following boundaries, to wit: Beginning at a point on the western boundary of the State of Missouri where the thirty-seventh parallel of north latitude crosses the same; thence west on said parallel to the twenty-fifth meridian of longitude west from Washington; thence north on said meridian to the fortieth parallel of latitude; thence east on said parallel to the western boundary of the State of Missouri; thence south with the western boundary of said State to the place of beginning: *Provided,* That nothing contained in the said Constitution respecting the boundary of said State shall be construed to impair the rights of person or property now pertaining to the Indians in said Territory, so long as such rights shall remain unextinguished by treaty between the United States and such Indians, or to include any territory which, by treaty with such Indian tribe, is not, without the consent of such tribe, to be included within the territorial limits or jurisdiction of any State or Territory; but all such territory shall be excepted out of the boundaries, and constitute no part, of the State of Kansas, until said tribe shall signify their assent to the President of the United States to be included within said State, or to affect the authority of the Government of the United States to make any regulation respecting such Indians, their lands, property, or other rights, by treaty, law, or otherwise, which it would have been competent to make if this act had never passed.

SEC. 2. *And be it further enacted,* That until the next general apportionment of Representatives, the State of Kansas shall be entitled to one Representative in the House of Representatives of the United States.

SEC. 3. *And be it further enacted,* That nothing in this act shall be construed as an assent by Congress to all or any of the propositions or claims contained in the ordinance of said Constitution of the people of Kansas, or in the resolutions thereto attached; but the following propositions are hereby offered to the said people of Kansas for their free acceptance or rejection, which, if accepted, shall be obligatory on the United States, and upon the said State of Kansas, to wit:

First: That sections numbered sixteen and thirty-six, in every township of public lands in said State, and where either of said sections or any part thereof has been sold or otherwise been disposed of, other lands, equivalent thereto and as contiguous as may be, shall be granted to said State for the use of schools.

Second: That seventy-two sections of land shall be set apart and reserved for the use and support of a State University, to be selected by the Governor of said State, subject to the approval of the Commissioner of the General Land Office, and to be appropriated and applied in such manner as the Legislature of said State may prescribe for the purpose aforesaid, but for no other purpose.

Third: That ten entire sections of land, to be selected by the Governor of said State, in legal subdivisions, shall be granted to the said State for the purpose of completing the public buildings, or for the erection of others at the seat of government, under the direction of the Legislature thereof.

Fourth: That all salt springs within said State, not exceeding twelve in number, with six sections of land adjoining or as contiguous as may be to each, shall be granted to said State for its use, the same to be selected by the Governor thereof within one year after the admission of said State, and when so selected to be used or disposed of on such terms, conditions and regulations as the Legislature shall direct: *Provided,* That no salt spring or land, the right whereof is now vested in any individual or individuals, or which may be hereafter confirmed or adjudged to any individual or individuals, shall, by this article, be granted to said State.

Fifth: That five per centum of all sales of all public lands lying within said State, which shall be sold by Congress after the admission of said State into the Union, after deducting all the expenses incident to the same, shall be paid to said State for the purpose of making public roads and internal improvements, or for other purposes, as the Legislature shall direct: *Provided,* That the foregoing propositions hereinbefore offered are on the condition that the people of Kansas shall provide by an ordinance, irrevocable without the consent of the United States, that said State shall never interfere with the primary disposal of the soil within the same by the United States, or with any regulations Congress may find necessary for securing the title in said soil to bona fide purchasers thereof.

Sixth: And that the said State shall never tax the lands or property of the United States in said State: *Provided, however,* That in case any of the lands herein granted to the State of Kansas have heretofore been confirmed to the Territory of Kansas for the purposes specified in this act, the amount so confirmed shall be deducted from the quantity specified in this act.

SEC. 4. *And be it further enacted,* That from and after the admission of the State of Kansas, as hereinbefore provided, all the laws of the United States, which are not locally inapplicable, shall have the same force and effect within that State as in other States of the Union; and the said State is hereby constituted a Judicial District of the United States, within which a District Court, with like powers and jurisdiction as the District Court of the United States for the District of Minnesota, shall be established; the Judge, Attorney and Marshal of the United States, for the said District of Kansas, shall reside within the same, and shall be entitled to the same compensation as the Judge, Attorney and Marshal of the District of Minnesota; and in all cases of appeal or writ of error heretofore prosecuted and now pending in the Supreme Court of the United States, upon any record from the Supreme Court of Kansas Territory, the mandate of execution or order of further proceedings shall be directed by the Supreme Court of the United States to the District of Kansas, or to the Supreme Court of the State of Kansas, as the nature of such appeal or writ of error may require; and each of those courts shall be the successor of the Supreme Court of Kansas Territory as to all such cases, with full power to hear and determine the same, and to award mesne or final process therein.

SEC. 5. *And be it further enacted,* That the Judge of the District Court for the District of Kansas shall hold two regular terms of the said Court annually, at the seat of government of the said State, to commence on the second Mondays of April and October in each year.

Approved 29th of January, 1861.

The signing of the bill by Buchanan is made known in Leavenworth by a despatch from Marcus J. Parrott to the Conservative. That paper prints an Extra, and D. R. Anthony carries it to Lawrence. The Legislature thanks the paper for its enterprise. Captain Frank B. Swift, Caleb S. Pratt, Edward Thompson, and James C. Horton, with a large company, go to Captain Bickerton's farm, where the "Old Sacramento" is buried, dig it up, take it to Lawrence, and consume the night in saluting the admission of Kansas. It is also a holiday in Leavenworth, all parties joining in salutes, speeches and songs.

The portion of the State of Kansas which came from Mexico, and did not form a part of the Louisiana Purchase, is bounded on the north by the Arkansas river, on the east by the twenty-third meridian, on the south by the thirty-seventh parallel, and on the west by the twenty-fifth meridian. The estimated area is 7,776 square miles. The counties in this southwestern part of the State are now (1875) called: Kansas, Stevens, Seward, Meade, Stanton, Grant, Arapahoe; with parts of Clark, Ford, Foote, Sequoyah, Kearney, and Hamilton. The United States Census Report for 1870 (p. 592) says this tract was "ceded by the State of Texas, and was not included in the Territory of New Mexico."

JANUARY 29.—The report of the Special Committee on Claim Bonds is published in the House Journal, pages 316 to 347.

JANUARY 29.—Ed. F. Schneider, Editor of the Times, gives a sketch of Leavenworth papers. The Weekly Herald was started in September, 1854, by Adams & Osborne. In December, Lucien J. Eastin became the editor, the publishers being Eastin & Adams. The Daily Herald appeared May 17, 1859; Wm. H. Gill, Editor, and Gill, Eastin, W. H. Adams and C. H. McLaughlin publishers. The paper was discontinued in October, 1860, but was revived the next month by Satterlee & Wilson, with Chas. W. Helm as editor. The Weekly Register was started in the spring of 1855, by Delahay & Sevier, with Mark W. Delahay as editor. It was a Free-State paper, and was mobbed and thrown into the Missouri on the night of Dec. 22, 1855. The Weekly Journal, Pro-Slavery, was started in the spring of 1856, by J. D. Henderson. The Daily Journal, by McLaughlin & Hutchison, came out in May, '58. It was short-lived. In the latter part of 1857, Geo. W. McLane issued The Young America. It died in January, 1858, and the Daily Ledger was born. This paper died early in July, '59. L'Estafette du Kansas, a French paper, by Frank Barclay, was born and died in '59. The Despatch began in July, '59, and lived about eighteen months. Jeff. L. Dugger started the State Register in August, 1859. It died early. There have been several German papers. The Weekly Times was issued March 7, 1857; the Daily Times, Feb. 15, 1858.

FEBRUARY 1.—Both houses pass a resolution "to elect two U. S. Senators from the State of Kansas."

FEBRUARY 2.—Adjournment of the Legislature. The general laws passed by the last Territorial Legislature, in 1861, fill 35 pages; the private laws of the same session fill 68 pages. They are bound in one volume. One excellent law declares how many clerks each house shall have, fixes their salary, and declares that no extra compensation shall be allowed to any one of them. The only other general law of importance pronounced illegal the bonds issued in payment of claims for losses. Of the private laws, twenty are "divorces;" one incorporates the Lawrence University of Kansas; one the Episcopal Female Seminary, at Topeka, and one incorporates the city of Marysville.

FEBRUARY 4.—Rebel delegates meet at Montgomery, Ala., to organize a Confederate Government.

FEBRUARY 9.—Gov. Robinson sworn into office. He asks the Legislature to meet on the 26th of March. He appoints M. F. Conway, Thos. Ewing, jr., Henry J. Adams and James C. Stone to represent Kansas in the "Peace Conference," at Washington. Ewing and Stone voted for "peace" and compromise.

FEBRUARY 9.—Jefferson Davis and Alex. H. Stephens elected Provisional President and Vice President of the Confederacy, by the Montgomery Convention.

FEBRUARY 11.—President Lincoln leaves Springfield for Washington.

FEBRUARY 15.—The New York Legislature appropriates $50,000 for the relief of Kansas sufferers.

FEBRUARY 16.—Trask & Lowman buy the Herald of Freedom office, and issue the Lawrence State Journal. John P. Greer has bought the Topeka Tribune.

FEBRUARY 18.—The Arapahoe and Cheyenne Indians cede all their land to the United States except a tract between the Sandy Fork of the Arkansas and the Purgatory river.

FEBRUARY 20.—Captain James Montgomery writes to the Governor that the southern border is in danger.

FEBRUARY 22.—President Lincoln's night journey from Harrisburg to Washington, in order to prevent an anticipated outrage at Baltimore.

MARCH 2.—

"*Amendment of the Constitution.*—The two chambers of Congress jointly *Resolved*, That the following article be proposed to the Legislatures of the several States as an amendment to the Constitution of the United States, which, when ratified by three-fourths of said Legislatures, shall be valid to all intents and purposes, as part of the said Constitution, viz.:

"'ARTICLE 13. No amendment shall be made to the Constitution which will authorize or give to Congress the power to abolish or interfere, within any State, with the domestic institutions thereof, including that of persons held to labor or service by the laws of said State.'

"Approved March 2, 1861."

Kansas did not ratify this amendment. It did not become a part of the National Constitution.

MARCH 4.—Inauguration of Abraham Lincoln.

MARCH 5.—Election to fill vacancies in the Legislature, in the Eighth, Tenth, Eleventh and Twelfth districts. Werter R. Davis is elected in the Eighth, over L. L. Jones, J. W. Scott in the Tenth, and H. S. Sleeper in

17

the Twelfth. In the Third district, Samuel Lappin is elected in place of
Mr. Torrey. The following is the vote of the Ninth district:

Towns and Precincts.	Updegraff.	Dutton.	Miller.
BOURBON COUNTY.			
Fort Scott	48	2	114
Mapleton	84	1	1
Franklin	46		
Marmaton	75		
Marion	50		
Dry Wood	25		
Freedom	75		
Osage	40		
Total	443	3	115
LINN COUNTY.			
Mound City	56	36	33
Centreville	44		26
Potosi	40		3
Moneka	14	6	16
Paris	48		79
Trading Post	32		45
Twin Springs	43	9	21
Total	277	51	183
LYKINS COUNTY.			
Osawatomie	145		2
Stanton	59	1	1
Paola	64		135
Osage	62		27
Total	330	1	165

Middle Creek gave 20 majority for Miller; Mound 17 for Updegraff.

MARCH 6.—Treaty of the Sacs and Foxes of Missouri and the Iowas,
with the United States.

MARCH 8.—Archibald Williams, of Illinois, appointed United States
District Judge of Kansas.

MARCH 10.—Linn county organizes the first militia regiment in the
State. Among the Captains are Charles R. Jennison and J. F. Broadhead.

MARCH 25.—The Republicans are said to have 86 and the Democrats 14
members of the Legislature.

MARCH 26.—Meeting of the first State Legislature.

MEMBERS AND OFFICERS OF THE SENATE.

Names.	P. O. Address.	County.	Born.	From.	Age.	Avocat'n.	Pol.	†
J. P. Root*	Wyandotte	Wyandotte	Mass.	Conn.	34	Phys'n.	Rep.	M
E. P. Bancroft	Emporia	Breckinridge	N. Y.	Mich.	32	L'nd Ag	Rep.	M
J. F. Broadhead	Mound City	Linn	N. Y.	N. Y.	30	Lawyer	Rep.	M
J. C. Burnett	Mapleton	Bourbon	Vt	Vt	35	Lawyer	Rep.	M
J. Connell	Leavenw'th	Leavenw'th	Ky	Ky	42	Farmer	Dem	M
H. B. Denman	Leavenw'th	Leavenw'th	Ohio	Ohio	32	Lawyer	Dem	S
H. R. Dutton	Hiawatha	Brown	N. Y.	Iowa	34	Surv'y'r	Rep.	S
P. P. Elder	Ohio City	Franklin	Me	Me	38	Attor'y.	Rep.	M
H. W. Farnsworth	Topeka	Shawnee	Vt	Conn.	44	Miller	Rep.	M
O. B. Gunn	Wyandotte	Wyandotte	Mass.	Ind	32	Civ. E'g	Rep.	M
S. E. Hoffman	Neosho Falls	Woodson	Penn.	Iowa	26	Lawyer	Rep.	S
S. D. Houston	Manhattan	Riley	Ohio	Iowa	42	Farmer	Rep.	M
J. M. Hubbard	Wabaunsee	Wabaunsee	Conn.	Conn.	28	Farmer	Rep.	S
S. Lappin	Seneca	Nemaha	Ohio	La	30	Farmer	Rep.	M

MEMBERS AND OFFICERS OF THE SENATE — *Concluded.*

Names.	P. O. Address.	County.	Born.	From.	Age	Avocat'n.	Pol.	†
J. Lockhart.........	Hibbard.......	Johnson	Scot'd	Ill	28	Farmer	Rep..	M
E. Lynde............	Grassh'r F'ls	Jefferson......	Conn..	Ohio..	40	Farmer	Rep..	M
J. A. Martin........	Atchison......	Atchison......	Penn..	Penn..	23	Editor...	Rep..	S
J. H. McDowell....	Leavenw'th.	Leavenw'th..	Va......	Ky....	36		Dem	M
Josiah Miller.......	Lawrence.....	Douglas......	S. C...	S. C...	31	Lawyer	Rep..	M
R. Morrow..........	Lawrence.....	Douglas......	N. J ..	Wis....	35	Specul'r	Rep..	M
T. A. Osborn	Elwood.........	Doniphan....	Penn..	Mich..	24	Lawyer	Rep..	S
J. A. Phillips.......	Paola	Lykins	N. C...	Ind	24	Lawyer	Rep..	S
H. N. Seaver.......	Highland	Doniphan....	N. Y..	N. Y..	50	Farmer	Rep..	M
H. S. Sleeper.......	Neosho R'p's	Breckinridge	N. Y..	Ill......	28	Surv'y'r	Rep..	S
W. Spriggs..........	Garnett.......	Anderson.....	Ky	Ind	34	Lawyer	Rep..	M
S. N. Wood..........	C'ncil Grove.	Morris	Ohio..	Ohio..	35	Farmer	Rep..	M
J. J. Ingalls, Secretary...............	Atchison	Atchison......	Mass..	Mass..	26	Lawyer	Rep..	S
J. Stotler, Assistant Secretary....	Emporia	Breckinridge	Md.....	Ohio..	26	Editor...	Rep..	M
J. R. Lambdin, Journal Clerk...	Chelsea	Butler..........	Va......	Ky....	26	Clerk ...	Rep..	S
D. Wilson, Docket Clerk..............	Ogden	Riley...........	Ohio..	Ohio..	31	Lawyer	Rep..	S
A. W. Pickering, Engross'g Clerk	Neosho Falls	Woodson	Ohio..	Ill	23	Student	Rep..	S
T. S. Wright, S'g't-at-Arms	Seneca..........	Nemaha.......	Penn..	Ind	52	Lawyer	Rep..	M
H. M. Robinson, Door Keeper.....	Hiawatha.....	Brown	Ind ...	Ind	27	Mech'ic	Rep..	M
F. R. Davis, Messenger..............	Lawrence.....	Douglas........	N. Y..	N. Y..	11	Mess'g'r	Rep..	S

* President. † Married or single.

MEMBERS AND OFFICERS OF THE HOUSE.

Name.	P. O. Address.	County.	Born.	From.	Age	Avocat'n.	Pol.	†
W. W. Updegraff*	Osawatomie..	Lykins	Penn..	Ind....	39	Phys'n..	Rep..	M
W. F. M. Arny.....	Hyatt..........	Anderson.....	D. C...	Ill	48	Farmer.	Rep..	M
J. B. Abbott........	Lawrence	Douglas.......	Conn..	Conn..	42	Mech'ic	Rep..	M
P. M. Alexander..	Lawrence	Douglas.......	Ill	Ill	34	Farmer	Rep..	M
A. Allen.............	Wabaunsee ..	Wabaunsee ..	Ohio..	Ohio..	33	Farmer	Rep..	M
D. C. Auld..........	Nottingham	Marshall......	Penn..	Ohio..	51	Farmer	Rep..	M
D. E. Ballard.......	Washington	Washington..	Vt......	Iowa..	24	Farmer	Rep..	S
O. Barber...........	Kanwaka.....	Douglas	Penn..	Ohio..	44	Farmer	Rep..	M
J. C. Bartlett.......	Topeka........	Shawnee	Ohio..	Ind....	31	Merch..	Rep..	M
J. J. Bentz..........	Leavenw'th..	Leavenw'th..	Ger'y..	Mo.....	34	Merch..	Rep..	M
W. D. Blackford...	Lawrence	Douglas.......	Penn..	Penn..	26	Lawyer	Rep..	S
F. N. Blake.........	Junct'n City.	Davis..........	Me.....	Ill	36	Editor ..	Rep..	S
N. B. Blanton	Humboldt ...	Allen...........	Mo.....	Mo.....	30	Farmer	Rep..	M
W. E. Bowker......	Indianola	Shawnee	Me.....	Me.....	31	Farmer	Rep..	S
E. J. Brown........	LeRoy	Coffey	N. Y..	Ohio..	33	Farmer	Dem..	S
H. Buckmaster.....	Oskaloosa	Jefferson......	Penn..	Ohio..	46	Phys'n..	Rep..	M
T. Butcher.........	Atchison......	Atchison......	Penn..	Wis....	50	Cont'or.	Rep..	M
J. M. Calvert......	Kickapoo.....	Leavenw'th..	Ky.....	Mo.....	46	Farmer	Dem..	M
S. R. Caniff........	Burlingame.	Osage	N. Y..	N. Y..	28	Manuf ..	Rep..	M
A. J. Chipman	C'ncil Grove.	Morris	Vt......	Mich..	26	Merch..	Rep..	S
R. W. Cloud........	Waterloo	Breckinridge	Ohio..	Ohio..	45	Farmer	Rep..	M
G. A. Colton........	Paola..........	Lykins.........	Vt......	Ill	31	Lawyer	Rep..	M
J. E. Corliss........	Shawnee	Johnson	Vt......	Iowa..	53	Farmer	Rep..	M
J. D. Crafton.......	Leavenw'th.	Leavenw'th..	Va......	Ky	40	Merch..	Dem	M
S. J. Crawford.....	Garnett.......	Anderson.....	Ind	Ill	26	Lawyer	Rep..	S
H. W. Curtis.......	Topeka........	Shawnee	Ohio..	Ill	39	Farmer	Rep..	M
G. A. Cutler........	LeRoy	Coffey	Tenn..	Mo.....	30	Phys'n..	Rep..	M
W. R. Davis........	Baldwin City	Douglas.......	Ohio..	Ill	46	Prof	Rep..	M
A. Ellis.............	New Lanc'r..	Lykins	Ohio..	Ohio..	44	Farmer	Rep..	M
I. E. Eaton........	Leavenw'th.	Leavenw'th..	Ohio..	Ohio..	40	Cont'or.	Dem	M
A. Elliott...........	Pardee........	Atchison......	S. C...	Mo.....	54	Farmer	Rep..	M
F. W. Emery.......	Palermo.......	Doniphan....	Me.....	Me.....	25	Editor ..	Rep..	S
W. P. Gambell.....	Leavenw'th.	Leavenw'th..	N. Y..	N. Y..	29	Lawyer	Dem	M
W. H. Grimes......	Atchison......	Atchison......	Md.....	Ohio..	57	Phys'n..	Rep..	M
A. Gray.............	Quindaro	Wyandotte...	N. Y..	N. Y..	29	Lawyer	Rep..	M
A. K. Hawkes......	Hartford......	Breckinridge	Mass..	Mass..	32	Farmer	Rep..	M

* Speaker. † Married or single.

MEMBERS AND OFFICERS OF THE HOUSE—*Concluded.*

Name.	P. O. Address.	County.	Born.	From.	Age	Avocat'n.	Pol.	†
J. E. Hayes..........	Olathe	Johnson.......	N. H..	Ill	42	Merch...	Rep..	M
H. H. Heberling...	Ridgeway.....	Osage	Va....	Ohio ..	52	Farmer	Rep..	M
T. P. Herrick.......	Highland	Doniphan ..	N. Y..	N. Y..	28	Lawyer	Rep..	M
E. Hoheneck.......	Wabaunsee ..	Wabaunsee...	Prus..	Ohio ..	32	Distil'r.	Rep..	S
N. Humber..........	Easton..........	Leavenw'th..	Ky....	Mo....	46	Farmer	Dem	M
J. H. Jones..........	Twin Sp'ngs.	Linn.....	Va....	Iowa..	35	Farmer	Rep..	M
W. C. Kimber......	Palermo......	Doniphan	Ohio ..	Mo	33	Miller ...	Dem	M
C. B. Keith........	Muscotah	Atchison......	Vt.....	Mich..	29	Merch...	Rep..	M
H. Knowles........	Marmaton	Bourbon	Me....	Wis....	40	Merch...	Rep..	M
J. Kunkel............	Lecompton ...	Douglas	Penn.	Penn.	42	Merch...	Rep..	M
W.W.H.Lawrence	Peoria City..	Franklin	Ohio ..	Ohio ..	34	Lawyer	Rep..	S
J. F. Legate........	Lexington	Johnson......	Mass.	Miss ..	31	Lawyer	Rep..	M
E. P. Lewis........	Sumner........	Atchison......	Penn.	Penn.	24	Lawyer	Rep..	S
E. J. Lines..........	Wabaunsee..	Wabaunsee ..	Conn.	Conn.	31	Lawyer	Dem	M
A. Low..............	Doniphan	Doniphan....	Md....	Ohio ..	49	Merch...	Rep..	M
J. McGrew..........	Wyandotte..	Wyandotte...	Penn.	Iowa..	39	Merch...	Rep..	M
S. B. Mahurin......	Fort Scott...	Bourbon	Ky....	Texas	30	Farmer	Rep..	M
J. A. Marcell........	Minneola	Franklin	N. J..	N. Y..	43	Farmer	Rep..	M
J. E. Moore.........	Auburn	Shawnee	N. J..	Ill	32	Clergy...	Rep..	M
P. G. D. Morton....	Chelsea	Butler........	Me....	Mass..	35	Lawyer	Rep..	S
A. U. Mussey.......	St. George...	Pottawato'e..	Vt.....	Vt......	27	Farmer	Rep..	M
J. T. Neal............	Barnesville ..	Bourbon	Tenn.	Ill	30	Phys'n..	Rep..	M
T. Pierce............	Henryville...	Riley...........	Ohio ..	Ohio ..	38	Farmer	Rep..	M
J. S. Rackliff.......	Medoc..........	Platte..........	Me....	Me......	39	Farmer	Rep..	M
A. Ray...............	Holton	Jackson.......	Ohio ..	Ohio ..	46	Farmer	Rep..	M
G. H. Rees	Americus	Breckinridge	Ohio ..	Iowa.	42	Farmer	Rep..	M
W. R. Saunders.....	LeRoy	Coffey	N. Y..	N. Y..	40	Farmer	Rep..	M
J. W. Scott.........	Carlyle	Allen	Penn.	Ind....	36	Phys'n..	Rep..	M
O. H. Sheldon......	Superior.......	Osage	N. Y..	N. Y..	27	Farmer	Rep..	M
J. H. Smith..........	Robinson.....	Brown	Conn.	Conn.	45	Farmer	Rep..	M
L. T. Smith..........	Leavenw'th ..	Leavenw'th..	N. Y..	Mich..	33	Hotel P.	Dem	M
W. H. Smyth........	Manhattan ..	Riley..........	Me....	Iowa..	26	Civ. En.	Rep..	S
C. Starns............	Leavenw'th ..	Leavenw'th..	Tenn.	Mo.....	48	Farmer	Dem	M
A. Stark.............	Moneka.......	Linn..........	Conn.	Conn.	27	Farmer	Rep..	M
J. W. Stewart.......	Baldwin City	Douglas........	Ohio ..	Iowa..	40	Clergy ..	Rep..	M
E. D. Thompson...	Lawrence	Douglas........	N. Y..	N. Y..	23	Banker.	Rep..	S
B. Wheat............	LeRoy	Coffey	Va....	Va......	52	Farmer	Rep..	M
R. P. C. Wilson.....	Leavenw'th.	Leavenw'th ..	Mo....	Texas	25	Lawyer	Dem	S
L. Woodard	Eudora	Douglas........	Ind....	Ind....	30	Farmer	Rep..	M
D. B. Emmert, Chief Clerk.......	Auburn........	Shawnee	Penn.	Ill	24	Editor...	Rep..	S
A. R. Banks, Ass't Ch'f Clerk.........	Minneola......	Franklin	Ohio ..	Penn..	25	Lawyer	Rep..	S
Arthur Gunther, Journal Clerk...	Lawrence	Douglas	Sax'n.	Wis ...	23	Clerk....	Rep..	S
T. Hopkins, Docket Clerk......	Miami..........	Lykins..........	Penn.	Iowa..	27	Mech...	Rep..	S
D. M. Adams, En- grossing Clerk...	Zeandale......	Wabaunsee ..	N. H..	N. H..	28	Farmer.	Rep..	M
B. P. Noteman, Enrolling Clerk.	Olathe	Johnson.......	N. Y..	Ill	36	Merch...	Rep..	M
C. Clarkson, Ser- geant-at-Arms..	Leavenw'th ..	Leavenw'th ..	Penn.	N. Y...	49	Merch...	Rep..	M
F. House, Assist. Serg't-at-Arms..	Wyandotte..	Wyandotte ..	Vt.....	N. Y...	31	Lawyer	Rep..	S
W. V. Barr, Door- keeper..............	Iowa Point...	Doniphan......	N. J...	N. Y...	46	Mech....	Rep..	M
C. T. K. Prentice, Messenger	McKinney ...	Douglas	Conn.	N. Y..	14	Clerk.?	Rep..	S
A. L. Bartlett, Messenger	Topeka.........	Shawnee	Ohio ..	Ind ...	9	Clerk....	Rep..	S

† Married or single.

MARCH 26.—Seven Slave States have seceded from the Union. South Carolina led, passing her Ordinance of Secession, without any dissenting votes, Dec. 20th, 1860.

—William Tholen, of Leavenworth, elected State Treasurer, entered the volunteer service, and did not act as Treasurer. H. R. Dutton, of Brown county, was appointed Treasurer by the Governor.

MARCH 30.—Message from Gov. Robinson. It is comprehensive and able.

APRIL.—Mark W. Delahay appointed Surveyor General.

APRIL 1.—Suspension of the Lecompton Democrat.

APRIL 1.—Fred. P. Stanton gets the vote of the Senate for U. S. Senator "from the south side of the Kaw."

APRIL 3.—Heavy rain, all over the State, the first of any importance for months.

APRIL 4.—Election of United States Senators, by the following vote:

James H. Lane	55	S. D. Houston	1
S. C. Pomeroy	52	S. A. Kingman	3
Marcus J. Parrott	49	A. J. Isacks	11
F. P. Stanton	21	M. F. Conway	1
M. W. Delahay	2		

There was only one ballot. The voting continued two hours, in which interval Lane fluctuated between 45 and 64, Pomeroy between 49 and 57, Parrott between 47 and 60, Stanton between 10 and 32, Delahay between 2 and 11, and Kingman between 3 and 18. Fifty-eight members changed their votes. This vote-changing precedent has been faithfully followed, in Legislatures and Conventions, up to the time of going to press.

In the spring, Driggs, Faris and Moore moved the Lecompton Democrat office to Atchison, and issued the Bulletin. It died that year.

APRIL 8.—Judge Williams opens the United States Court, at Topeka.

APRIL 9.—Lane endorsed in Leavenworth. All the politicians go to Washington to get office.

APRIL 12.—Bombardment of Fort Sumter by Rebels. Beginning of the Pro-Slavery Rebellion.

APRIL 13.—Illinois and Wisconsin currency no longer in use as a circulating medium. Great losses occasioned by Wild-Cat banks.

APRIL 15.—President Lincoln calls for 75,000 men to enforce the laws, and asks Congress to meet July 4th.

APRIL 16.—Dinner given to Judge John Pettit by the Leavenworth bar.

—W. F. M. Arny reports to the Legislature that relief goods have passed through his hands weighing 9,197,300 pounds. Of this amount, 3,051,304 pounds were for seed. The money furnished by the Legislatures of New York and Wisconsin, and the New York City Committee, and $22,481.93 in addition, has been expended. No details are given. Wagons are still taking relief goods from Atchison.

APRIL 17.—Governor Claib. Jackson, of Missouri, replies to the President's call for 75,000 men: "Not one man will the State of Missouri furnish to carry on such an unholy crusade."

—Captain Samuel Walker, of Lawrence, tenders to Governor Robinson a company of 100 men. A meeting is held in Atchison to form a military company. "Coercion" is voted down, and the Union company is not organized.

APRIL 18.—The steamboat "New Sam Gaty" arrives at Leavenworth, from St. Louis, with a Rebel flag flying. An immense crowd collects on the Levee, and the Captain is compelled to take down the traitor ensign and run up the Stars and Stripes. This was the decisive day for Leavenworth.

APRIL 20.—Seven military companies in Douglas county; nine in Leavenworth; one is ordered to Fort Leavenworth for thirty days' service.

—The Rebels seize the United States Arsenal at Liberty, Missouri.

—Samuel Walker and James C. Stone made Major Generals of the State militia.

APRIL 25.—Military companies organized in nearly every county.

APRIL 26.—M. Jeff. Thompson takes into St. Joseph the arms stolen at Liberty.

—A night guard is organized by citizens of Leavenworth to defend the town. This service continues to be voluntarily performed, whenever necessary, during the whole war.

APRIL 27.—Destructive fire in Leavenworth.

APRIL 29.—Report of Legislative Committee on Blue Mont Central College. The Trustees of the College voted, February 28, to give it to the State.

—Captain J. L. Reno has charge of the arsenal at Fort Leavenworth. He became a Major General, and was killed at Gettysburg. Reno county bears his name.

MAY 1.—A rebel camp in St. Joseph remains unmolested. Rebel flags wave in St. Joseph, Kansas City, Iatan, Weston, Platte City, and Independence, Mo.

MAY 1.—The following appointments are announced: Chester Thomas, Mail Agent; J. C. Burnett, Register Fort Scott Land Office; A. Low, Register Kickapoo Land Office; Ira Smith, Receiver Kickapoo Land Office; F. G. Adams, Register Lecompton Land Office; C. B. Lines, Receiver Lecompton Land Office; H. W. Farnsworth, Kaw Indian Agent; G. A. Colton, Miami Indian Agent; Charles B. Keith, Kickapoo Indian Agent; D. R. Anthony, Postmaster at Leavenworth; James Fletcher, Postmaster at Topeka; John A. Martin, Postmaster at Atchison; Jacob Stotler, Postmaster at Emporia.

MAY 2. – Extra Session of the Missouri Legislature. The following is copied from the Message of Governor Claiborne F. Jackson:

"Our interests and sympathies are identical with those of the Slaveholding States, and necessarily unite our destiny with theirs. The similarity of our social and domestic institutions, our industrial interests, our sympathies, habits and tastes, our common origin, territorial congruity, all concur in pointing out our duty in regard to the separation now taking place between the States of the old Federal Union."

There were 114,965 slaves in Missouri.

MAY 6.—George H. Fairchild elected Mayor of Atchison, by 100 majority, over Ike Hascall, Border-Ruffian.

—John T. Burris is appointed United States District Attorney; W. W. Ross, Pottawatomie Agent; P. P. Elder, Osage Agent at Fort Scott; Josiah Miller, Postmaster at Lawrence; S. D. Houston, Receiver at Junction City; John Hutchinson, Secretary of Dakota.

MAY 9.—Death of H. F. Otis, Mayor of Topeka.

MAY 10.—A Topeka letter of Ingalls, in the Conservative, has this description of Lane:

"It would be hard to give a rational and satisfactory analysis of the causes of Gen. Lane's popularity as an orator. Destitute of all graces of the art, he possesses but few even of its essentials; he writhes himself into more contortions than Gabriel Ravel in a pantomime; his voice is a series of transitions from the broken scream of a maniac to the hoarse rasping gutturals of a Dutch butcher in the last gasp of inebriation; the construction of his sentences is loose and disjointed; his diction is a pudding of slang, profanity and solecism; and yet the electric shock of his extraordinary eloquence thrills like the blast of a trumpet; the magnetism of his manner, the fire of his glance, the studied earnestness of his utterance, find a sudden response in the will of his audience, and he sways them like a field of reeds shaken in the wind. Devoid of those qualities of character which excite esteem and cement the enduring structure of popular regard, he overcomes the obstacles in the path of achievement by persistent effort and indomitable will."

MAY 10.—Capt. Nathaniel Lyon and Col. Francis P. Blair, at the head of 6,000 Union volunteers, many of them Germans, surround the Rebel State Guard, at St. Louis, and take them prisoners. Gen. D. M. Frost was in command of the Rebels. This movement saved Missouri to the Union.

MAY 14.—A. M. Clark and J. C. Stone write to the Governor that they cannot negotiate the Kansas bonds.

—Stampede of Union men from Western Missouri.

MAY 15.—Topeka letter of J. J. Ingalls:

"Mr McDowell, from the Committee on State Library, submitted a new report on the subject of a State seal this morning. The device represents a mountain horizon, and a prairie foreground traversed by a 'schooner' bound for the Peak; a rising sun illuminates a retreating herd of buffalo, and a farmer following the plough. The motto suggested is the terse, emphatic and appropriate legend, 'WE WILL.' The design is decidedly the most original and suggestive which has yet been presented, though Mr. Denman suggests that it might be better to change the motto to 'WE WON'T.'"

—George W. Brown, late of the Herald of Freedom, becomes a resident of Paola.

MAY 20.—

"The vexed question of a State seal has at last received its quietus at the hands of a conference committee. The new design embraces a prairie landscape, with buffalo pursued by Indian hunters, a settler's cabin, and a ploughman with his team, a river with a steamboat, a cluster of thirty-four stars surrounding the legend, 'AD ASTRA PER ASPERA,' the whole encircled by the words, 'Great Seal of the State of Kansas, 1861.'"—*J. J. Ingalls, in Conservative.*

MAY 21.—

"Directly after General Butler's accession to command at Fortress Monroe, three negro slaves came within his lines from the Rebel lines adjacent, stating that they were held as property by Colonel Mallory, of the Confederate forces in his front, who was about to send them to the North Carolina seaboard, to work on the Rebel fortifications there in progress, intended to bar that coast against our arms. General Butler heard their story, was satisfied of its truth, and said: 'These men are contraband of war; set them at work.'"—*Greeley's Conflict, vol. II, p. 238.*

MAY 21.—

"Judge Lambdin, who is just from Butler county, states that the reports of damage done by grasshoppers are not exaggerated. The insects have travelled a belt of country about six miles wide, devouring every green thing. Young fields of wheat have been completely destroyed by their ravages, not one blade remaining; early corn and vegetables and the foliage of trees have suffered with equal severity; and the evil seems to be on the increase, with no means of prevention."—*Topeka Letter in Conservative.*

MAY 22.—Republican Congressional Convention at Topeka. Thirty

counties send 55 delegates. Called to order by A. C. Wilder. On motion
of Wm. A. Phillips, Dr. R. Gilpatrick was made temporary Chairman, and
J. H. Signor, Secretary.

Committee on Credentials: T. D. Thacher, F. G. Adams, L. R. Palmer,
R. Crozier, James Montgomery. *Committee on Permanent Organization:*
C. P. Twiss, F. A. Bliss, J. A. McCall, A. D. Brown, C. V. Eskridge.

Officers: President, R. Gilpatrick; Vice Presidents, A. L. Lee, James L.
McDowell, R. M. Fish, T. W. Satchel; Secretaries, D. R. Anthony, J. H.
Signor.

Ballot for Member of Congress: M. F. Conway 37, Ed. Lynde 8, R. M.
Williams 6; Montgomery, Watson and Updegraff, one each.

The following resolutions, offered by D. R. Anthony, are adopted:

"*Resolved by the Republican Party of the State of Kansas in Convention assembled*, That the
existing condition of national affairs demands the emphatic and unmistakable expression of the convictions of the people of the State, and that Kansas allies herself with
the uprising Union hosts of the North to uphold the policy of the Administration.

"*Resolved*, That the grave responsibilities of this hour could not have been safely
postponed, and that they have not arrived too soon, and that in the present war between
Government and Anarchy the mildest compromise is treason against humanity.

"*Resolved*, That we spurn as specious sophistries all suggestions for the peaceful dis-
memberment of the Union, and pledge our fortunes and our honor to its maintenance,
intact and inviolate."

The following State Committee was appointed: A. C. Wilder, T. D. Thacher,
W. C. Dunton, J. F. Newlon, Ed. Russell, D. W. Houston, Loring Farnsworth.

MAY 23.—A. C. Wilder elected Chairman, and T. D. Thacher Secretary,
of the Republican State Committee.

MAY 24.—Railroad completed to Weston, Missouri; a line of boats from
Leavenworth to Weston.

MAY 28.—The First Kansas organizing, in the western part of Leavenworth.

JUNE 1.—F. P. Stanton appointed to take charge of military affairs in
New Mexico.

—Col. Emory and Maj. S. D. Sturgis arrive at Fort Leavenworth from
the South with United States troops.

JUNE 3.—Gen. Lyon in command of the Military Department of the West.

—Death of Stephen A. Douglas. He had given warm and efficient support to the Union cause and to President Lincoln.

—A Rebel flag captured at Iatan, Mo., and brought to Leavenworth by
Frank H. Drenning, Frank M. Tracy, Thos. Merrick, G. Mellen Lewis, Richard D. Lender, Wm. Smart, James Liddle, Emil Umfried, Mr. Voeth, Fred.
Amerine, Theo. Kroll, and Henry Laurenzier. These men were all from
the Elwood Guards, and the Leavenworth Steuben Guards, a German company, and all soldiers of the First Kansas. Drenning was struck by two
balls; two bullets entered Umfried's body and one his leg, and Voeth was
shot in the leg. It was the first Rebel flag captured, and created intense excitement, many prominent men opposing the act as illegal. A public meeting in Lawrence endorsed the act of the soldiers, and the Leavenworth
Conservative for sustaining them.

JUNE 4.—Adjournment of the Legislature.

—The name of Lykins county was changed by the Legislature to Miami; of Dorn to Neosho, and of Godfrey to Seward. An act was passed providing for the election of a District Attorney in each Judicial District, and an act calling an election for the permanent location of the State capital. The acts authorizing the issue of bonds created much discussion.

JUNE 4.— Organization of the First Kansas.

JUNE 10.— Captain Alfred Sully goes from Fort Leavenworth to St. Joseph, with a force of regulars, to organize a Home Guard.

JUNE 11.— Conway elected to Congress.

—The Second Kansas organized at Lawrence.

—Capt. Prince leaves Fort Leavenworth with regulars for Kansas City.

JUNE 13.— Seven companies of the First Kansas leave Leavenworth for Kansas City. The Second Kansas starts from Lawrence for Kansas City.

JUNE 13.— Sol. Miller publishes Legislative Sketches in the White Cloud Chief. This is one of them:

"W. F. M. &c. ARNY.— Mr. Arny is one of the Representatives from the Anderson District. He was born on the Peak of Teneriffe, in a very dry season;' and the soothsayers who were present upon the melancholy occasion, predicted that wherever he went drought would follow him. Such has been his experience in Kansas. His name originally was 'Nary,' and is supposed to have signified that 'nary' thing would grow where he cast his lot. Thus, Kansas has recently experienced the calamity of 'nary' corn, 'nary' wheat, 'nary' beans, 'nary' grass seed, 'nary' clothing for volunteers, etc. By some means, the letters forming his name have become transposed, and he is now called 'Arny.' His parents found great difficulty in deciding upon a name for him —they had so many from which to choose, and so many letters of the alphabet looked well in a name. They finally hit upon a plan to settle the question. The old man resolved to fashion all the letters of the alphabet out of potter's clay, then throw them against the side of the house, and as many of them as stuck to the wall, those letters should form initials of his name; but those that fell off, should be discarded. He carried out his design — it was a good day for the business, and nearly all the letters stuck!"

JUNE 13.— An article by R. C. Satterlee, in the Leavenworth Herald, on the Iatan flag matter, charging D. R. Anthony, of the Conservative, with falsehood, led to a shooting affray between the two men, in which Satterlee was killed. Anthony was tried before Judge McDowell, and acquitted.

JUNE 17.— Gov. Robinson calls for more troops.

—Gen. Lyon defeats Claib. Jackson at Booneville, Mo.

JUNE 20.— Second Kansas organized.

—The remainder of the First Kansas go to Kansas City.

JUNE 22.— Fall of a brick block at Wyandotte.

JUNE 24.— The First Kansas and regulars, under Maj. Samuel D. Sturgis, leave Kansas City for Springfield, Mo.

JUNE 25.— James H. Lane publishes a statement in the Conservative in which he says: "On the 20th instant I was duly appointed a Brigadier General in the volunteer force of the United States."

JUNE 26.— The Second Kansas leaves Kansas City.

JULY 2.— Treaty between the United States and the Delawares. Delaware lands pledged by the Leavenworth, Pawnee and Western R. R. Co. to secure its bonds.

JULY.— Surveyor General's office removed from Nebraska City to Leavenworth.

JULY 4.—The printers in the First and Second regiments issue a paper from a Rebel office, in Clinton, Mo.

JULY 7.—The Kansas troops, under Sturgis, meet Gen. Nathaniel Lyon, at Grand River.

JULY 9.—Gen. Fremont in command of the Western Department, at St. Louis.

JULY 12.—Organization of the Fifth Kansas begins.

JULY 12.—Senator Foot, of Vermont, presents the credentials of Frederick P. Stanton, from Gov. Robinson, as Senator from Kansas, in place of Lane. They are referred to the Judiciary Committee, after a statement from Lane that "this looks like an attempt to bury a man before he is dead." Stanton was appointed because Lane had accepted a commission as Brigadier General.

JULY 14.—O. E. Learnard, of the Fifth District, having resigned, Gov. Robinson appoints Robert M. Ruggles, of Emporia, Judge of that district.

JULY 15.—M. S. Adams, C. S. Lambdin, and Charles Starns, Commissioners to determine the location of the Penitentiary, take the oath of office, at Leavenworth. They bought a site in that county, November 25th.

JULY 15.—The Third Kansas organized; James Montgomery, Colonel.

JULY 18.—The first Overland coach arrives; seventeen days from San Francisco.

JULY 21.—Panic and retreat of the Union army from the Bull Run battle-field.

JULY 24.—Organization of the First Battery.

JULY 25.—By the vote of a Union meeting in Leavenworth, business houses close in time every day to allow all citizens time to drill.

AUGUST.—During the summer the State lands were selected by S. E. Hoffman, E. P. Bancroft and H. B. Denman. Their Report, dated January 14, 1862, is published in the State Documents. The following is copied from it:

"The following list will show the quantity of lands the State is entitled to under the provisions of the act of admission, and under the provisions of other acts of Congress:

"1st. In section 3d of the act of admission, 'sections number 16 and 36 in every township of public lands in the State are granted for the use of schools, and where either of said sections, or any part thereof, have been sold or otherwise disposed of, other lands equivalent thereto.' The quantity of land that would inure to the State under this provision, estimating the quantity from the number of surveyed townships taken from the records of the Surveyor General's office, would be, in the aggregate, 800,292 acres.

"2d. For the use and support of a State University, 46,080 acres.

"3d. For the purpose of completing or erecting public buildings at the seat of government, 6,400 acres.

"4th. Twelve salt springs, with six sections of land to each, 46,080 acres.

"5th. Under the act of Congress, approved September 4th, 1841, 500,000 acres.

"6th. Amount of land selected under the provisions of an act entitled 'An act to authorize settlers upon the 16th and 36th sections, who settle before the surveys of the public lands, to pre-empt their settlements,' approved February 26, A. D. 1859, to make up deficiencies where either townships or sections are fractional, 60,988 acres.

"Making the aggregate amount of lands to which the State is entitled under the provisions of the act of admission and other acts of Congress, 1,459,840 acres."

AUGUST 3.—Captain Sully takes Independence, Missouri.

AUGUST 9.—The Rebel John Matthews drives sixty Union families from the Neutral Lands.

AUGUST 10.—Battle of Wilson's Creek, ten miles south of Springfield, Missouri.

The following is copied from Greeley's Conflict:

"The First Missouri, First and Second Kansas, and First Iowa regiments, with Steele's battalion of Regulars, won immortal honor by the persistent and heroic gallantry with which they for hours maintained their ground against immense odds. The Rebels were repeatedly driven back in confusion, and the firing would be nearly or quite suspended for ten or twenty minutes; when, perceiving their decided superiority in numbers, since the rout and flight of Sigel's command, the Confederate officers would rally their men and bring them once more to the charge. Meantime, Gen. Lyon, who had led out his own little army to fight, against his own judgment, upon the representation of Gen. Sweeny that to abandon all southwest Missouri without a battle would be worse than a defeat, and who had evinced the most reckless bravery throughout, had been twice wounded, and had had his horse killed under him. The second ball struck him in the head, and seemed for the moment to confuse him. He walked a few paces to the rear, saying to Major Schofield, his Adjutant, 'I fear the day is lost;' to which Schofield responded, 'No, General; let us try them once more.' Major Sturgis offered him his own horse, which Lyon at first declined, but soon after mounted, and, bleeding from his two wounds, swung his hat in the air, and called upon the troops nearest him to prepare for a bayonet charge on the lines of the enemy. The Second Kansas rallied around him, but in a moment its brave Col. Mitchell fell severely wounded, and his soldiers cried out: 'We are ready to follow—who will lead us?' 'I will lead you!' replied Lyon; 'come on, brave men!' and at that moment a third bullet struck him in his breast, and he fell mortally wounded."

The fight opened at 5 A. M., and closed at 11:30. Gen. Ben. McCulloch's Report admits a loss of 265 killed, 800 wounded, and 30 missing. Our reports make our loss 223 killed, 721 wounded, and 292 missing. McCulloch says his force numbered 11,300, and 15 pieces of artillery. We had 5,000 troops in the beginning of the engagement, and less than 4,000 during the last four hours.

AUGUST 14.—Fremont declares martial law in Missouri.

AUGUST 17.—Gen. Lane fortifies at Camp Lincoln, Bourbon county.

AUGUST 18.—Organization of the Sixth Kansas begins.

AUGUST 31.—Gen. Fremont issues a General Order, from which the following is copied:

"The property, real and personal, of all persons in the State of Missouri who shall take up arms against the United States, or shall be directly proven to have taken active part with their enemies in the field, is declared to be confiscated to the public use; and their slaves, if any they have, are hereby declared free men."

SEPTEMBER.—George W. Kingsbury starts, at Junction City, the Smoky Hill and Republican Union.

—H. T. Geery starts the Frontier, at Junction City. Geo. E. Dummer soon succeeds him. In March, 1862, two companies of Kansas soldiers destroyed the office.

SEPTEMBER 2.—Battle of Dry Wood. Rebels under Rains; Union men under Cols. Montgomery, Jennison, and Johnson, and Capts. Moonlight, Ritchie, Williams and Stewart.

SEPTEMBER 3.—Platte River Bridge massacre. Barclay Coppoc and others were killed. Coppoc was with John Brown at Harper's Ferry, and was a Lieutenant in Montgomery's regiment when killed. His remains were given a military burial at Leavenworth, on the 6th. Nineteen persons were killed in this Rebel massacre.

SEPTEMBER 4.—St. Joseph in the hands of Rebels.

—Skirmish at Shelbina, Mo. Capt. J. R. McClure, of the Second Kansas, has his foot shot off.

SEPTEMBER 7.—Atchison in danger. Five companies go to her assistance from Jefferson, Jackson and Doniphan counties.

SEPTEMBER 8.— The First Kansas at Hannibal.

SEPTEMBER 11.— President Lincoln orders Gen. Fremont to so modify his Emancipation Order as to make it conform with the provisions of the act of Congress on the same subject.

SEPTEMBER 12.—Humboldt sacked by Rebels.

SEPTEMBER 15.— The Second Kansas arrives in Leavenworth. The regiment given a public reception on the 16th.

SEPTEMBER 20.—Siege of Lexington, Mo. Surrender of Cols. Mulligan, Peabody and Marshall, with 2,500 men, after four days' struggle.

SEPTEMBER 17.—Battle of Morristown, Mo. Col. H. P. Johnson, of Leavenworth, killed.

SEPTEMBER 20.—The John Brown song first sung in Leavenworth.

SEPTEMBER 21.—Col. Judson, of the Sixth Kansas, returns from the Neutral Lands, having routed the marauders and killed Matthews.

SEPTEMBER 23.—Lane takes Osceola and burns it.

SEPTEMBER 25.—Gen. Prentiss takes command at St. Joseph.

SEPTEMBER 26.—Vanity Fair, the New York humorous paper, publishes the following:

K. T. DID.

"We learn from Kansas Territory, that Captain Jennison, of border fame, has offered six hundred of his well-known 'Jayhawkers,' all bold riders and well mounted, to the Union cause; also, that other mounted regiments will shortly be organized. Good for K. T.!"—*Western Paper.*

From her borders, far away,
   Kansas blows a trumpet call,
Answered by the loud "hurrah!"
   Of her troopers, one and all.
"Knife and pistol, sword and spur!"
      Cries K. T.—
"Let my troopers all concur
   To the old flag, no demur—
      Follow me!"
Hence the song of jubilee,
Platyphillis from the tree,
High among the branches hid,
Sings all night so merrily—
      "K. T. did,
      . She did—she did!"

Thirty score JAYHAWKERS bold,
   Kansas men of strong renown,
Rally round the banner old,
   Casting each his gauntlet down.
"Good for Kansas," one and all
      Cry to her;
Riding to her trumpet call,
Blithe as to a festival,
      All concur!
Hence the revel and the glee,
As the chanter from the tree,
High among the branches hid,
Sings all night so merrily—
      "K. T. did!
      She did—she did!"

SEPTEMBER 30.—Lane's brigade arrives in Kansas City. Sturgis is there.

OCTOBER.—Organization of the Third Battery. Seventh Kansas organized.

OCTOBER 8.—Col. D. R. Anthony Provost Marshal of Kansas City.

OCTOBER 9.—First Annual Meeting of the State Temperance Society, at Topeka.

OCTOBER 11.—Sturgis and Lane leave for Springfield, Mo.

OCTOBER 16.—Humboldt burned by Rebels.

—The following petition led to a meeting of the Republican State Committee at Topeka, and the nomination of a State ticket:

"We, the undersigned citizens, suffering in common with others from the impotency or malice of the present State Executive, and earnestly desiring a State Government that will in a patriotic and energetic manner defend our people from invasion—knowing that by the plain and emphatic provisions of the State Constitution the term of our State officers expires on the first day of January, and that the legislative enactment continuing the State officers beyond that time is null and void, and that there is not sufficient time, before the election, to hold a Nominating Convention, do respectfully pray your honorable body to nominate a full State ticket of efficient Union men, without reference to their political antecedents—men who will conduct the State Government with reference to the good of the whole country, and not upon mere personal grounds."

The Committee made the following ticket and platform:

For Governor, George A. Crawford, of Bourbon county; for Lieutenant Governor, Joseph L. Speer, of Jefferson county; for Secretary of State, J. W. Robinson, of Riley county; for Attorney General, Samuel A. Stinson, of Leavenworth county; for Treasurer, H. R. Dutton, of Brown county; for Auditor, James R. McClure, of Davis county; for Superintendent of Public Instruction, H. D. Preston, of Osage county.

"*Resolved*, That the vigorous prosecution of the present war, the earnest and hearty support of the Administration in its efforts to crush out the rebellion, the maintenance of the Constitution, the enforcement of the laws, and the preservation of the Union, are the issues upon which these nominations are made."

OCTOBER 24.—Organization of the Ninth Kansas begins.

OCTOBER 25.—Gardner, Johnson county, sacked.

OCTOBER 30.—Settlers driven from Mine creek, Linn county.

NOVEMBER 2.—Lane and Sturgis reach Springfield.

—Gen. Fremont removed.

NOVEMBER 5.—Election. Vote on State Capital: Topeka, 7,996; Lawrence, 5,291; all others, 1,184. The State Board did not canvass the vote given for the George A. Crawford State ticket.

ATTORNEY GENERAL (to fill vacancy.)

Samuel A. Stinson received 11,971 votes, and is elected.

STATE TREASURER (to fill vacancy.)

H. R. Dutton.................................... 11,748 | J. H. Lane... 8

H. R. Dutton elected.

STATE SENATORS (to fill vacancies.)

SECOND DISTRICT—ATCHISON AND BROWN COUNTIES.

W. B. Barnett............. 1284 | John J. Ingalls............. 814 | George W. Bowman......... 705

W. B. Barnett and John J. Ingalls elected.

FOURTH DISTRICT—CLAY, RILEY, AND POTTAWATOMIE COUNTIES.

M. L. Essicks .... 454 | J. D. Adams............,........................... 18

M. L. Essicks elected.

SIXTH DISTRICT — SHAWNEE, JACKSON, JEFFERSON, AND OSAGE COUNTIES.

C. K. Holliday.. 980 | D. L. Lakin.. 230
J. C. Bartlett.. 884 | W. A. Shannon...................................... 1
C. K. Holliday elected.

EIGHTH DISTRICT — DOUGLAS, JOHNSON, AND WYANDOTTE COUNTIES.

John Speer.. 1357 | Robert S. Stevens.............................. 1687
James F. Legate .... 1141 | Charles G. Keeler................................ 1828
Charles G. Keeler and Robert S. Stevens elected.

NINTH DISTRICT — BOURBON, LINN, AND MIAMI COUNTIES.

Alonzo Curtis............... 856 | Thomas Roberts............ 849 | Horatio Knowles......... 830
Alonzo Curtis elected.

TENTH DISTRICT — ALLEN, ANDERSON, AND FRANKLIN COUNTIES.

Jacob G. Reese..................................... 442 | A. Stewart.. 383
Jacob G. Reese elected.

REPRESENTATIVES.

FIRST DISTRICT — DONIPHAN COUNTY.

Sol. Miller .... 670 | Franklin Grube.................................... 698
Ed. Russell.. 680 | Lyman Nash...................................... 212
Joseph Penny..................................... 534
Sol. Miller, Ed. Russell, Joseph Penny, and Franklin Grube elected.

SECOND DISTRICT — ATCHISON AND BROWN COUNTIES.

Thomas Murphy............................... 1247 | M. C. Willis.. 435
A. W. Johnson.................................. 1164 | P. H. Fay 231
R. A. Van Winkle.............................. 1139 | A. W. Robertson............................... 173
James B. Church................................... 28 | James D. Church................................ 922
C. H. McCauley.................................... 28 | O. H. McCauley.................................. 888
John Keen.. 513 | J. J. Patterson................................... 968
J. B. Reynolds..................................... 450 | S. B. Davis.. 478
F. Roache... 453
Thomas Murphy, A. W. Johnson, R. A. Van Winkle, Jas. D. Church, O. H. McCauley, and J. J. Patterson elected.

THIRD DISTRICT — NEMAHA, WASHINGTON, AND MARSHALL COUNTIES.

Harrison Foster................................... 427 | N. J. Leland.. 276
J. C. Smith.. 94 | S. F. Snider.. 26
F. P. Baker.. 353 | John E. Smith 80
D. C. Auld 168
Harrison Foster and F. P. Baker elected.

FOURTH DISTRICT — CLAY, RILEY, AND POTTAWATOMIE COUNTIES.

I. T. Goodnow..................................... 463 | Welcome Wells................................... 448
Davies Wilson .... 510 | O. J. Grover...................................... 505
I. T. Goodnow, Davies Wilson, Welcome Wells, and O. J. Grover elected.

FIFTH DISTRICT — DICKINSON, DAVIS, AND WABAUNSEE COUNTIES.

A. G. Robinson................................... 228 | J. B. Ingersoll.................................... 272
Geo. Montague................................... 189 | A. C. Pierce...................................... 278
Geo. Freeman..................................... 181 | T. F. Hersey...................................... 317
J. B. Ingersoll, T. F. Hersey, and A. C. Pierce elected.

SIXTH DISTRICT—SHAWNEE, JEFFERSON, JACKSON, AND OSAGE COUNTIES.

H. W. Martin	1562	J. M. Huber	1752
Golden Silvers	1533	Jeremiah Sabin	1420
P. E. Havens	1630	J. B. Parrott	199
C. H. Welch	1519	Jesse Hendrickson	183
M. Anderson	1539	J. W. Mann	154
A. Spaulding	1559		

H. W. Martin, Golden Silvers, P. E. Havens, C. H. Welch, M. Anderson, A. Spaulding, J. M. Huber, and Jeremiah Sabin elected.

SEVENTH DISTRICT—LEAVENWORTH COUNTY.

M. S. Adams	1236	Charles Starns	1209
T. J. Logan	1041	John P. Huesgen	1078
G. W. Gardiner	770	B. B. Moore	1067
E. McCrillus	1195	Thos. O'Guartney	1128
Geo. Gosling	1076	Chas. H. Grover	1106
James Medill	1189	John P. Mitchell	984
Geo. W. Baird	1039	J. H. Canady	1004
Thos. Carney	1307	John McCarthy	1232
Jas. A. McGonigle	1297		

M. S. Adams, E. McCrillus, Jas. Medill, Thos. Carney, Jas. A. McGonigle, Chas. Starns, Thos. O'Guartney, Chas. H. Grover, and John McCarthy elected.

EIGHTH DISTRICT—DOUGLAS, JOHNSON, AND WYANDOTTE COUNTIES.

Sidney Clarke	1367	B. W. Hartley	2515
R. L. Williams	1679	W. M. Shean	2692
A. Thoman	2685	Jas. McGrew	2710
Samuel Black	2677	W. W. Dickinson	2204
Chauncey L. Steel	2594	Geo. W. Smith	1424
E. G. Macy	2554	Geo. W. Benum	620
J. L. Jones	2554	Eli McKee	475
D. T. Mitchell	2693	John Giffen	485
W. H. M. Fishback	2498	L. D. Williams	386

G. W. Smith, W. W. Dickinson, Jas. McGrew, W. M. Shean, B. W. Hartley, W. H. M. Fishback, D. T. Mitchell, J. L. Jones, R. L. Williams, E. G. Macy, Chauncey L. Steel, Samuel Black, and A. Thoman elected.

NINTH DISTRICT—BOURBON, LINN, AND MIAMI COUNTIES.

James C. Marshall	481	George A. Reynolds	874
J. B. McGrew	468	Eli G. Jewell	864
Josiah Lamb	482	William T. Jones	865
W. R. Wagstaff	746	F. Muse	381
Henderson Rice	862	George E. Dennison	372
William Carr	837	A. Stark	334

William T. Jones, James C. Marshall, J. B. McGrew, Josiah Lamb, William R. Wagstaff, Henderson Rice, William Carr, George A. Reynolds, and Eli G. Jewell elected.

TENTH DISTRICT—ALLEN, ANDERSON, AND FRANKLIN COUNTIES.

Jacob A. Marcell	952	T. B. Killen	560
D. M. Valentine	830	J. N. Phillips	261
W. H. McClure	597	J. S. Pile	312
J. B. Lowrie	399	Mathew Porter	252
—— Lowrie	135	John T. Lanter	220
C. S. Clark	781		

Jacob A. Marcell, D. M. Valentine, W. H. McClure, J. B. Lowrie, C. S. Clark, and T. P. Killen elected.

ELEVENTH DISTRICT — WOODSON AND MADISON COUNTIES.

Benjamin F. Van Horn........................ 112 | A. K. Hanks.. 14
E. J. Brown.. 123 |
Benjamin F. Van Horn and E. J. Brown elected.

TWELFTH DISTRICT — OSAGE, COFFEY, AND BRECKINRIDGE COUNTIES.

O. H. Sheldon................................... 865 | Watson Foster.................................... 383
J. H. Leard....................................... 654 | Charles Morse.................................... 382
P. B. Plumb...................................... 591 | A. G. Miller...................................... 373
P. B. Maxson.................................... 581 | C. V. Eskridge.................................... 539
J. Jenks.. 211 | H. W. Watrous.................................... 332
F. W. Potter..................................... 592 |

O. H. Sheldon, J. H. Leard, P. B. Plumb, P. B. Maxson, F. W. Potter, and C. V. Eskridge elected.

THIRTEENTH DISTRICT — MORRIS, BUTLER, AND CHASE COUNTIES.

H. S. Hunt....................................... 106 | M. R. Leonard 189
C. Columbia.................................... 303 | A. R. Page.. 92
C. Columbia and M. R. Leonard elected.

FOURTEENTH DISTRICT — ARAPAHOE, GODFREY, GREENWOOD, HUNTER, WILSON, DORN, M'GEE, AND SALINE COUNTIES.

Horace L. Jones, 24. Horace L. Jones elected.

JUDGE (to fill vacancy).

FIFTH JUDICIAL DISTRICT — COFFEY, CHASE, BRECKINRIDGE, MORRIS, MADISON, AND OSAGE COUNTIES.

R. M. Ruggles..................................... 965 | W. R. Saunders.................................... 589
R. M. Ruggles elected.

DISTRICT ATTORNEYS.

FIRST JUDICIAL DISTRICT — WYANDOTTE, JACKSON, JEFFERSON, AND LEAVENWORTH COUNTIES.

J. C. Douglass.................................... 1665 | Thomas P. Fenlon.............................. 1966
Thomas P. Fenlon elected.

SECOND JUDICIAL DISTRICT — ATCHISON, DONIPHAN, BROWN, NEMAHA, AND MARSHALL COUNTIES.

Joseph F. Babbitt, 2,376. Joseph F. Babbitt elected.

THIRD JUDICIAL DISTRICT — CLAY, DAVIS, RILEY, WABAUNSEE, POTTAWATOMIE, DICKINSON, SHAWNEE, AND SALINE COUNTIES.

A. H. Case... 732 | W. P. Douthitt.................................... 240
L. McArthur...................................... 663 |
A. H. Case elected.

FOURTH DISTRICT — ANDERSON, ALLEN, BOURBON, DOUGLAS, LINN, MIAMI, JOHNSON, AND FRANKLIN COUNTIES.

Samuel A. Riggs................................. 2389 | W. F. Woodworth 1703
Samuel A. Riggs elected.

FIFTH DISTRICT — COFFEY, CHASE, BRECKINRIDGE, MORRIS, MADISON, BUTLER, WOODSON, AND OSAGE COUNTIES.

George H. Lillie......... 878 | Silas Fearl.................. 520 | P. B. Plumb.............. 49
George H. Lillie elected.

AMENDMENT TO CONSTITUTION AND BANKING LAW.

COUNTIES.	For Bank-ing Law...	Ag'st Bank-ing Law...	COUNTIES.	For Amend't to Sec. 7, Ar. 13, Const.....	Ag'st Am'd't to Sec. 7, Ar. 13, Const.....
Allen	....	....	Allen	....	....
Anderson	....	....	Anderson	....	....
Atchison	533	287	Atchison	558	276
Brown.......................	226	16	Brown	235	7
Butler.......................	8	....	Butler.......................	8	....
Breckinridge.............	218	165	Bourbon	86	33
Bourbon....................	93	33	Breckinridge.............	200	134
Chase........................	93	18	Chase........................	75	23
Coffey.......................	97	119	Coffey	95	8
Cherokee	....	....	Cherokee	....	....
Davis	....	....	Davis	....	....
Dickinson..................	4	63	Dickinson	239	64
Doniphan..................	278	123	Doniphan..................	239	71
Douglas....................	128	187	Douglas....................	229	180
Franklin....................	26	41	Franklin	220	79
Jackson.....................	88	173	Jackson.....................	118	97
Jefferson...................	....	....	Jefferson...................	....	....
Johnson	386	56	Johnson	379	14
Linn..........................	274	90	Linn..........................	314	58
Leavenworth.............	1,221	276	Leavenworth.............	139	1,324
Miami.......................	156	50	Miami	95	65
Madison....................	28	7	Madison....................	25	3
Morris.......................	49	46	Morris	36	50
Marshall...................	88	50	Marshall...................	83	90
Nemaha.....................	178	218	Nemaha	212	169
Osage	38	95	Osage	60	61
Riley	87	87	Riley	83	91
Pottawatomie............	7	177	Pottawatomie............	49	91
Shawnee....................	179	312	Shawnee....................	154	246
Saline.......................	....	33	Saline	1	13
Wabaunsee	89	31	Wabaunsee	75	43
Wyandotte	99	43	Washington...............	13	12
Washington	22	....	Wyandotte	103	36
Woodson....................	62	7	Woodson	53	7
Total..................	**4,655**	**2,807**	**Total**..................	**3,733**	**3,343**

The amendment made to the Constitution is as follows:

"No banking institution shall issue circulating notes of a less denomination than one dollar."

NOVEMBER 8.—D. R. Anthony sells the Conservative to D. W. Wilder. On the 16th of January, 1862, Mathew Weightman became a partner in its publication.

NOVEMBER 11.—General Halleck in command at St. Louis.

NOVEMBER 12.—Creation of the Department of Kansas, with Major General David Hunter in command.

NOVEMBER 15.—Return of the Kansas Brigade to Fort Scott.

—Treaty by which the Pottawatomies are to dispose of their land to the Leavenworth, Pawnee and Western Railroad Company.

NOVEMBER 19.—The Missouri Rebel Legislature pass an Ordinance of Secession.

NOVEMBER 25.—General Hunter arrives at Fort Leavenworth.

NOVEMBER 30.—General James W. Denver ordered to report at Fort Scott.

DECEMBER 6.—The Lawrence Republican says:

"In the following table we give the vote on all the candidates for State officers. The candidates voted for, as all our readers will recollect, are as follows: For Governor, George A. Crawford; for Lieutenant Governor, Joseph L. Speer; for Secretary of State,

18

J. W. Robinson; for Treasurer, H. R. Dutton; for Auditor, J. R. McClure; for Attorney General, S. A. Stinson; for Superintendent of Public Instruction, H. D. Preston.

Counties.	Crawford...	Speer...	Robinson...	Stinson...	Dutton...	Preston...	McClure...
Allen	208	205	207	209	209	208	205
Douglas *							
Dickinson	83	83	83	82	83	83	
Chase	83	73	72	132	133	68	68
Atchison *							
Coffey	532	527	529	533	530	530	531
Breckinridge	55	55	55			56	55
Morris	80	78	78			83	
Miami	274	284	286	286	291	288	287
Madison	58	58	58	58	58	58	58
Johnson	392	353	357	417	514	357	366
Riley	245	253	229	244	241		235
Saline	12	12	12	12	12	12	11
Linn	383	387	383	372	383	386	383
Wabaunsee	93	93	91	90	80	88	89
Brown	22	21	21			21	21
Nemaha	15	14	14			11	2
Jefferson *							
Jackson	207	211	216	224	208	222	221
Washington	44	45	45	45	45	45	45
Doniphan	311	285	237	625	652	258	252
Franklin	263	265	265	202	202	294	264
Butler *							
Pottawatomie	270	269	269	270	273	273	250
Davis	211	211	202	213	210	212	208
Woodson	78	74	74	77	80	74	74
Wyandotte	347	344	349	390	391	348	341
Osage	102	122	125	111	101	128	124
Leavenworth *							
Marshall	67	81	81	54	53	79	81
Cherokee	11	11	11	11	11	11	11
Bourbon	177	185	182	69	69	186	184
Anderson	195	191	181	191	191	191	191
Shawnee	608	595	617	676	677	622	594

* No returns from the above five counties.

"In the above table, it will be observed, George A. Crawford had 5,436 votes, with Atchison, Douglas, Leavenworth and Jefferson unreturned—the canvassers refusing to recognize the vote. Douglas county, which was not counted by the judges, gives Crawford 551 votes; Lawrence counted would add at least 200 to that. Let us estimate the unreturned counties, and see how the vote stands:

Vote returned, as per table	5,436	Atchison (estimated)	400
Douglas, as returned by township judges, except Lawrence	551	Leavenworth (estimated)	750
		Jefferson (estimated)	100
Lawrence (estimated)	200		
		Total	7,437

"The entire vote on the State Capital is 14,461. This would show that Crawford received 200 more than half the votes cast even upon the Capital question, which called out a very large vote."

DECEMBER 7.—Carl Horne sentenced to be hanged in Leavenworth— the first capital conviction in Kansas.

DECEMBER 11.—Rebel raid on Potosi, Linn county.

DECEMBER 14.—Major H. H. Williams, of the Third Kansas, takes Papinsville and Butler, Missouri.

DECEMBER 17.—General Lane receives a new military appointment.

DECEMBER 20.—The Eighth Kansas at Westport, Missouri. One hundred contrabands, freed by Col. Anthony, at Independence, arrive at Leavenworth in gay procession.

DECEMBER 31.—First Kansas ordered to Kansas City and Fort Scott.

DECEMBER 31.—The State printing for the coming year has been given out to the following persons:

Laws and Journals—J. H. Bennet, of Grasshopper Falls.

Documents and Blanks—Trask & Lowman, of Lawrence.

Legislative Printing—J. F. Cummings.

The binding was let to John Dodsworth and J. H. Bennet.

—The following facts relating to Kansas regiments are copied from the Report printed while Thomas J. Anderson was Adjutant General. Volume I contains 1,116 pages; volume II, 1,146 pages. The compilation was made from the original rolls by Samuel S. McFadden and Henry L. Isbell, who had both been soldiers in the Second Kansas. The volumes were printed by W. S. Burke, at Leavenworth, in 1867.

FIRST REGIMENT KANSAS VOLUNTEERS—INFANTRY.

Name and Rank.	Date of Muster.	Remarks.
COLONEL.		
George W. Deitzler........	May 28, 1861	Wounded in action, August 10, 1861, at Wilson's Creek, Mo.; prom. Brig. Gen., Nov. 29, 1862.
William Y. Roberts......	June 15, 1863	Mustered out with regiment, June 17, 1864.
LIEUT. COLONEL.		
Oscar E. Learnard.........	May 28, 1861	Resigned, July 25, 1862.
Otto M. Tennison........	Aug. 16, 1862	Dismissed, May 10, 1863.
Newell W. Spicer	June 15, 1863	Mustered out with regiment.
MAJOR.		
John A. Halderman......	May 28, 1861	Resigned, April 30, 1862.
William Y. Roberts	May 12, 1862	Promoted Colonel, June 15, 1863.
James Ketner..............	June 19, 1863	Mustered out with regiment.
ADJUTANT.		
Edwin S. Nash	June 1, 1861	Promoted Captain Co. G, June 1, 1862.
John A. Henry..............	Nov. 21, 1862	Assigned to Co. B, Veteran Batt., May 26, 1864.
QUARTERMASTER.		
George H. Chapin........	June 3, 1861	Resigned, October 25, 1861.
Charles F. Garrett........	....	Promoted Captain and A. Q. M., April 26, 1862.
John H. W. Mills..........	May 12, 1862	Promoted Captain and A. C. S., Feb. 19, 1863.
Martin H. Dickenson....	July 1, 1863	Mustered out with regiment.
SURGEON.		
George E. Budington.....	July 24, 1861	Resigned, March 12, 1863.
Mahlon Bailey..............	June 1, 1863	Mustered out with the regiment.
ASST. SURGEON.		
Samuel D. Smith..........	June 1, 1861	Resigned, April 16, 1862.
Mahlon Bailey	May 27, 1862	Promoted Surgeon, June 1, 1863.
Charles King...............	....	Resigned, December 10, 1862.
Joseph Speck...............	June 3, 1863	Assigned to Veteran Batt., May 28, 1864; mustered out, August 30, 1865.
CHAPLAIN.		
Ephraim Nute, jr.........	June 10, 1861	Mustered out with regiment.

COMPANY A.

Name and Rank.	Date of Muster.	Remarks.
CAPTAIN.		
Bernard P. Chenoweth..	May 30, 1861	Mustered out with regiment.
FIRST LIEUT.		
Peter A. Josephs	May 30, 1861	Resigned, August 14, 1861.
Charles O. Smith	Sept. 1, 1861	Resigned, October 29, 1862.
Robert Tracy	Feb. 1, 1863	Mustered out with regiment.
SECOND LIEUT.		
Charles O. Smith............	June 3, 1861	Promoted First Lieutenant, September 1, 1861.
Frank M. Tracy.............	Sept. 1, 1861	Promoted First Lieutenant Co. I, April 12, '62.
Robert Tracy	May 30, 1862	Promoted First Lieutenant, February 1, 1863.
Christopher H. Ford......	Nov. 17, 1863	Mustered out with regiment.

COMPANY B.

Name and Rank.	Date of Muster.	Remarks.
CAPTAIN.		
William Y. Roberts......	May 28, 1861	Promoted Major, May 12, 1862.
John P. Alden..............	May 12, 1862	Promoted Captain and A. C. S. Vols., July 2, '63.
Michael Mack...............	Feb. 21, 1864	Assigned to Co. B, Veteran Battalion.
FIRST LIEUT.		
John P. Alden............'..	May 28, 1861	Wounded in action, Aug. 10, 1861, Wilson's C'k, Mo.; promoted Captain, May 12, 1862.
Michael Mack...............	July 27, 1862	Promoted Captain, February 21, 1864.
SECOND LIEUT.		
John W. Dyer..............	June 8, 1861	Killed in action, Aug. 10, 1861, Wilson's Creek.
Hubbard H. Sawyer......	Sept. 1, 1861	Resigned, July 5, 1862.
Aaron W. Merrill.........	July 8, 1862	Mustered out with regiment.

COMPANY C.

Name and Rank.	Date of Muster.	Remarks.
CAPTAIN.		
Peter McFarland..........	May 29, 1861	Severely wounded, August 10, 1861, Wilson's Creek; resigned, December 11, 1862.
James Reed..................	Jan. 23, 1863	Mustered out with regiment.
FIRST LIEUT.		
James Phillips	May 29, 1861	Resigned, December 5, 1861.
Mathew Malone...........	Dec. 1, 1861	Resigned, February 14, 1862.
James Reed..................	Mar. 1, 1862	Promoted Captain, January 23, 1863.
Edward Reiley..............	Nov. 20, 1863	Mustered out with regiment.
SECOND LIEUT.		
Mathew Malone...........	May 29, 1861	Promoted First Lieutenant, December 1, 1861.
James Reed..................	Dec. 4, 1861	Promoted First Lieutenant, March 1, 1862.
Edward Reiley..............	May 10, 1862	Promoted First Lieutenant, November 20, '63.

COMPANY D.

Name and Rank.	Date of Muster.	Remarks.
CAPTAIN.		
Frank B. Swift..............	June 3, 1861	Wounded in action, Aug. 10, 1861, Wilson's C'k; resigned May 26, 1862.
Newell W. Spicer..........	May 26, 1862	Promoted Lieutenant Colonel, June 1, 1863.
Milton Kennedy...........	Dec. 8, 1863	Assigned to Veteran Company D, June 16, 1864.
FIRST LIEUT.		
Newell W. Spicer..........	June 3, 1861	Promoted Captain, May 26, 1862.
John W. Stone..............	May 26, 1862	Resigned, January 19, 1863
Milton Kennedy...........	April 13, 1863	Promoted Captain, December 8, 1863.
William H. Earl	Dec. 8, 1863	Assigned to Veteran Company D, June 16, 1864.
SECOND LIEUT.		
Caleb S. Pratt.............	June 3, 1861	Killed in action, Aug. 10, 1861, Wilson's Creek.
John W. Stone	Sept. 12, 1861	Promoted First Lieutenant, May 26, 1862.
Milton Kennedy...........	May 26, 1862	Promoted First Lieutenant, April 13, 1863.
William H. Earl.............	April 13, 1863	Promoted First Lieutenant, December 8, 1863.

COMPANY E.

Name and Rank.	Date of Muster.	Remarks.
CAPTAIN.		
Powell Clayton	May 29, 1861	Promoted Lieut. Col. Fifth Kas. Cav., Feb. 1, '62.
Lewis Stafford...............	Feb. 1, 1862	Accidentally killed, Young's Pt., La., Jan. 31, '63.
George M. Reeder.........	May 1, 1863	Resigned, October 8, 1863.
William C. Barnes	Jan. 18, 1864	Mustered out with regiment.
FIRST LIEUT.		
Lewis Stafford	May 29, 1861	Promoted Captain, February 1, 1862.
Alexander C. Soley	Feb. 1, 1862	Resigned, April 28, 1862.
George M. Reeder.........	May 1, 1862	Promoted Captain, May 1, 1863.
James H. Cowan	May 1, 1863	Resigned, August 1, 1863.
William C. Barnes.........	Dec. 10, 1863	Promoted Captain, January 17, 1864.
James Fitzpatrick.........	Jan. 18, 1864	Killed—shot by Adjutant Henry, May 21, 1864, Vicksburg, Miss.
SECOND LIEUT.		
Azel W. Spaulding	June 5, 1861	Resigned, October 31, 1861.
Alexander C. Soley	Nov. 12, 1861	Promoted First Lieutenant, February 1, 1862.
Lindsay Knapp.............	Feb. 1, 1862	Resigned, April 28, 1862.
James H. Cowan...........	April 29, 1862	Promoted First Lieutenant, May 1, 1863.
William C. Barnes	May 1, 1863	Promoted First Lieut., Dec. 10, 1863; wounded in action, Aug. 10, 1861, Wilson's Creek.

COMPANY F.

Name and Rank.	Date of Muster.	Remarks.
CAPTAIN.		
Samuel Walker.............	June 1, 1861	Promoted Major Fifth Kas. Cav., May 24, 1862.
Theron Tucker...........	May 26, 1852	Wounded in action, Feb. 10, 1863, near Lake Providence, La.; must'd out with regiment.
FIRST LIEUT.		
Levant L. Jones............	June 1, 1861	Killed in action, Aug. 10, 1861, Wilson's Creek.
Theron Tucker	Aug. 10, 1861	Promoted Captain, May 26, 1862.
Joseph Gilliford............	May 26, 1862	Resigned, June 14, 1862.
Shubal P. Thompson.....	July 1, 1862	Promoted Captain 16th Kas. Cav., Jan. 13, 1864.
Frederick W. Paetz......	Apr. 17, 1864	Wounded, Aug. 10, 1861, Wilson's Crk., Mo., and May, 1863, Lake Providence, La.; mustered out with regiment.
SECOND LIEUT.		
Edwin S. Nash.............	June 1, 1861	Promoted First Lieut. and Adjt., June 1, 1861.
Theron Tucker	June 1, 1861	Promoted First Lieutenant, August 10, 1861.
Joseph Gilliford............	Sept. 1, 1861	Promoted First Lieutenant, May 26, 1862.
Shubal P. Thompson.....	May 26, 1862	Promoted First Lieutenant, July 1, 1862.
Frederick W. Paetz......	Aug. 10, 1862	Promoted First Lieutenant, April 17, 1864.

COMPANY G.

Name and Rank.	Date of Muster.	Remarks.
CAPTAIN.		
Job B. Stockton............	May 23, 1861	Resigned, July 15, 1862.
Ed. S. Nash.................	Nov. 21, 1862	Resigned, March 17, 1863.
Abraham Funk............	June 25, 1863	Mustered out with regiment.
FIRST LIEUT.		
James Ketner..............	May 23, 1861	Promoted Captain Co. K, August 19, 1861.
Hugh D. McCarty........	Oct. 1, 1861	Wounded in action, August 10, 1861, Wilson's Creek, Mo.; resigned July 15, 1862.
Abraham Funk...........	July 30, 1862	Promoted Captain, June 25, 1863.
Alonzo J. Brown.........	June 25, 1863	W. in action —; prom. Capt. Co. H, July 8, 1863.
Calvin G. Beach...........	July 8, 1863	Mustered out with regiment, June 17, 1864.
SECOND LIEUT.		
Hugh D. McCarty........	May 29, 1861	Promoted First Lieutenant, October 1, 1861.
Abraham Funk...........	Oct. 1, 1861	Promoted First Lieutenant, July 30, 1862.
Alonzo J. Brown.........	July 30, 1862	Promoted First Lieutenant, May 25, 1863.
Joseph Pennock............	May 30, 1863	Mustered out with regiment, June 17, 1864.

COMPANY H.

Name and Rank.	Date of Muster.	Remarks.
CAPTAIN.		
Daniel McCook............	May 31, 1861	Resigned, November 10, 1861.
Otto M. Tennison..........	Nov. 10, 1861	Promoted Lieutenant Colonel, Aug. 16, 1862.
Sylvester T. Smith........	Oct. 24, 1862	Resigned, February 27, 1863.
Henry M. Howard	Mar. 31, 1863	Dismissed, May 31, 1863, per special order War Dept., Adjt. General's Office, May 18, 1863.
Alonzo J. Brown............	July 11, 1863	Resigned, Mar. 21, 1864, to accept appointment in Veteran Reserve Corps.
Curtis M. Benton..........	Apr. 27, 1864	Mustered out with regiment, June 16, 1864.
FIRST LIEUT.		
James A. McGonigle......	May 31, 1861	Resigned, October 3, 1861.
Otto M. Tennison..........	Oct. 3, 1861	Promoted Captain, November 10, 1861.
Michael Bransfield........	Nov. 10, 1861	Resigned, May 1, 1862.
Henry M Howard.........	May 1, 1862	Promoted Captain, March 31, 1863.
George M. Dilworth......	Mar. 31, 1863	Killed in action, May 10, 1863, at Pinhook, La.
Curtis M. Benton..........	July 11, 1863	Promoted Captain, April 27, 1864.
SECOND LIEUT.		
Michael Bransfield........	June 5, 1861	Promoted First Lieutenant, Nov. 10, 1861.
Sylvester T. Smith........	Feb. 11, 1862	Promoted Captain, October 24, 1862.
George M. Dilworth......	Aug. 16, 1862	Promoted First Lieutenant, March 31, 1863.
Martin H. Dickenson....	May 1, 1863	Prom. First Lt. and Reg. Qr. Mastr., July 1, '63.

COMPANY I.

Name and Rank.	Date of Muster.	Remarks.
CAPTAIN.		
Gustavus Zesch............	May 27, 1861	Mustered out with regiment.
FIRST LIEUT.		
Henry Sarstedt............	May 27, 1861	Resigned, February 2, 1862.
Emil Umfried............	Feb. 2, 1862	Resigned, April 12, 1862.
Frank M. Tracy............	April 12, 1862	Resigned, October 29, 1862.
Frederick Hubert........	Oct. 29, 1862	Mustered out with regiment.
SECOND LIEUT.		
Emil Umfried............	May 27, 1861	Promoted First Lieutenant, February 2, 1862.
Frederick Hubert........	May 1, 1862	Promoted First Lieutenant, October 29, 1862.
Francis Becker............	Oct. 29, 1862	Killed in action, June 9, 1863, Lake Provid., La.

COMPANY K.

Name and Rank.	Date of Muster.	Remarks.
CAPTAIN.		
George H. Fairchild......	May 31, 1861	Resigned, August 9, 1861.
James Ketner............	Sept. 1, 1861	Promoted Major, June 19, 1863.
John W. Murphy..........	June 27, 1863	Mustered out with regiment.
FIRST LIEUT.		
Camille Aguiel............	May 31, 1861	Killed in action, Aug. 10, 1861,Wilson's Ck., Mo.
Rinaldo A. Barker........	Sept. 1, 1861	Resigned, April 1, 1862, Lawrence, Kansas.
Jerome G. Miner..........	May 1, '62	Killed in action, Oct. 5, 1862, near Corinth, Miss.
John W. Murphy..........	Oct. 28, 1862	Promoted Captain, June 27, 1863.
George W. Hutt............	June 27, 1863	Mustered out with regiment.
SECOND LIEUT.		
Rinaldo A. Barker........	May 31, 1861	Prom. First Lieut., Sept. 1,'61 ; wounded in act'n in head, foot, left hand, Aug. 10, '61,Wils. Ck.
Jerome G. Miner..........	Oct. 1, 1861	Promoted First Lieutenant, May 1, 1862.
John W. Murphy..........	May 1, 1862	Promoted First Lieutenant, October 28, 1862.
George W. Hutt............	Oct. 28, 1862	Promoted First Lieutenant, June 27, 1863.
Joseph W. Martin........	July 10, 1863	Transferred to Co. B, Vet. Bat., May 29, 1864.

NEW COMPANY B—VETERAN MOUNTED INFANTRY.

Name and Rank.	Date of Muster.	Remarks.
CAPTAIN.		
Michael H. Mack........	Feb. 21, 1864	Resigned, July 19, 1864.
John A. Henry............	Aug. 25, 1865	Mustered out, Aug. 30, 1865, Lit. Rk., Ark., per S. O. No. 2, Hdqrs. Dept. La. & Tx., July 19,1865.
FIRST LIEUT.		
John A. Henry	Nov. 21, 1862	Promoted Captain, August 25, 1865.
SECOND LIEUT.		
Joseph W. Martin........	July 10, 1863	Killed at Atchison, Kas., Nov. 8, 1864, while absent on sick leave.
Van Buren Rice............	Feb. 1, 1865	Mustered out, August 30, 1865, Little Rock, Ark.

NEW COMPANY D—VETERAN MOUNTED INFANTRY.

Name and Rank.	Date of Muster.	Remarks.
CAPTAIN.		
Milton Kennedy..........	Dec. 8, 1863	Mustered out, August 30, 1865, Little Rock, Ark.
FIRST LIEUT.		
William H. Earl............	Dec. 8, 1863	Resigned April 26, 1865.
John McCoach..............	July 1, 1865	Mustered out, August 30, 1865, Little Rock, Ark.
SECOND LIEUT.		
John A. Henry............	July 1, 1865	Promoted Captain Veteran Co. B, Aug. 25, 1865.

The following is a list of the battles and skirmishes in which the First Kansas Volunteer Infantry were, in whole or in part, engaged:

Dug Springs, Mo., August 3, 1861; Wilson's Creek, August 10, 1861; Brownsville, Tenn., September, 1862; Trenton, Tenn., September 17, 1862;

Chewalla, Miss., October 5, 1862; Tuscumbia Mount, Miss., October 5, 1862; Lumpkin's Mills, Miss., December, 1862; Tallahatchie, Miss., December, 1862; Old River, La., February 10, 1863; Hood's Lane, La., February 10, 1863; Black Bayou, La., February 10, 1863; near Lake Providence, La., Feb. 10, 1863; Caledonia, La., May 10, 1863; Pinhook, La., May 10, 1863; Bayou Tensas, La., May 17, 1863; Holly Brook, La., June 9, 1863; Lake Providence, La., June 9, 1863; Lake Providence, June 29, 1863; Baxter's Bayou, La., June 9, 1863; Cross Bayou, La., September 14, 1863; Alexandria, La., September 20, 1863; Big Black river, Miss., October 8, 1863; Tallahatchie, Miss., November 30, 1863; Columbia, Ark., June 2, 1864; Atchafaluya Bayou, Ark., October 4, 1864; Salem, Miss.; Richmond, La.; Bayou Macon, La.; Yazoo City, Miss.; Benton, Miss.

SECOND REGIMENT KANSAS VOLUNTEERS—INFANTRY.

Name and Rank.	Date of Muster.	Remarks.
COLONEL. Robert B. Mitchell.........	June 20, 1862	Retained in service and transferred to the Second Kansas Volunteer Cavalry.
LIEUT. COLONEL. Charles W. Blair...........	June 20, 1861	Resigned, October 9, 1861.
MAJOR. William F. Cloud..........	June 20, 1861	Retained in service and transferred to the Second Kansas Cavalry.
ADJUTANT Edward D. Thompson...	June 20, 1861	Mustered out with regiment October 31, 1861.
QUARTERMASTER. Shaler W. Eldridge........	June 20, 1861	Mustered out with regiment.
SURGEON. Aquila B. Massey..........	June 20, 1861	Absent on detached service at time of muster-out of regiment.
ASSISTANT SURGEON. Eliphalet L. Pattee........	June 20, 1861	Absent on detached service at time of muster-out of regiment.
CHAPLAIN. Randolph C. Brant........	June 20, 1861	Mustered out with regiment.

COMPANY A.

Name and Rank.	Date of Muster.	Remarks.
CAPTAIN. Leonard W. Hone.........	June 20, 1861	Mustered out with regiment, October 31, 1861.
FIRST LIEUT. Thomas Fulton	June 20, 1861	Mustered out with reg't, Oct. 31, '61; wounded in action Aug. 10, 1861, at Wilson's Creek, Mo.
SECOND LIEUT. Luther H. Wentworth...	June 20, 1861	Mustered out with reg't Oct. 31, 1861; wounded in action Aug. 10, '61, at Wilson's Creek, Mo.
THIRD LIEUT. James C. French............	June 20, 1861	Disch'd by order of Gen. Fremont, Aug. 31, '61.

COMPANY B.

Name and Rank.	Date of Muster.	Remarks.
CAPTAIN. James R. McClure.........	June 20, 1861	Mustered out with reg't, Oct. 31, 1861; wounded in action, September 4, 1861, at Shelbina, Mo.
FIRST LIEUT. Anson R. Spinner..........	June 20, 1861	Resigned, August 31, 1861.
SECOND LIEUT. James P. Downer..........	June 20, 1861	Mustered out with regiment, October 31, 1861; promoted First Lieutenant, Sept. 1, 1861.
Edward C. D. Lines........	Aug. 31, 1861	Mustered out with regiment, October 31, 1861.
THIRD LIEUT. Edward C. D. Lines........	June 20, 1861	Promoted Second Lieut., Aug. 31, 1861; wounded in action, Aug. 10, 1861, at Wilson's Creek, Mo.

COMPANY C.

Name and Rank.	Date of Muster.	Remarks.
CAPTAIN. Simeon F. Hill.............	June 20, 1861	Mustered out, October 31, 1861.
FIRST LIEUT. James W. Parmeter.......	June 20, 1861	Mustered out with regiment, October 31, 1861.
SECOND LIEUT. Warren Kimball...........	June 20, 1861	Resigned, July 20, 1861.
John K. Rankin............	Sept. 1, 1861	Mustered out with regiment, October 31, 1861.
THIRD LIEUT. John K. Rankin.............	June 20, 1861	Promoted Second Lieutenant, Sept. 1, 1861.

COMPANY D.

Name and Rank.	Date of Muster.	Remarks.
CAPTAIN. Joseph Cracklin............	June 20, 1861	Resigned, October 1, 1861.
FIRST LIEUT. Thomas J. Sternbergh...	June 20, 1861	Mustered out with regiment, October 31, 1861.
SECOND LIEUT. Lucius J. Shaw.............	June 20, 1861	Died, September 5, 1861, of injury received at Platte river bridge, Mo., September 2, 1861.
THIRD LIEUT. Edward D. Thompson...		Promoted First Lieut. and Adj't, May 25, 1861.

COMPANY E.

Name and Rank.	Date of Muster.	Remarks.
CAPTAIN. Samuel J. Crawford.......	June 20, 1861	Retained in service and transferred to Second Kansas Cavalry.
FIRST LIEUT. John G. Lindsay...........	June 20, 1861	Mustered out with regiment, October 31, 1861.
SECOND LIEUT. A. R. Morton................	June 20, 1861	Absent without leave since August 7, 1861.
Samuel K. Cross............	Sept. 1, 1861	Mustered out with regiment, October 31, 1861.
THIRD LIEUT. Samuel K. Cross............	June 20, 1861	Promoted Second Lieutenant, Sept. 1, 1861.

COMPANY F.

Name and Rank.	Date of Muster.	Remarks.
CAPTAIN. Byron P. Ayers.............	June 20, 1861	Mustered out with regiment.
FIRST LIEUT. Ezekiel Bunn...............	June 20, 1861	Mustered out with regiment.
SECOND LIEUT. Barnett B. Mitchell.......	June 20, 1861	Mustered out with regiment.
THIRD LIEUT. David R. Coleman.........	June 20, 1861	Disch'd by order Gen. Fremont, Aug. 31, 1861.

COMPANY G.

Name and Rank.	Date of Muster.	Remarks.
CAPTAIN. Avra P. Russell............	June 20, 1861	Mustered out with regiment; wounded accidentally, Sept. 11, 1861, at Shelbina, Mo.
FIRST LIEUT. Charles P. Wiggins........	June 20, 1861	Mustered out with regiment; wounded in action, Aug. 10, 1861, Wilson's Creek.
SECOND LIEUT. Jacob A. Graham..........	June 20, 1861	Absent without leave since August 30, 1861.
THIRD LIEUT. Robert Newell...............	June 20, 1861	Killed in action, Aug. 10, 1861, Wilson's Creek.

COMPANY H.

Name and Rank.	Date of Muster.	Remarks.
CAPTAIN. William F. Cloud	....	Promoted Major, May 22, 1861.
Andrew J. Mitchell........	June 20, 1861	Promoted from First Lieut. to Captain, May 23, 1861; mustered out with regiment.
FIRST LIEUT. Charles S. Hills.............	June 20, 1861	Promoted from Sergeant May 23, 1861; mustered out with regiment.
SECOND LIEUT. Joseph A. Fuller ...•......	June 20, 1861	Mustered out with regiment.
THIRD LIEUT. William T. Galliher......	June 20, 1861	Discharged by order Gen. Fremont, Aug. 31, '61.

COMPANY I.

Name and Rank.	Date of Muster.	Remarks.
CAPTAIN. Samuel N. Wood	June 20, 1861	Transferred to Fremont's Battalion.
FIRST LIEUT. Charles Dimon..............	June 20, 1861	Mustered out with regiment.
SECOND LIEUT. Edward G. Pierce	June 20, 1861	Mustered out with the regiment.

COMPANY K.

Name and Rank.	Date of Muster.	Remarks.
CAPTAIN. William Tholen.............	June 25, 1861	Mustered out with regiment.
FIRST LIEUT. Gustavus Schreyer	June 25, 1861	Mustered out with regiment.
SECOND LIEUT. Ferdinand Jaedicke......	June 25, 1861	Mustered out with regiment.
THIRD LIEUT. James C. Bunch.............	June 20, 1861	Discharged at St. Louis, Mo., August 31, 1861.

SECOND REGIMENT KANSAS VOLUNTEERS — CAVALRY.

Name and Rank.	Date of Muster.	Remarks.
COLONEL. Robert B. Mitchell	June 20, 1861	Promoted Brigadier General United States Volunteers, April 8, 1862.
William F. Cloud..........	June 1, 1862	Mustered out, Jan. 19, 1865, Leavenworth, Kas.
LIEUT. COLONEL. Owen A. Bassett............	Aug. 1, 1862	Mustered out, Jan. 19, 1865, at Little Rock, Ark.
MAJOR. Charles W. Blair	Feb. 28, 1862	Promoted Colonel 14th Kansas Volunteer Cavalry, October 13, 1863.
Julius G. Fisk..............	Jan. 1, 1862	Mustered out, April 18, 1865, at Little Rock, Arkansas; wounded in action, November 28, 1862, at Cane Hill, Ark.
William F. Cloud..........	June 20, 1861	Promoted Colonel 10th Kansas Volunteer Infantry, March 27, 1862.
James M. Pomeroy.......	Feb. 28, 1862	Transferred to Ninth Kansas Cavalry by General Order No. 1, dated Headquarters Kansas State Militia, March 27, 1862.
Thomas B. Eldridge......	Jan. 4, 1862	Mustered out, March 20, 1862, at Camp Blair, Kansas, as supernumerary.
Henry Hopkins............	Nov. 13, 1863	Mustered out, Jan. 13, 1865, Leavenworth, Kas.
John Johnston..............	May 11, 1865	Mustered out, June 22, 1865, Fort Gibson, C. N.
ADJUTANT. John Pratt....................	Nov. 11, 1861	Promoted Captain and Assistant Adjutant General United States Volunteers, Feb. 6, 1863.
Morris Enright..............	Feb. 7, 1863	Dismissed the service by S. O. No. 387, dated W. D., A. G. O., November 7, 1864.

SECOND REGIMENT KANSAS VOLUNTEERS—CAVALRY—*Continued.*

Name and Rank.	Date of Muster.	Remarks.
ADJUTANT. Henry L. Isbell	Mar. 26, 1865	Mustered in to date prior to discharge as Serg. Maj. by S. O. 649, W. D., A. G. O.; mustered out August 11, 1865, at Lawrence Kansas.
BATTALION ADJUTANT. David R. Coleman.........	Feb. 28, 1862	Mustered out, September 6, 1862, General Order No. 126, W. D., A. G. O.
Joseph Cracklin............	Mar. 20, 1865	Mustered out, September 6; 1862, General Order No. 126, W. D., A. G. O.
William B. Parsons.......	Mar. 20, 1865	Transferred to 9th Kansas Cav., June 17, 1862.
QUARTERMASTER. Cyrus L. Gorton............	Nov. 2, 1861	Promoted Captain and Assistant Quartermaster United States Volunteers, June 11, 1864.
Clarence J. Williams	Dec. 8, 1864	Mustered out, June 22, 1865, at Ft. Gibson, C. N.
BATTALION Q. M. Elizur T. Goodrich........	....	Ordered to report at Ft. Leavenworth, Kansas, May, 1862; no further record of him.
COMMISSARY. Luther H. Wood...........	Jan. 1, 1862	Resigned on account of disability, October 19, 1864, at Fort Smith, Ark.
SURGEON. Joseph P. Root..............	Dec. 28, 1861	Mustered out, Apr. 18, 1865, at Little Rock, Ark.
ASST. SURGEON. George B. Wood............	Jan. 1, 1862	Resigned on account of ill health, September 27, 1862, in the field, Missouri.
John W. Robinson........	Oct. 23, 1862	Died of chronic dysentery at Fort Smith, Ark., December 10, 1863.
Valentine V. Adamson..	Sept. 27, 1861	Mustered out, June 22, 1862, at Ft. Gibson, C. N.
CHAPLAIN. Charles Reynolds..........	Jan. 1, 1862	Mustered out, Dec. 31, 1864, at Fort Scott, Kas.

COMPANY A.

Name and Rank.	Date of Muster.	Remarks.
CAPTAIN. Samuel J. Crawford......	June 20, 1861	Promoted Col. 2d Kas. Col'd Vols., Dec. 6, 1863.
John Johnston..............	Jan. 8, 1864	Mustered out, April 14, 1865, Little Rock, Ark.
FIRST LIEUT. John Johnston..............	Nov. 15, 1861	Promoted Captain, January 8, 1864.
Samuel K. Cross...........	Jan. 8, 1864	Mustered out, April 14, 1865, Little Rock, Ark.
SECOND LIEUT. Samuel K. Cross...........	Apr. 10, 1862	Promoted First Lieutenant, January 8, 1864.
Charles A. Archer.........	Feb. 8, 1864	Must'd in to date prior to dis'ge as Serg't by S. O. 447, W. D., A. G. O.; must'd out, April 14, 1864.

COMPANY B.

Name and Rank.	Date of Muster.	Remarks.
CAPTAIN. Elias S. Stover	Nov. 19, 1863	Mustered out, June 22, 1865, Fort Gibson, C. N.
FIRST LIEUT. William P. Phillips	Jan. 11, 1864	Mustered out, June 22, 1865, Fort Gibson, C. N.
SECOND LIEUT. Robert D. Watts............	Apr. 21, 1865	Mustered out, June 22, 1865, Fort Gibson, C. N.

COMPANY C.

Name and Rank.	Date of Muster.	Remarks.
CAPTAIN. Daniel S. Whittenhall...	Dec. 31, 1861	Resi'd for disability, Apr. 4, '63, Springfield, Mo.
Edward C. D. Lines	Feb. 23, 1863	Transferred from Co. K, May 4, 1863; killed in action, Sept. 1, '63, Backbone Mountain, Ark.
Edgar A. Barker	Nov. 1, 1863	Assigned to new Co. C, March 18, 1865.
FIRST LIEUT. Samuel C. Harrison......	Dec. 31, 1861	Deserted to the enemy, February 8, 1862.
Edward C. D. Lines.......	Feb. 20, 1862	Promoted Captain Co. K, February 23, 1863.
Edgar A. Barker	May 4, 1863	Promoted Captain, November 1, 1863.
Henry S. Jenks............	Jan. 11, 1864	Mustered out, Jan. 11, 1865, Fort Leavenworth.
SECOND LIEUT. William M. Hook	Dec. 31, 1861	Resigned, March 27, 1863, Springfield, Mo.
Henry S. Jenks............	May 4, 1863	Promoted First Lieutenant, January 11, 1864.
Alfred B. Hopkins.........	Jan. 11, 1864	Mustered out, Jan. 10, 1865, Fort Leavenworth.

COMPANY D.

Name and Rank.	Date of Muster.	Remarks.
CAPTAIN.		
Amaziah Moore	Dec. 11, 1861	Resigned on acc't of physical dis., Aug. 12, 1863.
John A. Lee	May 30, 1864	Assigned to new Company D, March 18, 1865.
FIRST LIEUT.		
Amaziah Moore............	Nov. 20, 1861	Promoted Captain, December 11, 1861.
Robert White........,......	Dec. 11, 1861	Resigned, April 30, 1862, at Fort Riley, Kas.
Horace L. Moore...........	May 1, 1862	Promoted Lt. Col. of 4th Ark. Cav., Feb. 18, 1864.
George W. Stabler........	May 1, 1864	Assigned to new Company D, March 18, 1865.
SECOND LIEUT.		
Horace L. Moore..........	Dec. 11, 1861	Promoted First Lieutenant, May 1, 1862.
John B. Dexter............	May 1, 1862	Promoted Capt. and A. Q. M. U. V., June 4, 1864.

COMPANY E.

Name and Rank.	Date of Muster.	Remarks.
CAPTAIN.		
John Gardner..............	Dec. 16, 1861	Mustered out, January 26, 1865, at Leavenworth.
FIRST LIEUT.		
John Gardner..............	Nov. 4, 1861	Promoted Captain, December 16, 1861.
Elias S. Stover.............	Dec. 16, 1861	Promoted Captain Company B, Nov. 29, 1863.
SECOND LIEUT.		
Augustus T. Lovelette...	Dec. 16, 1861	Mustered out, January 26, 1865, at Leavenworth.

COMPANY F.

Name and Rank.	Date of Muster.	Remarks.
CAPTAIN.		
Hugh Cameron,...........	Dec. 27, 1861	Promoted Lieut. Col. 2d Ark. Cav., Feb. 17, 1864.
James C. French..........	March 2, 1864	Mustered out, January 18, 1865, at Leavenworth.
FIRST LIEUT.		
Hugh Cameron............	Nov. 7, 1861	Promoted Captain, December 27, 1861.
James C. French..........	Dec. 27, 1861	Promoted Captain, March 2, 1864.
George W. Morgan........	Aug. 1, 1864	Assigned to duty as First Lieutenant of new Company D, March 18, 1865.
SECOND LIEUT.		
Albert Schroeder..........	Dec. 27, 1861	Resigned, March 7, 1862, at Leavenworth, Kas.
John A. Lee	Mar. 13, 1862	Promoted Captain Company D, May 30, 1864.

COMPANY G.

Name and Rank.	Date of Muster.	Remarks.
CAPTAIN.		
Austin W. Matthews......	Jan. 7, 1862	Mustered out, Jan. 13, '65, at Leavenworth, Kas.
FIRST LIEUT.		
Austin W. Matthews......	Jan. 3, 1862	Promoted Captain, January 7, 1862.
Patrick Cosgrove...........	Jan. 7, 1862	Promoted Captain Co. L, March 21, 1864.
SECOND LIEUT.		
Gideon M. Waugh.........	Jan. 7, 1862	Promoted Lieut. Col. 2d Ark. Cav., Jan. 7, 1864.
Philander W. Straw......	May 23, 1864	Assigned to duty as Second Lieutenant in new Co. D, March 18, 1865; prisoner of war, captured near Fort Gibson, C. N., Sept. 16, 1864.

COMPANY H.

Name and Rank.	Date of Muster.	Remarks.
CAPTAIN.		
Arthur Gunther............	Mar. 8, 1862	Must. out, March 18, 1865, at Little Rock, Ark.
FIRST LIEUT.		
David E. Ballard	Jan. 10, 1862	Resigned, Feb. 15, 1865, at Little Rock, Ark.
SECOND LIEUT.		
John K. Rankin	Mar. 8, 1862	Mustered out, March 18, 1865.

COMPANY I.

Name and Rank.	Date of Muster.	Remarks.
CAPTAIN.		
Samuel A. Williams......	Nov. 22, 1861	Resigned, March 28, 1862, at Shawnee. Kansas.
Byron P. Ayers............	Mar. 28, 1862	Resigned, March 27, 1863, at Springfield, Mo.
Charles Dimon.............	Nov. 4, 1863	Must. out, Jan. 10, 1865, at Leavenworth, Kas.
FIRST LIEUT.		
Robert H. Hunt............	Nov. 23, 1861	Resigned, September 3, 1862.
Clarence J. Williams.....	Oct. 20, 1863	Prom. First Lt. and Regt'l Qr. Mr., Dec. 7, '64; wounded in left shoulder Dec. 20, '63, in Ark.
SECOND LIEUT.		
Harvey A. Smith	Nov. 28, 1861	Resigned, March 28, 1862, at Shawnee, Kansas.
Charles Dimon.............	Mar. 28, 1861	Commissioned First Lieut., April 11, 1863, and placed on duty as such, but not mustered ; promoted Captain Co. I, November 4, 1863.
Edward Ross................	May 4, 1863	Assigned to duty as 2d Lt. new Co. C, Mar. 18,'65

COMPANY K.

Name and Rank.	Date of Muster.	Remarks.
CAPTAIN.		
Avra P. Russell............	Apr. 5, 1862	Died, December 12, 1862, in Field Hospital near Prairie Grove, Ark., of wounds received in battle Dec. 7, 1862, at Prairie Grove, Ark.
Edward C. D. Lines.......	Feb. 23, 1863	Transferred to Co. C, May 4, 1864.
John M. Mentzer..........	June 3, 1863	Must. out, Apr. 17, 1865, at Leavenworth, Kas.; W. in right limb near Camden, Ark., Apr. 20,'64.
FIRST LIEUT.		
Avra P. Russell............	Dec. —, 1861	Promoted Captain, April 5, 1862.
Pamett B. Mitchell........	Apr. 5, 1862	Mustered out, Apr. 17, '65, at Leavenworth, Kas.
SECOND LIEUT.		
John M. Mentzer	Apr. 5, 1862	Promoted Captain, June 3, 1863.

COMPANY L.

Name and Rank.	Date of Muster.	Remarks.
CAPTAIN.		
Patrick Cosgrove...........	Mar. 2, 1864	Mustered out, June 22, 1865, Fort Gibson, C. N.
FIRST LIEUT.		
Joseph Hutchison..........	Mar. 1, 1864	Mustered out, June 22, 1865, Fort Gibson, C. N.
SECOND LIEUT.		
John O. Miller..............	Mar. 1, 1864	Must. out, Sept. 8, '65, Leav., to date Aug. 11, '65.

NEW COMPANY C.

Name and Rank.	Date of Muster.	Remarks.
CAPTAIN.		
Edgar A. Barker............	Nov. 1, 1863	Resigned, May 23, 1865, at Fort Gibson, C. N.
George W. Stabler..........	June 9, 1865	Mustered out, June 22, 1865, Fort Gibson, C. N.
FIRST LIEUT.		
George W. Stabler.........	May 1, 1864	Promoted Captain, June 9, 1865.
Henry L. Isbell.............	June 9, 1865	Must.-in as First Lt. new Co. C revkd., and must. as First Lt. & Adjt. 2d Ks. Cv., date Mch. 26,'65.
SECOND LIEUT.		
Edward Ross................	May 4, 1863	Resigned, May 8, 1865, at Lewisburg, Ark.
Nathan W. Mott............	June 9, 1865	Mustered out, June 22, 1865, Fort Gibson, C. N.

NEW COMPANY D.

Name and Rank.	Date of Muster.	Remarks.
CAPTAIN.		
John A. Lee..................	May 30, 1864	Mustered out, June 22, 1865, Fort Gibson, C. N.
FIRST LIEUT.		
George W. Morgan........	Aug. 1, 1864	Resigned, May 1, 1865, at Lewisburg, Ark.
SECOND LIEUT.		
Philander W. Straw......	May 23, 1864	Mustered out, June 14, 1865, Leavenworth, Kas.

List of battles, etc., in which this regiment participated, showing loss reported in each:

Little Santa Fe (Cos. D and M)—Killed, E. M., 1. Coon Creek—Missing, E. M., 5. Newtonia (October 5, 1862,)—No loss. Hazel Bottom (B and M)—Missing, E. M., 1. Elk Horn Tavern—No loss. Sugar Creek—No loss. Cross Hollow—No loss. Old Fort Wayne—Killed, E. M., 4; wounded, E. M., 2; missing, E. M., 1. Boonesboro'—Wounded, E. M., 1. Cove Creek—No loss. Pineville (C and M)—Killed, E. M., 1. Cane Hill—Killed, E. M., 1. Carthage (November 27, 1862)—Killed, E. M., 1; missing, E. M., 1. Boston Mountain—No loss. Reed's Mountain—Killed, E. M., 2; wounded, E. M., 5. Prairie Grove—Killed, E. M., 3; wounded, O. 1, E. M. 11; missing, E. M., 1. Dripping Spring—Killed, E. M., 2. Bentonville (May 22, 1863)—H and M—No loss. Carthage (May 24, 1863)—No loss. Honey Springs—Killed, E. M., 1; wounded, E. M., 1. Bentonville (August 15, 1863)—No loss. Perryville—No loss. Devil's Backbone—Killed, O. 1, E. M. 2; wounded, E. M., 4. Dardanelle—No loss. Newtonia (September 27, 1863)—E and M—No loss. Choctaw Nation—Missing, E. M., 1. Fouche le Faix Mountain (D and M)—No loss. Roseville (November 12, 1863)—E and M—Killed, E. M., 1; missing, E. M., 5. Clarksville—Killed, E. M., 1. Caddo Gap (December 4, 1863)—B and M—No loss. Waldron (December 30, 1863)—Killed, E. M., 2; wounded, E. M., 6. Baker's Spring—Killed, E. M., 1; wounded, E. M., 2. Little Missouri River (A, D, and M)—No loss. Sulphur Springs (G and M)—No loss. Caddo Gap (January 26, 1864)—Missing, E. M., 1. Dallas (F, H, K, and M)—No loss. Waldron (February 1, 1864)—Wounded, E. M., 1. Mountain Fork—No loss. Caddo Mountain—Wounded, E. M., 1. Scott's Farm—Wounded, E. M., 1. Caddo Gap (Feb. 16, 1864)—Wounded, E. M., 1. Danville—Killed, E. M., 1; wounded, E. M., 1. Roseville (March 29, 1864)—B, E, and M - Killed, E. M., 1. Roseville (April 4, 1864)—D, E, and M—Killed, E. M., 5; wounded, E. M., 11. Prairie D'Ann—No loss. Roseville (April 15, 1864)—A and M—Wounded, E. M., 1. Poison Springs—Killed, E. M., 1; missing, E. M., 5. Jenkins's Ferry—No loss. Fort Smith (July 29, 1864)—Killed, E. M., 1. Crawford County—Killed, E. M., 2. Fort Smith (September 1, 1864)—Killed, E. M., 1. Fort Gibson—Killed, E. M., 2; missing, O., 2, E. M., 46. Cabin Creek—Killed, E. M., 1; missing, E. M., 2. Dardanelle (January 14, 1865)—A, B, and M—No loss.

This list is copied from the United States Official Army Register of Volunteers, issued by the Adjutant General, at Washington, July 16, 1867. "E. M." means Enlisted Men; "O," Commissioned Officers.

FIFTH REGIMENT KANSAS VOLUNTEERS—CAVALRY.

Name and Rank.	Date of Muster.	Remarks.
COLONEL.		
Hampton P. Johnson ...	....	Killed in action, Sept. 17, 1861, Morristown, Mo.
Powell Clayton............	Mar. 7, 1862	Promoted Brig. Gen. U. S. V., August 1, 1864.
LIEUT. COLONEL.		
John Ritchie...............	....	Prom. Col. Second Indian H. G., March 28, 1862.
Powell Clayton............	Dec. 28, 1861	Promoted Colonel, March 7, 1862.
Wilton A. Jenkins........	May 1, 1862	Mustered out, May 7, 1864, Fort Leavenworth, Kas., per S. O. 171, Headquarters Dep. Ark.
Thomas W. Scudder......	Oct. 29, 1864	Mustered out, January 4, 1865.

FIFTH REGIMENT KANSAS VOLUNTEERS—CAVALRY—*Continued.*

Name and Rank.	Date of Muster.	Remarks.
MAJOR.		
James H. Summers.......	....	Resigned, March 16, 1862.
Wilton A. Jenkins........	Feb. 28, 1862	Promoted Lieutenant Colonel, May 1, 1862.
S. E. Hoffman..............	April 10, 1862	Resigned, August 6. 1862.
Samuel Walker.............	May 24, 1862	Promoted Lt. Col. 16th Kas. Cav., Oct. 29, 1864.
Thomas W. Scudder......	Sept. 1, 1862	Promoted Lieut. Col., October 29, 1864; wounded in action, Oct. 26, 1863, Pine Bluff, Arkansas.
Stephen R. Harrington..	Oct. 29, 1864	Mustered out, January 10, 1865.
ADJUTANT.		
Stephen R. Harrington..	....	Promoted Captain Company K, July 1, 1862.
George W. DeCosta.......	Sept. 15, 1862	Promoted Paymaster U. S. A., April 21, 1864.
Lawrence Murphy........	July 9, 1864	Mustered out, January 4, 1865.
QUARTERMASTER.		
James Davis.................	Aug. 16, 1861	Prom. Capt. and A. C. S., U. S. V., Aug. 1, 1862.
Alfred Gray.................	April 19, 1861	Resigned on account of disability, March 24, 1864; was on detached service with Gen. Vandever from June 30, 1863, to date of discharge.
E. D. Hillyer...............	Mar. 1, 1863	Resigned, August 16, 1864.
COMMISSARY.		
George W. Stevens........	Mar. 3, 1863	Resigned, May 17, 1864.
James F. Vaughn.........	June 3, 1864	Mustered out, Jan. 10, 1865, Leavenworth, Kas.
SURGEON.		
E. B. Johnson.............	....	Discontinued as Surgeon upon reorganization of regiment in spring of 1862.
A. J. Huntoon..............	Jan. 5, 1862	Dismissed, March 30, 1863, Helena, Arkansas.
William B. Carpenter...	May 8, 1863	Mustered out, Sept. 7, 1864, Leavenworth, Kas.
ASSISTANT SURGEON.		
E. P. Sheldon.............	Jan. 1, 1862	Died of disease at Fort Scott, Kas., April 3, '62.
William B. Carpenter...	May 27, 1862	Promoted Surgeon, May 8, 1862.
Samuel Whitehorn.......	May 13, 1863	Resigned, October 30, 1863.
David R. Porter............	Aug. 1, 1863	Mustered out, Aug. 10, 1865, Leavenworth, Kas.
CHAPLAIN.		
Hugh D. Fisher...........	....	Mustered out, 1864, Leavenworth, Kansas.

COMPANY A.

Name and Rank.	Date of Muster.	Remarks.
CAPTAIN.		
John Ritchie.................	July 16, 1861	Promoted Lieutenant Colonel, Sept. 10, 1861.
William F. Creitz..........	Sept. 11, 1861	Mustered out, Aug. 11, 1864, Leavenworth, Kas.
FIRST LIEUT.		
William F. Creitz..........	July 16, 1861	Promoted Captain, September 11, 1861.
Thomas W. Scudder......	Sept. 11, 1861	Promoted Major, September 1, 1862.
Stephen J. Jennings......	Sept. 15, 1862	Mustered out, April 6, 1865, Leavenworth; captured by enemy, Mark's Mills, Ark., Apr. 25, '64.
SECOND LIEUT.		
Reuben A. Randlett......	July 16, 1861	Resigned, June 11, 1862.
Stephen J. Jennings......	Jan. 1, 1862	Promoted First Lieutenant, September 15, 1862.
Joseph McCarty............	....	Promoted Captain Company C, April 8, 1864.

COMPANY B.

Name and Rank.	Date of Muster.	Remarks.
CAPTAIN.		
John R. Clark..............	Aug. 12, 1861	Died, May 21, 1862, of gun-shot wound received from provost guard, Springfield, Mo.
Harrison Kelly.............	Oct. 11, 1862	Mustered out, September 3, 1864, Leavenworth.
FIRST LIEUT.		
John McIntosh	Aug. 12, 1861	Resigned, October 11, 1862.
Alfred Gray.................	Apr. 19, 1862	Transferred to staff as Regim'l Quartermaster.
Melton F. Clark............	Oct. 24, 1863	Mustered out, September 3, 1864, Leavenworth.
SECOND LIEUT.		
Hadley J. Alley............	Aug. 12, 1861	Resigned, March 14, 1862.
Melton F. Clark............	Apr. 1, 1862	Promoted First Lieutenant, October 24, 1863.
Samuel Cargo	Aug. 1, 1863	Dishonorably mustered out, February 22, 1864, per S. O. 87, W. D., A. G. O., Feb. 22, 1864.

COMPANY C.

Name and Rank.	Date of Muster.	Remarks.
CAPTAIN.		
Garret Gibson..............	Aug. 12, 1861	Resigned May 25, 1863.
Joseph McCarty............	Apr. 18, 1864	Mustered out, September 7, 1864, Leavenworth.
FIRST LIEUT.		
James H. Summers.......	Aug. 12, 1861	Promoted Major, September 10, 1861.
Charles G. Bridges........	Sept. 10, 1861	Resigned, April 8, 1862.
Jeremiah Sanders.........	Apr. 8, 1862	Resigned, April, 1864; wounded in action, May 25, 1863. Pope's Plantation, near Helena, Ark.
SECOND LIEUT.		
Charles G. Bridges........	Aug. 12, 1861	Promoted First Lieutenant, September 10, 1861.
Oliver H. P. Cox	Sept. 10, 1861	Resigned, July 14, 1862.
David D. Dailey............	Dec. 31, 1862	Mustered out, December 18, 1863.

COMPANY D.

Name and Rank.	Date of Muster.	Remarks.
CAPTAIN.		
Henry C. Seaman.........	July 24, 1861	Dismissed, Aug. 24, 1863, per S. O. 410, W. D., A. D. O., Sept. 12, '63, for absence without leave.
Orlin E. Morse..............	May 13, 1863	Mustered out, September 5, 1864, Leavenworth.
FIRST LIEUT.		
Joseph H. Trego...........	July 24, 1861	Resigned, October 17, 1864, Helena, Ark.
Orlin E. Morse..............	Dec. 31, 1862	Promoted Captain, May 13, 1863.
Asa D. Perrin...............	May 13, 1863	Mustered out, September 5, 1864, Leavenworth.
SECOND LIEUT.		
Orlin E. Morse.............	July 24, 1861	Promoted First Lieutenant, December 31, 1862.
Asa D. Perrin...............	Dec. 31, 1862	Promoted First Lieutenant, May 13, 1863.
Lawrence Murphy........	May 13, 1863	Promoted First Lieut. and Adjt., July 9, 1864.

COMPANY E.

Name and Rank.	Date of Muster.	Remarks.
CAPTAIN.		
James S. Hunt..............	Aug. 9, 1861	Res'd on acct. of dis., Apr. 16, '62, Carthage, Mo.
John F. Young........... ...	Apr. 10, 1862	Mustered out, Sept. 8, 1864, Leavenworth, Kas.
FIRST LIEUT.		
John F. Young..............	Aug. 9, 1861	Promoted Captain, April 16, 1862.
Ebenezer J. Barnes.......	June 12, 1862	Promoted Captain Company I, October 1, 1862.
Edwin D. Hillyer..........	....	Promoted Reg. Quartermaster, May 7, 1864.
James M. Lane.............	May 17, 1864	Mustered out, Sept. 8, 1864, Leavenworth, Kas.
SECOND LIEUT.		
James M. Heddens........	Aug. 9, 1861	Promoted First Lieutenant Co. K, Sept. 1, 1862.
Henry A. Simons..........	Nov. 17, 1862	Dishonorably mustered out, Feb. 22, 1864, Pine Bluff, Ark., by order of General Steele.

COMPANY F.

Name and Rank.	Date of Muster.	Remarks.
CAPTAIN.		
James M. Williams........	July 12, 1861	Resigned, May 15, 1862.
Henry Moore................	Dec. 13, 1861	Mustered out, Aug. 11, '64, Leav., Kas.; wounded in right wrist in action, May 11, 1863, at Mt. Vernon, Mo.
FIRST LIEUT.		
Henry Moore................	July 12, 1861	Promoted Captain, December 31, 1862.
Ansel D. Brown............	Dec. 31, 1862	Mustered out, Aug. 11, 1864, Leavenworth, Kas.
SECOND LIEUT.		
Ansel D. Brown............	July 12, 1861	Promoted First Lieutenant, Dec. 31, 1862.
Grover Youngs.............	Dec. 31, 1862	Mustered out, August 11, 1864.

COMPANY G.

Name and Rank.	Date of Muster.	Remarks.
CAPTAIN.		
Wilton A. Jenkins........	Nov. 8, 1861	Promoted Major, February 28, 1862.
Edward G. Pierce..........	Mar. 3, 1862	Resigned, June 23, 1864.
FIRST LIEUT.		
Wilton A. Jenkins........	Oct. 10, 1861	Promoted Captain, November 8, 1861.
Joseph E. McComas.......	Nov. 8, 1861	Res'd, acct. of ill health, Oct. 14,'62, Helena, Ark.
Edwin W. Jenkins........	Oct. 17, 1862	Mustered out, Dec. 3, 1864, Leavenworth, Kas.
SECOND LIEUT.		
Harrison Kelly............	Nov. 8, 1861	Promoted Captain Co. B, October 11, 1862.
Aaron J. Totten............	Oct. 17, 1862	Resigned, August 24, 1863.
Deloss Miller.................	Nov. 1, 1863	Mustered out, April 6, '65, Leav., Ks.; prisoner war, capt'd near Pine Bluff, Ark., Mar. 9, '64.

COMPANY H.

Name and Rank.	Date of Muster.	Remarks.
CAPTAIN.		
Samuel C. Thompson....	Nov. 14, 1861	Was mustered out as Captain and mustered as First Lieut., Feb. 9, 1862, and again mustered as Captain, March 17, 1862; mustered out, December 8, 1864, Leavenworth, Kansas.
FIRST LIEUT.		
William E. Rowe..........	Nov. 16, 1861	Mustered out, January 28, 1862.
Samuel C. Thompson....	Feb. 9, 1862	Promoted Captain, March 17, 1862.
Alfred Brant.................	Mar. 17, 1862	Mustered out, Dec. 8, 1864, Leavenworth, Kas.
SECOND LIEUT.		
George R. Huston..........	Nov. 16, 1861	Mustered out, January 28, 1862.
Mason W. Benjamin.......	Mar. 17. 1862	Resigned, March 19, 1864, Pine Bluff, Arkansas; wounded in action, May 11, 1863, Mount Vernon, Missouri.

COMPANY I.

Name and Rank.	Date of Muster.	Remarks.
CAPTAIN.		
John Lockhart..............	Mar. 17, 1862	Died of disease, Helena, Ark., Sept. 14, 1862.
Ebenezer J. Barnes........	Oct. 1, 1862	No date of muster-out appears on muster-out rolls.
FIRST LIEUT.		
James B. Harvey...........	....	Mustered out, February 7, 1862, Fort Lincoln, Kansas.
John Lockhart..............	Feb. 7, 1862	Promoted Captain, March 17, 1862.
James L. Stewart...........	Mar. 18, 1862	Resigned, August 1, 1862.
Andrew Fyfe.................	Dec. 31, 1862	Discharged for disability, August 23, 1864.
SECOND LIEUT.		
James L. Stewart...........	....	Promoted First Lieutenant, March 18, 1862.
Andrew Fyfe.................	Mar. 18, 1862	Promoted First Lieutenant, Dec. 31, 1862.
Thomas Stevenson.........	Dec. 31, 1862	Mustered out, June 22, 1865, DeVall's Bluff, Ark.

COMPANY K.

Name and Rank.	Date of Muster.	Remarks.
CAPTAIN.		
Adoniram J. Miller........	Mar. —, 1862	Resigned, July, 1862; was sworn into service Oct. 1, 1861; was commissioned and mustered Feb. 8, 1862, to cover previous service, and on same date mustered out on account of Company being below the minimum; was again commissioned and mustered March —, 1862.
Stephen R. Harrington..	July 1, 1862	Promoted Major, October 29, 1864.
FIRST LIEUT.		
William E. McGinnis.....	....	Mustered out, Feb. 9, 1862; cause unknown.
Jeremiah C. Johnson.....	Feb. 2, 1862	Resigned, April 16, 1862.
James M. Heddens........	Sept. 1, 1862	Resigned, April 28, 1865.
SECOND LIEUT.		
Alexander Rush.............	....	Mustered out, Feb. 9, 1862; cause unknown.
Edwin W. Jenkins.........	April 1, 1862	Promoted First Lieut. Co. G, October 17, 1862.
William J. Brewer.........	Oct. 17, 1862	Resigned, December 8, 1862.
James C. Wood..............	Dec. 31, 1862	Resigned, February 18, 1865.

COMPANY L.

Name and Rank.	Date of Muster.	Remarks.
CAPTAIN.		
James H. Young	May 14, 1863	Transferred to Fifteenth K. V. C., July 20, 1865.
FIRST LIEUT.		
James H. Young	April 22, 1863	Promoted Captain, May 14, 1863.
Tobias J. Hadley...........	June 4, 1863	Resigned, September 13, 1865.
SECOND LIEUT.		
William F. Goble	May 30, 1863	Transf'd to new Co. B, 16th K. V. C., July 20, '65.

COMPANY M.

Name and Rank.	Date of Muster.	Remarks.
CAPTAIN.		
William H. Lindsey......	July 23, 1863	Resigned, February 20, 1865.
Livingston G. Parker....	April 29, 1863	Transf'd to new Co. B, 15th K. V. C., July 20, '65.
FIRST LIEUT.		
Livingston G. Parker....	Sept. 25, 1863	Promoted Captain, April 29, 1865.
Henry N. Dunlap	June 1, 1865	Transf'd to new Co. B, 15th K. V. C., July 20, '65.
SECOND LIEUT.		
Henry N. Dunlap.........	Sept. 24, 1863	Promoted First Lieutenant, June 1, 1865.

List of battles, etc., in which this regiment participated, showing loss reported in each:

Harrisonville—No loss. Ball's Mills—No loss. Fort Scott (Sept. 1, 1861)—No loss. Fort Scott (Sept. 3, 1861)—Wounded, E. M., 1. Dry Wood—Wounded, E. M., 7; missing, E. M., 1. Papinsville—No loss. Morristown—Killed, O., 1; E. M., 1; wounded, E. M., 3. Osceola—Wounded, E. M., 1; missing, E. M., 1. West Point—Killed, E. M., 1. Butler—Killed, E. M., 1. Little Santa Fe—No loss. Turnback Creek—Killed, E. M., 1. Eminence—Killed, E. M., 1. Salem—No loss. Black Run—Killed, E. M., 1; wounded, E. M., 3. Trenton—Killed, E. M., 1. Parkersville—No loss. Oakland—No loss. Little Rock Road (G)—Killed, E. M., 1; wounded, E. M., 1. Mount Vernon—Killed, E. M., 1; wounded, E. M., 1. Polk's Plantation—Killed, E. M., 3; wounded, E. M., 7. Helena (May 25, 1863)—Killed, E. M., 5; wounded, E. M., 7; missing, O., 2, E. M., 20. Helena (July 4, 1863)—Killed, E. M., 3; wounded, E. M., 2. Little Rock—Killed, O., 1. Brownsville—Killed, E. M., 1. Tulip—No loss. Pine Bluff (Oct. 25, 1863)—Killed, E. M., 7; wounded, E. M., 9; missing, E. M., 1. Monticello—Missing, E. M., 1. Pine Bluff (Jan. 19, 1864)—Missing, E. M., 1. Blancheville—Missing, E. M., 7. Long View—No loss. Mount Elba—Missing, E. M., 1. Swan Lake—Killed, E. M., 1. Mark's Mills—Killed, E. M., 5; wounded, E. M., 7; missing, O., 2, E. M., 42. Brewer's Lane—Wounded, E. M., 1. Lexington—Wounded, E. M., 1. Little Blue—No loss. Independence—No loss. Big Blue—No loss. Osage—No loss. Newtonia—Killed, E. M., 1.—*Official Army Register of the Volunteer Force of the United States Army.*

19

SIXTH REGIMENT KANSAS VOLUNTEERS—CAVALRY.

Name and Rank.	Date of Muster.	Remarks.
COLONEL.		
William R. Judson........	July 27, 1861	Mustered out, March 11, '65, Leavenworth, Kas.
LIEUT. COLONEL.		
Lewis R. Jewell............	July 27, 1861	Died, November 30, 1862, of wounds received in action November 28, 1862, Cane Hill, Ark.
William T. Campbell.....	Dec. 1, 1862	Mustered out, March 18, '65, DeVall's Bluff, Ark.
MAJOR.		
William T. Campbell.....	July 27, 1861	Promoted Lieut. Colonel, December 1, 1862.
Wyllis C. Ransom.........	Mar. 14, 1862	Mustered out.
George W. Veale	Dec. 1, 1862	Resigned, October 10, 1863.
John A. Johnson..........	July 1, 1863	Mustered out, March 18, '65, DeVall's Bluff, Ark.
David Mefford	July 27, 1864	Mustered out, July 18, 1865, DeVall's Bluff, Ark.; prisoner of war, captured at Muzzard Prairie, Ark., July 27, 1864.
ADJUTANT.		
Charles O. Judson..........	Sept. 10, 1862	Resigned, March 7, 1862, Ft. Leavenworth, Kas.
Isaac Stadden...............	Mar. 7, 1862	Mustered out, Aug. 15, '62, Ft. Leavenworth, Kas.
William Burgoyne........	Sept. 6, 1862	Mustered out, July 18, 1865, DeVall's Bluff, Ark.
BATTALION ADJUTANT.		
William R. Judson, jr...	May 15, 1862	Mustered out, September 6, 1862.
QUARTERMASTER.		
George J. Clarke	Sept. 10, 1861	Assigned to duty as 1st Lt. Co. H, March 3, '62.
Simeon B. Gordon.........	Mar. 14, 1862	Mustered out, August 15, 1862.
Charles W. Jewell........	Nov. 7, 1864	Resigned, October 14, 1864.
Levi Bronson	Jan. 12, 1865	Mustered out, July 18, 1865, DeVall's Bluff, Ark.
COMMISSARY.		
John S. Lane................	Jan. 8, 1863	Mustered out, March 18, '65, DeVall's Bluff, Ark.
SURGEON.		
John S. Redfield............	July 27, 1861	Mustered out, Feb. 21, 1865, Clarksville, Ark.
Wesley Mellick.............	Mar. 17, 1865	Mustered out, July 18, 1865, DeVall's Bluff, Ark.
ASSISTANT SURGEON.		
Joseph R. Smith............	Jan. 6, 1862	Died of disease, Fort Scott, Kas., Aug. 2, 1862.
Stephen A. Fairchilds.....	Aug. 25, 1862	Killed by guerillas, April 5, '64, Roseville, Ark.
Wesley Mellick.............	Sept. 9, 1862	Promoted Surgeon, March 17, 1865.
CHAPLAIN.		
Richard Duvall	Mar. 7, 1862	Resigned, June 18, 1863.
William Willson	July 18, 1863	Mustered out, March 11, 1865, Leavenworth, Kas.

COMPANY A.

Name and Rank.	Date of Muster.	Remarks.
CAPTAIN.		
George W. Veale..........	July 21, 1861	Promoted Major, December 1, 1862.
John A. Johnson	Dec. 1, 1862	Promoted Major, July 1, 1863.
Thomas Crooks..............	Sept. 1, 1863	Mustered out, March 27, 1865, Leavenworth, Kas.
FIRST LIEUT.		
Matthew Clary..............	July 21, 1861	Resigned, September 1, 1862.
John A. Johnson	Sept. 1, 1862	Promoted Captain, December 1, 1862; wounded in left lung while charging enemy's battery at Cane Hill, Ark., November 28, 1862.
Thomas J. Darling........	Feb. 1, 1863	Discharged on account of physical disability, March 19, 1864.
SECOND LIEUT.		
John A. Johnson	July 21, 1861	Promoted First Lieutenant, September 1, 1862.
Thomas J. Darling........	Sept. 1, 1862	Promoted First Lieutenant, February 1, 1863.
Thomas Crooks.............	Feb. 1, 1863	Promoted Captain, September 1, 1863.
Thomas G. Howell........	Sept. 1, 1863	Transferred to new Company A, April 8, 1865.

COMPANY B.

Name and Rank.	Date of Muster.	Remarks.
CAPTAIN.		
Elijah E. Harvey...........	Aug. 12, 1861	Mustered out, November 18, 1864, Leavenworth.
FIRST LIEUT.		
Jacob Morehead.............	Aug. 12, 1861	Mustered out, November 18, 1864, Leavenworth.
SECOND LIEUT.		
Reason R. McGuire.......	Aug. 12, 1861	Mustered out, November 18, 1864, Leavenworth.

COMPANY C.

Name and Rank.	Date of Muster.	Remarks.
CAPTAIN. Harris S. Greeno...........	Aug. 24, 1861	Prom. Major 4th Ark. C., Oct. 16, 1864; wounded in action, July 2, 1862; also Aug. 24, 1862.
FIRST LIEUT. Reese J. Lewis..............	Aug. 24, 1861	Mustered out, Dec. 1, 1864, Little Rock, Ark.
SECOND LIEUT. David Mefford..............	Aug. 24, 1861	Promoted Captain Company H, March 3, 1862.
Richard L. Phillips........	Mar. 7, 1862	Mustered out, December 1, 1864, Leavenworth.

COMPANY D.

Name and Rank.	Date of Muster.	Remarks.
CAPTAIN. John W. Orahood.........	Aug. 25, 1861	Dismissed the service, September 22, 1863, for absence without leave.
David Goss...................	Jan. 4, 1864	Mustered out, Jan. 5, 1865, at Leavenworth.
FIRST LIEUT. Joseph Hall..................	Aug. 25, 1861	Resigned, June 1, 1863.
David Goss...................	July 15, 1863	Promoted Captain, January 4, 1864.
Hiram P. Barrick..........	Jan. 4, 1864	Mustered out, Jan. 5, 1865, at Leavenworth.
SECOND LIEUT. John S. Lane	Aug. 25, 1861	Promoted First Lt. and R. C., January 8, 1863.
David Goss...................	Jan. 8, 1863	Promoted First Lieutenant, July 15, 1863.
Hiram P. Barrick.........	July 15, 1863	Promoted First Lieutenant, January 4, 1864.
William H. Shattuck.....	Jan. 4, 1864	Assigned to duty as Second Lieutenant in new Co. A, March 21, 1865.

COMPANY E.

Name and Rank.	Date of Muster.	Remarks.
CAPTAIN. Henry M. Dobyns.........	Sept. 2, 1861	Killed in action, Oct. 23, '64, at Cow Creek, Mo.
FIRST LIEUT. Brainard D. Benedict....	Sept. 2, 1861	Died of consumption, at Mound City, Kansas, February 20, 1863.
Anson J. Walker...........	Mar. 13, 1863	Mustered out, March 27, 1865.
SECOND LIEUT. Herbert Robinson.........	Sept. 2, 1861	Mustered out, March 9, 1862.
Anson J. Walker...........	Mar. 12, 1862	Promoted First Lieutenant, March 13, 1863.
John M. Defriese	Mar. 13, 1863	Mustered out, March 27, 1865.

COMPANY F.

Name and Rank.	Date of Muster.	Remarks.
CAPTAIN. Charles F. Clarke..........	Oct. 21, 1861	Promoted Capt. and Asst. Adjt. Gen. U. S. Vols.
Frederick W. Schuarte..	Mar. 28, 1862	Transferred as Second Lieutenant to the Second U. S. Cavalry, July, 1862.
William Gordon............	Sept. 15, 1862	Resigned, August 4, 1863.
Charles O. Judson.........	Sept. 18, 1863	Assigned to new Co. A, March 18, 1865.
FIRST LIEUT. Charles F. Clarke	Oct. 4, 1861	Promoted Captain, October 21, 1861.
Frederick W. Schuarte..	Oct. 21, 1861	Promoted Captain, March 28, 1862.
William Gordon............	July 1, 1862	Promoted Captain, September 15, 1862.
Charles W. Jewell.........	Sept. 15, 1862	Promoted First Lt. and R. Q. M., Nov. 7, 1862.
William R. Judson, jr...	Nov. 20, 1862	Mustered out, April 17, 1865, at Leavenworth.
SECOND LIEUT. William Gordon............	Oct. 20, 1861	Promoted First Lieutenant, July 1, 1862.
Charles King.................	July 1, 1862	Resigned, September 18, 1862.
John P. Grassberger......	Oct. 15, 1862	Mustered out, Nov. 19, 1864, at Leavenworth.

COMPANY G.

Name and Rank.	Date of Muster.	Remarks.
CAPTAIN.		
Nathaniel B. Lucas.......	Feb. 4, 1862	Transf. as Capt. to 18thU.S. Col.V., April 6, 1864.
Robert Henderson.........	Dec. 9, 1864	Mustered out, May 19, 1865, DeVall's Bluff, Ark.; wounded in action, April 18, 1864, Poison Springs, Ark.
FIRST LIEUT.		
John M. Laing.............	Dec. 30, 1861	Promoted Major 15th K.C., October 15, 1863.
Robert Henderson.........	Jan. 1, 1864	Promoted Captain, December 9, 1864.
Ebenezer W. Lucas	Mar. 15, 1865	Mustered out May 19, 1865, DeVall's Bluff, Ark.
SECOND LIEUT.		
John M. Dunn.............	May 26, 1862	Resigned September 15, 1862.
Robert Henderson.........	Sept. 15, 1862	Promoted First Lieutenant, January 1, 1864.
Ebenezer W. Lucas........	Jan. 1, 1864	Promoted First Lieutenant, March 15, 1865.
Daniel Braman	....	Commissioned and assigned to duty as Second Lieutenant, but never mustered.

COMPANY H.

Name and Rank.	Date of Muster.	Remarks.
CAPTAIN.		
David Mefford.............	Feb. 7, 1862	Promoted Major, July 27, 1864.
FIRST LIEUT.		
George J. Clark...........	Feb. 1, 1862	Prom. Capt. Company E, 14th K.C., Aug. 21, 1863.
SECOND LIEUT.		
Albert H. Campbell.......	Feb. 1, 1862	Prom. Capt. Company G, 14th K.C., Sept. 8, 1863.

COMPANY I.

Name and Rank.	Date of Muster.	Remarks.
CAPTAIN.		
John T. Blake	May 26, 1863	Mustered out April 1, 1866, to date July 18, 1865.
FIRST LIEUT.		
Silas D. Harris.............	May 26, 1863	Mustered out July 18, 1865, DeVall's Bluff, Ark.
SECOND LIEUT.		
Levi T. Stewart	May 26, 1863	Resigned May 2, 1865.

COMPANY K.

Name and Rank.	Date of Muster.	Remarks.
CAPTAIN.		
John Rogers.................	Aug. 15, 1861	Mustered out as Captain, March 7, 1862, Fort Scott, Kas., and mustered in as First Lieut.
John Rogers.................	April 1, 1862	Killed in skirmish June 2, 1864, near Ft. Scott.
FIRST LIEUT.		
Charles H. Haynes........	Aug. 15, 1861	Mustered out March 7, 1862, Fort Scott, Kas.
John Rogers.................	Mar. 7, 1862	Promoted Captain, April 1, 1862.
Charles H. Haynes........	April 1, 1862	Prom. Capt. Company B, 16th K.C., June 28, 1863.
John G. Harris..............	July 16, 1863	Resigned on account of disability, Feb. 11, 1864.
SECOND LIEUT.		
Levi Hatch	Aug. 15, 1861	Mustered out March 7, 1862, Fort Scott, Kas.
John G. Harris.............	April 1, 1862	Prom. First Lt., July 16, 1863; severely wounded in neck in action, Nov. 28, 1862, Cane Hill, Ark.
William M. Smalley......	July 16, 1863	Mustered out March 27, 1865, Leavenworth.

COMPANY L.

Name and Rank.	Date of Muster.	Remarks.
CAPTAIN.		
Henry P. Ledger...........	June 18, 1863	Mustered out, July 18, '65, DeVall's Bluff, Ark.
FIRST LIEUT.		
Henry P. Ledger...........	....	Promoted Captain, June 18, 1863.
Jefferson Denton...........	June 18, 1863	Died of small-pox, Ft. Scott, Kas., Nov. 20, '63.
Leonard J. Swingley.....	Feb. 15, 1864	Mustered out, July 18, 1865, DeVall's Bluff, Ark.
SECOND LIEUT.		
Leonard J. Swingley.....	June 18, 1863	Promoted First Lieutenant, February 15, 1864.
James Graham..............	Oct. 1, 1864	Mustered out, July 18, 1865, DeVall's Bluff, Ark.

COMPANY M.

Name and Rank.	Date of Muster.	Remarks.
CAPTAIN. John W. Duff	July 30, 1863	Mustered out, July 18, 1865, DeVall's Bluff, Ark.
FIRST LIEUT. James Brooks	July 30, 1863	Mustered out, July 18, 1865, DeVall's Bluff, Ark.
SECOND LIEUT. John C. Anderson	July 30, 1863	Mustered out, July 18, 1865, DeVall's Bluff, Ark.

NEW COMPANY A.

Name and Rank.	Date of Muster.	Remarks.
CAPTAIN. Charles O. Judson	Sept. 18, 1863	Mustered out, July 18, 1865, DeVall's Bluff, Ark.
FIRST LIEUT. Thomas G. Howell	Mar. 21, 1865	Mustered out, July 18, 1865, DeVall's Bluff, Ark.
SECOND LIEUT. William H. Shattuck	Jan. 4, 1864	Mustered out, July 18, 1865, DeVall's Bluff, Ark.

List of battles, etc., in which this regiment participated, showing loss reported in each:

Dry Wood (Sept. 2, 1861)—Killed, E. M., 1; wounded, E. M., 1. Morristown—Wounded, E. M., 2. Osceola—No loss. Carthage—Wounded, E. M., 1. Diamond Grove—Wounded, E. M., 1. Lost Creek—No loss. Tabourville—No loss. Clear Creek—Wounded, E. M., 4. Hickory Grove (Aug. 23, 1862)—No loss. Coon Creek—Killed, E. M., 2; wounded, O. 1, E. M. 21; missing, E. M., 1. Hickory Grove (Sept. 19, 1862,)—Killed, E. M., 1; wounded, E. M., 2. Granby—No loss. Newtonia (Sept. 30, 1862)—Wounded, E. M., 5; missing, E. M., 1. Newtonia (Oct. 4, 1862)—No loss. Old Fort Wayne—No loss. Bastin Mountain—No loss. Dry Wood (Nov. 9, 1862)—Killed, E. M., 1. Cane Hill—Killed, E. M., 1; wounded, O. 3, E. M. 9. Prairie Grove—Missing, E. M., 1. Webber Falls (April 11, 1863)—No loss. Webber Falls (April 26, 1863)—No loss. Fort Gibson—Killed, E. M., 1; missing, E. M., 2. Cabin Creek (July 1, 1863)—No loss. Honey Springs—Wounded, E. M., 5. Webber Falls (Oct. 12, 1863)—Killed, E. M., 1; missing, E. M., 1. Baker's Springs—Missing, E. M., 1. Roseville—Killed, E. M., 14. Stone's Farm—Killed, E. M., 6. Prairie D'Ann—No loss. Moscow—No loss. Dutch Mills—Missing, E. M., 9. Camden—Killed, E. M., 1; missing, E. M., 3. Poison Springs—Wounded, O. 1, E. M. 1; missing, O. 1, E. M. 3. Princeton—Missing, E. M., 2. Jenkins's Ferry—Missing, E. M., 1. Dardanelle—Killed, E. M., 2; wounded, E. M., 1. Clarksville—Missing, E. M., 1. Fayetteville—Killed, E. M., 1. Iron Bridge—Killed, E. M., 1. Mazard Prairie—Killed, E. M., 11; wounded, O. 1, E. M. 5; missing, O. 2, E. M. 151. Lee's Creek—Missing, E. M., 1. Van Buren—Killed, E. M., 1. Fort Smith—Missing, E. M., 1. Cabin Creek (Sept. 19, 1864)—Missing, E. M., 11. Fort Scott—Killed, E. M., 1. Cow Creek—Killed, O., 1. Training Post—No loss.—*U. S. Army Register.*

SEVENTH REGIMENT KANSAS VOLUNTEERS—CAVALRY.

Name and Rank.	Date of Muster.	Remarks.
COLONEL.		
Charles R. Jennison......	Oct. 28, 1861	Resigned, May 1, 1862.
Albert L. Lee..............	May 17, 1862	Promoted Brigadier General Vols., Nov. 29, '62.
Thomas P. Herrick.......	June 11, 1863	Mustered out, September 28, 1865.
LIEUT. COLONEL.		
Daniel R. Anthony.......	Oct. 29, 1861	Resigned, September 3, 1862.
Thomas P. Herrick.......	Sept. 3, 1862	Promoted Colonel, June 11, 1863.
David W. Houston........	July 1, 1863	Discharged for disability, February 1, 1864.
William S. Jenkins.......	Mar. 21, 1864	Mustered out, November 14, 1864.
Francis M. Malone........	Nov. 19, 1864	Mustered out with regiment, Sept. 29, 1865.
MAJOR.		
Daniel R. Anthony.......	Sept. 29, 1861	Promoted Lieutenant Colonel, Oct. 29, 1861.
Thomas P. Herrick.......	Oct. 28, 1861	Promoted Lieutenant Colonel, Sept. 3, 1862.
Albert L. Lee..............	Oct. 29, 1861	Promoted Lieutenant Colonel, May 17, 1862.
John T. Snoddy............	July 22, 1862	Resigned, March 6, 1863.
Clark S. Merriman........	Oct. 31, 1862	Resigned, July 13, 1863.
William S. Jenkins........	May 27, 1863	Promoted Lieutenant Colonel, March 21, 1864.
Francis M. Malone........	Aug. 12, 1863	Promoted Lieutenant Colonel, Nov. 19, 1864.
Charles H. Gregory.......	April 18, 1864	Mustered out with regiment, Sept. 29, 1865.
Levi H. Utt................	Nov. 17, 1864	Mustered out with regiment.
ADJUTANT.		
John T. Snoddy............	Oct. 14, 1861	Mustered out, July 17, 1862, per G. O. No. 26.
William O. Osgood.......	May 28, 1862	Mustered out, July 29, 1862.
Frederick W. Emery.....	Oct. 30, 1862	Promoted Capt. and A. A. Gen., June 30, 1863.
Simeon M. Fox............	Dec. 27, 1864	Mustered out with regiment.
QUARTERMASTER.		
Robert W. Hamer........	Oct. 15, 1861	Mustered out, July 17, 1862, per G. O. No. 25.
Ebenezer Snyder..........	July 23, 1863	Mustered out, December 3, 1864.
James Smith................	Jan. 9, 1865	Mustered out with regiment.
COMMISSARY.		
Lucius Whitney............	July 22, 1863	Mustered out with regiment.
SURGEON.		
Joseph L. Wever............	Jan. 10, 1862	Resigned, June 7, 1864.
Joseph S. Martin...........	July 18, 1864	Mustered out with regiment.
ASSISTANT SURGEON.		
Joseph S. Martin...........	Nov. 5, 1861	Promoted Surgeon, July 18, 1864.
Joel J. Crook................	Oct. 10, 1864	Mustered out with regiment.
CHAPLAIN.		
Samuel Ayers..............	Oct. 14, 1861	Resigned August 31, 1862.
Charles H. Lovejoy.......	April 19, 1863	Mustered out with regiment, Sept. 29, 1865.

COMPANY A.

Name and Rank.	Date of Muster.	Remarks.
CAPTAIN.		
Thomas P. Herrick........	Aug. 31, 1861	Promoted Major, October 28, 1861.
Levi H. Utt.................	Oct. 28, 1861	Promoted Major, November 17, 1864; wounded in action, April 2, 1863, Leighton, Ala.
Bazil C. Sanders............	Feb. 6, 1865	Mustered out, September 29, 1865.
FIRST LIEUT.		
Levi H. Utt.................	Aug. 31, 1861	Promoted Captain, October 28, 1861.
Aaron M. Pitts..............	Oct. 28, 1861	Promoted Captain Company D, October 3, 1862.
Bazil C. Sanders............	Dec. 5, 1862	Mustered out, January 3, 1865.
Henry M. Campbell......	Jan. 18, 1865	Mustered out with regiment.
SECOND LIEUT.		
Thomas H. Lohnes........	Aug. 31, 1861	Resigned, February 13, 1862.
Jacob M. Anthony........	Apr. 2, 1862	Promoted Captain Company I, May 16, 1863.
DeWitt C. Taylor..........	May 18, 1863	Mustered out, November 14, 1864.

COMPANY B.

Name and Rank.	Date of Muster.	Remarks.
CAPTAIN.		
Fred. Swoyer	Oct. 5, 1861	Killed in action, Jan. 3, 1864, Somerville, Tenn.
William S. Moorhouse...	June 23, 1863	Mustered out, March 7, 1865, St. Louis.
FIRST LIEUT.		
Fred. Swoyer	Sept. 15, 1861	Promoted Captain, October 5, 1861.
Isaac Gannett...............	Oct. 5, 1861	Mustered out with regiment, September 29, '65.
SECOND LIEUT.		
William S. Moorhouse...	Sept. 10, 1861	Promoted Captain, April 22, 1863.
Charles L. Thompson....	Apr. 22, 1863	Mustered out with regiment.

COMPANY C.

Name and Rank.	Date of Muster.	Remarks.
CAPTAIN.		
William S. Jenkins........	Sept. 5, 1861	Promoted Major, May 27, 1863.
James Smith	July 1, 1863	Mustered out with regiment.
FIRST LIEUT.		
Francis M. Ray	Oct. 10, 1861	Resigned, December 8, 1861.
James D. Snoddy	Dec. 22, 1861	Resigned, December 30, 1862.
John A Farmer............	Dec. 30, 1862	Resigned, July 23, 1863.
Bayless S. Campbell......	Oct. 31, 1863	Mustered out with regiment.
SECOND LIEUT.		
James Smith.................	Oct. 10, 1861	Promoted Captain, July 1, 1863.
Bayless S. Campbell......	July 23, 1863	Promoted First Lieutenant, October 31, 1863.
John H. Wildey............	May 2, 1864	Mustered out with regiment.

COMPANY D.

Name and Rank.	Date of Muster.	Remarks.
CAPTAIN.		
Clark S. Merriman........	Sept. 3, 1861	Promoted Major, October 3, 1862.
Aaron M. Pitts..............	Oct. 3, 1862	Mustered out with regiment.
FIRST LIEUT.		
Andrew Downing.........	Sept. 3, 1861	Mustered out, September 27, 1864.
William Henry..............	Dec. 28, 1864	Mustered out with regiment.
SECOND LIEUT.		
Isaiah J. Hughes...........	Sept. 3, 1861	Resigned, June 2, 1863.

COMPANY E.

Name and Rank.	Date of Muster.	Remarks.
CAPTAIN.		
George J. Yeager...........	Aug. 4, 1861	Resigned, October 8, 1861.
Charles H. Gregory.......	Oct. 9, 1861	Promoted Major, April 8, 1864.
John Noyes, jr..............	May 19, 1864	Mustered out with regiment.
FIRST LIEUT.		
Charles H. Gregory.......	Aug. 4, 1861	Promoted Captain, October 9, 1861.
Russell W. Maryhugh...	Oct. 18, 1861	Mustered out, October 12, 1864.
Edwin L. Saunders........	Jan. 6, 1865	Mustered out with regiment.
SECOND LIEUT.		
John Noyes, jr..............	Oct. 18, 1861	Promoted Captain, May 19, 1864.

COMPANY F.

Name and Rank.	Date of Muster.	Remarks.
CAPTAIN.		
Francis M. Malone........	Sept. 14, 1861	Promoted Major, August 12, 1863.
Edward Colbert............	Oct. 26, 1863	Mustered out with regiment.
FIRST LIEUT.		
Amos Hodgeman...........	Sept. 25, 1861	Promoted Captain Company H, July 23, 1863.
John Clark...................	Oct. 26, 1863	Resigned, February 15, 1865.
John W. Moore	July 17, 1865	Mustered out with regiment.
SECOND LIEUT.		
John A. Tanner............	Sept. 14, 1861	Promoted First Lieutenant Co. C, Oct. 31, 1862.
Edward Colbert............	Oct. 31, 1862	Promoted Captain, October 26, 1863.

COMPANY G.

Name and Rank.	Date of Muster.	Remarks.
CAPTAIN.		
Edward Thornton.........	Oct. 29, 1861	Mustered out, September 29, 1865.
FIRST LIEUT.		
Edward Thornton.........	Oct. 12, 1861	Promoted Captain, October 29, 1861.
David W. Houston........	Oct. 29, 1861	Promoted Captain Co. H, September 30, 1862.
Harmon D. Hunt..........	Apr. 2, 1863	Mustered out, November 30, 1864.
Zachariah Norris..........	Jan. 17, 1865	Mustered out with regiment.
SECOND LIEUT.		
Christr. C. Tompkins ...	Oct. 29, 1861	Resigned, February 1, 1862.
Richard H. Kerr...........	Feb. 11, 1862	Dismissed the service per G. O. No. 195, dated War Dept., Adjt. Gen.'s Office, Nov. 24, 1862.
Zachariah Norris..........	Aug. 31, 1863	Promoted First Lieutenant, January 17, 1865.
William A. Pease	July 1, 1865	Mustered out with regiment.

COMPANY H.

Name and Rank.	Date of Muster.	Remarks.
CAPTAIN.		
Marshall Cleveland *	Oct. 14, 1861	Resigned, November 1, 1861.
Horace Pardee............	Nov. 8, 1861	Resigned, May 15, 1862.
James L. Rafety..........	May 15, 1862	Discharged by S. O. No. 319, August 31, 1862.
David W. Houston........	Sept. 30, 1862	Promoted Lieutenant Colonel, July 1, 1863.
Amos Hodgeman...........	July 21, 1863	Died, October 16, 1863, near Oxford, Miss., of wounds received in action at Wyatt, Miss., October 10, 1863.
Charles L. Wall..........	Apr. 6, 1864	Mustered out with regiment.
FIRST LIEUT.		
James L. Rafety	Oct. 7, 1861	Promoted Captain, May 15, 1862.
John Kendall.............	May 15, 1862	Dismissed the service per G. O. No. 195, dated War Dept., Adjt. Gen.'s Office, Nov. 22, 1862.
Charles L. Wall..........	Sept. 1, 1862	Promoted Captain, April 6, 1864.
Samuel N. Ayers.........	May 28, 1864	Resigned, March 20, 1865.
Wallace E. Dickson......	July 17, 1865	Mustered out with regiment.
SECOND LIEUT.		
Charles E. Gordon........	Oct. 14, 1861	Resigned, February 11, 1862.
John Kendall.............	Mar. 15, 1862	Promoted First Lieutenant, May 15, 1862.
Charles L. Wall..........	May 15, 1862	Promoted First Lieutenant, September 1, 1862.
Samuel R. Doolittle......	Sept. 1, 1862	Resigned, March 3, 1863.
Joseph H. Nessel	Apr. 8, 1863	Dismissed the service, April 18, 1864.

* "Cleve," the Jayhawker.

COMPANY I.

Name and Rank.	Date of Muster.	Remarks.
CAPTAIN.		
John L. Merrick...........	Nov. 29, 1861	Resigned, November 27, 1862.
Jacob M. Anthony........	May 16, 1863	Mustered out with regiment.
FIRST LIEUT.		
Robert Hayes.............	Nov. 29, 1861	Died of disease, at Corinth, Miss., Sept. 20, 1862.
William W. Howe........	Sept. 20, 1862	Resigned, December 1, 1863.
William Weston	Apr. 8, 1864	Mustered out with regiment.
SECOND LIEUT.		
Edwin Miller	Nov. 23, 1861	Resigned, September 27, 1865.
William Weston...........	Oct. 18, 1862	Promoted First Lieutenant, April 8, 1864.

COMPANY K.

Name and Rank.	Date of Muster.	Remarks.
CAPTAIN.		
John Brown, jr.............	Jan. 10, 1862	Resigned on account of disability, May 27, 1862.
George H. Hoyt..........	May 27, 1862	Resigned on account of disability, Sept. 3, 1862.
Burr H. Bostwick........	Oct. 30, 1862	Mustered out with regiment.
FIRST LIEUT.		
Burr H. Bostwick........	Nov. 12, 1861	Promoted Captain, October 30, 1862.
William W. Crane........	Sept. 13, 1863	Mustered out with regiment.
SECOND LIEUT.		
George H. Hoyt...........	Nov. 11, 1861	Promoted Captain, May 27, 1862.
Frederick W. Emery.....	May 27, 1862	Promoted First Lieut. and Adjt., Oct. 30, 1862.
Thomas J. Woodburn...	Oct. 30, 1862	Killed in act., Dec. 5, '62, near Coffeeville, Miss.
William W. Crane........	Aug. 15, 1863	Promoted First Lieutenant, Sept. 13, 1863.

List of battles, etc., in which this regiment participated, showing loss reported in each:

Little Blue (Cos. A, B, and H)—Killed, E. M., 7; wounded, O. 1, E. M. 8. Little Santa Fe—Wounded, E. M., 1. Independence (November 26, 1861)—Killed, E. M., 1; wounded, E. M., 1. Columbus—Killed, E. M., 5. Kossuth—Killed, E. M., 5; wounded, E. M., 6. Rienzi (September 9, 1862)—Wounded, E. M., 1. Rienzi (September 18, 1862)—Wounded, E. M., 1; missing, E. M., 2. Baldwin—Killed, E. M., 1; missing, E. M., 2.

Corinth (Oct. 3-4, 1862)—Wounded, E. M., 1. Ruckersville—Wounded, E. M., 1. Jumpertown—No loss. Cold Water—No loss. Holly Springs—Wounded, E. M., 1. Oxford—No loss. Coffeeville—Killed, O. 2, E. M. 2; wounded, O. 2, E. M. 8; missing, E. M., 4. Somerville—Killed, O. 1, E. M. 3; wounded, E. M., 2; missing, E. M., 1. Germantown (Jan. 27, 1863)—No loss. Cold Water Station—No loss. Germantown (April 1, 1863)—Missing, E. M., 1. Salisbury—Killed, E. M., 1. Leighton—Wounded, O., 1. Tupelo (May 5, 1863)—Wounded, E. M., 2. Florence—Wounded, E. M., 3; missing, E. M., 3. Hamburg—Wounded, E. M., 2. Iuka (July 7, 1863)—No loss. Iuka (July 14, 1863)—Wounded, E. M., 1. Corinth (August 16, 1863)—No loss. Swallows' Bluff (A and C)—Killed, E. M., 1; wounded, E. M., 3. Byhalia—No loss. Wyatt—Killed, E. M., 3; wounded, O. 1, E. M. 6; missing, O. 1, E. M. 3. Ripley—Wounded, O., 1. King's Creek—Missing, E. M., 1. Memphis—Killed, E. M., 1. La Fayette—Killed, E. M., 1. New Albany—Wounded, E. M., 1. Tupelo (July 14, 1864)—Wounded, E. M., 1. Ellistown—Killed, E. M., 1. Tupelo (July 25, 1864)—No loss. Tallahatchie River—No loss. Hurricane Creek—Wounded, E. M., 2. Independence (October 22, 1864)—No loss. Big Blue—Wounded, E. M., 1. Little Osage River—No loss.—*U. S. Army Register.*

EIGHTH REGIMENT KANSAS VOLUNTEERS—INFANTRY.

Name and Rank.	Date of Muster.	Remarks.
COLONEL.		
Henry W. Wessels........	....	Promoted from Maj. 6th U. S. Inf.; ord. to rejoin com'd in U. S. A., per G. O. 4, W. D., series '62.
Robert H. Graham	....	Discharged, January 27, 1864, to date Nov. 11, 1862; died near St. Louis, Mo., Nov. 11, 1862.
John A. Martin.............	Nov. 1, 1862	Mustered out, November 15, 1864.
LIEUT. COLONEL.		
John A. Martin.............	Oct. 27, 1861	Promoted Colonel, November 1, 1862.
James L. Abernathy......	Nov. 1, 1862	Resigned, November 8, 1863.
Edward F. Schneider.....	Dec. 21, 1863	Resigned, June 11, 1864.
James M. Graham.........	June 26, 1864	Resigned, September 23, 1864, Atlanta, Ga.
John Conover..............	Oct. 21, 1864	Mustered out with regiment.
MAJOR.		
Edward F. Schneider.....	Sept. 17, 1861	Promoted Lieutenant Colonel, Dec. 21, 1863.
James M. Graham.........	Dec. 21, 1863	Promoted Lieutenant Colonel, June 26, 1864.
John Conover..............	Aug. 23, 1864	Promoted Lieutenant Colonel, Oct. 21, 1864.
Henry C. Austin	Nov. 16, 1864	Mustered out with regiment.
ADJUTANT.		
Sheldon C. Russell........	Oct. 23, 1861	Resigned, November 15, 1862.
James E. Love...............	Nov. 17, 1862	Promoted Captain Company K, July 16, 1863.
Solomon R. Washer......	July 31, 1863	Mustered out with regiment; wounded in action, September 19, 1863, Chicamauga, Ga.
QUARTERMASTER.		
E. P. Bancroft..............	Oct. 22, 1861	Promoted Major Ninth K. V. C., April 1, 1862.
Benjamin B. Joslin........	....	Mustered out Feb. 28, '62, date of consolidation.
Alfred Robinson...........	April 2, 1862	Absent without leave; name dropped from the rolls after three years' service; supposed to have been mustered out.
Adam Cosner...............	Sept. 1, 1864	Mustered out with regiment.
SURGEON.		
J. B. Woodward............	Oct. 4, 1861	Transferred to 9th K. V. C., February 28, 1862.
Oliver Chamberlain......	Dec. 10, 1861	Resigned, September 22, 1864.
Nathaniel C. Clark........	Nov. 14, 1864	Mustered out with regiment.
ASST. SURGEON.		
George W. Hogeboom ...	Oct. 23, 1861	Promoted Surgeon 11th K. Vols., Sept. 25, 1862.
John Butterbaugh.........	Nov. 9, 1862	Resigned, March 4, 1864.
Samuel E. Beach	May 25, 1863	Died of disease, Nashville, Tenn., Nov. 4, 1863.
Edwin J. Talcott..........	May 1, 1864	Resigned, February 15, 1865.
CHAPLAIN.		
John Paulson...............	June 17, 1863	Mustered out with regiment.

COMPANY A.

Name and Rank.	Date of Muster.	Remarks.
CAPTAIN.		
James L. Abernathy......	Aug. 28, 1861	Promoted Lieutenant Colonel, Nov. 1, 1862.
Samuel Laighton............	Oct. 1, 1862	Resigned, November 27, 1864.
FIRST LIEUT.		
Samuel Laighton............	Aug. 28, 1861	Promoted Captain, October 1, 1862.
Roland Risdon..............	Oct. 1, 1862	Resigned, April 13, 1864.
Eli Balderston..............	July 1, 1864	Promoted Captain Company G, Oct. 12, 1864.
Ferdinand A. Berger.....	Oct. 21, 1864	Mustered out with regiment; severely wounded in action, Dec. 16, 1864, Nashville, Tenn.
SECOND LIEUT.		
John Conover..............	Aug. 28, 1861	Promoted 1st Lieut. Co. F, December 12, 1861.
Seth Foot	Dec. 12, 1861	Died of disease, Farmersburg, Ia., May 14, 1864.

COMPANY B.

Name and Rank.	Date of Muster.	Remarks.
CAPTAIN.		
David Block..................	Sept. 2, 1861	Resigned on account of disability, Apr. 20, 1863.
Claudius Keifer............	May 14, 1863	Wounded in right thigh in action, Sept. 19, 1863, Chicamauga, Ga.; wounded in arm and thigh in action, August 4, 1864, Atlanta, Ga.; no evidence of muster-out on file.
FIRST LIEUT.		
Charles Alton..............	Sept. 2, 1861	Resigned, May 7, 1863.
Zacharias Burkhardt.....	May 27, 1863	Died, Atlanta, Ga., October 28, 1863, in Rebel prison of wounds received in action, September 19, 1863, Chicamauga, Ga.
August Schulz..............	Feb. 3, 1864	Mustered out with regiment.
SECOND LIEUT.		
Martin Manerhan.........	Sept. 3, 1861	Resigned, July 15, 1862.
Claudius Keifer............	July 21, 1862	Promoted Captain, May 14, 1863.
William Backer............	May 27, 1863	Deserted, Nashville, Tenn., Sept. —, 1863.
Zacharias Burkhardt.....	May 14, 1863	Promoted First Lieutenant, May 27, 1863.

COMPANY C.

Name and Rank.	Date of Muster.	Remarks.
CAPTAIN.		
James M. Graham.........	Nov. 7, 1861	Promoted Major, December 21, 1863.
Richard R. Bridgland....	Mar. 8, 1864	Resigned, October 12, 1864.
George H. Robb............	Mar. 1, 1865	Mustered out with regiment.
FIRST LIEUT.		
John G. Becktold...........	Sept. 20, 1861	Resigned, June 3, 1863.
Richard R. Bridgland....	June 19, 1863	Promoted Captain, March 8, 1864.
George H. Robb............	Apr. 17, 1864	Promoted Captain, March 1, 1865.
SECOND LIEUT.		
Richard R. Bridgland...	Sept. 20, 1861	Promoted First Lieutenant, June 19, 1863.
William Becker............	Oct. 24, 1863	Died of chronic diarrhœa, Chattanooga, Tenn., November 21, 1863.

COMPANY D.

Name and Rank.	Date of Muster.	Remarks.
CAPTAIN.		
Arthur W. Williams......	Nov. 9, 1861	Resigned, February 2, 1863.
Stephen B. Todd	April 29, 1863	Resigned on acc't of disability, August 12, 1863.
John L. Graham............	....	Killed in action September 19, 1863, Chicamauga, Ga., before being mustered in.
Philip Rockefeller.........	Nov. 4, 1861	Resigned, August 13, 1864.
FIRST LIEUT.		
Arthur W. Williams......	Oct. 10, 1861	Promoted Captain, November 9, 1861.
Stephen B. Todd	Nov. 9, 1861	Promoted Captain, April 29, 1863.
John L. Graham............	April 30, 1863	Promoted Captain, September 13, 1863.
Philip Rockefeller.........	Sept. 15, 1863	Promoted Captain, November 4, 1863.
Valentine S. Fisk	Nov. 24, 1863	Mustered out, January 27, 1865, Nashville, Tenn., by reason of having served three years.
Thomas Adamson.........	Sept. 2, 1865	Mustered out with regiment.
SECOND LIEUT.		
John L. Graham............	Nov. 9, 1861	Promoted First Lieutenant, April 30, 1863.
Philip Rockefeller.........	April 30, 1863	Promoted First Lieutenant, September 15, 1863.

COMPANY E.

Name and Rank.	Date of Muster.	Remarks.
CAPTAIN.		
John Greelish...............	Nov. 5, 1861	Resigned, June 6, 1864; wounded in action, September 19, 1863, Chicamauga, Ga.
Henry C. Austin...........	Jan. 30, 1862	Promoted Major, November 16, 1864.
FIRST LIEUT.		
John Greelish...............	....	Promoted Captain, November 5, 1861.
Milton Rose..................	Nov. 5, 1861	Mustered out, Dec. 5, 1864, Nashville, Tenn.
Elisha D. Rose..............	Dec. 6, 1864	Mustered out with regiment.
SECOND LIEUT.		
Daniel D. Rooks	Nov. 5, 1861	Resigned, July 13, 1862.
Solomon R. Washer......	July 28, 1862	Prom. First Lieut. and Adjutant, July 31, 1863.

COMPANY F.

Name and Rank.	Date of Muster.	Remarks.
CAPTAIN.		
A. W. J. Brown	Jan. 1, 1862	Mustered out, Feb. 28, 1862, Osawatomie, Kas.
John Conover...............	Mar. 15, 1862	Promoted Major, August 23, 1864.
A. Earl Beardsley.........	Jan. 20, 1865	Dismissed, July 24, 1865, for absence without leave.
FIRST LIEUT.		
William S. Newbery......	Aug. 28, 1861	Resigned, April 29, 1864, Leavenworth, Kas.
John Conover...............	Dec. 12, 1861	Promoted Captain, March 15, 1862.
James A. Neff..............	Aug. 23, 1864	Mustered out with regiment.
SECOND LIEUT.		
J. Milton Hadley	Mar. 15, 1862	Promoted First Lieut. 9th K.V.C., June 25, 1863.
W. J. Larimer..............	Jan. 1, 1862	Mustered out as supernumerary, February 28, 1862, Leavenworth, Kas.
A. Earl Beardsley.........	Aug. 23, 1863	Promoted Captain, Jan. 10, 1865; wounded in action, Sept. 20, 1863, Chicamauga, Ga.; also July 2, 1864, Kenesaw, Ga.

COMPANY G.

Name and Rank.	Date of Muster.	Remarks.
CAPTAIN.		
Nicholas Harrington.....	Dec. 1, 1861	Resigned, Sept. 9, 1863, Murfreesboro, Tenn.
Robert Flickenger.........	Oct. 5, 1863	Resigned, April 6, 1864, Leavenworth, Kas.
Eli Balderston..............	Oct. 12, 1864	Mustered out with regiment.
FIRST LIEUT.		
Nicholas Harrington.....	Oct. 2, 1861	Promoted Captain, December 1, 1861.
Robert Flickenger.........	Dec. 1, 1861	Promoted Captain, October 5, 1863.
David Baker	Sept. 10, 1863	No evidence of muster-out on file; wounded in action, Sept. 19, 1863, Chicamauga, Ga.
SECOND LIEUT.		
Joseph Randolph..........	Dec. 1, 1861	Resigned, July 24, 1863, Murfreesboro, Tenn.

COMPANY H.

Name and Rank.	Date of Muster.	Remarks.
CAPTAIN.		
Edgar Trego	Jan. 30, 1862	Killed in action, Sept. 19, '63, Chicamauga, Ga.
Samuel R. Stanley	Sept. 1, 1864	Mustered out with regiment.
FIRST LIEUT.		
Frank Curtis................	Jan. 30, 1862	Discharged for disability, July 6, 1864; wounded in action, Sept. 20, 1863, Chicamauga, Ga.
Samuel R. Stanley	July 7, 1864	Promoted Captain, September 1, 1864.
Adam Cosner..................	Sept. 1, 1864	Transferred to Field and Staff as regimental Quartermaster, September 15, 1865.
SECOND LIEUT.		
Harvey C. Blackman.....	Jan. 30, 1862	Promoted Captain in U. S. Colored Troops.

COMPANY I.

Name and Rank.	Date of Muster.	Remarks.
CAPTAIN. Henry C. Austin	Jan. 30, 1862	Transferred to Co. E, to date July 4, 1864; wounded in action, September 19, 1863, Chicamauga, Ga.; captured July 4, 1864, while absent from his command.
Marion Brooks.............	Sept. 16, 1864	Mustered out with regiment.
FIRST LIEUT. Henry C. Austin	Oct. 24, 1861	Promoted Captain, January 30, 1862.
Marion Brooks..............	Jan. 30, 1862	Promoted Captain, September 16, 1864.
Charles Slawson............	Oct. 21, 1864	Mustered out with regiment.
SECOND LIEUT. Lewis B. Graham..........	Mar. 12, 1862	Mustered out August 1, 1862, Jacinto, Miss.
Byron Slemmons...........	Mar. 23, 1863	Resigned, July 17, 1865; wounded in action, September 19, 1863, Chicamauga, Ga.

COMPANY K.

Name and Rank.	Date of Muster.	Remarks.
CAPTAIN. William S. Herd............	Oct. 24, 1861	Resigned on account of disability, June 16, '63.
James E. Love...............	July 16, 1863	Mustered out, May 15, 1865.
FIRST LIEUT. James E. Love...............	Oct. 10, 1861	Promoted 1st Lieut. and Adjutant, Nov. 17, '62.
William H. Babcock......	Mar. 23, 1863	Resigned, June 28, 1864.
Jacob Niuffer	Aug. 30, 1864	Mustered out with regiment.
SECOND LIEUT. Fred. R. Neat...............	Jan. 1, 1862	Resigned, February 22, 1862.
William H. Babcock......	April 19, 1862	Promoted First Lieutenant, March 23, 1863.
Augustin J. Quinn........	Mar. 23, 1863	Discharged for disability, Dec. 28, '64, Cin., O.

List of battles, etc., in which this regiment participated, showing loss reported in each:

Rocky Bluff—No loss. Chaplin Hills—No loss. Lancaster—No loss. Chicamauga—Killed, O. 2, E. M. 34; wounded, O. 7, E. M. 141; missing, E. M., 19. Chattanooga—Killed, E. M., 5; wounded, O. 2, E. M. 25. Resaca——. Peachtree Creek—Wounded, E. M., 1. Atlanta—Killed, E. M., 1; wounded, O. 2, E. M. 17; missing, O. 1, E. M. 1. Nashville— Killed, E. M., 8; wounded, O. 1, E. M. 27.—*U. S. Army Register.*

NINTH REGIMENT KANSAS VOLUNTEERS—CAVALRY.

Name and Rank.	Date of Muster.	Remarks.
COLONEL. Edward Lynde..............	Mar. 24, 1862	Mustered out, Nov. 25, 1864, DeVall's Bluff, Ark.
LIEUT. COLONEL. Charles S. Clarke..........	Jan. 2, 1862	Mustered out, Jan. 16, 1865, DeVall's Bluff, Ark.
Willoughby Doudna......	May 15, 1865	Mustered out, July 17, 1865, DeVall's Bluff, Ark.
MAJOR. James M. Pomeroy.........	Feb. 28, 1862	Mustered out, Jan. 16, 1865, DeVall's Bluff, Ark.
Edward P. Bancroft......	April 1, 1862	Resigned, February 19, 1863.
Willoughby Doudna......	Aug. 21, 1863	Promoted Lieutenant Colonel, May 15, 1865.
Luin K. Thacher............	Jan. 5, 1863	Mustered out, Nov. 25, 1864, DeVall's Bluff, Ark.; wounded in skirmish, Osage river, Mo., 1863.
J. Milton Hadley..........	May 15, 1865	Mustered out, July 17, 1865, DeVall's Bluff, Ark.
ADJUTANT. Luin K. Thacher...........	Oct. 14, 1862	Promoted Major, January 5, 1863.
Albert D. Searl..............	July 9, 1863	Resigned, October 10, 1864.
BATTALION ADJT. John W. Hatcher..........	April 1, 1862	Promoted Reg'l Commissary, October 14, 1862.
Hayden M. Thompson...	May 28, 1862	Mustered out, July 29, 1862.
QUARTERMASTER. William Rosenthal........	Feb. 5, 1863	Resigned, September 12, 1864.
Jonathan B Snider........	Oct. 31, 1864	Mustered out, July 17, 1865, DeVall's Bluff, Ark.

NINTH REGIMENT KANSAS VOLUNTEERS—CAVALRY—*Continued.*

Name and Rank.	Date of Muster.	Remarks.
COMMISSARY.		
John W. Hatcher	Oct. 14, 1862	Resigned, August 12, 1864.
Isaac O. Pickering	Sept. 3, 1864	Mustered out, July 17, 1865, DeVall's Bluff, Ark.
SURGEON.		
Henry C. Bostwick	Mar. 27, 1862	Resigned, January 2, 1863.
William Wakefield	April 4, 1863	Mustered out, March 8, 1865, DeVall's Bluff, Ark.
ASSIST. SURGEON.		
William Wakefield	Sept. 2, 1862	Promoted Surgeon, April 4, 1863.
Norman T. Winans	April 6, 1863	Mustered out, Nov. 25, 1864, DeVall's Bluff, Ark.
Abijah J. Beach	Jan. 14, 1864	Mustered out, July 17, 1865, DeVall's Bluff, Ark.
CHAPLAIN.		
Gilbert S. Northup	Mar. 27, 1862	Resigned, March 9, 1863.
Strange Brooks	Mar. 24, 1864	Mustered out, Nov 25, 1864, DeVall's Bluff, Ark.

COMPANY A.

Name and Rank.	Date of Muster.	Remarks.
CAPTAIN.		
George F. Earl	Oct. 24, 1861	Mustered out, November 19, 1864, Leavenworth.
FIRST LIEUT.		
George F. Earl	Sept. 13, 1861	Promoted Captain, October 24, 1861.
Joshua A. Pike	Oct. 24, 1861	Promoted Capt. Company K, January 24, 1863.
Albert D. Searl	Jan. 1, 1863	Promoted Adjutant, July 9, 1863.
Amzi J. Steele	July 19, 1863	Assigned to new Company A.
SECOND LIEUT.		
Albert D. Searl	Oct. 24, 1861	Promoted First Lieut., January 24, 1863.
Benton Smith	Jan. 27, 1863	Resigned, April 8, 1864.
Henry C. Davis	June 23, 1864	Mustered out, November 19, 1864, Leavenworth.

COMPANY B.

Name and Rank.	Date of Muster.	Remarks.
CAPTAIN.		
Asaph Allen	Nov. 20, 1861	Mustered out Nov. 19, 1864, Leavenworth, Kas.
FIRST LIEUT.		
Asaph Allen	Oct. 12, 1861	Promoted Captain, November 20, 1861.
Lemuel T. Heritage	Nov. 20, 1861	Resigned, March 28, 1862.
Robert Madden	April 5, 1862	Resigned, April 19, 1863.
Henry Brandley	May 17, 1863	Assigned to new Company B.
SECOND LIEUT.		
Robert Madden	Nov. 20, 1861	Promoted First Lieutenant, April 5, 1862.
Henry Brandley	June 1, 1862	Promoted 1st Lieut., May 17, 1863; wounded by Indians, Feb. 27, 1863, near Ft. Halleck, Col.
Hugh W. Williams	May 17, 1863	Resigned, April 8, 1864.
William T. Kirby	June 24, 1864	Mustered out, Nov. 19, '64, Leavenworth, Kan.

COMPANY C.

Name and Rank.	Date of Muster.	Remarks.
CAPTAIN.		
John E. Stewart	July 24, 1861	Mustered out, Oct. 25, '64, Leavenworth, Kan.
FIRST LIEUT.		
John Bowles	July 24, 1861	Prom. Lt. Col. 1st Kas. Col'd Inft., Jan. 29, '63.
Lorendus B. Conant	Jan. 29, 1863	Assigned to duty as 1st Lieut. new Company A.
SECOND LIEUT.		
Wash. J. Buchanan	July 24, 1861	Resigned, April 12, 1862.
Lorendus B. Conant	Apr. 12, 1862	Promoted First Lieutenant, January 29, 1863.
Robert C. Philbrick	Mar. 3, 1863	Assigned to duty as 2d Lieut. new Company A.

COMPANY D.

Name and Rank.	Date of Muster.	Remarks.
CAPTAIN. Charles F. Coleman.......	Oct. 19, 1861	Mustered out, Dec. 19, 1864, Little Rock, Ark.
FIRST LIEUT. Anderson C. Smith........	Oct. 19, 1861	Resigned, May 20, 1862.
Austin G. Carpenter......	May 20, 1862	Mustered out, Dec. 19, 1864, Little Rock, Ark.
SECOND LIEUT. Avery T. Spencer..........	Oct. 19, 1861	Killed in action, Feb. 19, 1863, Spring River, Mo.
Jeremiah R. Sencenich..	Mar. 2, 1863	Assigned to new Company D.

COMPANY E.

Name and Rank.	Date of Muster.	Remarks.
CAPTAIN. Henry Flesher..............	Oct. 19, 1861	Mustered out, Jan. 16, 1865, DeVall's Bluff, Ark.
FIRST LIEUT. Claudius M. Meek.........	Oct. 19, 1861	Resigned, May 22, 1862.
Nimrod Hankins...........	June 10, 1862	Mustered out, Jan. 16, '65, DeVall's Bluff, Ark.
SECOND LIEUT. Jesse Parsons................	Oct. 19, 1861	Mustered out, Jan. 16, '65, DeVall's Bluff, Ark.

COMPANY F.

Name and Rank.	Date of Muster.	Remarks.
CAPTAIN. Benjamin F. Goss.........	Jan. 16, 1862	Mustered out, Jan. 16, 1865, DeVall's Bluff, Ark.
FIRST LIEUT. Isaac W. Dow..............	Jan. 16, 1862	Mustered out, Jan. 16, 1865, DeVall's Bluff, Ark.
SECOND LIEUT. Henry H. Opdyke	Jan. 16, 1862	Mustered out, Jan. 16, 1865, DeVall's Bluff, Ark.

COMPANY G.

Name and Rank.	Date of Muster.	Remarks.
CAPTAIN. Willoughby Doudna......	Dec. 17, 1861	Promoted Major, August 21, 1863.
J. Milton Hadley..........	Nov. 1, 1863	Assigned to new Company C.
FIRST LIEUT. Lewis C. Thompson	Oct. 15, 1861	Resigned, May 16, 1862.
Luin K. Thacher..........	May 1, 1862	Promoted Adjutant. October 14, 1862.
J. Milton Hadley..........	June 25, 1863	Promoted Captain, November 1, 1863.
Samuel M. Stansbury ...	Dec. 15, 1863	Mustered out, Jan. 16, 1865, DeVall's Bluff, Ark.
SECOND LIEUT. John N. Walkup..........	Oct. 15, 1861	Died of disease, Easton, Kansas, June 6, 1862.
Henry B. Hall..	June 10, 1862	Mustered out, Jan. 16, 1865, DeVall's Bluff, Ark.

COMPANY H.

Name and Rank.	Date of Muster.	Remarks.
CAPTAIN. Thomas P. Killen.........	Jan. 2, 1862	Mustered out, Jan. 16, 1865, DeVall's Bluff, Ark.
FIRST LIEUT. James W. Christian......	Jan. 2, 1862	Resigned, August —, 1862.
James Crane................	Mar. 17, 1863	Mustered out, Jan. 16, 1865, DeVall's Bluff, Ark.
SECOND LIEUT. Horatio N. F. Reed	Jan. 2, 1862	Promoted Captain Co. I, May 28, 1862.
James Crane................	May 28, 1862	Promoted First Lieutenant, March 17, 1863.
John M. Singer.............	Mar. 21, 1863	Resigned, January 12, 1865.

COMPANY I.

Name and Rank.	Date of Muster.	Remarks.
CAPTAIN. Horatio N. F. Reed	May 28, 1862	Mustered out, March 22, '65, DeVall's Bluff, Ark.
FIRST LIEUT. Matthew Cowley...........	Mar. 6, 1862	Died of disease, Little Rock, Ark., Oct. 7, 1864.
Jeremiah D. Conner.......	Jan. 9, 1865	Mustered out, March 22, '65, DeVall's Bluff, Ark.
SECOND LIEUT. Albert S. W. Knapper...	Nov. 6, 1861	Prom. Captain Co. B, 16th K. V. C., Dec. 19, 1863.
Jeremiah D. Conner	Jan. 31, 1864	Promoted First Lieutenant, January 9, 1865.

COMPANY K.

Name and Rank.	Date of Muster.	Remarks.
CAPTAIN. Thomas M. Bowen........	July 30, 1862	Prom. Col. Thirteenth K. V. I., Sept. 20, 1862.
Joshua A. Pike.............	Jan. 24, 1863	Resigned, September 20, 1864.
Wm. J. Houghawout.....	Nov. 3, 1864	Mustered out, June 24, 1865.
FIRST LIEUT. Thomas M. Bowen........	July 11, 1862	Promoted Captain, July 30, 1862.
John D. Wells..............	Aug. 4, 1862	Resigned, June 24, 1863.
John K. Whitson..........	Sept. 25, 1863	Mustered out, June 24, 1865.
SECOND LIEUT. Francis N. Sales............	Aug. 4, 1862	Resigned, March 9, 1863.
Wm. J. Houghawout.....	April 19, 1863	Promoted Captain, Nov. 3, 1864; was wounded in action, Oct. 23, 1864, Hurricane Creek, Ark.
Charles Johns..............	Dec. 6, 1864	Mustered out, June 24, 1865.

COMPANY L.

Name and Rank.	Date of Muster.	Remarks.
CAPTAIN. John I. DeLashmutt......	Aug. 31, 1863	Resigned, April 18, 1865.
James L. Arnold...........	May 15, 1865	Mustered out, July 17, 1865, DeVall's Bluff, Ark.
FIRST LIEUT. John I. DeLashmutt.....	May 2, 1863	Promoted Captain, August 31, 1863.
James L. Arnold...........	Sept. 21, 1863	Promoted Captain, March 15, 1865.
Willard Raymour..........	May 15, 1865	Mustered out, July 17, 1865, DeVall's Bluff, Ark.
SECOND LIEUT. Charles C. Southard	Aug. 15, 1863	Resigned, December 31, 1864.

COMPANY M.

Name and Rank.	Date of Muster.	Remarks.
CAPTAIN. Wm. W. P. McConnell...	Aug. 21, 1863	Resigned, Sept. 30, 1864, Little Rock, Arkansas.
John L. Price..............	Dec. 24, 1864	Mustered out, July 17, 1865, DeVall's Bluff, Ark.
FIRST LIEUT. Stephen L. Kenyon	Dec. 20, 1863	Mustered out, July 17, 1865, DeVall's Bluff, Ark.
SECOND LIEUT. John L. Price..............	Dec. 3, 1863	Promoted Captain, December 24, 1864.

NEW COMPANY A.

Name and Rank.	Date of Muster.	Remarks.
CAPTAIN. Amzi J. Steele	Feb. 16, 1863	Mustered out, July 17, '65, at DeVall's Bluff, Ark.
FIRST LIEUT. Lorendus B. Conant......	Jan. 29, 1863	Resigned, January 7, 1865.
Robert C. Philbrick.......	May 20, 1865	Mustered out, July 17, '65, at DeVall's Bluff, Ark.
SECOND LIEUT. Robert C. Philbrick.......	Mar. 3, 1863	Promoted First Lieutenant, May 20, 1865.

NEW COMPANY B.

Name and Rank.	Date of Muster.	Remarks.
CAPTAIN. Henry Brandley............	May 15, 1865	Mustered out, July 17, '65, at DeVall's Bluff, Ark.
FIRST LIEUT. Henry Brandley	May 17, 1863	Promoted Captain, May 15, 1865.
Joseph L. Denison	May 20, 1865	Mustered out, July 17, '65, at DeVall's Bluff, Ark.
SECOND LIEUT. Lewis McHone.............	May 15, 1865	Mustered out, July 17, '65, at DeVall's Bluff, Ark.

NEW COMPANY C.

Name and Rank.	Date of Muster.	Remarks.
CAPTAIN. J. Milton Hadley...........	Dec. 5, 1863	Promoted Major, May 15, 1865.
FIRST LIEUT. David M. Hester	Mar. 14, 1865	Mustered out, July 17, '65, at DeVall's Bluff, Ark.
SECOND LIEUT. Henry B. Hall...............	June 10, 1862	Resigned, February 10, 1865.
Edwin G. Parker...........	May 13, 1865	Mustered out, July 17, '65, at DeVall's Bluff, Ark.

NEW COMPANY D.

Name and Rank.	Date of Muster.	Remarks.
CAPTAIN. Jeremiah R. Sencenich..	May 15, 1865	Mustered out, July 17, '65, at DeVall's Bluff, Ark.
FIRST LIEUT. Lewis Edmundson.........	May 15, 1865	Mustered out, July 17, '65, at DeVall's Bluff, Ark.
SECOND LIEUT. Jeremiah R. Sencenich..	Mar. 2, 1863	Promoted Captain, May 15, 1865.
Aaron M. Thomas.........	May 15, 1865	Mustered out, July 17, '65, at DeVall's Bluff, Ark.

List of battles, etc., in which this regiment participated, showing loss reported in each:

Medoc (Co. C) — No loss. Ball's Mills (C) — No loss. Dry Wood (C) — Killed, E. M., 3; wounded, E. M., 1. Morristown (C) — No loss. Osceola (C) — No loss. Locust Grove (D, E, and H) — Killed, E. M., 1. Newtonia (D, E, F, and H) — Killed, E. M., 2; wounded, E. M., 5; missing, E. M., 2. Cane Hill (November 28, 1862) — No loss. Cane Hill (January 2, 1863, H) — Missing, E. M., 2. Spring River (D) — Killed, O., 1; wounded, E. M., 1. Fort Halleck (B) — Wounded, O., 1. Westport (E and K) — Killed, E. M., 14; wounded, E. M., 6. Blue River (K) — No loss. Cabin Creek (C) — Killed, E. M., 1; wounded, E. M., 1. Grand Pass (B) — Wounded, E. M., 6. Honey Springs (C) — No loss. Brooklyn (K) — No loss. Baxter Springs — Killed, E. M., 1. Harrisonville (G) — Killed, E. M., 1. Fayetteville (C) — Killed, E. M., 1. Frog Bayou — No loss. Bull Bayou — Killed, E. M., 1. Bull Creek (I) — No loss. Whitlen's Mills — Killed, E. M., 1; wounded, E. M., 1. Hurricane Creek — . Killed, E. M., 1; wounded, O., 1. — *U. S. Army Register.*

TENTH REGIMENT KANSAS VOLUNTEERS—INFANTRY.

Name and Rank.	Date of Muster.	Remarks.
COLONEL.		
James Montgomery	July 24, 1861	Transferred to Second Regiment South Carolina Colored Volunteers.
William Weer	June 20, 1861	Dismissed the service by G. O. No. 123, dated Headq'rs Dept. of Mo., St. Louis, Aug. 20, '64.
William F. Cloud	Mar. 28, 1862	Transferred to Second K. V. C., June 1, 1862.
LIEUT. COLONEL.		
James G. Blunt	July 24, 1861	Promoted Brig. Gen. U. S. Vols., April 8, 1862.
John T. Burris	July 24, 1861	Mustered out with regiment, August 20, 1865; promoted Brevet Colonel, March 13, 1865.
Charles S. Hills	Mar. 1, 1865	Promoted Brevet Colonel, March 25, 1865; mustered out, Aug. 30, 1865, at Montgomery, Ala.
MAJOR.		
Otis B. Gunn		Resigned, May 5, 1862.
Henry H. Williams	July 24, 1861	Mustered out with regiment, August 20, 1864.
ADJUTANT.		
Casimio B. Zulavsky	July 24, 1861	Mustered out, date unknown.
James A. Phillips	July 24, 1861	Promoted Major Third Indian H.G., July 20, '63.
Thomas McGannon	May 29, 1863	Mustered out with the regiment, Aug. 20, 1864.
QUARTERMASTER.		
Alfred Larzelere	Aug. —, 1861	Assigned to Third Indian Home Guards.
Alfred Gray	Feb. 11, 1862	Transferred to Co. B, Fifth Kansas Cavalry.
John G. Haskell	July 24, 1861	Prom. Capt. and A.Q.M., U.S. Vols., June 11, '62.
Alfred J. Lloyd	Aug. 13, 1862	Prom. Capt. and A.Q.M., U.S. Vols., April 7, '64.
SURGEON.		
Albert Newman	July 24, 1861	Mustered out, February 14, 1862.
Mahlon Bailey		Resigned, May 2, 1862.
John W. Scott	Aug. 15, 1861	Resigned, May 9, 1863.
J. B. Woodward	Oct. 4, 1861	Resigned, May 20, 1864.
Henry H. Tuttle	June 7, 1864	Mustered out, Aug. 30, '65, at Montgomery, Ala.
ASST. SURGEON.		
Edwin H. Grant		Mustered out, date unknown.
Richard W. Shipley		No evidence of muster-out on file.
George A. Miller	Aug. 28, 1862	Resigned, date unknown.
P. Gould Parker	Mar. 20, 1862	Resigned, July 23, 1864.
Henry H. Tuttle	Sept. 10, 1862	Promoted Surgeon, June 7, 1864.
CHAPLAIN.		
H. H. Moore	July 24, 1861	Mustered out, February 14, 1862.
Reeder M. Fish	Sept. 4, 1861	No evidence of muster-out on file.
John H. Drummond	May 1, 1862	Mustered out with regiment, August 20, 1864.

COMPANY A.

Name and Rank.	Date of Muster.	Remarks.
CAPTAIN.		
Josiah E. Hayes	July 16, 1861	Resigned, June 12, 1862.
Thomas E. Milhoan	June 23, 1862	Mustered out, Aug. 18, 1864, at Leavenworth.
FIRST LIEUT.		
Thomas E. Milhoan	July 16, 1861	Promoted Captain, June 23, 1862.
Stephen J. Willes	Aug. 26, 1862	Transferred as First Lt. Co. F, Fourth Reg. V. R. C., Nov. 7, 1863; severely wounded in right hip in action, Dec. 7, '62, at Prairie Grove, Ark.
William B. Stone	Nov. 10, 1863	Assigned to duty to new Co. C.
SECOND LIEUT.		
Fernando H. Burris	July 16, 1861	Resigned, April 16, 1862.
William B. Stone	May 24, 1862	Promoted First Lieutenant, Nov. 10, 1863.

COMPANY B.

Name and Rank.	Date of Muster.	Remarks.
CAPTAIN.		
Matthew Quigg	July 16, 1861	Mustered out, Aug. 19, 1864, Leavenworth, Kas.
FIRST LIEUT.		
Seth M. Tucker	July 16, 1861	Transferred to Company I, August 19, 1864.
SECOND LIEUT.		
David Whittaker	July 16, 1861	No evidence of muster-out on file; absent on det. service date of muster-out of company.

20

COMPANY C.

Name and Rank.	Date of Muster.	Remarks.
CAPTAIN.		
John A. Foreman........	....	Promoted Major 3d Indian Regt., July 11, 1862.
William R. Allen..........	July 30, 1861	Mustered out, February 13, 1862.
George D. Brooke	July 12, 1863	Assigned to new Company C.
FIRST LIEUT.		
George D. Brooke	July 24, 1861	Promoted Captain, June 12, 1863.
Joseph K. Hudson.........	....	No evidence of muster-out on file.
SECOND LIEUT.		
Isaac M. Ruth...............	July 24, 1861	No evidence of muster-out on file.

COMPANY D.

Name and Rank.	Date of Muster.	Remarks.
CAPTAIN.		
Eli Snyder...................	....	Resigned, May 27, 1862.
Charles S. Hills.............	May 11, 1862	Assigned to new Company A.
FIRST LIEUT.		
John Downing..............	Feb. —, 1862	Mustered out, Feb. 11, 1862, per G. O., W. D., series of 1862.
George D. Brooke.........	July 24, 1861	Transferred to Company C, September 28, 1862.
Frederick A. Smalley....	Sept. 1, 1862	Assigned to new Company D.
SECOND LIEUT.		
Frederick A. Smalley...	July 24, 1861	Promoted First Lieutenant, September 1, 1862.
Robert W. Wood...........	Sept. 1, 1862	Assigned to new Company A.

COMPANY E.

Name and Rank.	Date of Muster.	Remarks.
CAPTAIN.		
John F. Broadhead.......	July 25, 1861	Mustered out with regiment, August 18, 1864.
Samuel Stevenson..........	Aug. 2, 1861	Died of disease, Mound City, Kas., 1861.
FIRST LIEUT.		
David Schorn	....	Died, Dec. 18, 1862, Fayetteville, Ark., of wounds rec'd in action, Dec. 7, 1862, Prairie Grove, Ark.
James McArthur...........	Aug. 2, 1861	Mustered out, February 14, 1862.
William B. Keith..........	Mar. 1, 1863	Mustered out with regiment.
SECOND LIEUT.		
William B. Keith..........	Aug. 2, 1861	Promoted First Lieutenant, March 1, 1863.
Solomon Smith.............	May 20, 1863	Mustered out with regiment.

COMPANY F.

Name and Rank.	Date of Muster.	Remarks.
CAPTAIN.		
John J. Boyd...:.............	Aug. 6, 1861	Resigned, August 11, 1862.
Nathan Price	Sept. 15, 1862	Mustered out with regiment, August 19, 1864.
FIRST LIEUT.		
Nathan Price...............	Aug. 13, 1861	Promoted Captain, September 15, 1862.
Cyrus Leland, jr............	Sept. 15, 1862	Resigned, January 1, 1865.
SECOND LIEUT.		
Cyrus Leland, jr............	Aug. 6, 1861	Promoted First Lieutenant, September 15, 1862.
John Bryan...................	Oct. 28, 1862	Assigned to new Company B.

COMPANY G.

Name and Rank.	Date of Muster.	Remarks.
CAPTAIN.		
James H. Harris............	July 15, 1861	Must. out, March 4, 1862, and remust. as 1st Lt.
James M. Harvey..........	Aug. 7, 1861	Mustered out with regiment.
FIRST LIEUT.		
John U. Parsons...........	Aug. 7, 1861	Died of measles, Lawrence, Kas., Dec. 22, 1861.
William C. Harris.........	....	Mustered out, March 4, 1862.
James H. Harris...........	Mar. 4, 1862	Mustered out with regiment.
SECOND LIEUT.		
Josephus D. Warner......	Aug. 7, 1861	Resigned, December 30, 1862.
Andrew G. Ege	Aug. 16, 1861	No evidence of muster-out on file.
Gregor Wohlwend........	April 23, 1862	Died of consumption, Alton, Ill., March 10, 1864.
John C. Anderson.........	....	Mustered out, March 4, 1862.

COMPANY H.

Name and Rank.	Date of Muster.	Remarks.
CAPTAIN.		
Napoleon B. Blanton.....	Mar. 4, 1862	Resigned, February 2, 1863.
Samuel J. Stewart.........	Feb. 15, 1863	Mustered out with regiment, August 18, 1864.
FIRST LIEUT.		
Samuel J. Stewart.........	Aug. 7, 1861	Promoted Captain, January 15, 1863.
James H. Signor............	Feb. 15, 1863	Mustered out with regiment, August 18, 1864.
SECOND LIEUT.		
James H. Signor............	....	Promoted First Lieut., February 15, 1863.
Levi Rittenhouse..........	Mar. 8, 1863	Mustered out with regiment, August 18, 1864.

COMPANY I.

Name and Rank.	Date of Muster.	Remarks.
CAPTAIN.		
Charles P. Twiss............	July 24, 1861	Resigned, July 18, 1862.
William C. Jones...........	July —, 1862	Assigned to new Company B.
FIRST LIEUT.		
William C. Jones...........	July 24, 1861	Promoted Captain, July —, 1862.
James A. Pope..............	....	Resigned, February 15, 1863.
John F. Hill.................		Prom. Major 14th Kas. Vol. Cav., Sept. 18, 1863.
John E. Thorp..............	April 26, 1864	Assigned to new Company B.
Seth M. Tucker.............	July 16, 1861	Mustered out with regiment, August 19, 1864; transferred from Company B.
SECOND LIEUT.		
James R. McClelland.....	July 24, 1861	Died, Fort Scott, Kansas, December 11, 1861.
Pemberton R. Eves.......	July 24, 1861	Mustered out, March 15, 1862.
James A. Pope	Feb. 27, 1862	Promoted First Lieutenant.
John E. Thorp..............	Mar. 10, 1863	Promoted First Lieutenant, April 26, 1864.

COMPANY K.

Name and Rank.	Date of Muster.	Remarks.
CAPTAIN.		
Greenville Watson.........	Aug. 12, 1861	Resigned, March 23, 1863.
Jerome T. Kelly............	....	Mustered out, July 12, 1862, St. Louis, Mo., by order of General Halleck.
Charles S. Hills	May 11, 1862	Transferred to Company D, May 25, 1863.
Horace G. Loring	April 3, 1863	Mustered out, August 19, 1864.
FIRST LIEUT.		
Elijah Fleming..............	Aug. 12, 1861	Resigned, August 1, 1862.
Horace G. Loring..........	Aug. 1, 1862	Promoted Captain, April 3, 1863.
John Sherrin................	April 3, 1863	Mustered out with regiment.
SECOND LIEUT.		
James Davis..................	Aug. 12, 1861	Promoted Regimental Quartermaster Fifth K. V. C., September 2, 1861.
Horace G. Loring	Sept. 2, 1861	Promoted First Lieutenant, August 1, 1862.
John Sherrin................	Aug. 1, 1862	Promoted First Lieutenant, April 3, 1863.
Thomas McGannon.......	April 3, 1863	Promoted Adjutant, May 29, 1863.
George W. May............	May 30, 1863	Assigned to new Company D.

NEW COMPANY A.

Name and Rank.	Date of Muster.	Remarks.
CAPTAIN.		
Charles S. Hills	May 11, 1862	Promoted Lieutenant Colonel, March 1, 1865.
Robert W. Wood	Mar. 1, 1865	Mustered out with regiment, August 30, 1865.
FIRST LIEUT.		
Cyrus Leland................	Sept. 13, 1862	Resigned, December 29, 1864, per S. O. No. 360, Department of Missouri, 1864.
Robert W. Wood............	Jan. 25, 1865	Promoted Captain, March 1, 1865.
Porter W. Phillips........	Mar. 1, 1865	Mustered out with regiment, August 30, 1865.
SECOND LIEUT.		
Robert W. Wood............	Sept. 1, 1862	Promoted First Lieutenant, January 25, 1865.
Henry Banblitts	July 1, 1865	Mustered out with regiment, August 30, 1865.

NEW COMPANY B.

Name and Rank.	Date of Muster.	Remarks.
CAPTAIN. William C. Jones...........	July —, 1862	Mustered out with regiment, August 30, 1865.
FIRST LIEUT. John E. Thorp..............	April 26, 1864	Mustered out with regiment, August 30, 1865.
SECOND LIEUT. John Bryan.................	Oct. 28, 1862	Died, May 14, '65, New Orleans, La., of wounds received in action, April 9, '65, Ft.Blakely,Ala.
William M. Wicks	May 14, 1865	Mustered out with regiment, August 30, 1865.

NEW COMPANY C.

Name and Rank.	Date of Muster.	Remarks.
CAPTAIN. George Brooke	June 12, 1863	Mustered out, June 16, 1865.
FIRST LIEUT. William B. Stone..........	Nov. 10, 1863	Mustered out with regiment, August 30, 1865.
SECOND LIEUT. George W. May	May 30, 1863	Transferred to new Company D.

NEW COMPANY D.

Name and Rank.	Date of Muster.	Remarks.
FIRST LIEUT. Frederick A. Smalley ...	Sept. 1, 1862	Mustered out, January 20, 1865.
SECOND LIEUT. George W. May	May 30, 1863	Mustered out with regiment, August 30, 1865.

List of battles, etc., in which this regiment participated, showing loss reported in each:

Prairie Grove—Killed, E. M., 7; wounded, O. 2, E. M. 58. Franklin—Wounded, E. M., 6. Nashville—Wounded, E. M., 17. Fort Blakely—Killed, E. M., 5; wounded, O. 1, E. M. 10.—*U. S. Army Register.*

FIRST KANSAS BATTERY—LIGHT ARTILLERY.

Name and Rank.	Date of Muster.	Remarks.
CAPTAIN. Thomas Bickerton.........	July 24, 1861	Mustered out, February 15, 1862, orders W. D.
Norman Allen................	Feb. 25. 1862	Died of pneumonia, St. Louis, Mo., July 10, '63.
Marcus D. Tenney.........	Aug. 27, 1863	Mustered out, July 17, 1865, Leavenworth, Kas.
FIRST LIEUT. Norman Allen..............	July 24, 1861	Promoted Captain, February 25, 1862.
Alonzo Kent.................	July 20, 1861	Resigned, May 14, 1862.
Marcus D. Tenney........	Jan. 15, 1862	Promoted Captain, August 27, 1863.
John C. Stoneburner.....	May 15, 1862	Resigned, September 11, 1862.
Moses D. Baldwin.........	Sept. 11, 1862	Resigned June 13, 1863.
Thomas Taylor.............	July 10, 1863	Mustered out, July 17, 1865, Leavenworth, Kas.
John B. Cook................	Aug. 27, 1863	Mustered out, July 17, 1875, Leavenworth, Kas.
SECOND LIEUT. Hartson R. Brown	July 24, 1861	Mustered out, February 15, 1862, orders W. D.
Thomas Taylor.............	Aug. 1, 1861	Promoted First Lieutenant, July 10, 1863.
Moses D. Baldwin.........	Feb. 25, 1862	Promoted First Lieutenant, September 11, 1862.
John B. Cook................	Sept. 11, 1862	Promoted First Lieutenant, August 27, 1863.
Michael Kearney..........	July 10, 1863	Mustered out, July 17, 1865, Leavenworth, Kas.
James N. Nolan............	Aug. 27, 1863	Mustered out, March 4, 1865.

List of battles, etc., in which this battery participated, showing loss reported in each:

Ball's Mills — No loss. Dry Wood — No loss. Morristown — No loss.

Osceola—no loss. Newtonia—No loss. Prairie Grove—Killed, E. M.,
1; wounded, E. M., 8.—*U. S. Army Register.*

OFFICERS FROM KANSAS COMMISSIONED BY THE PRESIDENT.

MAJOR GENERAL.

Names.	Date of Commission.
James G. Blunt	November 29, 1862.

BRIGADIER GENERALS.

Robert B. Mitchell	April 8, 1862.
James G. Blunt	April 8, 1862.
Albert L. Lee	November 29, 1862.
George W. Deitzler	November 29, 1862.
Thomas Ewing, jr	March 13, 1863.
Powell Clayton	August 1, 1864.

AIDES-DE-CAMP.
Majors.

T. J. Weed	January 29, 1862.
Champion Vaughan	January 29, 1862.
John Ritchie	January 29, 1862.

Captains.

James R. McClure	January 29, 1862.
William A. Phillips	January 29, 1862.
Avra P. Russell	January 29, 1862.

ASSISTANT ADJUTANTS GENERAL.
Majors.

Charles Mundee	August 16, 1862.
Thomas J. Anderson	May 25, 1863.
Frederick W. Emery	February 6, 1865.

Captains.

Marcus J. Parrott	August 3, 1861.
Charles Mundee	August 24, 1861.
Daniel McCook	November 9, 1861.
Thomas Moonlight	April 14, 1862.
W. W. H. Lawrence	April 14, 1862.
Charles F. Clarke	June 12, 1862.
John Pratt	October 29, 1862.
Sidney Clarke	February 9, 1863.
Thomas J. Anderson	February 27, 1863.
William Tholen	March 13, 1863.
Frederick W. Emery	March 13, 1863.
John Willans	May 22, 1863.

ASSISTANT QUARTERMASTERS.
Captains.

Martin H. Insley	August 6, 1861.
Charles F. Garrett	April 25, 1862.
Theodore S. Case	June 9, 1862.
John G. Haskell	June 11, 1862.
Prince G. D. Morton	June 11, 1862.
Edmund B. Whitman	July 18, 1862.
George F. Warren	July 30, 1862.
Oliver S. Coffin	September 24, 1862.
Edward B. Grimes	September 29, 1862.
George W. McLane	October 20, 1862.
James A. Finley	November 26, 1862.
Samuel Hipple	November 26, 1862.

ASS'T QUARTERMASTERS — (CONCLUDED.)

Names.	Date of Commission.
S. Lappin	November 26, 1862.
Chester Thomas	February 9, 1863.
Willis C. Goff	February 19, 1863.
Adam Fisher	February 19, 1863.
George Alden	March 12, 1863.
William A. Rankin	July 30, 1863.
James E. Jones	February 23, 1864.
John B. Dexter	February 29, 1864.
Alfred J. Lloyd	April 7, 1864.
Cyrus L. Gorton	May 18, 1864.
Henry H. Gillum	August 22, 1864.
Franklin F. Bruner	February 25, 1865.

COMMISSARIES OF SUBSISTENCE.
Captains.

A. Carter Wilder	August 7, 1861.
Harvey A. Smith	April 25, 1862.
Robert Graham	June 11, 1862.
Oliver Barber	June 11, 1862.
Edmund N. Morrill	August 9, 1862.
Robert W. Hamer	August 9, 1862.
James Davis	September 5, 1862.
James Christian	September 5, 1862.
M. S. Adams	September 5, 1862.
Erastus Heath	September 30, 1862.
John E. Gould	November 26, 1862.
George L. Gaylord	February 9, 1863.
George W. Gardiner	February 19, 1863.
J. H. W. Mills	February 19, 1863.
John P. Alden	July 2, 1863.
David G. Peabody	July 30, 1863.
Demas M. Alexander	July 30, 1863.
Stephen A. Cobb	May 18, 1864.
Rufus R. Edwards	July 2, 1864.
H. Miles Moore	July 7, 1864.
Henry W. Fick	July 7, 1864.
Nelson Z. Strong	February 25, 1865.

SURGEONS.
Majors.

Henry Buckmaster	June 28, 1862.
Samuel B. Davis	February 19, 1863.
Geo. W. Hogeboom	July 19, 1863.

ADDITIONAL PAYMASTERS.
Majors.

Henry Foote	June 1, 1861.
Henry J. Adams	September 5, 1861.
Daniel M. Adams	February 19, 1863.
Hiram S. Sleeper	February 19, 1863.
Shaler W. Eldridge	March 11, 1863.
Josiah Miller	July 28, 1863.
George W. De Costa	April 21, 1864.

FIRST INDIAN REGIMENT.

Names.	Rank.	Date of Commission.
William A. Phillips	Major	June 2, 1862.
James A. Phillips	Major	July 10, 1862.
J. H. Gillpatrick	First Lieutenant and Adjutant	November 1, 1862.
Salmon S. Prouty	First Lieutenant and R. Q. M.	June 21, 1862.
John T. Cox	First Lieutenant and R. Q. M.	February 28, 1863.
John Chess	First Lieutenant and Adjutant	May 28, 1863.
Alfred F. Bicking	First Lieutenant	September 10, 1862.
Ferdinand R. Jacobs	First Lieutenant	September 10, 1862.
Robert T. Thompson	First Lieutenant	April 1, 1863.

FIRST INDIAN REGIMENT—Concluded.

Names.	Rank.	Date of Commission.
Francis J. Fox	First Lieutenant	September 10, 1862.
Albert Flanders	First Lieutenant	July 1, 1863.
Benj. F. Ayres	First Lieutenant	March 29, 1863.
Milford J. Burlingame	First Lieutenant	December 28, 1863.
Frederick Crafts	First Lieutenant	September 10, 1862.
Eli C. Lowe	First Lieutenant	September 10, 1862.
William Roberts	Second Lieutenant	July 1, 1863.
John D. Young	Second Lieutenant	August 25, 1864.

SECOND INDIAN REGIMENT.

Names.	Rank.	Date of Commission.
John Ritchie	Colonel	——
Fred. W. Schuarte	Lieutenant Colonel	——
E. W. Robinson	First Lieutenant and Adjutant	——
John C. Palmer	First Lieutenant and Adjutant	——
George Huston	First Lieutenant and R. Q. M	——
A. J. Ritchie	Surgeon	——
M. A. Campdorus	Assistant Surgeon	——
James H. Bruce	Captain	May 27, 1863.
Joel Moody	Captain	Unknown.
Charles Lenhart	First Lieutenant	October 15, 1862.
John M. Hunter	First Lieutenant	September 14, 1862.
James H. Bruce	First Lieutenant	Unknown.
William H. Kendall	First Lieutenant	December 8, 1862.
John Moffit	First Lieutenant	Unknown.
E. P. Gillpatrick	First Lieutenant	Unknown.
A. J. Waterhouse	First Lieutenant	
Silas Hunter	First Lieutenant	June 2, 1862.
David A. Painter	First Lieutenant	June 2, 1862.
—— Scott	First Lieutenant	June —, 1862.

THIRD INDIAN REGIMENT.

Names.	Rank.	Date of Commission.
William A. Phillips	Colonel	July 11, 1862.
John A. Foreman	Major	July 11, 1862.
William Galliher	First Lieutenant and Adjutant	July 11, 1862.
Alfred Larzelere	First Lieutenant and R. Q. M	July 11, 1862.
A. C. Spillman	Captain	November 4, 1862.
Henry S. Anderson	Captain	November 15, 1862.
Maxwell Phillips	Captain	May 28, 1863.
Solomon Kaufman	Captain	May 28, 1863.
Luke F. Parsons	First Lieutenant	July 11, 1862.
John S. Hanway	First Lieutenant	July 11, 1862.
Andrew W. Robb	First Lieutenant	July 11, 1862.
Harmon Scott	First Lieutenant	July 11, 1862.
Benjamin Whitlow	First Lieutenant	July 11, 1862.
Charles Brown	First Lieutenant	April 1, 1863.
William McCulloch	Second Lieutenant	December 31, 1862.
Basil G. McCrea	Second Lieutenant	December 31, 1862.
Jule C. Cayott	Second Lieutenant	May 28, 1863.

ONE HUNDRED AND THIRTEENTH U. S. COLORED TROOPS.

Names.	Rank.	Date of Commission.
James M. Steele	Lieutenant Colonel	December 10, 1863.
Josiah Sample	Captain	March 1, 1864.
E. P. Gillpatrick	Captain	March 1, 1864.
William H. Smith	Captain	March 1, 1864.
John Hayes, jr	Captain	March 1, 1864.
James W. Gilgus	Captain	March 1, 1864.
Thomas Prastor	First Lieutenant	March 1, 1864.

ONE HUNDRED AND THIRTEENTH U. S. COLORED TROOPS—Concluded.

Names.	Rank.	Date of Commission.
Wm. H. T. Wakefield	First Lieutenant	January 22, 1864.
Ben. B. Thompson	First Lieutenant	March 1, 1864.
Theodore C. Weaver	First Lieutenant	April 1, 1865.
Abram Smith	Second Lieutenant	March 1, 1864.
Wm. C. Kern	Second Lieutenant	March 1, 1864.
Alanson Simons	Second Lieutenant	January 26, 1864.

EIGHTEENTH U. S. COLORED TROOPS.

Names.	Rank.	Date of Commission.
John J. Sears	Lieutenant Colonel	August 18, 1864.
Lewis D. Joy	Major	September 10, 1864.
Nathaniel B. Lucas	Captain	April 2, 1864.
L. O. Snoddy	First Lieutenant and Adjutant	June 4, 1864.
Wm. H. Dodge	First Lieutenant and R. Q. M.	June 4, 1864.
Solomon Smith	Captain	October 7, 1864.
George J. Drew	First Lieutenant	June 20, 1864.
Charles H Goodier	First Lieutenant	September 9, 1864.
Josiah R. Drew	Second Lieutenant	August 8, 1864.
Wm. H. Dunlap	Second Lieutenant	September 16, 1864.
Thomas B. Murdock	Second Lieutenant	October 8, 1864.

FIFTY-SEVENTH U. S. COLORED TROOPS.

Name.	Rank.	Date of Commission.
SHas Hunter	Lieutenant Colonel	February 20, 1866.

SIXTY-FIFTH U. S. COLORED TROOPS.

Name.	Rank.	Date of Commission.
Abner Doane	First Lieutenant	February —, 1864.

SEVENTY-SECOND U. S. COLORED TROOPS.

Name.	Rank.	Date of Commission.
James M. Iliff	First Lieut. and R. Q. M.	June 24, 1864.

SECOND ARKANSAS INFANTRY.

Names.	Rank.	Date of Commission.
G. M. Waugh	Lieutenant Colonel	March —, 1864.
J. K. Klinefelter	First Lieutenant and Adjutant	April —, 1864.
Ira D. Bronson	Captain	May —, 1864.
M. A. Payne	First Lieutenant	May —, 1864.
Wm. W. Tibbs	Second Lieutenant	May —, 1864.

FOURTH ARKANSAS INFANTRY.

Names.	Rank.	Date of Commission.
Horace L. Moore	Lieutenant Colonel	May —, 1864.
H. S. Greeno	Major	September 8, 1864.
Henry Wood	Captain	
Wm. J. Hunter	Captain	July 29, 1864.
Howard Schuyler	Captain	December —, 1864.
Hugh Quinn	First Lieutenant	
John Tenant	Second Lieutenant	October 16, 1864.

FIFTH U. S. VOLUNTEERS.

Names.	Rank.	Date of Commission.
Thomas Hughes.........................	First Lieutenant......................	April 15, 1865.
Henry M. Herman.....................	First Lieutenant......................	April 18, 1865.
Chas. H. Hoyt	First Lieutenant......................	May 1, 1865.
Wm. M. Harshberger.................	Second Lieutenant....................	April 8, 1865.

DECEMBER 31.—Expenditures of the State for the year:

Governor's Department.............	$4,150 00	Miscellaneous accounts..............	$6,306 07
Secretary's Department..............	2,525 00	Commissioners to select lands.....	1,500 00
Auditor's Department.................	2,510 00	Adjutant General's Department..	586 79
Treasurer's Department.............	1,420 00	Quartermaster's Department......	261 75
Sup't of Public Instruction........	1,700 00	War expenses...........................	3,450 54
Attorney General.......................	963 31	Exp. issu'g and negotiat'g bonds.	1,087 20
Judiciary Department................	13,203 00	Comm'rs to locate Penitentiary..	182 50
Legislative exps. and Journals...	26,291 53		
State Printing	18,684 30	Total expenses for 1861............$84,821 99	

1862.

JANUARY 1.—The following papers are now published in the State: Independent, Oskaloosa, John W. Day and J. W. Roberts; Gazette, Grasshopper Falls, P. H. Hubbell; Express, Manhattan, James Humphrey; Frontier News, Junction City, Geo. E. Dummer; State Record, Topeka, E. G. Ross; Tribune, Topeka, Cummings & Shepherd; News, Emporia, Jacob Stotler; Herald, Osawatomie, C. E. Griffith; Republican, Lawrence, John Speer; State Journal, Lawrence, Trask & Lowman; Gazette, Wyandotte, R. B. Taylor; Post (German), Wyandotte; Shield & Banner, Mansfield, Linn county, J. Lyman; Neosho Valley Register, Burlington, S. S. Prouty; Smoky Hill and Republican Union, Junction City, George W. Kingsbury; Mirror, Olathe, John Francis; Chief, White Cloud, Sol. Miller; Union, Hiawatha, J. G. Parker; Union, Atchison, William H. Adams; Champion, Atchison, John A. Martin; Zeitung (German), Semi-weekly, Leavenworth, L. Sousman; Times, Daily and Weekly, Leavenworth, J. Kemp Bartlett; Conservative, Daily, Tri-Weekly and Weekly, Leavenworth, D. W. Wilder. There are twenty-three in the list; eight still live.

JANUARY 9.— Capt. John Brown, jr., arrives at Leavenworth with enough men to fill up his company.

JANUARY 9.—Judge Saunders W. Johnston presents to the Supreme Court the petition of Geo. A. Crawford praying for a peremptory writ of mandamus to compel the Board of Canvassers to count the votes cast for him for Governor.

—Major Chas. G. Halpine ("Miles O'Reilly") is Adjutant for General Hunter, at Fort Leavenworth.

JANUARY 14.—Meeting of the Legislature. *Members of the Senate:* E. P. Bancroft, J. F. Broadhead, Alonzo Curtis, J. Connell, H. B. Denman, Jacob G. Rees, C. K. Holliday, O. B. Gunn, S. E. Hoffman, M. L. Essick, J. M. Hubbard, S. Lappin, Chas. G. Keeler, Ed. Lynde, John J. Ingalls, Wm. B. Barnett, Robert S. Stevens, R. Morrow, T. A. Osborn, J. A. Phillips, H. N. Seaver, W. Spriggs, H. S. Sleeper, S. N. Wood.

Officers of the Senate: A. R. Banks, Secretary; C. K. Gilchrist, Assistant Secretary; J. G. Kelsey, Journal Clerk; O. F. Ingraham, Engrossing Clerk; J. R. Montgomery, Docket Clerk; J. S. Pigman, Sergeant-at-Arms; S. H. Fairfield, Doorkeeper; F. Jackson, Messenger.

Members of the House: Adams, Anderson, Baker, Brown, Carney, Church, Columbia, Dickinson, Eskridge, Fishback, Foster, Goodnow, Grover (4th District), Grover (7th District), Grube, Havens, Hersey, Huber, Ingersoll, Jewell, Johnson, Jones (8th District), Jones (9th District), Jones (14th District), Karr, Lamb, Leard, Leonard, Lowry, Macy, McAuley, Marcell, Martin, Medill, Maxson, Miller, Mitchell, Murphy, McCarthy, McClure, McCrillus, McGonigle, McGrew (8th District), McGrew (9th District), O'Guartney, Patterson, Penney, Pierce, Plumb, Potter, Reynolds, Rice, Russell, Sabin, Shean, Spaulding, Silvers, Smith, Starns, Steele, Thoman, Valentine, Van Horn, Van Winkle, Welch, Wells, Wilson, Williams.

Officers of the House: M. S. Adams, Speaker; John Francis, of Johnson county, Chief Clerk; Charles Clarkson, Sergeant-at-Arms; G. W. Griffith, Assistant Clerk; Dan. M. Adams, Engrossing Clerk; Mr. Moffit, Assistant Sergeant-at-Arms; Mr. McKinney, Docket Clerk; Mr. Watson, Journal Clerk; Robt. S. Parham, Enrolling Clerk.

JANUARY 15.—Union Indians defeated in the Indian Territory and driven to Kansas. They are encamped on Fall River.

JANUARY 21.—Sidney Clarke, contestant, admitted to the seat of George W. Smith, in the House.

JANUARY 21.—Publication of the decision of the Supreme Court overruling the motion of Geo. A. Crawford. The Court declares the election of Governor in 1861 illegal; opinion by Chief Justice Ewing. (*State of Kansas, ex rel. Crawford, vs. Robinson,* 1 Kan., 17.)

JANUARY 23.—Opotheyoholo, Chief of the Creek Nation, meets General Hunter and tells him the condition of affairs in the Indian Territory.

—The Thirteenth Wisconsin arrives in Leavenworth.

JANUARY 23.—The Legislature accepts a present of twenty acres of land, from the Topeka Town Association, as a site for the Capitol.

JANUARY 27.—Gen. Lane arrives in Leavenworth, as a Major General, to take command of an expedition to the Gulf.

JANUARY 29.—The Ninth Wisconsin reaches Leavenworth.

FEBRUARY 1.—Organization of the Tenth Kansas.

FEBRUARY.—Wm. S. Blakely and George W. Martin become the publishers of the Union, at Junction City.

FEBRUARY 4.—Reception of the First Kansas, in Leavenworth.

—Investigation by the Legislature of the bond negotiations made by Robert S. Stevens. The State reported to have lost $40,000.

FEBRUARY 12.—Death of W. R. Griffith, Superintendent of Public Instruction, at Topeka.

FEBRUARY 12.—An interesting printing swindle is exposed by Sol. Miller and P. B. Plumb. See House Journal, pp. 213 to 224.

FEBRUARY 14.—The report of the House Committee on the negotiation of State bonds is published. It concludes with a resolution impeaching the Governor, Secretary of State, and Auditor. The report is signed by Martin Anderson, H. L. Jones, B. W. Hartley, Sidney Clarke, and Thomas Carney. The House adopted the resolution by sixty-five votes in the affirmative, and none in the negative.

FEBRUARY 15.—The Impeachment Managers, on the part of the House, are P. B. Plumb, of Lyon; F. W. Potter, of Coffey; A. Spaulding, of Jefferson; W. R. Wagstaff, of Miami; D. Wilson, of Riley. Attorney General, S. A. Stinson.

FEBRUARY.—The Supreme Court holds that acts of the Territorial Legislature, passed after the admission of the State into the Union, are valid; opinion by Judge Kingman. (*State of Kansas, ex rel. Hunt, vs. Meadows,* 1 Kan., 90.)

FEBRUARY 20.—Kansas now has 9,000 soldiers in the field.

FEBRUARY 21.—Thos. Roberts admitted to the seat in the Senate made vacant by the resignation of James A. Phillips.

FEBRUARY 26.—Wilson Shannon, Fred. P. Stanton and Nathan P. Case appear as counsel for the impeached officers.

FEBRUARY 26.—James H. Lane writes to the Legislature that he has failed to make a satisfactory arrangement with Gen. Hunter; that he will not lead a military expedition to the Gulf; that he has resigned his Brigadiership, and that he will return to the Senate.

FEBRUARY 28.—The Daily Inquirer started in Leavenworth, by Adams & Driggs; Burrell E. Taylor, Editor. A meeting called to mob the paper was addressed by M. W. Delahay and D. W. Wilder, favoring free speech, and the meeting of argument with argument.

MARCH 1.—The seats in the Senate of Bancroft, Broadhead and Gunn are declared vacant, ostensibly because they had accepted commissions in the volunteer service. They were friends of Robinson and enemies of Lane.

Horatio Knowles is admitted to Broadhead's seat, and J. M. Rankin to Bancroft's seat.

MARCH 5.—Jas. C. Horton elected Assistant Journal Clerk of the Senate.

MARCH 5.—Formation of the State Agricultural Society. Meeting in the hall of the House of Representatives, Topeka.

Officers: President, Lyman Scott, of Leavenworth; Secretary, F. G. Adams, of Shawnee; Treasurer, Isaac Garrison, of Shawnee; Executive Committee, E. B. Whitman, of Douglas; F. P. Baker, of Nemaha; W. A. Shannon, of Lyon; C. B. Lines, of Wabaunsee; J. C. Marshall, of Linn; Martin Anderson, of Jackson; Thos. Arnold, of Coffey; J. W. Sponable, of Johnson; Welcome Wells, of Riley; R. A. Van Winkle, of Atchison.

No Fair was held.

MARCH 6.—Adjournment of the Legislature. This Legislature compiled the laws; the volume of laws fills 1116 pages. Among the acts passed were the following: Accepting the terms imposed by Congress upon the admission of the State; Apportioning the State for Senators and Representatives; Codes of civil and criminal procedure; Establishing a Criminal Court in

Leavenworth county; Organizing the county of Greenwood; Changing the
name of Breckinridge county to Lyon; Creating a State Board of Equali-
zation; Homestead exemption law; Providing for the management of the
School fund and the University fund; Repealing the law of Feb. 9, 1858,
establishing the office of Land District Recorder; Establishing the salaries
of State officers, Judges, and Members and Clerks of the Legislature.

MARCH 6, 7, 8.—Battle of Pea Ridge, Arkansas.

MARCH 7.—"The notorious Quantrell, alias Hart," plunders Aubrey and
kills three citizens.

MARCH 9.—Arthur Gunther, of Lawrence, having been commissioned as
a Captain in the Second Kansas, the Conservative publishes the following
copy of a certificate which Gunther carries in his pocket:

 HEADQUARTERS KANSAS VOLUNTEERS.

LAWRENCE CITY, Dec. 12, 1855.

This is to certify that A. GUNTHER faithfully and gallantly
served as Private in the *Wakarusa Liberty Guards*, Kansas Volunteers, from the 27th day of November, 1855, to the 13th day of
December, 1855, in defending the City of Lawrence, in Kansas
Territory, from demolition by foreign invaders; when he was
honorably discharged from said service.

H. F. SANDERS, *Captain.*

LYMAN ALLEN, *Col. Com. 1st Reg. Kas. Vols.*

J. H. LANE, *Gen. 1st Brig. Kas. Vols.*

C. ROBINSON, *Major General.*

MARCH 13.—Treaty with the Kansas Indians; improvements by certain
settlers to be paid for.

MARCH 14.—John A. Martin, Lieutenant Colonel of the Eighth Kansas,
is appointed Provost Marshal of Leavenworth.

MARCH 15.—Kansas soldiers at Fort Riley destroy the office of the Kansas
Frontier News, a disloyal paper published at Junction City.

—Gen. Denver ordered to take command in Kansas; Gen. Deitzler to
join Curtis, in Arkansas.

—The Conservative says:

"The Ninth, Twelfth and Thirteenth Wisconsin, the First, Third, Fifth and Sixth
Kansas, and Capt. Rabb's Battery, are now at Fort Scott. The Fourth is at Wyandotte,
the Seventh at Humboldt, and the Second at Shawneetown. The headquarters of the
Eighth are here, but the regiment is widely scattered."

MARCH 25.—

"There are now in southern Kansas between six and seven thousand Indians, refugees from the Rebels within the Indian Territory. A large number of these are encamped
at Leroy, Coffey county, on the Neosho river, at which place is established the headquarters of their Superintendent, and various agents. Leroy is also the depot from
which supplies are issued. The principal tribes to which these refugees belong are the
Creeks, Seminoles, Cherokees and Chickasaws, with a few scattered Wichitas and other
prairie tribes, whose location is west of Forts Cobb and Arbuckle. They have now been
in Kansas since the middle of January, a period of two months. Much suffering
has been endured by them. Before relief was afforded by Gen. Hunter, scores of these
people died of hunger, cold, and the diseases superinduced by these causes. Among
these Indians (whose numbers have lately been augmented by the arrival of several
fragmentary tribes of Quapaws, Senecas, etc.) are about 2,000 warriors, good and effective
braves, who only need arms and ammunition to make them a useful force."—*Conservative.*

MARCH 26.—Defeat of the First Colorado, at Pigeon's Ranch, New Mexico. John P. Slough is the Colonel, Samuel F. Tappan Lieutenant Colonel, and the regiment is largely made up of Kansas men.

MARCH 28.—Der Deutsche Krieger is the name of a German paper issued by the Ninth Wisconsin, at Fort Scott.

—Prof. S. M. Thorp, of Lawrence, is appointed Superintendent of Public Instruction.

APRIL 1.—Robt. B. Mitchell and James G. Blunt are appointed Brigadier Generals.

APRIL 6.—Battle of Pittsburgh Landing.

MAY 2.—Gen. Blunt commands the Department of Kansas.

—The First Indian regiment organized at Leroy.

MAY 8.—Congress appropriates $100,000 to pay the Lane Brigade.

MAY 9.—Gen. Hunter, in South Carolina, issues an emancipation proclamation.

MAY 11.—The Jayhawker Cleveland, alias Moore, alias Metz, killed at the Marais des Cygnes, by Lieut. Walker's men, of the Sixth Kansas. His body was taken to Osawatomie. He had been in Kansas twelve months. Was mustered in as a Captain in Jennison's regiment, but very soon mustered out. He stole in the name of Liberty.

MAY 17.—Kansas troops ordered to Corinth, Mississippi.

MAY 19.—Lincoln revokes Hunter's proclamation.

MAY 20.—Passage of the homestead law. It is chapter 75 of the U. S. Statutes of 1862.

MAY 22.—Organization of the First Indian regiment.

MAY 24.—Wm. A. Barstow, Colonel Third Wisconsin, Provost Marshal General of the State; Maj. Elias A. Calkins, of the Third Wisconsin, Provost Marshal of Leavenworth.

MAY 27, 28, 29.—The First, Seventh and Eighth Kansas, the Second Kansas Battery, and the Twelfth and Thirteenth Wisconsin, sail from Leavenworth towards Corinth.

MAY 27.—Capt. John Brown, jr., resigns, and Lieut. Geo. H. Hoyt is appointed Captain.

MAY 30.—Col. Wm. Weer, of the Tenth Kansas, given command of the Indian expedition.

JUNE 2.—The Senate meets as a Court of Impeachment. Counsel for defence, Wilson Shannon, Fred. P. Stanton, and N. P. Case; prosecution, Samuel A. Stinson, Azel Spaulding, Davies Wilson, and W. R. Wagstaff.

JUNE 3.—The Conservative is printed on a Hoe Cylinder Press, the first one brought to the State. Francis J. Nutz puts it up.

JUNE 3.—Stephen A. Cobb sworn in as the successor of Senator O. B. Gunn.

—Thos. A. Osborn elected President *pro tem.* of the Senate over John J. Ingalls, on the fourteenth ballot.

—The trial of John W. Robinson, Secretary of State, begins.

JUNE 6.—Byron Sherry elected Journal Clerk, and Richard J. Hinton and Robert Parham, Reporters.

JUNE 11.—The following is copied from the argument of Attorney General Stinson:

"Now, may it please this honorable Court, where is the first word of legal or competent testimony tending to show that Hillyer and Robinson might not have sold these bonds without the assistance or intervention of Stevens? We have the unsupported and somewhat interested opinion of Stevens on the point. We have the testimony of counsel in their Congressional experiences.

"MR. STANTON: I did not testify.

"MR. STINSON: I meant this remark in no disrespectful sense. I referred to the Congressional experiences which I understood you and Gov. Shannon to favor the Court with.

"MR. STANTON: The Attorney General is mistaken; I gave no Congressional experiences.

"MR. STINSON: Then I will throw the burden on Gov. Shannon. He must stand it, for he is not here to defend himself.

"The only reason seems to be that they understood from Senator Pomeroy that they better not try. Take this testimony together, and if it all be true, that distinguished Senator seems to have been drawn into the meshes of this web of conspiracy and fraud. He testified, in his deposition, that he is 'a laborer.' The Scripture says 'the laborer is worthy of his hire.' Let us, for the honor of the State, if we can, so liberally and charitably construe this testimony as to exclude the idea that the laborer received his hire in this transaction. Even this allusion may do injustice to an innocent man; but he who touches pitch must be defiled. The people of the State will gratefully accept, and at the same time earnestly insist upon, a full explanation of Mr. Pomeroy's connexion with this transaction."

JUNE 12.—The following is copied from the Report of the Trial:

"The first Article of Impeachment was read by the Secretary *pro tem.*

"ARTICLE 1. That the said John W. Robinson was, prior to the third day of June, A. D. 1861, ever since has been, and still is, Secretary of State of said State of Kansas. That on the fifth day of June, A. D. 1861, the said John W. Robinson, as Secretary of State, together with the Governor and Auditor of said State, was authorized and empowered to negotiate and sell the bonds of the State, the issuance of which was provided for in the act authorizing the negotiation of one hundred and fifty thousand dollars of the bonds of the State of Kansas, to defray the current expenses of the State, approved May 1, 1861.

"That bonds of the State of Kansas, to defray the current expenses of said State as aforesaid, were prepared, executed, and issued according to law.

"That the said John W. Robinson, being so empowered to sell and negotiate said bonds, did authorize and empower one Robert S. Stevens to negotiate and sell said bonds, to the amount of eighty-seven thousand two hundred dollars, at any price over sixty per centum upon the amount of said bonds, he, the said Stevens, paying to the State no more than sixty per centum of said amount; that under said agreement, and with the full knowledge and consent of said Robinson, said Stevens proceeded to sell and deliver a large amount of said bonds, to wit, the amount of fifty-six thousand dollars of said bonds, at the rate of eighty-five per centum on said amount of fifty-six thousand dollars, all of which was well known to said Robinson; and under the said agreement, with the full knowledge and consent of said Robinson, said Stevens paid over and accounted to said State for only the amount of sixty per centum on said bonds so sold as aforesaid, which said agreement, so made and entered into by said Robinson, was in direct violation of the laws of said State in this, that under the said laws said bonds could not be sold for less than seventy per centum on the amount of said bonds; and was in violation of the official duties of the said Robinson in this, that the said State was, by said agreement, defrauded out of its just rights, in that said State was entitled to receive the full amount for which said bonds were sold, while in truth and in fact, with the full knowledge and consent of the said Robinson, said bonds were sold for eighty-five per centum upon the dollar of the amount of said bonds, while in truth and in fact the said State did not receive more than sixty per centum upon the whole amount of said bonds so sold: whereby said John W. Robinson betrayed the trust reposed in him by the State of Kansas, subjected said State to great pecuniary loss, and has thereby been guilty of a high misdemeanor in said office of Secretary of State aforesaid."

"The President *pro tem.* then took the opinion of the members of the Court respectively, in the form following:

"Mr. ——, how say you? Is the respondent, John W. Robinson, Guilty or Not Guilty of a High Misdemeanor, as charged in this Article of Impeachment?

"The following gentlemen voted GUILTY, in response to the Chair: Messrs. Bayless, Cobb, Connell, Curtis, Essick, Holliday, Hubbard, Keeler, Knowles, Lambdin, McDowell, Osborn, Rankin, Rees, Roberts, Sleeper, and Spriggs—17.

"Those voting NOT GUILTY were: Messrs. Barnett, Ingalls, Denman, and Lappin—4."

"The President then arose, and recapitulated the votes thus:

"On the first Article of Impeachment, seventeen gentlemen having voted *Guilty*, and four *Not Guilty;* on the second, ten gentlemen having voted *Guilty*, and eleven gentlemen *Not Guilty;* on the third, eight gentlemen having voted *Guilty*, and thirteen *Not Guilty;* on the fourth, five gentlemen having voted *Guilty*, and sixteen *Not Guilty;* on the fifth, seven gentlemen having voted *Guilty*, and fourteen gentlemen *Not Guilty;* on the sixth, twenty-one gentlemen having voted *Not Guilty;* on the seventh, twenty-one gentlemen having voted *Not Guilty;* on the eighth, twenty-one gentlemen having voted *Not Guilty*—it therefore appears, that John W. Robinson is found Guilty of High Misdemeanor in office, as charged in the first Article of Impeachment, and is acquitted on the second, third, fourth, fifth, sixth, seventh and eighth Articles."

The Senate then voted to remove Secretary Robinson from office, by 18 to 3. The trial of Geo. S. Hillyer, Auditor, followed.

JUNE 15.—The Leavenworth Inquirer suppressed by Gen. Blunt.

JUNE 16.—The following is copied from page 396 of the Trial:

"The President then arose, and recapitulated the vote thus:

"On the first Article of Impeachment, seventeen gentlemen having voted *Guilty*, and four *Not Guilty;* on the second, nine gentlemen having voted *Guilty*, and twelve *Not Guilty;* on the third, six gentlemen having voted *Guilty*, and fifteen *Not Guilty;* on the fourth, five gentlemen having voted *Guilty*, and sixteen *Not Guilty;* on the fifth, no gentleman having voted *Guilty*, and nineteen *Not Guilty;* on the sixth, four gentlemen having voted *Guilty*, and seventeen *Not Guilty;* on the seventh, twenty-one gentlemen having voted *Not Guilty*—it therefore appears, that George S. Hillyer is found Guilty of High Misdemeanor in office, as charged in the first Article of Impeachment, and is Acquitted on the second, third, fourth, fifth, sixth and seventh Articles."

The Senate then voted, by 18 to 2, to remove Auditor Hillyer from office. The following is the Article on which he was found guilty:

"ARTICLE 1. That the said George S. Hillyer, as Auditor of State of the State of Kansas, was, together with the Secretary of State and Governor of said State, by the laws of said State, authorized and empowered to negotiate and sell the bonds of the State, the issuance of which was provided for in the act authorizing the negotiation of one hundred and fifty thousand dollars of the bonds of the State of Kansas, to defray the current expenses of the State, approved May 1, 1861.

"That bonds of the State of Kansas, to defray the current expenses of the State as aforesaid, were prepared, executed, and issued according to law.

"That the said George S. Hillyer, being so empowered to sell and negotiate said bonds, did authorize and empower one Robert S. Stevens to negotiate and sell said bonds to the amount of eighty-seven thousand two hundred dollars, at any price over sixty per centum upon the amount of said bonds, he, said Stevens, paying to the State no more than sixty per centum of said amount; that under said agreement, and with the full knowledge and consent of said Hillyer, said Stevens proceeded to sell and deliver a large amount of said bonds, to wit, the amount of fifty-six thousand dollars of said bonds, at the rate of eighty-five per centum on said amount of fifty-six thousand dollars, all of which was well known to said Hillyer; and under the said agreement, with the full knowledge and consent of said Hillyer, said Stevens paid over and accounted to said State for only the amount of sixty per centum upon said bonds so sold, which said agreement so made and entered into by said Hillyer, was in direct violation of the laws of said State in this, that under said laws said bonds could not be sold for less than seventy per centum on the amount of said bonds; and was in violation of the official duty of said Hillyer in this, that said State was by said agreement defrauded out of its just rights, in that said State was entitled to receive the full amount for which said bonds were sold, while in truth and in fact, with the full knowledge and consent of said Hillyer, said bonds were sold for eighty-five per centum upon the dollar, and the State did not receive therefrom more than sixty per centum upon the bonds so sold: whereby said Hillyer betrayed the trust reposed in him by the State of Kansas, subjected said State to great pecuniary loss, and has thereby been guilty of high misdemeanor in his said office of Auditor of State aforesaid."

The trial of Gov. Robinson followed, and was concluded the same day. His acquittal is thus announced:

"The President then arose, and recapitulated the votes thus:

"On the first Article, two gentlemen have pronounced *Guilty*, and nineteen *Not Guilty*; on the second Article, there is an unanimous vote of *Not Guilty*; on the third Article, there is an unanimous vote of *Not Guilty*; on the fourth Article, there is an unanimous vote of *Not Guilty*; on the fifth Article, one has said *Guilty*, and twenty *Not Guilty*: hence it appears that there is not a constitutional majority of votes finding Charles Robinson Guilty on any one Article. It therefore becomes my duty to declare that Charles Robinson stands Acquitted of all the Articles exhibited by the House of Representatives against him."

The Court adjourns. The volume of "Proceedings in the Impeachment Cases" contains 425 pages. The printing was superintended by Senator Ingalls. The report was made by R. J. Hinton.

June 18.—D. R. Anthony, Lieutenant Colonel of the Seventh Kansas, issued an Order concluding as follows:

"Any officer or soldier of this command who shall arrest and deliver to his master a fugitive slave, shall be summarily and severely punished, according to the laws relative to such crimes."

For issuing this Order, Col. Anthony was arrested and deprived of his command in Tennessee.

June 20.—Decision of Attorney General Edward Bates published. Gov. Robinson had commissioned A. L. Lee as Colonel of the Seventh. Lieut. Gov. Root gave Chas. W. Blair a commission for the same position. Gen. Blunt referred the question to the U. S. Attorney General, and received this reply:

"The absence of Governor Robinson from the State did not create the disability contemplated by the Constitution of Kansas, by which the Lieutenant Governor would be authorized to perform the duties of Governor."

Since this time the Private Secretary of the Governor has acted as Governor when the Governor has been absent.

June 22.—Organization of the Second Indian regiment.

June 24.—Treaty with the Ottawa Indians. The Ottawas to become citizens in five years; lands to be divided between them; 20,000 acres set apart for the purpose of endowing a school; ten acres for the benefit of the Ottawa Baptist Church, etc. C. C. Hutchinson is the Ottawa Indian Agent.

June 28.—Treaty with the Kickapoos. A portion of their lands to be set apart and held in severalty; the remainder to be sold. New homes to be purchased in the Indian country. The Atchison & Pike's Peak R. R. Co. may buy the lands, to be sold at $1.25 an acre.

JUNE 30.—Bill and Jim Anderson, Quantrell and others, make a raid into the State, shoot A. I. Baker and Segur, and set fire to the building they are in. Segur escapes and dies, while Baker dies immediately, and his body is burned to ashes. The Emporia News publishes the report.

JULY 1.—Incorporation by Congress of the Union Pacific Railroad Company. The following is a summary of the law—chapter 120 of the U. S. Statutes:

"3. There is granted to the Company every alternate section of public land, designated by odd numbers, to the amount of five alternate sections per mile on each side of said railroad, on the line thereof, and within the limits of ten miles on each side, not sold, reserved, or otherwise disposed of by the United States, and to which a pre-emption or homestead claim may not have attached, at the time the line of said road is definitely fixed.

"5. When 40 miles are finished, the Secretary of the Treasury shall issue to said Company bonds of the United States of $1,000 each, payable in thirty years, bearing six per cent. interest (payable semi-annually), which interest may be paid in United States Treasury notes, or any other money or currency which the United States have or shall declare lawful money and a legal tender, to the amount of sixteen bonds per mile for each section of forty miles; and to secure the repayment to the United States, all such bonds constitute a first mortgage in favor of the United States.

"8, 9. The Leavenworth, Pawnee and Western Railroad Company of Kansas are authorized to construct a railroad and telegraph line from the Missouri river, at the mouth of the Kansas, to connect with the Pacific Railroad of Missouri, to the one hundredth meridian of longitude, upon the same terms and conditions as provided for the construction of the Pacific Railroad, and to meet and connect with the same at the meridian aforesaid; and said railroad through Kansas shall be so located that the several roads from Missouri and Iowa, authorized to connect with the same, can make connexion within the limits prescribed in this act, provided the same can be done without deviating from the general direction of the whole line to the Pacific coast.

"10. The Kansas Company shall complete 100 miles of road in two years, and 100 miles a year thereafter; the California Company 50 miles in two years, and 50 miles a year thereafter; and after either or both companies have finished their own roads, they may unite on equal terms in the construction of the main line. The same is permitted to the Hannibal and St. Joseph, and the Pacific Railroad Company of Missouri, so far as to assist the Kansas Company to construct the Leavenworth branch.

"13. The Hannibal and St. Joseph Company may extend their road via Atchison, to unite with the road through Kansas; and the Leavenworth, Pawnee and Western Railroad Company may construct their road from Leavenworth to unite with the road through Kansas."

By the act there is to be a continuous railroad ready for use, from the Missouri to the Sacramento, by July 1, 1876.

JULY 2.—Passage of the act giving lands for Agricultural Colleges. It is chapter 130 of the U. S. Statutes, and is thus summarized:

"Public lands (not mineral), not exceeding 30,000 acres for each Senator and Representative in Congress, are apportioned to the several States; the proceeds of the sale of such lands shall be invested in stocks of the United States, or of the States, or some other safe stocks, yielding not less than five per cent.; and the moneys so invested shall constitute a perpetual fund, the capital of which shall remain forever undiminished, and the interest of which shall be inviolably appropriated, by each State which may take and claim the benefit of this act, to the endowment, support and maintenance of at least one college where the leading object shall be, without excluding other scientific and classical studies, and including military tactics, to teach such branches of learning as are related to agriculture and the mechanic arts, in such manner as the Legislatures of the States may respectively prescribe, in order to promote the liberal and practical education of the industrial classes in the several pursuits and professions in life."

July 15.—The Bourbon County Monitor issued at Marmaton, by D. B. Emmert.

July 23.—Ex-Governor Reeder visits Kansas.

August 4.—J. H. Lane opens an office in Leavenworth as a Recruiting Commissioner, to enlist colored as well as white soldiers, receiving his authority from Washington. The colored men are at first enlisted as laborers.

August 8.—Gen. Blunt leaves Leavenworth to take command of the Indian Expedition, now in the Indian Territory.

August 12.—P. B. Plumb and E. G. Ross begin enlisting men for the Eleventh.

August 15.—Orders are issued in Missouri, signed Upton Hays and W. C. Quantrile, declaring that all men going to Federal posts to enlist in the Federal army will be shot where taken.

August 19.—John Ross, Chief of the Cherokees, arrives in Leavenworth.

—E. G. Ross sells the Topeka Record to S. D. Macdonald and F. G. Adams.

September.—Organization of the Twelfth and Thirteenth Kansas.

September 6.—The Judicial Convention at Hiawatha unanimously renominates Albert H. Horton for Judge.

September 7.—Quantrell enters Olathe with a large force, kills several men, robs the stores, and destroys the offices of the Mirror and the Herald.

—Governor Robinson issues an order for a complete organization of the Militia. The name of S. R. Shepherd appears as Secretary of State.

September 10.—Organization of the Second Battery.

September 12.—T. Dwight Thacher resumes the publication of the Lawrence Republican.

September 13.—Thos. Ewing, jr., resigns, as Chief Justice, to take command of the Eleventh regiment.

—John A. Halderman is appointed Major General of the Militia of northern Kansas.

September 16.—Organization of the Third Indian regiment.

September 17.—Battle of Antietam.

September 17.—Republican State Convention at Topeka. Called to order by T. Dwight Thacher. *Vote for Chairman:* F. P. Baker, of Nemaha, 41; James Scott, of Linn, 28. M. R. Dutton was chosen Secretary.

Committee on Credentials: Legate, Murdock, Burnett, Odell, Wheeler, Bishop, and Wakefield.

Committee on Permanent Organization: Colton, McDowell, Thomas, Empie, Maxson, Drinkwater, and Pound.

Officers: President, F. P. Baker, of Nemaha; Vice Presidents, George W. Gardiner of Leavenworth, Coldman of Coffey, Shipley of Miami; Secretaries, M. R. Dutton of Jefferson, Griffith of Franklin, D. B. Emmert of Bourbon.

The call for the Convention placed the nomination of the Member of

21

Congress before that of Governor. Ed. Russell, of Doniphan, moved to nominate in that order. Lost, by 27 to 41. This was a triumph of Lane and Carney, and the defeat of George A. Crawford.

Committee on Resolutions: Woodworth, of Atchison; Sherry, of Nemaha; Crosby, of Jefferson; McKee, of Leavenworth; and Scott, of Linn.

Committee to Investigate Charges of Corruption Against Certain Candidates: McDowell, Russell, Fairchild, Thomas, Riggs, Burnett, and Reynolds.

Adjourned till morning. On reassembling, the Committee reported that there were no charges worthy of consideration.

Ballot for Governor: Thomas Carney, 42; George W. Collamore, 22; William A. Phillips, 9. *Ballot for Lieutenant Governor:* Thomas A. Osborn, of Doniphan, 50; John J. Ingalls, of Atchison, 22; George A. Crawford, of Bourbon, 2. On motion of James F. Legate, of Johnson, George A. Crawford was nominated for Secretary of State by acclamation. A committee appointed to wait on Mr. Crawford reported that he accepted the nomination unconditionally. In fact, he absolutely refused the nomination. *Ballot for Auditor:* Asa Hairgrove, of Linn, 39; Samuel Lappin, of Nemaha, 24; C. S. Lambdin, of Butler, 9; Martin Anderson, of Jackson, 3. *Ballot for Treasurer:* William Spriggs, of Anderson, 40; Judge John A. Wakefield, of Douglas, 32; John R. Swallow, of Lyon, 3. *Ballot for Superintendent of Public Instruction:* Isaac T. Goodnow, of Riley, 34; John Francis, of Johnson, 17; S. W. Greer, of Leavenworth, 2; S. M. Thorp, of Douglas, 3; Wm. A. Bishop, of Saline, 6; Abram Ellis, of Miami, 9; H. D. Preston, of Osage, 2; Watson, 1. Prof. Goodnow was, on motion, declared the nominee. *Ballot for Attorney General:* Warren W. Guthrie, of Brown, 42; C. K. Gilchrist, of Shawnee, 29; Mr. Lowe, 1. *Associate Justice:* L. D. Bailey, of Lyon, 31; Azel Spaulding, of Jefferson, 13; J. H. Watson, of Lyon, 21; Judge McKay, of Wyandotte, 8. On the second ballot Bailey received 44, Watson 28.

EVENING SESSION.—*First ballot for Congress:* A. C. Wilder 29, M. F. Conway 25, T. D. Thacher 10, W. W. H. Lawrence 10, Wm. A. Phillips 1. *Second ballot:* Wilder 34, Conway 27, Thacher 11, Lawrence 4. *Sixth ballot:* Wilder 37, Conway 23, Thacher 15. *Seventh ballot:* Wilder 41, Conway 20, Thacher 14. A letter is read from Thos. Ewing, jr., in which he says he will not resign as Chief Justice, unless he receives a commission as Colonel of the Eleventh.

State Central Committee: Samuel F. Atwood of Leavenworth, John J. Ingalls of Atchison, Sidney Clarke of Douglas, W. R. Saunders of Coffey, J. F. Newlon of Lyon, Chester Thomas of Shawnee, L. R. Palmer of Pottawatomie.

Speeches were made by Thos. Carney, A. C. Wilder, J. H. Lane, J. C. Vaughan, C. R. Jennison, and John A. Wakefield. The following platform was adopted:

"*Resolved,* That, as the representatives of the people of Kansas, we do most heartily endorse the administration of the President of the United States; that, having implicit confidence in the integrity of his character, and the steadfastness of his purpose, we will co-operate with him to the extent of our ability in his efforts to preserve and perpetuate the Union; that we desire a vigorous prosecution of the war, and a speedy and effectual vindication of a just and liberal Government, sought to be overthrown.

"*Resolved*, That we have full confidence in the ability and integrity of the nominees of this Convention; that we pledge to them our united support; and that we invite all friends of the Union, and advocates of the sentiments above enunciated, to co-operate with us in securing their election."

SEPTEMBER 18.—D. R. Anthony, Lieutenant Colonel of the Seventh, resigns and returns to Leavenworth, from Mississippi.

—Appearance of the Leavenworth Evening Bulletin, published by Henry Buckingham, A. N. Hamilton and George F. Prescott.

—The Conservative, during the campaign, edited by Ward Burlingame.

—Burrell B. Taylor is again editing the Inquirer.

SEPTEMBER 22.—President Lincoln's first Emancipation Proclamation. The Chicago Tribune says: "So splendid a vision has hardly shone upon the world since the day of the Messiah."

SEPTEMBER 24.—The body of Capt. John Lockhart, of the Fifth, reaches Leavenworth, from Helena, Ark. He was one of the truest and worthiest of the young pioneers and soldiers of Kansas. His family resided at McCamish, Johnson county.

—Capt. P. B. Plumb, of Company C, Eleventh Regiment, is elected Major.

SEPTEMBER 29.—Union State Convention at Lawrence. Called to order by Mr. Graves, of Woodson. W. W. Updegraff, of Miami, temporary Chairman, J. K. Goodin, of Franklin, Secretary.

Committee on Permanent Organization: Thos. Murphy of Atchison, A. J. Mead of Riley, Benj. F. Simpson of Miami, Hadley of Wyandotte, Ford of Douglas, Samuel A. Stinson of Leavenworth, N. S. Goss of Woodson.

Officers: President, W. W. Updegraff; Vice Presidents, Chas. G. Keeler of Johnson, Graves of Woodson, Benton of Atchison; Secretary, Hovey E. Lowman, of Douglas.

Committee on Platform: Stinson, Mead, Benton, Goss, Hadley, Roberts of Miami, and Ford of Douglas.

The following platform is adopted:

"*First:* That the condition of our country and State imperatively demands that all good and loyal citizens should, without distinction of party, unite in supporting the National Government in its efforts to crush the rebellion, and in maintaining the liberties of our people against threatened assaults from powerful and tyrannical political demagogues.

"*Second:* That there are now no open questions in regard to the present policy of the National Administration; its only policy should be to maintain the integrity of the Government, and re-establish the authority of the Constitution and the laws at every sacrifice.

"*Third:* That while there are among us differences of opinion upon minor questions of policy in the prosecution of the war, we are all agreed that the measures adopted should be those which will bear with the most crushing effect upon the Rebellion.

"*Fourth:* That the people, absorbed in the dangers which menace the country and the State, have neglected and abandoned the old political organizations, and these organizations have become the exponents of the schemes and ambition of demagogues and cliques. They present no issues of principles or policy, and only serve as the machinery to corrupt the elective franchise, and divide the loyal men of the nation.

"*Fifth:* That recent events in our own State have demonstrated the danger and disgrace attendant upon the active continuance of party organizations at this time. Federal patronage imprudently entrusted to dishonest politicians; open pecuniary bribery, and every species of corruption, have notoriously controlled the action of a recent political convention in this State, and placed in nomination candidates for office tainted with the disgrace of the assembly which presented them. To defeat this scheme, devised to control the destinies of the State by bribery, we pledge ourselves to use our most earnest and determined efforts.

"*Sixth:* That the people of Kansas love their liberties too dearly, and prize the elective franchise too highly, tamely to submit to the threatened attempt to control the coming election by violence from any quarter. Against corruption we will appeal to the honesty and integrity of the people; but at the sacrifice of life itself we will defend the purity and the freedom of the ballot box from armed interference."

The following nominations were made by acclamation: Governor, W. R. Wagstaff, of Miami; Lieutenant Governor, John J. Ingalls, of Atchison; Secretary of State, James Humphrey, of Riley; Treasurer, D. L. Lakin, of Jefferson; for Congress, M. J. Parrott, of Leavenworth; Attorney General, David P. Lowe, of Linn; Chief Justice, Willard P. Gambell, of Leavenworth; Associate Justice, Ed. S. Lowman, of Douglas. *Ballot for Auditor:* N. S. Goss, 22; C. G. Keeler, 13. *For Superintendent of Public Instruction:* E. D. Brown, of Wyandotte, 22; S. M. Thorp, of Douglas, 8. *State Central Committee:* James C. Horton, of Douglas, A. J. Mead of Riley, M. R. Benton of Atchison, J. M. Roberts of Miami, A. L. Williams of Shawnee. There were delegates in the Convention from eleven counties: Nemaha, Leavenworth, Atchison, Wyandotte, Johnson, Miami, Douglas, Franklin, Woodson, Riley, and Shawnee.

OCTOBER 1.—Democratic State Convention at Topeka. A. G. Ege, of Doniphan, President; Wm. Roy, of Johnson, and Wm. Shepherd, of Leavenworth, Secretaries. A resolution was passed to make no nominations. *State Committee:* H. B. Denman, N. J. Marvin, A. G. Ege, Hugh S. Walsh, Robt. Reynolds, Chas. Sims, N. S. Goss, John Martin, Robt. Graham. The following platform was adopted:

"*Whereas,* The Democratic party stands to-day where it has always stood, on the Constitution and Laws of the land, and an economical administration of the Government thereof; and

"*Whereas,* We believe that the Democratic party by its time-honored policy made this country great, powerful and prosperous, and the people happy; and

"*Whereas,* We still have abiding faith in its power and willingness to save: therefore,

"*Resolved,* 1st. That to the Democratic party we look for the political salvation of the country, the maintenance of the Constitution inviolate, and a faithful administration of the Government, and the liberty of citizenship.

"2d. That we will uphold and defend the principles of the Democratic party, the Constitution of our country, and the laws of the land made in pursuance thereof.

"3d. That we deeply regret the present unfortunate condition of our beloved country, and hope that such measures may be adopted by the Government so that the Constitution may be preserved as it is, and that the country may be restored as it was, and the States again united in one common sisterhood.

"4th. That the Constitution, and laws made in pursuance thereof, are and must remain the *supreme law of the land,* and as such must be preserved and maintained in their proper and rightful supremacy; that the rebellion now in arms against them must be suppressed, and it is the duty of all good citizens to aid the General Government in all legal and constitutional measures necessary and proper to the accomplishment of this end.

"5th. That we recommend to the Democracy of the several counties of this State to organize immediately, and in every Senatorial and Representative District run a candidate or candidates (as the case may be) for the State Legislature.

"6th. That this Convention appoint a State Democratic Central Committee, with usual powers."

OCTOBER 1.—Chester Thomas elected Chairman and Samuel F. Atwood Secretary of the Republican Committee. W. W. H. Lawrence, of Franklin county, put on the Republican ticket for Secretary of State. The Republican State ticket is supported by eighteen papers; the Union ticket by four, viz.: Leavenworth Times, Lawrence State Journal, Atchison Champion and Manhattan Express. The Leavenworth Inquirer, Atchison Union and Fort Scott Bulletin are straight Democratic or neutral.

OCTOBER 4.— Rebels defeated at Corinth.

OCTOBER 8.—Battle of Perryville, Kentucky.

OCTOBER 10.—James F. Legate, U. S. Assessor, enters upon his duties; office at Lawrence. Wm. G. Mathias is a straight Democratic candidate for Congress.

OCTOBER 16.—The Union Crusader, edited by Benj. F. Simpson, is issued at Paola.

OCTOBER 17.—Quantrell and his gang make a foray into Johnson county, kill three men and burn thirteen buildings. They killed two teamsters a few miles south of Shawnee, and stole their loaded wagons.

OCTOBER 17.—An Address to the People, issued by the Republican Committee.

—The First Kansas Colored is organized near Fort Lincoln, Bourbon county, and ordered to Baxter Springs. The Thirteenth is at Fort Scott, the Twelfth on the eastern border, and the Eleventh has left to join Blunt.

OCTOBER 21.—D. P. Lowe declines the Union nomination for Attorney General, and Louis Carpenter, of Lawrence, is nominated.

OCTOBER 22.—J. H. Watson is placed on the Republican ticket as the candidate for Chief Justice. The Convention made no nomination.

OCTOBER 27.—Thomas Ewing, senior, makes an argument in a land case at Topeka. The suit was brought by the United States against John Conner, Chief of the Delaware Tribe, and others, to set aside and cancel a patent issued by the United States for a large tract of land, known as the Government Farm, adjoining Leavenworth. Crozier and Gambell appeared for the United States; Ewing, Stinson and Isacks for the defence

OCTOBER 30.—Joseph Killerman, his wife and two children burned to death in a prairie fire, near Cresco, Anderson county.

NOVEMBER 1.—John A. Martin promoted to Colonel of the Eighth.

NOVEMBER 4.—State election. On the following page will be found the vote on the State tickets.

VOTE OF CANDIDATES.

NAMES.	TOTAL	Wyandotte	Woodson	Washington	Wabaunsee	Shawnee	Saline	Riley	Pottawatomie	Osage	Nemaha	Morris	Miami	Marshall	Lyon	Linn	Leavenworth	Johnson	Jefferson	Jackson	Greenwood	Franklin	Doniphan	Douglas	Dickinson	Davis	Coffey	Chase	Bourbon	Butler	Brown	Atchison	Anderson	Allen
Governor:																																		
Thomas Carney	10,090	183	61	42	156	455	60	177	200	126	313	72	415	235	427	463	1,612	368	504	203	98	322	682	879	54	134	324	107	413	23	229	232	190	231
W. R. Wagstaff*	5,463	123	50	15	16	145	10	96	41	52	64	74	361	61	66	171	1,033	238	294	151	27	175	287	627	22	83	121	11	86	14	22	759	96	122
Lieut. Governor:																																		
Thomas A. Osborn	9,023	48	54	45	136	262	62	178	152	118	290	72	430	270	425	466	1,336	368	251	186	108	327	750	866	30	131	319	107	438	23	227	148	192	228
John J. Ingalls*	5,685	251	52	11	35	332	9	97	83	55	93	67	351	29	65	159	883	230	534	169	6	155	105	617	35	86	123	10	49	12	24	794	93	121
Secretary of State:																																		
W. W. H. Lawrence	9,507	195	56	45	138	451	63	171	173	129	303	72	431	174	420	449	1,311	368	431	195	107	337	694	870	40	130	326	107	430	23	228	213	186	241
James Humphrey*	5,430	101	51	11	34	138	9	103	66	45	88	67	337	71	64	160	1,040	232	363	157	20	143	208	636	37	88	123	11	49	11	22	768	95	98
Auditor of State:																																		
Asa Hairgrove	9,584	190	24	45	157	462	63	180	175	118	304	71	432	243	423	488	1,314	366	433	194	107	331	694	874	40	131	293	107	456	23	230	219	188	209
N. S. Goss*	5,615	110	185	11	16	137	9	96	62	45	81	78	347	58	65	123	1,252	232	352	160	20	168	221	628	38	87	154	11	26	14	22	762	99	146
State Treasurer:																																		
William Spriggs	9,095	47	70	45	138	272	64	179	176	126	302	72	428	253	422	472	1,023	365	277	184	106	331	679	876	39	134	314	107	428	23	196	213	243	215
David L. Lakin*	6,294	258	34	11	34	327	9	98	63	54	83	78	350	49	67	156	1,343	231	520	172	20	169	236	629	39	87	129	11	54	14	56	769	19	123
Attorney General:																																		
Warren W. Guthrie	9,553	51	40	45	157	463	64	179	167	118	310	72	427	266	424	469	1,311	365	435	195	107	332	751	852	43	135	320	107	438	23	228	226	189	218
Louis Carpenter*	5,376	38	38	11	15	132	9	96	58	56	76	34	319	29	57	155	1,042	231	360	158	17	147	154	642	36	76	125	13	48	12	28	757	56	52
Supt. Public Instruction:																																		
Isaac T. Goodnow	9,530	51	54	45	154	464	64	172	164	135	317	72	424	276	423	468	1,317	363	429	195	105	331	695	872	54	131	321	107	440	23	229	225	192	218
E. D. Brown*	5,497	243	53	11	16	134	9	96	66	35	76	72	352	24	65	154	1,038	234	364	158	20	152	206	636	23	82	125	11	47	12	22	755	94	122
Chief Justice Supreme Court:																																		
John H. Watson	9,176	155	54	45	157	442	63	181	177	100	301	73	427	266	405	463	1,120	351	427	195	100	312	681	871	41	130	316	106	417	23	194	231	182	218
Willard P. Gambell*	6,016	151	45	11	16	152	9	97	62	45	88	99	348	35	70	159	1,521	233	365	159	22	171	235	629	39	88	129	11	67	14	52	685	79	131
Associate Justice Supreme Court:																																		
Lawrence D. Bailey	9,197	52	54	45	157	471	64	181	150	120	305	73	426	226	385	470	1,288	366	435	194	107	329	692	852	42	131	320	107	275	23	231	220	189	217
E. S. Lowman*	5,751	246	53	11	16	126	9	97	62	47	80	70	323	45	86	155	1,052	231	361	157	20	172	198	649	37	86	121	11	213	13	21	763	96	124
Representative in Congress:																																		
A. C. Wilder	9,076	191	60	41	154	446	62	175	188	116	293	71	464	202	420	461	1,340	360	438	193	105	330	679	893	39	133	325	107	460	23	228	255	191	223
Marcus J. Parrott*	4,066	98	30	15	16	106	11	95	52	52	85	14	289	35	71	163	948	212	296	119	8	133	192	556	40	85	101	1	32	7	24	624	94	58
Wm. G. Mathias†	930	4	20			37		4	4	6		60	11	60			348	5	52	35	14	33	40	19			4	11	1	6		100		63

*Union. †Democrat.

The following is the Legislative and Judicial vote:

First District.—Whole number of votes cast, 1,574; of which Sol. Miller received 651, Abraham Bennett 661, Robert J. Nesbitt 206, John Bayless 51. Sol. Miller and Abraham Bennett were elected.

Second District.—Whole number of votes cast, 1856; C. G. Foster received 743, Joshua Wheeler 736, C. A. Woodworth 153, W. J. Mason 58, R. St. Clair Graham 166. C. G. Foster and Joshua Wheeler were elected.

Third District.—Whole number of votes cast, 7,895; C. B. Pierce received 1,362, John Wilson 1,573, F. P. Fitzwilliam 1,388, Henry B. Keller 1,274, H. Miles Moore 1,208, H. Markson 1,090. C. B. Pierce, John Wilson and F. P. Fitzwilliam were elected.

Fourth District.—Whole number of votes cast, 785; Azel W. Spalding received 499, C. A. Buckmaster 286. Azel W. Spalding was elected.

Fifth District.—Whole number of votes cast, 632; Byron Sherry received 632, and was elected.

Sixth District—Whole number of votes cast, 543; Rufus Ousley received 233, Rufus Ousler 193, A. J. Francis 117. Rufus Ousley was elected.

Seventh District.—Whole number of votes cast, 620; T. H. Baker received 610, Peter From 7, T. S. Vail 1, F. Paulson 1, James Bromwell 1. T. H. Baker was elected.

Eighth District.—Whole number of votes cast, 591; David Brockway received 265, F. W. Giles 158, L. McArthur 142, Erastus Tefft 26. David Brockway was elected.

Ninth District.—Whole number of votes cast, 2,899; W. F. Woodworth received 1,378, John A. Beam 760, S. M. Thorp 751. W. F. Woodworth and John A. Beam were elected.

Tenth District.—Whole number of votes cast, 550; W. H. M. Fishback received 343, John M. Giffen 197, William Holmes 10. W. H. M. Fishback was elected.

Eleventh District.—Whole number of votes cast, 771; Johnson Clark received 418, J. H. Pratt 353. Johnson Clark was elected.

Twelfth District.—Whole number of votes cast, 295; James McGrew received 293, A. J. Reeves 1, Byron Judd 1. James McGrew was elected.

Thirteenth District.—Whole number of votes cast, 612; David P. Lowe received 418, J. W. Garnett 194. David P. Lowe was elected.

Fourteenth District.—Whole number of votes cast, 464; Isaac Ford received 431, E. Williams 33. Isaac Ford was elected.

Fifteenth District.—Whole number of votes cast, 276; M. R. Leonard received 162, W. B. Hernill 105, E. H. Sanford 9. M. R. Leonard was elected.

Sixteenth District.—Whole number of votes cast, 461; Orlin Thurston received 256, S. D. Redos 205. Orlin Thurston was elected.

Seventeenth District.—Whole number of votes cast, 780; D. M. Valentine received 565, James Y. Campbell 215. D. M. Valentine was elected.

Eighteenth District.—Whole number of votes cast, 589; F. W. Potter received 583, A. Lane 3. F. W. Potter was elected.

Nineteenth District.—Whole number of votes cast, 564; P. B. Maxson received 564, and was elected.

Twentieth District.—Whole number of votes cast, 517; S. M. Strickler received 386, L. B. Perry 131. S. M. Strickler was elected.

First District.—Votes cast, 179; F. E. Armstrong received 1, J. P. Johnson 178, and was elected.

Second District.—Votes cast, 126; S. F. Soller received 15, N. C. Clark 111, and was elected.

Third District.—Votes cast, 186; Lyman Nash received 41, Ed. Russell 145, and was elected.

Fourth District.—Votes cast, 201; Frederick Lyman received 60, William H. Hanson 141, and was elected.

Fifth District.—Votes cast, 156; Hazel Frick received 56, John W. Forman 100, and was elected.

Sixth District.—Votes cast, 234; C. W. Edgar received 6, W. C. Smith 25, G. W. Glick 203, and was elected.

Seventh District.—Votes cast, 237; W. P. Lamb received 38, G. W. Bowman 199, and was elected.

Eighth District.—Votes cast, 264; F. M. Williams received 123, Samuel Hollester 141, and was elected.

Ninth District.—Votes cast, 125; A. B. Wakefield received 20, S. J. H. Snyder 105, and was elected.

Tenth District.—Votes cast, 102; H. Perry received 4, F. Roach 41, H. S. Baker 57, and was elected.

Eleventh District.—Votes cast, 103; D. H. Babbitt 6, Noah Hanson 1, F. T. Neal 3, Ira J. Lacock 93, and was elected.

Twelfth District.—Votes cast, 138; Noah Hanson received 60, George E. Irwin 78, and was elected.

Thirteenth District.—Votes cast, 182; Samuel Lappin received 1, J. C. Hibbard 73, Richard Bradley 108, and was elected.

Fourteenth District.—Votes cast, 210; F. P. Baker received 96, John S. Hidden 114, and was elected.

Fifteenth District.—Votes cast, 312; scattering 11, R. R. Edwards 142, Jacob Weisbach 159, and was elected.

Sixteenth District.—Votes cast, 58; H. G. Hollenberg received 58 votes, and was elected.

Seventeenth District.—Votes cast, 172; S. V. Lee received 172 votes, and was elected.

Eighteenth District.—Votes cast, 344; John B. Hubbell received 151, R. S. Craft 192, and was elected.

Nineteenth District.—Votes cast, 289; E. Bailey received 2, Isaac Hall 105, G. M. Lee 182, and was elected.

Twentieth District.—Votes cast, 189; John Hays received 1, George Barrett 188, and was elected.

Twenty-first District.—Votes cast, 292; D. McElvey received 4, S. Kerr 75, James Peterson 103, J. H. Jones 110, and was elected.

Twenty-second District.—Votes cast, 491; E. Welsh received 241, Abraham Brown 250, and was elected.

Twenty-third District.—Votes cast, 512; M. Solleder received 135, Josiah Kellogg 377, and was elected.

Twenty-fourth District.—Votes cast, 356; R. H. Housley received 146, H. W. Ide 210, and was elected.

Twenty-fifth District.—Votes cast, 334; Allen Pierce received 121, Warren A. Lattin 213, and was elected.

Twenty-sixth District.—Votes cast, 222; R. E. Petherbridge received 86, Chas. H. Grover 136, and was elected.

Twenty-seventh District.—Votes cast, 128; H. C. Branch received 43, Thos. O. Gwartney 85, and was elected.

Twenty-eighth District.—Votes cast, 164; John Wright received 76, D. F. Walker 88, and was elected.

Twenty-ninth District.—Votes cast, 200; J. L. Wallace received 93, James Medill 107, and was elected.

Thirtieth District.—Votes cast, 164; D. H. Mitchell received 52, R. Cole Foster 112, and was elected.

Thirty-first District.—Votes cast, 293; James Halland received 1, M. W. Bottom 292, and was elected.

Thirty-second District.—Votes cast, 267; W. N. Kerr received 74, C. H. Stratton 193, and was elected.

Thirty-third District.—Votes cast, 114; A. H. Gregg received 43, D. G. Campbell 71, and was elected.

Thirty-fourth District.—Votes cast, 195; S. Bradbury received 83, William Williams 112, and was elected.

Thirty-fifth District.—Votes cast, 368; T. D. Thacher received 163, George Ford 205, and was elected.

Thirty-sixth District.—Votes cast, 257; Joel Grover received 105, J. S. Emery 152, and was elected.

Thirty-seventh District.—Votes cast, 201; D. W. Pingree received 86, John W. Vaughn 115, and was elected.

Thirty-eighth District.—Votes cast, 240; —— Zelvey received 61; C. S. Steele, 179, and was elected.

Thirty-ninth District.—Votes cast, 230; Henry Monson received 104, D. T. Mitchell 126, and was elected.

Fortieth District.—Votes cast, 204; A. Curtiss received 70, W. Foster 134, and was elected.

Forty-first District.—Votes cast, 344; T. G. Thornton received 1, J. A. Steele 149, W. P. Douthitt 195, and was elected.

Forty-second District.—Votes cast, 238; Henry Fox received 96, John T. Ward 142, and was elected.

Forty-third District.—Votes cast, 228; T. Roberts received 70, Isaac Christie 158, and was elected.

Forty-fourth District.—Votes cast, 302; M. F. Holaday received 117, John M. Ellis 185, and was elected.

Forty-fifth District.—Votes cast, 211; Samuel Jackson received 102, S. C. Convoy 109, and was elected.

Forty-sixth District.—Votes cast, 97; scattering 2; Daniel Underhill received 95 votes, and was elected.

Forty-seventh District.—Votes cast, 219; W. L. Henderson received 85, Fontley Muse 48, George E. Dennison 86, and was elected.

Forty-eighth District.—Votes cast, 140; A. H. Smith received 29, J. M. Sayer 111, and was elected.

Forty-ninth District.—Votes cast, 151; J. W. Babb received 22, T. F. Wilson 48, J. F. Broadhead 81, and was elected.

Fiftieth District.—Votes cast, 67; L. D. Clevenger received 26, D. B. Jackman 41, and was elected.

Fifty-first District.—Votes cast, 112; scattering 13; W. T. Jones received 37, J. Hawkins 62, and was elected.

Fifty-second District.—Votes cast, 97; David R. Cobb received 97 votes, and was elected.

Fifty-third District.—Votes cast, 205; Charles F. Drake received 205 votes, and was elected.

Fifty-fourth District.—Votes cast, 248; James Falkner received 86, A. W. T. Brown 162, and was elected.

Fifty-fifth District.—Votes cast, 91; J. A. Christie received 43, J. H. Campbell 48, and was elected.

Fifty-sixth District.—Votes cast, 155; G. W. Iler received 1 vote, C. W. Fraker 48, Isaac Hiner 106, and was elected.

Fifty-seventh District.—Votes cast, 116; S. Marsh received 43, Jackson Means 73, and was elected.

Fifty-eighth District.—Votes cast, 260; J. K. Goodin received 128, G. W. E. Griffith 136, and was elected.

Fifty-ninth District.—Votes cast, 231; B. C. Sanford received 74, H. B. Beeson 157, and was elected.

Sixtieth District.—Votes cast, 174; scattering 26; P. C. Schuyler received 71, James Rogers 77, and was elected.

Sixty-first District.—Votes cast, 223; H. McMahan received 92, Horace Tucker 131, and was elected.

Sixty-Second District.—Votes cast, 215; F. Robinson received 87, W. R. Saunders 128, and was elected.

Sixty-third District.—Votes cast, 110; A. McCartney received 110 votes, and was elected.

Sixty-fourth District.—Votes cast, 182; C. V. Eskridge received 182 votes, and was elected.

Sixty-fifth District.—Votes cast, 161; G. J. Tallman received 66, F. R. Page 95, and was elected.

Sixty-sixth District.—Votes cast, 122; W. A. Shannon received 46, John W. Loy 76, and was elected.

Sixty-seventh District.—Butler county, no returns.

Sixty-eighth District.—Votes cast, 114; E. A. Alford received 114 votes, and was elected.

Sixty-ninth District.—Votes cast, 155; J. E. Bryan received 77, William Downing 78, and was elected.

Seventieth District.—Votes cast, 171; J. B. Ingersoll received 77, D. M. Johnston 83, and was elected.

Seventy-first District.—Votes cast, 183; G. F. Gordon received 96, W. H. McKinley 69, J. C. Kennet 18. G F. Gordon was elected.

Seventy-second District.—Votes cast, 381; A. Todd received 110, R. E. Fullington 271, and was elected.

Seventy-third District.—Votes cast, 77; Robert S. Miller received 77, and was elected.

Seventy-fourth District.—Votes cast, 72; H. L. Jones received 20, R. H. Bishop 52, and was elected.

Seventy-fifth District.—Votes cast, 121; B. F. Van Horn received 46, J. Kinner 75, and was elected.

DISTRICT JUDGE.

Second District.—Whole number of votes cast for Judge of the District Court, 2,657; scattering 28; Albert H. Horton received 2,629 votes, and was elected.

NOVEMBER 15.—Completion of the survey of the Pottawatomie Reserve, by the Interior Department.

NOVEMBER 20.—The New York Tribune of November 20th publishes the following:

"*Cotton from Kansas.*—Garbutt, Black & Hendricks, Nos. 87 and 89 Warren street, have a bale of good, fair, short-staple cotton, unginned, grown in Kansas this year. A sample before us shows the seeds well ripened, and quality of lint equal to Tennessee Upland.

"A manufacturer says of a sample from Madison, Indiana:

"'As to quality, but little more could be desired than is shown in the specimen, of which the fibre, though not long, is fine, strong, silky and uniform. The same is true of the Kansas sample.'"

NOVEMBER 28.—Battle of Cane Hill, Arkansas.

NOVEMBER 30.—Expenditures of the State for the year:

Governor's Department	$3,437 92	State Library	2,000 00
Secretary's Department	3,428 21	Legislative exp. and Journals	27,861 71
Auditor's Department	2,892 07	Printing	25,288 25
Treasurer's Department	1,653 50	Impeachment case	7,171 58
Sup't of Public Instruction	1,512 64	Commissioners to select lands	2,871 60
Attorney General	1,087 98	Educating deaf and dumb	294 25
Quartermaster General	500 00	Miscellaneous expenses	4,077 45
Adjutant General	711 79		
Judiciary Department	15,254 21	Total for 1862	$100,043 16

DECEMBER 6.—Claiborne F. Jackson, Rebel Governor of Missouri, dies at Little Rock, Ark.   Thos. C. Reynolds, Lieutenant Governor, assumes to be Governor.

DECEMBER 7.—Gen. Blunt gains a victory at Prairie Grove, near Fayetteville, Ark.   The Kansas troops with Blunt are: part of the Ninth, Col. Lynde; the Sixth, Col. Judson; the Tenth, Col. Weer; the Eleventh, Col. Ewing; the Thirteenth, Col. Bowen; part of Blair's Battery, under Lieut. Ed. A. Smith; Allen's Battery, under Taylor and Tenney, and Stockton's Battery.   The battle is called Prairie Grove.

The following is copied from Greeley's Conflict, vol. II, p. 40:

"At 1:45 P.M., Gen. Blunt, in advance of his division, came into full view of the field where the battle was fiercely raging. The Rebels were very strongly posted on high, rolling ground, covered by timber, and only approached from the north over large, open fields, which afforded no cover, save that a part of them bore a crop of ripe corn. Blunt's eccentric advance had brought him in front of the enemy's left, where they had been massing a large force for the purpose of flanking Herron's position. The flankers found an enemy much nearer than they expected, and were at once hotly engaged with Blunt's division. Its three batteries, firing shell and case-shot at short range, soon proved an overmatch for the two Rebel batteries opposed to them, driving them and their supports back into the woods, where they were charged by Col. Weer, leading the Tenth, Thirteenth, and part of the Second and Eleventh Kansas and Twentieth Iowa, and a musketry fight of three hours was maintained with equal energy by the contending hosts. Meantime, our batteries were advanced at various points, and served with rare efficiency; Lieut. Tenney, with six 10-pound Parrotts, repelling with shell and canister, while unsupported, a formidable infantry attack. Here fell the Rebel Gen. Stein, of Missouri. A battery of ten guns, well supported, opening upon Tenney, he in ten minutes silenced its clamor, dismounting two of the guns, and driving off the residue. An attempt to capture Rabb's and Hopkins's batteries, which were supported by the Eleventh Kansas, Lieut. Col. Moonlight, was defeated with fearful slaughter. . . . Our loss in this battle was 167 killed, 798 wounded, and 183 missing—total, 1,148."

—Blunt gained a victory at Newtonia, October 4th; at Old Fort Wayne, October 22d; and at Cane Hill, November 28th.

DECEMBER 16.—M. S. Adams is appointed Brigade Commissary, and Judge Geo. W. Gardiner Quartermaster.

DECEMBER 29.—Blunt takes Van Buren, Arkansas.

—Gov. Carney appoints Ward Burlingame Private Secretary.

DECEMBER 31.—Battle of Stone River.

DECEMBER 31.—S. R. Shepherd, appointed Secretary of State to succeed J. W. Robinson, makes the Annual Report.

—The Supreme Court declared valid the action of the Senate sitting as a Court of Impeachment; opinion by Kingman, Ewing and Bailey concurring. The information states that Auditor Hillyer and Secretary Robinson have held office since the 16th day of June, 1862. The respondents assert that the Senate had no constitutional existence. The report of the case gives the facts and dates in the Impeachment proceedings. (*The State, ex rel. Adams, vs. Hillyer,* 2 Kan., 17.)

—Chas. Chadwick, Adjutant General, makes a report to Gov. Robinson. A list is given of all the officers of the militia. The Report fills 50 pages, and is published with the State documents.

—S. M. Thorp, appointed Superintendent of Public Instruction in place of W. R. Griffith, deceased, makes the Annual Report.

—George W. Collamore, Q. M. General of the Militia, makes a Report.

—The Auditor's Annual Report is made by David L. Lakin, appointed to succeed Geo. S. Hillyer.

ELEVENTH REGIMENT KANSAS VOLUNTEERS—CAVALRY.

Name and Rank.	Date of Muster.	Remarks.
COLONEL.		
Thomas Ewing, jr..........	Sept. 15, 1862	Promoted Brig. Gen. U.S. Vols., March 13, 1863.
Thomas Moonlight........	Apr. 25, 1864	Mustered out, July 17, '65, at Ft. Kearney, N. T.
LIEUT. COLONEL.		
Thomas Moonlight........	Sept. 20, 1862	Promoted Colonel, April 25, 1864.
Preston B. Plumb..........	May 17, 1864	Must. out, Sept. 13, 1865, at Fort Leavenworth.
MAJOR.		
Preston B. Plumb.........	Sept. 25, 1862	Promoted Lieutenant Colonel, May 17, 1864.
Martin Anderson...........	Nov. 22, 1863	Mustered out, Sept. 18, '65, at Ft. Leavenworth; promoted Colonel by brevet, March 13, 1865.
Edmund G. Ross...........	Apr. 24, 1864	Mustered out, Sept. 20, '65, at Ft. Leavenworth; prom. Lieut. Colonel by brevet, March 13, '65.
Nathaniel A. Adams.....	May 19, 1864	Mustered out, August 9, 1865.
ADJUTANT.		
John Willans...............	Sept. 4, 1862	Promoted Captain and Assistant Adjutant General U. S. Volunteers, May 31, 1863.
James E. Greer	Nov. 2, 1863	Promoted Captain Co. I, August 20, 1864.
Ira I. Taber..................	Oct. 12, 1864	Mustered out, August 19, 1865.
QUARTERMASTER.		
James R. McClure	Sept. 10, 1862	Mustered out, August 10, 1865.
COMMISSARY.		
Robert J. Harper	Oct. 8, 1863	Mustered out, August 19, 1865.
SURGEON.		
George W. Hogeboom ...	Sept. 27, 1862	Resigned, June 2, 1863.
Richard M. Ainsworth..	June 23, 1863	Dismissed by order of President, July 21, 1865.
ASSISTANT SURGEON.		
Richard M. Ainsworth..	Sept. 20, 1862	Promoted Surgeon, June 23, 1863.
Josiah D. Adams..........	Oct. 11, 1862	Mustered out, September 20, 1865.
Granville C. Taylor	Apr. 19, 1864	Mustered out, August 19, 1865.
CHAPLAIN.		
James S. Cline...............	Oct. 11, 1862	Mustered out, July 7, 1865.

COMPANY A.

Name and Rank.	Date of Muster.	Remarks.
CAPTAIN.		
Lyman Scott.................	Aug. 27, 1862	Resigned, February 20, 1863.
Henry E. Palmer..........	Mar. 24, 1863	No evidence of muster-out on file.
FIRST LIEUT.		
John Owens	Aug. 27, 1862	Died of pneumonia at Camp Babcock, Arkansas, November 19, 1862.
Henry E. Palmer	Dec. 31, 1862	Promoted Captain, March 24, 1863.
Joseph L. Thornton......	May 17, 1863	Mustered out, September 26, 1865.
SECOND LIEUT.		
Henry E. Palmer	Aug. 27, 1863	Promoted First Lieutenant, December 31, 1862.
Collins T. Slane.............	May 2, 1863	Mustered out, September 26, 1865.

COMPANY B.

Name and Rank.	Date of Muster.	Remarks.
CAPTAIN.		
Martin Anderson	Aug. 30, 1862	Promoted Major, November 22, 1863.
Louis F. Greene............	Nov. 23, 1863	Mustered out with company, August 31, 1865.
FIRST LIEUT.		
Amos C. Smith..............	Aug. 30, 1862	Resigned on account of disability, Feb. 3, 1863.
Louis F. Greene............	Mar. 29, 1863	Promoted Captain, November 23, 1863.
Ira I. Taber..................	Dec. 8, 1863	Promoted Adjutant, October 12, 1864.
John B. Parrott.............	Dec. 15, 1864	Mustered out with company, August 31, 1865.
SECOND LIEUT.		
Louis F. Greene............	Aug. 30, 1862	Promoted First Lieutenant, March 29, 1863.
Ira I. Taber..................	June 19, 1863	Promoted First Lieutenant, December 8, 1863.
John B. Parrott.............	Dec. 9, 1863	Promoted First Lieutenant, December 15, 1864.
James B. Hastings........	Dec. 30, 1864	Mustered out with company, August 31, 1865.

COMPANY C.

Name and Rank.	Date of Muster.	Remarks.
CAPTAIN.		
Preston B. Plumb.........	Sept. 10, 1862	Promoted Major, September 25, 1862.
Lemuel T. Heritage......	Sept. 25, 1862	Resigned on account of disability, September 7, 1863; wounded in knee in action, December 2, 1862, Prairie Grove, Ark.
Henry Pearce................	Sept. 19, 1863	Mustered out with company, August 7, 1865.
FIRST LIEUT.		
Henry Pearce................	Sept. 10, 1862	Promoted Captain, September 19, 1863.
William V. Phillips	Sept. 19, 1863	Mustered out with company, August 7, 1865.
SECOND LIEUT.		
William V. Phillips	Sept. 10, 1862	Promoted First Lieutenant, September 19, 1863.
George M. Walker	Sept. 20, 1863	Mustered out, September 22, 1865.

COMPANY D.

Name and Rank.	Date of Muster.	Remarks.
CAPTAIN.		
Jerome Kunkel............	Sept. 13, 1862	Cashiered by sentence G. C. M., G. O. No. 52, dated W. D., A. G. O., Oct. 7, 1864.
Peleg Thomas................	Dec. 13, 1864	Mustered out with company, Sept. 13, 1865.
FIRST LIEUT.		
Elias Gibbs..................	Sept. 13, 1862	Cashiered by sentence G. C. M., G. O. No. 52, dated W. D., A. G. O., Oct. 7, 1864.
Green A. Dewey............	Dec. 13, 1864	Mustered out with company.
SECOND LIEUT.		
Peleg Thomas................	Sept. 13, 1862	Promoted Captain, December 13, 1864.
Wm. B. Godfrey............	Dec. 13, 1864	Mustered out with company.

COMPANY E.

Name and Rank.	Date of Muster.	Remarks.
CAPTAIN.		
Edmund G. Ross............	Sept. 13, 1862	Promoted Major, April 29, 1864.
John D. Walker............	June 18, 1864	Mustered out with company, August 7, 1865.
FIRST LIEUT.		
Charles Drake	Sept. 13, 1862	Resigned, March 15, 1864.
George T. Robinson.......	July 7, 1864	Mustered out, July 17, 1865.
SECOND LIEUT.		
Nathan P. Gregg............	Sept. 13, 1862	Promoted Captain Company M, April 19, 1864.
Caleb S. Smith...............	Jan. 18, 1864	Mustered out with company.

COMPANY F.

Name and Rank.	Date of Muster.	Remarks.
CAPTAIN.		
Jacob G. Rees...............	Sept. 11, 1862	Resigned, February 23, 1865.
John G. Lindsay............	May 1, 1865	Mustered out with company, August 31, 1865.
FIRST LIEUT.		
John G. Lindsay............	Sept. 11, 1862	Promoted Captain, May 1, 1865.
George W. Simons.........	June 30, 1865	Mustered out with company, August 31, 1865.
SECOND LIEUT.		
George W. Simons.........	Sept. 11, 1862	Promoted First Lieutenant, June 30, 1865.
Marvin H. Payne	July 1, 1865	Mustered out with company, August 31, 1865.

COMPANY G.

Name and Rank.	Date of Muster.	Remarks.
CAPTAIN.		
Nathaniel A. Adams......	Sept. 13, 1862	Promoted Major, May 19, 1864.
Grenville L. Gove..........	May 19, 1864	Died of brain fever, Olathe, Kas., Nov. 7, 1864.
Alfred C. Pierce............	Dec. 26, 1864	Mustered out, August 18, 1865.
FIRST LIEUT.		
Grenville L. Gove	Sept. 13, 1862	Promoted Captain, May 19, 1864.
Alfred C. Pierce............	May 19, 1864	Promoted Captain, December 26, 1864.
Thomas Huey................	Dec. 26, 1864	Mustered out with company, June 13, 1865.
SECOND LIEUT.		
Alfred C. Pierce............	Sept. 13, 1862	Promoted First Lieutenant, May 19, 1864.
Samuel Long.................	May 29, 1864	Mustered out with company, June 13, 1865.

COMPANY H.

Name and Rank.	Date of Muster.	Remarks.
CAPTAIN. Joel Huntoon..............	Sept. 15, 1862	Mustered out with company, Sept. 13, 1865; promoted Colonel by brevet, Sept. 24, 1865.
FIRST LIEUT. Harrison Hannahs........	Sept. 15, 1862	Promoted Captain 50th Mo. Inf., Nov. 15, 1864.
John W. Ridgway.........	Dec. 24, 1864	Mustered out with company, Sept. 13, 1865.
SECOND LIEUT. John W. Ridgway.........	Sept. 15, 1862	Promoted First Lieut., December 24, 1864.
Sherman Bodwell..........	Jan. 1, 1865	Mustered out with company, Sept. 13, 1865.

COMPANY I.

Name and Rank.	Date of Muster.	Remarks.
CAPTAIN. Lewis D. Joy................	Sept. 15, 1862	Prom. Major 18th U.S. Col.V. Inf., Sept. 13, 1864.
James E. Greer..............	Aug. 20, 1864	Mustered out with company, Sept. 26, 1865.
FIRST LIEUT. Josiah B. McAfee..........	Sept. 16, 1862	Resigned, February 19, 1863.
William Y. Drew...........	Mar. 7, 1863	Mustered out with company, Sept. 26, 1865.
SECOND LIEUT. William Y. Drew...........	Sept. 15, 1862	Promoted First Lieutenant, March 7, 1863.
James J. Clancy............	Mar. 7, 1863	Mustered out with company, Sept. 26, 1865.

COMPANY K.

Name and Rank.	Date of Muster.	Remarks.
CAPTAIN. John M. Allen..............	Sept. 15, 1862	Mustered out with company, Sept. 13, 1865.
FIRST LIEUT. Josiah M. Hubbard.......	Sept. 15, 1865	Mustered out with company, Sept. 13, 1865.
SECOND LIEUT. Henry C. Haas.............	Sept. 15, 1862	Promoted Major 15th K.V.C., October 20, 1863.
Paul P. Grim................	Sept. 26, 1864	Mustered out with company, Sept. 13, 1865.

COMPANY L.

Name and Rank.	Date of Muster.	Remarks.
CAPTAIN. Henry Booth................	Apr. 18, 1864	Mustered out with company, September 26, 1865; wounded in left shoulder and right arm, in action, Walnut Creek, Kansas.
FIRST LIEUT. Henry Booth................	Mar. 23, 1864	Promoted Captain, April 18, 1864.
Jacob Van Antwerp.......	Apr. 18, 1864	Mustered out with company, Sept. 26, 1865.
SECOND LIEUT. William Booth..............	Apr. 18, 1864	Mustered out with company, Sept. 26, 1865.

COMPANY M.

Name and Rank.	Date of Muster.	Remarks.
CAPTAIN. Nathan P. Gregg...........	Apr. 19, 1864	Mustered out with company, Sept. 26, 1865.
FIRST LIEUT. Joseph D. Greer...........	Apr. 19, 1864	Mustered out with company, Sept. 26, 1865.
SECOND LIEUT. Henry C. Lindsey.........	Apr. 19, 1864	Mustered out with company, Sept. 26, 1865.

List of battles, etc., in which this regiment participated, showing loss reported in each:

Old Fort Wayne—No loss. Cane Hill—Wounded, E. M., 3. Boston

Mountain—Wounded, E.M., 3. Prairie Grove—Killed, E.M., 2; wounded, O. 1, E. M. 19. Scott's Ford—Wounded, E. M., 1. Deep Water Creek— No loss. Lexington—Killed, E. M., 1; wounded, E. M., 1; missing, E. M., 1. Little Blue—Killed, E. M., 5; wounded, O. 2, E. M. 14; missing, E. M., 1. Independence—Wounded, E. M., 1. Big Blue—Killed, E. M., 3; wounded, O. 1, E. M. 8. Cold Water Grove—No loss. Mine Creek — No loss. Sage Creek—No loss. Deer Creek—Killed, E. M., 1. Platte Bridge (June 3, 1865)—Killed, E. M., 1. White River—No loss. Rock Creek —No loss. Fort Halleck—No loss. Platte Bridge (July 26, 1865)— Killed, E. M., 26; wounded, E.M., 2.—*U. S. Army Register.*

TWELFTH REGIMENT KANSAS VOLUNTEERS—INFANTRY.

Name and Rank.	Date of Muster.	Remarks.
COLONEL. Charles W. Adams.........	Sept. 30, 1862	Promoted Brev. Brig. Gen., Feb. 13, '65; wounded in action, Apr. 30, '64, Jenkins' F'ry, Ark.; mustered out with regiment, June 30, '65.
LIEUT. COLONEL. Josiah E. Hayes.............	Sept. 30, 1864	Promoted Brev. Brig. Gen.; wounded in action and captured by the enemy, Apr. 30, '64, Jenkins' F'ry, Ark.; limb amputated above knee; exch'ged Feb. 25, '65; must'd out, July 15, '65.
MAJOR. Thomas H. Kennedy......	Sept. 30, 1862	Mustered out with regiment.
ADJUTANT. Charles J. Lovejoy.........	Sept. 30, 1862	Resigned, April 28, 1865, Little Rock, Ark.
QUARTERMASTER. Andrew J. Shannon......	Sept. 30, 1862	Promoted Captain and Assistant Provost Marshal, March —, 1864.
Joshua Clayton.............	May 22, 1864	Mustered out with regiment.
SURGEON. Cyrus R. Stuckslager.....	Sept. 30, 1862	Mustered out with regiment, June 30, 1865; captured by the enemy, April 30, 1864, Jenkins' Ferry, Ark.; exchanged, June 28, 1864.
ASST. SURGEON. Thomas Lindsay...........	Sept. 30, 1862	Mustered out with regiment.
John F. Everhart...........	Sept. 30, 1862	Resigned, November 4, 1863.
CHAPLAIN. Werter R. Davis.............	Sept. 30, 1862	Resigned, January 26, 1864.
William Sellers..............	Mar. 26, 1864	Resigned, April 13, 1865.

COMPANY A.

Name and Rank.	Date of Muster.	Remarks.
CAPTAIN. James D. Chesnut.........	Sept. 25, 1862	Mustered out with regiment.
FIRST LIEUT. John H. Tullis..............	Sept. 25, 1862	Resigned, Feb. 9, 1865, Little Rock, Ark.
SECOND LIEUT. Nathan R. Stone...........	Sept. 25, 1862	Died of disease, Westport, Mo., Oct. 13, 1862.
Andrew Hooper.............	Oct. 13, 1862	Mustered out, April 10, 1864, per S. O. No. 200, from Headquarters Dept. of Arkansas.

COMPANY B.

Name and Rank.	Date of Muster.	Remarks.
CAPTAIN. Thomas H. Kennedy.....	Sept. 25, 1862	Promoted Major, September 30, 1862.
George W. Umbarger.....	Sept. 30, 1862	Mustered out with regiment.
FIRST LIEUT. Lewis W. Hover............	Sept. 25, 1862	Dismissed the service, August 4, 1864.
Martin L. Town..............	Mar. 6, 1865	Mustered out with regiment.
SECOND LIEUT. George W. Umbarger......	Sept. 25, 1862	Promoted Captain, September 30, 1862.
Martin L. Town.............	Sept. 30, 1862	Promoted First Lieutenant, March 6, 1865.

COMPANY C.

Name and Rank.	Date of Muster.	Remarks.
CAPTAIN.		
Nick L. Benter..............	Sept. 26, 1862	Assassinated, April 2, 1864, Hot Springs, Ark.
William O. Hubbell	July 19, 1864	Mustered out with regiment.
FIRST LIEUT.		
William O. Hubbell......	Sept. 26, 1862	Promoted Captain, July 19, 1864.
William B. Nichols........	July 19, 1864	Resigned, August 3, 1864.
William A. Wells	Oct. 30, 1864	Resigned, May 9, 1865.
SECOND LIEUT.		
William B. Nichols........	Sept. 26, 1862	Promoted First Lieutenant, July 19, 1864.
Samuel S. Kirkham......	Oct. 30, 1864	Mustered out with regiment.

COMPANY D.

Name and Rank.	Date of Muster.	Remarks.
CAPTAIN.		
George W. Ashby.........	Sept. 25, 1862	Resigned, May 29, 1865, Arkansas.
FIRST LIEUT.		
Henry Shively..............	Sept. 25, 1862	Resigned, August 4, 1864, Arkansas.
Alfred Johnson.............	Jan. 5, 1865	Mustered out with regiment.
SECOND LIEUT.		
Alfred Johnson	Sept. 25, 1862	Promoted First Lieutenant, January 5, 1865.
Wm. H. Baker..............	Jan. 5, 1865	Died of disease, in Hospital, Little Rock, Ark., May 30, 1865.

COMPANY E.

Name and Rank.	Date of Muster.	Remarks.
CAPTAIN.		
James M. Steele............	Sept. 26, 1862	Promoted Lieut. Colonel 113th U. S. Colored Troops, January 16, 1864.
A. Jackson Jennings.....	Jan. 16, 1864	Mustered out with regiment.
FIRST LIEUT.		
A. Jackson Jennings.....	Sept. 26, 1862	Promoted Captain, January 16, 1864.
James H. Pleasants	Jan. 16, 1864	Mustered out with regiment.
SECOND LIEUT.		
James H. Pleasants	Sept. 16, 1862	Promoted First Lieutenant, January 16, 1864.
Henry S. Crumrine	May 24, 1864	Mustered out with regiment.

COMPANY F.

Name and Rank.	Date of Muster.	Remarks.
CAPTAIN.		
Clark McKay	Sept. 26, 1862	Resigned, April 11, 1864.
George W. S. Bell..........	Dec. 7, 1864	Mustered out with regiment.
FIRST LIEUT.		
George W. S. Bell..........	Sept. 26, 1862	Promoted Captain, December 7, 1864.
Charles Cochrane..........	Jan. 5, 1865	Mustered out with regiment.
SECOND LIEUT.		
Allen Crocker...............	Sept. 26, 1862	Resigned, July 23, 1864, Arkansas.

COMPANY G.

Name and Rank.	Date of Muster.	Remarks.
CAPTAIN.		
Ezekiel Bunn..............	Sept. 30, 1862	Resigned, February 10, 1865, Little Rock, Ark.
Alexander McAuthor...	Mar. 22, 1865	Mustered out with regiment.
FIRST LIEUT.		
Alexander McAuthor ...	Sept. 30, 1862	Promoted Captain, March 22, 1865.
Franklin Newell...........	Mar. 22, 1865	Resigned, May 25, 1865, Little Rock, Ark.
SECOND LIEUT.		
Franklin Newell..........	Sept. 30, 1862	Promoted First Lieutenant, March 22, 1865.

COMPANY H.

Name and Rank.	Date of Muster.	Remarks.
CAPTAIN.		
James W. Parmeter......	Sept. 30, 1862	Dismissed, July 7, 1864.
Augustus W. Burton.....	Jan. 26, 1865	Mustered out with company, August 6, 1865, Fort Riley, Kas.
FIRST LIEUT.		
Augustus W. Burton.....	Sept. 30, 1862	Promoted Captain, January 26, 1865.
William Pellett............	Mar. 10, 1865	Mustered out with company.
SECOND LIEUT.		
William Pellett............	Sept. 30, 1862	Promoted First Lieutenant, March 10, 1865.

COMPANY I.

Name and Rank.	Date of Muster.	Remarks.
CAPTAIN.		
Joseph T. Gordon	Sept. 30, 1862	Mustered out with regiment.
FIRST LIEUT.		
George Ellis.................	Sept. 30, 1862	Killed in act'n, Ap'l 30, 1864, Jenkins' Ferry, Ark.
James H. Berkshire.......	Aug. 13, 1864	Mustered out with regiment.
SECOND LIEUT.		
Demas M. Alexander.....	Sept. 30, 1862	Promoted Captain and A. C. S., July 30, 1863.
William H. Lindsey.......	Oct. 15, 1862	Prom. 1st Lt. Co. M, 16th K.V. C., June 25, 1863.
James H. Berkshire.......	Sept. 15, 1863	Promoted First Lieutenant, August 13, 1864.

COMPANY K.

Name and Rank.	Date of Muster.	Remarks.
CAPTAIN.		
John J. Sears................	Sept. 30, 1862	Promoted Major 3d Mo. Col.Vol., Feb. 16, 1864.
Peter J. Miserez............	May 26, 1864	Mustered out with regiment.
FIRST LIEUT.		
Peter J. Miserez............	Sept. 30, 1862	Promoted Captain, May 26, 1864.
William Barrett............	May 26, 1864	Resigned, May 20, 1865.
SECOND LIEUT.		
William Barrett............	Sept. 30, 1862	Promoted First Lieutenant, May 26, 1864.
Horace A. B. Cook.........	May 26, 1864	Mustered out with regiment.

List of battles, etc., in which this regiment participated, showing loss reported in each:

Baxter Springs—Killed, E. M., 1; wounded, E. M., 1. Prairie D'Ann —Wounded, E. M., 2. Jenkins' Ferry—Killed, O. 1, E. M. 7; wounded, O. 4, E. M. 25; missing, O. 2, E. M. 10. Fort Smith—Wounded, E. M., 1. —*U. S. Army Register.*

THIRTEENTH REGIMENT KANSAS VOLUNTEERS—INFANTRY.

Name and Rank.	Date of Muster.	Remarks.
COLONEL.		
Thomas M. Bowen	Sept. 20, 1862	Brevet Brigadier General, January 13, 1865; mustered out, June 28, 1865.
LIEUT. COLONEL.		
John B. Wheeler............	Sept. 20, 1862	Mustered out with regiment, June 26, 1865.
MAJOR.		
Caleb A. Woodworth	Sept. 20, 1862	Mustered out, June 26, 1865, Little Rock, Ark.
ADJUTANT.		
William P. Badger	Sept. 20, 1862	Resigned, October 10, 1863.
George W. Smith	Oct. 13, 1863	Mustered out, June 26, 1865, Little Rock, Ark.
QUARTERMASTER.		
Cyrus Leland	Sept. 20, 1862	Mustered out, June 26, 1865, Little Rock, Ark.
SURGEON.		
William H. Grimes.........	Sept. 20, 1862	Resigned, October 20, 1864, Arkansas.
Amos H. Calfee	Feb. 13, 1865	Mustered out, June 26, 1865, Little Rock, Ark.
ASSISTANT SURGEON.		
John Becker.................	Sept. 20, 1862	Resigned, February 27, 1864, Arkansas.
Richard W. Shipley.......	Oct. 1, 1862	Resigned, October 6, 1863, Departm't Missouri.
CHAPLAIN.		
Daniel A. Murdock.......	Sept. 20, 1862	Died of disease, April 28, 1863, Springfield, Mo.
Ozem B. Gardner..........	Sept. 1, 1863	Killed in action, Nov. 25, '64, Timber Hill, C. N.

COMPANY A.

Name and Rank.	Date of Muster.	Remarks.
CAPTAIN.		
Samuel Flickinger.........	Sept. 20, 1862	Mustered out with regiment, June 26, 1865, Little Rock, Ark.
FIRST LIEUT.		
Joseph A. Nixon...........	Sept. 20, 1862	Resigned, September 29, 1863.
Alfred A. Clutter...........	Dec. 22, 1863	Mustered out with regiment.
SECOND LIEUT.		
Alfred A. Clutter...........	Sept. 20, 1862	Promoted First Lieutenant, December 22, 1863.
Alexander Berry...........	Jan. 25, 1864	Resigned, September 26, 1864.
Harvey L. McAdams......	Jan. 11, 1865	Mustered out with regiment.

COMPANY B.

Name and Rank.	Date of Muster.	Remarks.
CAPTAIN.		
Henry Haverkorst........	Sept. 20, 1862	Resigned, April 20, 1863, St. Louis, Mo.
Marion N. Beeler...........	May 19, 1863	Died, August 13, 1864, Van Buren, Arkansas, of wounds received in skirmish, August 1, 1864.
Edward P. Perkins........	Dec. 6, 1864	No evidence of muster-out on file.
FIRST LIEUT.		
Marion N. Beeler...........	Sept. 20, 1862	Promoted Captain, May 19, 1863.
John F. Kotsch.............	May 27, 1863	Resigned, May 20, 1864, Van Buren, Ark.
Antoine Brentano..........	Sept. 27, 1864	Mustered out with regiment.
SECOND LIEUT.		
August Langehemeken..	Sept. 20, 1862	Resigned, March 27, 1863, Springfield, Mo.
Edward P. Perkins........	May 23, 1863	Promoted Captain, December 6, 1864.

COMPANY C.

Name and Rank.	Date of Muster.	Remarks.
CAPTAIN.		
Hugh Robertson...........	Sept. 20, 1862	Resigned, July 12, 1863.
Jeremiah Frankhouse ..	Nov. 1, 1863	Mustered out with regiment.
FIRST LIEUT.		
Jeremiah Frankhouse...	Sept. 20, 1862	Promoted Captain, November 1, 1863.
Alfred C. Low...............	Nov. 1, 1863	Mustered out with regiment.
SECOND LIEUT.		
Alfred C. Low	Sept. 20, 1862	Promoted First Lieutenant, November 1, 1863.

COMPANY D.

Name and Rank.	Date of Muster.	Remarks.
CAPTAIN.		
Henry R. Neal...............	Sept. 19, 1862	Resigned, January 16, 1865.
Robert Manville	Mar. 9, 1865	Mustered out with regiment.
FIRST LIEUT.		
John Batsell..................	Sept. 19, 1862	Resigned, December 5, 1863.
Robert Manville.............	Mar. 12, 1863	Promoted Captain, March 9, 1865.
John L. McCully............	Mar. 9, 1865	Mustered out with regiment.
SECOND LIEUT.		
Robert Manville.............	Sept. 19, 1862	Promoted First Lieutenant, March 12, 1863.
John L. McCully............	Mar. 12, 1863	Promoted First Lieutenant, March 9, 1865.

COMPANY E.

Name and Rank.	Date of Muster.	Remarks.
CAPTAIN.		
Perry Hutchinson	Sept. 20, 1862	Resigned, July 17, 1863.
James H. McDougall.....	Dec. 4, 1863	Dismissed the service per special order No. 127, dated Little Rock, Arkansas, May 29, 1865.
FIRST LIEUT.		
James H. McDougall.....	Sept. 20, 1862	Promoted Captain, December 4, 1863.
William W. Griffin........	Jan. 1, 1864	Mustered out with regiment.
SECOND LIEUT.		
John N. Cline...............	Sept. 20, 1862	Resigned, October 12, 1863.

COMPANY F.

Name and Rank.	Date of Muster.	Remarks.
CAPTAIN. John E. Hayes	Sept. 20, 1862	Resigned, May 3, 1865.
FIRST LIEUT. Archimedes S. Speck	Sept. 20, 1862	Resigned, July 12, 1863.
William J. May	Dec. 1, 1863	Mustered out with regiment.
SECOND LIEUT. William J. May	Oct. 4, 1862	Promoted First Lieutenant, December 1, 1863.
Robert B. Grimes	Dec. 1, 1863	Mustered out with regiment.

COMPANY G.

Name and Rank.	Date of Muster.	Remarks.
CAPTAIN. William S. Blackburn	Sept. 20, 1862	Mustered out with regiment.
FIRST LIEUT. Levi Hensel	Sept. 20, 1862	Mustered out with regiment.
SECOND LIEUT. Daniel C. Auld	Sept. 20, 1862	Resigned, April 2, 1863, at Springfield, Mo.
Nathaniel Slosson	Apr. 22, 1863	Mustered out with regiment.

COMPANY H.

Name and Rank.	Date of Muster.	Remarks.
CAPTAIN. Orlando H. Macauley	Sept. 20, 1862	Mustered out with regiment.
FIRST LIEUT. James C. McElroy	Sept. 20, 1862	Mustered out with regiment.
SECOND LIEUT. Theodore Collins	Sept. 20, 1862	Resigned, April 28, 1863.
John F. Shields	June 10, 1863	Mustered out with regiment.

COMPANY I.

Name and Rank.	Date of Muster.	Remarks.
CAPTAIN. John Shilling	Sept. 20, 1862	Mustered out with regiment.
FIRST LIEUT. Alonso Bradner	Sept. 20, 1862	Resigned, August 20, 1864, Little Rock, Ark.
John H. Croft	Jan. 6, 1865	Mustered out with regiment.
SECOND LIEUT. Langden M. Risley	Sept. 20, 1862	Died, January 22, 1863, Fayetteville, Ark., of wounds received in action, December 7, 1862, Prairie Grove, Ark.
John H. Croft	Mar. 2, 1863	Promoted First Lieutenant, January 6, 1865.

COMPANY K.

Name and Rank.	Date of Muster.	Remarks.
CAPTAIN. Patrick McNamara	Sept. 20, 1862	Discharged, May 15, 1865, Little Rock, Ark., per G. O. No. 8, W. D., series of 1865.
FIRST LIEUT. Daniel C. O'Keefe	Sept. 20, 1862	Resigned, August 15, 1863, St. Louis, Mo.
Hugh Dougherty	Feb. 8, 1864	Resigned, May 29, 1865, Little Rock, Ark.
SECOND LIEUT. Hugh Dougherty	Sept. 20, 1862	Promoted First Lieutenant, February 8, 1864.

List of battles, etc., in which this regiment participated, showing loss reported in each:

Cane Hill—No loss. Prairie Grove—Killed, E. M., 7; wounded, O. 2, E. M. 33; missing, E. M., 6.—*U. S. Army Register.*

FIRST REGIMENT KANSAS COLORED VOLUNTEERS—INFANTRY.

Name and Rank.	Date of Muster.	Remarks.
COLONEL.		
James M. Williams........	May 2, 1863	Promoted Brevet Brig. General, Feb. 13, 1865; mustered out, Pine Bluff, Ark., Oct. 1, 1865.
LIEUT. COLONEL.		
James M. Williams........	Jan. 13, 1863	Promoted Colonel, May 2, 1863.
John Bowles	May 2, 1863	Mustered out per S. O. No. 335, W. D., dated June 1, 1865, to take effect December 17, 1864.
Richard G. Ward..........	April 22, 1865	Mustered out with regiment, October 1, 1865.
MAJOR.		
John Bowles.................	Jan. 13, 1863	Promoted Lieutenant Colonel, May 2, 1863.
Richard G. Ward..........	May 2, 1863	Promoted Lieutenant Colonel, April 22, 1865.
ADJUTANT.		
Richard J. Hinton	Jan. 13, 1863	Promoted Captain 2d K.V. C. I., Oct. 21, 1863.
William C. Gibbons.......	Jan. 27, 1864	Mustered out, May 15, 1865.
QUARTERMASTER.		
Elijah Hughes...............	Jan. 13, 1863	Mustered out with regiment, October 1, 1865.
SURGEON.		
Samuel C. Harrington...	Jan. 15, 1863	Resigned, January 26, 1864.
J. Fulton Ensor............	Nov. 1, 1864	Mustered out with regiment, October 1, 1865.
ASSISTANT SURGEON.		
Eliab G. Macy..............	Jan. 26, 1863	Resigned, June 15, 1864, Fort Smith, Ark.
Abijah D. Tenny..........	May 2, 1863	Resigned, July 20, 1864, Fort Smith, Ark.
Chauncey S. Burr.........	April 23, 1865	Mustered out with regiment, October 1, 1865.
CHAPLAIN.		
George W. Hutchinson..	May 2, 1863	Resigned, June 18, 1864, Fort Smith, Ark.

COMPANY A.

Name and Rank.	Date of Muster.	Remarks.
CAPTAIN.		
Richard G. Ward..........	Jan. 13, 1863	Promoted Major, May 2, 1863.
Elkanah Huddleston.....	May 2, 1863	Mustered out on detachment-roll, Leavenworth, Kas., Oct. 31, 1865, to date Oct. 26, 1865.
FIRST LIEUT.		
Elkanah Huddleston.....	Jan. 13, 1863	Promoted Captain, May 2, 1863.
Benjamin G. Jones........	May 2, 1863	Promoted Captain Company B, Feb. 11, 1865.
William R. Smith	July 10, 1865	Mustered out with regiment.
SECOND LIEUT.		
Ezekiel A. Coleman......	Jan. 13, 1863	Dismissed the service per S. O. No. 99, W. D., 1865, to date February 1, 1864.
William R. Smith..........	April 22, 1865	Promoted First Lieutenant, July 10, 1865.

COMPANY B.

Name and Rank.	Date of Muster.	Remarks.
CAPTAIN.		
George J. Martin...........	Jan. 13, 1863	Resigned, April 10, 1864.
Benjamin G. Jones........	Feb. 11, 1865	Mustered out with regiment.
FIRST LIEUT.		
William G. White.........	Jan. 13, 1863	Resigned, February 23, 1863, Fort Scott, Kas.
Luther Dickinson..........	Feb. 24, 1863	Resigned, September —, 1865.
Walter J. Dallas............	Sept. 14, 1865	Mustered out with regiment.
SECOND LIEUT.		
Luther Dickinson..........	Jan. 13, 1863	Promoted First Lieutenant, February 24, 1863.
John Topping...............	Feb. 24, 1863	Killed in action, April 18, 1864, Poison Sp., Ark.
Walter J. Dallas	July 12, 1865	Promoted First Lieutenant, Sept. 14, 1865.

COMPANY C.

Name and Rank.	Date of Muster.	Remarks.
CAPTAIN.		
John R. Graton.............	Jan. 13, 1863	Mustered out with regiment.
FIRST LIEUT.		
Augustus T. Sholes........	Jan. 13, 1863	Promoted Captain Company K, July 21, 1865.
SECOND LIEUT.		
Benjamin W. Welch......	Jan. 19, 1863	Promoted Captain Company K, May 2, 1863.
Eberle Q. Macy..............	May 6, 1863	Killed in action, November 19, 1864, Timber Hills, C. N.
Alfred T. Jackson..........	Aug. 18, 1865	Mustered out with regiment.

COMPANY D.

Name and Rank.	Date of Muster.	Remarks.
CAPTAIN.		
Andrew J. Armstrong...	Jan. 13, 1863	Mustered out with regiment.
FIRST LIEUT.		
Daniel D. McFarland ...	Jan. 13, 1863	Resigned, July 20, 1864, Fort Smith, Arkansas.
James A. McGinnis	Feb. 20, 1865	Mustered out with regiment.
SECOND LIEUT.		
G. Mellen Lewis	Jan. 13, 1863	Promoted Captain Company I, Feb. 11, 1865.

COMPANY E.

Name and Rank.	Date of Muster.	Remarks.
CAPTAIN.		
Luther A. Thrasher......	Dec. 14, 1863	Mustered out with regiment.
FIRST LIEUT.		
John Overdeaw............	Jan. 13, 1863	Resigned, July 4, 1864.
Eli F. Bowton..............	April 23, 1865	Mustered out with regiment.
SECOND LIEUT.		
William C. Gibbons	Jan. 13, 1863	Promoted First Lieut. and Adj., Jan. 27, 1864.

COMPANY F.

Name and Rank.	Date of Muster.	Remarks.
CAPTAIN.		
Ethan Earle.................	Jan. 13, 1863	Resigned, June 21, 1864, Fort Smith, Ark.
Shabua S. Creps...........	Feb. 11, 1865	Mustered out with regiment.
FIRST LIEUT.		
Joseph Gardner............	Jan. 13, 1863	Died of chronic diarrhœa, Camp Davis, C. N., August 24, 1864.
Shebua S. Creps...........	Aug. —, 1863	Promoted Captain, February 11, 1865.
SECOND LIEUT.		
Asa Reynard.................	Jan. 13, 1863	Resigned, May 2, 1863.

COMPANY G.

Name and Rank.	Date of Muster.	Remarks.
CAPTAIN.		
William H. Smallwood..	Mar. 9, 1863	Resigned, April 19, 1865, Little Rock, Ark.
Bethuel Hitchcock........	Aug. 16, 1865	Mustered out with regiment.
FIRST LIEUT.		
Bethuel Hitchcock........	Mar. 9, 1863	Promoted Captain, Aug. 16, 1865; was captured April, 1864, Poison Springs, Ark.; exchanged.
SECOND LIEUT.		
Andrew J. Smith...........	May 2, 1863	Mustered out with regiment.

COMPANY H.

Name and Rank.	Date of Muster.	Remarks.
CAPTAIN.		
Ransom Ward...............	May 1, 1863	Mustered out with regiment,
FIRST LIEUT.		
Charles J. Coleman.......	May 1, 1863	Killed in ac'n, Apr. 18, '64, Poison Springs, Ark.
John H. Mockett..........	Sept. 14, 1865	Mustered out with regiment.
SECOND LIEUT.		
Wm. T. Edgerton..........	May 1, 1863	Resigned, November 14, 1863.
John H. Mockett...........	April 22, 1865	Promoted First Lieutenant, Sept. 14, 1865.

COMPANY I.

Name and Rank.	Date of Muster.	Remarks.
CAPTAIN.		
Benjamin F. Van Horn.	May 1, 1863	Resigned, January 19, 1864, Fort Smith, Ark.
G. Mellen Lewis............	Feb. 11, 1865	Mustered out with regiment.
FIRST LIEUT.		
Ransom L. Harris.........	June 27, 1863	Resigned, June 18, 1864, Fort Smith, Ark.
Dyer W. Hitchcock.......	April 26, 1865	Mustered out with regiment.
SECOND LIEUT.		
Horace H. Johnson.......	Dec. 24, 1863	Resigned, October 20, 1864.

COMPANY K.

Name and Rank.	Date of Muster.	Remarks.
CAPTAIN.		
Benjamin W. Welch......	May 2, 1863	Killed in skirmish with guerillas, November 19, 1864, Timber Hills, C. N.
Augustus T. Sholes........	July 21, 1865	No evidence of muster-out on file.
FIRST LIEUT.		
David M. Sutherland.....	May 2, 1863	Mustered out with regiment.
SECOND LIEUT.		
Albert E. Saviers...........	May 2, 1863	Discharged for disability, February 25, 1865, Fort Smith, Ark.

SECOND KANSAS BATTERY—LIGHT ARTILLERY.

Name and Rank.	Date of Muster.	Remarks.
CAPTAIN.		
Edward A. Smith..........	July 4, 1863	Mustered out, August 11, 1865.
FIRST LIEUT.		
Edward A. Smith..........	Aug. 25, 1862	Promoted Captain, July 4, 1863.
David C. Knowles.........	Sept. 19, 1862	Mustered out, August 11, 1865.
Andrew G. Clark...........	Aug. 8, 1863	Mustered out, August 11, 1865.
SECOND LIEUT.		
Andrew G. Clark...........	Sept. 10, 1862	Promoted First Lieutenant, August 8, 1863.
Aristarchus Wilson.......	Sept. 19, 1862	Mustered out, August 11, 1865.
William Requa.............	Aug. 8, 1863	Mustered out, August 11, 1865.

List of battles, etc., in which this battery participated, showing loss reported in each:

Newtonia—No loss. Cane Hill—No loss. Sherwood—Killed, E. M., 3. Cabin Creek—No loss. Honey Springs—Wounded, O., 1. Fort Smith—No loss.—*U. S. Army Register.*

1863.

JAN. 1.—Emancipation confirmed by President Lincoln's Proclamation.

JAN. 1.—The Lawrence Weekly Tribune started, by John Speer.

—Col. William A. Phillips in possession of Fort Gibson.

JAN. 3.—Dr. R. Gillpatrick arrives from Washington, with commissions for the officers of the Second and Third Indian Regiments.

JAN. 12.—State officers sworn in.

JAN. 13.—Meeting of the Legislature.

—The First Colored Regiment mustered, at Fort Scott.

—Officers of the Twelfth commissioned.

JAN. 13.—Message from Gov. Carney.

MEMBERS AND OFFICERS OF THE SENATE.

Names.	Age.	P. O. Address.	County.	Avocation.
Thomas A. Osborn, President.....	26	Elwood	Doniphan.....	Lawyer.
Thomas H. Baker......................	35	Irving...................	Marshall	Lawyer.
S. M. Thorp...........................	32	Lawrence	Douglas	Lawyer.
A. Bennett.............................	44	Troy....................	Doniphan.....	Minister.
David Brockway......................	32	Topeka.................	Shawnee	Lawyer.
Johnson Clark........................	34	Osawatomie..........	Miami	Farmer.
W. H. M. Fishback..................	30	Olathe	Johnson	Lawyer.
F. P. Fitzwilliam....................	26	Leavenworth	Leavenworth..	Lawyer.
Isaac Ford.............................	46	Rockford	Bourbon......	Farmer.
Cassius G. Foster....................	25	Atchison..............	Atchison......	Lawyer.
M. R. Leonard.......................	35	Bazaar	Chase.........	Physician.
D. P. Lowe............................	40	Mound City..........	Linn............	Lawyer.
P. B. Maxson.........................	34	Fremont...............	Lyon..........	Farmer.
James McGrew........................	41	Wyandotte............	Wyandotte...	Merchant.
Sol. Miller	32	White Cloud..........	Doniphan	Printer.
Rufus Oursler.........................	36	Circleville	Jackson........	Merchant.
C. B. Pierce..........................	31	Leavenworth	Leavenworth..	Lawyer.
F. W. Potter..........................	29	Burlington............	Coffey........	Laborer.
Byron Sherry.........................	28	Seneca.................	Nemaha	Lawyer.
Azel W. Spalding....................	25	Grasshopper Falls..	Jefferson.....	Lawyer.
Samuel M. Strickler.................	31	Junction City........	Davis	Merchant.
Orlin Thurston.......................	28	Humboldt.............	Allen..........	At'y-at-Law.
D. M. Valentine......................	32	Peoria City	Franklin.....	Lawyer.
Joshua Wheeler......................	36	Pardee	Atchison......	Farmer.
John Wilson..........................	34	Leavenworth	Leavenworth..	Merchant.
Wilbur F. Woodworth...............	35	Baldwin City.........	Douglas	Lawyer.
John Francis, Secretary............	30	Olathe	Johnson	Printer.
John G. Otis, Assistant Secretary,	24	Topeka.................	Shawnee	Lawyer.
Wm. Boulton, Journal Clerk......	41	Seneca.................	Nemaha	Carpenter.
Davies Wilson, Docket Clerk......	32	Emporia................	Lyon..........	At'y-at-Law.
Jno. Van Horn, Engrossing Clerk,	26	Baldwin City.........	Douglas	Mechanic.
Hugh A. Cook, Sergeant-at-Arms,	35	Minneola.............	Franklin......	Farmer.
Le Roy Crandall, Doorkeeper......	36	Fremont................	Lyon..........	Farmer.
Albert L Bartlett, Messenger......	10	Topeka.................	Shawnee	Clerk.

MEMBERS AND OFFICERS OF THE HOUSE OF REPRESENTATIVES.

Names.	Age	P. O. Address.	County.	Avocation.
Josiah Kellogg, Speaker............	32	Leavenworth	Leavenworth.......	Lawyer.
E. A. Alford	34	Bazaar	Chase..............	Farmer.
H. S. Baker	29	Atchison.............	Atchison	Farmer.
H. V. Beeson.........................	54	Stanton	Franklin...........	Farmer.
G. W. Barrett	30	Mount Florence..	Jefferson...........	Farmer.
R. H. Bishop.........................	34	Salina................	Saline.............	Farmer.
M. W. Bottom........................	52	Quindaro	Wyandotte.........	Builder.
G. W. Bowman.......................	46	Atchison.............	Atchison..........	Farmer.
R. Bradley............................	41	Ash Point...........	Nemaha	Farmer.
J. F. Broadhead......................	36	Mound City.........	Linn...............	Farmer.
A. Brown..............................	52	Leavenworth	Leavenworth.......	Land Agent
A. W. J. Brown......................	45	Iola...................	Allen..............	Farmer.
D. G. Campbell......................	42	Shawnee	Johnson	Farmer.
J. H. Campbell.......................	44	Carlyle.	Allen..............	Farmer.
N. C. Clark...........................	41	Columbus	Doniphan	Physician.
J. Christie.............................	34	Stanton	Miami	Farmer.
D. R. Cobb............................	35	Marmaton...........	Bourbon............	Co. Officer.
L. C. Conrey..........................	53	Osawatomie.........	Miami	Physician.
R. S. Craft............................	32	Holton................	Jackson............	Physician.
G. E. Dennison	43	Moneka	Linn	Physician.
W. P. Douthitt.......................	34	Topeka...............	Shawnee	Lawyer.
Wm. Downing.........................	41	Council Grove......	Morris	Farmer.
C. F. Drake...........................	29	Fort Scott...........	Bourbon............	Merchant.
J. M. Ellis............................	39	Paola.................	Miami	Farmer.
J. S. Emery...........................	32	Lawrence	Douglas	Lawyer.
C. V. Eskridge.......................	28	Emporia..............	Lyon	Merchant.
George Ford...........................	51	Lawrence	Douglas............	Merchant.
J. W. Forman.........................	44	Doniphan	Doniphan	Miller.
W. Foster.............................	41	Clinton	Douglas............	Farmer.
R. C. Foster..........................	28	Delaware City......	Leavenworth	Teamster.
B. E. Fullington.....................	43	Batchelor............	Riley	Farmer.

MEMBERS AND OFFICERS OF THE HOUSE OF REPRESENTATIVES—CONCL'D.

Names.	Age	P. O. Address.	County.	Avocation.
G. W. Glick	34	Atchison	Atchison	Lawyer.
G. F. Gordon	37	West Point	Davis	Farmer.
G. W. E. Griffith	29	Minneola	Franklin	Lawyer.
C. H. Grover	32	Leavenworth	Leavenworth	Farmer.
T. O'Gwartney	39	Easton	Leavenworth	Farmer.
W. P. Hanson	31	Palermo	Doniphan	Carpenter.
William Harrison	49	Chelsea	Butler	Farmer.
J. Hawkins	56	Mapleton	Bourbon	Physician.
J. S. Hidden	42	Centralia	Nemaha	Physician.
J. Hiner	48	Garnett	Anderson	Farmer.
H. G. Hollinberg	34	Marysville	Washington	Farmer.
S. Hollister	33	Sumner	Atchison	Miller.
H. W. Ide	29	Leavenworth	Leavenworth	Lawyer.
G. E. Irwin	32	Hamlin	Brown	Physician.
D. B. Jackman	38	Fort Lincoln	Bourbon	Teacher.
J. P. Johnson	40	Highland	Doniphan	Farmer.
D. M. Johnston	36	Mission Creek	Wabaunsee	Farmer.
J. H. Jones	35	Kaw City	Jefferson	Farmer.
J. Kinner	47	Eureka	Greenwood	Farmer.
I. J. Lacock	27	Hiawatha	Brown	Lawyer.
W. A. Lattin	36	Leavenw'th City.	Leavenworth	Farmer.
S. V. Lee	37	Manhattan	Pottawatomie	Farmer.
G. M. Lee	28	Winchester	Jefferson	Farmer.
J. W. Loy	32	Americus	Lyon	Farmer.
J. Means	30	Cresco	Anderson	Farmer.
A. McCartney	24	Neosho Falls	Woodson	Physician.
J. Medill	35	Springdale	Leavenworth	Farmer.
R. S. Miller	24	Abilene	Dickinson	Surveyor.
D. T. Mitchell	31	Lecompton	Douglas	Lawyer.
F. R. Page	32	Neosho Rapids	Lyon	Farmer.
J. Rogers	34	Burlingame	Osage	Lawyer.
Ed. Russell	30	Elwood	Doniphan	Farmer.
W. R. Saunders	42	LeRoy	Coffey	Lawyer.
J. N. Sayer	37	Blooming Grove	Linn	Farmer.
S. J. H. Snyder	50	Monrovia	Atchison	Farmer.
C. S. Steel	32	Willow Springs	Douglas	Farmer.
C. H. Stratton	34	Lexington	Johnson	Farmer.
H. Tucker	38	Ottumwa	Coffey	Physician
D. Underhill	37	Jackson	Linn	Farmer.
J. W. Vaughn	44	Baldwin City	Douglas	Farmer.
D. F. Walker	58	Springdale	Leavenworth	Merchant.
J. T. Ward	44	Tecumseh	Shawnee	Farmer.
J. Weisbach	31	Marysville	Marshall	Merchant.
W. Williams	33	Gardner	Johnson	Mechanic.
A. R. Banks, Chief Clerk	27	Topeka	Shawnee	Clerk.
J. W. Day, Assistant Clerk	29	Oskaloosa	Jefferson	Lawyer.
H. P. Welsh, Journal Clerk	28	Minneola	Franklin	Lawyer.
A. Ellis, Engrossing Clerk	47	Miami	Miami	Farmer.
C. S. Lambdin, Enrolling Clerk	53	Plymouth	Lyon	Paper M'kr.
Wm. Wilson, Docket Clerk	40	Lecompton	Douglas	Clergyman.
H. A. Burgess, Serg't-at-Arms	31	Lexington	Johnson	Farmer.
E. Cobb, Ass't Serg't-at-Arms	47	Junction City	Davis	Carpenter.
E. Downard, Doorkeeper	21	Elwood	Doniphan	Teacher.
M. B. Crawford, Ass't D'rkeeper	25	Topeka	Shawnee	House J'r.
Joseph Farren, Page	14	Lawrence	Douglas	——
William Griffith, Page	14	Topeka	Shawnee	——

JANUARY 13.—Meeting of the State Agricultural Society, at Topeka.

Officers: President, L. D. Bailey, Lyon county; Secretary, F. G. Adams, Shawnee county; Treasurer, F. P. Baker, Nemaha county.

Executive Committee: J. P. Johnson, Doniphan county; G. W. Collamore, Douglas county; David L. Lakin, Jefferson county; Abram Ellis, Miami county; S. M. Strickler, Davis county; J. S. Hidden, Nemaha county; C. Starns, Leavenworth county; J. R. Swallow, Lyon county; J. C. Marshall, Linn county; C. B. Lines, Wabaunsee county.

JANUARY 14.—The Senate passes unanimously a resolution introduced by D. P. Lowe, thanking the officers and soldiers of Blunt's command for their victories at Newtonia, in Missouri; at old Fort Wayne, in the Indian Nation; and at Cane Hill, Prairie Grove, and Van Buren, in Arkansas.

JANUARY 14.—The Fort Scott Bulletin publishes a letter written by Geo. A. Reynolds, in Washington, in which he says:

"About a month since, Sidney Clarke, Esq., while on his way to Washington, with the audited accounts of the irregular claims of Lane's Brigade, had the misfortune to lose his carpet-bag with all the papers connected with that service. The bag was stolen from him while in Baltimore. Since then he has used every effort to recover them, but without any success. I fear it will greatly delay the payment of the claims, and perhaps the business will all have to be done over again."

JANUARY 19.—Benj. P. Shillaber writes a poem for the Printers' Festival, given at Leavenworth.

JANUARY 24.—The new Board of State Canvassers declare John H. Watson Chief Justice, he having received 8,918 votes, to 6,006 for W. P. Gambell. The old Board declined to canvass the vote, and the Supreme Court sustained the old Board. The Court holds that the acceptance of an office under the United States by a judicial officer does not of itself work a vacancy in the office; that the vacancy in the office of Chief Justice occurred November 28th, 1862, when Ewing resigned; that the vacancy was properly filled by the Governor, who appointed Nelson Cobb Chief Justice on that day.

On the 4th of November, 1862, John H. Watson received a majority of all the votes cast for Chief Justice.

Opinion by Judge Kingman. (*The State, ex rel. Watson, vs. Cobb*, 2 Kan., 32.)

JANUARY 17.—Fort Scott re-established as a permanent military post.

—The President appoints Samuel Lappin, Geo. F. Warren and Chester Thomas, jr., Quartermasters.

JANUARY 27.—A book is printed in Leavenworth, called The Philosophy of Truth; written by F. Holiday Burris.

FEBRUARY 4.—S. M. Thorp admitted to the Senate, in place of John A. Beam.

FEBRUARY 10.—The Leavenworth Daily Inquirer, a Secession paper, ceases to exist. The presses were destroyed at 10:30 A. M., the type thrown out of the window, and the cases burned, on Shawnee street, near Main. Burrell B. Taylor, the editor, ran away.

FEBRUARY 13.—Execution of Carl Horne.

MARCH 1.—Guilford Dudley is appointed Adjutant General.

—Dan. M. Adams and H. S. Sleeper appointed Paymasters.

MARCH 2.—Geo. W. Collamore elected Mayor of Lawrence.

MARCH 3.—Adjournment of the Legislature. The important acts of the Legislature were as follows: A joint resolution accepting the act of Congress giving land for an Agricultural College; Establishing the Agricultural College in Riley county, provided that the Trustees of Bluemont College cede its land to the State in fee simple; An act for the government of the Agricultural College; Providing for the selection of the College lands; Giving Prof. P. A. Emery a salary for teaching the deaf and dumb; Funding the Territorial debt; Procuring temporary buildings for State offices; Making unorganized counties municipal townships; Providing for an Insane Asylum at Osawatomie; Changing the name of Grasshopper Falls to Sautrell Falls; Providing for building a Penitentiary; Paying a premium on the manufacture of salt; Establishing a State Normal School at Emporia; Authorizing two school districts in Lyon county to issue bonds (this seems to be the first act of this kind); Establishing the State University at Lawrence.

The volume of laws contains 128 pages. Since the admission of the State, public and private laws are published in the same volume.

MARCH 3.—The following is a summary of chapter 98, laws of Congress of 1863, granting lands to Kansas railroads:

"Grants to Kansas, to aid the construction: First, of a railroad and telegraph from the city of Leavenworth, by the way of the town of Lawrence, and via the Ohio City crossing of the Osage river, to the southern line of the State, in the direction of Galveston Bay in Texas, with a branch from Lawrence by the valley of the Wakarusa river, to the point on the Atchison, Topeka and Santa Fe railroad where said road intersects the Neosho river. Second, of a railroad from the city of Atchison, via Topeka, the capital of said State, to the western line of the State, in the direction of Fort Union and Santa Fe, New Mexico, with a branch from where this last-named road crosses the Neosho, down said Neosho valley to the point where the said first-named road enters the said Neosho valley; every alternate section of land, designated by odd numbers, for ten sections in width on each side of said roads, and each of its branches. If any such lands are sold or pre-empted, other as near as possible shall be given in lieu, but in no case further than twenty miles from the line of road; the granted lands to be applied exclusively to aid the roads. The sections among these lands remaining to the United States are not to be sold for less than double the minimum price, nor subject to private entry until first offered at public sale, except in case of actual settlers, who may buy at minimum price; the homestead law also applies to all these lands. The roads are to be free to the United States for carrying troops or any property. Rules for disposing of the lands are set down. If no part of the roads is done in ten years, the grant is void."

—Passage of an act by Congress for the removal of Indians from Kansas.

MARCH 8.—Rev. C. C. Hutchinson reappointed Ottawa Indian Agent.

MARCH 18.—Governor Carney goes to Washington, and Lieut. Gov. Osborn goes to Topeka, to act in his absence.

—E. N. Morrill is appointed Commissary; Oliver S. Coffin and Geo. Allen, Quartermasters; S. W. Eldridge and John B. Wheeler, Paymasters.

MARCH 13.—Thos. Ewing, jr., is made a Brigadier General; Captain Wm. Tholen, Adjutant General, and Captain M. H. Insley is appointed Quartermaster in the Regular Army.

APRIL.—Organization of the Fourteenth Kansas begins.

APRIL 6.—D. R. Anthony elected Mayor of Leavenworth.

APRIL 14.—T. Dwight Thacher becomes the proprietor of the Kansas City (Mo.) Journal.

APRIL 25.—Dr. Rufus Gillpatrick killed at Webber's Falls, Cherokee Nation, while dressing the wounds of a Rebel soldier.

APRIL 28.—C. W. Babcock makes arrangements for bridging the Kaw at Lawrence.

APRIL 30.—The Commissioners appointed by the Governor report to him that they have selected forty acres of land near Lawrence as a site for the University buildings.

MAY 1.—The Kansas Farmer founded by Lawrence D. Bailey, Topeka. The size of the printed page is 4½ by 7½ inches.

MAY 1.—Governor Carney sells State bonds in New York at 95¼.

MAY 2.—Battle of Chancellorsville.

MAY 18.—A ruffian and thief named Sterling hung by the citizens of Atchison. On the 23d, about 800 men from the country went into Atchison, took Mooney and Brewer, two other members of the gang, and hung them.

MAY 20.—Col. William A. Phillips has an engagement with Col. Coffey, at Fort Gibson (now called Fort Blunt.)

JUNE 1.—Sidney Clarke appointed Provost Marshal for Kansas, Nebraska and Colorado.

JUNE 3.—Two desperadoes, James Melvine and William Cannon, hung at Highland by citizens.

JUNE 11.—Col. James Montgomery, of Kansas, with his colored regiment, leaves Hilton Head for a raid in Georgia.

—Vallandigham nominated for Governor of Ohio.

JULY 1.—Col. James M. Williams, of the First Kansas Colored, 800 strong, and 500 Indians, has a fight at Cabin creek with a force of Texans and Indians under Stand Waitie. Complete Union victory.

JULY 3.—Final battle of Gettysburg; retreat of Lee.

JULY 4.—Surrender of Vicksburg. The rebellion reaches its climax.

JULY 8.—The Mississippi opened.

—James McCahon and A. R. Banks made Provost Marshals of Kansas; Ed. Russell and A. J. Shannon, Commissioners.

JULY 12.—John Morgan's raid in Ohio.

JULY 13.—Great draft riot in New York.

JULY 17.—Blunt gains a victory over Cooper, at Honey Springs, south of the Arkansas, in the Indian Territory.

JULY 27.—Organization of the Agricultural College; the first term to begin September 2.

AUGUST.—Death of Archibald Williams, United States District Judge.

AUGUST 17.—The Commissioners appointed by the Governor report to him that they have selected twenty acres of land adjoining Emporia as a site for the Normal School.

AUGUST 21.—The Quantrell Massacre, at Lawrence. The following account, by Rev. Richard Cordley, D.D., is copied from Blackburn's Gazetteer of Kansas. Dr. Cordley wrote a longer sketch for the Annual Register. A pamphlet of considerable length, describing the Massacre, was written by Hovey E. Lowman.

"Early in the summer of 1863, a large band entered Olathe, one night, about midnight. They took most of the citizens prisoners, and kept them till their work was done. They plundered the town, carried off what they wanted, and destroyed other property, and left before daylight. They killed some seven men.

"Some time after, they sacked the town of Shawnee twice. In addition to robbery, they here burned most of the town. Several were killed here also. Individual murders and house-burning were common.

"On the 20th of August, a body of between three and four hundred crossed the

State line at sundown. Riding all night, they reached Lawrence at daybreak. They dashed into the town with a yell, shooting at everybody they saw. The surprise was complete. The hotel, and every point where a rally would be possible, was seized at once, and the ruffians then began the work of destruction. Some of the citizens escaped into the fields and ravines, and some into the woods, but the larger portion could not escape at all. Numbers of these were shot down as they were found, and often brutally mangled. In many cases the bodies were left in the burning buildings and were consumed. The Rebels entered the place about five o'clock, and left between nine and ten. Troops for the relief of the town were within six miles when the Rebels went out. One hundred and forty-three were left dead in the streets, and about thirty desperately wounded. The main street was all burned but two stores. Thus, about seventy-five business houses were destroyed, and nearly one hundred residences. They destroyed something near two millions of property, left eighty widows and two hundred and fifty orphans, as the result of their four hours' work. Scenes of brutality were enacted, which have never been surpassed in savage warfare. The picture is redeemed only by the fact that women and children were in no case hurt."

The first news of the event was brought to Leavenworth by James F. Legate. The first full newspaper description of it was written by George T. Isbell, for the Leavenworth Conservative, and telegraphed thence through the country.

A book called "Shelby and his Men; or the War in the West," was printed in Cincinnati in 1867. It is a Confederate history. The following is copied from pages 400, 401:

"About daylight on the morning of August 21, 1863, Quantrell, with three hundred men, dashed into the streets of Lawrence, Kansas. Flame and bullet, waste and pillage, terror and despair, were everywhere. Two hundred were killed. Death was a monarch, and men bowed down and worshipped him. Blood ran in rivulets. The guerillas were unerring shots with revolvers, and excellent horsemen. General Lane saved himself by flight; General Collamore took refuge in a well, and died there. Poor Collamore! He should have kept away from the well, upon the principle that actuated the mother who had no objection to her boy's learning how to swim, if he didn't go near the water. Printers and editors suffered. Speer of the Tribune, Palmer of the Journal, Trask of the State Journal, hadn't time even to write their obituaries. Two camps of instruction for white and negro soldiers, on Massachusetts street (of course), were surrounded and all their occupants killed. Every hotel, except the City Hotel, was burned. Other property, valued at two million dollars, was also fired and consumed. . . . . Massachusetts street was made a mass of smouldering ruins. Sometimes there is a great deal in a name—in this instance more than is generally the case. After killing every male inhabitant who remained in Lawrence, after burning the houses in the town and those directly around it, Quantrell very quietly withdrew his men into Missouri and rested there, followed, however, at a safe distance, by General Lane, who made terrible threats, but miserable fulfilments. Two hundred white abolitionists, fifty or sixty negroes, and two millions of dollars worth of property were fearful aggregates of losses."

AUGUST 22.—The citizens of Leavenworth raise $10,000 for the relief of Lawrence.

AUGUST 23.—Blunt crosses the Arkansas.

—The following order issued by Gen. Thomas Ewing, jr.:

"GENERAL ORDER No. 11.] KANSAS CITY, Mo., Aug. 23d, 1863.

"All persons living in Jackson, Cass and Bates counties. Missouri, and that part of Vernon county included in this district, except those living within one mile of the limits of Independence, Hickman's Mill, Pleasant Hill and Harrisonville, and except those in Kaw Township, Jackson county, north of this creek and west of the Big Blue, embracing Kansas City and Westport, are hereby ordered to remove from their places of residence within fifteen days from the date hereof.

"Those who within that time prove their loyalty to the satisfaction of the commanding officer of the military station nearest their present places of residence, will receive from him certificates stating the fact of their loyalty, and the names of the witnesses by whom it can be sworn. All who have received such certificates will be permitted to remove to any military station in this district, or to any part of Kansas except the counties on the eastern border of the State. All others shall remove out of this district. Officers commanding companies and detachments serving in companies will see that this paragraph is promptly obeyed.

"All hay or grain in the field or under shelter, in the district from which the inhabitants are required to remove, within reach of the military stations after the 9th of September next, will be taken to such stations and turned over to the proper officers there, and a report of the amount so turned over made to the district headquarters, specifying the names of all loyal owners and the amount of such produce taken from them. All grain and hay found in such districts after the 9th of September next, not convenient to such stations, will be destroyed."

SEPTEMBER.—Organization of the Fifteenth Kansas begins.

SEPTEMBER 7.—M. M. Murdock founds the Burlingame Chronicle. W. F. Chalfant, the present proprietor, bought it in January, 1872.

SEPTEMBER 8.—Convention at Paola. President, T. A. Osborn; Vice Presidents, A. H. Dean, D. P. Lowe, I. Ford, W. H. M. Fishback, Johnson Clark, J. A. Woodworth, D. M. Valentine; Secretaries, D. W. Wilder, D. B. Emmert, Henry Buckingham, James C. Horton. Resolutions adopted asking the removal of Generals Schofield and Ewing, and the establishment of a new military department.

SEPTEMBER 10.—Samuel Hallett at work on the Kansas Pacific Railway at Wyandotte.

SEPTEMBER 19.—Battle of Chicamauga.

OCTOBER 6.—First State Fair, held at Leavenworth.

OCTOBER 6.—The following account of the massacre at Baxter Springs, Kansas, is copied from Greeley's Conflict, vol. II, p. 452:

"General Blunt, having been on business to Kansas, was returning with a small cavalry escort to Fort Smith, when he was struck, near Baxter's Springs, Cherokee Nation, by Quantrell, with 600 guerillas, and most of his small escort killed or disabled: among the eighty killed — nearly all after they had been captured — were Major H. Z. Curtis, son of Major General S. R. Curtis, and several civilians. [General Curtis named Fort Zarah for this son.] General Blunt, rallying some fifteen of his guard, escaped capture and death by great coolness and courage; their persistency in boldly fighting creating a belief that they were the van of a heavy force. A considerable train that accompanied them was sacked and burned. The attack was made very near the little post known as Fort Blair, which was next assailed; but its defenders, though few, were brave, and well led by Lieutenant Pond, Third Wisconsin Cavalry, who beat the enemy off, inflicting a loss of eleven killed and many more wounded. General Blunt and his remnant of escort kept the prairie till night, then made their way to the post. They had not ventured thither before, apprehending that it had been taken."

OCTOBER 6.—The Provost Marshal General writes that Kansas has furnished for the United States service the number of 4,440 troops in excess of all calls. Her white soldiers number 9,613. Colonel Fry's statement does not include the colored regiment, nor 2,262 Indians enrolled in three regiments, in Kansas, in 1862.

OCTOBER 7.—Meeting of State Editors at Leavenworth. D. H. Bailey, President; F. P. Baker, Secretary. On the 8th a Society was formed, with the following officers: President, John Speer; Vice President, Hovey E. Lowman; Secretary, D. H. Bailey; Treasurer, D. W. Wilder.

—Mark W. Delahay appointed United States District Judge.

OCTOBER 8.—The Republican State Committee meets in Leavenworth, and nominates Robert Crozier for Chief Justice.

—D. W. Wilder appointed Surveyor General of Kansas and Nebraska.

OCTOBER 16.—The Fifteenth Regiment mustered.

OCTOBER 21.—Henry C. F. Hackbusch appointed Chief Clerk of Surveyor General.

OCTOBER 23.—Discontinuance of the Delaware Land District—office at Atchison.

OCTOBER 25.—Battle of Pine Bluff.

"Pine Bluff, on the south bank of the Arkansas, fifty miles below Little Rock, was occupied, early in October, by Colonel Powell Clayton, Fifth Kansas Cavalry, with 350 men and four guns. Marmaduke, at Princeton, forty-five miles south, resolved to retake it. By the time he advanced to do so, Clayton had been re-enforced by the First Indiana Cavalry; so that now he had 600 men and nine light guns.

"Marmaduke, with twelve guns and a force estimated at 2,500, advanced in three columns, and poured in shell and canister for five hours, setting fire to the place; but Clayton had organized 200 negroes to barricade the streets with cotton bales, by whose services the fire was stopped without subtracting from his slender fighting force. The Rebel shells burned the Court House and several dwellings, battering most of the residue; but they could not take the town, and at 2 P. M. drew off, having lost 150 killed and wounded, beside 33 prisoners. Our loss was but 17 killed and 40 wounded—five of the former and twelve of the latter among the negro volunteers."—*Greeley's Conflict, vol. II, p. 453.*

NOVEMBER 1.—A book published, called "History of American Conspiracies." By Orville J. Victor. New York: James D. Torrey. 1863. One chapter is given to the "Kansas-Nebraska troubles," and one to "John Brown's Conspiracy." It contains a steel engraving by John Rogers, designed by Felix O. C. Darley, "Missourians going to Kansas to 'vote.'" The "voters" are well-armed assassins, and the engraving spirited.

NOVEMBER.—Organization of the Sixteenth Kansas begins.

—Location of the Insane Asylum, at Osawatomie.

NOVEMBER 2.—The conditions of the act of February 20 having been complied with, Governor Carney issues a proclamation declaring the State University to be permanently established at Lawrence.

NOVEMBER 3.—Election. The following is the canvass of the vote:

JUDICIAL VOTE.
CHIEF JUSTICE OF THE SUPREME COURT.

Robert Crozier.................................12,731 | Scattering..14

DISTRICT ATTORNEY FOR FIRST JUDICIAL DISTRICT.

Counties.	H. W. Ide.	T. P. Fenton	Total.	Majority for Ide.
Jackson	147	....	147	147
Jefferson	784	....	784	784
Leavenworth	1995	10	2005	1985
Wyandotte	307	36	343	271
Total	....	....	3279	3187

DISTRICT ATTORNEY FOR SECOND JUDICIAL DISTRICT.

Counties.	E. J. Jenkins	F. P. Babbitt	Scattering	Total	Majority for Jenkins
Atchison	929			929	929
Brown	303			303	303
Doniphan	855			855	855
Marshall	337			337	337
Nemaha	284	9	10	303	
Total				2727	2689

DISTRICT ATTORNEY FOR THIRD JUDICIAL DISTRICT.

Counties.	C. K. Gilchrist	A. H. Case	N. P. Case	Total	Maj. for C. K. Gilchrist	Majority for A. H. Case
Davis	113	109		222	4	
Dickinson	57	13		70	44	
Pottawatomie	131	24	6	161	107	
Saline	42	23		65	19	
Shawnee	276	240		516	36	
Wabaunsee	51	85		136		34
Riley	114	108		222	6	
Total				1392	182	

DISTRICT ATTORNEY FOR FOURTH JUDICIAL DISTRICT.

Counties.	Samuel A. Riggs	D. P. Lowe	Scattering	Total	Majority for Riggs
Allen	290			290	
Anderson	138			138	
Bourbon	239	187		426	52
Douglas	821	58	12	891	763
Franklin	181	1		182	180
Johnson	271	85		356	186
Linn	467			467	467
Miami	426			426	426
Total				3176	2502

DISTRICT ATTORNEY FOR FIFTH JUDICIAL DISTRICT.

Counties.	A. S. Howard	G. H. Lillie	Silas Pearl	Total	Maj. for Howard	Maj. for Pearl
Chase	55	52	2	109	3	
Coffey	86	6	248	340		162
Greenwood	31	11	39	81		8
Lyon	137	309	62	508		
Morris	89		30	119	59	
Osage	169	1	29	199	140	
Woodson	85			85	85	
Butler	21	1	1	23	20	
Total				1464	262	

VOTE FOR MEMBERS OF THE LEGISLATURE.
REPRESENTATIVES.

District.	Counties.	Names.	Votes	Maj.......	Vote of District.	Vote of County....
1	Doniphan............	J. P. Johnson.................	133	58	....	
		W. R. Parker.................	75	....		
		T. C. Shreve.................	50	....	258	
2	....	W. J. Orem.................	99	31	....	
		E. Fleming.................	68	....	167	
3	....	F. H. Drenning............	104	104	104	
4	....	C. C. Camp............	175	175	175	
5	....	J. W. Forman............	105	44		
		S. W. Lloyd............	61	....	176	880
6	Atchison............	G. W. Glick............	189	183		
		J. Saqui............	6	....	195	
7	....	Jacob Saqui............	208	132		
		William Dean............	76	....	284	
8	....	Asa Barnes	232	231		
		Samuel Hollister........	1	....	233	
9	....	B. W. Williams............	124	122		
		Scattering	2	....	126	
10	....	J. C. Batsell	83	83	83	921
11	Brown	Ira J. Lacock............	115	53		
		L. C. Dunn............	62	....		
		Scattering............	1	....	178	
12	....	George E. Irwin............	73	28		
		M. L. Savin	45	....	118	296
13	Nemaha	Richard Bradley............	133	39		
		George Graham............	94	....	227	
14	....	J. S. Hidden............	134	69		
		J. Hodgins............	65	....	199	426
15	Marshall	J. D. Brumbaugh............	224	117		331
		T. S. Vail............	107	....	331	
16	Washington............	G. H. Hollinberg............	48	48	48	48
17	Pottawatomie	O. J. Grover............	131	99		
		F. N. Sales............	32	....	163	163
18	Jackson............	J. W. Williams............	190	69		
		J. Rippetoe............	121	....	311	311
19	Jefferson............	C. A. Buck............	103	20		
		Thomas Hodges............	83	....		
		G. M. Lee............	61	....		
		N. Leaventon	25	....	272	
20	....	E. M. Hutchins	116	18		
		Robert Riddle............	98	....	214	
21	....	M. Barnes............	149	51		
		G. W. Gray............	98	....	247	733
22	Leavenworth............	William Freeland............	340	182		
		W. P. Gambell............	158	....	498	
23	....	Josiah Kellogg............	492	492	492	
24	....	George A. Moore............	390	301		
		John L. Pendery............	89	....	479	
25	....	James B. Laing............	251	71		
		W. A. Lattin............	180	....	431	
26	....	Jacob W. Craig	121	66		
		Charles H. Grover	55	....	176	
27	....	George R. Houts............	60	14		
		P. E. Thornton............	46	....	106	
28	....	David F. Walker............	62	18		
		John Wright............	44	....		
		Isaac M. Pierce	15	....	121	
29	....	Thomas Trower............	113	61		
		James L. Wallace............	52	....	165	
30	....	Ben. H. Twombly	97	21		
		H. T. Green............	76	....	173	2641
31	Wyandotte............	M. W. Bottom............	190	84		
		B. B. Hadley............	106	....		
		A. Guthrie............	45	....	341	341
32	Johnson............	C. H. Stratton............	126	103		
		W. D. Butt............	23	....	149	
33	....	D. G. Campbell............	71	22		
		S. B. Bell.........	49	....	120	
34	....	Harry McBride............	75	75	75	344
35	Douglas............	T. J. Sternberg............	254	254	254	
36	....	J. S. Emery............	114	63		
		S. J. Willes............	51	....	165	

VOTE FOR REPRESENTATIVES — (CONTINUED).

District.	Counties.	Names.	Votes.	May.	Vote of District.	Vote of County.
37	Douglas (concluded)........	Clarkson Reynolds................	71	41	....	
		W. G. Piper..........................	30	....	101	
38	....	A. Thoman...........................	66	3	....	
		Levi Woodard.............	63	....	129	
39	....	J. A. Wakefield....................	114	59	....	
		William Brass......................	55	....	169	
40	....	William Draper	90	88	....	
		Scattering	2	....	92	910
41	Shawnee..............	J. F. Cummings	194	83	....	
		W. P. Douthitt.....................	111	....		
		Scattering	3	....	• 308	
42	....	Henry Fox...........................	107	11	....	
		J. L. Weightman.................	95	....		
		Scattering	1	....	203	511
43	Miami..............	William Chesnut..................	84	39	....	
		Thomas Roberts..................	45	....	129	
44	....	T. H. Ellis..........................	134	134	134	
45	....	W. G. McCollock	93	29	....	
		R. Hiner..............................	64	....	157	420
46	Linn..............	William Snooks....................	45	1	....	
		Richard Hill........................	44	....	89	
47	....	J. H. Belding.......................	87	87	87	
48	....	Samuel Ayres......................	53	53	53	
49	....	Jeff. Fleming	102	102	102	331
50	Bourbon	William Stone......................	55	47	....	
		A. Warner...........................	8	....	63	
51	....	R. P. Stevens	51	28	....	
		M. T. Jones........................	23	....		
		J. Hawkins.........................	19	....	93	
52	....	D. R. Cobb.........................	87	87	87	
53	....	J. G. Miller........................	176	174	....	
		G. A. Reynolds....................	2	....	178	421
54	Allen..............	D. Rogers...........................	142	42	....	
		J. R. Goodin........................	100	....	242	
55	....	J. M. Evans	35	3	....	
		J. W. Scott..........................	32	....	67	309
56	Anderson..............	Henry Cavender...................	86	14	....	
		Isaac Hince.........................	72	....		
		James Adams.......................	7	....	165	
57	....	B. M. Lingo.........................	72	59	....	
		R. Kirkland........................	13	....	85	250
58	Franklin..............	Isaiah Pile..........................	81	78	....	
		Scattering...........................	3	....	84	
59	....	James N. Smith....................	80	80	80	164
60	Osage..............	James Rogers.......................	99	1	....	
		P. C. Schuyler	98	....	197	197
61	Coffey...............	Job Throckmorton................	137	111	....	
		Joseph Jenks	26	....	163	
62	....	William R. Saunders............	98	23	....	
		Abijah Jones........................	75	....	173	336
63	Woodson..............	A. W. Pickering....................	80	80	80	80
64	Lyon	C. V. Eskridge....................	135	17	....	
		Jacob Stotler.......................	118	....	253	
65	....	A. K. Hawks........................	62	16	....	
		G. H. Lillie.........................	46	....	....	
		Isaiah Booth........................	26	....	....	
		E. H. Sanford......................	29	....	....	
		W. H. Mickel.......................	4	....	167	
66	....	Joseph Frost........................	56	10	....	
		R. H. Abraham	46	....	102	522
67	Butler.......	G. T. Donaldson.................	19	4	....	
		L. M. Pratt.........................	15	....	34	34
68	Chase	A. L. Alford........................	76	44	....	
		H. L. Scribner	32	....	108	108
69	Morris..............	S. N. Wood..........................	96	46	....	
		William Downing.................	50	....	146	146
70	Wabaunsee..............	D. M. Johnston	109	85	....	
		F. Weir...............................	24	....		
		W. Mitchell.........................	2	....	135	135
71	Davis	P. Z. Taylor.........................	130	19	....	
		W. S. Gilbert...............	111	....	241	241

23

VOTE FOR REPRESENTATIVES — (CONCLUDED.)

District	Counties.	Names.	Votes ...	Maj.	Vote of District.	Vote of County...
72	Riley	B. E. Fullington	150	66		
		Robert Fleming	84		234	234
73	Dickinson	G. F. Hersey	69	69	69	69
74	Saline	H. L. Jones	42	20		
		H. Whiteley	22		64	64
75	Greenwood	James Kenner	63	51		
		Jochan Keyes	12		75	75
	Total					12,992

VOTE FOR SENATOR OF THE NINTH DISTRICT, DOUGLAS COUNTY, TO FILL A VACANCY.

Robert G. Elliott...906

RECAPITULATION OF VOTES.
CHIEF JUSTICE.

Robert Crozier...12,731
Scattering.. 14
  Total..12,745

DISTRICT ATTORNEYS.

First District..3,279
Second District...2,727
Third District...1,892
Fourth District...3,176
Fifth District 1,464
  Total..12,038

REPRESENTATIVES.

Total vote for all the candidates 12,992

NOVEMBER 19.—Speech of Abraham Lincoln at Gettysburg, on the occasion of dedicating a National Cemetery.*

"Fourscore and seven years ago our fathers brought forth on this continent a new nation, conceived in Liberty, and dedicated to the proposition that all men are created equal. Now, we are engaged in a great civil war, testing whether that nation, or any nation so conceived and so dedicated, can long endure. We are met on a great battlefield of that war. We have come to dedicate a portion of that field as a final resting-place for those who here gave their lives that that nation might live. It is altogether fitting and proper that we should do this.

"But, in a larger sense, we cannot dedicate, we cannot consecrate, we cannot hallow, this ground. The brave men, living and dead, who struggled here, have consecrated it far above our poor power to add or detract. The world will little note nor long remember what we say here, but it can never forget what they did here. It is for us the living, rather, to be dedicated here to the unfinished work that they have thus far so nobly advanced. It is rather for us to be here dedicated to the great task remaining before us; that from these honored dead we take increased devotion to that cause for which they gave the last full measure of devotion; that we here highly resolve that these dead shall not have died in vain; that this nation, under God, shall have a new birth of freedom, and that government of the people, by the people, for the people, shall not perish from the earth."

NOVEMBER 24.—Capture of Lookout Mountain—the "fight above the clouds."

---

*"There is what I call the American Idea. . . . . This Idea demands, as the proximate organization thereof, a Democracy; that is, a government of all the people, by all the people, for all the people; of course, a government of the Principles of Eternal Justice, the unchanging Law of God: for shortness' sake I will call it the Idea of Freedom."—THEODORE PARKER. *Speech at the New England Anti-Slavery Convention, Boston, May 29, 1850.*

NOVEMBER 30.—Expenditures of the State for the year:

Governor's Department	$4,230 00	Judiciary Department	15,243 58
Secretary's Department	5,025 84	Legislature and Journals	26,918 23
Auditor's Department	3,340 83	Printing Department	9,132 89
Treasurer's Department	2,116 00	Educating deaf and dumb	913 85
Superintendent of Public In-		Capitol grounds	1,000 00
struction	1,648 30	Selecting agricultural lands	1,000 00
Attorney General	1,120 58	Miscellaneous accounts	13,723 14
Quartermaster General	500 00		
Adjutant General	957 00	Total for 1863	$86,869 24

DECEMBER 1.—Death of Lyman Allen, at Lawrence. He came to Kansas in March, 1855, filled many public positions, and was a man of high character.

—The Lawrence bridge is nearly completed. It is 690 feet in length. It has been built by C. W. Babcock, E. D. Thompson, Josiah Miller, and M. J. Parrott.

DECEMBER 10.—The State "capitol building," so called, built by Mills, Farnsworth, Gordon, and Gage, completed and leased to the State.

DECEMBER 11.—Death of J. W. Robinson, Surgeon of the Second Kansas, at Fort Smith. He was generally believed to be innocent of intentional wrong-doing in the sale of the State bonds—an illegal act for which he was impeached, as Secretary of State, and removed from office. No other Kansas politician has died of a broken heart.

DECEMBER 16.—The Conservative reviews a pamphlet published by M. Neidner & Co., St. Louis, 1854. It is entitled "Negro Slavery No Evil, or the North and the South," and is a "Report Made to the Platte County Self-Defensive Association, by a Committee, through B. F. Stringfellow, Chairman." To the men sent to Kansas by the Emigrant Aid Societies the writer says: "We offer no argument but that of the strong arm;" "they are to us as would be a band of Blackfeet or Camanches;" "we would be justified in marching to their camp, and driving them back to their dens, without waiting for their attack;" "robbers and murderers have no right to call on the law for protection." The pamphlet contains forty pages.

—The Second Kansas (colored) is in camp at Fort Smith, Ark.

—Mr. Brinkerhoff, the pioneer conductor of the K. P., arrives.

DECEMBER 18.—Col. Wm. A. Phillips defeats a Rebel force near Fort Gibson.

DECEMBER 19.—Fort Gibson attacked by Stand Waitie; he is repulsed.

DECEMBER 22.—Wilkes Booth plays Richard III at the Leavenworth Theatre.

DECEMBER 22.—The following is copied from the report made to I. T. Goodnow, Superintendent of Public Instruction, by Joseph Denison, President of the Agricultural College:

"The commissioners, appointed to locate the lands donated by Congress to the Kansas State Agricultural College, have done their work very faithfully, as we have good evidence to believe, having visited and inspected each quarter-section in person; and they affirm that each quarter-section is suitable to make a good farm. The 90,000 acres of land for the endowment of the College are mostly located (76,000 acres) and designated, and their minimum value cannot be less than $2.50 per acre, making the minimum value of the endowment two hundred and twenty-five thousand dollars ($225,000.) Add to this the value of the College buildings, with the library, etc., and one hundred acres of land adjoining, estimated in July last at $25,000, and since increased by donations in musical instruments, electrical machines, furniture, etc., about $900, and you have the present assets of the institution. About $600 more are already pledged to the institution, by subscription, and this amount is expected to be still largely increased."

DECEMBER 31.—The Directors of the Penitentiary report that they have made a contract for building a Penitentiary.

DECEMBER 31.—W. W. Guthrie, Attorney General, makes a report which is published with the State documents — a good precedent.

DECEMBER 31.—The report of the Secretary of State contains a list of the lands selected by E. P. Bancroft, H. B. Denman and S. E. Hoffman for the State. They are: 46,080 acres, containing twelve salt springs, granted by Congress by the Act of Admission and confirmed to the State by the Secretary of the Interior; 6,376.36 acres for public buildings; 48,886.35 acres for the State University; 17,638.59 acres confirmed to the State in lieu of sections 16 and 36 which had been settled upon and disposed of before the surveys — total number of acres selected, 115,981.50.

DECEMBER 31.—P. A. Emery reports fifteen pupils in his deaf-mute school at Baldwin City, Douglas county.

FOURTEENTH REGIMENT KANSAS VOLUNTEERS—CAVALRY.

Name and Rank.	Date of Muster.	Remarks.
COLONEL. Charles W. Blair	Nov. 20, 1863	Mustered out on detached roll, Leavenworth, Kansas, Aug. 21, 1865, to date Aug. 11, 1865.
LIEUT. COLONEL. Charles W. Blair	Sept. 26, 1863	Promoted Colonel, November 20, 1863.
John G. Brown	May 5, 1864	Resigned, August 5, 1864, Fort Smith, Ark.
J. Finn Hill	Nov. 22, 1864	Died of pulmonary consumption, St. Louis, Missouri, May 11, 1865.
Albert J. Briggs	June 3, 1865	Mustered out with regiment, June 25, 1865.
MAJOR. Daniel H. David	Sept. 26, 1863	Dismissed, January 7, 1864, Fort Smith, Ark.
Charles Willetts	Nov. 12, 1863	Resigned, April 28, 1865, Pine Bluff, Arkansas.
John G. Brown	Nov. 20, 1863	Promoted Lieutenant Colonel, March 5, 1864.
J. Finn Hill	Jan. 20, 1864	Promoted Lieutenant Colonel, Nov. 22, 1864.
William O. Gould	Mar. 19, 1864	Mustered out on detached roll, Leavenworth, Kansas, Aug. 22, 1865, to date Aug. 11, 1865.
Albert J. Briggs	May 4, 1865	Promoted Lieutenant Colonel, June 3, 1865.
William N. Bixby	June 3, 1865	Mustered out with regiment.
ADJUTANT. William O. Gould	Nov. 1, 1863	Promoted Major, March 19, 1864.
Alexander D. Nieman	July 29, 1864	Promoted Captain Company D, June 4, 1865.
George W. Williams	June 10, 1865	Mustered out with regiment.
QUARTERMASTER. George W. Huston	Oct. 17, 1863	Prisoner of war from June 18, 1864, to May 27, 1865; mustered out with regiment.
COMMISSARY. Josiah C. Haskell	Nov. 9, 1863	Mustered out with regiment.
Count S. Steel	June 3, 1865	Died of pneumonia on board steamer, on the Arkansas river, May 4, 1865.
SURGEON. Albert W. Chenoweth	Jan. 1, 1864	Mustered out with regiment.
ASST. SURGEON. Albert W. Chenoweth	Aug. 21, 1863	Promoted Surgeon, January 1, 1864.
Willis J. Peak	Aug. 20, 1864	Mustered out with regiment.

COMPANY A.

Name and Rank.	Date of Muster.	Remarks.
CAPTAIN. William Larimer, jr.	Aug. 12, 1863	Mustered out with regiment.
FIRST LIEUT. Colden C. Whitman	May 19, 1863	Killed by guerillas, near Waldron, Arkansas, September 19, 1864.
Alexander D. Nieman	Nov. 11, 1863	Promoted Adjutant, July 29, 1864.
SECOND LIEUT. Robert H. Pierce	Aug. 24, 1863	Mustered out with regiment.

COMPANY B.

Name and Rank.	Date of Muster.	Remarks.
CAPTAIN. Charles H. Haynes........	June 18, 1863	Mustered out with regiment.
FIRST LIEUT. James Morris..............	June 18, 1863	Dismissed, March 4, 1865, Pine Bluff, Ark., per S. O. 36, from Headq'rs Dept. of Arkansas.
Judson B. Taylor	Mar. 4, 1865	Mustered out with regiment.
SECOND LIEUT. Andrew M. Anderson...	June 18, 1863	Discharged, Dec. 2, 1864, Fort Smith, Ark., per S. O. 99, Dept. of Arkansas.

COMPANY C.

Name and Rank.	Date of Muster.	Remarks.
CAPTAIN. Charles Willetts.............	Aug. 6, 1863	Promoted Major, November 12, 1863.
Benjamin F. Henry......	Feb. 23, 1864	Mustered out with regiment.
FIRST LIEUT. John G. Brown	Aug. 6, 1863	Promoted Major, November 20, 1863.
William C. Smith..........	Feb. 23, 1864	Mustered out with regiment.
SECOND LIEUT. J. F. Dalton..................	Aug. 6, 1863	Dishonorably mustered out of service, Aug. 26, 1864, to date Jan. 21, 1864, Fort Smith, Ark.
Pemberton R. Eves........	July 29, 1864	Mustered out, April 13, 1865.
Andrew J. Mowry.........	June 4, 1865	Mustered out with regiment.

COMPANY D.

Name and Rank.	Date of Muster.	Remarks.
CAPTAIN. William N. Bixby.........	Sept. 5, 1863	Promoted Major, June 3, 1865.
Alexander D. Nieman...	June 4, 1865	Mustered out with regiment.
FIRST LIEUT. Samuel L. Jennings......	Sept. 5, 1863	Mustered out with regiment.
William N. Bixby.........	Aug. 14, 1863	Promoted Captain, September 5, 1863.
SECOND LIEUT. James H. Berry............	Sept. 5, 1863	Dismissed the service, January 27, 1864.

COMPANY E.

Name and Rank.	Date of Muster.	Remarks.
CAPTAIN. George J. Clark.............	Aug. 21, 1863	Mustered out on detached roll, Fort Scott, Kas., August 11, 1865.
FIRST LIEUT. Benjamin F. Josling......	Aug. 21, 1863	Mustered out with regiment.
SECOND LIEUT. William B. Clark..........	Sept. 16, 1863	Mustered out with regiment.

COMPANY F. *

Name and Rank.	Date of Muster.	Remarks.
CAPTAIN. Albert J. Briggs.......... .	Aug. 26, 1863	Promoted Major, June 3, 1865.
John A. Huff..............	June 4, 1865	Mustered out with regiment.
FIRST LIEUT. John A. Huff	Aug. 26, 1863	Promoted Captain, June 4, 1865.
William D. Parish.........	June 7, 1865	Mustered out with regiment.
SECOND LIEUT. William D. Parish..........	Aug. 26, 1863	Promoted First Lieutenant, June 7, 1865.

COMPANY G.

Name and Rank.	Date of Muster.	Remarks.
CAPTAIN. Albert H. Campbell	Sept. 8, 1863	Mustered out, March 20, 1865.
FIRST LIEUT. Count S. Steel...............	Sept. 8, 1863	Promoted Regimental Commissary, June 3, '65.
John A. English	June 4, 1865	Mustered out with regiment.
SECOND LIEUT. James M. Kilgore.........	Sept. 8, 1864	Mustered out, July 1, 1864, at Little Rock, Ark.

COMPANY H.

Name and Rank.	Date of Muster.	Remarks.
CAPTAIN. Thomas Stephenson......	Sept. 26, 1863	Mustered out with regiment.
FIRST LIEUT. James A. Ogan..............	Sept. 26, 1863	Dismissed the service, August 2, 1865, at Lawrence, Kansas.
SECOND LIEUT. Dudley Sawyer............	Sept. 26, 1863	Mustered out, August 2, 1865.

COMPANY I.

Name and Rank.	Date of Muster.	Remarks.
CAPTAIN. Merimoth O. Teeple......	Nov. 4, 1863	Mustered out with regiment.
FIRST LIEUT. George L. Bowen...........	Nov. 4, 1863	Resigned, February 11, 1865.
Joseph Rickabaugh........	Apr. 20, 1865	Mustered out with regiment.
SECOND LIEUT. Joseph Rickabaugh........	Nov. 4, 1863	Promoted First Lieutenant, April 20, 1865.

COMPANY K.

Name and Rank.	Date of Muster.	Remarks.
CAPTAIN. Godfrey B. Nuzum........	Feb. 19, 1864	Mustered out with regiment.
FIRST LIEUT. Josephus Utt	Nov. 5, 1863	Resigned, July 28, 1864, at Fort Smith, Ark.
David Handley	Sept. 26, 1864	Mustered out with regiment.
SECOND LIEUT. Henry Minton..............	Feb. 7, 1864	Must. out with reg't, June 25, '65; was prisoner of war from April 26, 1864, to April 15, 1865.

COMPANY L.

Name and Rank.	Date of Muster.	Remarks.
CAPTAIN. Charles Harris..............	Oct. 20, 1863	Dismissed the service, June 3, '65, Little Rock, Ark.
FIRST LIEUT. Charles Harris	July 30, 1863	Promoted Captain, October 20, 1863.
Joseph Pratt.................	Oct. 20, 1863	Discharged, Fort Smith, Ark., April 28, 1865, to date November 29, 1864
William Jones	Apr. 18, 1865	Mustered out with regiment.
SECOND LIEUT. William Writtenberry...	Oct. 19, 1863	Resigned, February 11, 1865.

COMPANY M.

Name and Rank.	Date of Muster.	Remarks.
FIRST LIEUT. Alexander F. Barnes......	July 1, 1864	Killed in Cherokee Nation, date unknown.
George Patterson..........	May 31, 1865	Mustered out with regiment.
SECOND LIEUT. William L. Trott...........	....	Deserted, Fort Gibson, C. N., Sept. 2, 1864.

List of battles, etc., in which this regiment participated, showing loss reported in each:

Waldron (Co. A)—Killed, Q., 1; wounded, E. M., 2; missing, E. M., 1. Baxter Springs (A)—Killed, E. M., 17; wounded, E. M., 3; missing, E. M., 5. Flint Creek—Killed, E. M., 1. Prairie D'Ann—Missing, E. M., 2. Poison Springs—Missing, E. M., 4. Jenkins's Ferry—No loss. Ozark—Killed, E. M., 2; missing, E. M., 1. Camp Verdigris (M)—No loss. Cabin Creek—Missing, E. M., 3. Vache Grass—Killed, E. M., 8; wounded, O. 1, E. M. 1; missing, E. M., 4. Big Blue—Killed, E. M., 1.—*U. S. Army Register.*

FIFTEENTH REGIMENT KANSAS VOLUNTEERS — CAVALRY.

Name and Rank.	Date of Muster.	Remarks.
COLONEL.		
Charles R. Jennison......	Oct. 17, 1863	
Wm. F. Cloud..............	July 26, 1865	Mustered out, Oct. 19, 1865, at Leavenworth.
LIEUT. COLONEL.		
George H. Hoyt............	Oct. 17, 1863	Resigned, July 19, 1865; promoted Brev. Brig. Gen., March 13, 1865.
Henry C. Haas..............	Sept. 3, 1865	Mustered out, Oct. 19, 1865, Leavenworth.
MAJOR.		
Robert H. Hunt............	Oct. 2, 1863	Promoted Brev. Lt. Col., June 19, 1865.
John M. Laing..............	Oct. 19, 1863	
Henry C. Haas..............	Oct. 20, 1863	Promoted Lieutenant Colonel, Sept. 3, 1865.
Benj. F. Simpson..........	June 7, 1865	Mustered out, October 19, 1865.
Leroy J. Beam	Sept. 27, 1865	Mustered out, October 19, 1865.
ADJUTANT.		
Joseph Mackle..............	Sept. 1, 1863	Mustered out, October 19, 1865.
QUARTERMASTER.		
George W. Carpenter.....	Sept. 1, 1863	Promoted Captain and A. Q. M., U. S. Vols., November 22, 1864.
Samuel P. Warren.........	Mar. 22, 1864	Mustered out, October 19, 1865.
COMMISSARY.		
John Francis................	Oct. 27, 1863	Resigned, June 12, 1865.
George E. Clark............	Aug. 20, 1865	Mustered out, October 19, 1865.
SURGEON.		
Aug. E. Denning...........	Sept. 28, 1863	Died, Leavenworth, January 6, 1864.
Edward Twiss..............	June 14, 1864	Mustered out, October 19, 1865.
ASSIST. SURGEON.		
Edward Twiss...............	Oct. 31, 1863	Promoted Surgeon, June 14, 1864.
Samuel Ashmore...........	Sept. 27, 1864	Mustered out, October 19, 1865.
CHAPLAIN.		
Benj. L. Read...............	Oct. 23, 1863	Mustered out, October 19, 1865.

COMPANY A.

Name and Rank.	Date of Muster.	Remarks.
CAPTAIN.		
John A. Wanless...........	Nov. 23, 1863	
Wm. H. Morris	June 9, 1865	Mustered out with regiment, October 19, 1865.
FIRST LIEUT.		
James Wilson...............	Sept. 17, 1863	Mustered out with regiment.
SECOND LIEUT.		
D. W. Wallingford.........	Aug. 29, 1863	Honorably discharged, April 28, 1865.

COMPANY B.

Name and Rank.	Date of Muster.	Remarks.
CAPTAIN.		
John L. Thompson........	Oct. 6, 1863	Dismissed the service, March 20, 1865.
FIRST LIEUT.		
John Murphy...............	Sept. 17, 1863	Transferred to Company C, August 22, 1865.
SECOND LIEUT.		
David J. M. Wood.........	Mar. 18, 1863	Mustered out with regiment.

COMPANY C.

Name and Rank.	Date of Muster.	Remarks.
CAPTAIN.		
Benjamin F. Simpson.....	Oct.　6, 1863	Promoted Major, June 7, 1865.
James H. Young...........	May 14, 1863	Mustered out with regiment.
FIRST LIEUT.		
Joseph Phillips.............	Sept. 18, 1863	Resigned, May 20, 1865, Paola, Kas.
John Murphy...............	Sept. 17, 1863	Mustered out with regiment.
SECOND LIEUT.		
Isom Smith	Oct.　6, 1863	Resigned, April 30, 1864.
Ralph J. Farnsworth ...	June 15, 1864	Mustered out with regiment.

COMPANY D.

Name and Rank.	Date of Muster.	Remarks.
CAPTAIN.		
Tyrus J. Hurd...............	Nov. 19, 1863	Resigned, June 13, 1865.
Leroy J. Beam..............	Aug. 15, 1865	Promoted Major, September 27, 1865.
Darius J. Lobdell..........	Sept. 26, 1865	Mustered out with regiment.
FIRST LIEUT.		
Abram Ellis.................	Sept. 11, 1863	Resigned, February 22, 1865.
Leroy J. Beam..............	May 10, 1865	Promoted Captain, August 15, 1865.
Edward Thomes	Oct.　4, 1865	Mustered out with regiment.
SECOND LIEUT.		
Leroy J. Beam..............	Oct.　2, 1863	Promoted First Lieutenant, May 10, 1865.
Darius J. Lobdell..........	May 10, 1865	Promoted Captain, September 26, 1865.

COMPANY E.

Name and Rank.	Date of Muster.	Remarks.
CAPTAIN.		
Curtiss Johnson............	Nov. 24, 1863	Mustered out with regiment.
FIRST LIEUT.		
John T. Smith	Dec. 11, 1863	Resigned, May 30, 1865.
William H. H. Grinter..	Oct.　10, 1865	Mustered out with regiment.
SECOND LIEUT.		
William H. Bisbee.........	Nov.　9, 1863	Mustered out, May 18, 1865.

COMPANY F.

Name and Rank.	Date of Muster.	Remarks.
CAPTAIN.		
Orren A. Curtis............	Oct.　2, 1863	Mustered out, to date April 27, 1865.
Robert F. Bowman........	June　9, 1865	Mustered out with regiment.
FIRST LIEUT.		
Thomas J. Bragg...........	Oct.　2, 1863	Dismissed the service, July 25, 1864, per sentence G. C. M.
Luther H. Wentworth...	Sept.　8, 1865	Mustered out with regiment.
SECOND LIEUT.		
Robert F. Bowman........	Oct.　2, 1863	Promoted Captain, June 7, 1865.
Allison J. Pliley	Sept.　1, 1865	Discharged, July 31, 1865, per S. O. No. 9, Headquarters Dept. Missouri.

COMPANY G.

Name and Rank.	Date of Muster.	Remarks.
CAPTAIN.		
Charles O. Smith...........	Sept. 26, 1863	Mustered out with regiment.
FIRST LIEUT.		
Francis M. Hall............	Sept. 16, 1863	Resigned, August 14, 1865.
SECOND LIEUT.		
Henry L. Barker...........	Nov. 14, 1863	Resigned, September 22, 1865.

COMPANY H.

Name and Rank.	Date of Muster.	Remarks.
CAPTAIN.		
Oscar F. Dunlap............	Oct. 2, 1863	Resigned, June 10, 1865.
Jacob A. Sloneker.........	Oct. 7, 1865	Mustered out, Dec. 7, 1865, Fort Leavenworth.
FIRST LIEUT.		
Reeder M. Fish	Oct. 2, 1863	Dismissed the service per S. O. No. 232, W. D., A. G. O., July 9, 1864.
L. Craig Shields............	Nov. 23, 1864	Mustered out with company.
SECOND LIEUT.		
Francis E. Smith...........	Oct. 2, 1863	Dismissed the service per G. O. No. 232, W. D., A. G. O., June 9, 1864.
Edward Gill................	Sept. 20, 1864	Mustered out with company.

COMPANY I.

Name and Rank.	Date of Muster.	Remarks.
CAPTAIN.		
Samuel W. Greer..........	Oct. 14, 1863	Mustered out with regiment.
FIRST LIEUT.		
Stutely S. Nichols.........	Oct. 14, 1863	Mustered out with regiment.
SECOND LIEUT.		
William H. Morris........	Oct. 14, 1863	Promoted Captain Co. A, June 9, 1865.
Zena A. Mason..............	July 19, 1865	Mustered out with regiment.

COMPANY K.

Name and Rank.	Date of Muster.	Remarks.
CAPTAIN.		
Joseph B. Swain............	Oct. 10, 1863	Dismissed the service, March 20, '65; reinstated, to date March 20, 1865, per S. O. 224, W. D.
Anson J. Walker...........	May 24, 1865	Mustered out with regiment.
FIRST LIEUT.		
George W. Roberts........	Oct. 10, 1863	Dismissed, May 23, '64, by gen'l court martial.
Hiram E. Turner.........	July 8, 1864	Mustered out with regiment.
SECOND LIEUT.		
John H. Roberts	Oct. 10, 1863	Dismissed, May 23, '64, by gen'l court martial.
Justin N. Ayers............	July 9, 1864	Mustered out with regiment.

COMPANY L.

Name and Rank.	Date of Muster.	Remarks.
CAPTAIN.		
Dick D. Rooks	Oct. 16, 1863	Died of pneumonia, Ft. Scott, Kan., March 15,'64.
Orloff Norton..............	Mar. 28, 1864	Killed by guerillas, Cane Hill, Ark., Nov.11,'64.
Alonzo Donovan...........	Jan. 14, 1865	Mustered out with regiment.
FIRST LIEUT.		
Alonzo Donovan...........	Sept. 29, 1863	Promoted Captain, January 14, 1865.
Henry Gronheim..........	Jan. 14, 1865	Mustered out with regiment.
SECOND LIEUT.		
Orloff Norton..............	Nov. 14, 1863	Promoted Captain, March 28, 1864.
Henry Gronheim	April 8, 1864	Promoted First Lieutenant, January 14, 1865.
David M. Wood............	Nov. 18, 1863	Mustered out with regiment.

COMPANY M.

Name and Rank.	Date of Muster.	Remarks.
CAPTAIN.		
Edward B. Metz............	Oct. 17, 1863	Dismissed the service, May 12, 1865, per sentence of G. C. M.
William A. Johnson	June 9, 1865	Mustered out with regiment.
FIRST LIEUT.		
Emmett Goss...............	Oct. 8, 1863	Killed by guerillas, November 12, 1864, near Cane Hill, Arkansas.
Jacob A. Sloneker.........	Dec. 27, 1864	Promoted Captain Company H, October 7, 1865.
SECOND LIEUT.		
William A. Johnson......	Oct. 17, 1863	Promoted Captain, June 9, 1865.
Edmund Mercer............	July 20, 1865	Mustered out with regiment.

NEW COMPANY B.

Name and Rank.	Date of Muster.	Remarks.
CAPTAIN. Livingston G. Parker....	April 29, 1865	Mustered out with regiment.
FIRST LIEUT. Henry N. Dunlap.........	June 1, 1865	Mustered out with regiment.
SECOND LIEUT. William F. Goble	May 30, 1863	Mustered out with regiment.

· List of battles, etc., in which this regiment participated, showing loss reported in each:

Clear Creek (Cos. D and L)—Wounded, E. M., 2. Lexington— Wounded, E. M., 1; missing, E. M., 1. Little Blue—Killed, E. M., 3; wounded, O. 2, E. M. 35. Independence—Wounded, E. M., 2; missing, E. M., 6. Big Blue—Killed, E. M., 2; wounded, O. 1, E. M. 21; missing, E. M., 3. Osage—Missing, E. M., 1. Newtonia—Wounded, E. M., 10.— *U. S. Army Register.*

SIXTEENTH REGIMENT KANSAS VOLUNTEERS—CAVALRY.

Name and Rank.	Date of Muster.	Remarks.
COLONEL. Werter R. Davis............	Oct. 8, 1864	Mustered out with regiment, Nov. 28, 1865.
LIEUT. COLONEL. Werter R. Davis............	Mar. 10, 1864	Promoted Colonel, October 8, 1864.
Samuel Walker	Oct. 8, 1864	Mustered out with regiment, Dec. 6, 1865.
MAJOR. James A. Price..............	Feb. 29, 1864	Resigned, October 7, 1864.
Wilber F. Woodworth...	April 27, 1864	Resigned, June 20, 1865.
James Ketner..............	Oct. 8, 1864	Mustered out with regiment, December 6, 1865; promoted Brevet Colonel, March 13, 1865.
Clarkson Reynolds........	Oct. . 8, 1864	Mustered out with regiment, December 6, 1865.
ADJUTANT. Philip Doppler..............	Nov. 18, 1863	Promoted Captain Company E, Feb. 4, 1865.
Jonas G. Dodge	Mar. 20, 1865	Mustered out, November 28, 1865.
QUARTERMASTER. William B. Halyard......	Nov. 24, 1863	Mustered out, November 28, 1865.
COMMISSARY. William P. Miller.........	June 30, 1864	Mustered out, November 28, 1865.
SURGEON. James P. Erickson	July 1, 1864	Died of chronic dysentery, Fort Conner, D. T., September 21, 1865.
John A. Hart	Nov. 16, 1865	Mustered out, November 28, 1865.
ASSIST. SURGEON. George A. Benjamin	Mar. 6, 1865	Dismissed for incompetency, March 18, 1865, to date from muster-in.
John A. Hart...............	May 20, 1865	Promoted Surgeon, November 16, 1865.
CHAPLAIN. Thomas J. Ferril..........	Oct. 8, 1864	Mustered out, November 28, 1865.

COMPANY A.

Name and Rank.	Date of Muster.	Remarks.
CAPTAIN. Nathan Ames..............	Nov. 12, 1863	Mustered out with regiment, Dec. 6, 1865.
FIRST LIEUT. Alexander Montgomery	Feb. 13, 1864	Mustered out with regiment.
SECOND LIEUT. Alfred Thornbrugh......	Jan. 23, 1864	Discharged for disability, May 8, 1865.

COMPANY B.

Name and Rank.	Date of Muster.	Remarks.
CAPTAIN. Albert S. W. Knapper...	Dec. 19, 1863	Cashiered per S. O. No. 45, Dept. of Kansas, dated Leavenworth, Kansas, August 19, 1864.
John K. Wright............	Oct. 1, 1864	Mustered out with regiment.
FIRST LIEUT. McGinly M. Neely.........	Jan. 21, 1864	Promoted Captain Co. E, October 9, 1865.
SECOND LIEUT. John K. Wright............	Feb. 2, 1864	Promoted Captain, October 1, 1864.

COMPANY C.

Name and Rank.	Date of Muster.	Remarks.
CAPTAIN. Shubial P. Thompson...	Jan. 13, 1864	Mustered out with regiment.
FIRST LIEUT. James W. Hendrix.........	Dec. 22, 1863	Mustered out with regiment.
SECOND LIEUT. William R. Lambdin	Jan. 9, 1864	Resigned, March——, 1864.
Charles Ballance...........	Mar. 15, 1864	Promoted First Lieut. Co. G, October 7, 1865.

COMPANY D.

Name and Rank.	Date of Muster.	Remarks.
CAPTAIN. John Kendall..............	Feb. 4, 1864	Dismissed the service per special order No. 276, Department Missouri, series of 1865.
FIRST LIEUT. Henry T. Stith..............	Dec. 29, 1863	Dismissed the service per special order No. 15, War Department, dated January 10, 1865.
James L. Walker...........	Mar. 31, 1865	Died, October 22, 1865, of gunshot wounds.
SECOND LIEUT. Silas Dexter..................	Feb. 5, 1864	Discharged per S. O. 433, W. D., dated August 11, 1865, to take effect January 10, 1865.
James A. Spencer.........	Feb. 11, 1865	Mustered out with regiment.

COMPANY E.

Name and Rank.	Date of Muster.	Remarks.
CAPTAIN. Philip Doppler..............	Feb. 4, 1865	Resigned, June 20, 1865.
McGinly M. Neely.........	Oct. 9, 1865	Mustered out with regiment.
FIRST LIEUT. Charles Guenther.........	Jan. 7, 1864	Promoted Captain Co. M., November 3, 1864.
Esculapius Buckmaster.	Nov. 1, 1864	Resigned, July 17, 1865.
Thomas E. Mills............	Nov. 22, 1865	Mustered out with regiment.
SECOND LIEUT. Esculapius Buckmaster.	Mar. 16, 1864	Promoted First Lieutenant, November 1, 1864.
Thomas E. Mills............	Jan. 12, 1865	Promoted First Lieutenant, Nov. 22, 1865.

COMPANY F.

Name and Rank.	Date of Muster.	Remarks.
CAPTAIN. Adoniram J. Miller	April 27, 1864	Resigned, June 15, 1865.
Andrew J. Barber.........	Sept. 25, 1865	Mustered out with regiment.
FIRST LIEUT. Hiram Malotte..............	Jan. 21, 1864	Dismissed the service, March 8, 1865.
Andrew J. Barber.........	April 14, 1865	Promoted Captain, September 25, 1865.
Franklin Ellis.............	Nov. 16, 1865	Mustered out with regiment.
SECOND LIEUT. Jeremiah H. Malcomb...	April 29, 1864	Discharged, January 27, 1865, per S. O. No. 23, from Headquarters Department of Kansas.

COMPANY G.

Name and Rank.	Date of Muster.	Remarks.
CAPTAIN.		
John W. Hall..............	Mar. 2, 1864	Resigned, June 28, 1865.
Euphrates Shepherd	Oct. 7, 1865	Mustered out with regiment.
FIRST LIEUT.		
John W. Hall................	Jan. 22, 1864	Promoted Captain, March 2, 1864.
Jacob H. Cassidy...........	Mar. 2, 1864	Resigned, June 30, 1865.
Charles Ballance...........	Oct. 7, 1865	Mustered out with regiment.
SECOND LIEUT.		
Euphrates Shepherd......	Mar. 1, 1864	Promoted Captain, October 7, 1865.
Samuel C. Gilliland.......	Oct. 7, 1865	Mustered out with regiment.

COMPANY H.

Name and Rank.	Date of Muster.	Remarks.
CAPTAIN.		
H. W. Stubblefield.........	April 2, 1864	Mustered out with regiment.
FIRST LIEUT.		
Wesley T. Smith...........	Mar. 16, 1864	Mustered out with regiment.
SECOND LIEUT.		
David J. Keller..............	April 2, 1864	Resigned, July 27, 1865.

COMPANY I.

Name and Rank.	Date of Muster.	Remarks.
CAPTAIN.		
Absalom Hyde..............	June 18, 1864	Mustered out with company, Nov. 28, 1865.
FIRST LIEUT.		
George R. Barricklow...	April 13, 1864	Mustered out with company, Nov. 28, 1865.
SECOND LIEUT.		
Charles Byer.................	June 10, 1864	Resigned, November 22, 1865.

COMPANY K.

Name and Rank.	Date of Muster.	Remarks.
CAPTAIN.		
Nathaniel C. Cradit	Oct. 1, 1864	Discharged April 21, 1865, per S. O. 178, W. D.
Bradford S. Bassett	May 17, 1865	Mustered out with regiment.
FIRST LIEUT.		
Michael C. Clary..........	May 5, 1864	Resigned, September 6, 1865.
John S. Edie.................	Nov. 25, 1865	Mustered out with regiment.
SECOND LIEUT.		
John S. Edie	Oct. 12, 1864	Promoted First Lieutenant, November 25, 1865.

COMPANY L.

Name and Rank.	Date of Muster.	Remarks.
CAPTAIN.		
William B. Tompkins ...	Oct. 7, 1864	Mustered out with regiment.
FIRST LIEUT.		
George Wolfe	May 4, 1864	Mustered out with regiment.
SECOND LIEUT.		
Ira G. Robertson..........	Oct. 15, 1864	Promoted Captain Co. M, February 4, 1865.
William A. F. Ahrberg..	Feb. 10, 1865	Mustered out with regiment.

COMPANY M.

Name and Rank.	Date of Muster.	Remarks.
CAPTAIN.		
Thomas Hughes............	May 21, 1864	Dismissed the service, October 14, 1864.
Charles Guenther	Nov. 3, 1864	Resigned, June 21, 1865.
Ira G. Robertson...........	Feb. 4, 1865	Dismissed the service, June 14, 1865, per S. O. No. 300, War Department.
Thomas Flanagan.........	Sept. 26, 1865	Mustered out with regiment.
FIRST LIEUT.		
Thomas Hughes	Mar. 10, 1864	Promoted Captain, May 21, 1864.
Thomas Flanagan.........	May 21, 1864	Promoted Captain, September 26, 1865.
Joshua Mitchell............	Sept. 26, 1865	Mustered out with regiment.
SECOND LIEUT.		
Samuel P. Curtis...........	June 4, 1864	Resigned, August 23, 1865.

List of battles, etc., in which this regiment participated, showing loss reported in each:

Camden Point (Co. F)—No loss. Lexington—No loss. Little Blue—Wounded, E. M., 3. Independence—Wounded, E. M., 1. Big Blue—Wounded, E. M., 2. Little Osage River—No loss. Newtonia—Killed, E. M., 3. Powder River—Killed, E. M., 1; wounded, E. M., 1.—*U. S. Army Register.*

SEVENTEENTH REGIMENT KANSAS VOLUNTEERS—INFANTRY.

Name and Rank.	Date of Muster.	Remarks.
LIEUT. COLONEL.		
Samuel A. Drake...........	July 28, 1864	No evidence of muster-out on file.
ADJUTANT.		
D. C. Strandridge...........	July 28, 1864	No evidence of muster-out on file.
QUARTERMASTER.		
B. D. Evans	July 28, 1864	No evidence of muster-out on file.
ASSISTANT SURGEON.		
George E. Budington......	July 28, 1864	No evidence of muster-out on file.

COMPANY A.

Name and Rank.	Date of Muster.	Remarks.
CAPTAIN.		
John W. Murphy...........	July 28, 1864	Mustered out with regiment, Nov. 16, 1864.
FIRST LIEUT.		
George DeSanno............	July 28, 1864	Mustered out with regiment.
SECOND LIEUT.		
James Kelsey................	July 28, 1864	Mustered out with regiment.

COMPANY B.

Name and Rank.	Date of Muster.	Remarks.
CAPTAIN.		
William C. Barnes.........	July 28, 1864	Mustered out with regiment.
FIRST LIEUT.		
Isaac W. Houts	July 28, 1864	Mustered out with regiment.
SECOND LIEUT.		
Thomas G. Peppard......	July 28, 1864	Mustered out with regiment.

COMPANY C.

Name and Rank.	Date of Muster.	Remarks.
FIRST LIEUT.		
Asa R. Bancroft.............	July 28, 1864	Mustered out with regiment.
SECOND LIEUT.		
Mincher Condray.........	July 28, 1864	Mustered out with regiment.

COMPANY D.

Name and Rank.	Date of Muster.	Remarks.
CAPTAIN. Richard D. Mobley	July 28, 1864	Mustered out with regiment.
FIRST LIEUT. Mason M. Hovey	July 28, 1864	Mustered out with regiment.
SECOND LIEUT. Albion H. Whitcomb	July 28, 1864	Mustered out with regiment.

COMPANY E.

Name and Rank.	Date of Muster.	Remarks.
CAPTAIN. Herbert Robinson	Aug. 18, 1864	.Mustered out with regiment.
FIRST LIEUT. Perry G. Noel	Aug. 18, 1864	Mustered out with regiment.
SECOND LIEUT. John T. McKown	Aug. 20, 1864	Mustered out with regiment.

SECOND REGIMENT KANSAS COLORED VOLUNTEERS—INFANTRY.

Name and Rank.	Date of Muster.	Remarks.
COLONEL. Samuel J. Crawford	Nov. 1, 1863	Resigned, December 2, 1864; promoted Brigadier General by brevet, March 13, 1865.
LIEUT. COLONEL. Horatio Knowles	Nov. 1, 1863	Resigned, May 24, 1864, Little Rock, Ark.
James H. Gillpatrick	Nov. 9, 1864	Mustered out with regiment, October 9, 1865.
MAJOR. James H. Gillpatrick	Oct. 1, 1863	Promoted Lieutenant Colonel, Nov. 9, 1864.
Jerome A. Soward	Dec. 1, 1864	Mustered out with regiment.
ADJUTANT. John R. Montgomery	July 14, 1863	Promoted Captain Company E, January 1, 1865.
William D. Clark	Apr. 8, 1865	Mustered out with regiment.
QUARTERMASTER. Edwin Stokes	Aug. 12, 1863	Resigned, April 22, 1865, Little Rock, Ark.
George E. Hutchinson	Apr. 11, 1863	Transferred to Company D, September 17, 1865.
Reuben F. Playford	Sept. 6, 1863	Mustered out with regiment.
SURGEON. George W. Wolgamott	Jan. 27, 1864	Resigned, April 22, 1864, Camden, Ark.
D. A. Morse	Mar. 28, 1865	Resigned, July 11, 1865, Little Rock, Ark.
ASST. SURGEON. Francis P. Thomas	July 27, 1863	Discharged per S. O. 181, W. D., dated April 20, 1866, on account of insanity, to take effect May 5, 1865.
Jesse D. Wood	Nov. 1, 1863	Mustered out with regiment.
CHAPLAIN. Josiah B. McAfee	Nov. 6, 1863	Resigned, January 16, 1865.

COMPANY A.

Name and Rank.	Date of Muster.	Remarks.
CAPTAIN. Samuel Sanders	Aug. 19, 1863	Resigned, June 2, 1864.
Charles Scofield	Apr. 11, 1865	Mustered out with regiment.
FIRST LIEUT. Ralph E. Cook	Aug. 19, 1863	Killed in action, Oct. 6, '63, Baxter Springs, C. N.
John R. F. Shull	Nov. 10, 1863	Resigned, March 8, 1865.
Jesse Buckman	July 12, 1865	Mustered out with regiment.
SECOND LIEUT. Charles Scofield	Aug. 19, 1863	Promoted Captain, April 11, 1865.

COMPANY B.

Name and Rank.	Date of Muster.	Remarks.
CAPTAIN.		
Richard J. Hinton..........	Oct. 21, 1863	No evidence of muster-out on file.
FIRST LIEUT.		
John M. Cain	Sept. 2, 1863	Promoted Captain Co. G, October 9, 1864.
James M. Trant.............	Jan. 16, 1865	Resigned, March 8, 1865.
Joshua J. Locker..........	July 12, 1865	Mustered out with regiment.
SECOND LIEUT.		
James M. Trant.............	Sept. 2, 1863	Promoted First Lieutenant, January 16, 1865.
Joshua J. Locker...........	Nov. 10, 1864	Promoted First Lieutenant, July 12, 1865.

COMPANY C.

Name and Rank.	Date of Muster.	Remarks.
CAPTAIN.		
James A. Soward..........	Aug. 26, 1863	Promoted Major, December 1, 1864.
Marcus F. Gillpatrick ...	Dec. 1, 1864	Mustered out with regiment.
FIRST LIEUT.		
John E. Hayes.............	Aug. 26, 1863	Mustered out, to date December 11, 1864, per S. O. No. 60, W. D., A. G. O., Feb. 10, 1866.
George E. Hutchinson...	Apr. 15, 1865	Promoted Regt'l Quartermaster, April 23, 1865.
Thomas Adair	July 8, 1865	Mustered out with regiment.
SECOND LIEUT.		
Thomas Adair	Aug. 26, 1863	Promoted First Lieutenant, July 8, 1865.

COMPANY D.

Name and Rank.	Date of Muster.	Remarks.
CAPTAIN.		
Frank Kister	Sept. 4, 1863	Mustered out with regiment.
FIRST LIEUT.		
Reuben F. Playford......	Sept. 6, 1863	Transferred to field and staff as Regimental Quartermaster, September 17, 1865.
George E. Hutchinson...	Apr. 11, 1865	Mustered out with regiment.
SECOND LIEUT.		
William M. Mercer........	Sept. 4, 1863	Promoted First Lieutenant Co. H, Dec. 1, 1864.
Benjamin B. B. Reppert	Apr. 23, 1865	Mustered out with regiment.

COMPANY E.

Name and Rank.	Date of Muster.	Remarks.
CAPTAIN.		
George W. Sands..........	Sept. 10, 1863	Resigned, August —, 1864.
John R. Montgomery...	Jan. 1, 1865	Mustered out on det. roll, Little Rock, Ark., January 10, 1866.
FIRST LIEUT.		
Henry De Villiers.........	Sept. 10, 1863	Resigned, April 19, 1865.
Irenæus C. Myers.........	July 11, 1865	Mustered out with regiment.
SECOND LIEUT.		
William J. Brown.........	Sept. 10, 1863	Resigned, February 12, 1864.
Henry F. Best..............	Nov. 10, 1864	Promoted First Lieut. Co. G, July 11, 1865.

COMPANY F.

Name and Rank.	Date of Muster.	Remarks.
CAPTAIN.		
James Adams..............	Oct. 20, 1863	Mustered out with regiment.
FIRST LIEUT.		
Samuel Kaisennan........	Oct. 20, 1863	Resigned, April 10, 1864, Little Rock, Ark.
Isaiah Nichols.............	Dec. 1, 1864	Mustered out with regiment.
SECOND LIEUT.		
Isaiah Nichols	Oct. 20, 1863	Promoted First Lieutenant, December 1, 1864.

COMPANY G.

Name and Rank.	Date of Muster.	Remarks.
CAPTAIN.		
Ebenezer H. Curtiss......	Nov. 1, 1863	Resigned, April 22, 1864, Camden, Ark.
John M. Cain	Oct. 9, 1864	Mustered out with regiment.
FIRST LIEUT.		
David E. Westervelt	Nov. 1, 1863	Dismissed the service per S. O No. 322, dated Headquarters Dep't Arkansas, Dec. 31, 1864.
Henry F. Best..............	July 11, 1865	Mustered out with regiment.
SECOND LIEUT.		
George E. Hutchinson...	Nov. 1, 1863	Prom. 1st Lt. and Reg'l Q. M., April 23, 1865.

COMPANY H.

Name and Rank.	Date of Muster.	Remarks.
CAPTAIN.		
Alexander Rush	Nov. 1, 1863	Killed in action April 30, 1864, Jenkins's Ferry, Ark.
Orlando S. Bartlett........	Nov. 10, 1864	Mustered out with regiment.
'FIRST LIEUT.		
Orlando S. Bartlett........	Nov. 1, 1863	Promoted Captain, November 10, 1864.
William M. Mercer........	Dec. 1, 1864	Mustered out with regiment.
SECOND LIEUT.		
Daniel K. Harden.........	Nov. 1, 1863	Resigned.

COMPANY I.

Name and Rank.	Date of Muster.	Remarks.
CAPTAIN.		
James L. Rafety...........	Nov. 1, 1863	Dismissed the service per G. O. No. 71, dated Headquarters Dep't of Ark., July 13, 1865.
FIRST LIEUT.		
Marcus F. Gillpatrick...	Nov. 1, 1863	Promoted Captain Company C, Dec. 1, 1864.
Harry C. Chase	Dec. 1, 1864	No evidence of muster-out on file.
SECOND LIEUT.		
Harry C. Chase.............	Nov. 1, 1863	Promoted First Lieutenant, Dec. 1, 1864.
Irenæus C. Myers.........	Nov. 10, 1864	Promoted First Lieutenant Co. E, July 11, 1865.

COMPANY K.

Name and Rank.	Date of Muster.	Remarks.
CAPTAIN.		
John Branson..............	Nov. 1, 1863	Mustered out with regiment.
FIRST LIEUT.		
William G. White.........	Nov. 1, 1863	Mustered out with regiment.
SECOND LIEUT.		
Jesse Buckman.............	Nov. 1, 1863	Promoted First Lieut. Co. A, July 11, 1865.

THIRD KANSAS BATTERY—LIGHT ARTILLERY.

Name and Rank.	Date of Muster.	Remarks.
CAPTAIN.		
Henry Hopkins.............	Nov. 27, 1861	Promoted Major 2d Kan. Cav., Oct. 15, 1863.
John F. Aduddell.........	Jan. 26, 1864	Mustered out, January 19, 1865.
FIRST LIEUT.		
John F. Aduddell.........	Oct. 28, 1861	Promoted Captain, January 26, 1864.
Bradford S. Bassett........	Jan. 26, 1864	Mustered out, April 17, 1865, Leavenworth.
SECOND LIEUT.		
Oscar F. Dunlap...........	Oct. 28, 1861	Resigned, May 15, 1862.
Bradford S. Bassett	May 15, 1862	Promoted First Lieutenant, January 26, 1864.
Levinus Harris.............	Mar. 21, 1864	Mustered out, January 19, 1865.

List of battles in which this battery was engaged:

Hazel Bottom—Wounded, E. M., 1; missing, E. M., 1. Shell's Mills—No loss. Old Fort Wayne—No loss. Cane Hill—No loss. Prairie Grove—No loss. Van Buren—No loss. Honey Springs—Killed, E. M., 2.—*U. S. Army Register.*

INDEPENDENT COLORED KANSAS BATTERY—LIGHT ARTILLERY.

Name and Rank.	Date of Muster.	Remarks.
CAPTAIN. Hezekiah F. Douglass...	Feb. 27, 1865	Mustered out, July 22, 1865, Leavenworth.
FIRST LIEUT. William D. Mathews.....	Feb. 27, 1865	Mustered out, July 22, 1865, Leavenworth.
SECOND LIEUT. Patrick H. Minor	Feb. 27, 1865	Died of disease, Leavenworth, March 22, 1865.

1864.

JANUARY.—Publication of the first number of the Kansas Educational Journal. It continued to be published in book form through nine volumes and years, and was then continued about one year in a quarto form, ceasing to exist about the end of 1874. It was mainly supported by an annual appropriation made by the State. The first volume contains 344 pages. It is edited by H. D. McCarty, and printed at the Bulletin office, Leavenworth. The Associate Editors are D. P. Mitchell and B. L. Baldridge, Leavenworth; Richard Cordley and Miss Lois Reynolds, Lawrence; Peter McVicar and Mrs. E. H. Mabie, Topeka; James Rogers, Burlingame; R. K. McCartney, Grasshopper Falls; Isaac T. Goodnow, Manhattan; Miss H. A. Earhart, Pardee; Miss A. J. Ellinwood, Chicago, Ill.; and Miss Mary J. Watson, Emporia. The State Teachers' Association was formed at Leavenworth, September 29, 1863. The first Teachers' Association in the State was formed at Leavenworth, March 14, 1863. The Journal published 32 pages a month. The April number gives the State Geological Corps: B. F. Mudge, State Geologist; Frederick Hawn, Assistant; G. C. Swallow, Paleologist; Tiffin Sinks, Chemist and Meteorologist; C. A. Logan, Botanist, with charge of the Sanitary Relations of the State.

JANUARY 1.—Kansas made a military department, with Gen. Samuel R. Curtis in command.

JANUARY 12.—Meeting of the State Agricultural Society, at Topeka. *Officers:* President, L. D. Bailey, of Douglas; Secretary, F. G. Adams, of Shawnee; Treasurer, Wm. Spriggs, of Anderson. *Executive Committee:* R. G. Elliott, of Douglas; J. W. Sponable, of Johnson; S. M. Strickler, of Davis; P. B. Maxson, of Lyon; S. S. Tipton, of Anderson; J. L. McDowell, of Leavenworth; J. L. Hidden, of Nemaha; C. Starns, of Leavenworth; J. P. Johnson, of Douglas; D. L. Lakin, of Jefferson.

No Fair was held this year.

JANUARY 12.—Meeting of the Legislature.

STATE SENATORS.

Dist.	Names.	P. O. Address.	County.
1	Abram Bennett	Troy	Doniphan.
1	Sol. Miller	White Cloud	Doniphan.
2	Cassius G. Foster	Atchison	Atchison.
2	Joshua Wheeler	Pardee	Atchison.
3	F. P. Fitzwilliam	Leavenworth	Leavenworth.
3	Claudius B. Pierce	Leavenworth	Leavenworth.
3	John Wilson	Leavenworth	Leavenworth.
4	A. W. Spalding	Grasshopper	Jefferson.
5	Byron Sherry	Seneca	Br'wn and Nemaha.
6	Rufus Oursler	Circleville	Jackson and Pottawatomie.
7	Thomas H. Baker	Irving	Marshall, Riley and Washington.
8	David Brockway	Topeka	Shawnee.
9	Robert G. Elliott	Lawrence	Douglas.
9	Wilber F. Woodworth	Baldwin City	Douglas.
10	W. H. M. Fishback	Olathe	Johnson.
11	Johnson Clark	Osawatomie	Miami.
12	James McGrew	Wyandotte	Wyandotte.
13	David P. Lowe	Mound City	Linn.
14	Isaac Ford	Rockford	Bourbon.
15	M. R. Leonard	Bazaar	Morris, Chase and Butler.
16	Orlin Thurston	Humboldt	Allen and Woodson
17	David M. Valentine	Peoria City	Anderson and Franklin.
18	F. W. Potter	Burlington	Coffey and Osage.
19	Perry B. Maxson	Fremont	Lyon and Greenw'd
20	Samuel M. Strickler	Junction City	Wabaunsee, Davis, D'kinson, Saline.

MEMBERS OF THE HOUSE OF REPRESENTATIVES.

Dist.	Name.	Vote	County.	Dist.	Names.	Vote	County.
1	J. P. Johnson	258	Doniphan.	39	J. A. Wakefield	169	Douglas.
2	W. J. Orem	167	Doniphan.	40	Wm. Draper	92	Douglas.
3	F. H. Drenning	104	Doniphan.	41	J. F. Cummings	308	Shawnee.
4	C. C. Camp	175	Doniphan.	42	Henry Fox	203	Shawnee.
5	J. W. Forman	166	Doniphan.	43	Wm. Chestnut	129	Miami.
6	George W. Glick	195	Atchison.	44	Thomas H. Ellis	134	Miami.
7	Jacob Saqui	284	Atchison.	45	W. G. McColloch	157	Miami.
8	Asa Barnes	233	Atchison.	46	Wm. Snooks	89	Linn.
9	Boaz W. Williams	126	Atchison.	47	J. H. Belding	87	Linn.
10	J. C. Batsell	83	Atchison.	48	Samuel Ayers	53	Linn.
11	Ira J. Lacock	178	Brown.	49	Jefferson Fleming	102	Linn.
12	Geo. E. Irwin	118	Brown.	50	Wm. Stone	63	Bourbon.
13	Richard Bradley	227	Nemaha.	51	R. P. Stevens	93	Bourbon.
14	J. S. Hidden	199	Nemaha.	52	D. R. Cobb	87	Bourbon.
15	J. D. Brumbaugh	331	Marshall.	53	J. G. Miller	178	Bourbon.
16	G. H. Hollinberg	48	Washington.	54	D. Rogers	142	Allen.
17	O. J. Grover	163	Pottaw'mie.	55	J. M. Evans	35	Allen.
18	J. W. Williams	311	Jackson.	56	H. Cavender	165	Anderson.
19	C. A. Beach	272	Jefferson.	57	Benj. M. Lingo	85	Anderson.
20	E. M. Hutchins	214	Jefferson.	58	Isaiah Pile	84	Franklin.
21	M. Barnes	247	Jefferson.	59	James N. Smith	80	Franklin.
22	Wm. Freeland	498	Leavenw'th.	60	James Rogers	197	Osage.
23	Josiah Kellogg	492	Leavenw'th.	61	Job Throckmorton	163	Coffey.
24	Geo. A. Moore	479	Leavenw'th.	62	Wm. R. Saunders	173	Coffey.
25	James B. Laing	431	Leavenw'th.	63	A. W. Pickering	80	Woodson.
26	J. W. Craig	176	Leavenw'th.	64	C. V. Eskridge	253	Lyon.
27	G. R. Houts	110	Leavenw'th.	65	A. K. Hawks	167	Lyon.
28	D. F. Walker	121	Leavenw'th.	66	Joseph Frost	102	Lyon.
29	Thomas Trower	165	Leavenw'th.	67	G. T. Donelson	....	Butler.
30	B. H. Twombley	173	Leavenw'th.	68	A. L. Alford	108	Chase.
31	M. W. Bottom	341	Wyandotte.	69	S. N. Wood	146	Morris.
32	C. H. Stratton	149	Johnson.	70	D. M. Johnston	135	Wabaunsee.
33	D. G. Campbell	120	Johnson.	71	P. Z. Taylor	241	Davis.
34	Harry McBride	75	Johnson.	72	B. E. Fullington	234	Riley.
35	T. J. Sternbergh	254	Douglas.	73	T. F. Hersey	69	Dickinson.
36	James S. Emery	165	Douglas.	74	H. L. Jones	64	Saline.
37	Clarkson Reynolds	101	Douglas.	75	James Kenner	74	Greenwood.
38	Alois Thoman	129	Douglas.				

Officers of the Senate: John T. Morton, Secretary; John T. Weaver, Assistant Secretary; Alson I. Sherwood, Journal Clerk; W. F. Cotton, Docket Clerk; John Van Horn, Engrossing Clerk; H. A. Cook, Sergeant-at-Arms; Leroy Crandall, Doorkeeper; A. L. Bartlett, Messenger.

Officers of the House: Josiah Kellogg, Speaker; W. R. Saunders, Speaker pro tem.; A. R. Banks, Chief Clerk; J. B. Oliver, Assistant Clerk; H. P. Welsh, Journal Clerk; H. B. Waldron, Docket Clerk; C. S. Lambdin, Enrolling Clerk; D. F. Drinkwater, Engrossing Clerk; H. A. Burgess, Sergeant-at-Arms; Edward Cobb, Assistant Sergeant-at-Arms; —— Detrick, Doorkeeper.

JANUARY 13.—Message from Governor Carney.

JANUARY 18.—Robt. G. Elliott takes his seat in the Senate, as the successor of S. M. Thorp, killed in the Lawrence Massacre.

JANUARY 25.—Burning of Stockton's Hall, the Union Theatre building, Leavenworth.

JANUARY 29.—General Thayer succeeds General McNeil in command of the District of the Frontier.

JANUARY 30.—A wagon train, loaded with Fort Scott coal, arrives in Leavenworth.

—The Annual Register gives the following list of the Baptist Ministers in the State:

Names.	Post Office.	County.
Alderson, L. A.	Atchison	Atchison.
Alward, E.	Topeka	Shawnee.
Alvord, Nelson	Wathena	Doniphan.
Brant, R. C.	Leavenworth City	Leavenworth.
Barrett, T. W.	Leavenworth City	Leavenworth.
Bell, G. W. S.	Ottumwa	Coffey.
Curtis, Alonzo	Hiawatha	Brown.
Cabal, H.	Elizabethtown	Allen.
Dooley, Wm.	Ottumwa	Coffey.
Dean, A. H.	Paola	Miami.
Evans, R. P.	Lanesfield	Johnson.
Freeman, ——	Fort Scott	Bourbon.
Gibson, ——	Garnett	Anderson.
Hutchinson, C. C.	Lawrence	Douglas.
Harris, Israel	Humboldt	Allen.
Jones, J. T.	Ottawa Creek	Franklin.
Kermott, W. J.	Leavenworth City	Leavenworth.
Lackey, J. M.	Manhattan	Riley.
Pratt, J. G.	Leavenworth City	Leavenworth.
Perkins, A.	Atchison	Atchison.
Patterson, ——	Forest Hill	Lyon.
Ritter, Joseph	Paris	Linn.
Sands, G. W.	Elizabethtown	Allen.
Taylor, J. B.	Waterloo	Lyon.
Upham, W. P.	Lawrence	Douglas.
Veatch, E.	Lawrence	Douglas.
Waddell, D.	Atchison	Atchison.
Webb, S. M.	Humboldt	Allen.

"The aggregate number of Baptist churches in Kansas is about forty-eight, and number of members, 1,231."

JANUARY.—Indian Agents in the State: H. W. Farnsworth, of the Kaws; G. A. Cutler, of the Creeks; G. A. Colton, of the Weas, Peorias, Piankeshaws, Kaskaskias, and Miamis; P. P. Elder, of the Osages; H. W. Martin, of the Sac and Foxes; C. C. Hutchinson, of the Ottawas; C. B. Keith, of the Kickapoos; Fielding Johnson, of the Delawares; J. B. Abbott, of the Shawnees; W. W. Ross, of the Pottawatomies.

—The Annual Register says the first Minister of the Presbyterian Church (O. S.), who settled in Kansas, was Rev. S. M. Irvin. He was appointed by the Foreign Board to superintend the Iowa (Indian) Mission, near what is now Highland, in Doniphan county. This was in 1835.   •

In the year 1857, the General Assembly, in session at Lexington, Ky., constituted two Presbyteries within the Territory, under the names of "Highland" and "Kansas." The former met and organized, November 6, at Highland, with three Ministers present, and two churches represented. The Ministers were S. M. Irvin, W. H. Honnell and D. A. Murdock; the churches represented were Highland and Lodiana, the latter in Brown county, near Kennekuk. The Presbytery of Kansas failed to organize, and was, by the Assembly of 1858, merged in that of Highland, which now covers the whole of Kansas and Colorado.

There are now (1864) under its care twenty-two churches, with sixteen Ministers. The Presbytery at its last meeting, held in Leavenworth, adopted a paper by which their whole field is thrown into Missionary districts.

Special attention is given to education, and the University of Highland, Mapleton Academy and Iola High School are affording excellent advantages to the youth of the State.

Organized and growing churches may be found in Leavenworth, Lawrence, Atchison, Topeka, Highland, Lecompton, Salina, Bethel, Fort Scott, Carlyle, Burlingame, Twin Springs, Elm Grove, Denver City, and in other towns.   •

—An article by Rev. James H. Defouri, of Topeka, in the Annual Register, says "the Catholic population of Kansas is from 15.000 to 20,000 souls, spread all over the State, in a great many congregations, large and small. The Right Rev. J. B. Miege, D. D., is the Bishop of the Diocese. Under him, to minister to the wants of Catholics, are eighteen priests and several religious communities."

Leavenworth has the Cathedral, St. Mary's Academy, the largest boarding-school for young ladies in the State, directed by the Sisters of Charity, and a large Hospital under the care of the same Sisters. There is also a German Catholic Church.

"*Atchison County.*—St. Benedict's Church, Rev. Augustin Wirth, Pastor; Assistants, R. R. Thomas and X. Attached to the Church is St. Benedict's College, for young men, Very Rev. Wirth, Principal; also, a boarding-school for young ladies, under the direction of the Benedictine Sisters. The counties of Atchison, Doniphan and Brown are attended from Atchison.

"*Pottawatomie County.*—St. Mary's Mission Church of the Immaculate Conception, Very Rev. J. F. Deils, S. Y., Pastor; Assistants, R. R. Galland, Dumortier, and Laigniel, S. Y. A large school for Indian boys is under the direction of the Company of Jesus, Very Rev. J. F. Deils, Principal. Another school, for Indian girls, is under the direction of the ladies of the Sacred Heart of Jesus. Both schools are very numerous and flourishing. The counties of Pottawatomie, Wabaunsee, Riley, Morris, Davis, Dickinson, Saline, Chase, Lyon and Clay are attended from St. Mary's Mission.

"*Nemaha County.*—Seneca Church of St. Patrick, Rev. John Meurs, Pastor. Under his direction is a Catholic school, and also the district school. The counties of Nemaha, Marshall, Jackson and Washington are attended from Seneca.

"*Shawnee County.*—Topeka, Church of the Assumption of the B. V. M., Rev. James H. Defouri, Pastor. Attached to the Church is a select school, in a prosperous condition; Principal, Rev. J. H. Defouri; Assistant, James J. Kennedy, Esq. The counties of Shawnee, Osage, Jefferson, and part of Douglas, are attended from Topeka.

"*Douglas County.*—Lawrence, Church of St. John, Rev. Sebastian Farre, Pastor. The counties of Douglas, Johnson, Lykins and Franklin are attended from Lawrence.

"*Anderson County.*—Near Scipio, Church of St. Boniface, Rev. Oloys Meyer, Pastor. The counties of Linn, Anderson and Coffey are attended from Scipio.

"*Osage Indian Land.*—Catholic Mission, under the direction of the Fathers of the Company of Jesus. Church of St. Francis de Hieronymo, Very Rev. J. Schoenmakers, Pastor; Assistants, R. R. X. Hocken, and P. Ponzilione and X. .The Jesuit Fathers, notwithstanding the losses sustained by them on account of the Southern Rebellion, direct a large school for boys. The Mission has also a large school for Indian girls, under the direction of the Sisters of Loretto. The counties of Bourbon, Allen, Woodson, Greenwood, etc., are attended from the Osage Mission."

The Annual Register gives the following list of Ministers in the Church of the United Brethren in Christ:

Josiah Terrel............Mound City.	W. R. Eggleston............Centralia.
W. A. Cardwell............Big Springs.	J. Rogers............Mount Florence.
J. S. Gingerich............Lawrence.	S. B. McGrew............Mound City.
Samuel Kretsinger............Black Jack.	H. C. Dennison............Greeley.
Martin Seiler............Ridgeway.	L. O. Mouer............Burlingame.
W. Huffman............Lancaster.	T. W. Jessup............Burlingame.
H. A. Bell............Mound City.	A. P. Floyd............Fremont.
A. Prescott............Oskaloosa.	B. F. Lewis............Holton.
Wm. Phillips............Humboldt.	J. H. Bonebrake............Auburn.
George Bonebrake............Auburn.	H. M. Greene............Twin Mound.
N. Bixler............Emporia.	B. F. Moore............Lecompton.
C. Zook............Holton.	M. Husted............Burlington.
A. M. Thornton............Richfield.	D. Kling............Manhattan.
S. G. Elliott............Fremont.	H. D. Healey............Tecumseh.
E. Lewis............Holton.	Aaron Silver............Big Blue.

The following facts in regard to Marshall county are copied from the Annual Register:

"Marshall county was first settled by A. G. Woodward, in 1848. He kept a trading post at Independence Crossing, on Big Blue, six miles south of Marysville. The next settler was F. J. Marshall, who settled where the present military road crosses Big Blue river, and where the present town site of Marysville is situated, in the year 1850, and established a ferry and trading post, and sold articles of merchandise to the California emigrants, and traded goods for furs with the different tribes of Indians, when the Big Blue valley was the hunting ground for the Pawnees, Cheyennes, Otoes, and Sioux Indians. The next settlements were made by John D. Wells on Black Vermilion, George Manley on Manley's creek, and George Guittard, sen., where Guittard's Station is now situated, on the military road, twelve miles east of Marysville. The county in 1860 contained a population of 2,280.

"The first Probate Judge was James Doniphan, who held the first term on the 10th day of October, 1855, when the Probate Courts had jurisdiction in civil and criminal cases.

"The first Sheriff was Alexander Clark, commissioned in October, 1855, and was killed in June, 1856, while attempting to arrest two horse thieves.

"The first board of County Commissioners was W. N. Glenn, John D. Wells and A. M. L. Duncan. Their first session was in October, 1855."

FEBRUARY 5.—Hawkins Taylor appointed Mail Agent.

FEBRUARY 6.—Reception of the Seventh Kansas in Leavenworth.

— John T. Snoddy and James D. Snoddy buy the Elwood Press of H. D. Hunt, and remove it to Mound City.

FEBRUARY 6.—The following Senators protest against the election of a U. S. Senator this winter: Abram Bennett, R. G. Elliott, M. R. Leonard, Jas. McGrew, Rufus Oursler, F. W. Potter, S. M. Strickler, and D. M. Valentine. Nineteen members of the House sign a similar protest.

FEBRUARY 9.—Joint Convention of the two Houses to elect a U. S. Senator for the term beginning March 4, 1865. The result of the vote was: For Thos. Carney, 68; "Against a fraud," 1; Excused and declined to vote, 27; Blank, 2. Governor Carney was declared elected.

FEBRUARY 20.—Battle of Olustee, Fla. Colonel James Montgomery, of Kansas, and Colonel Thos. W. Higginson, of Massachusetts, commanding colored regiments, were in this engagement.

"Our left column, Colonel Montgomery, came last into the fight, just in time to stop a Rebel charge. The Fifty-fourth Massachusetts went in first, followed by the First North Carolina (both Black). They were of course overpowered; but the latter left its Lieut. Colonel, Major and Adjutant dead on the field. It was admitted that these two regiments had saved our little army from being routed."— *Greeley's Conflict, vol. II, p. 531.*

FEBRUARY 29.—Reception of the Eighth Kansas in Leavenworth.

MARCH 1.—Adjournment of the Legislature. Among the acts passed were the following: Allowing each county along the line of the Atchison, Topeka & Santa Fe Railroad to issue $200,000 in bonds for that road; Authorizing school districts to issue bonds; Providing for the election of County Attorneys; Appointing commissioners to locate a Blind Asylum in Wyandotte county; Authorizing Wyandotte county to issue $100,000 in bonds to the Union Pacific Railway Company, Eastern Division; Proposing an amendment to the Constitution, allowing soldiers and others to vote; Locating the Deaf and Dumb Asylum at Olathe; Authorizing the Governor to appoint a State Geologist; Abolishing grand juries; Amending the act incorporating the Leavenworth, Lawrence & Fort Gibson Railroad Company (it authorizes a branch from Lawrence through the Wakarusa Valley, to the A. T. & S. F. R. R.); Establishing a Bureau of Immigration; Accepting the grant of lands for railroads made by Congress March 3, 1863; Changing the name of Sautrell Falls to Grasshopper Falls; Changing the site of the Penitentiary; Organizing the State Normal School; Organizing the University; Refunding to certain counties the Territorial taxes paid by them for 1860; and a law submitting to the people in November the question whether the School Lands shall be sold.

MARCH 12.— Gen. Grant Commander-in-Chief.

APRIL 10.— The first volume of Horace Greeley's American Conflict issued. It contains several chapters giving important events in our annals.

APRIL 12.—William W. Bloss becomes one of the editors of the Conservative.

APRIL 20.—The War Department credits the State with 1,529 colored troops.

APRIL 20.—Thomas A. Osborn appointed U. S. Marshal.

APRIL 21.—Republican State Convention at Topeka. Gov. Carney sends a letter to the Convention resigning all claims to the office of United States Senator. Called to order by Sidney Clarke. John W. Scott temporary Chairman, M. M. Murdock Secretary.

Committee on Credentials: Foster, Irvin, Hoaglin, Reynolds, and Jones.

Committee on Permanent Organization: McGrew, Guthrie, Thornton, Sherry, and Camp.

Officers: President, John W. Scott, of Allen; Vice Presidents, S. H. Glenn of Atchison, A. G. Procter of Lyon, S. C. Russell of Douglas, W. S. Hoaglin of Jackson; Secretaries, M. M. Murdock, of Osage; J. W. Roberts, of Jefferson.

Committee on Resolutions: Bowen, Foster, Sternberg, Hofmann, Danford, Procter, Strickler, McDowell, Snoddy.

Vote for Delegates to the Baltimore National Convention: James H. Lane 44, A. Carter Wilder 49, Thomas M. Bowen 49, W. W. H. Lawrence 49, Martin H. Insley 51, F. W. Potter 49. *Alternates:* C. W. Babcock 50, S. A. Cobb 50, John M. Price 49, Robert McBratney 48, G. A. Colton 50, H. W. Farnsworth 50.

State Central Committee: Sidney Clarke, J. C. Burnett, J. M. Rankin, A. Low, James McCahon, W. S. Hoaglin, Jacob Stotler.

The following resolutions were adopted:

"*Resolved,* That the people of the State of Kansas have implicit confidence in the integrity, ability, prudence and patriotism of Abraham Lincoln. That he is their unqualified choice for re-election, and that a change in the Chief Executive at this critical time would prove detrimental to the cause of the Union and endanger our liberties as a people.

"*Resolved,* That the delegates from this State to the Baltimore Convention be instructed to cast their votes, and exert their entire influence, to secure the renomination of Abraham Lincoln to the Presidency.

"*Resolved,* That Slavery was the cause and now constitutes the strength of the Rebellion, and that we see no hope of permanent peace until the principles of Liberty enunciated in the Declaration of Independence are carried into practice, and that we subscribe to the doctrine of Universal Human Freedom.

"*Resolved,* That the question whether Slavery is to be perpetuated or not is no longer exclusively a State, but a National one, and it is therefore proper that the Constitution of the United States should be so amended as to secure Freedom to every human being within its jurisdiction.

"*Resolved,* That at this, the first Convention which has met since the session of the Legislature which perpetrated the Senatorial Swindle, we, the representatives of the people, for them and in their name, do set the seal of condemnation upon said act, and denounce it as a Fraud unparalleled in the history of political frauds.

"*Resolved,* That we regard the law giving to our citizens in the United States volunteer service the privilege of exercising the elective franchise as an act of justice to those who are willing to imperil life in defence of our liberties.

"*Resolved,* That the letter of Gov. Carney to this Convention, declining to consider himself a Senator, is another evidence of the weakness of any policy to obtain power under a Republican Government without the consent of the people."

—Death of John T. Snoddy, recently Major in the Seventh Kansas, at Mound City.

APRIL 30.—Battle at Jenkins's Ferry, the crossing of the Saline, Arkansas. Greeley's Conflict says:

"We had one section of a battery on the field, but could not use it. A section of a Rebel battery appeared and fired one round, when the Twenty-ninth Iowa and Second Kansas charged across the field, and brought away the guns.

"When all was over, and our men had crossed the river, Kirby Smith sent a flag of truce; but, finding only a burial party, instead of an army, he made haste to capture these and claim a victory."

MAY 3.—Grant crosses the Rapidan.

MAY 4.—A despatch from Washington says Kansas has raised 4,500 troops in excess of all calls, and that there will be no draft.

MAY 11.—Grant proposes "to fight it out on this line if it takes all summer."

MAY 13.—S. A. Cobb is appointed Commissary, C. C. Willetts Paymaster, and C. L. Gorton Quartermaster.

MAY.—Publication of the Second Annual Catalogue of Baker University, at Baldwin City.

Board of Trustees: First year, H. D. Fisher, G. W. Paddock, S. Brooks, S. Parker; second year, S. Kieffer, J. W. Frame, S. N. Walker, W. G. Piper; third year, R. P. Duval, H. Barricklow, C. Steuckeman, S. H. Watson; fourth year, L. B. Dennis, N. Taylor, D. P. Mitchell, Geo. H. Weaver.

The number of pupils is 204. The second annual address is delivered by Rev. D. P. Mitchell.

The Kansas and Nebraska Annual Conference, held at Nebraska City, April 16, 1857, took the initiative in the establishment of Baker University. Rev. A. Still and Rev. L. B. Dennis were authorized to assign to the Methodist Episcopal Church bonds for 700 acres of land given by the Palmyra Town Company for an institution of learning. The building was begun in the winter of 1858. In September, 1858, Rev. Werter R. Davis was elected President. He resigned June 25, 1862, and Rev. G. W. Paddock was elected President.

JUNE 1.—Democratic State Convention at Topeka. Wilson Shannon, President; John R. Goodin, Secretary. *Committee on Credentials:* W. G. Mathias, Hugh S. Walsh, Isaac E. Eaton, J. P. Taylor, Judge Miller.

The following delegates to the Chicago National Convention were elected: W. C. McDowell, Wilson Shannon, Orlin Thurston, L. B. Wheat, H. J. Strickler, J. P. Taylor.

Presidential Electors: Nelson Cobb, Thomas Bridgens, John W. Forman. State Committee, W. P. Gambell, Isaac E. Eaton, Edward Carroll, E. J. Lines, H. S. Walsh, Dr. Milligan, Allen White, O. P. Haughawout, A. G. Otis.

The Convention passed a resolution declaring it expedient to establish a Democratic journal in Leavenworth, and the following, offered by Mr. Gambell:

"*Resolved,* That we are in favor of making Kansas a free white State."

JUNE 1.—Railroad Convention of the Border Tier counties, at Paola; W. R. Wagstaff, President. The Convention asks for a land grant and appropriations for a railroad from the Missouri river to the Gulf.

JUNE 4.—Neosho Valley Railroad Convention, at Emporia; S. M. Strickler, President. Articles of Association were drawn up for a railroad from a point near Fort Riley, through the Neosho Valley, in the direction of Galveston. Robert M. Ruggles was made President of the Association.

JUNE.—The first catalogue published of the Agricultural College; there are 108 pupils.

JUNE 7, 8.—National Republican Convention at Baltimore. Nomination of Abraham Lincoln and Andrew Johnson.

JULY 1.—Act of Congress (chapter 198, U. S. Stats.) giving every alternate section of land designated by odd numbers, for ten sections in width on each side of the road, for a railroad and telegraph from Emporia, via Council Grove, to Fort Riley. The Wakarusa branch road is changed to run from Lawrence to Emporia, and is to receive the same grant made by the act of March 3, 1863. The Leavenworth, Lawrence & Ohio City road is required to run via Baldwin City.

JULY 2.—The following is copied from the act of Congress (chapter 216, U. S. Stats.) relating to Pacific railroads:

"SEC. 9. . . *And provided further,* That any company authorized by this act to construct its road and telegraph from the Missouri river to the initial point aforesaid, may construct its road and telegraph line so as to connect with the Union Pacific Railroad at any point westwardly of such initial point, in case such company shall deem such westward connexion more practicable or desirable; and in aid of the construction of so much of its road and telegraph line as shall be a departure from the route hereinbefore provided for its road, such company shall be entitled to all the benefits, and be subject to all the conditions and restrictions of this act: *Provided further, however,* That the bonds of the United States shall not be issued to such company for a greater amount than is hereinbefore provided, if the same had united with the Union Pacific Railroad on the 100th degree of longitude; nor shall such company be entitled to receive any greater amount of alternate sections of public lands than are also herein provided.

"SEC. 12 *And be it further enacted,* That the Leavenworth, Pawnee & Western Railroad Company, now known as the Union Pacific Railroad Company, Eastern Division, shall build the railroad from the mouth of the Kansas river, by way of Leavenworth; or, if that be not deemed the best route, then the said Company shall, within two years, build a railroad from the city of Leavenworth to unite with the main stem at or near the city of Lawrence; but to aid in the construction of said branch the said Company shall not be entitled to any bonds. And if the Union Pacific Railroad Company shall not be proceeding in good faith to build the said railroad through the Territories when the Leavenworth, Pawnee & Western Railroad Company, now known as the Union Pacific Railroad Company, Eastern Division, shall have completed their road to the 100th degree of longitude, then the last-named Company may proceed to make said road westward until it meets and connects with the Central Pacific Railroad on the same line. And the said railroad from the mouth of Kansas river to the one hundredth meridian of longitude shall be made by the way of Lawrence and Topeka, or on the bank of the Kansas river opposite said towns: *Provided,* That no bonds shall be issued or land certified by the United States to any person or company for the construction of any part of the main trunk-line of said railroad west of the one hundredth meridian of longitude and east of the Rocky Mountains, until said road shall be completed from or near Omaha, on the Missouri river, to the said one hundredth meridian of longitude."

JULY 2.—Report that Colonel Dan McCook, formerly of the First Kansas, is fatally wounded.

—Captain William D. Mathews begins to raise a Colored Battery.

—General Curtis authorized to raise a regiment of Hundred Days Men. It was called the Seventeenth.

—Gold quoted 276.

JULY 24.—Indian raids on Cow Creek and Fort Larned; stock and wagons stolen.

JULY 27.—Samuel Hallett killed at Wyandotte. He was building the Pacific Railroad.

—General Curtis in the Arkansas Valley, in southwestern Kansas, establishing posts to protect the Santa Fe mail route.

·JULY 27.—

"General Gano, with 1,500 Rebels, surprised an outpost of Fort Smith, held by Captain Mefford, with 200 of the Fifth Kansas, whom he captured, with 82 of his men, after we had lost 10 killed, 15 wounded, to 12 killed, 20 wounded, of the enemy. Gano, of course, got away before he could be reached from Fort Smith."—*Greeley's Conflict, vol. II, p. 555.*

AUGUST 3.—State Convention of colored men to ask that the word "white" be struck out of the Constitution.

AUGUST 5.—Farragut's victory at Mobile Bay.

AUGUST 10.—Serious Indian raid on the Little Blue, near Marysville.

AUGUST 14.—Death of Judge Elmore.

AUGUST 29.—Four companies of the Fifth Kansas, under Major Samuel Walker, arrive in Leavenworth from Pine Bluff, Arkansas.

AUGUST 29.—National Democratic Convention, at Chicago. McClellan and Pendleton nominated for President and Vice President.

SEPTEMBER 1.—Hood evacuates Atlanta.

—In the fall, Frank G. Adams started the Atchison Daily Free Press. It was consolidated with the Champion in August, 1868.

SEPTEMBER 6.—Fort Zarah established, by Gen. Curtis.

SEPTEMBER 8.—Republican State Convention, at Topeka. Called to order by Jacob Stotler. M. R. Dutton, temporary Chairman; John T. Cox, Secretary.

Committee on Credentials: Emmert, of Bourbon; Tholen, of Leavenworth; Hunt, of Lyon; Ballard, of Washington; Riddle, of Jefferson.

Committee on Permanent Organization: Sears, of Franklin; Shepherd, of Wabaunsee; McGrew, of Wyandotte; Low, of Doniphan; Limbocker, of Pottawatomie.

Officers: President, J. T. Cox, of Coffey; Vice Presidents, Wm. M. Inman of Franklin, Capt. Bowman of Atchison, Wm. Tholen of Leavenworth, W. E. Bowker of Shawnee, Thaddeus Prentice of Douglas; Secretaries, R. B. Lockwood of Morris, F. G. Adams of Atchison.

Voted to admit three delegates from each white regiment.

First ballot for Governor: George A. Crawford, 23; Samuel J. Crawford, 16; W. W. H. Lawrence, 21; T. A. Osborn, 12; S. D. Houston, 3; J. C. Burnett, 3; J. W. Scott, 3; R. Riddle, 1.

Sixth ballot: S. J. Crawford, 51; G. A. Crawford, 31.

Ballot for Member of Congress: Sidney Clarke, 46; A. C. Wilder, 35; D. R. Anthony, 3; Blank, 1.

For Lieutenant Governor: James McGrew, 38; J. W. Scott, 20; S. M. Strickler, 16.

R. A. Barker, of Atchison, was nominated for Secretary of State by acclamation.

For Auditor: John R. Swallow, 39; J. C. Lambdin, 22; C. L. Palmer, 7; Chester Thomas, 4.

Wm. Spriggs, of Anderson, was nominated for Treasurer by acclamation.

For Attorney General: J. D. Brumbaugh, 51; John T. Burris, 25.

I. T. Goodnow was renominated for Superintendent of Public Instruction.

Jacob Safford was nominated by acclamation for Associate Justice.

For Presidential Electors: Ellsworth Cheeseborough, of Atchison; Nelson McCracken, of Leavenworth; Robert McBratney, of Davis.

Mr. Cheeseborough and Mr. McCracken died before election day. The electors finally voted for were Robert McBratney, Thomas Moonlight and W. F. Cloud.

SEPTEMBER 13.—The Republican Union State Convention at Topeka made the following nominations: For Governor, Solon O. Thacher, of Douglas; Lieutenant Governor, John J. Ingalls, of Atchison; Secretary of State, William R. Saunders, of Coffey; Treasurer, J. R. McClure, of Davis; Auditor, Asa Hairgrove, of Linn; Attorney General, Hiram Griswold, of Leavenworth; Superintendent of Public Instruction, Peter McVicar, of Shawnee; Associate Justice, Samuel A. Kingman, of Brown; for Congress, Albert L. Lee, of Donipban.

The following platform was adopted:

"*Resolved*, That we are in favor of a vigorous prosecution of the war against the Rebellion, and no compromise with traitors against the Government.

"*Resolved*, That as Kansas in the past has been most lavish of her men and means in sustaining the country against treason, so in the future she will ever be found among the foremost in standing by and supporting the Government.

"*Resolved*, That we endorse the platform of the Baltimore Convention, and most earnestly recommend that all loyal voters in Kansas give to Lincoln and Johnson their undivided support.

"*Resolved*, That the corruptionists and plunderers who are robbing the nation of the material aid necessary to carry on the war with success are the most efficient aiders of Jeff. Davis and the Rebellion, and must be put down.

"*Resolved*, That the practice of the utmost economy consistent with an efficient administration of the affairs of the Government is imperatively the duty of both National and State Administrations.

"*Resolved*, That the noble sons of Kansas, who have been and are now in the field, asserting the supremacy of the nation over armed treason, and conferring brilliant renown upon our young State, deserve and receive the most hearty sympathy and support of the people of the State.

"*Resolved*, That the people have the right to assemble in a peaceful manner, to consult for all lawful purposes, and that the threats of violent interference by a faction of corrupt revolutionists with the exercise of the elective franchise receive our unqualified disapprobation.

"*Resolved*, That we believe it to be the duty of all good men, irrespective of party, to unite in putting down the 'one-man power' in Kansas, the corrupt and tyrannical exercise of which has brought disgrace and untold evil upon the State."

SEPTEMBER 13.—The Democratic State Convention at Topeka adopted the following platform:

" *Whereas*, The Delegate Convention of the Republican party, this day assembled at the Capital, has passed a resolution reaffirming the principles and re-establishing the rights guaranteed by the Constitution of the United States to every citizen thereof, and has declared that liberty of speech and of the press shall remain inviolate, and shall be maintained inviolate at all hazards throughout this State, and have moreover nominated candidates for the various offices to be filled at the next election, men who have given evidence of devotion to those principles, and whose past record affords ample guarantee that their principles will be faithfully carried out in the administration of the government of the State: therefore,

"*Resolved*, That this Convention deem it inexpedient for the Democratic party of Kansas to nominate a State ticket, to be supported at the ensuing election, and we deem it impolitic for any Democrat in the State to permit his name to be used as a candidate for any State office or member of Congress.

"*Resolved*, That we hereby ratify the nomination of George B. McClellan, of New Jersey, for President, and George H. Pendleton, of Ohio, for Vice President, and pledge them our undivided support.

"*Resolved*, That we hereby ratify and adopt the Chicago platform as understood and construed by General George B. McClellan in his letter accepting the nomination of the Chicago Convention for President of the United States.

"*Resolved*, That we believe, in justice to our brave soldiers from this State, who are periling their lives in defence of the Constitution, the Union, and our homes, that the Constitution of the State should be so amended as to permit such soldiers to exercise the right of suffrage, and that we, as a party, are heartily in favor of the proposed amendment to our Constitution for that purpose.

"*Resolved*, That all Democratic papers in the State publish the following ticket: For President, George B. McClellan, of New Jersey. For Vice President, George H. Pendleton, of Ohio. For State Electors, Nelson Cobb, of Douglas; Thomas Bridgens, of Bourbon; and Andrew G. Ege, of Doniphan county."

SEPTEMBER 20.—W. W. Bloss becomes the editor of the Leavenworth Times. D. R. Anthony and Sidney Clarke buy the Bulletin.

—Government train burned at Cabin Creek.

SEPTEMBER 27.—General Ewing arrives at Rolla, Mo., after being surrounded at Harrison by Price's forces.

OCTOBER 1.—General Sterling Price reported advancing towards Kansas with 15,000 men. He crossed the Arkansas, coming north at Dardanelles, Pope county, Arkansas, with from 5,000 to 15,000 men. His army was greatly increased in Arkansas and Missouri. Rosecrans was in command at St. Louis, and Steele at Little Rock. A supply train from Fort Scott to Fort Gibson was captured September 19, by General Gano, at Cabin Creek. Governor Carney learned of the Rebel advance September 24. General Thomas Ewing, jr., commanded the southeast Missouri district. He reached Pilot Knob with 1,051 men, September 26, and had an engagement with Marmaduke on the 27th. He then retreated, marching north and west. He was attacked at Harrison on the 29th and 30th, and withdrew to Rolla October 1st.

OCTOBER 2.—General Samuel R. Curtis, at Fort Leavenworth, learns that Price is coming west.

OCTOBER 8.—General Alfred Pleasonton takes command at Jefferson City. He sends General John B. Sanborn with 4,100 mounted men to follow Price.

OCTOBER 8.—Governor Carney calls out the State Militia. George W. Deitzler, Major General of the Militia; John T. Morton, Adjutant General.

OCTOBER 9.—General Curtis calls all United States troops into the field to resist Price.

OCTOBER 9.—General Blunt arrives at Olathe.

OCTOBER 10.—General Curtis proclaims martial law in Kansas. James H. Lane assigned to duty on his staff.

OCTOBER 11.—General Blunt takes command at Olathe, relieving General Sykes.

The Militia assembled at Olathe number 6,816; at Atchison, 1,154; at Paola, 1,872; at Mound City, 1,180; at Fort Scott, 1,050; at Wyandotte, 550. All are soon concentrated on the border.

OCTOBER 20.—Engagement at Lexington, Mo., and retreat to the Little Blue.

OCTOBER 21.—Battle along the Little Blue; fall back to the Big Blue, six miles east of Kansas City. Price and his whole army engaged.

OCTOBER 22.—Battle of the Big Blue; Union victory. Generals Pleasonton and Sanborn reach the Little Blue, and occupy Independence at night.

General Curtis's command consists of the Eleventh, Fourteenth, Fifteenth, Sixteenth, and Seventeenth Kansas, a battalion of the Third Wisconsin, a section of the Second Kansas battery, McLain's Colorado battery, and Captain Dodge's Ninth Wisconsin battery—in all, about 4,500 men.

Citizens of Kansas now under arms estimated to number 20,000.

OCTOBER 23.—Battle of Westport. Defeat and retreat of Price. Colonel Moonlight moves down the Kansas border in advance.

A raid is made on Marmaton, Bourbon county, six citizens killed, and the town sacked and fired.

Price enters Kansas in Linn county, a few miles south of West Point, Mo., and remains in the State, in that county and Bourbon, until he crosses the Marmaton, reaching the farthest point west in Linn county.

OCTOBER.—Publication of the first volume of Supreme Court Reports. Elliot V. Banks, Reporter. Preston B. Plumb, appointed the first Reporter, resigned in October, 1862. Louis Carpenter was appointed in January, 1863, and was killed in the Lawrence Massacre, August 21, 1863. The second and third volumes were issued in 1866; the fourth in 1868; the fifth in 1871—all by Banks. William C. Webb was appointed Reporter, and the sixth volume appeared in May, 1872, the seventh in November, 1872; the eighth and ninth in 1873; the tenth, eleventh and twelfth in 1874; the thirteenth in 1875.

The following facts are obtained from these volumes: Archibald Williams, United States District Judge, died in September, 1863. Robert Crozier was United States District Attorney until elected Chief Justice, in 1863. James S. Emery succeeded him as Attorney. John T. Morton was succeeded as United States Clerk by Frank G. Adams, in 1863. Nelson Cobb was appointed Chief Justice December 28, 1862. Clark J. Hanks succeeded F. G. Adams as United States District Clerk in 1863; in 1865, Adolphus S. Thomas succeeded Mr. Hanks. Andrew Stark was the Clerk of the Supreme Court in 1865. David J. Brewer was Judge of the Leavenworth Criminal Court in 1864, and was succeeded in 1865 by Peter McFarland. Samuel A. Riggs was appointed United States District Attorney in 1867, and Charles C. Whiting, United States Marshal. Hiram Griswold was appointed Commissioner in Bankruptcy. E. B. Fowler was appointed Clerk of the Supreme Court in 1868. He was succeeded by A. Hammatt in July, 1870. J. F. Broadhead succeeded Judge Lowe in March, 1871. D. W. Houston was appointed United States Marshal May 13, 1869. Albert H. Horton became United States District Attorney. Henry G. Webb was appointed Judge of the Eleventh District November 17, 1870. William C. Webb was appointed Reporter April 1, 1871. Charles Chadwick · was appointed Attorney General July 30, 1860, B. F. Simpson having resigned and entered the service. John F. Dillon was appointed United States Circuit Judge December 22, 1869, and held his first term of court here in May, 1870. Cyrus O. French was appointed Register in Bankruptcy in 1871. B. W. Perkins was appointed Judge of the Eleventh

District in March, 1873. C. I. Scofield was appointed United States District Attorney in June, 1873; he was succeeded by George R. Peck, in January, 1874. William S. Tough was appointed United States Marshal in April, 1873. J. Jay Buck was appointed Register in Bankruptcy in 1874.

OCTOBER 24.—The force in pursuit of Price numbers 10,000. There is a skirmish at Coldwater Grove, fifteen miles below Santa Fe. Pleasonton takes the right. Moonlight reaches Mound City at midnight, after a march of sixty-five miles. A part of the Rebel army encamps at the Trading Post. They murder and burn as they run.

OCTOBER 25.—Decisive day for Kansas. Battle near Mound City. Price commands the Rebels. We capture Gens. Marmaduke and Cabel, with nine guns and 800 men. Rebels retreat across Mine Creek. Two hundred Rebels buried there. Mound City made a hospital for the wounded of both armies.

Another engagement on the Little Osage. McNeil and Pleasonton in advance. Rebels retreat eastward, leaving Fort Scott to the right.

The Rebels make another stand on the Marmaton, six miles east of Fort Scott. The battle is called Charlott, from a creek and farm on the field. It is a Union victory.

Gen. Curtis reaches Fort Scott, and rescinds the order proclaiming martial law.

OCTOBER 26.— Gen. Curtis leaves Fort Scott with Moonlight's brigade, moving towards Lamar and Carthage. Gen. Blunt follows with the brigades of Jennison and Ford. McNeil had followed the retreating foe.

OCTOBER 27.—The brigades of Sanborn and Benteen leave Fort Scott, and join in the pursuit. Curtis camps at Shanghai.

OCTOBER 27.—Gov. Carney orders the Militia to return to their homes.

OCTOBER 28.— Curtis reaches Carthage.

OCTOBER 28.—Fight at Newtonia. Blunt begins alone. Sanborn comes up. Another struggle, and the Rebels abandon the field.

OCTOBER 29.—Rosecrans orders all the troops of his Department to return to their districts.

Congratulatory order from Gen. Deitzler.

OCTOBER 30.—Lieut. Gen. Grant orders the pursuit of Price to be resumed.

NOVEMBER 1.—Curtis at Pea Ridge.

NOVEMBER 3.—March to Sugar Creek.

NOVEMBER 4.—Curtis at Fayetteville.

NOVEMBER 5.— Our army encamps on the Prairie Grove battle-field.

NOVEMBER 6.—Cane Hill reached. Price crosses the Arkansas.

NOVEMBER 8.—Generals Curtis and Blunt reach the Arkansas. The object of the campaign is accomplished. Both Generals issue congratulatory orders. General Curtis said:

"The pursuit of Price in 1864, and the battles of Lexington, Little Blue, Big Blue, Westport, Marais des Cygnes, Osage, Charlott and Newtonia, will be borne on the banners of the regiments who shared in them; and the States of Missouri, Iowa, Kansas, Colorado, Illinois, Indiana, Wisconsin and Arkansas may glory in the achievement of their sons in this short but eventful campaign."

General Blunt said :

"On the 16th of October, the brigades of Colonel Jennison and Colonel Moonlight, numbering in all but 2,000 men, marched from Hickman's Mills, Mo., to Pleasant Hill, Holden and Lexington, to make a reconnoissance. . . . .

"On the 19th of October, at 11 A. M., we were attacked at Lexington by the enemy, 26,000 strong, and held the position until their entire army was developed, when our little force retired fighting and in good order, until the darkness of night put an end to the contest. . . . .

"On the 21st, the brigades of Colonels Jennison, Ford and Moonlight, numbering only 3,500 men, fought the battle of the Little Blue, contesting stubbornly every foot of ground with an enemy five to one against them, with the most glorious results. In this contest the Second Brigade, under Colonel Moonlight, is entitled to special commendation for the gallant manner in which they fought the enemy's advancing columns until re-enforcements arrived.

"On the 22d, the brigades of Colonels Jennison and Moonlight stubbornly contested the advance of the enemy at the crossing of the Big Blue, and at the State Line (after the enemy had forced a passage at Byrom's Ford), checking his right flank, and punishing him severely.

"Thus by striking the enemy in front, and by three days' severe fighting, he was firmly held in check until the command of Major General Pleasonton was enabled to check and attack his rear at Independence, and co-operate with us in obtaining the glorious results of the battle of Westport on the 23d, when the entire Division (including Colonel C. W. Blair's brigade of Kansas State Militia) attacked the enemy's front, and, after a severe conflict, turned his right flank, which resulted in his complete defeat and rout.

"In this day's contest credit is due to several regiments of Kansas State Militia for the gallant part they bore, which will be appropriately noticed in official reports."

General Blunt gives credit to the Second Colorado and to General Pleasonton for the courage displayed "in the battles of the Osage, on the 25th," and to Colonel Moonlight for the victory at Mound City.

All was honorable to the Militia in this campaign. Their sacrifices and heroism were not less glorious and patriotic than the deeds of the fathers of the country at Lexington, Bunker Hill, and on the other fields of the Revolution. All was honorable until the question of their pay came up in Congress, and until the scrip was hawked about by speculators in Kansas. Dishonor marked these transactions. Delay was made in Congress in order that the scrip might be depreciated. The Militiamen sold it for nearly nothing. When the money reached Kansas it was so disbursed as to call for the following censure—made by the Legislative Committee, March 2, 1874:

"Owing to the brief time allotted to your Committee in which to perform the work assigned them, they have been unable to make a detailed examination of the vouchers, papers, and accounts of the office of the Treasurer, and have not been able to count all of the Military scrip returned by the Treasurer to the Auditor as vouchers for the payment of money thereon; but your Committee, from their examination of the scrip, cannot but express the opinion that payments by the Treasurer out of this fund were carelessly and negligently made. In numerous instances, payments were made on scrip presented without the signature of the Treasurer thereto, and scrip was accepted and paid without the name of the payee being endorsed thereon. Such a practice necessarily opened the way to an improper disbursement of this fund, and an opportunity for money to be wrongfully drawn from the Treasury."

This report is signed by Albert H. Horton, T. F. Robley, S. N. Latta, and E. K. Townsend, and is found on page 4 of Proceedings of the Court of Impeachment, published in 1874.

NOVEMBER 8.—Election. Abraham Lincoln re-elected President.

VOTE FOR STATE OFFICERS, AND CONGRESSMAN.

Counties.	Governor.		Lieut. Gov.		Sec. of State.		Auditor.	
	S. J. Craw-ford...	*S. O. Thacher*	*J. McGrew...*	*J. J. Ingalls.*	*R. A. Barker.*	*W. R. Saun-ders.*	*J. R. Swal-low...*	*Asa Hair-grove.*
Allen	225	96	226	94	225	93	224	39
Anderson	239	57	229	60	224	60	229	60
Atchison	555	622	525	644	681	498	531	644
Bourbon	864	166	866	150	865	145	868	148
Butler	35	25	35	25	35	25	35	25
Brown	207	156	214	147	210	152	211	152
Coffey	278	149	285	142	280	144	282	147
Chase	60	67	63	66	64	65	66	69
Douglas	959	595	1,009	576	1,010	571	1,018	565
Doniphan	634	516	593	543	668	481	595	545
Davis	134	91	134	91	133	92	134	91
Dickinson	44	20	43	20	42	20	42	20
Franklin	320	127	331	113	331	112	330	113
Greenwood	96	18	41	8	97	8	97	22
Jefferson	635	379	628	371	631	374	628	376
Jackson	620	112	259	113	258	115	258	113
Johnson	258	179	264	265	260	264	254	276
Linn	299	448	254	487	234	500	301	406
Lyon	440	113	449	101	447	104	436	106
Leavenworth	1,350	2,077	1,343	2,079	1,360	2,063	1,348	2,071
Miami	439	266	434	264	431	263	431	263
Morris	50	105	48	106	48	104	47	108
Marshall	170	146	170	145	172	145	173	145
Nemaha	250	131	253	127	255	123	254	124
Neosho	2	24	....	27	....	26	....	27
Osage	121	68	120	68	88	89	119	69
Pottawatomie	173	87	168	94	167	92	168	92
Riley	160	111	159	111	161	110	157	114
Shawnee	427	132	384	275	387	272	359	279
Saline	50	55	55	57	48	57	40	66
Washington	59	43	56	47	57	46	56	47
Wilson	19	7	19	7	19	7	19	7
Woodson	56	46	56	46	55	47	56	46
Wabaunsee	116	63	102	75	102	75	106	72
Wyandotte	176	339	234	278	176	335	194	314
Total home vote	10,196	7,840	10,047	7,822	10,225	7,676	10,066	7,833
Soldiers' vote	2,191	608	2,047	671	1,996	587	1,967	657
Total vote	13,387	8,448	12,094	8,493	12,221	8,263	12,033	8,490

Counties.	Treasurer.		Att'y Gen.		Supt. Inst'n.		Ass'te Just.		Rep. in Cong.	
	William Spriggs.	*J. R. McClure*	*J. D. Brun-baugh.*	*H. Gris-wold.*	*I. T. Good-now.*	*J. S. Brown.*	*Jacob Stafford.*	*S. A. Kingm'n*	*Sidney Clarke.*	*A. L. Lee.*
Allen	218	101	224	93	224	93	224	93	192	126
Anderson	207	76	190	60	200	59	227	60	220	63
Atchison	531	641	519	644	555	609	533	647	508	659
Bourbon	865	146	862	146	863	145	864	146	760	243
Butler	35	25	35	25	35	25	35	25	26	30
Brown	249	114	122	165	281	80	184	169	146	219
Coffey	285	143	284	145	281	146	280	146	265	164
Chase	64	65	63	65	63	64	64	65	59	67
Douglas	1,022	561	1,010	575	929	617	987	597	977	598
Doniphan	586	622	540	581	617	527	537	612	495	655
Davis	·116	108	134	91	134	90	134	91	128	92
Dickinson	43	18	43	20	45	18	45	18	41	19
Franklin	341	102	331	191	335	101	331	113	317	125
Greenwood	97	13	9	13	27	13	97	7	96	13
Jefferson	629	372	608	385	627	362	606	382	597	302
Jackson	259	113	256	114	259	113	259	112	254	117
Johnson	258	275	261	265	266	163	261	265	235	288
Linn	239	503	127	503	265	468	235	482	191	541
Lyon	451	97	447	99	456	91	448	99	413	132
Leavenworth	1,346	2,076	1,324	2,100	1,353	2,063	1,342	2,080	1,162	2,230

VOTE FOR STATE OFFICERS, AND CONGRESSMAN—Concluded.

Counties.	Treasurer.		Att'y Gen.		Supt. Inst'n.		Ass'te Just.		Rep. in Cong.	
	William Spriggs.	J. R. McClure.	J. D. Brum-baugh.	H. Gris-wold.	Isaac T. Good-now.	J. S. Brown.	Jacob Safford.	S. A. Kingm'n.	Sidney Clarke.	A. L. Lee.
Miami	435	261	....	261	435	261	434	262	413	277
Morris	48	105	44	503	56	93	47	103	36	118
Marshall	172	146	190	122	176	139	167	148	149	167
Nemaha	257	122	212	143	261	120	227	152	227	152
Neosho	....	20	....	26	....	26	....	26		
Osage	117	72	115	72	122	53	113	76	114	73
Pottawatomie	166	93	165	93	166	94	173	86	158	98
Riley	154	112	150	119	167	94	168	102	145	135
Shawnee	394	268	376	281	395	263	373	278	379	280
Saline	48	57	45	59	51	44	49	55	42	62
Washington	57	46	46	46	64	37	55	41	57	46
Wilson	19	7	19	7	19	7	....	7	19	7
Woodson	56	46	56	46	56	46	56	46	55	47
Wabaunsee	104	73	105	71	104	72	104	72	102	77
Wyandotte	176	335	176	332	190	314	174	339	168	343
Total home vote	10,044	7,935	9,229	7,984	10,119	7,608	9,833	8,002	9,156	8,668
Soldiers' vote	2,007	591	1,870	593	2,027	555	1,988	634	1,674	1,042
Total vote	12,051	8,526	11,099	8,577	12,146	8,163	11,821	8,636	10,830	9,710

VOTE ON AMENDMENTS TO CONSTITUTION, AND SALE OF SCHOOL LAND.

Counties.	Amendments to Const'n.				Sale of School Land.	
	Sec. 3, Art. 1.		Sec. 12, Art. 2.			
	For.	Agst.	For.	Agst.	For.	Agst.
Allen	284	....	260	3	251	7
Anderson	76	1	35	1	92	30
Atchison	786	44	648	96	389	221
Bourbon	860	....	861	....	92	3
Butler	....	....	....	....	....	....
Brown	344	1	236	53	208	65
Coffey	286	....	279	....	65	1
Chase	117	9	117	9	117	9
Douglas	1,066	101	1,057	103	50	528
Doniphan	889	3	765	3	343	145
Davis	197	2	197	2	126	8
Dickinson	60	....	60	....	43	33
Franklin	275	4	275	2	74	....
Greenwood	69	....	69	....	45	....
Jefferson	....	....	....	....	....	....
Jackson	....	....	....	....	....	....
Johnson	215	1	151	34	113	15
Linn	534	1	504	30	21	10
Lyon	533	20	496	49	501	46
Leavenworth	1,017	109	717	183	36	555
Miami	434	2	35	....	72	15
Morris	142	12	138	13	150	2
Marshall	238	10	239	9	225	27
Nemaha	306	2	299	4	153	24
Neosho	....	....	....	....	....	....
Osage	157	3	149	11	....	....
Pottawatomie	....	....	....	....	....	....
Riley	....	....	....	....	....	....
Shawnee	607	....	533	11	104	398
Saline	100	....	100	....	19	....
Washington	64	....	64	....	71	....
Wilson	....	....	....	....	....	....
Woodson	....	....	....	....	....	....
Wabaunsee	164	2	154	9	77	44
Wyandotte	....	....	....	....	....	....
Total home vote	9,870	329	8,438	625	3,437	2,186
Soldiers' vote	886	....	270	1	75	145
Total vote	10,756	329	8,708	626	3,512	2,331

25

VOTE FOR MEMBERS OF THE SENATE.

District.	Counties.	Names.	Home vote.	Soldiers' vote.
1	Doniphan	F. H. Drenning	631	6
		N. Price	562	5
		J. T. Lane	542	76
		W. J. Orem	504	55
2	Atchison	M. Quigg	673	......
		Thomas Murphy	571	83
		J. Wheeler	545	......
		J. J. Patterson	509	1
3	Leavenworth	H. Foote	2,008	15
		J. F. Legate	1,979	32
		W. P. Gambell	1,895	15
		M. L. Grant	1,479	79
		G. D. Parks	1,422	98
		F. Wellhouse	1,384	93
4	Jefferson	J. H. Jones	974	20
5	Brown	Samuel Spear	221	......
		James A. Pope	131	......
	Nemaha	Samuel Spear	254	......
		James A. Pope	120	......
6	Jackson	O. J. Grover	242	7
	Pottawatomie	O. J. Grover	239	......
		Scattering	2	......
7	Marshall	E. C. Manning	181	42
		W. A. Adams	131	28
	Riley	E. C. Manning	128	......
		W. A. Adams	138	......
	Washington	E. C. Manning	61	......
		W. A. Adams	39	......
8	Shawnee	Dan Horne	361	14
		G. W. Veale	293	1
9	Douglas	John Speer	1,008	104
		Oliver Barber	993	73
		R. W. Ludington	585	15
		C. S. Warren	572	15
10	Johnson	T. C. Milhoan	292	3
		J. T. Weaver	236	8
11	Miami	G. A. Colton	420	59
		J. H. Pratt	270	4
12	Wyandotte	William Weer	271	......
		Byron Judd	237	22
13	Linn	—— Smith	453	4
		—— Jones	264	1
14	Bourbon	A. Danford	817	76
		Scattering	10	......
15	Morris	H. L. Hunt	101	......
		R. B. Lockwood	61	21
	Chase	H. L. Hunt	69	......
		R. B. Lockwood	55	......
	Butler	H. L. Hunt	23	......
		R. B. Lockwood	34	......
16	Allen	C. P. Twiss	227	3
		J. L. Fletcher	84	......
	Woodson	C. P. Twiss	58	......
		J. L. Fletcher	43	......
	Wilson	C. P. Twiss	26	......
	Neosho	C. P. Twiss	1	......
		J. L. Fletcher	29	......
17	Anderson	D. W. Houston	254	90
		Scattering	2	......
	Franklin	D. W. Houston	368	......
		—— Blair	67	......
18	Coffey	F. W. Potter	283	36
		James Rogers	142	......
	Osage	F. W. Potter	85	......
		James Rogers	99	......
19	Lyon	C. V. Eskridge	351	......
		P. B. Maxson	188	13
	Greenwood	C. V. Eskridge	44	42
		P. B. Maxson	63	......
20	Wabaunsee	W. K. Bartlett	110	22
		R. S. Miller	67	23
	Davis	W. K. Bartlett	144	......

VOTE FOR MEMBERS OF THE SENATE—Concluded.

District.	Counties.	Names.	Home vote.	Soldiers' vote.
20	Davis	R. S. Miller.	30	......
	Dickinson	W. K. Bartlett	47	......
		R. S. Miller	15	......
	Saline	W. K. Bartlett	59	......
		R. S. Miller	40	......

VOTE FOR MEMBERS OF THE HOUSE.

District.	Counties.	Names.	Home vote.	Soldiers' vote.
1	Doniphan	E. Detrick	156	7
		J. Dillon	122	......
2		D. L. Payne	134	......
		R. George	74	......
		J. Normelle	11	......
3		E. Russell	112	1
		E. Downard	82	4
4		C. Leland	152	......
		W. H. Wilson	81	......
5		A. Low	137	......
		R. Flickinger	59	......
6	Atchison	G. W. Glick	132	......
		E. K. Blair	112	12
7		G. H. Fairchild	144	4
		G. W. Bowman	119	17
8		M. R. Benton	150	......
		Dr. Larry	73	......
9		S. J. H. Snyder	99	......
		B. H. Williams	89	......
10		George Storch	71	......
		H. C. Purcell	46	......
11	Brown	W. P. Rawlings	119	......
		R. B. Ransom	93	......
12		D. Sutherland	87	3
		J. S. Tyler	61	......
13	Nemaha	J. D. Sammons	107	......
		J. M. Hicks	88	......
14		C. C. Coffinbury	129	......
		—— Nicolson	46	......
15	Marshall	J. D. Wells	173	34
		S. B. Todd	133	......
16	Washington	R. Darby	52	......
		G. H. Hollinberg	50	......
17	Pottawatomie	Russell Church	137	......
		J. E. Clardy	120	......
18	Jackson	James McLelan	213	......
		J. J. Preston	98	......
		W. Granger	49	......
19	Jefferson	M. R. Dutton	167	......
		Lewis Trower	159	......
20		Robert Riddle	143	......
		C. Hicks	68	......
21		A. B. Hendricks	186	......
		M. D. Baldwin	112	......
		T. R. Bayn	39	......
		—— Hawthorn	36	......
		Scattering	32	......
22	Leavenworth	T. M. O'Brien	478	7
		S. McFarland	225	31
		J. M. Brown	39	1
23		H. Smith	320	8
		C. H. Robinson	164	30
24		S. F. Atwood	296	2
		C. J. Hanks	256	6
25		M. Jordon	328	4
		J. Walkinshaw	220	9
26		L. Kennedy	116	......

VOTE FOR MEMBERS OF THE HOUSE—Continued.

District.	Counties.	Names.	Home vote …	Soldiers' vote …
26	Leavenworth (concluded)	J. Mize	107	11
27		T. O'Gwartney	94	
		W. S. Marvin	62	9
28		E. Stafford	94	8
		D. F. Walker	70	
29		J. T. Salsbury	135	5
		Thomas Kincaid	93	
		Scattering	4	
30		R. C. Foster	124	
		H. Brandt	76	
31	Wyandotte	C. S. Glick	267	
		T. A. Gruiter	240	14
32	Johnson	C. H. Stratton	135	5
		J. E. Corliss	101	1
33		D. G. Campbell	82	
		J. D. Tinderson	60	
34		C. L. Dillie	92	
		L. Bradbury	49	
35	Douglas	F. B. Swift	253	23
		R. A. Hays	222	
36		J. R. Kennedy	127	1
		J. M. Shepherd	103	
37		W. Craig	184	
		L. L. Hartman	40	14
38		E. S. Scudder	140	
		E. H. Vanhœsen	96	
39		W. Morrow	117	1
		R. Young	83	
40		W. Draper	149	20
		J. C. Steele	38	
41	Shawnee	S. D. Macdonald	223	4
		W. W. Ross	174	
42		James Fletcher	120	
		A. M. Thornton	117	1
		S. Parker	62	
43	Miami	H. Rice	154	8
		J. W. Jennison	79	
44		W. L. Houts	131	21
		R. W. Massey	127	2
45		W. Carr	109	6
		W. Hoffman	94	17
46	Linn	A. J. Loomis	118	
47		J. Hodson	89	
		W. H. Weatherman	67	
		S. J. Addis	66	
		C. Clark	15	
48		W. Goss	56	25
		T. J. Coseboom	40	
		E. A. Deland	25	
49		J. F. Broadhead	90	9
		E. Smith	73	
50	Bourbon	L. D. Clevinger	95	
		D. B. Jackman	48	
51		D. L. Campbell	123	2
		T. S. Brockman	1	
52		W. Griswold	203	
		D. R. Cobb	10	
		— Green	2	
53		W. Z. Strong	348	54
		Scattering	21	
54	Allen	W. Stewart	144	
		J. McClure	50	
		Scattering	2	
55		J. A. Christy	79	
56	Anderson	H. Cavender	96	
		J. H. Hiner	73	
57		A. G. West	68	
		J. Gibson	26	
		Scattering	2	
58	Franklin	H. A. Cook	141	2
		J. Parkinson	71	
59		J. Hanway	144	8

VOTE FOR MEMBERS OF THE HOUSE— Concluded.

District.	Counties.	Names.	Home vote.	Soldiers' vote.
59	Franklin (concluded)...............	H. F. Sheldon.....................	71	......
60	Osage	O. H. Browne.....................	98	8
		C. Becker	86	......
61	Coffey	J. Throckmorton..................	176	212
		Scattering	5	......
62	....	W. B. Perry.....................	104	3
		A. Stewart......................	100	......
		Scattering	5	......
63	Woodson	J. Foster.......................	56	......
		J. Moody	45	......
64	Lyon	J. Stotler	210	33
		T. Anner.......................	30	......
65	....	F. R. Page	97	4
		G. J. Tallman	52	......
		D. H. Baker...................	36	......
66	....	R. Abraham...................	65	3
		O. King.......................	33	3
		W. Grinnell....................	24	1
67	Butler.........................	J. R. Mead....................	31	3
		A. Ellis	24	......
68	Chase..........................	E. A. Alford..................	69	......
		M. R. Leonard................	85	16
69	Morris	J. Spencer....................	104	5
		J. Carey	56	5
70	Wabaunsee....................	H. D. Shepherd...............	108	2
		G. Swanzinger................	65	8
71	Davis	A. W. Callen.................	198	28
72	Riley	J. M. Harvey	178	20
		R. Nehaukee.................	81	6
73	Dickinson	C. Kohler....................	41	......
		J. Irwin.....................	23	......
74	Saline	R. H. Bishop	49	2
		N. B. Hues..................	50	......
75	Greenwood	W. Martindale................	58	......
76	Wilson........................	D. C. Finn	25	......
77	Neosho........................	—— Rogers..................	32	......

VOTE FOR ELECTORS OF PRESIDENT AND VICE PRESIDENT, NOVEMBER 8, 1864.

Counties.	R. McBratney.	W. F. Cloud.	T. Moonlight.	M. J. Parrott.	Nelson Cobb.	J. Bridgens.	A. G. Eye.	E. Chesebrough.
Allen...........................	250	250	211	39	73	73	72	......
Anderson.......................	257	256	238	18	37	37	37	......
Atchison........................	785	785	522	275	380	378	380	......
Bourbon	955	960	894	63	126	126	126	......
Brown	362	362	195	167	3	3	3	......
Butler..........................	41	39	9	32	19	19	19	2
Chase...........................	79	79	17	64	47	47	47	......
Coffey..........................	307	307	283	25	124	124	124	......
Davis...........................	151	153	90	63	65	65	65	......
Dickinson *.....................	42	42	....	42	20	20	20	......
Doniphan.......................	1,084	1,081	338	748	19	19	21	......
Douglas	1,349	1,353	1,032	328	198	194	192	......
Franklin........................	391	395	350	67	42	23	44	......
Greenwood	162	106	....	7	15	16	16	74
Jackson *.......................	266	267	238	21	105	106	104	......
Jefferson.......................	831	855	601	270	178	178	178	......
Johnson.........................	411	437	282	159	105	105	106	......
Leavenworth....................	2,122	2,139	1,440	749	1,379	1,371	1,371	......
Linn............................	704	689	370	332	62	62	62	......
Lyon	488	487	462	27	69	69	69	......

* The votes of those counties with a * attached to their names were not canvassed, owing to the fact that the returns were not sent in the time prescribed by law.

VOTE FOR ELECTORS OF PRESIDENT AND VICE PRESIDENT, NOVEM-
BER 8, 1864 — CONCLUDED.

Counties.	R. McBratney.	W. F. Cloud.	T. Moonlight.	M. J. Parrott.	Nelson Cobb.	J. Bridgens.	A. G. Ege.	E. Cheese-borough.
Marshall	260	260	....	260	59	59	59	......
Miami	621	614	462	174	79	80	80	......
Morris	70	70	....	70	98	98	98	......
Nemaha	*341	341	12	330	30	30	30	......
Neosho *	24	24	....	24	11	11	11	......
Osage	166	167	115	51	27	27	27	......
Pottawatomie	212	213	150	71	35	35	34	......
Riley	213	220	76	149	51	50	51	......
Saline *	75	75	....	75	34	34	34	......
Shawnee	574	573	391	186	75	75	75	......
Washington	93	93	....	56	....	....	....	36
Wabaunsee	163	163	50	113	7	7	7	......
Wilson *	21	21	....	21	5	5	5	......
Wyandotte	285	285	7	279	190	190	190	......
Woodson	67	67	45	22	35	35	35	......
Total	14,162	14,228	8,888	5,375	3,802	3,871	3,782	112

Abstract of the Soldier vote for Electors of President and Vice President,
not canvassed; the returns were not in the time prescribed by law:

"*Soldier Vote.*— Robt. McBratney, 2,867; Wm. F. Cloud, 2,586; Thos. Moonlight, 1,543;
M. J. Parrott, 828; Nelson Cobb, 34; J. Bridgens, 34; A. G. Ege, 36; E. Cheeseborough, 543.

RECAPITULATION.

Vote.	R. McBratney.	Wm. F. Cloud.	T. Moonlight.	M. J. Parrott.	Nelson Cobb.	J. Bridgens.	A. G. Ege.	E. Cheese-borough.
Home vote	14,162	14,228	8,880	5,375	3,802	3,871	3,782	112
Soldier vote	2,867	2,586	1,543	828	34	34	36	543
Total	17,029	16,814	10,423	6,203	3,836	3,905	3,818	655

VOTE FOR DISTRICT JUDGES.

FIRST JUDICIAL DISTRICT.

Counties.	D. J. Brewer.	A. M. Sawyer.	Total.	Total Soldier vote.
Leavenworth	2,009	1,362	....	
Wyandotte	335	170	3,876	
Soldier vote	19	95	....	114

SECOND JUDICIAL DISTRICT.

Counties.	A. H. Horton.	Scattering.	Total.	Total Soldier vote.
Atchison	589	....	....	
Brown	297	....	....	
Doniphan	857	....	....	
Marshall	157	....	....	
Nemaha	371	2	2,273	
Soldier vote	24	....	....	24

VOTE FOR DISTRICT JUDGES — Concluded.

THIRD JUDICIAL DISTRICT.

Counties.	C. K. Gil- christ	David Brock- way	J. P. Greer	White	Scattering	Total	Total Soldier vote
Davis	24	35	36	37			
Dickinson	9		4	35			
Jackson	164	37	33				
Jefferson	559	349	43	16			
Pottawatomie	126	80	33	12			
Riley	132	60	57	15			
Saline		19	2	19			
Shawnee	218	334	95	1			
Wabaunsee	25	86	43	2	22	2,812	
Soldier vote	49	9	11	2			71

FOURTH JUDICIAL DISTRICT.

Counties.	D. M. Valen- tine	G. W. Smith	Scattering	Total	Total Soldier vote
Anderson	204	22			
Allen	226	35			
Bourbon	865				
Douglas	856	702			
Franklin	396	21			
Johnson	279	4			
Linn	102	469			
Miami	403	263			
Neosho		29	39	4,915	
Soldier vote	459	14			473

FIFTH JUDICIAL DISTRICT.

Counties.	J. H. Wat- son	R. M. Rug- gles	Scattering	Total	Total Soldier vote
Butler	29	30			
Chase	64	64			
Coffey	257	167			
Greenwood	77	21			
Lyon	354	181			
Morris	41	121			
Osage	71	114			
Wilson	19	7			
Woodson	55	47	9	1,728	
Soldier vote	50	21			71

The vote given to Marcus J. Parrott as a Presidential Elector was Republican, but Anti-Lane. That was the issue between Republicans during the canvass. The Price Raid made Lane successful.

NOVEMBER 9.—Gen. Curtis moves toward Fort Scott, by way of Fort Gibson. Gen. Blunt moves to Fort Smith. Gens. Blunt and Herron soon arrive in Leavenworth, by way of Gibson and Scott.

NOVEMBER 16.—Sherman leaves Atlanta.

NOVEMBER 16.—Joseph Bond starts the Herald, at Humboldt—the first paper printed there. J. H. Young soon became one of the publishers. John R. Goodin was one of the editors. The Herald lived a year.

NOVEMBER 28.—First excursion train from Wyandotte to Lawrence.

NOVEMBER 30.—Battle of Franklin.

NOVEMBER 30.— Expenditures of the State for the year:

Governor's Department	$5,549 72	Visiting regts. and def'g border..	11,800 00
Secretary's Department	4,906 32	Deaf and Dumb Asylum	2,115 14
Auditor's Department	3,032 90	Agricultural College	3,778 28
Treasurer's Department	1,981 47	Normal School	1,013 00
Supt. of Public Instruction	1,685 00	Immigration fund	1,509 00
Attorney General	1,330 62	State Geologist	2,956 77
Judiciary	12,901 79	Rent of Capitol Building	1,500 00
Printing	21,214 64	Capitol grounds	851 35
Legislature and Journals	23,023 38	Land offices	1,640 50
Penitentiary	31,693 06	Miscellaneous expenses	1,809 01
Adjutant General	3,553 51		
Quartermaster	750 00	Total for 1864	$143,595 46

—Price crossed the Red River, halted at Bonham, and finally selected Clarksville, Texas, for his headquarters. Thos. C. Reynolds, who claimed to be the Confederate Governor of Missouri, published a long letter reviewing the Raid, and severely censuring Gen. Price for its failure.

DECEMBER 9.—Chivington's Indian fight and Indian massacre near Fort Lyon.

DECEMBER 13.—Hazen captures Fort McAllister.

—Sherman's report of his great March to the Sea.

DECEMBER 15.—Victory of Thomas, near Nashville.

DECEMBER 21.—Sherman occupies Savannah.

DECEMBER.— B. F. Mudge, State Geologist, makes his first Annual Report. It is a pamphlet of 56 pages.

—Publication of the Kansas Annual Register for 1864. Andrew Stark editor. The plan of the Register originated with Judge L. D. Bailey, and he hoped to have it published annually. This number is printed at the Bulletin office, Leavenworth, and contains 265 pages of interesting matter. The history of religious societies in the State, and of counties, is peculiarly valuable. Dr. Richard Cordley writes a sketch of Lawrence, twenty pages long. The book contains lithographic pictures of Thomas Carney, Thomas Ewing, jr., James H. Lane, A. C. Wilder, George W. Deitzler, and James G. Blunt.

DECEMBER 31.—The report of W. W. H. Lawrence, Secretary of State, gives a list of 495,552 1-5 acres of land selected for the State under the act of Congress of September 4, 1841.

DECEMBER 31.—Publication of the report of C. K. Holliday, Adjutant General. It is a book of 714 pages, contains a history of the Price Raid, and gives a roster and brief history of the volunteer regiments. The following list of the Militia engaged in the Price Raid is copied from the report:

COMMANDER-IN-CHIEF AND STAFF.

Names.	Rank.	Date of Commission.	Residence.	Remarks.
Thomas Carney....	Com'der-in-Chief...	Jan. 12, 1863	Leavenworth	In'g'd Jan. 12, '63.
Guilford Dudley...	Adjutant General...	Mar. 2, 1864	Topeka..........	Res., Apr. 30, 64.
C. K. Holliday......	Adjutant General...	May 2, 1864	Topeka..........	....
Edward Russell....	Lieut. Colonel........	Mar. 2, 1864	Elwood..........	....
David Brockway...	Lieut. Colonel........	Mar. 2, 1864	Topeka..........	....
Jas. A. McGonigle	Lieut. Colonel........	Mar. 2, 1864	Leavenworth	....
F. H. Drenning...	Lieut. Colonel........	Mar. 2, 1864	Elwood..........	....
W. H. M. Fishback	Lieut. Colonel........	Mar. 2, 1864	Olathe..........	Pro'ed Brig. Gen.
W. P. Dutton.......	Lieut. Colonel........	Mar. 2, 1864	Paola..........	....
J. R. Swallow.......	Lieut. Colonel........	Mar. 2, 1864	Emporia..........	....
D. P. Lowe........	Lieut. Colonel........	Mar. 2, 1864	Mound City ..	Resigned.
S. F. Atwood........	Lieut. Colonel........	April 29, 1864	Leavenworth	Resigned.
R. A. Randlett....	Lieut. Colonel........	May 18, 1864	Topeka..........	....
Wm. C. Crawford..	Lieut. Colonel........	Oct. 10, 1864	Topeka..........	....
A. S. Hughes.......	Lieut. Colonel........	Oct. 10, 1864	Atchison	....
Wm. Rosenthal....	Lieut. Colonel........	Oct. 10, 1864	Atchison	....
John W. Brown...	Lieut. Colonel........	Oct. 10, 1864	Auburn..........	....

MAJOR GENERAL AND STAFF.

Names.	Rank.	Date of Commission.	Residence.	Remarks.
Geo. W. Deitzler....	Major General.......	Feb. 29, 1864	Lawrence......	....
John T. Morton...	Asst. Adjt. General	April 20, 1864	Topeka..........	....
R. A. Randlett.....	Asst. Quar'master..	May 13, 1864	Topeka..........	Resigned.
Sam. F. Atwood...	Asst. Quar'master..	May 18, 1864	....	....
Chas. Chadwick...	Major................	May 13, 1864	Lawrence......	....
Geo. T. Robinson.	Major................	May 13, 1864	Topeka..........	Resigned.
Lewis C. Wilmarth	Major................	July 15, 1864	Topeka..........	....
John J. Ingalls.....	Major................	May 13, 1864	Atchison	....
Thomas White.....	Major................	May 13, 1864	Council Gr've	Deceased.
Elisha G. Moon....	Major................	Sept. 7, 1864	Topeka..........	....
H. Stein.............	Major................	May 13, 1864	Leavenworth	....
John A. Leffker...	Major................	May 13, 1864	Moneka......	....

FIRST BRIGADE K. S. M.

Names.	Rank.	Date of Commission.	Residence.	Remarks.
S. A. Drake............	Brig. General..........	Feb. 29, 1864	Leavenworth	Com. Lt. Col. Vol.
M. S. Grant............	Brig. General..........	Aug. 22, 1864	Leavenworth	....
Alonzo Hastings ..	Capt. and A. A. G...	April 13, 1864	Leavenworth	....
George O. Eddy....	Capt. and A. Q. M..	April 13, 1864	Leavenworth	Resigned.
E. H. Marsh........	Capt. and A. Q. M..	Oct. 17, 1864	Leavenworth	....
Ed. D. Thompson..	Capt. and A. C......	April 13, 1864	Lawrence	Resigned.
Peter Ridenour....	Capt. and A. C......	Oct. 17, 1864	Lawrence	....
J. H. Dubois..........	1st Lt. and A. D. C.	April 13, 1864	Leavenworth	....
John Gray	1st Lt. and A. D. C.	April 13, 1864	Atchison	Resigned.
David Stettauer ...	1st Lt. and A. D. C.	Oct. 17, 1864	Leavenworth	....
G. M. Lee..............	1st Lt. and A. D. C.	Oct. 17, 1864	Leavenworth	....

SECOND BRIGADE K. S. M.

Names.	Rank.	Date of Commission.	Residence.	Remarks.
Byron Sherry.......	Brig. General..........	Feb. 29, 1864	Seneca..........	....
John E. Smith......	Capt. and A. A. G..	May 13, 1864	Seneca..........	....
J. Weisbach..........	Capt. and A. Q. M..	May 13, 1864	Marshall Co...	....
G. H. Hollinberg..	Capt. and A. Com..	May 13, 1864	Wash'g'n Co..	....
H. M. Robinson ...	Capt. and A. D. C..	May 13, 1864	Brown Co.....	....
Alfred Saxey........	1st Lt. and A. D. C.	May 13, 1864	Doniphan	....

THIRD BRIGADE K. S. M.

Names.	Rank.	Date of Commission.	Residence.	Remarks.
W. H. M. Fishback	Brig. General..........	June 9, 1864	Olathe..........	....
Harry McBride ...	Capt. and A. A. G..	Aug. 22, 1864	Johnson Co....	....
James P. Way......	Capt. and Com......	Aug. 22, 1864	Johnson Co....	....
John P. Weaver....	Capt. and A. Q. M..	Aug. 22, 1864	Olathe	Resigned.
James B. Hovey....	Capt. and A. Q. M..	Oct. 8, 1864	Spring Hill....	....
J. B. Hovey	1st Lt. and A. D. C.	Aug. 22, 1864	Spring Hill...	Pr. C. & A. Q. M.
Horace Pardee......	1st Lt. and A. D. C.	Aug. 22, 1864	Spring Hill....	....
H. A. Burgess.......	1st Lt. and A. D. C.	Aug. 22, 1864	Spring Hill....	....
W. W. Updegraff..	1st Lt. and A. D. C.	Oct. 20, 1864	Osawatomie ..	....

FOURTH BRIGADE K. S. M.

Names.	Rank.	Date of Commission.	Residence.	Remarks.
John B. Scott........	Brig. General..........	Feb. 29, 1864	Le Roy..........	....
E. Robinson	Capt. and A. A. G ..	Mar. 22, 1864	Le Roy..........	....
James F. Walker..	Capt. and A. Q. M..	Mar. 22, 1864	Garnett..........	....
M. E. Grimes........	Capt. and Com.......	June 14, 1864	Le Roy..........	....

FIFTH BRIGADE K. S. M.

Names.	Rank.	Date of Commission.	Residence.	Remarks.
John T. Snoddy....	Brig. General	Feb. 29, 1864	....	Deceased.
S. N. Wood...........	Brig. General	Feb. 29, 1864	Council Grove..	....
H. C. Akin.........	Capt.&A.A.G.	Mar. 24, 1864	Council Grove..	....
R. A. Randlett......	Cpt. & A.Q.M.	Mar. 14, 1864	Topeka...........	Resigned.
W. R. Frost.........	Cpt. & A.Q.M.	May 24, 1864	Topeka...........	....
Amos D. Craigue..	Cpt. & A.Q.M.	Mar. 25, 1864	Topeka...........	....
G. T. Donaldson....	1stLt.&A.D.C.	Mar. 25, 1864	Chelsea...........	Resigned.
T. F. Hersey........	1stLt.&A.D.C.	May 24, 1864	Abilene...........	....
Asa R. Bancroft...	1stLt.&A.D.C.	May 25, 1864	Emporia...........	....
E. Woodman........	1stLt.&A.D.C.	May 25, 1864	Manhattan	....

FIRST REGIMENT K. S. M.

S. A. Drake...........	Colonel..........	Sept. 17, 1863	Leavenworth ..	Promoted Brig. Gen.
C. H. Robinson......	Colonel..........	Mar. 19, 1864	Leavenworth ..	....
Jas. A. McGonigle	Lieut. Col......	Sept. 17, 1863	Leavenworth ..	Promoted Gov. Staff.
H. D. McCarty.....	Lieut. Col......	Mar. 19, 1864	Leavenworth ..	....
L. Shindling.........	Major...........	Sept. 17, 1863	Leavenworth ..	....
Alonzo Hastings...	Adjutant	Nov. 23, 1863	Leavenworth ..	Resigned.
Francis S. Drake..	Adjutant	May 24, 1864	Leavenworth ..	....
A. J. Angell.........	Quar'master.	Sept. 17, 1863	Leavenworth ..	Resigned.
Henry S. Burr......	Quar'master.	July 18, 1864	Leavenworth ..	Resigned.
W. S. Vandoren...	Quar'master.	Oct. 10, 1864	Leavenworth ..	....
C. A. Logan	Surgeon.......	June 29, 1864	Leavenworth ..	....

COMPANY A.

Wm. Shepherd.....	Captain	Sept. 17, 1863	Leavenworth ..	Resigned.
H. P. Scott...........	Captain	July 21, 1864	Leavenworth ..	....
H. P. Scott...........	First Lieut...	Sept. 17, 1863	Leavenworth ..	Promoted Captain.
E. F. Root	First Lieut...	July 21, 1864	Leavenworth ..	....
A. D. Nieman......	Second Lieut	Sept. 17, 1863	Leavenworth ..	Resigned.
H. C. Keller.........	Second Lieut	July 21, 1864	Leavenworth ..	....

COMPANY B.

Jas. McCahon.......	Captain	Sept. 17, 1863	Leavenworth ..	Com. rev. June 23, '64.
H. D. McCarty	First Lieut...	Sept. 17, 1863	Leavenworth ..	Promoted.
John R. Bailey......	Second Lieut	Sept. 17, 1863	Leavenworth ..	Resigned.
D. R. Churchill.....	Second Lieut	Oct. 15, 1864	Leavenworth ..	....

COMPANY C.

C. R. Robinson.....	Captain	Sept. 17, 1863	Leavenworth ..	Resigned.
O. C. Beeler........	Captain	Sept. 14, 1864	Leavenworth ..	....
George Einstein...	First Lieut...	Sept. 17, 1863	Leavenworth ..	Resigned.
E. Hallett............	First Lieut...	Sept. 14, 1864	Leavenworth ..	....
H. W. Kastor.......	Second Lieut	Sept. 17, 1863	Leavenworth ..	Resigned.
D. Sibbett............	Second Lieut	Sept. 14, 1864	Leavenworth ..	....

COMPANY D.

W. S. Vandoren....	Captain	Sept. 17, 1863	Leavenworth ..	Resign'd, April 28,'64.
L. B. Wheat........	Captain	July 1, 1864	Leavenworth ..	....
L. B. Wheat........	First Lieut...	Sept. 17, 1863	Leavenworth ..	Promoted Captain.
Edward Carroll ...	First Lieut...	July 1, 1864	Leavenworth ..	....
Edward Carroll ...	Second Lieut	Sept. 17, 1863	Leavenworth ..	Promoted First Lt.
James S. Crow......	Second Lieut	July 22, 1864	Leavenworth ..	....

COMPANY E.

M. Bransfield	Captain	Sept. 17, 1863	Leavenworth ..	....
D. N. Mitchell......	First Lieut...	Sept. 17, 1863	Leavenworth ..	....
Simon Shaw.........	Second Lieut	Sept. 17, 1863	Leavenworth ..	....

COMPANY F.

Henry Sarsted	Captain	Sept. 17, 1863	Leavenworth ..	....
Joseph Walters ...	First Lieut...	Sept. 17, 1863	Leavenworth ..	....
Charles Schiller...	Second Lieut	Sept. 17, 1863	Leavenworth ..	....

COMPANY G, FIRST REGIMENT K. S. M.

Names.	Rank.	Date of Commission.	Residence.	Remarks.
Martin Smith......	Captain	Sept. 17, 1863	Leavenworth ..	....
John Berringer ...	First Lieut...	Sept. 17, 1863	Leavenworth ..	....
Philip Depper	Second Lieut	Sept. 17, 1863	Leavenworth ..	....

COMPANY H.

AugustusM.Sattig	Captain	Sept. 17, 1863	Leavenworth ..	....
Thomas Hughes...	First Lieut...	Sept. 17, 1863	Leavenworth ..	Resigned.
H. S. McClelland..	First Lieut...	Aug. 24, 1864	Leavenworth ..	....
H. S. McClelland..	Second Lieut	Sept. 17, 1863	Leavenworth ..	Promoted First Lt.
Henry Frank	Second Lieut	Aug. 24, 1864	Leavenworth ..	....

COMPANY I.

F. Lathy..............	Captain	Sept. 17, 1863	Leavenworth ..	....
Philip Doyle	First Lieut...	Sept. 17, 1863	Leavenworth ..	....
D. Bishop.............	Second Lieut	Sept. 17, 1863	Leavenworth ..	....

COMPANY K.

Harvey W. Ide......	Captain	Sept. 17, 1863	Leavenworth ..	Resigned.
J. C. Walkinshaw	Captain	May 16, 1864	Leavenworth ..	Resigned.
John Hollusk	Captain	Oct. 14, 1864	Leavenworth ..	....
John Holland......	First Lieut...	Sept. 17, 1863	Leavenworth ..	Resigned.
Henry Teeple......	First Lieut...	Oct. 14, 1864	Leavenworth ..	....
Charles N. Palmer	Second Lieut	Sept. 17, 1863	Leavenworth ..	....

BATTERY.

Henry Mehl.........	Captain	Sept. 17, 1863	Leavenworth ..	....
Charles Besser......	First Lieut...	Sept. 17, 1863	Leavenworth ..	....
Henry Deckelman	Second Lieut	Sept. 17, 1863	Leavenworth ..	....

COMPANY L.

F. M. Christian....	Captain	June 29, 1864	Delaware City..	....
F. S. Churchill.....	First Lieut...	June 29, 1864	Delaware City..	....
A. J. Nuckles	Second Lieut	June 29, 1864	Delaware City..	....

SECOND REGIMENT K. S. M.

W.W.H.Lawrence	Colonel.........	Sept. 19, 1863	Topeka	Resigned, Nov. 18,'63.
R. A. Randlett	Colonel.........	Nov. 30, 1863	Topeka	Resigned.
Geo. W. Veale......	Colonel.........	May 9, 1864	Topeka	....
R. A. Randlett	Lieut. Col.....	Sept. 19, 1863	Topeka	Promoted Colonel.
Henry M. Greene.	Lieut. Col.....	July 15, 1864	Monmouth......	Wounded, battle of Blue, Oct. 22, 1864.
Andrew Stark......	Major............	Sept. 19, 1863	Topeka	....
E. P. Kellam.......	Adjutant.......	Sept. 21, 1863	Topeka	....
Sam'l J. Reeder ...	Quar'master	Nov. 4, 1863	Indianola	Taken pris., battle of Blue, Oct. 22, 1864.
S. E. Martin..........	Surgeon	Sept. 21, 1863	Topeka	....

COMPANY A.

L. Farnsworth	Captain	Sept. 19, 1863	Topeka	Resigned.
Geo. W. Veale......	Captain	April 20, 1864	Topeka	Promoted Colonel.
Daniel H. Horne..	Captain	May 14, 1864	Topeka	....
S. R. Remington...	First Lieut...	Sept. 17, 1863	Topeka	....
D. A. Hunter	Second Lieut	Sept. 19, 1863	Topeka	Resigned.
Geo. O. Wilmarth.	Second Lieut	April 20, 1864	Topeka	....

COMPANY B.

R. A. Randlett	Captain	Aug. 25, 1863	Topeka	Promoted Lieut. Col.
A. J. Huntoon......	Captain	Nov. 27, 1863	Topeka	Prisoner battle Blue.
A. J. Huntoon......	First Lieut...	Aug. 25, 1863	Topeka	Promoted Captain.
James R. Parker..	First Lieut...	Nov. 27, 1863	Topeka	....
Andrew Stark......	Second Lieut	Aug. 25, 1863	Topeka	Promoted Major.
S. W. Higby.........	Second Lieut	Nov. 27, 1863	Topeka	Prisoner battle Blue.

COMPANY C, SECOND REGIMENT K. S. M.

Names.	Rank.	Date of Commission.	Residence.	Remarks.
J. B. Hammon	Captain	Aug. 26, 1863	Tecumseh.........	....
J. Tyler.............	First Lieut...	Aug. 26, 1863	Tecumseh.........	Resigned.
C. S. Pyle.............	First Lieut...	May 16, 1864	Tecumseh.........	Removed to Ft. Scott.
J. Tyler...............	First Lieut...	Oct. 10, 1864	Tecumseh.........	....
Hiram Ward.........	Second Lieut	Aug. 26, 1863	Tecumseh	....

COMPANY D.

O. A. Curtis	Captain	Sept. 2, 1863	Indianola	Resigned.
Sterling B. Miles..	Captain	Sept. 17, 1863	Indianola	Wounded battle Blue.
Sterling B. Miles..	First Lieut...	Sept. 2, 1863	Indianola	Promoted Captain.
G. P. Clark...........	First Lieut...	Sept. 19, 1863	Indianola	Resigned.
Samuel J Reeder.	Second Lieut	Sept. 2, 1863	Indianola	Resigned.
Thos. H. Heller ...	Second Lieut	Sept. 19, 1863	Indianola	....

COMPANY E.

John H. Banks......	Captain	June 9, 1864	Topeka	....
Wm. P. Douthitt..	First Lieut...	....	Topeka	....
John H. Banks......	Second Lieut	Dec. 21, 1863	Topeka	Promoted Captain.
Samuel Harriott...	Second Lieut	June 9, 1864	Topeka	....

COMPANY F.

James Thompson.	Captain	Sept. 2, 1863	Big Springs......	....
Dennis Mariatty...	First Lieut...	Sept. 2, 1863	Big Springs......	....
P. H. Glenn.........	Second Lieut	Sept. 2, 1863	Big Springs......	....

COMPANY G.

Harvey McCaslin.	Captain	Sept. 5, 1863	Auburn............	Resigned.
H. E. Bush...........	Captain	Sept. 18, 1863	Auburn............	Wounded Oct. 22, '64.
H. E. Bush...........	First Lieut...	Sept. 18, 1863	Auburn............	Promoted Captain.
H. L. Shumway...	First Lieut...	Sept. 18, 1863	Auburn............	....
W. H. DeLong......	Second Lieut	Sept. 18, 1863	Auburn............	Died of wounds.

COMPANY H.

Charles C. Neal....	Captain	Sept. 7, 1863	Williamsport...	Resigned.
Perry Tice...........	Captain	June 4, 1864	Willliamsport...	....
Perry Tice...........	First Lieut...	Sept. 7, 1863	Williamsport...	Promoted Captain.
Joseph Young......	First Lieut...	June 4, 1864	Williamsport .	....
Henry K.Winans.	Second Lieut	Sept. 7, 1863	Williamsport...	....

COMPANY I.

J. L. Wightman...	Captain	Sept. 9, 1863	Richland	Resigned.
William Disney...	Captain	May 20, 1864	Richland	....
William Disney...	First Lieut...	Sept. 9, 1863	Richland	Promoted Captain.
John Helton........	First Lieut...	May 20, 1864	Richland	....
John Helton........	Second Lieut	Sept. 9, 1863	Richland	Promoted First Lt.
William Reed......	Second Lieut	May 20, 1864	Richland	....

COMPANY K.

Alexander Bailey	Captain	June 4, 1863	Osage county...	⎫
J. B. Stewart........	Captain	May 16, 1864	Burlingame.....	⎬ Transferred to S. F.
Edwin Timms......	First Lieut...	May 4, 1863	Burlingame.....	⎪ Battalion.
Geo. W. Berrill....	Second Lieut	May 4, 1863	Burlingame.....	⎭

COMPANY L.

D. B. Burdick......	Captain	Nov. 14, 1863	Ridgeway........	....
R. Clark..............	First Lieut...	Nov. 14, 1863	Ridgeway........	....
Wm. McNaught..	Second Lieut	Nov. 14, 1863	Ridgeway........	....
M. Heils	Second Lieut	May 16, 1864	Ridgeway........	....

COMPANY M.

J. W. Mossman....	Captain	Sept. 26, 1863	Wabaunsee......	....
Peter S. Wemple...	First Lieut...	Sept. 26, 1863	Mission Creek.	....
T. K. Thompson...	Second Lieut	Sept. 26, 1863	Mission Creek.	....

BATTERY SECOND REGIMENT K. S. M.

Names.	Rank.	Date of Commission.	Residence.	Remarks.
W. W. H. Lawrence	Captain	Aug. 24, 1863	Topeka	Resigned.
Ross Burns	Captain	Sept. 19, 1863	Topeka	Wounded.
Ross Burns	First Lieut.	Aug. 24, 1863	Topeka	Promoted Captain.
Samuel Hall	First Lieut.	Sept. 19, 1863	Topeka	Resigned.
Tobias Billings	First Lieut.	July 19, 1864	Topeka	
Samuel Hall	Second Lieut	Aug. 24, 1863	Topeka	Promoted First Lt.
Chas. H. Wyckoff.	Second Lieut	Sept. 19, 1863	Topeka	Prisoner.

THIRD REGIMENT K. S. M.

Names.	Rank.	Date of Commission.	Residence.	Remarks.
F. B. Swift	Colonel	Nov. 2, 1863	Lawrence	Resigned.
Chas. Willemsen	Colonel	Feb. 13, 1864	Lawrence	
James S. Moore	Lieut. Col.	Nov. 13, 1863	Lawrence	Resigned.
Newell W. Spicer	Lieut. Col.	Oct. 13, 1864	Lawrence	
Andrew Still	Major	Nov. 13, 1863	Lawrence	Resigned.
Joseph E. Riggs	Major	Oct. 17, 1864	Lawrence	
S. S. Horton	Adjutant	Nov. 13, 1863	Lawrence	
Paul R. Brooks	Quar'master	Nov. 13, 1863	Lawrence	

COMPANY A.

Holland Wheeler.	Captain	Aug. 17, 1864	Lawrence	
Richard Huggard	First Lieut.	Feb. 13, 1864	Lawrence	Removed.
R. W. Sparr	First Lieut.	Aug. 17, 1864	Lawrence	
R. A. Watts	Second Lieut	Aug. 17, 1864	Lawrence	

COMPANY C.

John H. Wilder	Captain	Dec. 12, 1863	Lawrence	
Samuel J. Kimball	First Lieut.	Dec. 12, 1863	Lawrence	
C. A. Faris	Second Lieut	Oct. 4, 1864	Lawrence	

COMPANY D.

James Brandon	Captain	Sept. 17, 1863	Lecompton	
John Hornback	First Lieut.	Sept. 17, 1863	Lecompton	
Jas. D. Todhunter	Second Lieut	Aug. 2, 1864	Lecompton	

COMPANY E.

Frank B. Swift	Captain	Oct. 13, 1864	Lawrence	
James D. Faxon	First Lieut.	Oct. 13, 1864	Lawrence	
Eph. W. Baker	Second Lieut	Oct. 13, 1864	Lawrence	

COMPANY F.

W. T. Hindman	Captain	Dec. 12, 1863	Wakarusa	
W. B. Kennedy	First Lieut.	Dec. 12, 1863	Wakarusa	
Wm. Meairs	Second Lieut	Dec. 12, 1863	Wakarusa	

COMPANY G.

L. G. Anderson	Captain	Oct. 14, 1864	Franklin	
J. D. Herrington	First Lieut.	Oct. 12, 1864	Franklin	
John McFarland	Second Lieut	Aug. 10, 1864	Franklin	

COMPANY H.

Whitford Thurber	Captain	Dec. 12, 1863	Wakarusa	
David C. Adams	First Lieut.	Dec. 12, 1863	Wakarusa	
Wm. B. Baker	Second Lieut	Dec. 12, 1863	Wakarusa	

COMPANY I.

J. C. Vincent	Captain	July 5, 1864	Lecompton	
Chas. H. Rand	First Lieut.	July 5, 1864	Lecompton	
Jacob Redinger	Second Lieut	July 5, 1864	Lecompton	

COMPANY K.

A. R. Leonard	Captain	June 25, 1864	Kanwaka	
Robert J. Barber	First Lieut.	June 25, 1864	Kanwaka	
John Barber	Second Lieut	June 25, 1864	Kanwaka	

COMPANY L, THIRD REGIMENT K. S. M.

Names.	Rank.	Date of Commission.	Residence.	Remarks.
R. A. Steele	Captain	July 12, 1864	Bloomington	
William Draper	First Lieut	July 12, 1864	Bloomington	
C. W. Ferrier	Second Lieut	July 12, 1864	Bloomington	

COMPANY M.

C. M. Meek	Captain	Aug. 2, 1864	Lawrence	
Benton Smith	First Lieut	Aug. 2, 1864	Lawrence	
B. D. Palmer	Second Lieut	Aug. 2, 1864	Lawrence	

FOURTH REGIMENT K. S. M.

S. S. Cooper	Colonel	Nov. 4, 1863	Oskaloosa	Removed from dist.
Wm. D. McCain	Colonel	Nov. 16, 1864	Oskaloosa	
J. B. Hubbell	Lieut. Col	Nov. 4, 1863	Oskaloosa	Prom. Colonel 20th.
N. F. Hewitt	Lieut. Col	Oct. 17, 1863	Oskaloosa	
G. B. Carson	Quar'master	Nov. 16, 1864	Oskaloosa	
C. B. McClellan	Adjutant	Nov. 16, 1864	Oskaloosa	
J. B. Divilbiss	Surgeon	Nov. 16, 1864	Oskaloosa	

COMPANY A.

Company A transferred to Twentieth Regiment.

COMPANY B.

Company B transferred to Twentieth Regiment.

COMPANY C.

Jerome B. Hazen	Captain	Sept. 2, 1863	Oskaloosa	
Wm. D. McCain	Captain	Dec. 7, 1863	Oskaloosa	Promoted Colonel.
Wm. D. McCain	First Lieut	Sept. 2, 1863	Oskaloosa	Promoted Captain.
W. L. Demming	First Lieut	Dec. 7, 1863	Oskaloosa	
W. L. Demming	Second Lieut	Sept. 2, 1863	Oskaloosa	Promoted First Lt.
Eli Evans	Second Lieut	Dec. 7, 1863	Oskaloosa	

COMPANY D.

John W. Rodgers	Captain	Sept. 5, 1863	Winchester	
W. P. Wilt	First Lieut	Sept. 5, 1863	Winchester	Resigned.
Hiram Webb	First Lieut	Oct. 15, 1863	Winchester	
A. J. Gafford	Second Lieut	Sept. 5, 1863	Winchester	Resigned.
John H. Webb	Second Lieut	Jan. 26, 1864	Winchester	

COMPANY E.

William Estes	Captain	Sept. 10, 1863	Kentucky Tp	Resigned.
Andrea Dehort	Captain	July 1, 1864	Kentucky Tp	
William Cather	First Lieut	Sept. 10, 1863	Kentucky Tp	
Joseph Culton	Second Lieut	Sept. 10, 1863	Kentucky Tp	

COMPANY F.

E. M. Hutchins	Captain	Sept. 16, 1863	Grassh. Falls	Resigned.
N. F. Hewitt	Captain	Sept. 29, 1864	Grassh. Falls	Promoted Lieut. Col.
Wm. A. Cowen	Captain	Oct. 17, 1863	Grassh. Falls	
John Beland	First Lieut	Sept. 16, 1863	Grassh. Falls	
Sam'l D. Divilbiss	Second Lieut	Sept. 16, 1863	Grassh. Falls	Resigned.
George Riffert	Second Lieut	July 6, 1864	Grassh. Falls	

COMPANY G.

James H. Jones	Captain	Sept. 19, 1863	Kaw City	
James M. Huber	First Lieut	Sept. 19, 1863	Kaw City	
John J. Townsend	Second Lieut	Sept. 19, 1863	Kaw City	

COMPANY H.

Golden Silvers	Captain	Sept. 22, 1863	Mt. Florence	
Newell Colby	First Lieut	Sept. 22, 1863	Mt. Florence	
John Rippetoe	Second Lieut	Sept. 22, 1863	Mt. Florence	

COMPANY I, FOURTH REGIMENT K. S. M.

Names.	Rank.	Date of Commission.	Residence.	Remarks.
A. G. Patrick	Captain	Sept. 22, 1863	Mt. Florence...	Removed out of Dist.
W. C. Butts	Captain	July 1, 1864	Grassh. Falls...	....
W. C. Butts	First Lieut...	Sept. 22, 1863	Grassh. Falls...	Promoted Captain.
W. G. Keech........	First Lieut...	July 1, 1864	Grassh. Falls...	....
S. B. Hogan..........	Second Lieut	Sept. 22, 1864	Grassh. Falls...	....

COMPANY K.

| J. W. Houtz.......... | Captain ...... | Sept. 22, 1863 | Winchester ..... | .... |
| J. J. Martin.......... | Second Lieut | Sept. 22, 1863 | Winchester ..... | .... |

COMPANY L.

Ephraim Bainter..	Captain	Dec. 7, 1863	Osawkee	Resigned.
John Freek..........	Captain	Nov. 14, 1864	Osawkee	....
John Freek..........	First Lieut...	Dec. 7, 1863	Osawkee	Promoted Captain.
Johnson Kennedy	First Lieut...	Nov. 14, 1864	Osawkee	....
Horace C. Deming	Second Lieut	Dec. 7, 1863	Osawkee	Resigned.
Jas. D. Nesbitt.....	Second Lieut	Nov. 14, 1864	Osawkee	....

COMPANY M.

Henry Morley......	Captain	Jan. 13, 1864	Oskaloosa........	Resigned.
John L. Patterson	Captain	May 14, 1864	Sarcoxie	....
J. O. Reed............	First Lieut...	Dec. 7, 1863	Oskaloosa........	Resigned.
Moses D. Baldwin	First Lieut...	May 14, 1864	Sarcoxie	Resigned.
D. M. Smith.........	First Lieut...	July 6, 1864	Oskaloosa........	....
David M. Smith...	Second Lieut	Dec. 7, 1863	Oskaloosa........	Promoted First Lt.
Jesse D. Miller......	Second Lieut	May 14, 1864	Sarcoxie	Resigned.
Amos M. Fawcett.	Second Lieut	July 6, 1864	Oskaloosa........	....

COMPANY N.

F. M. Whitlow	Captain	Dec. 7, 1863	Sarcoxie..........	....
Thomas R. Bayne	Captain	Oct. 15, 1864	....	....
M. J. Bundy.........	First Lieut...	Dec. 7, 1863	Sarcoxie..........	Removed from Dist.
H. B. Hatton........	First Lieut...	June 14, 1864	Sarcoxie..........	....
William Williams	Second Lieut	Dec. 7, 1863	Sarcoxie..........	Removed from Dist.
Thomas J. Hare...	Second Lieut	June 14, 1864	Sarcoxie..........	....

COMPANY O.

J. M. Hawthorne..	Captain	Nov. 1, 1864	Jefferson Co....	....
Noah W. Moon....	First Lieut...	Nov. 1, 1864	Jefferson Co....	....
Sylvester Alton...	Second Lieut	Nov. 1, 1864	Jefferson Co....	....

FIFTH   REGIMENT   K. S. M.

G. A. Colton	Colonel........	Sept. 28, 1863	Paola	....
G. H. Hume.........	Lieut. Col....	Sept. 28, 1863	Paola	....
Assail Hunt.........	Major..........	Sept. 28, 1863	Paola	....
T. J. Hedges	Adjutant......	Sept. 28, 1863	Paola	....
B. Snyder............	Quar'master	Sept. 28, 1863	Paola	....

COMPANY A.

John P. Dodd......	Captain	Sept. 4, 1863	Osage	....
S. Underhill.........	First Lieut...	Sept. 4, 1863	Osage	....
W. G. McCollock..	Second Lieut	Sept. 4, 1863	Osage	....

COMPANY B.

Charles Rice..........	Captain	Sept. 5, 1863	Stanton	Resigned.
J. K. Landers	Captain	July 25, 1864	Stanton	....
P. P. Bingham	First Lieut...	July 25, 1864	Stanton	....
Joel Goodrich......	Second Lieut	Sept. 5, 1864	Stanton	Resigned.
W. P. Bowen........	Second Lieut	July 25, 1864	Stanton	....

COMPANY C.

G. H. Hume.........	Captain	Oct. 4, 1863	New Lancaster	....
John Massey........	First Lieut...	Oct. 4, 1863	New Lancaster	....
R. S. Hiner	Second Lieut	Oct. 4, 1863	New Lancaster	....

COMPANY D, FIFTH REGIMENT K. S. M.

Names.	Rank.	Date of Commission.	Residence.	Remarks.
H. Pardee............	Captain	Sept. 28, 1863	Paola............	....
Jacob Snyder........	First Lieut...	Sept. 28, 1863	Paola............	....
W. W. Childer......	Second Lieut	Sept. 28, 1863	Paola............	....

COMPANY E.

Elias Snyder........	Captain	Sept. 28, 1863	Osawatomie	Resigned.
Thomas Roberts...	Captain	July 18, 1864	Osawatomie	Resigned.
W. R. Wagstaff....	Captain	Aug. 22, 1864	Paola............	....
James Bell............	First Lieut...	Aug. 28, 1864	....	Resigned.
Henry Smith	First Lieut...	July 18, 1864	....	Resigned.
Martin Dale.........	First Lieut...	Aug. 22, 1864	....	....
Matt Stephens......	Second Lieut	Sept. 28, 1863	Osawatomie......	Resigned.
C. M. Stephens.....	Second Lieut	July 18, 1864	....	Resigned.
M. D. Gossett.......	Second Lieut	July 8, 1864	....	....

COMPANY F.

| L. A. Arnott......... | First Lieut... | Sept. 28, 1863 | Indianapolis ... | Resigned. |
| W. J. Ellis .... | Second Lieut | Sept. 28, 1863 | Indianapolis ... | .... |

COMPANY G.

G. B. Trayler........	Captain	Sept. 9, 1863	St. Marysville..	....
H. L. Lyon..........	First Lieut...	Sept. 9, 1863	St. Marysville..	....
S. W. Spear	Second Lieut	Sept. 9, 1863	St. Marysville..	Resigned.
James V. Lyon.....	Second Lieut	Aug. 2, 1864	Lyons.............	....

COMPANY H.

James Ray...........	Captain	Sept. 28, 1863	Richland.........	....
F. N. Dodd...........	First Lieut...	Sept. 28, 1863	Richland.........	....
J. W. Pile............	Second Lieut	Sept. 28, 1863	Richland.........	Removed from Dist.
Charles N. White.	Second Lieut	April 25, 1864	Richland.........	....

COMPANY I.

G. W. Raney	Captain	Nov. 5, 1863	Wea.................	Resigned.
W. B. Keith..........	Captain	Sept. 19, 1864	Paola	....
G. W. Wise	First Lieut...	Nov. 5, 1863	Wea.................	Resigned.
Peter Reynolds....	First Lieut...	Sept. 19, 1864	Paola	....
J. A. Hicks...........	Second Lieut	Nov. 5, 1863	Wea.................	....

COMPANY K.

Seth Clover..........	Captain	Sept. 8, 1863	Paola	Resigned.
Thomas Roberts...	Captain	July 18, 1864	Osawatomie.....	....
Thos. J. Hedges...	First Lieut...	Sept. 8, 1863	Osawatomie.....	Promoted.
Henry B. Smith...	First Lieut...	July 8, 1864	Osawatomie.....	....
M. D. Gossett.......	Second Lieut	Sept. 8, 1863	Osawatomie.....	Resigned.
C. M. Stephens.....	Second Lieut	July 18, 1864	Osawatomie.....	....

SIXTH REGIMENT K. S. M.

James D. Snoddy..	Colonel	June 13, 1864	Mound City.....	....
H. Robinson	Major	June 30, 1864	Mound City.....	....
E. R. Smith	Adjutant	June 30, 1864	Mound City.....	....
James L. Scott.....	Quarterm'r ..	June 30, 1864	Mound City.....	....
L. B. Hiatt............	Surgeon	June 30, 1864	Mound City.....	....

COMPANY A.

Justin N. Ayres...	Captain	Sept. 4, 1863	Centreville......	....
Charles Barnes....	Captain	Aug. 2, 1864	Centreville......	....
H. Robinson	First Lieut...	Sept. 4, 1863	Centreville......	Promoted Major.
D. F. Park...........	First Lieut...	Aug. 2, 1864	Centreville......	....
Benj. F. Bradley...	Second Lieut	Sept. 4, 1863	Centreville......	Resigned.
Jesse Brown........	Second Lieut	Aug. 28, 1864	Centreville......	....

COMPANY B, SIXTH REGIMENT K. S. M.

Names.	Rank.	Date of Commission.	Residence.	Remarks.
M. P. McDaniels...	Captain	Sept. 10, 1863	Paris, Linn Co.	Removed.
W. S. McDowell....	Captain	June 3, 1864	Paris, Linn Co.	Resigned.
Nelson Knight.....	Captain	Aug. 2, 1864	Paris, Linn Co.	
Jeremiah Farris...	First Lieut...	Sept. 10, 1863	Paris, Linn Co.	Resigned.
Owen D. Botkin...	First Lieut...	Aug. 2, 1864	Paris, Linn Co.	
John M. Honnis...	Second Lieut	Sept. 10, 1863	Paris, Linn Co.	Resigned.
J. S. Corbin	Second Lieut	Aug. 2, 1864	Paris, Linn Co.	

COMPANY C.

J. H. Trego	Captain	Dec. 31, 1863	Linn county...	Resigned.
Theo. F. Wilson ...	Captain	Aug. 2, 1864	Linn county...	
Dennis Gray........	First Lieut...	Dec. 31, 1863	Linn county...	Resigned.
J. J. Calton........	First Lieut...	Aug. 2, 1864	Linn county...	
A. S. Potter	Second Lieut	Dec. 31, 1863	Linn county...	Resigned.
Lyman Strong......	Second Lieut	Aug. 2, 1864	Linn county...	

COMPANY D.

M. McDaniels......	Captain	Dec. 31, 1863		Resigned.
T. L. Wilson	Captain	Aug. 5, 1864		
Elias Snook	First Lieut...	Dec. 31, 1863		Resigned.
W. J. Brewer.......	First Lieut...	Aug. 5, 1864		
A. W. Long.........	Second Lieut	Dec. 31, 1863		Resigned.
John Rice............	Second Lieut	Aug. 5, 1863		

COMPANY E.

T. L. Wilson.........	Captain	Dec. 31, 1863	Linn county....	Resigned.
T. M. Crawford ...	Captain	Aug. 5, 1864	Linn county....	
W. J. Brewer.......	First Lieut...	Dec. 31, 1863	Linn county....	Resigned.
G. H. B. Hopkins..	First Lieut...	Aug. 5, 1864	Linn county....	
A. L. Hills...........	Second Lieut	Dec. 31, 1863	Linn county....	

COMPANY F.

Herbert Robinson	Captain	Dec. 31, 1863		Resigned.
William Lewis	Captain	Aug. 5, 1864		
John H. Belding...	First Lieut...	Dec. 31, 1863		Resigned.
Jeremiah Fanes...	First Lieut...	Sept. 10, 1863		
James P. Way......	Second Lieut	Dec. 31, 1863		

COMPANY G.

David Lindsey.....	Captain	Oct. 31, 1863	Linn county....	Res., June 13, 1864.
Isaac Morris.........	Captain	Dec. 15, 1863	Linn county....	
Robt. P. Stephens.	First Lieut...	Oct. 31, 1863	Linn county....	
Aaron Lamb	Second Lieut	Oct. 31, 1863	Linn county....	Resigned.
Asbury S. Potter..	Second Lieut	Dec. 15, 1863	Linn county....	

COMPANY H.

John F. Clippard.	Captain	Aug. 5, 1864		
B. F. Bradley.......	First Lieut...	Aug. 5, 1864		

COMPANY I.

Wm. Lounsbury...	Captain	Aug. 5, 1864		
Elias Snook	First Lieut...	Aug. 5, 1864		Resigned.
Nathaniel Oats ...	First Lieut...			
T. C. Crague.........	Second Lieut	Aug. 5, 1864		Resigned.
William C. Ryan ..	Second Lieut			

COMPANY K.

Zebadiah W. Lason	Captain	Aug. 5, 1864		
Elias Snook..........	First Lieut...	Aug. 5, 1864		
T. C. Crague	Second Lieut	Aug. 5, 1864		

COMPANY L.

David Lindsey.....	Captain	Oct. 31, 1863		
John H. Belding..	First Lieut...	Oct. 31, 1863		
Aaron Lamb	Second Lieut	Oct. 31, 1863		

26

COMPANY M, SIXTH REGIMENT K. S. M.

Names.	Rank.	Date of Commission.	Residence.	Remarks.
Amos W. Long.....	Captain	Aug. 5, 1864	....	....
Mark T. Phelps ...	First Lieut...	Aug. 5, 1864	....	....
Stephen B. Griffin	Second Lieut	Aug. 5, 1864	....	....

COMPANY N.

C. C. Hadsell	Captain	Aug. 5, 1864	....	....
William Goss........	First Lieut...	Aug. 5, 1864	....	....
A. H. Smith.........	Second Lieut	Aug. 5, 1864	....	....

SEVENTH REGIMENT K. S. M.

Peter McFarland..	Colonel	Dec. 9, 1863	Leavenworth ..	....
R. N. Hershfield...	Lieut. Col.....	Dec. 9, 1863	Leavenworth ..	....
E. L. Stanley........	Major	Dec. 9, 1863	Leavenworth ..	....
Chas. A. Clarke....	Adjutant.......	Dec. 9, 1863	Leavenworth ..	Res., Nov. 2, 1864.

COMPANY A.

T. C. Stevens........	Captain	Dec. 8, 1863	Leavenworth ..	Res., April 28, 1864.
W. C. Higginson...	Captain	July 15, 1864	Leavenworth ..	....
W. L. Easson........	First Lieut...	July 15, 1864	Leavenworth ..	....
W. C. Zentmeyer..	Second Lieut	July 15, 1864	Leavenworth ..	....

COMPANY B.

Kearney Cusick...	Captain	Sept. 22, 1863	Leavenworth ..	Resigned.
W. H. Hays..........	Captain	July 15, 1864	Leavenworth ..	....
Ed. Sherlock	First Lieut...	Sept. 22, 1863	Leavenworth ..	Resigned.
J. B. Ludlum.......	First Lieut...	Sept. 22, 1863	Leavenworth ..	....
John Dugan..........	Second Lieut	Sept. 22, 1863	Leavenworth ..	Resigned.
J. H. Lyon...........	Second Lieut	Sept. 22, 1863	Leavenworth ..	....

COMPANY C.

Smith D. Woods...	Captain	Sept. 22, 1863	Leavenworth ..	Resigned.
T. A. Hurd...........	Captain	July 15, 1864	Leavenworth ..	....
T. A. Hurd...........	First Lieut...	Sept. 22, 1863	Leavenworth ..	Promoted Captain.
S. Hastings.........	First Lieut...	July 15, 1864	Leavenworth ..	....
S. Hastings..........	Second Lieut	Sept. 22, 1863	Leavenworth ..	Promoted First Lieut
G. W. Foster	Second Lieut	July 15, 1864	Leavenworth ..	....

COMPANY D.

Oliver Diefendorf	Captain	Sept. 22, 1863	Leavenworth...	Resigned.
Edward Reilly......	Captain	July 5, 1864	Leavenworth...	....
John B. Ludlum...	First Lieut...	Sept. 22, 1863	Leavenworth...	....
J. H. Lyon...........	Second Lieut	Sept. 22, 1863	Leavenworth...	....

This Company transferred to Nineteenth Regiment, as Company E.

COMPANY E. •

A. C. Harlow........	Captain	Sept. 22, 1863	Leavenworth...	....
J. S. Spear	First Lieut...	Sept. 22, 1863	Leavenworth...	....
Frank Goble........	Second Lieut	Sept. 22, 1863	Leavenworth...	....

COMPANY F.

George Einstein...	Captain	July 5, 1864	Leavenworth...	....
Peter Huesgen.....	First Lieut...	Sept. 22, 1863	Leavenworth...	Resigned.
Morris Kayser......	First Lieut...	July 5, 1864	Leavenworth...	....
N. W. West	Second Lieut	Sept. 22, 1863	Leavenworth...	Resigned.
D. A. Comstock ...	Second Lieut	July 5, 1864	Leavenworth...	....

COMPANY G.

R. H. Kerr...........	Captain	Sept. 22, 1863	Leavenworth...	....
John Kaczynsky..	First Lieut...	Sept. 22, 1863	Leavenworth...	....
Thomas Kyle.......	Second Lieut	Sept. 22, 1863	Leavenworth...	....

COMPANY H, SEVENTH REGIMENT K. S. M.

Names.	Rank.	Date of Commission.	Residence.	Remarks.
Robert Ward	Captain	Sept. 22, 1863	Leavenworth...	Resigned.
Gust. Bayer.........	Captain	July 15, 1864	Leavenworth...	....
B. F. Toombley ...	First Lieut...	Sept. 22, 1863	Leavenworth...	Resigned.
Charles Schiller...	First Lieut...	July 15, 1864	Leavenworth...	....
S. J. McCown.......	Second Lieut	Sept. 22, 1863	Leavenworth...	Resigned.
Louis Brusher......	Second Lieut	July 5, 1864	Leavenworth...	....

COMPANY I.

Crawford Moore...	Captain	Sept. 22, 1863	Leavenworth...	Resigned.
James McCahon...	Captain	July 15, 1864	Leavenworth...	....
James J. Daniels..	First Lieut...	Sept. 22, 1863	Leavenworth...	Resigned.
George S. Smith...	First Lieut...	July 15, 1864	Leavenworth...	....
Richard Gilstrap..	Second Lieut	Sept. 22, 1863	Leavenworth...	Resigned.
A. McFarland......	Second Lieut	July 15, 1864	Leavenworth...	....

COMPANY K.

William Smith......	Captain	Sept. 22, 1863	Leavenworth...	....
Wm. V. French...	First Lieut...	Sept. 22, 1863	Leavenworth...	....
William Hills......	Second Lieut	Sept. 22, 1863	Leavenworth...	....

COMPANY M.

Geo. W. Baird......	Captain	Dec. 8, 1863	Easton............	....
J. J. Robinson.......	First Lieut...	Dec. 8, 1863	Easton............	....
J. C. Baird	Second Lieut	Dec. 8, 1863	Easton............	....

COMPANY N.

James Henderson	Captain	Dec. 8, 1863	Easton............	....
John Thornbury..	First Lieut...	Dec. 8, 1863	Easton............	....
Wm. T. Martin ...	Second.Lieut	Dec. 8, 1863	Easton............	....

COMPANY O.

Transferred to Nineteenth Regiment, as Company G.

COMPANY P.

Transferred to Nineteenth Regiment, as Company B.

COMPANY Q.

Edward Sherlock..	First Lieut...	Dec. 8, 1863	Leavenworth...	....
John Dugan	Second Lieut	Dec. 8, 1863	Leavenworth...	....

COMPANY R.

Ed. S. Menegar.....	Captain	Dec. 8, 1863	Delaware.........	....
Gilbert M. Piper...	First Lieut...	Dec. 8, 1863	Delaware.........	....
Joseph Drees........	Second Lieut	Dec. 8, 1863	Delaware.........	....

EIGHTH REGIMENT K. S. M.

S. N. Wood............	Colonel.........	Nov. 10, 1863	Council Grove	Promoted Brig. Gen.
Wm. S. Smith......	Colonel.........	July 4, 1864	Cot'nw'd Falls	....
W. S. Smith..........	Lieut. Col...	Nov. 10, 1863	Cot'nw'd Falls	Promoted Colonel.
R. B. Lockwood...	Lieut. Col...	July 14, 1864	Council Grove	....
R. B. Lockwood...	Major...........	Nov. 10, 1863	Council Grove	Promoted Lieut. Col.
A. S. Pollard	Major...........	July 14, 1864	Council Grove	....
Thomas White......	Adjutant	Dec. 21, 1863	Council Grove	Deceased.
John H. Scribner	Quar'master	Dec. 21, 1863	Council Grove	....
J. H. Bradford.......	Surgeon	Dec. 21, 1863	Council Grove	....

COMPANY A.

S. N. Wood	Captain	May 20, 1863	Council Grove	Promoted Colonel.
James Cairey.......	Captain	Nov. 14, 1863	Council Grove	....
R. B. Lockwood...	First Lieut...	May 20, 1863	Council Grove	Promoted Major.
James Cairey	First Lieut...	Oct. 1, 1863	Council Grove	Promoted Captain.
Joseph Dunlap.....	First Lieut...	Nov. 14, 1863	Council Grove	....
James Cairey.......	Second Lieut	May 20, 1863	Council Grove	Promoted First Lt.
Theodore Jones...	Second Lieut	Oct. 1, 1863	Council Grove	....

COMPANY B, EIGHTH REGIMENT K. S. M.

Names.	Rank.	Date of Commission.	Residence.	Remarks.
W. S. Smith.........	Captain	Sept. 16, 1862	Cot'nw'd Falls.	Promoted Lieut. Col.
A. S. Howard.......	Captain	Jan. 13, 1864	Cot'nw'd Falls.	
A. S. Howard.......	First Lieut...	Sept. 16, 1863	Cot'nw'd Falls.	Promoted Captain.
H. E. Snyder........	First Lieut...	Jan. 13, 1864	Cot'nw'd Falls.	
H. L. Hunt	Second Lieut	Sept. 16, 1863	Cot'nw'd Falls.	

COMPANY C.

William F. Lard ..	Captain	Sept. 8, 1863	Council Grove.	
James E. Bryan...	First Lieut...	Sept. 8, 1863	Council Grove.	
Jacob A. B. Bear...	Second Lieut	Sept. 8, 1863	Council Grove.	

COMPANY D.

Charles Gunter....	Captain	Sept. 22, 1863	Clark's Creek..	
Henry Baxter......	First Lieut...	Sept. 22, 1863	Clark's Creek..	
Cartney Holmes...	Second Lieut	Sept. 22, 1863	Clark's Creek..	

COMPANY E.

S. D. Price............	Captain	Sept. 22, 1863	Neosho Falls...	
T. J. Lambert.......	First Lieut...	Sept. 22, 1863	Neosho Falls...	
M. Clay................	Second Lieut	Sept. 22, 1863	Neosho Falls...	

COMPANY F.

H. H. Doolittle.....	Captain	Nov. 11, 1863	Cot'nw'd Falls.	Resigned.
Geo. W. Williams.	Captain	Mar. 17, 1864	Cot'nw'd Falls.	
O. H. Drinkwater.	First Lieut...	Nov. 11, 1863	Cot'nw'd Falls.	Resigned.
M. R. Leonard......	First Lieut...	Nov. 25, 1863	Cot'nw'd Falls.	
Asa Taylor...........	Second Lieut	Nov. 11, 1863	Cot'nw'd Falls.	

COMPANY G.

G. F. Donaldson...	Captain	Sept. 28, 1863	Chelsea............	
John Spencer	First Lieut...	Sept. 28, 1863	Chelsea	
D. Llewellyn........	Second Lieut	Sept. 28, 1863	Chelsea............	

NINTH REGIMENT K. S. M.

Frank M. Tracy...	Colonel	Feb. 17, 1864	Doniphan	
Sylvest. Bonesteel	Lieut. Col...	Feb. 17, 1864	Highland........	
Lewis Tracy	Major	Feb. 17, 1864	Elwood	
A. Saxey..............	Adjutant.......	Feb. 17, 1864	Troy...............	
A. J. Miner	Quar'master.	Feb. 17, 1864	Troy...............	
N. Harrington	Surgeon........	Feb. 17, 1864	Troy...............	

COMPANY A.

G. W. Barr...........	Captain	Oct. 17, 1863	Elwood	
T. A. Hays...........	First Lieut...	Oct. 17, 1863	Elwood	
Lewis Tracy	Second Lieut	Oct. 17, 1863	Elwood	Promoted Major.

COMPANY B.

S. Bonesteel.........	Captain	Sept. 19, 1863	Highland........	Promoted Lieut. Col.
John Dillon.........	Captain	Feb. 17, 1864	Highland........	
John Dillon.........	First Lieut...	Sept. 19, 1863	Highland........	Promoted Captain.
James Williams...	First Lieut...	Feb. 17, 1864	Highland........	
Jesse W. Jones......	Second Lieut	Sept. 19, 1863	Highland........	

COMPANY C.

Frank M. Fracy ..	Captain	June 20, 1863	Doniphan........	Promoted Colonel.
Robert J. Wynn...	Captain	Feb. 17, 1864	Doniphan........	
Robert J. Wynn...	First Lieut...	June 20, 1863	Doniphan........	Promoted Captain.
Cyrus C. Camp....	First Lieut...	Feb. 17, 1864	Doniphan........	
A. A. Gardner	Second Lieut	June 20, 1863	Doniphan........	Removed from Dist.
J. R. Plummer......	Second Lieut	Feb. 17, 1864	Doniphan........	

COMPANY D, NINTH REGIMENT K. S. M.

Names.	Rank.	Date of Commission.	Residence.	Remarks.
James Wake.........	Captain	Sept. 19, 1863	Wathena.........	Resigned.
Benj. Harding......	Captain	Apr. 13, 1864	Wathena.........	
Abrah'm Johnson	First Lieut...	Sept. 19, 1863	Wathena.........	Resigned.
Augustus Miller...	First Lieut...	Apr. 13, 1864	Wathena.........	
Young Guthery ...	Second Lieut	Sept. 22, 1863	Wathena.........	Resigned.
J. O. Larzelere......	Second Lieut	Apr. 13, 1864	Wathena.........	

COMPANY E.

F. W. Ledington...	Captain	Sept. 22, 1863	Doniphan.........	Resigned.
Elijah Fleming....	Captain	Aug. 5, 1864	Doniphan.........	
A. B. Symms........	First Lieut...	Sept. 22, 1863	Doniphan.........	Resigned.
C. Nahnung.........	First Lieut...	Aug. 5, 1864	Doniphan.........	
N. S. Sprowls	Second Lieut	Sept. 22, 1863	Doniphan.........	Resigned.
Daniel Jacks........	Second Lieut	Aug. 5, 1864	Doniphan.........	

COMPANY F.

A. S. Addis...........	Captain	Sept. 22, 1863	Doniphan.........	
Arthur Larkin....	First Lieut...	Sept. 22, 1863	Doniphan.........	
H. N. Short	Second Lieut	Sept. 22, 1863	Doniphan.........	

COMPANY G.

S. Anderson.........	Captain	Oct. 12, 1863	Palermo.........	
P. Grady.............	First Lieut...	Oct. 12, 1863	Palermo.........	
R. Myers.............	Second Lieut	Oct. 12, 1863	Palermo.........	

COMPANY H.

William Orem.......	Captain	Dec. 8, 1863	Syracuse	
James H. Long.....	First Lieut...	Dec. 8, 1863	Syracuse	
Patrick Kirwin.....	Second Lieut	Dec. 8, 1863	Syracuse	

COMPANY I.

J. T. Lane.............	Captain	Dec. 8, 1863	Iowa Point......	Resigned.
James M. Powell..	Captain	July 18, 1864	Iowa Point......	
W. H. Nesbitt......	First Lieut...	Dec. 8, 1863	Iowa Point......	Resigned.
A. H. Acton.........	First Lieut...	July 18, 1864	Iowa Point......	
C. W. McCoy........	Second Lieut	Dec. 8, 1863	Iowa Point......	Resigned.
Fred. Breckholter	Second Lieut	July 18, 1864	Iowa Point......	

COMPANY K.

C. W. Noyes	Captain	Dec. 8, 1863	White Cloud...	
H. F. Macy..........	First Lieut...	Dec. 8, 1863	White Cloud...	
Allen Hollencraft	Second Lieut	Dec. 8, 1863	White Cloud...	

COMPANY L.

Albert Perry........	Captain	July 1, 1864	Troy	
Joseph Hayton.....	First Lieut...	July 1, 1864	Troy.............	
J. L. Zimmerman.	Second Lieut	July 1, 1864	Troy.............	

COMPANY M.

James M. Tracy....	Captain	Oct. 19, 1864	Elwood...........	
D. B. Jones..........	First Lieut...	Oct. 19, 1864	Elwood...........	
Archibald Craig....	Second Lieut	Oct. 19, 1864	Elwood...........	

TENTH REGIMENT K. S. M.

William Pennock	Colonel.........	Nov. 18, 1863	Centropolis......	
Miles Morris........	Lieut. Col....	Nov. 18, 1863	Garnett	
A. Wiley.............	Major.........	Nov. 18, 1863	Garnett	
J. K. Goodin	Adjutant......	Dec. 1, 1863	Minneola.........	Pro. Captain Co. A.
Irwin C. Hughes ..	Quar'master	Dec. 1, 1863	Minneola	
M. F. Holaday......	Surgeon	Oct. 10, 1864	Lane.............	

COMPANY A, TENTH REGIMENT K. S. M.

Names.	Rank.	Date of Commission.	Residence.	Remarks.
William Pennock	Captain	Sept. 10, 1863	Centropolis	Promoted Colonel.
J. K. Goodin	Captain	Dec. 10, 1863	Minneola	Commis'n revoked.
James Harris	Captain	Dec. 8, 1863	Centropolis	Commis'n revoked.
W. S. Delano	Captain	Feb. 11, 1864		Entered U. S. service.
James W. Jane	Captain	June 7, 1864	Minneola	
James Harris	First Lieut	Sept. 10, 1864	Centropolis	Promoted Captain.
Charles Clark	First Lieut	Feb. 11, 1864		
W. S. Delano	Second Lieut	Sept. 10, 1683		Promoted Captain.
John Clark	Second Lieut	Mar. 14, 1864		

COMPANY B.

Miles Morris	Captain	Sept. 19, 1863	Garnett	Pro. Lieut. Colonel.
George W. Iler	Captain	Dec. 24, 1863	Garnett	
A. W. Jones	First Lieut	Sept. 19, 1863	Garnett	Resigned.
James Reynolds	First Lieut	May 16, 1864	Garnett	
Junius Reynolds	Second Lieut	Sept. 19, 1864	Garnett	Pro. First Lieut.
H. Cavender	Second Lieut	May 16, 1864	Garnett	

COMPANY C.

R. E. Jenness	Captain	Sept. 19, 1863	Peoria	
W. D. Springer	First Lieut	Sept. 19, 1863	Peoria	
G. B. Davidson	Second Lieut	Sept. 19, 1863	Peoria	

COMPANY D.

William Benton	Captain	Sept. 19, 1863	Peoria	
Anders'n Johnson	First Lieut	Sept. 19, 1863	Peoria	
S. Wheatly	Second Lieut	Sept. 19, 1863	Peoria	

COMPANY E.

Hardy Warren	Captain	Sept. 24, 1863	Mt. Gilead	
Harrison Lowrey	First Lieut	Sept. 24, 1863	Mt. Gilead	
John Fox	Second Lieut	Sept. 24, 1863	Mt. Gilead	

COMPANY F.

Milton Pettibone	Captain	Oct. 2, 1863	Ottawa	
Thomas Taylor	First Lieut	Oct. 2, 1863	Ottawa	
A. Rankin	Second Lieut	Oct. 2, 1863	Ottawa	

COMPANY G.

Mars Burrell	Captain	Oct. 12, 1863	Ohio City	
John W. Gannon	First Lieut	Oct. 12, 1863	Ohio City	
John Walruff	Second Lieut	Oct. 12, 1863	Ohio City	

COMPANY H.

S. H. Case	Captain	Oct. 28, 1863	Anderson Co	Removed from Dist.
J. A. Cunningham	Captain	Sept. 3, 1864	Berea	
John N. Bronell	First Lieut	Oct. 28, 1863		
D. W. Hoover	Second Lieut	Oct. 28, 1863		

COMPANY I.

Jas. McLaughlin	Captain	Nov. 10, 1863	Garnett	
Henry Fenerborn	First Lieut	Nov. 10, 1863	Garnett	Removed from Dist.
David Wright	First Lieut	June 27, 1864	Garnett	
James S. Smith	Second Lieut	Nov. 10, 1863	Garnett	

COMPANY K.

James B. Loury	Captain	Dec. 12, 1863	Reeder P. O	
David S. Easton	First Lieut	Dec. 12, 1863	Reeder P. O	Resigned.
Samuel Patton	First Lieut	July 22, 1864	Mineral Point	
W. H. Hooper	Second Lieut	Dec. 12, 1863	Reeder P. O	

COMPANY L, TENTH REGIMENT K. S. M.

Names.	Rank.	Date of Commission.	Residence.	Remarks.
W. H. H. Loury...	Captain	July 14, 1864	Ottawa	Resigned.
Edward Smith......	First Lieut...	July 14, 1864	Ottawa	
F. F. Johnson......	Second Lieut	July 14, 1864	Ottawa	Resigned.

ELEVENTH REGIMENT K. S. M.

A. J. Mitchell......	Colonel.........	Oct. 28, 1863	Emporia	
J. C. Bunch	Lieut. Col...	Oct. 28, 1863	Emporia	Resigned.
R. H. Abraham....	Major.........	Oct. 28, 1863	Emporia	
J. Stotler.............	Adjutant	Oct. 28, 1863	Emporia	
N. S. Storrs	Quar'master	May 30, 1864	Emporia	
J. A. Moore...........	Surgeon	April 18, 1864	Emporia	

COMPANY A.

A. R. Bancroft	Captain	Sept. 10, 1863	Emporia	
G. D. Humphrey...	First Lieut...	Sept. 10, 1863	Emporia	
J. D. Gilchrist......	Second Lieut	Sept. 10, 1863	Emporia	Resigned.
G. W. Frederick...	Second Lieut	Aug. 5, 1864	Emporia	

COMPANY B.

Malcolm Campbell	Captain	Sept. 26, 1863	Plymouth	
A. J. Reeves	First Lieut...	Sept. 26, 1863	Plymouth	
David McCool......	Second Lieut	Sept. 26, 1863	Plymouth	

COMPANY C.

Alfred B. Elliott ..	Captain	Sept. 26, 1863	Fremont.........	
J. W. Loy.............	Second Lieut	Sept. 26, 1863	Fremont.........	

COMPANY D.

J. C. Hill.............	Captain	Sept. 29, 1863	Americus........	
J. H. White.........	First Lieut...	Sept. 29, 1863	Americus........	
Joseph Kempton..	Second Lieut	Sept. 29, 1863	Americus........	

COMPANY E.

Transferred to Santa Fe Battalion.

COMPANY F.

P. H. Hunt...........	Captain	May 16, 1864	Emporia	
Ed. Borton...........	First Lieut...	May 16. 1864	Emporia	
M. B. Jacobs........	Second Lieut	May 16, 1864	Emporia	

COMPANY G.

Wm. E. McGinnis	Captain	Sept. 8, 1864	Hartford.........	
Wm. K. Maybury.	First Lieut...	Sept. 8, 1864	Hartford.........	
G. Griffith.............	Second Lieut	Sept. 8, 1864	Hartford.........	

TWELFTH REGIMENT K. S. M.

L. S. Treat...........	Colonel.........	Dec. 12, 1863	Atchison.........	
S. O. Hilton.........	Lieut. Col...	Dec. 12, 1863	Atchison.........	
J. C. Batsell.........	Major.........	Dec. 12, 1863	Atchison.........	Resigned.
Geo. H. Hawkins.	Adjutant	Jan. 30, 1864	Monrovia........	Resigned.
G. M. Woodworth.	Adjutant	Aug. 29, 1864	Monrovia........	
Junius F. Brown..	Quar'master	Jan. 30, 1864	Atchison.........	
Chas. Williamson..	Surgeon	July 8, 1864	Atchison.........	

COMPANY A.

Asa Barnes	Captain	Sept. 17, 1863	Mt. Pleasant...	
G. W. Thompson..	First Lieut...	Jan. 20, 1864	Mt. Pleasant...	
J. Maxwell...........	Second Lieut	Jan. 20, 1864	Mt. Pleasant...	

COMPANY B.

Sam'l M. Bowman	Captain	Sept. 18, 1863	Kickapoo	Resigned.
Sam'l L. Hollister	Captain	Dec. 7, 1863	Kickapoo	
Ferdin'd Jaedicke	First Lieut...	Sept. 18, 1863	W. Creek	Resigned.
Wm. H. Cook	First Lieut...	Sept. 3, 1864	W. Creek	
Fred. Christy.......	Second Lieut	Sept. 18, 1863	W. Creek	Resigned.
Wm. J. Bailey......	Second Lieut	Sept. 3, 1864	W. Creek	

COMPANY C, TWELFTH REGIMENT K. S. M.

Names.	Rank.	Date of Commission.	Residence.	Remarks.
Geo. J. Weaver.....	Captain	May 26, 1864	Atchison..........	....
Geo. J. Weaver.....	First Lieut...	Sept. 18, 1863	Atchison..........	Promoted Captain.
Henry F. Smith...	First Lieut...	May 26, 1864	Atchison..........	....
Henry F. Smith...	Second Lieut	May 18, 1863	Atchison..........	Promoted First Lt.
Jas. W. Truesdale	Second Lieut	May 26, 1864	Atchison..........	....

COMPANY D.

Hezekiah J. Crist.	Captain	Jan. 27, 1864	Huron	....
Sam. H. Cozard....	First Lieut...	Oct. 22, 1863	Monrovia	....
Eli Watson	First Lieut...	Jan. 27, 1864	Huron	....
Hezekiah J. Crist.	Second Lieut	Oct. 23, 1863	Monrovia	Promoted Captain.
G. M. Fuller........	Second Lieut	Jan. 27, 1864	Monrovia	Removed from Dist.
Wm. H. Sidner.....	Second Lieut	May 19, 1864	Huron	....

COMPANY E.

Robert White......	Captain	Oct. 3, 1863	Eden	....
John English	First Lieut...	Oct. 3, 1863	Eden	....
Milton F. Steeter..	Second Lieut	Oct. 3, 1863	Eden	....

COMPANY F.

A. S. Best	Captain	Nov. 5, 1863	Monrovia........	....
Benj. Walleck......	First Lieut...	Nov. 5, 1863	Monrovia........	Removed.
Henry Widner.....	First Lieut...	June 9, 1864	Monrovia........	Resigned.
John N. Holliday.	First Lieut...	Aug. 22, 1864	Monrovia........	....
Geo. W. Hawkins.	Second Lieut	Aug. 5, 1864	Monrovia........	Promoted Adjutant.
John Graves	Second Lieut	June 9, 1864	Monrovia........	....

COMPANY G.

William M. Ham..	Captain	Nov. 23, 1863	Kennekuk	Resigned.
Martin C. Willis...	Captain	May 18, 1864	Atchison Co....	....
Wm. P. Badger....	First Lieut...	Nov. 23, 1863	Atchison Co....	Resigned.
William M. Ham..	First Lieut...	Oct. 10, 1864	Atchison Co....	....
T. W. Carter........	Second Lieut	Nov. 23, 1863	Atchison Co....	....

COMPANY H.

A. J. Evans..........	Captain	Dec. 7, 1863	Atchison Co....	....
L. A. Wait	First Lieut...	Dec. 7, 1863	Atchison Co....	Resigned.
Orren D. Haskell.	First Lieut...	Oct. 6, 1864	Atchison Co....	....
J. R. Underwood..	Second Lieut	Dec. 7, 1863	Atchison Co....	....

COMPANY K.

William Jackson..	Captain	Dec. 7, 1863	Atchison Co....	....
G. L. Gove	First Lieut...	Dec. 7, 1863	Atchison Co....	....
Julius Newman...	Second Lieut	Dec. 7, 1863	Atchison Co....	....

THIRTEENTH REGIMENT K. S. M.

Julius A. Keeler...	Colonel	Oct. 13, 1863	Johnson Co.....	....
Alex. S. Johnson..	Lieut. Col.....	Oct. 13, 1863	Johnson Co.....	....
J. Nicholson.........	Major	Oct. 13, 1863	Johnson Co.....	....
W. A. Ocheltree...	Adjutant......	Oct. 13, 1863	Johnson Co.....	Resigned.
William Roy........	Adjutant......	Oct. 13, 1863	Johnson Co.....	....
Benj. B. Francis...	Quar'master.	Oct. 13, 1863	Johnson Co.....	....
W. D. Bull	Surgeon	Oct. 13, 1863	Johnson Co.....	....

COMPANY A.

Geo. F. Warnick...	Captain	Oct. 13, 1863	Lexington	....
John Johnson......	Captain	Oct. 8, 1864	DeSoto...........	....
J. R. Baldwin......	First Lieut...	Oct. 13, 1863	Lexington	....
J. D. Baird...........	First Lieut...	Oct. 8, 1864	....	....
G. W. Train.........	Second Lieut	Oct. 13, 1863	Lexington	....
Jonath'n Dowdle..	Second Lieut	Oct. 8, 1864	DeSoto...........	....

COMPANY B.

Jos. H. Gamble ...	Captain	Sept. 19, 1863	Westport	....
J. A. Pemberton..	First Lieut...	Sept. 19, 1863	Westport	....
A. Waldsmith......	Second Lieut	Sept. 19, 1863	Westport	....

COMPANY C, THIRTEENTH REGIMENT K. S. M.

Names.	Rank.	Date of Commission.	Residence.	Remarks.
J. C. Stuck..........	Captain	Oct. 13, 1863	Monticello	....
Samuel Garrett....	First Lieut....	Oct. 13, 1863	Monticello	....
A. Robards	Second Lieut	Oct. 13, 1863	Monticello	Resigned.
Wm. B. Cortin	Second Lieut	May 13, 1864	Monticello	....

COMPANY D.

A. S. Johnson.......	Captain	Sept. 19, 1863	Eastport	....
T. C. Porter........	First Lieut....	Sept. 19, 1863	Eastport	....
P. G. Cross...........	Second Lieut	Sept. 19, 1863	Eastport	....

COMPANY E.

Samuel McGinnis.	Captain	Sept. 19, 1863	Olathe	....
John James.........	First Lieut....	Sept. 19, 1863	Olathe	....
William Henry ...	Second Lieut	Sept. 19, 1863	Olathe	....

COMPANY F.

H. M. Dresher......	Captain	Nov. 20, 1863	McCamish......	....
David Martin......	Captain	Sept. 12, 1863	Lanesfield	....
S. K. Wilbite........	First Lieut....	Nov. 20, 1863	....	....
H. L. Ward	Second Lieut	Nov. 20, 1863	....	....

COMPANY G.

E. Davis	Captain	Oct. 13, 1864	Gardner	....
John Kizer..........	First Lieut....	Oct. 13, 1864	Gardner	....
John Bradbury....	Second Lieut	Oct. 13, 1864	Gardner	....

COMPANY H.

Wm. Waterhouse.	Captain	Oct. 13, 1863	Aubrey	....
Franklin Trekell.	First Lieut....	Oct. 13, 1863	Aubrey	Resigned.
Thos. Dougherty..	Second Lieut	Oct. 13, 1863	Aubrey	....

COMPANY I.

Thos. A. Parker...	Captain	Oct. 13, 1863	Spring Hill......	....
John Mosier	First Lieut....	Oct. 13, 1863	Spring Hill......	....
J. M. Galaway......	Second Lieut	Oct. 13, 1863	Spring Hill......	....

FOURTEENTH REGIMENT K. S. M.

D. W. Scott	Colonel..........	Nov. 9, 1863	Ogden	Resigned.
Jas. M. Harvey ...	Colonel..........	Oct. 19, 1864	Ogden	....
E. L. Patee..........	Lieut. Col.....	Oct. 9, 1863	Manhattan	Resigned.
Frank Mansfield..	Lieut. Col.....	Jan. 27, 1864	Manhattan	....
T. S. St. John.......	Major..........	Nov. 9, 1863	Zeandale..........	....
Joseph Carney.....	Adjutant	Nov. 24, 1864	Manhattan	....
Ephraim Warner.	Quar'master.	Nov. 24, 1864	Ogden	....
O. E. Dickenson...	Surgeon	Nov. 24, 1864	Manhattan	....

COMPANY A.

A. Todd..............	Captain	Jan. 27, 1864	Manhattan	....
Ambrose Todd.....	First Lieut....	Sept. 10, 1863	Manhattan	Promoted Captain.
A. Dodge.............	First Lieut....	Feb. 22, 1864	Manhattan	....
E. B. Sneyth	Second Lieut	Sept. 10, 1863	Manhattan	Resigned.
Asaph Browning..	Second Lieut	May 14, 1864	Manhattan	Resigned.
Geo. B. Brown	Second Lieut	Sept. 10, 1864	Manhattan	....

COMPANY B.

Martin Mauerhan	Captain	Sept. 16, 1863	Manhattan	....
John Fleming	First Lieut....	Sept. 16, 1863	Manhattan	Removed from Dist.
Geo. W. Wisner....	First Lieut....	July 14, 1864	Manhattan	....
Geo. W. Wisner...	Second Lieut	Feb. 4, 1864	Manhattan	Promoted First Lieut
Samuel Jack	Second Lieut	July 14, 1864	Manhattan	....

COMPANY C.

Chauncey Noyes..	Captain	Oct. 2, 1863	Wabaunsee	....
William Mitchell..	First Lieut....	Oct. 2, 1863	Wabaunsee	Promoted to Staff.
Geo. S. Burt........	First Lieut....	Mar. 14, 1864	Wabaunsee	....
Geo. S. Burt.........	Second Lieut	Oct. 2, 1863	Wabaunsee	Promoted First Lieut
Walter S. Griswold	Second Lieut	Mar. 14, 1864	Wabaunsee	....

COMPANY D, FOURTEENTH REGIMENT K. S. M.

Names.	Rank.	Date of Commission.	Residence.	Remarks.
Edward Knapp ...	Captain	Oct. 10, 1863	Wabaunsee	....
Joseph True	First Lieut...	Oct. 10, 1863	Wabaunsee	....
William Lange.....	Second Lieut	Oct. 10, 1863	Wabaunsee	....

COMPANY E.

F. N. Saus	Captain	Oct. 21, 1863	Westmoreland	Resigned.
Sargent Moody ...	Captain	July 11, 1864	Westmoreland	....
J. S. Betts............	First Lieut...	Oct. 21, 1863	Westmoreland	....
F. Blockskey.......	Second Lieut	Oct. 21, 1863	Westmoreland	....

COMPANY F.

John H. Curtis.....	Captain	Nov. 30, 1863	Ogden	....
J. M. Myres.........	First Lieut...	Dec. 30, 1864	Ogden	....
C. M. Dyche	Second Lieut	Dec. 7, 1864	Ogden	....

COMPANY G.

L. W. Craub	Captain	Oct. 31, 1863	St. George........	....
J. N. Linbocker...	Captain	May 26, 1864	Louisville.........	....
J. N. Linbocker...	First Lieut...	Oct. 31, 1863	St. George........	Promoted Captain.
J. H. Clark..........	First Lieut...	May 26, 1864	Louisville.........	....
John H. Clark	Second Lieut	Oct. 31, 1863	Louisville.........	Promoted First Lieut
F. J. Crawford	Second Lieut	May 26, 1864	Louisville.........	....

COMPANY H.

C. W. Knapp	Captain	Nov. 4, 1863	Wild Cat.........	....
D. C. Pierce.........	First Lieut...	Nov. 4, 1863	Riley county:..	....
B. H. Fuller..........	Second Lieut	Nov. 4, 1863	Riley county...	....

COMPANY I.

Mincher Coudray.	Captain	Mar. 26, 1864	Shawnee Tp....	....
Mincher Coudray.	First Lieut...	Nov. 9, 1863	Shawnee Tp....	Promoted Captain.
S. M. Wilhite	First Lieut...	May 16, 1864	Manhattan	....
John Dial.............	Second Lieut	Nov. 9, 1863	Shawnee Tp....	....

COMPANY K.

C. P. McDonald ...	Captain	July 14, 1864	Zeandale.........	....
C. P. McDonald ...	First Lieut...	Dec. 9, 1863	Wabaunsee Co.	Promoted Captain.
W. F. Smith	First Lieut...	July 14, 1864	Wabaunsee Co.	....
W. F. Smith	Second Lieut	Dec. 9, 1863	Wabaunsee Co.	Promoted First Lieut

COMPANY L.

Charles Webber...	First Lieut...	Dec. 9, 1863	Mill Creek	....
William Horn	Second Lieut	Dec. 9, 1863	Wabaunsee Co.	....

FIFTEENTH REGIMENT K. S. M.

John T. Price......	Colonel	Nov. 4, 1863	Junction City..	....
William Gordon ..	Lieut. Col	Nov. 4, 1863	Junction City..	....
Wm. S. Blakely ...	Major	Nov. 4, 1863	Junction City..	....
R. E. Laurenson ..	Adjutant......	Nov. 17, 1863	Junction City..	....
P. Z. Taylor.........	Quar'master	Nov. 17, 1863	Junction City..	....
E. W. Seymour.....	Surgeon	Nov. 17, 1863	Junction City..	....

COMPANY A.

A. W. Callen	Captain	Oct. 31, 1863	Junction City..	....
J. F. Schmidt	First Lieut...	Nov. 24, 1863	Junction City..	....
John Gross..........	Second Lieut	Feb. 15, 1864	Junction City..	....

COMPANY B.

George Ware........	Captain	Oct. 31, 1863	Junction City..	....
Wm. Mullhayen...	First Lieut...	Oct. 31, 1863	Junction City..	....
J. Fred. Staats	Second Lieut	Oct. 31, 1863	Junction City..	....

COMPANY C, FIFTEENTH REGIMENT K. S. M.

Names.	Rank.	Date of Commission.	Residence.	Remarks.
Moses Younkin...	Captain	Oct. 31, 1861	Gatesville........	En. in U. S. service.
Marshall Barry ...	Captain	May 20, 1864	....	....
Maxwell Saunders	First Lieut...	Oct. 31, 1863	Gatesville........	Removed to Ky.
S. D. Kirby	First Lieut...	May 20, 1864	Gatesville........	....
Lewis Laftice	Second Lieut	Oct. 31, 1863	Gatesville........	En. in U. S. service.
D. H. Meyers	Second Lieut	May 20, 1864	Gatesville........	....

COMPANY D.

Names.	Rank.	Date of Commission.	Residence.	Remarks.
C. H. Thompson....	Captain	Nov. 4, 1863	Dickins'n Co....	....
John Irwin..........	First Lieut...	Nov. 4, 1863	Dickins'n Co....	....
Samuel Richards..	Second Lieut	Nov. 4, 1863	Dickins'n Co....	....

COMPANY E.

Names.	Rank.	Date of Commission.	Residence.	Remarks.
David Church......	Captain	Jan. 12, 1864	Junction City..	....
David Church......	First Lieut...	Jan. 9, 1864	Junction City..	Promoted Captain.
Charles Salcheo...	First Lieut...	Jan. 12, 1864	Junction City..	....
Samuel Orr..........	Second Lieut	Jan. 9, 1864	Junction City..	....

COMPANY F.

Names.	Rank.	Date of Commission.	Residence.	Remarks.
George A. Taylor.	Captain	Nov. 24, 1863	Kenton	....
P. Z. Taylor.........	First Lieut...	Nov. 24, 1863	Junction City..	Promoted Quar'm'r.
R. D. Mobley.......	First Lieut...	Feb. 17, 1864	Junction City..	....
James H. Brown...	Second Lieut	Nov. 24, 1863	Kenton	....

COMPANY G.

Names.	Rank.	Date of Commission.	Residence.	Remarks.
H. L. Jones..........	Captain	Nov. 24, 1863	Salina	....
C. Harver...........	First Lieut...	Nov. 24, 1863	Salina	....
Timothy Rioridan	Second Lieut	Nov. 24, 1863	Salina	....

COMPANY H.

Names.	Rank.	Date of Commission.	Residence.	Remarks.
Charles Briggs	First Lieut...	Nov. 30, 1863	Ashland..........	....
W. B. Mead..........	Second Lieut	Nov. 30, 1863	Ashland..........	....

COMPANY I.

Names.	Rank.	Date of Commission.	Residence.	Remarks.
A. H. Rose...........	Captain	June 8, 1864	Solomon City...	....
E. Schaltenbrund.	First Lieut...	June 8, 1864	Solomon City...	....
And. J. Ingersoll..	Second Lieut	June 8, 1864	Solomon City...	....

SIXTEENTH REGIMENT K. S. M.

Names.	Rank.	Date of Commission.	Residence.	Remarks.
F. W. Potter.........	Colonel.........	Dec. 24, 1863	Burlington......	....
A. S. Goss............	Lieut. Col.....	Dec. 24, 1863	Neosho Falls...	....
Wm. B. Perry......	Major..........	Dec. 24, 1863	Le Roy...........	....
S. C. Jenkins.......	Adjutant.......	Dec. 24, 1863	Le Roy...........	....
Orson Kent.........	Quar'master	Dec. 24, 1863	Burlington......	....
W. Manson..........	Surgeon	Dec. 24, 1863	Le Roy...........	....

COMPANY A.

Names.	Rank.	Date of Commission.	Residence.	Remarks.
Joseph Jenks.......	Captain	Oct. 12, 1863	Ottumwa	....
D. H. Houtt.........	First Lieut...	Oct. 12, 1863	Ottumwa	....
N. C. Terrill........	Second Lieut	Oct. 12, 1863	Ottumwa	....

COMPANY B.

Names.	Rank.	Date of Commission.	Residence.	Remarks.
F. W. Potter	Captain	Oct. 3, 1863	Burlington......	Promoted Colonel.
A. A. Burr...........	Captain	Dec. 24, 1863	Burlington......	....
A. A. Burr...........	First Lieut...	Oct. 12, 1863	Burlington......	Promoted Captain.
George Gisey.......	First Lieut...	Dec. 24, 1863	Burlington......	....
Theodore O'Leary	Second Lieut	Oct. 3, 1863	Burlington......	....

COMPANY C, SIXTEENTH REGIMENT K. S. M.

Names.	Rank.	Date of Commission.	Residence.	Remarks.
Curtis Phillips......	Captain	Oct. 12, 1863	Le Roy............	....
John A. Robinson	First Lieut...	Oct. 12, 1863	Le Roy............	....
Wm. B. Perry......	Second Lieut	Oct. 12, 1863	Le Roy............	....

COMPANY D.

James A. Stewart.	Captain	Oct. 12, 1863	Le Roy............	....
Payton Casner......	First Lieut...	Oct. 12, 1863	Le Roy............	....
Asa Whitney........	Second Lieut	Oct. 12, 1863	Le Roy............	....

COMPANY E.

Mark McLeese	Captain	Oct. 28, 1863	Ottumwa	....
J. S. Harrell........	First Lieut...	Oct. 28, 1863	Ottumwa	....
Joseph Leabo........	Second Lieut	Oct. 28, 1863	Ottumwa	....

COMPANY F.

Wm. W. Brazell...	Captain	Oct. 28, 1863	Greenwood	....
Oscar Coy............	First Lieut...	Oct. 28, 1863	Pleasant Gr've	....
John Estess........	Second Lieut	Oct. 28, 1863	Pleasant Gr've	....

COMPANY G.

Joseph H. Gunby.	Captain	Oct. 28, 1863	Belmont..........	Resigned.
James E. Walkins	First Lieut...	Oct. 28, 1863	Belmont..........	....
Robt. N. Daniels...	Second Lieut	Oct. 28, 1863	Belmont..........	....

COMPANY H.

B. R. Smith..........	Captain	Dec. 12, 1863	Neosho Falls...	....
Owen Deveny......	First Lieut...	Oct. 28, 1863	Neosho Falls...	....
B. R. Smith..........	Second Lieut	Oct. 28, 1863	Neosho Falls...	Promoted Captain.
G. L. Wait...........	Second Lieut	Oct. 28, 1863	Neosho Falls...	Resigned.
Nathan Keller	Second Lieut	Oct. 14, 1864	Neosho Falls...	....

COMPANY I.

John Douglas	Captain	Nov. 2, 1863	Le Roy	....
Samuel J. Carter..	First Lieut...	Nov. 2, 1863	Le Roy	....
Warren Crandal...	Second Lieut	Nov. 2, 1863	Le Roy	....

COMPANY K.

Charles Puffer......	Captain	Nov. 2, 1863	Burlington......	....
J. Throckmorton..	First Lieut...	Nov. 2, 1863	Burlington......	....
Thomas Ormald...	Second Lieut	Nov. 2, 1863	Burlington......	....

COMPANY L.

A. Williams........	Captain	Dec. 11, 1863	Eureka	....
H. J. Cantrell......	First Lieut...	Dec. 11, 1863	Eureka	....
T. J. Jones............	Second Lieut	Dec. 11, 1863	Eureka	....

COMPANY M.

John Duncan	Captain	Dec. 11, 1863	Shell Rock......	....
Chas. H. Norton...	First Lieut...	Dec. 11, 1863	Shell Rock......	....
Wm. W. Duncan...	Second Lieut	Dec. 11, 1863	Shell Rock......	....

SEVENTEENTH REGIMENT K. S. M.

E. C. Manning	Colonel	Nov. 14, 1863	Marysville	....
H. G. Hollenburg.	Lieut. Col....	Nov. 14, 1863	Washington	....
John D. Wells......	Major...........	Nov. 14, 1863	Washington	....
J. D. Brumbaugh..	Adjutant......	Nov. 14, 1863	Marysville	....
E. Putney............	Quar'master	Nov. 14, 1863	Nottingham	....
C. J. Lee	Surgeon	Nov. 14, 1863	Marysville	....

COMPANY A, SEVENTEENTH REGIMENT K. S. M.

Names.	Rank.	Date of Commission.	Residence.	Remarks.
William Henry....	Captain	Nov. 27, 1863	Marysville	....
Wm. McClosky.....	First Lieut...	Feb. 22, 1864	Marysville	....
Henry Ogle.........	Second Lieut	Oct. 31, 1863	Marysville	....

COMPANY B.

Andrew D. Lane ..	Captain	Nov. 14, 1863	Irving	
Theodore S. Vaile.	Captain	Aug. 13, 1864	Irving	
Wm. A. McLain...	First Lieut...	Nov. 14, 1863	Irving	
Thomas Baker......	Second Lieut	Nov. 14, 1863	Irving	
Sidney H. Warren	Second Lieut	Aug. 13, 1864	Irving	

COMPANY C.

Isaac M. Schooley.	Captain	Dec. 2, 1863	Clifton	
Jas. M. Hagaman.	First Lieut...	Dec. 2, 1863	Clifton	
Samuel C. Chester	Second Lieut	Dec. 2, 1863	Clifton............	

COMPANY D.

J. McNulty...........	Captain	May 24, 1864	Washington......	Removed from Dist.
A. S. Vaught.........	Captain	June 28, 1864	Washington......	....
Henry Clark........	First Lieut...	June 9, 1864	Washington......	....
Joel Snyder..........	Second Lieut	June 9, 1864	Washington......	....

COMPANY E.

James Kelley.......	Captain	Dec. 14, 1864	Nottingham	....
Robert Morrison..	First Lieut...	Dec. 14, 1864	Nottingham	....
John D. Wilson.....	Second Lieut	May 24, 1864	Nottingham ,...	....

COMPANY F.

Frank Schmidt.....	Captain	May 24, 1864	Marysville	....
R. Y. Shubley......	First Lieut...	May 24, 1864	Marysville	....
H. P. Wells..........	Second Lieut	May 24, 1864	Marysville	....

EIGHTEENTH REGIMENT, K. S. M.

P. L. Hubbard......	Colonel	Mar. 7, 1864	Atchison..........	Resigned.
Matthew Quigg....	Colonel	Sept. 10, 1864	Atchison..........	....
G. M. Kuhl...........	Lieut. Col...	Mar. 7, 1864	Atchison..........	....
J. M. Crowell	Major	Nov. 23, 1864	Atchison..........	....
A. S. Hughes........	Adjutant......	Apr. 13, 1864	Atchison..........	Resigned.
S. Heselberger......	Adjutant......	Aug. 11, 1864	Atchison..........	....
Virgil W. Parker..	Quar'master	Apr. 13, 1864	Atchison..........	....
W. W. Cochrane...	Surgeon.........	Apr. 13, 1864	Atchison..........	....

COMPANY A.

E. Butcher............	Captain	Sept. 2, 1863	Atchison..........	....
F. W. McLaughlin	Second Lieut	Sept. 2, 1863	Atchison..........	....

COMPANY B.

Wm. Bowman......	Captain	Sept. 8, 1863	Atchison..........	Resigned.
Thomas Murphy..	Captain	July 8, 1864	Atchison..........	....
Jacob Saqui.........	First Lieut...	Sept. 8, 1863	Atchison..........	Resigned.
A. H. Whitcomb...	First Lieut...	July 8, 1864	Atchison..........	Resigned.
A. J. L. Philbrick.	First Lieut...	Aug. 16, 1864	Atchison..........	....
C. Neal.................	Second Lieut	June 3, 1864	Atchison..........	....

COMPANY C.

Geo. W. Taylor.....	Captain	Sept. 11, 1863	Atchison..........	....
John Heartha......	First Lieut...	Sept. 11, 1863	Atchison..........	....
Henry Buchanan.	Second Lieut	Sept. 11, 1863	Atchison..........	....

COMPANY D.

Lewis Higby........	Captain	Sept. 17, 1863	Atchison..........	....
S. T. Walter.........	First Lieut...	Sept. 17, 1863	Atchison..........	....
P. Doland............	Second Lieut	Sept. 17, 1863	Atchison..........	....

COMPANY E, EIGHTEENTH REGIMENT K. S. M.

Names.	Rank.	Date of Commission.	Residence.	Remarks.
Robert Breedlore.	Captain	Oct. 12, 1863	Pardee	....
B. F. Whittaker...	Captain	Sept. 16, 1864	Pardee	....
D. M. Stillman	First Lieut...	Oct. 12, 1863	Pardee	....
S. P. Griffin..........	Second Lieut	Oct. 12, 1863	Pardee	....

NINETEENTH REGIMENT K. S. M.

M. S. Grant..........	Colonel..........	May 13, 1864	Leavenworth ..	Promoted Brig. Gen.
B. F. Akers..........	Colonel..........	Sept. 3, 1864	Leavenworth ..	Resigned.
A. C. Hogan	Colonel..........	Oct. 14, 1864	Leavenworth ..	
J. A. Neice............	Lieut. Col.....	June 3, 1864	Leavenworth ..	Resigned.
A. C. Hogan	Lieut. Col.....	Sept. 3, 1864	Leavenworth ..	Resigned.
John Wright........	Lieut. Col.....	Oct. 14, 1864	Leavenworth ..	
William Smith......	Major..........	June 3, 1864	Leavenworth ..	
John Freeland......	Adjutant......	June 3, 1864	Leavenworth ..	
E. M. Marsh..........	Quar'master	May 13, 1864	Leavenworth ..	Resigned.
J. W. Skinner......	Quar'master	Oct. 14, 1864	Leavenworth ..	
Tiffin Sinks..........	Surgeon	May 13, 1864	Leavenworth ..	

COMPANY A.

Benj. F. Akers......	Captain	June 3, 1864	Leavenworth ..	Promoted Colonel.
Thomas R. Clark..	Captain	Nov. 1, 1864	Leavenworth ..	
Thomas R. Clark..	First Lieut...	June 3, 1864	Leavenworth ..	Promoted Captain.
Joseph Kesler......	First Lieut...	Nov. 1, 1864	Leavenworth ..	
A. O. Bangs..........	Second Lieut	June 3, 1863	Leavenworth ..	Resigned.
Patrick McGraw..	Second Lieut	Nov. 1, 1864	Leavenworth ..	

COMPANY B.

Joseph Goble........	Captain	Dec. 8, 1863	Kickapoo..........	....
C. F. Lublin	First Lieut...	Dec. 8, 1863	Kickapoo	....
J. W. Craig	Second Lieut	Dec. 8, 1863	Kickapoo	....

COMPANY C.

Nels'n McCracken	Captain	June 3, 1864	Leavenworth ..	Resigned.
Jas. L. McDowell..	Captain	Oct. 12, 1864	Leavenworth ..	
Peter Huesgen......	First Lieut...	June 3, 1864	Leavenworth ..	Resigned.
John W. Spratley.	First Lieut...	Oct. 14, 1864	Leavenworth ..	
N. W. West	Second Lieut	June 3, 1864	Leavenworth ..	Resigned.
Chas. Schincke.....	Second Lieut	Oct. 14, 1864	Leavenworth ..	

COMPANY D.

Thomas Trower...	Captain	June 3, 1864	Springdale......	....
A. D. McCune......	First Lieut...	June 3, 1864	Springdale	....
Crayton Carney...	Second Lieut	June 3, 1864	Springdale	....

COMPANY E.

John Wright.........	Captain	Dec. 8, 1863	Springdale......	....
E. D. Bowen	First Lieut...	June 3, 1864	Springdale	....
David N. Gilbert..	Second Lieut	Dec. 8, 1863	Springdale	....

COMPANY F.

John Francis.......	Captain	July 3, 1864	Stranger	....
William Franck...	First Lieut...	July 3, 1864	Stranger	Resigned.
Lorenzo Wallace..	First Lieut...	Oct. 14, 1864	Stranger	
Lorenzo Wallace ..	Second Lieut	July 3, 1864	Stranger	Promoted First Lt.
David C. Morrow..	Second Lieut	Oct. 14, 1864	Stranger	....

COMPANY G.

A. C. Hogan	Captain	Dec. 8, 1863	Salt Creek........	Promoted.
Jesse Connell......	Captain	Oct. 14, 1864	Salt Creek.......	
John Duffin.........	First Lieut...	Dec. 8, 1863	Salt Creek.......	....
J. Harris..............	Second Lieut	Dec. 8, 1863	Salt Creek.......	....

COMPANY H, NINETEENTH REGIMENT K. S. M.

Names.	Rank.	Date of Commission.	Residence.	Remarks.
Crawford Moore...	Captain	June 3, 1864	Stranger	
Sam'l F. Burdett..	First Lieut...	June 3, 1864	Stranger	
Richard Gilstrap..	Second Lieut	June 3, 1864	Stranger	

COMPANY I.

F. Wellhouse........	Captain	June 3, 1864	Pleasant Ridge	
W. I. Johnson	First Lieut...	June 3, 1864	Pleasant Ridge	
R. E. Petherborge	Second Lieut	June 3, 1864	Pleasant Ridge	

COMPANY K.

A. C. Harlow........	Captain	June 3, 1864	Delaware	
James L. Spears...	First Lieut...	June 3, 1864	Delaware	
Frank M. Goble...	Second Lieut	June 3, 1864	Delaware	

COMPANY L.

Walter S. Kerr.....	Captain	June 3, 1864	Springdale	
A. W. Walker......	First Lieut...	June 3, 1864	Springdale	
H. G. Talcott........	Second Lieut	June 3, 1864	Springdale	

COMPANY M.

William Orr.........	Second Lieut	Oct. 14, 1864		

COMPANY O.

J. E. Bauserman ..	Captain	Oct. 17, 1864	Leav'worth Co.	
E. S. Dunham	First Lieut...	Oct. 17, 1864	Leav'worth Co.	
Abner Haskins ...	Second Lieut	Oct. 17, 1864	Leav'worth Co.	

COMPANY N.

James McCune.....	Captain	Oct. 18, 1864		
J. L. Hamby........	First Lieut...	Oct. 18, 1864		
H. W. Harrison...	Second Lieut	Oct. 18, 1864		

TWENTIETH REGIMENT K. S. M.

John B. Hubbell..	Colonel.........	June 28, 1864	Holton...........	
James McClellan..	Lieut. Col.....	June 28, 1864	Holton...........	
William Knipe.....	Major...........	June 28, 1864	Circleville......	
W. L. Burns.........	Adjutant	Oct. 13, 1864		
P. M. Hodges.......	Quar'master.	Oct. 13, 1864		
B. F. Fuller..........	Surgeon	Oct. 10, 1864		

COMPANY A.

J. F. M. Walters...	Captain	June 14, 1864	Holton...........	
J. N. Walton........	First Lieut...	June 14, 1864	Holton...........	
Wm. Behtsker......	First Lieut...	Sept. 19, 1864	Holton...........	
Hugh McBride.....	Second Lieut	June 14, 1864	Holton...........	

COMPANY B.

W. S. Hoaglin......	Captain	June 1, 1864	Holton...........	
J. Taylor.............	First Lieut...	June 1, 1864	Holton...........	
Wm. L. Burns	Second Lieut	June 1, 1864	Holton...........	

COMPANY C.

S. J. Foster	First Lieut...	June 29, 1864	Circleville........	Promoted Capt. Co. F.
Homer Heathman	Second Lieut	June 29, 1864	Circleville........	Pro'ted 1st Lt. Co. F.
J. B. Coffin............	Second Lieut	June 29, 1864	Circleville........	

COMPANY D, TWENTIETH REGIMENT K. S. M.

Names.	Rank.	Date of Commission.	Residence.	Remarks.
James McLellan...	Captain	July 30, 1863	Cedar Creek ...	Promoted.
J. L. Finnicum....	Captain	Aug. 9, 1864	Holton..........	
Stephen J. Elliott	First Lieut...	July 30, 1863	Cedar Creek....	
John Coleman	Second Lieut	July 29, 1863	Cedar Creek....	

COMPANY E.

R. J. Tolin...........	Captain	Feb. 4, 1864	Aurora City.....	
C. C. Branhan......	First Lieut...	Feb. 4, 1864	Aurora City.....	
A. C. Cochran......	Second Lieut	Feb. 4, 1864	Aurora City.....	

COMPANY F.

S. J. Foster..........	Captain	Oct. 10, 1864	Circleville	
H. Heathman......	First Lieut...	Oct. 12, 1864	Circleville......	
B. F. Niswander...	Second Lieut	Oct. 12, 1864	Circleville........	

COMPANY G.

O. J. Grover.........	Captain	Oct. 13, 1864	Vienna, Pott'ie	
R. S. Wooley........	First Lieut...	Oct. 13, 1864	Vienna, Pott'ie	
Moses Day	Second Lieut	Oct. 13, 1864	Vienna, Pott'ie	

TWENTY-FIRST REGIMENT K. S. M.

Sandy Lowe.........	Colonel.........	Sept. 23, 1864	Willow Springs	
F. L. Robinson.....	Lieut. Col....	Sept. 23, 1864	Baldwin City...	
A. T. Still............	Major...........	Sept. 23, 1864	Baldwin City...	
George F. Smith...	Adjutant	Sept. 23, 1864		
E. A. Barrett........	Quar'master.	Sept. 23, 1864		
Wm. D. Martin....	Surgeon	Sept. 23, 1864	Baldwin City...	

COMPANY A.

| C. Tefft................ | Captain .... | Oct. 14, 1862 | | |

COMPANY B.

Sylvester Creel.....	Captain	Sept. 16, 1863	Wash. Creek ...	
R. N. Woodward..	First Lieut...	Sept. 16, 1863	Wash. Creek....	
D. C. Holbert........	Second Lieut	Sept. 16, 1863	Wash. Creek....	

COMPANY C.

J. H. Lafland.......	Captain	Dec. 12, 1863	Blue Mound......	
H. R. Saunders.....	First Lieut...	Oct. 16, 1863		
Daniel Street........	Second Lieut	Oct. 16, 1863		

COMPANY D.

J. W. Pingree	Captain	May 7, 1864	Baldwin City...	
H. E. Badwell......	First Lieut...	Oct. 10, 1864	Baldwin City...	
Daniel F. Feye.....	Second Lieut	Oct. 10, 1864	Baldwin City...	

COMPANY E.

Henry Webber......	Captain	Aug. 2, 1864	Clinton..........	
Sam'l W. Metsker	First Lieut...	Aug. 2, 1864	Clinton..........	
Wm. M. Baldwin..	Second Lieut	Aug. 2, 1864	Clinton..........	

COMPANY G.

Barton Andrews..	Captain	Sept. 21, 1863		
Silas Dexter.........	First Lieut...	Oct. 14, 1864		
David Foster........	Second Lieut	Oct. 14, 1864		

COMPANY H.

W. A. David..........	Captain	Sept. 5, 1863	Prairie City.....	
James Skaggs......	First Lieut...	Sept. 5, 1863	Prairie City.....	
Elisha Brown	Second Lieut	Sept. 5, 1863	Prairie City.....	

COMPANY K, TWENTY-FIRST REGIMENT K. S. M.

Names.	Rank.	Date of Commission.	Residence.	Remarks.
G. F. Sprague	Captain	June 29, 1864	Prairie City......	....
James Ashley......	First Lieut...	June 29, 1864	Prairie City......	....
Joseph Meadow...	Second Lieut	June 29, 1864	Prairie City......	....

COMPANY L.

Jackson Bell........	Captain	Dec. 31, 1863	Black Jack......	....
John McKilip......	First Lieut...	Dec. 31, 1863	Black Jack......	....
M. Thompson......	Second Lieut	Dec. 31, 1863	Black Jack......	....

COMPANY M.

Julius Fisher.......	Captain	Sept. 16, 1863	Eudora............	....
Christian Stroble.	First Lieut...	Sept. 16, 1863	Eudora............	....
Freder'k Galfkon	Second Lieut	Sept. 16, 1863	Eudora............	....

TWENTY-SECOND REGIMENT K. S. M.

James P. Taylor ..	Colonel	Sept. 7, 1864	Seneca............	....
Lewis Shecly	Lieut. Col.....	Sept. 7, 1864	Nemaha Co......	....
Isaac E. Coleman..	Major...........	Sept. 7, 1864	Nemaha Co......	....
William F. Wells..	Major...........	Sept. 7, 1864	Nemaha Co......	....
J. S. Hidden	Adjutant.......	Sept. 7, 1864	Nemaha Co......	....
Bolivar Scofield...	Surgeon	Sept. 7, 1864	Nemaha Co......	....

COMPANY A.

Lew. J. McGowan	Captain	Sept. 25, 1863	Seneca	....
Asa Titus............	First Lieut...	Sept. 22, 1863	Seneca	....
William Forbion..	Second Lieut	Sept. 25, 1863	Seneca	....

COMPANY B.

Robert Little.......	Captain	Sept. 19, 1863	Muddy Creek...	....
Jacob Shoemaker.	First Lieut...	Sept. 19, 1863	Brown County	....
Josiah Travis	Second Lieut	Sept. 19, 1863	Brown County	....

COMPANY C.

J. H. Higgins	Captain	June 22, 1864	Red Vermil'n ..	....
Ephr'm Blankley.	First Lieut...	June 22, 1864	Red Vermil'n ..	....
M. N. Shepherd...	Second Lieut	June 22, 1864	Red Vermil'n ..	....

COMPANY D.

Wm. C. Vasser......	Captain	June 9, 1864	Albany	....
Nicholas Vasser...	First Lieut...	June 9, 1864	Albany	....
Rob't Williamson.	Second Lieut	June 9, 1864	Albany	....

COMPANY E.

Morton Cave........	Captain	Jan. 22, 1864	Nemaha Tp.....	....
William Weaks ...	First Lieut...	Jan. 22, 1864	Nemaha Tp.....	....
George Frederick.	Second Lieut	Jan. 22, 1864	Nemaha Tp.....	....

COMPANY F.

T. S. Wright........	Captain	Aug. 25, 1864	Grenada	....
John Stanley.......	First Lieut...	Aug. 25, 1864	Grenada	....
Daniel Woodman.	Second Lieut	Aug. 25, 1864	Grenada	....

COMPANY G.

J. N. Cline	Captain	Sept. 27, 1863	Lincoln	....
N. Hocker	First Lieut...	June 22, 1863	Lincoln	....
J. G. Jones...........	Second Lieut	June 22, 1863	Lincoln	....

27

COMPANY H, TWENTY-SECOND REGIMENT K. S. M.

Names.	Rank.	Date of Commission.	Residence.	Remarks.
Aaron Magill	Captain	Sept. 21, 1864	Sabetha..........	....
Michael McGenty	First Lieut...	Dec. 7, 1863	Sabetha..........	....
Coga Fox.............	Second Lieut	Dec. 7, 1863	Sabetha..........	....

COMPANY I.

N. W. Dressy.......	Captain	Oct. 1, 1864	Centralia	....
H. Smith.............	First Lieut...	Oct. 1, 1864	Centralia	....
L. Lochmuller......	Second Lieut	Oct. 1, 1864	Centralia	....

TWENTY-THIRD REGIMENT K. S. M.

William Weer......	Colonel.........	Oct. 15, 1864	Wyandotte......	....:...................
Joseph Gilliford...	Lieut. Col.....	Oct. 15, 1864	Wyandotte......	....
Isaiah Walker	Quar'master	Oct. 15, 1864	Wyandotte......	....
George B. Wood...	Surgeon	Oct. 15, 1864	Wyandotte......	....

COMPANY A.

J. G. McKibban...	Captain	Oct. 28, 1863	Quindaro	....
Theodore Bartles..	Captain	July 18, 1863	Quindaro	....
Isaac Lemons......	First Lieut...	Oct. 28, 1863	Quindaro	....
Joseph Turk........	Second Lieut	Oct. 28, 1863	Quindaro	....

COMPANY B.

Jas. M. Chinault...	Captain	Nov. 9, 1863	Muncytown.....	....
Patrick Reedy	First Lieut...	Nov. 9, 1863	Muncytown.....	....
Michael Collins...	Second Lieut	Nov. 9, 1863	Muncytown.....	Resigned.
John E. Johnson..	Second Lieut	Aug. 16, 1864	Muncytown.....	....

COMPANY C.

Matthew Clarry...	Captain	June 23, 1864	Wyandotte......	....
Isaac N. White.....	First Lieut...	June 23, 1864	Wyandotte......	....
Robert Halford....	Second Lieut	June 23, 1864	Wyandotte......	....

COMPANY D.

Philip Hascher....	Captain	June 23, 1864	Wyandotte	....
Hermann Stach...	First Lieut...	June 23, 1864	Wyandotte	....
J. Muenzewmier..	Second Lieut	June 23, 1864	Wyandotte	....

COMPANY E.

Joseph Gilliford...	Captain	July 21, 1864	Wyandotte	Promoted.
Philip Knoblock..	Captain	Oct. 10, 1864	Wyandotte	....
Rynear Morgan...	First Lieut...	July 21, 1864	Wyandotte	....
Martin Stewart....	Second Lieut	July 21, 1864	Wyandotte	....

COMPANY F.

Thos. A. Gruiter..	Captain	Aug. 13, 1864	Muncytown	....
L. B. Pratt...........	First Lieut...	Aug. 13, 1864	Muncytown	....
Jacob Maigly.......	Second Lieut	Aug. 13, 1864	Muncytown	....

COMPANY G.

Hiram Wood........	Captain	Oct. 14, 1864	Wyandotte	....
N.A.Reicheneck'r	First Lieut...	Oct. 14, 1864	Wyandotte	....
Jas. Brown	Second Lieut	Oct. 14, 1864	Wyandotte	....

COMPANY H.

Chas. S. Glick......	Captain	Oct. 14, 1864	Wyandotte	....
Wm. J. Huffaker..	First Lieut...	Oct. 19, 1864	Wyandotte	....
Francis House.....	Second Lieut	Oct. 19, 1864	Wyandotte	....

COMPANY I.

S. S. Sharp...........	Captain	Oct. 17, 1864		.
Wm. J. Fulton.....	First Lieut...	Oct. 17, 1864		....
T. W. Packs.........	Second Lieut	Oct. 17, 1864		....

TWENTY-FOURTH REGIMENT K. S. M.

Names.	Rank.	Date of Commission.	Residence.	Remarks.
Isaac Staddin	Colonel.........	Oct. 22, 1864	Fort Scott	....
John Van Fossen..	Lieut. Col.....	Oct. 22, 1864	Bourbon Co.....	....
Joseph Ury..........	Major...........	Oct. 22, 1864	Bourbon Co.....	....
A. Danford..........	Adjutant	Oct. 22, 1864	Fort Scott	....
J. T. Bridgens......	Quar'master	Oct. 22, 1864	Bourbon Co.....	....

COMPANY A.

John T. White.....	First Lieut...	Oct. 22, 1864	Fort Scott	....
C. B. Hayward.....	Second Lieut	Oct. 22, 1864	Fort Scott	....

COMPANY B.

W. C. Dennison...	First Lieut...	Oct. 22, 1864	Bourbon Co.....	....
R. D. Lender........	Second Lieut	Oct. 22, 1864	Bourbon Co.....	....

COMPANY C.

James B. Skeen...	Captain	Oct. 22, 1864	Bourbon Co.....	....
Thomas Barnes ...	First Lieut...	Oct. 22, 1864	Bourbon Co.....	....
C. B. Maurice.......	Second Lieut	Oct. 22, 1864	Bourbon Co.....	....

COMPANY D.

J. C. Hinkley	Captain	Oct. 22, 1864	Bourbon Co.....	....
Robert Stalker.....	First Lieut...	Oct. 22, 1864	Bourbon Co.....	....

COMPANY E.

Henry T. Coffman	Captain	Oct. 22, 1864	Bourbon Co.....	....
Robert Adams......	First Lieut...	Oct. 22, 1864	Bourbon Co.....	....
Wm. P. Gray.......	Second Lieut	Oct. 22, 1864	Bourbon Co.....	....

COMPANY F.

J. C. Ury..............	Captain	Oct. 22, 1864	Bourbon Co.....	....
J. B. Cabiniss	First Lieut...	Oct. 22, 1864	Bourbon Co.....	....
S. Streeter............	Second Lieut	Oct. 22, 1864	Bourbon Co.....	....

SANTA FE BATTALION, K. S. M.

M. M. Murdock....	Colonel.........	May 26, 1864	Burlingame	....
W. F. Aderholt....	Major...........	May 26, 1864	Wilmington ...	....

COMPANY A.

John Hodgson	Captain	May 14, 1864	Wilmington	....
E. H. Sanford......	First Lieut...	May 14, 1864	Wilmington	....
Levi Smith	First Lieut...	May 30, 1864	Wilmington ...	....
W. F. Aderholt ...	Second Lieut	May 14, 1864	Wilmington ..	....
R. J. Murs	Second Lieut	May 30, 1864	Wilmington ...	....

COMPANY B.

J. B. Stewart........	Captain	May 16, 1864	Burlingame	....
Edward Timms ...	First Lieut...	June 4, 1863	Burlingame	....
Geo. W. Perrill.....	Second Lieut	June 4, 1863	Burlingame	....

BOURBON COUNTY BATTALION, K. S. M.

Geo. P. Eaves.......	Lieut. Col.....	June 13, 1864	Marmaton........	....

COMPANY A.

David D. Roberts.	Captain	Oct. 12, 1863	Fort Lincoln...	....
Isaac Burton........	First Lieut...	Oct. 12, 1863	Fort Lincoln...	....
C. W. Campbell.....	Second Lieut	Oct. 12, 1863	Fort Lincoln...	....

COMPANY B.

Dyer Smith..........	Captain	Oct. 28, 1863	Marmaton	....
D. R. Radden	First Lieut...	Oct. 28, 1863	Marmaton	....
B. R. Wood	Second Lieut	Oct. 28, 1863	Marmaton	....

COMPANY C, BOURBON COUNTY BATTALION, K. S. M.

Names.	Rank.	Date of Commission.	Residence.	Remarks.
John J. Stewart...	Captain	Oct. 28, 1863	Mill Creek......	....
John Blair...........	First Lieut...	Oct. 28, 1863	Mill Creek......	....
Elias M. Marshall	Second Lieut	Oct. 28, 1863	Mill Creek......	....

COMPANY D.

S. B. Mahurn	Captain	Nov. 4, 1863	Fort Scott......	....
John Hamilton ...	First Lieut...	Nov. 4, 1863	Fort Scott......	....
John C. Audrick...	Second Lieut	Nov. 4, 1863	Fort Scott......	....

COMPANY E.

Benj. F. Gumm ...	Captain	Dec. 11, 1863	Marion Prec't..	....
Benj. F. Gumm ...	Captain	July 13, 1864	Turkey Creek..	....
Nathan Baker	First Lieut...	July 13, 1864	Turkey Creek..	....
William Goff........	Second Lieut	July 13, 1864	Turkey Creek..	....

COMPANY F.

Isaac Morris........	Captain	Dec. 15, 1863	Xenia	....
Robert S. Stevens..	First Lieut...	Dec. 15, 1863	Xenia	....
Asbury S. Potter..	Second Lieut	Dec. 15, 1863	Xenia	....

COMPANY G.

W. A. Shannon....	Captain	June 20, 1864	Fort Scott......	....
N. J. Roscoe	First Lieut...	June 20, 1864	Fort Scott......	....
David McComas...	Second Lieut	June 20, 1864	Fort Scott......	....

1865.

JANUARY 1.—John A. Martin returns to the Atchison Champion. It had been edited by John J. Ingalls about three years.

JANUARY 9.— State officers sworn in.

JANUARY 10.—Meeting of the Legislature.

LIST OF MEMBERS AND OFFICERS OF THE SENATE.

Members and Officers.	Age	Post Office Address.	County.	Avocation.
James McGrew, President...............	43	Wyandotte	Wyandotte	Merch't.
Bartlett, H. W. K	40	Junction City......	Davis	Merch't.
Barber, Oliver	48	Kanwaka............	Douglas..........	Farmer.
Colton, Gustavus A	35	Paola	Miami	Farmer.
Danford, A......................................	35	Fort Scott...........	Bourbon	Lawyer.
Drenning, Frank H.........................	28	Elwood...............	Doniphan........	Lawyer.
Eskridge, Chas. V...........................	30	Emporia	Lyon...............	Merch't.
Foote, Henry	36	Leavenworth	Leavenworth ..	
Gambell, W. P.................................	33	Leavenworth	Leavenworth ..	Attorney
Grover, O. J....................................	37	Neuchatel...........	Nemaha	Farmer.
Houston, D. W................................	37	Garnett..............	Anderson.........	Lawyer.
Horne, Daniel H.............................	36	Topeka	Shawnee	Farmer.
Jones, J. H	37	Kaw City............	Jefferson.........	Farmer.
Legate, Jas. F................................	36	Leavenworth.......	Leavenworth ..	Farmer.
Lane, J. T	33	Iowa Point.........	Doniphan........	Merch't.
Manning, E. C	26	Marysville	Marshall.........	Printer.
Milhoan, T. E.................................	32	Olathe	Johnson	Farmer.
Murphy, Thomas.............................	36	Atchison	Atchison	Hotel k'r
Potter, F. W....................................	31	Burlington	Coffey	Laborer.
Quigg, Mathew...............................	28	Atchison	Atchison	Clerk.
Spear, S..	48	Hiawatha	Brown..............	Farmer.
Speer, John.....................................	47	Lawrence	Douglas...........	Printer.
Smith, A. H....................................	37	Blooming Grove ..	Linn...............	Farmer.
Twiss, Charles P.............................	31	Iola..................	Allen..............	Lawyer.
Weer, William................................	40	Wyandotte	Wyandotte......	Lawyer.
A. Smith Devenney, Secretary........	30	Olathe	Johnson..........	Lawyer.
W. S. Newberry, Assistant Secretary	30	Iola..................	Allen..............	Lawyer.
M. M. Murdock, Docket Clerk........	29	Burlingame.........	Osage	Editor.
Ira H. Smith, Journal Clerk...........	49	Topeka..............	Shawnee	Land Agt
L. M. Benedict, Engrossing Clerk....	34	Vienna...............	Pottawatomie..	Farmer.
W. B. Bowman, Enrolling Clerk......	35	Wyandotte..........	Wyandotte	Lawyer.
T. Mills, Sergeant-at-Arms.............	51	Topeka..............	Shawnee	Mason.
Wm. Thompson, Doorkeeper...........	32	Topeka..............	Shawnee	Farmer.
Wm. Young, Assistant Doorkeeper..	23	Topeka..............	Shawnee	Mason.
Clarence Walrod, Page...................	12	Paola	Miami	Student.
Charles Horne, Page......................	11	Topeka..............	Shawnee	Student.

MEMBERS AND OFFICERS OF HOUSE OF REPRESENTATIVES.

Members.	Age.	Post Office Address.	County.	Avocation.
Jacob Stotler, Speaker	30	Emporia	Lyon	Printer.
Abraham, R. H	37	Emporia	Lyon	Farmer.
Atwood, Samuel F	34	Leavenworth	Leavenworth	Convey'cer
Benton, Milton R	49	Atchison	Atchison	Farmer.
Broadhead, J. F	34	Mound City	Linn	Lawyer.
Browne, O. H	45	Ridgeway	Osage	Farmer.
Callen, A. W	32	Junction City	Davis	Lawyer.
Campbell, D. G	44	Shawnee	Johnson	Farmer.
Campbell, D. L	40	Mapleton	Bourbon	Merchant.
Cavender, Henderson	31	Garnett	Anderson	Merchant.
Christy, J. A	52	Iola	Allen	Farmer.
Church, R	55	Westmoreland	Pottawatomie	Farmer.
Cleavenger, L. D	44	Fort Scott	Bourbon	Physician.
Coffinberry, Chas. C	36	Lincoln	Nemaha	Farmer.
Cook, Hugh A	37	Minneola	Franklin	Farmer.
Craig, Warner	28	Black Jack	Douglas	Farmer.
Darby, Rufus	49	Washington	Washington	Farmer.
Detrick, D	49	Highland	Doniphan	Farmer.
Dille, C. L	48	Lanesfield	Johnson	Farmer.
Draper, William	33	Clinton	Douglas	Farmer.
Dutton, M. R	34	Oskaloosa	Jefferson	Farmer.
Fairchild, G. H	31	Atchison	Atchison	Banker.
Finn, Daniel C	28	Syracuse	Wilson	Lawyer.
Foster, Robert Cole	30	Leavenworth	Leavenworth	Laborer.
Fletcher, James	35	Tecumseh	Shawnee	Farmer.
Glick, Charles S	32	Wyandotte City	Wyandotte	Lawyer.
Glick, G. W	38	Atchison	Atchison	Attorney.
Goss, William	34	Blooming Grove	Linn	Farmer.
Griswold, Nelson	44	Turkey Creek	Bourbon	Farmer.
Hanway, James	56	Lane	Franklin	Farmer.
Harvey, James M	31	Fort Riley	Riley	Farmer.
Hendrick, A. B	35	Rising Sun	Jefferson	Farmer.
Hodgson, J	59	Paris	Linn	Farmer.
Houts, W. L	33	Paola	Miami	Merchant.
Hughes, N. B	31	Salina	Saline	Physician.
Jordan, Michael	45	Leavenworth	Leavenworth	Hotel k'per
Karr, William	51	New Lancaster	Miami	Farmer.
Kennedy, J. R	41	Lawrence	Douglas	Farmer.
Kennedy, Lawrence	47	Pleasant Ridge	Leavenworth	Farmer
Kohler, C	30	Junction	Dickinson	Smith.
Leland, Cyrus, jr	23	Troy	Doniphan	Soldier.
Leonard, M. R	37	Bazaar	Chase	Physician.
Loomis, A. J	39	Twin Springs	Linn	Farmer.
Low, A	53	Doniphan	Doniphan	Farmer.
Macdonald, S. D	39	Topeka	Shawnee	Printer.
Martindale, Wm	29	Madison	Greenwood	Farmer.
McClellan, J	44	Holton	Jackson	Farmer.
Mead, James R	28	Towanda	Butler	Merchant.
Moody, Joel	31	Belmont	Woodson	Lawyer.
Morrow, William	37	Lecompton	Douglas	Merchant.
O'Brien, T. M	34	Leavenworth	Leavenworth	Mil. Att'y.
O'Gwartney, Thos	42	Easton	Leavenworth	Farmer.
Page, F. R	34	Neosho Rapids	Lyon	Farmer.
Payne, D. L	28	Columbus	Doniphan	Farmer.
Perry, William B	24	LeRoy	Coffey	Merchant.
Rawlings, N. P	39	Robinson	Brown	Farmer.
Riddle, Robert	36	Grasshopper Falls	Jefferson	Farmer.
Rice, H	39	Osawatomie	Miami	Farmer.
Rogers, H. D	33	Humboldt	Neosho	Laborer.
Russell, Ed	32	Elwood	Doniphan	Farmer.
Sammons, I. D	30	Albany	Nemaha	Stock rais'r
Salisbury, J. P	40	Leavenworth	Leavenworth	Farmer.
Scudder, E. S	47	Willow Springs	Douglas	Farmer.
Shepherd, H. D	26	Wilmington	Wabaunsee	Merchant.
Smith, Henry	34	Leavenworth	Leavenworth	Merchant.
Snyder, S. J. H	52	Monrovia	Atchison	Farmer.
Stafford, E	36	Springdale	Leavenworth	Physician.
Spencer, J	34	Council Grove	Morris	Farmer.
Stewart, Watson	38	Humboldt	Allen	Farmer.
Storch, George	30	Kennekuk	Atchison	Merchant.
Stratton, C. H	36	DeSoto	Johnson	Farmer.
Strong, N. Z	37	Fort Scott	Bourbon	Lawyer.
Sutherland, D. H	46	New Eureka	Brown	Farmer.

MEMBERS AND OFFICERS OF THE HOUSE OF REPRESENTATIVES — CONCL'D.

Members and Officers.	Age	P. O. Address.	County.	Avocation.
Swift, Frank B...............................	30	Lawrence	Douglas........	Printer.
Throckmorton, Job............................	30	Burlington......	Coffey	Farmer.
Wells, John D	34	Barrett	Marshall	Farmer.
West, A. G.................................	43	Ozark.............	Anderson	Farmer.
D. B. Emmert, Chief Clerk.............	28	Fort Scott.......	Bourbon......	Publisher.
Freeman Bell, Assistant Clerk	31	Topeka...........	Shawnee	Farmer.
C. S. Lambdin, Journal Clerk...............	56	Plymouth........	Lyon	Farmer.
John MacReynolds, Docket Clerk.........	32	Paola	Miami.......	Printer.
D. F. Drinkwater, Engrossing Clerk......	27	Cedar Point.....	Chase	Farmer.
John T. Cox, Enrolling Clerk..............	44	Ottumwa	Coffey	Lawyer.
J. E. Follansbee, Ass't Journal Clerk.....	25	Topeka...........	Shawnee	Teacher.
J. D. Farren, Sergeant-at-Arms............	54	Lawrence	Douglas	Teacher.
Thos. Archer, Ass't Sergeant-at-Arms....	31	Topeka...........	Shawnee	Merchant.
M. B. Crawford, Doorkeeper...............	28	Topeka...........	Shawnee	Carpent'r.
C. T. K. Prentice, Assistant Doorkeeper	17	McKinney's....	Douglas........	Farmer.
William Miller, Page.......................	18	Ridgeway.......	Osage	Farmer.
Albert L. Bartlett, Page.....................	12	Neosho Rapids	Lyon.............	Farmer.
Wm. R. Griffith, Page	16	Topeka...........	Shawnee	Farmer.

JANUARY 11.—Free Missouri sends greeting to the Kansas Legislature.
—Message from Gov. Crawford.

JANUARY 12.—James H. Lane elected U. S. Senator, for the term beginning March 4, 1865. Lane received 82 votes, Wm. A. Phillips 7, Wm. C. McDowell 4, C. B. Brace 2, W. Y. Roberts 2, B. M. Hughes 1. The election is followed by a banquet.

JANUARY 12.—Meeting of the State Agricultural Society, at Topeka. *Officers:* President, L. D. Bailey, of Douglas county; Secretary, John S. Brown, of Douglas; Treasurer, Wm. Spriggs, of Anderson. *Executive Committee:* R. G. Elliott, of Jefferson; H. B. Keller, of Leavenworth; S. Hubbard, of Wyandotte; A. W. J. Brown, of Allen; James B. Maynard, of Doniphan; C. B. Lines, of Wabaunsee; J. W. Sponable, of Johnson; S. M. Strickler, of Davis; P. B. Maxson, of Lyon; S. S. Tipton, of Anderson. No Fair was held this year.

JANUARY 16.—Joel Moody admitted to the seat in the House, of Jonathan Foster, from the Sixty-third District, Woodson county.

JANUARY 17.—C. K. Holliday, Adjutant General, makes the following statement in regard to Kansas troops, to Gov. Crawford:

No. of Regiment.	Arm of service.	Period.	Date of organization.	Original strength.	Recruits.	Aggregate.	Veterans re-enlisted.
First Regiment..........	Infantry...	3 years	May, 1861	986	206	1,192	116
Second Regiment........	Infantry...	3 m'ths	May, 1861	650	....	650	....
Second Regiment	Cavalry....	3 years	Fall, 1861	870	403	1,273	56
Fifth Regiment..........	Cavalry....	3 years	Fall, 1861	900	420	1,320	29
Sixth Regiment..........	Cavalry....	3 years	Fall, 1861	851	654	1,505	79
Seventh Regiment......	Cavalry....	3 years	Oct., 1861	902	356	1,258	455
Eighth Regiment........	Infantry...	3 years	Oct., 1861	719	243	962	218
Ninth Regiment........	Cavalry....	3 years	Spring, 1862	817	710	1,527	31
Tenth Regiment........	Infantry...	3 years	Aug., 1861	777	250	1,027	182
Eleventh Regiment....	Cavalry....	3 years	Sept., 1862	916	498	1,414	....
Twelfth Regiment......	Infantry...	3 years	Sept., 1862	910	103	1,013	....
Thirteenth Regiment..	Infantry...	3 years	Sept., 1862	890	93	983	....
Fourteenth Regiment.	Cavalry....	3 years	Dec., 1863	1,070	53	1,125	....
Fifteenth Regiment...	Cavalry....	3 years	Oct., 1863	1,015	208	1,223	....
Sixteenth Regiment....	Cavalry....	3 years	Oct., 1864	1,000	42	1,042	....
Seventeenth Reg't......	Infantry...	100 dys	July, 1864	455	....	455	....
First Regiment (Col'd)	Infantry...	3 years	Jan., 1863	869	223	1,092	....
Second Reg't (Col'd)....	Infantry...	3 years	Nov., 1863	901	36	937	....

COL. HOLLIDAY'S REPORT — *Concluded.*

No. of Regiment.	Arm of service	Period	Date of organization	Original strength	Recruits	Aggregate.	Veterans re-enlisted.
First Battery	Artillery	3 years	——, 1861	150	23	173	43
Second Battery	Artillery	3 years	Aug., 1862	140	12	152	....
Third Battery	Artillery	3 years	March, 1863	126	20	146	....
Inde'dent Bat. (Col'd)	Artillery	3 years	——	54	....	54	....
Cr. by enl'nts in other States				74	....	74	....
Total					....	20,597	1,209
Add Veterans					....	1,209	....
Grand aggregate					....	21,806	

"The foregoing exhibit shows the number of the several regiments of Kansas volunteers in the service of the United States since the commencement of the war; the arm of service with which they were connected; term of service; date of organization; original strength of regiments; number of recruits added since organization; aggregates of regiments, and veterans re-enlisted: making in all a grand aggregate of 21,806 men.

"Of the foregoing aggregate of 21,806 men, the Second Infantry was in the service for a period of only three months, and the Seventeenth Infantry for one hundred days. The Second numbered 650 men; the Seventeenth 455 men; making a total of 1,105 men. These reduced to three-years men—the standard of measurement adopted by the Department of War—would lessen the foregoing aggregate 1,009 men, and render it equal to 20,797 three-years men.

"The foregoing exhibit embraces all the white and colored troops enlisted in the volunteer service of which this office has any *official* information.

"It embraces also a number of Indians who were regularly recruited in the white regiments. These were our home Indians, such as the Delawares, Shawnees, Pottawatomies, etc.; many of them having been made citizens of the United States by act of Congress. It is impossible to separate these home Indians, or distinguish them from other members of the regiments, as they are reported here the same as other volunteers. Of this number, 2,083 are colored.

"In addition to the foregoing, there are three regiments of Indians in the service, officered, originally, almost exclusively by citizens from Kansas. These regiments have never reported to this office, consequently I can make no estimate of their numbers.

"The First and Second of the Indian Regiments, and part of the Third, were recruited in Kansas; the credits, however, consisting chiefly of refugee Indians, from the Cherokee and Creek Nations. A part, however, were resident Indians whose lands were, and still are, within the limits of our State, and whose homes and firesides are still here."

JANUARY 19.—Legislature adjourns to the 23d, to take a railroad excursion to Lawrence and Wyandotte.

—Report of Senate Committee to the petition of Nathan Price, that J. T. Lane is elected Senator from the First District.

JANUARY 26.—Overland mail line from Atchison reopened, after having been closed three weeks.

JANUARY 27.—A cotton gin at Burlington is doing a good business.

JANUARY 30.—Report of Senate Committee that the Auditor has drawn warrants to pay claims of officers and men in service in the State Militia, amounting to $62,800.

JANUARY 30.—Alex. H. Stephens, R. M. T. Hunter and Judge Campbell come within Grant's lines as Peace Commissioners.

FEBRUARY 1.—Congress passes the Constitutional Amendment abolishing Slavery.

FEBRUARY 1.—The mail service in this State, for the year ending June 30, 1864, cost $83,736; receipts, $58,644.

FEBRUARY 2.—Lincoln and Seward meet the Peace Commissioners at Fortress Monroe.

—Gold in Richmond, 4,400 per cent. premium.

FEBRUARY 6.—A Special Committee reports in favor of relocating the Penitentiary.

FEBRUARY 7.—Gen. Samuel R. Curtis leaves Fort Leavenworth, and is succeeded by Gen. G. M. Dodge.

FEBRUARY 10.—Report of House Special Committee, that D. Rogers is not entitled to a seat from Neosho county:

"In the organization of Neosho county, we find on file in the Secretary of State's office the necessary papers to complete such organization. We find from the evidence before us that D. Rogers, S. E. Beach and Rufus Estes, who filed the affidavit as to the number of inhabitants of the county of Neosho, are residents of Allen county. That of the thirty-one persons representing themselves as resident freeholders of Neosho county, a large majority are residents of Allen county; and that J. L. Fletcher, who was appointed Special Clerk, and the three persons appointed County Commissioners, are residents of Allen county."

FEBRUARY 15.—A draft begins, for the first time in the State, and because full credits have not been given.

—Much talk in the newspapers about cattle stolen from the Indian Territory.

FEBRUARY 17.—Sherman occupies Columbia, South Carolina.

FEBRUARY 18.—Gov. Crawford appoints the following Militia officers: Wm. F. Cloud, Major General, K. S. M.; D. E. Ballard, Quartermaster General, K. S. M.; John K. Rankin, Inspector General and Paymaster General; N. T. Winans, Surgeon General.

FEBRUARY 20.—Adjournment of the Legislature. It was a very short session. Among the laws made were the following: Authorizing counties and cities to issue bonds to railroad companies; Providing for taking the first census; To encourage the growth of forest trees; For a geological survey; For the incorporation and regulation of railroad companies; For the payment of claims arising out of the Price Raid and the expeditions of Gen. Curtis against the Indians, in July and August, 1864; For the government of the Insane Asylum; To prevent the bringing of Texas stock into the State.

FEBRUARY 21.—The Eleventh Kansas, Col. Plumb, leaves Fort Riley for Fort Kearney.

FEBRUARY 25.—G. C. Swallow appointed State Geologist.

—Gen. Thos. Ewing, jr., leaves the army.

MARCH 3.—Summary of a law passed by Congress, chapter 88 of U. S. Statutes:

"Allows the Central Pacific Railroad Company, and the Western Pacific Railroad Company, of California; the Union Pacific Railroad Company; the Union Pacific Railroad Company, Eastern Division; and all other Companies provided for in Pacific Railroad Act of July 2, 1864 (see Statutes 1864, ch. 210), to issue their six per centum thirty years' bonds upon their separate roads, and to issue their bonds respectively to the extent of 100 miles in advance of a continuous completed line of construction. The assignment made by the Central Pacific Railroad Company of California, to the Western Pacific Railroad Company of that State, of the right to construct all that portion of the railroad and telegraph from San Jose to Sacramento, is ratified. The first twenty miles of the road must be completed one year from July 1, 1865, and the entire road within four years thereafter."

MARCH 4.—Reinauguration of Lincoln. Conclusion of his Address:

"Neither party expected for the war the magnitude or the duration which it has already attained. Neither anticipated that the cause of the conflict might cease with, or even before the conflict itself should cease. Each looked for an easier triumph, and a result less fundamental and astounding.

"Both read the same Bible, and pray to the same God; and each invokes his aid against the other. It may seem strange that any men should dare to ask a just God's assistance in wringing their bread from the sweat of other men's faces; but let us judge not, that we be not judged. The prayers of both could not be answered. That of neither has been answered fully. The Almighty has his own purposes. 'Woe unto the world because of offences, for it must needs be that offences come; but woe to that man by whom the offence cometh.' If we shall suppose that American Slavery is one of these offences, which, in the providence of God, must needs come, but which, having continued through his appointed time, he now wills to remove, and that he gives to both North and South this terrible war as the woe due to those by whom the offence came, shall we discern therein any departure from those divine attributes which the believers in a living God always ascribe to him? Fondly do we hope, fervently do we pray, that this mighty scourge of war may soon pass away. Yet, if God wills that it continue until all the wealth piled by the bondman's two hundred and fifty years of unrequited toil shall be sunk, and until every drop of blood drawn with the lash shall be paid with another drawn by the sword; as was said three thousand years ago, so still it must be said, 'The judgments of the Lord are true and righteous altogether.'

"With malice towards none, with charity to all, with firmness in the right as God gives us to see the right, let us strive on to finish the work we are in; to bind up the Nation's wounds; to care for him who shall have borne the battle, and for his widow and his orphans; to do all which may achieve and cherish a just and a lasting peace among ourselves and with all nations."

MARCH 10.—Major Thos. J. Anderson appointed Adjutant General.

MARCH 15.—The draft in Kansas suspended.

—Hiram S. Sleeper appointed Surveyor General of Kansas and Nebraska. Henry C. Fields Chief Clerk.

MARCH 17. —Death of L. A. Maclean, staff officer of Gen. Sterling Price; formerly chief clerk of John Calhoun, at Lecompton.

MARCH 18.—Geo. A. Crawford orders machinery for a Woollen Factory, at Fort Scott.

—All the Kansas regiments at Fort Smith, Ark., five in number, leave there.

APRIL.—Geo. W. Martin revives the Union, and calls it the Junction City Union.

APRIL 1.—Battle of Five Forks; great victory of Sheridan.—Grant closing around Petersburg.

APRIL 2.—Advance on Petersburg. Petersburg and Richmond evacuated. Departure of Jeff. Davis.

APRIL 3.—Weitzel occupies Richmond.

APRIL 4.—Lincoln in Richmond.

APRIL 8.—Great Jubilee in Leavenworth over the Union victories and the end of the war. There were similar celebrations all over the State.

APRIL 9.—Surrender of Lee at Appomattox Court House.

APRIL 10.—Hiram T. Beman appointed Assistant Adjutant General.

APRIL 14.—Assassination of President Lincoln, by John Wilkes Booth, at Ford's Theatre, at 10 o'clock P. M. *Murderous attack upon Secretary Seward, by Payne.*

APRIL 15.—President Lincoln dies, at 22 minutes past 7 o'clock A. M.

—Andrew Johnson takes the oath of office as President.

APRIL 15.—Gov. Crawford appoints April 23d as a day of fasting and prayer, on account of the assassination of President Lincoln.

APRIL 18.—Terms of surrender by Johnston to Sherman.

APRIL 22.—Elijah Sells appointed Superintendent of Indian Affairs, vice William G. Coffin, resigned.

MAY 4.—Burial of Abraham Lincoln in Oak Ridge Cemetery, Springfield, Illinois.

MAY 5.—E. C. K. Garvey and C. K. Holliday buy the Topeka Tribune of Andrew Stark.

—Gen. R. B. Mitchell appointed to command the District of Kansas.

MAY 10.—Capture of Jeff. Davis, at Irwinville, Georgia.

—A census taken in this month gives the State a population of 135,807.

MAY 13.—Artemus Ward thanks the Leavenworth Typographical Union for electing him an honorary member. Among other things, he says: "It is the first time I was ever elected to anything. I once ran for County Clerk in this State, (Ohio,) but an ignorant and ruffianly people defeated me by some three thousand five hundred scattering votes. The civil war soon followed. Events since that *there* time are matters of history. I need not speak of them."

JUNE 1.—James Christian and Milton W. Reynolds buy the Lawrence State Journal.

JUNE 2.—Kirby Smith and Magruder formally surrender their forces at Galveston.

JUNE 26.—Work begun on the Leavenworth and Lawrence Railroad.

—The Home Journal started in Ottawa, by I. S. Kalloch and Charles T. Evans. Ottawa is one year old.

JULY 1.—"The Army of the Border" published by Church & Goodman, Chicago. It is a book of 351 pages, written by Richard J. Hinton, and is a history of the Price Raid of 1864. The pursuit and defeat of Gen. Price was the most important event in the history of the State, and it is fortunate that this record was made. The writer spent ten years in Kansas in unselfish and heroic service, and his name is gratefully remembered.

The rebel account of this campaign is given in the book called "Shelby and his Men; or the War in the West." The author says:

"No prisoners were taken, and why should there be? . . . Shelby was leaving Kansas and taking terrible adieus. He was fighting the devil with fire, and smoking him to death. Hay stacks, houses, barns, produce, crops and farming implements were consumed before the march of his squadrons, and what the flames spared the bullet finished. On those vast plains out west there, the jarring sabre-strokes were unheard, and the revolvers sounded as the tapping of woodpeckers. Shelby was soothing the wounds of Missouri by stabbing the breast of Kansas. For the victims of Lane and Jennison he demanded life for life and blood for blood. The interest had been compounded, but he gathered it to the uttermost farthing. Fort Scott lay before him like a picture, mellowed by haze and distance, and the orders for its destruction had gone forth. . . . I know not what feelings this exultation over fire and pillage may awaken in the breasts of Yankees, and I care not."—*pp. 447, 448.*

JULY 12.—Railroad meeting in behalf of the Leavenworth, Lawrence & Fort Gibson road, at Ottawa. Called to order by Gen. Lane, President of the road. The amount of bonds to be voted by each county fixed upon.

JULY 13.—Return of the Twelfth Kansas to Lawrence, where the regiment is to be mustered out.

—Gen. John Pope ordered to Fort Leavenworth.

JULY 17.—The Lawrence Journal appears as a Daily.

—Petroleum excitement in Miami and Bourbon counties.

JULY 26.—Second Annual Meeting of the State Teachers' Association, at Atchison.

JULY 26.—Books opened at Lawrence for the St. Louis, Lawrence & Denver Railroad.

—Damaging floods in different parts of the State.

—Escort train of Company H, Eleventh Kansas, burned at Red Buttes by Indians, and several soldiers killed.

—Mathews's Colored Battery mustered out.

JULY 28.—A. T. & S. F. R. R. meeting in Topeka. Atchison, Jefferson, Shawnee, Osage, Lyon and Chase counties agree to vote bonds September 12th; the same day that bonds are to be voted for the L. L. & F. G. R. R.

AUGUST 3.—Gov. Crawford writes to Secretary Harlan that the Osages and Cherokees are holding land in Kansas to which they have no title.

AUGUST 4.—Capt. E. A. Smith's Second Kansas Battery arrives at Fort Leavenworth, to be mustered out.

AUGUST 7.—Isaac E. Eaton reports from Denver to D. A. Butterfield that the Smoky Hill expedition is successful, and that route the best.

—Col. Thos. Moonlight resigns.

AUGUST 16.—The steamboat E. Hensley, Capt. Burke, built at Leavenworth, makes a trip to Lawrence.

AUGUST 21.—Kansas U. S. Provost Marshal offices abolished.

AUGUST 28.—Election, at Olathe, of Directors of the Kansas and Neosho Valley R. R. Co. Col. Kersey Coates elected President.

—Col. S. W. Eldridge is building, for the third time, the Eldridge House, at Lawrence.

AUGUST 31.—J. M. Edmunds, Commissioner of the General Land Office, replies to Gov. Crawford that his views in regard to the boundaries of the Osage and Cherokee lands are erroneous. Some time later, G. J. Endicott made a new survey; his conclusion was that the authorities at Washington were wrong. The correspondence is given in the Message of Gov. Crawford, January 10, 1866. One point of the dispute was the location of "White Hair's Village."

SEPTEMBER 10.—All Kansas troops ordered to be mustered out as soon as they can reach home.

SEPTEMBER 29.—Treaty with the Great and Little Osage Indians. The Osages sell to the United States the lands bounded as follows:

"Beginning at the southeast corner of their present reservation, and running thence north with the eastern boundary thereof fifty miles to the northeast corner; thence west with the northern line thirty miles; thence south fifty miles, to the southern boundary of said reservation; and thence east with said southern boundary to the place of beginning."

The United States agree to pay $300,000 for the land. They also cede to the United States a tract of land twenty miles in width from north to south, off the north side of the remainder of their present reservation, and extending its entire length from east to west.

OCTOBER 14.—Treaty with the Cheyennes and Arapahoes.

OCTOBER 15.—George T. Isbell becomes the publisher of the Grasshopper Falls Jeffersonian.

OCTOBER 17.—The claims before the Price Raid Commission amount to nearly $2,000,000.

OCTOBER 18.—Public reception of Gen. W. T. Sherman in Leavenworth. He was received in Lawrence on the 19th.

—The pontoon bridge at Topeka completed.

—Major B. S. Henning takes up his residence at Lawrence, and superintends the Leavenworth and Lawrence Railroad.

OCTOBER 30.—President Johnson, after a long controversy, accepts the first forty miles of the Kansas branch of the Pacific Railroad.

—Death of Lewis Tracy, Esq., in Doniphan county. He was one of the earliest citizens of Kansas and of the Platte Purchase, in Missouri. He joined the Union army when more than sixty years old.

NOVEMBER 2.—Annual election.

SENATORS TO FILL VACANCIES.

Counties.	1ST DIST.		2D DIST.		9TH DIST.	11TH DIST.		14TH DIST.			15TH DIST.	
	Sol. Miller	Abram Bennett	Joshua Wheeler	Geo. W. Martin	Eugene L. Akin	David Anderson	A. S. McGuffin	D. B. Emmert	E. A. Smith	Scattering	Reuben Riggs	Mahlon Stubbs
Doniphan..	680	538										
Atchison....			730	519								
Douglas......					1,575							
Miami........						723	21					
Bourbon ...								459	415	1		
Butler											22	25
Chase........											78	65
Morris											105	75
Marion......											25	
											230	165

MEMBERS OF THE HOUSE.

District.	Counties.	Names.	Votes.	Maj.	Total.	Vote of County.
1	Doniphan..............	Charles E. Fox........................	180			
		John H. Utt............................	139	41	319	
2	....	Robert H. Montgomery............	121			
		William J. Orem	64	57	185	
3	....	Lyman Nash	119			
		W. H. Smallwood....................	98	21	217	
4	....	W. Harrington	141			
		Robert Myles	125	16	266	

MEMBERS OF THE HOUSE—CONTINUED.

District.	Counties.	Names.	Votes.	Maj.	Total.	Vote of County.
5	Doniphan (continued)..	E. M. Stratton	64			
		F. E. Micks	50			
		F. E. Mix	42			
		E. A. Beauchary	8		164	1,151
6	Atchison	G. W. Glick	185			
		E. K. Blair	165	20	350	
7		William Jackson	217			
		Robert Manville	141	76	358	
8		W. S. Cain	154			
		M. R. Benton	69	85	223	
9		Milo Carlton	145			
		Joseph Dousbough	9	136	154	
10		George W. Stabler	55	19		
		Orvill Lee	36			
		W. K. Shimp	29		120	1,205
11	Brown	Ira J. Lacock	143		143	
12		Chase E. Parker	110	66		
		John M. Meidith	44			
		P. B. Rust	4			
		C. B. Sanders	1		159	302
13	Nemaha	George Graham	129		129	
14		James K. Gross	114	30		
		Joseph Hanners	84			
		S. H. Andrews	1		199	328
15	Marshall	James Smith	187	42		
		S. B. Todd	145		332	332
16	Washington	G. H. Hollenberg	90	47		
		R. H. West	43		133	133
17	Pottawatomie	H. P. Smith	202	50		
		S. Moody	152		354	354
18	Jackson	James McLellan	189	85		
		John Rippetoe	104			
		Golden Silvers	78		371	371
19	Jefferson	Walter N. Allen	189	40		
		J. M. Johnson	149		338	338
20		George Van Gaasbeek	134			
		Robert Riddle	94	40	228	
21		Jerome Kunkel	119	5		
		A. Venard	114			
		B. W. Whitlow	40			
		J. N. O. P. Wood	80			
		M. D. Baldwin	85		438	1,004
22	Leavenworth	T. M. O'Brien	230	112		
		E. N. O. Clough	118			
		W. G. Mathias	113		461	
23		Josiah Kellogg	233		233	
24		C. R. Jennison	289	5		
		W. F. Cloud	284		537	
25		Auley McAuley	362		362	
26		Fred. Wellhouse	84	50		
		Will. F. Goble	34		118	
27		N. Humber	81	23		
		J. C. Baird	58		139	
28		J. Knight	137	23		
		Walker Kerr	114		251	
29	.:	Jos. P. Bauserman	71	28		
		J. M. Orr	11			
		Milton Sloan	43		125	
30		R. Cole Foster	92	49		
		J. D. Ross	43		135	2,397
31	Wyandotte	Isaiah Walker	325	167		
		James D. Chestnut	158			
		Scattering	9			492
32	Johnson	John T. Burris	239	80		
		John C. Collins	159		389	
33		A. S. Johnson	157	95		
		R. N. Pursell	62			
		F. Strausser	35		254	
34		Garret C. Rue	122	22		
		Thomas A. Parker	100			
		—— Young	2		224	876
35	Douglas	John K. Rankin	654		654	

MEMBERS OF THE HOUSE—Continued.

District.	Counties.	Names.	Votes......	Maj......	Total......	Vote of County.
36	Douglas (concluded)......	George W. Smith........................	101	23		
		E. R. Falley........................	78		179	
37	....	Warner Craig........................	113		113	
38	....	Levi Woodard........................	188		188	
39	....	J. H. Bonebrake........................	98	52	98	
		A. J. Parrish	46		46	
		W. S. Kirby	21		165	
40	....	James H. Kelley	135		135	1,434
41	Shawnee	C. K. Holliday........................	334	132		
		W. W. H. Lawrence ...:........................	202		536	
42	....	James Fletcher	155	58		
		John S. Ward........................	97		252	788
43	Miami	H. B. Smith........................	150	116		
		Z. Baker........................	34		184	
44	....	R. W. Massey........................	189	30		
		John McReynolds	159		348	
45	....	Sylvester Underhill........................	231		231	763
46	Linn	O. D. Harmon........................	62	12		
		R. Hill	50		112	
47	....	J. M. Arthur........................	101	5		
		Jonathan Hodgson........................	96			
		Scattering........................	....		197	
48	....	J. C. Quinn........................	111	52		
		John S. Leave	59		170	
49	....	J. M. Brice	94	44		
		James D. Snoddy	50			
		Scattering........................	....		144	623
50	Bourbon........................	W. H. Green........................	79	28		
		T. L. Wilson........................	51		130	
51	....	Joseph L. Wilson........................	136	99		
		H. Goff........................	37		173	
52	....	Nelson Griswold........................	141	139		
		Scattering........................	2		143	
53	....	C. W. Blair........................	264	119		
		W. A. Shannon	145		409	855
54	Allen	Joseph Bond	161	73		
		W. C. Jones........................	88			
		—— Christy........................	1		250	
55	....	F. W. Power........................	66	18		
		John A. Christy........................	48		114	364
56	Anderson	H. Cavender........................	99	1		
		—— McShane........................	98			
		J. Hiver........................	48		245	
57	....	J. W. Stewart........................	52	21		
		D. L. Duff........................	31			
		John Smith........................	13			
		S. L. Fullenwider........................	20		116	361
58	Franklin........................	William Pennock........................	78	22		
		Alfred Johnson........................	56			
		A. Johnson........................	2		136	
59	....	Jacob G. Reese	189	186		
		James Hanway........................	3		192	328
60	Osage........................	H. D. Preston	129	53		
		P. C. Schuyler	76			
		S. P. Hart	39		244	244
61	Coffey	Charles Cochrane........................	174	61		
		J. M. Rankin	113		287	
62	....	A. N. Coffin........................	123			
		A. Jones........................	111	12		
		W. A. Ela........................	16		150	537
63	Wilson	Isaac W. Dow........................	92	52		
		W. B. Stines........................	40			
		Scattering........................	1		133	133
64	Lyon........................	Jacob Stotler........................	251	250		
		Scattering........................	1		252	
65	....	E. H. Sanford........................	155	152		
		Scattering........................	3		158	
66	....	Charles Drake........................	77	38		
		S. L. Loy........................	39			
		Scattering........................	4		120	530
67	Butler	D. L. McCabe........................	37	25		
		L. M. Pratt........................	12			
		S. W. Satchell........................	5		54	54

MEMBERS OF THE HOUSE—Concluded.

District.	Counties.	Names.	Votes.	Maj.	Total.	Vote of County.
68	Chase	S. N. Wood	105	59		
		O. H. Drinkwater	46		249	249
69	Morris	J. H. Bradford	101	23		
		R. B. Lockwood	78		179	179
70	Wabaunsee	H. D. Shepherd	77		77	77
71	Davis	A. W. Callen	248	238		
		J. P. Wiley	5			
		L. B. Perry	3			
		Scattering	2		258	258
72	Riley	J. M. Harvey	282	281		
		J. H. Phelps	1		283	283
73	Dickinson	C. H. Kohler	39	3		
		Dan. Jones	36		75	75
74	Saline	W. A. Phillips	74	1		
		H. L. Jones	73		147	147
75	Greenwood	William Martindale	84	31		
		W. B. Godfrey	53			
		W. W. Brazel	11		148	148
76	Woodson	Henry Pearman	69	23		
		A. Thompson	46		115	115
77	Neosho	Darius Rogers	50			
		Scattering			50	50
78	Marion	A. A. Moore	28		28	28

NOVEMBER 15.—Telegraph completed to Topeka.

—Prof. Swallow discovers marble at Fort Scott.

—The Eighth Kansas is at San Antonio, Texas.

—Grading in progress on the railroad between Leavenworth and Wyandotte.

NOVEMBER 16.—The Sixteenth Kansas arrives at Fort Leavenworth, from the Plains.

NOVEMBER 20.—Col. Vliet leaves Lawrence to survey the L. L. & Ft. G. R. R., and the Emporia branch.

NOVEMBER 23.—The first rail laid on the Atchison and Pike's Peak R. R.

—Major B. F. Simpson returns to the practice of law, in Miami county.

—The Lawrence and Pleasant Hill Railroad is surveyed.

NOVEMBER 27.—Major O. B. Gunn leaves Atchison to survey the A. T. & S. F. R. R.

NOVEMBER 30.—Expenditures of the State for the year:

Governor's Department	$6,325 00	Legislature and Journals	23,287 95
Secretary's Department	5,421 45	State Normal School	2,000 00
Auditor's Department	2,960 54	Penitentiary	21,506 22
Treasurer's Department	2,767 00	Geological Survey	7,500 00
Sup't of Public Instruction	1,866 85	Deaf and Dumb Asylum	2,041 11
Attorney General	1,031 48	Agricultural College	3,316 50
Adjutant General	6,042 50	Capitol grounds and building	42,492 15
Quartermaster General	1,480 94	Military purposes	2,992 19
Paymaster General	1,000 00	Taking census	2,997 07
Judiciary Department	15,691 95	Rent of Capitol building	3,000 00
Printing	24,979 74	Miscellaneous expenses	3,715 72
Military Companies	2,789 23		
Total for 1865			$187,105 59

DECEMBER 9.—The Topeka Leader issued, by J. F. Cummings & Co.; Ward Burlingame Editor.

—Western Home Journal, at Ottawa, edited by I. S. Kalloch and C. C. Hutchinson.

DECEMBER 13.—Col. Wm. A. Barstow, of the Third Wisconsin, dies in Leavenworth.

DECEMBER 14.—The Adjutant General reports that Kansas furnished the General Government during the war 19,812 men.

—A telegraph office is established at Troy.

—Robert B. Mitchell appointed Governor of New Mexico.

DECEMBER 15.—The Report of R. A. Barker, Secretary of State, says the census taken in May is not yet classified and arranged. It contains a list of the bonds issued under the act of March 1, 1864, to refund taxes, amounting to $39,675; a list of the bonds issued to fund the Territorial debt, under the act of Feb. 20, 1863, amounting to $57,300 issued to date; and a list of the land selected by Johnson Clark, P. B. Maxson and Daniel Mitchell for the Agricultural College, amounting to 82,313.53 acres.

DECEMBER 15.—The report of President Denison, of the Agricultural College, to Superintendent Goodnow, says the Catalogue contains the names of 113 students.

—G. W. Paddock, Regent, reports that the Regents of the University held their first meeting March 21. R. W. Oliver was elected Chancellor; G. W. Paddock, Secretary; G. W. Deitzler, Treasurer; and Jas. S. Emery, Librarian. The officers, with Solon O. Thacher and Charles Robinson, were made an executive committee. James H. Lane and the City of Lawrence have given an additional site of eight acres of land. A new building, fifty feet square, is in process of erection.

—Prof. Joseph Mount has charge of the Deaf and Dumb school, at Baldwin City.

—The Normal School opened at Emporia, February 15, with 18 students. L. B. Kellogg and H. B. Norton are the teachers.

—Fifty miles of the Kansas Pacific road are completed.

—The Leavenworth Conservative publishes long military histories, written by Col. Moonlight and Col. Jennison.

1866.

JANUARY 3.—Officers of the State Agricultural Society, elected at Topeka: President, L. D. Bailey, of Douglas; Secretary, John S. Brown, of Douglas; Treasurer, Wm. Spriggs, of Anderson; Superintendent, J. L. McDowell. *Executive Committee:* C. B. Lines of Wabaunsee county, J. W. Sponable of Johnson, H. J. Strickler of Shawnee, G. W. Deitzler of Douglas, S. S. Tipton of Anderson, R. G. Elliott of Jefferson, H. B. Keller of Leavenworth, Alfred Gray of Wyandotte, A. W. J. Brown of Allen, Jas. B. Maynard of Doniphan. State Fair held at Lawrence.

JANUARY 5.—James H. Lane returns to Leavenworth from Washington, and makes a speech on Reconstruction, and endorsing President Andrew Johnson.

—The Eighth Kansas arrives in Atchison.

JANUARY 8.—Report of G. C. Swallow, State Geologist, 94 pages; of Maj. F. Hawn, Assistant, 28 pages; of C. A. Logan, on the Sanitary Relations of Kansas, 50 pages; of Tiffin Sinks, on the Climatology of Kansas, 20 pages.

The following tables are copied from Dr. Sinks's Report:

TABLE OF MEAN TEMPERATURE FOR SEASONS AND YEARS.

Location.	Latitude	Longitude	Altitude (feet)	Spring	Summer	Autumn	Winter	Maximum	Minimum	Year
Fort Leavenworth...	39°21'	94°44'	896	53°76	74°05	53°66	29°76	108°	—30°	52°81
Fort Riley.............	39 00	96 30	1,180	55 85	79 12	56 09	27 98	106	—23	53 47
Fort Scott.............	37 45	94 35	1,000	54 75	74 95	55.27	32 93	98	—10	54 48
Fort Larned..........	38 15	99 20	1,780	50 76	77 43	54 34	32 12			53 66
Fort Kearney........	40 38	98 57	2,360	46 81	71 47	49 35	23 04	102	—28	47 66
St. Louis.............	38 40	90 05	450	54 15	76 19	55 44	32 27	107	—18	54 51
Cincinnati.............	39 05	84 29	500	53 80	73 70	53 60	33 80	106	—17	53 70
Pittsburgh.............	40 32	80 02	704	49 97	71 47	51 43	30 59	100	—18	50 86

TABLE OF MEAN TEMPERATURE FOR MONTHS.

Location.	January	February	March	April	May	June	July	August	September	October	November	December
Fort Leavenworth.	28°00	31°15	42°22	55°47	63°64	71°31	76°67	74°16	66°16	54°46	40°36	29°77
Fort Riley	24 73	31 49	44 66	56 03	67 47	76 40	82 26	78 71	72 55	55 60	40 13	27 73
Fort Scott.............	32 91	34 98	43 13	55 72	65 48	72 11	77 22	75 53	68 62	55 23	41 91	31 09
Fort Larned..........	27 18	35 09	43 03	52 92	56 43	73 49	79 84	78 98	70 28	52 36	40 39	34 09
Fort Kearney........	21 14	26 11	34 50	47 13	58 81	68 51	73 56	72 33	64 42	49 56	34 07	21 87
St. Louis.............	35 44	33 43	42 30	55 08	65 07	74 20	78 22	76 16	69 58	54 20	42 55	31 93
Cincinnati	38 50	34 10	43 40	54 50	63 50	71 10	76 30	73 70	65 50	53 00	42 30	33 80
Pittsburgh	29 25	31 16	39 02	49 96	60 92	69 22	72 98	71 21	63 58	50 91	39 80	31 35

MEAN PRECIPITATION OF RAIN, CALCULATED FOR SEASONS AND YEARS.

Places of Observation.	Spring	Summer	Autumn	Winter	Year	No. Years.
Fort Leavenworth	7.32	13.03	7.57	3.42	31.34	30
Fort Riley	5.62	10.68	5.87	2.72	24.90	5
Fort Scott	12.57	16.37	8.39	4.79	42.12	10
Fort Larned	5.36	8.45	4.01	.81	18.63	4
Fort Kearney	6.80	10.62	4.85	1.50	23.77	13
St. Louis	12.30	14.14	8.94	6.94	42.32	19
Cincinnati	12.14	13.70	9.90	11.15	46.89	20
Pittsburgh	9.38	9.87	8.23	7.48	34.96	18
Athens, Illinois	12.20	13.30	9.20	7.10	41.80	10

"Taking the records at Forts Leavenworth, Riley and Scott as a basis for calculation, the mean annual precipitation of rain for the eastern half of the State is 32 78-100 inches. The mean for the western half is about 24 inches.

"The mean for Minnesota is 30 inches, for Wisconsin 32 inches, and for Michigan 30 inches."

28

JANUARY 9.—Meeting of the Legislature.

MEMBERS AND OFFICERS OF THE SENATE.

Members and Officers.	Age.	P. O. Address.	County.	Avocation.
James McGrew, President	44	Wyandotte	Wyandotte	Merch't.
Akin, Eugene L	28	Lawrence	Douglas	Lawyer.
Anderson, David	41	Paola	Miami	Farmer.
Bartlett, W. K	40	Junction City	Davis	Merch't.
Barber, Oliver	49	Kanwaka	Douglas	Farmer.
Drenning, F. H	28	Wathena	Doniphan	Lawyer.
Emmert, D. B	29	Fort Scott	Bourbon	Publis'r.
Eskridge, C. V	31	Emporia	Lyon	Merch't.
Foote, Henry	36	Leavenworth	Leavenworth	Farmer.
Gambell, W. P	33	Leavenworth	Leavenworth	Attor'ey.
Grover, O. J	38	America City	Nemaha	Farmer.
Houston, D. W	37	Garnett	Anderson	Lawyer.
Horne, D. H	36	Topeka	Shawnee	Land Ag.
Jones, J. H	38	Kaw City	Jefferson	Farmer.
Legate, J. F	37	Leavenworth	Leavenworth	Farmer.
Manning, E. C	27	Marysville	Marshall	Printer.
Miller, Sol	35	White Cloud	Doniphan	Printer.
Milboan, T. E	33	Olathe	Johnson	Farmer.
Wheeler, Joshua	39	Pardee	Atchison	Farmer.
Potter, F. W	32	Burlington	Coffey	Laborer.
Quigg, M	29	Atchison	Atchison	Clerk.
Riggs, Reuben	56	Marion Centre	Marion	Lawyer.
Spear, S	49	Hiawatha	Brown	Farmer.
Smith, A. H	38	Blooming Grove	Linn	Farmer.
Twiss, Charles P	32	Iola	Allen	Lawyer.
Weer, William	41	Wyandotte	Wyandotte	Lawyer.
A. R. Banks, Secretary	30	Lawrence	Douglas	Lawyer.
A. Hitchcock, Assistant Secretary	38	Lawrence	Douglas	Minister.
W. F. Goble, Docket Clerk	27	Pleasant Ridge	Leavenworth	Book'er.
Ira H. Smith, Journal Clerk	49	Topeka	Shawnee	Land Ag.
L. M. Benedict, Engrossing Clerk	34	Vienna	Pottawatomie	Farmer.
W. B. Bowman, Enrolling Clerk	35	Wyandotte	Wyandotte	Lawyer.
T. Mills, Sergeant-at-Arms	51	Topeka	Shawnee	Mason.
Wm. Thompson, Doorkeeper	32	Topeka	Shawnee	Farmer.
G. Y. Arnold, Assistant Doorkeeper	23	Topeka	Shawnee	Merch't.
Clarence Walrod, Page	12	Paola	Miami	Student.
J. T. Miller, Page	14	Topeka	Shawnee	Student.

MEMBERS AND OFFICERS OF THE HOUSE OF REPRESENTATIVES.

Members.	Age.	P. O. Address.	County.	Avocation.
John T. Burris, Speaker	37	Olathe	Johnson	Lawyer.
Allen, W. N	32	Oskaloosa	Jefferson	Lawyer.
Arthur, J. M	49	Centreville	Linn	Farmer.
Bauserman, J. P	25	Leavenworth	Leavenworth	Farmer.
Blair, C. W	37	Fort Scott	Bourbon	Lawyer.
Bradford, J. H	37	Council Grove	Morris	Physician.
Brice, S. M	51	Mound City	Linn	Physician.
Bond, Joseph	45	Humboldt	Allen	Printer.
Bonebrake, J. H	35	Lecompton	Douglas	Physician.
Cain, W. S	29	Atchison	Atchison	Farmer.
Callen, A. W	33	Junction City	Davis	Lawyer.
Carlton, Milo	51	Pardee	Atchison	Farmer.
Cavender, H	32	Garnett	Anderson	Merchant.
Craig, Warner	29	Baldwin City	Douglas	Farmer.
Cochrane, Charles	32	Ottumwa	Coffey	Farmer.
Coffin, A. V	46	Le Roy	Coffey	Everyth'g.
Drake, C	29	Americus	Lyon	Farmer.
Dow, Isaac W	33	Neosho Falls	Woodson	Mechanic.
Fletcher, James	36	Tecumseh	Shawnee	Farmer.
Foster, R. C	31	Leavenworth	Leavenworth	Teamster.
Fox, Charles E	31	Highland	Doniphan	Farmer.
Graham, George	45	Seneca	Nemaha	Merchant.
Green, W. H	38	Fort Lincoln	Bourbon	Farmer.
Glick, G. W	38	Atchison	Atchison	Attorney.

MEMBERS AND OFFICERS OF THE HOUSE OF REPRESENTATIVES—Concl'd.

Members and Officers.	Age.	P. O. Address.	County.	Avocation.
Griswold, Nelson	45	Turkey Creek	Bourbon	Farmer.
Gross, James R	34	America City	Nemaha	Freighter.
Harmon, O. D	37	Twin Springs	Linn	Farmer.
Harrington, N	42	Palermo	Doniphan	Physician.
Harvey, J. M	32	Fort Riley	Riley	Farmer.
Hollenberg, G. H	38	Marysville	Washington	Farmer.
Holliday, C. K	38	Topeka	Shawnee	Lawyer.
Humber, N	50	Easton	Leavenworth	Farmer.
Jackson, W	32	Atchison	Atchison	Farmer.
Jennison, C. R	32	Leavenworth	Leavenworth	Farmer.
Johnson, A. S	33	Shawnee	Johnson	Farmer.
Kellogg, Josiah	33	Leavenworth	Leavenworth	Lawyer.
Kelly, James H	40	Willow Springs	Douglas	Farmer.
Knight, Jonathan	32	Tonganoxie	Leavenworth	Farmer.
Kohler, C	31	Junction City	Dickinson	Mechanic.
Kunkel, Jerome	38	Rising Sun	Jefferson	Lumber'n.
Lacock, Ira J	31	Hiawatha	Brown	Lawyer.
Martindale, Wm	30	Madison	Greenwood	Farmer.
Massey, R. W	43	Paola	Miami	Lawyer.
Montgomery, R. H	27	Columbus	Doniphan	Teacher.
Mix, F. E	27	Atchison	Doniphan	Farmer.
Moore, A. A	54	Marion Centre	Marion	Rancher.
McAuley, A	54	Leavenworth	Leavenworth	Lawyer.
McCabe, David L	34	Eldorado	Butler	Bl'ksmith.
McLellan, James	45	Holton	Jackson	Farmer.
Nash, Lyman	45	Wathena	Doniphan	Mechanic.
O'Brien, T. M	35	Leavenworth	Leavenworth	Mil. att'y.
Parker, C. E	41	Carson	Brown	Farmer.
Pearman, H	43	Belmont	Wilson	Farmer.
Pennock, Wm	35	Minneola	Franklin	Farmer.
Preston, H. D	36	Burlingame	Osage	Farmer.
Phillips, Wm. A	39	Salina	Saline	Journalist.
Power, F. M	34	Iola	Allen	Farmer.
Quinn, J. C	56	Mound City	Linn	Farmer.
Rankin, Jno. K	28	Lawrence	Douglas	Laborer.
Rees, J. G	40	Mount Gilead	Franklin	Farmer.
Rogers, D	34	Humboldt	Neosho	Merchant.
Rue, G. C	42	Gardner	Johnson	Merchant.
Sanford, Eph. H	43	Allen	Lyon	Lawyer.
Stabler, Geo. W	30	Huron	Atchison	Stock r'ser.
Shepard, H. D	27	Wilmington	Wabaunsee	Merchant.
Stewart, J. W	45	Garnett	Anderson	Miller.
Smith, James	28	Barrett	Marshall	Farmer.
Smith, H. P	35	Rock Creek	Pottawatomie	Miller.
Smith, Geo. W	60	Lawrence	Douglas	Lawyer.
Smith, H. B	33	Osawatomie	Miami	Merchant.
Stotler, Jacob	31	Emporia	Lyon	Printer.
Underhill, S	42	Osawatomie	Miami	Farmer.
Van Gaasbeck, Geo	50	Grasshopper Falls	Jefferson	Farmer.
Walker, Isaiah	40	Wyandotte	Wyandotte	Merchant.
Wellhouse, F	37	Pleasant Ridge	Leavenworth	Farmer.
Wilson, Joseph S	49	Mapleton	Bourbon	Farmer.
Wood, S. N	40	Cottonwood Falls	Chase	Farmer.
Woodard, Levi	35	Eudora	Douglas	Farmer.
John T. Morton, Chief Clerk	44	Topeka	Shawnee	Lawyer.
John E. Thorpe, Assistant Clerk	26	Iola	Allen	Farmer.
Wm. R. Brown, Journal Clerk	25	Lawrence	Douglas	Lawyer.
J. A. Soward, Docket Clerk	31	Wyandotte	Wyandotte	Merchant.
Dwight G. Hull, Engrossing Clerk.	24	Atchison	Atchison	Bookk'per.
W. H. Cowan, Enrolling Clerk.	24	Topeka	Shawnee	Clerk.
Thos. Archer, Sergeant-at-Arms	32	Topeka	Shawnee	Trader.
L. W. Graham, Ass't Serg.-at-Arms	33	Elmendaro	Lyon	Farmer.
G. Pharaoh, Doorkeeper	24	Lawrence	Douglas	File cutter.
C. T. K. Prentice, Ass't Doork'per.	18	Lawrence	Douglas	Farmer.
Wm. R. Griffith, Page	17	Topeka	Shawnee	Farmer.
Wm. Miller, Page	19	Ridgeway	Osage	Student.
Francis J. Rice, Page	12	Topeka	Shawnee	Student.

JANUARY 9.—The following is copied from Gov. Crawford's Message:

"Baker University, located at Baldwin City, Douglas county, is under the control of the Methodist Episcopal Church; Lane University, in the same county, is under the supervision of the United Brethren Church; Ottumwa College, at Ottumwa, Coffey county, is under the management of the Christian Church; Highland University, at Highland, Doniphan county, is under the control of the Presbyterian Church; Ottawa University, at Ottawa City, Franklin county, is under the care of the Baptist Church; Lincoln College, at Topeka, belongs to the Congregational Church; the Episcopal Church has a Female Seminary at Topeka; Wetmore Institute, at Irving, Marshall county, is under the control of the Presbyterian Church; the Methodists are erecting one at Circleville, in Jackson county, which will soon be ready for occupation; they also own Hartford Institute, at Hartford, Lyon county."

—There are about 300 miles of railroad in the State.

—Baker University, at Baldwin City, has 202 students.

JANUARY 11.—The Price Raid Commission have audited claims amounting to $400,000.

—Lawrence has a woollen factory nearly completed.

—Thos. Murphy, Indian Superintendent, pays the Ottawa Indians their last annuity. Of their lands, 87,000 acres are to be sold to settlers; 20,000 acres are given to the College now in process of erection.

—Senator Lane addresses the citizens of Topeka in behalf of Andrew Johnson's policy; his resolutions are adopted, as they had been in Leavenworth.

JANUARY 12.—T. J. Anderson, Adjutant General, reports that we lost 472 officers and 7,344 enlisted men during the war.

JANUARY 17.—Meeting in Topeka to form a State Editors' and Publishers' Association. R. B. Taylor Chairman, John A. Martin Secretary. Eighteen papers represented.

—The Burlington Woollen Factory is in operation.

JANUARY 26.—A bill has passed the Senate giving 500,000 acres of State lands to railroads. It passes the House February 17th, by 44 to 27, and against the written protest of twenty-three members. See House Journal, p. 483. The Attorney General declares the bill constitutional. House Journal, pp. 494-8.

FEBRUARY 12.—Theodore C. Sears, by invitation, addresses the Legislature on the life and character of Abraham Lincoln.

—Wool-growing becomes an important interest in Anderson county.

FEBRUARY 20.—Death of Samuel A. Stinson, of Leavenworth, at Wiscasset, Maine. Mr. Stinson was a member of the Wyandotte Convention, had been Attorney General of the State, and was one of the most brilliant, successful and popular lawyers in the State.

FEBRUARY 27.—Adjournment of the Legislature. Among the acts passed were the following: Apportioning the State for Senators and Representatives; Seventeen acts relating to bonds; Defining the boundaries of Neosho county; Providing temporary buildings at Olathe for a Deaf and and Dumb Asylum; Encouraging the growth of forest trees; Giving the 500,000 acres of land granted to Kansas under the act of Sept. 4, 1841, to the following railroad companies: The Northern Kansas, from Elwood; the Kansas and Neosho Valley (for a road through Johnson, Miami, Linn, and Bourbon counties); the Union Pacific Railway, Southern Branch, from Fort Riley along the Neosho Valley; and to the Leavenworth, Lawrence and Fort Gibson Railroad Company—the lands to be sold for the benefit of these companies, by an Agent appointed by the Governor;—An act for the protection of State and county treasuries; Changing the name of the Leavenworth, Lawrence and Fort Gibson Railroad Company to the Leavenworth, Lawrence and Galveston Railroad Company; Issuing bonds to build the Penitentiary; For the erection of a State House, and the sale of public lands; For the sale of Normal School lands; For the sale of University lands; For the sale of Agricultural College lands.

MARCH 1.—A coal mine is in successful operation near Ridgeway, Osage county.

MARCH 8.—Proposals are published for building a portion of a State Penitentiary.

MARCH 10.—Col. John W. Horner is elected President of Baker University.

MARCH 19.—Jas. L. McDowell becomes Postmaster at Leavenworth.

—E. C. Manning revives the Big Blue Union.

—The track on the Pacific road is laid to Silver Lake, twelve miles west of Topeka.

MARCH 20.—The names of five soldiers who were buried at Andersonville are published. They belonged to the Eighth Kansas.

MARCH 29.—Proposals are published for building a portion of the State Capitol.

APRIL.—Gov. Crawford sells in New York $60,000 Penitentiary and $70,000 Public Improvement State bonds, at 91 cents on the dollar.

APRIL 6.—J. H. Lane, in the Senate, makes a bitter speech supporting the President's policy, but indignantly denying that he wears Andrew Johnson's collar.

APRIL 12.—Ira J. Lacock takes charge of the Hiawatha Sentinel.

APRIL 14.—A public meeting in Lawrence strongly condemns the course of Senator Lane. The resolutions were reported by Major E. G. Ross.

—Gen. John W. Whitfield writes from Austin, Texas: "We got whipped, and there is no use to talk. I am the most loyal man now you ever saw."

APRIL 14.—A meeting in Fort Scott, called to support Johnson and Lane, denounces both.

APRIL 18.—The Humboldt Union started: W. T. McElroy, Publisher; Orlin Thurston, Editor. T. C. Sherman, W. R. Spooner and D. B. Emmert have been partners of Mr. McElroy.

APRIL 20.—First National Bank of Topeka organized.

—The Ben. Holladay Overland Mail runs from the terminus of the Pacific road to Denver.

—G. A. Colton takes charge of the Paola Free Press.

MAY 12.—Meeting in Hiawatha to take measures to consolidate the Northern Kansas R. R. Co. with the St. Joseph and Denver. Samuel Lappin President, F. H. Drenning Secretary.

MAY 13.—A farmer killed by Indians on the Solomon.

MAY 14.—Ward Burlingame succeeds T. C. Sears as editor of the Conservative.

—R. St. Clair Graham appointed Judge, vice Albert H. Horton, resigned.

MAY 15.—Trains begin running on the Leavenworth branch, to Lawrence. R. H. Shoemaker is Superintendent of the road.

MAY 20.—Six men killed by Indians, fifteen miles west of Lake Sibley.

TABLE SHOWING THE POPULATION OF THE STATE, MAY, 1865.

Counties.	White.	Colored.	Indian.	Total.
Allen	2,450	287	....	2,737
Anderson	2,544	115	....	2,659
Atchison	8,316	613	....	8,929
Butler	276	18	....	294
Brown	2,784	107	....	2,891
Bourbon	7,174	787	....	7,961
Eight-mile strip neutral lands, south of Bourbon county.	595	1	....	596
Clay	238	....	....	238
Coffey	3,127	256	....	3,383
Chase	870	....	....	870
Douglas	13,736	2,078	....	15,814
Doniphan	8,787	808	....	9,595
Davis	1,167	22	....	1,189
Dickinson	442	....	....	442
Franklin	3,583	112	....	3,695
Greenwood	1,187	1	....	1,188
Jefferson	5,584	269	....	5,853
Jackson	2,940	22	....	2,962
Johnson	5,469	342	382	6,093
Linn	5,853	690	....	6,543
Lyon *	2,200	48	....	2,248
Leavenworth	20,882	3,374	....	24,256
Miami	5,842	309	....	6,151
Morris	1,115	26	....	1,141
Marion	161	1	....	162
Marshall	2,346	3	....	2,349
Nemaha	2,615	23	....	2,638
Neosho	698	79	....	777
Ottawa	178	....	....	178
Osage	1,140	29	....	1,169
Pottawatomie	2,022	97	....	2,119
Riley	1,802	11	....	1,813
Shawnee	3,201	257	....	3,458
Saline	472	1	....	473
Washington †	....	....	....	....
Woodson	1,108	199	....	1,307
Wabaunsee	1,043	38	....	1,081
Wyandotte	3,323	1,504	....	4,827
Wilson †	....	....	....	....
Total	127,270	12,527	382	140,179

* Sixty-fifth District not returned.   † Not reported.

At a meeting of the State Central Democratic Committee at Leavenworth, the following preamble and resolutions were adopted:

"*Whereas*, In the present crisis in public affairs it becomes the duty of every political organization and every individual who has the interest of his country at heart, so far as its or his action can influence public opinion, to faithfully, honestly, and fearlessly express that opinion: be it, therefore, by the State Central Committee of the State of Kansas,

"*Resolved*, 1. That, representing and speaking in behalf of eight thousand Democratic voters of the State, we hold as fundamental principles that the Federal Constitution and the laws passed in pursuance thereof, ever are supreme throughout the limits of the United States, and in each and every State, North, South, East and West; and that all men, President, Senators, Congressmen, and private individuals, are bound by them, and as officers and citizens, should, in every act, submit to and be guided by their spirit.

2. That we cordially uphold and stand by the administration of President Johnson, in so far as his public policy has indicated that his purpose has been and is to uphold the principles upon which the Government was founded, and to sustain the rights of the people and all the States equally.

3. That without regard to past political differences, we invite the co-operation of all men in the State in securing to our State Government officers of acknowledged capacity and integrity.

4. That we distinctly repudiate all idea of permitting any longer our party organization to become in any way submissive to the political or personal fortunes of any man or set of men outside of the party, and, upon the principles heretofore set forth, whether victory or defeat be the result.

5. That the interests of the party imperatively require the establishing of a Democratic organ at Leavenworth City.

6. That the chairman be authorized and requested to call a State Convention, at such time and place as he shall deem proper, to select a ticket for State officers and Member of Congress, to be voted for at the ensuing election.

T. P. FENLON, *Secretary pro tem.*   W. P. GAMBELL, *Chairman.*

JUNE.—The Educational Journal is published at Topeka.

—In the summer, Samuel N. Wood starts the Chase County Banner. Theodore Alvord published it from August 3, 1867, till November, 1868. In 1870, the Banner stopped, and the press went to Winfield. F. E. Smith published the Banner one year.

JUNE 1.—Bridge over the Kaw, at Wyandotte, nearly completed.

—The towns of Chetopa, Wamego, Solomon and Montana begin to be talked about.

—Survey begun on the Fort Scott and Sedalia road.

JUNE 8.—J. H. Lane votes with the rest of the Republican Senators, for the Constitutional Amendment.

JUNE 10.—M. F. Conway nominated as Consul to Marseilles. He sustains Johnson's policy.

JUNE 11.—Senator Lane obtains leave of absence. He arrives in Lawrence on the 16th.

JUNE 20.—Meeting of the Republican Committee at Topeka. State Convention to be held September 5th.

—Gen. Lane passes Leavenworth on his way East.

JUNE 23.—The Fenian company raised in Leavenworth returns to that city.

—Robert Tracy enlarges the Troy Reporter.

JUNE 25.—Gen. Lane reported seriously ill, at the Lindell Hotel, St. Louis.

JUNE 25.—The Missouri Pacific completed to Kansas City.

JUNE 27.—Neosho county is receiving a very large immigration.

—The L. L. & G. is located to nearly the southern boundary of the State.

—The season is a very wet one.

—Lawrence city and Douglas county have voted bonds to the Pleasant Hill road.

—Doniphan county has voted bonds to the Denver road.

—Steamboats still running from Weston to Kansas City.

—Judge Bailey asks the poet Whittier to be present at the State Fair, at Lawrence.

JUNE 28.—Gen. Lane arrives at Kansas City.

—John Speer confirmed as Collector.

JUNE 29.—Gen. Lane arrives in Leavenworth, and stops with his brother-in-law, Gen. McCall, at the Government farm, on the Fort Reservation.

—Santa Fe coaches now start from Junction City.

JULY 1.—The Conservative of Tuesday, July 3d, says:

"On Sunday evening, (July 1st,) being apparently in comparative good health and sound mind, Senator Lane rode out with Mr. McCall from the Farm House. During the time he made excuse to leave the carriage several times, seemingly having a morbid plan of self-destruction, until, arriving at a gate, McCall alighted to open it. As the latter reached the gate, Senator Lane sprang from the carriage and, being then in the rear of it, exclaimed, 'Good-bye, Mac.,' and immediately fired a pistol, the muzzle being placed in his mouth. The ball struck the roof of the mouth and emerged from about the upper centre of the cranium, having passed through the brain and almost perpendicularly through the head. With a convulsive spring into the air, the Senator fell, apparently lifeless, to the earth. The evidently pulseless body was immediately placed in the carriage by those accompanying—McCall and Capt. Adams, (a brother of Gen. Lane's son-in-law)—and taken to the house, and surgeons summoned as speedily as possible, who proceeded to make examination as to the nature and extent of the wound. At present writing (12 M.) the Senator is still unconscious, and no hopes are entertained of his recovery."

On the 6th the same paper said: "Gen. Lane recognizes persons, and converses to some extent with his friends."

The Senator died on Wednesday, July 11th, at 11:55 A. M. James Henry Lane was the son of Amos Lane, and was born in Lawrenceburg, Indiana, June 22, 1814. In 1846, he became Colonel of a regiment raised to engage in the Mexican war; in 1847, he became Colonel of another Indiana regiment; in 1849, he was elected Lieutenant Governor; in 1852, he was a Democratic Presidential Elector, and was elected to Congress; in April, 1855, he came to Kansas. In this State, in politics, he was the King.

JULY 1.—The first through passenger train leaves Leavenworth for St. Louis, on the Missouri River and Missouri Pacific lines.

—E. C. Manning starts the Radical, at Manhattan.

JULY.—Indian raid on White Rock river; they rob citizens and violate women.

JULY 3.—State Teachers' Association meets at Lawrence. *Officers:* President, P. McVicar; Recording Secretary, L. B. Kellogg; Corresponding Secretary, John S. Brown; Treasurer, Miss Carrie Collins. *Executive Committee:* D. J. Brewer, B. F. Mudge, R. K. McCartney, Orlando Sawyer.

JULY 3.—Chapter 159 of the U. S. Statutes authorizes the U. P. R. R., Eastern Division, to designate its general route and file a map before December 1. The road is to unite with the Union Pacific at a point not more than fifty miles west of the meridian of Denver.

Heretofore the line followed the Republican valley; now it goes up the Smoky Hill.

JULY 4.—At the Soldiers' Celebration, at Topeka, Gen. Blunt makes a speech formally presenting the battle-flags to Gov. Crawford. The oration is delivered by Samuel A. Kingman.

JULY 4.—Treaty with the Delawares. The Secretary of the Interior is authorized to sell the remainder of the Delaware lands to the Missouri River R. R. Co., at not less than $2.50 an acre.

JULY 9.—Work begun on the St. Joseph and Denver road.

JULY 19.—Treaty with the Cherokees. The right of way granted to a railroad from the east, and to one from the north. The Cherokees cede to the United States the tract of land in Kansas sold to the Cherokees in 1835 ; also that strip of land in Kansas ceded to the Cherokees in that treaty. These lands are to be sold at not less than $1.25 an acre. The United States agrees to run the boundary line between the Cherokee country and the States of Arkansas, Missouri and Kansas. The Senate added a proviso to the treaty, allowing the lands to be sold in a body at $1 an acre.

JULY 20.—Governor Crawford appoints Major Edmund G. Ross United States Senator.

—W. F. Cloud, Major General of the Militia, calls for a cavalry regiment to protect the frontier against Indians.

JULY 21.—Major W. C. Ransom shot by bushwhackers, in Kansas City, and severely wounded. The attempted assassination was caused by Major Ransom's gallant service on the border during the war.

JULY 23.—Congress (Chap. 212, U. S. Statutes) grants lands to aid in the construction of a railroad and telegraph from Elwood, westwardly, via Marysville, so as to effect a junction with the Union Pacific Railroad, with the usual guarantees to settlers under the homestead and other laws. The sections within ten miles of the road which are not granted shall not be sold for less than double the minimum price of the public land. For every ten consecutive miles of road completed, patents shall issue for so many sections of land as lie opposite and coterminous with said completed sections. If the road is not completed within ten years, the land remaining unpatented shall revert to the United States.

JULY 25.—The National Union Club, at Leavenworth, elects the following delegates to the Philadelphia Convention of August 14th: Hugh Ewing, Charles W. Blair, V. Nicholas Smith, James L. McDowell, Hiram S. Sleeper, G. A. Colton.

JULY 25.—Congress (Chap. 241, U. S. Statutes) grants lands to the State of Kansas to aid in the construction of the Kansas and Neosho Valley Railroad and its extension to Red river.

This road became the Missouri River, Fort Scott and Gulf.

JULY 26.—Congress (Chap. 270, U. S. Statutes) grants land to aid in the construction of a Southern Branch of the Union Pacific Railway and Telegraph, from Fort Riley, Kansas, to Fort Smith, Arkansas.

This road became the Missouri, Kansas and Texas.

JULY 28.—Bayard Taylor returns east, after a lecturing tour and visit in Kansas and Colorado.

—The Democrats elect the following delegates to the Philadelphia Convention: W. P. Gambell, G. W. Glick, J. L. Pendery, Orlin Thurston, T. P. Fenlon, E. F. Campbell. Alternates: F. P. Fitzwilliam, Isaac Sharp, W. A. Tipton, R. M. Ruggles, Charles Rubicam.

JULY 30.—The President sends Victoria a message by the Atlantic cable.

AUGUST 1.—The Second Annual Report of the Superintendent of Public Schools of Leavenworth is published. It fills 56 pages, and is an admirably prepared document. David J. Brewer is the Superintendent.

AUGUST 1.—Work begun on the L. L. & G., at Lawrence.

AUGUST 4.—Gen. Albert L. Lee returns to the State. He makes a speech in Leavenworth, on the 11th.

—Secretary Harlan agrees to have the Neutral Lands surveyed.

AUGUST 16.—Col. Wm. A. Phillips speaks in Leavenworth.

AUGUST.—Settlers on Lulu creek, a branch of the Solomon, driven off by Indians. Settlers' fields destroyed on the upper Republican.

AUGUST 18.—McReynolds & Simpson issue the Paola Republican.

—Trains are running to Manhattan.

—Jack Henderson visits Leavenworth. He is appointed Indian Agent, at Santa Fe, by Andy Johnson.

AUGUST 31.—The National Union Committee hold a meeting in Leavenworth, and issue a call for a State Convention at Topeka. The Democrats join in the call.

SEPTEMBER 5.—Major General John Pope erects the initial stone of the Neosho Valley R. R., at Junction City. Speeches by Robert McBratney, N. S. Goss, and others.

SEPTEMBER 5.—State Republican Convention, at Topeka. Called to order by Jacob Stotler. *Vote for temporary Chairman:* J. P. Root, 47; Geo. Graham, 33. M. R. Dutton, Secretary.

Committee on Credentials: Geo. T. Isbell of Jefferson, Lulell of Saline, Crane of Shawnee, Leland of Doniphan, Harden of Lyon.

Committee on Permanent Organization: Russell of Cherokee, Beates of Davis, Cavender of Anderson.

A despatch was sent to the Loyal Southern Convention, at Philadelphia.

J. P. Root was elected President; M. R. Dutton and Dr. Lulell, Secretaries.

Samuel J. Crawford was renominated for Governor, receiving 64 votes, to 18 for Andrew Akin, of Morris county.

Committee on Resolutions: Speer, Keith, Pearsall, Anthony and Prouty.

Vote for Lieutenant Governor—first ballot: McGrew 12, Strickler 14, Green 20, Updegraff 3, Barr 6, Elder 12, Burris 9, Larimer 6.

Second ballot: McGrew 11, Strickler 16, Green 27, Barr 1, Elder 15, Burris 11.

Third ballot: Green 55, Elder 17, Strickler 10.

Vote for Secretary of State—first ballot: Barker 40, Emmert 29, Moonlight 12, Day 1.

Second ballot: Barker 44, Emmert 32, Moonlight 6.

J. R. Swallow was renominated for Auditor by acclamation.

Vote for Treasurer—first ballot: Anderson 30, Lappin 22, Johnson 22, Twiss 6, Mills 2.

Second ballot: Anderson 50, Lappin 17, Johnson 14, Twiss 1.

For Superintendent of Public Instruction: McVicar 51, Hartman 31.

For Attorney General: Geo. H. Hoyt 59, J. D. Brumbaugh 15, J. M. Rankin 8.

For Chief Justice: Samuel A. Kingman 43, David P. Lowe 39.

Sidney Clarke was nominated for Congress by acclamation.

A. D. Richardson, of the New York Tribune, made a brief speech.

State Committee: H. D. Fisher, R. B. Taylor, Geo. W. Gardiner, Frank H. Drenning, Jacob Stotler, D. B. Emmert, Chas. C. Whiting. F. H. Drenning was elected Chairman, and C. C. Whiting Secretary.

The following platform was adopted:

"To give expression to the sentiment and opinion of the loyal people of Kansas, we the delegates assembled in State Convention, do hereby adopt the following resolutions:

"*Resolved*, That with devout thankfulness and gratitude to God, who has delivered us from the anarchy and desolation of war—who has overthrown and broken the cursed power and crime-creating institution of Slavery—and with unfaltering faith and trust in the eternity of Good, and in the divinity of Justice—we hereby reaffirm our devotion to liberty and to the sacred and inalienable rights of man.

"*Resolved*, That in the great and awful wickedness which our President has perpetrated in making treason a virtue and loyalty a crime; in giving to Rebels the protection, and to their anarchy the sanction of law; in casting upon the noble and sacrificing Unionists of the South the scorn and the insolence of tyrannic power; in fostering and encouraging the spirit of disaffection among the Rebels, and in crushing the dawning hopes of the freedmen; in usurping and overriding the authority of Congress, and in trampling upon the sovereignty of States; and in his audacious and crowning wickedness in calling our Representatives 'An assumed Congress,' meaning the tyrant's threat at anarchy or absolute power—has lost our confidence and respect, and to his insolence and threats we hurl back our defiance and scorn.

"*Resolved*, That our Congress, for their unwavering fidelity to duty, to the freedmen, and the Government; for their undaunted heroism in resisting the encroachments of the President; for their stern and unswerving purpose to reward loyalty and punish treason, and for their love of justice, we extend to them the gratitude and thanks of a grateful people. And to our Senator and Member of Congress, because they have obeyed the wishes and not trifled with the conscience of their constituents—from the bottom of our hearts we extend to them the hand of greeting, and say, 'Well done, good and faithful servants.'

"*Resolved*, That we recommend to the next Legislature the submission of the question of impartial suffrage to a vote of the people of Kansas."

SEPTEMBER 9.—Northwestern Kansas and Fort Kearney, Neb., overrun with grasshoppers. They are in Nemaha and Marshall counties. The Wyandotte Gazette is quoted in the Conservative as saying: "Between Topeka and Wamego they fill the air like snow-flakes in a winter storm."

—The Conservative gives a list of thirty-seven newspapers published in the State; thirty-one support the Republican ticket, five oppose it, and one is doubtful.

—Survey of the Neutral Lands is soon to be made.

SEPTEMBER 12.—Grasshopper visitation at Osage Mission. "Most all the crops were saved." In the spring of 1867 they hatched, but "a sudden freshet swept them all away."

SEPTEMBER 12.—Dedication of the State University. Solon O. Thacher delivers the oration.

SEPTEMBER 14.—Grasshoppers reach Lawrence.

SEPTEMBER 15.—Grasshoppers in Leavenworth county.

—Colonel Charles W. Blair Postmaster at Fort Scott.

SEPTEMBER 20.—Prospectus issued of the Leavenworth Commercial, to be published by George F. Prescott, George C. Hume and A. F. Callahan.

—The Right Reverend Thomas H. Vail, Bishop of Kansas, resigns the Rectorship of the Atchison Episcopal church, and is succeeded by Reverend John Bakewell.

—National Union State Convention at Topeka. Called to order by James L. McDowell. G. A. Colton, temporary chairman. Secretaries, M. W. Reynolds, Charles Hayward, A. F. Callahan, and Bond of Allen.

Committees: Permanent Organization—James Ketner, Royal Baldwin,

Charles W. Adams, Charles Thompson, Richard Burr; Resolutions—G.
W. Glick, W. C. McDowell, S. H. Fletcher, James L. McDowell, Edwards;
Credentials—J. L. Pendery, T. J. Dolan, L. R. Palmer, H. G. Wilson,
Wilkinson. *President:* Wm. C. McDowell. *Vice Presidents:* Hiram S.
Sleeper, J. W. Forman, J. R. McClure, James Christian, Richard Burr.
Secretaries: M. W. Reynolds, Charles Hayward, A. F. Callahan, Bond of
Allen, and Campbell of Morris.

On motion of L. B. Wheat, J. L. McDowell was nominated for Governor
by acclamation.

On motion of G. W. Glick, J. R. McClure, of Davis, was nominated for
Lieutenant Governor by acclamation.

On motion of Mr. Bridgens, of Bourbon, Colonel M. Quigg, of Atchison,
was nominated for Secretary of State by acclamation.

On motion of T. P. Fenlon, Ross Burns, of Shawnee, was nominated for
Attorney General by acclamation.

On motion of Charles S. Glick, I. S. Walker, of Wyandotte, was nominated for Treasurer by acclamation.

On motion of R. C. Foster, N. S. Goss, of Woodson, was nominated for
Auditor by acclamation.

On motion of G. W. Glick, Joseph Bond, of Allen, was nominated for
Superintendent of Public Instruction by acclamation.

H. T. Wilson, of Bourbon, nominated Wilson Shannon for Chief Justice.
Governor Shannon declined in favor of Nelson Cobb, who was nominated
by acclamation.

On motion of L. B. Wheat, Charles W. Blair, of Bourbon, was nominated
for Member of Congress by acclamation.

State Central Committee: G. W. Glick, J. B. Sharp, George A. Reynolds,
Samuel H. Fletcher, J. L. Pendery, James A. McGonigle, James Ketner,
F. P. Fitzwilliam, H. S. Sleeper.

The following platform was adopted:

"*Whereas,* The exigencies of the times, so startling that wise men fear revolution—so
pregnant with the destiny of constitutional government that patriotism and statesmanship alike tremble for the future—so alarming that the fundamental principles of our
Republican Government are in danger of being disowned and repudiated and substituted by the caprice of revenge and the madness of fanaticism—demand of all who
love the Constitution and the Government of our fathers, that in a spirit of patriotism
which places our country and our cherished institutions above party, they should
earnestly and zealously labor for the speedy restoration of the Union under the Constitution: therefore, be it

"*Resolved,* 1. That we heartily endorse the resolutions and address of the National
Union Convention that met at Philadelphia.

"2. That inasmuch as the war is over and peace is again restored to our recently dis-
tracted country, and inasmuch as the blood and treasure expended by those who
cherished the Union of the States and the supremacy of the Constitution, were poured
out so freely in vindication of constitutional government, it becomes the bounden duty
of all good men to see to it that the great sacrifices of the war were not made in vain,
but that the triumph of our arms becomes the triumph of those great principles of
government bequeathed to us by our ancestors.

"3. That in the great crisis of our country growing out of the disagreement between
Congress and the Administration, we heartily endorse the policy of President Johnson

in his manly defence of the Constitution and the Union against the assaults of a partisan Congress and a fanatical party to destroy the Government bequeathed to us by our fathers.

"4. That it is the constitutional right of every State in the Union, through its loyal representatives in both houses of Congress, to participate in the National Legislature, subject alone to the right of each house to judge of the election and qualification of its members; and States cannot legally be disfranchised or punished for the actions of any of their citizens.

"5. That inasmuch as the Southern States lately in rebellion have repealed their ordinances of secession, repudiated the so-called Confederate debt, and accepted the constitutional amendment abolishing Slavery throughout the jurisdiction of the United States, the continued refusal of Congress, through its session of eight months, to recognize the right of Congressional representation to ten States in the Union, and subject to the Constitution, is at war with the genius and spirit of our institutions, and revolutionary in its character.

"6. That the war has definitely settled the question that the right of secession is a political heresy; and that no State nor combination of States can throw off their primal allegiance to the General Government; and that the Constitution, and the laws passed in pursuance thereof, are the supreme law of the land, ordinances and statutes to the contrary notwithstanding.

"7. That the officers and soldiers of the war have our unfeigned thanks for their patriotic defence of the Union, and their glorious triumphs in the conflict of arms; and with them we join in denouncing the meanness of Congress in voting to its members an increase of pay at the rate of thirty-three dollars per day, while voting to the soldiers who periled their lives for the Union, a bounty of only fifty dollars for two years' service in fighting for the Union.

"8. That the prodigality, corruption and imbecility of the present officials of this State merits and ought to receive the severest reprobation of the honest, tax-ridden people of the State.

"9. That we condemn the criminal conduct of the present Executive in neglecting or refusing to extend the protection of the State to the hardy pioneers of our western borders against Indian hostilities and savage barbarities daily and notoriously committed against them.

"10. That in its revolutionary action the Congress of the United States, demanding as a condition precedent to the right of representation, the recognition of negro equality and negro suffrage, has promulgated a dogma abhorrent to the feelings of the American people, and arrogated to itself a power that, under the Constitution, belongs exclusively to the States; and that we, in opposition to the real policy of the Radicals, declare our unalterable determination to oppose negro suffrage in the State of Kansas."

—A resolution was adopted asking the removal from office of men who opposed the President; and another sympathizing with the Irish people in their effort to restore their lost liberties.

OCTOBER.—State Musical Convention at Lawrence.

—P. McVicar is the editor of the Educational Journal.

OCTOBER.—Settler killed by Indians west of Lake Sibley.

OCTOBER 2.—State Fair at Lawrence.

—Hugh Ewing appointed Minister to the Hague, and credited to Kansas.

—M. J. Parrott and A. L. Lee are on the stump for the Republican ticket.

OCTOBER 7.—The Kansas Pacific track laid to the old town of Pawnee; the United States Commissioners inspect 130 miles of the road.

OCTOBER 16.—General George A. Custer leaves Leavenworth to take command at Fort Riley.

OCTOBER 17.—Laying of the corner-stone of the State Capitol by the Grand Lodge of Masons.

OCTOBER 18.—John Speer turns over the United States Collector's office to Edward Carroll, of Leavenworth.

OCTOBER 20.—James M. Harvey, a member of the House last winter, is nominated for the Senate.

OCTOBER 27.—Topeka Daily Tribune issued.

—H. B. Denman, of Leavenworth, appointed Indian Superintendent of the Northern Superintendency.

NOVEMBER 1.—The Junction City Union published as a Daily to August 1st, 1867.

—Leavenworth has six daily papers.

NOVEMBER 6.—Election. The following is the vote on State tickets:

Counties.	GOVERNOR.		LIEUT. GOV.		SEC. OF STATE		STA. AUDIT'R		STATE TREAS	
	S. J. Crawford.	J. L. McDowell	Nehemiah Green	J. R. McClure.	R. A. Barker.	Mathew Quigg.	J. R. Swallow.	N. S. Goss	M. Anderson.	J. Walker.
Allen	407	168	406	169	404	169	397	168	405	168
Anderson	367	56	371	58	371	56	348	57	369	56
Atchison	1,120	609	1,134	604	1,128	608	1,134	605	1,134	604
Bourbon	855	404	856	405	855	405	855	404	856	402
Brown	452	36	453	36	451	36	453	36	450	36
Butler	61	27	61	27	61	27	63	26	60	27
Chase	155	31	156	24	157	24	156	24	157	24
Cherokee	272	49	271	49	272	49	272	49	271	49
Clay	102	4	101	4	102	4	102	4	102	4
Coffey	402	228	405	229	404	228	403	229	405	227
Davis	341	200	338	187	341	201	341	203	341	201
Dickinson	101	93	99	96	100	95	100	94	100	94
Doniphan	1,233	366	1,248	349	1,238	360	1,245	351	1,234	351
Douglas	1,729	459	1,787	402	1,817	397	1,817	394	1,816	394
Franklin	747	112	750	110	725	111	729	110	751	110
Greenwood	168	4	168	4	168	4	168	4	168	4
Jackson	371	149	365	125	368	139	367	138	276	148
Jefferson	829	423	840	432	836	425	837	426	772	442
Johnson	846	404	846	401	848	421	848	417	840	424
Leavenworth	1,944	2,247	2,016	2,191	2,034	2,179	2,019	2,172	2,018	2,188
Linn	781	185	805	181	804	182	805	182	803	182
Lyon	647	61	651	51	652	51	649	54	649	52
Marshall	560	33	556	25	534	25	556	25	553	25
Marion	41	14	21	34	20	29	32	18	34	14
Miami	778	362	778	362	781	359	783	360	781	361
Morris	113	133	112	132	112	132	111	128	112	132
Nemaha	384	177	385	177	385	177	385	177	379	179
Neosho	266	61	261	66	259	67	256	70	261	66
Osage	272	46	272	40	282	39	282	40	280	40
Ottawa	92	......	89	4	93	......	93	......	93	......
Pottawatomie	389	162	388	159	389	159	389	159	383	161
Riley	369	24	363	27	366	24	369	24	368	24
Saline	210	37	210	37	210	37	210	37	208	37
Shawnee	886	200	885	198	894	193	898	189	905	178
Shirley	48	......	48	......	48	......	48	......	46	......
Washington	115	......	115	......	116	......	116	......	116	......
Wabaunsee	245	23	253	13	257	13	254	14	255	14
Wilson	157	53	144	53	151	53	149	54	150	53
Woodson	117	53	117	53	118	53	86	84	118	52
Wyandotte	398	458	393	463	393	460	393	461	373	480
Total	19,370	8,152	19,517	7,977	19,571	7,991	19,516	7,988	19,392	8,008

VOTE ON STATE OFFICERS — *Concluded.*

Counties.	SUPT. PUB. INS.		ATT'Y GENERAL.		CHIEF JUSTICE.		MEM. OF CONG.	
	P. McVicar......	*Joseph Bond......*	*Geo. H. Hoyt......*	*Ross Burns......*	*S. A. Kingman......*	*Nelson Cobb......*	*Sidney Clarke......*	*C. W. Blair......*
Allen..................	402	158	393	169	404	168	394	169
Anderson	370	56	299	60	370	56	366	58
Atchison............	1,136	602	1,125	602	1,149	588	1,133	608
Bourbon	852	406	852	405	856	408	841	407
Brown	454	36	430	36	436	36	448	38
Butler	60	27	32	49	60	27	58	27
Chase	156	22	126	24	97	16	153	30
Cherokee	273	49	274	48	272	49	269	50
Clay..................	101	4	101	4	102	4	99	4
Coffey	405	228	394	228	404	226	405	226
Davis.................	340	201	339	202	340	200	340	201
Dickinson	100	94	99	95	100	94	79	94
Doniphan	1,245	351	1,238	353	1,247	350	1,225	366
Douglas	1,816	389	1,762	407	1,660	414	1,758	429
Franklin............	749	109	742	110	752	108	741	112
Greenwood	168	4	168	4	167	4	168	....
Jackson.............	367	137	332	149	360	141	361	152
Jefferson...........	833	424	494	537	732	426	820	435
Johnson.............	849	398	805	448	851	417	836	427
Leavenworth	2,016	2,182	1,963	2,193	2,008	2,179	1,982	2,206
Linn..................	803	182	695	236	793	182	777	187
Lyon	648	52	174	270	651	51	643	62
Marshall	533	24	555	25	551	22	560	32
Marion	20	29	18	30	20	29	18	35
Miami	783	361	746	370	782	362	765	367
Morris	112	132	104	132	112	131	104	134
Nemaha	384	176	383	176	378	175	378	179
Neosho	259	62	252	70	259	65	206	79
Osage	282	39	269	42	282	40	272	44
Ottawa..............	93	....	90	....	93	....	92	1
Pottawatomie	388	159	381	161	389	162	390	159
Riley	367	24	352	26	368	24	368	24
Saline................	211	37	201	37	210	37	209	37
Shawnee.............	895	189	810	248	907	178	868	204
Shirley	48	....	48	....	48	....	48	....
Washington........	116	....	101	....	115	....	114	....
Wabaunsee	258	11	198	48	253	14	259	12
Wilson...............	149	54	149	54	148	53	148	94
Woodson............	117	52	116	52	118	52	115	54
Wyandotte..........	391	465	313	481	386	466	392	462
Total.............	19,549	7,945	17,916	8,581	19,236	7,955	19,201	8,106

NOVEMBER 6.—Vote for District Judge in the Second District:

Names of Counties.	CANDIDATES.	
	R. S. Graham...	*C. C. Camp...*
Atchison	1,579	.....
Brown	456	.....
Doniphan	1,228	.....
Marshall	529	1
Washington	55	60
Nemaha	513	.....
Total..	4,360	61

VOTE FOR MEMBERS OF THE SENATE.

District.	Counties.	Names.	Votes.	Maj.	Vote of District.
1	Doniphan	A. Low	1,177		
		N. G. Clarke	1,155		
		D. M. Johnston	367		
		J. W. Jenkins	232		
		W. Ellsworth	75		
2	Atchison	J. M. Price	1,149		
		J. K. Fisher	1,124		
		F. M. McLaughlin	605		
		M. R. Benton	574		
3	Leavenworth	P. McFarland	2,264		
		R. C. Foster	2,052		
		H. C. Haas	2,020		
		J. Medill	1,875		
		T. O'Gwartney	1,685		
		C. R. Jennison	1,591		
		W. S. Jenkins	396		
4	Jefferson	S. S. Cooper	739	247	
		A. G. Patrick	492		1,231
5	Nemaha	George Graham	347		
		J. E. Smith	179		
	Brown	George Graham	410	523	
		J. E. Smith	55		
		Scattering	1		992
6	Jackson	W. H. Dodge	276		
		Golden Silvers	221		
	Pottawatomie	W. H. Dodge	380	275	
		Golden Silvers	160		
		J. E. Clardy	3		1,040
7	Washington	J. M. Harvey	116		
		G. H. Hollenberg	2		
	Marshall	J. M. Harvey	553		
	Riley	J. M. Harvey	360	1,065	
		D. S. Chandler	9		
	Shirley	J. M. Harvey	47		1,087
8	Shawnee	G. W. Veale	621	154	
		C. K. Holliday	467		1,088
9	Douglas	S. A. Riggs	1,820		
		L. F. Greene	1,814		
		Homer Hays	20		
		John Speer	4		
10	Johnson	J. B. Abbott	697	123	
		A. S. Johnson	574		
		Scattering	1		1,372
11	Miami	B. F. Simpson	756	393	
		J. W. Gossett	363		1,119
12	Wyandotte	J. B. Sharp	559	269	
		L. L. Hartman	290		849
13	Linn	D. Underhill	748	577	
		J. Hodgson	171		
		Scattering	6		925
14	Bourbon	D. B. Emmert	826		
		J. H. Couch	419		
	Cherokee	D. B. Emmert	263	588	
		J. H. Couch	82		1,590
15	Butler	S. N. Wood	59		
		Reuben Riggs	28		
	Chase	S. N. Wood	130		
		Reuben Riggs	51		
	Marion	S. N. Wood	12		
		Reuben Riggs	39		
	Morris	S. N. Wood	75	7	
		Reuben Riggs	151		545
16	Allen	J. W. Scott	335		
		W. Doudna	198		
	Neosho	John W. Scott	225		
		W. Doudna	82		
	Wilson	John W. Scott	80		
		W. Doudna	117		
	Woodson	John W. Scott	104	285	
		W. Doudna	62		1,203
17	Anderson	A. Wiley	249		
		H. P. Welch	163		
	Franklin	A. Wiley	577	407	

VOTE FOR MEMBERS OF THE SENATE—Concluded.

District.	Counties.	Names.	Votes....	Maj......	Vote of District.
18	Franklin (concluded).........	H. P. Welch	256		1,245
	Coffey..............................	James Rogers.................................	427		
		Orlando Walking	145		
	Osage	James Rogers.................................	213	437	
		Orlando Walking..........................	58		
		Scattering	1		844
19	Lyon	P. B. Maxson	644		
		E. H. Sanford	83		
		Scattering	1		
	Greenwood......................	P. B. Maxson	88		
		E. H. Sanford	79		900
20	Davis..............................	W. S. Blakely	345		
		Abram Barry	197		
	Dickinson	W. S. Blakely	103		
		Abram Barry	91		
	Saline..............................	W. S. Blakely	105	472	
		Abram Barry	37		
		L. F. Parsons.	100		
	Ottawa	W. S. Blakely	76		
		L. F. Parsons.	16		
	Wabaunsee	W. S. Blakely	124		
		L. F. Parsons.	134		
		Abram Barry..............................	4		
		W. M. S. Blakely........................	8		
	Clay	W. S. Blakely	35		
		Abram Barry	4		
		L. F. Parsons.	66		1,442

VOTE FOR MEMBERS OF THE HOUSE.

District.	Counties.	Names.	Votes	Maj......	Vote of District.	Vote of County.
1	Doniphan......................	W. R. Parker	220	51		
		N. M. Keith....................................	169		389	
2	....	G. H. Robb......................................	130	39		
		J. Normille....................................	91			
		R. Small..	79		300	
3	....	B. D. Evans....................................	255	210		
		A. J. Haskell..................................	45		300	
4	....	E. J. Jenkins	227	137		
		A. Perry..	90		317	
5	....	R. Flickinger..................................	186	103		
		A. G. Ege..	83		269	1,575
6	Atchison......................	Wm. Bowman..............................	233	59		
		E. Button	174		· 407	
7	....	G. W. Bowman................................	356	238		
		W. Jackson....................................	118			
		L. S. Treat	2		476	
8	....	G. W. Thompson............................	205	31		
		J. Howell.......................................,	174		379	
9	....	W. J. May......................................	188	158		
		S. Pardee..	30		218	
10	....	M. J. Cloyce	113	59		
		D. W. Cozard..................................	54			
		J. W. Perry....................................	40		207	1,687
11	Brown	M. C. Willis....................................	192			
		J. W. Overholzer............................	114	78	306	
12	....	C. E. Parker..................................	158	149		
		Robert Rhea..................................	9		167	473
13	Nemaha	T. B. Collins	148	14		
		J. P. Taylor....................................	134			
		Scattering	5		287	
14	....	Joseph Hanemum............................	107	44		
		J. S. Hidden....................................	63			
		P. Hamilton....................................	60			
		A. S. Kenoyer..................................	31			
		Scattering ....:	1		262	549
15	Marshall......................	J. D. Wells....................................	307	3		
		J. W. Bollinger ....,........	304		611	

29

MEMBERS OF THE HOUSE—Continued.

District.	Counties.	Names.	Votes.	Maj.	Vote of District.	Vote of County.
16	Washington	D. E. Ballard	69	17		
		G. H. Hollenberg	52		121	121
17	Pottawatomie	R. W. Jenkins	373	284		
		F. M. Sales	89			
		H. Smith	61		523	523
18	Jackson	P. Bryant	207	138		
		R. Hogg	69		276	
		J. B. Oliver	89	30		
		J. W. Williams	59			
79		J. Rippetoe	45			
		A. C. Beckwith	30		231	507
		Scattering	8			
19	Jefferson	F. M. Johnson	280	161		
		C. A. Buck	119		399	
20		W. C. Butts	161	25		
		L. Prentice	136			
		H. Smith	39		336	
21		A. Venard	341	161		
		S. R. Bayne	180		521	1,256
22	Leavenworth	John Harrison	323	79		
		T. J. Darling	244			
		Ira Taylor	102			
		Scattering	1		670	
23		M. Przybylowicz	282	103		
		G. A. Moore	179			
		H. Miles Moore	156		617	
24		H. Allen	412	410		
		Scattering	2		414	
25		John Dugan	269	24		
		Levi Houston	245			
		A. McAuley	240		754	
26		L. Kennedy	198	55		
		F. Wellhouse	143		341	
27		J. Turner	131	72		
		G. W. Baird	59		190	
28		J. F. Knight	190	59		
		B. B. Moore	131		321	
29		John Faulkner	198	63		
		S. S. Nichols	135		333	
30		S. D. Lecompte	144	33		
		W. Dunlap	111			
		H. Brandt	51		306	3,946
31	Wyandotte	Dan. Killen	217	97		
		J. A. Soward	120		337	
80		T. J. Barker	305	110		
		Alfred Gray	195			
		Scattering	2		502	839
32	Johnson	M. B. Lyon	282	56		
		H. McBride	226		508	
33		Albert Johnson	229	19		
		D. G. Campbell	210			
		Scattering	2		441	
34		J. W. Sponable	202	92		
		R. Addy	110		312	1,261
35	Douglas	Josiah Miller	716		716	
36		T. H. Kennedy	158	9		
		C. W. Babcock	149		307	
37		J. K. Goodin	152	2		
		G. C. Snow	150		302	
38		Sam. Hindman	135	36		
		Allen Pierce	99		234	
39		T. H. Clark	137	12		
		W. M. Nace	125		262	
40		W. Draper	126	46		
		J. C. Coleman	80		206	2,027
41	Shawnee	J. M. Spencer	398	79		
		A. H. Case	319			
		J. B. Whitaker	39		756	
42		S. E. A. Palmer	185	111		
		J. A. Powell	74			
		Ben. Stees	65	.	324	1,080
43	Miami	W. W. Updegraff	248		248	
44		J. A. Kendall	286	11		

MEMBERS OF THE HOUSE—CONTINUED.

District.	Counties.	Names.	Votes.	Maj.	Vote of District.	Vote of County.
44	Miami (concluded).........	A. G. McKenzie...............	275		561	
45	....	William Huffman............	225	141		
		D. M. Sheldon...............	84		309	1,118
46	Linn................	O. D. Harmon...............	118	111		
		Scattering...................	7		125	
47	....	Enoch Estep...................	218	141		
		J. N. Hight..................	77		295	
48	....	J. S. Lane....................	268	265		
		N. McCord	3		271	
49	....	J. P. Way....................	202	199		
		Scattering...................	3		205	896
50	Bourbon	W. A. McIntosh...............	104	23		
		A. W. Burton.................	81			
		Scattering...................	34		219	
51	....	Joseph Wilson...............	170	132		
		M. E. Hudson	38		208	
52	....	W. F. Travers...............	204	150		
		B. F. Gumm	54			
		Scattering...................	6		264	
53	....	S. A. Manlove	271	1		
		B. P. McDonald...............	270		541	1,232
54	Allen	J. R. Goodin.................	233	52		
		H. D. Parsons...............	180			
		J. Sansom...................	2		415	
55	....	F. M. Bower..................	74	13		
		E. Fisk......................	61		135	550
56	Anderson	Thomas Lindsay...............	133	4		
		C. P. Alvey.................	129		262	
57	....	W. M. Hamby.................	124	83		
		J. S. Johnson...............	41		165	427
58	Franklin	J. M. Luce...................	194	100		
		H. Bell......................	94		288	
59	....	W. E. Kibbee.................	502	461		
		M. F. Holaday...............	41		543	831
60	Osage	H. C. Sheldon	130	24		
		D. B. Foster	106			
		S. R. Caniff.................	183			
		Scattering...................	1		320	320
61	Coffey	Job Throckmorton...............	201	112		
		William Gans	89		290	
62	....	Allen Crocker.................	177	25		
		R. Burr......................	152			
		E. E. Coffin.................	1		330	620
63	Woodson	H. J. Gregory	95	39		
		O. Devinney.................	56			
		Scattering...................	15		166	166
64	Lyon	P. B. Plumb.................	223	114		
		C. V. Eskridge	109		332	
65	....	G. R. Harper.................	80	9		
		D. K. Hardin.................	71			
		Dan. Hendricks...............	58			
		S. C. Martin.................	21		230	
66	....	J. D. Jaquith...............	132	128		
		Scattering...................	4		136	698
67	Butler................	J. D. Conner.................	37	10		
		J. P. Goodale...............	27			
		J. H. Adams.................	24		88	88
68	Chase	H. Brandley.................	117	53		
		H. E. Snyder	64			
		H. L. Scribner...............	9		190	190
69	Morris	C. Columbia.................	134	23		
		Thomas Collins...............	111		245	245
70	Wabaunsee	H. J. Loomis.................	168	74		
		D. M. Adams.................	94		262	262
71	Davis	E. S. Stover.................	339	154		
		H. F. Hale ...:...............	185		524	524
72	Riley................	H. Booth.................	361		361	361
73	Dickinson	C. H. Thompson...............	98	3		
		D. R. Emery.................	95		193	193
74	Saline................	A. C. Spilman...............	158	83		
		H. L. Jones.................	75			
		C. H. Martin	5		238	238
75	Greenwood	E. Tucker...................	129	94		

MEMBERS OF THE HOUSE — Concluded.

District.	Counties.	Names	Votes	Maj.	Vote of District.	Vote of County.
75	Greenwood (concluded)...	G. H. Lillie..................	35		164	164
76	Marion..........................	A. A. Moore.................	39	27		
		C. R. Roberts..............	12		51	
77	Wilson.........................	J. W. Jewitt................	112	17		
		J. Keys......................	95		207	207
78	Neosho	D. Rogers...................	297	278		
		J. C. Weibley..............	19			
		M. C. Wright..............	4		320	320
81	Ottawa........................	R. D. Mobley..............	94	93		
		Scattering..................	1		95	95
82	Clay	L. Gates....................	67	32		
		J. P. Byon..................	35		102	102
83	Cherokee.....................	D. C. Finn..................	129	6		
		H. Harryman...............	123			
		J. Sherwood................	75			
		J. M. Reed.................	25		352	352
84	Shirley........................	J. P. Rupe.................	27	6		
		D. M. Hagarman	21		48	48
		Total........................				26,753

NOVEMBER 30.—Expenditures of the State for the year:

Governor's Department............	$5,803 06	Agricultural College.................	5,673 00
Secretary's Department............	5,825 68	State University......................	2,885 98
Auditor's Department..............	3,932 00	Normal School........................	13,000 00
Treasurer's Department...........	2,980 88	Deaf and Dumb Asylum.............	6,200 00
Supt. of Public Instruction.......	1,751 86	Insane Asylum........................	3,500 00
Attorney General....................	1,021 53	Military companies...................	2,621 00
Adjutant General....................	9,474 60	Legislature and Journals	25,204 05
Judiciary	14,582 99	Miscellaneous expenses............	2,899 60
Printing................................	17,405 11	Railroad Land Agent...............	1,236 28
Penitentiary..........................	68,926 66		
Capitol Building......................	41,540 88	Total for 1866.....................$236,465 16	

NOVEMBER 30.—The following statement of Price Raid claims is copied from the report of T. J. Anderson, Adjutant General:

"The claims audited by the Board of Commissioners up to November 1, 1866, are as follows:

Services rendered... $197,327 34
Materials, supplies, and transportation furnished.. 152,530 54
Damages sustained... 106,806 05
Miscellaneous claims.. 36,290 90

Total $492,644 83

"There are in the possession of the Board a number of claims received *after* the 1st day of November, which they could not act upon."

The United States Senate passed a bill to pay $259,474.13 of Price Raid claims. The House failed to pass it.

—During the year Paola has erected buildings valued at $108,300.

DECEMBER.—The trade of Leavenworth for the year is estimated at $32,440,000.

DECEMBER 1.—The Directory and Shippers' Guide, for Kansas and Nebraska, issued by Holland & Co.

DECEMBER 7.—State Encampment of the Veteran Brotherhood meets in Topeka. John A. Martin elected Commander-in-Chief.

DECEMBER 8.—The Leavenworth Board of Trade condemns the County Board for subscribing $300,000 to the stock of the P. C. & F. D. R. R. Co.

—John Willans succeeds Geo. W. Martin as Register of the Junction City Land Office.

DECEMBER 15.—The Normal School Visitors report that the new building is nearly completed. It is forty by sixty feet on the ground, and two stories high. A boarding-house is also nearly finished.

President Denison, of the Agricultural College, reports 150 students, and the completion of the boarding-house.

E. J. Rice, President of University Faculty, says the first session opened September 12, with three Professors and forty students.

Board of Regents, State Agricultural College: L. D. Bailey, S. D. Houston, J. G. Reaser, John Pipher, T. H. Baker, W. L. Woodworth, R. Cordley, E. Gale, D. Earhart.

Board of Directors, State Normal School: James Rogers, T. S. Huffaker, C. V. Eskridge, J. W. Roberts, G. C. Morse, J. M. Rankin.

Board of Regents, State University: Chas. Robinson, J. D. Liggett, Wm. A. Starrett, T. C. Sears, J. S. Emery, D. P. Mitchell, S. O. Thacher, C. B. Lines, Joseph S. Wever, E. M. Bartholow, G. W. Paddock, C. K. Holliday.

DECEMBER 18.—R. A. Barker, Secretary of State, says in his Report:

"It appears from the records in this office, that during the year ending November 30, 1866, there was issued and registered, under the provisions of 'An act entitled 'An act to fund the Territorial debt,' approved February 20, 1863,' the sum of $4,900 in bonds, making the total amount of bonds issued and registered, $62,200."

—Opening of the Wyandotte bridge.

DECEMBER 28.—The military commission have allowed Price and Curtis Raid claims, amounting to $492,944.83; claims audited by previous commissions, $224,200.46; total claims against the United States, $717,145.59.

1867.

JANUARY 1.—Catalogue issued of Lincoln College. Number of students, 92. *Trustees:* Lewis Bodwell, President; S. D. Storrs, J. D. Liggett, Ira H. Smith, Richard Cordley, Harrison Hannahs, John Ritchie, H. D. Rice, William E. Bowker, J. W. Fox, H. W. Farnsworth.

JANUARY 1.—Dedication of the Normal School building, at Emporia. H. B. Norton writes a Dedication Hymn, of which the following is the concluding stanza:

"By all the progress and the might
Which other ages shall unfold—
By all the brilliant beams that light
The Future's skies of morning gold—
By all that sheds a cheering ray
Upon the path the Past has trod—
We dedicate its walls, this day,
To Truth, to Freedom, and to God!"

JANUARY.—The Report of Provost Marshal General Fry shows the proportion per thousand men which each loyal State contributed to the item of mortality. Kansas heads the column; her proportion was 61.01; Vermont is second, 58.22; and Massachusetts third, 47.76. Gen. Fry says:

"Kansas shows the highest battle mortality of the table. . . . The same singularly martial disposition which induced above half of the able-bodied men of the State to enter the army without bounty, may be supposed to have increased their exposure to the casualties of battle after they were in the service."

Among the Kansas troops, the number of officers killed in battle was 36; enlisted men, 923. Number of officers died of wounds, 8; enlisted men, 259. Number of officers died of disease, 24; enlisted men, 2,170.

—The first term of the present Governor does not conclude until the Legislature has been in session six days.

—The State Record issues a Daily.

JANUARY 8.—Meeting of the Legislature.

STATE OFFICERS.

Names.	Former P. O.	County.	Where Born.	Age	Avocation.
S. J. Crawford, Governor.	Garnett.........	Anderson......	Indiana.........	31	Lawyer.
N. Green, Lieut. Gov.......	Manhattan....	Riley.............	Ohio	29	Minister.
R. A. Barker, Sec. of State	Atchison.........	Atchison.........	Vermont......	36	Attorn'y.
J. R. Swallow, Auditor....	Emporia.........	Lyon.............	New Jersey..	46	Printer.
M. Anderson, Treasurer..	Circleville......	Jackson..........	Ohio.............	49	Farmer.
P. McVicar, Sp't Pub.Inst.	Topeka	Shawnee	NewBrunsw.	37	Minister.
G. H. lloyt, Att'y General	Leavenworth	Leavenworth	Massach'tts ..	29	Attorn'y.

JUDGES OF THE SUPREME COURT.

Names.	Former P.O.	County.	Where Born.	Age	Avocation.
S. A. Kingman, Chief Justice.	Atchison...	Atchison...	Massachusetts	48	Attorn'y.
J. Safford, Associate Justice.	Topeka	Shawnee ...	Vermont.........	39	Lawyer.
L. D. Bailey, Associate Justice	Clinton	Douglas.....	New Hampsh...	47	Lawyer.

JUDGES OF DISTRICT COURTS.

Names.	Districts.	P. O. Address.	County.
D. J. Brewer............................	First.............	Leavenworth	Leavenworth.
R. St. Clair Graham	Second...........	Atchison...........	Atchison.
C. K. Gilchrist.........................	Third............	Topeka	Shawnee.
D. M. Valentine	Fourth..........	Ottawa.............	Franklin.
J. H. Watson...........................	Fifth..............	Emporia	Lyon.
D. P. Lowe..............................	Sixth	Mound City........	Linn.
Wm. Spriggs............................	Seventh..........	Garnett.............	Anderson.
Jas. Humphrey.........................	Eighth...........	Manhattan	Riley.
S. N. Wood.............................	Ninth.............	Cottonwood Falls	Chase.

MEMBERS AND OFFICERS OF THE SENATE.

Names.	P. O. Address.	County.	Where Born.	Age.	Avocation.
N. Green, President.........	Manhattan......	Riley............	Ohio........	29	Minister.
Abbott, James B.............	DeSoto............	Johnson........	Conn......	48	Mechanic.
Blakely, William S...........	Chapman Cr'k.	Dickinson....	New York.	28	Merchant.
Clark, N. C..................	Wathena........	Doniphan....	Ohio........	44	Physician.
Cooper, S. S.................	Oskaloosa......	Jefferson......	Illinois......	40	Physician.
Dodge, William H............	Holton............	Jackson......	Kentucky..	32	Lawyer.
Emmert, D. B................	Fort Scott......	Bourbon......	Penn......	30	Publisher.
Fisher, J. K.................	Huron............	Atchison......	Penn......	42	Farmer.
Foster, R. C.*...............	Leavenworth ..	Leavenw'th.	Kentucky..	32	Lawyer.
Graham, George.............	Seneca............	Nemaha......	New York.	46	Merchant.
Greene, L. F.................	Baldwin City...	Douglas........	Ohio........	31	Farmer.
Haas, H. C..................	Leavenworth ..	Leavenw'th.	Germany ..	32	Carpenter.
Harvey, James M............	Fort Riley......	Riley............	Virginia....	33	Farmer.
Low, A.......................	Doniphan........	Doniphan....	Maryland ..	55	Farmer.
McFarland, P................	Leavenworth ..	Leavenw'th ..	Ireland......	34	Farmer.
Maxson, P. B................	Emporia..........	Lyon............	R'de Island	39	Farmer.
Price, J. M..................	Atchison........	Atchison......	Kentucky..	37	Lawyer.
Rogers, James	Burlingame	Osage............	New Hamp.	38	Lawyer.
Riggs, Samuel A.............	Lawrence........	Douglas........	Ohio........	31	Lawyer.
Scott, J. W..................	Iola................	Allen............	Penn......	42	Physician.
Sharp, J. B..................	Wyandotte......	Wyandotte...	Ohio........	31	Lawyer.
Simpson, B. F...............	Paola..............	Miami..........	Ohio........	30	Lawyer.
Underhill, D.................	Jackson............	Linn..........	Indiana......	40	Farmer.
Veale, G. W.................	Topeka............	Shawnee......	Indiana......	33	Freighter.
Wiley, A.....................	Ottawa............	Franklin......	Ohio........	42	Physician.
Wood, S. N..................	Cotton'd Falls.	Chase	Ohio........	41	Farmer.
A. R. Banks, Secretary.....	Lawrence........	Douglas........	Ohio........	31	Lawyer.
Jos. Speck, Assist. Sec'y *	Wyandotte	Wyandotte...	Penn......	—	Physician.
M. R. Dutton, Jour. Clerk.	Grantville......	Jefferson......	Conn......	37	Farmer.
W. F. Goble, Docket Cl'k *	Pleasant Ridge	Leavenw'th.	Iowa......	29	Book-k'per
A. J. Simpson, Eng. Cl'k *	Carlyle	Allen............	Indiana......	25	Carpenter.
Geo. B. Holmes, Enr. Cl'k.	Topeka............	Shawnee......	Mass......	50	Clerk.
D.L. Payne,Ser.-at-Arms *	Troy................	Doniphan......	Indiana......	30	Farmer.
J.Drew, As't Ser.-at-Arms	Burlingame	Osage............	New York.	65	Farmer.
Geo. W. Weed, Doork'r *..	Pardee............	Atchison......	New York.	31	Farmer.
G.Pharaoh,Ass't Doork'r *	Louisville........	Pottawato'ie.	Prussia......	27	None.
Clarence Walrod, Page *...	Paola	Miami..........	Illinois......	14	Student.
Wm. R. Griffin, Page *......	Topeka............	Shawnee......	Ohio........	18	Student.
Wm. H. Fletcher, Page *...	Topeka	Shawnee......	Indiana......	14	Student.

MEMBERS AND OFFICERS OF THE HOUSE OF REPRESENTATIVES.

Names.	P. O. Address.	County.	Where Born.	Age.	Avocation.
P. B. Plumb, Speaker *.....	Emporia..........	Lyon	Ohio........	30	Farmer.
Allen, Harvey..................	Leavenworth ..	Leavenw'th.	Ohio	42	Cab't m'kr.
Barker, Thomas J............	Wyandotte......	Wyandotte...	Virginia....	38	Farmer.
Booth, Henry *................	Manhattan......	Riley............	England....	28	Farmer.
Bowman, George W.†........	Atchison..........	Atchison......	Penn......	52	Farmer.
Bowman, William............	Atchison..........	Atchison......	New Hamp	38	Miller.
Brandley, Harry..............	Bazaar	Chase	Switzerl'd..	25	Farmer.
Bryant. Peter.................	Banner............	Jackson........	Illinois......	29	Farmer.
Butts, W. C..................	Grass'per Falls	Jefferson......	New York.	33	Farmer.
Bent, C. H.*.................	Oswego..........	Labette........	New York.	28	Farmer.
Clark, T. H.*................	Big Springs....	Douglas........	New Hamp	37	Farmer'
Cloyes, M. J.................	Lancaster	Atchison......	Vermont...	40	Farmer.
Collins, T. B.................	Albany..........	Nemaha	Ohio........	33	Farmer.
Columbia, Charles *..........	Council Grove..	Morris	Ohio........	40	Blacksm'h.
Conner, J. D.*...............	Eldorado........	Butler..........	Ireland......	29	Farmer.
Crocker, Allen...............	Burlington......	Coffey..........	Indiana......	42	Farmer.
Draper, William.............	Clinton............	Douglas........	New York.	35	Farmer.
Dugan, John..................	Leavenworth ..	Leavenw'th.	Ireland......	26	Contractor
Estep, Enoch.................	Paris..............	Linn............	Illinois......	41	Farmer.
Evans, B. D..................	Elwood	Doniphan....	Penn......	37	Mechanic.
Faulkner, J. K...............	Stranger........	Leavenw'th.	Virginia....	32	Farmer.
Finn, D. C...................	Pleasant View.	Cherokee	New York.	30	Lawyer.
Flickinger, R.................	Geary City......	Doniphan....	Penn......	33	Lumber'n.
Gates, Lorenzo...............	Gatesville........	Clay	New York.	44	Farmer.
Goodin, Joel K...............	Baldwin City...	Douglas........	Ohio........	42	Attorney.
Goodin, J. R.................	Humboldt......	Allen	Ohio........	27	Lawyer.
Gregory, H. J................	Belmont	Woodson......	Tennessee	40	Farmer.

The names marked thus * are single.   Those marked thus † are widowers.

MEMBERS AND OFFICERS OF THE HOUSE OF REPRESENTATIVES—Concl'd.

Names.	P. O. Address.	County.	Where Born.	Age	Avocation.
Hamby, William N...........	Garnett	Anderson	N.Carolina	52	Farmer.
Hannon, J..................	Leavenworth ..	Leavenwo'th	Ireland......	29	——
Hannum, J.................	America City...	Nemaha......	Ohio	52	Farmer.
Harmon, O. D..............	Twin Springs...	Linn............	Ohio	38	Farmer.
Harper, G. R..............	Neosho Rapids	Lyon	Penn.........	41	Merchant.
Hindman, S................	Willow Springs	Douglas.......	Ohio	52	Farmer.
Hollenberg, G. H..........	Marysville	Washington	Hanover	41	Farmer.
Huffman, William..........	New Lancaster	Miami........	Ohio	51	Minister.
Jaquith, J. D..............	Americus.......	Lyon	Vermont.....	45	Lawyer.
Jenkins, E. J..............	Troy	Doniphan.....	Ohio	33	Lawyer.
Jenkins, R. W..............	Vienna	Pottawat'mie	Kentucky.	36	Farmer.
Jewitt, J. W...............	Coyville.	Wilson..........	Illinois	23	Farmer.
Johnson, A................	Shawnee	Johnson......	New York.	56	Farmer.
Johnson, F. M..............	Winchester.....	Jefferson.....	Indiana	40	Tradesman
Kendall, J. A..............	Squiresville	Miami	Kentucky..	—	Farmer.
Kennedy, L................	Pleasant Ridge	Leavenwo'th	Ireland	50	Farmer.
Kennedy, T. H.............	Lawrence.......	Douglas.......	Ohio	34	Farmer.
Kibbe, William F..........	Ohio City.......	Franklin	New York.	33	Farmer.
Killen, Daniel.............	Wyandotte	Wyandotte ..	Penn	49	R.R. Cont'r
Knight, Jonathan..........	Tonganoxie.....	Leavenwo'th	Penn	34	Various.
Lane, J. S.................	Blooming G've	Linn..........	New York.	34	Merchant.
Luce, J. M.................	Centropolis	Franklin	New York.	36	Laborer.
Lecompte, S. D.............	Leavenworth ..	Leavenwo'th	Maryland..	52	Lawyer.
Lindsay, Thomas...........	Garnett	Anderson	Ohio	40	Physician.
Loomis, H. J..............	Mission Creek.	Wabaunsee..	Ohio	38	Farmer.
Lyon, M. B................	Monticello	Johnson......	Ohio	45	Farmer.
Manlove, S. A.............	Fort Scott......	Bourbon	Illinois......	27	Merchant.
May, William J............	Monrovia	Atchison......	Indiana	28	Farmer.
McIntosh, W. A...........	Barnesville	Bourbon	New York.	32	Farmer.
Miller, Josiah.............	Lawrence.......	Douglas.......	S. Carolina	37	Merchant.
Mobley, R. D.*.............	Salina	Ottawa.......	Kentucky..	32	Farmer.
Moore, A. A...............	Marion Center.	Marion	Ohio	32	Merchant.
Oliver, J. B...............	Rossville........	Jackson	Penn	25	Merchant.
Palmer, S. E. A	Auburn	Shawnee	Penn	33	Farmer.
Parker, C. E	Carson..........	Brown........	Maine	42	Farmer.
Parker, W. R	Iowa Point.....	Doniphan.....	N.Carolina	66	Farmer.
Power, F. M	Carlyle	Allen.........	Indiana.....	35	Farmer.
Przybylowicz, M...........	Leavenworth ..	Leavenwo'th	Poland......	40	Butcher.
Robb, George H...........	Troy	Doniphan.....	Penn	32	Farmer.
Rogers, D.................	Rogers's Mill..	Neosho	New York.	35	Merchant.
Rupe, J. B.*..............	Elk Creek.......	Shirley	Indiana.....	32	Farmer.
Sheldon, H. C.............	Burlingame....	Osage	New York.	37	Farmer.
Spencer, James M..........	Topeka	Shawnee	New York.	35	Lawyer.
Spillman, A. C.............	Salina	Saline	Miss..........	29	Farmer.
Sponable, J. W............	Gardner	Johnson......	New York.	35	Farmer.
Stover, E. S.*.............	Junction City..	Davis	Maine	30	Mechanic.
Thompson, C. H...........	Abilene	Dickinson ...	Virginia ...	36	Farmer.
Thompson, G. W...........	Atchison..........	Atchison......	Kentucky..	39	Farmer.
Throckmorton, Job.........	Burlington......	Coffey	Ohio	32	Farmer.
Travis, W. F..............	Marmaton......	Bourbon	Ohio	37	Minister.
Tucker, Edwin.............	Eureka	Greenwood ..	Vermont.....	30	Farmer.
Turner, Joshua............	Easton	Leavenwo'th	Missouri....	38	Farmer.
Updegraff, W. W..........	Osawatomie....	Miami........	Penn	45	Physician.
Venard, A.................	Osawkee	Jefferson.....	Ohio	38	Physician.
Way, James P.............	Mound City...	Linn..........	Indiana	40	Merchant.
Wells, J. D................	Barrett's P. O..	Marshall......	Kentucky..	39	Farmer.
Willis, M. C...............	Kennekuk	Brown........	Tennessee	36	Farmer.
Wilson, J. S...............	Mapleton	Bourbon......	Kentucky..	50	Farmer.
John T. Morton, Chief Cl'k	Topeka	Shawnee	Mass	45	Lawyer.
J. H. Prescott, Ass't Cl'k*	Salina	Saline	N. H.........	26	Farmer.
Wm. R. Brown, Jour. Cl'k*	Emporia..........	Lyon	New York.	26	Lawyer.
G.D.Stinebaugh,Enr.Cl'k*	Ohio City	Franklin	Ohio	26	Clerk.
Asa Hairgrove, Eng. Cl'k*	Topeka	Shawnee	Georgia	41	Mechanic.
D.B. Jackman, Dock. Cl'k*	Fort Lincoln...	Bourbon	Mass	42	Lawyer.
J. A. Hunter, Ser.-at-Arms	Topeka	Shawnee	Ohio	35	Farmer.
M.B.Crawford,As.S.-at-A's	Topeka	Shawnee	Ohio	30	Carpenter.
J. M. Adair, Doorkeeper †..	Burlington......	Coffey	Kentucky..	65	Wagonm'r.
M. R. Moore, Ass't Doork'r	Topeka	Shawnee	Indiana	20	Bummer.
Frank Rice, Page *.........	Topeka	Shawnee	Indiana	13	Student.
Charlie Painter, Page *.....	Emporia..........	Lyon	Ohio	11	Student.
Willie Miller, Page *.......	Ridgeway	Osage	Ohio	20	——
C. N. Norton, Page *........	Topeka	Shawnee	New York.	16	None.

The names marked thus * are single.　Those marked thus † are widowers.

JANUARY 15.—Meeting of the veterans of 1855-6, in the Senate Chamber. Henry J. Adams presides. Speeches are made by M. J. Parrott, Charles Robinson, and C. B. Lines.

JANUARY 16.—Election of the following officers of the State Agricultural Society: President, R. G. Elliott, of Douglas; Secretary, H. J. Strickler, of Shawnee; Treasurer, C. B. Lines, of Shawnee; Superintendent, J. L. McDowell. *Executive Committee:* M. J. Alkire, of Shawnee; H. C. Cross, of Lyon; S. S. Tipton, of Anderson; W. G. Coffin, of Leavenworth; J. W. Sponable, of Johnson; G. W. Deitzler, of Douglas; B. W. Williams, of Atchison; M. R. Dutton, of Jefferson; W. A. Phillips, of Saline; Alfred Gray, of Wyandotte.

A Fair was held at Lawrence.

JANUARY 17.—Colonel John C. Vaughan delivers the address before the Publishers' and Editors' Association, at Topeka. The Association asks the Legislature to create the office of State Printer.

—General W. W. Wright, Superintendent of the Kansas Pacific, writes to Governor Crawford that the work was begun in August, 1863; forty miles were built in 1864; in 1865-6, 110 miles were completed, including the line from Leavenworth to Lawrence; the track is now laid to the 155th mile-post, twenty miles beyond Fort Riley; Shoemaker, Miller & Co. are to complete the road to the 385th mile-post.

JANUARY 18.—The town of Osage Mission laid out, by George A. Crawford, Chas. D. Drake and others.

—The Insane Asylum at Osawatomie has four inmates.

JANUARY 22.—The Senate votes for United States Senator for the long term, as follows: S. C. Pomeroy, 16; A. L. Lee, 8; D. R. Anthony, 1. For the short term, the vote stands: Thos. Carney, 9; S. O. Thacher, 5; E. G. Ross, 5; I. S. Kalloch, 3; George A. Crawford, 1; J. P. Root, 1; S. D. Houston, 1.

JANUARY 22.—The House votes as follows for United States Senator for the short term: Thomas Carney, 32; E. G. Ross, 24; S. O. Thacher, 14; I. S. Kalloch, 8; Werter R. Davis, 3; Charles Robinson, 2; George A. Crawford, 1.

JANUARY 23.—Election of United States Senators. Vote for the long term, beginning March 4, 1867: S. C. Pomeroy, 84; A. L. Lee, 25. For the short term: Edmund G. Ross, 68; Thomas Carney, 40; Samuel A. Riggs, 1. There is only a single ballot for each Senator.

—A movement on foot to cause the State to purchase a building at Olathe for the Deaf and Dumb School.

—The town of Ellsworth laid out.

—Charles G. Leland, of the Philadelphia Press, writes a song: "Hans Breitmann vent to Kansas."

FEBRUARY 1.—Coaches make the trip from Junction City to Santa Fe in seven days.

—A suspension bridge is to be built at Ottawa.

—The foundation of the Capitol is reported to be worthless, being made of rotten stone.

—John N. Holloway, of Indiana, is collecting materials for a History of Kansas.

FEBRUARY 6.—Douglas county votes bonds to the L. L. & G. Road.

—Ed. D. Thompson, of Lawrence, is appointed Register of the Santa Fe Land Office.

FEBRUARY 9.—The Legislature votes to investigate the Senatorial election.

FEBRUARY 12.—George A. Crawford, by invitation, addresses the Legislature on the life and services of Abraham Lincoln.

—The Marais des Cygnes bridged at Osawatomie.

—Bridges swept away at Wyandotte, Topeka (pontoon), Manhattan, and Fort Riley.

—The Lawrence Tribune published a letter from S. C. Pomeroy to Geo. W. Deitzler. Of Wm. Sturges, of Chicago, the Senator says: "I hope you will not distrust him, but use him and his associates in the most confiding and liberal spirit." Mr. Sturges is announced as President of the L. L. & G. R. R.

FEBRUARY 15.—The Atchison and Pike's Peak R. R., 40 miles, receives $640,000 in Government bonds; the Union Pacific, Eastern Division, 155 miles, $2,480,000.

—The Freedmen's University, at Quindaro, is said to be in a flourishing condition.

FEBRUARY 18.—Treaty with the Sacs and Foxes. Lands ceded to the United States. New reservation provided in the Indian country.

FEBRUARY 21.—The Legislature elects Wm. Bowman, John Hammond and Daniel Killen State House Commissioners.

—The Salina Herald issued, by B. J. F. Hanna.

FEBRUARY 23.—Treaty with the Senecas, Mixed Senecas and Shawnees, Quapaws, Confederated Peorias, Kaskaskias, Weas and Piankeshaws, Ottawas of Blanchard's Ford and Roche de Bœuf, Miamies, and certain Wyandottes. It is provided that these Indians, now residing in Kansas, shall remove to new homes in the Indian Territory.

—Treaty with the Pottawatomies, to provide a new home in the Indian country. The Leavenworth, Pawnee and Western Railroad Company having failed to buy their lands, they may be purchased by the Atchison, Topeka and Santa Fe Railroad Company.

—The State Senate discusses a bill which proposes a five-million State railroad debt.

—Hiawatha has a flour mill driven by wind.

—Judge Greer retires from the Topeka Daily Tribune.

—The United States Senate rejects the nomination of Edward Carroll as United States Collector, John Ritchie, Register at Topeka, and John Willans, Register at Junction City.

—The Legislature makes four new judicial districts.

FEBRUARY 25.—The Investigating Committee conclude their report as follows:

"And while this testimony is not sufficient of itself to authorize your Committee to make a special recommendation for definite action on the part of the Senate, they here record their convictions that money has been used for the base purposes of influencing members of the Legislature to disregard the wishes of their constituents, and to vote as money dictated, and regret their failure to procure the evidence necessary to demonstrate the facts to the people of the State."—*Senate Journal, pp. 755 to 767.*

FEBRUARY 26.—The gopher bill was changed by the Senate into a grasshopper bill, giving a bounty for all scalps of grasshoppers furnished with the ears.—Judge Lecompte, of the House, delivers a poem.—S. A. Riggs, James McCahon and John M. Price are appointed to codify the laws; Geo. A. Crawford and L. D. Bailey, Commissioners of Immigration.

FEBRUARY 26.—The Governor makes the following appointments: *Regents of the State University:* D. P. Mitchell, G. W. Paddock, W. A. Starrett, J. L. Wever, T. C. Sears.

FEBRUARY 28.—Death at Wyandotte of Col. Wm. Weer. He had been U. S. District Attorney and Colonel of the Tenth Regiment. He was a man of unusual intellectual power. His remains were taken to Illinois for burial.

MARCH 1.—Young grasshoppers appear near Leavenworth. The Oskaloosa Independent reports early hatching and premature death of the gryllus.

MARCH 2.—Congress passes a joint resolution for the reduction of the Fort Riley Military Reservation, and granting land to build a bridge over the Republican.

MARCH 2.—State Historical Society organized. Samuel A. Kingman, President; C. K. Holliday, Vice President; D. W. Stormont, Treasurer; Andrew Stark, Librarian; S. D. Bowker, Corresponding Secretary; George A. Crawford, Recording Secretary.

MARCH 3.—Adjournment of the Legislature. Among the acts passed were the following: Ratifying the 14th Amendment to the Constitution of the United States; For building a Blind Asylum at Wyandotte; Issuing $100,000 in bonds for the Penitentiary; Issuing $15,500 in bonds for the Deaf and Dumb Asylum; Issuing $100,000 in bonds for the State House; Changing or defining the boundaries of Wilson, Labette, Dickinson, Bourbon, Crawford and Cherokee counties; Defining the boundaries of Montgomery, Greenwood, Howard, Butler, Cowley, Marion, McPherson, Sedgwick, Sumner, Jewell, Mitchell, Lincoln, Ellsworth, Rice, Reno, Harper, Smith, Osborne, Russell, Barton, Stafford, Pratt, Barbour [should be spelled Barber], Phillips, Rooks, Ellis, Rush, Pawnee, Kiowa, Comanche, Norton, Graham, Trego, Ness, Hodgeman, Ford and Clark counties; Accepting a grant of land for bridging the Republican, at Fort Riley; Providing for the assumption by the State of the Price Raid claims, and referring them again to a special committee; Changing the name of Shirley county to Cloud; Making the Freedmen's University, at Quindaro, a present of State taxes. Three amendments to the Constitution were submitted to the people; one on negro suffrage, one on woman suffrage, and one disfranchising certain soldiers.

MARCH 3.—J. R. McClure is confirmed as Register at Junction City, and C. W. Blair as Postmaster at Fort Scott. H. W. Martin is rejected as Agent of the Sacs and Foxes. H. L. Taylor, for the Shawnees, and Geo. C. Snow, for Osages, are confirmed. Nathan Price, for the Kickapoos, and Forrest R. Page, for the Kaws, are rejected.

—"Beyond the Mississippi," by Albert D. Richardson, published at

Hartford, Conn. Another edition was issued in 1869. It is a book of 620 pages, about one-third of it made up of letters written by Mr. Richardson from Kansas, to the Boston Journal and New York Tribune, between 1857 and 1867. It is profusely illustrated, and gives a graphic picture of affairs in Kansas—men, scenery, events. It is not history, but an entertaining story, well preserving the spirit of the times. Its exaggerations are characteristic of the people and the period, but they prevail to such an extent that nothing can be copied here.

MARCH 4.—D. P. Lowe is appointed Judge of the Sixth District, Wm. Spriggs of the Seventh, Jas. Humphrey of the Eighth, Samuel N. Wood of the Ninth.

MARCH 8.—Thos. Moonlight is confirmed as U. S. Collector.

—Chas. C. Whiting is confirmed as U. S. Marshal, vice Thos. A. Osborn, removed.

MARCH 13.—The Platte Country R. R. is completed from Weston to a point opposite Leavenworth.

—Joel Huntoon is confirmed as Register at Topeka.

—Court House burned at Troy.

MARCH 18.—E. S. Stover is confirmed as Agent for the Kansas Indians, and A. Wiley for the Sacs and Foxes.

—John W. Scott is rejected as Register at Humboldt.

MARCH 19.—The Atchison Champion says there are 6,866 Indians in the State. Treaties have been made for their land—1,071,946 acres.

MARCH 20.—The Missouri Valley Press Association organized; sixteen dailies represented. D. R. Anthony, of the Bulletin, elected President; John W. Wright, of the Conservative, Secretary; John Speer, of the Lawrence Tribune, Treasurer.

MARCH 26.—Governor Crawford appoints D. E. Ballard, W. H. Fitzpatrick and Wm. N. Hamby, Commissioners, to re-audit and correct the Price Raid awards.

APRIL 1.—Rev. Hiram R. Revels, afterwards United States Senator from Mississippi, is the pastor of the African Methodist Church, Leavenworth.

—John A. Halderman is elected Mayor of Leavenworth, Samuel Kimball of Lawrence, and Cassius G. Foster of Atchison.

APRIL 2.—The Kansas Pacific sells Delaware lands at Lawrence, at auction, at good figures.

APRIL.—Gov. Crawford sells $30,000 of State bonds to the School Commissioners, at 91 cents on the dollar. In New York, he sells $100,000 at the same price. The remaining $70,000 are sold in New York by Auditor Swallow, in September, at 90 cents on the dollar.

APRIL 2.—John G. Haskell appointed Quartermaster General.

APRIL 3.—Impartial Suffrage Convention at Topeka. Lucy Stone Blackwell, Mr. Blackwell and Mrs. C. I. H. Nichols make speeches. A State Association formed. President, Gov. S. J. Crawford; Vice President, Lieut. Gov. N. Green; Corresponding Secretary, Samuel N. Wood; Recording Secretary, Miss Minnie Otis; Treasurer, John Ritchie.

APRIL 8.—Samuel A. Riggs confirmed as United States District Attorney, vice James S. Emery.

—The locomotive within five miles of Salina.

—Colorado had grasshoppers in 1864 and 1865. They did not come to Kansas.

APRIL 17.—A. F. Callahan retires from the Leavenworth Commercial.

—Death, in New York, of George L. Stearns, the early friend of Kansas and John Brown.

APRIL 22.—Death of George Dimon, ex-Mayor, and proprietor of the Wilder House, Fort Scott.

—Marriage of Bishop Vail, in Philadelphia.

—D. J. Silver & Son, State House contractors, have removed the defective stone, and are putting in new foundations.

APRIL 24.—Earthquake shock, at 2:45 P. M., in eastern Kansas and western Missouri. A second shock soon followed. A few chimneys fell.

APRIL 29.—Trains run to Salina.

—James F. Legate appointed Mail Agent for Kansas and New Mexico.

APRIL 30.—Gens. Hancock and Custer lead an expedition against Indians, in western Kansas.

MAY 1.—John K. Rankin takes possession of the Lawrence Post Office.

—A. H. Hallowell is succeeded, on the Kansas City Journal, by John Wilder.

—Emporia ships 20,000 pounds of flour, by flatboat, to Fort Gibson.

—Grasshoppers destroying crops in some localities.

MAY 6.—A. Anderson succeeds W. W. Wright as Superintendent of the Kansas Pacific.

—The Atchison Daily Free Press, L. R. Elliott, Editor, enters upon its fifth volume.

—Lucy Stone is stumping the State for woman suffrage.

—Geo. T. Isbell removes the Jeffersonian from Grasshopper to Oskaloosa.

MAY 14.—Laying of the corner-stone of Odd Fellows' Hall, Leavenworth.

MAY 15.—Meeting of the Republican State Committee, at Topeka. Steps taken to canvass the State in behalf of negro suffrage.

—Grasshoppers industrious.

—Bourbon county votes bonds to the Sedalia road.

MAY 22.—M. H. Insley's name is published as one of the proprietors of the Leavenworth Conservative.

—That paper says: "It is believed that the grasshoppers will do no damage. The birds are eating them, and they are otherwise mysteriously disappearing."

MAY 23.—Subscription books of the Atchison and Nebraska City R. R. opened.

—Miami county issues bonds to the Border Tier road.

—Robert Tracy sells the Wathena Reporter to Ed. H. Snow and Geo. W. Larzelere.

JUNE.—Third Annual Catalogue issued of the Agricultural College. Number of students, 178.

June 1.—The Leavenworth Medical Herald, a monthly, issued by Drs. C. A. Logan and Tiffin Sinks.

—Hiram Griswold is appointed Register in Bankruptcy.

—Contract let for a court house in Jefferson county.

—Grasshoppers leave Coffey and Greenwood counties; no damage done since the recent heavy rains; crops fine.

June 6.—Simon Cameron and other Eastern men make a journey to the end of the Kansas Pacific track.

June 9.—Ben. F. Wade, Z. Chandler, J. A. J. Creswell, Richard Yates, Lyman Trumbull, John Covode, and others, arrive in Leavenworth.

—Twenty-three houses burned in Atchison.

June 10.—Wade, Covode and George Francis Train make speeches in Lawrence. They pass on to the end of the track.

—Leavenworth county and Platte county, Mo., overrun with grasshoppers.

June 14.—Death of Jacob Saqui, a leading Mason, at Atchison. He had been Grand Master of the Grand Lodge for six years.

—Great flood at Salina and Ellsworth.

—There are 10,000 Sunday school children in the State, and over 1,000 teachers.

—No grasshoppers south of Ottawa.

—A poem called "Osseo, the Spectre Chieftain," by Evander C. Kennedy, is published in Leavenworth.

—Indian raid in western Kansas.

June 24.—Grasshoppers begin to fly.

—Murders by Indians daily reported. Gen. Hancock starts for Denver, to open the route.

—There have been no grasshoppers in Junction City, or west of that place. They laid eggs and hatched only in the northeastern counties, and in Missouri.

—Gen. Custer loses sixty men in a fight with Indians, near the head-waters of the Republican.

June 29.—The Leavenworth Bulletin sold by D. R. Anthony. Geo. T. Anthony ceases to be its editor.

June 29.—Gen. W. T. Sherman authorizes Gov. Crawford to call out a volunteer battalion to protect the frontier. Four companies were raised — the Eighteenth Kansas Cavalry — for four months' service.

July 1.—The Examining Commissioners of the Price Raid Claims, D. E. Ballard, W. N. Hamby, and W. H. Fitzpatrick, make a report to Governor Crawford, of which he speaks as follows in his Message, in January, 1868:

"On the 1st day of April last, the Commission met, organized, and entered upon the laborious task to be performed.

"After a thorough and careful investigation and re-examination, which consumed the entire time allowed by law, the Commission made their report to me, on the 1st day of July, 1867; which report I herewith transmit, and from which I deduce the following:

Amount allowed for services.. $218,393 75
Amount allowed for services, supplies and transportation........................... 81,682 32
Amount allowed for services—damages sustained................. .... 131,693 83
Amount allowed for services, property lost, and miscellaneous.................... 35,518 47

Whole amount allowed by Examining Commission............................ $467,293 37

Amount allowed by Price Raid Commission for supplies, transportation, property lost, and miscellaneous $367,548 70
Amount allowed by Examining Commission for supplies, transportation, damages, property lost, and miscellaneous..................................... 248,894 62

  Difference $118,654 08

"It will thus be seen that the awards of the Examining Commission are one hundred and eighteen thousand six hundred and fifty-four dollars and eight cents ($118,654.08) less than the amount allowed by the Price Raid Commission. A portion of this discrepancy can doubtless be accounted for by an honest difference of opinion between the two Boards in regard to the prices of material, supplies, &c.; while another portion, I regret to say, can only be accounted for by a package of forged or fabricated vouchers, amounting to some eighteen thousand dollars, which were placed in my possession by the Examining Commission when they made their report, in compliance with the law. These forged or fabricated claims purport to have been sworn to before the Secretary of the Price Raid Commission. Whether he has been imposed upon by unknown parties is not for me to determine; but I respectfully refer the whole subject to the Legislature, with the earnest recommendation that a thorough and searching investigation be made of the entire affair, so as to prevent undue suspicion from attaching to those who might be farthest from the commission of such a crime. Besides, if the Commission should have been mistaken in judging these claims to be forged when in fact they were genuine, then an investigation is due, in order that the innocent may not suffer."

July 1.—Governor Crawford issues a proclamation calling for eight companies of cavalry to fight Indians.

—Theodore Alvord & Co. publish the Banner, at Cottonwood Falls.

—Death of Delos F. Drinkwater, a pioneer, in West Virginia.

—M. C. Wheeler Postmaster of Paola, vice John McReynolds, of the Republican.

—George A. Crawford becomes one of the editors of the Kansas Farmer.

July 4.—State Teachers' Association, at Topeka. President, B. F. Mudge; Recording Secretary, Miss M. J. Watson; Corresponding Secretary, D. L. Bradford; Treasurer, H. D. McCarty; Executive Committee: Kellogg, Horner, Rice, Pierce, and Putnam.

July 5.—The cars are running to Ellsworth.

July 6.—Coffey county has voted $200,000 in bonds for the Neosho Valley road.

July 9.—Grasshoppers all gone from Leavenworth. Their presence in a part of the State created no panic or alarm.

—Colonel George H. Hoyt edits the Conservative.

—R. B. Taylor returns to the Wyandotte Gazette.

July 15.—The Eighteenth Kansas mustered into the United States service. The Report of Adjutant General McAfee says:

"During the month of July a battalion of four companies was organized by authority from Lieutenant General Sherman, to protect the western settlements; to guard the employés of the Union Pacific Railway, Eastern Division, and the travel on the great highways leading to the west and southwest. The Battalion was commanded by Major H. L. Moore, of Lawrence, formerly Lieut. Colonel of the Fourth Arkansas Cavalry; Company A, by Captain Henry Lindsey, of Topeka, with Lieutenants Thomas Hughes and John H. Wellman; Company B, Captain Edgar A. Barker, with Lieutenants John W. Price and Samuel L. Hybarger, succeeded by Francis M. Stahl; Company C, by Captain Geo. B. Jenness, with Lieutenants Peleg Thomas and James Reynolds; Company D, by Captain David L. Payne, with Lieutenants John M. Cain and Henry Hegwer. The Battalion consisted of 358 officers and enlisted men."

July 16.—Death of Judge Wm. C. McDowell, of Leavenworth, in St. Louis. He fell from the top of a coach while riding from the Southern

Hotel to the Pacific depot; one wheel passed over his body. The Kansas friends with him were Thos. Carney, E. Stillings, J. C. Burnett, W. P. Gambell, J. W. Scott, John Speer, and Wm. Spriggs. Judge McDowell was a member of the Wyandotte Convention, and the first Judge of the Leavenworth district. He was a man of very brilliant talents, of spotless integrity, and was universally beloved.

July 17.—Rev. Olympia Brown and Miss Bessie Bisbee are speaking in the State for woman suffrage.

—A post office is established at Ellsworth, and letters are no longer detained at Fort Harker.

July 18.—The Topeka Record says the Price Raid Commissioners threw out $118,000 of the $360,000 claims allowed. "A large number of the claims are said to be marked on the margin of the rolls, 'Forged or fabricated.'"

—The News started at Holton, by A. W. Moore.

—The cholera is raging at Fort Harker.

—Crops good all over the State.

—Davis county votes bonds to the Neosho Valley road. The counties have voted that road $800,000.

July.—Second Annual Catalogue issued of the State University. John Fraser, President and Chancellor. Number of students, 105.

July 24.—Silver & Son, contractors, withdraw from work on the State House; the contract is given to Bogert and Babcock.

—Cholera at Ellsworth. Fifteen Kansas soldiers have died at Fort Larned, of cholera. The Eighteenth Battalion is at Larned.

August 1.—Seven men of a railroad grading party killed by Indians, twenty miles east of Fort Hays.

August 2.—The Agricultural College lands offered for sale.

—John S. Brown, of Lawrence, retires from the Kansas Farmer.

—W. K. McCoy & Bros., of Springfield, Ill., establish a stock-yard for Texas cattle, at Abilene.

August 10.—A new bridge is completed at Wyandotte.

—Maj. W. F. Downs, of the Central Branch, is selling the Kickapoo lands, of which the Company owns 152,417 acres.

August 12.—The men who burned the Platte river bridge, in 1861, are arrested in St. Joseph.

August 15.—First passenger train over the Valley road, opposite Leavenworth.

—The Eighteenth Battalion ordered from Fort Dodge to Fort Hays.

August 18.—Thomas J. Anderson resigns, and J. B. McAfee is appointed Adjutant General. Ward Burlingame succeeds Capt. McAfee as Gov. Crawford's Private Secretary.

August 20.—Gen. Sheridan ordered to Kansas.

August 21.—Corner-stone laid of the first abutment of a bridge across the Missouri, at Kansas City. Octave Chanute, Chief Engineer.

—Fight with Indians on the Solomon.

—Capt. J. K. Fisher, of Atchison, is appointed Revenue Inspector.

AUGUST 23.—Arrangements made with Dull & Gowan, and others, to build the Neosho Valley road.

—Mr. Bogert has a large force at work on the basement of the State House.

—The building of J. E. Hays, Olathe, has been bought for the Deaf and Dumb Asylum.

AUGUST 29.—Susan B. Anthony and Elizabeth Cady Stanton leave New York to advocate woman suffrage in Kansas.

SEPTEMBER 1.—George T. Anthony enlarges the Kansas Farmer.

SEPTEMBER 3.—John B. Irvin dies, at Jonesboro', Ill. Dr. Irvin lived at Kennekuk, had been a member of the Legislature, and was an early and leading citizen of Atchison county.

SEPTEMBER.—Kellogg and Norton become the Editors of the Educational Journal. It is published at Emporia.

SEPTEMBER 5.—Leading Republicans meet at Lawrence, and organize a campaign in favor of negro and against woman suffrage. D. W. Houston is Chairman, and John A. Martin, Secretary, of the meeting. An Anti-Female Suffrage State Committee appointed: C. V. Eskridge, Chairman; E. C. Manning, Secretary. The members of the State Committee are as follows: S. A. Kingman, Jno. A. Martin, C. G. Foster, T. C. Sears, G. H. Hoyt, H. C. Haas, J. G. Blunt, S. A. Riggs, G. W. Deitzler, E. M. Bartholow, T. B. Eldridge, Geo. W. Smith, J. W. Roberts, R. J. Harper, Martin Anderson, Geo. W. Martin, D. W. Parker, B. F. Simpson, J. D. Snoddy, S. A. Manlove, D. W. Houston, I. S. Kalloch, C. C. Whiting, J. R. Swallow, J. F. Cummings, O. H. Sheldon, J. B. Orwig, Jacob Weisbach, C. G. Allen, Andrew Akin, P. B. Plumb, J. Stotler, H. N. Bent.

—Grasshoppers leave Omaha. Since they left Kansas they have done much damage in western Missouri and southwestern Iowa.

—National Cemeteries are to be established at Forts Leavenworth and Scott.

SEPTEMBER 11.—Reception of General P. H. Sheridan in Leavenworth.

SEPTEMBER 18.—Iron received at Atchison for the next section of the Central Branch.

—Indians continue their attacks on railway men, beyond Hays.

—Grasshoppers appear on the Cottonwood river. They are seen in the air in Leavenworth, flying southwest "in great numbers."

SEPTEMBER 18.—Democratic State Convention at Leavenworth. F. P. Fitzwilliam, President; P. Z. Taylor, Vice President; J. A. Berry and A. A. Tousley, Secretaries. The following platform is adopted:

"*Resolved*, That, in the opinion of this Convention, public credit can only be sustained, public confidence in our institutions preserved, and the general prosperity of all classes of our people maintained, by a return to a system of rigid economy and retrenchment in national, state and county expenses.

"2. That, as charity should always begin at home, so should economy and the cutting-down of expenses begin in the curtailment of our national, state and county extravagances, and in abolishing all useless expenditures; and we demand the same at the hands of our national, state and county authorities.

"3. That we are in favor of a system of equal taxation, predicated upon all property and valuables, that the burden of labor may be lightened.

"4. That we are opposed to an aristocracy exempted by partial legislation from taxation or bearing any portion of the burdens of government.

30

"5. That we demand the redemption of the United States Government bonds in the same currency by which they were contracted, that there may be no unjust discrimination between the citizen and the bondholder.

"6. That equal and exact justice to all men, of whatever sect, rank or condition, is a cardinal doctrine of Democracy, and that unequal taxation is one of the sources of the discontent which now prevails throughout the land; that we demand that the three thousand millions of bonds on which no state, county or municipal taxes are paid shall be placed upon the duplicate in every state and county in the land, so that all men shall stand equal before the laws, and that the children of the rich and poor may start fairly in the race of life, without governmental favor or governmental oppression.

"7. That we do not regard a national debt as a national blessing, but, on the contrary, as a sore and great calamity to any people. The down-trodden masses of the Old World, suffering for ages the oppression and penalty, caused by the ambition of rulers, and the wars of privileged dynasties, have no reason to love the tyrants who saddled upon their backs ponderous national cumbrances. Such debts are constant drains upon the manhood of nations, and pander alone to the passions of the non-producer and the worthless. As citizens we desire to see our national debt paid to the last dollar—paid without delay—in the same national currency that the farmer gets for his products, the artisan for the work of his hands, the laborer for his toil and sweat, and the merchant for his goods. When the people of the United States do this, they will have fully discharged their duty, and none but moneyed Shylocks, or their tools and apologists, will ask for more.

"8. That we are opposed to all the proposed amendments to our State Constitution, and to all unjust, intolerant, and proscriptive legislation, whereby a portion of our fellow-citizens are deprived of their social rights and religious privileges."

SEPTEMBER 23.—German Convention at Topeka. H. C. Haas, President; August Tauber, Secretary. The sentiment of the Convention in favor of adhering to the Republican party, allowing full latitude of individual opinion and action, and opposition to sumptuary laws.

—Gov. Crawford tenders a regiment to Gen. Sherman, the Indian hostilities still continuing.

—P. H. Hubbell starts the Grasshopper Falls Gazette.

—J. W. Cook is building a woollen factory at Wathena.

—Lyon county is building a court house.

—The Hutchinson Family singing for woman suffrage.

OCTOBER 1.—Henry Buckingham buys an interest in the Leavenworth Times.

—Jefferson county votes on two railroad propositions.

—Doniphan county votes on the Nebraska and Denver roads.

—The Central Branch is graded to the Blue.

OCTOBER 3.—Two men hung by a Vigilance Committee at Ellsworth.

—Spring Hill, Johnson county, growing rapidly.

—Samuel N. Wood leads the woman suffrage campaign.

—Blind Asylum at Wyandotte completed.

OCTOBER 11.—General Sherman telegraphs that the United States will pay the Eighteenth, when it is mustered out.

—Excellent crops in every county.

OCTOBER 14.—The Leavenworth Commercial says the State funds are in Dan. M. Adams's keeping, and are now invested in cattle.

OCTOBER 15.—The Kansas Pacific has completed 338 miles of its road.

—W. F. Goble starts the Kansas Central paper, at Olathe.

—Basil M. Simpson edits the Paola Republican.

OCTOBER 15.—Ground broken at Junction City for the Neosho Valley road. Speeches by Thaddeus H. Walker, Geo. T. Anthony and others.

—Heavy Texas cattle trade at Abilene.

OCTOBER 21.—Treaty made with the Kiowas and Comanches, on Medicine Lodge Creek. New reservation defined.

OCTOBER 28.—By treaty with the Cheyennes and Arapahoes, made on Medicine Lodge Creek, these tribes are located on a reservation in the Indian Territory.

OCTOBER 28.—Frank H. Drenning, Chairman of the State Committee, issues an address to Republican voters, in behalf of negro suffrage.

—Indian Peace Commissioners at Medicine Lodge Creek.

OCTOBER 29.—The Eighteenth Battalion ordered to Fort Harker, to be mustered out.

NOVEMBER 4.—Geo. Francis Train concludes his campaign for female suffrage, and leaves the State.

NOVEMBER 5.—Annual election.

VOTE ON THE VARIOUS PROPOSITIONS TO AMEND THE CONSTITUTION OF THE STATE.

Counties.	Striking out the word "White."		Striking out the word "Male."		Restricting the elective franchise.	
	For.	Against.	For.	Against.	For.	Against.
Allen	324	266	243	303	454	163
Anderson	258	259	218	275	393	138
Atchison	412	1,161	345	1,235	736	884
Bourbon	550	725	464	736	1,350	33
Brown	265	346	248	341	342	222
Butler	33	70	28	76	39	64
Chase	120	123	118	125	164	83
Clay	47	53	39	58	78	32
Crawford	50	199	45	150	150	41
Cherokee	200	186	249	239	254	110
Coffey	239	434	299	350	272	364
Davis	183	383	167	364	281	304
Dickinson	89	95	34	140	151	44
Doniphan	338	1,425	355	1,390	576	1,126
Douglas	1,017	1,147	652	1,464	1,484	635
Franklin	280	539	120	709	652	175
Greenwood	133	198	99	198	234	56
Jackson	173	445	162	387	301	310
Jefferson	392	1,159	335	1,158	649	894
Johnson	400	852	325	866	655	438
Labette	115	213	95	217	207	134
Leavenworth	890	2,703	1,588	1,775	1,135	2,289
Linn	340	798	253	791	737	178
Lyon	503	273	209	565	701	92
Marion	13	58	16	59	16	56
Marshall	167	427	160	410	304	229
Miami	486	865	243	970	850	413
Morris	48	212	66	203	71	190
Nemaha	251	421	227	427	396	178
Neosho	151	322	101	367	236	180
Osage	207	143	121	238	225	113
Ottawa	44	27	34	32	57	15
Pottawatomie	226	456	155	501	352	336
Riley	351	277	218	378	329	267
Shawnee	494	670	439	731	900	234
Saline	162	219	132	233	252	123
Wabaunsee	149	108	114	152	230	28
Washington	39	118	19	143	93	78
Wilson	36	138	43	170	132	81
Woodson	88	149	94	141	187	56
Wyandotte	159	826	168	798	235	779
Total	10,483	19,421	9,070	19,857	16,860	12,165

SENATORS TO FILL VACANCIES.

Dist.	Counties.	Names.	Vote in Co.	Vote in Dis.	Maj.
2	Atchison	Samuel Hipple	966		246
		R. A. Van Winkle	726	1,692	
9	Douglas	O. E. Learnard	1,315		342
		John W. Horner	972	2,286	
14	Bourbon	W. M. Matheny	814		
	Crawford		197		
	Cherokee		403		561
	Bourbon	C. F. Drake	612		
	Crawford		201		
	Cherokee		45	2,277	
15	Butler	A. A. Moore	46		
	Chase		108		
	Marion		66		
	Morris		162		63
	Butler	J. W. McMillan	55		
	Chase		139		
	Marion		7		
	Morris		118	701	
17	Anderson	P. P. Elder	500		
	Franklin		812	1,312	1,312

MEMBERS OF THE LEGISLATURE.

District.	Counties.	Names.	Votes	Maj.	Vote of District.	Vote of County.
1	Doniphan	Thos. J. Vanderslice	158	36		
		Israel May	122			
		Wm. R. Parker	100			
		H. N. Seaver	100		480	
2		H. C. Moore	229	148		
		George Flemming	81			
		W. D. Rippey	14			
		John P. Bitner	11		335	
3		W. H. Smallwood	129	10		
		E. D. McClelland	119			
		E. G. Westcott	54			
		N. Abbey	10		312	
4		E. J. Jenkins	350	346		
		Daniel Bursk	4			
		John Martin	2		356	
5		J. H. Philbrick	181	90		
		Wm. Kirby	91		272	
6	Atchison	Geo. W. Glick	323	160		1,755
		W. W. Guthrie	163		486	
7		A. Byram	189	52		
		John Gray	136		325	
8		George W. Thompson	197	155		
		J. Potter	45		242	
9		B. W. Williams	140	4		
		J. W. Breadlove	136			
		Scattering	2		278	
10		W. L. Johnson	113	8		
		Wm. Martin	95		208	1,539
11	Brown	E. Bierer	217	84		
		Ira J. Lacock	133			
		Scattering	3		353	
12		John Downs	185	154		
		J. S. Tyler	29		212	565
13	Nemaha	Philip Rockefeller	201	44		
		J. P. Taylor	157			
		Scattering	2		360	
14		John Hodgins	195	31		
		J. F. Hocker	164		359	719
15	Marshall	A. G. Patrick	339	339	339	339
16	Washington	S. F. Snyder	91	50		
		R. P. West	41			
		Vernon Parker	40		172	172
17	Pottawatomie	R. W. Jenkins	368	4		
		Martin Mannerhan	364		732	732

MEMBERS OF THE LEGISLATURE—Continued.

District.	Counties.	Names.	Votes.	Maj.	Vote of District.	Vote of County.
18	Jackson	D. W. C. Locke	19₈	115		
		Peter Dickson	83			
		Scattering	4		285	
79		George W. Miller	145	81		
		George Ewbank	64			
		Golden Silvers	56		265	550
19	Jefferson	John B. Johnson	238	62		
		Thomas Housh	176			
		Stephen Stiers	69		483	
20		W. C. Butts	179	24		
		D. H. Frazier	155		334	
21		Robert Armstrong	491	191		
		J. D. Rollins	300		791	1,608
22	Leavenworth	W. P. Gambell	232	24		
		James McCahon	308		640	
23		H. Miles Moore	315	53		
		C. D. Roys	262		577	
24		C. R. Jennison	319	12		
		M. S. Adams	307		626	
25		Mathew Ryan	411	200		
		Daniel Shire	211		622	
26		W. H. Hastings	189	116		
		J. R. Deland	73		262	
27		James Cooley	121	60		
		William Kincaid	61		182	
28		Seth Hollingsworth	260	90		
		Jos. Wright	110		310	
29		J. L. Wallace	188	87		
		J. B. Pickering	101		289	
30		Thos. L. Towne	136	6		
		S. D. Lecompte	130		266	3,774
31	Wyandotte	Vincent J. Lane	239	28		
		Stephen A. Cobb	211		450	
80		Richard Hewitt	434	302		
		Thom A. Grinter	132		566	1,016
32	Johnson	J. P. Robinson	325	93		
		C. E. Lewis	232		557	
33		D. G. Campbell	249	40		
		Abner Arrasmith	207			
		J. McAuley	1		455	
34		J. B. Bruner	180	52		
		Dan Martin	128		308	1,220
35	Douglas	George W. Smith	432	58		
		Wilson Shannon, jr	374			
		T. H. Lescher	135			
		Wm. Haseltine	10		951	
36		Joel Grover	135	13		
		James Bryson	122		257	
37		Joel K. Goodin	230	158		
		Amos Walton	72		302	
38		C. M. Sears	300		300	
39		G. W. Zinn	216		216	
40		Horace Tucker	145	63		
		Henry Webber	82		227	2,253
41	Shawnee	John Guthrie	657	438		
		A. L. Williams	219		876	
42		James Fletcher	201	32		
		L. J. Beam	169		370	1,248
43	Miami	H. H. Williams	230	137		
		W. B. Keith	93		323	
44		J. W. Gosset	332	21		
		E. H. Topping	311		643	
45		Wm. Huffman	210	10		
		W. H. Wilhite	179		398	1,364
46	Linn	A. A. Smith	155	83		
		W. J. Fray	72			
		Richard Hill	1		223	
47		Henry Blackburn	178	88		
		Sam. Ayres	90			
		John Fletcher	1		269	
48		J. W. Garret	246	83		
		B. J. Long	162		408	
49		James D. Snoddy	121	53		

MEMBERS OF THE LEGISLATURE—Continued.

District.	Counties.	Names.	Votes.	Maj.	Vote of District.	Vote of County.
49	Linn (concluded)	T. J. Baskerville	68			
		Joel Moody	1		100	1,096
50	Bourbon	Wm. Hinton	169	105		
		S. M. Allen	64		233	
51		B. F. Smalley	161	67		
		—— Taylor	97		251	
52		J. B. Moore	218	140		
		B. F. Gumm	78		296	
53		E. M. Hulett	323	49		
		W. C. Webb	274		597	1,387
54	Allen	N. B. Blanton	292	159		
		J. N. Phillip	137		436	
		Scattering	3			
55		Lewis Edmunson	88	14		
		Wm. O. Keith	54		180	616
		J. H. Campbell	38			
56	Anderson	T. G. Headley	182	40		
		D. W. Houston	142		324	
57		W. N. Hamby	111	8		
		P. T. Mathews	103		214	538
58	Franklin	James Foster	127	50		
		Capt. James	77			
		T. Jones	53			
		E. D. Coburn	33		290	
59		H. P. Welsh	448	51	448	738
60	Osage	J. R. Stewart	123			
		S. R. Caniff	72			
		M. Rambo	62			
		M. Hupp	61			
		D. B. Burdick	58			
		M. W. Richardson	1		377	377
61	Coffey	Harrison Kelley	172	16		
		H. N. F. Read	156		328	
62		P. H. Smith	363	361		
		—— Read	2		365	693
63	Woodson	David W. Finney	125	5		
		John H. Bayer	120		245	245
64	Lyon	P. B. Plumb	332	258		
		Mark Patty	74			
		Scattering	2		408	
65		A. J. Andrews	118	10		
		D. K. Hardin	108		226	
66		J. D. Jaquith	133	86		
		Watson Grinnell	47		180	814
67	Butler	G. T. Donaldson	42	2		
		L. M. Pratt	40			
		H. D. Kellogg	19			
		D. M. Bronson	10			
		Scattering	2		113	113
68	Chase	O. H. Drinkwater	141	13		
		Henry Brandley	125		266	266
69	Morris	Isaac Sharp	177	71		
		A. B. Spencer	106		283	283
70	Wabaunsee	William Mitchell	259		259	259
71	Davis	John K. Wright	327	41		
		David Monfort	286		613	613
72	Riley	D. M. Johnson	246	15		
		Gottlieb Schauble	231			
		Henry Booth	192			
		Scattering	2		671	671
73	Dickinson	William Lamb	101	18		
		Eliphalet Barber	83		184	184
74	Saline	E. F. Millard	227	97		
		L. F. Parsons	130			
		H. L. Jones	46		403	403
75	Greenwood	Edwin Tucker	132	19		
		L. Clogton	113			
		J. J. Barrett	63			
		J. C. Clogston	1		309	309
76	Marion	C. O. Fuller	67	59		
		G. H. Costello	8		75	75
77	Wilson	P. Fay	175	150		
		Dr. McCartney	25		200	200

MEMBERS OF THE LEGISLATURE—Concluded.

District.	Counties.	Names.	Votes.	Maj.	Vote of District.	Vote of County.
78	Neosho	Thomas H. Butler	237	83		
		D. T. Mitchell	154			
		A. F. Neely	154		545	545
81	Ottawa	R. D. Mobley	50	9		
		H. H. Tucker	41		91	91
82	Clay	Magnus H. Ristine	113		113	113
83	Cherokee	N. D. Ingraham	328	130		
		C. C. McDowell	198		526	526
84	Cloud	James M. Hagaman	32			
85	Labette	W. C. Watkins	206	10		
		J. S. Waters	196		402	402
86	Crawford	John Hamilton	217	43		
		J. Warmley	174		391	391
88	Ellis	W. E. Webb	212	73		
		R. M. Fish	139			
		W. J. Ohler	128			
		J. G. Duncan	2		481	481
	Total vote in State					31,413

VOTE CAST FOR JUDGES OF THE DISTRICT COURTS, FOR THE SIXTH,
SEVENTH, EIGHTH AND NINTH JUDICIAL DISTRICTS.

District.	Counties.	Names.	Vote of County.	Vote of District.	Maj.
6	Bourbon	D. P. Lowe	1,432		
	Crawford	D. P. Lowe	393		
	Cherokee	D. P. Lowe	416		
	Linn	D. P. Lowe	1,223		
	Miami	D. P. Lowe	1,376	4,840	4,840
	Anderson	John R. Goodin	205		
	Allen	John R. Goodin	378		
	Labette	John R. Goodin	196		
	Neosho	John R. Goodin	290		
	Wilson	John R. Goodin	152		
	Woodson	John R. Goodin	163		207
7	Allen	Nelson F. Acres	263		
	Anderson	Nelson F. Acres	304		
	Labette	Nelson F. Acres	201		
	Neosho	Nelson F. Acres	228		
	Wilson	Nelson F. Acres	102		
	Woodson	Nelson F. Acres	79		
	Woodson	William Spriggs	1	2,562	
	Clay	James Humphrey	109		
	Cloud	James Humphrey	61		
	Davis	James Humphrey	313		
	Dickinson	James Humphrey	199		
8	Ottawa	James Humphrey	54		
	Riley	James Humphrey	515		
	Saline	James Humphrey	312		131
	Davis	S. B. White	219		
	Saline	S. B. White	25		
	Riley	Scattering	4	1,811	
	Butler	W. R. Brown	33		
	Chase	W. R. Brown	139		
9	Marion	W. R. Brown	65		43
	Butler	S. N. Wood	71		
	Chase	S. N. Wood	115		
	Marion	S. N. Wood	8	431	

November 5.—Ross, Steele & Co. bring suit against the U. P. R. R., E. D.
They were the contractors before the road was sold to Hallett and Fremont.

—On negro suffrage, the State followed the saying of a well-known politician: "Talk for it; vote agin it."

—The L. L. & G. done one mile south of Lawrence.

—A coal company is formed at Burlingame.

—The Hays City Advance issued, by Joseph Clarke, W. H. Bisbee and Willis Emery.

November 6.—O. H. Browning, Secretary of the Interior, writes to Geo. A. Crawford that James F. Joy has bought the Cherokee Neutral Lands. They have been appraised by Wm. A. Phillips and John T. Cox. Mr. Joy represents the Border Tier railroad.

—Woodson county voted against railroad bonds.

November 22.—Completion of the Kansas City and Cameron railroad.

November 30.—

In obedience to your orders [Gov. Crawford's], I have had duplicate copies of all pay-rolls made, which are now ready for binding. The claims arising out of the Price Raid are as follows:

On pay-rolls	$218,398 75
Material, supplies, and transportation	81,682 32
Damages	131,693 83
Miscellaneous claims	35,518 47
Total	$467,293 37

Amount justly due the State of Kansas from the U. S. Government:

Claims for expenditures for 1861 and 1862	$12,351 04
Allowed on the above claim	9,360 82
Balance due the State	$2,990 22
Military bonds of 1864	$100,000 00
Military bonds of 1866	40,000 00
Interest on the above, about	30,000 00
Miscellaneous claims, about	12,000 00
Arising out of Price Raid	467,293 37
Aggregate	$652,283 59

—*Report of Adjutant General McAfee.*

November 30.—Expenditures of the State for the year:

Governor's Department	$8,191 23	Normal School	13,997 97
Secretary's Department	7,434 70	University	9,380 26
Auditor's Department	3,927 17	Insane Asylum	7,759 00
Treasurer's Department	2,831 05	Deaf and Dumb Asylum	9,930 90
Sup't of Public Instruction	2,030 58	Agricultural Society	6,000 00
Attorney General	2,055 15	Agricultural College	12,138 90
Adjutant General	4,764 34	Railroad Land Agent	1,641 90
Judiciary Department	22,839 36	Blind Asylum	10,034 00
Legislature and Journals	28,473 50	Military expenses	1,860 00
Printing Department	13,891 02	Miscellaneous expenses	2,683 60
Capitol building and grounds *	91,487 61		
Penitentiary †	155,946 49	Total for 1867	$419,298 73

* Of State Capitol expenditure, $89,513.01 is from the sale of $100,000 in bonds.

† Of Penitentiary expenditure, $89,329.16 is from the sale of $100,000 in bonds.

November 30.—The following facts in regard to Lincoln College—afterwards changed to Washburn—are copied from a statement of S. D. Bowker to Superintendent McVicar:

"The purpose of founding an institution of learning of a high literary and religious character early took possession of the minds of the people of Kansas. The project first came up for general discussion in 1857, at which time measures were adopted to secure a fitting location for such an enterprise. Unforeseen difficulties, however, attended the settlement of the Territory and the formation of a State Government. Repeated hostile invasions, the hardships of the year of famine, and the tumult arising from the war, compelled the suspension, for a time, of all active effort for the establishment of the College. On the return of peace, the interest hitherto manifested took a tangible form, and on the 6th of February, 1865, an act of incorporation was secured under the name of 'Lincoln College.'

"Lincoln College is located at Topeka, Kansas. Topeka, the Capital of the State, is situated on the Kansas river, about sixty miles from its junction with the Missouri, at a point on the Pacific Railroad, 350 miles west of St. Louis. The city is built on elevated prairie ground, about one mile south of the river.

"An elegant stone edifice for the Preparatory Department was completed in the autumn of 1865. The building is located at the southeast corner of the Capitol Square, one of the most sightly positions in the city. Its rooms for recitations and general exercises will accommodate some 150 students; besides these it has rooms for library and cabinet. The first term of the College opened January, 1866, with five teachers and over thirty students; among the latter were representatives from six or seven different counties of the State."

DECEMBER.—Report of the Codifying Commissioners. It fills an octavo volume of 1021 pages.

DECEMBER 6.—Topeka Daily Tribune re-issued, under the management of J. P. Greer and A. L. Williams.

—Lawrence is made headquarters of the K. P. road. George Noble is Division Superintendent.

DECEMBER 10.—Geo. T. Anthony becomes editor of the Conservative.

—The Smoky Hill is bridged at Salina.

DECEMBER 10.—First annual meeting of the State Horticultural Society, at Lawrence. President, Wm. Tanner; Vice President, Charles B. Lines; Secretary, G. C. Brackett; Treasurer, S. T. Kelsey.

DECEMBER 18.—Last payments made, at Paola, to the confederated tribes, Peoria, Kaskaskia, Wea and other Indians. They number 204 persons. When they came to Kansas, in 1846, they numbered about 800. They go to the Indian Territory.

—The K. P. done to the 335th mile-post.

DECEMBER 20.—Completion of the Republican river bridge, at Junction City.

—John Severance is to receive $55,000 for completing the St. Jo. & D. R. R. to Troy.

DECEMBER 21.—Stock books opened of the Kansas and Missouri Bridge Co., at Leavenworth, and $59,100 subscribed.

DECEMBER 23.—Gov. Hayes appoints Ed. F. Schneider Adjutant General of Ohio. He had been Major of the Eighth Kansas, and editor of the Leavenworth Times.

DECEMBER 29.—Last rail laid on the 100th mile of the Central Branch.

DECEMBER 30.—There are 523 miles of railroad in the State. The K. P. is within 35 miles of the western boundary—main line completed, 335 miles; Leavenworth branch, 33 miles. The Central Branch is operating 90 miles. The L. L. & G. is done to Ottawa, 27 miles.

—A book appears with this title: "History of Kansas, from the First Exploration of the Mississippi Valley to its Admission into the Union. By J. N. Holloway, A. M. Lafayette, Ind. James, Emmons & Co., Journal Buildings." pp. 584. This is the most bulky of the books on Kansas, but probably contains less reading matter than Mrs. Robinson's. Like the other histories, it has no index; the important facts published in it are badly arranged, and it is not easy to find any special subject in regard to which the reader may want information. The opinions, the grammar, and the spelling, especially of proper names, might be criticised. The author was a non-resident, and it is really surprising that the book is so complete. It ends with the admission of the State into the Union. The book had a large sale, but Mr. Holloway has not received the credit which his industry justly entitled him to.

EIGHTEENTH KANSAS CAVALRY BATTALION.

Name and Rank.	Date of Muster.	Remarks.
MAJOR. Horace L. Moore............	July 15, 1867	Mustered out with battalion, Nov. 15, 1867.

COMPANY A.

Name and Rank.	Date of Muster.	Remarks.
CAPTAIN. Horace L. Moore............	July 15, 1867	Promoted Major, July 15, 1867.
Henry C. Lindsey.........	July 15, 1867	Mustered out with battalion.
FIRST LIEUT. Thomas Hughes	July 15, 1867	Mustered out with battalion.
SECOND LIEUT. John H. Wellman.........	July 15, 1867	Mustered out with battalion.

COMPANY B.

Name and Rank.	Date of Muster.	Remarks.
CAPTAIN. Edgar A. Barker............	July 15, 1867	Mustered out with battalion.
FIRST LIEUT. John W. Price	July 15, 1867	Mustered out with battalion.
SECOND LIEUT. Samuel L. Hybarger	July 15, 1867	Died of cholera, Fort Larned, Kas., July 26, '67.
Francis M. Stahl............	Aug. 8, 1867	Mustered out with battalion.

COMPANY C.

Name and Rank.	Date of Muster.	Remarks.
CAPTAIN. George B. Jenness.........	July 15, 1867	Mustered out with battalion.
FIRST LIEUT. Peleg Thomas...............	July 15, 1867	Mustered out with battalion.
SECOND LIEUT. Janius Reynolds...........	July 15, 1867	Mustered out with battalion.

COMPANY D.

Name and Rank.	Date of Muster.	Remarks.
CAPTAIN. David L. Payne.............	July 15, 1867	Mustered out with battalion.
FIRST LIEUT. John M. Cain	July 15, 1867	Mustered out with battalion.
SECOND LIEUT. Henry Hegwer.............	July 15, 1867	Mustered out with battalion.

1868.

JANUARY 1.—Die Fackel, a German paper, removed from Wyandotte to Atchison.

JANUARY 7.—Jefferson county votes bonds to the A. T. & S. F., and the Lawrence, Oskaloosa and Atchison road, by 64 majority. At a previous election the propositions were defeated.

—The Olathe Central and Paola Republican publish county histories.

JANUARY 7.—In reply to a resolution, Secretary Browning sends a message to Congress on Indian land sales in Kansas. The Cherokee Neutral Lands were sold to James F. Joy, October 9th, at a dollar an acre, without an official notice that bids would be received for the land. The patent will be issued when the purchase-money is received. The Atchison and Pike's Peak Railroad Company gave $1.25 an acre for 123,832 acres of Kickapoo land. The Leavenworth, Pawnee and Western Railroad Company bought 223,966.78 acres of Delaware lands, known as the Delaware Diminished Reserve. Of these lands, 92,589.22 acres have been paid for and patented to Leonard T. Smith, President of the Missouri River Railroad Company. Other land sales, under treaties, are mentioned in the communication.

JANUARY 10.—State officers pass over the L. L. & G., preparatory to giving it 125,000 acres of State land.

JANUARY 11.—Mrs. Stanton publishes an article in the Revolution, on the woman suffrage campaign in Kansas. She believes the vote cast for female suffrage was in the main Democratic.

JANUARY 14.—Meeting of the Legislature.

STATE OFFICERS.

Names.	P. O. Address.	County.	Where Born.	Age	Avocation.
S. J. Crawford, Governor.....	Garnett	Anderson	Indiana.....	32	Lawyer.
N. Green, Lieut. Governor...	Manhattan...	Riley	Ohio	30	Minister.
R. A. Barker, Sec. of State...	Atchison......	Atchison......	Vermont ...	37	Attorney.
J. R. Swallow, Auditor	Emporia	Lyon	N. Jersey..	47	Printer.
M. Anderson, Treasurer......	Circleville ...	Jackson........	Ohio	49	Farmer.
P. McVicar, Supt. Pub. Inst.	Topeka.......	Shawnee......	N. Bruns'k	38	Minister.
Geo. H. Hoyt, Att'y General	Leavenworth	Leavenworth	Mass........	30	Attorney.

JUDGES OF THE SUPREME COURT.

Names.	P. O. Address.	County.	Where Born.	Age	Avocation.
S. A. Kingman, Chief Justice...	Atchison......	Atchison	Mass..........	50	Attorney.
Jacob Safford, Associate Justice	Topeka........	Shawnee	Vermont...	40	Lawyer.
L. D. Bailey, Associate Justice ..	Clinton	Douglas..	New Hamp	46	Lawyer.

JUDGES OF DISTRICT COURTS.

Names.	Dist.	Post Office Address.	County.
D. J. Brewer..	1	Leavenworth	Leavenworth.
R. St. Clair Graham..............................	2	Atchison.....................	Atchison.
C. K. Gilchrist.......................................	3	Topeka........................	Shawnee.
D. M. Valentine....................................	4	Ottawa.......................	Franklin.
J. H. Watson..	5	Emporia......................	Lyon.
D. P. Lowe...	6	Mound City.................	Linn.
John R. Goodin......................................	7	Humboldt	Allen.
James Humphrey	8	Manhattan	Riley.
William R. Brown..................................	9	Cottonwood Falls	Chase.

MEMBERS AND OFFICERS OF THE SENATE.

Names.	P. O. Address.	County.	Where Born.	Age	Avocation.
N. Green, President........	Manhattan	Riley	Ohio	29	Minister.
Abbott, James B.............	DeSoto...........	Johnson......	Conn	67	Convey'cer
Blakely, William S.........	Junction City..	Davis	New York.	38	Merchant.
Clark, N. C.................	Columbus.......	Doniphan.....	Ohio	34	Physician.
Cooper, S. S.................	Oskaloosa	Jefferson......	Illinois	26	Physician.
Dodge, William H...........	Holton...........	Jackson.......	Kentucky..	51	Lawyer.
Elder, P. P.................	Ottawa...........	Franklin	Maine.......	34	Banker.
Foster, R. C.................	Leavenworth ..	Leavenw'th.	Kentucky..	31	Lawyer.
Graham, George	Seneca...........	Nemaha	New York.	66	Merchant.
Greene, L. F	Baldwin City...	Douglas........	Ohio	32	Farmer.
Haas, H. C.................	Leavenworth ..	Leavenw'th.	Germany...	28	Carpenter.
Harvey, James M............	Fort Riley......	Riley.........	Virginia.....	16	Farmer.
Hipple, Samuel	Monrovia.......	Atchison......	Penn	19	Farmer.
Learnard, O. E.............	Lawrence	Douglas......	Vermont...	14	Farmer.
Low, A......................	Doniphan........	Doniphan.....	Maryland..	30	Farmer.
Matheny, W. M.............	Baxter Springs	Cherokee	Kentucky..	49	Lawyer.
Maxson, P. B	Emporia	Lyon	R'de Island	29	Farmer.
McFarland, P...............	Leavenworth ..	Leavenw'th.	Ireland......	45	Farmer.
Moore, A. A.................	Marion Centre	Marion	Ohio	41	Merchant.
Price, John M...............	Atchison.........	Atchison......	Kentucky.	33	Lawyer.
Rogers, James	Burlingame.....	Osage	New Hamp	45	Lawyer.
Scott, J. W.................	Iola.............	Allen.........	Penn	33	Physician.
Sharp, Isaac B.............	Wyand'te City.	Wyandotte..	Ohio	47	Lawyer.
Simpson, B. F.............	Paola............	Miami.........	Ohio	32	Lawyer.
Underhill, D...............	Jackson..........	Linn..........	Indiana......	33	Farmer.
Veale, G. W.................	Topeka..........	Shawnee	Indiana.....	34	Freighter.
E. C. Manning, Secretary..	Manhattan	Riley	New York.	47	Printer.
Jos. Speck, Assist. Sec'y..	Wyandotte......	Wyandotte ..	Penn	35	Physician.
M. R. Dutton, Jour. Clerk.	Grantville......	Jefferson......	Conn	56	Farmer.
J. H. Titsworth, Dock. Cl'k	Pardee	Atchison......	New Jers'y	35	Farmer.
A. J. Simpson, Eng. Clerk.	Carlyle	Allen..........	Indiana......	40	Carpenter.
Geo. B. Holmes, Enr. Cl'k.	Topeka	Shawnee	Mass.......	35	Land Ag't.
M.W. Reynolds, Offic'l Rep	Lawrence	Douglas......	New Jers'y	32	Journalist.
D. L Payne, Ser.-at-Arms.	Troy.............	Doniphan.....	Indiana......	38	Soldier.
J. Drew, As't Ser.-at-Arms.	Burlingame	Osage	New York.	39	Farmer.
Geo. W. Weed, Doork'per..	Pardee	Atchison......	New York.	43	Farmer.
G. Pharaoh, As't Doork'per	Louisville.......	Pottawat'ie ...	Prussia	32	Farmer.
Clarence J. Walrod, Page..	Paola.............	Miami.........	Illinois.....	32	Clerk.
William R. Griffith, Page..	Topeka	Shawnee	Ohio	41	Teamster.
Wm. H. Fletcher, Page.....	Erie	Neosho	Indiana.....	34	Farmer.

MEMBERS AND OFFICERS OF HOUSE OF REPRESENTATIVES.

Names.	P. O. Address.	County.	Where Born.	Age	Avocation.
Geo. W. Smith, Speaker...	Lawrence	Douglas........	Pennsylv...	62	Attorney.
Andrews, A. J.................	Neosho Rapids	Lyon	Ohio	42	Farmer.
Armstrong, Robert...........	Perry............	Jefferson	Indiana......	43	Farmer.
Bierer, Everard	Hiawatha.......	Brown	Penn	41	Lawyer.
Blackburn, Henry...........	Linnville	Linn............	England....	54	Farmer.
Blanton, N. B.................	Humboldt	Allen	Missouri ...	38	Farmer.
Bruner, J. B.................	Gardner..........	Johnson	Penn	30	Merchant.
Butler, T. H.................	Erie	Neosho	Ohio	45	Farmer.
Butts, W. C.................	Grassh'r Falls..	Jefferson......	New York.	34	Farmer.
Byram, A...................	Atchison.........	Atchison......	Kentucky..	75	Farmer.
Campbell, D. G.............	Shawnee	Johnson	Tennessee	47	Farmer.
Cooley, James.............	Mt. Pleasant ...	Leavenw'th.	Kentucky..	44	Farmer.
Donaldson, G. T	Chelsea..........	Butler	Ohio	36	Farmer.
Downs, John...............	Albany...........	Brown	New York.	39	Farmer.
Drinkwater, O. H...........	Cedar Point.....	Chase	Penn	32	Farmer
Duncan, Charles C..........	Ellsworth	Ellsworth....	Ohio	24	Grocer.
Edmundson, Lewis...........	Iola..............	Allen	Penn	36	Plasterer.
Fay, P......................	New Albany.....	Wilson..........	New York.	49	Miller.
Finney, D. W...............	Neosho Falls....	Woodson	Indiana.....	26	Merchant.
Fletcher, James.............	Tecumseh	Shawnee	Penn .....:..	38	Farmer.
Foster, James N.............	Peoria City.....	Franklin	Indiana.....	30	Farmer.
Fuller, C. O	Marion Centre.	Marion	New York.	39	Farmer.
Gambell, W. P.............	Leavenworth...	Leavenw'th.	New York.	34	Attorney.
Garrett, J. W...............	Potosi	Linn............	New York.	58	Farmer.
Glick, G. W.................	Atchison.........	Atchison......	Ohio	40	Attorney.
Goodin, Joel K.............	Baldwin City...	Douglas........	Ohio	45	Attorney.
Gossett, J. W...............	Paola	Miami.........	Kentucky..	39	Physician.

MEMBERS AND OFFICERS OF HOUSE OF REPRESENTATIVES—Concluded.

Names.	P. O. Address.	County.	Where Born.	Age.	Avocation.
Grover, Joel	Lawrence	Douglas	New York·	43	Farmer.
Guthrie, John	Topeka	Shawnee	Indiana	38	Attorney.
Hagaman, James M	Elk Creek	Cloud	New York.	37	Farmer.
Hamby, W. N	Garnett	Anderson	North Car.	52	Farmer.
Hamilton, John	Hamilton	Crawford	Pennsylv.	52	Farmer.
Hastings, W. H	Pleasant Ridge	Leavenw'rth	North Car.	38	Farmer.
Headley, T. G	Garnett	Anderson	Indiana	49	Farmer.
Hewitt, Richard	Wyandotte	Wyandotte	New York.	63	Physician.
Hinton, William	Fort Lincoln	Bourbon	Kentucky.	40	Farmer.
Hodgins, I.	Centralia	Nemaha·	New York.	38	Dairyman.
Hollingsworth, S.	Tonganoxie	Leavenw'rth	Ohio	42	Farmer.
Huffman, William	New Lancaster	Miami	Ohio	52	Minister.
Hulett, E. M	Fort Scott	Bourbon	New York.	28	Attorney.
Ingraham, Nathan D.	Baxter Springs	Cherokee	Ohio	42	Nurs'yman
Jaquith, J. D.	Americus	Lyon	Vermont.	46	Farmer.
Jenkins, E. J.	Troy	Doniphan	Ohio	34	Lawyer.
Jenkins, R. W	Vienna	Pottawato'ie	Kentucky.	37	Farmer.
Jennison, C. R.	Leavenworth	Leavenw'rth	New York.	33	Farmer.
Johnston, D. M	Manhattan	Riley	New York.	41	Laborer.
Johnson, J. B.	Oskaloosa	Jefferson	Illinois	25	Lawyer.
Johnson, W. S.	Lancaster	Atchison	Virginia	34	Farmer.
Kelley, Harrison	Ottumwa	Coffey	Ohio	30	Farmer.
Lamb, William	Detroit	Dickinson	North Car.	61	Farmer.
Lane, Vincent J	Wyandotte	Wyandotte	Pennsylv.	70	R. R. contr.
Lecompte, Samuel D.	Leavenworth	Leavenw'rth	Maryland.	53	Lawyer.
Locke, D. W. C.	Holton	Jackson	Vermont.	31	Farmer.
Millard, Ed. F.	Salina	Saline	Michigan.	25	Merchant.
Miller, G. W	South Cedar	Jackson	Kentucky.	32	Farmer.
Mitchell, William	Wabaunsee	Wabaunsee	Scotland.	42	Farmer.
Mobley, R. D.	Minneapolis.	Ottawa	Kentucky.	33	Farmer.
Moore, J. B.	Fort Scott	Bourbon	Illinois	34	Farmer.
Moore, H. C.	Troy	Doniphan	Kentucky.	38	Farmer.
Moore, H. Miles	Leavenworth	Leavenw'rth	New York.	38	Attorney.
Patrick, A. G.	Irving	Marshall	Indiana	40	Printer.
Philbrick, J. L.	Doniphan	Doniphan	New Hamp.	42	Insur. ag't.
Plumb, P. B.	Emporia	Lyon	Ohio	30	Attorney.
Ristine, M. H.	Clay Centre	Clay	Indiana	49	Carpenter.
Robinson, J. P.	DeSoto	Johnson	Indiana	34	Physician.
Rockefeller, Philip	Albany	Nemaha	New York.	46	Mechanic.
Ryan Mathew	Leavenworth	Leavenw'rth	Ireland	49	T.cattle t'r.
Sears, Charles M.	Eudora	Douglas	New York.	38	St'e mason.
Sharp, Isaac	Council Grove	Morris	Pennsylv.	36	Attorney.
Smalley, B. F.	Xenia	Bourbon	Ohio	40	Farmer.
Smallwood, W. H	Wathena	Doniphan	Kentucky.	26	Farmer.
Smith, A. A	Twin Springs	Linn	Ohio	38	Physician.
Smith, P. H	Leroy	Coffey	New York.	40	Merchant.
Snoddy, James D.	Mound City	Linn	Pennsylv.	29	Attorney.
Snyder, S. F.	Washington	Washington	Kentucky.	69	Farmer.
Stewart, J. R.	Burlingame	Osage	Pennsylv.	38	Lawyer.
Thompson, G. W	Atchison	Atchison	Kentucky.	40	Farmer.
Tucker, Edwin	Eureka	Greenwood	Vermont.	31	Farmer.
Tucker, Horace	Sigel	Douglas	Conn.	43	Hortic'st.
Vanderslice, Thomas J.	Highland	Doniphan	Kentucky.	40	Farmer.
Wallace, James L.	Leavenworth	Leavenw'rth	North Car.	52	Physician.
Watkins, W. C.	Oswego	Labette	Tennessee.	33	Lawyer.
Webb, W. E.	Hays City	Ellis	New York.	29	Op. in land
Welsh, H. P.	Ottawa	Franklin	Ohio	34	Attorney.
Williams, B. W	Monrovia	Atchison	North Car.	51	Farmer.
Williams, H. H	Osawatomie	Miami	New York.	39	Merchant.
Wright, John K	Junction City.	Davis	Indiana	33	Merchant.
Zinn, George W	Lecompton	Douglas	Ohio	58	Farmer.
John T. Morton, Chief C'k	Topeka	Shawnee	Mass.	46	Lawyer.
E. C. Kennedy, Ass't Clerk	Leavenworth.	Leavenw'rth	Indiana	26	Lawyer.
J. M. Mahan, Journal Cl'k	Junction City.	Davis	Ohio	29	Lawyer
M. R. Moore, Docket Cl'k	Topeka	Shawnee	Indiana	21	Stud't L. C.
Emma Hunt, Enroll'g C'k	Emporia	Lyon	Indiana	—	Student.
N. Merchant, Engross. C'k	Peoria City	Franklin	New York.	37	Farmer.
H. C Hollister, Reporter..	Leavenworth	Leavenw'rth	New York.	34	Stenogr.
H. H. Sawyer, S.-at-Arms.	Wyandotte	Wyandotte	Vermont.	87	Trader.
M. B. Crawford, A. S.-at-A.	Topeka	Shawnee	Ohio	31	House car.
Horace Gibbs, Doorkeeper	Oskaloosa	Jefferson	Ohio	41	Farmer.
C. S. Norton, Asst. Doork'r	Topeka	Shawnee	New York.	17	Student.
Frank J. Nice, Page	Topeka	Shawnee	Indiana	14	Merchant.
Chas. F. Painter, Page	Emporia	Lyon	Ohio	11	Student.
Edwin S. Eldridge, Page	Lawrence	Douglas	Mass	15	Printer.

JANUARY 14.—The Commissioners to codify the laws make a statement of their work to the Legislature.

JANUARY 15.—Election of the following officers of the State Agricultural Society, at Topeka: President, R. G. Elliott, of Douglas; Secretary, H. J. Strickler, of Shawnee; Treasurer, C. B. Lines, of Wabaunsee; Superintendent, P. G. Lowe. *Executive Committee:* M. J. Alkire of Shawnee, W. G. Coffin of Leavenworth, J. W. Sponable of Johnson, B. W. Williams of Atchison, Josiah Miller of Douglas, M. R. Dutton of Jefferson, Alfred Gray of Wyandotte, W. L. Harrison of Franklin, A. B. Whiting of Riley, J. W. Scott of Allen. A Fair was held at Leavenworth.

JANUARY 17.—Meeting of the Editorial Association, at Topeka. Address by Milton W. Reynolds, of the Lawrence Journal. *Officers elected:* President, R. B. Taylor; Vice Presidents, John A. Martin, M. W. Reynolds, Geo. W. Martin; Secretary, S. D. Macdonald; Treasurer, P. H. Peters. John A. Martin was elected to deliver the next address. John A. Martin, John Speer and James D. Snoddy were appointed to memorialize the Legislature to so amend the Constitution as to create the office of State Printer.

JANUARY 17.—Report of State House Commissioners. (House Journal, pp. 98 to 104.)

JANUARY 18.—Report on Blind Asylum building. (House Journal, pp. 125 to 129.)

—The Delaware Indians pass through Lawrence, to their new home in the Indian Territory.

JANUARY 23.—Message from the Governor, on the Penitentiary. (House Journal, pp. 192–4.)

JANUARY 23.—In the contest of Stephen A. Cobb against Vincent J. Lane, the House decides that Lane is entitled to his seat.

JANUARY 31.—A fire in Leavenworth burned the Mercantile Library. Besides many valuable books, it contained files of the Leavenworth Herald (presented to the Library by Eugene F. Havens), and many other State newspapers. The generous enterprise of the citizens soon supplied a new Library, equal in size to the one destroyed. In 1869, Alonzo L. Callahan wrote a history and compiled a Catalogue of the Library. It was published by the Times and Conservative.

—A Legislative Committee, investigating the original Price Raid awards, finds that many claims were dishonestly allowed.

—Jackson county is building a Court House.

FEBRUARY 1.—There are eleven Daily and fifty Weekly papers in the State.

FEBRUARY 3.—T. Dwight Thacher issues the Evening Republican, at Lawrence.

FEBRUARY 4.—Meeting of the Historical Society, at Topeka. Address by Judge Kingman, the President. George A. Crawford read a paper on the Calhoun Candle-box. *Officers elected:* President, S. A. Kingman; Vice President, J. R. Swallow; Recording Secretary, George H. Hoyt; Corresponding Secretary, George A. Crawford; Treasurer, D. W. Stormont; Librarian, P. McVicar.

FEBRUARY 4.—Governor Crawford makes a statement of the money due the State by the United States. (See Senate Journal, pp. 220-1.)

FEBRUARY 5.—Death of Willard P. Gambell, a member of the House, from Leavenworth. Mr. Gambell had lived in Kansas about ten years, and probably had no superior among our citizens as a lawyer.

FEBRUARY 6.—S. D. Macdonald retires from the Topeka Record, and F. P. Baker becomes sole proprietor.

FEBRUARY 13.—Meeting of the Republican Committee, at Topeka. Frank H. Drenning, Chairman; George A. Crawford, Secretary *pro tem.* Convention called for March 25th.

FEBRUARY 14.—Reports of State officers begin to appear.

FEBRUARY 15.—A Senate Committee reports in favor of concentrating the State institutions at Topeka. (Senate Journal, pp. 319-21.)

FEBRUARY 17.—Report of Joint Legislative Committee on the action of the different Price Raid Commissions. (Senate Journal, pp. 339 to 345.)

FEBRUARY 18.—Report of Superintendent McVicar on school lands lost to the State. (Senate Journal, pp. 364 to 370.)

FEBRUARY 19.—James McCahon elected to the seat made vacant by the death of Willard P. Gambell.

FEBRUARY 21.—Report of Committee on building Penitentiary. (Senate Journal, 416 to 423, and 449 to 452.) The testimony is given in House Journal, pp. 658 to 689.

FEBRUARY 24.—The lower house of Congress passes a resolution to impeach President Johnson, by 126 to 46.

FEBRUARY 25.—P. B. Plumb's resolution, endorsing the impeachment of Johnson, passes the House by 47 to 28.

FEBRUARY 26.—Democratic State Convention, at Topeka. A. J. Mead, President; Jos. Oliver, Geo. F. Prescott, and H. C. Hollister, Secretaries. *Delegates elected to the National Convention:* Wilson Shannon, jr., Lawrence; Thos. P. Fenlon, Leavenworth; Chas. W. Blair, Fort Scott; Geo. W. Glick, Atchison; A. J. Mead, Manhattan; Isaac Sharp, Council Grove. The following resolutions were adopted:

"*Resolved*, That we regret the unhappy differences between the Radical party in Congress and the President, and condemn the attempt on the part of Congress to strip the Presidential office of its constitutional authority, and the Supreme Court of its proper functions, in order that they may carry out their unprecedented schemes of negro supremacy in certain States, in violation of the Constitution of the United States, and contrary to the sentiments and feelings of the great bulk of the population of the Union.

"*Resolved*, That we are in favor of guaranteeing to each State in this Union a republican form of government, under the control of the white race.

"*Resolved*, That we have full confidence in the sober second thought of the people, and feel confident that, at the next election, they will so decide as to do justice to the fundamental law, promote the ends of justice, and reunite the States of this once glorious Union in harmony and peace.

"*Resolved*, That the distrust of business men throughout the Union, and want of confidence in pecuniary matters, caused by the neglect of the Congress of the United States to present and perfect measures in regard to taxation and currency, is evidence of want of capacity to appreciate the situation, or indifference to the general welfare.

"*Resolved*, That an equal and uniform rate of taxation upon all property and valuable assets, of both rich and poor alike, is the true doctrine of a republican government.

"*Resolved*, That gold for the rich and paper for the poor is oppressive and unjust, and an equal and uniform currency for the whole people is demanded by both honor and justice, and the Congress of the United States would be more properly engaged in relieving the burthens of the people than in struggles for political power.

"*Resolved*, That the flag of our country should protect the rights of persons and property of all our citizens, both native and foreign-born, in all parts of the world, and the Government should take prompt measures to make that protection certain and effective."

Speeches were made by Chas. W. Blair, Geo. W. Glick, and Thomas P. Fenlon.

FEBRUARY 27.—Report of Committee in relation to Governor Crawford and the Kansas Pacific. (House Journal, pp. 835, 841, 847.)

MARCH 2.—

"The following gentlemen were confirmed as Regents of the State University: C. B. Lines, of Wabaunsee county; Rev. John Ekin, of Shawnee county; and Bishop Thomas H. Vail, of Douglas county.

"*For Regents of the Agricultural College:* Thomas H. Baker and E. C. Manning, of Riley county; and Rev. Charles Reynolds, of Davis county.

"*For Directors of the State Normal School:* G. C. Morse, of Lyon county; James Rogers, of Osage county; T. S. Huffaker, of Morris county; L. D. Bailey, of Douglas county; and S. S. Prouty, of Coffey county.

"*For Adjutant General:* J. B. McAfee, of Jefferson county.

"*For Quartermaster General:* J. G. Haskell, of Douglas county.

"*For Directors of the Penitentiary:* T. C. Sears, of Leavenworth county; A. Low, of Doniphan county; and M. R. Dutton, of Jefferson county."—*Senate Journal, p. 609.*

MARCH 2.—Maj. Gen. P. H. Sheridan resumes command of the Department of the Missouri, at Fort Leavenworth.

MARCH 3.—Last business of the Legislature—passing a new Price Raid bill, and the code.

MARCH 4.—Adjournment of the Legislature. Two volumes of laws are published, one called the General Statutes, (as revised by Price, Riggs and McCahon,) containing 1270 pages, and one called Special Laws, (although general laws are published in it,) containing 104 pages. Among the laws made were the following: State bonds for Penitentiary, $50,000; State bonds for Capitol, $150,000; State bonds for Insane Asylum, $20,000; Defining the boundaries of Gove and Wallace counties; A resolution for the protection of settlers on the Cherokee Neutral Lands.

The Laws were printed by John Speer, at Lawrence. Edward P. Harris superintended the printing, and the General Laws and Special Statutes of 1868 are the best specimens of legal printing, the most accurate and handsome volumes, we have in the State.

MARCH 4.—Legislative excursion to Hays City and the end of the track, at Coyote.

MARCH 5.—The two German papers of Leavenworth consolidate, and take the name Zeitung.

—Senator Ross is reported by telegraph as opposed to impeachment.

—P. H. Hubbell stops the Grasshopper Falls Gazette, and starts the Ellsworth Advocate.

—Meetings of settlers on the Osage and Neutral Lands, demanding a chance to buy their homes at the price established by law.

—Douglas county twice enjoined from issuing bonds to the L. L. & G.

MARCH 25.—Republican State Convention, at Topeka. John W. Scott temporary Chairman, and E. C. Manning Secretary.

Committee on Credentials: James C. Horton, Byron Sherry, Benjamin F. Simpson, A. J. Huntoon, E. S. Stover.

On Organization: J. A. Johnson, P. P. Elder, Charles Drake, A. Low, J. W. McMillan, R. D. Mobley, John Speer, F. W. Potter, Henry Booth.

On Resolutions: I. S. Kalloch, Albert H. Horton, Ed. R. Smith, J. B. Johnson, P. C. Schuyler, A. J. Bell, John W. Scott.

Officers: President, John T. Burris; Vice Presidents, Wm. A. Phillips, T. C. Sears, J. B. Johnson, P. P. Elder, J. W. McMillan, A. Low, J. T. Lanter, A. J. Huntoon, A. H. Horton; Secretaries, F. G. Adams, W. A. Cormany, John Speer.

The following were elected delegates to the National Convention: C. W. Babcock, B. F. Simpson, S. S. Prouty, John A. Martin, N. A. Adams, Louis Weil. *Alternates:* A. Danford, C. P. Twiss, F. P. Baker, Cyrus Leland, jr., J. W. McMillan, J. A. Weisbach.

The following resolutions were adopted:

"*Resolved*, That the Republican party of Kansas, through its delegates assembled in State Convention, hereby reaffirms its devotion to the principles of justice, equality and nationality which were triumphantly vindicated in the late war, and that the reconstruction of the Union upon the basis of the equality of all men before the law, the complete extirpation of Slavery and the ideas which gave it birth, the speedy restoration of permanent peace and prosperity, and the preservation of the public faith and national credit untarnished and inviolate, are all dependent upon the triumph of the great Republican party of the country at the ensuing Presidential election.

"*Resolved*, That regarding the splendid military record of Gen. Ulysses S. Grant with unfeigned admiration, having faith in his wisdom, integrity, prudence and firmness; believing his name synonymous with our cause, and that he is emphatically the man for the times, we cheerfully add our voice to the loud acclaim in his behalf, and instruct the delegates from Kansas to the National Republican Convention at Chicago to cast their votes as a unit in favor of his nomination for the office of President of the United States.

"*Resolved*, That while recognizing the ability and public services of others whose names have been presented to the country, we hereby declare Hon. S. C. Pomeroy as the first choice of the Republican party in this State for the office of Vice President. His early and consistent identification with the cause of human freedom, his patriotic services in Congress, his earnest and uniform devotion to the wants and interests of his constituents, as well as his great prudence and firmness, give assurance that his nomination would inspire universal confidence and enthusiasm, and in his election the loyal people of the nation would have for Vice President 'a man we can trust.'

"*Resolved*, That this Convention express thanks to the soldiers and sailors of the Union who fought and conquered armed Rebels, and stood true to the principles which they vindicated and the flag which floated over them and led them to victory; and that their heroic sacrifices and services will forever be remembered with gratitude by the people of the country which has been saved through their valor and patriotism.

"*Resolved*, That every American citizen, whether by birth or adoption, is entitled to the protection of the nation and its flag; and while it is incumbent on the Government to institute negotiations for the establishment of an international law for expatriation, recognizing naturalization by one nation as terminating allegiance due to another, and conferring all rights of citizenship, it is no less its duty to vindicate its people, of all classes, whether native or naturalized, from oppression or interference, either at home or abroad, when in the legitimate exercise or defence of their personal rights.

"*Resolved*, That we tender our most cordial thanks to Edwin M. Stanton, the statesman of the old Roman type, stern, steadfast and true, for the firmness and patriotism with which he has maintained the majesty of the law and the rights of the people against the attempted invasion of a faithless and wicked Executive.

31

"*Resolved*, That we approve the action of the House of Representatives in its arraignment of Andrew Johnson for high crimes and misdemeanors in office, and we earnestly call upon the Senate of the United States, sitting as a Court of Impeachment, to proceed with the trial of the President without fear, favor or affection, and we pledge the people of Kansas to stand by and maintain the just judgment of the law.

"*Resolved*, That, believing the ensuing Presidential election will settle finally and conclusively, if rightly determined, the great issues brought upon us by the Rebellion, and being convinced that the work which was done in putting down the Rebellion was well and righteously done, and should stand, we exhort our fellow-Republicans throughout the State to perfect and complete their party organizations, and to provide forthwith for the systematic diffusion of political intelligence, by journals and otherwise, and to organize for a vigorous and efficient canvass henceforth to the close of the polls in November next."

MARCH 28.—Nat. G. Barter buys the Border Sentinel, Linn county, of Joel Moody.

. MARCH.—S. T. Kelsey's forest at Ottawa attracts general attention. He has cultivated twenty-five acres.

—Cheese-making has become an important industry at Centralia, Nemaha county.

MARCH 30.—Methodist Conference at Lawrence. Bishop Thompson presides. D. P. Mitchell and W. R. Davis elected to the General Conference. Presiding Elders, A. B. Leonard, C. R. Rice, J. D. Knox.

APRIL.—A book published called "History and Directory of Doniphan County; Sketches of Each Village in the County; Citizens' and Business Directory. R. F. Smith, Editor. Smith, Vaughan & Co., Publishers." pp. 348. The book contains many important facts, is not well printed, and its main purpose is advertising, not history.

APRIL 6.—Burning of the Leavenworth Zeitung office; it was owned by Louis Weil.

APRIL 7.—The Douglas county bonds are to be given to the Leavenworth, Lawrence and Galveston Railroad Company.

— Contract for building the east wing of the Insane Asylum, at Osawatomie, let to S. M. Larkins, of Paola, at $25,934.

— Kansas Pacific done to the 385th mile-post.

APRIL.—A resolution passed by Congress to enable settlers to buy the Osage Ceded Lands.

APRIL 16.—Alex. McDonald, formerly of Fort Scott, is elected United States Senator from Arkansas. Powell Clayton, formerly of Leavenworth, is Governor, and Thomas M. Bowen, formerly of Marysville, is Chief Justice.

APRIL 23.—Meeting at Emporia of the "Wichita Town and Land Company." W. W. H. Lawrence, President; E. P. Bancroft, Secretary. The Secretary was authorized to make a map of Wichita.

APRIL 27.—Supplemental treaty with the Cherokees. On the 30th of August, 1866, Secretary Harlan made a contract with the American Emigrant Company, of Connecticut, for the sale of the Cherokee Neutral Lands. Secretary Browning regarded this sale as illegal, and, on the 9th of October, 1867, he made a contract to sell the lands to James F. Joy. It is now agreed, April 27th, 1868, that the American Emigrant Company shall assign its contract to Joy, and the contract is reaffirmed and declared valid, as herein modified; the contract between Browning and Joy is cancelled.

May 5.—D. W. Wilder returns to the Leavenworth Conservative.

May 5.—D. L. Moody, the famous Chicago revivalist, speaks in Laing's Hall, Leavenworth, to immense audiences.

May 14.—Wm. A. Phillips announces that the Cherokee Neutral Land Commissioners have finished their labors in the field, and will send their plats to Washington.

May 16.—President Johnson acquitted. Senator Ross voted against impeachment.

May 20.—Republican Convention at Chicago. Grant and Colfax nominated for President and Vice President.

May 20.—Houston Nesbitt and H. H. Stafford begin the publication of the Jefferson County Democrat, at Oskaloosa.

May 27.—Treaty with the Osage Indians, selling their land to the L. L. & G. R. R. Co., at twenty cents an acre. There are 8,000,000 acres.

June 3.—F. P. Baker starts the Daily Record, at Topeka.

June 4.—E. S. Stover, Agent of the Kaws, informs Gov. Crawford that the Cheyennes are fighting the Kaws, on the Kaw reservation.

June 9.—E. R. Trask starts the Register, at Oswego.

June.—The Senate confirms a supplemental treaty selling the Neutral Lands to James F. Joy.

—The State officers memorialize the United States Senate against confirming the Osage treaty.

June 26.—Centre College, Kentucky, confers the degree of Doctor of Divinity on Rev. J. G. Reaser, of Leavenworth.

June 29.—Dr. Hartwell Carver makes a journey over the Nebraska-Pacific, and sends the editor of the Conservative his "blessing and benediction." Dr. Carver is called the Father of the Pacific road, having advocated it before Whitney and Benton. His first article urging a road across the continent was published in the New York Courier and Enquirer, August 11th, 1837.

June 29.—A letter of R. J. Hinton, in the Worcester (Mass.) Spy, gives the following statement of sales by the Government, of Kansas Indian land:

Reservation.	When Sold.	To Whom.	Acres Sold.	Per Acre.
Delaware	August 31, 1866	Len. T. Smith	92,598.33	$2 50
Kickapoo	August 16, 1865	Atchison & P. P. R. R.	123,832.61	1 25
Ottawa	June, 1864, to July, 1866	Different persons	18,405.63	2 31
Sac & Fox	Since January 1, 1864	Hugh McCulloch	2,220.76	1 73
Sac & Fox		Carney & Stevens	2,490.36	1 84
Sac & Fox		Wm. R. McKean	29,677.21	64
Sac & Fox		Fuller & McDonald	39,058.27	73
Sac & Fox		Robert S. Stevens	51,689.31	71
Sac & Fox		John McManus	142,915.90	1 09
Sac & Fox		Other persons	20,667.85	2 42
Kaw	Since January 1, 1864	J. W. McMillan	2,946.59	1 16
Kaw		Northrup & Chick	7,519.66	1 28
Kaw		Other persons	23,505.07	1 50
Cherokee Neutral	October 9, 1867	James F. Joy	800,000.00	1 00

July 2.—State Teachers' Association at Emporia. *Officers:* President, D. J. Brewer, Leavenworth; Recording Secretary, Mrs. J. H. Gorham, Emporia; Corresponding Secretary, Joseph Denison, Manhattan; Treasurer, Miss E. D. Copley, Paola; Executive Committee, B. F. Mudge, Man-

hattan; D. T. Bradford, Atchison; D. H. Robinson, Lawrence; M. D. Gage, Junction City; E. F. Heisler, Wyandotte.   L. B. Kellogg and H. B. Norton continued as editors of the Journal.

JULY 6.— National Democratic Convention in New York. On the 9th, Horatio Seymour was nominated for President, on the twenty-second ballot. Frank P. Blair was unanimously nominated for Vice President. Thomas Ewing, jr., was a candidate for Vice President, and was defeated by Order No. 11.

JULY 9.—The United States Senate passes a bill to pay the Price Raid claims.

JULY 14.—A pamphlet reporting the Impeachment investigation reaches Kansas. It is claimed that a letter signed by S. C. Pomeroy and sent to James F. Legate, was forged by Mr. Luce. Thurlow Weed and Edmund Cooper, Johnson's Private Secretary, seem to have declared that the letter was genuine. The committee acquit Pomeroy of trying to sell his vote to President Johnson.

JULY.—S. G. Mead starts the Eureka Herald.

JULY 15.—Republican State Convention called, to meet September 9th.

JULY 16.—Generals Grant and Sherman arrive in Leavenworth, and are received by General Sheridan. On the 17th there was a public reception at the Club Rooms. On the 18th the three Generals started for Denver.

JULY 20.—Congress authorizes the sale of twenty acres of the Fort Leavenworth reservation, for coal-mining purposes.

JULY 20.— Congress grants the right to bridge the Missouri at Leavenworth, and at St. Joseph.

JULY 22.—Dr. Wm. H. Saunders sends the Lawrence Republican the following analysis of our upland prairie soil:

Organic matter	11.00	Silica 69.83
Alumina	8.66	Sesquioxide of iron 2.05
Potassa	1.15	Soda ....a trace
Lime	3.23	Magnesia.................. 2.00
Chlorine	0.00	Sulphuric acid..........a trace
Phosphoric acid	2.08	
		100.00

"The lower or bottom prairie contains more organic matter. We have a soil rich in all the chemical elements necessary for a vigorous growth of vegetation."

JULY 29.—Democratic State Convention at Topeka. Called to order by Thomas P. Fenlon. W. R. Wagstaff, of Miami, temporary Chairman; P. Z. Taylor, of Davis, Secretary.

Committee on Credentials: Wilson Shannon, jr., of Douglas, J. E. Clardy, of Pottawatomie, George Kingsley of Miami, P. Chitwood of Linn, Thomas P. Fenlon of Leavenworth.

Committee on Organization: T. M. O'Brien of Leavenworth, R. Aldy of Johnson, John Martin of Shawnee, Adam Dobson of Franklin, Seth Clover of Miami, C. H. Armes of Ellis, A. G. Ege of Doniphan, R. C. Whitney of Davis, Samuel Hipple of Atchison.

Officers: President, Daniel Vanderslice, of Doniphan; Vice Presidents, F. P. Fitzwilliam of Leavenworth, W. T. Shirley of Miami, John B. Scott of Coffey, Thomas Dixon of Riley, D. G. Campbell of Johnson, A. Byram of Atchison, N. Hoysradt of Douglas, John A. Miller of Bourbon, S. C.

Gephart of Jefferson, Reuben Riggs of Marion, J. P. Taylor of Nemaha, G. W. Miller of Jackson, John L. Rice of Shawnee; Secretaries, P. Z. Taylor of Davis, P. H. Tiernan of Leavenworth, P. G. Parker of Johnson, Isaac B. Sharp of Wyandotte, Thomas Dolan of Atchison, A. Dobson of Franklin, P. Chitwood of Linn, A. O. Robbins of Ellsworth, W. S. Kanugh of Chase; Sergeant-at-Arms, James A. Cornell of Shawnee; Pages, Frank Rice and Charles Prodnell.

Committee on Resolutions: J. W. Morris, A. G. Otis, H. S. Walsh, D. G. Campbell, J. M. Jarboe, W. H. Warner, A. McCartney, C. H. Armes, Reuben Riggs.

Isaac E. Eaton read the report of the caucus on a plan of organization, as follows:

"The committee of the Democratic caucus to whom was referred the subject of party organization, make the following recommendations:

"1. That a committee consisting of one from each county, to be designated by the respective delegations, shall be appointed to constitute a committee on party organization, and that the postoffice address of such committee shall be reported to the Convention.

"2. That a Central Committee of nine be appointed to serve as a State Central Committee for the ensuing year.

"3. That the Committee on Party Organization be instructed to cause a thorough organization of the party in the several counties of the State, and have made out a list of all the voters in their respective counties, under the designation of 'Democrat,' 'Radical,' and 'Doubtful,' and that they forward, on or before the 1st day of September next, a copy of said list, and such other information as they think may tend to advance the interests of the Democratic cause, to the Chairman of the State Central Committee."

Geo. W. Glick was nominated for Governor by acclamation.

Maxwell McCaslin was unanimously nominated for Lieutenant Governor.

Wilson Shannon, jr., was nominated for Secretary of State.

Gottlieb Schauble, of Riley, was nominated for Auditor.

For Treasurer, Adam Brenner, of Doniphan, received 42 votes; Allen McCartney, of Bourbon, 93.

Ross Burns, of Shawnee, was nominated for Attorney General by acclamation.

Archibald Beatty, of Wyandotte, was nominated for Superintendent of Public Instruction, by acclamation.

W. R. Wagstaff was nominated for Associate Justice.

Charles W. Blair, of Bourbon, was nominated for Congress, by acclamation.

The following Presidential Electors were selected: Leonard T. Smith, Leavenworth; P. Z. Taylor, Davis; Orlin Thurston, Allen.

The following platform was adopted:

"*Resolved,* That the Democracy of the State of Kansas in convention assembled, do hereby ratify and reaffirm the platform of principles adopted by the National Democratic Convention of July 4th, 1868, and we heartily and cheerfully endorse the nomination of Horatio Seymour, of New York, for President, and Frank P. Blair, of Missouri, for Vice President, and pledge to them our earnest and energetic support.

"*Resolved,* That the bonded debt of the United States should be paid according to the terms of its creation, and all that portion thereof which is not designated to be paid in coin should be paid in greenbacks; that whatever money is received by the laborer for his work, by the farmer for his produce, by the soldier's widow as her pension, should also be received by all other creditors of the United States where express provision is not made by law to the contrary."

"*Resolved*, That the National Bank currency should be called in, and the bonds pledged for their redemption cancelled, and lawful money of the United States substituted in their place, thereby saving some eighteen millions of coin interest per annum for the redemption of the bonded debt.

"*Resolved*, That while we are in favor of education for all, we are opposed to mixed schools of black and white children, and are in favor of separate schools for each race.

"*Resolved*, That we are in favor of the speedy removal of all Indians from the State, and the extinction of all Indian titles as speedily as possible, and that in the making of all treaties for the Indian reservations in the State of Kansas, we demand that the same shall be opened to actual settlers under the homestead and pre-emption laws, and that sections 16 and 36 be secured and set apart for the public.

"*Resolved*, That we hereby denounce the profligate expenditures of the public money of the people of the State of Kansas by the Radical party, and that we denounce as oppressive and unjust the excessive taxation that has been levied on the people of this State by that party.

"*Resolved*, That we owe a debt of lasting gratitude to the soldiers and sailors of the United States for their services in suppressing the rebellion, and that their services will be held in grateful remembrance by the American people.

Committee on Organization: Allen, W. E. Grover, Humboldt; Atchison, W. P. Waggener, Atchison; Bourbon, W. H. Warner, Fort Scott; Chase, H. L. Hunt, Cottonwood Falls; Crawford, C. H. Strong; Cherokee, Wm. W. Cooke; Davis, Robert Reynolds; Dickinson, H. C. Brown, Abilene; Doniphan, Daniel Vanderslice, Highland; Douglas, Ely Moore, Lawrence; Ellis, M. W. Soule, Hays City; Ellsworth, J. H. Kimkle, Ellsworth; Franklin, Adam Cobson, Ottawa; Jackson, Z. G. Williams, Holton; Jefferson, S. C. Gephart, Oskaloosa; Johnson, W. B. White, Olathe; Labette, —— Watkins, Chetopa; Leavenworth, J. L. McDowell; Linn, J. H. Barlow, Paris; Marion, Reuben Riggs, Marion Centre; Miami, Geo. Kinsley, Paola; Morris, James A. Robbins, Council Grove; Nemaha, James Taylor, Seneca; Neosho, John O'Grady, Osage Mission; Osage, N. L. Wyatt, Burlingame; Pottawatomie, J. E. Clardy, Wamego; Riley, A. B. Brookfield, Ogden; Shawnee, H. E. Norton, Topeka; Wabaunsee, E. J. Lines, Wabaunsee; Wilson, Wm. M. Brown, New Albany; Woodson, O. P. Haughawout, Neosho Falls; Wyandotte, Chas. S. Glick, Wyandotte.

State Central Committee: J. L. McDowell, Leavenworth; T. M. O'Brien, Leavenworth; Robert Ferberger, Atchison; A. Byram, Atchison; Isaac B. Sharp, Wyandotte; Nicholas Hoysradt, Douglas; Hugh S. Walsh, Jefferson; A. J. Mead, Riley; N. S. Goss, Woodson.

JULY 31.—Frank P. Blair is serenaded, and makes a speech in Leavenworth. He is one of the Pacific Railroad Commissioners.

AUGUST 10.—Indian outrage on Spillman's Creek. Cheyennes and Arapahoes reported in the Solomon Valley.

AUGUST 11.—The Atchison Champion and Free Press consolidated; John A. Martin and Frank A. Root, Publishers; Frank G. Adams retires.

AUGUST 13, 14.—Ten settlers killed and four wounded, in the Solomon Valley, by Indians. Raids along the Republican and Saline.

AUGUST 18.—Gen. Alfred Sully in pursuit of Indians on the Solomon. —J. B. McAfee reports eight men killed at Asher Creek.

AUGUST.—Geo. T. Anthony appointed United States Collector.

AUGUST 20.—Gen. Sheridan and Col. Forsyth leave Fort Leavenworth for Fort Harker.

AUGUST 23.—Gen. Sheridan reports that the Indians have killed twenty citizens of Kansas, and wounded many more. He directs their forcible removal to their reservations.

AUGUST 27.—Prof. Louis Agassiz, Roscoe Conkling, Ward Hunt, and other Eastern men, visit Leavenworth. Agassiz said he had never seen such good soil as he had seen in Kansas and Missouri. The peaches, apples, pears and grapes, he thought equal to any he had ever tasted. Of the Catholic Cathedral he said: "It is an anachronism; it represents the past. That great free-school building pleases me better; that represents the future. Mankind will probably continue to worship, but not in this way." He speaks of Prince Neuwied, who explored the Missouri up to the Yellowstone, and says his report is marvellous for its accuracy and ability. His *Reise durch Nordamerika* was published at Coblentz in 1838–43, and an English version in London, in 1843. The report is second to Lewis and Clarke in time, but first in geological importance.

The Conservative reprints Longfellow's poem on Agassiz:

"And he wandered away and away
With Nature, the dear old nurse,
Who sang to him night and day
The rhymes of the universe."

AUGUST 31.—An immense army of grasshoppers comes down to the ground in Leavenworth. No harm is done; it is a year of the greatest prosperity.

SEPTEMBER 9.—Republican State Convention at Topeka. Called to order by F. H. Drenning. Temporary Chairman, George Graham; Secretary, Alfred Gray.

Committee on Credentials: S. A. Cobb, J. Stotler, J. H. Gillpatrick, C. C. Whiting, A. Low, J. T. Lanter, Alfred Spear.

Committee on Permanent Organization: J. E. Hayes, Dr. Hathaway, D. Carmichael, J. S. Hidden, Gregory of Woodson, W. P. Douthitt, P. B. Maxson.

Officers: President, D. R. Anthony; Vice President, Josiah E. Hayes; Secretaries, M. M. Murdock and B. J. F. Hanna.

Committee on Resolutions: Joshua Wheeler, John Schott, A. G. Chase, A. Danford, J. Stotler, J. H. Gillpatrick, I. S. Kalloch, Jos. Clarke, F. W. Potter.

First ballot for Governor: Geo. A. Crawford 35, James M. Harvey 31, Thos. Carney 23, T. H. Walker 1.

Second ballot: Crawford 36, Harvey 30, Carney 22, Walker 1, Deckelman 1.

Third ballot: Crawford 37, Harvey 28, Carney 23, Phillips 1, Walker 1.

Fourth ballot: Crawford 40, Harvey 25, Carney 24, Hayes 1.

T. A. Osborn withdrew the name of Thos. Carney.

Fifth ballot: Harvey 50, Crawford 39, Carney 1.

Ballot for Congressman: Sidney Clarke 55, S. J. Crawford 12, Jas. D. Snoddy 7, T. D. Thacher 11, J. W. Scott 3.

First ballot for Lieutenant Governor: C. V. Eskridge 40, C. G. Foster 31, Geo. H. Hoyt 12, Jos. L. Speer, 5.

Second ballot: Eskridge 50, Foster 31, Hoyt 5, Speer 2.

Convention adjourned to the 10th.

First ballot for Associate Justice: C. K. Gilchrist 22, L. D. Bailey 18, A. M. Sawyer 9, D. M. Valentine 23, John T. Burris 11, Geo. W. Gardiner 3, A. H. Horton 1.

Second ballot: Valentine 36, Gilchrist 24, Bailey 11, Sawyer 1, Burris 9, Gardiner 1.

Third ballot: Valentine 54, Gilchrist 27, Burris 6, Bailey 3, Gardiner 1.

For Secretary of State: Thomas Moonlight received 71 votes, and J. B. McAfee 19.

For Auditor: A. Thoman 63, S. S. Prouty 23, J. R. Swallow 1.

For Treasurer: George Graham 50, M. Anderson 29, John Hosick 5, John M. Funk 5, S. S. Prouty 1.

First ballot for Attorney General: E. J. Jenkins 33, A. Danford 18, D. J. Brewer 18, A. L. Williams 5, John Q. Porter 5, Johnson 3, D. B. Hadley 1.

Second ballot: Danford 37, Jenkins 34, Brewer 11, Williams 3, Johnson 1.

Third ballot: Danford 48, Jenkins 34, Williams 3.

P. McVicar was nominated for Superintendent of Public Instruction by acclamation.

Presidential Electors: I. S. Kalloch, D. R. Anthony, A. H. Horton.

State Committee: George W. Martin, E. J. Jenkins, B. F. Simpson, P. P. Elder, T. A. Osborn, E. L. Akin, J. M. Spencer, I. N. Dow, M. M. Murdock.

The following resolutions were adopted:

"1. The Union Republican party of the State of Kansas, in Delegate Convention assembled, pledges its earnest and positive adherence to the principles and platform of the National Union Republican Party, adopted at Chicago, and to the nominees of the Convention, Gen. U. S. Grant and Schuyler Colfax, its most cordial and enthusiastic support.

"2. The history of the Democratic party in Kansas, from its earliest attempt to force the system of human Slavery upon a reluctant people, its systematic violation of the ballot, its perfidious apathy during the struggle for national existence, is a record of violence, cowardice and fraud. Its leaders and its principles are unchanged, and deserve alike the unqualified opposition of every citizen who believes in the supremacy of the law and the perpetuity of free institutions.

"3. The studied and persistent hostility of the Democratic party to the prosecution of the war for the preservation of the Union, its constant and malignant efforts in the North to perplex the Government and dishearten the people, and its open and undisguised treason in the South; its position of uncompromising opposition to every measure originated for the safety of the nation; its nomination of candidates for President and Vice President who propose, if elected, to trample in the dust laws duly enacted, to disperse State governments constitutionally established, and undo the work of reconstruction with violence and blood, impel all friends of the Republic, with renewed energy, to rally in ardent support of the Republican party, around which the hopes of the Nation clustered in its darkest hours.

"4. During the eight years of its possession of National power, the Republican party has proved itself equal to the sacred trust which the Nation confided to its charge, and achieved results which have no parallel in the annals of the political organizations of the world. Its career has been one of beneficence to the poor, justice to the oppressed, and fidelity to those immutable principles without which a Republic is impossible. By the development of the Pacific Railroad system, it has incalculably augmented our resources, and enlarged the national domain; by the Homestead enactments it has increased the wealth and population of the West; by the eight-hour law it has proved its loyalty to labor; by its assertion of the doctrine of expatriation it has evinced its devotion to the rights of our foreign-born citizens; by the adoption of the Fourteenth Constitutional Amendment it has irrevocably secured the results of the war, elevated citizenship, established the national credit, emancipated and enfranchised a race, and dedicated a continent to Freedom. In the future, as in the past, it will continue to advocate those measures which will promote economy, national honesty, domestic concord, and friendly relations with foreign powers, to the end that we may have a government of laws and not of men.

"5. In the distribution of public lands and Indian reserves we demand the full protection of the rights of settlers, and the reservation of the 16th and 36th sections, to which the State is justly entitled, for educational purposes. Wholesale grants of territory to speculators and foreign corporations are unfavorable to the interests of the community, and inconsistent with the objects for which the National domain should be distributed. We especially condemn the policy of disposing of Indian reservations to railroad or land monopolies, and insist that such lands be immediately opened to actual settlers, at not more than one dollar and twenty-five cents per acre. We demand, in the name of our frontier settlers, that the uncivilized Indians be driven from the State, and the civilized tribes be speedily removed to the Indian country.

"6. To our Member of Congress, who favored and labored for the arraignment of Andrew Johnson, for high treason and misdemeanors in office, and to our Senator, who promptly pronounced him guilty thereof by his recorded vote, we extend the gratitude and thanks of a grateful people."

SEPTEMBER 14.—W. S. Burke buys the Leavenworth Bulletin.

—In the fall, Nelson Abbott established the Atchison Daily Patriot.

SEPTEMBER 14.—Governor Crawford calls for five companies of Cavalry, for three months' service on the frontier. They were soon raised, and sent to Lake Sibley, Ayersburg (in the Solomon valley), Salina, and Marion Centre.

SEPTEMBER 17.—Wilder & Sleeper buy the Times, and the consolidated paper is called the Times and Conservative.

SEPTEMBER 17.—Colonel Geo. A. Forsyth is surrounded by Indians, on the North Fork of the Republican, receives two nearly fatal wounds, and loses several men. Among the killed are Lieut. F. H. Beecher and Surgeon John H. Mooers. The fight lasted eight days.

—P. P. Elder is elected Chairman, and M. M. Murdock Secretary, of the Republican Committee.

SEPTEMBER 18.—Execution of Melvin Baughn, at Seneca. He killed Jesse S. Dennis, in 1866.

—L. R. Elliott buys and consolidates the Manhattan Radical and Independent. The new paper is called the Standard.

SEPTEMBER 23.—A company of Militia, raised by Governor Crawford, is marching southwest.

SEPTEMBER 29.—State Fair at Leavenworth.

SEPTEMBER 30.—Meeting of the Missouri Valley Associated Press. D. W. Wilder is elected President, and Geo. F. Prescott, Secretary.

—Colonel T. J. Peter makes arrangements to build the A. T. & S. F. R. R.

OCTOBER 1.—It is announced that the General Statutes will be delivered October 31st, and take effect after that date.

—Indian outrages near Ellsworth and Fort Zarah.

OCTOBER 9.—General Sheridan, near Fort Hays, calls on the Governor for a regiment to fight Indians.

OCTOBER 10.—Proclamation of Governor Crawford, calling for a regiment of volunteers, for six months' service.

OCTOBER 13.—Eleventh Annual Session of the Odd Fellows, at Atchison; membership, 1,575.

OCTOBER 13.—Four men killed and one wounded by Indians, in the Solomon valley. Two women have been carried into captivity by Indians.

OCTOBER 15.—The Leavenworth Call issued, by Joseph Clarke, Henry Buckingham, and W. H. Bisbee.

SEPTEMBER 19.—Mrs. Bassett and infant child captured by Indians, on the Solomon.

OCTOBER 20.—Company A, of the Nineteenth Kansas, mustered in, at Topeka.

OCTOBER 30.—John M. Haeberlein starts the Freie Presse, Daily, in Leavenworth.

—A despatch from Grinnell says the Indians tore up the track, thirty-five miles from Sheridan, and threw off six cars.

NOVEMBER.—Wm. Tanner, Leavenworth, has chestnut trees eight years old fifteen feet high.

NOVEMBER.—The Springfield, Mass., Republican says:

"Prof. Agassiz is fairly seething with enthusiasm over his visit to Kansas. All Brazil was nothing to what he has seen of natural beauty and scientific revelations."

NOVEMBER 3.—Annual election.

VOTE FOR PRESIDENTIAL ELECTORS.

Counties.	A. H. Horton...	D. R. Anthony	I. S. Kalloch...	Len. T. Smith.	P. Z. Taylor...	Orlin Thurston
Allen	693	691	690	200	191	202
Anderson	612	611	610	130	130	130
Atchison	1,297	1,295	1,295	934	934	934
Bourbon	1,443	1,441	1,442	486	486	486
Brown	691	689	690	178	178	178
Butler	135	135	135	93	93	93
Chase	243	243	243	71	71	71
Clay	175	175	175	21	21	21
Crawford	479	479	480	265	264	264
Coffey	637	637	636	261	261	261
Cloud	100	100	100	11	11	11
Davis	371	372	373	256	258	256
Dickinson	194	194	194	98	98	98
Doniphan	1,549	1,573	1,573	721	721	721
Douglas	2,434	2,427	2,418	609	609	609
Ellis	68	68	68	171	171	171
Ellsworth	159	161	161	135	138	135
Franklin	1,030	1,028	1,060	319	317	316
Greenwood	341	341	341	98	98	98
Jackson	553	553	553	313	313	313
Jefferson	1,268	1,268	1,266	724	724	721
Johnson	1,487	1,485	1,487	723	723	723
Labette	617	617	617	166	166	166
Leavenworth	2,671	2,623	2,664	2,330	2,315	2,315
Linn	1,310	1,310	1,310	415	416	416
Lyon	946	941	942	110	110	110
Marion	52	52	52	47	47	47
Marshall	514	514	514	228	228	228
Miami	1,250	1,248	1,243	557	557	557
Morris	155	154	155	172	171	171
Nemaha	591	591	590	272	272	272
Neosho	708	707	707	409	411	411
Osage	422	422	422	83	83	83
Ottawa	136	136	136	....	....	....
Pottawatomie	613	613	613	300	300	299
Republic	62	62	62	3	3	3
Riley	587	587	586	130	129	130
Shawnee	1,351	1,348	1,345	450	450	450
Saline	348	345	345	117	116	114
Wabaunsee	333	332	333	41	41	41
Washington	202	202	202	52	52	52
Wilson	368	368	368	192	192	192
Woodson	263	264	263	81	81	81
Wyandotte	569	568	568	628	628	628
Total	30,028	29,968	30,027	13,620	13,578	13,571

VOTE FOR STATE OFFICERS.

Counties.	GOVERNOR.		LIEUT. GOV.		SEC. OF STATE.		AUDITOR.	
	Jas. M. Harvey.	Geo. W. Glick.	Chas. V. Eskridge	Maxwell McCaslin	Thos. Moonlight.	W. Shannon, jr.	Alois Thoman.	Gottlieb Schauble
Allen	684	206	682	204	683	204	683	203
Anderson	609	134	606	134	613	131	613	131
Atchison	1,221	1,012	1,272	960	1,285	953	1,281	956
Bourbon	1,433	492	1,434	292	1,435	491	1,435	491
Brown	681	185	684	182	683	181	685	182
Butler	135	96	133	96	136	93	137	92
Chase	243	73	218	81	243	72	243	73
Clay	173	22	172	22	167	22	168	22
Crawford	478	267	475	267	473	266	412	333
Coffey	630	269	624	264	631	263	635	264
Cloud	100	11	100	11	100	10	100	11
Davis	374	253	366	260	366	261	369	258
Dickinson	196	97	196	97	194	98	194	98
Doniphan	1,547	743	1,555	734	1,562	715	1,563	733
Douglas	2,398	631	2,357	626	2,366	646	2,374	627
Ellis	49	135	40	140	48	135	49	134
Ellsworth	164	133	161	137	161	137	161	137
Franklin	1,065	320	1,043	320	1,068	278	1,066	320
Greenwood	340	102	334	101	342	100	344	101
Jackson	536	332	547	320	545	319	547	319
Jefferson	1,247	749	1,245	744	1,255	741	1,260	737
Johnson	1,480	735	1,480	732	1,478	732	1,482	732
Labette	615	168	613	168	....	....		
Leavenworth	2,657	2,348	2,660	2,343	2,657	2,334	2,664	2,328
Linn	1,289	438	1,289	430	1,293	427	1,288	426
Lyon	937	115	891	114	939	110	937	112
Marion	52	47	52	47	52	47	52	47
Marshall	497	238	507	234	506	232	509	232
Miami	1,272	570	1,166	619	1,237	568	1,244	566
Morris	155	172	155	171	154	173	156	171
Nemaha	579	287	585	280	586	280	586	280
Neosho	706	410	706	411	708	403	707	410
Osage	421	83	412	83	417	83	421	83
Ottawa	180	5	178	6	177	6	179	6
Pottawatomie	597	315	595	315	599	313	599	312
Republic	63	3	63	....	63	....	63	....
Riley	588	129	581	133	583	133	562	457
Shawnee	1,340	453	1,093	453	1,337	438	1,328	450
Saline	350	115	345	116	349	114	349	116
Wabaunsee	341	43	318	40	333	37	345	41
Washington	202	56	202	66	201	57	201	56
Wilson	340	184	341	185	343	185	343	185
Woodson	264	81	259	82	264	81	264	81
Wyandotte	567	624	566	629	568	629	571	627
Total	29,795	13,809	29,301	13,849	29,200	13,498	29,169	13,640

STATE OFFICERS, ASSOCIATE JUSTICE, AND MEMBER OF CONGRESS.

Counties.	TREASURER.		ATT'Y GEN'L.		SUP. PUB. IN.		ASSOC. JUS.		MEM. OF CON.	
	George Graham	A. M'Cartney	Addison Danford.	Ross Burns.	Peter McVicar.	Archibald Beatty.	David M. Valentine.	Wm. R. Wagstaff	Sidney Clarke.	Chas. W. Blair.
Allen	683	204	683	204	687	204	681	204	662	214
Anderson	614	131	613	133	613	130	606	133	601	131
Atchison	1,278	956	1,279	956	1,281	956	1,279	905	1,269	965
Bourbon	1,435	491	1,435	487	1,434	491	1,435	491	1,417	507
Brown	685	182	684	180	686	181	685	181	687	181
Butler	137	92	133	96	137	92	137	92	138	98
Chase	243	73	139	76	243	73	240	76	240	75
Clay	172	22	171	22	163	22	172	22	172	9
Crawford	474	267	465	267	478	267	474	267	476	265
Coffey	634	264	635	264	632	266	634	264	624	270
Cloud	100	10	100	11	101	10	100	5	99	10
Davis	366	260	365	260	366	260	366	260	365	260
Dickinson	194	98	194	98	195	97	194	97	193	98
Doniphan	1,562	732	1,562	733	1,563	730	1,564	607	1,556	824

STATE OFFICERS, ASSOCIATE JUSTICE, AND MEMBER OF CONGRESS—CONCL'D.

Counties.	TREASURER.		ATT'Y GEN'L.		SUP. PUB. INS		ASSOC. JUS.		MEM. OF CON.	
	George Graham	A. M'Cartney	Addison Danford	Ross Burns...	Peter McVicar	Archibald Beatty...	David M. Valentine	Wm. R. Wagstaff	Sidney Clarke.	Chas. W. Blair...
Douglas	2,404	625	2,406	625	2,388	634	2,399	704	2,191	671
Ellis......................	49	134	49	134	50	134	49	134	51	142
Ellsworth	161	137	160	138	161	135	162	137	162	137
Franklin..............	1,067	320	1,067	319	1,067	320	1,065	323	1,040	327
Greenwood	342	100	342	100	344	101	341	99	340	101
Jackson...............	550	320	546	323	551	319	544	319	543	321
Jefferson.............	1,261	734	1,260	739	1,258	736	1,260	739	1,244	738
Johnson...............	1,482	737	1,483	730	1,482	732	1,880	732	1,475	733
Labette..............	....	....	....	....	....	....	....	....	589	158
Leavenworth	2,672	2,339	2,676	2,323	2,665	2,327	2,662	2,329	2,618	2,352
Linn....................	1,300	425	1,291	429	1,296	420	1,291	434	1,291	426
Lyon	939	112	938	115	939	111	939	113	926	118
Marion	52	47	52	47	52	47	52	39	47	47
Marshall	508	233	509	213	502	232	510	232	508	231
Miami	1,254	566	1,253	566	1,257	567	1,193	611	1,230	572
Morris	155	171	155	172	156	171	155	170	149	173
Nemaha	587	271	587	278	586	280	587	280	584	282
Neosho	708	409	708	410	707	410	707	409	679	420
Osage	421	83	421	83	422	83	421	83	413	84
Ottawa................	184	6	184	6	184	6	184	5	184	6
Pottawatomie	598	313	597	314	595	315	598	314	598	314
Republic	63	....	63	....	63	....	63	....	62	3
Riley	585	133	385	134	587	132	585	134	574	136
Shawnee..............	1,331	439	1,293	485	1,333	440	1,325	451	1,272	461
Saline.................	350	115	349	116	350	109	349	115	348	116
Wabaunsee	345	40	233	53	346	41	344	41	340	42
Washington.........	201	57	201	57	201	57	201	57	202	54
Wilson.................	336	191	343	185	343	185	343	185	341	183
Woodson.............	262	83	264	81	262	82	265	80	264	81
Wyandotte..........	570	627	571	626	563	633	568	628	560	633
Total..............	29,338	13,544	29,247	13,588	29,289	13,547	29,209	13,500	29,324	13,969

VOTE FOR JUDGES OF THE DISTRICT COURT, IN THE FIRST, SECOND, THIRD, FOURTH, AND FIFTH JUDICIAL DISTRICTS.

District.	Counties.	H. W. Ide...	T. A. Hurd	District.	Counties.	J. T. Morton...	S. Clarke...
First.........	Leavenworth	2,599	2,376	Third......	Jefferson..............	1,261	....
	Wyandotte.........	571	624		Shawnee..............	1,752	5
					Wabaunsee..........	384	....
	Total...............	3,170	3,000		Pottawatomie.....	910	....
					Jackson...............	846	....
					Total..............	5,153	5

District.	Counties.	N. Price...	A. G. Otis.	District.	Counties.	O. A. Bassett	James Christian...
Second......	Atchison.............	1,009	1,218				
	Brown	621	225				
	Doniphan............	1,363	833				
	Washington	191	67				
	Republic............	63	....	Fourth ...	Douglas.............	2,137	826
	Nemaha	533	327		Franklin	1,038	341
	Marshall............	387	343		Johnson	1,409	793
	Total...............	4,167	3,013		Total	4,584	1,960

District.	Counties.	J. H. Watson...	W. B. Parsons.	R. M. Ruggles...	District.	Counties.	J. H. Watson...	W. B. Parsons...	R. M. Ruggles...
Fifth	Lyon	808	93	......	Fifth	Greenwood...	309	49	......
	Osage............	396	99	......		Morris	149	....	174
	Coffey	496	379	......		Total	2,158	620	174

VOTE FOR STATE SENATORS.

Dist.	Counties.	Names.	Votes.	Maj.	Dist.	Counties.	Names.	Votes.	Maj.
1	Doniphan ...	E. J. Jenkins......	1452	718	14	Bourbon ...	M. V. Voss.........	1423	1123
	Doniphan ...	W. H. Smallwood....	1518	764		Crawford...	M. V. Voss.........	448	
	Doniphan ...	D. Vanderslice....	754			Cherokee..	....		
	Doniphan ...	W. J. Stout........	734			Bourbon ...	J. E. McKeighan	481	
2	Atchison....	W. H. Grimes....	1260	252		Crawford...	J. E. McKeighan	271	
	Atchison....	S. J. H. Snyder...	1214	253		Cherokee..	....		
	Atchison....	J. W. Forman.....	1018		15	Butler........	J. R. Mead........	128	135
	Atchison....	Samuel Hipple...	961			Chase	J. R. Mead........	216	
3	Leavenw'th.	John McKee......	2690	196		Marion	J. R. Mead........	47	
	Leavenw'th	Wm. Larimer....	2579	232		Morris........	J. R. Mead........	138	
	Leavenw'th	M. Smith........	2542	271		Butler........	Isaac Sharp....	82	
	Leavenw'th	J. A. Halderman.	2494			Chase	Isaac Sharp....	81	
	Leavenw'th	J. W. Morris......	2347			Marion	Isaac Sharp....	45	
	Leavenw'th	T. O'Gwartney...	2271			Morris........	Isaac Sharp....	186	
4	Jefferson ...	J. C. Bailey......	1253	514	16	Allen	J. C. Carpenter..	686	1695
	Jefferson ...	G. B. Carson....	739			Labette	J. C. Carpenter..	653	
5	Brown.........	Albert G. Spear.	631	699		Neosho......	J. C. Carpenter..	615	
	Nemaha......	Albert G. Spear...	557			Wilson	J. C. Carpenter..	363	
	Brown........	J. Martin............	186			Woodson ...	J. C. Carpenter..	265	
	Nemaha......	J. Martin............	303			Allen	F. M. Frost	197	
	Brown........	Scattering..........	4			Neosho......	F. M. Frost	449	
	Nemaha......	Scattering..........	2			Wilson	F. M. Frost	161	
6	Jackson......	O. J. Grover........	549	452		Woodson ...	F. M. Frost	80	
	Pottawat'ie	O. J. Grover........	556			Labette	C. F. Hutchings.	9	
	Jackson......	J. Richey............	317		17	Anderson ..	E. S. Niccolls....	307	334
	Pottawat'ie	J. Richey............	366			Franklin...	E. S. Niccolls....	897	
7	Cloud.........	A. A. Carnahan..	81	932		Anderson ..	D. W. Houston..	391	
	Marshall.....	A. A. Carnahan..	505			Franklin...	D. W. Houston..	479	
	Republic.....	A. A. Carnahan..	58			Anderson ..	Scattering.........	1	
	Riley..........	A. A. Carnahan..	555		18	Coffey.......	M. M. Murdock..	641	1051
	Washington	A. A. Carnahan..	196			Osage.........	M. M. Murdock..	410	
	Cloud.........	A. Smith........	20		19	Greenwood	E. Tucker........	326	1270
	Marshall.....	A. Smith........	232			Lyon..........	E. Tucker........	945	
	Republic.....	A. Smith........	3			Greenwood	Scattering........	1	
	Riley..........	A. Smith........	151		20	Clay..........	J. H. Prescott...	168	779
	Washington	A. Smith........	57			Davis.........	J. H. Prescott...	332	
	Riley.........	B. F. Mudge........	2			Dickinson..	J. H. Prescott...	177	
8	Shawnee	W. H. Fitzpatrick	1087	479		Ellis..........	J. H. Prescott...	43	
	Shawnee	John Martin......	608			Ellsworth..	J. H. Prescott...	147	
9	Douglas	Levi Woodard...	2399	1756		Ottawa	J. H. Prescott...	174	
	Douglas	O. E. Learnard ...	2355	1718		Saline........	J. H. Prescott...	263	
	Douglas	S. K. Huson......	643			Wabaunsee	J. H. Prescott...	369	
	Douglas	W. M. Nace........	637			Clay..........	R. E. Laurenson	15	
10	Johnson......	Abner Arrasmith	1445	688		Davis.........	R. E. Laurenson	296	
	Johnson......	D. G. Campbell...	757			Dickinson..	R. E. Laurenson	113	
11	Miami.........	H. H. Williams...	1217	642		Ellis..........	R. E. Laurenson	136	
	Miami.........	E. Darniello......	575			Ellsworth..	R. E. Laurenson	141	
12	Wyandotte..	C. S. Glick......	581	5		Ottawa......	R. E. Laurenson	8	
	Wyandotte..	S. A. Cobb.......	576			Saline........	R. E. Laurenson	166	
13	Linn...........	J. F. Broadhead..	1270	838		Wabaunsee	R. E. Laurenson	19	
	Linn...........	R. S. Kelso, jr.....	432			Scattering..	....	1	
	Linn...........	Scattering	1						

VOTE FOR MEMBERS OF THE HOUSE OF REPRESENTATIVES.

District.	Counties.	Names.	Votes.	Maj.	Vote of District.	Vote of County.
1	Doniphan......................	J. S. Martin................	430	245		
		T. J. Vanderslice..................	185		615	
2	....	G. W. Wood................	280	118		
		Charles Ladwick...........	162		442	
3	....	A. J. Mowry	214	30		
		M. Bryant.................	184		398	
4	....	H. C. Hawkins.............	202	22		
		Joseph Randolph............	180			
		David Lee.................	80		462	
5	....	David Whitaker	175	17		
		L. A. Hoffman	158		333	2,250
6	Atchison......................	Oliver Davis	309	41		
		J. S. Galbraith	268		557	

VOTE FOR MEMBERS OF THE HOUSE OF REPRESENTATIVES—CONTINUED.

District.	Counties.	Names.	Votes.	Maj.	Vote of District.	Vote of County.
7	Atchison (concluded)	A. J. Evans	276	110		
		H. Myer	166		442	
8		G. W. Thompson	258	39		
		S. Hollister	219		477	
9		Joseph Logan	280	154		
		J. Kirkpatrick	126		406	
10		W. M. Hamm	188	82		
		W. Martin	106		294	2,196
11	Brown	M. B. Bowers	428	298		
		S. Smouse	130			
		Scattering	1		559	
12		George E. Irwin	130	11		
		J. S. Tyler	119			
		John Meredith	42		291	850
13	Nemaha	Samuel Lappin	291	161		
		J. P. Koelzer	130			
		Scattering	1		422	
14		Daniel Helphrey	241	58		
		W. S. Mathews	183		424	846
15	Marshall	William Smith	444	160		
		Thomas Wells	284		728	728
16	Washington	Rufus Darby	179	113		
		W. Lovering	66		245	245
17	Pottawatomie	P. Y. Baker	546	218		
		J. W. Weiler	328		874	874
18	Jackson	J. L. Williams	319	101		
		J. B. McComas	218		537	
79		N. J. Allen	184	61		
		G. W. Miller	123		307	844
19	Jefferson	J. B. Johnson	403	233		
		A. J. Miller	172		577	
20		William Crosby	250	90		
		W. C. Butts	160		410	
21		F. Gilluly	560	165		
		H. S. Walsh	395		955	1,942
22	Leavenworth	P. H. Tiernan	353	38		
		H. P. Scott	315		668	
23		Josiah Kellogg	379	67		
		G. F. Prescott	312		691	
24		M. S. Adams	538	210		
		J. McCarthy	322		860	
25		R. V. Flora	483	180		
		C. Currier	303		786	
26		R. N. Palmer	209	69		
		George B. Coffin	140		349	
27		N. Humber	126	25		
		A. G. Chase	101		227	
28		T. McIntosh	301	73		
		David Smith	228		529	
29		Joseph Howell	239	44		
		J. L. Wallace	195		434	
30		James J. Larimer	225	46		
		J. D. Reynerson	179		404	4,948
31	Wyandotte	H. W. Cook	250	71		
		D. Ryers	179		429	
80		Thomas Feeney	426	114		
		D. B. Hadley	312			
		Scattering	4		742	1,171
32	Johnson	R. E. Stephenson	641	358		
		J. P. Robinson	283		724	
33		D. B. Johnson	495	164		
		J. Watts	331		826	
34		J. T. Rankin	290	134		
		J. M. Willis	156		446	1,996
35	Douglas	James Blood	867	590		
		E. B. Chadwick	277		1,114	
36		Joel Grover	265	207		
		J. J. McGhee	58			
		N. Cameron	46		369	
37		Amos Walton	188	17		
		H. E. Cowgill	171			
		G. W. Wood	44		403	
38		A. Brundage	365	326		

VOTE FOR MEMBERS OF THE HOUSE OF REPRESENTATIVES — CONTINUED.

District.	Counties.	Names.	Votes.....	Maj......	Vote of District.	Vote of County...
38	Douglas (continued)	J. Deskins	39		404	
39		J. L. Jones	165	40		
		W. Pennington	125		270	
40		L. D. Bailey	236	165		
		H. Webber	71		307	2,663
41	Shawnee	J. Guthrie	854	510		
		George L. Young	344		1,198	
42		Perry Tice	345	201		
		E. Carriger	142		487	1,685
43	Miami	S. Hymer	327	156		
		W. H. Willhoit	171		498	
44		T. J. Taylor	536	164		
		P. G. Parker	372		908	
45		Reuben Smith	333	291		
		L. D. Williams	42		375	1,781
46	Linn	A. G. Seaman	223	205		
		G. Hart	18		241	
47		J. H. Madden	225	74		
		J. Chitwood	151		376	
48		S. R. Hungerford	486	303		
		R. S. Kelso	183		669	
49		J. D. Snoddy	258	145		
		H. P. Clay	113		371	1,657
50	Bourbon	D. D. Roberts	248	204		
		E. G. Morrell	44			
		Scattering	3		295	
51		L. Roberts	263	176		
		J. B. Groesbeck	87		350	
52		J. B. Moore	407	341		
		E. Williams	66		473	
53		W. Simpson	460	149		
		E. M. Hulett	311		771	1,880
54	Allen	J. Q. Porter	267	63		
		M. Neal	204			
		W. S. Newbury	146		617	
55		G. B. Inge	221	189		
		A. Allen	32			
		Scattering	1		254	871
56	Anderson	John Butterbaugh	251	77		
		E. P. Gilpatrick	174			
		Scattering	1		426	
57		Charles Gregg	275	275	275	701
58	Franklin	J. McClenahan	400	262		
		G. W. Ashby	138		538	
59		T. C. Bowles	646	468		
		A. W. Adams	178		824	1,362
60	Osage	M. B. Hupp	277	184		
		J. Law	93			
		G. B. Jackson	84		454	454
61	Coffey	J. A. McGinnes	298	156		
		W. J. Sanders	142		440	
62		E. E. Coffin	279	119		
		W. Crandall	160			
		Scattering	8		447	887
63	Woodson	B. F. Johnson	264	186		
		Peter Yohon	78		342	342
64	Lyon	J. Stotler	484	483		
		Scattering	1		485	
65		J. M. Hunter	141	26		
		S. G. Britton	115			
		R. Best	75		331	
66		C. Drake	193	193	193	1,009
67	Butler	T. R. Wilson	134	48		
		W. C. Black	86		220	220
68	Chase	E. B. Crocker	223	139		
		A. Miller	84		307	307
69	Morris	H. W. McNay	162	1		
		M. Conn	161		323	323
70	Wabaunsee	S. R. Weed	262	139		
		W. Mitchell	123			
		Scattering	2		387	387
71	Davis	A. C. Pierce	361	105		
		J. H. Brown	256		617	617

VOTE FOR MEMBERS OF THE HOUSE OF REPRESENTATIVES—Concluded.

District.	Counties.	Names.	Votes.	Maj.	Vote of District.	Vote of County.
72	Riley	Ed. Secrest	584	451		
		J. T. Pritner	133		717	717
73	Dickinson	Cyrus Kilgore	188	86		
		E. Barber	102		290	290
74	Saline	J. Maltby	198	60		
		J. Hambarger	138			
		T. Anderson	116		452	452
75	Greenwood	W. F. Osborn	306	181		
		B. F. Humphrey	125			
		Scattering	1		432	432
76	Marion	A. E. Case	56	13		
		R. Riggs	43		99	99
77	Wilson	W. F. Travis	315	122		
		R. M. Nelson	193		508	508
78	Neosho	Thomas H. Butler	629	176		
		S. L. Coulter	453		1,082	1,082
81	Ottawa	Wallace W. Lambert	96	4		
		James Gable	92		188	188
82	Clay	M. H. Ristine	98	3		
		J. B. McLaughlin	95		193	193
84	Cloud	J. N. Dalrymple	93	93	93	93
85	Labette	D. D. McGeath	567	361		
		W. C. Watkins	206		773	773
86	Crawford	James Wamsley	467	202		
		John Hamilton	265		732	732
87	Ellis	J. F. Wright	138	100		
		U. E. Thurmond	38			
		Scattering	8		184	184
88	Ellsworth	Z. Jackson	185	74		
		J. E. New	111			
		J. Miller	1		297	297
90	Republic	R. P. West	37	9		
		M. Schooley	28		65	65

VOTE CAST FOR AMENDMENT TO SECTION 4, ARTICLE 15, OF THE CONSTI-
TUTION OF THE STATE OF KANSAS.

Counties.	For.	Ag'nst	Counties.	For.	Ag'nst
Allen	448	31	Leavenworth	393	262
Anderson	130	207	Linn	1,246	41
Atchison	431	17	Lyon	81	3
Bourbon	54	1,128	Marion	36	1
Brown	431	158	Marshall	......	......
Butler	36	10	Miami	......	......
Chase	......	......	Morris	88	55
Clay	139	4	Nemaha	657	144
Crawford	......	......	Neosho	262	361
Cherokee	......	......	Osage	141	155
Coffey	549	297	Ottawa	......	......
Cloud	......	......	Pottawatomie	700	73
Davis	......	......	Republic	......	......
Dickinson	258	9	Riley	236	323
Doniphan	......	......	Shawnee	1,421	161
Douglas	943	590	Saline	158	101
Ellis	......	......	Wabaunsee	345	37
Ellsworth	172	7	Wallace	......	......
Franklin	273	278	Washington	165	6
Greenwood	196	33	Wilson	......	......
Jackson	238	242	Woodson	264	33
Jefferson	793	144	Wyandotte	250	177
Johnson	1,677	294			
Labette	260	33	Total	13,471	5,415

NOVEMBER 4.—Gov. S. J. Crawford resigns, to take command of the
Nineteenth Regiment. Lieutenant Governor Green takes the oath as Governor. The regiment left camp, at Topeka, on the 5th.

NOVEMBER 15.—Gen. Sheridan makes a report to Gen. Sherman, in which a complete history is given of the Indian campaign in Kansas. He demands that the War Department "have sole and entire charge of the Indians."

"It is the interest of the nation and humanity to put an end to this inhuman farce. The Peace Commission, and the Indian Department, and the Military and the Indians, make a 'balky team.' The public treasury is depleted, and innocent people murdered, in the quadrangular management, in which the public treasury and the unarmed settlers are the greatest sufferers."

NOVEMBER 19.—Lincoln College, Topeka, takes the name of Washburn, from its benefactor, Hon. Ichabod Washburn, of Worcester, Mass.

NOVEMBER 27.—Gen. Custer defeats the Cheyennes in a battle on the Washita river, near the Antelope Hills, Indian Territory.

NOVEMBER 30.—Expenditures of the State for the year:

Governor's Department	$5,518 73	Insane Asylum	30,952 13
Secretary's Department	6,631 07	Deaf and Dumb Asylum	10,300 00
Auditor's Department	3,321 45	Blind Asylum	14,222 11
Treasurer's Department	5,050 07	Agricultural College	8,275 00
Attorney General	1,250 00	Agricultural Society	3,500 00
Supt. of Public Instruction	2,100 00	State University	6,966 00
Adjutant General	5,085 25	Normal School	5,186 00
Judiciary	20,350 00	Transcribing Journals	1,286 00
Printing	35,251 10	Military expenses	1,140 27
Capitol building and grounds*	141,333 39	Miscellaneous expenses	1,455 80
Legislative expenses	31,068 00		
Penitentiary †	116,906 72	Total for 1868	$457,149 09

*$150,000 in bonds issued for Capitol; proceeds in above, $137,180.69.
†$50,000 in bonds issued for Penitentiary; proceeds in above, $45,588.35.

NOVEMBER 30.—First Annual Report of the Trustees of the Blind Asylum. The Trustees are F. P. Baker, Wm. Larimer and Frederick Speck.

NOVEMBER 30.—Report of the officers of the Deaf and Dumb Asylum. The Board of Trustees consists of: A. S. Johnson, President, Mission, Johnson county; Frank E. Henderson, Secretary, Olathe; G. H. Lawrence, Treasurer, Olathe; J. K. Goodin, Baldwin City; D. L. Lakin, Topeka.

NOVEMBER 30.—Superintendent McVicar, in his Report, says he has brought suit to test the constitutionality of the law giving 500,000 acres of lands to railroads; that of the 800,000 acres of Cherokee Neutral Lands, "not a single acre is reserved for the benefit of common schools;" and that no reservation was made in the Osage Treaty for the benefit of schools. He says:

The following is a summary of the amount of school lands lost to the State by Indian Reservations and Trust Lands within the limits of Kansas:
School lands on 16th and 36th sections of Indian Reservations—

In Topeka U. S. Land District	159,269.44
In Cherokee Neutral Tract	53,000
In Neosho and Labette counties	55,000
In Osage Reserve, Trust Lands	500,000
Total acres	767,269.44

DECEMBER 1.—Perry Fuller is Collector of the Port, at New Orleans.

—Judge A. H. Horton, Presidential Elector, carries the vote to Washington.

DECEMBER 2.—A building at Salina robbed of forty-three stand of Spencer arms and several thousand rounds of ammunition, owned by the State.

32

DECEMBER 4.—State officers accept ten miles of the St. Joseph and Denver R. R. Geo. W. Veale, State Agent, sells 104,632 acres to Dudley M. Steele, at $1.25 per acre — being the remainder unsold of the 125,000 acres given to the road. The railroad company draw the money ($130,790) from the State Treasurer.

DECEMBER 8.—The Catholic Cathedral, at Leavenworth, dedicated.

—F. P. Baker enlarges the Topeka Daily Record.

DECEMBER 13.—The Fort Scott road is completed twenty-three miles. State officers visit and accept it, and it is now entitled to 125,000 acres of State land.

DECEMBER 15.—James Hanway, Daniel Underhill, and S. L. Adair, Trustees, make the Fourth Annual Report of the Insane Asylum, at Osawatomie. The new building is now occupied. W. W. Updegraff is the Steward.

DECEMBER 30.—The following is copied from the Report of J. B. McAfee, Adjutant General:

"The killed, as far as can be ascertained, on the border and on the plains, within the limits of this State, during the year, number from eighty to one hundred persons.

"Claims of the State of Kansas against the United States Government:

Military bonds of 1864	$100,000 00
Military bonds of 1866	40,000 00
Military bonds of 1868	30,000 00
Balance due from 1861 and 1862	2,990 22
Interest on above, about	40,000 00
Miscellaneous claims, about	12,000 00
Price Raid claims	490,000 00
Military claims of 1868, about	100,000 00
Whole amount	$814,990 22

"The great famine in Sweden has been causing tens of thousands to immigrate to this country; a great portion of them might, with proper effort, be secured to this State. Large purchases have already been made in Republic, Jewell, Cloud, Mitchell, Ottawa, Lincoln, Saline and McPherson counties. Those having already settled in Republic county are very apprehensive of Indian troubles, and one raid might break up entirely the settlement and deter the others from coming to it."

NINETEENTH REGIMENT KANSAS VOLUNTEERS—CAVALRY.

Name and Rank.	Date of Muster.	Remarks.
COLONEL.		
Samuel J. Crawford	Nov. 4, 1868	Resigned; resignation accepted, Feb. 12, 1869.
Horace L. Moore	Mar. 23, 1869	Mustered out, April 18, 1869.
LIEUT. COLONEL.		
Horace L. Moore	Oct. 30, 1868	Promoted Colonel; date of com., Mar. 8, 1869.
William C. Jones	Mar. 23, 1869	Mustered out, April 18, 1869.
MAJOR.		
William C. Jones	Oct. 26, 1868	Promoted Lt. Col.; date of com., Mar. 8, 1869.
Charles Dimon	Oct. 30, 1868	Mustered out, April 18, 1869.
Richard W. Jenkins	Nov. 4, 1868	Mustered out, April 18, 1869.
Milton Stewart	Mar. 23, 1869	Mustered out, April 18, 1869.
SURGEON.		
Mahlon Bailey	Oct. 16, 1868	Mustered out, April 18, 1869.
ASSISTANT SURGEON.		
Ezra P. Russell	Oct. 20, 1868	Mustered out, April 18, 1869.
Robert Aikman	Nov. 11, 1868	Mustered out, April 18, 1869.
ADJUTANT.		
James M. Steele	Oct. 20, 1868	Mustered out, April 18, 1869.
QUARTERMASTER.		
Luther A. Thrasher	Oct. 17, 1868	Mustered out, April 18, 1869.
COMMISSARY.		
John Johnston	Oct. 20, 1868	Mustered out, April 18, 1869.

COMPANY A.

Name and Rank.	Date of Muster.	Remarks.
CAPTAIN. Allison J. Pliley	Oct. 20, 1868	Mustered out with regiment, April 18, 1869.
FIRST LIEUT. B. D. Wilson	Oct. 20, 1868	Mustered out with regiment, April 18, 1869.
SECOND LIEUT. Raleigh C. Powell		Resigned, and resignation accepted, Jan 5, '69.
Joseph Beacock	Mar. 23, 1869	Mustered out with regiment, April 18, 1869.

COMPANY B.

Name and Rank.	Date of Muster.	Remarks.
CAPTAIN. Charles E. Reck	Oct. 23, 1868	Mustered out with regiment, April 18, 1869.
FIRST LIEUT. Henry H. McCollister	Oct. 28, 1868	Mustered out with regiment, April 18, 1869.
SECOND LIEUT. Charles H. Champney	Oct. 23, 1868	Mustered out with regiment, April 18, 1869.

COMPANY C.

Name and Rank.	Date of Muster.	Remarks.
CAPTAIN. Charles P. Twiss	Oct. 26, 1868	Mustered out with regiment, April 18, 1869.
FIRST LIEUT. Walter J. Dallas	Oct. 26, 1868	Mustered out with regiment, April 18, 1869.
SECOND LIEUT. Jesse E. Parsons	Oct. 26, 1868	Mustered out with regiment, April 18, 1869.

COMPANY D.

Name and Rank.	Date of Muster.	Remarks.
CAPTAIN. John Q. A. Norton	Oct. 26, 1868	Mustered out with regiment.
FIRST LIEUT. John S. Edie	Oct. 26, 1868	Mustered out with regiment.
SECOND LIEUT. Charles H. Hoyt	Oct. 26, 1868	Mustered out with regiment.

COMPANY E.

Name and Rank.	Date of Muster.	Remarks.
CAPTAIN. Thomas J. Darling	Oct. 26, 1868	Mustered out with regiment.
FIRST LIEUT. Wm. B. Bidwell	Oct. 26, 1868	Mustered out with regiment.
SECOND LIEUT. Charles T. Brady	Nov. 4, 1868	Mustered out with regiment.

COMPANY F.

Name and Rank.	Date of Muster.	Remarks.
CAPTAIN. George B. Jenness	Nov. 4, 1868	Mustered out with regiment.
FIRST LIEUT. DeWitt C. Jenness	Oct. 27, 1868	Mustered out with regiment.
SECOND LIEUT. John Fellows	Oct. 27, 1868	Mustered out with regiment.

COMPANY G.

Name and Rank.	Date of Muster.	Remarks.
CAPTAIN.		
Charles Dimon.............	Oct. 28, 1868	Promoted Major, October 30, 1868.
Richard D. Lender........	Nov. 4, 1868	Mustered out with regiment.
FIRST LIEUT.		
Richard D. Lender........	Oct. 28, 1868	Promoted Captain.
Myron A. Wood............	Nov. 4, 1868	Mustered out with regiment.
SECOND LIEUT.		
Myron A. Wood	Oct. 28, 1868	Promoted First Lieutenant.
Henry C. Litchfield......	Nov. 4, 1868	Resigned, and resignation accepted Jan. 22, '69.
James W. Brown...........	Mar. 23. 1868	Mustered out with regiment.

COMPANY H.

Name and Rank.	Date of Muster.	Remarks.
CAPTAIN.		
David L. Payne	Oct. 29, 1868	Mustered out with regiment.
FIRST LIEUT.		
Mount A. Gordon	Oct. 29, 1868	Mustered out with regiment.
SECOND LIEUT.		
Robert M. Steele............	Oct. 29, 1868	Mustered out with regiment.

COMPANY I.

Name and Rank.	Date of Muster.	Remarks.
CAPTAIN.		
Roger A. Elsworth..........	Oct. 29, 1868	Mustered out with regiment.
FIRST LIEUT.		
James J. Clancy............	Oct. 29, 1868	Mustered out with regiment.
SECOND LIEUT.		
James M. May	Oct. 29, 1868	Mustered out with regiment.

COMPANY K.

Name and Rank.	Date of Muster.	Remarks.
CAPTAIN.		
Milton Stewart..............	Oct. 29, 1868	Promoted Major. Date of com., March 8, 1869.
Emmet Ryus.................	Mar. 23, 1869	Mustered out with regiment.
FIRST LIEUT.		
Emmet Ryus.................	Oct. 29, 1868	Promoted Captain.
Charles H. Hallett.........	Mar. 23, 1869	Mustered out with regiment.
SECOND LIEUT.		
Charles H. Hallett.........	Oct. 29, 1868	Promoted First Lieutenant.
Robert I. Sharp.............	Mar. 23, 1869	Mustered out with regiment.

COMPANY L.

Name and Rank.	Date of Muster.	Remarks.
CAPTAIN.		
Charles H. Finch	Oct. 29, 1868	Mustered out, April 18, 1869.
FIRST LIEUT.		
Henry E. Stoddard........	Oct. 29, 1868	Mustered out, April 18, 1869.
SECOND LIEUT.		
Winfield S. Tilton.........	Oct. 29, 1868	Mustered out, April 18, 1869.

COMPANY M.

Name and Rank.	Date of Muster.	Remarks.
CAPTAIN.		
Sargent Moody..............	Oct. 29, 1868	Mustered out, April 18, 1869.
FIRST LIEUT.		
James Graham..............	Oct. 29, 1868	Mustered out, April 18, 1869.
SECOND LIEUT.		
James P. Hurst	Oct. 29, 1868	Mustered out, April 18, 1869.

1869.

JANUARY.—Sheridan's Indian campaign is described at length in a book called: "Sheridan's Troopers on the Borders: A Winter Campaign on the Plains, by DeB. Randolph Keim. With numerous engravings. Philadelphia: Claxton, Remsen & Haffelinger." pp. 308. It is a well-written and handsomely-printed book. It begins with the writer's arrival in Leavenworth, in the summer of 1868, and ends with the completion of Sheridan's campaign against the Indians, in March, 1869. Forsyth's fight at Arrickaree Fork, Sept. 17, 1868, the massacres on the Saline and the Solomon, the battle of Washita, and many other interesting events, are narrated.

—During the past year, Baker University has had 181 students, Washburn College 57, Episcopal Female Seminary 90.

JANUARY 1.—Ward Burlingame, who was the Private Secretary of Govs. Carney and Crawford, receives the appointment from Gov. Harvey.

JANUARY 12.—Meeting of the Legislature.

STATE OFFICERS.

Names.	Former P. O.	County.	Where Born.	Age.	Avocation.
J. M. Harvey, Governor..	Fort Riley......	Riley............	Virginia........	35	Farmer.
C. V. Eskridge, Lt. Gov...	Emporia........	Lyon............	Virginia.......	37	Mercha't.
T. Moonlight, Sec. of State	Leavenworth	Leavenworth	Scotland	35	
A. Danford, Att'y Gen....	Fort Scott......	Bourbon........	New Hamp..	39	Attorn'y.
P. McVicar, Sp't Pub.Inst.	Topeka	Shawnee	New Brunsw.	39	Minister.
Geo. Graham, Treasurer..	Seneca	Nemaha	New York....	49	Mercha't.
A. Thoman, Aud. of State	Lawrence	Douglas.........	Switzerland..	39	Farmer.

JUDGES OF THE SUPREME COURT.

Names.	Former P.O.	County.	Where Born.	Age.	Avocation.
S. A. Kingman, Chief Justice.	Atchison...	Atchison...	Massachusetts	51	Attorn'y.
J. Safford, Associate Justice.	Topeka	Shawnee ...	Vermont.........	41	Lawyer.
D. M. Valentine, Asso. Justice	Ottawa	Franklin...	Ohio..............	38	Lawyer.

JUDGES OF DISTRICT COURTS.

Names.	Districts.	P. O. Address.	County.
H. W. Ide..............................	First............	Leavenworth	Leavenworth.
Nathan Price..........................	Second............	Troy..................	Doniphan.
John T. Morton.......................	Third............	Topeka	Shawnee.
Owen A. Bassett......................	Fourth............	Lawrence..........	Douglas.
J. H. Watson..........................	Fifth............	Emporia	Lyon.
D. P. Lowe.............................	Sixth	Mound City.......	Linn.
John R. Goodin.......................	Seventh..........	Humboldt..........	Allen.
James Humphrey......................	Eighth.............	Manhattan	Riley.
William R. Brown....................	Ninth............	Cottonwood Falls	Chase.
John T. Burris........................	Tenth............	Olathe...............	Johnson.

—Barzillai Gray, Judge Criminal Court, Leavenworth county.

MEMBERS AND OFFICERS OF THE SENATE.

Names.	P. O. Address.	County.	Where Born.	Age.	Avocation.
Eskridge, C. V., President	Emporia	Lyon	Virginia	37	Merchant.
Arrasmith, Abner	Olathe	Johnson	Kentucky	56	Farmer.
Bailey, J. C.	Perryville	Jefferson	Penn	34	Merchant.
Broadhead, J. F.	Mound City	Linn	New York.	38	Lawyer.
Carnahan, A. A.	Clyde	Cloud	Ohio	30	Attorney.
Carpenter, John C.	Erie	Neosho	Penn	30	Attorney.
Cobb, Stephen A.	Wyandotte	Wyandotte	Minnesota.	35	Attorney.
Fitzpatrick, W. H.	Topeka	Shawnee	Kentucky	47	Farmer.
Grimes, W. H.	Atchison	Atchison	Maryland	65	Physician.
Grover, O. J.	Savannah	Pottawato'ie.	New York.	41	Farmer.
Jenkins, E. J.	Troy	Doniphan	Ohio	35	Lawyer.
Larimer, William	Delaware T'p	Leavenw'th.	Penn	59	Farmer.
Learnard, O. E.	Lawrence	Douglas	Vermont	36	Farmer.
Mead, James R.	Towanda	Butler	Vermont	31	Farmer.
Murdock, M. M.	Burlingame	Osage	Virginia	31	Editor.
McKee, John	Leavenworth	Leavenw'th.	Missouri	41	Civil Eng.
Niccolls, E. S.	Garnett	Anderson	Penn	39	Farmer.
Prescott, J. H.	Salina	Saline	New Hamp	38	Attorney.
Schmidt, Martin	Leavenworth	Leavenw'th.	Germany	35	—
Smallwood, W. H.	Wathena	Doniphan	Kentucky	27	Farmer.
Snyder, S. J. H.	Monrovia	Atchison	Maryland	56	Farmer.
Spear, A. G.	Hiawatha	Brown	Ohio	33	Farmer.
Tucker, Edwin	Eureka	Greenwood	Vermont	32	Farmer.
Voss, M. V.	Fort Scott	Bourbon	Ohio	30	Attorney.
Williams, H. H.	Osawatomie	Miami	New York.	40	Merchant.
Woodard, Levi	Eudora	Douglas	Indiana	38	Farmer.
Geo. C. Crowther, Sec'y	Irwin	Marshall	Conn	21	Editor.
J. D. Gilchrist, As't Sec'y.	Oskaloosa	Jefferson	New Hamp	28	Attorney.
D. M. Bronson, Jour'l Cl'k	Eldorado	Butler	New York.	31	Attorney.
L. M. Benedict, Dock't Cl'k	Vienna	Pottawato'ie	New York.	38	Farmer.
H. H. Carr, Engros'g Cl'k	Eudora	Douglas	Ohio	34	Attorney.
N. Merchant, S'gt-at-Ar's	Prairie City	Franklin	New York.	38	Farmer.
George W. Weed, Doork'r	Pardee	Atchison	New York.	33	Farmer.
A. A. House, As't Doork'r	Junction City	Davis	Ohio	18	Student.
Edwin C. Eldridge, Page	Lawrence	Douglas	Ohio	16	Student.
William H. Fletcher, Page	Erie	Neosho	Indiana	15	Student.
William R. Griffith, Page	Topeka	Shawnee	Ohio	...	Student.

MEMBERS AND OFFICERS OF THE HOUSE OF REPRESENTATIVES.

Names.	P. O. Address.	County.	Where Born.	Age.	Avocation.
Adams, M. S., Speaker	Leavenworth	Leavenw'th.	New Hamp	42	Lawyer.
Allen, N. J.	North Heder	Jackson	Penn	27	Farmer.
Bailey, L. D.	Clinton	Douglas	New Hamp	49	Farmer.
Baker, P. Y.	Westmoreland.	Pottawato'ie	Illinois	26	Farmer.
Blood, James	Lawrence	Douglas	Wisconsin	48	Farmer.
Bowers, M. B.	White Cloud	Brown	Penn	38	Farmer.
Bowles, T. C.	Ottawa	Franklin	Ohio	40	Lawyer.
Brundage, A.	Prairie City	Douglas	Penn	68	Farmer.
Butterbaugh, J.	Garnett	Anderson	Maryland	36	Farmer.
Butler, T. H.	Erie	Neosho	Ohio	45	Farmer.
Case, Alexander E.	Marion Centre	Marion	Penn	...	Cattle D'r.
Coffin, E. E.	Le Roy	Coffey	Indiana	30	Cattle D'r.
Cook, H. W	Wyandotte	Wyandotte	Ohio	36	Lawyer.
Crocker, E. B.	Bazaar	Chase	Michigan	30	Farmer.
Crosby, William	Grass'per Falls	Jefferson	Maine	36	Merchant.
Dalrymple, J. N.	Clyde	Cloud	Ohio	31	Farmer.
Darby, Rufus	Washington	Washington.	Ohio	52	Farmer.
Davis, Oliver	Atchison	Atchison	Mass	33	—
Drake, C	Americus	Lyon	Ohio	32	Farmer.
Evans, A. J	Atchison	Atchison	Ohio	40	Farmer.
Feeney, T.	Wyandotte	Wyandotte	Ireland	32	Farmer.
Flora, R. V.	Leavenworth	Leavenw'th.	Virginia	55	Bricklayer.
Gilluly, Francis	Oskaloosa	Jefferson	Mass	51	Farmer.
Gregg, Charles	Mineral Point.	Anderson	New York.	41	Farmer.
Grover, Joel	Lawrence	Douglas	New Jers'y	44	Farmer.
Guthrie, John	Topeka	Shawnee	Indiana	39	Attorney.
Hamm, W. M.	Muscotah	Atchison	Kentucky	34	Farmer.
Hawkins, H. C.	Troy	Doniphan	New York.	38	Attorney.
Helphrey, D.	America	Nemaha	Ohio	37	Farmer.
Howell, Joseph	Leavenworth	Leavenw'th.	New Jers'y	35	Farmer.

MEMBERS AND OFFICERS OF HOUSE OF REPRESENTATIVES—Concluded.

Names.	P. O. Address.	County.	Where Born.	Age	Avocation.
Humber, N..............	Easton............	Leavenwo'th	Kentucky..	53	Farmer.
Hungerford, S. R.............	Blooming G've	Linn............	Vermont...	38	Miller.
Hunter, J. M..............	Forest Hill	Lyon............	Penn	31	Farmer.
Hupp, M. B..............	Ridgeway.......	Osage..........	Ohio	33	Farmer.
Hymer, Samuel.............	Rockville.........	Miami..........	Indiana ..	39	Farmer.
Inge, J. B..............	Geneva..........	Allen..........	Virginia ..	43	Farmer.
Irwin, G. E.............	Hamlin..........	Brown	Kentucky..	30	Physician.
Jackson, Z.............	Fort Harker....	Ellsworth	Penn	42	Merchant.
Jones, J. L.............	Lecompton	Douglas.......	Mass	38	Farmer.
Johnson, J. B.............	Oskaloosa.......	Jefferson	Illinois...	26	Lawyer.
Johnson, D. B.............	Shawnee.........	Johnson.......	Ohio	28	Farmer.
Johnson, B. F.............	Neosho Falls...	Woodson	Virginia....	28	Carpenter.
Kellogg, Josiah.............	Leavenworth...	Leavenwo'th	New York.	32	Lawyer.
Kilgore, Cyrus.............	Abilene.........	Dickinson.....	Penn	55	Lawyer.
Lambert, W. W.............	Lindsey..........	Ottawa......	New York.	34	Farmer.
Lappin, Samuel.............	Seneca..........	Nemaha......	Ohio	38	Farmer.
Larimer, J. I.............	Leavenworth...	Leavenwo'th	Penn	49	Farmer.
Logan, Joseph.............	Monrovia........	Atchison......	Indiana ..	35	Farmer.
Madden, J. H.............	Mound City.....	Linn............	Illinois ...	27	Farmer.
Maltby, Joel.............	Salina..........	Saline..........	Conn	55	Farmer.
Martin, J. S.............	Highland.........	Doniphan......	Ohio	38	Physician.
Moore, J. B.............	Fort Scott......	Bourbon	Illinois...	35	Farmer.
Mowry, A. J.............	Wathena.........	Doniphan......	New York.	36	Farmer.
McClenahan, John............	Ottawa..........	Franklin	Ohio	35	Farmer.
McDowell, C. C.............	Wirtonia........	Cherokee......	Virginia ...	48	Physician.
McGinnis, J. A.............	Hartford........	Coffey	Indiana ...	32	Farmer.
McGrath, —.............	....	....	....	...	...
McIntosh, T.............	Tonganoxie.....	Leavenwo'th	....	...	...
McNay, H. W.............	Council Grove..	Morris..........	Ohio	43	Saddler.
Osborn, W. F.............	Virgil..........	Greenwood ..	Indiana ...	41	Farmer.
Palmer, R. E.............	Kickapoo........	Leavenwo'th	Virginia....	24	Farmer.
Pierce, A. C.............	Junction City..	Davis..........	New York.	33	Lawyer.
Porter, J. Q.............	Humboldt........	Allen..........	Indiana		Lawyer.
Rankin, J. T.............	Spring Hill.....	Johnson......	Tennessee	46	Merchant.
Ristine, M. H.............	Clay Centre....	Clay..........	Indiana.....	50	Carpenter.
Roberts, D. D.............	Fort Lincoln....	Bourbon	Indiana	31	Farmer.
Roberts, L.............	Dayton..........	Bourbon	New York.	60	Farmer.
Seaman, A. G.............	Jackson.........	Linn............	New York.	34	Farmer.
Secrest, E.............	Randolph........	Riley	Switzerl'd..	36	Farmer.
Simpson, William............	....	Crawford	Illinois ...	31	Farmer.
Smith, W. H.............	Barrett........	Marshall......	Penn	26	Loafer.
Smith, R.............	Osawatomie...	Miami..........	England....	36	Farmer.
Snoddy, J. D.............	Mound City.....	Linn............	Penn	30	Attorney.
Stevenson, R. E.............	Olathe..........	Johnson......	Illinois ...	29	Farmer.
Stotler, Jacob	Emporia	Lyon	Maryland...	35	Printer.
Taylor, T. J.............	Paola..........	Miami..........	Virginia....	67	Minister.
Tice, Perry..............	Topeka..........	Shawnee	Penn	47	Farmer.
Tiernan, P. H.............	Leavenworth....	Leavenwo'th	Missouri ..	27	Printer.
Thompson, G. W.............	Atchison.........	Atchison......	Kentucky..	41	Farmer.
Travis, W. F.............	Coyville.........	Wilson........	Ohio	38	Farmer.
Uhler, William.............	Fort Wallace....	Wallace......	Penn	41	Wheel'ght.
Wamsley, James.............	Crawfordsville..	Crawford	Ohio	...	Blacks'th.
Walton, Amos.............	Vinland..........	Douglas... ...	Penn	30	Farmer.
Weed, S. R.............	Alma..........	Wabaunsee...	Miss	36	Clerk.
West, R. P.............	Salt Marsh......	Republic......	Indiana....	38	Minister.
Whitaker, David............	Doniphan........	Doniphan......	Penn	...	Farmer.
Williams, J. L.............	Holton..........	Jackson......	Ohio	48	Physician.
Wilson, T. R.............	Eldorado........	Butler	Penn	38	Farmer.
Wood, G. W.............	Troy..........	Doniphan......	Missouri ..	27	Farmer.
Wright, J. F.............	Hays City.......	Ellis	New York..	...	Merchant.
H. C. Olney, Chief Clerk...	Atchison.......	Atchison......	New York.	27	Editor.
J. C. Pratt, Ass't Clerk......	Madison, Wis..	Potter	Penn	24	Surveyor.
J. H. Mayhan, Jour. Clerk	Abilene.........	Dickinson ...	Ohio	30	Lawyer.
W. H. Cox, Ass't Jour. Cl'k	Abilene..........	Dickinson ...	Kentucky..	27	Dentist.
M. R. Moore, Docket Clerk	Topeka..........	Shawnee	Indiana	22	Clerk.
Miss H. R. Henry, Enr.C'k	Holton	Jackson.......	Illinois......	24	Teacher.
Joshua Mitchell, Engr. C'k	Centralia	Nemaha	Maine	27	Farmer.
G.A. Schreiner, Serg.-at-A.	Wyandotte	Wyandotte ..	Germany...	37	Pilot.
John Drew, Ass't S.-at-A...	Burlingame.....	Osage..........	England....	62	Farmer.
Adam H. Beck, Doorkeep'r	Ottawa..........	Franklin	Ohio	26	Silvers'th.
C. S. Norton, Ass't Doork.	Topeka..........	Shawnee	New York.	18	Printer.
Francis J. Rice, Page	Topeka..........	Shawnee	Indiana	15	Student.
Willie H. Davis, Page	Topeka..........	Shawnee	Indiana	12	Student.
Willie H.Weymouth, Page	Topeka..........	Shawnee	Kansas	13	Carpenter.
Harry Finity, Page	Topeka..........	Shawnee	Illinois	17	

JANUARY 13.   Election of the following officers of the State Agricultural Society, at Topeka: President, R. G. Elliott, of Douglas; Secretary, H. J. Strickler, of Shawnee; Treasurer, C. B. Lines, of Wabaunsee; Superintendent, Alfred Gray. *Executive Committee:* M. J. Alkire of Shawnee, Jas. Larimer of Leavenworth, J. W. Sponable of Johnson, Josiah Miller of Douglas, A. B. Whiting of Riley, J. N. Insley of Jefferson, Alfred Gray of Wyandotte, S. T. Kelsey of Franklin, J. W. Scott of Allen.   Fair held at Lawrence.

JANUARY 19.—Election of State Printer:

First ballot: S. S. Prouty 23, S. D. Macdonald 6, Sol. Miller 13, W. S. Burke 7, John A. Martin 5, Jacob Stotler 12, Geo. C. Crowther 4, John Speer 12, Geo. W. Martin 7, Geo. F. Prescott 5, R. B. Taylor 3.

Second ballot: Prouty 38, Macdonald 21, Miller 20, Speer 18, Prescott 5, Taylor 3, Stotler 1.

Third ballot: Prouty 42, Macdonald 22, Speer 22, Miller 19, Prescott 2.

Fourth ballot: Prouty 69, Macdonald 19, Speer 16, Miller 4.

JANUARY 20.—State Convention of colored people, at Topeka.   They ask the Legislature to memorialize Congress to provide for negro suffrage. Wm. D. Mathews, of Leavenworth, was made Chairman of a State Committee.

JANUARY 20.—The seat of Charles S. Glick, Senator from Wyandotte county, is given to S. A. Cobb, contestant.

FEBRUARY 4.—Woman Suffrage Convention, at Topeka.   President, Mrs. E. Bliss; Vice Presidents, Rev. W. A. Starrett and Rev. D. H. Johnston; Secretaries, Mrs. D. Ogden and A. L. Winans.

FEBRUARY 6.—R. D. Mobley, of Ottawa county, is appointed State Agent for the sale of railroad lands.

FEBRUARY 9.—Death of Wm. Y. Roberts, at Lawrence.   The Senate passes appropriate resolutions.

FEBRUARY 9.—Report of Committee on Penitentiary.   (Senate Journal, pp. 294 to 300, and 526 to 529; and House Journal, pp. 524 to 530.)

—Report of Adjutant General of troops raised under all calls during the war.   (House Journal, pp. 506 to 516.)

FEBRUARY 12.—Report of Committee on State House building expenses. (Senate Journal, pp. 359 to 363, and 608, 609.)

FEBRUARY 23.—Report of Senate Committee on State Treasurer:

"Your Committee beg respectfully to direct attention to the unsatisfactory character of the late Treasurer's last annual report.   By that report it would appear that the permanent school fund invested is only $86.613.50, whereas your Committee found in the hands of the Treasurer, belonging to said fund, bonds amounting to $186,950, which had been turned over to the present Treasurer by the late incumbent in that office. They would further state that they found in the hands of the present Treasurer, received from the same source, bonds, belonging to the State University fund, amounting to $10,300, of which no mention whatever is made in the late Treasurer's last annual report.   Your Committee are of the opinion that section 48 of 'An act relating to the forms and duties of the State officers of the Executive Department,' chapter 102 of General Statutes, clearly makes it the duty of the State Treasurer, in his annual report, to present a full exhibit of the State funds of every kind and character in the custody of the State Treasurer, instead of simply an exhibit of his receipts and disbursements during the year, as presented in the late Treasurer's last annual report. . . . ."

Your Committee desire to call attention to section 52, chapter 102 of the compiled statutes, which provides that the Governor, Secretary of State and Auditor shall constitute a board of examination, whose duty it shall be, once a month at least, without previous notice, to make a thorough and complete examination of all the books, vouchers, accounts, records, bonds, securities, claims, assets, and effects, which are or should be in the treasury. And shall count all moneys in the treasury, and compare the books, vouchers, accounts, and records of the same.

"Your Committee are of the opinion that the provisions of this section should be strictly complied with, as the intention of the section was to prevent any State Treasurer from loaning, speculating in, or otherwise using, the funds of the State. By making this examination, the exact condition of the treasury, each month, would be known, and be an answer to the rumors constantly afloat of parties speculating with the funds of the State."—*Senate Journal, pp. 493 to 497.*

FEBRUARY 27.—The Legislature ratifies the Fifteenth Amendment to the Constitution of the United States. The ratification is defective, and the amendment goes over to the next Legislature.

MARCH 3.—*Appointments:* William S. Moorhouse, of Atchison county, Adjutant General; H. T. Beman, of Shawnee county, Assistant Adjutant General; William Burgoyne, William C. Jones, and Frank H. Drenning, Aides-de-Camp to the Commander-in-Chief; Frederick Speck, F. P. Baker, and William Larimer, Trustees of the Blind Asylum; H. H. Sawyer, Superintendent of the Blind Asylum; J. M. McClenahan, of Franklin county, and B. J. F. Hanna, of Saline county, Regents of the State Agricultural College; Harrison Kelley, of Coffey county, and E. Hensley, of Leavenworth county, Directors of the Penitentiary.

MARCH.—Gov. Harvey appoints Z. Jackson, of Ellsworth county, Edson Baxter, of Saline county, and James F. Tallman, of Washington county, Commissioners under the act of March 3, to audit and report claims for losses, in 1867 and 1868, from Indian depredations.

MARCH 4.—S. S. Prouty and J. B. Davis buy the Topeka Leader of J. F. Cummings. This was No. 13, vol. 4. Mr. Cummings had published this paper and the Topeka Tribune, and was in the office with Mr. Garvey when the first Topeka paper was issued—the Kansas Freeman, July 4, 1855. The last number of the Leader was probably the one issued April 8th.

MARCH 4.—Legislature adjourns. Among the acts are the following: Issuing $75,000 State bonds for military expenses of 1868; Issuing $100,000 State bonds "for the purpose of providing a military contingent fund, to be used in protecting the frontier of the State" (the Attorney General, Adjutant General and Auditor are to audit the claims presented); Issuing $70,000 State bonds to aid in completing the east wing of the Capitol; Issuing $14,000 State bonds to defray expense of raising the Nineteenth Regiment; A joint resolution for a committee of five to investigate all the accounts connected with the building of the Capitol; Providing for a commission to audit Price Raid and Curtis Expedition claims; Providing for the election of a Public Printer; For the settlement of losses from Indian raids in 1867 and 1868; Giving certain salt lands to the Normal School; For the investigation of Penitentiary accounts; Making County Clerks assessors of railroad property; Authorizing the Governor to appoint an Agent to buy seed wheat for destitute citizens on the western frontier, and appropriating $15,000.

MARCH 23.—The Secretary of State and Treasurer meet under the act of February 9, and issue bonds to pay the military expenses incurred in 1868.

MARCH 30.—The first locomotive, the "C. K. Holliday," passes over the A. T. & S. F. R. R. bridge, at Topeka.

MARCH 31.—The Nineteenth Regiment is ordered to Hays City, to be mustered out.

APRIL 3.—Burning of the Topeka Record office. The paper was re-issued, April 6th.

APRIL 7.—Congress passes a resolution, for the relief of the settlers on the Shawnee absentee lands.

APRIL 10.—

By an act of Congress, in the form of a joint resolution, approved April 10, 1869, sections 16 and 36 on that part of the Osage reservation known as the Osage ceded and trust lands, have been secured to the State, for the support of public schools. This provision of the act referred to includes all of sections 16 and 36, or their equivalents, in Labette and Neosho counties, and, by a construction of the Commissioner of the General Land Office, all of sections 16 and 36, or their equivalents, on what is known as the "Twenty-mile strip," on the north of the Osage diminished reserve, and extending from the west line of Neosho county through the south part of Wilson, Greenwood and Butler counties, to the west line of the Osage reserve, a distance of about two hundred and fifty miles. The amount of school lands thus secured to the State by the act of Congress of the 10th of April last, is as follows:

In Labette county... 22,408 acres
In Neosho county... 20,480 acres
On the Twenty-mile strip...177,777 acres

Total..220,665 acres
—Supt. McVicar's Report.

APRIL 13.—C. W. Babcock is appointed Surveyor General; Geo. W. Martin, Register of the Junction City Land office; Watson Stewart, Register at Humboldt, and G. E. Beates, of Junction City, U. S. Assessor.

APRIL 14.—Henry C. F. Hackbusch, of Leavenworth, appointed Chief Clerk of Surveyor General.

APRIL.—Levi Woodard, David Whitaker and T. J. Taylor meet at Topeka, to audit claims growing out of the Price Raid and the Indian Expedition under General Curtis, in July and August, 1864.

MAY.—Surveyor General's office removed from Leavenworth to Lawrence.

MAY 1.—Issue of the Topeka Daily Commonwealth, by Prouty, Davis & Crane.

MAY 10.—Capt. Henry King and Maj. A. W. Edwards, partners of F. P. Baker in the State Record, arrive from Illinois.

MAY 14.—Geo. H. Hoyt is appointed U. S. Mail Agent, and D. W. Houston U. S. Marshal.

MAY 20.—Grasshoppers in Leavenworth; reported in the Times and Conservative; no report of their appearance in other parts of the State.

MAY 21.—Indian raid on the Republican. Killing and plundering of settlers on White Rock creek, Republic county. Six men and one woman killed, and two boys captured.

MAY 25.—Albert H. Horton sworn in as U. S. District Attorney, succeeding Samuel A. Riggs.

—Gov. Harvey asks Gen. Schofield to send troops to preserve peace on the Neutral Lands.

MAY 30.—Indian raid on the Saline; thirteen persons killed and wounded.

MAY 31.—Gov. Harvey issues a proclamation enjoining the people of Cherokee and Crawford counties to yield obedience to the officers of the law. He asks that a detachment of troops be sent to the Cherokee Neutral Lands to assist the civil officers in the preservation of peace.

JUNE.—W. S. Moorhouse, Adjutant General, stations Militia on Plum creek, Fisher creek, Spillman creek, on the Saline, on Beaver creek, on the Republican, and on Turkey creek, near the Little Arkansas. The following is copied from his Report, dated December 20th:

"The following is the battalion, as originally mustered in:

"Company A—Captain, A. J. Pliley; First Lieutenant, C. B. Whitney; Second Lieutenant, John Marshall; fifty-four men.

"Company B—Captain, W. A. Winsell; First Lieutenant, Joseph Becock; Second Lieutenant, B. C. Lawrence; sixty-one men.

"Company C—Captain, I. N. Dalrymple; First Lieutenant, H. H. Tucker; seventy men.

"Company D—Captain, Richard Stanfield; First Lieutenant, Herod Johnson; sixty-five men.

"Detachment—Second Lieutenant, C. Stinson; thirty men.

"Making an aggregate of eleven commissioned officers, and three hundred enlisted men; considerable more than the number authorized by law. This excess was caused from the fact that during the high water all communication with the frontier was cut off, and men were recruited more rapidly than I anticipated. The number was gradually reduced to one hundred and fifteen, at the final muster-out, on Nov. 20th, 1869.

"The total expense of the battalion is $82,833.26."

JUNE 25.—The Fifth Annual Report of the Board of Education of the City of Leavenworth is a book of 270 pages, printed by John C. Ketcheson, and the best specimen of printing yet seen in the State. The Superintendent of the schools is P. J. Williams, recently of New York.

JUNE 26.—Flood in Chapman creek; thirteen lives lost. Water four feet deep on the bottoms, at Junction City. It is a very wet and fruitful year.

JUNE 29.—State Teachers' Association, at Manhattan. *Officers elected:* President, I. J. Banister, of Paola. *Executive Committee:* E. F. Heisler of Wyandotte, Mrs. J. H. Gorham of Emporia, Miss E. M. Dickinson of Atchison, P. J. Williams of Leavenworth, and P. Fales of Franklin county. Recording Secretary, Miss Alice L. Norton, of Manhattan; Corresponding Secretary, Thomas C. Dick, of Jefferson county; Treasurer, Miss Lizze Ela, of Emporia.

JUNE 30.—Association of County and City Superintendents, at Manhattan. *Officers:* President, Peter McVicar; Vice Presidents, Philetus Fales, A. D. Chambers, P. J. Williams; Secretary, E. Gale. *Executive Committee:* I. J. Banister, E. F. Heisler, T. C. Dick.

JULY.—Publication of "The Discovery of the Great West," by Francis Parkman. It is a history of French discovery, exploration and dominion in North America. The heroes of the volume are Robert Cavalier de La Salle (born at Rouen, in 1643), Jean Nicollet (first Frenchman who penetrated to one of the northern tributaries of the Mississippi), Louis Joliet (born in Quebec, in 1645), Father Marquette, Father Hennepin, Tonty, and the Sieur de la Motte.

JULY 28.—Neutral Land Settlers' meeting at Jacksonville, Neosho county. *President:* Dr. C. C. McDowell. *Vice Presidents:* Dr. Moore, of Crawford;

William R. Laughlin, of Cherokee; William Logan, of Labette; and Bryant Purcell, of Neosho. *Secretaries:* C. D. Sayrs, of Crawford; J. N. Ritter, of Cherokee; J. C. Coulter, of Labette; and William H. Maguire, of Neosho. Resolutions were passed against the land-grant system; requesting Senators Ross and Pomeroy to resign; and against the claim of James F. Joy to a title in the Neutral Lands.

AUGUST 4.—The Monitor and the Post, Fort Scott Dailies, are admitted to the Associated Press, and entitled to receive despatches.

—United States soldiers are guarding railroad graders in Crawford county.

—This is one of the railroad-bond-voting years.

AUGUST.—Sale of Agricultural College lands during the month, 5,720 acres, at $4.75 per acre. The whole amount received from sales to date, $164,000.

SEPTEMBER 1.—The third Price Raid Commission reports to Governor Harvey that it has allowed claims amounting to $72,380.54. These were in part Price Raid claims, and in part claims arising from the Indian Expedition of Major General Samuel R. Curtis, in July and August, 1864.

—E. R. Trask starts the Pioneer, at Independence, Montgomery county.

SEPTEMBER 10.—Railroad open from Leavenworth to Atchison.

SEPTEMBER 15.—The National Pomological Society, at Philadelphia, by a unanimous vote, awards to Kansas its great gold medal "for a collection of fruit unsurpassed for size, perfection and flavor."

SEPTEMBER 18.—Charles B. Lines writes from Philadelphia that the Kansas fruit has received the highest award.

SEPTEMBER.—A "Manifesto of the People of the Cherokee Neutral Lands" issued. It is a pamphlet of twenty-two pages, and is signed by C. C. McDowell and W. R. Laughlin, of Cherokee county, and A. Perry and C. Dana Sayrs, of Crawford county. The following is copied from the pamphlet:

"In 1803, our Government bought from France what has since been known as the 'Louisiana Purchase,' of which the Cherokee neutral land is an integral part.

"After Missouri became a State, and its western counties were being settled, for the protection of its inhabitants, the Government treated, in 1827, with the Osage Indians, for this tract of land, with the stipulation that neither the Indians nor the whites should occupy the same, thus placing a strip fifty miles north and south by twenty-five east and west as a barrier between the white and the red men. So it remained until the treaty-making power gave the Cherokee Nation the right to occupy the tract.

"In 1866, by a 'treaty,' they gave back the land to the United States, and attempted to do so 'in trust,' and to empower the Secretary of the Interior to sell the neutral land.

"One of the last official acts of the then Secretary of the Interior (Harlan) was to sell as much of the tract as was not 'occupied by actual settlers at the date of the treaty,' to the 'American Emigrant Company,' for one dollar per acre.

"But Secretary Browning, on assuming the office, procured the opinion of Attorney Stanbery that Harlan's sale was 'illegal and void;' and on that 'opinion' set the sale aside. Browning then proceeded to sell the residue of the tract not 'occupied by actual settlers at the date of the treaty,' to James F. Joy, of Detroit, Michigan, at one dollar per acre, although Fremont had offered one dollar and a quarter per acre for it.

"The Emigrant Company threatened litigation, and matters remained secretly in negotiation until June 6, 1868, when, to the utter surprise of the settlers, a supplemental treaty was put through the Senate, which assumed to cancel Mr. Joy's contract with Browning, and to assign to him the contract of the Emigrant Company. Such is a very brief outline of the strange transactions by which the 'rings' cast lots for the garments of the settlers, and proposed to divide among themselves the gains of this most infamous of all 'jobs' for robbing the settlers of the West."

OCTOBER.—The North American Review of this date (vol. CIX, pp. 401, 402) contains a paper by Lewis H. Morgan, on Indian Migrations, from which the following is copied:

"The most perfect display of the prairies is found in the eastern parts of Kansas and Nebraska. It is no exaggeration to pronounce this region, as left by the hand of Nature, the most beautiful country in its landscape upon the face of the earth. Here the forest is restricted to narrow fringes along the rivers and streams, the courses of which are thus defined as far as the eye can reach, whilst all between is a broad expanse of meadow-lands, carpeted with the richest verdure and wearing the appearance of artistically graded lawns. They are familiarly called the rolling prairies, because the land rises and falls in gentle swells, which attain an elevation of thirty feet, more or less, and descend again to the original level, within the distance of one or more miles. The crest-lines of these motionless waves of land intersect each other at every conceivable angle, the effect of which is to bring into view the most extended landscape, and to show the dark green foliage of the forest trees skirting the streams in pleasing contrast with the light green of the prairie grasses. In their spring covering of vegetation these prairies wear the semblance of an old and once highly-cultivated country, from the soil of which every inequality of surface, every stone, and every bush has been carefully removed and the surface rolled down into absolute uniformity. The marvel is suggested how Nature could have kept these verdant fields in such luxuriance after man had apparently abandoned them to waste. This striking display is limited to about one hundred and thirty miles in the eastern part of Kansas, and a narrower belt in eastern Nebraska."

OCTOBER.—James McCahon, of Leavenworth, edits a volume of decisions of the Supreme Court of the Territory of Kansas. Published by Callaghan & Cockcroft, Chicago. pp. 298.

OCTOBER 1.—Excursion on the Neosho Valley Railroad from Junction City, twenty-five miles. The road is inspected by State officers preparatory to giving it 125,000 acres of land. Robert S. Stevens is the manager of the road.

—State Convention of Spiritualists, in Topeka. Dr. F. L. Crane, President; Secretary, Miss Jennie Crowe.

OCTOBER 4.—Excursion on the Santa Fe Railroad, from Topeka to Burlingame. Gov. Harvey accepts the twenty-six miles.

OCTOBER 27.—Railroad open to Council Grove.

—Convention of colored men at Topeka. Wm. D. Mathews, President; J. W. Scott and W. R. Conner, Secretaries.

NOVEMBER 2.—Annual election.

VOTE FOR JUDGE IN THE TENTH JUDICIAL DISTRICT.

Counties.	Hiram Stevens.	W.H.M. Fishba'k	Maj.
Johnson	773	728	45
Wyandotte	924	172	752
Miami	1,226	113	1,113
Total	2,923	1,013	1,910

VOTE FOR MEMBERS OF THE HOUSE OF REPRESENTATIVES.

District	Counties	Names	Votes	Maj	Vote of District	Vote of County
1	Doniphan	S. F. Nesbitt	319	304		
		George W. Neal	14		333	
2		A. Hazen	110	71		
		E. Fleming	39		149	
3		A. J. Mowry	252	252	252	
4		E. H. LeDuc	220	99		
		F. Hartley	121		341	
5		David Whitaker	132	2		
		William Ege	130		262	1,337
6	Atchison	Thomas Murphy	480	480	480	
7		A. J. Evans	273	270		
		R. A. Heim	2			
		W. J. Burge	1		276	
8		J. Parsons	234	60		
		James Stallons	174		408	
9		Joseph Logan	217	209		
		D. Campbell	8			
		J. Robinson	2			
		B. W. Williams	1		228	
10		E. H. Baliff	167	104		
		D. P. Erp	63		230	1,622
11	Brown	J. F. Babbitt	317	204		
		E. Bierer	113		430	
12		A. Curtis	102	46		
		D. L. Anderson	56		158	588
13	Nemaha	L. Hensel	204	18		
		G. W. Collings	186			
		Mrs. Hawley	3			
		William Barnes	2			
		P. McQuaid	1			
		J. Maston	1		397	
14		William Morris	245	117		
		F. A. Stickle	128		373	770
15	Marshall	John D. Wells	378	172		
		J. J. Sheldon	206		584	584
16	Washington	Andrew S. Wilson	182	70		
		Rufus Darley	112		294	294
17	Pottawatomie	John H. Clark	387	82		
		Charles C. Duncan	305		692	692
18	Jackson	J. L. Williams	267	44		
		W. H. Dodge	223		490	
79		Byron Stewart	151	41		
		N. Y. Allen	110		261	751
19	Jefferson	Levi Wilhelm	332	46		
		E. D. Russell	286		618	
20		W. C. Butts	213	157		
		Calvin Smith	56			
		R. Riddle	5			
		—— Cowan	1		275	
21		David Rorick	392	82		
		D. E. L. Kretsinger	310			
		A. F. Magrew	132		834	1,727
22	Leavenworth	Byron Sherry	444	270		
		William Freeland	174		618	
23		Josiah Kellogg	294	57		
		J. B. Zeigler	237		531	
24		J. A. Halderman	343	103		
		E. Russell	240		583	
25		Daniel Shire	284	17		
		R. V. Flora	267		551	
26		Charles H. Grover	134	25		
		J. F. Hathaway	109		243	
27		W. F. Ashley	130	30		
		R. A. Kelsey	100		230	
28		S. B. Stewart	210	50		
		E. M. Harkins	160			
		Seth Hollingsworth	49		419	
29		John K. Faulkner	227	4		
		Joseph Howell	223		450	
30		J. I. Larimer	194	3		
		James Bauserman	191		385	4,010
31	Wyandotte	Vincent J. Lane	273	147		
		H. W. Cook	126		399	

VOTE FOR MEMBERS OF THE HOUSE OF REPRESENTATIVES—Continued.

District.	Counties.	Names.	Votes......	Maj......	Vote of District.	Vote of County......
80	Wyandotte (concluded)	John T. Makay......................	406	92		
		James Peak............................	314		720	1,119
32	Johnson.....................	John T. Burris.......................	489	210		
		John M. Giffen......................	279		768	
33	....	John Lusher	345	187		
		Amos A. Fay.........................	158			
		James McAuley......................	7			
		A. Payne...............................	1		511	
34	....	Frederick Ridlon....................	140	21		
		William Maxwell....................	119		259	1,538
35	Douglas	William H. Sells....................	434	118		
		Josiah Miller........................	316		750	
36	....	George Benson.......................	67	21		
		E. D. Ladd...........................	46		113	
37	....	Elijah Sells..........................	176	105		
		Amos Walton	71		247	
38	....	A. J. Jennings.......................	111	111	111	
39	....	W. H. Peckham......................	100	3		
		J. H. Bonebrake.....................	97		197	
40	....	William B. Disbrow	90	90	90	1,508
41	Shawnee	John Guthrie	895	895	895	
42	....	John W. Brown......................	291	204		
		James Fletcher......................	87		378	
79	....	Byron Stewart	23	23	23	1,296
43	Miami	Reuben Smith........................	188	74		
		Johnson Clark.......................	114		302	
44	....	E. H. Topping.......................	510	314		
		J. W. Gossett........................	196			
		H. Torrey.............................	110		816	
45	....	C. W. Green..........................	153	85		
		A. Ellis................................	68		221	1,339
46	Linn	John Dixon	103	82		
		O. D. Harmon........................	21			
		Lander Redfield.....................	6		130	
47	....	William B. Scott....................	93	15		
		Herbert Robinson....................	78		171	
48	....	J. W. Babb	175	67		
		Morris Howard......................	108			
		N. C. Gunn...........................	2		285	
49	....	James D. Snoddy....................	171	170		
		J. H. Stearns........................	1			
		T. J. Bakerville.....................	1			
		J. L. Carter..........................	1		174	760
50	Bourbon.....................	J. A. Tiffany	135	91		
		D. D. Roberts........................	44			
		D. B. Jackman	14		193	
51	....	C. W. Libby	135	129		
		J. B. Britton.........................	6			
		S. N. Northway......................	2			
		John Brown...........................	1			
		J. A. Casteel.........................	1		145	
52	....	George P. Eves	136	121		
		Scattering	15		151	
53	....	W. C. Webb...........................	434	209		
		J. S. Miller	225			
		Scattering	1		660	1,149
54	Allen	J. C. Redfield........................	281	25		
		H. D. Parsons	256		537	
55	....	J. D. Hosley..........................	126	101		
		A. Cozine..............................	25			
		E. C. Bray	12		163	700
56	Anderson.....................	John G. Lindsay.....................	188	14		
		George W. Cooper...................	174		362	
57	....	J. H. Whitford.......................	107	49		
		Jackson Means......................	58		165	527
58	Franklin.....................	George T. Pierce.....................	242	242	242	
59	....	James Hanway.......................	465	206		
		William H. Clark....................	259			
		D. Holaday...........................	14		738	980
60	Osage.....................	J. Wilkins.............................	323	8		
		John Russell	315			
		Ellis Lewis...........................	138		776	776
61	Coffey.....................	Elihu E. Coffin......................	245	181		

VOTE FOR MEMBERS OF THE HOUSE OF REPRESENTATIVES—Concluded.

District.	Counties.	Names.	Votes.	Maj.	Vote of District.	Vote of County.
61	Coffey (concluded)	James L. Ward	64			
		J. M. Cole	12		321	
62		Hardin McMahon	223	46		
		Silas Fearl	179			
		Miss Upton	1		405	726
63	Woodson	H. J. Gregory	184	71		
		C. B. Graves	113		297	297
64	Lyon	Jacob Stotler	559	486		
		R. M. Ruggles	73		632	
65		J. M. Hunter	122	28		
		Oliver Phillips	94		216	
66		Charles Drake	153	152		
		T. C. Hill	1			
		William Null	1		155	1,003
67	Butler	H. Small	113	38		
		H. D. Lamb	75			
		D. W. Boutwell	31			
		L. B. Snow	2			
		—— Small	2			
		—— Boutwell	2			
		J. Boswell	1			
		—— Lamb	1		227	227
68	Chase	F. B. Hunt	90	6		
		H. Brandley	84			
		A. S. Howard	73			
		H. L. Hunt	1		248	248
69	Morris	Charles G. Parker	191	27		
		H. W. McNay	164		355	355
70	Wabaunsee	J. H. Pinkerton	234	209		
		L. H. Pillsbury	25			
		H. C. McKey	1		260	260
71	Davis	John K. Wright	317	126		
		R. Howard	191		508	508
72	Riley	Edward Secrest	372	41		
		George W. Higinbotham	331			
		William Higinbotham	1		704	704
73	Dickinson	Conrad Kohler	188	22		
		J. F. Staatz	166		354	354
74	Saline	J. H. Snead	302	72		
		Thomas Anderson	230		532	532
75	Greenwood	W. F. Osborn	139	4		
		J. R. Bullion	135		274	274
76	Marion	Levi Billings	74	73		
		William Layer	1		75	75
77	Wilson	No returns.				
78	Neosho	Thomas H. Butler	557	211		
		A. T. Filley	346			
		A. H. Holeman	216		1,119	1,119
81	Ottawa	Wallace W. Lambert	112	34		
		Elijah Smith	78		190	190
82	Clay	L. Gates	197	165		
		George Taylor	32			
		J. B. McLaughlin	4		233	233
83	Cherokee	No returns.				
84	Cloud	A. L. Shelhamer	108	34		
		B. H. McEckron	74		182	182
85	Labette	No returns.				
86	Crawford	S. J. Langdon	546	396		
		John T. Voss	150			
		A. A. Fletcher	111			
		Isaac Ford	21		828	828
87	Ellis	J. V. Macintosh	114	16		
		J. F. Wright	98		212	212
88	Ellsworth	John H. Edwards	199	90		
		Z. Jackson	109			
		William N. Anderson	1		309	309
89	Wallace	Simon Motz	137	58		
		Joseph Speck	79		216	216
90	Republic	R. P. West	68	13		
		John Manning	55		123	123
	Montgomery (new Co.)	John E. Adams	158	48		
		E. Fitch	110		268	268
	Total vote					33,310

NOVEMBER 6.—Amos Sanford starts the Workingman's Journal, at Columbus, Cherokee county.

NOVEMBER 10.—Noble L. Prentis arrives in Topeka, from Illinois, and takes a position on the Daily Record.—The Fort Scott Monitor appears as a daily.—Our New Home, a Scandinavian paper, is started at Frankfort, Marshall county.

—The Kansas City Times says Quantrell was born in Maryland, "where his mother and two sisters now reside:" that while he and his brother were going through Kansas to Pike's Peak, his brother was killed, and Quantrell wounded; that Quantrell "came back to remember and avenge;" that he was shot in a skirmish, in Kentucky, and died at Louisville, in a hospital.

NOVEMBER 11.—W. H. Warner and E. A. Wasser establish the Girard Press. July 14, 1871, the office was burned by a mob. The paper reappeared three weeks afterwards. A. P. Riddle bought Dr. Warner's interest, June 16, 1873. Crawford county has had three other short-lived papers.

—Ex-Governor Robert J. Walker dies, in Washington, aged sixty-eight.

NOVEMBER 15.—The Kansas Farmer publishes the picture called "Droughty Kansas," designed by Henry Worrall, of Topeka, and photographed by J. Lee Knight.

NOVEMBER 25.—A. D. Richardson fatally shot in New York City, by Daniel McFarland.

NOVEMBER 30.—The Auditor's Report says:

"The State of Kansas has, for the protection of her frontiers, already expended an amount of $346,000, and besides this assumed Price Raid claims to the amount of half a million, making a total of $846,000, which ought to be paid by the General Government."

NOVEMBER 30.—Expenditures of the State for the year:

Governor's Department	$5,483 50	Capitol building and grounds*..	117,005 01
Secretary's Department	8,440 54	Penitentiary	106,644 83
Auditor's Department	4,010 10	Sheriffs conveying prisoners to	
Treasurer's Department	3,017 93	Penitentiary	2,566 49
Attorney General	4,325 00	State House Commissioners	1,500 00
Sup't of Public Instruction	1,951 06	Horticultural Society	500 00
Adjutant General	1,552 13	Price Raid Commissioners	1,269 22
Judiciary Department	29,230 66	Rent of Capitol Building	2,000 00
Legislative expenses	26,102 91	Printing	54,012 25
Blind Asylum	10,092 80	Transcribing Journals	1,343 18
Insane Asylum	28,707 37	Agricultural Society	3,500 00
Deaf and Dumb Asylum	12,815 23	Indian Raid Commissioners	477 40
State University	11,993 60	Seed wheat:	14,117 10
Normal School	9,930 62	Miscellaneous accounts	2,287 84
Agricultural College	9,394 22	Total for 1869	$471,270 99

*Seventy thousand dollars in bonds were issued, and sold for $66,442.57, which is included in this amount.

DECEMBER.—J. W. Foster's new book on the Mississippi Valley gives the annual rainfall in different parts of the country, as follows:

Cincinnati, Ohio	46.69	San Francisco, Cal	21.95
New York City	42.23	El Paso, New Mexico	11.21
Fort Scott, Kansas	42.12	Fort Yuma	3.15
Ann Arbor, Mich	28.60		

DECEMBER.—The State University has had, during the year, 143 students; the Agricultural College, 173; the Normal School, 198. Prisoners in the Penitentiary, 186; patients in the Insane Asylum, 31; pupils in the Blind Asylum, 20; pupils in the Deaf and Dumb Asylum, 34.

—General Phil. Sheridan makes an official report of his Indian campaign, from October 15, 1868, to March 27, 1869.

—Leavenworth county paid school teachers, during the year, $34,506.96; value of school houses in the county, $131,336.

DECEMBER 7.—The locomotive arrives in Emporia.

DECEMBER 10.—John F. Dillon appointed United States Circuit Judge.

DECEMBER 14.—Colonel Hoyt resigns as Mail Agent. A. Low, of Doniphan, appointed.

—Adjutant General Moorhouse pays the militia.

DECEMBER 14.—Third Annual Meeting of the State Horticultural Society, at Ottawa. *Officers elected:* President, William Tanner, of Leavenworth; Vice President, C. B. Lines, of Wabaunsee; Secretary, G. C. Brackett, of Lawrence; Treasurer, S. T. Kelsey, of Ottawa.

DECEMBER 15.—John W. Delaney retires from the Junction City Union, and George W. Martin becomes sole proprietor.

—State House ready for occupancy.

DECEMBER 15.—The following is copied from the Report of Superintendent McVicar:

"The whole number of school houses reported is 1,213; a gain of 260 over last year. A fine edifice was completed in the city of Atchison during the year, at a cost, including furniture, of about $40,000. This edifice was recently destroyed by fire. It was insured, however, for $30,000, and upon the ruins another edifice will soon stand complete. Wathena, in Doniphan county, has erected a school building at a cost of $10,000. At Troy, an edifice is in process of erection, at a cost of $8,000. Seneca, the county seat of Nemaha county, completed an edifice valued at $15,000. The city of Fort Scott has taken steps to build a house worth about $30,000. Topeka has laid the foundation for an edifice at a cost of $34,000. At Leroy, an edifice has been erected, at a cost of nearly $10,000. School houses have been built at Irving, Manhattan, Neosho Falls, Oswego, Washington, Alma, Olathe, and at many other central points in the State. In addition to these, a greater number of good school houses have been built in rural communities than in any previous year."

On "the 500,000-acre case," the Report says the Supreme Court "has declined to give any decision on the main point involved, on the ground of alleged informalities in the presentation of the case."

The Report says the school lands lost to the State on the Cherokee Neutral Lands amount to 50,000 acres.

DECEMBER 20.—R. S. Stevens receives a patent from the Governor for lands set apart for the Neosho Valley R. R. Trains are running regularly to Emporia.

DECEMBER.—The Missouri River, Fort Scott and Gulf road completed to Fort Scott.

DECEMBER 25.—The State officers leave the old buildings on Kansas Avenue, and go into the new building on Capitol Square, the east wing of which is completed.

DECEMBER 30.—The State House Commissioners report that $417,588.29 has already been expended on the State House.

1870.

JANUARY.—B. F. Mudge writes to the Kansas Farmer of a visit to Fort Scott:

"At the farm of John G. Stuart, on the Marmaton, southwest of Fort Scott, I saw a remarkable natural curiosity, in the form of a boiling, burning spring. In sinking an artesian boring, Mr. Stuart, at a depth of 230 feet, struck a stream of gas. After he discontinued the boring, water filled the basin; but the gas continued to rise in large quantities. This was accidentally set on fire, and has continued to burn without interruption for over two months. The gas rises with such force that the water is in a state of violent agitation, as if from the most intense heat. The flames rise from the surface of the water to the height of four to six feet, and three feet in diameter. It presents a novel and beautiful appearance."

The supply of gas seems inexhaustible. Many years before, near the old Fort, the same result followed a similar experiment.

JANUARY 1.—The L. L. & G. is graded nearly to Garnett.

—Frank A. Root starts the Waterville Telegraph.

—The Osage Mission Journal says White Hair, the head chief of the Osages, died on Christmas eve, at his camp on the Verdigris.

JANUARY 11.—Meeting of the Legislature.

STATE OFFICERS.

Names.	Former P. O.	County.	Where Born.	Age	Avocation.
J. M. Harvey, Governor..	Fort Riley......	Riley............	Virginia........	36	Farmer.
C. V. Eskridge, Lt. Gov...	Emporia........	Lyon............	Virginia........	38	Mercha't.
T. Moonlight, Sec. of State	Leavenworth.	Leavenworth	Scotland	36	
A. Danford, Att'y Gen...	Fort Scott......	Bourbon......	New Hamp...	40	Attorn'y.
P. McVicar, Sp't Pub.Inst.	Topeka	Shawnee........	New Brunsw.	40	Minister.
Geo. Graham, Treasurer..	Seneca...........	Nemaha......	New York....	50	Mercha't.
A. Thoman, Aud. of State	Lawrence	Douglas........	Switzerland..	46	Farmer.
S. S. Prouty, State Printer	Topeka..........	Shawnee	New York....	38	Printer.
D. Whitaker, Adj. Gen	Doniphan......	Doniphan......		34	

JUDGES OF THE SUPREME COURT.

Names.	Former P.O.	County.	Where Born.	Age	Avocation.
S. A. Kingman, Chief Justice.	Atchison...	Atchison...	Massachusetts	52	Attorn'y.
J. Safford, Associate Justice.	Topeka	Shawnee ...	Vermont.........	42	Lawyer.
D. M. Valentine, Asso. Justice	Ottawa	Franklin...	Ohio..............	39	Lawyer.

JUDGES OF DISTRICT COURTS.

Names.	Districts.	P. O. Address.	County.
H. W. Ide................................	First..............	Leavenworth	Leavenworth.
Nathan Price............................	Second............	Troy................	Doniphan.
John T. Morton........................	Third.............	Topeka............	Shawnee.
Owen A. Bassett.......................	Fourth............	Lawrence..........	Douglas.
J. H. Watson............................	Fifth..............	Emporia	Lyon.
D. P. Lowe...............................	Sixth..............	Mound City......	Linn.
John R. Goodin.........................	Seventh..........	Humboldt..........	Allen.
Wm. H. Canfield.......................	Eighth............	Junction City....	Davis.
William R. Brown......................	Ninth.............	Cottonwood Falls	Chase.
Hiram Stevens..........................	Tenth.............	Paola..............	Johnson.
Wm. C. Webb...........................	Eleventh..........	Fort Scott..........	Bourbon.

—Barzillai Gray, Judge Criminal Court, Leavenworth county.

MEMBERS AND OFFICERS OF THE SENATE.

Names.	P. O. Address.	County.	Where Born.	Dist.	Avocation.
Eskridge, C. V., President	Emporia	Lyon	Virginia		Merchant.
Arrasmith, Abner	Olathe	Johnson	Kentucky	10	Farmer.
Bailey, J. C	Perryville	Jefferson	Penn	4	Merchant.
Broadhead, J. F	Mound City	Linn	New York.	13	Lawyer.
Carnahan, A. A	Clyde	Cloud	Ohio	7	Attorney.
Carpenter, John C	Erie	Neosho	Penn	16	Attorney.
Cobb, Stephen A	Wyandotte	Wyandotte	Minnesota.	12	Attorney.
Fitzpatrick, W. H	Topeka	Shawnee	Kentucky	8	Farmer.
Grimes, W. H	Atchison	Atchison	Maryland	2	Physician.
Grover, O. J	Savannah	Pottawato'ie.	New York.	6	Farmer.
Jenkins, E. J	Troy	Doniphan	Ohio	1	Lawyer.
Larimer, William	Delaware T'p	Leavenw'th.	Penn	3	Farmer.
Learnard, O. E	Lawrence	Douglas	Vermont.	9	Farmer.
Mead, James R	Towanda	Butler	Vermont	15	Farmer.
Murdock, M. M	Burlingame	Osage	Virginia	18	Editor.
McKee, John	Leavenworth	Leavenw'th.	Missouri	3	Civil Eng.
Niccolls, E. S	Garnett	Anderson	Penn	17	Farmer.
Prescott, J. H	Salina	Saline	New Hamp	20	Attorney.
Schmidt, Martin	Leavenworth	Leavenw'th.	Germany	3	
Smallwood, W. H	Wathena	Doniphan	Kentucky	1	Farmer.
Snyder, S. J. H	Monrovia	Atchison	Maryland	2	Farmer.
Spear, A. G	Hiawatha	Brown	Ohio	5	Farmer.
Tucker, Edwin	Eureka	Greenwood	Vermont	19	Farmer.
Voss, M. V	Fort Scott	Bourbon	Ohio	14	Attorney.
Williams, H. H	Osawatomie	Miami	New York.	11	Merchant.
Woodard, Levi	Eudora	Douglas	Indiana	9	Farmer.
Geo. C. Crowther, Sec'y	Irwin	Marshall	Conn		Editor.
J. D. Gilchrist, As't Sec'y.	Oskaloosa	Jefferson	New Hamp		Attorney.
D. M. Bronson, Jour'l Cl'k	Eldorado	Butler	New York.		Attorney.
L. M. Benedict, Dock't Cl'k	Vienna	Pottawato'ie	New York.		Farmer.
H. H. Carr, Engros'g Cl'k	Eudora	Douglas	Ohio		Attorney.
N. Merchant, S'gt-at-Ar's	Prairie City	Franklin	New York.		Farmer.
George W. Weed, Doork'r	Pardee	Atchison	New York.		Farmer.
A. A. House, As't Doork'r	Junction City	Davis	Ohio		Student.
Edwin C. Eldridge, Page	Lawrence	Douglas	Ohio		Student.
William H. Fletcher, Page	Erie	Neosho	Indiana		Student.
William R. Griffith, Page	Topeka	Shawnee	Ohio		Student.

MEMBERS AND OFFICERS OF THE HOUSE OF REPRESENTATIVES.

Names.	Dist.	P. O. Address.	County.
Adams, John E			Montgomery.
Ashley, W. F	27	Easton	Leavenworth.
Baliff, E. H	10	Lancaster	Atchison.
Babbitt, J. F	11	Hiawatha	Brown.
Babb, J. W	48		Linn.
Benson, George	36		Douglas.
Bishop, W. P	85	Oswego	Labette.
Billings, Levi	76	Marion Center	Marion.
Butts, W. C	20	Grasshopper Falls	Jefferson.
Burris, John T	32	Olathe	Johnson.
Butler, Thomas H	78	Erie	Neosho.
Brown, John W	42	Auburn	Shawnee.
Clark, John H	17	Louisville	Pottawatomie.
Coffin, Elihu E	61	Le Roy	Coffey.
Curtis, A	12	Carson	Brown.
Disbrow, William B	46	Clinton	Douglas.
Dixon, John	46	La Cygne	Linn.
Drake, Charles	66	Americus	Lyon.
Edwards, John H	88	Ellsworth	Ellsworth.
Evans, A. J	7	Atchison	Atchison.
Eves, George P	52	Turkey Creek	Bourbon.
Faulkner, John K	29	High Prairie	Leavenworth.
Gates, L	82	Gatesville	Clay.
Green, C. W	45	Fontana	Miami.
Gregory, H. J	63	Belmont	Woodson.
Grover, Charles H	26	Salt Creek Valley	Leavenworth.
Guthrie, John	41	Topeka	Shawnee.
Hazen, A	2	Columbus	Doniphan.
Halderman, J. A	24	Leavenworth City	Leavenworth
Hanway, James	59	Ohio City	Franklin.
Hensel, L	13	Seneca	Nemaha.

MEMBERS AND OFFICERS OF HOUSE OF REPRESENTATIVES — CONCLUDED.

Names.	Dist.	P. O. Address.	County.
Hosley, J. D	55	Ozark	Allen.
Hunt, F. B	68	Cottonwood Falls	Chase.
Hudson, T. J	77		Wilson.
Hunter, J. M	65	Forest Hill	Lyon.
Jennings, A. J	38	Eudora	Douglas.
Kellogg, Josiah	23	Leavenworth City	Leavenworth.
Kohler, Conrad	73	Lyons	Dickinson.
Lambert, Wallace W	81	Lindsay	Ottawa.
Langdon, S. J	86	Iowa City	Crawford.
Lane, Vincent J	31	Wyandotte City	Wyandotte.
LeDuc, E. H	4	Troy	Doniphan.
Larimer, J. I	30	Leavenworth City	Leavenworth.
Libby, C. W	51	Xenia	Bourbon.
Lindsay, John G	56	Garnett	Anderson.
Logan, Joseph	9	Monrovia	Atchison.
Lusher, John	33	Aubrey	Johnson.
Macintosh, J. V	87	Hays City	Ellis.
Makay, John T	80	Quindaro	Wyandotte.
McMahon, H	62	Ottumwa	Coffey.
Morris, William	14	Wetmore	Nemaha.
Mowry, A. J	3	Wathena	Doniphan.
Motz, Simon	89	Sheridan	Wallace.
Murphy, Thomas	6	Atchison	Atchison.
Nesbitt, S. F	1	Highland	Doniphan.
Osborn, W. F	75	Virgil	Greenwood.
Parson, J	8	Mount Pleasant	Atchison.
Parker, Charles G	69	Council Grove	Morris.
Peckham, W. H	39	Big Springs	Douglas.
Pierce, George T	58	Ottawa	Franklin.
Pinkerton, J. H	70	Wabaunsee	Wabaunsee.
Redfield, J. C	54	Humboldt	Allen.
Ridlon, Frederick	35	McCamish	Johnson.
Rorick, David	21	Perryville	Jefferson.
Sanford, Amos	83	Columbus	Cherokee.
Scott, William B	47	Oakwood	Linn.
Secrest, Edward	72	Randolph	Riley.
Sells, William H	35	Lawrence	Douglas.
Sells, Elijah	37	Baldwin City	Douglas.
Sherry, Byron	22	Leavenworth City	Leavenworth.
Shire, Daniel	25	Leavenworth City	Leavenworth.
Shelhamer, A. J	84		Cloud.
Small, H	67		Butler.
Smith, Reuben	43	Osawatomie	Miami.
Snead, J. H	74	Salina	Saline.
Snoddy, James D	49	Mound City	Linn.
Stewart, Byron	79	Mount Florence	Jackson.
Stewart, S. B	28	Tonganoxie	Leavenworth.
Stotler, Jacob	64	Emporia	Lyon.
Tiffany, J. A	50	Barnesville	Bourbon.
Topping, E. H	44	Paola	Miami.
Webb, W. C	53	Fort Scott	Bourbon.
Wells, John D	15	Barrett's Mill	Marshall.
West, R. P	90	Salt Marsh	Republic.
Whitaker, David	5	Doniphan	Doniphan.
Whitford, J. H	57		Anderson.
Wilson, A. S	16	Washington	Washington.
Williams, J. L	18	Holton	Jackson.
Wilhelm, Levi	19	Winchester	Jefferson.
Wilkins, J	60	Valley Brook	Osage.
Wright, John K	71	Junction City	Davis.
H. C. Olney, Chief Clerk		Atchison	Atchison.
A. W. Hayes, Assistant Clerk		Topeka	Shawnee.
H. Brandley, Journal Clerk			Johnson.
F. W. Watson, Docket Clerk			Coffey.
Miss Emma D. Campbell, Enr. Clerk		Topeka	Shawnee.
H. H. Tucker, Engrossing Clerk		Lawrence	Douglas.
Mrs. Sarah J. Neal, Ass't Eng. Clerk		Atchison	Atchison.
Geo. A. Schriner, Sergeant-at-Arms		Wyandotte	Wyandotte.
M. B. Crawford, Ass't Ser.-at-Arms		Topeka	Shawnee.
A. H. Beck, Doorkeeper		Ottawa	Franklin.
John Helwig, Assistant Doorkeeper			Leavenworth.
Willie Davis, Messenger		Topeka	Shawnee.
Ephie Smith, Messenger		Wyandotte	Wyandotte.
Edward Matthews, Messenger		Leavenworth	Leavenworth.
Thomas Parks, Messenger		Wyandotte	Wyandotte.

JANUARY 17.—Annual meeting of the Editorial Association. Address by R. B. Taylor, of the Wyandotte Gazette.

JANUARY 19.—Annual meeting of the Kansas and Missouri Associated Press, at Leavenworth. The seventeen daily papers in the Association pay for their regular despatches $14,295 a year. D. W. Wilder re-elected President, and Geo. F. Prescott Secretary.

JANUARY 21.—Hiram R. Revels is elected to the United States Senate from Mississippi. He had been a resident of Leavenworth.

JANUARY 26.—Disclosure in regard to ex-Collector Speer made in the Topeka Record.

JANUARY 26.—Auditor Thoman makes the following statement to the House:

STATE PENITENTIARY.

Total amount expended during the years 1863 to 1869, inclusive.................. $442,502 72

INSANE ASYLUM.

Total amount expended during the years 1867 to 1869, inclusive.................. 67,423 50

DEAF AND DUMB ASYLUM.

Total amount expended during the years 1862 to 1869, inclusive.................. 44,457 49

BLIND ASYLUM.

Total amount expended during the years 1867 to 1869................................. 31,814 91

Total expended.......... .... $586,198 62

JANUARY 26.—Report of House Committee that the State Treasurer lends the State money to the Topeka Bank, and receives four per cent. on current balances. (House Journal, pp. 319 to 341.) ·

JANUARY 31.—Report of State-House Investigating Committee. (Senate Journal, pp. 173 to 177.)

JANUARY 31.—Report of Penitentiary Investigating Committee. (Senate Journal, p. 178.)

FEBRUARY 1.—The Commonwealth defends the Treasurer. The Record says: "Here is a clearly-established case of open, persistent, and flagrant disobedience — virtual defiance, indeed — of the law; and a prima facie case of collusion between the Treasurer and his bankers to use the surplus money of the State for purposes of private speculation."

FEBRUARY 4.—The House appoints a Committee of five to visit the Neutral Land, and investigate the matter of sending United States troops there. The Report made fills 164 pages.

FEBRUARY 14.—The House is visited by Thomas Warren, born in Virginia, February 14, 1770, and one hundred years old to-day. He came to Kansas in 1854. With Mr. Warren were Thomas C. Hannum, born in Pennsylvania, aged 84; Amos Morris, born in Pennsylvania, aged 82; Gamaliel Garlinghouse, born in New Jersey, aged 78; John Callaham, born in South Carolina, aged 75; Lewis Buckingham, born in New York, aged 72; and Sabin Kellam, born in Vermont, aged 80. (House Journal, pp. 652-3.)

FEBRUARY 16.—*Appointments confirmed:* John A. Halderman and J. G. Reaser of Leavenworth county, Charles Robinson of Douglas county, George A. Crawford of Bourbon county, and F. W. Giles of Shawnee county, Regents of the State University; David Whitaker of Doniphan county, Adjutant General.

FEBRUARY 17.—Report of House Committee on Cherokee Neutral Lands. (House Journal, pp. 735 to 894.) J. H. Snead makes a special report. (House Journal, pp. 916 to 920.)

FEBRUARY 22.—The Treasurer reports that the money deposited with the Topeka Bank "has this day been withdrawn therefrom."

FEBRUARY 23.—Legislative excursion to Burlington, over the M. K. & T. R. W. The Committee on Resolutions consisted of M. V. Voss, Josiah Kellogg, John T. Burris, E. J. Jenkins, J. A. Halderman, John McKee, John R. Goodin, Jacob Stotler, V. J. Lane, S. S. Prouty, Henry King, T. D. Thacher, M. M. Murdock, J. S. Redfield, Isaac Sharp, J. W. Horner, John K. Wright, and Jos. Clarke.

FEBRUARY 24.—V. P. Wilson starts the Chronicle, at Abilene.

FEBRUARY 26.—Secretary Moonlight makes a report on the issue of State bonds. (Senate Journal, pp. 476-8.)

FEBRUARY 28.—Report of Committee investigating Treasurer and Auditor. The majority report says:

"We find that there is no authority in law for depositing the funds of the State in any local or State bank; that State funds have been so deposited by the Treasurer in the Topeka Bank, in the city of Topeka; that the Treasurer claims that it is impossible for him to perform his duties as such officer with safety to the State, and maintain the credit of the State, without making such deposits, in order to keep the funds in a secure place, and meet the interest on the bonds of the State as it falls due in New York. [See concluding portions of Graham's testimony submitted.] Whether the necessity claimed to exist by Mr. Graham justifies the failure to comply with the law on the statute books by Mr. Graham, we do not attempt to pronounce; we simply state it is in the course of established precedent.

"We find that, by the testimony, there was no agreement between the Treasurer and the Topeka Bank, or any person for the bank, for the Treasurer, or either of them, whereby Mr. Graham was to receive interest on deposits of funds of the State; that there does appear upon the books of said bank a credit to Mr. Graham, to the amount of $1,056.70, arising from interests on deposits of State funds, which, if credited at all, should have been placed to the credit of the State; but that such credit was made to the individual account of Mr. Graham, without the knowledge or consent of said Graham, and that he immediately caused such credit to be erased from his personal account on the books of said bank, as soon as he learned of its existence." [See testimony of Geo. G. Corning, President, J. R. Swallow, Cashier, and Geo. Graham.]

The minority report says:

"The undersigned is of opinion that any toleration of a disregard of the provisions of law governing public officers is demoralizing in its tendency, and destructive of that security which is absolutely essential for the protection of the funds of the State. If the law is obnoxious, the best way to get rid of it is, as has been well said by General Grant, to enforce it strictly. Official bonds are not sufficient security to protect the State, where there is not integrity and a faithful adherence to the oath of office in the discharge of the important duties imposed by law. Without the most scrupulous respect for laws by the officers charged with their execution, security is gone and legislation a farce."—*Senate Journal, pp. 525 to 560.*

MARCH.—Beck, Follett and McClure start the Index, at Cottonwood Falls. It was published nine months, when Yale & Gifford moved it to Wichita and started the Tribune.

—Publication of a book with this title: "The Early History of St. Louis and Missouri, from its first Exploration by white men, in 1673, to 1843.

By Elihu H. Shepard, formerly Professor of Languages in St. Louis College. St. Louis: Southwestern Book and Publishing Company." pp. 170.

MARCH 3.—Adjournment of the Legislature. Among its acts are the following: Providing a room in the Capitol for the Agricultural Society; Authorizing Lawrence to issue $100,000 in bonds, to aid in erecting a building for the University; Authorizing the State School Commissioners to buy the Lawrence University bonds, (eighteen acts relate to bonds); Establishing a Normal School in Northern Kansas (Leavenworth); Creating the office of State Librarian, and a Board of Directors of the State Library; Incorporating the city of Wathena; Ratifying the Fifteenth Amendment to the Constitution of the United States.

MARCH 4.—T. B. Murdock establishes the Walnut Valley Times, at Eldorado. It is the oldest paper south of Emporia and west of Eureka.

MARCH 24.—Annual Conference M. E. Church, at Topeka, Bishop Clark presiding.

—The K. P. road is finished to Kit Carson, eighty-two miles west of Sheridan.

MARCH 16.—William C. Webb appointed Judge of the new judicial district—Crawford, Cherokee, Labette, Montgomery, and Howard counties.

APRIL 1.—Sidney Clarke reports to the House the arguments of James F. Joy and W. R. Laughlin, on the Cherokee Neutral Land question. It is Report No. 53, 2d Session 41st Congress, and contains 32 pages.

APRIL.—The vote of the five principal cities in the State at the city election, the first week in April, stood as follows: Leavenworth, 2,859; Topeka, 1,374; Lawrence, 1,217; Atchison, 1,069; Fort Scott, 1,026.

—George T. Isbell becomes local editor of the Leavenworth Conservative.

APRIL 20.—Celebration at Humboldt of the arrival of the M. K. & T. R. W.

APRIL 20.—John S. Gilmore starts the Wilson County Citizen.

APRIL 24.—The Topeka Record says of the ex-Collector case that the defalcation is about $160,000, and that there has been "perjury and forgery on the part of somebody." Supervisor Marr is removed from this district, and McDonald and Joyce, of the St. Louis whiskey ring, sent here.

MAY 3.—The Normal School for Northern Kansas established at Leavenworth.

MAY 5.—Three men killed by Indians on Limestone creek, Mitchell county. No other lives lost by Indian raids during the year. United States troops are stationed in the Republican, Solomon and Saline valleys.

MAY 10.—Indians reported in Jewell county.

MAY 10.—Seven outlaws from the Indian Territory break into the house of J. N. Roach, at Ladore, Neosho county, dangerously wound him, and outrage his two daughters. One of the ruffians was killed by his own party, in a quarrel; five others were caught by the citizens and hung on one tree.

MAY 11.—Episcopalian Convention at Junction City.

—Congress establishes the Arkansas Land District.

—Congregationalists meet at Leavenworth.

MAY 12.—Baxter Springs celebrates the completion of the Missouri River, Fort Scott and Gulf Railroad.

—Corner-stone of Methodist church laid at Atchison.

MAY 19.—Fort Scott entertains the Missouri editors.

MAY 29.—The Chronicle reports 150,000 head of cattle on the way from Texas to Abilene.

—Burning of the old Topeka House.

MAY 31.—Henry Buckingham starts the Republican Valley Empire, at Clyde. It was the first paper printed in either the Republican or Solomon valleys. It was removed to Concordia, December 24, 1870. H. E. Smith, the present publisher, bought the Empire in November, 1872. Cloud county has had five other papers, all short-lived.

JUNE.—An illustrated political pamphlet of 32 pages, published at Topeka. It bears this title: "Political Affairs in Kansas. A Review of the Official Acts of our Delegation in Congress. Shall Inefficiency and Corruption be Sustained? The Issues of the Coming Political Campaign. A new Deal and less Steal." It contains eleven wood cuts. The tract is especially aimed at S. C. Pomeroy and Sidney Clarke.

JUNE 3.—Major Henry J. Adams dies, at Waterville. He was the first Free-State Mayor of Leavenworth, and one of our best public men.

JUNE 4.—The Champion says Atchison has fifteen public and secret societies.

JUNE 8.—Eleventh Annual Baptist Convention, at Lawrence.

—The Salina Herald is enlarged.

—The New Hampshire Agricultural Society grants a diploma for Kansas fruit.

JUNE 13.—The first court in Sedgwick county, held by Judge Wm. R. Brown.

JUNE 14.—Abram Burnett, a Pottawatomie Chief, of 406 pounds, dies, near Topeka.

—Perry Fuller gives a bond, in the sum of $50,000, for his appearance to answer certain Custom-House charges against him, in New Orleans.

JUNE 18.—The United States House of Representatives passes a bill to pay citizens of Kansas for losses during the Border-Ruffian war, in 1855–1856. It makes the United Circuit Judge the Commissioner to receive and examine claims, and appropriates $500,000.

JUNE 20.—The Sons of Temperance pass resolutions eulogizing the late Dr. Amory Hunting.

—The La Cygne Journal issued.

There are 1,283 miles of railroad in the State; Kansas Pacific, 454; Missouri, Kansas and Texas, 182; Union Pacific, Central Branch, 100; Leavenworth, Lawrence and Galveston, 64; Missouri River, Fort Scott and Gulf, 102; Atchison, Topeka and Santa Fe, 27; Leavenworth, Atchison and Northwestern, 21; Missouri River, 28; St. Joseph and Denver, 40.

By the acts of Congress of July 1, 1862, and July 2, 1864, the Kansas Pacific Railway received, in bonds, from the Government $6,303,000; and the Central Branch, $1,600,000. The bonds given by the Government to all the Pacific roads (under acts bearing these dates) amounted to $64,618,-832.

JUNE 21.—Col. Bernard P. Chenoweth, formerly Captain of Company A, First Kansas Regiment, dies at Canton, China, where he was United States Consul.

JUNE 27.—The Leavenworth Coal Company begins to take out coal.

JUNE 28.—Annual Meeting of the State Teachers' Association, at Wyandotte. *Officers elected*: President, J. Evans Platt, of Manhattan; Recording Secretary, Miss E. M. Dickinson, of Quindaro; Corresponding Secretary, D. J. Evans, of Topeka; Treasurer, Miss Matilda J. Upton, of Burlington; Executive Committee, David Donovan, of Leavenworth; State Superintendents, M. D. Gage, of Junction City, Frank H. Snow, of Lawrence, and A. D. Chambers, of Hartford.

JUNE.—U. S. Census taken.

County.	Population in 1860.	Population in 1870.	No. Acres of improved land.	Of Farms.	Of Farming Implements and Machinery.	Estimated value of all Farm productions, includ. betterm'ts and additions to stock.
				VALUE.		
Allen	3,082	7,023	30,288	$1,392,595	$64,060	$424,468
Anderson	2,393	5,204	29,433	1,318,618	82,400	450,763
Atchison	7,729	15,472	72,788	3,405,515	207,415	1,128,633
Bourbon	6,101	15,102	105,972	4,371,975	248,070	1,289,676
Brown	2,607	6,823	50,189	2,272,272	118,468	457,283
Butler	437	3,072	11,054	451,955	40,804	147,568
Chase	808	1,992	9,137	853,082	36,400	160,882
Cloud		2,323	94,460	552,819	40,476	166,851
Cherokee		11,047	55,682	1,041,239	131,420	812,638
Clay	163	2,942	10,805	619,585	49,395	184,761
Coffey	2,842	6,335	34,420	1,874,810	86,555	512,758
Cowley		1,174	2,327	317,120	19,461	133,817
Crawford		8,005	60,044	2,393,155	133,646	705,495
Davis	1,163	5,600	23,915	782,110	36,695	275,628
Dickinson	378	3,037	10,924	629,707	29,712	171,882
Doniphan	8,083	13,971	71,275	220,982	149,189	895,582
Douglas	8,637	20,582	94,775	3,177,403	148,326	1,432,014
Ellis		2,041				
Ellsworth		1,350	2,449	111,390	9,880	51,946
Franklin	3,030	10,406	75,587	3,322,930	177,247	947,565
Greenwood	759	3,485	20,130	979,153	40,502	312,922
Howard		2,706	2,251	89,280	7,205	50,677
Jackson	1,936	6,053	41,388	2,305,240	84,995	844,801
Jefferson	4,459	12,526	91,004	4,218,363	172,187	1,001,762
Jewell		205	960	37,050	3,008	21,620
Johnson	4,364	13,725	129,435	4,545,235	210,167	1,195,923
Labette		9,979	39,029	1,664,181	92,141	449,369
Leavenworth	12,606	32,472	106,221	5,131,173	148,581	1,395,865
Lincoln		516	1,226	68,050	4,931	4,710
Linn	6,336	12,198	89,557	3,547,218	154,509	944,887
Lyon	3,197	8,016	19,163	1,271,622	55,518	324,045
Marion	74	767	3,201	182,650	13,479	105,527
Marshall	2,280	7,228	34,988	1,549,220	79,013	518,177
McPherson		917	3,129	169,499	119,778	37,231
Miami	4,980	11,729	95,138	3,965,724	143,810	871,316
Mitchell		498	33,322	102,355	19,282	5,131
Montgomery		7,613	18,743		32,364	240,261
Morris	770	2,218	7,821	415,496	22,460	144,818
Nemaha	2,436	7,296	40,416	1,956,530	112,877	539,341
Neosho		1,223	38,320	1,445,508	77,897	446,042
Ness		125				

UNITED STATES CENSUS — *Concluded.*

| County. | Population in 1860.... | Population in 1870.... | No. Acres of improved land.... | VALUE. | | |
				Of Farms	Of Farming Implements and Machinery....	Estimated value of all Farm productions, includ. betterm'ts and additions to stock....
Osage	1,113	7,631	28,649	$1,903,211	$106,895	$401,276
Ottawa...................		2,130	11,342	541,510	33,791	168,554
Pawnee		179				
Pottawatomie	1,529	7,888	31,642	1,883,120	107,908	746,095
Republic		1,290	11,180	334,200	19,401	131,500
Rice			8	1,800		
Riley.....................	1,124	5,104	26,076	1,614,165	83,216	
Rooks....................		45				461,340
Rush		75				
Saline....................		4,206	23,197	1,121,462	69,130	309,777
Sedgwick.................		1,096	3,422	259,374	2,137	144,051
Shawnee	3,513	13,035	47,512	4,415,410	176,062	983,160
Smith		66	407	25,200	875	9,600
Wabaunsee	1,023	3,373	325	963,008	62,825	219,465
Wallace		378				
Washington...............	333	3,970	9,781	413,490	26,054	165,751
Wilson...................	27	6,494	12,8J8	766,070	52,301	272,242
Woodson.................	1,488	3,827	10,026	485,170	20,960	149,700
Wyandotte...............	2,609	10,066	26,553	1,411,087	36,371	384,439
Total	107,204	362,307	1,920,610	$78,891,098	$4,202,272	$24,351,585

The increase per cent. in population of Kansas from 1860 to 1870 was 235.99. Maine and South Carolina increased less than one per cent. each in that decade. The average increase for all the States and Territories was 21.52 per cent.

JULY.—A book issued, called "Gazetteer and Directory of the State of Kansas: Containing Concise Descriptions of the Cities, Towns and Villages of the State, with the Names of Professional and Business Men. With a Map. Lawrence, Kansas: Blackburn & Co., Publishers. 1870." pp. 303. The historical sketch is written by Richard Cordley. Milton W. Reynolds writes the paper on "Kansas as a Field for Immigration." Jas. R. McClure Register at Junction City, writes a land article. The following list of newspapers is given:

Place.	Name of Paper.	Issue.	Publisher or Proprietor.
Abilene.................	Chronicle...................	Weekly	V. P. Wilson.
Alma...................	Herald....................	Weekly	Sellers & Fairfield.
Altoona................	Union	Weekly	Bowser & Brown.
Atchison...............	Champion and Press...	Daily and Weekly.	John A. Martin.
Atchison...............	Patriot	Daily and Weekly.	Nelson Abbott.
Baxter Springs......	Sentinel.................	Weekly	Lyons & Coulter.
Burlingame	Chronicle...................	Weekly	M. Marshall Murdock.
Burlington...........	Patriot ..	Weekly	A. D. Brown.
Chetopa...............	Advance	Weekly	Horner & Fitch.
Columbus.............	Workingman's Journ'l	Weekly	Printing Company.
Council Grove......	Advertiser	Weekly	Wallace H. Johnson.
Cottonwood Falls.	Banner....................	Weekly	Frank E. Smith.
Detroit	Western News	Weekly	A. W. Robinson.
Eldorado..............	Walnut Valley Times..	Weekly	Murdock & Danford.
Emporia..............	News	Weekly	Stotler & Williams.
Emporia..............	Tribune	Weekly	Main & Nixon.
Erie	Dispatch..................	Weekly	Kimball & Benton.
Eureka	Herald....................	Weekly	S. G. Mead.
Frankfort............	Our New Home..........	Weekly	J. Andersen.
Fort Scott............	Monitor	Daily and Weekly.	George A. Crawford.

LIST OF NEWSPAPERS—*Concluded.*

Place.	Name of Paper.	Issue.	Publisher or Proprietor.
Fort Scott............	Post	Daily and Weekly.	Schiller & Herrington.
Fredonia.............	Courier	Weekly	J. R. Jennings.
Garnett	Plaindealer	Weekly	D. E. Olney.
Girard	Press	Weekly	Warner & Wasser.
Hiawatha............	Sentinel	Weekly	David Downer.
Holton	Press	Weekly	A. W. Moore
Humboldt	Union	Weekly	W. T. McElroy.
Independence......	Pioneer	Weekly	E. R. Trask.
Irving.................	Recorder	Weekly	Crowther & Smith.
Junction City......	Union	Weekly	Geo. W. Martin.
Lawrence	{ Republican Journal... Western Home Jour...	Daily .... } Weekly .... }	Kalloch,Thach'r& Reynolds.
Lawrence	Kansas Tribune	Daily and Weekly.	John Speer.
Leavenworth	Bulletin....................	Daily and Weekly.	Wm. S. Burke.
Leavenworth	Commercial..............	Daily and Weekly.	Prescott & Hume.
Leavenworth	Evening Call.............	Daily	J. Clarke & Co.
Leavenworth	Freie Presse	Daily	J. M. Haeberlein.
Leavenworth	Kansas Farmer..........	Monthly	George T. Anthony.
Leavenworth	Times & Conservative..	Daily and Weekly.	Wilder & Sleeper.
Louisville............	Gazette	Weekly	P. McClosky.
Lyndon	Signal.......................	Weekly	Leslie J. Perry & Co.
Manhattan..........	Standard...................	Weekly	L. R. Elliott.
Medina	New Era...................	Weekly	Solomon Weaver.
Mound City.........	Sentinel	Weekly	Nat. G. Barter.
Neosho Falls........	Democrat	Weekly	J. B. Boyle.
Netawaka............	Herald......................	Weekly•.................	Frank H. Stout.
Olathe	Mirror	Weekly	McKee & Dempsey.
Olathe................	News Letter	Weekly	J. A. & H. F. Canutt.
Osage Mission......	Journal	Weekly	J. H. Scott.
Oskaloosa	Independent..............	Weekly	J. W. Roberts.
Oskaloosa............	Statesman	Weekly	Ben. R. Wilson.
Oswego	Register	Weekly	E. R. Trask.
Ottawa	Journal	Weekly	Patterson & Hand.
Paola..................	Advertiser	Weekly	W. M. Mitchell.
Paola..................	Republican................	Weekly	Basil M. Simpson.
Pleasanton	Press........................	Weekly	Lewis & Winfree.
Salina..................	Herald......................	Weekly	B. J. F. Hanna.
Seneca.................	Independent Press......	Weekly	G. W. Collings.
Seneca.................	Courier	Weekly	John P. Cone.
Topeka	Advertiser	Monthly	Mills & Smith.
Topeka	Commonwealth	Daily and Weekly.	Prouty, Davis & Crane.
Topeka	State Record..............	Daily and Weekly.	Baker & King.
Troy....................	Republican................	Weekly	C. G. Bridges.
Wamego	Valley	Weekly	T. W. Lowe & Co.
Washington	Observer...................	Weekly	J. J. Tallman.
Waterville...........	Telegraph	Weekly	Frank A. Root.
Wathena.............	Reporter...................	Weekly	Drenning & Holt.
White Cloud........	Chief	Weekly	Sol. Miller.
Wyandotte...........	Gazette.....................	Weekly	F. A. Kessler.

The following is copied from page 106:

"The Most Worshipful Grand Lodge of Ancient, Free and Accepted Masons of Kansas will meet in Atchison, on the third Wednesday in October, 1870. M. W. John H. Brown, Grand Master; R. W. E. T. Carr, Grand Secretary, both of Leavenworth.

"Most Excellent Grand Royal Arch Chapter of the State of Kansas meets in Atchison on the third Tuesday in October, 1870. M. E. Owen A. Bassett, Grand High Priest, Lawrence; R. E. E. T. Carr, Grand Secretary.

"The Grand Commandery of Knights Templar of the State of Kansas meets in annual conclave, in Atchison, on the third Monday in October, 1870. Sir William O. Gould, R. E. Grand Commander, Leavenworth; Sir E. T. Carr, Grand Recorder."

There is a Masonic Lodge at Iowa Point, five at Leavenworth, one at Wyandotte, Pleasant Ridge, Atchison, three at Lawrence, Junction City, two at Fort Scott, Ottumwa, Emporia, America City, Oskaloosa, Tecumseh, Manhattan, two at Topeka, Ottawa, Olathe, Circleville, Grasshopper Falls, Paris, Baldwin City, Osawatomie, High Prairie, Le Roy, Mapleton, Humboldt, Doniphan, Auburn, Mound City, Silver Lake, Hiawatha, Council

Grove, Paola, Iola, Seneca, DeSoto, Blooming Grove, Holton, Monticéllo, Garnett, Easton, Xenia, Monrovia, Petersburg, Perryville, Granada, Shawnee, Troy, Spring Hill, Coyville, Mount Pleasant, Timber Ridge, Salina, Twin Springs, Oswego, Wathena, Gardner, Burlington, Frankfort, Pardee, Salt Lake City, Baxter Springs, Huron, Chetopa, Augusta, Wamego, Erie, Neosho Rapids, White Cloud, Burlingame, Cottonwood Falls, New Albany, Neosho Falls, Eudora, Lindsay, Waterville, Centralia, Clinton, Winchester, Montana, Pleasanton, and North Topeka.

There are Chapters at Atchison, Leavenworth, Fort Scott, Lawrence, Topeka, Wyandotte, Ottawa, Grasshopper Falls, Oskaloosa, Olathe, Humboldt, Emporia, Manhattan, Oswego, Troy, Doniphan, and Chetopa.

There are Commanderies at Leavenworth, Atchison, Fort Scott, Lawrence, and Topeka.

The following is copied from pages 111, 112:

"INDEPENDENT ORDER OF ODD FELLOWS.—The Grand Lodge of this order was instituted at Tecumseh, June 2, 1858. It is a movable body, meeting annually on the second Tuesday in October, at the place selected at its previous session, and composed of its officers and duly elected representatives from the subordinate Lodges. The present basis of representation is one from each Lodge of seventy-five members or less, and one for each additional fifty or fraction. The present number of Lodges is forty-eight, and number of members, three thousand. The following list will show where these Lodges are located, and the nights of meeting:

Place of Meeting.	Name of Lodge.	No.	Night.	Names of D. P. G. M.
Topeka	Shawnee	1	Tuesday	C. O. Smith.
Leavenworth	Leavenworth,	2	Tuesday	Sam. F. Burdett.
Wyandotte	Summonduwot	3	Monday	Fred. Speck, M. D.
Lawrence	Lawrence	4	Tuesday	H. O. Sholes.
Atchison	Friendship	5	Tuesday	Wm. L. Challiss.
White Cloud	White Cloud	6		
Leavenworth	Germania	9	Thursday	George Walter.
Paola	Paola	11	Friday	D. B. Wilson.
Burlingame	Burlingame	14	Friday	H. Dubois.
Emporia	Union	15	Tuesday	John Bay.
Garnett	Garnett	16	Tuesday	J. L. Kircheval.
Manhattan	Manhattan	17	Thursday	Edgar Rogers.
Lawrence	Halcyon	18	Wednesday	James S. Crew.
Seneca	Seneca	19	Thursday	
Mound City	Magnolia	20	Saturday	E. P. Bunn.
Iola	Iola	21	Tuesday	W. S. Newberry.
Fort Scott	Fort Scott	22	Monday	W. A. Shannon.
Gardner	Gardner	23	Tuesday	V. R. Ellis.
Ottawa	Ottawa	24	Saturday	H. F. Sheldon.
Junction City	Frontier	25	Monday	Geo. W. Martin.
Pardee	Pardee	26	Monday	John Davidson.
Leavenworth	Metropolitan	27	Friday	James S. Crow.
Salina	Salina	28	Thursday	B. J. F. Hanna.
Burlington	Burlington	29	Tuesday	W. H. Hickcox.
Humboldt	Humboldt	30	Wednesday	J. C. Chambers.
Baldwin City	Baldwin City	31	Monday	L. J. Dallas.
Oskaloosa	Eagle	32	Tuesday	L. J. Trower.
Atchison	Schiller	33	Wednesday	Jacob Pohler.
Holton	Holton	34	Tuesday	A. W. Moore.
Barnesville	Samaritan	35	Wednesday	D. K. Nickerson.
Oswego	Oswego	36	Wednesday	M. Read.
Coyville	Wildey	37	Saturday	T. J. Hudson.
Troy	Troy	38	Tuesday	X. K. Stout.
Le Roy	Prairie	39	Tuesday	Abijah Jones.
Topeka	Topeka	40	Wednesday	A. Cannon.
Wathena	Phœnix	41	Wednesday	P. M. Sturges.
Eudora	Eudora	42	Saturday	F. Bernitz.

NAMES AND LOCATION OF LODGES — *Concluded.*

Place of Meeting.	Name of Lodge.	No.	Night.	Name of D. P. G. M.
Council Grove............	Council Grove...........	43	Saturday...........	Isaac Sharp.
Erie	Erie	44	Saturday...........	John Smith.
Perry......................	Hope.....................	45	Monday.............	David Rorick.
....	Neosho Rapids..........	46	....	———
Clinton....................	Clinton..................	47	....	———
Chetopa...................	Chetopa..................	48	....	———
Neosho Falls..............	Grove....................	49	....	J. F. Cooper.
Jacksonville..............	Jacksonville	50	....	———
Baxter Springs...........	Baxter Springs.........	51	....	———
Eureka	Eureka..................	52	....	———

"*Degree Lodges:* Lawrence, Kaw Valley, No. 1; Topeka, Capital City, No. 2.

"*Rebekah Degree Lodges:* Topeka, Rebekah Degree Lodge, No. 1; Fort Scott, Rebekah, Degree Lodge, No. 2; Holton, Rebekah Degree Lodge, No. 3.

"*Grand Lodge:* The officers of the Grand Lodge for 1869-70 are: H. J. Canniff, M. W. Grand Master, Prairie City; John Pipher, R. W. D. Grand Master, Manhattan; D. B. McDougall, R. W. Grand Warden, Burlingame; Samuel F. Burdett, R. W. Grand Secretary, Leavenworth; James S. Crow, R. W. Grand Treasurer, Leavenworth; C. A. Logan, Leavenworth, Levi Empie, Burlingame, Representatives to G. L. U. S. The session of 1870 will be held at Fort Scott, on Tuesday, October 11.

"*Grand Encampment:* This body was organized October 9, 1866, with five subordinate Encampments, since which time they have increased to twelve. It is composed of its officers and duly-elected representatives, upon a similar basis to that of the Grand Lodge. It meets annually, at the same time and place as the Grand Lodge. The subordinate Lodges are located as follows: Leavenworth, Far West, No. 1; Leavenworth, Schiller, No. 2 (German); Topeka, Shawnee, No. 3; Lawrence, Mount Oread, No. 4; Burlingame, Osage, No. 5; Atchison, Hesperian, No. 6; Fort Scott, Rising Star, No. 7; Oskaloosa, Hebron, No. 8; Wyandotte, Wyandotte, No. 9; Ottawa, Lincoln, No. 10; Garnett, Wildey, No. 11; Junction City, Jerusalem, No. 12. The present number of members is about 450."

JULY.—The Oskaloosa Independent says: "The first type of the Kansas Freeman, at Topeka, was set on the open prairie, under a June sun."

JULY 1.—Salina ships beef to New York, in refrigerator cars.

JULY 4.—Large meeting at Ladore, of settlers on the Osage Lands.

JULY 7.—Death of Judge Josiah Miller, at Lawrence. He was a native of South Carolina, came here in August, 1854, and was an ardent Free-State man. In January, 1855, he established the "Free State" newspaper; it was destroyed May 21st, 1856.

JULY.—The cash value of photographed letters is determined.

—Geo. T. Anthony, U. S. Collector, travels over the State, in search of the "dead, insolvent, bankrupt, and absconded."

—Perry Fuller is living with Colonel E. P. Boudinot, in the Indian Territory, near Chetopa.

—A new College is building, at St. Mary's Mission.

JULY 7.—Congress establishes the Republican Land District.

JULY 12.—Meeting of the Presbyterian Synod, at Topeka.

—W. A. Shannon appointed Receiver of the Land Office at Augusta, and Thos. J. Sternberg Receiver of the Republican Land District.

JULY 15.—Congress provides for the removal of the Osage Indians, and the sale of their land.

JULY 20.—The Santa Fe R. R. completed to Emporia.

—Labor Union Convention, at Leavenworth. Amos Sanford and F. P.

Baker were elected delegates to the National Labor Congress. W. V. Barr, President; B. F. Sylvis, Secretary; H. B. Carter, Treasurer; Executive Committee, W. R. Laughlin, John C. Ketcheson, A. R. Johnson, Hugh Cameron, and S. Markham.

JULY 30.—Iowa editors visit Leavenworth and Topeka.

—Coal mining at Burlingame.

AUGUST.—"Kansas, as She Is," is the name of a pamphlet of 64 pages, printed in Lawrence by the "Kansas Publishing Company." The object of the book is to promote immigration.

AUGUST 1.—Judge David P. Lowe, of Fort Scott, addresses the "Fifteenth Amendment" Convention, at Leavenworth. Senator Revels is present.

AUGUST 9.—The Republican Committee, P. P. Elder, Chairman, and M. M. Murdock, Secretary, meets at Lawrence. State Convention to be held September 8th.

—A. J. and W. T. Lea issue the Independent, at Columbus.

—Mount St. Mary's Academy, near Leavenworth, completed.

AUGUST 13.—Senator E. G. Ross exposes the Black Bob Land Fraud, in the Topeka Record.

AUGUST.—Killing of John Sanderson, a notorious outlaw, by a mob, in Davis county. Three associates sent to the penitentiary, and several others driven out of the country.

AUGUST 19.—Railroad completed from Olathe to Ottawa.

AUGUST 27.—Colonel A. S. Johnson removes from Johnson county (which was named for his father) to Topeka. He is the first white male born in Kansas.

—E. G. Mains starts the Arkansas City Traveller.

SEPTEMBER 5.—State Natural History Society, at Lawrence. *Officers elected:* President, John Fraser; Vice President, B. F. Mudge; Secretary, J. D. Parker; Treasurer, F. H. Snow; Curators, B. F. Mudge and F. H. Snow.

—In the fall, Leslie J. Perry and A. A. Putnam started the Augusta Crescent. J. B. Davis bought the paper, and changed the name to Republican. U. A. Albin bought the office, and removed it to McPherson county.

SEPTEMBER 8.—Republican State Convention, at Topeka. Called to order by P. P. Elder. James D. Snoddy received 101 votes for temporary Chairman, and John A. Martin 76. J. B. Johnson, of Jefferson county, was elected temporary Secretary. On motion of Geo. A. Crawford, it was voted to make nominations by a viva voce vote. The temporary were made the permanent officers.

Informal ballot for Congressman: Sidney Clarke 77, D. P. Lowe 58, M. S. Adams 18, John Ritchie 6, Jacob Stotler 15, D. R. Anthony 12, W. P. Borland 1, S. J. Crawford 1, Thos. Moonlight 10.

First formal ballot: D. P. Lowe 84, Sidney Clarke 77, M. S. Adams 17, J. Stotler 3, T. Moonlight 8, D. R. Anthony 9. All the opponents of Clarke changed to Lowe, and the nomination was made unanimous.

The Convention reassembled on the 9th.

Ballot for Governor: James M. Harvey 125, D. R. Anthony 45, Thos. A. Osborn 24.

Ballot for Lieutenant Governor: P. P. Elder 92, E. C. Niccolls 18, David Gordon 48, J. C. Carpenter 35. P. P. Elder's nomination made unanimous.

Ballot for Associate Justice: David J. Brewer 113, James Rogers 22, Mr. Beale 5, W. W. Nevison 13, David Brockway 6, Judge Safford 30.

Ballot for Secretary of State: W. H. Smallwood 139, Wm. M. Twine 24, Thos. Moonlight 13.

Alois Thoman was unanimously nominated for Auditor.

Ballot for Treasurer: Josiah E. Hayes 89, George Graham 48, John Francis 34.

Ballot for Attorney General: A. L. Williams 70, J. B. Johnson 55, H. W. Cook 9, J. L. Stillwell 12.

H. D. McCarty was unanimously nominated for Superintendent of Public Instruction.

State Central Committee: D. R. Anthony, John A. Martin, H. T. Beman, Elijah Sells, Jacob Stotler, S. A. Manlove, John W. Scott, B. J. F. Hanna, T. B. Murdock, H. W. Cook, J. R. Hallowell, W. D. Mathews, W. R. McLain, David Gordon.

John A. Martin reported the following platform:

"1. The Union Republican party of Kansas, in delegate convention assembled, reaffirms its adherence to, and its faith in, the principles of universal liberty, justice and humanity, for which it has during ten years past zealously and successfully battled, and upon which it has now securely and forever established the foundations of the Government.

"2. It points with pride to a career of victory unsullied by a single act of national cowardice, wrong, or inhumanity. It has, during its administration of public affairs, crushed the most gigantic rebellion that ever assailed the Government, broken the shackles of a race long enslaved, and elevated them to the dignity and privileges of citizenship; enacted and put into operation a beneficent homestead law; originated and perfected a splendid system of highways across the continent; secured the recognition of the doctrine of expatriation; and in all things proved itself equal to the sacred trusts committed to its hands.

"3. The Republican party, with such a record, needs to make no flaunting promises of future fidelity to the great principles upon which its organization is based. But this convention of delegates, representing the Republicans of Kansas, takes occasion to express the conviction and purpose of the party: First, To maintain and defend the fruits of its victory in the field; namely, the unity of the republic, the abolition of slavery, the enfranchisement of the colored race, and equal rights for all. Second, To protect and preserve the fruits of its victory in legislation; namely, the homestead law in its whole letter and spirit, the law of expatriation, and a wholesome system of public improvements.

"4. In the future, as in the past, the Republican party will continue to advocate the measures which will promote economy, national honesty, domestic concord, and friendly relations with foreign powers — to the end that we may have a government of laws, and not of men.

"5. We cordially endorse the patriotic, honest, and economical administration of President Grant, and hail with satisfaction the rapid reduction of the national debt, which its faithful collection of public revenues and honest application of them brought about.

"6. In the struggle now going on in Europe our sympathies are heartily with the German people. Their triumph is a victory of liberal principles. We rejoice in the overthrow of the Napoleon dynasty, and earnestly pray that the war may result in the organization and permanent establishment of a republican form of government in France and other European nations.

"7. That the Republican party stands pledged to remove all disqualifications and restrictions imposed upon the late Rebels, in the same measure as the spirit of disloyalty may die out, and may be consistent with the safety of the loyal people.

"8. In the distribution of public lands and Indian reserves, we demand the full protection of the rights of settlers, and the reservation of the 16th and 36th sections to which the State is entitled for educational purposes. Wholesale grants of land to speculators and foreign corporations are unfavorable to the interests of the community, and inconsistent with the objects for which the national domain should be distributed. We especially condemn the policy of disposing of Indian reservations to railroad or land monopolies, and insist that such lands be immediately opened to actual settlement, at not more than one dollar and twenty-five cents per acre."

The following resolution, offered by John T. Voss, of Crawford county, was unanimously adopted:

"Resolved, That the policy of granting subsidies of public lands to capitalists and monopolies is condemned, and that we repudiate the action of certain of our Republican Representatives in Congress in the sale of the Cherokee Neutral Lands."

D. R. Anthony was made Chairman and Jacob Stotler Secretary of the State Committee.

SEPTEMBER 14.—Emporia celebrates the opening of the Santa Fe road.

SEPTEMBER 15.—Old settlers' meeting at Lawrence. *President:* Charles Robinson. *Vice President:* John A. Wakefield. *Secretary:* Joseph Savage. Speeches by William A. Phillips, Charles H. Lovejoy, Dan. Horne, S. C. Pomeroy, Rev. E. Nute, James F. Legate, D. R. Anthony, John Speer, J. B. Abbott, Captain Bickerton, S. O. Thacher, and S. N. Simpson. All united in singing the anthem, "John Brown."

SEPTEMBER 15.—Democratic State Convention, at Topeka. Called to order by Hugh S. Walsh. Isaac Sharp temporary Chairman, and C. C. Duncan Secretary.

Committee on Credentials: R. V. Flora, Wm. Evington, G. W. Miller, Dr. Bowen, T. C. Irwin, H. D. Wilson, J. D. Rush, Daniel Montfort, J. H. Castello, W. H. Brady, J. D. O'Conner.

Committee on Platform: Thomas P. Fenlon, J. L. Berry, H. J. Strickler, George A. Reynolds, J. R. Gates, S. A. Williams, O. Thurston, T. B. Bickersham, A. White, Charles S. Glick, M. V. B. Bennett.

Committee on Organization: W. N. Allen, T. P. Fenlon, Wm. Mitchell, Dr. Couch.

Officers of Convention: President, P. G. Parker, of Johnson; Vice Presidents, Isaac E. Eaton of Leavenworth, W. P. Hetherington of Atchison, S. C. Gephart of Jefferson, A. J. Allen of Franklin, H. T. Wilson of Bourbon, G. A. Bowlus of Allen, J. R. McClure of Davis; Secretaries, George F. Prescott of Leavenworth, Nelson Abbott of Atchison, J. L. Goode of Bourbon, Ely Moore of Douglas.

The Convention adopted the following platform:

"The Democratic party of Kansas submits to the voters of the State the following declaration of principles, to which it invites their earnest attention and support:

"The preservation of the rights of the States as members of the Federal Union intact.

"The speedy restoration of all the States to perfect equality and self-government.

"The immediate removal of all political disabilities incurred by citizens in the late war.

"The recognition of all amendments to the Constitution as of the same binding force as the original text; but as the autocratic method of ratifying the recent amendments by a partisan majority excited the alarm of all good citizens, it shall hereafter be understood as the law of the land that the Constitution of the United States is not to be

34

touched by any political party until the people shall have had a full, fair and honest hearing on the proposed change.

"That the substitution of treasury notes for the national bank currency is a measure of imperative necessity and economy.

"That as the confidence in the national bank currency only exists by reason of the Government bonds which are deposited as their security, it is an unnecessary extravagance to pay eighteen millions of gold per annum to those institutions for doing what might be better done by the Government itself.

"That the one hundred and forty-four millions of gold, equal to two hundred millions in currency, which has been paid to them in the last eight years, would have been better applied in payment of the national debt than paid to the bonded interests in these banks, which have escaped taxation, and taxation alike upon all species of property, whether gold, greenbacks, national currency, or bonds.

"Reduction, if not abolition, of the hateful and oppressive internal revenue tax.

"A thorough reform, and strict economy, in all the branches of the Government.

"Payment of the national debt in accordance with the law authorizing its creation. And we demand a repeal of the act of Congress providing for the payment of the Five-Twenties in coin.

"A national currency, secure against the effect of speculation, and distributed in a just ratio between the States.

"That, as a large part of the Territorial domain has been given away to railroad and other monopolies, and as large land estates are the evil and impoverishment of a nation, we oppose any further squandering of public lands; and we would reserve them for settlers, in good faith, and as a means of legitimate reward to the Government.

"We condemn, as dangerous to liberty, and subversive of the Constitution, the late military interference by the Federal administration in the State election in North Carolina. If such action be permitted to go unchallenged in one State, it is an invitation for a like outrage in another; a concession that the elective franchise — the basis of our Government — may, at the pleasure of the President, be controlled by the power of the bayonet.

"We welcome the birth of a new Republic in Europe, and extend sympathy to any people aspiring to or struggling for liberty and self-government; and we trust that the present struggle in Europe will result in the downfall of imperialism, and the establishment of a republican government.

"That the law of self-preservation — the first dictate of reason — the interests of the laboring and industrial class, demand that Chinese laborers shall not be colonized into this country.

"That no advantage that may seem to be in view from their cheap labor, almost of a servile character, will justify the grave consequences to be fairly apprehended from a systematic introduction of these people to our shores.

"That we deem the sessions of the Legislature too long and too expensive, producing in their legal enactments but poor equivalent for the taxes necessary to pay for their support; and in the name of a people taxed almost beyond endurance, we demand short sessions, small appropriations, and healthy constitutional legislation; and at the hands of all departments of the State Government, legislative, executive and judicial, the prompt, efficient and honest discharge of their duties.

"That the general history of the Radical administration in this State is one of fraud, corruption and imbecility; a disgrace and blot upon the fair fame of our gallant and heroic people; the journals of our Legislative Assembly are stained with the deeds of impeachments, of mislegislation, on account of bribery, corruption and malfeasance in office; and the evil has become so grievous that it behooves the people in their majesty to throw off the shackles that corrupt politicians have placed on them, and elect honest and competent men to office.

"That we condemn, as not only unauthorized by, but in direct violation of, the Federal and State Constitution, the quartering of United States troops upon the people of Cherokee and Crawford and other counties, in the interest of the person or persons claiming to own the lands in that vicinity. The question was and is a legal one, to be finally decided by the courts having jurisdiction thereon; and the quartering of Federal troops upon the settlers is not only an outrage upon their rights, but a gross violation of Federal and State supreme law, and a disgrace and shame upon the authorities of the State, who have thus invoked this unlawful and dangerous agency.

"*Resolved,* That we are in favor of a tariff for revenue only; and we demand that the burdens of taxation shall be fairly and equally adjusted. Recognizing labor as the foundation and source of our national prosperity, it is both the duty and interest of the Government to foster and protect it, and that no adjustment to that end can be made without striking from the statute books the present unjust and odious tariff laws, a system of taxation based upon favoritism, and which has destroyed American commerce and oppressed the people of the great agricultural regions; which has compelled the many to pay tribute to the few, and which has built up monopolies that control, not only every American market, but also the legislation of Congress; and we demand that the prime articles of necessity, such as tea, coffee, sugar, salt, and those fabrics which constitute the wearing apparel of the workingman and his family, shall be placed upon the free list.

"*Resolved,* That the legislation of the dominant party, by which the bondholder, 'who speculated in the blood of the soldier,' receives gold, and the soldier who shed his blood to preserve the Republic, his widow and orphans, receive greenbacks, is an unjust discrimination; and that we demand such legislation as will make no distinction between the creditors of the Government.

"*Resolved,* That the brave man's blood is worth more than the rich man's money, and that there should be but one currency for the rich and the poor, the bondholder and soldier; and that, if favors should be extended, they are due to the brave man who periled his life for our preservation, the widows and orphans of our dead heroes, and not the speculator.

"*Resolved,* That this Convention invite the fellowship and co-operation of earnest and good men, of all parties, to unite with us in the election of the nominees now put forward by this Convention, upon the platform submitted.

"*Resolved,* That the Democratic party recognize the necessity of organization among the laboring classes and their friends, as a means of their self-protection against the encroachments of capital, and that the 'Labor Union,' so called, have its largest sympathy; and we respectfully invite the attention of that organization and its members to the efforts of the Democratic party in behalf of the laboring classes, and earnestly desire and request their co-operation with us in the use of every means to foster and advance the best interests of the laboring classes."

For Secretary of State: Chas. C. Duncan, of Pottawatomie, received 130 votes; John M. Giffen, of Johnson, 10.

Hardin McMahon, of Coffey, unanimously nominated for Auditor.

For Treasurer: S. C. Gephart, of Jefferson, 119; A. C. Snell, of Davis, 22.

A. W. Rucker, of Cherokee, unanimously nominated for Attorney General, and Thomas S. Murray, of Douglas, for Superintendent of Public Instruction; Robt. M. Ruggles, of Lyon, for Associate Justice; R. Cole Foster, of Leavenworth, for Congress; and Isaac Sharp, of Morris, for Governor.

State Committee: Thos. P. Fenlon, H. Miles Moore, Geo. W. Glick, John Martin, S. G. Stoughton, Ellis Lewis, Samuel A. Williams, O. P. Houghawout, H. L. Hunt, P. G. Parker, M. V. B. Bennett.

SEPTEMBER 22.—Workingmen's State Convention, at Topeka. President, C. O. Smith; Vice Presidents, Douglas of Cherokee, Moore of Nemaha, and Pollock of Leavenworth; Secretaries, A. Sanford and B. F. Sylvis. The platform endorses the platform of the National Labor Reform party; demands that all acts of the Legislature shall be adopted by a popular vote before they become laws; favors exempting $1,000, instead of $200, from taxation; honest men for office; no treaty with Indians without an act of Congress; each human being born with a natural right to land; favors Republics in Europe; asks for the removal of political disabilities; condemns James M. Harvey, and his Neutral Land policy; sympathizes with the Black Bob and all other settlers, who are struggling for their rights.

Ballot for Candidate for Congress: John C. Vaughan 13, G. T. Pierce 5,

Geo. H. Hoyt 3. Col. Vaughan was nominated, but declined, and Hon. Amos Sanford was nominated. The other nominations, as follows: *Governor*, W. R. Laughlin; *Lieut. Governor*, T. Moore, of Nemaha; *Secretary of State*, G. T. Pierce; *Auditor*, W. C. Fowler, of Jefferson; *Treasurer*, T. S. Slaughter, of Johnson; *Superintendent of Public Instruction*, H. D. McCarty; *Attorney General*, Geo. H. Hoyt; *Associate Justice*, G. M. Harrison, of Montgomery. *State Committee:* J. S. Vincent of Cherokee, H. Cameron of Douglas, B. F. Sylvis of Leavenworth, Jos. Briggs of Franklin, L. W. Sargent of Nemaha, Isaac Fowler of Jefferson, H. H. Tillman of Bourbon, T. S. Slaughter of Johnson, E. Keller of Crawford, and C. O. Smith of Shawnee.

SEPTEMBER 21.—Jos. P. Root, of Wyandotte, appointed Minister to Chili.

SEPTEMBER 25.—The Democratic Standard started, at Lawrence.

SEPTEMBER 27.—State Fair at Ft. Scott. Annual Address by Senator Ross.

SEPTEMBER 30.—Election on the State Fair grounds, at Fort Scott, of the following officers of the State Agricultural Society: President, I. S. Kalloch, of Douglas; Vice President, O. E. Learnard, of Douglas; Secretary, H. J. Strickler, of Shawnee; Superintendent, Alfred Gray. *Executive Committee:* Alfred Gray, of Wyandotte; James I. Larimer, of Leavenworth; S. T. Kelsey, of Franklin; J. N. Insley, of Jefferson; J. W. Scott, of Allen; N. A. Adams, of Riley; E. S. Niccolls, of Anderson; Andrew Wilson, of Jefferson; John Inlow, of Johnson.

OCTOBER.—Emporia is building two large boarding-houses for the use of the students of the Normal School.

OCTOBER 8.—Horace Greeley lectures in Union Hall, Topeka. He also spoke in Lawrence.

—The candidates of the Labor Reform party withdraw. Mr. Sanford supports R. C. Foster.

OCTOBER 12.—Grand Lodge of Odd Fellows in session at Fort Scott.

OCTOBER 18.—The Kansas Pacific gives an excursion to Denver to Kansas editors.

—The New York Tribune publishes a letter from Mr. Greeley, dated Topeka, October 9th, in which he says:

"Settlers are pouring into eastern Kansas by car-loads, wagon-loads, horse-loads, daily, because of the fertility of her soil, the geniality of her climate, her admirable diversity of prairie and timber, the abundance of her living streams, and the marvellous facility wherewith homesteads may here be created. . . . . Having exposed freely the errors, as I see them, of all parties, I hardly need restate that Kansas, in spite of them all, is going ahead magnificently; and I predict that the child is born who will see her fifth if not fourth in population and production among the States of our Union."

OCTOBER 18.—The Grand Lodge of Good Templars meets at Lawrence.

OCTOBER 19.—The Grand Lodge of Masons meets at Atchison.

OCTOBER 20.—James W. Steele "takes some stock" in the State Record Company.

OCTOBER 26.—Iola celebrates the arrival of the L. L. G. & R. R.

OCTOBER 27.—Berry and Campbell start the Humboldt Statesman. It died in May, 1872.

NOVEMBER 1.—Great freshet all over the State. The streams reported higher than at any time since 1858.

—Isaac Sharp starts the Council Grove Democrat.

NOVEMBER 2.—The Emporia News issues a Daily.

NOVEMBER 4.—Senator Pomeroy writes from Muscotah to Joseph Savage, of his historical article in the New York Ledger, published in October, that it was written by a reporter for that paper, "as I am told." "I never saw it until it appeared, printed, in the Ledger."

NOVEMBER 8.—Annual election.

VOTE FOR GOVERNOR, LIEUT. GOVERNOR, AND SECRETARY OF STATE.

Counties.	GOVERNOR.			LIEUT. GOVERNOR.			SECRETARY OF STATE.		
	Jas. M. Harvey	Isaac Sharp	W. R. Laughlin	P. P. Elder	A. J. Allen	T. Moore	William H. Smallwood	C. C. Duncan	Geo. T. Pierce
Allen	913	334	....	909	335	....	913	335	......
Anderson	721	156	....	705	164	....	720	164	......
Atchison	1,292	911	....	1,290	910	....	1,288	914	......
Bourbon	1,252	784	....	1,276	768	....	1,282	767	......
Brown	612	191	....	611	192	....	608	193	......
Butler	925	228	....	926	227	....	927	227	......
Chase	194	50	....	189	49	....	189	49	......
Clay	438	30	....	446	21	....	416	36	......
Crawford	346	884	....	375	870	....	385	873	......
Cherokee	385	1,272	....	418	298	950	427	293	951
Coffey	824	301	....	819	303	....	782	301	......
Cloud	311	80	....	313	80	....	315	80	......
Cowley	255	92	....	254	88	....	254	94	......
Davis	520	259	....	489	286	....	483	292	......
Dickinson	327	180	....	323	180	....	324	180	......
Doniphan	1,339	674	....	1,339	678	....	1,322	675	......
Douglas	2,705	733	....	2,698	736	....	2,709	738	......
Ellis	109	312	....	105	313	....	104	313	......
Ellsworth	182	48	....	183	48	....	183	14	......
Franklin	1,105	343	....	1,049	391	13	1,105	366	16
Greenwood	320	101	....	317	105	....	319	104	......
Howard	505	110	....	500	115	....	511	109	......
Jackson	576	329	....	579	330	....	579	330	......
Jefferson	1,338	862	....	1,331	789	....	1,331	867	......
Johnson	1,472	749	....	1,476	746	....	1,484	738	......
Jewell	123	....	....	124	....	....	113		......
Labette	1,027	650	....	1,035	641	....	1,049	645	......
Leavenworth	2,625	2,076	....	2,633	2,080	....	2,635	2,072	......
Linn	1,291	295	....	1,288	296	....	1,291	297	......
Lyon	1,284	272	....	1,283	270	....	1,293	270	......
Lincoln	150	5	....	151	4	....	150	5	......
Marion	89	89	....	82	94	....	82	93	......
Marshall	1,028	384	....	1,020	387	....	1,022	387	......
Miami	1,057	562	....	1,048	564	....	1,059	561	......
Mitchell	120	20	....	107	35	....	101	39	......
Morris	243	261	....	262	245	....	261	246	......
Montgomery	868	688	97	889	680	89	895	678	85
McPherson	197	1	....	197	1	....	197	1	......
Nemaha	679	410	....	691	396	....	688	405	......
Neosho	709	1,292	11	823	1,246	....	873	1,222	......
Osage	1,608	317	....	1,609	315	....	1,615	313	......
Ottawa	395	2	....	391	2	....	394	2	......
Pottawatomie	632	521	....	636	519	....	631	524	......
Republic	316	9	....	317	9	....	316	9	......
Riley	693	146	....	690	151	....	684	158	......
Shawnee	1,689	440	....	1,694	438	....	1,702	445	......
Saline	819	189	....	809	189	....	809	187	......
Sedgwick	377	208	....	375	205	....	372	206	......
Wabaunsee	461	57	....	474	54	....	474	54	......
Wallace	34	97	....	32	96	....	33	99	......
Washington	882	152	....	882	152	....	883	150	......
Wilson	942	390	....	936	370	....	940	392	......
Woodson	459	190	....	460	189	....	461	190	......
Wyandotte	904	760	....	891	772	....	890	773	......
Total	40,666	20,469	108	40,749	19,422	1,052	40,873	19,475	1052

VOTE FOR AUDITOR, TREASURER, AND ATTORNEY GENERAL.

Counties.	AUDITOR.			TREASURER.			ATTORNEY GENERAL.		
	A. Thoman.	Hardin McMahon.	W. C. Fowler.	J. E. Hayes.	S. C. Gephart.	T. S. Slaughter.	A. L. Williams.	A. W. Rucker.	G. H. Hoyt.
Allen	913	335	....	913	335	......	912	336	......
Anderson	724	157	....	723	161	......	718	165	......
Atchison	1,286	914	....	1,283	918	......	1,285	918	......
Bourbon	1,213	765	....	1,282	765	......	1,280	766	......
Brown	611	192	....	611	192	......	609	192	......
Butler	907	227	....	925	228	......	918	227	......
Chase	188	50	....	190	50	......	187	50	......
Clay	447	35	....	447	221	......	447	21	......
Crawford	398	856	....	383	872	......	391	747	......
Cherokee	427	297	942	426	1,232	......	416	1,085	......
Coffey	800	318	....	823	300	......	819	300	......
Cloud	313	80	....	313	80	......	314	79	......
Cowley	254	94	....	254	94	......	274	94	......
Davis	490	287	....	483	294	......	485	292	......
Dickinson	324	180	....	323	180	......	323	180	......
Doniphan	1,340	679	....	1,339	680	......	1,341	678	......
Douglas	2,721	717	....	2,525	721	......	2,710	739	......
Ellis	105	312	....	104	312	......	104	313	......
Ellsworth	182	14	....	183	14	......	183	14	......
Franklin	1,116	364	10	1,110	365	11	1,109	365	......
Greenwood	321	103	....	320	103	......	320	103	......
Howard	507	110	....	500	110	......	509	110	......
Jackson	579	330	....	579	330	......	576	330	......
Jefferson	1,334	867	....	1,235	930	......	1,297	871	......
Johnson	1,469	745	....	1,554	619	......	1,483	736	......
Jewell	121	....	....	121	....	......	120	....	......
Labette	1,052	645	....	1,055	639	......	1,049	642	......
Leavenworth	2,639	2,067	....	2,634	2,077	......	2,629	2,076	......
Linn	1,291	296	....	1,292	295	......	1,292	295	......
Lyon	1,292	267	....	1,292	270	......	1,289	269	......
Lincoln	150	5	....	150	5	......	150	5	......
Marion	72	93	....	82	93	......	82	94	......
Marshall	1,023	387	....	1,022	387	......	1,022	387	......
Miami	1,057	562	....	1,058	562	......	1,056	563	......
Mitchell	104	35	....	98	34	......	100	35	......
Morris	263	244	....	263	244	......	263	244	......
Montgomery	898	677	84	911	675	74	896	675	77
McPherson	197	1	....	197	1	......	197	1	......
Nemaha	698	399	....	691	401	......	693	404	......
Neosho	882	1,213	....	863	1,214	......	880	1,213	......
Osage	1,614	314	....	1,611	314	......	1,614	314	......
Ottawa	394	1	....	394	2	......	319	2	......
Pottawatomie	637	517	....	636	519	......	635	520	......
Republic	316	9	....	316	9	......	316	9	......
Riley	690	152	....	688	153	......	690	150	......
Shawnee	1,732	408	....	1,698	440	......	1,745	351	......
Saline	809	189	....	810	188	......	810	188	......
Sedgwick	364	202	....	375	202	......	374	204	......
Wabaunsee	475	54	....	476	54	......	467	54	......
Wallace	33	96	....	33	96	......	33	96	......
Washington	881	152	....	871	167	......	880	152	......
Wilson	942	392	....	934	340	......	937	390	......
Woodson	462	189	....	460	190	......	461	189	......
Wyandotte	892	763	....	892	772	......	889	773	......
Total	40,949	19,362	1,036	40,651	20,449	85	40,898	20,006	77

VOTE FOR SUPERINTENDENT OF PUBLIC INSTRUCTION, ASSOCIATE JUSTICE, AND MEMBER OF CONGRESS.

Counties.	SUP. PUB. INS.		ASSOC. JUSTICE.		MEM. OF CON.	
	H. D. McCarty.	*Thomas S. Murray....*	*D. J. Brewer....*	*R. M. Ruggles.*	*D. P. Lowe....*	*R. C. Foster....*
Allen..................................	914	335	913	335	910	335
Anderson.............................	717	164	727	157	711	169
Atchison	1,287	918	1,287	923	1,286	914
Bourbon..............................	1,286	767	1,283	768	1,290	750
Brown	609	190	611	192	612	192
Butler	925	227	924	231	924	227
Chase	190	50	182	55	189	50
Clay	445	16	446	....	434	27
Crawford.............................	383	871	382	875	374	873
Cherokee.............................	1,370	293	1,368	297	424	1,256
Coffey.................................	827	299	810	311	823	301
Cloud	315	80	313	80	312	80
Cowley................................	254	94	254	94	254	94
Davis	487	289	484	293	482	293
Dickinson	324	180	323	180	321	181
Doniphan	1,342	676	1,337	676	1,340	680
Douglas	2,704	745	2,715	736	2,671	749
Ellis..................................	104	313	109	305	105	312
Ellsworth	183	14	....	....	182	48
Franklin	1,125	364	1,109	368	1,093	371
Greenwood	320	103	314	110	511	110
Howard	511	110	508	110	318	103
Jackson...............................	579	329	579	330	564	329
Jefferson	1,325	863	1,322	806	1,318	878
Johnson..............................	1,517	731	1,483	739	1,440	743
Jewell	119	....	122	....	113	10
Labette................................	1,051	636	1,046	646	1,027	650
Leavenworth	2,682	2,034	2,664	2,037	2,537	2,190
Linn	1,293	290	1,291	296	1,274	291
Lyon	1,296	268	1,265	295	1,282	275
Lincoln...............................	150	5	150	5	151	5
Marion................................	82	94	80	95	86	92
Marshall..............................	1,022	386	1,021	328	1,020	388
Miami.................................	1,058	561	1,057	562	1,064	555
Mitchell..............................	96	35	83	20	79	61
Morris.................................	263	244	263	243	266	242
Montgomery	974	681	897	678	883	770
McPherson	197	1	197	1	197	1
Nemaha...............................	687	404	693	405	687	408
Neosho................................	890	1,212	887	1,214	701	1,301
Osage.................................	1,615	313	1,608	321	1,005	319
Ottawa................................	395	2	394	2	382	2
Pottawatomie	637	518	635	519	629	523
Republic..............................	316	9	316	9	318	9
Riley	689	153	698	145	689	152
Shawnee..............................	1,700	415	1,698	441	1,646	457
Saline.................................	810	188	808	188	809	187
Sedgwick..............................	371	205	372	210	370	325
Wabaunsee	476	54	474	54	472	54
Wallace	33	87	34	92	33	100
Washington	882	155	880	151	878	151
Wilson	943	391	941	391	930	399
Woodson	460	190	465	190	456	196
Wyandotte	891	770	895	761	896	772
Total..............................	42,121	19,322	41,717	19,280	40,368	20,950

VOTE FOR JUDGES OF THE DISTRICT COURTS, FOR THE EIGHTH AND ELEVENTH JUDICIAL DISTRICTS.

District	Counties.	W. H. Canfield.	H. G. Webb.	W. M. Matheny.
8...	Clay	445		
	Cloud	395		
	Davis	772		
	Dickinson	326		
	Ellsworth	278		
	Ottawa	231		
	Riley	842		
	Jewell	92		
	Mitchell	42		
	Saline	902		
	McPherson	193		
	Republic	42		
11...	Crawford		859	372
	Cherokee		1,213	427
	Labette		1,358	325
	Montgomery		815	604
	Howard		347	51
	Total	4,560	4,592	1,779

VOTE FOR STATE SENATORS.

Dist.	Counties.	Names.	Votes.	Maj.	Dist.	Counties.	Names.	Votes.	Maj.
1	Doniphan	Sol. Miller	1787	1632	7	Riley	A. Simis, jr	148	
		I. Wood	1705	1550		Wash'gton.	A. Simis, jr	206	
		Adam Brenner	155		8	Shawnee	W.H.Fitzpatrick	1487	911
2	Atchison	John M. Price	1254	341		Shawnee	W. V. Barr	576	
		Joseph Logan	1201	208	9	Douglas	J. C. Vincent	2492	1669
		Samuel Hipple	993				L. J. Worden	1568	371
		W. Hetherington	913				Samuel A. Riggs	1197	
		George J. Martin.	16				W. M. Nace	823	
3	Leavenw'h	W. S. Van Doren.	2565	1165			S. K. Huson	650	
		H. C. Haas	2484	374	10	Johnson	G. M. Bowers	816	211
		Josiah Kellogg	2338	111			A. S. Devenney	605	
		B. B. Moore	2127				J. B. Marshall	494	
		Wm. Larimer	2110				D. G. Campbell	173	
		W. D. Mathews	1399				J. E. Corliss	127	
		G. W. Gardiner	41		11	Miami	E. H. Topping	965	315
		A. D. Moorehead.	3				W. D. Hoover	650	
4	Jefferson	G. W. Hogeboom.	1113	108			Johnson Clark	1	
		W. C. Garrett	1005		12	Wyandotte	George P. Nelson	881	128
		James H. Jones	67				Alfred Gray	753	
		Scattering	1				Scattering	7	
5	Brown	Joseph Cracraft	346	87	13	Linn	James D. Snoddy	849	175
	Nemaha	J. Cracraft	642				David Linton	674	
	Brown	W. B. Slosson	452				Scattering	8	
	Nemaha	W. B. Slosson	449		14	Bourbon	H. D. Moore	822	796
	Nemaha	A. W. Tracey	1			Crawford	H. D. Moore	836	
6	Jackson	James McLellan	459	153		Cherokee	H. D. Moore	1171	
	Shawnee	James McLellan	25			Bourbon	C. G. Hawley	1171	
	Pot'watmie	James McLellan	633			Crawford	C. G. Hawley	389	
	Jackson	C. G. Waynant	435			Cherokee	C. G. Hawley	473	
	Shawnee	C. G. Waynant	10			Bourbon	Scattering	38	
	Pot'watmie	C. G. Waynant	519			Cherokee	Scattering	2	
7	Cloud	Phil. Rockefeller.	217	568	15	Butler	E. S. Stover	912	1153
	Marshall	Phil. Rockefeller.	387			Chase	E. S. Stover	114	
	Republic	Phil. Rockefeller.	223			Cowley	E. S. Stover	322	
	Riley	Phil. Rockefeller.	303			Marion	E. S. Stover	75	
	Wash'gton.	Phil. Rockefeller.	743			Morris	E. S. Stover	278	
	Cloud	A. G. Barrett	80			Sedgwick	E. S. Stover	382	
	Marshall	A. G. Barrett	658			Butler	H. L. Hunt	245	
	Republic	A. G. Barrett	93			Chase	H. L. Hunt	107	
	Riley	A. G. Barrett	387			Cowley	H. L. Hunt	15	
	Wash'gton.	A. G. Barrett	87			Marion	H. L. Hunt	102	
	Cloud	A. Simis, jr	92			Morris	H. L. Hunt	227	
	Marshall	A. Simis, jr	347			Sedgwick	H. L. Hunt	234	
	Republic	A. Simis, jr	9			Butler	Scattering	1	

VOTE FOR STATE SENATORS—CONCLUDED.

Dist...	Counties.	Names.	Votes.	Maj...	Dist...	Counties.	Names.	Votes.	Maj...
16	Allen.........	H. C. Whitney...	373	1167	19	Greenwood	Jacob Stotler.....	319	1852
	Labette.....	H. C. Whitney...	903			Lyon.........	Jacob Stotler.....	1344	
	Montg'ery.	H. C. Whitney....	687			Lyon.........	T. G. Wibley.....	11	
	Neosho......	H. C. Whitney....	1791			Greenwood	O. Shannon.......	1	
	Woodson...	H. C. Whitney....	149			Lyon.........	Scattering.........	20	
	Wilson......	H. C. Whitney....	712		20	Clay.........	J. H. Prescott.....	445	2259
	Howard....	H. C. Whitney...	153			Davis	J. H. Prescott.....	429	
	Allen.........	J. H. Crichton...	773			Dickinson..	J. H. Prescott.....	274	
	Labette......	J. H. Crichton...	768			Ellis.........	J. H. Prescott.....	406	
	Montg'ery.	J. H. Crichton...	853			Ellsworth..	J. H. Prescott.....	159	
	Neosho......	J. H. Crichton...	327			Wallace....	J. H. Prescott.....	116	
	Woodson...	J. H. Crichton...	328			Ottawa.....	J. H. Prescott.....	254	
	Wilson	J. H. Crichton...	548			Saline......	J. H. Prescott.....	722	
	Howard....	J. H. Crichton...	4			Wabaunsee	J. H. Prescott.....	486	
	Allen.........	J. W. Richards ...	64			Mitchell....	J. H. Prescott.....	7	
	Montg'ery.	Scattering	2			McPherson	J. H. Prescott.....	185	
	Woodson...	Scattering	2			Clay.........	T. F. Hersey......	18	
	Howard	Scattering	1			Davis	T. F. Hersey......	347	
17	Anderson ..	T. C. Sears.........	542	612		Dickinson..	T. F. Hersey......	216	
	Franklin ..	T. C. Sears	838			Ellis.........	T. F. Hersey......	2	
	Anderson ..	Preston Bowen...	315			Ellsworth..	T. F. Hersey......	62	
	Franklin ...	Preston Bowen...	453			Ottawa.....	T. F. Hersey......	135	
	Franklin ...	A. M. Blair......	119			Saline......	T. F. Hersey......	257	
18	Coffey.......	M. M. Murdock...	490	283		Mitchell....	T. F. Hersey......	185	
	Osage	M. M. Murdock...	1066			McPherson	T. F. Hersey......	2	
	Coffey.......	Silas Fearl........	504			Ottawa.....	Z. Jackson........	1	
	Osage	Silas Fearl........	769			McPherson	Z. Jackson........	5	
	Coffey.......	Benjamin Wright	46			Wabaunsee	W. V. Barr	2	
	Osage	—— Rynerson.....	1			Saline......	—— Hersey......	1	

VOTE FOR MEMBERS OF THE HOUSE OF REPRESENTATIVES.

District...	Counties.	Names.	Votes....	Maj......	Vote of District...	Vote of County...
1	Doniphan..................	Thomas H. Moore	391	257		
		George Neal	134		525	
2	....	Abram Bennett	133	90		
		R. Morley.....................	43		176	
3	....	A. J. Mowry.....................	155	8		
		Edward Searcy.....................	147			
		J. G. Robertson..................	115			
		E. D. McClellan	36		453	
4	....	S. G. Whittaker.................	210	9		
		C. J. Jones...................	201		411	
5	....	J. B. Kennedy...................	176	10		
		Wm. M. Ege...................	166		342	1,907
6	Atchison....................	Thomas Murphy	422	123		
		J. H. Sawyer	299		721	
7	....	S. C. King.....................	210	15		
		J. M. Lindley..................	195		405	
8	....	Asa Barnes...................	235	122		
		John Parsons...................	113			
		J. Falkner.....................	3		351	
9	....	S. P. Griffin	236	103		
		G. A. Cushman	133		369	
10	....	Joseph C. Wilson................	204	115		
		J. G. McCannon...........	89		293	2,139
11	Brown.......................	J. F. Babbitt	225	24		
		Charles Knabb	201			
		A. G. Spear	132		558	
12	....	C. E. Parker...................	196	190		
		G. F. Irwin...................	6			
		O. Fountain...................	4		206	764
13	Nemaha....................	Richard Johnson................	310	13		
		W. W. Stewart	297			
		A. W. Stewart.................	2			
		M. Lanham	1		610	
14	....	A. Simons.....................	248	24		
		F. A. Stickle....................	224		472	1,082

VOTE FOR MEMBERS OF THE HOUSE OF REPRESENTATIVES—Continued.

District.	Counties.	Names.	Votes.....	Maj.....	Vote of District...	Vote of County....
15	Marshall.................	W. H. Smith	525	39		
		J. D. Wells...............................	486			
		Perry Hutchinson.....................	398		1,409	1,409
16	Washington..............	A. S. Wilson...........................	484	54		
		B. W. Williams........................	430			
		S. P. Botes............................	88		1,002	1,002
17	Pottawatomie	H. C. Linn	685	228		
		J. P. Shannon.........................	457		1,142	1,142
18	Jackson.....................	J. L. Williams.........................	369	127		
		D. H. Sutherland.....................	242		611	
79	....	C. R. Burns............................	148	23		
		G. W. McReynolds	125		273	884
19	Jefferson..................	John Willitts..........................	351	22		
		Henry Ogle	329		680	
20	....	William C. Butts	192	4		
		E. D. Hillyer..........................	188			
		J. B. Schaeffer.......................	56			
		C. S. Walter............................	4			
		W. J. Taylor............................	1		441	
21	....	Joseph L. Speer.......................	433	68		
		David Rorick...........................	368			
		J. C. Northrup	210			
		J. Rowrick	1		1,012	2,133
22	Leavenworth	Thomas J. Darling...................	397	18		
		J. B. Kitchen..........................	379		776	
23	....	R. D. Colley...........................	383	193		
		C. M. Williams	190		573	
24	....	J. F. Legate...........................	395	119		
		John Conover	276			
		Cole McCrea...........................	5		676	
25	....	T. P. Fenlon	408	181		
		F. Wellhouse...........................	227		635	
26	....	J. J. Crook.............................	158	7		
		J. F. Hathaway	151		309	
27	....	W. F. Ashby............................	132	24		
		J. W. Houts............................	108		240	
28	....	A. C. Williams........................	261	30		
		George M. Jewett....................	231		492	
29	....	Joseph Howell	254	21		
		J. F. Barrett...........................	233		487	
30	....	Levi Churchill.........................	210	11		
		John Johnson..........................	199			
		C. R. Jennison.........................	6		415	4,603
31	Wyandotte................	Rufus E. Cable........................	360	228		
		V. J. Lane..............................	132			
		William Richart.......................	107		599	
80	....	J. K. Hudson..........................	467	97		
		Alex. J. Campbell.....................	370			
		W. M. Donahoe........................	204		1,044	1,640
32	Johnson....................	William Williams.....................	360	33		
		H. L. Taylor	327			
		J. W. Haws............................	261		948	
33	....	D. B. Johnson.........................	464	273		
		B. F Hollenback.......................	191		655	
34	....	I. D. Clapp	252	37		
		T. E. Pearce...........................	215		467	2,070
35	Douglas	W. G. Melville.........................	729	98		
		H. S. Clarke...........................	631			
		Wilson Shannon, jr...................	226		1,586	
36	....	George W. Benson....................	159	28		
		R. L. Williams.........................	131			
		George A. Reynolds..................	75		365	
37	....	Elijah Sells............................	291	142		
		William Roe	149		440	
38	....	C. W. Ingle............................	193	106		
		O. G. Richards........................	87			
		Henry Fager...........................	57		337	
39	....	W. H. Peckham,......................	156	25		
		A. R. Greene	131			
		Charles Ingersoll.....................	25		312	
40	....	H. C. Fisher...........................	174	90		
		J. T. Mitchell	84			
		H. C. Hayden	33		291	3,331

VOTE FOR MEMBERS OF THE HOUSE OF REPRESENTATIVES—Continued.

District.	Counties.	Names	Votes	Maj.	Vote of District.	Vote of County.
41	Shawnee	G. W. Veale	1,194	916		
		George L. Young	2/8		1,472	
42		Jacob Haskell	208	11		
		E. Carriger	197			
		J. W. Brown	172		577	
70		George W. McReynolds	25	15		
		Charles R. Burns	10		35	2,384
43	Miami	H. B. Smith	211	120		
		B. F. Martin	91			
		Scattering	2		304	
44		B. F. Simpson	459	67		
		T. M. Carroll	392		851	
45		J. M. Carpenter	228	28		
		C. Eby	200		428	1,279
46	Linn	Scott Shattuck	119	48		
		J. S. Payne	71		190	
47		D. A. Crocker	190	76		
		J. Hodgson	114			
		William Taylor	2			
		Nelson Brown	1		307	
48		A. Barber	502	229		
		G. H. B. Hopkins	273			
		Henry Plumb	1		776	
49		S. M. Brice	221	206		
		D. Forrister	15			
		J. M. Die	1		237	1,510
50	Bourbon	W. H. Green	168	167		
		J. A. Tiffany	1		169	
51		C. W. Libby	158	24		
		L. Alsop	134		292	
52		C. S. Steele	202	84		
		E. Williams	118		320	
53		W. C. Webb	587	31		
		S. A. Williams	556		1,143	1,923
54	Allen	J. C. Redfield	554	119		
		H. D. Parsons	435		989	
55		J. F. Knowlton	125	41		
		L. Edmondson	84			
		N. F. Acres	42		251	1,240
56	Anderson	John G. Lindsay	272	13		
		Geo. W. Cooper	259		531	
57		Thomas Thompson	163	24		
		J. H. Whitford	139		302	833
58	Franklin	J. M. Luce	252	16		
		R. E. Jenness	236			
		Wm. Pennock	3		491	
59		H. P. Welsh	502	232		
		Wm. Pennock	270			
		W. H. Ambrose	169		941	1,432
60	Osage	Wm. Whistler	837	98		
		A. H. Jumper	739			
		Ellis Lewis	295			
		Scattering	14		1,885	1,885
61	Coffey	Charles Puffer	365	88		
		F. A. Atherly	277		642	
62		C. B. Butler	265	66		
		E. E. Coffin	199		464	1,106
63	Woodson	G. A. Bogart	248	58		
		Michael Redy	190			
		Thomas H. Davidson	184			
		Scattering	16		638	638
64	Lyon	R. M. Overstreet	529	108		
		C. V. Eskridge	421		950	
65		F. R. Page	179	32		
		W. F. Gould	147		326	
66		T. C. Hill	149	52		
		Charles Drake	97		246	1,522
67	Butler	L. S. Friend	687	227		
		T. H. Baker	410			
		John L. Pratt	47			
		D. M. Bronson	1		1,145	1,145
68	Chase	S. M. Wood	138	38		
		H. E. Snyder	100		238	238

VOTE FOR MEMBERS OF THE HOUSE OF REPRESENTATIVES—Concluded.

District.	Counties.	Names.	Votes...	Maj...	Vote of District.	Vote of County...
69	Morris	James Phinney	287	73		
		I. Hammond	214		501	501
70	Wabaunsee	J. H. Pinkerton	483	452		
		T. K. Thomson	31			
		H. L. Hunt	5			
		H. C. Tapscott	3		522	522
71	Davis	S. M. Strickler	432	88		
		John T. Price	344		776	766
72	Riley	J. M. Morris	351	50		
		W. S. Crump	182			
		M. D. Waters	301		834	834
73	Dickinson	Ephraim Warner	253	10		
		A. S. Davidson	243		496	496
74	Saline	J. H. Snead	466	9		
		R. H. Bishop	458			
		I. F. Clark	54			
		Scattering	2		981	981
75	Greenwood	W. F. Osborn	219	50		
		I. R. Phenis	169			
		Scattering	23		411	411
76	Marion	A. A. Moore	131	82		
		Thomas W. Bowm	49			
		Scattering	1		181	181
77	Wilson	A. McCartney	707	81		
		John Russell	626		1,333	1,333
78	Neosho	S. W. Irwin	892	296		
		John O'Grady	596			
		G. W. Gabriel	359			
		S. W. Foster	139			
		J. C. Blair	137			
		H. S. Dodd	53		2,176	2,176
81	Ottawa	Jacob Campbell	204	16		
		C. S. Wyeth	188			
		Scattering	1		393	393
82	Clay	J. B. McLaughlin	257	47		
		George Taylor	210		467	467
83	Cherokee	George W. Wood	1,159	690		
		J. R. Hallowell	469			
		J. D. O'Conner	21		1,649	1,649
84	Cloud	B. H. McEckron	238	81		
		Joseph Berry	157		395	395
85	Labette	J. M. Marsh	923	157		
		D. C. Hutchinson	766			
		Scattering	6		1,695	1,695
86	Crawford	S. J. Langdon	676	289		
		F. M. Mason	387			
		W. B. Bond	189		1,252	1,252
87	Ellis	H. H. Metcalf	293	169		
		H. J. McGaffigan	124		417	417
88	Ellsworth	A. W. Bayer	170	51		
		D. B. Long	119			
		M. Newton	7		296	296
89	Wallace	George E. Higday	115	55		
		Alonzo P. Wise	60		175	175
90	Republic	N. T. Van Natta	210	98		
		G. W. Johnson	112		322	322
...	Montgomery	T. L. Bond	863	170		
		Wm. H. Allison	693			
		W. H. Clark	94		1,650	1,650
...	Howard	James Reynolds	306	52		
		J. Y. Campbell	254			
		E. R. Cutler	95		655	655
...	Cowley	E. C. Manning	203	53		
		H. B. Norton	150		353	353
...	Sedgwick	J. M. Steele	376	65		
		E. W. Smith	311		687	687
...	McPherson	Olof Olson	117	35		
		J. M. Underwood	82		199	199
...	Lincoln	Ira C. Buzick	151	151	151	151
...	Mitchell	E. H. Cawker	134	80		
		John W. Rees	54			
		G. W. Stinson	46		234	234
...	Jewell	Felix T. Gandy	81	31		
		Dennis Taylor	50		131	131

The political standing of the Legislature is as follows:

	Senate.	House.	*Joint* Ballot.
Republicans	21	87	108
Democrats	2	8	10
Independents	2	3	5
Republican majority	17	76	93

NOVEMBER 8.—Chief Justice Chase writes to Samuel N. Wood: "I am glad to read such favorable accounts of the county with which you have done me the honor to associate my name."

NOVEMBER 8.—Rev. Pardee Butler visits Topeka.

—Excitement in Butler county; Vigilance Committee make arrests; Jack Corbin and Lewis Booth were hung; James Smith shot and killed. On the night of December 2, Mike Drea, Wm. G. Quimby, Dr. Morris, and his son, Aleck Morris, were hung, near Douglas. They were horse thieves and murderers. Adjutant General Whittaker went to Eldorado, with arms, and ordered the militia of the county to be called out, but afterwards countermanded the order.

NOVEMBER 10.—Conference of the United Brethren, at Lecompton.

NOVEMBER 22.—Railroad celebration at Humboldt.

NOVEMBER 24.—The Germans of Kansas collect and send to the Fatherland, $5,762.25, for the relief of sick and wounded soldiers.

NOVEMBER 30.—Expenditures of the State for the year:

Governor's Department	$5,009 80	Normal School	10,398 67
Secretary's Department	10,849 70	Capitol Building	23,598 52
Auditor's Department	4,312 50	Penitentiary	35,999 32
Treasurer's Department	3,050 00	Sheriffs conveying prisoners	2,838 05
Attorney General	1,181 00	Horticultural Society	291 75
Sup't of Public Instruction	2,699 34	Agricultural Society	2,500 00
Adjutant General	1,498 00	Sale of Agricult'l College lands,	
Judiciary	33,972 26	I. T. Goodnow	4,350 71
Legislative expenses	34,667 02	Transcribing Journals	1,300 00
Blind Asylum	8,900 00	Home for Friendless Women	10,000 00
Insane Asylum	13,067 00	Printing	35,605 50
Deaf and Dumb Asylum	13,193 38	Miscellaneous accounts	795 87
State University	14,570 33		
Regents	447 20	Total for 1870	$275,095 92

DECEMBER 6.—Fourth annual session of the State Horticultural Society, at Manhattan. *Officers elected:* President, Wm. M. Howsley, Leavenworth; Vice President, B. F. Mudge, Manhattan; Secretary, George C. Brackett, Lawrence; Treasurer, S. T. Kelsey, Pomona; Trustees, C. H. Cushing, Leavenworth, James Christian, Lawrence, S. S. Hougham, Manhattan.

DECEMBER 12.—The report of Adjutant General Whittaker gives the following table showing the number of persons drawing pensions from the United States at the office of C. B. Lines, Agent at Topeka:

Name of Regiment.	No. of Invalids......	No. of Widows, etc....
First Kansas Infantry..	38	15
Second Kansas Infantry and Cavalry..	18	13
Fifth Kansas Cavalry	15	24
Sixth Kansas Cavalry..	21	37
Seventh Kansas Cavalry..	14	7
Eighth Kansas Infantry..	46	32
Ninth Kansas Cavalry	17	44
Tenth Kansas Infantry..	12	16
Eleventh Kansas Cavalry..	28	40
Twelfth Kansas Infantry...	15	23
Thirteenth Kansas Infantry..	27	22
Fourteenth Kansas Cavalry...	6	11
Fifteenth Kansas Cavalry...	20	13
Sixteenth Kansas Cavalry..	7	10
Second Kansas State Militia...	10	9
First Kansas Battery...	4	3
Second Kansas Battery...	4	5
First Kansas Colored..	9	19
Second Kansas Colored	9	3
Eighteenth United States Colored Infantry.............................	....	4
Total...	320	350

DECEMBER 12.—

"The claims allowed by the second and third Boards of Commissioners (appointed for the purpose of auditing the Price Raid claims of 1864, and the Indian expedition under Major General Curtis, in July and August of the same year), up to September 1st, 1869, are as follows:

Services rendered...	$233,345 47
Materials, supplies and transportation furnished....................................	111,352 53
Damages sustained..	159,191 34
Miscellaneous claims...	36,627 64

"In addition to this amount allowed by these Commissioners, there have been audited by special committees of the Legislature, and by the Auditor and Treasurer of State, claims for services amounting to six thousand seven hundred and one dollars and thirteen cents ($6,701.13.) This will make the total amount of this debt five hundred and forty-seven thousand two hundred and eighteen dollars and eleven cents ($547,218.11.)

"The State has assumed five hundred thousand dollars of this debt, leaving the balance unassumed. I would therefore respectfully suggest that your Excellency recommend the assumption of this balance, by the State, of forty-seven thousand two hundred and eighteen dollars and eleven cents ($47,218 11.)

"The State has also expended for the protection of her frontiers three hundred and forty-six thousand dollars ($346,000), making the grand total of indebtedness eight hundred and ninety-three thousand two hundred and eighteen dollars and eleven cents ($893,218.11), which ought to be paid by the General Government."—*Report of Adjutant General Whittaker.*

DECEMBER 15.—The following is copied from the Report of Superintendent McVicar:•

"By a recent ruling of the Hon. J. D. Cox, Secretary of the Interior, dated August 16, 1870, all rights of the State to sections sixteen and thirty-six on the Osage Trust Lands are denied. The Secretary says: 'The lands embraced in the second article of the Osage Treaty of September 29th, 1865, are required to be sold in trust for the benefit of the Indians. The United States acquired no beneficial interest in them, and in no sense can they be considered public lands. The State, therefore, has acquired no right through the United States to any part of said lands, and is not entitled to equivalents for such of the sixteenth and thirty-sixth sections as may be disposed of to pre-emptors.'

"It seems strange that the Secretary should rule that the State has acquired no right through the United States to any part of said lands, when the joint resolution of Congress, approved April 10th, 1869, expressly provides, 'That the sixteenth and thirty-sixth sections *in each township of said lands* shall be reserved for State school purposes.' But the point on which the Secretary seemed to base his decision is, that the trust lands *are not public lands*, and therefore do not come within the provisions of the act of admission, in accordance with which the joint resolution grants the sixteenth and thirty-sixth sections. By this technical construction and decision, the State is deprived of nearly 200,000 acres of school lands on the trust tract, or about one million dollars of permanent school fund. It remains with the Legislature to determine what measure, if any, can be taken to test the rights of the State in the premises."

"The Diminished Osage Reserve embraces a tract of country thirty miles wide, north and south, by over two hundred miles east and west, and extending along the south line of the State from the west line of Labette county to the western boundary of the Osage Reserve. After two years and more of varied fortunes, commencing with the notorious 'Sturges Treaty,' and followed by amended bills and supplements to bills, this tract was finally opened to settlement by virtue of section fifteen of the Indian Appropriation Bill, approved July 15, 1870, which provides that the lands of the Osage Indians in Kansas, including the trust lands north of the Diminished Reservation, 'shall be opened to settlement after survey, excepting the sixteenth and thirty-sixth sections, which shall be reserved to the State of Kansas for school purposes.' The bill is silent in regard to questions that will probably arise soon. A large portion of these school lands on the Diminished Reserve, and the best of them, were settled upon prior to the passage of the act, and prior to survey, while the lands were in possession of the Indians. The bill does not open the lands to settlement until *after* the survey, which in the case of the Diminished Reserve has not yet been made. What then are the rights of the State in case of school lands already settled upon within the Diminished Reserve, and which will be settled upon before the survey can be made?"

"Owing to a reaction in the public mind in regard to the disposal of the Indian Reserves, there has been added to the common school endowment of the State during the past four years, by acts of Congress, approved April 10, 1869, and July 15, 1870:

In Labette county	22,408 acres.
In Neosho county	20,480 acres.
On Trust Lands	177,777 acres.
On Diminished Osage Reserve	266,666 acres.
Equivalents located and confirmed	7,404 acres.
Total	494,755 acres."

This year ends the second term of Superintendent McVicar, one of the ablest and most valuable men the State has had in any public office.

DECEMBER 15.—Senator Pomeroy writes from Washington to Robert Bonner, of the New York Ledger, restating his previous restatement. He now says the article was written by an amanuensis. Mr. Bonner gave Mr. Pomeroy $200 for the article, and publishes a receipt, every word of which "is in the handwriting of the distinguished Senator."

DECEMBER 16.—The M. K. & T. R. W. is laying track west of Fort Scott, and east of Parsons.

—The Lawrence Journal says that during the past two years the K. P. R. W. has sold 700,000 acres of land, for $2,000,000. The Swedish colony, in Saline county, has taken 22,000 acres; the Scotch colony, in Dickinson county, 47,000 acres; the English colony, in Clay county, 32,000 acres; and the Welsh colony, in Riley county, 19,000 acres.

DECEMBER 17.—Attempt in Leavenworth to recover the right of way through the city, granted to the Leavenworth, Atchison and Northwestern Railroad Company.

—Jefferson county has seventy-nine school houses.

DECEMBER 20.—Atchison is lighted by gas.

DECEMBER 24.—There are fifty-five school-houses in Franklin county.

DECEMBER 21.—Leslie J. Perry sells the Garnett Plaindealer.

—D. W. Wilder removes to Fort Scott, and becomes, January 1st, the Editor of the Monitor.

—Gov. Harvey, in his Message, in January, says the safety of the frontier during the year was mainly caused by the exertions of General John Pope, commanding the Department of the Missouri. He placed all available troops on the frontier, under the command of General Custer.

DECEMBER 27.—D. Dickinson, State Librarian, reports 6,306 volumes in the Library, 577 having been added during the year. He asks that "the whole matter of exchange with the several States be committed to the Librarian."

—Meeting of the State Teachers' Association, at Leavenworth. *Officers elected:* President, Philetus Fales, of Ottawa; Corresponding Secretary, F. H. Snow, of Lawrence; Recording Secretary, Mrs. H. A. Monroe, of Atchison; Treasurer, L. Emma Haynes, of Wabaunsee; Executive Committee, H. D. McCarty of Leavenworth, J. A. Banfield of Topeka, Flora L. Allen of Leavenworth, E. M. Dickinson of Wyandotte.

DECEMBER 30.—During the year, Lane University has had 130 students, Washburn College 45, Baker University 140, Hartford Institute 80, Wetmore Institute 125, Episcopal Female Seminary 148, Emporia Normal School 243, Leavenworth Normal School 61, State University 213, Agricultural College 286.

· 1 8 7 1.

JANUARY.—There are eighty papers in the State.

—The station-houses along the line of the M. K. & T. road are painted with Fort Scott paint, and the cement used for its bridges is made at Fort Scott.

—The Herald is started, at Ottawa, by Anderson & Tone.

—A. G. Chase is one of the editors of the Kansas Farmer.

—Scott & Howard publish the Osage Mission Journal. Peffer & Wellman publish the Fredonia Journal.

—The Kansas Annual and Farmer's Record, for 1871. By William A. Brice, Leavenworth. Pages, 76.

—Cash sales of coal in Fort Scott, $900 a day.

—Fifty new buildings in Osage Mission.

—Quarry of flagstone opened at Osage City.

—New Methodist church dedicated at Burlington. D. P. Mitchell and C. R. Rice conduct the services.

—The Republican Valley Empire, published by Henry Buckingham, removes from Clyde to Concordia.

—Major E. P. Bancroft's new Hall, in Emporia, is nearly finished.

JANUARY 9.—State officers sworn in, by Chief Justice Kingman.

JANUARY 10.—The A. & N. R. R. reaches White Cloud.

JANUARY 11.—Reported death of Perry Fuller, at Washington.

JANUARY 12.—Death of James McCahon, in Leavenworth, aged 37 years. He was twice appointed to codify our laws, was a leading lawyer, issued a volume containing the decisions of our Territorial courts, was Provost Marshal of the State during the war, a very prominent Republican, and a man of the highest character. He was born in Pennsylvania, and first settled in Doniphan county, and edited the Geary City Era.

—W. H. Johnson discontinues the Council Grove Advertiser, and goes to Salina.

JANUARY 12.—Nathan Cree becomes the editor of the Lawrence Standard, and retains the position until September 26, 1872.

—Meeting of the Legislature.

STATE OFFICERS.

Names.	P. O. Address.	County.
James M. Harvey, Governor	Fort Riley	Riley.
P. P. Elder, Lieutenant Governor	Ottawa	Franklin.
W. H. Smallwood, Secretary of State	Wathena	Doniphan.
A. L. Williams, Attorney General	Topeka	Shawnee.
H. D. McCarty, Supt. of Public Instruction	Leavenworth	Leavenworth.
J. E. Hayes, State Treasurer	Olathe	Johnson.
A. Thoman, Auditor of State	Topeka	Shawnee.
S. S. Prouty, State Printer	Topeka	Shawnee.
David Whittaker, Adjutant General	Doniphan	Doniphan.
D. Dickinson, State Librarian	Oskaloosa	Jefferson.
W. C. Webb, Supt. Insurance Department	Fort Scott	Bourbon.

JUDGES OF THE SUPREME COURT.

Names.	P. O. Address.	County.
S. A. Kingman, Chief Justice	Atchison	Atchison.
D. J. Brewer, Associate Justice	Leavenworth	Leavenworth.
D. M. Valentine, Associate Justice	Ottawa	Franklin.

JUDGES OF DISTRICT COURTS.

Names.	Districts.	P. O. Address.	County.
H. W. Ide	First	Leavenworth	Leavenworth.
Nathan Price	Second	Troy	Doniphan.
John T. Morton	Third	Topeka	Shawnee.
Owen A. Bassett	Fourth	Lawrence	Douglas.
J. H. Watson	Fifth	Emporia	Lyon.
J. F. Broadhead	Sixth	Mound City	Linn.
John R. Goodin	Seventh	Humboldt	Allen.
Wm. H. Canfield	Eighth	Junction City	Davis.
William R. Brown	Ninth	Cottonwood Falls	Chase.
Hiram Stevens	Tenth	Paola	Johnson.
H. G. Webb	Eleventh	Oswego	Labette.
A. S. Wilson	Twelfth	Washington	Washington.

—Barzillai Gray, Judge Criminal Court, Leavenworth county.

MEMBERS OF THE SENATE.

Names.	Dist.	P. O. Address.	County.
P. P. Elder, President	....	Ottawa	Franklin.
Bowers, G. M.	10	Lenexa	Johnson.
Cracraft, Joseph	5	Capioma	Nemaha.
Fitzpatrick, W. H.	8	Topeka	Shawnee.
Haas, H. C.	3	Leavenworth	Leavenworth.
Hogeboom, G. W.	4	Oskaloosa	Jefferson.
Kellogg, Josiah	3	Leavenworth	Leavenworth.

35

MEMBERS AND OFFICERS OF THE SENATE—Concluded.

Names.	Dist.	Post Office Address.	County.
Logan, Joseph	2	Effingham	Atchison.
Miller, Sol	1	White Cloud	Doniphan.
Moore, H. D	14	Monmouth	Crawford.
Murdock, M. M	18	Burlingame	Osage.
McLellan, James	6	Holton	Jackson.
Nelson, George P	12	Wyandotte	Wyandotte.
Prescott, J. H	20	Salina	Saline.
Price, John M	2	Atchison	Atchison.
Rockefeller, Philip	7	Washington	Washington.
Sears, T. C	17	Ottawa	Franklin.
Snoddy, James D	13	Mound City	Linn.
Stover, E. S.	15	Council Grove	Morris.
Stotler, Jacob	19	Emporia	Lyon.
Topping, F. H	11	Paola	Miami.
Van Doren, W. S.	3	Leavenworth	Leavenworth.
Vincent, J. C.	9	Lawrence	Douglas.
Whitney, H. C.	16	Humboldt	Allen.
Wood, J.	1	Doniphan	Doniphan.
Worden, L. J.	9	Lawrence	Douglas.
George C. Crowther, Secretary		New Chicago	Neosho.
Charles C. Prescott, Ass't Secretary		Salina	Saline.
William Bolton, Journal Clerk		Seneca	Nemaha.
J. Cary French, Docket Clerk		Dover	Shawnee.
Mrs. Sarah J. Neal, Engrossing Clerk		Atchison	Atchison.
Mrs. H. E. Holman, Enrolling Clerk			Greenwood.
George H. Schreiner, Sergeant-at-Arms.		Wyandotte	Wyandotte.
J. R. Kennedy, Ass't Sergeant-at-Arms.		Olathe	Johnson.
George W. Weed, Doorkeeper		Leavenworth	Leavenworth.
D. B. Aker, Assistant Doorkeeper			Marshall.
Ephie Smith, Page		Wyandotte	Wyandotte.
Harry Whitney, Page		Humboldt	Allen.
Jennie Griffith, Page		Topeka	Shawnee.

MEMBERS AND OFFICERS OF THE HOUSE OF REPRESENTATIVES.

Names.	Dist.	Post Office Address.	County.
Ashby, W. F.	27	Easton	Leavenworth.
Babbitt, J. F.	11	Hiawatha	Brown.
Barnes, Asa	8	Locust Grove	Atchison.
Barber, A	48	Paris	Linn.
Bayer, A. W.	88	Ellsworth	Ellsworth.
Bennett, Abram	2	East Norway	Doniphan.
Baker, T. H	67	Augusta	Butler.
Benson, George W	36	Lawrence	Douglas.
Bogart, G. A	63	Toronto	Woodson.
Bond, T. L.		Elk City	Montgomery.
Brice, S. M.	48	Mound City	Linn.
Burns, C. R	79	North Topeka	Shawnee.
Butts, William C	20	Grasshopper Falls	Jefferson.
Butler, C. B.	62	Leroy	Coffey.
Buzick, Ira C.		Elk Horn	Lincoln.
Cable, Rufus E.	31	Wyandotte	Wyandotte.
Carpenter, J. M.	45	New Lancaster	Miami.
Cawker, E. H.		Cawker City	Mitchell.
Campbell, Jacob	81	Summerville	Ottawa.
Churchill, Levi	30	Fairmount	Leavenworth.
Clapp, J. D.	34	Gardner	Johnson.
Colley, D. D	23	Leavenworth	Leavenworth.
Crook, J. J.	26	Kickapoo	Leavenworth.
Crocker, D. A	47	Mound City	Linn.
Darling, Thomas J.	22	Leavenworth	Leavenworth.
Fenlon, T. P.	25	Leavenworth	Leavenworth.
Fisher, H. C.	40	Marion	Douglas.
Gandy, Felix T.		Jewell City	Jewell.
Green, W. H.	50	Osaga	Bourbon.
Griffin, S. P.	9	Pardee	Atchison.
Haskell, Jacob	42	Dover	Shawnee.
Hill, T. C.	66	Americus	Lyon.
Higday, George E.	89	Wichita	Wallace.
Howell, Joseph	29	Leavenworth	Leavenworth.

MEMBERS AND OFFICERS OF THE HOUSE—CONTINUED.

Names.	Dist.	Post Office Address.	County.
Hudson, J. K	80	Glen Park	Wyandotte.
Ingle, C. W	38	Prairie City	Douglas.
Irwin, S. W	78	New Chicago	Neosho.
Johnson, D. B	33	Shawnee	Johnson.
Johnson, Richard	14	Seneca	Nemaha.
Kennedy, J. B	5	Doniphan	Doniphan.
King, C. S	7	Atchison	Atchison.
Knowlton, J. F	55	Geneva	Allen.
Langdon, S. J	86	Iowa City	Crawford.
Legate, J. F	24	Leavenworth	Leavenworth.
Libby, C. W	51	Xenia	Bourbon.
Lindsay, John G	56	Garnett	Anderson.
Linn, H. C	17	St. Mary's	Pottawatomie.
Luce, J. M	58	Centropolis	Franklin.
Manning, E. C		Winfield	Cowley.
Mahr, J. M	85	Montana	Labette.
Mellville, W. G	35	Lawrence	Douglas.
Metcalf, H. H	87	Ellis	Ellis.
Mowry, A. J	3	Wathena	Doniphan.
Morris, J. M	72	Ogden	Riley.
Moore, A. A	76	Marion Centre	Marion.
Moore, T. H	1	Iowa Point	Doniphan.
Murphy, Thomas	6	Atchison	Atchison.
McCartney, A	77	Neodesha	Wilson.
McEckron, B. H	84	Clyde	Cloud.
McLaughlin, J. B	82	Clay Center	Clay.
Olson, Olof		Lindsburg	McPherson.
Osborn, W. F	75	Virgil	Greenwood.
Overstreet, R. M	64	Emporia	Lyon.
Page, F. R	65	Neosho Rapids	Lyon.
Parker, C. E	12	Walnut Creek	Brown.
Peckham, W. H	39	Big Springs	Douglas.
Phinney, James	69	Council Grove	Morris.
Pinkerton, J. H	70	Alma	Wabaunsee.
Puffer, Charles	61	Burlington	Coffey.
Redfield, J. C	54	Humboldt	Allen.
Reynolds, James		Longton	Howard.
Sells, Elijah	37	Lawrence	Douglas.
Shattuck, Scott	46	Twin Springs	Linn.
Simons, A	14	Seneca	Nemaha.
Smith, W. H	15	Marysville	Marshall.
Smith, H. B	43	Osawatomie	Miami.
Snead, J. H	74	Salina	Saline.
Speer, Joseph L	21	Newman	Jefferson.
Steele, C. S	52	Uniontown	Bourbon.
Steele, J. M		Wichita	Sedgwick.
Strickler, S. M	71	Junction City	Davis.
Thompson, Thomas	57	Garnett	Anderson.
Van Natta, N. T	90	Belleville	Republic.
Veale, G. W	41	Topeka	Shawnee.
Warner, Ephraim	73	Detroit	Dickinson.
Webb, W. C	53	Fort Scott	Bourbon.
Welsh, H. P	59	Ottawa	Franklin.
Whittaker, S. G	4	Troy	Doniphan.
Whistler, William	60	Quenemo	Osage.
Wilson, A. S	16	Washington	Washington.
Wilson, J. C	10	Muscotah	Atchison.
Williams, J. L	18	Holton	Jackson.
Williams, William	32	Olathe	Johnson.
Williams, A. C	28	Tonganoxie	Leavenworth.
Willetts, John	19	Grove City	Jefferson.
Wood, S. M	68	Cottonwood Falls	Chase.
Wood, George W	83	Columbus	Cherokee.
Simpson, B. F., Speaker	44	Paola	Miami.
A. R. Banks, Chief Clerk		Lawrence	Douglas.
S. F. Burdett, Assistant Clerk		Leavenworth	Leavenworth.
D. W. Henderson, Journal Clerk			Saline.
William H. Price, Docket Clerk			Atchison.
Miss Carrie Sain, Enrolling Clerk		Topeka	Shawnee.
Miss Carol M. Crouse, Engrossing Clerk,		Oswego	Labette.
Mrs. R. Flower, Asst. Engrossing Clerk,		Topeka	Shawnee.
W. D. Knox, Sergeant-at-Arms		Junction City	Davis.
A. D. Johnson, Asst. Sergeant-at-Arms			Johnson.
A. H. Beck, Doorkeeper		Ottawa	Franklin.

MEMBERS AND OFFICERS OF THE HOUSE—Concluded.

Names.	Post Office Address.	County.
John Helwig, Assistant Doorkeeper		Atchison.
Miss Jennie Maxwell, Page	Topeka	Shawnee.
Miss Hattie Butler, Page	Topeka	Shawnee.
T. H. Earnest, Page	Ottawa	Franklin.
Frank Hunt, Page	Topeka	Shawnee.
Ed. Mathews, Page	Leavenworth	Leavenworth.
W. M. Young, Page	Wathena	Doniphan.
Mart. Reynolds	Longton	Howard.

JANUARY 13.—Ex-Gov. Thos. Carney says he is not a candidate for the Senate.

JANUARY 16.— Episcopal Convention at Atchison—the first of the Diocese of Kansas.

— C. B. Lines reappointed United States Pension Agent.

JANUARY 17.—Election of State Printer. *First ballot:* S. S. Prouty 41, Sol. Miller 31, F. P. Baker 27, George F. Prescott 13. Joseph Clarke 9, C. G. Patterson 1. *Second ballot:* Prouty 46, Miller 32, Baker 28, Prescott 11, Clarke 5. *Third ballot:* Prouty 67, Miller 25, Baker 24, Prescott 4, Clarke 2. Necessary to a choice, 62.

—Meeting of the State Temperance Society. Mr. Jenkins, President; Peter McVicar, Secretary.

—Meeting of the Editors' and Publishers' Association. *Officers elected:* President, Milton W. Reynolds, of the Lawrence Journal; Vice President, M. M. Murdock, of the Burlingame Chronicle; Treasurer, S. S. Prouty, of the Topeka Commonwealth; Secretary, S. D. Macdonald, of the Topeka Record; Orator, Henry King; Alternate, George A. Crawford. The Annual Address delivered by Ward Burlingame, of the Commonwealth. Speeches made by Col. John C. Vaughan, Sidney Clarke, S. O. Thacher, T. P. Fenlon, John Guthrie, and Gov. Harvey.

JANUARY 21.—Legislative excursion to Kansas City.

— The Commonwealth publishes a history of Topeka churches.

—The Columbus Independent claims that Cherokee county coal is the best in the State for manufacturing purposes.

JANUARY 24.—Meeting of the Society of Michigan in Lawrence. Address by W. C. Ransom; speeches by James D. Snoddy, M. W. Reynolds, and James M. Spencer.

— Incorporation of the Homœopathic Medical Society of the State. *Incorporators:* S. K. Huson, R. Huson, H. F. Klemp, J. N. Rubicon, John J. Edie.

JANUARY 24.—Vote of the Senate for a United States Senator, for the term beginning March 4, 1871: Alexander Caldwell, of Leavenworth county, 8 votes; Sidney Clarke, of Douglas, 6; S. J. Crawford, of Lyon, 5; E. G. Ross, of Douglas, 1; W. R. Laughlin, of Crawford, 1; T. H. Walker, of Shawnee, 1; W. A. Phillips, of Saline, 1; Jas. D. Snoddy, of Linn, 1; W. Shannon, of Douglas, 1.

Vote of the House: Mr. Caldwell received 30 votes, Mr. Crawford 22, Mr. Clarke 21, Mr. Ross 7, Mr. Snoddy 11, Mr. Fenlon 2, Mr. Vaughan 1, Mr. Laughlin 1, Mr. McVicar 1, Mr. Bennett 1, Mr. Sells 1.

JANUARY 25.—Election of U. S. Senator. Alexander Caldwell 87, Samue J. Crawford 34, Wilson Shannon 2.

JANUARY 26.—Meeting of the soldiers of the Army of the Frontier, at Topeka. President, Nathan Price; Secretary, David Whittaker. Voted to hold a reunion, at Emporia, December 7th. *Committee of Arrangements:* P. B. Plumb, Wm. A. Phillips, Mathew Quigg, Josiah E. Hayes, Owen A. Bassett, H. H. Williams, Geo. W. Veale.

JANUARY 26.—Reception of Senator Caldwell, in Leavenworth. Speeches by ex-Governor Carney, Senator Ross, Thos. P. Fenlon, Jas. F. Legate, and others.

FEBRUARY 1.—Peter McVicar elected President of Washburn College.

FEBRUARY 2.—Congress passes a bill to provide for auditing the Price Raid claims.

FEBRUARY 3.—Caldwell Senatorial Banquet at Leavenworth, to the Legislature.

—Atchison county has fifty-six school-houses.

—John Speer retires from the Lawrence Tribune. He says he has been connected with the Kansas press most of the time for sixteen years.

FEBRUARY 9.—Congress passes a bill to sell a part of the Fort Leavenworth Reserve to the Fair Association.

FEBRUARY 10.—L. J. Perry buys half of the Ottawa Journal.

FEBRUARY 14.—Crane & Byron, of Topeka, publish a book called "The Science of Evil," by Joel Moody, of Mound City.

—The Committee to investigate the State Treasurer report:

"From the above exhibit it is shown that over $200,000 of the revenue of the State is virtually deposited in banks in Kansas City, Missouri, or in Topeka, Kansas, in open violation of law.

"A disregard of the law for the custody and safe-keeping of the revenue of the State by the officer who is made the custodian of the people's money, raised by taxation for the payment of the expenses of the State Government, is an act of bad faith that demands the enforcement of the penalties prescribed.

"If the law had no moral power to restrain the officer sworn to its support, then security is gone, and the funds of the State have but little protection.

"This pernicious system of pretending to deal in drafts and certificates of deposit, to evade the law which prohibits depositing in a bank or other place, is one fraught with evil and danger. The certificates and drafts are held by the State Treasurer for an indefinite period, thereby releasing the drawer for want of diligence—a practice that no business man would adopt for himself—and if the banks in New York should fail, the State would be the loser for the amount drawn."—*House Journal, pp. 416 to 419.*

FEBRUARY 14.—

"Responsive to my letter of the 17th of October, 1870 (published in last Annual Message), I have been officially informed that the Secretary of the Interior has decided, in accordance with the claim asserted in the letter, that the State is entitled, for school purposes, to the sixteenth and thirty-sixth sections within the Osage Trust Lands, and their Diminished Reservation; the length of the correspondence precludes its insertion here; but it will be laid before you. The decision is dated February 14th, 1871, and was received at this office March 8th, 1871."—*Gov. Harvey's Message, January 9, 1872.*

FEBRUARY 15.—Henry King retires from the Topeka Record.

FEBRUARY 16.—Ward Burlingame retires from the Commonwealth, to become the Secretary of Senator Caldwell.

FEBRUARY 20.—The Chicago and Southwestern Railroad is completed to Leavenworth.

—The Atchison Champion begins its fourteenth year.

FEBRUARY 28.—Report of the Special Committee on Insurance Money received by the Auditor:

"From the law it will be seen that the Auditor had no authority whatever to receive this money from insurance companies, and much less to hold a large amount of it in his hands for a period of from six to eighteen months. From the law it will also appear that the payment into the Treasury, by the corporation seeking the certificate, of the sum of fifty dollars is a condition precedent to its right to demand and the Auditor's right to issue a certificate of authority. The facts show that all the certificates issued by Mr. Thoman have been issued without and prior to such payment, in nearly all cases many months."

MARCH 1.—John M. Crowell, of Atchison, appointed Special Agent of the Post Office Department, at large.

MARCH 3.—Adjournment of the Legislature. Among its acts are these: Apportioning the State for Senators and Representatives; Authorizing the School Commissioners to buy $50,000 of Lawrence bonds; Creating the Twelfth Judicial District; Establishing an Insurance Department; Providing for the settlement of losses on the frontier; Appropriating $6,000 for seed wheat and corn, for western counties; For the election of a Board of Railroad Assessors; To restrain State, County and City Treasurers from speculating in their offices. Nineteen acts were passed authorizing municipal bonds.

MARCH 6.—W. A. Morgan establishes the Chase County Leader, at Cottonwood Falls.

—Geo. C. Hume leaves the Leavenworth Commercial for the St. Louis Journal of Commerce, and changes it from a Weekly to a Daily.

MARCH 7.—W. H. Rossington succeeds Hume as editor of the Leavenworth Commercial, and remains till the fall of '72.

—The Tribune is established at Independence, by Humphrey & Yoe.

—The King bridge shops nearly completed, at Iola.

—John McReynolds removes from Paola to Emporia.

MARCH 14.—

"On the 14th of March, 1871, I proceeded to Leavenworth, and met James A. Hardee, Inspector General, U. S. A., J. D. Bingham, Quartermaster, U. S. A., and T. H. Stanton, Paymaster, U. S. A., members of the Commission appointed by the Secretary of War to examine and audit the Price Raid claims, pursuant to Act of Congress, approved February 2, 1871. The Commission, having been organized and qualified according to law, at Fort Leavenworth, was invited to meet at Topeka, for convenience of access to the necessary papers; and it accordingly met here on the 17th of March. It was afforded every possible facility for the discharge of the duty, and after a number of days of assiduous labor, went to Washington to report the result to the Secretary of War, to be by him communicated to Congress as a basis for an appropriation for the payment of the claims."—*Gov. Harvey's Message, Jan. 9, 1872.*

MARCH 19.—Wm. C. Webb appointed Superintendent of Insurance.

MARCH 19.—Andrew S. Wilson appointed Judge of the Twelfth District.

MARCH 20.—Joseph Logan distributes seed wheat in the northwest.

—George Merrill succeeds Col. Huntoon as Receiver in the Topeka Land Office.

—The Junction City Land Office is to be moved to Salina.

—Conference of the M. E. Church at Paola. Number of local preachers, 243; value of church property, $288,783; Sunday school children, 10,683.

MARCH 24.—The Governor appoints the following Railroad Assessors: Ed. Russell, George Graham, J. C. Bailey, John Walruff, H. N. Bent, C. W. Libby, F. M. Power, J. M. Allen, F. B. Hunt, H. H. Williams, R. W. Wright, Jacob Weisbach.

—M. W. Coulter becomes sole owner of the Baxter Springs Sentinel.

MARCH 28.—Incorporation of the Eclectic Medical Association of the State. *Incorporators:* George H. Field, Samuel E. Martin, Caleb D. Ward, Ansell M. Eidson, David Surber, Daniel B. Crouse.

APRIL 4.—T. Dwight Thacher becomes the sole owner of the Lawrence Republican Journal.

—The type on which the White Cloud Chief is printed has been in constant use sixteen years.

—A "Hand-Book of Progressive Philosophy," by Edward Schiller, of Fort Scott, is published by Redfield, New York.

—Frank H. Drenning becomes sole owner of the Wathena Reporter.

APRIL 27.—Isaac M. Ruth, business manager of the Lawrence Tribune, found dead in his bed. Mrs. Ruth was in Leavenworth. A dying statement by Mr. Ruth led to the arrest of Dr. Medlicott. May 5th the coroner's jury brings in a verdict that Mr. Ruth came to his death from the effects of a narcotic poison, administered by Dr. J. J. Medlicott.

MAY.—John A. Banfield edits the Educational Journal.

MAY 11.—Episcopal Convention at Fort Scott.

— The Congregational Association holds its fifteenth Annual Session at Emporia.

—The Missouri, Kansas and Texas Railway reaches Cabin Creek, Indian Territory.

MAY 15.—Appointment of D. D. Colley, Leavenworth, David Heller, Clyde, and Thomas W. Bown, Marion Centre, Commissioners to audit losses from Indian raids between the years 1861 and 1871.

MAY 16.—D. B. Emmert confirmed as Receiver of the Humboldt Land Office.

MAY 23.—The civil and criminal suits against John Speer are withdrawn:

"DEPARTMENT OF JUSTICE, WASHINGTON, MAY 15TH, 1871.

"*Albert H. Horton, Esq., United States Attorney, Atchison, Kansas:*

"SIR: I am directed by the Attorney General to inform you, in relation to the criminal cases of the United States vs. Speer and others, that you are authorized to enter a *nolle prosequi* in them. This direction is given you, as there is some doubt whether they are cases which came within the internal revenue act, and thus are under the control of the Commissioner of Internal Revenue, or whether directions in respect to them should come from this Department. Very respectfully, your obedient servant,

"CLEMENT HUGH HILL, *Assistant Attorney General.*"

JUNE 3.—The Emporia Ledger established. H. W. McCune, the present (1875) publisher, has been connected with the paper since March 20, 1873.

JUNE.—The Educational Journal publishes a catalogue of plants, native and naturalized, found in Kansas, by J. H. Carruth, with additions by F. H. Snow and E. Hall.

JUNE 6.—The Missouri Board of Agriculture visits Kansas.

JUNE 6.—J. B. Davis leaves the Commonwealth. . He is succeeded by S. D. Macdonald.

—Ed. H. Snow buys the Ottawa Journal.

—The Indian Depredation Commissioners meet at Topeka.

JUNE 10.—The Spirit is issued, at Paola, by Leslie J. Perry and C. M. Bright.

JUNE 15.—Baptist Convention in session, at Leavenworth.

—Wichita and Abilene are rival cattle markets.

JUNE 16.—Terrific tornado at Eldorado.

JUNE 20.—Texas cotton begins to arrive at Parsons.

JUNE 30.—Seventh Annual Report of the City of Leavenworth Board of Education. pp. 115. J. L. Wever is President of the Board, and P. J. Williams Superintendent of the Schools. In the "Questions for Promotion," Greek words, printed with Greek letters, are freely used—for the first time in a Kansas book.

JULY.—The total assessed valuation of property in the State, made in June, 1870, for the U. S. Census, was $89,905,470. The true valuation of property, made for the same purpose by County Clerks, was $183,998,744; or more than twice as much.

JULY.—A book appears with this title: "Resources of Kansas. Fifteen Years' Experience. By C. C. Hutchinson. With a new Map and forty Illustrations.

'The rudiments of Empire here
Are plastic yet, and warm;
The chaos of a mighty world
Is rounding into form.'

Topeka, Kansas: Commonwealth State Printing House." pp. 287.

The following is copied from the book:

" *Table showing the average rainfall of Kansas, in comparison with that of other States, for the five years from January 1, 1865, to January 1, 1870. By Professor F. H. Snow.*

States.	Spring.	Summer	Autumn	Winter.	March 1 to Oct. 1.	Year.
Kansas	10.82	18.06	9.79	5.42	34.15	44.09
Maine	13.74	10.55	13.33	9.99	28.23	47.61
New Hampshire	10.40	10.49	12.66	7.85	25.40	41.40
Vermont	10.31	10.44	11.82	7.32	25.01	39.89
Massachusetts	13.46	11.17	11.72	10.20	28.71	46.55
Connecticut	13.01	13.34	13.11	10.54	30.88	50.00
New York	11.16	11.19	12.41	9.92	26.85	44.68
New Jersey	13.18	13.88	12.53	11.39	31.81	50.98
Pennsylvania	12.04	12.46	11.17	10.01	29.05	45.68
Maryland	13.67	13.95	12.39	11.22	32.05	51.23
Kentucky	15.18	13.77	9.88	12.50	33.92	51.33
Ohio	12.34	11.73	9.80	8.09	29.24	41.96
Michigan	8.32	9.90	11.00	6.47	23.19	35.69
Indiana	14.35	12.84	10.32	9.27	32.94	46.78
Illinois	11.53	12.07	8.14	6.02	27.92	37.76
Wisconsin	8.92	13.23	8.16	5.87	25.53	36.18
Minnesota	6.09	13.39	8.42	3.78	24.43	31.68
Iowa	10.57	16.72	8.86	6.38	32.14	42.53
Missouri	12.67	13.34	9.29	6.42	30.74	41.72
Nebraska	8.76	12.56	6.25	5.09	24.93	32.62
Av'age rainfall in 20 States for 5 y'rs.	11.52	12.75	10.55	8.19	28.86	43.01

"I quote from a letter dated Topeka, January 27, 1871, received from W. H. Fisk, Superintendent of one of the coal companies working in Osage county, as follows:

"'We have two shafts at Osage City, some fifty feet in depth, and a mine at Carbondale, entered by a slope or drift, the main entry being some eight hundred feet long.

Our present force and facilities will enable us to take out twenty car-loads per day, six thousand bushels. We have contracts with the Kansas Pacific, and Atchison, Topeka and Santa Fe Railway Companies, to supply them with coal. Our Osage coal is pronounced by good judges to be equal to any in the State. The dimensions of the Osage shafts are 5x13 feet, 50 feet in depth.'

"Mining is prosecuted extensively by organized companies in Bourbon county, near Fort Scott, and in Crawford, Cherokee, Neosho, and Labette counties. Extensive mines are opened near Chetopa, in the latter county. One company ship from twenty-five to forty car-loads per day from Fort Scott, employing about two hundred and fifty men. The veins that are worked in this region range from two to four feet in thickness, and are but a few feet below the surface."

The book takes a rose-colored view of everything relating to Kansas, is well written, and is the best immigration document the State has published. Ten thousand copies were issued, the Legislature making an appropriation for the printing.

JULY.—A book issued with this title: "The Law of Estoppel. By Henry M. Herman, Counsellor at Law, Leavenworth, Kansas. Albany, W. C. Little & Co."

JULY 6.—The Leavenworth County Board give the K. P. stock to the "Kansas Central," or narrow-gauge road.

—The threats of assassination made by the "vigilants," in Butler county, against T. B. Murdock, of the Eldorado Times, lead to the insanity and death of his wife and child.

JULY 24.—Geo. A. Crawford says John Brown's "Parallel" was written in the house of Dr. A. B. Massey, at the Trading Post, Linn county, and read to Mr. Crawford by Kagi, the day it was written. Anderson and Stevens, then known as Hazlitt and Whipple, were also present.

—Completion of the Topeka Female Seminary building, built under the direction and through the exertions of Bishop Vail.

JULY 27.—Crane & Byron, of Topeka, publish "My Captivity Among the Sioux," a book written by Mrs. Kelley.

JULY 31.—Gov. Harvey offers a reward of $500 for the apprehension and conviction of the incendiaries who burned the Girard Press, on the 15th inst.

AUGUST.—Appearance of a "Guide to the Country along the line of the Missouri, Kansas and Texas Railway," by R. F. Smith. It is a book of 217 pages, filled with loud praise of the towns, men, and newspapers published between Fort Scott and Chetopa, and Junction City and Parsons. The early history of the towns is usually given.

AUGUST.—George W. Hoss, of Indiana, elected Principal of the Emporia Normal School.

AUGUST.—The Agricultural editors of New York visit Kansas.

AUGUST 14.—The Fort Scott Monitor Company publish for Rev. T. B. Taylor a book called, "Old Theology Turned Upside Down, or Right Side Up."

—Nearly every county in the State has one or more new railway projects.

AUGUST 21.—A writer in the Commonwealth says: "The air of Newton is tainted with the hot steam of human blood." Six persons are killed in that town.

AUGUST 24.—John A. Martin, of the Atchison Champion, and George

A. Crawford, of the Fort Scott Monitor, are appointed Centennial Commissioners, by Gov. Harvey.

—National Camp Meeting, near Topeka.

—The Educational Journal is removed from Emporia to Topeka.

—Geo. H. Hoyt returns to Athol, Mass.

SEPTEMBER 1.—The L. L. & G. reaches Coffeyville, on the southern boundary of the State.

—The Ottawa University case is tried before Judge Bassett.

—The Vedette says buffaloes come within ten miles of Wichita.

—The Emporia News says C. H. Withington built the first house in Lyon county, in 1854.

—Mr. Hanna, of the Salina Herald, is pronounced the champion chess-player of the State.

SEPTEMBER 3.—Cyrus O. French, of Fort Scott, is appointed Register in Bankruptcy.

—Dr. C. C. McDowell succeeds Amos Sanford on the Columbus Journal.

SEPTEMBER.—Fort Scott dedicates a school-building equalled, says the Educational Journal, by only three in the State—the "Morris," of Leavenworth, the "Lincoln," of Topeka, and the "Central Building," of Atchison.

SEPTEMBER 3.—A Kansas literary monthly is talked of by the Fort Scott Monitor, the project originating with Edward Schiller.

SEPTEMBER 4.—The American Pomological Society, at Richmond, Va., awards Kansas "the highest premium for the largest and best display of fruit, unequalled in size, beauty and excellence during the session of the American Pomological Society."

SEPTEMBER 5.—Methodist State Convention at Lawrence.

SEPTEMBER 10.—N. L. Prentis writes a history of the State Agricultural Society, for the Topeka Record.

— Paola has 747 school children.

—State Fair at Topeka.

SEPTEMBER 15.—Election, on the State Fair grounds at Topeka, of the following officers of the State Agricultural Society: President, I. S. Kalloch, of Douglas; Vice President, O. E. Learnard, of Douglas; Secretary, Alfred Gray, of Wyandotte; Treasurer, Thomas Murphy, of Atchison; Superintendent, J. L. McDowell. *Executive Committee:* J. I. Larimer of Leavenworth, S. T. Kelsey of Franklin, J. N. Insley of Jefferson, J. W. Scott, of Allen, N. A. Adams of Riley, E. S. Niccolls of Anderson, John Inlow of Johnson, Andrew Wilson of Shawnee, J. K. Hudson of Wyandotte, G. A. Crawford of Bourbon.

SEPTEMBER 15.—Old Settlers' meeting at Blanton's Crossing. President, Charles Robinson; Vice Presidents, Geo. W. Smith, J. A. Wakefield, A. Alquire, Capt. Bickerton, Capt. A. Cutler, and John Speer; Secretaries, Capt. W. I. R. Blackman, and W. L. G. Soule. Letters received from Geo. W. Brown, Rockford, Ill., and James Redpath, Boston.

—Geo. Tauber starts the Zeitung, at Topeka.

SEPTEMBER 26.—Excursion from Chicago to Leavenworth, over the

Southwestern Railroad. President Grant and General Beauregard in the party.

OCTOBER.—The St. Louis Fair gives Kansas a diploma "for the best exhibition of apples."

OCTOBER.—The New England Fair, at Lowell, Mass., awards a silver medal to Kansas for its display of fruit.

OCTOBER.—The Pennsylvania Horticultural Society awards Kansas a silver medal for its fruit.

OCTOBER 5.—Excursion from Atchison, over the A. & N. R. R. to the first crossing of the Nemaha, in Nebraska. This seems to have been the only excursion in which Sol. Miller ever took a part.

—Dr. John H. Stringfellow returns and becomes a citizen of Atchison.

OCTOBER 6.—Rev. Winfield Scott writes from Albany that the Kansas fruit obtained the highest award at the New York State Fair.

—Manufacture of ochre brick at Osage City.

OCTOBER 8.—Trial of Dr. Medlicott, at Garnett.

OCTOBER 10.—Grand Lodge I. O. O. F. meets at Lawrence.

OCTOBER 19.—Meeting of the Masonic Grand Lodge at Topeka.

—John Maloy takes charge of the Council Grove Democrat.

—The number of houses in Leavenworth is 3,084.

—The Synod of Kansas meets at Humboldt; sermon by Rev. Dr. J. G. Reaser.

—Catholic Church dedicated at Wathena.

—Several cities and societies contribute liberally to the sufferers by the great fire in Chicago.

OCTOBER 24.—Sixth Annual Convention of the Editors' and Publishers' Association, at Lawrence. Address by Henry King, of Topeka. *Officers:* President, M. W. Reynolds; Vice Presidents, Geo. F. Prescott, D. W. Wilder, G. C. Crowther, Albert Griffin; Secretary, S. D. Macdonald; Treasurer, S. S. Prouty; Orator, Geo. A. Crawford; Alternate, D. W. Wilder. The Convention encouraged the project of establishing the Kansas Magazine. There was an excursion to Humboldt, Fort Gibson, Fort Scott, Sedalia, (Mo.), and Chicago.

OCTOBER 28.—Mrs. Ruth arrested, at Lawrence, as an accomplice in the murder of her husband. Dr. Medlicott was found guilty of murder in the first degree, on the 26th.

OCTOBER 25.—The Natural History Society meets at Leavenworth.

—E. C. Manning, on his farm near Winfield, Cowley county, has raised a crop of corn on a field from which wheat was harvested in June. Last year he also raised a second crop.

—Railroad in progress from Cherryvale to Independence.

NOVEMBER.—The New York Independent says:

"Kansas is the best advertised and most favorably known of the Far-Western States. Her prestige is due to three causes: 1st. Her political troubles and warfare for Freedom, which elicited universal sympathy; 2d. The fertility of her soil, the superior of which does not exist in the West; and 3d. To the activity of her citizens."

NOVEMBER.—The Emporia News and Tribune are consolidated.

NOVEMBER 5.—Convention of Spiritualists, at Lawrence.

NOVEMBER 7.—Annual election.

VOTE FOR STATE SENATOR.

District.	Counties.	Names.	Votes.	Maj.	Vote of District.	Vote of County.
3	Leavenworth	C. R. Jennison	2,736	542		
		J. J. Crook	2,194		4,930	4,930

VOTE FOR MEMBERS OF THE HOUSE OF REPRESENTATIVES.

District.	Counties.	Names.	Votes.	Maj.	Vote of District.	Vote of County.
1	Doniphan	Thomas M. Pierce	490	193		
		Pryor Plank	297		787	
2		James A. Oder	303			
		Robert C. Mailler	305	2	608	
3		Ed. Searcy	252	24		
		A. J. Mowry	228		480	1,875
4	Atchison	G. W. Glick	294			
		C. I. Scofield	513	219	807	
5		J. C. Wilson	385	137		
		H. C. Baker	248		633	
6		C. T. Griffin	423	89		
		Benj. Wallack	334		757	2,197
7	Brown	C. F. Bowron	747	432		
		H. A. Parsons	315		1,062	1,062
8	Nemaha	Ira F. Collins	380	103		
		J. P. Taylor	277			
		J. E. Taylor	1			
		A. C. DeForrest	7		665	
9		A. C. DeForrest	443	266		
		A. M. Flint	177			
		J. W. McLaughlin	1		621	1,286
10	Marshall	Alvinza Jeffers	795	204		
		Charles B. Mathews	591		1,386	1,386
11	Washington	C. J. Aldrich	798	798	798	798
12	Riley	John E. Pinkerton	906	434		
		R. E. Fullington	472			
		Scattering	6		1,384	1,384
13	Pottawatomie	J. C. Lightcap	535	253		
		J. H. Chadsey	382			
		Scattering	6		923	
14		Welcome Wells	223	15		
		E. Aldrich	208			
		Scattering	6		437	1,360
15	Jackson	Jacob Laughmiller	516	176		
		E. L. Shields	340		856	856
16	Jefferson	Terry Critchfield	496	306		
		Geo. W. Gray	190		686	
17		Hugh S. Walsh	241			
		H. K. Kennedy	393	152	634	
18		Jno. W. Rogers	351	139		
		T. J. Housh	212		563	1,883
19	Leavenworth	L. M. Goddard	408	74		
		Dr. H. Stein	334		742	
20		J. W. Taylor	185			
		N. Marchand	413	228	598	
21		S. N. Latta	596	566		
		J. F. Legate	30		626	
22		Thomas P. Fenlon	439	54		
		M. J. Parrott	385		824	
23		James Cooley	365	52		
		Jacob Winter	313		678	
24		J. Bauserman	354			
		B. C. Barker	524	170	878	
25		J. E. Barrett	300			
		C. J. Halstead	385	85	685	5,031
26	Wyandotte	Hiram Mallott	777	15		
		Frank Betton	762		1,539	
27		S. A. Cobb	528	335		

VOTE FOR MEMBERS OF THE HOUSE OF REPRESENTATIVES—Continued.

District.	Counties.	Names.	Votes.	Maj.	Vote of District.	Vote of County.
27	Wyandotte (concluded)..	G. R. Todd............	193		721	2,260
28	Johnson................	D. B. Johnson.........	334			
		James H. Connelly..........	428	94	762	
29		T. G. Stevenson........	550	296		
		J. W. Buel............	254			
		Henry Hooker.........	80			
		E. Williams...........	1			
		E. W. Smith...........	133		1,018	
30		E. Clarke.............	243			
		A. Taylor.............	379	136		
		C. W. Batch..........	20			
		Scattering	2		644	2,424
31	Miami...............	D. H. Johnson........	691	147		
		J. E. Thayer.........	544		1,235	
32		H. B. Smith..........	546			
		F. M. Fain...........	571	25	1,117	2,352
33	Linn...............	J. M. Sayer..........	583	409		
		J. V. Donaldson......	174			
		W. C. Gibbons.......	39			
		Z. McFadden.........	1		797	
34		Wm. B. Scott........	227	26		
		Robert Ewing........	201		428	
35		A. W. Burton........	402	259		
		Henry Ham..........	143		545	1,770
36	Bourbon...........	W. H. Green.........	415	219		
		M. E. Hudson........	196			
		Scattering...........	13		624	
37		J. R. Greening	364	348		
		L. S. Humphreys......	16			
		Scattering...........	9		389	
38		T. F. Robley.........	520			
		L. G. Palmer........	539	19	1,060	2,073
		Scattering...........	1			
39	Crawford.............	S. D. Ashmore........	360	122		
		H. M. Kirkpatrick....	238		600	
		Scattering...........	2			
40		S. J. Langdon........	379	286		
		R. B. James.........	93			
		Scattering,..........	1		473	1,073
41	Cherokee	W. H. Clark.........	293			
		G. W. Wood.........	496	203	796	
		Scattering	7			
42		S. T. Kennedy........	472	35		
		W. H. Graves	437			
		W. H. Clark.........	28			
		G. W. Wood.........	40		979	1,775
		Scattering..........	2			
43	Labette.............	J. J. Wood..........	336	37		
		J. W. Richardson.....	299			
		J. M. Mahr..........	133		768	
44		D. C. Constant.......	473	9		
		Gilbert Cooper........	464			
		P. B. Clark..........	111		1,048	1,816
45	Neosho	O. S. Copeland	549	48		
		R. N. Baylies........	501		1,050	
46		E. H. Keables........	568	237		
		John C. Carpenter.....	331		899	1,949
47	Allen	G. H. Requa.........	261			
		T. B. Mills..........	351	90	612	
48		S. J. Stewart........	336			
		G. P. Smith..........	458	22	794	1,406
49	Anderson..........	J. H. Whitford.......	545	138		
		Geo W. Cooper	407		952	952
50	Franklin	W. H. Clark.........	537	203		
		C. R. Cook..........	334			
		S. Devore...........	4		875	
51		Wm. H. Schofield.....	481	294		
		H. Donohue.........	187			
		J. M. Foster.........	5		673	1,448
52	Douglas...........	C. Robinson.........	974	974	974	
53		Dudley Haskell......	450	173		
		C. H. Langston......	277			
		G. W. Benson........	169			

VOTE FOR MEMBERS OF THE HOUSE OF REPRESENTATIVES— CONTINUED.

District.	Counties.	Names.	Votes....	Maj.....	Vote of District....	Vote of County....
53	Douglas (concluded).....	Geo. A. Reynolds	137		1,033	
54	....	James H. Kelly	392	181		
		C. Ingersoll	211		603	
55		Elijah Sells	575	575	575	3,185
56	Shawnee....................	S. C. Gregg	440	211		
		C. W. Higinbotham	229		669	
57	....	C. K. Holliday	809	417		
		John Martin	392		1,201	
58	....	H. E. Bush	452	255		
		Perry Tice	76			
		John L. Price	197		725	2,595
59	Osage	J. R. Cowan	687	686		
		William Barnett	1		688	
60	....	A. Blake	472	408		
		N. C. Sweezey	64		536	1,224
61	Coffey.....................	David Grimes	514			
		Chas. B Butler	708	194	1,222	1,222
62	Woodson..................	B. F. Everett	358	33		
		G. W. Ashby	325			
		J. R. Gilbert	32		715	715
63	Wilson	S. S. Benedict	709	214		
		Capt. M. G. Averill	495		1,204	1,204
64	Montgomery.............	W. J. Harrod	301			
		E. B. Dunwell	539	238	840	
65	....	L. U. Humphreys	475			
		B. F. Devore	523	48	998	1,838
66	Howard....................	R. H. Nichols	673	108		
		N. B. Cartwell	565			
		E. Fuller	15			
		W. Pomeroy	6		1,259	1,259
67	Greenwood.................	Ira P. Nye	448	138		
		G. A. Gordon	310		758	758
68	Lyon	C. V. Eskridge	591	189		
		L. T. Heritage	402		993	
69	....	Chas. Drake	301	16		
		F. R. Page	285			
		Scattering	89		675	1,668
70	Wabaunsee	James M. Johnson	397	32		
		C. C. Little	365			
		Scattering	2		764	764
71	Davis.....................	S. M. Strickler	485	80		
		R. D. Laurenson	405			
		Scattering	2		892	892
72	Morris.....................	G. W. Clark	361	7		
		J. Stanley	354		715	715
73	Chase	S. N. Wood	222			
		J. W. McWilliams	297	75	519	519
74	Butler	Isaac Mooney	727	123		
		W. P. Campbell	604		1,331	1,331
75	Cowley	T. McIntyre	430	144		
		E. C Manning	286			
		S. M. Fall	244		960	960
76	Sedgwick...................	D. L. Payne	572	18		
		H. C. Sluss	554		1,126	1,126
77	Marion	Frank Doster	293	114		
		R. C. Bates	179		472	472
78	McPherson.................	O. Olson	204	152		
		L. C. Almond	52		256	256
79	Dickinson	Christian Hoffman	642	315		
		O. F. Searl	327		969	969
80	Clay........................	C. M. Kellogg	524	80		
		Richard Wake	444			
		C. W. Lindner	5		973	973
81	Republic	A. D. Wilson	275	112		
		R. P. West	163			
		P. McHucheon	154			
		D. C. Gamble	77			
		Scattering	2		671	671
82	Cloud......................	B. H. McEckron	575	550		
		Scattering	25		600	600
83	Ottawa.....................	E. Hollingsworth	336	177		
		R. D. Mobley	159			
		Scattering	1		496	496

VOTE FOR MEMBERS OF THE HOUSE OF REPRESENTATIVES—Concluded.

District.	County.	Names.	Votes	Maj.	Vote of District.	Vote of County.
84	Saline	J. Boynton	717	233		
		M. D. Sampson	484		1,201	1,201
85	Ellsworth	V. B. Osborne	200	92		
		H. L. Pestana	108		308	308
86	Lincoln	Frank A. Schermerhorn	155	44		
		T. F. Garver	111		266	266
88	Jewell	D. W. Pate	140	39		
		James A. Scarborough	101		241	241
89	Ellis	John H. Edwards	191	30		
		Simon Moatz	161		352	352
90	Wallace	Fred C. Gay	74	43		
		John A. McGinty	31		105	105
92	Rice	F. J. Griffith	85		85	85
93	Osborne	W. L. Bear	101	49		
		D. E. Tilden	38			
		Q. A. Gates	52			
		F. Thompson	22		213	213
	Total vote					69,599

VOTE FOR JUDGES OF THE DISTRICT COURTS IN THE SIXTH, SEVENTH
AND EIGHTH JUDICIAL DISTRICTS.

District.	Counties.	Names of Candidates.	Vote of County.	Total.
6...	Linn	M. V. Voss	762	
	Bourbon	M. V. Voss	1,230	1,992
	Linn	J. F. Broadhead	986	
	Bourbon	J. F. Broadhead	783	1,769
7...	Allen	John R. Goodin	1,124	
	Neosho	John R. Goodin	1,014	
	Wilson	John R. Goodin	845	
	Woodson	John R. Goodin	196	3,179
	Allen	H. W. Talcott	250	
	Neosho	H. W. Talcott	703	
	Wilson	H. W. Talcott	2	
	Woodson	H. W. Talcott	246	1,201
8...	Riley	William H. Canfield	308	
	Davis	William H. Canfield	858	
	Dickinson	William H. Canfield	352	
	Saline	William H. Canfield	591	
	Ellsworth	William H. Canfield	281	
	Ellis	William H. Canfield	324	
	Ottawa	William H. Canfield	267	
	Lincoln	William H. Canfield	242	
	McPherson	William H. Canfield	30	
	Rice	William H. Canfield	80	3,333
	Riley	H. G. Barner	1,076	
	Davis	H. G. Barner	38	
	Dickinson	H. G. Barner	531	
	Saline	H. G. Barner	614	
	Ellsworth	H. G. Barner	26	
	Ellis	H. G. Barner	4	
	Ottawa	H. G. Barner	225	
	Lincoln	H. G. Barner	22	
	McPherson	H. G. Barner	173	
	Wallace	H. G. Barner	25	2,734
	Dickinson	J. R. McClure	93	93

VOTE FOR RAILROAD ASSESSORS.

District.	County.	Names of Candidates.	Vote of County.	Total.
1...	Leavenworth	Jacob Vogel	2,193	2,193
	Leavenworth	James Medill	3,011	3,011

VOTE FOR RAILROAD ASSESSORS—Continued.

District.	Counties.	Names.	Vote of County.	Total.
	Nemaha	W. J. Robbins	141	141
	Atchison	George Graham	429	
	Brown	George Graham	343	
	Nemaha	George Graham	732	
	Doniphan	George Graham	225	1,729
2	Atchison	J. P. Johnson	706	
	Brown	J. P. Johnson	554	
	Nemaha	J. P. Johnson	38	
	Doniphan	J. P. Johnson	1,053	2,351
	Atchison	J. H. Sawyer	1,169	
	Nemaha	J. H. Sawyer	380	
	Doniphan	J. H. Sawyer	574	2,123
	Jefferson	Andrew Blevins	19	19
	Jefferson	Fred Bort	42	42
	Jackson	Charles Hayden	378	378
	Jefferson	V. Brown	1,015	
	Shawnee	V. Brown	226	1,241
3	Jackson	S. S. Cooper	399	
	Jefferson	S. S. Cooper	28	
	Shawnee	S. S. Cooper	1,934	
	Wabaunsee	S. S. Cooper	126	
	Pottawatomie	S. S. Cooper	880	3,367
	Wabaunsee	Samuel R. Weed	215	215
	Douglas	F. Gleason	2,949	
	Franklin	F. Gleason	716	
	Anderson	F. Gleason	608	4,273
4	Douglas	W. H. Carson	395	
	Franklin	W. H. Carson	354	
	Anderson	W. H. Carson	59	808
	Coffey	H. N. Bent	901	
	Lyon	H. N. Bent	793	
	Osage	H. N. Bent	241	1,935
5	Coffey	R. M. Wright	232	
	Lyon	R. M. Wright	859	
	Morris	R. M. Wright	483	
	Osage	R. M. Wright	307	1,881
	Linn	Ed. R. Smith	1,072	
6	Bourbon	Ed. R. Smith	1,140	2,212
	Linn	T. W. Wattles	697	
	Bourbon	T. W. Wattles	955	1,652
	Neosho	J. Moffit	370	
	Wilson	J. Moffit	219	589
	Allen	J. A. Stevens	106	
	Neosho	J. A. Stevens	1,022	
	Wilson	J. A. Stevens	544	
	Woodson	J. A. Stevens	213	1,885
7	Allen	Eli Gilbert	631	
	Neosho	Eli Gilbert	21	
	Wilson	Eli Gilbert	72	724
	Allen	I. L. Fletcher	432	
	Neosho	I. L. Fletcher	549	
	Wilson	I. L. Fletcher	344	
	Woodson	I. L. Fletcher	171	1,496
	Rice	Charles Kingman	19	19
	Ottawa	D. C. Jones	117	117
	Ellis	J. N. Allen	21	21
	Davis	A. Cameron	1	
	Dickinson	A. Cameron	93	
	Saline	A. Cameron	30	
	Ellsworth	A. Cameron	306	430
	Riley	John Danielson	954	
	Dickinson	John Danielson	637	
8	Saline	John Danielson	1,141	
	Ellis	John Danielson	5	
	Ottawa	John Danielson	303	
	Lincoln	John Danielson	118	
	McPherson	John Danielson	174	
	Wallace	John Danielson	5	3,337
	Riley	J. M. Allen	368	
	Davis	J. M. Allen	893	
	Dickinson	J. M. Allen	246	
	Ellis	J. M. Allen	306	1,813

VOTE FOR RAILROAD ASSESSORS—Concluded.

District.	Counties.	Names of Candidates.	Vote of County.....	Total.....
	Chase	C. R. Roberts	5	
	Marion	C. R. Roberts	181	186
	Chase	S. M. Wood.....................	368	
	Marion	S. M. Wood.....................	272	
9...	Sedgwick	S. M. Wood.....................	97	737
	Chase	R. M. Spivey.....................	149	
	Sedgwick	R. M. Spivey.....................	527	676
	Butler	Stephen J. Wood.....................	1,326	1,326
	Wyandotte	Emmot Ryus	721	721
	Wyandotte	J. R. Perkins.....................	395	395
	Wyandotte	James McGrew.....................	186	186
	Johnson.....................	W. W. Williams.....................	209	209
	Johnson.....................	B. Nicholson.....................	216	216
10...	Johnson.....................	Thomas Roberts	96	
	Miami	Thomas Roberts	1,131	1,227
	Johnson.....................	H. H. Williams	1,424	
	Miami	H. H. Williams	1,172	
	Wyandotte	H. H. Williams	40	2,636
	Labette	E. C. Wells.....................	742	
	Cherokee.....................	E. C. Wells.....................	1,133	
	Crawford	E. C. Wells.....................	692	
	Montgomery.....................	E. C. Wells.....................	977	3,544
11...	Labette	R. W. Wright	976	
	Cherokee	R. W. Wright	640	
	Crawford	R. W. Wright	212	
	Montgomery	R. W. Wright	899	
	Howard	R. W. Wright	609	
	Cowley	R. W. Wright	333	3,669
	Republic.....................	H. C. Sprengle.....................	596	
	Washington	H. C. Sprengle.....................	455	
	Marshall.....................	H. C. Sprengle.....................	755	
	Clay	H. C. Sprengle.....................	2	
	Cloud	H. C. Sprengle.....................	236	2,044
12...	Jewell	D. E. Ballard.....................	160	
	Republic.....................	D. E. Ballard.....................	36	
	Washington	D. E. Ballard.....................	285	
	Marshall.....................	D. E. Ballard.....................	631	
	Clay	D. E. Ballard.....................	1,003	
	Cloud	D. E. Ballard.....................	339	
	Osborne	D. E. Ballard.....................	98	2,552

NOVEMBER 8.—The corporators of the Kansas Magazine Company are S. S. Prouty, H. King, D. W. Wilder, C. W. Babcock, Thos. A. Osborn, John A. Martin, D. M. Valentine, M. W. Reynolds, and W. H. Smallwood.

NOVEMBER 13.—D. R. Anthony consolidates the Bulletin with the Leavenworth Times.

NOVEMBER 15.—The Independence Tribune says: "The raising of a second crop is a task easily accomplished in this locality. We have corn and potatoes in this office of good quality, which were planted in June and July."

NOVEMBER 20.—Completion of the Insane Asylum building, at Osawatomie.

NOVEMBER 21.— Old Settlers' excursion from Lawrence, East.

NOVEMBER 25.—Lawrence has in operation the first street railway in the State.

—W. W. Updegraff, Superintendent of the Blind Asylum, at Wyandotte, resigns, and J. D. Parker succeeds him.

—The coal trade of Fort Scott now reaches half a million dollars, annually.

—The whole press of the State says good words for the proposed Magazine.

36

NOVEMBER 30.—Expenditures of the State for the year:

Governor's Department............	$5,222 67	State University.........................	16,915 00
Secretary's Department............	12,259 15	Deaf and Dumb Asylum...............	14,800 00
Auditor's Department..............	4,216 00	Blind Asylum...........................	7,633 43
Treasurer's Department...........	4,550 00	Normal School, Emporia...........	8,424 85
Attorney General......................	1,525 00	Normal School, Leavenworth....	6,377 80
Supt. of Public Instruction.......	3,050 50	Capitol building and grounds....	8,198 49
Adjutant General.....................	1,601 30	Neutral Land Defense Com'tee..	2,000 00
Judiciary	31,588 55	Agricultural College................	2,700 00
Librarian...............................	1,450 00	Military purposes.....................	1,581 91
Transcribing Journals..............	1,789 22	Regents.................................	294 60
Printing *...............................	41,692 01	C. C. Hutchinson, Book on Kan..	2,500 00
Immigration fund	5,000 00	Protestant and Catholic Asy-	
Sheriffs, conveying prisoners to		lums, Leavenworth...............	5,000 00
Penitentiary.........................	3,513 40	Seed wheat.............................	6,000 00
Penitentiary.............................	35,072 00	Miscellaneous expenses............	857 44
Legislative expenses...................	38,562 54		
Insane Asylum.........................	53,931 00	Total for 1871....................$329,293 42	

* $5,971.48 more than appropriated.

DECEMBER 1.—M. W. Reynolds is appointed Receiver of the Humboldt Land Office.

—The telegraph is completed to Seneca.

DECEMBER 1.—Ross's Paper, by E. G. Ross, is issued at Coffeyville.

—Over thirty new school-houses have been built in Washington and Republic counties during the year.

—Election of Directors of the Lawrence and Topeka Railroad. President, C. K. Holliday; Vice President, John Guthrie; Secretary, Jacob Safford.

DECEMBER 6.—Daily State Record discontinued. F. P. Baker, in his "Farewell," says he became connected with the Record in February, 1863, when Topeka had about 1,000 inhabitants. The Daily was started in June, 1868.

—West E. Wilkinson, of the Courier, wins the Seneca jack-knife; "carries it off triumphantly."

DECEMBER 6.—Col. James Montgomery dies, in Linn county.

—P. B. Maxson becomes Register of the Humboldt Land Office.

DECEMBER 11.—Noble L. Prentis becomes one of the editors of the Lawrence Journal.

—The streets of Fort Scott are macadamized.

DECEMBER 13.—Librarian Dickinson reports 7,341 volumes in the State Library.

DECEMBER 15.—James W. Steele goes over the State in behalf of the Magazine.

—A new town, called Hutchinson, is laid out on the Santa Fe road, 261 miles from Atchison.

DECEMBER 17.—Capt. Samuel J. Gilmore dies, at Osage Mission. He was the first white settler of that place, and the second pioneer in Neosho county.

DECEMBER 26.—The State Horticultural Society holds its Annual Meeting at Lawrence.

DECEMBER 29.—Eighth Annual Meeting of the State Teachers' Association, at Topeka. Address by Philetus Fales. *Officers elected:* President,

John Fraser, Lawrence; Corresponding Secretary, Joseph Denison, Manhattan; Recording Secretary, C. B. Isham, Council Grove; Executive Committee, John A. Banfield, Topeka; P. J. Williams, Leavenworth; J. N. Lee, Topeka; J. A. Barrows, Osage county; James B. Smith, Humboldt.

DECEMBER 31.—The Report of Superintendent McCarty, in addition to the usual statistics, gives a history of the Kansas Academy of Science, which was organized September 1, 1868.

1872.

JANUARY 1.—There are one hundred and twenty-one newspapers in the State.

—The Kansas Magazine is issued, from the Commonwealth office, Topeka; Henry King, Editor. The most noticeable articles, then and afterwards, were written by John J. Ingalls and James W. Steele. In this number Ingalls writes of A. D. Richardson, and the following is copied from his sketch:

"Kansas exercised the same fascination over him that she does over all who have ever yielded to her spell. There are some women whom to have once loved renders it impossible ever to love again. As the 'gray and melancholy main' to the sailor, the desert to the Bedouin, the Alp to the mountaineer, so is Kansas to all her children.

"No one ever felt any enthusiasm about Wisconsin, or Indiana, or Michigan. The idea is preposterous. It is impossible. They are great, prosperous communities, but their inhabitants can remove and never desire to return. They hunger for the horizon. They make new homes without the *maladie du pays*. But no genuine Kansan can emigrate. He may wander. He may roam. He may travel. He may go elsewhere, but no other State can ever claim him as a citizen. Once naturalized the allegiance can never be forsworn."

The four volumes of the Magazine contain articles relating to Kansas written by Milton W. Reynolds, Charles B. Wilkinson, R. J. Hinton, A. W. Lyman, Charles Robinson, Fred. J. Stanton, John E. Rastall, Frederic Lockley, Frank B. Sanborn, James M. Harvey, Joseph G. Waters, William B. Parsons, Francis S. McCabe, William A. Phillips, James H. Defouri, John W. Roberts, F. W. Giles, H. B. Norton, D. B. Emmert, W. H. Smallwood, Charles Reynolds, James Hanway, Sam. M. Newhall, Mrs. Rosetta B. Hastings (a daughter of Rev. Pardee Butler), and others.

JANUARY 4.—Grand Army of the Republic Convention at Lawrence. W. S. Jenkins elected Department Commander, vice S. A. Cobb, resigned.

—The "Prying Proboscis" is the name given to an investigation by the Legislature.

JANUARY 5.—Wm. B. Craig, Geo. W. Barr, John L. Motter and Obe. Craig, of Wathena, are given the credit for building the Doniphan and Wathena Railroad.

—The Wyandotte Herald is issued.

—S. H. Dodge joins A. D. Brown, in the Burlington Patriot.

JANUARY 6.—The Leavenworth Times says the debt of St. Joseph, Mo., is $1,416,700; of Kansas City, Mo., $1,000,000, and of Leavenworth, $700,000.

JANUARY 9.—Meeting of the Legislature.

STATE OFFICERS.

Names.	P. O. Address.	County.
James M. Harvey, Governor..	Fort Riley	Riley.
P. P. Elder, Lieutenant Governor...................................	Ottawa	Franklin.
W. H. Smallwood, Secretary of State.............................	Wathena	Doniphan.
A. L. Williams, Attorney General...................................	Topeka...........	Shawnee.
H. D. McCarty, Superintendent of Public Instruction...	Leavenworth...	Leavenw'th.
J. E. Hayes, State Treasurer..	Olathe	Johnson.
A. Thoman, Auditor of State..	Topeka...........	Shawnee.
S. S. Prouty, State Printer,..	Topeka...........	Shawnee.
David Whittaker, Adjutant General...............................	Doniphan........	Doniphan.
D. Dickinson, State Librarian...	Oskaloosa.......	Jefferson.
W. C. Webb, Superintendent Insurance Department....	Fort Scott........	Bourbon.

JUDGES OF THE SUPREME COURT.

Names.	P. O. Address.	County.
S. A. Kingman, Chief Justice..	Atchison.........	Atchison.
D. J. Brewer, Associate Justice.....................................	Leavenworth...	Leavenworth.
D. M. Valentine, Associate Justice................................	Ottawa	Franklin.

—Barzillai Gray, Judge Criminal Court, Leavenworth county.

JUDGES OF THE DISTRICT COURTS.

Names.	District.	P. O. Address.	County.
H. W. Ide	First............	Leavenworth City..	Leavenworth.
P. L. Hubbard.................................	Second........	Atchison..............	Atchison.
John T. Morton..............................	Third	Topeka	Shawnee.
Owen A. Bassett............................	Fourth........	Lawrence............	Douglas.
J. H. Watson.................................	Fifth............	Emporia	Lyon.
M. V. Voss...................................	Sixth...........	Mound City...........	Linn.
John R. Goodin.............................	Seventh.......	Humboldt	Allen.
William H. Canfield........................	Eighth.........	Junction City........	Davis.
William R. Brown	Ninth..........	Cottonwood Falls...	Chase.
Hiram Stevens	Tenth	Paola	Miami.
H. G. Webb	Eleventh......	Oswego	Labette.
A. S. Wilson.................................	Twelfth........	Washington...........	Washington.
W. P. Campbell..............................	Thirteenth..	Eldorado..............	Butler.
J. H. Prescott................................	Fourteenth...	Salina..................	Saline.

MEMBERS OF THE SENATE.

Names.	Dist.	P. O. Address.	County.
P. P. Elder, President...........................	......	Ottawa....................	Franklin.
Bowers, G. M......................................	10	Lenexa....................	Johnson.
Cracraft, Joseph.................................	5	Hiawatha..................	Brown.
Fitzpatrick, W. H................................	8	Topeka	Shawnee.
Haas, H. C...	3	Leavenworth	Leavenworth.
Hogeboom, G. W................................	4	Oskaloosa.................	Jefferson.
Jennison, C. R....................................	3	Leavenworth	Leavenworth.
Kellogg, Josiah...................................	3	Leavenworth.............	Leavenworth.
Logan, Joseph....................................	2	Effingham	Atchison.
Miller, Sol...	1	White Cloud	Doniphan.
Moore, H. D.......................................	14	Monmouth	Crawford.
Murdock, M. M	18	Burlingame................	Osage.
McLellan, James.................................	6	Holton	Jackson.
Nelson, George P................................	12	Wyandotte	Wyandotte.
Prescott, J. H.....................................	20	Salina	Saline.
Price, John M.....................................	2	Atchison..................	Atchison.
Rockefeller, Philip...............................	7	Washington	Washington.
Sears, T. C	17	Ottawa	Franklin.
Snoddy, James D................................	13	Mound City...............	Linn.
Stover, E. S.......................................	15	Council Grove	Morris.
Stotler, Jacob.....................................	19	Emporia	Lyon.

MEMBERS AND OFFICERS OF THE SENATE—Concluded.

Names.	Dist.	Post Office Address.	County.
Topping, E. H.	11	Paola	Miami.
Vincent, J. C.	9	Lawrence	Douglas.
Whitney, H. C.	16	Humboldt	Allen.
Wood, J.	1	Doniphan	Doniphan.
Worden, L. J.	9	Lawrence	Douglas.
George C. Crowther, Secretary		New Chicago	Neosho.
Charles C. Prescott, Ass't Secretary		Salina	Saline.
William Bolton, Journal Clerk		Seneca	Nemaha.
Wm. H. Price, Docket Clerk		Topeka	Shawnee.
Mrs. Sarah J. Neal, Engrossing Clerk.		Atchison	Atchison.
Mrs. H. E. Holman, Enrolling Clerk		Eureka	Greenwood.
George H. Schreiner, Sergeant-at-Arms.		Wyandotte	Wyandotte.
J. R. Kennedy, Ass't Sergeant-at-Arms.		Olathe	Johnson.
George W. Weed, Doorkeeper		Leavenworth	Leavenworth.
D. B. Aker, Assistant Doorkeeper			Marshall.
Ephie Smith, Page		Wyandotte	Wyandotte.
Harry Whitney, Page		Humboldt	Allen.
Jennie Griffith, Page		Topeka	Shawnee.

MEMBERS OF THE HOUSE OF REPRESENTATIVES.

Names.	Dist.	Post Office Address.	County.
Cobb, S. A., Speaker	27	Wyandotte	Wyandotte.
Aldrich, C. J.	11	Brantford	Washington.
Ashmore, S. D.	39	Girard	Crawford.
Barker, B. C.	24	Springdale	Leavenworth.
Bear, W. L.	93	Osborne City	Osborne.
Benedict, S. S.	63	Guilford	Wilson.
Blake, Alexander	60	Melvern	Osage.
Bowron, C. F.	6	White Cloud	Doniphan.
Boynton, J.	84	Salina	Saline.
Burton, A. W.	35	Mound City	Linn.
Bush, H. E.	58	Auburn	Shawnee.
Butler, C. B.	61	Leroy	Coffey.
Clark, G. W.	72	Parkerville	Morris.
Clark, Wm. H.	50	Ottawa	Franklin.
Connely, J. H.	28	New Santa Fe	Johnson.
Constant, D. C.	44	Chetopa	Labette.
Collins, Ira F.	8	Sabetha	Nemaha.
Cooley, James	23	Kickapoo	Leavenworth.
Copeland, O. S.	46	Osage Mission	Neosho.
Cowen, John R.	59	Carbondale	Osage.
Critchfield, Terry	16	Oskaloosa	Jefferson.
DeForest, H. C.	9	Wetmore	Nemaha.
DeVore, B. F.	65	Independence	Montgomery.
Doster, Frank	77	Marion Centre	Marion.
Drake, C.	69	Americus	Lyon.
Dunwell, E. B.	64	Parker	Montgomery.
Edwards, John H.	89	Ellis	Ellis.
Everett, B. F.	62	Neosho Falls	Woodson.
Eskridge, C. V.	68	Emporia	Lyon.
Fain, F. M.	32	Fontana	Miami.
Fenlon, Thos. P.	22	Leavenworth	Leavenworth.
Gay, F. C.	90	Wallace	Wallace.
Goddard, L. M.	19	Leavenworth	Leavenworth.
Green, W. H.	36	Osaga	Bourbon.
Greening, J. R.	37	Fort Scott	Bourbon.
Gregg, S. C.	56	North Topeka	Shawnee.
Griffin, C. T.	6	Atchison	Atchison.
Griffith, F. J.	91	Atlanta	Rice.
Halstead, C. J.	25	Reno	Leavenworth.
Haskell, D. C.	53	Lawrence	Douglas.
Hoffman, C.	79	Detroit	Dickinson.
Holliday, C. K.	57	Topeka	Shawnee.
Hollingsworth, E.	83	Lindsey	Ottawa.
Hackney, W. P.	92	Belle Plain	Sumner.
Hutchinson, C. C.	94	Hutchinson	Reno.
Jeffers, Alvinza	10	Irving	Marshall.
Johnson, D. H.	31	Paola	Miami.

MEMBERS AND OFFICERS OF HOUSE OF REPRESENTATIVES—CONCLUDED.

Names.	Dist.	Post Office Address.	County.
Johnson, J. M	70	Wilmington	Wabaunsee.
Keables, E. H	45	Thayer	Neosho.
Kellogg, C. M	80	Clay Centre	Clay.
Kelley, J. H	54	Willow Springs	Douglas.
Kennedy, H. K	17	North Topeka	Shawnee.
Kennedy, S. T	42	Columbus	Cherokee.
Latta, S. N	21	Leavenworth	Leavenworth.
Langdon, S. J	40	Iowa City	Crawford.
Loughmiller, Jacob	15	Buck's Grove	Jackson.
Lightcap, J. M	13	Wamego	Pottawatomie.
Malott, H	26	Wyandotte	Wyandotte.
Marchand, N	20	Leavenworth	Leavenworth.
Mailler, Robert	2	Troy	Doniphan.
McEckron, B. H	82	Clyde	Cloud.
McIntyre, T	75	Arkansas City	Cowley.
Mills, T. B	47	Iola	Allen.
McWilliams, J. W	73	Cottonwood Falls	Chase.
Mooney, Isaac	74	Towanda	Montgomery.
Nichols, R. H	66	Longton	Howard.
Nye, Ira P	67	Eureka	Greenwood.
Olson, O	78	Lindsburg	McPherson.
Osborne, V. B	85	Ellsworth	Ellsworth.
Palmer, L. G	38	Fort Scott	Bourbon.
Pate, D. W	88	Jewell City	Jewell.
Payne, D. L	76	Wichita	Sedgwick.
Pierce, T. M	1	Iowa Point	Doniphan.
Pinkerton, J. H	12	Manhattan	Riley.
Rees, John	87	Beloit	Mitchell.
Robinson, C	52	Lawrence	Douglas.
Rodgers, J. W	18	Winchester	Jefferson.
Sayer, J. M	33	Blooming Grove	Linn.
Schofield, Wm. H	51	Williamsburg	Franklin.
Scofield, C. I	4	Atchison	Atchison.
Schermerhorn, F. A	86	Rocky Hill	Lincoln.
Scott, W. B	34	Mound City	Linn.
Searcy, Ed	3	Elwood	Doniphan.
Sells, E	55	Lawrence	Douglas.
Smith, G. P	48	Humboldt	Allen.
Stevenson, T. G	29	Monticello	Johnson.
Strickler, S. M	71	Junction City	Davis.
Taylor, A	30	Gardner	Johnson.
Wells, W	14	Manhattan	Riley.
Whitford, J. H	49	Garnett	Anderson.
Wilson, A. D	81	Belleville	Republic.
Wilson, J. C	5	Muscotah	Atchison.
Wood, G. W	41	Columbus	Cherokee.
Wood, J. J	43	Montana	Labette.
A. R. Banks, Chief Clerk		Lawrence	Douglas.
S. F. Burdett, Assistant Clerk		Leavenworth	Leavenworth.
H. Brandley, Journal Clerk		Matfield Green	Chase.
E. E. Bacon, Docket Clerk		Leroy	Coffey.
Mrs. Rebecca Hays, Ass't Docket Clerk		Topeka	Shawnee.
Miss Carrie Sain, Enrolling Clerk		Topeka	Shawnee.
Miss Lizzie Ela, Ass't Enrolling Clerk		Emporia	Lyon.
Mrs. R. Flower, Engrossing Clerk		Topeka	Shawnee.
Miss K. Reck, Ass't Engrossing Clerk		Atchison	Atchison.
James M. Matheny, Sergeant-at-Arms		St. Mary's	Pottawatomie.
Thos. Sanders, Ass't Sergeant-at-Arms			Osage.
A. H. Beck, Doorkeeper		Ottawa	Franklin.
Dora Scott, Page			
Hattie Butler, Page			
Robert Miller, Page			
Frank Blake, Page			
William Wakefield, Page			
Thomas Parks, Page			
Frank Morgan, Page			

JANUARY 9.—

"The corrupt use of money in elections of all kinds, and the consequent peculation and demoralization, together with the fact that legislation and administration have sometimes been influenced by corrupt appliances, demand and are beginning to receive the attention of upright officials and patriotic citizens throughout the nation."

"The frequent appearance of money as an element of corrupt political power, is appalling to patriotic and thoughtful men everywhere. Its tendency is to create and perpetuate an oligarchy of the very wealthy and unscrupulous, with their base and mercenary adherents."

. . . .

"I recommend the passage of a law providing that any corporation, against which it shall be proven that money has been contributed for the election or defeat of any candidate for any public office, shall forfeit its charter; and that all managing officers of such corporations, if residents of this State, shall be disfranchised, and if non-residents, they shall be rendered incapable of doing any official act within the jurisdiction of this State."—*Gov. Harvey's Message.*

JANUARY 17.—The Lawrence Standard gives the names of nineteen members of the last Legislature who are charged with having been bribed to vote for Senator Caldwell; about half of them are Democrats.

—During the past year the M. K. & T. build a railroad from Holden, Mo., to Paola; the A., T. & S. F. completed the road-bed from Atchison to Topeka; the St. Louis, Lawrence & Denver road was built from Pleasant Hill, Mo., to Lawrence, fifty-eight miles; and the St. Joseph & Denver was extended from Marysville to Fairbury, Neb.

JANUARY 18. — Resolutions introduced in the Legislature to investigate the Caldwell election.

JANUARY 22.—The Russian Grand Duke Alexis received by the Legislature.

—The Presbyterians of the State contributed last year to the Memorial Fund of that Church, $72,212.40.

JANUARY 24.—A committee of five members of the House and three of the Senate appointed to investigate charges of bribery and corruption connected with the Senatorial elections of 1867 and 1871.

JANUARY 31.—W. H. Green, Chairman of House Special Committee, reports:

"Your committee find that there have been audited claims for which the scrip commonly known as the Price Raid Scrip has been issued or ordered to be issued, of the class of claims arising from—

Material, supplies, transportation	$111,352 53
Service of Militia	256,761 20
Miscellaneous	36,627 64
Total	$404,741 37

"Your committee also find that of the class of claims arising from damages done by Rebel and Federal troops to property, and for which the scrip of the State has been issued to the amount of $159,191.34, no action was taken by the Commissioners sent from Washington last spring.

"And your committee find that all the scrip issued for any of the above classes is of the date of June 1, 1867, and bears interest at the rate of seven per cent. per annum."
—*House Journal, pp. 373-4.*

JANUARY 31.—Marcus J. Parrott accepts an invitation to address the House on Commercial Politics.

—During the year, Crane & Byron, Topeka, publish two pamphlets — the Kansas Road Laws, and the Kansas Bond Laws, by Hugh M. Spalding. The Commonwealth prints Ravenia, a novel, by Annie Nellis.

FEBRUARY 1.—

"STATE OF KANSAS, ATTORNEY GENERAL'S OFFICE, }
TOPEKA, KANSAS, February 1, 1872. }

"To THE SENATE: Your Secretary has furnished me the following resolution, adopted by you on the 30th day of January, 1872:

"'*Resolved,* That the Attorney General be, and is hereby instructed, to enquire into the Missouri River, Fort Scott and Gulf Railroad, the Kansas Pacific Railroad, the Leavenworth, Lawrence and Galveston Railroad, and the Missouri River Railroad, whether said roads are located and operated according to their grants and as provided by their charters, and report the same to the Senate within one week.

"'Adopted January 30, 1872.　　　　　　　　　GEO. C. CROWTHER, *Secretary.*'

"And in response thereto I submit the following digest of the legal status of the roads mentioned in the resolution:

"1. *The Missouri River, Fort Scott and Gulf Road.* This road was originally called the 'Kansas and Neosho Valley Railroad Company,' and by that name filed its charter of incorporation in the office of the Secretary of State, on the 8th day of March, A. D. 1865. Its northern terminus, as fixed by its charter, was 'the eastern terminus of the Union Pacific Railroad, E. D.' (now the Kansas Pacific), 'on the State line dividing Kansas and Missouri.' The southern terminus was 'the southern boundary of the State of Kansas, in the valley of the Neosho river.'

"On the 25th of July, A. D. 1866, Congress granted to this Company (by its name of Kansas and Neosho Valley Railroad Company) certain public land to aid in the construction of a railroad 'from the eastern terminus of the Union Pacific Railroad, Eastern Division, at the line between Kansas and Missouri, at or near the mouth of the Kansas river, on the south side thereof, southwardly through the eastern tier of counties in Kansas,' to Preston, Texas. (U. S. Statutes at Large, vol. 14, p. 236.)

"On the 5th of October, 1868, the probate court of Johnson county, under section 15, chapter 57, Laws of 1866, page 129, granted a decree changing the name of the 'Kansas and Neosho Valley Railroad Company' to the 'Missouri River, Fort Scott and Gulf Railroad.' This decree was filed with the Secretary of State October 10, 1868.

"2. On the 12th of October, 1865, another company, named the '*Missouri River, Fort Scott and Gulf Railroad,*' filed a charter of incorporation with the Secretary of State. Its northern terminus is 'the eastern terminus of the Union Pacific Railroad, E. D.' (now the Kansas Pacific), 'in Kansas.' Its southern terminus is 'a point on the southern boundary of Kansas at or near Baxter Springs, south of Fort Scott, and in the direction of Fort Gibson.'

"3. *Kansas Pacific Railway Company.* This company was originally called the Leavenworth, Pawnee and Western Railroad, and was incorporated by act of the Territorial Legislature, in 1855. (Laws of 1855, page 914.) Its eastern terminus was 'the town of Leavenworth,' and its western was 'Pawnee or Fort Riley, with the right to extend to the western boundary of the Territory' of Kansas. The land grant of this road (Statutes at Large, vol. 12, p. 494) provides for the building of a road from the Missouri river, at the mouth of the Kansas river, on the south side thereof. The name of this road was changed by its directors to that of the 'Union Pacific Railway, Eastern Division.' The name was subsequently changed to the 'Kansas Pacific Railway.'

"4. The charter of the *Missouri River Railroad Company* was filed with the Secretary of State on the twentieth day of February, A. D. 1865. The charter provides the termini as follows: 'Commencing on the line between the State of Missouri and the State of Kansas, at the terminus of the Missouri Pacific Railroad, thence along or near the Missouri river to the city of Leavenworth, thence to Fort Leavenworth.'

"5. *The Leavenworth, Lawrence and Fort Gibson Railroad Company* was incorporated by act of the Territorial Legislature, February 12, 1858. (Private Laws of 1858, page 123.) Its charter provides for building a railroad from 'Leavenworth City to Fort Gibson, or the highest point of steamboat navigation of Grand River.'

"On the third of March, 1863 (Statutes at Large, vol. 12, page 772), Congress made a grant of land to this company to aid the building of a railroad 'from the City of Leavenworth by the way of the town of Lawrence to the southern line of the State, in the direction of Galveston Bay, in Texas, with a branch from Lawrence by the valley of the Wakarusa river, to the point on the Atchison, Topeka and Santa Fe Railroad, where said road intersects the Neosho river.' On the twenty-third of February, 1866, the State granted to the road the proceeds of one-fourth of the five hundred thousand acres, which section three of article six of our Constitution describes as a part of the 'perpetual school fund of the State.' On the 24th of February, 1866, the name of this road was changed by the Legislature (Laws of 1866, page 191), to the 'Leavenworth, Lawrence and Galveston Railroad Company.'

"I forgot, in the proper place, to mention the fact that the Kansas and Neosho Valley Railroad also got one-fourth of the proceeds of the five hundred thousand acres aforesaid to aid in building a road, 'commencing at or near the mouth of the Kansas river, in the State of Kansas, opposite the city of Wyandotte, and running through the counties of Johnson, Miami, Linn and Bourbon, in the direction of the southern boundary of the State.'

"This is the legal status of these roads. Not being empowered by law or by your resolution to hear and determine questions of fact by the ordinary modes of taking testimony, I am unable to state whether, as a matter of fact, these roads are 'located and operated according to their grants, and as provided by their charters.'

"Respectfully submitted.   A. L. WILLIAMS, *Attorney General.*"
—*Senate Journal, pp. 253 to 256.*

FEBRUARY 1.—Rev. J. Boynton invited to address the Legislature on "A pure Christianity the only basis of a free and stable Government."

—W. L. Chalfant buys the Osage Chronicle.

FEBRUARY 21.—Republican State Convention at Lawrence. Called to order by D. R. Anthony. *Temporary Officers:* J. D. Snoddy, Chairman; J. C. Horton, Secretary. *Committee on Credentials:* D. B. Emmert, J. B. Davis, M. Cracraft, M. Stephenson, A. L. Williams, H. L. Taylor, C. G. Hawley. *Committee on Organization:* B. F. Simpson, W. J. Bawden, E. S. Stover, J. C. Carpenter, E. S. Niccolls, W. M. Matheny, John Speer. *Committee on Resolutions:* Albert H. Horton, L. H. Vanschieck, H. H. Williams, Joseph Steel, James McClellan. *Officers of Convention:* President, James D. Snoddy; Vice Presidents, J. J. Wood, M. Cracraft, E. J. Jenkins; Secretaries, J. C. Horton, J. S. Wilson. Judge A. H. Horton reported the following resolutions, which were adopted:

"*Whereas,* The Republicans of Kansas, assembled in Convention for the purpose of electing delegates to unite with delegates of other States, on June 5th ensuing, for the purpose of nominating the next President and Vice President of the United States, desire to give renewed and most emphatic expression to their confidence in the principles, their pride in the record, and their faith in the future of that national political organization which carried the country through the difficulties and preserved it amid the disasters of one of the stormiest conflicts of all history; and which has addressed itself to the solution of those delicate and difficult problems which are the general legacy of all wars, and more especially of such a civil strife as ours, in such a manner as—with such local exceptions as would be inseparable from any policy of pacification—to secure to the country at large a degree of internal peace, organic unity, financial standing and credit, and general business prosperity, which are the wonder and admiration of all the nations of the earth; and believing, as this Convention does, that this satisfactory condition of affairs is largely attributable to the patient courage and wisdom of the man who was first the trusted Commander-in-Chief of the armies, and then the honored President of the councils of the Republic: it is therefore

"*Resolved,* That the delegates this day chosen to attend the Philadelphia National Convention be and they are hereby instructed to cast their votes for the patriot President and citizen and soldier, Ulysses S. Grant, who in the dark and disastrous days of the Republic displayed those qualities of courage, wisdom, loyalty and unyielding persistency which inspired the friends of Freedom with new energy and hope, filled and fired the gallant soldiers of the Union with the spirit to fight, and, if need be, to die in its defence, and which crowned our long conflict with the inestimable boon of complete victory and permanent peace; and who in the less dangerous but more difficult duties to which a grateful people called him, has proved himself an able, steady and successful pilot of the ship of state; amid conflicting opinions and trying exigencies, the earnest advocate of all judicious attempts at political reform; the foremost friend of all oppressed and distressed peoples, of whatever condition or color, who are struggling for the inalienable rights of perfect equality before the law; the undaunted defender of our national claims and equities in the great parliament of the nations; whose administration, in short, has brought us a degree of prosperity at home and respect and dignity abroad, which it would be suicidal to interrupt or interfere with until time has been given to complete and cement the work so well begun and so auspiciously prosecuted to the present time."

570　　　　　*ANNALS OF KANSAS.*　　　　　[1872.

The following delegates were chosen to the Philadelphia Convention: Henry Buckingham of Concordia, Benjamin F. Simpson of Paola, John A. Martin of Atchison, Wm. Baldwin of Wichita, H. C. Cross of Emporia, Charles A. Morris of Fort Scott, George Noble of Lawrence, John C. Carpenter of New Chicago, and Josiah Kellogg and John M. Haeberlein of Leavenworth. The following alternates were chosen: S. F. Ayres, E. S. Niccolls, J. V. Fairbanks, Frederic Close, A. A. Thomas, Percy Daniels, R. E. Stephenson, Thomas Newton, S. J. Smith, and M. S. Thomas.

The following resolution, introduced by A. A. Carnahan, of Cloud county, was adopted:

"*Resolved*, That we hereby denounce any man in public life who will dare to employ corrupt means in politics, and we, the Republicans of Kansas, will set our faces steadfastly against all such, and will endeavor to make the future of Kansas pure and good."

There were 174 delegates in the Convention, and the National delegates were elected by ballot.

FEBRUARY 22.—President Denison, of Manhattan, and Rev. Dr. Chas. Reynolds, of Fort Riley, go to Washington to attend the Convention of officers of Agricultural Colleges.

—The Missouri, Kansas and Texas road is running to Muskogee.

—Soldiers' Reunion at Topeka.

FEBRUARY 23.—A caucus of Opposition or Liberal Republicans is held at Topeka.

FEBRUARY 24.—Unanimous report from the joint committee to investigate Senatorial elections. The report is as follows:

"*Mr. President of the Senate, and Speaker of the House of Representatives:* The committee appointed under the foregoing resolution met on the twenty-sixth day of January, 1872, and organized and issued subpœnas for witnesses, and adjourned until Tuesday, the thirtieth day of January, and on that day met and proceeded to take the testimony of witnesses, and continued from day to day, and ceased the taking of testimony on the twenty-third day of February, 1872. We summoned to appear before us persons within the State, of whom it was alleged that they knew something of the subject-matter of the enquiry, and the testimony of those who appeared was taken. Under the authority of a concurrent resolution, the committee employed James Chew as their clerk, who reduced to writing all the testimony taken, which testimony is herewith submitted, and made a part of our report.

"From the testimony taken, your committee find: That at the Senatorial election of 1867 a large sum of money was used, and attempted to be used, in bribing, and in attempting to bribe and influence the members of the Legislature, to secure the election of S. C. Pomeroy, E. G. Ross and Thomas Carney, by S. C. Pomeroy, Thomas Carney, Perry Fuller, and others in their employ. (See the report of a committee appointed in 1867, in House Journal of 1867, from page 957 to page 971, inclusive. Also, see testimony herewith submitted, of G. A. Reynolds, I. S. Kalloch, R. D. Mobley, S. D. Macdonald, T. A. Osborn, Joshua Wheeler, William Spriggs, D. R. Anthony, Edward Russell, and others.)

"It also appears in reference to that election that S. C. Pomeroy and Sidney Clarke, in March, 1866, jointly paid one thousand dollars, and promised to pay the further sum of two thousand dollars, for which they executed their joint notes to M. W. Reynolds, who has been recently appointed Receiver of the Land Office at Neodesha, in consideration that he would use the columns of his paper, the Journal, at Lawrence, to secure the election of S. C. Pomeroy to the United States Senate in 1867, and Sidney Clarke to Congress, in the fall of 1866. It also appears that S. C. Pomeroy paid, in addition, the further sum of two hundred and fifty dollars to the said M. W. Reynolds. It further appears that M. W. Reynolds sued upon these notes in the Douglas county district court, and the defendants, Pomeroy and Clarke, pleaded therein an illegal consideration for the notes, and that the findings of the court upon trial upon the merits were for the defendants, and the judgment against the plaintiff Reynolds. That Reynolds had the case prepared for the Supreme Court, and then directed his counsel not to proceed further in the cause, and that shortly thereafter he was appointed to the public office he now holds. From the depositions of Pomeroy and Clarke, taken and used in that case, it would seem that the payment of the one thousand dollars, and the promise of two thousand dollars, to M. W. Reynolds, were to advance Republicanism in Kansas, and to secure a Republican victory at the election in the fall of 1866.

"When such testimony as this is viewed in the light of the then well-known fact, and the subsequently demonstrated truth, that the State was then Republican by a majority of eleven thousand, without the aid of the Lawrence Journal, its falsity is apparent. That the one thousand dollars was paid, and the two thousand dollars promised to be paid was so paid and promised to be paid to subsidize the Journal in the interests of S. C. Pomeroy and Sidney Clarke personally, is a fair conclusion from the testimony. (See the testimony of Geo. A. Reynolds, W. W. Nevison, and the depositions of S. C. Pomeroy, Sidney Clarke, Geo. A. Reynolds, and the findings of the court.) As a thorough investigation of the Senatorial election of 1867, by reason of the lapse of time since that date, absolutely required for its preparation and completion much more time than the ordinary length of a Legislative session, the committee were forced to be content in that regard with what they could glean from the witnesses brought before them for the proof of other facts. Yet, from all the testimony before the committee on that question, we have no hesitation in recording our well-established conclusions, that money was used in a large amount and in a corrupt and criminal way by candidates for United States Senator, and by their friends with their knowledge.

"In relation to the election of 1871, the committee find that the testimony shows that Sidney Clarke was a candidate for election to the office of United States Senator in 1871, and that his friends engaged for him, which act he afterwards ratified, some eighty rooms at the Tefft House; that, in addition thereto, he rented and fitted up on the opposite side of the street from the Tefft House, and on the corner of Kansas avenue and Sixth avenue, a suit of five rooms, which was during that canvass designated as 'the soup house,' and 'the bread riot,' where refreshments were kept. That he deposited with the Kansas Valley National Bank, when he came here, twenty-five hundred dollars, which was drawn out by Mr. Adams upon authority from Clarke.

"That Sidney Clarke overdrew his account about sixteen hundred dollars. (See testimony of Clarke, Adams and Abell et al.) That he offered to members of the Legislature appointments to office and payment of expenses of the election of members of the Legislature, for their votes for himself for United States Senator. (See testimony of King, Phinney, Bond and Wheeler.) That he told R. S. Stevens to make whatever arrangements he pleased with Caldwell in regard to his (Clarke's) expenses. (See testimony of Clarke.) That Stevens paid out for Sidney Clarke, during that canvass, about twenty-six hundred dollars. (See testimony of George A. Reynolds.)

"That his friend, D. M. Adams, with the knowledge of Clarke, undertook to purchase Senator Wood's vote with the promise of an office, which promise was secured by a certificate of deposit of the Kansas Valley National Bank for the sum of three thousand dollars, actually issued. (See the testimony of King, Abell and Adams.) That Mr. Wheaton, of Fort Scott, a friend of Mr. Clarke's, who was here endeavoring to secure Clarke's election, offered to buy the vote of W. C. Webb for Mr. Clarke, for the sum of two thousand dollars, at Fort Scott, in December, 1870. (See testimony of Webb.) These things all conspire to place the fact beyond question that Mr. Clarke intended to use, used, and was endeavoring to use, and with his knowledge permitted his friends to use and endeavor to use, money and other valuable considerations, in an illegal, corrupt and criminal way, to secure votes for himself for the United States Senate. (See testimony of Clarke, Adams, Phinney, King, P. T. Abell, W. C. Webb, and W. Shannon.) It also appears that R. S. Stevens, who is a resident of Attica, New York, and General Manager of the Missouri, Kansas and Texas Railroad, and whose business headquarters were then, as now, in Sedalia, Missouri, was here in the interest of Mr. Clarke, and expended an amount of money for his use in the canvass. Also that P. T. Abell was here and spent a sum of money in the interest of Mr. Clarke, and was at that time in the employment of James F. Joy in his railroad business in this State. (See testimony of George A. Reynolds and P. T. Abell.) Also that John McDonald, a resident of St. Louis, Missouri, who had a peculiar interest in Mr. Clarke's election, was here in Clarke's interest. It also appears that Adams paid out of Clarke's money the entire expense of 'the soup house.' That a part of the moeny paid by Stevens went to pay the expenses of 'the soup house.' And that Col. P. T. Abell paid two or three hundred dollars as a part of the expenses of 'the soup house.' May it not be that the disgraceful 'soup house' is made the *ledger scape-goat* of greater sins of these men? (See testimony of Adams, Abell and Reynolds.) It can hardly be supposed, even by the most verdant, that Mr. Adams would issue the paper of the Kansas Valley National Bank for three thousand dollars, and Mr. Wheaton offer to pay two thousand dollars for a vote for Mr. Clarke, without the authority of Mr. Clarke.

"In the case of the certificate for the three thousand dollars, the testimony of Mr. King shows that the transaction, which was a direct attempt to obtain a vote for Mr. Clarke by bribery (the bribery being a mail agency, or its cash equivalent—three thousand dollars), was with the knowledge and consent of Mr. Clarke, if not by his positive direction. The fact that Mr. Wheaton came here and labored for Mr. Clarke, and was at the time he made the offer to Mr. Webb, and had been before, the strong friend of Mr. Clarke, leaves but little doubt, even with the most sceptical, that it was an effort directed and assented to by Clarke, to bribe Webb with two thousand dollars. The offers made to Phinney by Clarke himself and S. C. King, as shown by Wheeler's testimony, are of the same character, except that in the latter it does not appear that any money was to be used in connexion with the appointment. (See testimony of Clarke, Wheeler, King, Phinney, and Abell.)

"In relation to the matters affecting Alexander Caldwell, the testimony shows that Len. T. Smith was his particular friend, and was a Democrat, and here working earnestly in the interest of Mr. Caldwell, and recognized by him as his confidential adviser and agent. That J. L. McDowell was here working for and on confidential terms with Alexander Caldwell, in consideration of the promise of Caldwell to remove Mrs. Johnson, a widow, whose husband was killed early in the war, at Morristown, Missouri, from the post office at Leavenworth. (See testimony of McDowell, Thomas, et al.)

"That a large lobby of Leavenworth men were here in the interest of Caldwell. That Thomas Carney was here upon confidential relations with Caldwell. That some kind of a written agreement existed between Caldwell and Carney in relation to the Senatorial election. (See testimony of McDowell, et al.)

"That Carney stated, but about two weeks ago, that he was coming before the committee to testify, and sent such message to the committee; that he was notified by telegraph, as well as by summons, to appear; that he was going to tell all he knew, and that he knew that Caldwell and those in his interest had purchased the votes of members of the Legislature to vote for Caldwell (see the testimony of Osborn); that a check for *seven thousand dollars*, drawn by Len. T. Smith in favor of Thomas Carney, went into the hands of T. J. Anderson, which was by Mr. Anderson presented and cashed at the Kansas Valley National Bank, January 23, 1871. (See testimony of D. M. Adams.

"That another check for the sum of *five thousand dollars*, drawn by J. W. Morris, was cashed under very suspicious circumstances by the Topeka Bank, on the night of the 23d day of January, 1871. (See the testimony of Morris, Mulvane, and Jacob Smith.)

"That another check for *one thousand two hundred dollars* was drawn by Robert Crozier, and cashed at the Topeka Bank on the 24th or 25th day of January, 1871, and the cash delivered to Len. T. Smith. (See testimony of Mulvane and Crozier.)

"That Len. T. Smith borrowed an amount of money from Thomas A. Osborn to pay his hotel bill. (See testimony of Osborn.)

"That a draft upon the Treasurer of the Kansas Pacific Railway Company for *ten thousand dollars* was presented by T. J. Anderson, and cashed at the Kansas Valley National Bank, on the 23d day of January, 1871.

"It will be borne in mind that the first vote for United States Senator, in 1871, was upon the 24th day of January, 1871, and the joint convention and final vote on the next day, being on the 25th day of January.

"There is now a note for three thousand five hundred dollars in the Kansas Valley National Bank, made by Anderson and endorsed by Caldwell, for transactions in this canvass, which note is for the benefit of T. J. Anderson.

"That Mr. Caldwell claims that the Kansas Pacific Railway Company, by its agents, at or about the time of the Senatorial election of 1871, promised to give to him thirty thousand dollars as its share of the election expenses of that election, or as its bonus for his influence as United States Senator. That Caldwell demanded of and importuned Mr. Perry, the President of the Kansas Pacific Railway Company, to pay to Mr. Caldwell the said sum of $30,000, at Leavenworth, after his election, and that by an arrangement with Mr. Perry, Mr. Caldwell and his faithful friend, Len. T. Smith, came to

Topeka from Leavenworth to see about and settle up this *thirty-thousand-dollar* transaction, and that the agents of the company here did not admit the promise, as alleged by Caldwell, but did not stand as square on the subject as the President of the Company wished. (See testimony of J. P. Usher.) That Len. T. Smith wanted to arrange with Jacob Smith, President of the Topeka Bank, to cash checks given in the canvass. (See testimony of Jacob Smith.) That Len. T. Smith wished to be informed of any members of the Legislature who could be bought. (See testimony of Greeno.) That Len. T. Smith said they were dead broke on the morning of the 23d or 24th, but as soon as Major Anderson came, they would have plenty of greenbacks again, and that he would be back in a few moments. That Anderson did come back and apparently had something, and went into Caldwell's private room with Caldwell. (See testimony of Raymond.) That W. H. Carson got one thousand dollars of this corruption fund. (See testimony of Shannon and Spriggs.) That money was paid and offered to be paid to various members of the Legislature by Caldwell's agents and friends. (See testimony of Spriggs, Hammond, Greeno, Melville, Neal, Osborn, Thomas Floyd, Chase, G. W. Wood, Manning, Burke, H. D. Baker, and others.) That George Smith paid out to members of the Legislature, for Mr. Caldwell, and with an understanding that it should be refunded to him by Caldwell, over twenty thousand dollars. (See testimony of Spriggs.) That Caldwell promised appointments to office and other favorable official acts for votes. (See testimony of Bond, and others.) That Caldwell said after his election, at different times, that his election cost him more than any one was aware of, and clearly indicated by his conversation, and in fact said, that he paid for his seat in the United States Senate from this State, twice as much as the salary of the office for the full term of six years would amount to, or about sixty thousand dollars, and that he paid Carney's election expenses, amounting to more than ten per cent. of the whole sum, or over six thousand dollars. (See Burke's testimony, also Adams and Davis.) That Caldwell offered twice or oftener to pay all of Sidney Clarke's election expenses, and that he did agree with R. S. Stevens to pay them upon consideration of Clarke's withdrawal and Clarke's friends' support of Caldwell in the Joint Convention. From all the testimony your committee find that Alexander Caldwell used bribery, and other corrupt and criminal means, by himself and his friends, with his full knowledge and consent, to secure his election in 1871, to the U. S. Senate, from the State of Kansas.

"Your committee have also to report that the most important witnesses, Thomas Carney, Len. T. Smith, W. H. Carson, and T. J. Anderson, are now fugitives from the State, for the purpose of depriving this committee of their testimony, and that their absence is in contempt of proper processes issued and served upon them, and, as your committee is convinced, from all the circumstances surrounding their sudden and clandestine hegira, for a cash consideration paid to at least two of them, (see Burke's and Osborn's testimony.) W. A. Martin and Joel Thomas, important witnesses as we believe, have failed to appear, and we have been unable to learn of their whereabouts since they were served—Thomas being served by copy, Martin twice with personal service, once with a subpœna and once with the rule of the Senate. Thomas Moonlight and John Fletcher have failed to appear in obedience to process. Every reasonable effort has been used to get these witnesses. Diligent enquiry does not discover that R. S. Stevens has been in the State during the pendency of this enquiry. Ever since this enquiry began, there has been an organized effort of persons in the interest of Mr. Caldwell, and perhaps others, to keep out of the reach of the committee witnesses whose attendance was greatly desired. Every obstruction that could be has been thrown in our way by these persons.

"The secrecy with which the crimes which the testimony we submit discover, the interest of all concerned to conceal them and the disgrace which attaches to all the parties implicated, even remotely, make the labor of proving them very difficult. Men who have been guilty of giving or taking a bribe, or in anywise connected therewith, as a general rule do not hesitate to hide their own and confederates' infamy behind the less odious crime of perjury.

"The time left us after our assignment to this duty before the close of the session was entirely too short to permit us to go entirely through the work we have had in hand, especially when it is remembered that we had our ordinary legislative duties to perform as well as this extraordinary duty. The magnitude of our labors, and of the subject referred to us, can be fully appreciated by those only who have met the enquiry face to face. When the testimony which we herewith submit is read in the light of the facts that Len. T. Smith left the State about the time this investigation was ordered, and remains away; that Carney, Anderson and Carson are fugitives who have sought refuge beyond the territorial limits of the State; that Fletcher, Thomas and Martin are skulking, secreted or absent from the State, there can be but one conclusion, and that is, that some person or persons are guilty of the offences into which we are enquiring, and that they know it. (See testimony of Osborn, Burke, Adams, Spriggs, and others.)

"From the testimony, all will see that the full and complete exposition of these high crimes is the incessant labor of months instead of the few days we have had. As our report must of necessity be made before this session closes, and as adjournment is near at hand, we are compelled to close our labors with the testimony of the sixty-four witnesses which we have examined and the documents attached to their testimony, all of which we respectfully submit.   J. D. SNODDY, *Chairman on part of Senate.*
                                                     E. S. STOVER.
                                                     H. C. WHITNEY.
                                                     WM. H. CLARK, *Chairman on part of House.*
                                                     G. W. CLARK.
                                                     J. J. WOOD.
                                                     J. BOYNTON.
                                                     D. H. JOHNSON."
                                                     —*Senate Journal, pp. 561 to 569.*

FEBRUARY 26.—

"STATE OF KANSAS, EXECUTIVE DEPARTMENT, TOPEKA, February 26, 1872.

"TO THE LEGISLATURE: I have just received from Hon. D. P. Lowe, M. C., the enclosed letter and accompanying documents relating to the Price Raid Claims. I place them before you with the recommendation that you take such action as you deem proper to secure an equitable adjustment and prompt payment of the claims.

                                                     "JAMES M. HARVEY, *Governor.*"

"HOUSE OF REPRESENTATIVES, WASHINGTON, D. C., Feb. 22, 1872.

"HON. JAMES M. HARVEY—*Dear Sir:* I have heretofore sent you a copy of the report and bill approved by the Committee on Claims, to appropriate $337,054 on the Price Raid Claims. The Committee unanimously voted to report the bill favorably, and have been ready for three weeks to report it, but the Committee has not been called. I expect the bill to pass, but nothing is certain until it is done. It has occurred to me that possibly some State legislation might be necessary to enable the Treasurer to pay the money to the parties whose claims are approved by the Commission, inasmuch as all the amount which the State has partially assumed is not allowed by the Commission. What the case may be as to the disbursement of the money by the State under existing laws I cannot tell, as I have not all the legislation of the State before me, but thought I had better call your attention to it. Possibly it might be desirable to pass an act authorizing the Treasurer to pay to each of the parties in whose favor the Commission report the amount found due them. I do not know that it is necessary, but simply invite attention to it. Yours, truly,   D. P. LOWE."
—*House Journal, pp. 1066-7.*

The Legislature took no action. Had such a law been passed, all illegal disbursement of the money would have been prevented.

FEBRUARY 28.—M. J. Parrott, S. A. Riggs, N. A. Adams, S. N. Wood, A. Thoman, H. C. Haas and E. G. Ross issue an address to the people of Kansas. It takes ground against the renomination of President Grant. It opposes "absolutism," "imperialism" and "personalism," and favors civil service reform and revenue reform. The signers call themselves Republicans, and give no name to the new party,

FEBRUARY 29.—J. J. Wood, of Labette county, appointed Regent of the University; John D. Parker, Superintendent of the Blind Asylum; H. J. Strickler, Regent of the Agricultural College; T. C. Bowles, Trustee of the Insane Asylum.

MARCH 1.—W. C. Tenney appointed Regent of the State University; T. J. Sternberg, Regent of the Agricultural College.

—Nathan Price, Judge of the Second Judicial District, resigns. P. L. Hubbard was appointed his successor.

—B. F. Simpson is elected Chairman, and George Noble Secretary, of the Philadelphia delegation.

—During the winter Rev. E. P. Hammond held revival meetings in several towns in the State, with very important results.

MARCH.—The length of the Leavenworth bridge over the Missouri is 994 feet; of approaches, 5,500; height above high-water, 51 feet 6 inches.

MARCH 2.—Adjournment of the Legislature. Among its laws were thirty-eight to authorize or legalize issues of municipal bonds; An act creating the State Board of Agriculture; Appropriating $3,000 for the relief of western settlers; Appropriating $2,500 for the Freedmen's University of Quindaro; For the issue and registration of bonds; Defining the boundary of Kingman and Harvey counties; Creating the Thirteenth and Fourteenth Judicial Districts; Providing for the settlement of losses from Indian depredations from 1860 to 1871; Creating a Commission to audit and allow Price Raid and Curtis Expedition muster-rolls; Regulating the infliction of the death penalty; Increasing the salaries of State officers and Supreme and District Court Judges; Providing for the sale of Normal School land.

MARCH 6.—M. E. Conference meets, at Emporia.

—Dr. W. E. Webb, of Topeka, has a book in press entitled "Buffalo Land."

MARCH 7.—The following Commissioners appointed under the act of February 28, 1872, to provide for settlement of losses from Indian depredations between 1860 and 1871: David Kelso, Oswego, Labette county; F. P. Baker, Topeka, Shawnee county; Henry Brandley, Bazaar, Chase county. The following award was made by this Commission:

Number.	Tribes who Committed Depredations.	Amount Claimed.	Amount Allowed.
1	Cherokee	$38,528 40	$3,165 00
2	Osage	22,894 96	18,290 96
3	Cheyenne	35,407 00	34,785 00
4	Cheyenne and Arapaho	24,363 70	18,963 70
5	Wichita	775 00	775 00
6	Arapaho	17,715 00	9,165 00
7	Kiowa	4,897 00	4,880 00
8	Sac and Fox	675 00	675 00
9	Sioux	2,813 00	2,813 00
10	Caddo	665 00	665 00
11	Cheyenne and Sioux	4,152 00	4,152 00
12	Kiowa and Comanche	4,359 00	200 00
13	Cheyenne and Pawnee	5,573 00	5,573 00
14	Cheyenne, Arapaho and Kiowa	560 00	560 00
15	Pawnee	475 00	475 00
16	Cheyenne and Kiowa	4,930 00	1,430 00
17	Creek	4,425 00	
18	Kiowa and Arapaho	6,730 00	6,730 00
19	Cherokee and Osage	2,469 00	
20	Sioux, Cheyenne and Pawnee	3,000 00	
21	Cheyenne and Comanche	6,510 00	6,510 00
	Total	$191,917 06	$119,807 66

In 1874, the Legislature ordered the Auditor to send the papers of this Commission, and other records of like character, to the Secretary of the Interior. They were sent.

MARCH 20.—State Convention of colored men at Lawrence.

—The Concordia Empire says 932,175 acres of land were entered under the homestead law at that place, during the year 1871.

APRIL.—The Beloit Gazette is started, by Chaffee & Johnson; the Holton Express by Frank A. Root.

APRIL.—The Educational Journal publishes a catalogue of the birds of Kansas, by Frank H. Snow, assisted by Edwin A. Popenoe, of Topeka, and Geo. F. Gaumer and Nelson J. Stephens, of Lawrence.

The Journal says: "The all-absorbing topic everywhere in Kansas to-day is the Revival. . . . May every teacher in Kansas study and practise Mr. Hammond's methods!"

APRIL 1.—Leslie J. Perry appointed Postmaster at Paola.

APRIL 9.—State Medical Society meets, at Lawrence.

APRIL 10.—Liberal Republican convention at Topeka. Called to order by Marcus J. Parrott. *Officers of the Convention:* President, Samuel J. Crawford; Vice Presidents, Byron Sherry, H. B. Horn, A. Thoman, C. Willemsen, H. E. Shepherd, W. H. Morris, T. S. Floyd, E. L. Buesche, F. R. Russell, J. E. Martin, and J. F. Clark; Secretaries, M. Benas, W. S. Smith, Joseph G. Waters. *Committee on Resolutions:* S. A. Riggs, C. A. Birnie, J. R. Hallowell, H. H. Labhere, J. T. Clark, E. G. Ross, T. Sandford, P. J. Carmichael, J. Baker, George Tauber, J. Y. Hewitt. *Committee to select Delegates to Cincinnati:* M. J. Parrott, A. Thoman, M. A. Wood, J. T. Warwich, A. R. Bancroft, G. T. Pierce, E. H. Sanford. Speeches were made by A. Thoman, Byron Sherry, J. R. Hallowell, and Samuel N. Wood. The committee on resolutions reported the following, which was adopted:

"*Resolved,* That the Liberal Republicans of Kansas, mindful of the early record of our State, so closely involved with the history of the Republican party and the struggle of national existence, still steadfast and true to the vital principles which called that party into existence, would ever maintain as a part of our birthright 'the rightful sovereignty of the Union, emancipation, equality of civil rights, and enfranchisement.' With a loyalty to principles that is higher and stronger than a loyalty to party or party leaders, jealous and watchful of the fair fame of our young State, earnest and resolute now as in the struggle to save the soil from the encroachment of the Slave power, we call upon the people of Kansas to unite in an effort to put a stop to the attempted absorption of the civil functions of the Government by the military, and the encroachment of Executive power; to inaugurate a thorough and genuine reform of the civil service that shall put a stop to the shameful abuse of official patronage for the control of conventions, whether in the interest of an individual, a faction, or a party; to effect a modification of our revenue system, so that no class or special interest of the country shall be encouraged at the expense of the rest; to secure a wise and just system of taxation which shall place no needless burden on the people; to save the public lands of the nation to actual settlers under the principles of the homestead laws; to establish general amnesty as a correlative of impartial suffrage; and to extend our national sympathies to all people who are struggling to emulate our example of popular enfranchisement."

Over one hundred names were suggested as delegates to Cincinnati—among them the following: M. J. Parrott, S. J. Crawford, A. Thoman, T. H. Walker, C. C. McDowell, S. J. Langdon, E. G. Ross, A. R. Bancroft, S. A. Riggs, F. W. Giles, S. N. Wood, C. B. Butler, Byron Sherry, G. T. Pierce, J. F. Cottrell, C. F. Hutchings, W. L. Parkinson, J. F. McDowell, W. B. Hutchison, and J. G. Waters. Hon. B. Gratz Brown, of Missouri, made an elaborate address. The following Central Committee was appointed: C. A. Birnie, J. Butler, A. Thoman, J. Walruff, A. R. Bancroft, L. G. Palmer, Alfred Taylor, Judge Humphrey, S. N. Wood, J. E. Deitze, F. R. Russell, G. H. Hollenbach, J. E. Martin, and R. H. Bishop. A. Thoman was made Chairman and S. N. Wood Secretary of the Committee.

April 13.—M. M. Murdock founds the Wichita Eagle.

April 18.—Leavenworth celebrates the completion of the bridge across the Missouri; thirty thousand people present.

April 23.—A terrific tornado at Coffeyville destroys the office of Ross's Paper.

April.—A book issued called "Buffalo Land," by W. E. Webb. It describes the country between Topeka and the Rocky Mountains. It is profusely illustrated by Henry Worrall, of Topeka. Published by E. Hannaford & Co., Cincinnati and Chicago.

May.—Investigation of Caldwell and Pomeroy, at Washington, called out by the Legislative investigation.

May 1.—Thos. Hughes, of Fort Scott, joins Judge F. G. Adams in the publication of the Waterville Telegraph.

May 3.—Horace Greeley is nominated for President, and B. Gratz Brown for Vice President, at Cincinnati.

May.—Ottawa prepares to erect a new central school building.

—Garnett is to have a College, under the charge of the United Presbyterian Church.

May 8.—Act of Congress for the removal of the Kaw Indians.

May 9.—Acts of Congress for the relief of settlers on the Osage lands, and on the Cherokee strip.

May 15.—Railroad completed to Wichita.

May 16.—First train through between Atchison and Topeka.

May 23.—Excursion from Atchison to Topeka.

May 28.—Laying of the first rail on the Lawrence and Topeka Railroad, at Topeka.

—New Land Office at Cawker City.

—Major Fielding Johnson fatally injured in jumping from a railroad train, at Topeka.

May 28.—Editorial Convention, at Emporia. *Officers elected:* President, T. Dwight Thacher; Vice Presidents, Albert Griffin, D. W. Wilder, W. D. Walker; Secretary, J. S. Wilson; Treasurer, W. F. Chalfant; Orator, I. S. Kalloch; Alternate, Geo. W. Martin; Poet, James W. Steele. The Annual Address was delivered by D. W. Wilder, of the Fort Scott Monitor. An excursion to Wichita followed. Resolutions were reported by R. B. Taylor.

May 31.—State Convention of Universalists, at Lawrence.

June.—The Fort Scott Monitor says of the University building: "There is not a structure on the American continent, erected for educational purposes, equal to this in size, or surpassing it in its adaptedness for the purposes of the higher education. . . . . The building will be heated with steam and lighted with gas, and every room will be supplied with water. An electrical clock will give the hour in every room at the same instant, and electricity will also be made a useful and instructive servant in various other ways."

37

June 2.—The Kansas Central open from Leavenworth to Grasshopper Falls.

—George W. Deitzler, of Lawrence, goes to California to live.

—The White Cloud Chief removes to Troy.

—An editorial article in the Atchison Champion gives the county bonded debt as $525,200, and the city $357,250, crediting the figures to County Clerk Galé and City Clerk Wagenhals.

June 3.—Mr. Logan, in the Senate, reports that the Committee on Privileges and Elections have ascertained no facts sufficient to sustain the charges of bribery and corruption against Senator Pomeroy. Senator Caldwell's case was not considered for want of time.

June 5.—Act of Congress to carry into effect the treaty with the Seneca and other tribes of Indians.

June 6.—The Philadelphia Convention nominates U. S. Grant for President and Henry Wilson for Vice President.

—Grading begins on the Junction City and Fort Kearney Railroad.

June 8.—Congress (Chap. 366 of U. S. Stats.) appropriates $337,054 to reimburse the State of Kansas for disbursements in aid of suppressing the Rebellion. The money was disbursed by the State Treasurer, in paying Price Raid scrip, in the summer and fall of 1872.

—This Congress (Chaps. 11 and 239 of U. S. Stats.) increases the number of Congressmen to 292, and gives Kansas three members.

June 10.—Santa Fe road completed to Hutchinson.

June 11.—Democratic Convention at Topeka. Ex-Gov. Wilson Shannon, President. He counselled the party to unite with all friends of reform and opponents of centralization and plunder. Thos. P. Fenlon was made Chairman of the Committee on Resolutions. Marcus J. Parrott made a speech, cordially inviting the union of Democrats with the supporters of Horace Greeley. The following platform was adopted:

"The Democrats of Kansas, in Convention assembled, do declare—

"*First,* That the paramount duty of every citizen, as such, is devotion and obedience to the Constitution and laws of the Republic, made, as they are, with the design and purpose to perpetuate individual liberty to its utmost limit consistent with good government and public order.

"*Second,* That political organizations are useful and beneficial only when their purpose and action demonstrate that love of country controls their councils and dictates their policy; but when lawless ambition, imbecility, corruption and man-worship dominate a political party, it is the duty of all citizens, without regard to previous political affiliations, forgetful of past differences, to join hands and hearts in the effort to crush such party, and to drive its leaders from power.

"*Third.* Believing as we do that the Chief Executive of the nation and the nominee of the Republican party for re-election is utterly unfitted for the high position he holds; that his administration of the Government stands alone in the history of the nation for shameless ignorance, nepotism and gift-taking; for reckless disregard of law and forgetfulness of the honor of the Republic; for utter want of that dignity and statesmanship which should characterize the executive government of the first Republic of the earth, and that his continuance in power would degrade the nation and be dangerous to the liberties of the people; so believing, we are willing to join with all good citizens in the pending campaign in the effort to drive him from place.

"*Fourth.* As this, in our judgment, can be most surely accomplished by accepting and supporting the platform and candidates of the Cincinnati Convention, the delegates this day accredited to the National Convention at Baltimore are hereby instructed that it is the desire of the Democracy of Kansas that the National Council of the party shall not place a ticket in the field, but that it shall, in the interest of the country, and to the end that a shameless administration shall be driven from power, give its sanction to and its powerful voice in favor of the nominees and platform of the Cincinnati Convention. And our delegates are directed to vote and act in accordance with these resolutions."

The following delegates were elected: Wilson Shannon, Thos. P. Fenlon, E. M. Hulett, R. B. Morris, Geo. B. Wood, W. R. Wagstaff, John Martin, Isaac Sharp, B. F. Devore, and T. W. Waterson.

JUNE 12.—Arkansas river bridge, at Wichita, opened for travel.

JUNE 13.—Geo. P. Smith starts the Humboldt Southwest. His son, Byron C. Smith, was one of the editors. In the fall the paper stopped. The office was removed to Neodesha, Wilson county.

JUNE 20.—Republican ratification meeting at Topeka addressed by Senator Matt. H. Carpenter, of Wisconsin.

JUNE 23.—Congress creates a new Land District in the Northwest.

JUNE 25.—Republican State Conventions called to meet at Lawrence and Topeka, Sept. 4—two delegates and two alternates from each district to each Convention.

JUNE 26.—The State Committees of the Democratic and Liberal Republican parties·meet at Lawrence, and call the State Convention, at Topeka, Sept. 11.

JUNE 29.—Completion of the Chicago and Southwestern to Atchison.

JUNE 29.—C. M. Taylor, City Marshal of Baxter Springs, shot and killed by Mayor J. R. Boyd.

. JUNE.—Eugene F. Ware becomes the editor of the Fort Scott Monitor, and that paper advocates Greeley and Brown.

JULY 1.—Excursion from Wichita to Atchison.

JULY 4.—Work begun on the Manhattan and Northwestern Railroad.

—J. A. Halderman presides at the American banquet given in London.

JULY 10.—The Democratic Convention at Baltimore adopts the Cincinnati platform and nominates Greeley and Brown.

—The Hutchinson News issued, by Perry Bros. & Co.

—Bridge over the Kaw completed at Wamego.

—A straight Democratic Convention is called to meet at Louisville, September 3d.

—W. S. Jenkins is appointed Register, and J. C. Redfield Receiver, of the Wichita Land Office.

JULY 15.—A correspondent of the Kansas Farmer tells what he knows of the organization called "The Patrons of Husbandry," or the "Grange."

—John H. Tice, of St. Louis, publishes a book on Kansas and Colorado. It is called, "Over the Plains and on the Mountains."

—The Leavenworth Medical Herald reaches its third volume; Tiffin Sinks, editor and proprietor.

JULY 15.—Judge Philip C. Schuyler, one of the most prominent of the early citizens of Kansas, dies at Burlingame.

—Dr. Medlicott is in the Anderson county jail.

JULY 30.—Charles M. Foster, of Topeka, Charles F. Koester, of Marysville, and P. R. Brooks, of Lawrence, are appointed to revise the tax laws.

—The Topeka Republicans erect a Wigwam and hold frequent meetings.

August 2.—John A. Logan speaks at Atchison.

August 13.—Gov. Harvey receives the Price Raid money in Washington.

August 14.—Milton R. Moore and James L. King issue the Topeka Tanner & Cobbler.

August 20.—Rev. N. Green publishes a card, saying he is a candidate for Congress.

—George W. Larzelere edits the Troy Republican.

August 22.—H. C. Ashbaugh establishes the Newton Kansan.

August 27.—Straight-out Democratic State Convention at Topeka. W. H. Peckham, Chairman; J. M. Margrave, Secretary. The following delegates were elected to the National Convention at Louisville: W. H. Peckham, J. H. Oliver, S. W. Brooks, J. M. Margrave, R. E. Lawrence. Alternates: Morris Holmes, George E. Williams, J. V. Holt, H. H. Stafford, J. T. Curran. The following platform was adopted:

"*Resolved*, That we believe in equal freedom and equal rights for all citizens, and that injustice consists in the restriction of such equality.

"2. We believe in the equal dignity of the several States of the Union; in the inherent right of local self-government, to be limited only by the constitutional powers delegated to the Federal Government for specific purposes; in the largest liberty for each citizen consistent with the equal liberty of all.

"3. We believe in the doctrine that governments were instituted among men to secure freedom to the right by restricting only the wrong, and that people, therefore, are best governed who govern themselves.

"4. In the proposition that the offices of the Government belong to the people, and not to the office-holders, and that the use of official patronage to reward political friends or punish political enemies is a crime against the people, which ought to be restrained and punished.

"5. In the right of the Government to assess and collect taxes, whether excise or tariff, for no purpose whatever but the support of the Government; that what is called 'protection' is but a name to designate robbery; and that equal rights of trade and exchange should be free from Government restriction.

"6. We recognize the validity and binding force of the 13th, 14th and 15th Amendments to the National Constitution; but we denounce as revolutionary, and as subversive of the Constitution and the traditions of free government, the means that were used to bring about those amendments.

"7. We are opposed to the policy practised by the Government for the last ten years, in giving away the public domain to rich conspirators, and declare that the public lands belong to the homeless.

"8. That the Convention at Baltimore having shamefully nominated uncompromising and unrepentant Radicals for the high offices of President and Vice President, the Democracy of the country, true to their convictions of right and the traditions of the party, would be false to themselves and false to the country in following the treachery of the politicians who participated in this shameful bargain and sale, in which the attempt is made to sell the principles of three million voters.

"9. We approve and endorse the call for a National Democratic Convention to be held on the 3d of September, in Louisville, Ky.

"10. That our delegates are instructed to cast the vote of Kansas for that pure and incorruptible statesman, Charles O'Conor, for President of the United States."

The following State Committee was appointed: W. H. Peckham, J. M. Margrave, J. K. Wells, H. H. Stafford, H. C. Retiker.

August 28.—The A. & N. R. R. completed to Lincoln, Neb.

August 30.—The Second Judicial District Convention, at Hiawatha, unanimously nominates P. L. Hubbard for Judge.

SEPTEMBER.—Osage Mission is building a $15,000 school house.

SEPTEMBER 4.—Charles O'Conor nominated for President and John Q. Adams for Vice President, at Louisville.

SEPTEMBER.—Election, on the State Fair Grounds at Topeka, of the following officers of the State Agricultural Society: President, H. J. Strickler, of Shawnee; Vice President, G. W. Veale, of Shawnee; Secretary, Alfred Gray, of Wyandotte; Treasurer, Thomas Murphy, of Atchison; Superintendent, H. T. Beman. *Executive Committee:* J. K. Hudson, of Wyandotte; S. T. Kelsey, of Franklin; J. I. Larimer, of Leavenworth; J. N. Insley, of Jefferson; E. S. Niccolls, of Anderson; G. L. Young, of Shawnee; James Rogers, of Osage; Martin Anderson, of Jackson; Wm. Martindale, of Greenwood; Malcolm Conn, of Morris.

SEPTEMBER 4.—Republican State Convention, at Topeka. Called to order by H. T. Beman. John A. Martin, Secretary *pro tem.* For temporary Chairman, Josiah Kellogg received 108 and John Guthrie 77 votes.

Committee on Credentials: J. D. Brumbaugh, Geo. Graham, W. W. Creighton, Bas. M. Simpson, H. D. Baker, J. A. Wells, E. E. Custer, William Burgoyne, G. C. Clemens, T. B. Fletcher, Frank Doster, L. N. Robinson, C. G. Hawley, David Gordon.

Committee on Resolutions: D. B. Emmert, P. P. Elder, W. Jay, N. Marchand, W. W. Guthrie, E. Smith, A. J. Shellhammer, Albert Griffin, H. Brandley, C. G. Hawley, J. A. Helphingstine, M. Baldwin, R. D. Mobley.

Committee on Permanent Organization: T. C. Jones, O. Y. Hart, J. O. Pickering, J. W. Stover, H. C. Hawkins, G. C. Clemens, J. C. Wilson, Mr. Hunt, H. Brandley.

Committee on Order of Business: B. W. Perkins, Ed. Russell, Mr. Burris, L. L. Ryan, D. Campbell, Mr. St. Clair, D. C. Wilson, Thomas Murphy, H. G. Evans.

The following officers were elected: President, Josiah Kellogg, Vice Presidents, W. Jay, P. W. Pickering, J. D. Brumbaugh; Secretaries, G. C. Crowther, H. Brandley.

First ballot for Governor: John M. Price, 65; Thomas A. Osborn, 60; John C. Carpenter, 32; Charles V. Eskridge, 21; R. B. Taylor, 9; G. W. Smith, 8.

Second ballot: Price, 69; Osborn, 63; Carpenter, 35; Eskridge, 24; Taylor, 3; Smith, 1.

Third ballot: Price, 69; Osborn, 63; Carpenter, 36; Eskridge, 21; Taylor, 3.

Fourth ballot: Price, 72; Osborn, 66; Carpenter, 36; Eskridge, 22.

Fifth ballot: Price, 71, Osborn, 63; Carpenter, 38; Eskridge, 20.

Sixth ballot: Price, 73; Osborn, 63; Carpenter, 32; Eskridge, 14.

Seventh ballot: Price, 75; Osborn, 74; Carpenter, 31; Eskridge, 15.

Eighth ballot: Price, 75; Osborn, 90; Carpenter, 29.

Ninth ballot: Price, 96; Osborn, 90; Carpenter, 29.

Tenth ballot: Osborn, 103; Price, 71; Carpenter, 20.

For Lieutenant Governor, Elias S. Stover, of Council Grove, was nominated, over E. S. Niccolls, of Garnett. William H. Smallwood was renominated for Secretary of State, by acclamation.

The candidates for State Treasurer were Josiah E. Hayes, R. H. Graham, James C. Horton, Samuel G. Hoyt, and Alexander R. Banks. Col. Hayes was renominated on the fourth ballot.

Daniel W. Wilder, of Fort Scott, was nominated for Auditor by acclamation.

Samuel A. Kingman, of Atchison, was renominated for Chief Justice by acclamation.

The candidates for Attorney General were Archibald L. Williams, J. B. Johnson, C. I. Scofield, and W. M. Matheny. On the third ballot, A. L. Williams was renominated.

Hugh D. McCarty, R. W. Putnam, John W. Horner, and Philetus Fales, were candidates for Superintendent of Public Instruction. Col. McCarty was renominated.

The following State Committee was selected: W. W. Creighton, John A. Martin, John Guthrie, Wm. Spriggs, A. M. F. Randolph, James D. Snoddy, D. B. Emmert, G. E. Beates, R. W. P. Muse, Bas. M. Simpson, B. W. Perkins, A. W. Campbell, Linus J. Webb, H. B. Baker. Chairman, John Guthrie; Secretary, John A. Martin.

The following platform was adopted:

"*Resolved*, That the Republicans of Kansas, in delegate convention assembled, hereby heartily approve and endorse the platform of the National Republican party adopted at Philadelphia on the 5th day of June, 1872, and we pledge our unswerving support to the nominees of that Convention, U. S. Grant and Henry Wilson.

"*Resolved*, That we hold that the laws protecting the rights of the citizens ought to be rigidly enforced, and that in all cases where the local governments are powerless or inefficient, it is the imperative duty of the National Government to see that the laws are enforced, and here we squarely take issue with the fourth resolution of the Cincinnati platform.

"*Resolved*, That the Republican party of Kansas, now, as in the past, is in favor of the free and uncorrupted exercise of the right of the elective franchise, both at the polls and in legislative election; and it condemns in unmeasured terms the use of any corrupt policies to procure election to any elective office, and here pledges uncompromising hostility to all men who have or may use any corrupting influences to secure any position of profit or honor.

"*Resolved*, That as there is a question at issue between the settlers upon the lands recently acquired from the Indians in this State and railroad corporations, which leaves no apparent recourse except through the courts, a resort to which must necessarily involve much litigation and expense that the occupants, on account of their poverty, are illy prepared to meet, we ask that the Government itself test the question to its fullest extent; and as a tangible solution of the question, should it be decided finally that the title to the lands in issue rests in the corporations, by virtue of grants and treaties, then our Senators and Representatives in Congress are earnestly requested to use their utmost endeavors to secure the adoption of measures that will result in satisfying all reasonable demands of the corporations, quiet the title, and vest the same in the occupying claimants, under the homestead and pre-emption laws."

SEPTEMBER 4.—Republican State Congressional Convention at Lawrence. Called to order by D. R. Anthony. John J. Ingalls received 118 and Geo. W. Veale 66 votes for temporary Chairman. *Committee on Credentials:* L. Loughmiller, B. S. Campbell, Judge Hoagland, H. P. Welsh, H. Kelly, W. R. Biddle, F. M. Powers, Mr. McDonald, J. A. Pike, I. S. Slaughter, F. A. Bettis, J. A. Jones, J. M. Steele, and J. G. Mohler. *Committee on Permanent Organization:* T. B. Murdock, J. H. Knight, B. H. McEckron, G. W. Burchard, C. Leland, jr., G. M. Waugh, and D. L. Kretsinger.

Committee on Resolutions: H. W. Cook, A. McAllister, Mr. Dunsmore, Geo. W. Veale, Mr. Stevenson, Geo. R. Peck, Ira J. Lacock, A. H. Horton, and A. M. Morgan. The following officers were elected: President, John J. Ingalls; Vice Presidents, Elijah Sells, Samuel Lappin, H. C. Cross, Thos. B. Eldridge, John H. Edwards, J. D. Dixon; Secretaries, H. P. Welsh, Isaac Isbell, and John S. Gilmore. The platform adopted is in substance the same as that adopted by the Topeka Convention. *Ballot for candidates for Congress:* D. P. Lowe, 132; Wm. A. Phillips, 122; Sidney Clarke, 59; S. A. Cobb, 54; S. M. Strickler, 36; Nathan Price, 43; H. W. Gillett, 25; E. J. Jenkins, 24; P. B. Maxson, 24; D. C. Haskell, 23; N. Green, 18; D. R. Anthony, 9; G. W. Veale, 7; J. J. Ingalls, 6; S. D. Houston, 6; T. D. Thacher, 4; B. F. Simpson, 4; J. D. Snoddy, 2. Lowe and Phillips were declared nominated by acclamation. *Ballot for a third candidate:* Stephen A. Cobb, 75; Nathan Price, 42; Sidney Clarke, 47. Mr. Clarke's name was withdrawn, and Col. Cobb received the nomination on the next ballot. *Presidential Electors:* Charles H. Langston, of Lawrence; John Guthrie, of Topeka; W. W. Smith, of Waterville; J. S. Merritt, of Pottawatomie county; and Louis Weil, of Leavenworth.

SEPTEMBER 11.—Liberal Republican Convention at Topeka. Charles Robinson, President; Pardee Butler, J. H. Watson, J. H. Peckham, Sam'l A. Manlove, Alfred Taylor and George W. Gardiner, Vice Presidents; Secretaries, C. A. Berrill, Johnson Barker, J. R. Hallowell. The following committee was appointed to confer with the Democratic Convention: L. A. Potter, Joshua Wheeler, B. F. Kelley, P. H. Peters, J. W. Beck, J. Critchfield, Byron Sherry, A. Robinson, A. S. Deming, H. S. Campbell, Joel Moody, L. G. Palmer, S. J. Langdon, J. F. McDowell, J. M. Mahr, Thos. H. Butler, Geo. P. Smith, M. E. Chaney, Robt. Morrow, F. W. Giles, John Meigs, Silas Burrell, C. J. Peckham, S. J. Crawford, H. Craik, N. A. Adams, E. A. Eaton, J. H. Sneed, M. J. Ennessy.

Committee on Credentials: Parrott, Philbrick, Ingersoll, Graham, and Pellett.

Speeches were made by S. N. Wood, Pardee Butler, General William Larimer, and Capt. Wm. D. Mathews.

Committee on Platform: Geo. W. Gardiner, R. S. Graham, A. Thoman, Sam'l A. Riggs, W. E. Copeland, David Linton, Geo. P. Smith, A. C. Pierce, S. N. Wood, Alfred Taylor, E. G. Ross, T. McIntyre, J. H. Snead.

Robt. Morrow reported from the conference committee that the Liberals were to have the nomination of Governor, two Members of Congress, three Presidential Electors, the Attorney General, Auditor, and Superintendent of Public Instruction; the Democrats one Member of Congress, the Secretary of State, Judge of the Supreme Court, and Lieutenant Governor. Report agreed to.

The Committee on Resolutions reported that the joint committee had agreed upon the following platform:

"*Resolved,* That the Liberal Republican and Democratic parties of the State of Kansas, in delegate convention assembled, accept and endorse the platform of principles adopted by the Convention of Cincinnati, of May 3d, and that of Baltimore, of July 9, 1872, and especially do we approve and reaffirm the fourth section of said platform.

"*Resolved,* That we hereby ratify the nomination of Horace Greeley for President and B. Gratz Brown for Vice President of the United States, and we pledge to them our unfaltering support.

"*Resolved,* That we are opposed to all further grants of land to railroad or other corporations. The public domain should be held sacred to actual settlers; and we hereby pledge the Liberal Republican and Democratic parties of Kansas to such legislation, State and National, as may be or become necessary to secure to all settlers on public lands, within the State of Kansas, their full, just and equitable rights.

"*Resolved,* That now, as in the past, we as Republicans are in favor of the free and uncorrupted exercise of the elective franchise at the polls and in Legislative elections, and we condemn in unmeasured terms the corrupt practices, and the use of money before resorted to, to procure seats in the Senate of the United States, and pledge continued hostility to all men who have attempted to procure, or in the future may attempt to obtain, positions by these most disgraceful and corrupting influences. And in the coming election for Senator we are determined to support no man to whom the least taint or suspicion of the use of money or other improper means attaches, and to that end we urge the voters of the State to oppose every candidate for the Legislature whose character for integrity is not entirely above suspicion.

"*Resolved,* That labor is the true wealth of the State, and that we demand such legislation as will protect and build up the agricultural and industrial interests of our whole State.

"*Resolved,* That we pledge the Liberal Republican and Democratic parties of the State of Kansas to untiring opposition to extravagance and corruption in the administration of national, State, county and municipal affairs; to the practice of strict economy, and to the reduction of the burdens of taxation upon property and labor.

"*Resolved,* That we are in favor of an equal, uniform rate of valuation of all the property in the State.

"*Resolved,* That the interest of civilization demands that the Indian Territory lying between the States of Kansas and Texas be opened to settlement, under the principles of the pre-emption and homestead laws of the United States, at the earliest practicable period.

"*Resolved,* That the Indian policy of the Administration has been a fraud and a failure, and that we demand for the settlers upon the frontier full protection against the outrages of Indian tribes."

The committee of conference reported the following list of candidates: For Governor, Thaddeus H. Walker, of Topeka; Congressmen, Robert B. Mitchell of Paola, M. J. Parrott of Leavenworth, and N. A. Adams of Manhattan; Lieutenant Governor, John Walruff, of Ottawa; Treasurer, M. S. Beach, of Lawrence; Auditor, C. H. Pratt, of Humboldt; Secretary of State, J. F. Waskey, of Labette county; Attorney General, B. P. Waggener, of Atchison; Superintendent of Public Instruction, L. J. Sawyer, of Osage county; Chief Justice, H. C. McComas of Fort Scott; Presidential Electors, William Larimer, N. A. English, G. H. Hollenberg, Samuel A. Riggs, A. W. Rucker.

The following candidates were then selected by ballot: Governor, T. H. Walker; Congressmen, W. R. Laughlin, of Cherokee, and S. A. Riggs, of Douglas; Presidential Electors, Pardee Butler, Wm. Larimer, and Alois Thoman; Auditor, V. B. Osborne; Treasurer, C. H. Pratt; Superintendent of Public Instruction, L. J. Sawyer. The other nominations, made by the Democrats, were ratified. The following State Committee was appointed: Charles A. Birney, J. L. Philbrick, T. J. Anderson, Mr. Mills, H. H. Jordan, J. D. McCleverty, G. P. Smith, W. A. Kiser, Hewett Craig, A. S. Devenney, R. N. Donnelly, P. H. Peters, J. D. Martin, J. H. Snead, Wm. D. Mathews. The members of the Democratic Convention then marched into Union Hall. Speeches were made by T. H. Walker, M. V. B. Bennett, S. N. Wood, John Martin, and H. Miles Moore.

SEPTEMBER 11.—State Democratic Convention, at Topeka. Called to order by T. P. Fenlon. *Temporary Officers:* President, John Martin; Secretaries, H. Hiles Moore, Nathan Cree, Nelson Abbott.

Committee on Credentials: Wilson Shannon, jr., H. Miles Moore, Samuel A. Williams, H. E. Norton, and Asa Hairgrove.

Committee on Permanent Organization: M. V. B. Bennett, Hayden, Clover, Leonard, Lane.

Officers of the Convention: President, Wilson Shannon, of Douglas; Vice Presidents, Charles Sprague of Jackson, John Hanlon of Leavenworth J. C. Frazier of Montgomery, C. Durfee of Doniphan, Hiero T. Wilson of Bourbon, A. P. McMillin of Pottawatomie, J. H. Conolly of Johnson, Isaac Sharp of Morris, T. W. Waterson of Marshall, P. T. Pendleton of Ellsworth, T. J. Dolan of Atchison, E. H. Keables of Neosho; Secretaries, H. Miles Moore of Leavenworth, Nathan Cree of Douglas, George F. Prescott of Leavenworth, Nelson Abbott of Atchison, Solon Goode of Bourbon, W. H. Ellis of Miami, G. H. Peacock of Montgomery.

· *Committee on Resolutions:* Charles W. Blair, T. P. Fenlon, John Martin, M. V. B. Bennett, P. T. Pendleton.

Committee of Conference with Liberal Republicans on State ticket, and other matters: B. S. Cash, T. J. Dolan, J. P. Taylor, A. Sims, A. M. Crockett, W. N. Allen, T. P. Fenlon, T. J. Lane, D. G. Campbell, T. H. Ellis, P. Chitwood, S. A. Williams, J. R. Gathright, J. D. O'Conner, J. J. Brown, G. W. McMillin, M. Neal, J. Deskins, N. Cree, J. Martin, J. Merryberry, A. M. Van Slyke, G. W. Houston, H. E. Norton, A. A. Jackson, I. Sharp, G. W. Murphy, T. T. Curtis, J. Foster.

The joint platform was adopted.

State Central Committee: H. M. Moore, R. B. Morris, John Martin, Ely Moore, E. W. Burton, J. S. Bentley, M. S. Gast, Robert Reynolds, J. M. Gordon, J. H. Conolly, M. V. B. Bennett, T. F. Pursey, R. B. Safford, P. T. Pendleton.

SEPTEMBER 16.—The letter of S. C. Pomeroy to W. W. Ross is published in the Lawrence Standard.

—The "Greeley Executive State Committee" is as follows: Isaac E. Eaton, Samuel A. Riggs, Wilson Shannon, jr., Byron Sherry, M. S. Beach, John C. Shea, and T. J. Anderson; headquarters at Lawrence.

—Dr. C. A. Logan, of Leavenworth, elected Grand Sire of the Grand Lodge I. O. O. F., of the United States, at Baltimore.

SEPTEMBER 19.—Old Settlers' meeting in Douglas county.

SEPTEMBER 27.—Death of Hovey E. Lowman, at Waverley, New York. [H]e was the editor and one of the publishers of the Lawrence State Journal [wh]en it was destroyed, and his partner, Josiah C. Trask, killed, by Quan[trel]l. Soon after this loss he removed to New York; thence to Saginaw, [Mic]higan; returning to Kansas, and editing the Lawrence Tribune and [Le]avenworth Times, in 1870. As a logical writer, he has had no superior [on th]e Kansas press. Mr. Lowman was a man of the purest character, and [chiva]lrous in his warm-hearted devotion to friends and principles. He [wrote] and published in a pamphlet a history of the Quantrell Massacre. [The as]sassination of his friends, and the sleepless nights and constant alarms that followed that murderous morning, struck him a blow from which he never recovered.

OCTOBER 3.—O'Conor Electors appointed.

OCTOBER 5.—Kansas Yearly Meeting of Friends, at Lawrence. Proceedings published in a pamphlet of 55 pages, by the Lawrence Journal.

OCTOBER 6.—Street railroad completed in Leavenworth.

OCTOBER 12.—Thos. Hughes buys the Marysville Locomotive, and changes the name to Marshall County News.

OCTOBER 17.—Death of Wm. H. Seward, at Auburn.

OCTOBER 17.—Floyd & Sowers issue the Wichita Daily Beacon, the first daily in the Arkansas valley, in this State. The daily edition ceased December 10th. Milton Gable bought the Beacon in the summer of 1874. A Daily was also issued in the summer of 1873.

OCTOBER 20.—Temperance Electors appointed: Geo. S. Evarts, of Topeka; H. N. Elliot, of Manhattan; M. J. Firey, of Emporia; L. D. Myers, of Humboldt, and F. Coates, of Solomon City.

—The M. K. & T. is completed to Caddo.

—Terrible prairie fire in Butler county.

OCTOBER 25.—Benj. F. Stringfellow presides at a Republican meeting in Atchison.

OCTOBER 30.—Death of the wife of Horace Greeley.

NOVEMBER.—Parsons and Eldorado have built large school-houses.

NOVEMBER.—W. H. Rossington becomes one of the editors of the Commonwealth.

NOVEMBER 5.—Annual election.

VOTE FOR RAILROAD ASSESSORS.

Dist.	Counties.	Names of Candidates.	Votes.	Total.	Maj.
8...	Davis	J. L. Noble	603		
	Dickinson	J. L. Noble	246		
	Morris	J. L. Noble	398		
	Riley	J. L. Noble	421	1,668	
	Davis	John P. Swenson	351		
	Dickinson	John P. Swenson	804		
	Morris	John P. Swenson	505		
	Riley	John P. Swenson	971	2,631	963
13...	Butler	W. B. Hutchison	1,027		
	Cowley	W. B. Hutchison	538		
	Howard	W. B. Hutchison	2		
	Sumner	W. B. Hutchison	79	1,646	
	Butler	J. M. Steele	870		
	Cowley	J. M. Steele	1,242		
	Greenwood	J. M. Steele	1		
	Howard	J. M. Steele	335		
	Sedgwick	J. M. Steele	1,094		
	Sumner	J. M. Steele	1,043	4,585	2,(
	Sedgwick	W. H. Vigus	275	275	
14...	Barton	D. N. Heizer	173		
	Ellis	D. N. Heizer	214		
	Ellsworth	D. N. Heizer	155		
	McPherson	D. N. Heizer	450		
	Saline	D. N. Heizer	1,366		
	Wallace	D. N. Heizer	56	2,414	(22
	Barton	A. Green	47		
	Ellis	A. Green	4		
	Ellsworth	A. Green	308		
	Lincoln	A. Green	83		
	McPherson	A. Green	37		
	Saline	A. Green	13	492	

VOTE FOR THREE MEMBERS OF CONGRESS AT LARGE.

Counties.	D. P. Lowe.	Wm. A. Phillips.	Stephen A. Cobb.	Samuel A. Riggs.	Robert B. Mitchell.	W. R. Laughlin.
Allen	1,175	1,165	1,147	555	542	536
Anderson	927	912	911	326	334	324
Atchison	1,945	1,937	1,914	1,403	1,379	1,370
Barton	162	162	161	53	50	50
Bourbon	2,058	1,942	1,986	1,385	1,389	1,399
Brown	1,135	1,132	1,134	371	372	375
Butler	1,454	1,459	1,218	757	516	512
Chase	489	487	443	245	195	194
Cherokee	930	824	866	1,219	1,247	1,275
Clay	747	750	746	182	181	178
Cloud	922	921	922	272	269	272
Coffey	1,050	1,043	1,034	478	477	474
Cowley	1,250	1,256	1,204	580	534	531
Crawford	647	558	577	1,081	1,113	1,073
Davis	550	552	548	443	444	443
Dickinson	856	855	855	231	232	231
Doniphan	1,777	1,781	1,781	1,017	1,017	1,017
Douglas	3,077	3,102	2,850	1,543	1,392	1,215
Ellis	162	166	173	119	117	111
Ellsworth	241	240	231	249	238	236
Franklin	1,671	1,692	1,643	693	684	656
Greenwood	855	850	850	350	353	352
Harvey	573	572	570	202	198	203
Howard	1,751	1,739	1,735	909	919	921
Jackson	901	900	901	91	91	91
Jefferson	1,731	1,727	1,721	926	922	931
Jewell	686	686	686	115	118	115
Johnson	1,875	1,855	1,808	1,189	1,224	1,172
Labette	1,790	1,770	1,770	998	986	996
Leavenworth	3,051	2,939	2,868	2,576	2,577	2,515
Lincoln	327	322	327	102	109	108
Linn	1,636	1,676	1,651	723	804	717
Lyon	1,635	1,605	1,586	452	417	402
Marion	683	683	683	156	155	156
Marshall	1,378	1,378	1,378	626	626	626
McPherson	455	455	457	35	36	34
Miami	1,433	1,528	1,530	869	1,003	862
Mitchell	712	709	712	191	191	194
Montgomery	1,812	1,800	1,809	1,396	1,427	1,415
Morris	544	521	536	405	389	378
Nemaha	1,111	1,107	1,108	459	462	458
Neosho	1,367	1,407	1,415	1,354	1,381	1,339
Norton	34	34	34	....	....	.....
Osage	1,842	1,833	1,806	509	538	537
Osborne	430	431	430	30	30	30
Ottawa	611	603	611	139	133	132
Phillips	153	153	153	32	32	32
Pottawatomie	1,307	1,305	1,303	726	722	719
Reno	266	266	266	89	89	89
Republic	1,111	1,111	1,111	....	....	....
Rice	193	192	192	38	38	38
Riley	1,063	1,067	1,016	356	335	329
Russell	144	148	146	15	15	15
Saline	1,089	1,053	1,093	387	367	355
Sedgwick	992	992	988	490	487	437
Shawnee	2,449	2,521	2,501	1,033	1,018	1,000
Smith	309	365	365	112	72	72
Sumner	731	727	725	407	401	402
Wabaunsee	637	639	622	188	190	185
Wallace	34	29	34	40	40	40
Washington	995	995	995	462	462	462
Wilson	1,383	1,374	1,379	548	551	552
Woodson	793	790	784	272	266	264
Wyandotte	1,303	1,300	1,344	1,180	1,176	1,117
Total	67,400	67,114	66,345	34,450	33,985	33,264

VOTE FOR ELECTORS OF PRESIDENT AND

Counties.	REPUBLICAN.				
	C. H. Langston....	*John Guthrie......*	*Louis Weil........*	*Jas. S. Merrill ...*	*Wm. W. Smith....*
Allen	1,154	1,157	1,157	1,157	1,157
Anderson..............................	919	926	926	925	926
Atchison	1,951	1,954	1,953	1,953	1,952
Barton	160	160	160	160	160
Bourbon	2,002	2,005	2,006	2,006	2,006
Brown	1,131	1,132	1,132	1,132	1,132
Butler	1,452	1,452	1,452	1,452	1,452
Chase...................................	480	482	481	482	480
Cherokee..............................	887	892	892	891	955
Clay	747	744	744	744	744
Cloud	919	920	920	920	920
Coffey..................................	1,023	1,035	1,035	1,035	1,035
Cowley.................................	1,241	1,241	1,241	1,241	1,241
Crawford..............................	584	585	585	585	584
Davis	546	547	547	547	546
Dickinson.............................	846	846	846	846	846
Doniphan.............................	1,777	1,787	1,787	1,787	1,787
Douglas	3,009	3,058	3,059	3,058	3,058
Ellis	163	163	163	163	163
Ellsworth.............................	233	234	234	234	234
Franklin...............................	1,648	1,658	1,658	1,658	1,658
Greenwood............................	857	857	856	857	857
Harvey.................................	563	563	563	563	563
Howard	1,724	1,738	1,737	1,737	1,733
Jackson	895	895	895	895	895
Jefferson	1,711	1,725	1,724	1,723	1,724
Jewell	687	684	686	684	686
Johnson................................	1,821	1,837	1,839	1,839	1,839
Labette	1,688	1,778	1,779	1,779	1,779
Leavenworth..........................	2,990	2,929	2,917	2,927	2,930
Lincoln	320	321	321	321	....
Linn	1,704	1,704	1,704	1,704	1,704
Lyon	1,633	1,623	1,623	1,623	1,625
Marion.................................	676	677	676	676	678
Marshall...............................	1,378	1,378	1,377	1,379	1,370
McPherson............................	439	443	443	443	443
Miami	1,537	1,544	1,545	1,544	1,544
Mitchell	717	718	718	718	718
Montgomery	1,795	1,797	1,795	1,797	1,797
Morris	529	529	529	529	529
Nemaha	1,100	1,107	1,106	1,106	1,106
Neosho.................................	1,405	1,402	1,408	1,409	1,409
Norton.................................	34	34	34	34	34
Osage...................................	1,804	1,813	1,812	1,812	1,812
Osborne................................	423	423	423	423	423
Ottawa	596	605	605	605	605
Phillips.................................	147	147	147	147	147
Pottawatomie	1,303	1,307	1,308	1,305	1,307
Reno....................................	266	266	....	266	266
Republic	1,028	1,028	1,028	1,028	1,028
Rice.....................................	196	196	196	196	196
Riley	1,055	1,055	1,055	1,055	1,055
Russell.................................	146	146	146	146	146
Saline...................................	1,068	1,081	1,082	1,082	1,081
Sedgwick	988	992	986	986	987
Shawnee	2,514	2,521	2,517	2,519	2,522
Smith	366	366	366	366	366
Sumner.................................	727	728	728	728	728
Wabaunsee............................	629	631	632	627	629
Wallace	54	54	54	54	54
Washington...........................	982	984	985	985	984
Wilson	1,358	1,358	1,362	1,362	1,362
Woodson...............................	780	782	782	782	782
Wyandotte............................	1,300	1,304	1,303	1,304	1,304
Total........................	66,805	67,048	66,770	66,942	66,783

VICE PRESIDENT OF THE UNITED STATES.

	LIBERAL.						STRAIGHT-OUT.				
Pardee Butler......	*Wm. H. Larimer.*	*F. W. Giles........*	*N. A. English....*	*A. W. Tucker.....*	*A. Thomas.........*	*W. H. Peckham.*	*L. R. Brooks......*	*G. E. Williams...*	*R. E. Laurence..*	*J. C. Canaan......*	*Wm. Palmer......*
516	516	515	515	517	....	....	....	....	....	....	......
316	314	314	314	314	....	....	....	....	....	....	......
1,358	1,358	1,358	1,357	1,358	....	....	....	....	....	....	......
64	....	....	64	64	64	....	....	....	....	....	......
1,339	1,339	1,339	1,339	1,337	....	15	15	15	15	15	......
381	381	381	381	381	....	....	....	....	....	....	......
468	468	450	469	469	....	....	....	....	....	....	......
187	187	58	190	187	132	....	....	....	....	....	......
1,187	1,186	813	1,172	1,138	413	....	....	....	....	....	......
188	187	187	188	187	....	....	....	....	....	....	......
260	260	....	260	260	260	....	....	....	....	....	......
470	471	470	470	471	....	....	....	....	....	....	......
517	516	517	517	517	....	4	4	....	4	....	......
1,028	1,027	1,028	1,028	1,029	....	7	7	....	7	....	......
441	440	440	440	440	....	2	2	2	2	2	......
222	222	222	222	222	....	2	2	2	2	2	......
1,094	1,096	1,094	1,094	1,094	....	....	....	....	....	....	......
1,327	1,321	1,319	1,319	1,319	....	....	....	....	....	....	......
114	114	114	114	114	....	5	5	5	5	5	......
239	239	215	239	239	23	....	....	....	....	....	......
154	153	154	154	154	....	....	....	....	....	....	......
346	346	346	346	346	....	....	....	....	....	....	......
187	187	187	187	187	....	....	....	....	....	....	......
1,007	1,007	....	1,006	1,006	1,007	....	....	....	....	....	......
441	441	441	441	441	....	....	....	....	....	....	......
911	910	829	828	907	63	1	1	1	1	1	......
115	115	....	115	115	115	....	....	....	....	....	......
1,193	1,193	1,193	1,193	1,193	....	1	1	1	1	1	......
1,014	1,014	987	1,014	992	49	....	....	....	....	....	......
2,516	2,523	2,520	2,527	2,495	13	....	....	....	....	....	......
114	114	....	114	114	114	....	....	....	....	....	......
632	632	632	632	632	....	43	43	43	....	43	......
418	416	379	415	414	....	....	....	....	....	....	......
148	148	148	145	148	....	....	....	....	....	....	......
622	622	580	622	614	42	....	....	....	....	....	......
48	40	48	48	48	....	....	....	....	....	....	......
868	865	865	865	865	....	....	....	....	....	....	......
183	183	....	183	183	183	....	....	....	....	....	......
1,397	1,399	1,397	1,397	1,397	....	....	....	....	....	....	......
335	335	335	385	335	....	....	....	....	....	....	......
444	444	445	444	444	....	23	23	23	23	23	......
1,325	1,325	1,265	1,325	1,214	71	6	6	6	6	6	......
529	532	44	535	534	488	8	8	8	8	8	......
38	38	31	36	38	8	1	1	1	1	1	......
127	127	....	127	127	127	....	....	....	....	....	......
32	32	....	32	32	32	....	....	....	....	....	......
692	694	692	690	683	....	....	....	....	....	....	......
90	90	90	90	90	....	....	....	....	....	....	......
48	48	48	48	48	....	....	....	....	....	....	......
36	36	....	36	36	36	3	3	3	3	3	......
338	338	334	338	338	....	....	....	....	....	....	......
16	16	16	16	16	....	....	....	....	....	....	......
356	356	269	355	357	87	....	....	....	....	....	......
484	....	482	483	484	....	....	....	....	....	....	440
979	978	981	976	975	....	5	5	5	5	5	......
75	75	....	74	70	75	....	....	....	....	....	......
402	402	....	402	402	402	3	3	3	3	3	......
186	187	2	188	186	186	....	....	....	....	....	......
44	44	44	44	44	....	....	....	....	....	....	......
446	446	110	446	446	335	....	....	....	....	....	......
524	523	479	515	571	44	27	27	22	26	22	......
238	250	174	250	248	57	....	....	....	....	....	......
1,156	1,155	1,154	1,153	1,155	....	....	....	....	....	....	......
32,970	32,421	23,535	32,679	32,781	4,426	156	156	140	112	140	440

VOTE FOR GOVERNOR, LIEUT. GOVERNOR, AND SECRETARY OF STATE.

Counties.	GOVERNOR. Thomas A. Osborn	GOVERNOR. Thaddeus H. Walker	LIEUT. GOV. E. S. Stover	LIEUT. GOV. John Walruff	SEC. OF STATE. William H. Smallwood	SEC. OF STATE. J. F. Waskey	AUDITOR. D. W. Wilder	AUDITOR. V. B. Osborne
Allen	1,154	516	1,166	545	1,168	539	1,162	538
Anderson	910	335	923	325	929	327	927	325
Atchison	1,857	1,436	1,942	1,379	1,943	1,373	1,944	1,373
Barton	162	53	163	63	164	62	164	63
Bourbon	1,979	1,398	2,008	1,385	2,008	1,387	2,037	1,351
Brown	1,122	391	1,133	382	1,135	382	1,134	374
Butler	1,444	529	1,458	515	1,461	515	1,457	514
Chase	463	221	489	173	490	195	490	195
Cherokee	903	1,220	891	1,250	890	1,233	906	1,232
Clay	732	200	739	197	751	180	755	177
Cloud	920	273	924	266	924	266	924	266
Coffey	1,043	482	1,046	479	1,047	479	1,046	481
Cowley	1,233	543	1,224	537	1,245	539	1,245	537
Crawford	594	1,087	593	1,087	593	1,089	593	1,092
Davis	539	453	553	439	549	413	548	443
Dickinson	852	234	859	228	855	231	857	223
Doniphan	1,737	1,116	1,777	1,121	1,818	1,081	1,794	1,112
Douglas	3,024	1,361	3,065	1,318	3,073	1,312	3,060	1,318
Ellis	166	119	165	121	165	120	165	120
Ellsworth	242	236	239	239	239	239	230	247
Franklin	1,648	703	1,641	713	1,686	666	1,680	670
Greenwood	856	366	858	366	856	369	856	368
Harvey	574	106	574	185	566	196	566	187
Howard	1,744	926	1,741	925	1,746	921	1,747	921
Jackson	805	495	902	490	902	488	903	488
Jefferson	1,674	974	1,726	929	1,729	925	1,731	925
Jewell	688	117	688	117	687	117	688	117
Johnson	1,832	1,216	1,851	1,196	1,859	1,186	1,854	1,191
Labette	1,788	1,013	1,878	1,021	1,752	1,050	1,873	1,018
Leavenworth	3,143	2,357	2,952	2,553	2,966	2,518	3,018	2,481
Lincoln	328	124	303	119	327	118	298	146
Linn	1,640	750	1,683	722	1,687	721	1,685	721
Lyon	1,630	447	1,642	433	1,640	441	1,553	427
Marion	661	157	682	157	683	156	682	156
Marshall	1,360	658	1,386	626	1,388	626	1,333	637
McPherson	452	37	452	36	451	36	452	36
Miami	1,489	910	1,548	878	1,552	875	1,553	875
Mitchell	710	197	714	193	713	194	713	189
Montgomery	1,801	1,431	1,809	1,438	1,806	1,439	1,808	1,438
Morris	540	382	547	368	545	380	545	380
Nemaha	1,080	486	1,109	460	1,106	462	1,068	459
Neosho	1,433	1,340	1,433	1,337	1,424	1,336	1,435	1,337
Norton	34	....	34	....	34	....	34	....
Osage	1,816	562	1,840	544	1,843	544	1,842	540
Osborne	428	37	430	36	430	34	430	36
Ottawa	605	133	613	131	613	131	614	131
Phillips	153	32	153	32	153	32	153	32
Pottawatomie	1,271	743	1,305	724	1,338	689	1,287	742
Reno	265	90	268	89	266	90	266	90
Republic	1,000	25	1,069	25	1,069	4	1,069	4
Rice	190	38	193	35	190	38	190	38
Riley	1,040	351	1,059	339	1,062	335	1,059	340
Russell	148	15	148	15	149	15	149	15
Saline	1,078	379	1,095	363	1,093	363	1,096	362
Sedgwick	1,070	391	991	483	993	481	991	492
Shawnee	2,645	1,144	2,503	1,029	2,539	983	2,514	1,007
Smith	367	74	367	74	366	74	367	74
Sumner	717	400	728	410	726	412	728	410
Wabaunsee	600	218	635	190	637	187	637	186
Wallace	56	44	56	44	56	44	56	44
Washington	987	472	995	465	987	....	988	290
Wilson	1,374	549	1,378	559	1,378	548	1,378	561
Woodson	781	273	786	271	786	270	792	265
Wyandotte	1,277	1,193	1,302	1,175	1,304	1,173	1,308	1,171
Total	66,715	34,608	67,324	34,345	67,535	33,665	67,387	33,978
Majorities	32,011	....	32,979	....	33,870	....	33,165	....

VOTE FOR TREASURER OF STATE, ATTORNEY GENERAL, SUPERINTEND-
ENT OF PUBLIC INSTRUCTION, AND CHIEF JUSTICE.

Counties.	TREASURER.		ATT'Y GEN'L.		SUP. PUB. INS.		CHIEF JUST'E.	
	J. E. Hayes.	*Chas. H. Pratt.*	*A. L. Williams.*	*B. P. Wagener.*	*H. D. McCarty.*	*L. G. Sawyer.*	*Samuel A. Kingman.*	*H. C. McComas.*
Allen	1,065	641	1,166	537	1,174	527	1,124	583
Anderson	920	327	928	323	927	323	922	328
Atchison	1,945	1,380	1,873	1,415	1,945	1,367	1,957	1,344
Barton	163	63	165	62	164	60	163	61
Bourbon	1,985	1,404	2,007	1,383	2,014	1,382	1,963	1,425
Brown	1,133	382	1,141	381	1,140	383	1,140	377
Butler	1,272	698	1,456	516	1,456	516	1,456	516
Chase	455	228	489	194	486	198	490	195
Cherokee	890	1,249	892	1,094	832	1,279	878	1,260
Clay	753	175	750	181	754	176	751	181
Cloud	923	267	924	266	926	264	923	267
Coffey	1,041	482	1,043	481	1,042	435	1,043	481
Cowley	1,211	568	1,244	537	1,245	537	1,244	536
Crawford	591	1,094	591	1,090	591	1,083	571	1,114
Davis	547	443	552	439	551	441	550	440
Dickinson	854	233	855	232	852	231	857	228
Doniphan	1,771	1,119	1,783	1,113	1,776	1,113	1,786	1,113
Douglas	3,010	1,359	3,066	1,328	3,081	1,308	3,066	1,311
Ellis	165	120	166	120	165	120	165	120
Ellsworth	240	236	252	226	240	233	238	239
Franklin	1,678	671	1,678	668	1,678	667	1,682	668
Greenwood	548	376	856	368	856	368	856	369
Harvey	562	192	565	197	565	197	566	197
Howard	1,714	952	1,747	923	1,745	919	1,746	920
Jackson	903	489	903	489	903	485	904	490
Jefferson	1,731	925	1,732	920	1,734	920	1,732	925
Jewell	689	117	691	116	689	116	691	117
Johnson	1,894	1,121	1,856	1,189	1,857	1,187	1,855	1,189
Labette	1,763	1,031	1,778	1,024	1,784	1,009	1,779	1,029
Leavenworth	2,914	2,570	2,960	2,538	3,049	2,437	2,960	2,519
Lincoln	326	109	314	110	318	113	326	110
Linn	1,689	720	1,687	722	1,687	722	1,685	726
Lyon	1,652	430	1,652	427	1,629	421	1,631	446
Marion	683	156	603	156	682	156	683	156
Marshall	1,383	637	1,379	643	1,386	629	1,383	637
McPherson	451	36	453	36	452	36	453	36
Miami	1,549	873	1,551	876	1,552	874	1,547	880
Mitchell	711	193	713	194	713	195	712	194
Montgomery	1,784	1,437	1,809	1,438	1,803	1,430	1,810	1,437
Morris	345	370	545	380	547	379	545	380
Nemaha	1,109	459	1,107	460	1,107	460	1,112	456
Neosho	1,382	1,390	1,431	1,173	1,438	1,326	1,425	1,182
Norton	34	....	34	....	34		34	
Osage	1,827	560	1,843	542	1,851	457	1,842	543
Osborne	431	35	429	35	430	36	430	36
Ottawa	612	131	611	132	614	131	612	132
Phillips	153	32	153	32	153	32	153	32
Pottawatomie	1,300	725	1,303	720	1,307	715	1,305	721
Reno	265	91	266	90	266	89	266	90
Republic	1,069	3	1,069	4	1,070	4	1,069	4
Rice	190	38	191	38	190	38	190	38
Riley	1,060	339	1,062	334	1,061	336	1,060	349
Russell	149	15	149	10	149	15	149	15
Saline	1,094	364	1,123	329	1,095	364	1,097	364
Sedgwick	986	489	934	485	993	484	988	473
Shawnee	2,521	1,006	2,536	987	2,540	992	2,540	986
Smith	359	74	367	74	367	74	367	74
Sumner	722	417	728	410	729	406	725	411
Wabaunsee	636	189	633	190	640	184	636	189
Wallace	56	44	56	44	56	44	56	44
Washington	989	267	997	466	998	458	996	466
Wilson	1,378	548	1,300	538	1,391	548	1,378	551
Woodson	757	301	786	271	787	250	790	266
Wyandotte	1,298	1,176	1,305	1,174	1,311	1,164	1,304	1,174
Total	66,277	34,866	67,458	33,860	67,567	33,843	67,357	34,131
Majority	31,232	....	33,480	....	33,720	....	33,064	....

VOTE FOR MEMBERS OF THE SENATE.

District.	Counties.	Names of Candidates.	Vote of County.	Total.	Maj.
1...	Doniphan	Nathan Price	1,137	1,137	
	Doniphan	F. H. Drenning	851	851	
	Doniphan	J. A. Leonard	864	864	
2...	Atchison	Wm. H. Grimes	1,866	1,866	403
	Atchison	Joseph C. Wilson	1,928	1,928	465
	Atchison	Wm. C. Smith	1,463	1,463	
	Atchison	Joseph Logan	1,355	1,355	
3...	Brown	E. N. Morrill	1,100		
	Brown	J. S. Tyler	300		
	Brown	John Kirk	31	31	
	Nemaha	E. N. Morrill	1,096	2,196	1,410
	Nemaha	J. S. Tyler	452	752	
4...	Marshall	Frank Schmidt	1,113		
	Marshall	G. H. Hollenberg	871		
	Washington	Frank Schmidt	756	1,869	309
	Washington	G. H. Hollenberg	689	1,560	
5...	Jackson	L. R. Palmer	903		
	Jackson	Henry Hegner	486		
	Pottawatomie	L. R. Palmer	1,087	1,990	620
	Pottawatomie	Henry Hegner	884	1,370	
6...	Jefferson	J. W. Rogers	1,372	1,372	120
	Jefferson	G. B. Carson	1,129	1,129	
	Jefferson	J. A. Amos	123	123	
7...	Leavenworth	Thomas Moonlight	2,913	2,913	356
	Leavenworth	Jacob Winter	2,617	2,617	60
	Leavenworth	J. T. McWhirt	2,594	2,594	37
	Leavenworth	C. A. Birnie	2,557	2,557	
	Leavenworth	C. R. Jennison	2,242	2,242	
	Leavenworth	James F. Legate	2,070	2,070	
	Leavenworth	W. G. Coffin	623	623	
8...	Wyandotte	Byron Judd	1,343	1,343	198
	Wyandotte	D. B. Hadley	1,145	1,145	
9...	Johnson	John P. St. John	1,772	1,772	527
	Johnson	L. F. Greene	1,245	1,245	
10...	Miami	E. H. Topping	1,533	1,533	632
	Miami	J. W. Gossett	901	901	
11...	Linn	Andrew Ely	1,546	1,546	732
	Linn	Joel Moody	814	814	
12...	Bourbon	W. E. Guerin	1,570	1,570	311
	Bourbon	F. R. Boyle	1,258	1,258	
	Bourbon	William Simpson	274		
	Bourbon	Stephen Alberty	264		
13...	Crawford	William Simpson	1,061	1,335	444
	Crawford	Stephen Alberty	627	891	
14...	Cherokee	W. M. Matheny	1,122	1,122	182
	Cherokee	C. C. McDowell	940	940	
15...	Labette	James A. Crichton	1,587	1,587	429
	Labette	Wm. Dick	1,157	1,157	
16...	Neosho	Walter L. Simons	1,513	1,513	286
	Neosho	R. N. Bayless	1,223	1,223	
17...	Anderson	W. A. Johnson	888		
	Anderson	Geo. P. Smith	324		
	Allen	W. A. Johnson	1,109	1,997	1,100
	Allen	Geo. P. Smith	573	897	
18...	Franklin	A. M. Blair	1,686	1,686	1,032
	Franklin	John A. Davenport	654	654	
19...	Douglas	Samuel Walker	2,979	2,979	1,176
	Douglas	M. A. O'Neil	2,532	2,532	729
	Douglas	O. E. Learnard	1,803	1,803	
	Douglas	W. C. Tenney	1,310	1,310	
20...	Shawnee	N. C. McFarland	2,371	2,371	1,243
	Shawnee	A. Thoman	1,128	1,128	
21...	Osage	C. S. Martin	1,309		
	Osage	H. D. Shepard	984		
	Osage	Wm. Whistler	6	6	
	Wabaunsee	C. S. Martin	420	1,729	338
	Wabaunsee	H. D. Shepard	401	1,385	
22...	Coffey	C. B. Butler	837		
	Coffey	A. D. Brown	664		
	Woodson	C. B. Butler	615	1,452	350
	Woodson	A. D. Brown	438	1,102	
23...	Wilson	A. M. York	1,371		
	Montgomery	A. M. York	1,811	3,182	1,268

VOTE FOR MEMBERS OF THE SENATE—*Concluded.*

District.	Counties.	Names of Candidates.	Vote of County.	Total.	Maj.
23...	Wilson	Frank Willis	496		
	Montgomery	Frank Willis	1,418	1,914	
24...	Lyon	Wm. Martindale	1,464		
	Greenwood	Wm. Martindale	824	2,288	1,356
	Lyon	Thomas Armor	538		
	Greenwood	Thomas Armor	394	932	
25...	Butler	M. M. Murdock	863		
	Cowley	M. M. Murdock	1,225		
	Harvey	M. M. Murdock	364		
	Howard	M. M. Murdock	1,195		
	Reno	M. M. Murdock	258		
	Sedgwick	M. M. Murdock	1,173		
	Sumner	M. M. Murdock	796	5,874	1,750
	Butler	David L. Payne	1,103		
	Cowley	David L. Payne	556		
	Harvey	David L. Payne	306		
	Howard	David L. Payne	1,432		
	Reno	David L. Payne	92		
	Sedgwick	David L. Payne	303		
	Sumner	David L. Payne	332	4,124	
26...	Chase	Henry Brandley	461		
	Marion	Henry Brandley	716		
	Morris	Henry Brandley	520	1,697	965
	Chase	E. A. Bruse	210		
	Marion	E. A. Bruse	121		
	Morris	E. A. Bruse	401	732	
27...	Riley	V. P. Wilson	642		
	Davis	V. P. Wilson	523		
	Dickinson	V. P. Wilson	716	1,881	344
	Riley	R. B. Spillman	722		
	Davis	R. B. Spillman	460		
	Dickinson	R. B. Spillman	352	1,534	
28...	Lincoln	E. Barker	371		
	Phillips	E. Barker	173		
	Smith	E. Barker	441		
	Republic	E. Barker	1,079		
	Ottawa	E. Barker	620		
	Osborne	E. Barker	458		
	Norton	E. Barker	34		
	Mitchell	E. Barker	903		
	Jewell	E. Barker	798		
	Clay	E. Barker	738		
	Cloud	E. Barker	923	6,533	6,533
29...	Saline	John H. Edwards	871		
	McPherson	John H. Edwards	327		
	Ellsworth	John H. Edwards	148		
	Ellis	John H. Edwards	209		
	Wallace	John H. Edwards	26		
	Rice	John H. Edwards	203		
	Barton	John H. Edwards	147		
	Russell	John H. Edwards	140	2,071	906
	Saline	J. H. Snead	460		
	McPherson	J. H. Snead	170		
	Ellsworth	J. H. Snead	318		
	Ellis	J. H. Snead	69		
	Wallace	J. H. Snead	20		
	Rice	J. H. Snead	25		
	Barton	J. H. Snead	71		
	Russell	J. H. Snead	15	1,148	

VOTE FOR MEMBERS OF THE HOUSE OF REPRESENTATIVES.

District.	County.	Names of Candidates.	Votes.	Maj.	Plur.
1	Doniphan	M. B. Bowers	524		168
		J. H. Long	356		
		J. F. Mauk	305		
2		B. O'Driscoll	407		14
		A. Low	393		
		A. Jeffs	46		

38

VOTE FOR MEMBERS OF THE HOUSE OF REPRESENTATIVES— CONTINUED.

District.	Counties.	Names of Candidates.	Votes.	Maj.	Plur.
3	Doniphan (concluded)....	E. Searcy	355	43	
		A. Larzelere	175		
		Lyman Nash	137		
4	Atchison	A. W. Spalding	672	253	
		Henry Brandner	419		
5		G. W. Gillespie	691	346	
		William H. Kemper	345		
6		M. E. Larkin	553	24	
		G. W. Thompson	529		
7	Brown	C. F. Bowron	1,122	764	
		B. F. Killey	351		
8	Nemaha	Cyrus I. Scofield	406	44	
		J. H. Peckham	347		
9		H. C. DeForrest	495	198	
		T. B. Gray	294		
10	Marshall	I. C. Legere	023	118	
		John D. Wells	1,905		
11	Washington	A. J. Banta	890	323	
		J. E. Barrett	567		
12	Riley	W. J. Hunter	795	220	
		Samuel Long	575		
13	Pottawatomie	R. A. Guffy	664	144	
		B. Hagan	484		
		W. H. Powell	36		
14		Welcome Wells	538	288	
		J. M. Johnson	250		
15	Jackson	P. M. Hodges	904	423	
		A. McKeever	481		
16	Jefferson	J. F. Willetts	481	146	
		J. I. Moore	335		
17		V. Brown	441	43	
		J. F. Hinton	398		
18		D. H. Frazier	473	23	
		E. K. Townsend	383		
		S. Stiers	67		
19	Leavenworth	W. S. Plummer	363	20	
		D. R. Anthony	343		
20		T. Morgan	315	14	
		Joseph Clarke	281		
		William Fairchild	20		
21		Josiah Kellogg	449	17	
		J. I. Larimer	432		
22		W. H. Bond	373	36	
		J. C. Murphy	337		
23		J. Turner	435	143	
		C. S. Foster	292		
24		H. C. Fields	517	93	
		M. J. Parrott	419		
25		T. Dillard	426	5	
		C. Moore	419		
26	Wyandotte	W. S. Tough	837	21	
		John Coon	816		
27		W. J. Buchan	387	17	
		James S. Bell	370		
28	Johnson	Thomas James	535	18	
		G. M. Bowers	517		
29		J. M. Miller	641	82	
		G. H. Lawrence	559		
30		D. Belden	363		77
		A. Taylor	286		
		J. T. Woodward	109		
31	Miami	J. W. Beaty	650	168	
		Robert Collett	482		
32		Reuben Smith	779	303	
		H. H. Patten	476		
33	Linn	S. R. Hungerford	475		85
		Seneca Johnson	121		
		Harvey Smith	390		
34		J. F. Ward	463	207	
		J. D. McRae	196		
35		L. H. Lane	449	129	
		J. W. Miller	320		
36	Bourbon	W. J. Cochrane	588	274	

VOTE FOR MEMBERS OF THE HOUSE OF REPRESENTATIVES—Continued.

District.	Counties.	Names of Candidates.	Votes.	Maj.	Plur.
36	Bourbon (concluded)......	Isaac Burton.................................	314		
37	....	Jacob Brenner...............................	540	131	
		W. J. Stroud.................................	409		
38	....	B. P. McDonald.............................	774	48	
		Jacob D. Rush...............................	725		
39	Crawford.....................	A. J. Vickers................................	486	205	
		Joseph Fetters...............................	281		
40	....	S. J. Langdon...............................	389		131
		G. W. Brown................................	258		
		N. W. Taylor................................	194		
41	Cherokee	William Givins...............................	509		
		A. F. Childs.................................	541		32
		G. W. Wood.................................	110		
42	....	C. W. Harvey...............................	450	3	
		T. A. Rucker................................	447		
43	Labette.....................	W. W. Harper...............................	956	521	
		George A. Reynolds	433		
44	....	W. H. Mapes................................	807	324	
		Christian Leib...............................	483		
45	Neosho	Elijah Cravens..............................	648		
		C. F. Hutchings.............................	827	116	
		J. N. Beach.................................	60		
46	....	Frank Bacon.................................	580		1
		A. L. Taylor................................	579		
47	Allen	Edward H. Funston.........................	500	108	
		Nelson F. Acres.............................	392		
48	....	William Wakefield..........................	440	87	
		J. W. Pine	353		
49	Anderson...................	John T. Lanter..............................	785	356	
		William Gear................................	429		
50	Franklin.....................	E. J. Nugent................................	604	57	
		M. E. Cheney...............................	547		
51	....	William Bateman...........................	643	192	
		J. H. Harrison..............................	421		
		J. T. Burt..................................	30		
52	Douglas.....................	James S. Crew	789	426	
		Samuel Kimball.............................	363		
53	....	I. S. Kalloch................................	987	586	
		Turner Sampson	317		
		William Sells...............................	84		
54	....	A. K. Lowe..................................	354		48
		William H. Christian........................	306		
		J. L. Jones..................................	255		
55	....	N. Henshaw.................................	444	120	
		E. E. Geddes................................	324		
56	Shawnee.....................	Daniel M Adams............................	537	158	
		A. J. Arnold................................	379		
57	....	George W. Veale............................	840	177	
		John Martin................................	663		
58	....	Wesley Gregg................................	630	306	
		J. M. Harvey................................	324		
59	Osage	S. R. Shoemaker............................	829	500	
		William P. Deming	328		
		H. DuBois	1		
60	....	A. B. Cooper................................	425		59
		Thomas Donnell.............................	353		
		E. W. Burton................................	366		
61	Coffey.......................	J. A. Kennedy	593		
		J. M. Sheafor...............................	249		
		S. K. Cross.................................	660		67
62	Woodson.....................	William Peck................................	588	142	
		J. W. Turner................................	446		
63	Wilson.......................	J. Z. Sexton.................................	1,314	722	
		J. N. Halstead..............................	588		
64	Montgomery.................	T. B. Eldridge..............................	832	17	
		E. B. Dunwell...............................	815		
65	....	M. S. Bell..................................	888	202	
		B. F. Devore................................	686		
66	Howard.....................	Charles Barbour	885		
		E. S. Cummings.............................	1,128		243
		John Rambo.................................	612		
67	Greenwood...................	S. P. Huntington............................	806	371	
		John Gage...................................	435		

VOTE FOR MEMBERS OF THE HOUSE OF REPRESENTATIVES — Concluded.

District.	Counties.	Names of Candidates.	Votes	Maj.	Plur.
68	Lyon	L. N. Robinson	617	180	
		S. P. Young	329		
		S. G. Brown	108		
69		J. M. Hunter	567	177	
		R. W. Randall	390		
70	Wabaunsee	Abraham Sellers	522	263	
		E. H. Sanford	131		
		J. M. Bisbey	125		
71	Davis	W. S. Blakely	641	289	
		James Humphrey	351		
72	Morris	J. A. Wallace	451		
		C. H. Titus	471	20	
73	Chase	Wm. Jeffrey	325	9	
		W. S. Smith	316		
74	Butler	Thomas H. Baker	1,688	1,540	
75	Cowley	James McDermott	1,214	639 ·	
		A. N. Demming	575		
76	Sedgwick	E. B. Allen	890	296	
		N. A. English	594		
77	Marion	J. K. McLean	755	744	
78	McPherson	J. E. Simpson	348	204	
		L. P. Peershawl	144		
79	Dickinson	S. J. Kabler	864	651	
		Jos. G. McCoy	213		
80	Clay	S. L. Stratton	538	451	
		M. H. Ristine	387		
81	Republic	Alman Shaw	724	312	
		R. P. West	412		
82	Cloud	H. C. Snyder	665	144	
		Wm. English	521		
83	Ottawa	W. B. Davis	562	389	
		Frank Philbrick	70		
		J. K. Osborne	103		
84	Saline	Eric Forsee	752	82	
		H. D. Baker	670		
85	Ellsworth	H. F. Hoseman	181		17
		A. Homeson	164		
		Paul T. Carlett	110		
		Wm. King	19		
86	Lincoln	George Green	221	5	
		John Harshbarger	182		
		W. T. Eubank	34		
87	Mitchell	John Curtain	561	243	
		Wm. C. Ingram	318		
88	Jewell	Geo. S. Bischop	660	492	
		W. H. Cammeron	168		
89	Ellis	Simon Motz	174	86	
		Michael Sweeney	88		
90	Wallace	Alex. Ross	80	60	
		A. T. Bisel	20		
91	Rice	Wm. Lourey	94		8
		F. J. Griffith	59		
		H. P. Ninde	86		
92	Sumner	Geo. M. Miller	552		
		C. A. Rohrabacher	555		3
		Peter Fish	5		
93	Osborne	W. L. Bear	152		
		C. Reasoner	263	60	
		John Rathbun	51		
94	Reno	C. C. Hutchinson	223	92	
		J. H. Lawson	131		
95	Smith	J. T. Morrison	255	85	
		W. H. Porter	170		
96	Harvey	H. E. Ensign	406	42	
		J. J. Barker	171		
		Wm. N. Congdon	191		
97	Barton	J. L. Brinkman	168	108	
		D. R. Smith	60		
98	Russell	David Adams	152	137	
		D. B. Waterman	15		
99	Phillips	Noah Weaver	99	10	
		Felix T. Gandy	89		
100	Norton	N. H. Billings	21	10	
		S. D. Reed	11		

VOTE FOR JUDGES OF THE DISTRICT COURTS.

District.	Counties.	Names of Candidates.	Vote of County.	Total.	Maj.
1...	Leavenworth	H. W. Ide	2,922	2,922	455
	Leavenworth	J. W. English	2,467	2,467	
	Atchison	P. L. Hubbard	2,063		
	Brown	P. L. Hubbard	1,074		
	Doniphan	P. L. Hubbard	1,728		
	Nemaha	P. L. Hubbard	1,116	5,981	2,700
2...	Atchison	Chas. W. Johnson	1,249		
	Brown	Chas. W. Johnson	409		
	Doniphan	Chas. W. Johnson	1,163		
	Nemaha	Chas. W. Johnson	459	3,280	
	Jackson	John T. Morton	1,385		
	Jefferson	John T. Morton	1,442		
3...	Pottawatomie	John T. Morton	1,263		
	Shawnee	John T. Morton	3,503		
	Wabaunsee	John T. Morton	767	8,360	8,359
	Anderson	Owen A. Bassett	879		
	Douglas	Owen A. Bassett	3,008		
4...	Franklin	Owen A. Bassett	1,268	5,155	2,431
	Anderson	C. B. Mason	360		
	Douglas	C. B. Mason	1,306		
	Franklin	C. B. Mason	1,058	2,724	
	Coffey	E. B. Peyton	957		
	Lyon	E. B. Peyton	1,565		
5...	Osage	E. B. Peyton	1,238	3,760	1,649
	Coffey	Ellis Lewis	572		
	Lyon	Ellis Lewis	436		
	Osage	Ellis Lewis	1,103	2,111	
	Bourbon	James D. Snoddy	1,789		
6...	Linn	James D. Snoddy	1,455	3,244	3,241
	Davis	W. H. Canfield	657		
	Dickinson	W. H. Canfield	1,079		
8...	Morris	W. H. Canfield	930		
	Ottawa	W. H. Canfield	644		
	Riley	W. H. Canfield	1,398	4,708	4,704
	Chase	W. R. Brown	489		
	Harvey	W. R. Brown	383		
	Marion	W. R. Brown	232		
	Reno	W. R. Brown	194		
9...	Rice	W. R. Brown	201	1,499	251
	Chase	Frank Doster	187		
	Harvey	Frank Doster	347		
	Marion	Frank Doster	579		
	Reno	Frank Doster	92		
	Rice	Frank Doster	35	1,240	
	Clay	A. S. Wilson	738		
	Cloud	A. S. Wilson	924		
	Jewell	A. S. Wilson	796		
	Marshall	A. S. Wilson	2,015		
	Mitchell	A. S. Wilson	900		
12...	Norton	A. S. Wilson	34		
	Osborne	A. S. Wilson	458		
	Phillips	A. S. Wilson	173		
	Republic	A. S. Wilson	1,088		
	Smith	A. S. Wilson	441		
	Washington	A. S. Wilson	1,450	9,017	9,014
	Butler	W. P. Campbell	819		
	Cowley	W. P. Campbell	1,173		
	Greenwood	W. P. Campbell	874		
	Howard	W. P. Campbell	1,360		
	Sedgwick	W. P. Campbell	802		
13...	Sumner	W. P. Campbell	499	5,527	824
	Butler	J. M. Atwood	1,135		
	Cowley	J. M. Atwood	633		
	Greenwood	J. M. Atwood	352		
	Howard	J. M. Atwood	1,289		
	Sedgwick	J. M. Atwood	674		
	Sumner	J. M. Atwood	620	4,703	
	Barton	J. H. Prescott	222		
	Ellis	J. H. Prescott	220		
14...	Ellsworth	J. H. Prescott	371		
	Lincoln	J. H. Prescott	373		
	McPherson	J. H. Prescott	481		
	Russell	J. H. Prescott	158		

VOTE FOR JUDGES OF THE DISTRICT COURTS— Concluded.

District.	Counties.	Names of Candidates.	Vote of County...	Total ...	Maj ......
14...	Saline.............................	J. H. Prescott......................	1,415		
	Wallace	J. H. Prescott......................	56	3,296	3,185
	Ellis	John G. Spivey..................	3		
	Ellsworth	John G. Spivey..................	90	93	

The political standing of the Legislature is as follows:

	Senate.	House.	Joint Ballot.
Republicans	27	75	102
Democrats..	4	11	15
Independents	2	14	16
Republican majority..	21	50	71

NOVEMBER 5.—

"Our vote at the late election was larger than the vote of either of the States of Maine, New Hampshire, Vermont, Connecticut, Rhode Island, Arkansas, Delaware Florida, Nebraska, Nevada, Oregon, South Carolina, West Virginia, California or Minnesota—larger than the vote of any New England State except Massachusetts, and larger than the combined vote of Nebraska, Delaware, Nevada, Rhode Island and Oregon."— Gov. Osborn's Message, January, 1873.

The message contained the following statement in regard to railroads:

"In 1862, not a mile of railroad was in operation in the State. Now we have 2,039 miles in actual operation, while several new roads are in process of construction. Kansas has more miles of railroad than either of the twenty-six States named below: Maine, New Hampshire, Vermont, Massachusetts, Rhode Island, Connecticut, New Jersey, Delaware, Maryland, West Virginia, Wisconsin, Minnesota, Virginia, North Carolina, South Carolina, Florida, Alabama, Mississippi, Louisiana, Texas, Kentucky, Tennessee, Arkansas, California, Oregon, and Nevada. Of all the Southern States which opposed the admission of Kansas into the Union, only one, Georgia, has more miles of railroad. She exceeds us but sixty-nine miles, and will not lead us many weeks longer."

NOVEMBER. —Eugene F. Ware retires from the Monitor. —The Fort Scott Daily Republican suspends.—George J. Clark wheels a sack of Goodlander flour to J. S. Redfield's house, Fort Scott, on an election bet. Charles W. Blair makes the speech.

NOVEMBER 20.—The M. K. and T. reaches the Red river and Texas.

NOVEMBER 26.— Dedication of the Atchison Odd Fellows' Hall.

NOVEMBER 29.— Death of Horace Greeley. Of all the friends of Free Kansas he was the most powerful.

NOVEMBER 30.—

"Here I must call attention to the fact that Wallace county has again made no returns of taxable property. It does not possess a proper county organization, and the only sign of life that is given annually are the election returns, showing the election of some person as Representative, drawing pay for mileage and per diem as member of the Legislature for representing nobody. If 'no taxation without representation,' is not a myth, then this Wallace county farce ought to be stopped after four years' trial." Report of Auditor Thoman.

The farce is continued, and has become a fraud.

NOVEMBER 30.—Expenditures of the State for the year:

Governor's Department	$5,000 00	Agricultural College	15,032 28
Secretary's Department	17,073 96	Railroad Assessors	2,667 35
Auditor's Department	8,033 92	Sheriffs conveying prisoners to	
Treasurer's Department	8,495 00	Penitentiary	5,032 11
Attorney General	1,580 60	Regents State Institutions	1,996 60
Sup't of Public Instruction	2,876 28	Horticultural Society	1,000 00
Adjutant General	1,400 00	Agricultural Society	3,825 85
Judiciary Department	39,092 16	Freedmen's University	1,372 00
Legislative expenses	42,518 53	Transcribing Journals	1,963 40
Printing	57,362 53	Arresting fugitives from justice	425 65
Normal School, Emporia	61,522 66	Military purposes	1,180 40
Normal School, Leavenworth	7,567 53	Commission on Indian Claims	500 00
State University	68,290 00	Library	4,157 55
Penitentiary	104,040 09	Seed wheat	2,476 25
State House and Grounds	30,486 67	Miscellaneous	251 50
Insane Asylum	22,713 00		
Blind Asylum	10,088 96	Total for 1872	$544,192 83
Deaf and Dumb Asylum	14,200 00		

DECEMBER 2.—The new University building, at Lawrence, opened for instruction.

—A recent decision of the Supreme Court declares good the title of Jas. F. Joy to the Neutral Lands.

DECEMBER 4.—Meeting of Presidential Electors, at Topeka. The vote is taken to Washington by John Guthrie.

DECEMBER 6.—Destructive fire at St. Mary's.

DECEMBER 10.—The epizootic horse disease in the State.

DECEMBER 11.—The Report of Adjutant General Whittaker contains a statement showing the general account of debits and credits for arms, etc., issued to Kansas by the General Government under the law for arming the Militia. It foots up as follows:

Value of arms issued to Kansas... $107,049 75
Amount of apportionment... 57,564 79

Balance due United States... $49,488 96

DECEMBER 12.—Librarian Dickinson reports 8,473 books in the State Library. Only four books have been lost since he took charge of the Library.

DECEMBER 18.—The Report of Secretary Smallwood gives the date of the organization of new counties as follows: Reno, January 1, 1872; Smith, Feb. 1; Harvey, April 10; Barton, May 16; Russell, July 18; Phillips, July 26; Norton, August 22; Pawnee, Nov. 4; Rooks, Nov. 26.—In 1871, Sumner, Osborne and Rice were organized.

DECEMBER 24.—Destructive fire at Fontana, Miami county.

DECEMBER 25.—Burlington is building a $25,000 school-house.—Independence has erected a large school building, designed for eight departments.—Wilson county has forty-two school-houses, those at Altoona and Neodesha being very large, the one at Neodesha costing $15,000.—Chetopa is building a $25,000 school-house.—Paola has erected one of the largest and finest public school buildings in the State, at a cost of $50,000.

DECEMBER 25.—State Teachers' Association, at Humboldt. *Officers elected:* President, John W. Horner, of Chetopa; Recording Secretary, S.

B. Lemon, of Independence; Corresponding Secretary, S. M. Gaston, of Lawrence; Treasurer, Mrs. H. A. Monroe, of Atchison. *Executive Committee:* Wm. Wheeler of Ottawa, Geo. W. Hoss of Emporia, R. H. Jackson of Atchison, Miss Collins of Iola, and Frank H. Snow of Lawrence. The next Convention to be held at Ottawa.

DECEMBER 26.— Great fire at Concordia.

DECEMBER 30.—

"On the seventeenth of August, I received the sum of $336,817.37, which had been appropriated by act of Congress to the State of Kansas, in payment for a certain class of military claims; while for the interest on the debt thus paid, and for other classes of claims contracted at the same time, and for which Union Military scrip had been issued, no provision was made. There being no law governing my action in case of partial payment, and believing that it would be wronging the claimants, either to wait action by the Legislature or to pay those first presented in full, I decided to pay without interest that class of scrip only which had been allowed by Congress, and to issue certificates showing the amount of interest then due on the same.

"The scrip issued for the Curtis Expedition against the Indians, and for the services of certain irregular companies in the Price Raid, although not allowed by Congress, has been paid, as it was found impossible to distinguish by the warrants for what kind of service they had been issued. There will, therefore, be a deficiency in the funds for the payment of scrip issued for services, transportation, supplies and miscellaneous, including the Curtis Expedition, to the amount of $94,348.48, exclusive of interest; in addition to which there still remains outstanding interest certificates issued on scrip paid, to the amount of $124,000, and scrip given for damages, $159,191.34—to all of which I would respectfully call your attention, and recommend that some early and final disposal be made of the same."—*Report of Treasurer Hayes.*

DECEMBER 31.—Superintendent McCarty reports the school fund as $769,395.99. He gives a list of the bonds bought during the year.

—The new Normal School building nearly completed. The State gave $50,000, and the city of Emporia $10,000.

—The State House Commissioners report that $30,506 has been expended on the east portico of the east wing, and ask for $12,500 more.

DECEMBER 31.—Annual Report of the State Board of Agriculture, pp. 432, including the History and Transactions of the Academy of Science. The Report contains tables of State products; a list of the newspapers of the State; proceedings of the Farmers' Convention in April, 1873; lists of clubs and societies in all parts of the State; a detailed account of the Eighth State Fair; articles by Charles V. Riley, George T. Anthony, J. K. Hudson, R. S. Elliott, and J. G. Haskell, with many illustrations.

In the part devoted to the Academy of Science, are J. H. Carruth's catalogue of plants seen in Kansas, and essays by Wm. H. Saunders, B. F. Mudge, F. H. Snow, and Lizzie J. Williams.

The Transactions of the Horticultural Society are published in the same volume, making 199 more pages. The officers of the Society are: President, Wm. M. Howsley, Leavenworth; Vice President, J. C. Vincent, Lecompton; Secretary, G. C. Brackett, Lawrence; Treasurer, S. T. Kelsey, Pomona; Trustees, E. Gale of Manhattan, E. Snyder of Highland, William Maxwell of Lanesfield.

Essays are published by E. Gale, John H. Tice, J. Stayman, B. L. Kingsbury, Chas. V. Riley, S. T. Kelsey, John A. Warder, William M. Howsley, James Christian, and F. H. Snow.

DECEMBER.—A book issued, entitled "The Sons of the Border. Sketches of the Life and People of the Far Frontier. By James W. Steele ('Deane Monahan'). Topeka, Kansas: Commonwealth Printing Company. 1873." pp. 260. An introduction is written by Henry King. The book is made up of eighteen stories written by Steele and published in the Kansas Magazine. The sketches as they appeared in that Monthly were copied by the best newspapers in every part of the country, from Boston to New Orleans. They described the new life of the extreme West with grace, vigor and brilliancy, and stamped the young author as a man of genius. The book was admirably reviewed in the Magazine by John J. Ingalls.

DECEMBER.—Henry King retires and James W. Steele becomes the editor of the Kansas Magazine.

1873.

JANUARY 1.—A. T. & S. F. Railroad completed to the Colorado line.

JANUARY 3.—Robinson House burned, at Emporia.

JANUARY.—School Records for Kansas, by Peter McVicar, published by Geo. W. Crane.

—Township Officers' Guide, by Hugh M. Spalding, published by Geo. W. Crane, at Topeka.

JANUARY 10.—Examination of witnesses begins, in Washington, in the case of U. S. Senator Caldwell. The Senate had adopted the following resolution, May 11, 1872:

"*Resolved*, That the Committee on Privileges and Elections be authorized to investigate the election of Senator S. C. Pomeroy, by the Legislature of Kansas, in 1867, and the election of Senator Alexander Caldwell, in 1871; that the committee have power to send for persons and papers; that the chairman, or acting chairman, of said committee, or any sub-committee thereof, have power to administer oaths; and that the committee be authorized to sit in Washington, or elsewhere, during the session of Congress, and in vacation."

The witnesses now examined are: Sidney Clarke, J. M. Luce, Jonathan Hammond, William Spriggs, Wm. H. Carson, Thos. J. Anderson, Leonard T. Smith, Ira C. Buzick, Joel Thomas, James L. McDowell, Jacob Smith, Daniel R. Anthony, Wm. H. Peckham, John Fletcher, Fred. K. Hunt, J. M. Steele, Thos. L. Bond, Geo. W. Wood, Jas. Phinney, Thos. Carney, William S. Burke, Jas. H. Snead, C. H. Stilwell, Edwin C. Manning, Henry Foote, Claudius B. Brace, J. G. Reaser, Geo. S. Smith, John L. Pendery, Thos. P. Fenlon, Jeremiah Clark, S. J. Langdon, G. G. Gage, Frank H. Drenning, Chester Thomas, Sol. Miller, O. J. Hopkins, G. M. Simcock, M. H. Insley, L. J. Worden, Jas. F. Legate, Chas. Columbia, David A. Comstock, Robert Crozier, Theo. C. Sears, Isaac D. Clapp, Wm. Williams, D. W. Thomas, Geo. B. Sherwood, A. C. Van Duyn. The examination of witnesses ended February 5th. Senator Caldwell's attorneys were Caleb Cushing and Robert Crozier.

Senator Morton's report, as Chairman of the Committee, was submitted February 17. It concludes as follows:

"It has been a subject of discussion in the Committee whether the offences of which they believe Mr. Caldwell to have been guilty should be punished by expulsion or go to the validity of his election, and a majority are of the opinion that they go to the validity of his election, and had the effect to make it void. Wherefore the Committee recommend to the Senate the adoption of the following resolution:

"*Resolved*, That Alexander Caldwell was not duly and legally elected to a seat in the Senate of the United States by the Legislature of the State of Kansas.

"In conclusion, the Committee remark that, while Mr. Caldwell did things to procure his election which cannot be tolerated by the Senate, they believe he was as much sinned against as sinning. He was a novice in politics, and evidently in the hands of men who encouraged him in the belief that Senatorial elections in Kansas were carried by the use of money."

The Report is contained in a book of 470 pages. It is Report No. 451, Senate, Forty-second Congress, Third Session.

JANUARY 14.—Thirteenth Annual Session of the Legislature.

STATE OFFICERS.

Names.	P. O. Address.	County.
Thomas A. Osborn, Governor	Leavenworth ..	Leavenworth.
E. S. Stover, Lieutenant Governor	Council Grove..	Morris.
W. H. Smallwood, Secretary of State	Wathena	Doniphan.
A. L. Williams, Attorney General	Topeka...........	Shawnee.
H. D. McCarty, Superintendent of Public Instruction..	Leavenworth...	Leavenw'th.
J. E. Hayes, State Treasurer	Olathe	Johnson.
Daniel W. Wilder Auditor of State	Fort Scott	Bourbon.
S. S. Prouty, State Printer	Topeka	Shawnee.
C. A. Morris, Adjutant General	Fort Scott	Bourbon.
D. Dickinson, State Librarian	Oskaloosa........	Jefferson.
Ed. Russell, Superintendent Insurance Department.....	Leavenworth ..	Leavenworth.

JUDGES OF THE SUPREME COURT.

Names.	P. O. Address.	County.
S. A. Kingman, Chief Justice	Topeka............	Shawnee.
D. J. Brewer, Associate Justice	Leavenworth...	Leavenworth.
D. M. Valentine, Associate Justice	Ottawa	Franklin.

—Byron Sherry, Judge Criminal Court, Leavenworth county.

JUDGES OF THE DISTRICT COURTS.

Names.	District.	P. O. Address.	County.
H. W. Ide	First............	Leavenworth City..	Leavenworth.
P. L. Hubbard	Second.........	Atchison..............	Atchison.
John T. Morton	Third	Topeka	Shawnee.
Owen A. Bassett	Fourth	Lawrence.............	Douglas.
E. B. Peyton	Fifth	Emporia	Lyon.
M. V. Voss	Sixth...........	Fort Scott............	Bourbon.
John R. Goodin	Seventh........	Humboldt	Allen.
William H. Canfield	Eighth..........	Junction City......	Davis.
William R. Brown	Ninth..........	Cottonwood Falls...	Chase.
Hiram Stevens	Tenth	Paola	Miami.
B. W. Perkins	Eleventh......	Oswego	Labette.
A. S. Wilson	Twelfth........	Washington.........	Washington.
W. P. Campbell	Thirteenth...	Eldorado..............	Butler.
J. H. Prescott	Fourteenth...	Salina.................	Saline.
A. J. Banta	Fifteenth	Beloit..................	Mitchell.

MEMBERS AND OFFICERS OF THE SENATE.

Names.	Dist.	Post Office Address.	County.
E. S. Stover, President....................	....	Council Grove.............	Morris.
Blair, A. M................................	18	Ottawa.......................	Franklin.
Brandley, H	26	Matfield Green............	Chase.
Butler, C. B	22	Leroy.........................	Coffey.
Barker, E..................................	28	Jewell City	Jewell.
Crichton, J. H............................	15	Chetopa	Labette.
Edwards, J. H............................	29	Ellis..........................	Ellis.
Ely, Andrew..............................	11	La Cygne	Linn.
Grimes, W. H	2	Atchison.....................	Atchison.
Guerin, W. E.............................	12	Fort Scott....................	Bourbon.
Johnson, W. A............................	17	Garnett	Anderson.
Judd, Byron..............................	8	Wyandotte	Wyandotte.
Martin, C. S..............................	21	Osage City..................	Osage.
Martindale, William	24	Madison	Greenwood.
Matheny, William M.....................	14	Baxter Springs.............	Cherokee.
McFarland, N. C..........................	20	Topeka........................	Shawnee.
McWhirt, J. T.............................	7	Leavenworth................	Leavenworth.
Moonlight, Thomas	7	Leavenworth	Leavenworth.
Morrill, E. N..............................	3	Hiawatha....................	Brown.
Murdock, M. M............................	25	Wichita......................	Sedgwick.
O'Neil, M. A..............................	19	Black Jack...................	Douglas.
Palmer, L. R..............................	5	St. Mary's...................	Pottawatomie.
Price, Nathan............................	1	Troy..........................	Doniphan.
Rogers, J. W..............................	6	Winchester	Jefferson.
Schmidt, Frank...........................	4	Marysville...................	Marshall.
Simons, W. L.............................	16	Osage Mission.............	Neosho.
Simpson, William	13	Pawnee Station............	Bourbon.
St. John, J. P.............................	9	Olathe	Johnson.
Topping, E. H.............................	10	Paola	Miami.
Walker, Samuel..........................	19	Lawrence	Douglas.
Wilson, J. C..............................	2	Muscotah	Atchison.
Wilson, V. P..............................	27	Abilene	Dickinson.
Winter, Jacob............................	7	Leavenworth................	Leavenworth.
York, A. M	23	Independence...............	Montgomery.
George C. Crowther, Secretary............	....	Osage Mission..............	Neosho.
T. H. Cavanaugh, Assistant Secretary...	....	Salina........................	Saline.
George W. Findlay, Sergeant-at-Arms...	....	Fort Scott....................	Bourbon.
J. R. Kennedy, Asst. Sergeant-at-Arms,	....	Olathe........................	Johnson.
George W. Weed, Doorkeeper...............	....	Leavenworth................	Leavenworth.
S. M. Lanham, Journal Clerk...............	....	Seneca........................	Nemaha.
W. H. Cowan, Docket Clerk...............	....	Topeka	Shawnee.
Miss Nellie Blake, Enrolling Clerk.......	....	Olathe	Johnson.
Mrs. Sarah J. Neal, Engrossing Clerk....	....	Atchison.....................	Atchison.
Jennie Griffith, Page....................	....	Topeka	Shawnee.
Allie Morris, Page.......................	....	Wichita......................	Sedgwick.
Janet Edwards, Page.....................	....	Paola.........................	Miami.

MEMBERS AND OFFICERS OF THE HOUSE OF REPRESENTATIVES.

Names.	Dist.	Post Office Address.	County.
Josiah Kellogg, Speaker......................	21	Leavenworth	Leavenworth.
Adams, David.............................	98	Bunker Hill	Russell.
Adams, D. M..............................	56	North Topeka..............	Shawnee.
Allen, E. B................................	76	Wichita......................	Sedgwick.
Bacon, F..................................	46	Chanute	Neosho.
Baker, Thomas H..........................	74	Augusta	Butler.
Banta, A. J...............................	11	Washington	Washington.
Bateman, William	51	Peoria City	Franklin.
Beaty, J. W...............................	31	Paola	Miami.
Belden, D.................................	30	DeSoto	Johnson.
Bell, M. S.................................	65	Independence...............	Montgomery.
Billings, N. H.............................	100	Norton Centre..............	Norton.
Bishop, George S..........................	88	White Rock..................	Republic.
Blakely, W. S.............................	71	Junction City	Davis.
Bond, W. H................................	22	Leavenworth	Leavenworth.
Bowers, M. B....................	1	White Cloud	Doniphan.
Bowron, C. F.............................	7	White Cloud	Doniphan.
Brenner, Jacob............................	37	Hepler.......................	Bourbon.
Brinkman, G. L............................	97	Great Bend..................	Barton.

MEMBERS AND OFFICERS OF HOUSE OF REPRESENTATIVES—CONTINUED.

Names.	Dist....	*Post Office Address.*	*County.*
Brown, V.	17	Medina	Jefferson.
Buchan, W. J	27	Wyandotte	Wyandotte.
Childs, A. F	41	Columbus	Cherokee.
Cochrane, W. J	36	Uniontown	Bourbon.
Cooper, A. B.	60	Osage City	Osage.
Crew, James S.	52	Lawrence	Douglas.
Cross, S. K.	61	Burlington	Coffey.
Cummings, E. S	66	Elk Falls	Howard.
Curtain, John	87	Beloit	Mitchell.
Davis, W. B.	83	Delphos	Ottawa,
DeForrest, H. C.	9	Wetmore	Nemaha
Dillard, Thomas	25	Hoge	Leavenworth.
Eldridge, T. B.	64	Coffeyville	Montgomery.
Ensign, H. A.	96	Newton	Harvey.
Fields, H. C.	24	Leavenworth	Leavenworth.
Forsee, E.	84	Falun	Saline.
Frazier, D. H.	18	Mt. Florence	Jefferson.
Funston, E. H.	47	Carlyle	Allen.
Gillespie, G. W	5	Atchison	Atchison.
Gregg, W	57	Topeka	Shawnee.
Green, George	86	Lincoln Centre	Lincoln.
Guffy, R. A.	13	Vienna	Pottawatomie.
Harper, W. W.	43	Mound Valley	Labette.
Harvey, C. W	42	Baxter Springs	Cherokee.
Henshaw, N	55	Hesper	Douglas
Hodges, P. M.	15	Holton	Jackson.
Hoesman, H. F.	85	Ellsworth	Ellsworth.
Hungerford, S. R.	33	LaCygne	Linn.
Hutchings, C. F.	45	Osage Mission	Neosho.
Hutchinson, C. C.	94	Hutchinson	Reno.
Huntington, S. P.	67	Eureka	Greenwood.
Hunter, J. M.	69	Emporia	Lyon.
Hunter, W. J.	12	Manhattan	Riley.
James, Thomas	28	Westport, Missouri	Johnson.
Jeffrey, William	73	Elmdale	Chase.
Kahler, S. J.	79	Abilene	Dickinson.
Kalloch, I. S.	53	Lawrence	Douglas.
Lane, L. H	35	Prescott	Linn.
Langdon, S. J.	40	Cherokee	Crawford.
Larkin, M. E.	6	Larkin	Atchison.
Lanter, J. T.	49	Garnett	Anderson.
Legere, I. C	10	Frankfort	Marshall.
Lowrey, William	91	Brookdale	Rice.
Lowe, A. K.	54	Lecompton	Douglas.
Mapes, W. H.	44	Oswego	Labette.
McDermott, James	75	Dexter	Cowley.
McDonald, B. P.	38	Fort Scott	Bourbon.
McLean, J. K.	77	Florence	Marion.
Miller, J. M.	29	Ocheltree	Johnson.
Miller, G. M.	92	Wellington	Sumner.
Morgan, Thomas	20	Leavenworth	Leavenworth.
Morrison, J. T.	95	Smith Centre	Smith.
Motz, Simon	89	Hays City	Ellis.
Nugent, E. J.	50	Ottawa	Franklin.
O'Driscoll, B	2	Doniphan City	Doniphan.
Peck, William	62	Toronto	Woodson.
Plummer, W. S.	19	Leavenworth	Leavenworth.
Reasoner, C.	93	Osborne City	Osborne.
Robinson, L. N.	68	Emporia	Lyon.
Ross, Alex	90	Wallace	Wallace.
Scofield, C. I.	8	Seneca	Nemaha.
Searcy, E.	3	Elwood	Doniphan.
Sellers, A.	70	Alma	Wabaunsee.
Sexton, J. Z.	63	Fredonia	Wilson.
Shaw, A.	81	Belleville	Republic.
Shoemaker, S. R.	59	Lyndon	Osage.
Simpson, T. E.	78	Lindsburg	McPherson.
Smith, Reuben	32	Osawatomie	Miami.
Snyder, H. C.	82	Glasco	Cloud.
Spalding, A. W	4	Atchison	Atchison.
Stratton, S. L.	80	Republican City	Clay.
Titus, Charles H.	72	Parkerville	Morris.
Tough, William S.	26	Leavenworth	Leavenworth.
Turner, J.	23	Easton	Leavenworth.

MEMBERS AND OFFICERS OF HOUSE OF REPRESENTATIVES—Concluded.

Names.	Dist.	Post Office Address.	County.
Veale, G. W.	57	Topeka	Shawnee.
Vickers, A. J.	39	Girard	Crawford.
Ward, J. F.	34	Goodrich	Linn.
Wakefield, Wm.	48	Humboldt	Allen.
Weaver, N.	99	Kirwin	Phillips.
Wells, Welcome	14	Manhattan	Riley.
Willetts, J. F.	16	Oskaloosa	Jefferson.
A. R. Banks, Chief Clerk		Lawrence	Douglas.
G. C. West, Assistant Clerk		Parsons	Labette.
W. Wirt Walton, Journal Clerk		Winfield	Cowley.
James M. Matheny, Sergeant-at-Arms		Newbury	Wabaunsee.
John H. Helwig, First Ass't S.-at-Arms.		Monrovia	Atchison.
D. W. Acker, Second Ass't Ser.-at-Arms.		Vermilion	Nemaha.
Wm. P. Ames, Docket Clerk		Olathe	Johnson.
Emma R. Bristol, Engrossing Clerk		Ladore	Neosho.
Lizzie Ela, Enrolling Clerk		Emporia	Lyon.
Russell B. Armstrong, Postmaster		Wyandotte	Wyandotte.
George E. Brown, Doorkeeper		Olathe	Johnson.
A. H. McWhorter, First Ass't Doork'per		Lawrence	Douglas.
M. F. Collins, Second Ass't Doorkeeper..		Olathe	Johnson.
Emma Bragg, Page			
Jennie Maxwell, Page			
Mary Fletcher, Page			
Charley Wakefield, Page			
Jennie Hosmer, Page,			
Hattie Butler, Page			
Milton Cummings, Page			
Frank Childs, Page			

JANUARY.—Election of the following officers of the State Board of Agriculture, at Topeka, by the Presidents of County Societies: President, E. S. Niccolls, of Anderson; Vice President, T. Murphy, of Atchison; Secretary, Alfred Gray, of Shawnee; Treasurer, G. W. Veale, of Shawnee; Superintendent, George Noble. *Executive Committee:* J. K. Hudson of Wyandotte county, G. L. Young of Shawnee, James Rogers of Osage, Martin Anderson of Jackson, Wm. Martindale of Greenwood, Malcolm Conn of Morris, G. T. Anthony of Leavenworth, R. P. Edgington of Butler, George Noble of Douglas. *Geologist:* B. F. Mudge, Manhattan, Professor of Natural Science, State Agricultural College. *Entomologist:* C. V. Riley, St. Louis, Mo., State Entomologist of Missouri. *Meteorologist:* Frank H. Snow, Lawrence, Professor of Natural History and Meteorology, University of Kansas. *Botanist:* James H. Carruth, Lawrence. *Signal Service Committee:* Frank H. Snow of Douglas county, B. F. Mudge of Riley, James H. Carruth of Douglas.

JANUARY 21.—Election of State Printer. *First ballot:* S. S. Prouty 65, Geo. W. Martin 62. *Second ballot:* S. S. Prouty 63, Geo. W. Martin 64. *Third ballot:* S. S. Prouty 58, Geo. W. Martin 68.

JANUARY 25.—The Anti-Pomeroy caucus is addressed by D. P. Lowe, W. A. Phillips, S. A. Cobb, J. M. Harvey, C. A. Logan, John M. Price, and others.

JANUARY 28.—*Vote for Senator, in the Senate:* D. M. Valentine 1, J. M. Harvey 6, S. C. Pomeroy 10, W. A. Phillips 2, D. P. Lowe 5, C. A. Logan 2, John M. Price 3, Thos. A. Osborn 2, John T. Morton 1, Chas. Robinson 1. *In the House:* S. C. Pomeroy 40, J. M. Harvey 19, D. P. Lowe 13, C. A. Logan 11, John M. Price 3, D. M. Valentine 2, John T. Morton 4, Chas. Robinson 3, John J. Ingalls 1, T. H. Walker 1.

JANUARY 29.—*Vote for Senator:* John J. Ingalls 115, D. P. Lowe 6, Sidney Clarke 2, A. M. York 2, Chas. Robinson 1, S. A. Kingman 1.

Before the vote was taken, Alexander M. York, Senator from Montgomery county, made a speech, in which he said:

"I visited Mr. Pomeroy's room, in the dark and secret recesses of the Tefft House, on Monday night [January 27th], and at that interview my vote was bargained for, for a consideration of $8,000; two thousand dollars of which were paid to me on that evening, five thousand dollars the next afternoon, and a promise of the additional one thousand when my vote had been cast in his favor. I now, in the presence of this honorable body, hand over the amount of $7,000 just as I received it, and ask that it be counted by the Secretary." [Col. York advanced and placed upon the Chief Clerk's desk two parcels of money, one open, and amounting to $2,000, and a brown paper parcel, tied with twine, which, upon examination, was found to contain $5,000 in greenbacks, of large denominations.] "I ask, Mr. President, that that money be used to defray the expenses of prosecuting the investigation of S. C. Pomeroy for bribery and corruption."

(The money was used to pay Pomeroy's lawyers, for acquitting him, two years afterwards.*)

The Commonwealth, which had favored Pomeroy's election, said:

"During the delivery of this astounding address, of which the foregoing is but a weak and incomplete abstract, the audience was deathly still. Every word fell with a thrill on the senses of the packed and spell-bound throng, like the dull and startling thud of clods on a coffin. In that coffin reposed the remains of the corruption that, since the organization of the State, has perched upon its back like the Old Man of the Sea."

A congratulatory meeting held that evening was participated in by E. S. Stover, A. M. York, W. A. Johnson, J. P. St. John, A. W. Spaulding, W. S. Plummer, B. F. Simpson, Paul R. Brooks, T. D. Thacher, D. P. Lowe, S. A. Cobb, W. A. Phillips, John J. Ingalls, Jas. D. Snoddy, James M. Harvey, J. H. Edwards, H. W. Cook, Byron Sherry, and others. A resolution was passed unanimously, and with rousing cheers, thanking Col. York for his courageous and patriotic course. A suit was instituted against Senator Pomeroy for bribery.

JANUARY 29.—A Topeka despatch in the Atchison Champion, signed J. A. M., says:

"Mr. Pomeroy's friends were overwhelmed with astonishment and shocked beyond measure. . . . His counsel, however, have refused to allow him to make any statements concerning the matter until the excitement at present existing subsides."

An editorial article in the Champion, on Ingalls, soon after this event, said:

"That terrible and overwhelming development gave him the almost unanimous vote of both branches of the Legislature."

Another editorial article in the Champion says:

"At last, as sudden and terrible as an earthquake which overwhelms a busy city in ruin and disaster, came the awful revelation and final end, crushing with defeat and disgrace the man who had so long represented the State with usefulness and capacity in the Senate, and who might have been, but for this shocking exposure, in one hour more, re-elected for a term of six years. . . . For his offence we have no excuse and no sympathy. He understood full well the consequences; he risked them, and he is suffering them."

JANUARY 31.—Senator Pomeroy's trial for bribery postponed till June.

*TOPEKA, KANSAS, March 12, 1875.—Received of A. M. York the sum of seven thousand dollars, less the amount of costs in the case of The State of Kansas against S. C. Pomeroy, now pending in the District Court in and for Osage county, Kansas, in full of amount paid by me to said A. M. York during the session of the Kansas State Legislature, in the year 1873.   S. C. POMEROY.

By ALBERT H. HORTON, his attorney.

FEBRUARY 4.—The House, by a vote of 64 to 8, asks Pomeroy to resign.

FEBRUARY 4.— The State Senate passes a resolution requesting the United States Senate to appoint a committee to investigate the charges against S. C. Pomeroy.

—Passage of a resolution to investigate the charges of bribery against S. C. Pomeroy.

FEBRUARY 5.—The Senate, by a vote of 21 to 9, passes a resolution requesting Pomeroy to resign.

—The House, by a vote of 51 to 39, asks Caldwell to resign.

—The joint committee to investigate the Pomeroy bribery case meets.

—Death of Seth. M. Hays, at Council Grove. He established a trading post there in 1847.

FEBRUARY 6.—The following is copied from an opinion of A. L. Williams, Attorney General, in regard to the legal obligations of the L. L. & G. R. R. Co. to the State:

"The L. L. & G. also has a grant of the proceeds of 125,000 acres of land from the State, under date of February 23, 1866. (See Laws of 1866, page 142, or General Statutes, page 888.) This land is part of 500,000 acres which the Legislature of 1865 wrested (I might use a harsher and more accurate word) from the school fund of the State, to which it had been solemnly devoted by the people in our Constitution, and divided it between four railroads in the State. To suppose that a law framed in the direct interest of these roads contained any serious restricting or forfeiting clause would be absurd, And a glance at its provisions will at once acquit its framers of any such intention."

FEBRUARY 8.—Death of ex-Governor John W. Geary, at Harrisburg.

FEBRUARY 9.—Mr. Pomeroy, in the Senate, denies the charges made against him, and asks for investigation.

FEBRUARY 11.—Gen. Pope informs Gov. Osborn that the President has complied with the Governor's request, and that the U. S. troops will be withdrawn from the Cherokee Neutral Lands.

FEBRUARY 15.—Report of committee that Auditor Thoman registered bonds of the cities of Budlong, Cloud and Gregory, Cherokee county, but that there were no such cities in existence.

FEBRUARY 15.—Henry G. Webb, Judge of the Eleventh District, resigns, and the committee investigating his alleged corruption in office is discharged.

—Farmers' Co-operative Convention in Topeka. Messrs. Aikin, Cramer, Otis, Downs and Ritchie take part.

FEBRUARY 17.—Investigation of Pomeroy by the United States Senate. The witnesses examined were Alexander M. York, William A. Johnson, James C. Horton, Frank Bacon, William H. Bond, B. O'Driscoll, William Simpson, W. M. Matheny, Edward Searcy, Wm. E. Guerin, David L. Payne, C. J. Hanks, D. W. Houston, Asa Low, J. P. Brown, J. S. Hoke, John A. Martin, George T. Anthony, Daniel H. Horne, R. W. Wright, J. L. Sharp, Thomas Murphy, J. Z. Sexton, W. R. Laughlin, Sidney Clarke, John J. Murphy, C. A. Rohrabacher, I. S. Kalloch, Asa Hairgrove, John M. Holmes, P. B. Maxson, John Q. Page, J. D. Liggett, Robert McBratney, F. M. Shaw, John McDonald, John A. Joyce, Chester Thomas, A. H. Horton, Samuel C. Pomeroy, Stephen A. Cobb.

The argument for A. M. York was made by B. F. Simpson; for S. C. Pomeroy, by Caleb Cushing and Albert H. Horton.

FEBRUARY 19.—T. D. Thacher elected President, and George F. Prescott Secretary, of the Associated Press, at Leavenworth.

—Candidates for Caldwell's seat are numerous.

FEBRUARY 22.—Farmers' Convention at Topeka.

FEBRUARY 25.—The following is Senator Pomeroy's account of the York transaction, given under oath to the committee, February 25. See pp. 233-5 of the Report:

"GENTLEMEN OF THE COMMITTEE: I submit herewith a true statement of the facts as they relate to my action in the cases of bribery and corruption now pending before this Committee.

"It is a gratification to me that all the material facts are well established by competent testimony, so that very little is at issue upon my own individual statement.

"And first, I deny that I gave at any time authority or permission to any man to use any money or other valuable thing to control or influence improperly the votes of any members of the Legislature in the State of Kansas, and specifically deny that I ever gave such authority to the gentlemen named or designated by the witnesses upon this trial, to wit: Mr. A. H. Horton, C. A. Rohrabacher, J. S. York, J. T. Brown, J. J. Murphy, A. Low, or to either one of them. And, secondly, that while I never delegated such authority to others, I positively never exercised it in any instance myself.

"Senator Simpson, from the Neutral Lands, often spoke to me of the condition of the settlers there, and as often I spoke of my desire to relieve them, not only by the passage of the bill pending before the Senate, but by every means in my power. When he spoke of a letter he had received from Mr. Laughlin, stating that his means of support in Washington had become reduced to '$2.50,' and they had no means of continuing him here save by voluntary contribution, I told him I was a friend of those poor settlers, and would, in any event, contribute to his support. And soon after reaching Washington I met Mr. Laughlin, and although his friends did not support me, and did not promise me any support, still I did what I said I would, and gave him, as he testified, $50; and hence it is certain that my contribution had no relation to any man's vote who represented those people, for I never even had the promise of a vote, or expected a vote from that locality.

"And if one well-established fact of bribery, outside of the charge of Mr. York, has been proved by witnesses testifying either here or at Topeka (where I have not pretended to have a man to defend or represent me), I do not know it, and do not believe it.

"And now as to the charge of this Mr. York, and his associate conspirators, I will say the true facts have been already stated by witnesses, and the transaction already seen to be a purely business one, having no relation whatever to *his vote*, which, on several occasions, I had learned of his pledging to me. About the last of the week before the Tuesday set for the first ballot, Mr. T. B. Eldridge, M. W. Reynolds, Mr. De Long, and others, all from his own county, assured me with more or less positiveness of York's support.

"But some days before I learned that, I had, after much deliberation, agreed to aid Mr. J. Q. Page and associates to start a National Bank at Independence, where Page had a private bank, and having satisfied myself of his ability, capacity, and fitness for the management of such an institution, I agreed to furnish him with money sufficient, when put with his $25,000, would make a sum sufficient to purchase thirty United States bonds, of the denomination of $1,000 each.

"Mr. Page urged and was anxious to procure the money before he left Topeka, and I told him it was inconvenient for me to furnish over $2,000 then, but would get it soon, and he might depend upon it, and make his arrangements accordingly.

"At this time I met at the Tefft House Mr. W. P. Borland, of Second National Bank of Leavenworth, who enquired of me if I should not need some currency before leaving Topeka, as he thought from appearances my hotel bills would be large. At first I told him no. The next day I met him, and said I should like to get $5,000, for forty or sixty days, as I had agreed to help a friend organize a National Bank, and he would refund it as soon as he got his currency from the Government.

"He then brought me a package, said to contain $5,000, which I never opened or counted, or even gave a note or receipt for at the time, and I put the same in my valise.

"Upon Monday night, the 27th, Mr. York came to my room, having seen me or sent me word several times that he would do so, and at once began to report what had been going on at the anti-Pomeroy caucus, and I heard him through. Before leaving he spoke of the favor I had granted his friend Page, and said Page had requested him to get the money and forward it to him at Independence, and that he, York, should leave soon after the election for home.

"I told him I was not prepared at that time to furnish it, although I had promised it to Page before I left the city. Mr. York spoke; said that perhaps I had no confidence in him. I assured him of my confidence, and told him I could furnish $2,000 at that time, and thought I should be able to furnish $5,000 more the next day. The amount necessary I had calculated would be from $5,000 to $8,000 to pay for the bonds and their premium, in addition to the $25,000 Mr. Page and his associates could furnish.

"I then paid him the first instalment of $2,000, and the next day I paid the package of $5,000 just as I had received the same from Mr. Borland, and neither gave Mr. Borland nor took a receipt. But during that day I had sent Mr. Knight at one time, and Mr. Lemuel Pomeroy at another time, to find Mr. Page, if he had not left the city, to inform him of the whole transaction. But these gentlemen both returned, saying that they were unable to find Mr. Page, and I rested in the belief that the transaction was all right until I heard of the misrepresentation of the facts by Mr. York upon the floor of the Joint Convention. I then denounced it as a conspiracy, a plot, and told my counsel here, Judge Horton, the whole story, and within a few days left Kansas for Washington.

"This, in brief, is the history of that *charge of bribery* for which I asked of the Senate a committee to investigate, and this *one act* (the transaction with Page and York), I now solemnly declare had no reference whatever to the vote of York, and was made and executed entirely independent of it.

"I make this statement upon my honor as a Senator, and upon my oath, and I further 'specifically deny,' as I stated in the Senate when I demanded this investigation, 'that I ever entered into any contract or agreement, directly or indirectly, with any man, a member of the Kansas Legislature or not, for a vote in my favor, or that I ever, directly or indirectly, paid or promised to pay any individual one dollar, or any other sum, for his vote for me in the late Senatorial election in Kansas.'   S. C. POMEROY."

FEBRUARY 28.—Banquet and ball, at Topeka, to the Nebraska Legislature.

MARCH.—Appointment of Regents and Trustees:

University: Chas. Robinson, Lawrence; Wm. Fairchild, Leavenworth; John A. Anderson, Junction City; Archibald Beatty, Independence; F. T. Ingalls, Atchison; Samuel A. Kingman, Topeka. V. P. Wilson and N. C. McFarland were soon after appointed in the places of Anderson and Kingman, who resigned.

Normal School: J. W. Horner, Chetopa; Chas. B. Butler, Burlington; H. C. Cross, Emporia; Geo. W. Wood, Doniphan county; M. M. Murdock, Wichita; Edwin Tucker, Eureka.

Insane Asylum: A. F. Childs, Columbus; Levi Woodard, Hesper; T. C. Bowles, Ottawa; D. W. Stormont, Topeka; Reuben Smith, Osawatomie; John T. Lanter, Garnett.

Deaf and Dumb Asylum: Archibald Shaw, Olathe; W. H. M. Fishback, Olathe; John Francis, Iola; E. S. Stover, Council Grove; W. B. Craig, Wathena; J. W. Rogers, Winchester.

Blind Asylum: Joseph Speck, Wyandotte; J. D. Brumbaugh, Marysville;

39

David Gordon, Fort Scott; Stephen M. Wood, Chase county; W. B. Slosson, Sabetha; Welcome Wells, Pottawatomie county.

Leavenworth Normal School: Thos. Moonlight, John H. Brown, Joseph L. Wever, Levi Houston, W. O. Gould, H. L. Newman.

MARCH 3.—The majority report in the Pomeroy case is presented by Senators Frelinghuysen, Buckingham, and Alcorn. They say:

"The committee, bearing in mind, while examining the evidence, that the whole transaction, whatever view be taken of it, is the result of a concerted plot to defeat Mr. Pomeroy, and remembering that the burden of proof is on the party making the accusation, have come to the conclusion that Mr. York has not sustained his charge by sufficient proof, contradicted as it is by the evidence of Mr. Page and Mr. Pomeroy."

Mark Twain's version of the report, in the Gilded Age, is as follows:

"It being plain that Senator Dilworthy's statement was rigidly true, and this fact being strengthened by his adding to it the support of 'his honor as a Senator,' the committee rendered a verdict of 'Not proven that a bribe had been offered and accepted.' This in a manner exonerated Noble, and let him escape."

Senator Vickers reports:

"I cannot decide that the guilt of Mr. Pomeroy is established beyond a reasonable doubt."

Senator Thurman reports:

"I also believe that the testimony convicts Mr. Pomeroy of having attempted to bribe Senator York, of that Legislature, to vote for him; that Pomeroy delivered to York $7,000 is not denied."

The book containing this investigation is a Senate document, Report No. 523, Forty-second Congress, Third Session. pp. 270.

Senator Pomeroy retained his seat until the end of the session, March 4.

—Mark Twain's book, published this year, contains 574 pages. It is a work of fiction. "Anything but history," says Robert Walpole, "for history must be false."

MARCH 3.— In the House of Representatives, Butler, Peters, and Potter were appointed to present to the Senate articles of impeachment against Judge Delahay. They appeared at the bar of the Senate, in obedience to the order. Judge Delahay resigned, and Cassius G. Foster, of Atchison, was appointed.

MARCH 4.—Inauguration of President Grant.

—The State Senate passes a resolution, authorizing the defendants to employ counsel in the suit of John Q. Page vs. E. S. Stover and J. E. Hayes, to recover the $7,000 paid by Pomeroy to York, by a vote of 14 to 8. In the House, the resolution was laid on the table.

MARCH 5.—B. W. Perkins, of Oswego, appointed Judge of the Eleventh District.

—Charles A. Morris appointed Adjutant General, and Hiram T. Beman Assistant Adjutant General.

MARCH 6.—Report of the Committee on the Pomeroy bribery charges:

"The Committee appointed to investigate charges of bribery and corruption against Hon. S. C. Pomeroy, United States Senator, during the Senatorial election in the State of Kansas, in January, A. D. 1873, to whom was referred the foregoing resolution, beg leave to submit the following report:

"*Whereas*, In pursuance to said resolution, the said Committee have carefully examined a large number of witnesses, and from said evidence have adduced the following facts:

"1. That S. C. Pomeroy, while a United States Senator, and during his candidacy for re-election to said position, did attempt to use money, both himself and by those professing to be his authorized agents, to corrupt members of the present Legislature in influencing and attempting to influence them to vote for said S. C. Pomeroy for United States Senator.

"2. That the said S. C. Pomeroy did, on the 28th and 29th days of January, 1873, pay to one A. M. York, a member of the Senate of the State of Kansas, the sum of $7,000, to influence his vote for the said S. C. Pomeroy for United States Senator.

"3. That Richard Stephens, professing to be a friend to the said S. C. Pomeroy, did attempt to bribe with money one Wm. Bateman, a member of the House of Representatives of the State of Kansas, to vote for S. C. Pomeroy for United States Senator.

"Therefore, we, the Committee, do find that the said S. C. Pomeroy is guilty of the crime of bribery, and attempting to corrupt, by offers of money, members of the Legislature of the State of Kansas.

"Therefore your Committee request to be discharged from further consideration of this subject.

W. E. GUERIN,
E. N. MORRILL,
Committee on part of the Senate.
S. K. CROSS,
E. J. NUGENT,
Committee on part of the House."

MARCH 6.—Senator Morton introduces a resolution, that Alexander Caldwell was not legally elected to a seat in the United States Senate by the Legislature of Kansas.

MARCH 7.—Adjournment of the Legislature. Among the acts passed were twenty-five authorizing municipal bonds; The "debenture law," (an act "to provide for the incorporation of Savings and Trust Companies"); Defining the boundaries of Decatur, Rawlins, Cheyenne, Sheridan, Thomas, Sherman, Clark, Ford, Hodgeman, Ness, Lane, Buffalo, Foote, Meade, Scott, Sequoyah, Arapaho, Seward, Wichita, Kearney, Grant, Stevens, Greeley, Hamilton, Stanton, Kansas, Pawnee, Rush and Stafford counties; Creating the Fifteenth Judicial District; Amending the occupying-claimant act; Creating a Price Raid Commission; Extending time of payment for school lands to ten years; Creating a State Board of Education; Providing an amendment to the Constitution to increase the number of members of the Legislature; For the appointment of Regents and Trustees for the control of the public institutions; For the collection of statistics; Exempting mortgages from taxation.

MARCH 8.—Wm. H. Fitzpatrick confirmed as Register of the Topeka Land Office.

—Texas Central Railroad completed to Red river.

MARCH 10.—Carmi W. Babcock reappointed and confirmed Surveyor General of Kansas.

MARCH 10.—Senator Morton addresses the Senate at length against Caldwell, his speech occupying over seven pages of the Congressional Record. (The Senate is in Special Session.) The debate continues from day to day, and is participated in by a large number of Senators.

MARCH 13.—A. J. Banta appointed Judge of the Fifteenth Judicial District.

MARCH 14.—Cornelius A. Logan, of Leavenworth, appointed Minister to Chili, vice Jos. P. Root.

—Lorenzo J. Worden confirmed as Postmaster, at Lawrence.

MARCH 19.—Cyrus I. Scofield appointed U. S. District Attorney.

MARCH 19.—A. T. Sharpe founds the Ottawa Republican. On the 26th of September, J. N. Murdock became one of the publishers, and continued in the paper about six months.

MARCH 20.—Henry King confirmed as Postmaster, at Topeka.

MARCH 22.—Wm. S. Tough confirmed as U. S. Marshal.

MARCH 24.—E. S. Niccolls, of Garnett, appointed Receiver, and W. W. Martin, of Fort Scott, Register, of the Independence Land Office.

MARCH 24.—

"The VICE PRESIDENT. The Chair will lay before the Senate the notification of the resignation of Mr. Caldwell as a Senator of the United States. The Secretary will read it.
"The Chief Clerk read as follows:
"'WASHINGTON, D. C., March 24, 1873.
"'SIR: I do hereby very respectfully notify you, and through you the Senate of the United States, that I have resigned, and do resign, my seat in that body as a Senator from the State of Kansas; and that I have forwarded by mail, postage prepaid, addressed to the chief executive officer of that State, at Topeka, Kansas, a resignation in the following form, to wit:
"'UNITED STATES SENATE CHAMBER, March 24, 1873.
"'SIR: I hereby respectfully tender you my resignation as a Senator of the United States from the State of Kansas, to take effect immediately.
"'Very respectfully, your obedient servant,   ALEXANDER CALDWELL.
"'His Excellency, the Governor of Kansas, Topeka, Kansas.'"
—*Congressional Record, p. 164.*

MARCH 26.—Eighteenth Annual Session of the Kansas Conference of the M. E. Church, at Ottawa, Bishop Bowman presiding. *Presiding Elders appointed:* Leavenworth, W. R. Davis; Lawrence, J. Boynton; Emporia, P. T. Rhodes; Manhattan, G. S. Dearborn; Fort Scott, D. P. Mitchell; Humboldt, A. K. Johnson; Salina, J. Laurence; Wichita, J. McQuiston. Number of members, 15,083; of churches, 79; value of churches, $277,500; Sunday School scholars, 14,184; volumes in libraries, 13,207.

MARCH 26.—Farmers' State Convention, at Topeka. Called to order by Alfred Gray. J. K. Hudson, temporary Chairman; Dr. A. G. Chase, Secretary. *Committee on Credentials:* Willis, Stiles, Galloway, Kilpatrick, and Miller. Speeches by Mr. Bronson of Douglas, C. W. Lawrence of Leavenworth, and R. A. Van Winkle of Atchison. *Committee on Permanent Organization:* V. P. Wilson, G. W. H. Moore, R. A. Van Winkle, J. N. Insley, H. Bronson, S. P. Hall, G. M. Moore, Mr. Shidler, C. W. Clapp, R. Morgan, A. H. Grass, G. M. Parks, C. S. Brodbent, F. Kingman, Chas. Williamson. *Officers:* President, John Davis, of Davis county; Vice Presidents, Jonathan Weaver of Saline, Alfred Taylor of Johnson; Secretaries, J. K. Hudson of Wyandotte, and J. T. Stevens of Douglas.

The Convention reassembled on the 27th, and adopted the following preamble and resolutions:

"*Whereas,* Agriculture in its various departments is the basis of all material prosperity; and whereas, the burdens and impositions under which it lies having become intolerable, therefore the farmers of Kansas, in convention assembled, do put forth this declaration of our desires and purposes, and state:

"1. Farmers desire to unite in the form of clubs, unions, or stock associations, for the purpose of showing that they can come together and co-operate like other folks for a common good, and for the moral effect it will have upon themselves and the rest of mankind.

"2. They desire association for the purpose of controlling the prices of their products through their own boards of trade or their own appointed agents, so that nothing need be thrown upon the market for less than the cost of production and a reasonable profit.

"3. They desire to unite for the purpose of getting their supplies at cost, with a reasonable per cent. added to pay for collecting and distributing, and the use of capital.

"4. They desire to co-operate for the purpose of securing a reduction in freights, and breaking the blockade between the different parts of the country, by argument, by legislative enactment, and by means of the courts.

"5. They desire tax reform, the abolition of sinecure offices, the reduction of salaries, rigid economy in public expenditures, and the repeal of our present iniquitous tax penalties.

"6. They desire home manufactures, so that the money paid for implements may be kept in the State, and our population increased by industrious operatives, engaged in creating wealth rather than in speculation.

"7. They desire that the balance of our public domain should be kept forever sacred to actual settlement, and in no contingency be allowed to fall into the hands of railroad monopolies and land sharks: therefore, be it

"*Resolved,* That organization is the great want of the producing classes at the present time, and we recommend every farmer in the State to become a member of some Farmers' Club, Grange of the Patrons of Husbandry, or other local organization.

"*Resolved,* That the taxes assessed and charged upon the people, both by National, State and local Governments, are oppressive and unjust, and vast sums of money are collected, far beyond the needs of an economical administration of government.

"*Resolved,* That we respectfully request our Senators and Members of Congress to vote for and secure an amendment to the tariff laws of the United States, so that salt and lumber shall be placed on the free list, and that there shall be made a material reduction on the duty on iron, and that such articles as do not pay the cost of collection be also placed on the free list.

"*Resolved,* That we earnestly request the Legislature of our State at its next session to enact a law regulating freights and fares on our railroads, upon a basis of justice, and that we further request our Members of Congress to urge the favorable action of that body, where the full power exists beyond all doubt, to the same end; and, if need be, to construct national highways at the expense of the Government.

"*Resolved,* That the act passed by the Legislature exempting bonds, notes, mortgages and judgments from taxation is unjust, oppressive, and a palpable violation of our State Constitution, and we call upon all assessors and the county boards to see that said securities are taxed at their fair value.

"*Resolved,* That the practice of voting municipal bonds is pernicious in its effect, and will inevitably bring bankruptcy and ruin on the people, and we therefore are opposed to all laws allowing the issuance of such bonds.

"*Resolved,* That giving banks a monopoly of the Nation's currency, thereby compelling the people to pay them such interest therefor as they may choose to impose, seven-tenths of which interest we believe is collected from the farmers, is but little less than legalized robbery of the agricultural classes.

"*Resolved,* That for the speedy and thorough accomplishment of all this, we pledge each other to ignore all political preferences and prejudices that have swayed us hitherto to our hurt, and support only such men for office as are known to be true to our interests, and in whose integrity and honesty we have the most implicit confidence."

A Constitution of the Farmers' Co-operative Association was formed, and the following officers elected: President, John Davis; Vice President, J. K. Hudson, of Wyandotte; Secretary, Alfred Gray, of Shawnee; Treasurer, H. Bronson, of Douglas. *Directors:* T. B. Smith of Douglas, John Mings of Osage, O. W. Bill of Riley, A. H. Grass of Montgomery, J. S. Van Winkle of Leavenworth.

APRIL 1.—W. H. Rossington, managing editor of the Commonwealth.

—Gen. James G. Blunt, and others, are charged with conspiracy to defraud the Government and a body of Cherokee Indians in North Carolina.

APRIL 8.—Annual Meeting of the Congregationalists of Southern Kansas, at Cottonwood Falls.

—The Burlington Patriot announces the death of Gen. John B. Scott, the founder of Leroy. "He came to Kansas in 1845, and resided at the old

Agency until 1854, when he and Col. Whistler came to this county and took claims."

APRIL 9.—Gov. Osborn offers a reward of $500 for the apprehension of the murderer of Dr. York, brother of Col. A. M. York. Dr. York disappeared some weeks ago, and is supposed to have been murdered between Osage Mission and Independence.

—In the spring the Coffeyville Courier was started, by Chatham & White. James J. Chatham soon became the sole publisher. In the fall of 1875, the Courier was removed to Independence and issued as a Daily.

APRIL 16.—Destructive fire at Paola.

APRIL 23.—A fire at Fort Scott destroys over thirty buildings, principally on Market street.

—State Senators' excursion to Galveston leaves Emporia.

APRIL 24.—Banquet to Senator Ingalls, at Leavenworth.

APRIL 27.—Birth of the Atchison Daily Globe. It died December 14th, 1873.

APRIL 28.—Col. D. W. Houston and C. N. Shaw buy the Leavenworth Commercial.

—Fire at Iola.

—Dr. Madison Mills, U. S. A., dies at Leavenworth.

APRIL 30.—Fire at Burlingame.

—Conference of the Liberal Christians of the Missouri Valley, at Kansas City.

MAY 4.—The remains of Dr. Wm. H. York, and other murdered men, found on the farm of the Bender family, in the northwest corner of Labette county, about ten miles from Thayer, and five miles from Cherryvale, on the road from Independence (where Dr. York resided) to Osage Mission. Among the victims were Benj. M. Brown, of Howard county, John Greary, W. F. McCrotty, H. F. McKegzie, G. W. Langchor, and a little girl. Three bodies were found beneath the house, and four graves in different parts of the field. All were killed by blows on the back of the head, and had their throats cut. Two hammers were found in the house. The Bender family consisted of Wm. Bender, sixty years old; his wife, fifty-five; their daughter, Kate, twenty-three, and son, John, twenty-five. They came to Kansas in December, 1870, and moved to this slaughter-pen in February, 1871. They were Germans, and kept a small stock of groceries and liquors. Kate was a "medium," and advertised her skill as a spiritual doctor. The family fled about three weeks ago, leaving their stock behind. At Thayer they bought tickets for Humboldt. The Independence Republican says:

" The generally-accepted theory of the manner of the killing is that travellers were seated in such a manner that their heads would lean against and indent the cloth partition, which crossed the room. Some one stationed behind the curtain would then strike them with a hammer, and some one in the front room was ready to finish the job. After that they were taken to the trap-door, where they were thrown in, their throats cut, and they were left until night, when they were carried out, and buried in the field."

MAY 7.—Death of Chief Justice Chase, in New York.

MAY 14.—The Wamego Blade issued by Cuningham & Goodwin.

MAY 14.—Railroad Assessors meet at Topeka.

MAY 16.—Death of John M. Haeberlein, of the Daily Freie Presse, Leavenworth — the only German Daily in the State.

—Louis Melius joins Edwin H. Snow, in publishing the Ottawa Journal.

—George Grant imports stock for his sixty-thousand-acre farm, at Victoria, Ellis county.

—W. H. Johnson consolidates the Abilene Chronicle and Journal.

MAY 20.—Editorial Convention, at Atchison. Address by I. S. Kalloch, poem by James W. Steele. T. Dwight Thacher was re-elected President; J. W. Steele, orator; W. S. Burke, of Leavenworth, alternate, and Noble L. Prentis, poet. Fort Scott was selected as the next place of meeting. There was a ball and banquet at Atchison, and an excursion to Lincoln, Neb., on the 21st. This is the seventh annual meeting.

MAY 25.—Thomas M. O'Brien, defaulting claim agent, arrested in Colorado.

MAY 30.—Soldiers' reunion at Lawrence; 8,000 people present.

MAY 31.—Bridge across the Missouri at St. Joseph completed.

—Midland Railroad Company organized at Topeka.

JUNE 2.—W. S. Burke starts the Leavenworth Argus.

JUNE 8.—Judge Dillon's Iola bond decision published.

JUNE 14.—Illinois editorial excursion to Topeka.

JUNE 16.—The case of The State against S. C. Pomeroy, for the bribery of A. M. York, came up before Hon. John T. Morton, Topeka. On motion of Pomeroy's counsel, the case was continued to the next term.

JUNE 18.—Funeral of Judge John A. Wakefield, at Lawrence. He came to Kansas in 1854, and was a leading member of the Free-State party.

JUNE.—A pamphlet of 40 pages, called "Farmers' Unions and Tax Reform," by Henry Bronson, President of the Douglas County Farmers' Union, is published at Lawrence, and goes through four editions. Mr. Bronson also published the Vox Populi, a weekly newspaper, at Lawrence.

JUNE.—An article on Osawatomie, by James Hanway, is published in the Kansas Magazine, vol. 3, p. 551. Mr. Hanway says the site of the Town was selected by the Massachusetts Aid Society. A grist and saw mill was built there by the Society in the Spring of 1856. A printing press, brought by Dayton & Gardner from New York, was concealed during the troubles of that year. Charles Griffith bought the material in 1857, and issued the Herald. John McReynolds was the next purchaser; the office was afterwards removed to Paola.

The 7th of June, 1856, is given as the date of the sacking of Osawatomie, by John W. Whitfield and 170 Missourians. The battle of Osawatomie took place August 30th, 1856. John Brown commanded the Free-State men, and kept the enemy at bay several hours. "The raiders then entered the town, took what property they could conveniently carry away, and applied the torch to the buildings, and by evening it was but a heap of ashes." The fight "was the most severe of any which took place during the troubles in Kansas."

"In the autumn of 1856, during the troubles which existed throughout Kansas, one morning before the sun was up an individual by the name of Pat Devlin was seen entering the village of Osawatomie. He was riding a horse, or mule, and loaded down with no inconsiderable amount of articles of various character, which entirely covered his beast. A neighbor met him and accosted him in a familiar manner: 'Pat, you look as if you had been out on an excursion.' 'Yes,' said Pat, 'I have been out Jayhawking,' Not fully understanding the meaning of the term 'Jayhawking,' he enquired of Pat what he meant. Pat, who was a bold Free-State Irishman, replied that he had been foraging off the enemy, meaning the Pro-Slavery party. He then, like a true lexicographer, explained the meaning of the word 'Jayhawker.' He said that in Ireland there was a bird called the jayhawk, which worried its prey before devouring it."

McReynolds first published, in 1858 or '59, this explanation of the word. "Jayhawker" did not become universally known until Charles R. Jennison assumed it for himself and his soldiers, the Seventh Kansas, in 1861. It is now synonymous with Kansan.

JULY.—A book issued with this title: "The Homestead Guide, describing the great Homestead Region in Kansas and Nebraska, and containing the Homestead, Pre-emption, and Timber-Bounty Laws, and a Map of the Country Described. Waterville, Kansas: F. G. Adams, Compiler and Publisher. 1873." pp. 312. The best summary of Judge Adams's admirable book is given in its Preface, which is copied below:

"The object of this publication is to give reliable information to homestead-seekers. The information relates to the broadest area of desirable homestead lands within the United States; it relates to the struggle by which those lands were wrested from the recent occupancy of ferocious savages; and now that the amplest safety is assured the settler, these pages show the mode by which, at the mere cost of entry fees, title from the Government can be acquired to these lands. An account of the progress of settlements within this region is also given, showing how a hitherto unpeopled wild, of most fertile soil, of most healthful climate and pleasing landscape, of gurgling brooks and rapid-flowing mill-streams, of grassy plains and prairie billows, of rocky cliffs, of timber-skirted water-courses, of broad alluvions, of exhaustless deposits of coal, and salt, and gypsum—is now, with marvellous rapidity, being covered with cultivated fields, with numberless domestic herds, and with thriving towns, springing up under the magic influence of the wand of enterprise—carrying trade and manufactures where, before, the murmur of traffic and the hum of machinery were never heard.

"In collecting the facts here presented, we have drawn largely from our own observations, but are much indebted to other publications relating to Kansas and Nebraska, to the authors of which we have, in the proper connexions, aimed to give just credit."

JULY 6.—Shooting affray in the Otis House, Atchison, between Jacob S. Hoke and W. W. Marbourg.

JULY 12.—Meeting of Osage Land Settlers at Thayer; 5,000 people present.

—County Treasury defalcation in Jefferson county.

JULY 17.—The Wellington Press established. John H. Folks is the publisher. Eight papers have died in Sumner county.

JULY 22.—Hon. Oliver P. Morton, U. S. Senator, visits Topeka.

—The trotting stallion, Smuggler, goes in 2:19¾, at Olathe.

JULY 28.—J. Q. Page, in the District Court, at Topeka, makes a motion to dismiss the case begun by himself against the State of Kansas and others, for the recovery of the $7,000 package of bribe money, he agreeing to pay all costs of action. Motion granted.

JULY 28.—Rev. John A. Anderson, of Junction City, elected President of the Agricultural College.

JULY 30.—Organization of the State Grange, at Lawrence. The following "History of the Kansas State Grange" is copied from The Patrons' Hand-Book, published by J. K. Hudson, at Topeka, in 1874. It is a book of 40 double-column pages:

"The material at hand with which to write anything like a history of the Kansas State Grange is very meagre. Hiawatha Grange, Brown county, was the first organized in the State, which occurred in April, 1872. Little was done beyond the organization of Osage Grange, in Crawford county, which was organized very early in the spring, and was the first Grange in the south part of the State.

"Up to December, 1872, there were only nine Granges in the State. The Order, during the winter, grew but little, many of the Granges being discouraged, not only for the want of the secret work, but also because of the little interest manifested throughout the State in the organization.

"The call to meet at Lawrence, July 30, 1873, to form a State Grange, gave a new impetus to the organization. It grew very rapidly during the spring and summer, and when the State Grange met, they numbered about four hundred. Brothers Dumbauld, Spurgeon and Cramer deserve much praise for their persistent efforts to organize the movement. The large amount of gratuitous pioneer work by these men entitles them to the consideration of every good Patron. They adhered while other men doubted; and now, when the Grange has become a great power in the State, their early struggles and labors in its behalf should not be forgotten.

"In December, 1872, William Duane Wilson, from Iowa, visited Kansas, and, in connexion with a few Granges in the south part of the State, effected a temporary organization of the State Grange, as follows: Master, F. H. Dumbauld; Overseer, —— Bell; Lecturer, J. A. Cramer; Secretary, G. W. Spurgeon; Treasurer, H. H. Angell.

"At the meeting of the State Grange, at Lawrence, July 30, 1873, for the first time, there were 409 organized Granges in the State. Dudley W. Adams, Master of the National Grange, was present, and assisted in forming the State Grange; also, T. A. Thompson, Lecturer of the National Grange, greatly aided in shaping the State Grange, and in giving the secret work of the Order to the delegates. The election of officers resulted as follows:

"Master, T. G. Boling, Leavenworth county; Overseer, M. E. Hudson, Bourbon county; Lecturer, John Boyd, Montgomery county; Steward, E. D. Smith, Jewell county; Assistant Steward, J. B. Richey, Franklin county; Chaplain, W. S. Hanna, Franklin county; Treasurer, H. H. Angell, Cherokee county; Secretary, G. W. Spurgeon, Neosho county; Gate Keeper, C. W. Lawrence; Ceres, Mrs. Mattie Morris; Flora, Mrs. M. H. Charles; Pomona, Mrs. Amanda C. Rippey; Lady Assistant Steward, Mrs. Jennie D. Ritchie; Executive Committee, F. H. Dumbauld, W. P. Popenoe, and J. B. Shaeffer.

"The constitution provided for the meeting of the State Grange the third Wednesday in February. The Executive Committee decided to hold the session at Topeka.

"At this meeting sixty counties were represented. The Secretary reported 975 Granges as organized, representing an actual membership of over 27,000. The constitution and by-laws were revised, and the declaration of purposes adopted by the National Grange at St. Louis adopted as the principles of the Kansas State Grange.

"The election for Master to fill the vacancy occasioned by the resignation of Master Boling resulted in the selection of M. E. Hudson, when the vacancy in the office of Overseer, caused by his promotion, was filled by the election of Wm. Sims. The term of W. P. Popenoe as a member of the Executive Committee having expired, he was re-elected. W. H. Fletcher, of Clay county, was elected Gate Keeper—Mr. Lawrence, elected at a previous meeting of the State Grange, having failed to accept and qualify. After installation of officers, conferring the fifth degree, hearing reports of committees, adopting resolutions, and transacting the necessary business for the ensuing year, the Grange adjourned *sine die.*

"Since the adjournment of the State Grange, the organization of Granges throughout the State has been more rapid than ever before—the number of Granges up to April 1st exceeding 1,200, with a total membership of over 30,000."

JULY 31.—Death of Hiram J. Strickler, near Tecumseh, Shawnee county. He was a native of Virginia, and came here in the winter of

1855. He was in the Council, in '55, and was Territorial Auditor from '58 to '61. He was also Territorial Adjutant General, and President of the State Agricultural Society. He was universally respected as a man of integrity and honor.

—The Atchison Champion publishes the following lines. They were copied all over the Union, and the general belief was and is that Senator Ingalls wrote them. They were entitled:

"A SERENADE; THE POLITICIAN TO HIS LOVE.

"'By the time we have reached home and got our cows milked, it will be dark.'— *Speech at Monrovia.*

"The moon is shining on the grange,
  The winds are hushed, the leaves are still,
The patient stars look softly down
  Upon my cot at Shannon Hill.
Then come, my horny-handed love,
  And wander through the dell with me,
And gaze upon the Durham bull
  And listen to his pedigree.

"My stores upon Commercial street
  Are empty; there's in trade a lull;
I've bartered off my house in town,
  And real estate is very dull;
I'm putting up a residence
  On Second street, above the mill,
But till it's finished I shall live
  Upon my farm at Shannon Hill.

"Once I was in the railroad ring,
  But now my hands are hard with toil;
I've scattered hay-seed in my hair
  And blacked my boots with harness oil.
My city cows have all gone dry,
  I am no longer in my prime;
My day is drawing to its close
  And it will soon be milking time.

"I think I know a new milch cow
  That's just exactly what I need;
She's thin from running out to grass
  But only wants a change of feed.
I'll mix a mash of free-trade bran,
  Swindles, high taxes, and back pay,
And coax her to the ballot-box
  And feed her till election day.

"Dear Snyder, grasp her by the horns!
  Sweet Wheeler, hold her by the tail!
Oh, let me safely sit between
  And calmly fill my milking pail.
And when November's breezes show
  'Tis time my Berkshire hogs to kill,
I'll move back into town again
  And sigh no more for Shannon Hill."

AUGUST 1.—Topeka Daily Blade started, by J. Clark Swayze.

— Noble L. Prentis edits the Junction City Union till March 1, 1875.

AUGUST 4.—The Catholic Publication Society, New York, issues a book on "Irish Emigration to the United States: What it has been and what it is. By the Rev. Stephen Byrne, O. S. D." It is an excellent and valuable book. The following relating to Kansas is copied from pages 124 to 128:

"The soil is very productive throughout, mostly presenting a rolling surface, thus affording superior drainage. Every kind of grain and fruit can be grown; it is especially adapted to the growing of the grape. The rich, black soil is generally from two to six feet and more thick.

"There are millions of acres of the best land for sale by the various railroads alone that run through Kansas; besides these, there are the 'homestead lands.'

"The climate is very salubrious throughout; new sections of the country are visited by intermittent fever in spring and fall, which disappears with the progress of the cultivation of the soil. Vast numbers of people, who have been in feeble health in the more eastern States, contend that they have been greatly benefitted by the climate. The summer heat is rendered less oppressive and excessive by a continual breeze, and the nights are very refreshing. . . . . .

"The land is of equally good quality almost everywhere. In the south and southwest the soil is sometimes a little deeper than in the north or northwest; the north sometimes has more woodland; so that, on the whole, I find little or no difference. I give below the offices of the various railroad land departments, with price of land and general terms:

"In the southeast, there is the Missouri River, Fort Scott and Gulf Railroad, owning and selling about three hundred and fifty' thousand acres in Bourbon, Crawford and Cherokee counties, the price ranging from four to twelve dollars per acre; sold on credit, running through ten years, at seven per cent. annual interest; twenty per cent. discount for cash. The land is excellent; plenty of coal in the neighborhood. Several Catholic congregations are already in existence in that neighborhood. For land, address Gen. John A. Clark, Land Commissioner, Fort Scott, Kansas. To find out what facilities for satisfying your spiritual wants before purchasing, address Rev. M. J. Doherty, at Fort Scott, or Rev. E. Bononcini, at Baxter Springs, or Rev. John Schoenmakers, S. J., at Osage Mission, Kansas.

"In the southeast is also the Leavenworth, Lawrence and Galveston Railroad land. In some portions of this land, the rocky stratum, underlying the soil, crops out, and forms the surface. Excepting such portions, the land is of very good quality, ranging at about the same price. Address John W. Scott, Land Commissioner, at Chanute. To find out, before making any purchases, where there is a church or Catholic settlement, address Very Rev. A. Heiman, at Scipio P. O. For land south of this, you may address Rev. R. Deusterman, at Humboldt.

"The southwest is traversed by the Atchison, Topeka and Santa Fe R. R., owning and selling over three millions of acres along its line; price of land ranging from two to eight dollars per acre; time for payment, eleven years, with 7 per cent. interest, besides other very favorable conditions. The land of this company is very superior, though there is scarcity of timber. For information about land, etc., address A. S. Johnson, Land Commissioner, at Topeka; but before, and for actual location, address Rev. F. Swembergh, at Wichita; Rev. Jos. Perrier, or Rev. J. H. Defouri, both at Topeka, Kansas.

"The west is traversed by the Kansas Pacific R. R. Along its line from east to west there are more Catholic settlements than on any other road at present. It owns and has for sale about six millions of acres, prices ranging from two to six dollars per acre, sold on five years' credit, with interest at six per cent., in this manner, one-fifth cash at time of purchase; for the next two years only the interest on the balance, etc. For information about land, address John P. Devereux, Land Commissioner, at Lawrence, Kansas. Where to find church and Catholic settlements, address Rev. John Fogarty, at Solomon City, Kansas, and Rev. P. Scholl, at Junction City, Kansas.

"The northwest: Two railroads run through the northern portion of the State from east to west, along which there are several Catholic settlements. The St. Joseph and Denver R. R. has about 100,000 acres in Marshall, Washington, Republic, Jewell, Cloud, Ottawa, and Riley counties, for sale at from three to six dollars, one-fifth of which is payable in cash at time of purchase, the balance in five equal annual payments, with ten per cent. interest. For information about land, address D. M. Steele, President Kansas Land Company, at St. Joseph, Missouri. To find out the location of Catholic settlements, address Rev. A. Weikmann, at Hanover, or Rev. Thos. O'Reiley, at Frankfort, or Rev. L. Mollier, at Concordia, Kansas.

"For information about land owned by the Central Branch U. P. R. R., address Major W. F. Downs and the Very Rev. Father Giles Christoph, O.S.B., at Atchison, or Rev. Th. Bartl, at Severance P. O., or Rev. Timothy Luber, at Seneca, Kansas.

"The Vicariate Apostolic of Kansas, established in 1851, has two vicars apostolic, residing at Leavenworth; forty-eight priests, and several clerical students; fifty-five churches built, and sixteen building. There are several religious institutions, both male and female. Catholic population, 30,000."

August 5.— Five Mennonite leaders visit Harvey, Sedgwick, Reno, Marion and McPherson counties, to select lands for a colony from Russia.

—Thos. J. Anderson chosen Superintendent of the Topeka Rolling Mills.

August 6.— Coal-oil excitement at Paola.

—Delegate convention of the various Catholic Societies of the State at Leavenworth. President, John Moffat, Osage Mission; Vice Presidents, P.

Connolly, Wyandotte, M. A. Wolfrom, Leavenworth; Secretary, Rev. T. A. Butler, Leavenworth; Treasurer, W. F. Dolan, Atchison. Among the resolutions passed was the following:

"*Resolved,* That it is the sense of the Catholic Union of Kansas that the present system of education is in opposition to the letter and spirit of the Constitution of the United States, and we claim it is unjust to impose a school upon Catholics in direct opposition to their wishes."

AUGUST 9.—R. B. Taylor, of the Wyandotte Gazette, arrested, on the charge of defaming the character of S. A. Cobb. He is afterwards tried for libel, and acquitted.

AUGUST 13.—Judge Samuel A. Williams dies, at Fort Scott. He was a member of the Legislature of 1855, and was appointed Probate Judge of Bourbon county by that body.

—Serious trouble at Osage Mission, caused by county-seat difficulties.

AUGUST 17.—S. S. Prouty retires from the Commonwealth, and Henry King becomes the publisher.

—Alvord & Farey start the Junction City Tribune.

AUGUST 19.—The free-delivery system ordered for the Leavenworth post-office.

AUGUST 20.—Kellar hung by citizens in Linn county. He had killed his wife, Mrs. Boyd and her two children, and then burned Boyd's house over their bodies. The tragedy occurred near Twin Springs.

SEPTEMBER 1.—The Agricultural College starts on a new career, with the following officers: *Board of Regents:* James Rogers, Burlingame; Chas. Reynolds, Fort Riley; N. A. Adams, Manhattan; J. K. Hudson, Wyandotte; Josiah Copley, Perryville; N. Green, Holton. J. A. Anderson, President, Manhattan; William Burgoyne, Secretary, Manhattan; E. B. Purcell, Treasurer, Manhattan; E. Gale, Loan Commissioner, Manhattan; L. R. Elliott, Land Agent, Manhattan.

—In the fall, W. H. Watkins started the Independence Kansan.

SEPTEMBER 3.—Burning of the Massasoit House, at Atchison.

SEPTEMBER 5.—The officers of the St. Joseph & Denver Railroad resign, and a committee is appointed to make an investigation into the affairs of the company.

—W. S. Tough sells Smuggler, in Boston.

SEPTEMBER 8.—Rich discoveries of lead near Baxter Springs.

SEPTEMBER 8, 9.—Meeting of the Kansas Academy of Science, at Lawrence. The following officers were elected for the current year: President, Frank H. Snow; Vice Presidents, John A. Banfield and John D. Parker; Secretary, John Wherrell; Treasurer, Robert J. Brown; Curators, Frank H. Snow, B. F. Mudge, and Edwin A. Popenoe. The following Commissioners were confirmed for the current year: Geology, B. F. Mudge; Ornithology, F. H. Snow; Entomology, F. H. Snow and Edwin A. Popenoe; Language, D. H. Robinson and J. H. Lee; Engineering, F. W. Bardwell; Technology, F. E. Stimpson; Astronomy, John Fraser; Meteorology, John D. Parker; Botany, J. H. Carruth, John Wherrell, and Frank H. Snow; Mineralogy, W. D. Kedzie; Chemistry, William H. Saunders.

SEPTEMBER 9.—Prof. B. F. Mudge lectures on the Mound Builders, before the Academy of Science, at Lawrence. He gives an account of an extensive ancient village within a short distance of the Solomon river, where a pottery covers half an acre of ground.

—The Secretary of the Interior orders a reappraisement of the Kaw lands.

SEPTEMBER 11.—The K. P. R. W. extended from Kit Carson to Fort Lyon, forty-two miles.

SEPTEMBER 15.—Carl Moller, cashier of the German Savings Bank, Leavenworth, a defaulter.

SEPTEMBER 22.—State Fair at Topeka. Governor Osborn makes the opening address.

—Financial panic; banks generally suspend, Kansas City taking the lead.

OCTOBER.—The last number of the Kansas Magazine is issued; it is the fourth number of Vol. IV.

OCTOBER 1.—Great meeting of Settlers at Osage Mission.

OCTOBER 11.—Martin F. Conway, in Washington, fires three shots at S. C. Pomeroy, one of which slightly wounds the ex-Senator. Conway is arrested, and says of Pomeroy: "He ruined myself and family." Pomeroy says he has never had any controversy or ground for difficulty with Conway.

OCTOBER 15.—Rev. Charles R. Pomeroy elected President of the Emporia Normal School.

—Irrigation Convention at Denver; the Western States and Territories represented.

OCTOBER 20.—Burning of the Commonwealth building.

—Samuel Fry, one of the old Free-State Guard of Lawrence, dies at Columbia, Texas, where he was a railroad contractor.

OCTOBER 28.—Eighth Annual Meeting of the State Sabbath School Association, at Emporia.

OCTOBER.—A Catalogue is published of the Topeka Library. It contains about 1,000 volumes.

NOVEMBER.—D. B. Emmert starts a Monthly, at Humboldt, called the Rural Kansan. It was published one year.

NOVEMBER 4.—Annual election.

VOTE ON PROPOSED AMENDMENT TO ART. 2, SEC. 2 OF THE CONSTITUTION.

Counties.	For.	Against.	Counties.	For.	Against.
Allen	166	722	Dickinson	1,024	18
Anderson	3	1,009	Doniphan	370	1,394
Atchison	462	597	Douglas	325	1,704
Barbour	52	....	Ellis	264	10
Barton	24	232	Ellsworth	501	2
Billings	52	37	Ford	59	158
Bourbon	608	1,859	Franklin	41	1,114
Brown	151	763	Greenwood	245	130
Butler	1,467	135	Harper	277	....
Chase	495	107	Harvey	529	7
Cherokee	401	636	Howard	729	318
Clay	754	189	Jackson	958	183
Cloud	875	40	Jefferson	132	1,595
Coffey	42	746	Jewell	874	64
Comanche	....	....	Johnson	825	1,838
Cowley	1,087	5	Labette	627	418
Crawford	8	827	Leavenworth	1,115	360
Davis	963	38	Lincoln	504	....

VOTE ON AMENDMENT TO CONSTITUTION—Concluded.

Counties.	For.	Against.	Counties.	For.	Against.
Linn	85	1,506	Rice	81	94
Lyon	603	257	Riley	776	427
Marion	415	8	Rooks	114	....
Marshall	1,218	74	Russell	256	....
McPherson	571	8	Saline	1,242	109
Miami	66	1,914	Sedgwick	1,352	15
Mitchell	887	17	Shawnee	437	1,889
Montgomery	362	489	Smith	369	22
Morris	470	65	Sumner	928	9
Nemaha	34	831	Wabaunsee	56	561
Neoso	360	501	Wallace (no return)	......	....
Ness	263	....	Washington	764	93
Osage	180	1,201	Wilson	702	341
Osborne	434	1	Woodson	149	359
Ottawa	665	19	Wyandotte	....	5
Pawnee	72	5			
Phillips	391	3	Total	32,240	29,189
Pottawatomie	91	1,011			
Reno	350	14	Majority	3,051	
Republic	988	36			

VOTE FOR RAILROAD ASSESSORS.

District.	Counties.	Names of Candidates.	Vote of County.	Total.	Maj.
1...	Leavenworth	Harry L. Bickford	2,494	2,494	291
	Leavenworth	Crawford Moore	1,260	1,260	
	Leavenworth	Charles Grover	943	943	
	Atchison	Frank M. Tracy	113		
	Brown	Frank M. Tracy	113		
	Doniphan	Frank M. Tracy	2,179		
	Nemaha	Frank M. Tracy	673	3,078	1,792
	Brown	N. Hanson	558		
	Nemaha	N. Hanson	37	595	
2...	Atchison	S. J. H. Snyder	148		
	Doniphan	S. J. H. Snyder	74	222	
	Atchison	D. E. Mervin	101	101	
	Atchison	Mr. Wilcox	91	91	
	Atchison	E Muldoon	96	96	
	Atchison	Scattering	158		
	Nemaha	Scattering	23	181	
	Jefferson	D. F. Eggers	1,213		
	Pottawatomie	L. F. Eggers	311		
	Shawnee	L. F. Eggers	2,993	4,517	2,888
	Jackson	John Carver	669		
3...	Jefferson	John Carver	34	703	
	Jackson	S. S. Cooper	53		
	Jefferson	S. S. Cooper	751	804	
	Shawnee	A. J. Huntoon	65	65	
	Jackson	A. M. Crockett	47	47	
	Anderson	Turner Sampson	2		
	Douglas	Turner Sampson	2,209		
4...	Franklin	Turner Sampson	685	2,896	2,735
	Douglas	F. Gleason	83		
	Franklin	F. Gleason	78	161	
	Coffey	J. L. Williams	72		
	Lyon	J. L. Williams	1,619		
	Osage	J. L. Williams	83	1,774	261
	Coffey	H. N. Bent	1,134		
5...	Lyon	H. N. Bent	22		
	Osage	H. N. Bent	59	1,215	
	Osage	J. A. Drake	175	175	
	Coffey	Scattering	46		
	Osage	Scattering	77	123	
	Bourbon	A. Shinn	1,657		
6...	Linn	A. Shinn	1,064	2,721	1,001
	Bourbon	Ed. R. Smith	899		
	Linn	Ed. R. Smith	821	1,720	

VOTE FOR RAILROAD ASSESSORS—Continued.

District.	Counties.	Names of Candidates.	Vote of County.	Total.	Maj. or Plur.
	Allen	Henry W. Talcott	744		
	Woodson	Henry W. Talcott	852	1,596	659
	Allen	John Moffit	350		
	Neosho	John Moffit	549	899	
	Neosho	John A. Gaston	687		
7...	Wilson	John A. Gaston	54	741	
	Neosho	J. A. Stevens	160		
	Wilson	J. A. Stevens	777	937	
	Allen	Scattering	48		
	Wilson	Scattering	26		
	Woodson	Scattering	15	89	
	Davis	John M. Allen	11		
	Dickinson	John M. Allen	243		
	Riley	John M. Allen	778	1,032	77
	Davis	P. Z. Taylor	617		
	Dickinson	P. Z. Taylor	72		
	Morris	P. Z. Taylor	75		
	Ottawa	P. Z. Taylor	191	955	
8...	Davis	John P. Swenson	109	109	
	Davis	A. J. Rodgers	24		
	Morris	A. J. Rodgers	145	169	
	Davis	Scattering	12		
	Morris	Scattering	2		
	Ottawa	Scattering	12		
	Riley	Scattering	82	108	
	Barton	Joel T. Davis	310		
	Harvey	Joel T. Davis	149		
	Reno	Joel T. Davis	312		
	Rice	Joel T. Davis	208	979	511
	Ford	J. Caller	143	143	
9...	Pawnee	T. J. Clark	78	78	
	Harvey	William Prouty	22	22	
	Chase	L. P. Allspaugh	1		
	Harvey	L. P. Allspaugh	21		
	Marion	L. P. Allspaugh	443	465	
	Chase	George W. Yeager	468	468	
	Johnson	Newton Ainsworth	998		
	Miami	Newton Ainsworth	1,276		
	Wyandotte	Newton Ainsworth	446	2,720	1,020
	Johnson	Daniel Killen	40		
	Miami	Daniel Killen	456		
10...	Wyandotte	Daniel Killen	1,204	1,700	
	Johnson	G. H. Beach	894		
	Miami	G. H. Beach	410		
	Wyandotte	G. H. Beach	54	1,358	
	Johnson	J. E. Corliss	695		
	Wyandotte	J. E. Corliss	25	720	
	Crawford	J. D. Emerson	220		
	Labette	J. D. Emerson	32		
	Montgomery	J. D. Emerson	1,089	1,341	137
	Cherokee	Samuel Fellows	4		
	Labette	Samuel Fellows	1,149	1,153	
	Cherokee	J. W. Doudna	46		
	Labette	J. W. Doudna	443	489	
	Montgomery	J. H. Ashbaugh	1,204	1,204	
	Cherokee	M. A. Wood	70		
11...	Crawford	M. A. Wood	592		
	Labette	M. A. Wood	28	690	
	Cherokee	E. C. Wells	705		
	Labette	E. C. Wells	2	707	
	Cherokee	A. T. Lea	574		
	Crawford	A. T. Lea	157		
	Labette	A. T. Lea	25	756	
	Crawford	J. T. Lea	31	31	
	Crawford	R. W. Doudna	35	35	
	Crawford	Scattering	16	16	
	Clay	P. Hutchinson	415		
	Cloud	P. Hutchinson	856		
	Marshall	P. Hutchinson	1,531		
12...	Republic	P. Hutchinson	854		
	Washington	P. Hutchinson	1,125	4,781	3,605
	Clay	J. B. Quimby	315		
	Cloud	J. B. Quimby	84		

VOTE FOR RAILROAD ASSESSORS—Concluded.

District	Counties.	Names of Candidates.	Vote of County...	Total	Maj......
12...	Marshall	J. B. Quimby	521		
	Republic	J. B. Quimby	164		
	Washington	J. B. Quimby	92	1,176	33
13...	Sedgwick	John M. Steele	42	42	
	Cowley	E. B. Allen	9	9	
14...	Ellis	W. F. Leslie	241		
	Ellsworth	W. F. Leslie	517		
	McPherson	W. F. Leslie	320		
	Russell	W. F. Leslie	293		
	Saline	W. F. Leslie	687	2,058	1,846
	Lincoln	J. F. Leslie	100	100	
	Lincoln	C. R. Buell	239		
	Saline	C. R. Buell	489	728	
	McPherson	W. W. Jones	323	323	
	Ellis	Scattering	56		
	Ellsworth	Scattering	2		
	Russell	Scattering	3	61	

VOTE FOR JUDGES OF THE DISTRICT COURTS.

District	Counties.	Names of Candidates.	Vote of County...	Total	Maj. or Plur...
10...	Miami	Hiram Stevens	2,025		
	Johnson	Hiram Stevens	2,300		
	Wyandotte	Hiram Stevens	862	5,187	3,470
	Miami	H. W. Cook	83		
	Johnson	H. W. Cook	342		
	Wyandotte	H. W. Cook	1,184	1,609	
	Miami	R. W. Murray	3	3	
	Johnson	S. E. McCracken	105	105	
11...	Cherokee	B. W. Perkins	778		
	Crawford	B. W. Perkins	453		
	Labette	B. W. Perkins	766		
	Montgomery	B. W. Perkins	1,198	3,195	689
	Cherokee	J. M. Scudder	327		
	Crawford	J. M. Scudder	378		
	Labette	J. M. Scudder	794		
	Montgomery	J. M. Scudder	1,007	2,506	
	Cherokee	H. W. Barnes	332		
	Crawford	H. W. Barnes	260		
	Labette	H. W. Barnes	386		
	Montgomery	H. W. Barnes	40	1,018	
	Cherokee	J. G. Parkhurst	17		
	Crawford	J. G. Parkhurst	47		
	Labette	J. G. Parkhurst	291		
	Montgomery	J. G. Parkhurst	20	375	
15...	Billings	Joel Holt	108		
	Jewell	Joel Holt	885		
	Mitchell	Joel Holt	917		
	Osborne	Joel Holt	433		
	Phillips	Joel Holt	443		
	Rooks	Joel Holt	114		
	Smith	Joel Holt	617	3,513	3,508

VOTE FOR STATE SENATOR, TO FILL VACANCY IN THE NINETEENTH SENATORIAL DISTRICT.

Names of Candidates.	Counties.	Vote of County...	Total	Maj......
H. Bronson	Douglas	2,105	2,105	639
D. C. Haskell	Douglas	1,466	1,466	

VOTE FOR MEMBERS OF HOUSE OF REPRESENTATIVES.

District.	Counties.	Names of Candidates.	Votes......	Maj. or Plur....
1	Doniphan....................	Nathan Springer...................	483	26
		B. A. Seaver....	300	
		D. W. Rippey....................	157	
2	....	X. K. Stout....	543	288
		B. O'Driscoll....	255	
3	....	F. H. Drenning....................	208	21
		Jacob Ramsel....	187	
		B. F. Bowman....	179	
4	Atchison....................	A. H. Horton	825	501
		L. S. Howe....	324	
5	....	Robert White....	469	
		Samuel Stoner....	487	18
6	....	D. G. Wilson....	476	21
		G. W. Thompson	455	
7	Brown	Joseph D. Hardy....................	922	455
		John D. Spencer....................	467	
8	Nemaha	J. E. Taylor....................	476	239
		George Graham	237	
9	....	C. S. Cummings	403	159
		Peter Hamilton	244	
10	Marshall....................	Allen Reed....................	1,128	248
		M. D. Tenney....................	880	
11	Washington	A. G. Baber....................	673	119
		Wm. H. Knight....................	554	
12	Riley	H. P. Dow....................	777	107
		Geo. T. Polsen....................	667	
13	Pottawatomie....................	O. J. Grover....................	470	19
		E. McKee....................	451	
14	....	Jas. H. Shehi....................	428	36
		Jas. P. Shannon	384	
15	Jackson....................	John Birkett	600	33
		A. L. Stevens	567	
16	Jefferson	M. C. Mowry....................	401	6
		J. B. Johnson....................	395	
17	....	V. Brown....................	468	125
		David Rorick....................	343	
18	....	E. K. Townsend	407	7
		E. M. Hutchins....................	269	
		J. A. Codey....................	131	
19	Leavenworth	D. R. Anthony....................	441	253
		Jas. McMichael	188	
20	....	Jos. W. Taylor....................	228	2
		Geo. A. Moore	226	
		G. F. Miller....................	85	
21	....	S. N. Latta....................	409	23
		Jas. F. Legate	386	
22	....	T. P. Fenlon....................	721	721
23	....	Watson Tucker	338	16
		J. S. Van Winkle....................	257	
		J. J. Crook....................	65	
24	....	James Medill....................	477	173
		A. F. Evans....................	303	
		J. M. Orr	1	
25	....	C. W. Lawrence....................	265	1
		W. H. Taylor....................	264	
		C. C. Duncan	190	
		F. M. Smith....................	2	
26	Wyandotte....................	Sanford Haff....................	535	86
		J. K. Hudson....................	449	
		James Peak....................	392	
27	....	R. B. Taylor....................	425	181
		Jno. D. Cruise	244	
28	Johnson....................	Thos. Hancock....................	403	94
		H. S. Carter....................	309	
		J. E. Thornton....................	198	
29	....	W. W. Maltby....................	475	122
		R. Aikman....................	353	
		J. M. Giffen....................	221	
30	....	Geo. Rogers....................	425	152
		W. M. Shean....................	241	
		Geo. Gensel....................	32	
31	Miami....................	J. C. Cusey.........,	658	245
		David Anderson	413	

40

VOTE FOR MEMBERS OF HOUSE OF REPRESENTATIVES — Continued.

District.	Counties.	Names of Candidates.	Votes...	Maj. or Plur...
32	Miami	L. Hendrickson	303	
		M. Tinkham	760	457
33	Linn	J. R. Van Zandt	475	87
		Wm. Mackey	388	
34		Herbert Robinson	318	200
		J. C. Marshall	117	
		L. Newell	1	
35		Charles Campbell	364	164
		James Walker	200	
36	Bourbon	S. Bird	451	170
		Wiley Bollinger	281	
37		David Johnson	532	347
		W. R. Griffin	185	
38		T. F. Robley	686	272
		J. D. Manlove	414	
39	Crawford	W. H. McGuire	402	134
		A. J. Vickers	267	
40		A. B. Mitchell	279	95
		A. M. Brown	184	
		S. J. Langdon	174	
41	Cherokee	L. Conklin	474	33
		M. Douglas	441	
42		L. T. Stowell	420	224
		T. Wells	196	
43	Labette	J. L. Williams	523	176
		G. C. West	347	
		J. S. Waters	209	
		G. W. Chess	184	
44		W. H. Mapes	564	76
		Isaac Butterworth	486	
45	Neosho	James M. Allen	508	58
		C. F. Hutchings	450	
		T. H. Butler	196	
46		T. P. Leech	595	312
		M. McLachlin	197	
		W. A. Nichols	86	
47	Allen	E. H. Funston	436	147
		J. A. Christie	287	
48		Eli Gilbert	301	35
		J. W. Ellis	246	
49	Anderson	J. L. White	550	111
		B. M. Lingo	439	
50	Franklin	C. B Mason	502	1
		H. M. Robb	320	
		Wm. H. Clark	181	
51		J. H. Harrison	655	363
		J. Hanway	292	
52	Douglas	J. C. Horton	510	42
		Alexander Love	468	
53		John C. Watts	715	424
		Alex. R. Banks	290	
54		L. H. Edson	733	644
		A. K. Lowe	89	
55		William Roe	702	702
56	Shawnee	Ira C. Johnson	530	57
		Daniel M. Adams	473	
57		John Martin	1,028	617
		J. B. McAfee	411	
58		Jacob Welchhans	376	169
		Lewis Hanback	207	
		John G. Otis	196	
59	Osage	D. B. Burdick	579	52
		W. W. Morris	525	
60		N. A. Perrill	577	72
		W. H. Wilson	505	
61	Coffey	F. W. Potter	542	48
		Jacob Baer	494	
		O. Walkling	334	
		H. Teachout	46	
62	Woodson	Frank Butler	517	163
		L. M. Olden	299	
		William Peck	53	
63	Wilson	J. A. Beam	774	112

VOTE FOR MEMBERS OF THE HOUSE OF REPRESENTATIVES—Continued.

District.	Counties.	Names of Candidates.	Votes	Maj. or Plur.....
63	Wilson (concluded)	Thomas Blakeslee	662	
64	Montgomery....................	John Boyd.........................:	570	2
		C. S. Brown	567	
65	....	A. A. Stewart......................	631	68
		J. S. Russum.......................	563	
66	Howard	James N. Young...................	788	21
		W. H. Guy.........................	767	
		O. D. Lemert......................	763	
67	Greenwood	J. W. Johnson	454	86
		J. B. Clogston	368	
68	Lyon........................	M. J. Firey	542	148
		Mark Patty........................	394	
69	....	H. F. McMillan	611	495
		P. P. Herrick......................	116	
70	Wabaunsee....................	Abram Sellers	486	258
		Arthur Reed.......................	228	
71	Davis........................	A. C. Stickney....................	497	154
		G. E. Beates.......................	343	
		John K. Wright....................	223	
72	Morris	Thomas S. Huffaker..............	534	114
		C. L. Thomas	369	
		W. A. McCollom..................	48	
73	Chase	T. S. Jones	330	34
		J. G. Winne.......................	290	
74	Butler........................	H. D. Hill.........................	963	270
		David Young	693	
75	Cowley	William Martin...................	738	70
		James McDermott	666	
76	Sedgwick	E. P. Thompson...................	904	409
		Z. McClung.......................	495	
77	Marion	B. Pinkney	745	733
78	McPherson....................	T. E. Simpson....................	331	
		J. M. Underwood	382	51
79	Dickinson	J. M. Hodge......................	613	174
		E. Barber.........................	439	
80	Clay........................	S. D. Beegle......................	622	103
		C. W. Lindner	519	
81	Republic....................	W. H. Pilkenton..................	522	81
		R. P. West........................	411	
		A. D. Wilson	90	
82	Cloud	B. H. McEckron	973	973
83	Ottawa.....................	R. F. Thompson	483	298
		J. J. Jenness	183	
84	Saline.....................	Jonathan Weaver.................	619	18
		M. D. Sampson....................	601	
.		J. H. Snead.......................	145	
85	Ellsworth....................	H. L. Pestana....................	306	90
		Perry Hodgden	216	
86	Lincoln.....................	Volney Ball.......................	287	80
		J. Harshbarger	186	
		David G. Bacon	21	
87	Mitchell	D. C. Everson....................	569	186
		Y. Douglass.......................	383	
88	Jewell	C. E Parker......................	685	317
		George S. Bishop..................	368	
89	Ellis	H. J. McGaffigan	152	1
		T. K. Hamilton	151	
90	Wallace	No returns.		
91	Rice.....................	M. J. Morse	131	28
		William Lowrey...................	103	
		T. H. Watt........................	98	
92	Sumner	W. P. Hackney....................	790	539
		W. H. Carter......................	249	
93	Osborne....................	Calvin Reasoner	266	99
		R. T. Osborne.....................	167	
94	Reno	C. C. Hutchinson	341	120
		J. W. Kanaga......................	221	
95	Smith.....................	J. T. Morrison....................	258	25
		L. N. Plummer	105	
		L. C. Uhl..........................	213	
96	Harvey	A. C. Richardson	511	481
		Charles Schaeffer	20	
97	Barton.....................	J. F. Cummings...................	201	38

VOTE FOR MEMBERS OF HOUSE OF REPRESENTATIVES—Concluded.

District.	Counties.	Names of Candidates.	Vote of County.	Maj.
97	Barton (concluded)...............	And. McKinney	163	
98	Russell	John Fritts	165	3
		B. W. Goodhue..........................	162	
99	Phillips	John Bissell	254	68
		J. T. Wood................................	186	
100	Billings	C. C. Vance	81	52
		Thos. Biermont..........................	29	
101	Pawnee	Henry Booth...............................	48	16
		W. R. Adams..............................	32	
102	Rooks.....................................	Henry Taylor..............................	110	105
103	Ford........................	James Hanrahan........................	163	107
		M. V. Cutler	55	
		John Taylor...............................	1	
104	Barbour	W. E. Hutchinson........................	278	278
105	Harper	Wm. H. Hornor...........................	256	235
		G. E. Phillips	21	
106	Ness	S. G. Rodgers............................	263	263
107	Comanche	A. J. Mowry	272	272
	Total.......................	....	89,443	......

NOVEMBER 18.—Stitzel and Blair, horse thieves, shot and killed at Grasshopper Falls.

NOVEMBER 19.—In a lecture delivered in Washington, Frederick Douglass says John Brown's Constitution for the government of the proposed insurrectionary Republic was written in his house, in Rochester, New York, and that he still possesses the original draft.

—The Death of the Kansas Magazine is announced.

NOVEMBER 22.—Gov. Osborn appoints Robert Crozier U. S. Senator.

NOVEMBER 25.—Major J. K. Hudson buys the Kansas Farmer. The Farmer had been published in quarto form from September 1, 1867, by George T. Anthony. The volumes contain the agricultural and industrial history of the State. They are well printed, and contain articles written by prominent citizens in every county. Major Hudson changed the form to folio.

NOVEMBER 30.—Fourth Annual Report of D. Dickinson, State Librarian. Volumes in the Library, 9,241.

NOVEMBER 30.—The following table of Land Grants to Kansas railroads is copied from Poor's Railroad Manual:

Date of Laws.	Name of Road.	Acres Certified.	Quantities Granted.
March 3, 1863...	Leavenworth, Lawrence and Galveston...............	168,189	800,000
July 1, 1864......	Atchison, Topeka and Santa Fe.......................	....	3,000,000
July 1, 1864......	Union Pacific, Southern Branch.......................	....	500,000
July 23, 1866.....	St. Joseph and Denver City...........................	....	1,700,000
July 25, 1866.....	Kansas and Neosho Valley, now known as Missouri River, Fort Scott and Gulf Railroad......	....	2,350,000
July 26, 1866.....	Southern Branch of the Union Pacific Railroad, now Missouri, Kansas and Texas Railroad......	508,342	1,520,000
July 1, 1862.......	Central Branch, Union Pacific }	227,941	245,166
July 2, 1864.......	Central Branch, Union Pacific }		
July 1, 1862.......	Kansas Pacific }	....	6,000,000
July 2, 1864.......	Kansas Pacific }		

NOVEMBER 30.—

"The following table shows the length of each railroad in the State, and the value per mile, as fixed by the Railroad Assessors. The total assessed value given in the table is too large, some of the roads running through unorganized counties where no tax is levied or collected:

Name of Road.	*No. miles operated.*	*Ass'd val. per mile.*	*Total Ass'd valuation.*
Kansas Pacific..	476.550	$7,900	$3,764,745
Leavenworth, Lawrence & Galveston....................	187.100	5,300	991,630
Missouri River, Fort Scott & Gulf....................	158.886	7,222	1,147,474
Atchison, Topeka & Santa Fe..........................	496.160	5,000	2,480,800
Missouri, Kansas & Texas.............................	252.980	4,700	1,189,006
Kansas Central.......................................	55.270	3,000	165,810
Junction City & Fort Kearney.........................	33.000	3,000	99,000
Central Branch.......................................	100.000	4,000	400,000
Leavenworth, Atchison & Northwestern.................	21.155	7,250	153,373
Saint Joseph & Denver................................	137.690	4,700	647,143
Missouri River.......................................	22.244	8,000	177,952
St. Louis, Lawrence & Denver, Carbondale Branch......	30.600	3,500	107,100
St. Louis, Lawrence & Denver.........................	39.250	4,000	157,000
Doniphan & Wathena...................................	13.500	3,000	40,500
Atchison & Nebraska..................................	38.213	4,779	182,619
Total...	2,062.598	....	$11,704,154

"The Kansas Pacific escapes payment on 30.85 miles in Trego county, $243,715; 31 miles in Gove county, $244,900; and 76.80 in Wallace county, $606,720; total, $1,095,333, on 138.65 miles. I suppose the tax is now paid on the parts of roads running through military reserves, Attorney General Williams having decided last year that it ought to be paid.

"The Atchison, Topeka and Santa Fe road escapes payment on 17.64 miles in Pawnee county, $88,200; on 24.28 miles in a tract of land now outside of any county, $121,400; on 38.32 in Ford county, $191,600; on 25.96 in Foote county, $129,800; on 25.31 in Sequoyah county, $126,550; on 26.34 in Kearney county, $131,700; and on 28.65 miles in Hamilton county, $143,250; or $932,500 on 186.50 miles.

"The railroads of Kansas are therefore assessed at $9,676,319.

"Poor's Railroad Manual, a high authority, says the railroads in Kansas have cost $53,258 per mile. On this estimate, the value of the 2,062 miles of railroad in Kansas is $109,817,996, or more than one hundred million dollars more than the amount for which they are assessed. Mr. Poor is friendly to the railroads."—*Auditor Wilder's Report.*

NOVEMBER 30.—Expenditures of the State for the year:

Governor's Department............	$8,075 00	Printing....................................	54,089 18
Secretary's Department...........	18,130 59	Agricultural College...............	23,225 96
Auditor's Department..............	5,369 50	Freedman's University.............	1,100 00
Treasurer's Department...........	6,551 00	State Librarian........................	1,881 60
Attorney General.....................	1,850 00	Transcribing Journals..............	2,054 45
Adjutant General.....................	550 00	Horticultural Society...............	1,000 00
Sup't of Public Instruction.......	4,211 95	Agricultural Society.................	5,290 00
Judiciary..............................	47,297 43	Regents...................................	2,558 90
Normal School, Emporia...........	16,976 03	State House and grounds..........	9,945 80
Normal School, Leavenworth...	5,988 65	Revising Tax Laws...................	450 00
Blind Asylum...........................	11,586 01	J.C.Douglass, Territorial Sup't...	850 00
Deaf and Dumb Asylum...........	35,078 17	Conveying prisoners to Peniten-	
Insane Asylum.........................	25,575 00	tiary.....................................	643 70
State University......................	24,531 53	J. M. Matheny..........................	5,000 00
Legislative expenses.................	50,172 24	Miscellaneous accounts............	1,908 75
Entertaining Neb. Legislature...	1,771 50		
Penitentiary...........................	71,200 00	Total for 1873...................$444,902 94	

DECEMBER.—Report of Joseph C. Wilson, C. S. Brodbent and Charles Puffer, Board of Commissioners on Public Institutions, under the act of March 6, 1873. W. P. Barnett, of Brown county, and P. P. Elder, of Franklin county, appointed Commissioners under the act, resigned.

The chapter on the University cites the statutes relating to the institution; gives a list of its lands, and says none have been sold.

"The amounts given by the city of Lawrence to the University are as follows:

Site of old building, valued at	$10,000
Value of old building	20,000
Site of new building, valued at	40,000
Amount given by Amos Lawrence to the city of Lawrence for educational purposes, and with his consent turned over to the University, and now bearing interest in Kansas State bonds	10,300
Amount voted by the city of Lawrence for new building	100,000
Total given by city of Lawrence	$182,300
The amount of cash received for the fifty thousand dollars State scrip appropriated in 1872, was	$48,097 20
From the one hundred thousand dollars of city bonds	90,500 00
Total cost of new building thus far, in cash	$138,597 20

In addition to this, there is an unpaid building account standing against the University of seven thousand four hundred and forty-four dollars and eighty-one cents, making the entire cost paid and unpaid.....$146,042 01

"Appropriations made by the State:

	Undrawn.	Appropriated.
1866	$4,114 02	$7,000 00
1867	3,714 58	13,094 84
1868	533 34	7,500 00
1869	....	11,670 00
1870	....	14,570 33
1871	7 50	17,665 00
1872 (exclusive of the $50,000 building fund)	....	18,290 00
1873	128 47	24,660 00
	$9,240 41	$114,450 17

Total drawn from State, aside from the $50,000 for building.....$105,209 76

"There was also an act passed in the year 1864, page 194, to refund to the citizens of Lawrence five thousand one hundred and sixty-seven dollars. This, it will be observed, was the year after the Quantrell raid.

"The University has always been fortunate in having an able Board of Managers—men noted for their superior qualifications in education, of intellectual attainments and financial and administrative experience; and the records show none of the humiliating bickerings and strife that have disgraced the meetings of the boards of some of our other State institutions."

The State Normal School at Emporia has received 38,400 acres of land from the State; only 486 acres have been sold.

"The following, taken from the books of the State Auditor, will show the amount of money drawn from the State for all purposes, except members of the Board:

1864—Salaries of teachers	$1,000 00
1865—Salaries of teachers	2,000 00
1866—For building	10,000 00
Salaries of teachers	3,000 00
1867—For building	5,650 00
For enclosure of grounds	1,000 00
For well and cistern	850 00
For salaries of teachers	4,000 00
For furniture, books, etc.	1,500 00
For Model School	1,000 00
1868—For salaries of teachers	1,500 00
For Associate Principal	6,000 00
For salaries of female teachers	1,000 00
(Not drawn, $50.)	
For Model School	900 00
(Not drawn, $275.)	
For extra work	50 00
For classifying lands	427 00
For deficit current expenses	290 00
For insurance	75 00
For diplomas	110 00
For catalogues	150 00
For chandeliers and lamps	60 00
For American Cyclopædia	100 00
For dictionary and maps	124 00
(Not drawn, $26.)	

1869—For current expenses.. 10,106 00
    (Not drawn, $175.38.)
1870—For current expenses.. 10,542 46
    (Not drawn, $143.79.)
1871—For miscellaneous... 8,475 00
    (Not drawn, $50.15.)
1872—For building 50,000 00
    For current expenses.. 11,940 00
    (Not drawn, $417.)
1873—For current expenses and extra cost of building............. 17,829 50
    (Not drawn, $854.47.)
    Total not drawn..$1,991 79

    Total amount expended by State.................................$142,297 17

"The above does not include pay of members of Board of Regents, as provided by law, but it does include other different items allowed by former Boards to its members for expenses, etc."

A list of its lands is given.

The following is copied from the brief account of the Leavenworth Normal School:

Appropriations made:		Undrawn balances:	
1871	$6,971 70	1871	$593 90
1872	7,581 03	1872	13 50
1873	6,000 00	1873	11 32

The Agricultural College is treated at length. The land given by the United States is supposed to be about 81,000 acres. The State did not receive the 90,000 acres, for the reason that some of the land selected was within railroad limits, and one acre within those limits counted for two outside of that limit. Mr. Goodnow sold 44,829 acres; Mr. Elliott has sold 640. Amount received from sales, $197,157.06.

"NUMBER OF ACRES UNSOLD IN EACH COUNTY.

Washington county	12,640.00	Riley county	2,691.50
Dickinson county	16,000.00	Clay county	480.00
Marshall county	4,320.00		
Total			36,131.50

"The amounts drawn from the State from year to year, according to the books of the State Auditor, are seen below:

1864	$2,892 25	1870	....
1865	3,316 50	1871	....
1866	....	1872	15,000 00
1867	18,011 10	1873	23,000 00
1868	6,420 00		
1869	8,919 00	Total	$77,468 85

"This amount, of course, is exclusive of the amounts paid the Land Agents, Loan Commissioner, and Regents."

The following is copied from the chapter on the Insane Asylum:

"The amounts drawn from the State, according to the State Auditor's books, are as follows:

1864...Locating Asylum	$5 00	1870...Current expenses	13,073 00
1866...Current exp. and building,	3,500 00	Undrawn balance	$6 20
1867...Current exp. and building,	7,775 00	1871...Current expenses	13,931 00
1868...Current exp. and building,	12,600 00	Building fund	40,000 00
Building fund	20,000 00	1872...Current expenses	21,000 00
1869...Current expenses	12,244 00	1873...Current expenses	25,575 00
Undrawn balance	$2 50		
Total for all purposes			$186,168 87

"Of the foregoing amount about $80,000 have been expended for buildings, repairs, barn, privies, well, trees, walks, and fencing."

In 1868, $20,000 were appropriated in State bonds. Cost of the main building, $74,677.

The following is copied from the chapter on the Blind Asylum:

The total amount drawn from the State for all purposes, except pay of Directors and Trustees, is shown by the State Auditor's books as follows:

1867	$10,000 00	1872	10,100 00
1868	11,722 11	1873	11,586 01
1869	10,150 00		
1870	8,900 00	Total	$70,161 48
1871	7,703 36		

There was a balance undrawn in—

1869	$57 20
1871	105 39
1872	11 04
1873	3 99
	$177 62

Total cash $69,983 86

The Deaf and Dumb Asylum appropriations are summed up in the following table:

The amount drawn from the State, not including Trustees' salaries, nor building fund, except for out-houses, cisterns, and general repairs, is shown by the Auditor's books, as follows:

Date.	Undrawn.	Appropriated.
1862	....	$500 00
1863	$484 15	1,500 00
1864	170 00	1,800 00
1865	2,828 89	4,500 00
1866	250 01	5,600 00
1867	622 28	10,517 18
1868	200 00	10,500 00
1869	125 00	12,940 23
1870	286 62	13,580 00
1871	....	14,800 00
1872	....	14,200 00
1873	1,526 41	16,604 58
Totals	$6,494 35	$107,941 99

Total cost of current expense	$101,447 64
Add cost of old building	15,500 00
Add cost of new building	20,000 00
Grand total	$136,947 64

The following relates to the Penitentiary:

The annexed statement, furnished by Auditor Wilder, gives the amount drawn from the State; but we believe that a full and exhaustive examination of the State records, appropriations, and Penitentiary records, will show that this statement will vary some:

1861...C. S. Lambdin, Commissioners	$153 00
1861...Cohen & Markson, clothing	100 00
1861...Leavenworth county, boarding	545 30
1861...Leavenworth county, boarding	739 50
1862...Leavenworth county, boarding	333 75
1862..Leavenworth county, boarding	600 00
1862...Cohen & Markson, clothing	112 50
1862...John McCarty	29 50
1863...From appropriations	7,279 74
1864...From appropriations	7,680 94
1865...From appropriations	14,336 39
1866...From appropriations	41,148 47
1867...From appropriations	115,540 55
1868...From appropriations	42,316 35
1869...From appropriations	103,275 93
1870...From appropriations	35,000 00
1871...From appropriations	35,000 00
1872...From appropriations	77,065 00
1873...From appropriations	71,200 00

Although not strictly within our jurisdiction, as specified in the law authorizing this Board, but simply for general information and at the request of several of the

State officers, we include as below given, the total expenditure upon the State House and grounds:

1863...	Fencing grounds, etc.		$958 50
1864...	Trees and fencing	$41 50	
	Improving grounds	809 85	851 35
1865...	Planting trees		299 50
1866...	Capitol		42,492 65
1867...	Bonds	100,000 00	
	Trees	82 00	
	Repairs	50 00	100,132 00
1868...	Bonds		150,000 00
1869...	Bonds	70,000 00	
	Commissioners Killen, Bowman, and Hammond	1,500 00	
	Building	49,997 30	121,497 30
1870...	Commissioners' services, Killen, Hammond, and Bowman,	375 00	
	Commissioners' travelling expenses, Killen, Bowman, and Hammond	1,325 25	
	J. G. Haskell, Architect	666 60	
	Tweeddale & Cook, privy	2,129 91	
	Tweeddale & Cook, building steps	300 00	
	Scott Bros., painting	152 50	
	Tweeddale & Cook, drains	64 00	
	Tweeddate & Cook, repairs	7 00	
	H. J. Miller, gas fixtures	4,500 00	
	John Goodin, heating	3,852 00	
	Tweeddale & Cook, extra work	174 62	
	M. B. Crawford, repairs	3 50	
	Excelsior Gas Co., fixtures	570 75	
	Building	4,707 16	18,828 35
1871...	W. Tweeddale	394 00	
	Improvement of grounds	5,000 00	5,394 00
1872...	Improvement of grounds	5,000 00	
	Building	559 16	
	Building east portico	25,000 00	30,559 16
1873...	Building east portico	9,500 00	
	Improvement of grounds	350 00	9,850 00
	Total		$480,862 81

RECAPITULATION.

State House building	$467,813 46
Improving grounds	13,049 35
	$480,862 81

DECEMBER 15.—The Leavenworth Times says United States Attorney Scofield has agreed not to prosecute Pomeroy for bribery; the trial is set for the first Monday in January.

—James F. Legate becomes Editor of the Leavenworth Call.

—George S. Smith, Treasurer of Leavenworth county, is a defaulter to the amount of $72,000.

DECEMBER 18.—Thomas S. Morrison, of the Surveyor General's office, says the centre of the State is in Rice county, viz.: the corner of sections 5, 6, 7, and 8, township 18, south, range 9, west.

DECEMBER 20.—Secretary Smallwood reports the organization of the following counties: Ford, April 5; Barbour, April 14; Harper, August 20; Ness, October 23; Comanche, October 28.

DECEMBER 31.—The Emporia Normal School has had 218 students; the Leavenworth Normal School 99. There are 121 patients in the Insane Asylum; 52 pupils in the Deaf and Dumb Asylum — the new building will be completed in February. The State University has had 239 students. There are 121,690 children enrolled in the public schools; value of school-houses, $3,408,956; the permanent school fund amounts to $1,003,688.99. St. Benedict's College, Atchison, has 95 students; Mount St. Mary's Female Academy, Leavenworth, 55. There are graded public schools at Atchison, Chetopa, Concordia, Fort Scott, Hiawatha, Independence, Junction City, Leavenworth, Louisville, Neosho Falls, Oswego, Parsons, Wichita, and Wamego.

1874.

JANUARY 1.—There are one hundred and forty-eight newspapers published in the State, representing the following counties: Allen, Anderson, Atchison, Barton, Bourbon, Brown, Butler, Chase, Cherokee, Clay, Cloud, Coffey, Cowley, Crawford, Davis, Dickinson, Doniphan, Douglas, Ellis, Ellsworth, Ford, Franklin, Greenwood, Harvey, Howard, Jackson, Jefferson, Jewell, Johnson, Labette, Leavenworth, Lincoln, Linn, Lyon, Marion, Marshall, McPherson, Miami, Mitchell, Montgomery, Morris, Nemaha, Neosho, Osage, Osborne, Ottawa, Pawnee, Phillips, Pottawatomie, Reno, Republic, Rice, Riley, Russell, Saline, Sedgwick, Shawnee, Smith, Sumner, Wabaunsee, Washington, Wilson, Woodson, and Wyandotte.

JANUARY 1.—V. P. Wilson buys the North Topeka Times, of J. V. Admire.

JANUARY 9.—The Kansas Farmer issued at Topeka.

—The Opposition members of the Legislature declare that the Caucus held on the 8th was not for the purpose of forming a new political party.

JANUARY 13.—Meeting of the Legislature.

STATE OFFICERS.

Names.	P. O. Address.	County.
Thomas A. Osborn, Governor	Leavenworth	Leavenworth.
E. S. Stover, Lieutenant Governor	Council Grove	Morris.
W. H. Smallwood, Secretary of State	Wathena	Doniphan.
A. L. Williams, Attorney General	Topeka	Shawnee.
H. D. McCarty, Superintendent of Public Instruction	Leavenworth	Leavenw'th.
J. E. Hayes, State Treasurer	Olathe	Johnson.
Daniel W. Wilder Auditor of State	Fort Scott	Bourbon.
Geo. W. Martin, State Printer	Junction City	Davis
C. A. Morris, Adjutant General	Fort Scott	Bourbon.
D. Dickinson, State Librarian	Topeka	Shawnee.
Ed. Russell, Superintendent Insurance Department	Leavenworth	Leavenworth.

JUDGES OF THE SUPREME COURT.

Names.	P. O. Address.	County.
S. A. Kingman, Chief Justice	Topeka	Shawnee.
D. J. Brewer, Associate Justice	Leavenworth	Leavenworth.
D. M. Valentine, Associate Justice	Ottawa	Franklin.

JUDGES OF DISTRICT COURTS.

Names.	Districts.	P. O. Address.	County.
H. W. Ide	First	Leavenworth	Leavenworth.
P. L. Hubbard	Second	Atchison	Atchison.
John T. Morton	Third	Topeka	Shawnee.
Owen A. Bassett	Fourth	Lawrence	Douglas.
E. B. Peyton	Fifth	Emporia	Lyon.
M. V. Voss	Sixth	Fort Scott	Bourbon.
John R. Goodin	Seventh	Humboldt	Allen.
James H. Austin	Eighth	Junction City	Davis.
William R. Brown	Ninth	Hutchinson	Reno.
Hiram Stevens	Tenth	Paola	Miami.
B. W. Perkins	Eleventh	Oswego	Labette.
A. S. Wilson	Twelfth	Washington	Washington.
W. P. Campbell	Thirteenth	Eldorado	Butler.
J. H. Prescott	Fourteenth	Salina	Saline.
Joel Holt	Fifteenth	Beloit	Mitchell.

—Byron Sherry, Judge Criminal Court, Leavenworth county.

MEMBERS OF THE SENATE.

Dist.	Names.	Age	Pol.	Post Office.	County.	Occupation.
	E. S. Stover, Pres..	39	Rep .	Council Grove ...	Morris	Merchant.
1	Nathan Price	36	Rep .	Troy...................	Doniphan........	Lawyer.
2	W. H. Grimes......	71	Rep .	Atchison...........	Atchison..........	Physician.
2	J. C. Wilson..........	29	Rep .	Muscotah	Atchison..........	Far & st'ck dea'r
3	E. N. Morrill....	40	Rep .	Hiawatha..........	Brown	Banker.
4	Frank Schmidt ...	43	Rep .	Marysville........	Marshall	Banker.
5	L. R. Palmer........	55	Rep .	St. Mary's..........	Pottawatomie..	Farmer.
6	J. W. Rogers........	53	Rep .	Doyle's Station..	Jefferson........	Farmer.
7	J. T. McWhirt....	45	Dem.	Leavenworth	Leavenworth ..	Farmer.
7	Jacob Winter	62	Rep .	Leavenworth	Leavenworth ..	Law. and farmer
7	Thos. Moonlight..	40	Rep .	Leavenworth ..	Leavenworth ..	Surveyor.
8	B. Judd...............	49	Dem.	Wyandotte	Wyandotte......	Banker.
9	John P. St. John..	41	Rep .	Olathe.............	Johnson..........	Lawyer.
10	E. H. Topping	43	Rep .	Somerset..........	Miami............	Farmer.
11	A. F. Ely..........	35	Rep .	La Cygne	Linn...............	Lawyer.
12	W. E. Guerin......	26	Rep .	Fort Scott........	Bourbon..........	Lawyer.
13	Wm. Simpson......	36	Lib..	Pawnee Station..	Bourbon..........	Farmer.
14	W. M. Matheny...	41	Rep .	Baxter Springs...	Cherokee	Lawyer.
15	J. H. Crichton	30	Rep .	Chetopa	Labette	Lawyer.
16	W. L. Simons......	35	Rep .	Osage Mission ...	Neosho	Lawyer.
17	W. A. Johnson....	42	Rep .	Garnett.............	Anderson........	Lawyer.
18	A. M. Blair.........	41	Rep .	Ottawa..............	Franklin........	Banker.
19	M. A. O'Neil......	42	Rep .	Black Jack........	Douglas..........	Physician.
19	Henry Bronson...	54	Ref .	Lawrence	Douglas..........	Farmer.
20	N. C. McFarland..	51	Rep .	Topeka.............	Shawnee	Lawyer.
21	C. S. Martin........	37	Rep .	Osage City..........	Osage	Farmer & miller.
22	Chas. B. Butler...	35	Far'r	Le Roy............	Coffey	Stock-grower.
23	A. M. York..........	35	Rep .	Independence.....	Montgomery....	Lawyer.
24	Wm. Martindale...	38	Rep .	Madison	Greenwood	Farmer.
25	M. M. Murdock...	37	Rep .	Wichita............	Sedgwick	Editor.
26	Henry Brandley...	33	Rep .	Matfield Green...	Chase	Farmer.
27	V. P. Wilson........	45	Rep .	Abilene	Dickinson.......	Editor.
28	E. Barker............	57	Rep .	Jewell City	Jewell	Farmer.
29	John H. Edwards.	49	Rep .	Ellis.................	Ellis..............	Farmer.

OFFICERS OF THE SENATE.

Names.	Age	Pol.	Post Office.	County.	Occupation.
Tom H. Cavanaugh, Secretary...	30	Rep...	Salina	Saline	Farmer.
D. B. Emmert, Ass't Secretary...	37	Rep...	Humboldt	Allen	Publisher.
Geo. W. Findlay, Serg't-at-Arms	32	Rep...	Fort Scott.....	Bourbon	Coal dealer.
Geo. W. Weed, Ass't Ser-at-Arms	38	Rep...	Leavenworth	Leavenworth	Farmer.
S. M. Lanham, Journal Clerk.....	26	Rep...	Seneca	Nemaha..........	Book-keeper.
W. H. Cowan, Docket Clerk.......	32	Rep...	Independe'ce	Montgomery	Farmer.
Nellie Blake, Enrolling Clerk.....	21	Rep...	Fort Scott.....	Bourbon	Teacher.
Sarah J. Neal, Engrossing Clerk..	45	Rep...	Atchison	Atchison	
C. J. Burk, Doorkeeper...........	54	Rep...	Waterville ...	Marshall	Farmer.
H. L. Burgess, Ass't Doorkeeper..	24	Rep...	Olathe...........	Johnson........	Book-keeper.
F. S. McCabe, Chaplain............	45	Rep...	Topeka..........	Shawnee	Minister.
Jennie A. Griffith, Messenger....	16	Rep...	Topeka..........	Shawnee	
Jennette Edwards, Messenger....	13	Rep...	Paola	Miami	
E. Halloch Morris, Messenger....	12	Rep...	Topeka..........	Shawnee	Student.
J. W. Edwards, Postmaster........	37	Rep...	Paola	Miami	Farmer.

MEMBERS OF THE HOUSE OF REPRESENTATIVES.

Dist.	Names.	Age	Pol.	Post Office.	County.	Occupation.
82	B. H. McEckron, Speaker...	39	Rep..	Shirley	Cloud	Farmer.
1	N. L. Springer.................	42	Ref...	Severance........	Doniphan...	Farmer.
2	Xerxes K. Stout.............	48	Lib..	Troy	Doniphan..	Law. and far.
3	F. H. Drenning.............	38	Rep..	Wathena..........	Doniphan..	Lawyer.
4	Albert H. Horton........	38	Rep..	Atchison........	Atchison...	Attorney.
5	Samuel Stoner...............	46	Far..	Lancaster........	Atchison...	Farmer.
6	D. G. Wilson................	38	Rep..	Effingham.......	Atchison...	Farmer.
7	J. D. Hardy.................	38	None	Hiawatha........	Brown	Farmer.

MEMBERS OF THE HOUSE OF REPRESENTATIVES—Continued.

Dist.	Names.	Age	Politics.	Post Office.	County.	Occupation.
8	J. E. Taylor............	34	Indep.....	Seneca	Nemaha	Lawyer.
9	C. S. Cummings	35	Rep........	Centralia	Nemaha	Blacksmith.
10	Allen Reed............	40	Rep........	Reedville	Marshall........	Farmer.
11	A. G. Baber	41	Rep........	Clifton	Washington ..	Farmer.
12	H. P. Dow.............	33	Rep........	Berlin	Riley	Farmer.
13	O. J. Grover...........	46	Rep........	Savannah	Pottawatomie	Farmer.
14	James Shehi	41	Rep........	Otter Lake	Pottawatomie	Farmer.
15	John Birkett.........	55	Rep........	Circleville	Jackson.........	Clergyman.
16	M. C. Mowry........	43	Ref	North Lawrence.	Jefferson........	Farmer.
17	Val. Brown	50	Farmer..	Medina	Jefferson........	Farmer.
18	E. K. Townsend.....	35	Ref	Grasshop'r Falls.	Jefferson........	Farmer.
19	D. R. Anthony......	50	Rep........	Leavenworth......	Leavenworth.	Editor.
20	J. W. Taylor	30	Dem	Leavenworth......	Leavenworth.	Att'y at law.
21	S. N. Latta	52	Rep........	Leavenworth	Leavenworth.	Real Estate.
22	Thos. P. Fenlon.....	36	Indep.....	Leavenworth	Leavenworth.	Attorney.
23	W. Tucker	54	Rep........	Leavenworth	Leavenworth.	Farmer.
24	James Medill.........	54	Rep........	Springdale	Leavenworth.	Farmer.
25	Chas. W. Lawrence	45	Farmer..	Lawrence	Leavenworth.	Farmer.
26	Sanford Haff........	35	Dem	Wyandotte	Wyandotte ...	Farmer.
27	R. B. Taylor	52	Ind. Rep.	Wyandotte	Wyandotte ...	Editor.
28	Thomas Hancock...	33	Liberal..	Stanley	Johnson.........	Farmer.
29	W. W. Maltby........	55	Indep.....	Olathe	Johnson.........	Farmer.
30	Geo. F. Rogers.......	42	Ref	Hesper	Johnson.........	Farmer.
31	J. C. Cusey...........	43	Ref	Paola	Miami...........	Farmer.
32	M. Tinkham	33	Farmer..	Lewisburg...........	Miami...........	Farmer.
33	J. R. Van Zandt.....	37	Rep........	Pleasanton.........	Linn...............	Merchant.
34	H. Robinson..........	37	Ref	Farlandville........	Linn...............	Farmer.
35	Charles Campbell...	37	Ref	Mapleton............	Linn...............	Farmer.
36	S. Bird.................	37	Rep........	Glendale............	Bourbon	Farmer.
37	David Johnson.......	55	Rep........	Uniontown	Bourbon	Farmer.
38	T. F. Robley..........	33	Rep........	Fort Scott..........	Bourbon	Lawyer.
39	W. H. McGuire.......	37	Liberal..	Jacksonville........	Neosho...........	Farmer.
40	A. B. Mitchell........	47	Liberal..	Girard	Crawford	Farmer.
41	L. Conklin............	40	Ref	Neutral City	Cherokee........	Farmer.
42	L. T. Stowell.........	58	Ref	Baxter Springs....	Cherokee........	Farmer.
43	J. L. Williams	26	Ref	Oswego	Labette	Nurserym'n
44	W. H. Mapes.........	43	Rep........	Oswego	Labette	Farmer.
45	James M. Allen......	31	Rep........	Urbana...............	Neosho	Farmer.
46	T. P. Leech	35	Indep.....	Thayer	Neosho	Farmer.
47	E. H. Funston........	37	Rep........	Iola	Allen	Farmer.
48	Eli Gilbert	51	I. R.......	Humboldt	Allen.............	Lawyer.
49	J. E White............	54	Rep........	Garnett	Anderson	Farmer.
50	C. B. Mason	40	Lib. Ind..	Ottawa	Franklin	Attorney.
51	J. H. Harrison	43	Ref	Wellsville...........	Franklin	Farmer.
52	James C. Horton....	36	Rep........	Lawrence	Douglas.....	Gen'l Agent.
53	John C. Watts	39	Ref	Lawrence	Douglas.........	Mason.
54	L. H. Edson...........	43	Ref	Belvoir	Douglas.........	Farmer.
55	William Roe.........	42	Farmer..	Vinland	Douglas.........	Farmer.
56	I. C. Johnson........	64	Ref	North Topeka......	Shawnee........	Farmer.
57	John Martin..........	40	Dem	Topeka	Shawnee.......	Attorney.
58	Jac. Welchhans......	39	Ref	Topeka	Shawnee........	Teacher.
59	D. B. Burdick........	43	Rep........	Burlingame	Osage	Farmer.
60	N. A. Perrill	30	Rep	Reading	Osage	Farmer.
61	F. W. Potter..........	41	Indep....	Burlington..........	Coffey	Farmer.
62	Frank Butler.........	33	Indep.....	Kalida	Woodson........	Farmer.
63	J. A. Beam............	65	Farmer..	Verdi	Wilson	Farmer.
64	C. S. Brown	33	Rep........	Independence......	Montgomery..	Lawyer.
65	A. A. Stewart........	37	Ref	Independence......	Montgomery..	Farmer.
66	James N. Young ...	58	Rep........	Pawpaw	Howard	Farmer.
67	James W. Johnson	32	Indep.....	Jauesville..........	Greenwood ...	Farmer.
68	M. J. Firey............	34	Farmer..	Emporia	Lyon	Farmer.
69	H. F. McMillan	37	Rep........	Agnes City.........	Lyon..............	Farmer.
70	A. Sellers	37	Rep........	Alma	Wabaunsee....	Editor.
71	A. C. Stickney.......	40	Rep........	Junction City......	Davis.............	Merchant.
72	T. S. Huffaker.......	48	Rep........	Council Grove.....	Morris	Farmer.
73	Thomas S. Jones...	33	Rep........	Cottonwood Falls	Chase	Lawyer.
74	H. D. Hill.............	34	Rep........	Augusta	Butler	Physician.
75	Wm. Martin...........	60	Farmer..	Winfield	Cowley	Farmer.
76	E. P. Thompson.....	56	Rep........	Wichita	Sedgwick	Farmer.
77	B. Pinckney	48	Rep........	Peabody	Marion	Farmer.
78	J. M. Underwood...	33	None.....	Marquette...........	McPherson	Farmer.
79	J. M. Hodge..........	48	Rep........	Abilene	Dickinson......	Physician.
80	S. D. Beegle.........	50	Ref	Clay Center........	Clay..............	Farmer.
81	W. H. Pilkenton.....	40	Rep........	Bellville	Republic........	Lawyer.

MEMBERS OF THE HOUSE OF REPRESENTATIVES—Concluded.

Dist.	Names.	Age.	Pol.	Post Office.	County.	Occupation.
83	R. F. Thompson	27	Rep..	Minneapolis.....	Ottawa.........	Lawyer.
84	Jonathan Weaver..	37	Fmr	Lesterville......	Saline...........	Farmer.
85	H. L. Pestana........	30	Ind..	Ellsworth	Ellsworth	Lawyer.
86	V. Ball..................	33	Rep..	Colorado..........	Lincoln..........	Farmer.
87	D. C. Everson	26	Rep..	Glen Elder	Mitchell........	Physician.
88	C. E. Parker	50	Rep..	Holmwood	Jewell...........	Farmer.
89	H. J. McGaffigan...	36	Rep..	Hays City........	Ellis	Merchant.
90	No election............	......	......	....	Wallace...........	————
91	M. J. Morse..........	42	Rep..†	Brookdale.......	Rice.............	Minister.
92	W. P. Hackney	31	Rep..	Wellington	Sumner	Attorney.
93	Calvin Reasoner....	36	Rep..	Osborne City.....	Osborne	Farmer.
94	C. C. Hutchinson...	40	Rep..	Hutchinson	Reno	Land Agent.
95	J. T. Morrison	32	Rep..	Cedarville.......	Smith	Farmer.
96	A. G. Richardson...	43	Rep..	Newton	Harvey	Farmer.
97	J. F. Cummings	42	Ind..	Great Bend......	Barton..........	Editor.
98	John Fritts...........	34	Rep..	Bunker Hill.....	Russell	Fmr.& stk.raiser.
99	John Bissell..........	44	Rep..	Phillipsburg....	Phillips.........	Farmer.
100	C. C. Vance...........	40	Rep..	Norton	Billings.........	Lawyer.
101	Henry Booth.........	35	Rep..	Larned	Pawnee	Farmer.
102	H. R. Taylor.........	32	Rep..	Stockton	Rooks	Stock raising.
103	James Hanrahan...	34	Ind..	Dodge City.......	Ford.............	Tradesman.
104	W. E. Hutchinson..	26	Rep..	Medicine Lodge	Barbour.........	Farmer.
105	Wm. H. Hornor...	32	Rep..	Bluff City.......	Harper	Lawyer.
106	S. G. Rodgers	40	Ref..	Smallwood City	Ness.............	Physician.
107	A. J. Mowry...........	40	Rep..	Smallwood	Comanche	Farmer.

OFFICERS OF THE HOUSE OF REPRESENTATIVES.

Names.	Office.	Age.	Pol.	Post Office.	County.
Alex. R. Banks	Chief Clerk..............	38	Rep..	Lawrence........	Douglas.
John C. Moseley......	Assistant Chief Clerk..	30	Rep..	Clay Centre.....	Clay.
O. W. Bromwell......	Journal Clerk	28	Lib..	Wichita.........	Sedgwick.
A. B. Ostrander	Docket Clerk.............	27	Rep..	Lawrence	Douglas.
Emma R. Bristol.....	Enrolling Clerk...........	22	Rep..	Humboldt	Allen.
Rebecca Flower......	Engrossing Clerk	35	Rep..	Topeka	Shawnee.
James M. Matheny..	Sergeant-at-Arms	31	Rep..	Topeka	Shawnee.
R. V. Kennedy.......	Ass't Sergeant-at-Arms	32	Rep..	Bunker Hill ...	Russell.
George E. Brown.....	Doorkeeper	27	Rep..	Olathe	Johnson.
A. H. McWhorter ...	First Ass't Doorkeeper	35	Rep..	Lawrence	Douglas.
Patrick Gilson	Sec'd Ass't Doorkeeper	60	Dem	Leavenworth...	Leavenworth
M. B. Crawford......	Postmaster	38	Rep..	Howard City....	Howard.
Emma Duncan.........	Page	13	....	Ottawa..........	Franklin.
Mary Fletcher........	Page	13	....	Topeka...........	Shawnee.
Jennie Maxwell......	Page	13	....	Topeka...........	Shawnee.
Augusta Nilson.......	Page	12	....	Topeka...........	Shawnee.
George W. Latham..	Page	12	....	Belleville........	Republic.
Lorin Cozine..........	Page	12	....	Iola...............	Allen.
Harland Cummings	Page	10	....	Great Bend.....	Barton.

JANUARY 14.—Election of officers of the State Board of Agriculture: President, Geo. T. Anthony, Leavenworth; Vice President, E. H. Funston, Carlyle; Treasurer, J. C. Wilson, Topeka; Secretary, Alfred Gray, Topeka.

Members of the Board: Joshua Wheeler, Pardee, Atchison county; C. S. Brodbent, Wellington, Sumner; S. J. Carter, Burlington, Coffey; H. R. Crowell, Baxter Springs, Cherokee; I. O. Savage, Belleville, Republic; L. Wilson, Leavenworth, Leavenworth; W. P. Popenoe, Topeka, Shawnee; S. T. Kelsey, Hutchinson, Reno; John H. Edwards, Ellis, Ellis.

Officers by Appointment: Geologist, B. F. Mudge, Manhattan; Entomologist, E. A. Popenoe, Topeka; Meteorologist, Prof. Frank H. Snow (Professor of Natural History and Meteorology, State University), Lawrence; Botanist, Prof. James H. Carruth, Lawrence; Chemist, Prof. W. K. Kedzie (Professor of Chemistry, State Agricultural College), Manhattan; Signal Service Commissioners, Frank H. Snow, Lawrence; B. F. Mudge, Manhattan; J. H. Carruth, Lawrence; Taxidermist, O. S. George, Topeka.

The Tenth Annual State Fair was held at Leavenworth.

—Meeting of the Farmers' Co-operative Association.

JANUARY 14.—George R. Peck, of Independence, appointed United States District Attorney.

JANUARY 15.—Albert H. Horton offers a resolution for the appointment of a committee to investigate the charges made by the Auditor against the Treasurer.

JANUARY 16.—Death of Peter T. Abell, the founder of Atchison.

JANUARY 19.—The United States Attorney General issues an order for the District Attorney of Kansas to begin a suit in the United States Circuit Court to test the validity of patents issued to railroad companies for any part of the Osage Ceded Lands.

—County-seat war in Howard county.

JANUARY 27.—Vote of the Senate for United States Senator, to fill the vacancy caused by the resignation of Alexander Caldwell: Thomas A. Osborn 4, Wm. A. Phillips 2, James M. Harvey 5, S. A. Kingman 4, P. B. Plumb 4, J. K. Hudson 2, John Davis 1, I. S. Kalloch 1, J. C. Carpenter 2, J. D. Snoddy 1, D. W. Wilder 1, W. R. Laughlin 1, W. I. Larimer 1, D. R. Anthony 1, W. L. Simons 1, George T. Anthony 1, Charles Sumner 1.

Vote of the House: Thomas A. Osborn 16, Wm. A. Phillips 17, J. C. Carpenter 3, J. M. Harvey 7, John R. Goodin 1, M. E. Hudson 5, N. Green 1, P. B. Plumb 13, Wilson Shannon 2, B. H. McEckron 1, Johnson Clark 5, D. W. Wilder 3, E. G. Ross 3, S. A. Kingman 9, M. M. Murdock 5, E. S. Stover 1, Charles Robinson 2, W. H. Smallwood 1, A. M. F. Randolph 1, Henry Bronson 2, J. K. Hudson 1, John Martin 1, W. D. Rippey 1, George T. Anthony 2, James D. Snoddy 1, James H. Crichton 1, D. R. Anthony 1.

JANUARY 28.—The Senate Journal, page 127, contains the opinion of A. L. Williams, Attorney General, on the 500,000-acre land case.

JANUARY 28.—Vote for Senator in Joint Convention:

In the Senate: J. M. Harvey 4, T. A. Osborn 3, P. B. Plumb 3, S. A. Kingman 3, E. S. Stover 8, W. R. Laughlin 2, John T. Morton 1, D. M. Valentine 1, J. Davis 1, Wm. Larimer 1, Charles Robinson 1, W. A. Phillips 5.

In the House: J. M. Harvey 10, T. A. Osborn 13, P. B. Plumb 18, S. A. Kingman 7, E. S. Stover 1, Charles Robinson 10, W. A. Phillips 19, W. L. Simons 5, Nathan Price 5, E. G. Ross 5, M. E. Hudson 2, B. H. McEckron 1, D. W. Wilder 2, C. C. Hutchinson 1, W. H. Smallwood 1, A. M. F. Randolph 1, Henry Bronson 2, J. K. Hudson 2, M. M. Murdock 1. Whole number of votes cast, 139. Necessary to a choice, 70.

JANUARY 29.—Vote for U. S. Senator:

In the Senate: E. S. Stover 12, J. M. Harvey 5, W. A. Phillips 3, J. K. Hudson 3, T. P. Fenlon 2, Chas. Robinson 1, J. D. Snoddy 1, N. C. McFarland 1.

In the House: E. S. Stover 8, P. B. Plumb 17, J. M. Harvey 13, W. A.

Phillips 18, J. K. Hudson 20, T. P. Fenlon 10, Chas. Robinson 8, E. G. Ross 4, Sam'l A. Kingman 3, W. H. Smallwood 2, Nathan Price 1, D. W. Wilder 1, A. M. F. Randolph 1.

JANUARY 31.—Vote for U. S. Senator:

In the Senate: J. M. Harvey 5, E. S. Stover 12, J. K. Hudson 3, P. B. Plumb 5, T. P. Fenlon 2, Chas. Robinson 1, W.·A. Phillips 3.

In the House: P. B. Plumb 20, J. M. Harvey 17, E. S. Stover 15, J. K. Hudson 15, W. A. Phillips 13, Chas. Robinson 10, T. P. Fenlon 9, E. G. Ross 2, N. Price 1, N. Green 1, S. A. Kingman 1, A. M. F. Randolph 1.

—The Topeka Blade discontinued.

FEBRUARY 2.—Vote for Senator:

In the Senate: J. M. Harvey 18, P. B. Plumb 4, W. L. Simons 2, E. S. Stover 2, J. D. Snoddy 2, D. M. Valentine 1, Charles Robinson 1.

In the House: J. M. Harvey 58, P. B. Plumb 17, W. L. Simons 14, E. S. Stover 6, Charles Robinson 3, T. P. Fenlon 2, N. Price 2, A. M. F. Randolph 1, D. R. Anthony 1.

FEBRUARY 3.—B. L. Kingsbury appointed Regent of the Agricultural College, in place of Rev. Dr. Charles Reynolds, resigned; Charles A. Bates, in place of Rev. N. Green, resigned; James H. Crichton, Regent of the Emporia Normal School, in place of John W. Horner, resigned.

—State Temperance Convention at Topeka.

FEBRUARY 10.—The House, by a vote of 57 to 26, asks for the speedy trial of ex-Senator Pomeroy.

FEBRUARY.—The Fort Scott Monitor publishes the following poem, written by Eugene F. Ware, of that city:

THE GEESE AND THE CRANES.

It is sunrise; in the morn
Stands a field of ripened corn,
  And the rich autumnal rays
  Of these Southern Kansas days
Fill that field of ripened corn
  With an opalescent haze.
And the flocks of geese and cranes,
Pick the fallen, golden grains.

It is noontime; and the rays
Of the Indian summer blaze,
  And the field of ripened corn,
  Much more shattered than at morn,
Seems emerging from the haze.
  Fewer geese, but far more cranes,
  Pick the fallen, golden grains.

It is evening; and the haze
Of the short, autumnal days
  Like a mantle seems to rest
  On the dark and leaden West.
Shattered is the field of maize.
  Homeward fly the geese; the cranes
  Linger, picking golden grains.

It is midnight; rains and sleet
On the blackened landscape beat;
  And there nothing now remains
Of that field of standing corn.
  But through darkness, sleet and rains
  Comes the crying of the cranes,
As they search through fields forlorn,
  Fighting for the final grains.

Hours the grains, and life the field
  Where the golden grains are had.
  And our habits, good and bad,
Represent the geese and cranes,
Eating up the golden grains.
  Few the habits that are best,
  And they early go to rest.
But through sleet and midnight rains
Heard the clamors are of cranes,
  Fighting for the final grains.

—*Ironquill.*

FEBRUARY 10.—John A. Anderson, President of the Agricultural College, invited to address the Legislature on the 13th.

FEBRUARY 12.—Dedication of the Masonic Temple, at Leavenworth.

—Burning of the Central Block, Atchison.

FEBRUARY 13.—W. H. Grimes appointed Trustee of the Insane Asylum.

FEBRUARY 17.—

"DEPARTMENT OF THE INTERIOR, OFFICE OF INDIAN AFFAIRS, }
"WASHINGTON, D. C., February 17, 1874. }

"SIR: I have the honor to acknowledge the receipt, by reference from the Hon. Commissioner of the General Land Office, of your communication dated the 4th instant, requesting a list of all Indian Reservations in Kansas, disposed of by the Government since the 29th of January, 1861, the date of the admission of Kansas as a State into the Union, out of which the State did not have reserved to it the sixteenth and thirty-sixth sections for school purposes, and the area of each such reservation.

"In compliance therewith, I have the honor to submit the following report:

		Acres.
CHEROKEE NEUTRAL LANDS....................................		793,288.80
CHIPPEWA AND MUNSEE LANDS:		
Chippewa and Munsee lands, sold.........................	3,801.31	
Chippewa and Munsee lands, reservation...............	4,395.31	8,196.62
DELAWARE LANDS:		
Sold to Leavenworth, Pawnee & Western Railroad Co...........	223,890.84	
Sold to Missouri River Railroad Co........................	92,598.33	
Reserved by treaty stipulations.........................	7,494.08	323,983.25
KANSAS TRUST AND DIMINISHED RESERVATION LANDS................		256,063.77
KICKAPOO LANDS:		
Sold to Atchison & Pike's Peak Railroad Co........................	123,832.61	
Allotments...	8,312.14	
Reservation...	20,272.53	152,417.28
MIAMI LANDS:		
Allotments...	60,023.85	
National Reserve...	10,608.13	70,631.98
NEW YORK LANDS—32 allotments		10,215.63
OSAGE CEDED LANDS*—under treaty of Sept. 29, 1865, (Stat. at Large, volume 14, p. 687,)...............................		960,000.00
OTTAWA LANDS:		
For schools...	19,997.76	
Buildings	640.00	
Allotments...	24,970.00	
Trust lands...	30,134.95	75,742.71
PEORIA, KASKASKIA, &c.:		
Allotments to Larrimer and Shields......................	321.55	
Sold April, 1868..	5,312.82	
Unsold April, 1868, and now allotted....................	641.61	
Seventy-four allotments, approved in 1858................	42,000.82	48,276.80
POTTAWATOMIE LANDS:		
Sold to Atchison, Topeka & Santa Fe Railroad Co....................	338,766.82	
Allotments...	150,444.41	
Mission lands..	1,654.62	
Diminished reserve.......................................	77,357.67	568,223.52
SHAWNEE LANDS—including Black Bob and Absentees..............		200,000.00
Grand total in acres.....................................		3,467,040.36

"The foregoing lands comprise all the Indian lands in Kansas held as such January 29, 1861, which have since been disposed of, either by sale or allotments, or are retained as reservations, from which the school sections (16th and 36th) were not reserved to the State.   Very respectfully, your obedient servant,

"EDWARD P. SMITH, *Commissioner.*

"To Hon. S. A. Cobb, House of Representatives."

FEBRUARY 17.—J. K. Hudson, Topeka, issues a pamphlet containing the Constitution of the Kansas State Grange. *Officers:* Master, M. E. Hudson, Mapleton, Bourbon county; Overseer, Wm. Sims, Topeka, Shawnee county; Lecturer, John Boyd, Independence; Steward, E. D. Smith, Jewell City, Jewell county; Assistant Steward, J. B. Richie, Franklin county; Chap-

---

*NOTE.—The 16th and 36th sections reserved for school purposes, in Trust Lands, (Statutes at Large, volume 17, p. 90.)

lain, W. S. Hanna, Ottawa ; Treasurer, H. H. Angell, Sherman City ; Secretary, G. W. Spurgeon, Jacksonville ; Gate Keeper, W. H. Fletcher, Clay county ; Ceres, Mrs. Mattie Morris ; Flora, Mrs. M. H. Charles ; Pomona, Mrs. Amanda C. Rippey ; Lady Assistant Steward, Mrs. Jennie D. Richie. *Executive Committee:* F. H. Dumbauld, Jacksonville, Neosho county ; I. B. Shaeffer, Grasshopper Falls ; W. P. Popenoe, Topeka. *State Agent:* John G. Otis, Topeka. These officers were elected February 17, at Topeka.

FEBRUARY 19.—W. H. Johnson starts the Hays City Sentinel.

—The Temperance Crusade reaches Kansas.

FEBRUARY 20.—Meeting in the Court House, Topeka, to form an "Anti-Monopoly and Reform party," participated in by John Davis, A. M. York, Henry Bronson, and others. Simpson, Robinson, Goodhue, Burnett, Beegle, Akin and Potter appointed a committee to call a State Convention.

FEBRUARY 23.—The State Treasury Investigating Committee make a report, and ask the impeachment of the Treasurer.

FEBRUARY.—Death of Gov. William Walker, of the Wyandotte tribe of Indians. He came with the tribe from Ohio, some thirty years ago.

FEBRUARY 25.—Suits begun to determine the question of the title to the Osage Ceded Lands.

FEBRUARY 26.—The Senate Journal, page 338, contains the report of Senator M. A. O'Neil on Price Raid claims:

"Whole amount of scrip for damages	$159,191 34
Interest on scrip for damages	78,000 00
Whole amount of scrip for all other purposes	94,338 48
Interest on scrip for all other purposes	46,000 00
Additional claims audited and allowed under the provisions of sec. 1 of the supplemental act of the laws of 1873	1,018 16
Amount due, to be provided for out of the consolidated military fund, as provided for under sec. 3 of the foregoing act	236 50
Total amount of interest certificates issued for scrip paid	124,000 00

RECAPITULATION.

Damage scrip	$159,191 34
Estimated interest on same	78,000 00
Service and other scrip	94,338 48
Estimated interest on same	46,000 00
Additional claims, 1872	1,018 16
Additional claims, 1873	236 50
Total outstanding scrip	$378,794 48

After deducting the amount of $336,817.37 of scrip cancelled with money appropriated by act of Congress."

MARCH 2.—

"The question recurring on the resolution charging Hon. Josiah E. Hayes with high crimes and misdemeanors in office, and that he be impeached, the roll was called with the following result: Yeas, 74 ; nays, 20."—*House Journal, p. 781.*

—James H. Austin appointed Judge of the Eighth District.

MARCH 3.—The House elects the following Impeachment Managers: A. H. Horton, C. B. Mason, John Martin, T. S. Jones, W. P. Hackney, T. P. Fenlon and F. W. Potter.

MARCH 4.—Message from Governor Osborn, from which the following is copied:

"It appears that the county seat of Howard county was, at an election held in September, 1873, located at Elk Falls, and that at a subsequent election it is claimed was voted to the town of Boston, but the county officers were temporarily enjoined from removing the records of the county to Boston by an order of the District Court of said county, under date of Dec. 11, 1873, and a motion to dissolve the injunction was heard at chambers on the 2d day of January, 1874, before Hon. W. P. Campbell, Judge of said District, and overruled. On the 20th day of January, 1874, a party of armed men, numbering one hundred and fifty, entered the town of Elk Falls, and with force and arms took possession of and carried away the books, papers, records, files and office furniture of the several county offices, and conveyed them to the town of Boston in said county."

MARCH 5.— Benj. B. Gale appointed Postmaster at Atchison.

—Frank H. Drenning appointed State Agent for the sale of railroad lands.

—Death of Wm. E. Bowker, at Los Angeles, Cal. He came to Kansas in 1855; was a member of the Territorial Legislature, of the Wyandotte Convention, Treasurer of Shawnee county, and was one of the incorporators of Lincoln, now Washburn, College.

MARCH 6.—The House Managers exhibit articles of impeachment against Josiah E. Hayes, State Treasurer, to the Senate. They are signed by A. H. Horton, C. B. Mason, F. Wm. Potter, Thomas S. Jones, and Wm. P. Hackney.

Wilson Shannon, B. F. Simpson, and A. Smith Devenney, Attorneys for the Treasurer, present an answer to the articles.

MARCH 7.—Senator Henry Bronson, of Douglas county, resigns.

—O. J. Grover appointed Director of the Penitentiary.

MARCH.—The new Chapel at the Penitentiary dedicated; services by Rev. Richard Cordley, of Lawrence, and Rev. B. L. Baldridge, Chaplain of the Penitentiary.

MARCH 10.—Cassius G. Foster, of Atchison, appointed United States District Judge.

—Normal School located at Concordia, Cloud county.

—Adjournment of the Legislature. Bond laws disappearing from the statute-book. Among the acts passed are the following: Apportioning the State into three Congressional Districts; Making an appropriation to test the title to the Osage Ceded Lands; Amending the bond-registration law and restricting the power to issue municipal bonds; Providing for the appointment of State Centennial Managers; A civil-rights protection law; Defining the boundaries of Edwards, Kiowa, Stafford, and Pawnee counties; Attaching Linn county to the Tenth Judicial District; Establishing a Fiscal Agency in New York; Authorizing Dickinson, Lincoln, Howard, Barbour, Clay, Saline, Pawnee, Reno, Ford, Harper, Jewell, and Barton counties to issue bonds to fund indebtedness; Reappropriating the military fund; Exempting Mennonites and Friends from military service; Prohibiting lotteries; Authorizing railroad companies to issue preferred stock; A railroad-assessment law, giving the assessment to township assessors; Requiring the education of all healthy children; Providing for the investment of sinking funds; repealing the act creating a Board of State House Commissioners; Repealing the act exempting mortgages from taxation; For the semi-annual payment of taxes.

MARCH 11.— Charles Sumner dies, in Washington.

MARCH 12.—Arms sent to Howard county.

—Senator Morrill, of Maine, reports that no obligation rests upon the United States to reimburse Kansas, or any State, for expenses incurred and damages sustained by reason of the incursions of hostile Indians. "The duty of protecting their citizens rests primarily with the States."

MARCH 14.—Pension Agent Lines, at Topeka, pays 1,515 pensioners in nine days, $50,000.

MARCH 16.—James W. Steele, of Topeka, appointed Consul at Matanzas.

MARCH 18.—David Dickinson reappointed State Librarian.

MARCH 20.—The Temperance Crusade at its height in the State.

MARCH 24.—T. F. Houts and Jas. S. Emery appointed Regents of the University.

—W. H. Pilkenton and Frederick Speck appointed Trustees of the Blind Asylum.

—Levi Woodard and Jacob Rhodes appointed Trustees of the Insane Asylum.

MARCH 27.—Osage City ships 1,000 tons of coal per week.

MARCH 30.—Centennial Managers appointed: George T. Anthony, Leavenworth; E. W. Dennis, Topeka; S. T. Kelsey, Hutchinson; A. J. North, Atchison; D. J. Evans, Topeka.

APRIL 3.—A Digest of Kansas Reports, issued by C. F. W. Dassler, of the Leavenworth bar. W. J. Gilbert, St. Louis, Publisher. The book embraces decisions in McCahon's, Dillon's and Woolworth's Reports, in ten volumes of Kansas State Reports, and Kansas cases in the U. S. Supreme Court. It contains 279 pages.

APRIL 10.—It is reported that there are 1,100 Granges in the State, and 30,000 members.

APRIL 11.—Track-laying begins at Topeka on the Midland road.

APRIL 13.—Seven buildings burned in Junction City. Among them the Hale House.

APRIL 14.—John Davis issues a circular letter preliminary to calling a Reform or Anti-Monopoly Convention. Convention to be held in June.

APRIL 15.—Samuel D. Lecompte, Cyrus Leland, jr., J. G. Mohler, John W. Pipher, C. J. Jones, H. W. Cook, H. C. Cross, G. W. Veale, T. B. Murdock, and John S. Gilmore, the Republican Congressional Committee, meet at Topeka. S. D. Lecompte was elected Chairman, and Cyrus Leland Secretary, of the First District Committee, and a meeting called at Manhattan. H. C. Cross was elected Chairman, and W. A. Morgan Secretary, of the Third District Committee, and a meeting called at Emporia, June 16. Messrs. Cook and Gilmore, of the Second District, called a meeting at Wyandotte, April 17th. The absent members were D. B. Dyer of Cherokee, and John E. Baer of Franklin.

APRIL 16.—Death of Anthony A. Ward. He came to the Shawnee Indian Agency, in Kansas, in 1841. In 1854, he selected a claim adjoining Topeka. He was probably the oldest white settler of Shawnee county, and his family is believed to have lived in the Territory and State longer than any other white family.

APRIL 17.—A Convention in Franklin county attempts to give birth to an Independent State party. Convention called at Topeka, May 27.

APRIL 17.—M. Reasoner, E. C. Snowden, H. E. Smith, M. McKinnod,

B. H. McEckron, F. W. Sturgis and W. E. Reid appointed Directors of the Concordia Normal School.

APRIL 23.—Donnell, Lawson & Co., New York, appointed State Fiscal Agents.

APRIL 24.—The first rail rolled in the Topeka Rolling Mills.

—Another fire in Emporia; seven buildings burned since January 1st.

APRIL 30.—Treasurer Hayes resigns.

MAY 1.—John Francis, of Iola, Allen county, appointed State Treasurer.

—Albert H. Horton writes to E. S. Stover that the Treasurer has resigned; that this is a "confession of his guilt;" that "the Board of Managers have decided that it is an unnecessary expense to call witnesses before the Senate, and ask you to recall the subpœnas issued, and notify the witnesses summoned that they need not appear." "On the convening of the Senate we shall announce to the Court the resignation, and shall state that we do not deem it advisable to proceed with an expensive trial."

MAY 12.—Meeting of the Senate as a Court of Impeachment. J. C. Vincent appears from Douglas county, in place of Henry Bronson, resigned, and Geo. W. Glick in place of Jos. C. Wilson, resigned, of Atchison county.

MAY 13.—Adjournment of Impeachment Court.

—John Fraser, Chancellor of the University, resigns.

MAY 26.—Editorial Convention at Fort Scott. Address by W. S. Burke of Leavenworth; Poem by Eugene F. Ware, of Fort Scott. *Officers:* President, D. R. Anthony; Vice Presidents, D. W. Houston, Albert Griffin, U. F. Sargent, W. T. McElroy; Secretary, W. R. Spooner; Treasurer, Geo. W. Martin; Orator, Geo. A. Crawford; alternate, Noble L. Prentis; Poet, Mrs. Louis Walker. Next Convention to be held at Manhattan. Excursion to St. Louis.

MAY 27.—Independent Reform Convention, at Topeka. W. C. Smith, of Atchison, Chairman; T. C. Nicholson, of Paola, Secretary. The Convention was adjourned to August 5th. The new call is signed by Louis Melius, Isaac E. Eaton, C. A. Buck, T. E. Smith, J. G. Searle, J. B. Scroggs, J. B. Rollinger, C. Davenport, J. G. Otis, E. P. Pomeroy, J. Robinson, Isaac Sharp, O. Shannon, T. Duston, A. McLouth, W. C. Smith, J. Y. Hewitt, J. A. Cody, T. W. Hutchinson, S. Haff, Nelson Abbott, E. K. Townsend.

MAY 27.—Mass meeting, at Parsons, of settlers on the Osage Ceded lands.

—Geo. W. Crane, Topeka, publishes Township Records and Printed Forms, by Hugh M. Spalding.

—A book published with this title: "The Trinity. By F. H. Burris, A. M., Member of the South Kansas Conference. With an Introduction by Prof. Joseph Haven, D.D., LL.D. Chicago: S. C. Griggs & Co. 1874." pp. 216.

—In the summer, the Kurtz brothers removed the Florence Pioneer to Augusta and started the Gazette, which they still publish.

JUNE 3.—Benj. F. Akers, of Lawrence, sells Ethan Allen, the trotting stallion.

—Special train over the Midland road, from Topeka to Lawrence.

June 7.—The Baccalaureate Sermon at the University is delivered by Rev. Dr. F. S. McCabe, of Topeka. George T. Anthony, of Leavenworth, delivers the Annual Address.

June 8.—The Osage Ceded Land case argued before the U. S. Circuit Court, at Leavenworth, by George W. Peck, H. C. McComas and Wilson Shannon.

—The Pomeroy bribery case brought up before Judge Morton, at Topeka, and Pomeroy's counsel suggested July 27th as the day they would go to trial. This day was agreed upon.

June 10.—The John Davis Reform Convention meets at Topeka, and joins the 5th-of-August movement.

June 17.—Republican State Convention to meet August 26.

—A bill passes Congress making two new Land Districts.

June 27.—Indian difficulties reported in the Southwest.

June 29.—Charles A. Morris appointed Register and Eli Gilbert Receiver of the Larned Land Office; John H. Edwards Register, John C. Carpenter Receiver, of the Hays City office.

—George S. Smith, the Leavenworth defaulting Treasurer, convicted at Atchison.

—The Kansas Home Cook-Book published. It is made up of recipes furnished by ladies of Leavenworth and other cities and towns in the State, and is published by the Board of Managers for the benefit of the Home for the Friendless, Leavenworth. Printed at Leavenworth by John C. Ketcheson. pp. 264. A second edition was issued in 1875.

July 7.—Arch. Shaw and W. A. Shannon appointed Trustees of the Deaf and Dumb Asylum.

July 7.—Snow, Melius & Bain buy the Lawrence Tribune.

— Fred. Sowers sells the Wichita Beacon to Milton Gabel.

July 20.—Appearance of a book containing the "Proceedings of the Court of Impeachment Sitting for the Trial of Josiah E. Hayes, Treasurer, together with the Testimony taken in New York, and a Detailed Statement of Price Raid Scrip Paid." pp. 352. The book contains the Report of the Investigating Committee, the action of the House upon it, the proceedings of the Senate, a list of the witnesses summoned, the depositions taken in New York by A. L. Williams and C. B. Mason, and a list of the Price Raid scrip made by P. B. Castle. This last-named list fills 212 pages.

July 22.—Orville H. Browne, a pioneer, dies at Peace, Rice county, aged 59 years.

July 27.—Pomeroy bribery case before Judge Morton. The motion to quash the information was overruled by Judge Morton, on the 29th. An application for a change of venue was then made by Pomeroy's counsel, and the cause was sent to Osage county.

—Three horse-thieves hung in Sumner county, by the Vigilance Committee.

July 30.—A letter from Jewell county gives the first intimation published in the Commonwealth of the grasshopper raid.

August.—

"Nothing more alarming than the usual predatoray forays of Indians occurred until

June 16, when a party of savages surprised a citizen of Ford county but a few miles from Fort Dodge, and murdered him; and this was followed by the murder of four others, in quick succession, in Barbour and Comanche counties. The bloody work thus inaugurated did not stop until twenty-six citizens had been brutally massacred within the boundaries of the State. To dwell upon the details of these atrocities is no part of my purpose; they are horrifying in their enormity, and their recital would chill the blood in the veins of the most stoical. Unhappily, the pictures are not new; they have been produced and reproduced on almost every page of our frontier history; all are drawn in bloody colors. Remembering all that our people have suffered from this source, it can scarcely be matter of wonder that among them forbearance toward the Indian has become nearly an extinct virtue.

"The United States troops on the borders of the State were, in July and August, nearly all withdrawn for the purpose of accompanying General Miles on his expedition against the Cheyennes, and the State was left comparatively without protection. The Osages, whose reservation lies immediately south of the State, were reported to be hostile, and evidence, almost conclusive, had been obtained of their participation in the murders in Ford, Barbour and Comanche counties. The appeals to me for protection were incessant and urgent. Homes were being abandoned, and interests vital to individuals and important to the State were in danger of annihilation. Feeling myself under obligations to protect peaceful citizens in the enjoyment of their rights of person and property, and the circumstances narrated rendering the necessity imperative, I reluctantly determined to call into active service a limited force of the State militia. This force was increased and diminished as the emergency seemed to require, and at no time exceeded the number that I deemed to be absolutely requisite to protect the State from invasion and the frontier settlers from the fury of the savage. The small force in the field was kept moving actively along the southern line, and I am glad to be able to state that since it was called into the service not a citizen has been killed by Indians on the line of its operations. That many valuable lives and much property were saved by the precautions taken, will not admit of a doubt. Confidence in the ability and disposition of the Government to defend the border was restored, and thousands of citizens who had fled in consternation at the rumored approach of the savages, returned to their homes."— *Governor Osborn's Message, January, 1875.*

AUGUST 5.—State Independent Reform Convention at Topeka. John Davis temporary chairman, Nelson Abbott, Secretary, U. A. Albin, Assistant Secretary.

Committee on Credentials: H. C. Squires, C. E. Harrington, A. H. Mussey, M. C. Howard, Peter Bell, Wm. Simpson, F. M. Powers, L. McKinzie, Joel Moody, J. Frank McDowell, C. Coddington, E. A. Carr, A. A. Alvord.

Committee on Permanent Organization: C. H. Grover, B. P. Waggener, J. H. Eshleman, H. Allen, Jos. Randolph, T. W. Tallman, G. P. Smith, Theodore Alvord, J. C. Cusey, J. H. Rudd, J. S. Vedder, A. Harris, J. R. Dean.

Speeches were made by M. J. Firey, H. C. McComas, U. F. Sargent, J. R. Hallowell, Mr. Black, David Linton, Mr. Tuttle, Mr. Christy, G. P. Smith, Mr. Poehler, Mr. Hurst, Nelson Abbott, John Davis, J. C. Cusey, Mr. Majors of Crawford, Mr. Scroggs, Isaac Sharp, Mr. Dean, Samuel A. Riggs, Alfred Taylor, and Marcus J. Parrott.

Officers: President, John Boyd of Montgomery; Vice Presidents, J. H. Watson, of Lyon, Wm. Kalhoefer of Washington, Sanford Haff of Wyandotte; Secretary, Nelson Abbott of Atchison; Assistant Secretaries, Theo. Alvord of Davis, Peter Bell of Coffey.

Committee on Platform: John Davis, N. Abbott, Isaac E. Eaton, H. Allen, H. C. McComas, W. H. Clark, M. J. Firey, J. R. Dean, Peter Bell.

On motion, candidates for Governor stated their views, J. C. Cusey and

Alfred Taylor making such speeches. U. F. Sargent vouched for M. E. Hudson.

The following platform was adopted:

"*Resolved*, That we, the delegates and representatives of the people of Kansas favorable to the organization of an independent political party, laying aside past differences of opinion, and earnestly uniting in a common purpose to secure needed reforms in the administration of public affairs, cordially unite in submitting these declarations:

"That all political power is inherent with the people; that no government is worthy of preservation, or should be upheld, which does not derive its powers from the consent of the governed; that by equal and just laws, the rights of life, liberty and the pursuit of happiness shall be assured to all men, without distinction of race, color or nationality; that the maintenance of these principles is essential to the perpetuity of our republican institutions, and that to this end the Federal Constitution, with all its amendments, the rights of the States, and the Union of the States, must be preserved.

"That the maintenance inviolate of the rights of the States, and especially the right of each State to order and control its own domestic institutions according to its own judgment exclusively, is indispensable to that balance of power in which the perfection and endurance of our political fabric depends.

"That the conduct of the present Administration in the bold defiance of public sentiment and disregard of the public good; in its prodigality and wasteful extravagance; in the innumerable frauds perpetrated under its authority; in its disgraceful partiality for and reward of unworthy favorites; in its reckless and unstable financial policy, and in its incapacity to meet the vital question of the day and provide for the general welfare, stands without a parallel in our national history, and the highest considerations of duty require the American people, in the exercise of their inherent sovereignty, to check the accumulation of evil, and bring the Government back to its ancient landmarks of patriotism and economy.

"That the faith of the Nation must be retained inviolate; that the public debt, of whatever kind, should be paid in strict accordance with the law under which it was contracted.

"That we favor the repeal of the tariff on lumber, and that the tariff on the necessities of common life be abolished or reduced to the lowest possible figure, and that the tax on incomes be restored.

"The railroad corporations should be made subservient to the public good; that while we shall discountenance any action calculated to retard the progress of railroad enterprises, or work injustice to these invaluable auxiliaries to commerce and civilization, yet we demand such constitutional legislation upon this subject, both State and Federal, as will effectually secure the industrial and producing interests of the country against all forms of corporate monopoly and extortion.

"That in view of the widespread corruption that has penetrated Kansas in every department of its organization as a State, we will support no man for office merely because he is the nominee of a party, but to obtain our votes in every instance he must possess the Jeffersonian standard of fitness—honesty, capacity, and fidelity to the Constitution.

"That the frequent cases of malfeasance in office which have been developed within the last four years upon the part of State and county officials—the losses sustained by the people through the defalcations of county treasurers—imperatively demand such legislation as will secure the tax-payers for all funds paid into the State and county treasuries, and all interest accruing thereon; and we denounce it an act of criminal neglect in the Legislature having failed to provide for the speedy removal of defaulting treasurers from office, and their punishment for malfeasance therein.

"That the act of the Legislature of Kansas of March 1, 1866, by which the five hundred thousand acres of land dedicated forever to the school fund by sec. 3, art. 8, of our State Constitution, was divided among and appropriated to four railroad corporations, is unconstitutional and void; that this land still in right and equity belongs to the State land school fund, and measures should be adopted for its recovery.

"That we hereby extend our sympathy to the settlers on the Osage lands, and to homestead settlers whose titles are contested by railroad companies, and we hereby declare that the Reform party of Kansas will use every honest means to aid these people in their struggle for their homes."

Convention reassembled August 6. *Vote for Governor:* M. E. Hudson 98, J. C. Cusey 52, Chas. Robinson 14, Alfred Taylor 12. Before the result was announced the statement was made that Mr. Hudson would not accept. The Convention was in a tumult, and votes changed from Hudson to Robinson, and from Robinson to Cusey. The vote was finally declared, James C. Cusey 146½, M. E. Hudson 26½, Davis 1, scattering 8. The name of ex-Governor Robinson was withdrawn by Joseph E. Riggs. E. Harrington was nominated for Lieutenant Governor by acclamation. *For Secretary of State:* Nelson Abbott 98, B. F. Little 7, G. P. Smith 60, Isaac E. Eaton 2, Pearcely 4. The candidates for Treasurer were James E. Watson of Douglas, A. J. Hopkins of Shawnee, Charles F. Koester of Marshall, and E. W. Majors of Crawford. Pending the roll call, Mr. Koester was nominated by acclamation. *For Auditor:* G. P. Smith, of Wilson, 87; A. J. Hopkins, 41; Jonathan Weaver, of Saline, 32. Col. Smith was nominated. *For Attorney General:* J. B. F. Cates, of Allen, 84; J. R. Hallowell, of Cherokee, 87. *For Superintendent of Public Instruction:* H. B. Norton, of Cowley, 140; J. E. Bryan, of Allen, 17; John Fraser, of Douglas, 6. *For Associate Justice:* W. P. Douthitt, of Shawnee, by acclamation. *State Committee:* F. P. Williams, N. Abbott, S. D. Macdonald, H. L. Moore, J. V. Randolph, John M. Galloway, F. M. Powell, Theodore Alvord, Alfred Taylor, J. F. McDowell, J. S. Vedder, George H. English, H. L. Jones.

The delegates from the First District nominated Marcus J. Parrott for Congress.

AUGUST 6.—Fire at Paola—the third within fourteen months. Burning of the Spirit and Republican offices.

—State Temperance Convention called, by John B. Campbell, G. W. C., Grand Lodge of Good Templars; J. Jay Buck, G. W. C. T.; and David C. Beach, G. W. S.

AUGUST 7.—The President locates the new Land Offices at Hays City and Larned.

—Expedition against Indians outfitting at Fort Dodge; to be commanded by General Miles.

—Grasshoppers reach Topeka, and stay till winter. W. P. Popenoe says: "They seem to cover the face of the earth."

AUGUST 9.—Prof. H. B. Norton, nominated for Superintendent of Public Instruction by the Reform Convention, and Charles F. Koester, nominated for Treasurer, decline the nominations.

AUGUST 20.—State Temperance Convention at Topeka. J. Jay Buck, temporary Chairman.

Committee on Credentials: Mr. Dearborn, Mr. Beach, Mrs. Flower, Mr. Blakesley, Col. Ritchie.

Committee on Permanent Organization: D. P. Mitchell, J. H. Clark, Dr. Newman, Dr. Callahan, Mrs. Wood.

Committee on Resolutions: Mr. Beach, W. K. Marshall, Miss A. M. Way, Dr. Ward, Mrs. Wilson, J. P. Root.

Speeches by Rev. H. D. Fisher, Rev. Dr. F. S. McCabe, Col. Ritchie, and Dr. J. P. Root.

Officers: President, J. Jay Buck; Vice Presidents, Rev. Mr. Dearbon, Dr. Coon, J. C. Miller; Secretary, D. C. Beach; Assistant Secretary, Mrs. J. H. Clark; Treasurer, Mrs. John Higinbotham.

The resolutions ask for the organization of a State Temperance Society; repudiate the licensing of crime; favor a national prohibitory law; regret that the recent Reform Convention refused to incorporate a Temperance plank in its platform, and repudiate all men and parties who ignore this great issue of the age; recommend an immediate amendment of our State Constitution, giving to woman the right of suffrage; state that there is an irrepressible conflict between the liquor interest and the interests of human society, and that toleration and compromise should not be allowed; protest against the elevation to office of any man addicted to the use of intoxicating liquors; if the Republican Convention ignores this issue, a Temperance Convention should be called for the purpose of organizing an independent party, and nominating an independent ticket. The Convention reassembled on the 21st. The State Temperance League was organized, with the following officers: President, Rev. Dr. Richard Cordley; Vice Presidents, J. P. Root, V. M. Garwood, N. C. McFarland; Secretary, D. C. Beach; Assistant Secretary, Mrs. J. H. Clark; Treasurer, Mrs. Willam Fairchild; Executive Committee, J. Jay Buck, Noble L. Prentis, Mrs. D. Wilson, Mrs. L. Sharon.

AUGUST 20.—Republican Congressional Convention, First District, at Leavenworth. Called to order by Samuel D. Lecompte, Chairman of Committee. For temporary chairman, D. L. Palmer, of Jewell county, received 43 votes, to 39 for George Storch, of Atchison county. R. R. Hays was elected Secretary. The following committees were appointed:

On Credentials: J. M. Hodge of Dickinson, C. C. Vance of Norton, Mr. Curtin of Mitchell, S. A. Couch of Leavenworth, J. S. Hidden of Nemaha, L. R. Palmer of Pottawatomie, George Storch of Atchison.

On Permanent Organization: D. R. Anthony of Leavenworth, John Collins of Pottawatomie, D. E. Ballard of Washington, W. P. Henderson of Jewell, F. J. Wendell of Atchison, Joseph Short of Cloud, Albert Brown of Osborne.

On Resolutions: Samuel M. Strickler of Davis, Ferd. J. Wendell of Atchison, D. Williamson of Washington, Henry Inman of Ellsworth, Cyrus Leland, jr., of Doniphan, J. A. Blackburn of Leavenworth, A. Wells of Nemaha.

Officers: President, O. J. Grover, of Pottawatomie; Vice President, H. A. Potts; Secretaries, H. Johnson, R. R. Hays.

Dr. Hodge nominated William A. Phillips for Congress; James F. Legate nominated D. W. Houston. Mr. Legate withdrew the name of Col. Houston, announced that Nathan Price had withdrawn, and moved that William A. Phillips be nominated by acclamation; motion carried unanimously. Speeches were made by Colonel William A. Phillips and Judge Nathan Price.

The following Congressional Committee was appointed: D. L. Palmer of

Jewell, D. R. Anthony of Leavenworth, J. S. Hidden of Nemaha, George Huyck of Ellsworth, J. B. Corbett of Russell, O. J. Grover of Pottawatomie.

The following resolutions were adopted:

"*Resolved*, That our Representative be instructed to work for the income tax.

"*Resolved*, That we call upon our Representative in Congress to assist the workingmen in the collection of their claims, due by the United States Government, on account of the evasion of the eight-hour law.

"*Resolved*, That this Convention, confiding in the Republican party as the true and only embodiment of the great fundamental principle upon which free government can safely rest, and recognizing in the consistent declarations and patriotic acts of that party the power which converted a country half slave and half free into a country altogether free, bringing it safely through the dark and trying hours of treason and rebellion to the end of peace at home and respect abroad, do hereby reaffirm our devotion to its principles; that the country gratefully recognizes, as we do, that to the Republican party we are indebted for each and every political reform in the past, and can trust it in unquestioned confidence in the future, for all the reforms demanded in this our progressive age.

"*Resolved*, That we respectfully submit to the Republican State Convention the work of preparing and enunciating a platform as a work properly incumbent upon it.

"*Resolved*, That the delegates of the First Congressional District, in convention assembled, respectfully request His Excellency, the Governor of Kansas, to call a special session of the Legislature, to take into consideration the condition of the State, in view of the prospect of the suffering of the inhabitants caused by the destruction of the grasshoppers."

AUGUST 22.—The Osage Ceded Land suits decided by Samuel F. Miller and John F. Dillon in favor of the settlers. A jubilee meeting at Parsons is addressed by G. C. West, T. C. Cory, M. W. Reynolds, Willard Davis, and others.

—Gov. Osborn asks the President for 2,000 carbines for the Indian war.

AUGUST 25.—The western delegates to the Republican State Convention hold a meeting and instruct that Convention to ask for an extra session of the Legislature.

AUGUST 26.—Republican State Convention at Topeka. Called to order by John Guthrie. For temporary Chairman, Nathan Price nominated John M. Price; B. F. Simpson nominated John C. Carpenter. Carpenter received 104 votes, Price 94. John A. Martin was unanimously elected Secretary.

Committee on Credentials: D. C. Haskell, D. Naylor, Henry Booth, T. L. Marshall, G. M. Waugh.

Committee on Resolutions: E. T. Carr, John A. Martin, Benj. F. Ricker, T. D. Thacher, J. Jay Buck, W. J. Bawden, John S. Gilmore, Noble L. Prentis, H. P. Ninde, Benj. F. Simpson, E. A. Wasser, M. E. Latham, Jas. Kelly, S. W. Henderson, A. J. Banta.

Committee on Permanent Organization: James D. Snoddy, R. R. Hayes, Josiah Kellogg, George W. Gillespie, W. M. McLaughton.

Whole number of delegates, 214.

Officers: President, T. Dwight Thacher; Secretaries, John A. Martin, W. T. McElroy. Voted to nominate candidates by a viva voce vote.

The following platform was adopted:

"The delegates of the Republican party of Kansas in convention assembled, confidently appealing to the people of the State for a continued support, point with pride to the record of the Republican achievements in the past as the best pledge that the party they represent will be true to every present or future obligation, and equal to every present or future emergency.

"The courage, patriotism and wisdom of the Republican party has been tested and proven; it came into being as the expression of the people against the iniquity of Slavery; it continued in power during the war as the embodiment of their devotion to the integrity of the Union; it abolished Slavery, suppressed armed rebellion, and conquered a permanent peace; it enfranchised the slaves, and secured for them equal political and civil rights; it made just provision for the nation's defenders; it enacted a beneficent homestead law; it organized a financial system whereby the nation was enabled to meet the emergencies of a great civil war, to furnish a sound and uniform currency, and to prevent the commercial depression and disasters usually attendant upon or succeeding civil strife. By successful diplomacy, it has established a principle of peaceful arbitration between nations. It has paid $356,000,000 of the war debt, and $5,000,000 during the last year of financial panic and prostration. It has relieved the products of industry and the necessaries of life from an annual levy and collection of more than $300,000,000 of taxes. Under its rule the national exports have increased from $300,000,000 to almost $650,000,000. It has restored the national credit and maintained the national reputation abroad. It has held in check the turbulent and reactionary forces of the late Rebellion, and has at the same time been tolerant beyond example to those who sought to destroy the Republic. And, finally, with rare courage, has addressed itself to the work of investigating official delinquencies and punishing official dishonesty in its own ranks.

"A party whose career has thus been signalized at every step by great achievements, has not only established the strongest title to public confidence, but has presented the best pledge that it is willing and able to satisfactorily and honorably adjust the new problems of legislation and administration that are pressing for consideration and settlement. We recognize the fact that parties cannot live upon glory. New issues are constantly arising, and the party that deserves to live must be ready to provide for their solution. The past only affords a guarantee that the intelligence which created the Republican party, and the patriotism and wisdom that have sustained it, are sufficient to provide for the emergencies of the present, and make this period date not only the death of Slavery, but as well the birth of a comprehensive Nationality, the strictest and firmest integrity in official trusts, a just protection of individual rights against corporate power, thorough practical reform in every department of the public service, honestly distributed burdens, and honestly exercised powers. Therefore,

"*Resolved*, That the powers of the General Government having been stretched to an unhealthy extent to meet the crisis of civil war and reconstruction, should now be restored to their normal action; that the public debt should be reduced not spasmodically, but gradually and surely, and in a way that will not burden the industries of the country by excessive exactions; that any and all schemes of taxation devised to meet the extraordinary demand, should be modified according to the dictates of the strictest principles of economy and justice; that official prodigality, recklessness and corruption incident to times of haste, irregularity and convulsion must give place to economy, stability and honesty, and finally that the only test of political preferment should be capacity and integrity in the discharge of official trust. That as the policy of the Republican party in relation to the finances has afforded the people not only a safe, sound and popular currency of equal and uniform worth in every portion of the commonwealth, but has greatly improved the credit of the country at home and abroad, we point with pride to its record and accomplishment in this regard, and while reaffirming the policy announced by the party in National Convention in 1868 and 1872, and triumphantly endorsed by the people at the polls, a policy which, while contributing to the public credit, has also enhanced the individual and collective prosperity of the American people, we favor such legislation as will make national banking free to all, under just and equal laws, based upon the policy of specie resumption at such time as is consistent with the material and industrial interests of the country, to the end that the volume of currency may be regulated by the natural laws of trade.

"*Resolved*, While all the necessary wants of the State Government should be supplied by a reasonable, just and uniform taxation, the labor and production of the commonwealth must not be crippled by the employment and maintenance of too many office-holders; hence, it becomes the duty of the Legislature to lessen the number of officials, and make such a revision of the laws of the State as to provide for a more economical administration of our State and county affairs. We are opposed to all official gratuities under the guise of an increase of pay or salaries during official terms.

"*Resolved*, That the peril of the Government lies not so much in high ambitions as in low dishonesties, and the pressing duty of the day is to secure honesty and purity in the public service. We commend the courage of the Republican party in instituting investigation of corruptions in office, sparing neither friends nor foes; and we demand such legislation as will bring to certain punishment any officer who, being entrusted with the charge of public funds, appropriates the same for his own use, or fails to properly account for them. Embezzlement is theft, and ought to be punished as such.

"*Resolved*, That all the railroad corporations of the State are the creatures of its Legislature, and it is the duty of that body to subject them to such wise and impartial enactments as will protect the people of the State from extortion, and will secure them transportation of products, merchandise and passengers at reasonable rates.

"*Resolved*, That a revision of the patent laws of the United States is imperatively demanded, so as to prevent a monopoly of useful inventions, and at the same time to give proper encouragement and remuneration to inventors.

"*Resolved*, That the present 'peace policy' of dealing with the Indians has failed to afford adequate protection to the frontier settlers, and we are in favor of transferring the Indian Bureau to the control of the War Department.

"*Resolved*, That we commend the action of Congress in repealing the act known as the back-pay law, and favor an amendment to the National Constitution which shall forever prohibit any Congress from increasing its own compensation.

"*Resolved*, That drunkenness is one of the greatest curses of modern society, demoralizing everything it touches, imposing fearful burdens of taxation upon the people, a fruitful breeder of pauperism and crime, and a worker of evil and only evil continually; hence we are in favor of such legislation, both general and local, as experience shall show to be most effectual in destroying this evil.

"*Resolved*, That we rejoice with the citizens residing on the Osage Ceded Lands over the late decision of the United States Circuit Court in their favor, and point to that decision as evidence that the rights of the people are safe in the hands of the courts.

"*Resolved*, That the unwritten law enacted by the example of the father of his country in declining a re-election to a third Presidential term, is as controlling as though it was incorporated in the National Constitution, and ought never to be violated.

"*Resolved*, That the public lands of the United States be sacredly held for the use and benefit of the actual settlers, and we condemn and disapprove of any further grants of the public domain to railroad or other corporations."

Ballot for Governor: Thomas A. Osborn 96, James C. Horton 51, W. H. Smallwood 42, George T. Anthony 12. *Second ballot:* Osborn 104, Horton 55, Smallwood 32, Anthony 12.

John C. Carpenter, James D. Snoddy, W. W. Sain, Benjamin F. Simpson and a few other delegates withdrew from the Convention.

Ballot for Lieutenant Governor: M. J. Salter 59, M. M. Murdock 52, E. N. Morrill 47, John H. Edwards 25, V. P. Wilson 6. *Second ballot:* Salter 62, Murdock 50, Morrill 38, Edwards 13. *Third ballot:* Salter 103, Morrill 50, Murdock 31, Edwards 2.

Ballot for Secretary of State: Thomas H. Cavanaugh 51, D. B. Emmert 35, O. J. Grover 32, W. Y. Drew 20, M. W. Coulter 20, W. Burlingame 6, James Scarborough 16. *Second ballot:* Cavanaugh 72, Emmert 41, Grover 34, Drew 15, Coulter 15, Scarborough 1. *Third ballot:* Cavanaugh 103, Grover 45, Emmert 38.

For Auditor: Daniel W. Wilder was renominated by acclamation.

Ballot for Treasurer: Samuel Lappin 98, John Francis 75.

Ballot for Attorney General: A. M. F. Randolph 107, J. B. Johnson 69.

Ballot for Superintendent of Public Instruction: John Fraser 93, H. B. Norton 87.

Ballot for Associate Justice: D. M. Valentine 106, A. L. Williams 47.

State Committee: Lucien Baker, Leavenworth; Nathan Price, Troy; John Guthrie, Topeka; E. A. Fisher, Lawrence; J. Jay Buck, Emporia; W. C. Webb, Fort Scott; J. L. Denison, Osage Mission; John K. Wright, Junction City; R. H. Ballinger, Larned; G. M. Waugh, Gardner; W. H. Whiteman, Columbus; F. G. Adams, Waterville; J M. Balderston, Wichita; Henry Inman, Leavenworth; A. J. Banta, Beloit. John Guthrie, Chairman; J. Jay Buck, Secretary.

AUGUST 28.—Gov. Osborn calls an extra session of the Legislature, to meet September 15th.

AUGUST 28.—Republican Congressional Convention, Third District, at Emporia. Called to order by H. C. Cross. Job Throckmorton, temporary Chairman, W. S. Jenkins, Secretary. *Committee on Credentials:* Lewis Hanback, J. E. Hudson, H. Whiteside, R. H. Nichols, J. R. Phenis, D. W. Finney. *Committee on Permanent Organization:* E. C. Manning, P. I. Bonebrake, J. W. Long, T. McCarthy, C. Cochran. *Committee on Resolutions:* Jacob Stotler, A. S. Redden, N. A. Perrill, T. M. James. Fifty-eight delegates present. *Officers:* President, William Sims; Vice President, Jacob Stotler; Secretaries, W. S. Jenkins, W. C. Tompkins. Three resolutions were adopted—endorsing the State platform and ticket; endorsing O. P. Morton's measure for the election of President and United States Senators by a direct vote of the people; asking an amendment to the homestead law to preserve their homes to actual settlers who may temporarily leave them. *Ballot for member of Congress:* Wm. R. Brown 20, Cyrus K. Holliday 14, P. B. Maxson 7, C. V. Eskridge 6, Harrison Kelly 6, W. P. Campbell 2, J. McDermott 2, H. C. Sluss 1. *Second ballot:* Brown 20, Holliday 15, Maxson 7, Eskridge 5, Kelly 6, Campbell 2, McDermott 2, Sluss 1. *Third ballot:* Brown 19, Holliday 15, Kelly 6, Maxson 7, Campbell 2, Eskridge 6, McDermott 2, Sluss 1. *Fourth ballot:* Brown 20, Holliday 15, Kelly 6, Maxson 7, Campbell 2, Eskridge 6, McDermott 2, Sluss 1. *Ninth ballot:* Brown 32, Holliday 17, Kelly 5, Campbell 4. *District Committee:* Jacob Stotler, of Lyon; A. G. Richardson, of Harvey; Duncan McDonald, of Morris; R. H. Nichols, of Howard; W. S. Jenkins, of Sedgwick; J. V. Admire, of Shawnee; Henry Booth, of Pawnee. It was voted that the Republican vote be made the basis of future conventions.

AUGUST 31.—John Francis declines the nomination for State Treasurer tendered by the Reform Committee. James E. Watson, of Lawrence, is placed on that ticket.

SEPTEMBER 1.—J. P. Bauserman declines the Reform nomination for Superintendent of Public Instruction.

SEPTEMBER 2.—Republican Congressional Convention, Second District, at Humboldt. Called to order by H. W. Cook. S. S. Benedict, of Wilson, temporary Chairman; F. B. McGill, of Labette, Secretary. Mr. Benedict received 41 votes, and Silas A. Day, of Bourbon, 22.

Committee on Credentials: T. B. Eldridge, G. W. Bowen, A. T. Lea, Watson Stewart, S. L. Patrick.

Committee on Permanent Organization: J. F. Broadhead, J. W. Wilson, H. C. Allen, I. H. Betton, J. S. Weaver.

Committee on Resolutions: J. H. Whison, Henry Shanklin, J. F. Hill, P. I. B. Ping, S. L. Self.

Officers: President, S. S. Benedict; Vice President, S. A. Day; Secretary, F. B. McGill; Assistant Secretary, W. A. Rankin.

First ballot for Member of Congress: Stephen A. Cobb 45, W. L. Simons 19. A speech was made by Colonel Cobb.

The following platform was adopted:

"Reaffirming the Republican National platforms of 1868 and 1872, and the Republican State platform of 1874, of Kansas, and believing that the Republican party has well performed its mission in the past, and will continue to be as it has been, the party of and for the people, trusted by and faithfully serving the people: therefore,

"*Resolved,* That we recognize that to be the true policy of the Government which shall harmonize all the diversified interests and pursuits necessarily existing in a country of such vast extent, and this can only be done by so directing legislation as to give a just protection and reward to every branch of our diversified industries, and we are in favor of giving precedence to those measures which shall recognize agricultural and mechanical pursuits as entitled to the most ample protection and the fullest development. We are in favor of the expenditure by Government of such sums as may be necessary to properly improve inland navigation, of such outlays as will secure cheap transportation to our seaboard, and provide such facilities as are needed at our nearest Gulf harbor for giving to the agriculturists of the West a port of shipment for their surplus products at that point, together with such encouragement to manufacturing interests as will bring producers and consumers in close proximity and establish a community of interest between them.

"*Resolved,* That the agricultural and commercial interests of the State of Kansas, and more especially of this Congressional District, imperatively demand the improvement of the harbor of Galveston, and the establishment of such means as will furnish cheap transportation for our products to that port, and thence to the great commercial marts of the world. We believe that to be the best commercial policy for Kansas which shall result in Galveston becoming her port of shipment and wholesale market, and we will cordially endorse and co-operate with our Congressional delegation in their efforts to shape legislation to this end.

"*Resolved,* That we oppose any continuation of the system inaugurated first by the Democratic party, of giving large grants of lands to railroad corporations. We are in favor of holding those in possession of corporate wealth and power to a strict conformity to law.

"*Resolved,* That we favor an amendment to the Constitution of the United States providing for the election of President and Vice President by a direct vote of the people without the intervention of the Electoral College, and also the election of United States Senators by the people of the State instead of by the Legislature.

"*Resolved,* That we most heartily approve of the policy of the Republicans in the radical departure the party has made from the practice of the Democratic party, by instituting investigations and exposing corruption in office, sparing neither political friend nor foe.

"*Resolved,* That the reduction of twenty-six millions of dollars in the estimated General Government expenses for the coming fiscal year meets our most hearty approval, and shows that on questions of retrenchment and economy the party is carrying out in good faith its pledges to the people; and that we regard as another evidence of the party's policy of economy and retrenchment the fact of the great reduction of the interest amount paid annually upon our national debt.

"*Resolved,* That while we realize the great benefits to the whole country arising from the railway system in its development of our vast resources, and while we accord to railway corporations their proper rights, we demand for and in behalf of the people a more reasonable tariff of freights and fares, and that the same shall be guaranteed by appropriate national legislation.

"*Resolved*, That the settlers on the Osage Ceded Lands are to be congratulated on the favorable issue of their contest for the possession of their homes, and that this result is a favorable augury of the future protection of settlers' rights, which we demand of our Congressional delegation to zealously and fearlessly guard, so as to prevent hereafter any recurrence of such contests.

"*Resolved*, That as citizens of Kansas we feel a just pride in the efforts and character of our present Congressional and Senatorial delegation, and believe that they have labored faithfully to protect and forward the truest interests of their constituents and State."

The following Congressional Committee was appointed: H. W. Cook, of Wyandotte county, Chairman; A. T. Lea, of Cherokee county, Secretary; T. Dwight Thacher, Douglas county; W. A. Johnson, Anderson county; L. Stillwell, Neosho county; F. R. Ogg, Johnson county; Daniel Grass, Montgomery county; George W. Findlay, Bourbon county; A. F. Sharpe, Franklin county; John S. Gilmore, Wilson county; F. B. McGill, Labette county.

SEPTEMBER 3.—Reform Congressional Convention of the Second District, at Ottawa. Called to order by William Simpson, of Bourbon, Chairman. U. F. Sargent, of Bourbon, Secretary. J. Frank McDowell, of Cherokee, and James Wilson, of Johnson, were elected Assistant Secretaries. The foregoing were made the permanent officers of the Convention. Speeches were made by A. M. York and W. W. Maltby. The Committee on Credentials reported twenty-five delegates present. Delegates from counties not fully represented were allowed to cast the full vote of their counties. The following list of the ballots for candidate for Congress is copied from the Paola Spirit:

Names of Candidates.	BALLOTS.													
	1st.	2d.	3d.	4th.	5th.	6th.	7th.	8th.	9th.	10th.	11th.	12th.	13th.	14th.
John R. Goodin......	12	18	20	20	27	21	27	26	48	38	27	36½	48	66
Hiram Stevens........	33	27	28	28	32	32	32	33	34	....	....	....	....	....
John Boyd..............	15	15	13	13	7	7	7	15	18	26	11	....	....	....
Sam'l A. Riggs........	9	11	6	20	20	17	17	7	....	....	....	....	....	....
H. C. McComas........	16	15	18	15	13	22	16	....	....	....	....	....	....	....
Sidney Clarke.........	14	13	14	3	....	....	....	14	....	....	....	....	....	....
M. E. Hudson.........	....	....	....	....	....	....	....	....	....	19	21	19	44	33
Chas. Robinson........	....	....	....	....	....	....	....	....	....	21	37	43½	6	....

The following Congressional Committee was appointed: A. M. York of Montgomery county, W. L. Parkinson of Franklin county, Sidney Clarke of Douglas county, W. W. Maltby of Johnson county, and P. H. Tiernan of Bourbon county.

The following resolution was adopted:

"*Resolved*, That it is the duty of Congress and the Legislature of our State to reduce the fees and salaries of public officers to such amounts as shall be a reasonable and fair compensation for the honest and faithful discharge of official duty, and we demand of Congress the unconditional repeal of the law properly and justly called the 'salary-grab law,' as applied to the President of the United States."

SEPTEMBER 4.—Reform Congressional Convention in the Third District, held at Emporia. The following is the official report, from the Topeka Record:

The Independent Reform Congressional Convention met at Emporia, as per adjournment. A. Harris, of Wichita, was chosen temporary Chairman, and J. V. Randolph, of Emporia, Secretary.

Committee on Permanent Organization: M. B. Ross, John Armstrong, O. P. Haughawout, G. W. Spencer, James Newlon.

Committee on Credentials: Samuel Dolman, David L. Payne, N. A. English, J. H. Watson, W. W. Cone.   •

Committee on Resolutions: J. J. Barker, Peter Bell, J. M. Miller, Frank Ross, A. Harris.

The following gentlemen were reported entitled to seats in the Convention: Fifty-sixth District, G. W. Spencer, S. D. Macdonald, J. C. Swayze; Fifty-seventh, Samuel Dolman, John Armstrong; Fifty-eighth, H. H. Wilcox, John Ritchie, John G. Otis; Sixty-first, Peter Bell, J. H. Noell; Sixty-second, O. P. Haughawout, D. Phillips, G. D. Carpenter; Sixty-eighth, W. B. Ross, J. H. Watson, J. A. Newlon; Sixty-ninth, J. M. Miller, Frank Ross, J. V. Randolph; Seventieth, W. W. Cone; Seventy-second, H. H. McArdell, John Maloy, E. S. Bertram; Seventy-third, Samuel N. Wood; Seventy-fourth, William Price; Seventy-sixth, N. A. English; Ninety-sixth, J. J. Barker, D. L. Payne.

Officers: A. Harris was elected President, and Peter Bell Secretary.

The Committee on Platform reported the following:

"*Resolved*, That the platform and principles enunciated by the State Convention of the Reform party, which met in Topeka on the 5th of August, meet our entire and hearty approbation.

"*Resolved*, That we announce our determination to support the nominees of that Convention, and declare our allegiance to that party of Reform."

Informal ballot for Congressman: J. K. Hudson 15, M. J. Firey 11, J. J. Barker 4, S. J. Crawford 2.

First ballot: J. K. Hudson 17, M. J. Firey 12, Samuel J. Crawford 7.

During the taking of the second ballot it was found that Joseph K. Hudson would be nominated, and a motion was made and carried to make the nomination unanimous.

The following Congressional District Committee was appointed: John G. Otis, Peter Bell, M. B. Ross, A. Harris, Mr. Edgerton.

SEPTEMBER 7.—State Fair opens in Leavenworth.

SEPTEMBER 8.—Six hundred Mennonites arrive in Topeka, and spend some time there before going to their homes in the Southwestern part of the State.

—Jacob Stotler appointed Postmaster at Emporia.

SEPTEMBER 10 and 11.—State Temperance Convention at Leavenworth. Rev. J. Boynton President, David C. Beach Secretary. There were 64 delegates, from nine counties.

The following nominations were made: Governor, Dudley C. Haskell; Lieutenant Governor, P. B. Maxson; Secretary of State, W. H. Robinson; Treasurer, William Fairchild; Auditor, C. B. Lines; Attorney General, A. A. Foote; Superintendent of Public Instruction, Mrs. M. J. Sharon; Associate Justice, D. M. Valentine.

Many of these candidates declined the nominations, and the ticket, as finally voted for at the polls, stood as follows: Governor, W. K. Marshall, of Lawrence; Lieutenant Governor, L. Brown, Girard, Crawford county; Secretary of State, W. H. Robinson, of Leavenworth; Auditor, David C. Beach, of Lawrence; Treasurer, William Fairchild, of Leavenworth; Attorner General, A. M. F. Randolph, of Coffey county; Superintendent of Public Instruction, Mrs. M. J. Sharon, of Marion county: Associate Justice Supreme Court, D. M. Valentine, Ottawa, Franklin county.

The following platform was adopted:

"The Temperance men and women of the State of Kansas, believing that the time has come when they ought to present a State ticket, composed of honest, temperate and capable men, hereby unite in the following declaration of principles:

"We are in favor of—

"1. The civil and political equality of all men and women.

"2. An economical administration of all departments of the Government.

"3. Political reform by selecting for office none but honest and capable men.

"4. The legal prohibition of the manufacture, importation and sale, for beverage use, of all intoxicating liquors.

"5. The fostering and improvement of our system of common schools.

"6. The speedy and exemplary punishment of all public officers guilty of embezzlement, the misappropriation of the public funds, or neglect to perform sworn duties.

"7. The immediate and complete protection of our exposed frontier from Indian outrages.

"8. The public assistance by all proper and legal means of the sufferers from the grasshoppers and drought in the newly-settled counties of the State.

"But we are inflexibly opposed—

"1. To all forms of repudiation, either State, National or municipal.

"2. To the appropriation of the public domain to the building of railroads."

SEPTEMBER 15.—Special Session of the Legislature. Ballot for Speaker: Thomas P. Fenlon 23, E. H. Funston 23, F. W. Potter 13. *Second ballot:* Fenlon 27, Funston 23, Potter 10. *Third ballot:* Fenlon 31, Funston 28.

Thanks were returned to Hon. Gerrit Smith for his recent donation for the relief of the destitute.

SEPTEMBER 22.—Adjournment of the Special Session of the Legislature. It passed a law requiring every corporation created by or existing under the laws of this State to keep a general office within the State; An act authorizing counties to issue bonds for relief purposes; An act authorizing the issue of bonds for the relief of the destitute people of the frontier, (only $7,500 in bonds were issued under this act); A law requiring county treasurers to make quarterly statements, and a few other acts.

SEPTEMBER 23.—Eleven hundred Mennonites arrive at Topeka.

OCTOBER.—Clay Centre is building a fine school-house.—Jewell county has 113 organized school districts.—Hutchinson has built a $14,000 school-house.—The Superintendent reports that "the graded schools of Wichita will compare favorably with any in the country."—Shawnee county has over 100 separate schools.—Alma has a graded school and a fine new building.—Wilson county had 75 schools in session in the fall and winter.—Miami county has expended $55,000 for schools this year.—The University has eleven instructors, and its students come from twenty-five counties.—The Agricultural College has thirteen instructors, and 208 students.—The Emporia Normal School has 236 students.—The Leavenworth Normal School has students from twenty-seven counties.—Baker University has 101

42

students; Rev. Dr. Joseph Denison is the President.—Mount St. Mary's Female Academy, Leavenworth, has 50 students; its buildings cost $85,500..

OCTOBER 5.—Seventh Annual Meeting of the Academy of Science, at Topeka.

OCTOBER.—John A. Anderson issues a Hand-book of the Agricultural College. It is an interesting and valuable book, containing 124 pages.

—N. A. Adams has been elected Secretary of the College Board.

OCTOBER 5.—Four Kansas railroads ship 122,914 head of Texas cattle in eight months.

OCTOBER 14.—The Mennonites buy 100,000 acres of land of the A. T. & S. F. Railroad Company, all lying north of Florence, Peabody, Walton, Newton, Halstead, Burrton, and Hutchinson.

OCTOBER 24.—C. G. Hawley appointed Postmaster at Girard.

OCTOBER 26.—J. C. Martin and W. E. Timmons start the Chase County Courant.

OCTOBER 27.—Ninth Annual Meeting of the State Sabbath School Association, at Atchison. President, S. B. Riggs, of Emporia; F. T. Ingalls and Henry Clarkson, Secretaries; Thomas J. White, Reporter.

NOVEMBER.—The Third Annual Report of the State Board of Agriculture contains tabular statistics from which the following facts are obtained: National Banks in the State, 26; capital, $1,983,000; deposits for the last six months, $2,994,330. Other Banks in the State, 86; deposits, $2,399,616; capital, $1,588,006.

"The following list of manufacturing establishments has been returned to the county boards during the year:

	No.	Capital.
Water-power saw mills	15	$54,272
Steam saw mills	50	196,522
Water-power flour mills	80	1,061,195
Steam flour mills	59	1,044,910
Water-power saw and grist mills	13	71,500
Steam-power saw and grist mills	14	63,892
Furniture and cabinet factories	13	157,820
Foundries and rolling mills	5	195,000
Woollen factories	6	111,600
Miscellaneous, embracing oil factories, cheese factories, gypsum, soap, and carriage factories	50	567,915
Total	305	$3,524,627

"This is exclusive of cigar manufactories, breweries, machine shops of the different railroads, and all the minor industries."

The following church statistics are given:

Denominations.	Organizations....	Membership	Church Edifices...	Value of Church Property.
Presbyterian	161	6,604	74	$294,855
Congregational	113	3,831	48	238,500
Baptist	229	9,789	53	226,900
United Presbyterian	39	1,313	14	49,200
Methodist	621	22,096	96	339,400
Episcopal	34	1,136	22	172,000
Catholic	191	32,311	72	415,200

The book has been prepared by Alfred Gray and George T. Anthony. The New York Times says it is the best Agricultural Report ever issued in this country.

NOVEMBER 3.—Annual election.

VOTE FOR GOVERNOR, LIEUT. GOVERNOR, AND SECRETARY OF STATE.

Counties.	GOVERNOR.			LIEUT. GOVERNOR.			SEC'Y OF STATE.		
	Thos. A. Osborn.	James C. Casey.	W. R. Marshall.	M. J. Salter.	E. Harrington.	L. Brown.	T. H. Cavanaugh.	Nelson Abbott.	W. H. Robinson.
Allen	541	736	23	718	595	2	666	619	5
Anderson	523	460	20	575	438	7	579	429	8
Atchison	1,594	1,294	13	1,614	1,291	...	1,624	1,273	3
Barbour	98	80	...	99	79	...	99	79	...
Barton	304	170	...	305	170	...	308	168	...
Bourbon	1,117	1,241	140	1,263	1,189	92	1,271	1,171	95
Brown	717	628	16	765	569	...	767	588	4
Butler	607	298	625	861	272	384	865	268	393
Chase	201	513	15	264	461	11	228	423	50
Cherokee	682	878	64	683	885	49	676	888	50
Clay	771	304	42	781	302	38	777	303	38
Cloud	875	180	...	911	158	...	912	158	...
Coffey	722	565	4	785	549	3	788	505	3
Cowley	1,000	494	22	942	541	...	1,010	456	5
Crawford	350	689	150	376	671	140	376	676	133
Davis	452	328	...	469	301	...	491	297	...
Dickinson	712	269	6	737	253	3	736	249	2
Doniphan	1,457	978	3	1,459	930	3	1,465	924	3
Douglas	1,446	1,618	169	1,534	1,610	110	1,538	1,605	109
Ellis	230	19	...	229	19	...	232	19	...
Ellsworth	357	9	...	369	...	...	368	...	...
Edwards	71	1	...	73	...	...	73	...	...
Ford	135	1	...	135	2	...	136	...	...
Franklin	798	1,117	23	928	1,032	10	931	1,021	16
Greenwood	646	489	17	732	443	...	733	440	...
Harvey	559	57	14	596	31	4	598	29	2
Howard	1,881	719	...	1,877	694	...	1,916	689	...
Jackson	633	497	...	634	500	...	642	490	...
Jefferson	869	1,064	43	915	1,043	27	92	944	82
Jewell	753	289	9	904	158	...	917	144	6
Johnson	1,012	1,528	84	1,064	1,490	66	1,086	1,453	71
Kingman	113	19	...	113	19	...	113	19	...
Labette	1,228	730	77	1,407	585	46	1,269	706	61
Leavenworth	3,076	1,247	128	2,378	1,889	122	2,039	2,224	124
Lincoln	356	134	...	357	134	...	354	135	...
Linn	702	950	180	798	929	3	807	922	125
Lyon	880	635	23	955	547	...	1,028	528	...
Marion	548	228	...	592	194	...	594	191	4
Marshall	1,348	528	33	1,301	505	20	1,374	504	22
McPherson	661	321	...	672	311	...	660	314	...
Miami	855	1,318	57	975	1,295	19	970	1,265	20
Mitchell	635	375	...	668	353	...	667	350	...
Montgomery	1,255	1,106	...	1,294	1,085	...	1,291	1,010	...
Morris	548	415	...	569	395	...	571	395	...
Norton	107	12	...	124	...	...	125	1	...
Nemaha	794	573	2	833	535	1	834	536	1
Neosho	557	1,178	16	1,090	739	3	1,074	725	4
Osage	972	752	45	1,068	720	1	1,082	687	1
Osborne	283	42	1	361	24	...	367	24	...
Ottawa	731	26	7	739	17	7	742	16	6
Pratt	39	43	...	40	42	...	40	42	...
Pawnee	110	64	...	110	65	...	107	64	...
Phillips	145	193	...	410	2	...	417	1	...
Pottawatomie	863	692	3	879	664	...	911	114	...
Reno	657	54	8	719	21	...	720	19	...
Republic	1,012	20	22	1,044	12	5	1,049	12	5
Rice	162	93	39	256	17	...	252	10	35
Riley	692	521	12	907	322	12	909	310	16
Rooks	92	21	...	92	22	...	93	21	...
Russell	257	...	10	269	...	...	270	...	10
Saline	795	285	...	762	336	...	844	239	...
Sedgwick	923	508	...	944	492	...	983	460	...
Shawnee	1,602	950	26	1,748	881	14	1,756	796	28
Smith	300	130	...	454	8	...	473	6	...
Sumner	480	439	...	485	433	...	499	400	...
Wabaunsee	506	242	...	533	237	...	539	227	...
Wallace	77	...	...	77	...	...	77	...	...
Washington	743	532	...	752	524	...	754	507	...
Wilson	592	820	28	869	606	3	868	601	3
Woodson	274	411	54	515	248	1	485	270	1
Wyandotte	706	1,181	4	874	1,043	1	891	1,008	1
Total	48,594	35,301	2,277	52,637	32,927	1,207	52,633	31,967	1,546

VOTE FOR AUDITOR, TREASURER, AND ATTORNEY GENERAL.

Counties.	AUDITOR.			TREASURER.			ATT'Y GEN'L.	
	D. W. Wilder	G. P. Smith	D. C. Beach	Samuel Lappin	James E. Watson	Wm. Fairchild	A. M. F. Randolph	J. R. Hallowell
Allen	675	606	2	538	715	....	632	681
Anderson	606	399	15	541	465	14	583	434
Atchison	1,626	1,297	3	1,636	1,274	3	1,610	1,307
Barbour	99	79	....	99	79	....	99	79
Barton	308	170		299	173	....	307	171
Bourbon	1,344	1,119	88	1,226	1,211	107	1,361	1,177
Brown	760	598	5	707	635	6	760	243
Butler	919	259	339	845	234	391	1,253	280
Chase	279	444	12	116	599	15	275	394
Cherokee	686	885	49	664	851	49	598	996
Clay	795	292	37	787	299	38	820	304
Cloud	909	159		898	173	....	909	154
Coffey	797	514	3	725	574	3	879	445
Cowley	966	536	11	744	728	14	970	545
Crawford	384	675	130	369	685	131	506	682
Davis	503	287	....	453	325	....	489	300
Dickinson	741	249	2	722	258	2	782	248
Doniphan	1,461	937	3	1,477	908	....	1,462	929
Douglas	1,552	1,604	119	507	2,663	81	1,675	1,594
Ellis	231	19	....	232	10	....	231	19
Ellsworth	370	....		358	....		370	....
Edwards	73			73			73	
Ford	135	2		134	2		134	2
Franklin	950	1,003	11	790	1,137	12	942	1,029
Greenwood	738	431		714	461	....	733	438
Harvey	600	3	2	580	39	6	600	32
Howard	1,919	692	....	1,909	697	....	1,918	690
Jackson	638	497		610	518	....	637	503
Jefferson	939	1,023	28	809	1,033	36	942	1,042
Jewell	881	158	....	886	181	6	921	146
Johnson	993	1,484	79	957	1,546	76	1,130	1,491
Kingman	113	19		108	24	....	113	19
Labette	1,320	647	57	1,098	867	61	1,335	710
Leavenworth	2,454	1,698	121	2,157	2,021	163	2,094	2,219
Lincoln	358	133		355	135	....	357	133
Linn	811	921	116	784	939	127	944	903
Lyon	1,063	525	2	817	718	24	1,032	446
Marion	596	190	4	465	300	5	602	189
Marshall	1,412	491	20	1,311	574	20	1,415	504
McPherson	674	315	....	673	316	....	671	317
Miami	983	1,285	18	932	1,312	28	249	1,297
Mitchell	667	349	....	609	356	....	665	352
Montgomery	1,217	1,088		1,212	1,169	....	1,273	1,112
Morris	571	396		430	511	....	570	389
Norton	106	....		125	....		126	....
Nemaha	839	533	1	749	570	3	835	534
Neosho	981	857	5	583	1,239	5	970	873
Osage	1,096	695	2	848	941	3	1,087	707
Osborne	365	23		192	192	....	368	24
Ottawa	745	11	6	739	16	7	752	12
Pratt	40	39	....	37	43	....	40	42
Pawnee	110	61	....	103	70	....	110	64
Phillips	417	2	1	396	7	....	419	....
Pottawatomie	889	681	....	822	734	....	995	641
Reno	720	15	....	709	16	11	719	18
Republic	1,048	11	5	1,044	14	5	1,053	11
Rice	253	11	4	251	26	4	297	11
Riley	918	313	10	727	489	16	920	318
Rooks	93	22	....	92	21	....	92	22
Russell	275	....	10	275	....	10	285	....
Saline	767	332	....	712	387	....	728	344
Sedgwick	950	481	....	912	517	....	962	478
Shawnee	1,787	854	12	1,450	1,136	22	1,767	882
Smith	478	1	....	451	11	....	480	....
Sumner	499	424	....	474	445	....	488	434
Wabaunsee	539	232	....	521	246	....	535	231
Wallace	77	....		77	....		77	....
Washington	750	524	....	749	531	....	745	525
Wilson	936	519	4	760	699	12	870	609
Woodson	499	267	1	286	460	10	484	284
Wyandotte	882	1,029	2	843	1,064	1	887	1,028
Total	53,175	32,448	1,339	47,333	37,589	1,530	52,881	33,137

VOTE FOR SUP'T OF PUBLIC INSTRUCTION, AND ASSOCIATE JUSTICE.

Counties.	SUP'T PUB. INSTRUCTION.			ASS'TE JUSTICE.	
	John Fraser	*W. B. Christopher*	*Mrs. M. J. Sharon*	*D. M. Valentine*	*W. P. Douthitt*
Allen	623	688	6	618	693
Anderson	586	434	....	565	447
Atchison	1,599	1,314	2	1,612	1,307
Barbour	98	79	....	100	79
Barton	306	171	....	307	171
Bourbon	1,262	1,177	115	1,365	1,196
Brown	763	598	3	761	602
Butler	600	269	396	1,239	290
Chase	271	455	10	271	490
Cherokee	680	853	56	699	911
Clay	778	291	53	826	298
Cloud	911	155	....	912	159
Coffey	801	503	3	811	507
Cowley	923	568	5	975	540
Crawford	380	676	128	509	678
Davis	504	285	....	490	299
Dickinson	744	231	....	743	247
Doniphan	1,459	932	3	1,462	933
Douglas	1,735	1,434	95	1,570	1,696
Ellis	235	9	....	230	20
Ellsworth	370	....	....	370	....
Edwards	73	....	....	73	....
Ford	135	2	....	138	....
Franklin	947	1,006	13	1,030	870
Greenwood	736	435	....	734	440
Harvey	598	30	3	598	33
Howard	1,911	688	....	1,920	687
Jackson	638	502	....	635	504
Jefferson	926	1,026	31	893	1,086
Jewell	913	....	5	920	146
Johnson	1,104	1,469	59	1,135	1,494
Kingman	113	19	....	113	19
Labette	1,201	655	59	1,342	696
Leavenworth	2,060	2,197	120	2,028	2,212
Lincoln	337	132	....	359	132 ·
Linn	801	914	137	936	917
Lyon	1,032	526	....	1,027	554
Marion	602	182	5	534	255
Marshall	1,399	495	24	1,425	499
McPherson	671	315	....	673	316
Miami	997	1,274	16	998	1,287
Mitchell	667	350	....	670	349
Montgomery	1,290	1,082	....	1,286	1,084
Morris	561	398	....	569	398
Norton	125	....	....	125	....
Nemaha	835	535	....	842	531
Neosho	984	861	1	970	870
Osage	1,086	701	3	1,067	729
Osborne	367	22	....	389	3
Ottawa	744	12	6	750	14
Pratt	40	42	....	40	43
Pawnee	111	64	....	111	62
Phillips	418	....	....	418	....
Pottawatomie	915	648	....	863	684
Reno	722	19	....	709	28
Republic	1,049	11	4	1,053	10
Rice	155	12	143	300	11
Riley	905	314	19	928	311
Rooks	93	21	....	92	22
Russell	270	....	10	284	....
Saline	765	323	....	759	347
Sedgwick	952	484	....	953	485
Shawnee	1,759	884	11	1,484	1,179
Smith	481	....	....	482	....
Sumner	490	431	....	485	436
Wabaunsee	515	239	....	526	241
Wallace	77	....	....	77	....
Washington	758	520	....	745	530
Wilson	874	603	3	878	584
Woodson	484	279	3	483	286
Wyandotte	894	1,016	8	883	1,029
Total	52,098	32,860	1,558	53,172	33,147

VOTE FOR MEMBERS OF THE SENATE.

District.	Counties.	Names of Candidates.	Vote of County	Total	Maj. or Plur.
1...	Doniphan	C. G. Bridges	1,439		505
	Doniphan	John L. Blair	934		
2...	Atchison	George W. Gillespie	1,739		432
	Atchison	S. P. Griffin	1,436		131
	Atchison	George W. Glick	1,307		
	Atchison	E. R. Brown	1,305		
	Brown	J. M. Miller	726		
3...	Nemaha	J. M. Miller	759	1,485	266
	Brown	Joseph Cracraft	630		
	Nemaha	Joseph Cracraft	589	1,219	
	Marshall	Boaz W. Williams	1,124		
4...	Washington	Boaz W. Williams	535	1,659	242
	Marshall	Charles Coddington	717		
	Washington	Charles Coddington	699	1,416	
	Jackson	J. S. Hopkins	456		
5...	Pottawatomie	J. S. Hopkins	856	1,312	29
	Jackson	James McLellan	659		
	Pottawatomie	James McLellan	617	1,276	
6...	Jefferson	J. B. Schaeffer	1,042		92
	Jefferson	Val. Brown	950		
	Leavenworth	J. A. Halderman	2,551		472
	Leavenworth	J. P. Bauserman	2,146		243
7...	Leavenworth	T. L. Johnson	2,167		298
	Leavenworth	J. B. Dutton	1,769		
	Leavenworth	E. Stillings	2,079		
	Leavenworth	J. C. Stone	1,903		
8...	Wyandotte	Byron Judd	979		47
	Wyandotte	H. W. Cook	932		
9...	Johnson	W. W. Maltby	1,410		268
	Johnson	V. R. Ellis	1,142		
10...	Miami	William Jones	1,276		271
	Miami	E. H. Topping	1,005		
11...	Linn	R. B. McMillan	979		161
	Linn	James D. Snoddy	816		
12...	Bourbon	J. W. Bainum	1,224		277
	Bourbon	C. W. Libby	947		
	Bourbon	D. M. Davis	209		
13...	Crawford	D. M. Davis	574	783	78
	Bourbon	E. Holt	127		
	Crawford	E. Holt	578	705	
14...	Cherokee	E. C. Wells	872		104
	Cherokee	H. R. Hubbard	768		
15...	Labette	J. H. Crichton	1,105		241
	Labette	J. M. Mahr	831		
	Labette	M. W. Reynolds	33		
16...	Neosho	Walter L. Simons	1,011		169
	Neosho	G. W. Spurgeon	840		
	Anderson	Thomas Bartlett	509		
17...	Allen	Thomas Bartlett	798	1,307	292
	Anderson	Louis Walker	504		
	Allen	Louis Walker	511	1,015	
18...	Franklin	W. L. Parkinson	1,211		455
	Franklin	James Hanway	756		
	Douglas	J. C. Horton	1,821		102
19...	Douglas	Charles Robinson	1,719		396
	Douglas	H. L. Moore	1,594		
	Douglas	Jeremiah Boynton	1,323		
20...	Shawnee	William Sims	2,082		1,589
	Shawnee	M. J. Alkire	493		
	Osage	C. S. Martin	1,134		
21...	Wabaunsee	C. S. Martin	402	1,536	544
	Osage	T. K. Thompson	637		
	Wabaunsee	T. K. Thompson	354	991	
	Coffey	D. W. Finney	488		
	Woodson	D. W. Finney	444	932	275
22...	Coffey	C. B. Butler	477		
	Woodson	C. B. Butler	180	657	
	Coffey	Charles Stoeltzing	347		
	Woodson	Charles Stoeltzing	141	488	
	Wilson	W. A. Peffer	709		
23...	Montgomery	W. A. Peffer	1,260	1,975	153
	Wilson	M. A. Brooks	724		
	Montgomery	M. A. Brooks	1,096	1,820	

VOTE FOR MEMBERS OF THE SENATE—Concluded.

District.	Counties.	Names of Candidates.	Vote of County.	Total.	Maj. or Plur.
24...	Greenwood	Wm. Martindale	689		
	Lyon	Wm. Martindale	1,062	1,751	774
	Greenwood	M. J. Firey	478		
	Lyon	M. J. Firey	498	976	
25...	Edwards	H. C. St. Clair	73		
	Ford	H. C. St. Clair	137		
	Pawnee	H. C. St. Clair	111		
	Barbour	H. C. St. Clair	178		
	Butler	H. C. St. Clair	1,355		
	Cowley	H. C. St. Clair	914		
	Harvey	H. C. St. Clair	618		
	Howard	H. C. St. Clair	2,011		
	Reno	H. C. St Clair	753		
	Sedgwick	H. C. St. Clair	954		
	Sumner	H. C. St. Clair	597		
	Kingman	H. C. St. Clair	131		
	Pratt	H. C. St. Clair	78	7,900	6,208
	Pawnee	R. B. Saffold	64		
	Butler	R. B. Saffold	177		
	Cowley	R. B. Saffold	591		
	Howard	R. B. Saffold	549		
	Sedgwick	R. B. Saffold	480		
	Sumner	R. B. Saffold	318	1,691	
26...	Chase	Samuel R. Peters	327		
	Marion	Samuel R. Peters	512		
	Morris	Samuel R. Peters	459	1,298	91
	Chase	B. Pinckney	407		
	Marion	B. Pinckney	293		
	Morris	B. Pinckney	506	1,206	
27...	Davis	H. P. Dow	559		
	Dickinson	H. P. Dow	671		
	Riley	H. P. Dow	869	2,099	1,216
	Davis	John Davis	233		
	Dickinson	John Davis	320		
	Riley	John Davis	325	878	
28...	Rooks	Horace Cooper	114		
	Clay	Horace Cooper	769		
	Cloud	Horace Cooper	745		
	Jewell	Horace Cooper	890		
	Lincoln	Horace Cooper	299		
	Mitchell	Horace Cooper	694		
	Norton	Horace Cooper	37		
	Ottawa	Horace Cooper	493		
	Osborne	Horace Cooper	375		
	Phillips	Horace Cooper	359		
	Republic	Horace Cooper	510		
	Smith	Horace Cooper	481	5,766	3,991
	Clay	R. P. West	59		
	Cloud	R. P. West	308		
	Jewell	R. P. West	176		
	Lincoln	R. P. West	123		
	Mitchell	R. P. West	246		
	Norton	R. P. West	27		
	Ottawa	R. P. West	195		
	Osborne	R. P. West	5		
	Phillips	R. P. West	100		
	Republic	R. P. West	491		
	Smith	R. P. West	41	1,771	
29...	Russell	Solomon Stephens	232		
	Saline	Solomon Stephens	818		
	McPherson	Solomon Stephens	708		
	Ellsworth	Solomon Stephens	370		
	Ellis	Solomon Stephens	238		
	Wallace	Solomon Stephens	78		
	Rice	Solomon Stephens	277		
	Barton	Solomon Stephens	434	3,205	2,888
	Saline	James H. Snead	275	275	

VOTE FOR MEMBERS OF THE HOUSE OF REPRESENTATIVES.

District.	Counties.	Names of Candidates.	Votes....	Maj. or Plur...
1	Doniphan	Giles A. Briggs	561	118
		F. J. Close	443	
2		M. T. Landon	365	23
		R. S. Hinkley	342	
3		John L. Motter	230	57
		T. H. Vorhies	173	
		A. J. Mowry	135	
		Jos. Randolph	84	
4	Atchison	Wm. C. Smith	554	26
		Edward Fleischer	528	
5		T. B. Tomlinson	478	68
		Samuel Stoner	410	
6		A. J. Sutton	441	19
		Alex. Walker	422	
7	Brown	M. C. Willis	699	58
		Jos. D. Hardy	641	
8	Nemaha	G. W. Brown	365	13
		A. P. Herrol	351	
9		S. P. Conrad	616	598
		A. Baujons	12	
10	Marshall	C. J. Brown	1,300	679
		M. D. Tenney	621	
11	Washington	J. W. Bell	725	169
		Clinton Hogue	556	
12	Riley	George Pickett	645	65
		C. L. Wilkins	578	
13	Pottawatomie	J. S. Codding	433	8
		E. McKee	425	
		P. McClosky	62	
14		P. Marvel	367	89
		Dr. Little	227	
15	Jackson	J. W. Williams	618	132
		B. H. Bradshaw	486	
16	Jefferson	Matt. Edmonds	321	24
		N. Simmons	297	
17		W. B. Spurlock	225	27
		J. N. O. P. Wood	198	
		H. C. Mains	197	
18		J. P. Barnes	392	46
		E. D. Russell	346	
19	Leavenworth	H. D. Mackay	347	149
		Wm. D. Matthews	198	
20		John C. Vaughan	267	97
		R. A. Lovitt	170	
21		Jas. F. Legate	440	209
		H. C. Keller	188	
		George A. Eddy	43	
22		F. P. Fitzwilliam	392	170
		Wm. O. Gould	222	
23		H. C. Squires	334	40
		Wm. Housley	294	
24		M. R. Mitchell	427	126
		C. R. Jennison	301	
25		Crawford Moore	360	88
		E. E. Hollenbeck	272	
26	Wyandotte	Sanford Haff	492	46
		J. L. Pritchard	446	
		H. N. Kerr	271	
27		W. J. Buchan	401	126
		John B. Scroggs	275	
28	Johnson	D. G. Campbell	334	59
		J. R. Thorp	275	
		David Warren	161	
		James W. Noel	102	
29		R. E. Stevenson	540	46
		George Black	494	
30		Z. Meredith	355	27
		Geo. T. Rogers	328	
31	Miami	T. E. Smith	587	27
		L. Bradbury	560	
32		F. M. Fain	654	195
		S. Underhill	459	
33	Linn	A. C. Dodd	404	30

VOTE FOR MEMBERS OF THE HOUSE OF REPRESENTATIVES—Continued.

District.	Counties.	Names of Candidates.	Votes.	Maj. or Plur.
33	Linn (concluded)............	Harvey Smith	374	
34	....	H. Robinson	289	77
		C. M. Vertrus......................	211	
		Walker Walker	1	
35	....	O. E. Morse........................	293	36
		H. P. Clay.........................	257	
36	Bourbon	John Raney.........................	397	102
		A. K. Hull	295	
37	....	A. Goucher	344	16
		Jacob Brenner	328	
38	....	E. M. Hulett.......................	552	63
		W. C. Webb.........................	489	
		J. M. Hiatt........................	136	
39	Crawford.....................	W. H. Merriwether..................	280	25
		E. P. Pomeroy......................	259	
40	....	George W. Brown	398	198
		Stephen Alberty....................	199	
41	Cherokee	H. H. Angell.......................	611	205
		C. Spencer	406	
42	....	W. E. Cowan........................	352	111
		L. T. Stowell	241	
43	Labette......................	J. J. Wood.........................	618	60
		William Dick.......................	558	
44	....	R. W. Wright	401	6
		J. C. McKnight.....................	395	
45	Neosho	C. F. Stauber......................	473	79
		Robert Brogan......................	394	
		Louis A. Reese.....................	110	
46	....	A. P. Gibson	486	192
		Frank Bacon	291	
47	Allen	E. H. Funston......................	402	108
		G. B. Inge.........................	291	
48	....	R. V Blair.........................	367	122
		G. W. Moon.........................	215	
49	Anderson.....................	H. Clay Reppert	631	251
		A. G. West	380	
50	Franklin.....................	P. P. Elder........................	598	232
		Jasper Robinson....................	366	
51	....	J. N. Foster.......................	549	114
		S. Topping.........................	435	
52	Douglas......................	T. D. Thacher......................	573	271
		H. H. Howard	278	
53	....	D. C. Haskell......................	565	195
		William B. Kennedy.................	352	
54	....	T. E. Tabor........................	419	124
		H. C. Fisher.......................	294	
55	....	L. H. Tuttle.......................	387	142
		J. M. Still	244	
56	Shawnee...........	James Burgess	393	136
		James Stearns	257	
		G. C. Clemens......................	195	
57	....	John Martin........................	1,035	1,031
58	....	F. R. Foster.......................	482	249
		F. P. Firey........................	233	
59	Osage	S. B. Bradford.....................	516	139
		Harrison Dubois....................	377	
60	....	F. Donnelly........................	503	131
		L. R. Adams	359	
61	Coffey.......................	B. L. Kingsbury....................	761	264
		J. F. Jones........................	497	
62	Woodson......................	A. B. Mann	461	157
		David Askern.......................	302	
63	Wilson.......................	S. S. Benedict	790	141
		C. J. Wright	644	
64	Montgomery...................	William Huston.....................	574	133
		A. J. Hersey.......................	441	
		L. Gladfelter	173	
65	....	L. A. Walker.......................	430	43
		B. M. Armstrong....................	353	
		James DeLong.......................	387	
66	Howard.......................	Edward Jaquins	1,521	370
		T. B. Rice.........................	1,151	
67	Greenwood....................	A. W. Scott........................	553	20

VOTE FOR MEMBERS OF THE HOUSE OF REPRESENTATIVES — Continued.

District.	Counties.	Names of Candidates.	Votes.	Maj. or Plur.
67	Greenwood (concluded)...	Wm. McBrown	533	
		J. P. Hillyard	94	
68	Lyon	Geo. Johnston	529	211
		S. J. Crawford	318	
69		John W. Loy	622	618
70	Wabaunsee	S. A. Baldwin	439	104
		Wm. Mitchell	335	
71	Davis	C. G. Cox	507	233
		H. C. McCarty	272	
72	Morris	F. M. Hooton	424	
		John Maloy	424	
		J. P. Burkhart	121	
73	Chase	S. M. Wood	446	162
		O. H. Drinkwater	283	
74	Butler	Jos. L. Ferguson	999	451
		Abram Leidy	547	
75	Cowley	Thos. R. Bryan	818	115
		A. S. Williams	703	
76	Sedgwick	E. B. Allen	954	496
		W. T. Jewett	458	
77	Marion	R. C. Bates	415	70
		F. Doster	345	
78	McPherson	A. W. Smith	677	369
		B. Evans	307	
79	Dickinson	Orrin A. Root	637	290
		W. H. Sutphen	324	
80	Clay	S. D. Beegle	441	29
		George Taylor	412	
		J. S. Harris	244	
81	Republic	W. H. Pilkenton	993	965
		W. H. Settles	12	
82	Cloud	C. K. Wells	736	426
		W. E. Reid	310	
83	Ottawa	R. D. Mobley	271	31
		J. W. McLaren	240	
		John Henry	164	
		D. M. Dunn	76	
		A. B. Murch	30	
84	Saline	G. C. Lockwood	1,074	1,071
85	Ellsworth	G. A. Atwood	190	6
		H. V. Faris	184	
86	Lincoln	James B. Goff	279	60
		Volney Ball	219	
87	Mitchell	H. C. Babcock	513	24
		W. T. S. May	480	
88	Jewell	D. L. Palmer	425	2
		S. E. Wilson	423	
		N. Gishweler	214	
89	Ellis	W. N. Morphy	144	40
		Hill P. Wilson	103	
90	Wallace	C. W. N. Ruggles	80	80
91	Rice	S. M. Wirt	185	67
		S. B. Terry	118	
92	Sumner	W. H. Carter	508	103
		J. W. Hamilton	405	
93	Osborne	S. B. Farwell	368	349
94	Reno	Thos. T. Taylor	742	742
95	Smith	C. S. Aldrich	293	103
		G. M. Edson	183	
96	Harvey	J. E. Duncan	641	637
97	Barton	G. L. Brinkman	320	156
		W. H. Odell	164	
98	Russell	A. B. Cornell	150	10
		E. A. Church	140	
99	Phillips	F. H. Jewett	218	12
		D. L. Smith	206	
100	Norton	C. C. Vance	100	42
		P. Hanson	58	
101	Pawnee	J. M. Miller	112	50
		Wm. White	62	
102	Rooks	F. McNulty	62	11
		Samuel S Boggs	51	
103	Ford	R. H. Wright	140	140

VOTE FOR MEMBERS OF THE HOUSE OF REPRESENTATIVES—Concluded.

District.	Counties.	Names of Candidates.	Votes	Maj. or Plur.
104	Barbour	H. E. Vantrees	95	14
		M. W. Sutton	81	
105	Harper			
106	Ness			
107	Comanche			
108	Kingman	W. H. Child	105	78
		A. R. Burgess	27	
109	Pratt	J. M. Moore	81	81
110	Edwards	C. L. Hubbs	46	18
		A. L. Kendall	28	

VOTE FOR MEMBER OF CONGRESS FROM THE FIRST CONGRESSIONAL DISTRICT.

COUNTIES OF THE FIRST DISTRICT.	Wm. A. Phillips	M. J. Parrott	N. Green
Atchison	1,504	1,268	142
Brown	755	597	6
Cloud	783	256	22
Clay	962	114	39
Davis	484	303	5
Dickinson	739	244	3
Doniphan	1,412	978	3
Ellis	228	18	2
Ellsworth	344	11	17
Graham			
Jewell	829	151	94
Jackson	434	425	275
Jefferson	898	986	81
Leavenworth	1,708	2,581	200
Lincoln	345	146	
Marshall	1,040	379	469
Mitchell	640	380	3
Nemaha	780	506	76
Norton	89	38	
Osborne	371	15	5
Ottawa	471	63	195
Phillips	291	47	81
Pottawatomie	929	590	24
Republic	961	26	83
Riley	957	212	68
Rooks	90	23	
Russell	265	13	
Saline	651	329	90
Smith	417	36	18
Washington	710	488	73
Total	20,087	11,223	2,074
Majority	6,777		

VOTE FOR MEMBER OF CONGRESS FROM THE SECOND CONGRESSIONAL
DISTRICT.

COUNTIES OF THE SECOND DISTRICT.	J. R. Goodin.	S. A. Cobb.
Allen	737	574
Anderson	425	564
Bourbon	1,232	1,321
Cherokee	878	742
Crawford	715	457
Douglas	1,646	1,596
Franklin	1,077	882
Johnson	1,561	1,028
Labette	749	1,300
Linn	962	888
Montgomery	1,066	1,313
Miami	1,286	983
Neosho	1,020	822
Wilson	585	883
Wyandotte	1,026	887
Total	14,965	14,240
Majority	713	

VOTE FOR MEMBER OF CONGRESS FROM THE THIRD CONGRESSIONAL
DISTRICT.

COUNTIES OF THE THIRD DISTRICT.	W. R. Brown.	J. K. Hudson.
Barbour	104	73
Barton	273	206
Butler	751	771
Comanche		
Chase	251	483
Coffey	733	587
Cowley	914	644
Edwards	73	
Ford	132	3
Greenwood	693	480
Harper		
Harvey	601	37
Howard	1,659	944
Kingman	123	9
Lyon	884	693
Marion	429	354
McPherson	637	362
Morris	506	461
Ness		
Osage	1,028	767
Pawnee	106	69
Pratt	43	39
Reno	695	45
Rice	226	68
Sedgwick	842	599
Shawnee	1,521	1,139
Sumner	462	456
Wabaunsee	498	272
Wallace *		
Woodson	397	371
Total	14,581	9,932
Majority	4,645	

* William A. Phillips received 77 votes.

VOTE FOR JUDGES OF THE DISTRICT COURT IN THE SIXTH, EIGHTH, AND ELEVENTH JUDICIAL DISTRICTS.

District.	County.	Names of Candidates.	Vote of County.	Total.	Maj.
6	Bourbon	W. C. Stewart	1,197	1,197	1,197
8	Davis	James H. Austin	790		
	Dickinson	James H. Austin	1,008		
	Morris	James H. Austin	953		
	Ottawa	James H. Austin	758		
	Riley	James H. Austin	1,231	4,740	4,733
11	Montgomery	B. W. Perkins	1,438		
	Labette	B. W. Perkins	1,036		
	Cherokee	B. W. Perkins	823		
	Crawford	B. W. Perkins	768	4,065	1,042
	Montgomery	J. D. McCue	951		
	Labette	J. D. McCue	891		
	Cherokee	J. D. McCue	798		
	Crawford	J. D. McCue	377	3,017	

NOVEMBER 6.—J. H. Folks appointed Regent of the Agricultural College.

NOVEMBER 7.—W. J. Bawden appointed Judge of the Sixth District.

NOVEMBER 10.—The Pomeroy bribery case comes on at Burlingame, before Judge Peyton. Gen. Stringfellow, for the defence, asked a continuance, and it was granted.

NOVEMBER 12.—Appointment of a State Relief Committee, at Topeka, consisting of E. S. Stover, F. S. McCabe, O. T. Welch, F. W. Giles, Henry King, Wm. Sims, S. T. Kelsey, A. L. Vorhees, Wm. C. Tenney, John Fraser, J. C. Cusey, C. H. Lebold, John Geise, B. H. McEckron, J. H. Edwards, Rev. Mr. McCobas, John A. Martin, Geo. W. Glick, M. J. Morse, G. A. Thompson, P. B. Plumb, M. M. Murdock, J. H. Crichton, Wm. Martindale, Horace Cooper, E. N. Morrill, M. E. Hudson, Charles W. Blair, Theo. C. Sears, D. J. Brewer, W. A. Johnson, Alfred Gray.

NOVEMBER 19.—Rev. Dr. Jas. Marvin elected Chancellor of the University.

NOVEMBER 19.—Organization of the State Central Relief Committee, at Topeka. President, E. S. Stover; Secretary, Henry King; Treasurer, F. W. Giles. *Executive Committee:* E. S. Stover, Henry King, F. W. Giles, O. T. Welch, F. S. McCabe, M. M. Murdock, Wm. C. Tenney, D. J. Brewer, Thos. Murphy. Voted that an address be prepared by Rev. Dr. McCabe, Gen. John Fraser, and M. M. Murdock.

NOVEMBER 30.—Expenditures of the State for the year:

Governor's Department	$7,097 40	Penitentiary	74,453 26
Secretary's Department	15,787 82	Agricultural College	28,012 08
Auditor's Department	5,312 62	Regents of State Institutions	5,979 23
Treasurer's Department	4,346 04	Conveying prisoners to Penitentiary	10,345 75
Attorney General	1,850 00		
Supt. of Public Instruction	4,916 71	Orphan Asylum, Leavenworth	7,000 00
Librarian	2,656 55	Publishing Const. Amendment	8,967 70
Adjutant General	800 00	State Board of Agriculture	16,735 42
Supreme Court	22,047 64	Settlers on Osage Lands	2,500 00
District Judges	38,588 76	Legislative expenses	35,130 45
Normal School, Emporia	12,595 56	Miscellaneous appropriations	14,067 77
Normal School, Leavenworth	5,990 40	Court of Impeachment	10,166 31
Blind Asylum	8,880 36	Legislative expenses, Special Session	9,027 90
Deaf and Dumb Asylum	16,413 54		
Insane Asylum	41,527 40	Investigating Committee	968 80
State University	29,244 81	Horticultural Society	1,000 00
Printing	37,866 01	Total for 1874	$432,212 34
Transcribing Journals	1,935 00		

—The following is the State debt:

Issued under act of	Date of Issue.	For What.	Rate per ct.	When Payable.	Where.	Face of Bonds.	Am't Sold For.	Bought by Perman't School Fund.	Bought by Sinking Fund.
1861	July 1, '61	Cur. Exp.	7	July 1, '76	N. Y...	$150,000	} $173,150 00	$18,100	$34,600
1863	Mar.20,'63	Cur. Exp.	7	July 1, '78	N. Y...	54,000			
1863	July 1, '63	F. Terr. D.	6	July 1, '83	Top'ka	61,600	61,600 00	15,700	21,000
1864	July 1, '64	Refund.T.	6	July 1, '84	Top'ka	39,675	39,675 00	36,425	1,200
1864	July 1, '64	Mil. Purp.	7	July 1, '84	N. Y...	100,000	87,586 00	11,000	....
1864	July 1, '64	Penit'y ...	7	July 1, '84	N. Y...	50,000	45,000 00	....	....
1866	July 1, '66	Penit'y ...	7	July 1, '86	N. Y...	60,000	54,600 00	....	....
1866	July 1, '66	Pub. Imp.	7	July 1, '96	N. Y...	70,000	63,210 00	....	38,000
1866	July 1, '66	Mil. Purp.	7	July 1, '86	Top'ka	40,000	38,220 00	40,000	....
1867	July 1, '67	Penit'y ...	7	July 1, '97	N. Y...	100,000	89,329 16	50,000	....
1867	July 1, '67	Cap. B'dg.	7	July 1, '97	N. Y...	100,000	89,513 00	30,000	5,000
1867	July 1, '67	D. & D.As.	7	July 1, '87	Top'ka	15,500	15,500 00	15,500	....
1868	July 1, '68	Cap. B'dg.	7	July 1, '98	N. Y...	150,000	137,180 00	66,000	....
1868	July 1, '68	Penit'y ...	7	July 1, '98	N. Y...	50,000	45,588 35	....	50,000
1868	July 1, '68	Mil. Purp.	7	July 1, '88	N. Y...	30,000	27,353 00	30,000	....
1868	July 1, '68	InsaneAs.	7	July 1, '98	N. Y...	20,000	18,352 33	20,000	....
1869	Jan. 1, '69	Mil. Purp.	7	July 1, '89	N. Y...	75,000	69,000 00	75,000	....
1869	Jan. 1, '69	Mil. Purp.	7	July 1, '99	N. Y...	89,000	83,200 00	89,000	....
1869	Jan. 1, '69	Mil. Purp.	7	July 1, '89	N. Y...	12,000	11,380 00	11,000	1,000
1869	Jan. 1, '69	Cap. B'dg.	7	July 1, '89	N. Y...	70,000	66,442 57	....	30,000
1874	Oct.15, '74	Rel'f B'ds.	7	Oct. 15,'94	N. Y...	5,000	5,000 00	5,000	....
						$1,341,775	$1,220,779 41	$512,725	$180,800

"The following bonds are held by the sinking fund:

Date of Issue.	For what Purpose.	Rate of Interest.	Amount of Bonds.
May 1, 1863	Funding Territorial debt...................................	6 per cent.	$11,000 00
July 1, 1863	Funding Territorial debt...................................	6 per cent.	10,000 00
July 1, 1864	Funding Territorial debt...................................	6 per cent.	1,200 00
July 1, 1861	Current expenses...	7 per cent.	4,600 00
Mar.20, 1863	Current expenses...	7 per cent.	30,000 00
July 1, 1868	Penitentiary buildings....................................	7 per cent.	50,000 00
July 1, 1867	Capitol building...	7 per cent.	5,000 00
July 1, 1869	Capitol building...	7 per cent.	30,000 00
July 1, 1866	Public improvements......................................	7 per cent.	38,000 00
Jan. 1, 1869	Military purposes..	7 per cent.	1,000 00
	Total..		$180,800 00

"The amount of the Kansas State debt held by the Permanent School Fund is $512,-725; by the Sinking Fund, $180,800; State bonds now outstanding and unpaid, $648,250."—*Auditor Wilder's Report.*

NOVEMBER 30.—The Insane Asylum, at Osawatomie, has steam water-works in successful operation.

NOVEMBER 30.—The following table is given to show what the State has attempted to raise each year by taxation:

Year.	Rate of tax on the dollar.	Tax levied.	Taxable property as fixed by the State Board.
1861	3 mills	$74,233	$24,774,333
1862	5 "	101,469	19,285,749
1863	5 "	127,302	25,460,400
1864	5 "	152,334	30,502,791
1865	5 "	181,136	36,227,200
1866	4 "	201,760	50,439,634
1867	5 "	281,381	56,276,360
1868	6½ "	435,407	66,949,549
1869	10 "	763,836	76,383,697
1870	8¾ "	809,620	92,528,099
1871	6 "	652,521	108,753,575
1872	8½ "	1,085,372	127,690,937
1873	6 "	754,105	125,684,176
1874	6 "	773,499	128,916,519
1875	6 "	729,266	121,544,344

—*Auditor Wilder's Report.*

The 1875 figures have been added to the above table. The Report says: "The whole of this tax is never collected, and only a fraction of the amount levied in any year is collected during that year."

—Librarian Dickinson says the State owns 4,278 volumes of Kansas Supreme Court Reports, worth $17,112. The number of books in the Library is 10,297.

DECEMBER.—Report of Charles Puffer, C. S. Brodbent, and Wm. W. Creighton, Commissioners of Public Institutions. It is a volume of 406 pages.

DECEMBER 1.—Secretary Smallwood reports the following counties organized during the year: Kingman, February 27; Pratt, March 14; Edwards, August 21.

DECEMBER.—

"There are now in the State 4,395 school districts, of which 391 were organized during the past year. In the number of pupils enrolled in the public schools there has been an increase, since the last report of the Superintendent, of 13,000; 5,043 teachers have been employed, an increase from 1873 of more than twenty per cent. The amount distributed to the various counties, on the semi-annual dividend of school money, is $261,952.61, an increase for the year of $30,035.34. The progress made by the higher educational institutions is none the less marked."—*Gov. Osborn's Message, Jan., 1875.*

DECEMBER 1.—

"It has been repeatedly asserted that the laws governing the State Treasury are impracticable, and that no person could perform the duties of the office and comply with the law. On the 19th of May, I issued a circular to the several county treasurers, reciting the sections of the statutes showing the kind of funds which should be received by the State Treasurer in payment of all moneys due the treasury, with a notice that hereafter no drafts or checks would be received. In some instances no attention was paid to said circular, but a prompt adherence to the law on my part produced the desired effect on the part of others; and after a period of more than six months I can truly say that the law governing the treasury of the State of Kansas is a good one for the people of the State, and ought not in any manner to be modified, but rather strengthened by additional safeguards."—*Treasurer Francis's Report.*

DECEMBER.—The St. Mary's Times issued. O. L. R. Sedgwick, publisher; H. G. Evans, editor.

DECEMBER 8.—The Lawrence Tribune suspends.

—The Kansas Pacific train robbed at Muncie, a few miles west of Kansas City, at 3 P. M. Five masked men flagged and stopped the train, cut off the passenger coaches, moved the engine and express car some distance forward, and robbed Wells, Fargo & Co.'s safe of about $27,000.

DECEMBER 10.—William McDaniels, one of the Muncie train robbers, arrested in Kansas City.

DECEMBER 10.—The new Deaf and Dumb Asylum, at Olathe, is completed; number of pupils in the school, 80. The Ninth Annual Report gives a history of legislation in Kansas for the Deaf and Dumb.

DECEMBER 15.—Eighth Annual Meeting of the State Horticultural Society, at Emporia. *Officers:* President, E. Gale, Manhattan; Vice President, Robert Milliken, Emporia; Secretary, G. C. Brackett, Lawrence; Treasurer, Fred. Wellhouse, Leavenworth. *Executive Board:* H. E. Van Deman, Geneva, Allen county; E. Snyder, Highland, Doniphan county; J. Stayman, Leavenworth.

DECEMBER 17.—A. M. Campbell confirmed as Postmaster at Salina, and Luther M. Eggers as Register of the Hays City Land Office.

DECEMBER 21.—Edward Russell resigns as Superintendent of Insurance, and Henry Clarkson is appointed.

—The Blue Rapids Woollen Mills manufacture cloth to clothe the convicts in the Penitentiaries of Kansas, Nebraska and Colorado.

DECEMBER 28.—Death of Gerrit Smith, in New York City.

—Burning of Drake's Block, in Fort Scott.

—M. M. Murdock appointed Postmaster at Wichita.

DECEMBER 29.—The Lawrence dam completed and utilized. The dam has cost $100,000, and furnishes between two and three thousand horse-power. It has been under construction since 1872.

DECEMBER 31.—The Report of Charles A. Morris, Adjutant General, gives a detailed account of Indian raids and military operations during the year. The following is copied from pages 33, 34, and 36: .

"The total number of persons known to have been murdered within the State, by Indians, since the 16th of June last, is twenty-seven, inclusive of the four citizens of Kansas, killed July 3d, on the Fort Sill trail, while engaged in transporting Indian supplies. . . . The following shows the force and term of service of the militia called into service during the present year to repel Indian invasion:

Name of Company.	Numerical strength.	When ordered into service...	When relieved from service...	Full time of service.
Co. A, Sedgwick County Mounted Militia	21	July 10, 1874	July 21, 1874	11 days.
Co. A, Barbour County Mounted Militia*	60	Aug. 7, 1874	Aug. 24, 1874	18 days.
Co. A, Barbour County Mounted Militia†	60	Aug. 24, 1874	Nov. 24, 1874	90 days.
Co. A, Cowley County Mounted Militia...	60	Aug. 28, 1874	Nov. 28, 1874	90 days.
Co. A, Reno County Mounted Militia......	40	Aug. 21, 1874	Oct. 14, 1874	54 days.
Barbour County Mounted Guards‡.........	50	Sept. 3, 1874	Dec. 22, 1874	109 days.

* Before reorganization. † Second organization. ‡ Ordered into service again, December 22, 1874, and still on duty.

. . . .

"The State has heretofore paid, for defence against Indians, $206,000, under the following acts, to wit:

An act to provide for the issuance and sale of the bonds of the State for the purpose of defraying the expenses of the Kansas militia; approved March 3, 1868 .... $30,000

An act to provide for the issuance and sale of bonds of the State of Kansas for the purpose of liquidating the indebtedness of the State, incurred for military purposes during the year 1868, in defending the citizens of the State against the ravages of hostile Indians on the frontier of Kansas; approved February 9, 1869.. 75,000

An act to provide for the issuance and sale of bonds of the State of Kansas to provide a military contingent fund for the protection of the frontier against hostile Indians; approved February 26, 1869 89,000

An act to provide for the issuance and sale of bonds for defraying the expenses in raising the Nineteenth Regiment Kansas Volunteer Cavalry; approved March 3, 1869.. 12,000

"There was also paid by the State $140,000, in addition to the above, for defensive purposes, under acts of February 22, 1864, and March 6, 1866, a portion of which was for defence against Indians.

"So much of this amount as has been paid to protect the State against Indian depredations, together with the military expenses of the present year, should be assumed by the General Government, and refunded to the State."

DECEMBER 31.—The following is copied from Superintendent McCarty's Report:

TABLE SHOWING THE GROWTH OF FREE SCHOOLS IN KANSAS.

Years.	Number of Counties reporting...	Number organized School Districts...	Number of School Districts report'g.	No. Children of School Age.			No. of Children enrolled.		
				Males.	Females.	Total.	Males.	Females.	Total.
1861	12	217	114	....	....	4,901	....	....	2,310
1862	28	534	304	7,911	6,065	13,976	4,721	3,872	8,595
1863	33	705	506	12,516	12,058	24,574	7,645	7,458	15,103
1864	33	823	640	....	....	37,979	....	....	22,667
1865	35	847	721	....	....	45,441	....	....	26,409
1866	37	986	871	28,104	26,621	54,725	....	....	31,528
1867	42	1,172	1,056	32,275	30,558	62,833	20,696	18,753	39,449
1868	43	1,372	1,232	40,246	35,904	76,150	23,640	21,500	45,140
1869	43	1,707	1,621	48,007	44,510	92,517	30,197	28,484	58,681
1870	47	2,068	1,950	52,254	56,988	119,244	32,183	31,035	63,218
1871	53	2,647	2,438	73,248	69,110	142,358	44,870	44,907	89,777
1872	60	3,419	3,170	85,095	80,887	165,982	53,666	52,997	106,663
1873	64	4,004	3,847	90,714	85,357	184,957	57,772	54,645	121,690
1874	68	4,395	4,181	101,872	87,138	199,019	68,978	66,620	135,598

COMPARATIVE TABLE—Continued.

Years.	Average daily attendance...	Average time school taught—Months.	No. Teachers employed.			Average salary per month.		Average paid Teachers...	Amount expended on fuel, repairs, etc.
			Males.	Females.	Total.	Males.	Females.		
1862	....	3.2	90	229	319	....	....	$14,009 67	$1,747 23
1863	5,549	3.8	164	400	564	....	....	21,845 27	....
1864	8,744	3.5	205	527	732	$27 00	$16 10	16,361 67	10,625 61
1865	14,210	3.4	247	652	899	46 74	34 41	86,898 92	....
1866	....	4.3	405	681	1,086	41 27	28 90	115,924 11	....
1867	20,573	4.4	541	664	1,205	39 44	26 41	170,046 39	42,824 42
1868	27,238	5	746	855	1,601	39 56	29 08	203,878 54	45,319 87
1869	31,124	5	896	1,118	2,014	37 07	28 93	292,719 94	79,343 76
1870	39,401	5.2	1,079	1,161	2,240	39 60	31 10	318,596 31	98,644 33
1871	52,891	5.8	1,453	1,625	3,078	41 54	31 75	449,273 05	44,690 58
1872	61,538	5.4	1,747	2,048	3,795	40 20	31 50	596,611 94	58,886 08
1873	71,062	5.34	1,880	2,144	4,675	38 43	30 64	716,056 08	51,504 06
1874	77,386	5.5	2,360	2,683	5,043	37 24	28 69	723,578 63	51,263 70

COMPARATIVE TABLE—Concluded.

Yrs.	Disbursement of State School Fund...	Disbursement of County Fund...	Amount raised by District Tax...	Number of School Houses.					Value of School Houses...
				Log.	Frame.	Brick.	Stone.	Total.	
1862	....	....	$10,381 81	....	....	....	....	....	$10,432 50
1863	$12,918 14	....	12,300 59	....	....	....	....	....	32,972 60
1864	24,193 01	....	58,343 29	....	....	....	....	....	76,500 71
1865	24,814 11	....	107,293 47	....	....	....	....	....	122,822 64
1866	31,054 24	....	192,620 17	....	....	....	....	....	318,897 31
1867	49,961 36	$21,353 33	273,057 18	241	339	15	108	703	573,690 08
1868	55,989 90	30,804 94	342,421 70	270	472	28	182	953	813,062 75
1869	116,235 80	19,259 93	428,983 98	348	606	35	224	1,213	1,031,892 00
1870	139,957 37	14,260 19	518,332 85	352	864	46	239	1,501	1,520,041 40
1871	182,377 20	30,000 88	534,261 69	266	1,197	61	263	1,820	2,024,594 33
1872	217,810 80	22,680 65	822,644 94	204	1,507	244	348	2,437	2,845,262 58
1873	231,917 28	27,404 54	931,958 69	263	2,263	246	461	3,134	3,408,956 00
1874	261,952 62	49,273 76	895,095 35	328	2,482	263	470	3,543	3,989,085 67

43

CENSUS TAKEN MARCH 1, 1875.

The following figures have been furnished by Alfred Gray, Secretary of the State Board of Agriculture. They are not official, but will not vary 500 from the official result:

Counties.	Population.	Counties.	Population.	Counties.	Population.
Allen	6,638	Harper	....	Phillips	2,817
Anderson	5,800	Harvey	5,050	Pottawatomie	10,342
Atchison	20,191	Jackson	6,684	Pratt*	....
Barbour	367	Jefferson	11,654	Reno	5,114
Barton	2,106	Jewell	7,652	Republican	8,050
Bourbon	16,879	Johnson	14,582	Rice	2,455
Brown	8,728	Kingman*	....	Riley	7,066
Butler	9,840	Labette	14,568	Rooks†	567
Chautauqua	7,634	Leavenworth	27,738	Rush	451
Chase	3,000	Lincoln	2,492	Russell	1,054
Cherokee	13,393	Linn	11,546	Saline	6,359
Clay	6,648	Lyon	9,578	Sedgwick	8,162
Cloud	7,195	Marion	5,904	Shawnee	15,389
Coffey	7,239	Marshall	10,818	Smith	3,915
Comanche*	....	McPherson	6,202	Sumner	4,925
Cowley	8,927	Miami	12,680	Wabaunsee	4,694
Crawford	9,383	Mitchell	5,182	Wallace*	....
Davis	4,765	Montgomery	12,177	Washington	8,548
Dickinson	6,911	Morris	4,595	Wilson	9,752
Doniphan	13,923	Nemaha	7,103	Woodson	4,472
Douglas	18,365	Neosho	9,763	Wyandotte	12,385
Edwards	234	Ness*	....	Unorganized Cos‡	500
Elk	5,300	Norton	901		
Ellis	942	Osage	10,281	Total	526,732
Ellsworth	1,761	Osborne	3,466		*4,424
Ford	813	Ottawa	4,430		
Franklin	10,039	Pawnee	1,006		531,156
Greenwood	6,642				

* The counties of Comanche and Ness polled 535 votes at the general election in 1873. The counties of Kingman, Pratt and Wallace polled 571 votes in 1874. Allowing four inhabitants to the voter, it will give to these counties, at the periods named, a population of 4,424. † Returns of 1874. ‡ Estimated.

INDEX.

M.

CPSIA information can be obtained
at www.ICGtesting.com
Printed in the USA
BVHW011348310820
587693BV00007B/104